# Managing
# Human
# Resources

## Productivity, Quality of Work Life, Profits

### Ninth Edition

**Wayne F. Cascio**
The Business School
University of Colorado Denver

McGraw-Hill
Irwin

MANAGING HUMAN RESOURCES:
PRODUCTIVITY, QUALITY OF WORK LIFE, PROFITS

Published by McGraw-Hill, a business unit of The McGraw-Hill Companies, Inc., 1221 Avenue of the Americas, New York, NY, 10020. Copyright © 2013 by The McGraw-Hill Companies, Inc. All rights reserved. Printed in the United States of America. Previous editions © 2010, 2006, and 2003. No part of this publication may be reproduced or distributed in any form or by any means, or stored in a database or retrieval system, without the prior written consent of The McGraw-Hill Companies, Inc., including, but not limited to, in any network or other electronic storage or transmission, or broadcast for distance learning.

Some ancillaries, including electronic and print components, may not be available to customers outside the United States.

♲ This book is printed on recycled and acid-free paper.

4 5 6 7 8 9 0 QVS/QVS 1 0 9 8 7 6 5 4

ISBN 978-0-07-802917-2
MHID 0-07-802917-1

Vice President & Editor-in-Chief: *Brent Gordon*
Vice President & Director, Specialized Publishing: *Janice M. Roerig-Blong*
Editorial Director: *Paul Ducham*
Sponsoring Editor: *Laura Spell*
Editorial Coordinator: *Jonathan Thornton*
Marketing Manager: *Donielle Xu*
Senior Project Manager: *Lisa A. Bruflodt*
Buyer: *Nicole Baumgartner*
Design Coordinator: *Margarite Reynolds*
Media Project Manager: *Prashanthi Nadipalli*
Cover Design: *Studio Montage, St. Louis, Missouri*
Cover photo credits: *Clockwise from top:* © ColorBlind Images/Blend Images LLC; Stockbyte/ Getty Images; Nikada/Getty Images
Typeface: *10/12 Melior*
Compositor: *Aptara®, Inc.*
Printer: *Quad/Graphics*

**Library of Congress Cataloging-in-Publication Data**

Cascio, Wayne F.
    Managing human resources / Wayne F. Cascio.—9th ed.
       p. cm.
    Includes bibliographical references and index.
    ISBN-13: 978-0-07-802917-2 (alk. paper)
    ISBN-10: 0-07-802917-1 (alk. paper)
    1. Personnel management.   I. Title.
HF5549.C2975 2012
658.3—dc23                                                    2011044070

To Tanni Lee
Endless Joy

# ABOUT THE AUTHOR

WAYNE F. CASCIO holds the Robert H. Reynolds Distinguished Chair in Global Leadership at the University of Colorado Denver. He earned his B.A. degree from Holy Cross College, his M.A. degree from Emory University, and his Ph.D. in industrial/organizational psychology from the University of Rochester.

Professor Cascio is past chair of the Society for Human Resource Management Foundation and the Human Resources Division of the Academy of Management, and past president of the Society for Industrial and Organizational Psychology. He is a Fellow of the National Academy of Human Resources, the Academy of Management, and the American Psychological Association, and he holds a Diplomate in industrial/organizational psychology from the American Board of Professional Psychology. He received the Distinguished Career award from the HR Division of the Academy of Management in 1999, an honorary doctorate from the University of Geneva, Switzerland, in 2004, and in 2008 he was named by the *Journal of Management* as one of the most influential scholars in management over the past 25 years. In 2010 he won the Michael R. Losey Human Resources Research Award from the Society for Human Resource Management.

Professor Cascio is a senior editor of the *Journal of World Business*. His editorial board memberships have included the *Journal of Applied Psychology, Academy of Management Review, Journal of Management, International Journal of Selection and Assessment, Human Performance, Organizational Dynamics,* and *Asia-Pacific Journal of Human Resources.* He has consulted with a wide variety of organizations on six continents, and periodically he testifies as an expert witness in employment discrimination cases. Professor Cascio is an active researcher and writer. He has published more than 165 articles and book chapters, and 24 books.

# CONTENTS IN BRIEF

# CONTENTS

# BOXES AND SPECIAL FEATURES

# PREFACE

I did not write this book for students who aspire to be specialists in human resource management (HRM). Rather, I wrote it for students of general management whose jobs inevitably will involve responsibility for managing people, along with capital, material, and information assets. A fundamental assumption, then, is that all managers are accountable to their organizations in terms of the impact of their HRM activities, and they are expected to add value by managing their people effectively. They also are accountable to their peers and to their subordinates in terms of the quality of work life that they are providing.

As a unifying theme for the text, I have tried to link the content of each chapter to three key outcome variables—productivity, quality of work life, and profits. This relationship should strengthen the student's perception of HRM as an important function affecting individuals, organizations, and society.

Each chapter incorporates the following distinguishing features:

- In keeping with the orientation of the book toward general managers, each chapter opens with "Questions This Chapter Will Help Managers Answer." This section provides a broad outline of the topics that each chapter addresses.
- Following the chapter opener is a split sequential vignette, often from the popular press, that illustrates "Human Resource Management in Action." Events in the vignette are designed to sensitize the reader to the subject matter of the chapter. The events lead to a climax, but then the vignette stops—like a two-part television drama. The reader is asked to predict what will happen next and to anticipate alternative courses of action.
- Then the text for the chapter appears—replete with concepts, research findings, court decisions, HR Buzz boxes, and international comparisons.
- Each chapter includes an "Ethical Dilemma." Its purpose is to identify issues relevant to the topic under discussion where different courses of action may be desirable and possible. The student must choose a course of action and defend the rationale for doing so.
- As in the eighth edition, "Implications for Management Practice" provides insights into the ways in which issues presented in the chapter affect the decisions that managers must make. "Impact" boxes in each chapter reinforce the link between the chapter content and the strategic objectives—productivity, quality of work life, and the bottom line—that influence all HR functions.
- Near the end of the chapter, the vignette introduced at the outset continues, allowing the reader to compare his or her predictions with what actually happened.

Ultimately the aim of each chapter is to teach prospective managers to *make decisions* based on accurate diagnoses of situations that involve people—in domestic as well as global contexts. Familiarity with theory, research, and practice enhances the ability of students to do this. Numerous real-world applications of concepts allow the student to learn from the experiences of others, and the dynamic design of each chapter allows the student to move back and forth from concept to evidence to practice—then back to evaluating concepts—in a continuous learning loop.

## WHAT'S NEW IN THE NINTH EDITION?

HR texts have sometimes been criticized for overemphasizing the HR practices of large organizations. There is often scant advice for the manager of a small business who "wears many hats" and whose capital resources are limited. To address this issue explicitly, I have made a conscious effort to provide examples of effective HRM practices in small businesses in almost every chapter.

This was no cosmetic revision. I examined every topic and every example in each chapter for its continued relevance and appropriateness. I added dozens of new HR Buzz boxes to illustrate current practices, updated legal findings from each area, and cited the very latest research findings in every chapter. I added literally hundreds of new references since the previous edition of the book, and removed older ones that are less relevant today. As in previous editions, I have tried to make the text readable, neither too simplistic nor too complex.

The book still includes 16 chapters, presented in the same order as in the previous edition. "Applying Your Knowledge" cases and exercises still appear in each chapter, and although many of the chapter-opening vignettes ("Human Resource Management in Action") retain the same titles, I have updated each one to reflect current information and content. As in the previous edition, I have boldfaced key terms as they are discussed in the text and included a consolidated list of them at the end of each chapter. A glossary at the back of the book also helps students to locate definitions of important terms quickly.

A final consideration is the treatment of international issues. While there are merits to including a separate chapter on this topic, as well as interspersing international content in each chapter, I do not see this as an either–or matter. I have done both, recognizing the need to frame domestic HR issues in a global context (e.g., recruitment, staffing, compensation, labor-management relations). At the same time, the book covers international issues (e.g., cultural differences, staffing, training, and compensation of expatriates) in more depth in a separate chapter.

## NEW TOPICS IN THE NINTH EDITION

- Chapter 1, on HR and the global business environment, includes the latest meta-analysis results on the relationship between investments in human capital and organizational performance, and also on the relationships between specific management practices and stock performance. It also identifies some key effects of globalization—that technical skills, while mandatory, will be less defining of the successful manager than the ability to work across cultures and to build relationships with many different constituents. With respect to technology, the chapter emphasizes that technology-driven job destruction does not decrease overall employment. Ultimately, the economic growth created by new jobs overwhelms the drag from jobs destroyed. What about technology? The chapter coveys the message that employees and prospective employees should recognize collaborative technology as a key component of firms' global hiring strategies. Learn to leverage social-networking sites, and to research which sites are most effective in each market.

- Chapter 2, on the financial impact of HRM, begins by presenting longitudinal meta-analysis data that support the causal link between employee attitudes and the bottom-line financial performance of firms. Building on the L-A-M-P model, the chapter stresses the critical role of logic, and uses Sysco Corporation as an example of how a compelling logic tells a story about potential causes and consequences, and also identifies measures that are most appropriate. More broadly, the chapter emphasizes application of the LAMP process as a powerful tool for educating leaders outside of HR, and for embedding HR measures in their mental frameworks. When that happens, meaningful data provide the basis for people-related business decisions. Updated examples of the processes used to cost out of absenteeism, turnover, work-life, and training programs complete the chapter.

- Chapter 3, on the legal context, includes updated case law and statistics in all areas relevant to employment. In addition, it considers the Americans with Disabilities Act (ADA), as amended in 2008; training for ADA compliance; the latest developments in the Uniformed Services Employment and Reemployment Rights Act (USERRA); the Family and Medical Leave Act (FMLA); and case law related to sexual harassment, seniority, retaliation, and preferential selection,

- Chapter 4, on diversity, includes more information on making the business case for diversity and inclusion, and for the increasingly diverse composition of workforces. The chapter also contains completely revised and updated information on African-American, Hispanic, and Asian buying power, as well as on women in the workforce. There is also a new company example—"Aetna: Embedding Diversity into the Fabric of the Business"—and also updated and revised information about characteristics and management strategies for Gen X, Gen Y, older workers, workers with disabilities, and gay workers.

- Chapter 5, "Planning for People," uses McDonald's to illustrate the alignment of strategy, formulation, analysis, and implementation. It also includes a detailed specification of "high-performance work practices," along with a new, integrative model of today's approach to job design. Strategic workforce planning is presented as the formal process that connects business and HR strategies, providing data, analytics, and insights to inform, and sometimes to challenge, executive decisions about strategy. To illustrate the challenges associated with extending the planning process across borders, the chapter cites 3M's experience with global workforce planning. An updated treatment of leadership succession completes the treatment of planning for people.

- Chapter 6, "Recruiting," begins with a new vignette, "The Perils and Promise of Social Media," treating recruitment as an important component of the staffing supply chain. It uses a new, integrated model of the recruitment process to serve as an overarching framework for many of the topics presented, and identifies many new company examples whose practices are consistent with the model. A feature new to this edition is a section entitled, "What's New in Employee Referrals?" that focuses on strategies firms are using to find passive candidates. Treatments of external recruitment sources, such as virtual job fairs, executive search firms, employment agencies, Web-based job boards, and recruitment advertising have all been updated thoroughly, as has the other side of recruitment, job search from the applicant's perspective.

- Chapter 7, "Staffing": Using Netflix as an example, the chapter emphasizes the critical role of corporate culture as the key to staffing "fit." It also includes newly updated treatments of screening methods, such as recommendations, references, and background checks (especially checks of social-networking sites), along with assessment methods, such as drug screening, integrity and mental ability tests, personality measures, personal-history data, and employment interviews. There are lots of new company examples, such as how Google uses "crowd-sourcing" in its hiring decisions. The chapter concludes with a review of recent findings with respect to situational judgment tests and assessment centers.

- Chapter 8, on training, incorporates updated examples and research findings about computer-based simulation games, executive coaching, and "rapid prototyping"—a method for creating, testing, and modifying training materials quickly. A new example is Boeing's use of laptop computers to train mechanics on its 787 Dreamliner airplanes. UPS driver training is also newly updated in this edition. Other new features include an ethical dilemma involving anger management, a description of IBM's approach to on-boarding new employees through simulation of a virtual world, and the use of gaming by other companies to orient new employees.

- Chapter 9, "Performance Management," begins with a recent poll of 750 HR executives about the use and effectiveness of performance management systems in their organizations. It also includes recent findings about the use and limitations of goal setting, the effectiveness of multisource feedback, and the use of social-networking–style systems that allow employees and managers to post Twitter-length questions and to receive immediate, rapid feedback about their performance. The chapter concludes with an updated international application on the impact of national culture on performance management processes.

- Chapter 10, "Managing Careers," includes newly updated information about the effect of downsizing on employee loyalty, bottom-line benefits for family friendly companies, and Cisco's use of an innovative retention program called "Cisco Choice" targeted at Gen Y employees. It also considers alternative approaches to mentoring—group-based, anonymous, and mentoring with micro-feedback (limited to 140 characters). New strategies for dealing with plateaued workers, 14 alternatives to downsizing, and updated findings regarding retirement decisions complete the chapter.

- Chapter 11, on pay and incentives, begins with updates to the opening vignette, "The Trust Gap," namely, the Dodd-Frank Wall Street Reform and

Consumer Protection Act and some of the causes of the global financial crisis. It identifies the growing trend toward variable pay programs, the use of flexibility as an important element of a total rewards program, IBM's changed pay strategy and pay system to support its changed business strategy, and a new law that permits "clawbacks" of pay that resulted from material misstatements of financial reports. The latest information on Web-based salary-comparison sources, incentives that encourage excessive risk taking, as well as updated treatments of executive compensation, profit-sharing, gain-sharing, and employee stock-ownership plans complete the chapter.

- Chapter 12, on benefits, begins with an updated version of the chapter-opening vignette, "The New World of Employee Benefits," which starts the student thinking about the cost and strategic purpose of employee benefits. We then consider some important changes in the legal requirements governing Social Security, unemployment insurance, and pensions. Every statistic with respect to security and health benefits, payments for time not worked, and employee services has been reviewed and updated to reflect the most current data and research findings. We present the major provisions of the new health-care law, the Patient Protection and Affordable Care Act, and also describe some current strategies companies are using to contain costs. With respect to benefit communications, the chapter describes how some firms are placing online interactive tools outside company intranet firewalls so employees and spouses can access them from home.

- Chapter 13, on unions, examines trends in union membership, as well as conditions in global product and service markets that make resurgence in union power unlikely. We also examine the 2011 National Football League lockout, updated statistics and trends in dispute resolution, and the movement toward labor-management cooperation, as reflected in the collective bargaining agreement between the United Steelworkers and Goodyear Tire & Rubber Company.

- Chapter 14, on justice and ethics, examines the latest research findings with respect to employee voice, as well as international norms about procedural and distributive justice. It also presents new findings with respect to alternative nonunion grievance procedures, the pros and cons of progressive discipline, social-media policies and "at-will" employment, termination procedures, how Facebook competes on privacy, fair information practices in the Internet Age, and the new incentives for whistle-blowers and enhanced antiretaliation protections under the Dodd-Frank Wall Street Reform and Consumer Protection Act. The chapter concludes with a new Case 14-1, "Blowing the Whistle."

- Chapter 15, on safety, health, and EAPs: All statistics and costs in the section "Extent and Cost of Safety and Health Problems" have been thoroughly updated, as have new OSHA requirements for training in the language that an employee understands. We use the example of the US Airways flight that made an emergency landing on the Hudson River in 2009 to show that safety pays. We also use the example of BP's 2010 Gulf oil spill to show the need for a company culture and incentives that emphasize safety, and the example of the worker suicides at Foxconn to show that multinationals have important stakes in the operations of their subcontractors in less-developed countries. Finally, the section of AIDS and business has been completely updated, as have the sections on alcoholism, drug abuse, and workplace violence.

■ Chapter 16, on international HR, begins with updated figures on the costs of expatriates, as well as changes in the patterns of foreign direct investment that make overseas assignments more likely for managers and employees. It also considers new findings on HR in the European Union, along with recent meta-analytic results of almost 600 studies based on Hofstede's cultural-value dimensions. Recent data on global talent risks are presented as a major concern for MNEs, yet few have taken action to address them. New findings also are presented with respect to global staffing methods, job aid for trailing spouses, cross-cultural training and development, pay adjustments and performance management, international labor relations, and the North American Free Trade Agreement.

## HELP FOR INSTRUCTORS AND STUDENTS

Several important supplements are available to help you use this book more effectively.

### Online Learning Center (*www.mhhe.com/cascio9e*)

■ The instructor's manual includes suggested course outlines for both 10- and 16-week terms, chapter outlines, answers to "Challenge" questions that follow the chapter-opening vignette, answers to end-of-chapter discussion questions, and comments on end-of-chapter cases and exercises.

■ A matrix of features (shown in the instructor's manual) helps distinguish this book from competitors. The grid shows the specific chapter coverage of important topics such as international applications, new technology, the Internet, ethical issues, the financial impact of HR activities, and workforce diversity.

■ The test bank contains true-false, multiple-choice, fill-in-the-blank, and short-answer questions for each chapter. Approximately 1,200 questions are included. Each is classified according to the level of difficulty and includes a text page reference.

■ PowerPoint–presentation software and slides include tables, figures, and content from each chapter of the text, thereby providing an easy-to-follow outline for classroom presentations.

■ Readers can access chapter reviews, self-grading quizzes, and additional exercises.

### Human Resource Management Video DVD Volume 3 (ISBN 007743718)

This DVD provides 16 HRM-related videos, including one new video produced by the SHRM Foundation ("Once the Deal is Done: Making Mergers Work").

Other new notable videos available for this edition include "Google Employee Perks," "Zappos.com," and "Recession Job Growth." Other video options include the Manager's Hot Seat series, interactive video exercises available at www.mhhe.com/mhs.

## ORGANIZATION AND PLAN OF THE BOOK

The text is based on the premise that three critical strategic objectives guide all HR functions: productivity, quality of work life, and profits. The functions—employment; development; compensation; labor-management accommodation; and safety, health, and international implications—in turn, are carried out in multiple environments: competitive, legal, social, and organizational.

Part 1, "Environment," includes Chapters 1 through 4. It provides the backdrop against which students will explore the nature and content of each HRM function. These first four chapters paint a broad picture of the competitive, legal, social, and organizational environments in which people-management activities take place. They also describe key economic and noneconomic factors that affect productivity, quality of work life, and profits. This is the conceptual framework within which the remaining five parts (12 chapters) of the book unfold.

Logically, "Employment" (Part 2) is the first step in the HRM process. Analyzing work, planning for people, recruiting, and staffing are key components of the employment process. Once employees are on board, the process of "Development" (Part 3) begins, with workplace training, performance management, and career management activities.

Parts 4, 5, and 6 represent concurrent processes. That is, "Compensation" (Part 4), "Labor-Management Accommodation" (Part 5), and "Support and International Implications" (Part 6) are all closely intertwined, conceptually and in practice. They represent a network of interacting activities such that a change in one of them (e.g., a new pay system or a collective-bargaining agreement) inevitably will have an impact on all other components of the HRM system. It is only for ease of exposition that the book presents them separately in Parts 4, 5, and 6.

## ACKNOWLEDGMENTS

Many people played important roles in the development of this edition of the book, and I am deeply grateful to them. Ultimately any errors of omission or commission are mine, and I bear responsibility for them.

Several people at McGraw-Hill/Irwin were especially helpful. Publisher Paul Ducham, Managing Developmental Editor Laura Spell, and Marketing Manager Jaime Halteman provided advice, support, and encouragement. Editorial Coordinator Jonathan Thornton, Project Manager Lisa Bruflodt, and Full-Service Project Manager Robin Bonner (of Aptara, Inc.) were ever vigilant to ensure that all phases of the book's production stayed on schedule.

It has been a pleasure to work with each of these individuals. Finally, the many reviewers of the current and previous editions of the text provided important insights and helped improve the final product. Their guidance and feedback have helped make the book what it is today, and they each deserve special thanks:

- James P. Gelatt, University of Maryland University College
- Karen Jacobs, LeTourneau University
- Jacqueline Landau, Salem State College
- Debbie Louise Mackey, University of Tennessee, Knoxville
- Gery Markova, Wichita State University
- Timothy P. Munyon, West Virginia University
- Robert Prescott, Rollins College
- Sarah Sanders Smith, Purdue University North Central
- Eugene F. Stone-Romero, University of Texas at San Antonio

**Wayne F. Cascio**

# ENVIRONMENT

To manage people effectively in today's world of work, one must understand and appreciate the significant competitive, legal, and social issues. The purpose of Chapters 1 through 4 is to provide insight into these issues. They provide both direction for and perspective on the management of human resources in the 21st century.

# 1

# HUMAN RESOURCES IN A GLOBALLY COMPETITIVE BUSINESS ENVIRONMENT

*Questions This Chapter Will Help Managers Answer*

1. What will 21st-century corporations look like?
2. What people-related business issues must managers be concerned about?
3. Which features will characterize the competitive business environment in the foreseeable future, and how might we respond to them?
4. What people-related problems are likely to arise as a result of changes in the forms of organizations? How can we avoid these problems?
5. What are the HR implications of our firm's business strategy?

# THE 21ST-CENTURY CORPORATION*

Sparked by new technologies, particularly the Internet, the corporation is undergoing a radical transformation that is nothing less than a new Industrial Revolution. This time around, the revolution is reaching every corner of the globe. The 21st-century corporation that emerges is, in many ways, the polar opposite of the 20th-century organizations that senior managers helped shape.

Many factors are driving change, but none is more important than the rise of Internet technologies. Like the steam engine or the assembly line, the Internet has already become an advance with revolutionary consequences, most of which we have only begun to feel. The Internet gives everyone in the organization, from the lowliest clerk to the chairman of the board, the ability to access a mind-boggling array of information—instantaneously from anywhere. Instead of seeping out over months or years, ideas can be zapped around the globe in the blink of an eye. That means that the 21st-century corporation must adapt itself to management via the Web. It must be predicated on constant change, not stability; organized around networks, not rigid hierarchies; built on shifting partnerships and alliances, not self-sufficiency; and constructed on technological advantages, not bricks and mortar.

The organization chart of the large-scale enterprise had long been defined as a pyramid of ever-shrinking layers leading to an omnipotent CEO at its apex. The 21st-century corporation, in contrast, is far more likely to look like a web: a flat, intricately woven form that links partners, employees, external contractors, suppliers, and customers in various collaborations. The players will grow more and more interdependent, and managing this intricate network will be as important as managing internal operations.

In contrast to factories of the past 100 years that produced cookie-cutter products, the company of the future will tailor its products to each individual by turning customers into partners and giving them the technology to design and demand exactly what they want. Mass customization will result in waves of individualized products and services, as well as huge savings for companies, which no longer will have to guess what and how much customers want.

Intellectual capital will be critical to business success. Bringing breakthrough products to market first will provide little advantage to companies because technology will let competitors match or exceed them almost instantly. To keep ahead of the steep new-product curve, it will be crucial for businesses to attract and retain the best thinkers. Companies will need to build a deep reservoir of talent—including both employees and free agents—to succeed in this new era. But attracting and retaining top talent will require more than just huge paychecks. Organizations will need to create the kinds of cultures and reward systems that keep the best minds engaged. The old command-and-control hierarchies

*Sources: World Economic Forum and Boston Consulting Group. (2011). *Global talent risk—Seven responses.* Cologny/Geneva, Switzerland: Author; Economist Intelligence Unit. (2010). *Global Firms in 2020: The Next Decade of Change for Organizations and Workers.* Alexandria, VA: SHRM; Colvin, G. (2009, March 16). The world's most admired companies. *Fortune,* pp. 75–78; Hamm, S. (2007, Mar. 27). Speed demons. *BusinessWeek,* pp. 67–76; Hamm, S. (2007, Apr. 16). People are his bottom line. *Fortune,* p. 30; Byrne, J. A. (2000, Aug. 28). Management by web. *BusinessWeek,* pp. 84–96; Colvin, G. (2000, Mar. 6). Managing in the info era. *Fortune,* pp. F6–F9; Pfeffer, J. and Veiga, J. F. (1999). Putting people first for organizational success. *Academy of Management Executive* 13(2), pp. 37–48.

are fast crumbling in favor of organizations that empower vast numbers of people and reward the best of them as if they were owners of the enterprise.

***It's Global.***    In the beginning, the global company was defined as one that simply sold its goods in overseas markets. Later, global companies assumed a manufacturing presence in numerous countries. The company of the future will call on talent and resources—especially intellectual capital—wherever they can be found around the globe, just as it will sell its goods and services around the globe. Indeed, the very notion of a headquarters country may no longer apply, as companies migrate to places of greatest advantage. The new global corporation might be based in the United States but do its software programming in Sri Lanka, its engineering in Germany, and its manufacturing in China. Every outpost will be connected seamlessly by the Internet, so that far-flung employees and freelancers can work together in real time.

***It's about Speed.***    Call it the innovation imperative. Competition is more intense than ever because of the rise of the Asian powerhouses and the spread of disruptive new Internet technologies and business models. If companies are to thrive in this hypercompetitive environment, they must innovate more and faster. Here's just one example: In the cell-phone business, Nokia, Motorola, and others used to take 12 to 18 months to develop basic models. Today, it's six to nine months. With everything from product cycles to employee turnover on fast-forward, there is simply not enough time for deliberation or bureaucracy.

The 21st-century corporation will not have one ideal form. Some will be completely disaggregated, wholly dependent on a network of suppliers, manufacturers, and distributors for their survival. Others, less so. Some of the most successful companies will be very small and very specialized. Others will be gargantuan in size, scope, and complexity. Table 1–1 presents a summary of these changes.

If people are so critical to business success in the 21st-century organization, what will it take to attract and retain the best? According to John T. Chambers, CEO of Cisco Systems, Inc.: "The reason people stay at a company is that it's a great place to work. It's like playing on a great sports team. Really good players want to be around other really good players. Secondly, people like to work for good leadership. So creating a culture of leaders that people like is key. And the third is, are you working for a higher purpose than an IPO or a paycheck? Our higher purpose is to change the way the world works, lives, and plays."[a]

So if firms are to produce profits through people, what should they do? In the case conclusion at the end of the chapter, we will examine seven practices of successful organizations.

## Challenges

1. In Table 1–1, which dimensions of the 21st-century prototype model require effective skills in managing people?
2. How might the Internet change the ways that employees and managers interact?
3. If the 21st-century prototype model of organizations is to be successful, how must companies change their approaches to managing people?

---

[a]Hamm, 2007 (April 16), op. cit.

## Table 1–1

### WHAT A DIFFERENCE A CENTURY CAN MAKE: CONTRASTING VIEWS OF THE CORPORATION

| Characteristic | 20th century | 21st century |
|---|---|---|
| Organization | The pyramid | The web or network |
| Focus | Internal | External |
| Style | Structured | Flexible |
| Source of strength | Stability | Change |
| Structure | Self-sufficiency | Interdependencies |
| Resources | Atoms (physical assets) | Bits (information) |
| Operations | Vertical integration | Virtual integration |
| Products | Mass production | Mass customization |
| Reach | Domestic | Global |
| Financials | Quarterly | Real-time |
| Inventories | Months | Hours |
| Strategy | Top-down | Bottom-up |
| Leadership | Dogmatic | Inspirational |
| Workers | Employees | Employees + free agents |
| Job Expectations | Security | Personal growth |
| Motivation | To compete | To build |
| Improvements | Incremental | Revolutionary |
| Quality | Affordable best | No compromise |

## THE ENTERPRISE IS THE PEOPLE

Organizations are managed and staffed by people. Without people, organizations cannot exist. Indeed, the challenge, the opportunity, and also the frustration of creating and managing organizations frequently stem from the people-related problems that arise within them. People-related problems, in turn, frequently stem from the mistaken belief that people are all alike, that they can be treated identically. Nothing could be further from the truth. Like snowflakes, no two people are exactly alike, and everyone differs physically and psychologically from everyone else. Sitting in a sports arena, for example, will be tall people, small people, fat people, thin people, people of color, white people, elderly people, young people, and so on. Even within any single physical category there will be enormous variability in psychological characteristics. Some will be outgoing, others reserved; some will be intelligent, others not so intelligent; some will prefer indoor activities, others outdoor activities. The point is that these differences demand attention so that each person can maximize his or her potential, so that organizations can maximize their effectiveness, and so that society as a whole can make the wisest use of its human resources.

This book is about managing people, the most vital of all resources, in work settings. Rather than focus exclusively on issues of concern to the human resource specialist, however, we will examine human resource management (HRM) issues in terms of their impact on management in general. A changing world order has forced us to take a hard look at the ways we manage people. Research has shown time and again that HRM practices can make an important, practical difference in terms of three key organizational outcomes: productivity, quality of work life, and profit. Each chapter in this book considers the impact of a different aspect of human resource management on these three broad themes. To study these impacts, we will look at the latest theory and research in each topical area, plus examples of actual company practices.

This chapter begins by considering what human resources management is all about, how it relates to the work of the line manager, and how it relates to profits. Then we will consider some current competitive challenges in the business environment, emphasizing the importance of business and human resources (HR) strategy—both of which have direct implications for productivity and quality of work life. Let's begin by considering the nature of HRM.

## MANAGING PEOPLE: A CRITICAL ROLE FOR EVERY MANAGER

Managers are responsible for optimizing all of the resources available to them—material, capital, and human.[1] When it comes to managing people, however, all managers must be concerned to some degree with the following five activities: staffing, retention, development, adjustment, and managing change.

**Staffing** comprises the activities of (1) identifying work requirements within an organization; (2) determining the numbers of people and the skills mix necessary to do the work; and (3) recruiting, selecting, and promoting qualified candidates.

**Retention** comprises the activities of (1) rewarding employees for performing their jobs effectively; (2) ensuring harmonious working relations between employees and managers; and (3) maintaining a safe, healthy work environment.

**Development** is a function whose objective is to preserve and enhance employees' competence in their jobs through improving their knowledge, skills, abilities, and other characteristics; HR specialists use the term "competencies" to refer to these items.

**Adjustment** comprises activities intended to maintain compliance with the organization's HR policies (e.g., through discipline) and business strategies (e.g., cost leadership).

**Managing change** is an ongoing process whose objective is to enhance the ability of an organization to anticipate and respond to developments in its external and internal environments, and to enable employees at all levels to cope with the changes.

Needless to say, these activities can be carried out at the individual, work-team, or larger organizational unit (e.g., department) level. Sometimes they are initiated by the organization (e.g., recruitment efforts or management development programs), and sometimes they are initiated by the individual or work team (e.g., voluntary retirement, safety improvements). Whatever the case, the responsibilities for carrying out these activities are highly interrelated. Together, these activities constitute the **HRM system.** To understand how each of the major activities within HRM relates to every other one, consider the following scenario.

As a result of a large number of unexpected early retirements, the Hand Corporation finds that it must recruit extensively to fill the vacated jobs. The firm is well aware of the rapid changes that will be occurring in its business over the next 5 to 10 years, so it must change its recruiting strategy in accordance with the expected changes in job requirements. It also must develop selection procedures that will identify the kinds of competencies required of future employees. Compensation policies and procedures may have to change because job requirements will change, and new incentive systems will probably have to be developed. Since the firm cannot identify all the competencies that will be required 5 to 10 years from now, it will have to offer new training and development programs along the way to satisfy those needs. Assessment procedures will necessarily change as well, because different competencies will be required in order to function effectively at work. As a result of carrying out all this activity, the firm may need to discharge, promote, or transfer some employees to accomplish its mission, and it will have to provide mechanisms to enable all remaining employees to cope effectively with the changed environment.

It is surprising how that single event, an unexpectedly large number of early retirees, can change the whole ballgame. So it is with any system or network of interrelated components. Changes in any single part of the system have a reverberating effect on all other parts of the system. Simply knowing that this will occur is healthy because then we will not make the mistake of confining our problems to only one part. We will recognize and expect that whether we are dealing with problems of staffing, training, compensation, or labor relations, all parts are interrelated. In short, the systems approach provides a conceptual framework for integrating the various components within the system and for linking the HRM system with larger organizational needs.

To some, the activities of staffing, retention, development, and adjustment are the special responsibilities of the HR department. But these responsibilities also lie within the core of every manager's job throughout any organization and because line managers have **authority** (the organizationally granted right to influence the actions and behavior of the workers they manage), they have considerable impact on the ways workers actually behave.

Thus a broad objective of HRM is to optimize the usefulness (i.e., the productivity) of all workers in an organization. A special objective of the HR department is to help line managers manage those workers more effectively. As Jack Welch, legendary former CEO of General Electric noted: "Look, HR should be every company's 'killer app.' What could possibly be more important than who gets hired, developed, promoted, or moved out the door? Business is a game, and as with all games, the team that puts the best people on the field and gets them playing together wins. It's that simple."[2]

This is consistent with the findings of a recent survey by the Economist Intelligence Unit (EIU), based on responses from 555 senior executives from 68 countries.[3] Findings revealed two of the most important human capital challenges that organizations everywhere are facing: (1) recruitment and retention of high-quality people across multiple territories, particularly as competition

| Table 1–2 | | |
|---|---|---|

**HRM ACTIVITIES AND THE RESPONSIBILITIES OF LINE MANAGERS AND THE HR DEPARTMENT**

| Activity | Line management responsibility | HR department responsibility |
|---|---|---|
| Staffing | Providing data for job or competency analyses and minimum qualifications; integrating strategic plans with HR plans; interviewing candidates, integrating information collected by the HR department, making final decisions on entry-level hires and promotions | Job/competency analysis, workforce planning, recruitment; compliance with civil rights laws and regulations; application forms, written tests, performance tests, interviews, background investigations, reference checks, physical examinations |
| Retention | Fair treatment of employees, open communication, face-to-face resolution of conflict, promotion of teamwork, respect for the dignity of each individual, pay increases based on merit | Compensation and benefits, employee relations, health and safety, employee services |
| Development | On-the-job training, job enrichment, coaching, applied motivational strategies, performance feedback to subordinates | Development of legally sound performance management systems, morale surveys, technical training; management and organizational development; career planning, counseling; HR research |
| Adjustment | Discipline, discharge, layoffs, transfers | Investigation of employee complaints, outplacement services, retirement counseling |
| Managing change | Provide a vision of where the company or unit is going and the resources to make the vision a reality | Provide expertise to facilitate the overall process of managing change |

for top talent grows more intense; and (2) improving the appeal of the company culture and working environment. Meeting these challenges is a responsibility that is shared by the HR department and line managers, as shown in Table 1–2.

In the context of Table 1–2, note how line and HR managers share people-related business activities. Generally speaking, HR provides the technical expertise in each area, while line managers (or, in some cases, self-directed work teams) use this expertise in order to manage people effectively. In a small business, however, line managers are responsible for both the technical and managerial aspects of HRM. In a 2011 survey of chief HR officers, one described his or her greatest challenge as follows: "Creating a true sense of ownership among the senior leaders regarding their roles as "Chief Talent Officers." Recognizing that having the right people in critical leadership roles is not an HR thing, or responsibility, but rather it is a business imperative and must be truly owned by the leaders of the respective businesses/functions."[4]

## WHY DOES EFFECTIVE HRM MATTER?

At a broad level, HRM is concerned with choices—choices that organizations make from a wide variety of possible policies, practices, and structures for managing employees.[5] More specifically, there exists a substantial and growing body of research evidence showing a strong connection between how firms manage their people and the economic results they achieve. For example, a 2011 meta-analysis (a quantitative summary of empirical results) included 66 studies with 68 samples involving 12,163 observations.[6] Results indicated that the average correlation between measures of human capital (e.g., the executive experience of the top-management team) and measures of performance (e.g., profitability, customer satisfaction), was 0.21. Results were even stronger for studies that used specific measures of human capital, as opposed to general measures, and for those that relied on operational performance measures (e.g., innovation, customer-service satisfaction) rather than global performance measures (e.g., return on assets, return on sales).

Another 2011 study done by accounting professors at Wharton and Stanford used data from 153 publicly traded companies to assess the impact of several HR management practices on stock returns 12 months later.[7] They found that a 10 percent increase in a measure of goal-setting activity at firms was associated with a 6 percent increase in industry-adjusted stock returns. A 6 percent stock boost also was associated with a 10 percent increase in a measure of the extent to which managers used the full spectrum of the rating scale when evaluating employees. In short, managers in companies that are clear with employees about work expectations and that provide honest feedback on a regular basis drive successful performance. Needless to say, the extent to which these practices actually will pay off depends on the skill and care with which the many HR practices available are implemented to solve real business problems and to support a firm's operating and strategic initiatives.

Such high-performance work practices provide a number of important sources of enhanced organizational performance.[8] People work harder because of the increased involvement and commitment that comes from having more control and say in their work. They work smarter because they are encouraged to build skills and competence. They work more responsibly because their employers place more responsibility in the hands of employees farther down in the organization. What's the bottom line in all of this? HR systems have important, practical impacts on the survival and financial performance of firms, and on the productivity and quality of work life of the people in them.

Now that we know what HRM is, and why it matters, the next step is to understand some significant features of the competitive business environment in which HRM activities take place. Four such features are globalization, technology, e-commerce, and demographic changes.

## FEATURES OF THE COMPETITIVE BUSINESS ENVIRONMENT

### Globalization

At its core, the **globalization** of business refers to the free movement of capital, goods, services, ideas, information, and people across national boundaries. Markets in every country have become fierce battlegrounds where both domestic and foreign competitors fight for market share. For example, Coca-Cola earns more than 75 percent of its revenues from outside the United States! The top 5 of the 500 largest firms in the world (Walmart Stores, Royal Dutch Shell, Exxon Mobil, BP, and Toyota) gross almost $1.5 trillion; the top 5 in profits (Gazprom, Exxon Mobil, Industrial and Commercial Bank of China, BP, and China Construction Bank) make more than $94 billion in profits; and the top 5 biggest employers (Walmart Stores, China National Petroleum, State Grid Corporation China, U.S. Postal Service, and Sinopec) employ more than 6.5 million people.[9]

***The Backlash against Globalization.***   In no small part, the booming economies of recent years in developed countries have been fueled by globalization. Open borders have allowed new ideas and technology to flow freely around the globe, accelerating productivity growth and allowing companies to be more competitive than they have been in decades. Yet there is a growing fear on the part of many people that globalization benefits big companies instead of average citizens, as stagnating wages and growing job insecurity in developed countries create rising disenchantment. In theory, less-developed countries win from globalization because they get jobs making low-cost products for rich countries. Rich countries win because, in addition to being able to buy inexpensive imports, they also can sell more sophisticated products like financial services to emerging economies. The problem, according to many experts, is that workers in the West are not equipped for today's pace of change, in which jobs come and go and skills can quickly become redundant.[10] In the public eye, multinational corporations are synonymous with globalization. In all of their far-flung operations, therefore, they bear responsibility to be good corporate citizens, to preserve the environment, to uphold labor standards, to provide decent working conditions and competitive wages, to treat their employees fairly, and to contribute to the communities in which they operate. Doing so will make a strong case for continued globalization.

***Implications of Globalization for HRM.***   Globalization is a fact of organizational life, as countries, companies, and workers are interconnected as never before. Global trade connects the fate of every industry and laborer, no matter how small or seemingly self-sufficient, to the decisions of bureaucrats in China, shipbuilders in Korea, and bankers everywhere.[11] To illustrate, consider how the ripple effects of the Japanese earthquake of 2011 affected auto manufacturers. When the quake shut down parts suppliers in Japan, assembly of General Motors vehicles in Shreveport, LA, and Buffalo, NY, also shut down, and workers were laid off. Production slowdowns in Spain, France, and Germany affected GM, Toyota, and PSA Peugeot-Citroën.[12]

Another feature of globalization is that cheap labor and plentiful resources, combined with ease of travel and communication, have created global labor markets. This is fueling mobility as more companies expand abroad and people consider foreign postings as a natural part of their professional development. Beyond the positive effects that such circulation of talent brings to both developed and developing countries, it enables employment opportunities well beyond the borders of one's home country. This means that competition for talent will come not only from the company down the street, but also from the employer on the other side of the world. It will be a seller's market, with talented individuals having many choices. Countries as well as companies will need to brand themselves as employers of choice in order to attract this talent.[13]

Along with these trends, expect to see three more. The first is increasing workforce flux, as more roles are automated or outsourced, and more workers are contract-based, are mobile, or work flexible hours. This may allow companies to leverage global resources more efficiently, but it also will increase the complexity of management's role. Second, expect more diversity as workers come from a greater range of backgrounds. Those with local knowledge of an emerging market, a global outlook, and an intuitive sense of the corporate culture will be particularly valued. Not surprisingly, talented young people will more frequently choose their employers based, at least in part, on opportunities to gain international experience. Finally, technical skills, while mandatory, will be less defining of the successful manager than the ability to work across cultures and to build relationships with many different constituents.[14]

## Technology

It is no exaggeration to say that modern technology is changing the ways we live and work. Consider the number of mobile phone users in just three nations: China (900 million), India (800 million), and the United States (303 million). That is more than 2 billion in just three countries![15] The information revolution will transform everything it touches—and it will touch everything. Information and ideas are keys to the new creative economy because every country, every company, and every individual depends increasingly on knowledge. People are cranking out computer programs and inventions, while lightly staffed factories churn out the sofas, the breakfast cereals, and the cell phones. Fortunately, history shows that technology-driven job destruction does not decrease overall employment—even while making some jobs obsolete. Ultimately,

New technology has changed the ways we work.

the economic growth created by new jobs overwhelms the drag from jobs destroyed.[16] Perhaps author Thomas Friedman of *The World Is Flat* expressed the effects of technology best when he wrote:

> You know the "IT revolution" that the business press has been touting for the last 20 years? Sorry, but that was only the prologue. The last 20 years were just about forging, sharpening, and distributing all the new tools with which to collaborate and connect. *Now* the real IT revolution is about to begin, as all the complementarities between these tools start to really work together to level the playing field.[17]

In the creative economy, however, the most important intellectual property is not software or music. Rather, it is the intellectual capital that resides in people. When assets were physical things like coal mines, shareholders truly owned them. But when the most vital assets are people, there can be no true ownership. The best that corporations can do is to create an environment that makes the best people want to stay.[18] Therein lies the challenge of managing human resources.

***Impact of New Technology on HRM.*** If they have not done so already, HR professionals will need to recognize collaborative technology as a key component of their firms' global hiring strategy—leveraging social-networking sites and researching which sites are most effective in each market. However, the most central use of technology in HRM is an organization's **human resources information system** (HRIS). Indeed, as technology integrates with traditionally labor-intensive HR activities, HR professionals are seeing improvements in response time and efficiency of the report information available. Dozens of vendors offer HRIS applications ranging from benefits enrollment to applicant tracking, time and attendance records, training and development, payroll, pension plans, and employee surveys. Such systems are moving beyond simply storing and retrieving information to include broader applications such as report generation, succession planning, strategic planning, career planning, and evaluating HR policies and practices.[19] In that sense, today's HRIS tools help with management control and decision making.

### E-Commerce

Consider this forecast:

> The Internet will change the relationship between consumers and producers in ways more profound than you can yet imagine. The Internet is not just another marketing channel; it's not just another advertising medium; it's not just a way to speed up transactions. The Internet is the foundation for a new industrial order. The Internet will empower consumers like nothing else ever has. . . . The Web will fundamentally change customers' expectations about convenience, speed, comparability, price, and service.[20]

Today, electronic commerce (e-commerce) encompasses a very wide range of business activities and processes, from e-banking to offshore manufacturing to e-logistics. In fact, the ever-growing dependence of modern industries on electronically enabled business processes gave impetus to the growth and development of supporting systems, for example, broadband and fiber-optic networks, supply-chain management software, customer-relationship management software, inventory-control systems, and financial-accounting software.[21]

Whether it's business-to-business (B2B) or business-to-consumer (B2C), e-commerce has taken off, with a compound annual growth rate exceeding 20 percent from 2000–2009 in the United States alone.[22] E-commerce companies that understand what consumers want and can deliver it are growing at a rate that few other consumer businesses their size have ever attained. As an example, consider search engine Google. Google makes hundreds of millions of dollars selling advertising that is keyed to the words that people search for. Advertisers only pay if people click. Advertisers like that model because they know exactly who looked at their ads, and they only pay if their ads are seen. As of 2011, online advertising generated $55 billion in revenues—and it is gaining momentum.[23]

The Internet is now a major factor in pricing. Retail e-commerce sites cut consumer prices by pitting a multitude of sellers against one another, allowing Web-surfing buyers to identify quickly the lowest possible price for any good. Web-based search engines provide buyers with more information—and bargaining power—about products than ever before. Industries like books, music, and travel led the way. Jewelry, online bill payments, telecom, hotels, real estate, and software are following close behind.[24]

As you read this, however, and as you ponder the future of e-commerce, consider one inescapable fact: All of the people who make e-commerce possible are knowledge workers. The organizations they work for still have to address the human resource challenges of attracting, retaining, and motivating them to perform well.

## Demographic Changes and Increasing Cultural Diversity

The number as well as the mix of people available to work is changing rapidly, as Figures 1–1 and 1–2 illustrate. As Figure 1–1 shows, there will be a precipitous drop in the growth of the labor force among prime-age employees between 2006 and 2016. Over the next four decades, non-Hispanic whites will be a slim majority of the U.S. population. Hispanics will make up nearly a quarter of the population, with Asians, African Americans, and, to a much lesser extent, Native Americans, comprising the rest (see Figure 1–2). Currently, female participation has jumped to 60 percent from 50 percent two decades ago, and the long-term trend toward earlier retirement has recently

**Figure 1–1**

Projected percentage change in labor force by age, 2006–2016. (*Source:* U.S. Bureau of Labor Statistics (July 31, 2008). *Projected growth in labor force participation of seniors, 2006–2016*. Retrieved from *http://www.bls. gov/opub/ted/2008/ jul/wk4/art04.htm*.)

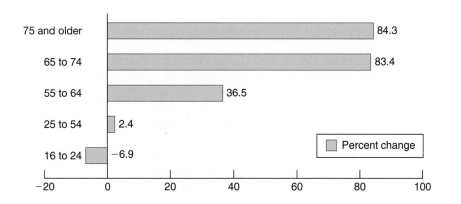

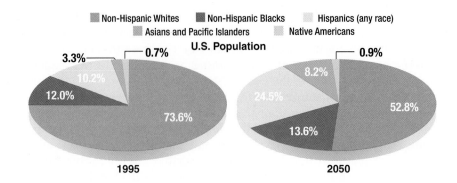

**Figure 1–2**

U.S. population by age and race, 2000 and 2050. (*Source:* U.S. Census Bureau.)

been reversed. The average retirement age is now 64. Seventy-five percent of retirees want to launch new careers after that, and 42 percent of those want to cycle between periods of work and leisure.[25]

***Implications for HRM.*** These trends have two key implications for managers: (1) The reduced supply of workers (at least in some fields) will make finding and keeping employees a top priority. (2) The task of managing a culturally diverse workforce, of harnessing the motivation and efforts of a wide variety of workers, will present a continuing challenge to management.

The organizations that thrive will be the ones that embrace the new demographic trends instead of fighting them. That will mean even more women and minorities in the workforce—and in the boardrooms as well. Workforce diversity is not just a competitive advantage. Today it's a competitive necessity.

## RESPONSES OF FIRMS TO THE NEW COMPETITIVE REALITIES

In today's world of fast-moving global markets and fierce competition, the windows of opportunity are often frustratingly brief.[26] "Three-C" logic (i.e., command, control, compartmentalized information) dominated industrial society's approach to organizational design throughout the 19th and 20th centuries, but trends such as the following are accelerating the shift toward new forms of organization in the early part of the 21st century:[27]

- The shift from vertically integrated hierarchies to networks of specialists.
- The decline of routine work (sewing-machine operators, telephone operators, word processors) coupled with the expansion of complex jobs that require flexibility, creativity, and the ability to work well with people (managers, software-applications engineers, artists, and designers).
- Pay tied less to a person's position or tenure in an organization and more to the market value of his or her skills.
- A change in the paradigm of doing business from making a product to providing a service, often by part-time or temporary employees.
- Outsourcing of activities that are not core competencies of a firm (e.g., payroll, benefits administration, relocation services).
- The redefinition of work itself: constant learning, more higher-order thinking, less nine-to-five mentality.

In response to these changes, many firms are doing one or more of the following: developing new forms of organization, restructuring (including downsizing), adopting quality-management programs, reengineering work processes, and building flexibility into work schedules and rules. Let's briefly consider each of these.

## New Forms of Organization

One example of a new organizational form that is evolving from these changes is the **virtual organization,** where teams of specialists come together to work on a project—as in the movie industry—and then disband when the project is finished. Virtual organizations are already quite popular in consulting, in legal defense, and in sponsored research. They are multisite, multiorganizational, and dynamic.[28] More common in the information age, however, is the **virtual workplace** in which employees operate remotely from each other and from managers.[29] They work anytime, anywhere—in real space or in cyberspace. The widespread availability of e-mail, teleconferencing, collaborative software, and intranets (within-company information networks) facilitates such arrangements. Compelling business reasons, such as reduced real estate expenses, increased productivity, higher profits, improved customer service, access to global markets, and environmental benefits drive their implementation. Jobs in sales, marketing, project engineering, and consulting seem to be best suited for virtual workplaces because individuals in these jobs already work with their clients by phone, or at the clients' premises. Such jobs are service- and knowledge-oriented, dynamic, and evolve according to customer requirements.

A third example of a new organizational form is the *modular corporation*—that's right, modular. The basic idea is to focus on a few core competencies—those a company does best, such as designing and marketing computers or copiers—and to outsource everything else to a network of suppliers.[30] If design and marketing are core competencies, then manufacturing or service units are modular components. They can be added or taken away with the flexibility of switching parts in a child's LEGO set. Companies are outsourcing work within their home countries (onshore), near their home countries (nearshore), and far from their home countries (offshore). At a global level, firms are spending enormous sums of money on outsourcing and offshoring (offshore outsourcing), as Figure 1–3 shows.

The fact is, the work processes in practically every big department of a corporation can now be outsourced and managed to some degree offshore. Here is an example of how truck-leasing company Penske and India's Genpact collaborate on one process.[31]

1. When Penske buys a truck and leases it in the United States, Genpact's Indian staff remotely secures state titles, registrations, and permits electronically.
2. After the truck is returned, the driver's log and taxes, fuel, and toll documents are sent to Genpact. The paperwork is forwarded to Genpact's office in Juarez, Mexico. There, the staff enters data from the driver's logs in Penske's computer system.
3. Workers in Genpact's office in Hyderabad, India, then process all the data for tax filings and accounting.

## Figure 1–3

The modular corporation.

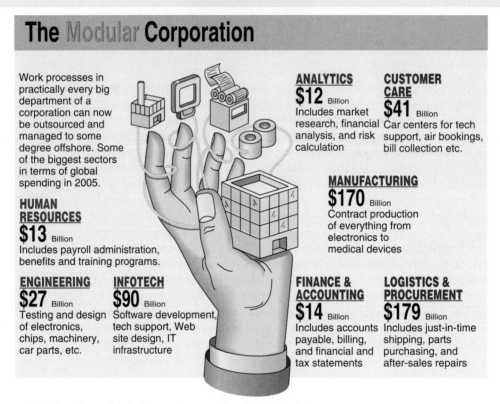

# The Modular Corporation

Work processes in practically every big department of a corporation can now be outsourced and managed to some degree offshore. Some of the biggest sectors in terms of global spending in 2005.

**ANALYTICS**
**$12** Billion
Includes market research, financial analysis, and risk calculation

**CUSTOMER CARE**
**$41** Billion
Car centers for tech support, air bookings, bill collection etc.

**HUMAN RESOURCES**
**$13** Billion
Includes payroll administration, benefits and training programs.

**MANUFACTURING**
**$170** Billion
Contract production of everything from electronics to medical devices

**ENGINEERING**
**$27** Billion
Testing and design of electronics, chips, machinery, car parts, etc.

**INFOTECH**
**$90** Billion
Software development, tech support, Web site design, IT infrastructure

**FINANCE & ACCOUNTING**
**$14** Billion
Includes accounts payable, billing, and financial and tax statements

**LOGISTICS & PROCUREMENT**
**$179** Billion
Includes just-in-time shipping, parts purchasing, and after-sales repairs

*Source:* Engardio, P. (2006, Jan. 30). The future of outsourcing. *BusinessWeek,* p. 55.

The number of people involved in the remote, global workforce is staggering. According to one estimate, it comprises hundreds of millions of people, and it is growing at many times the rate of the traditional workforce.[32] The implication? The global search for talent must focus increasingly on building remote capacity, as opposed to recruiting foreign talent to domestic shores. Leaders need to focus laser-like attention on attracting, deploying, and keeping a workforce that is as good as or better than that of the competition. In the long run, all other threats and opportunities pale by comparison. As an example, consider General Electric. In 2000, about 30 percent of GE's business was overseas; today, 60 percent is. In 2000, 46 percent of GE employees were overseas; today, 54 percent are.[33]

### Restructuring, Including Downsizing

**Restructuring** can assume a variety of forms, of which employment downsizing is probably the most common. Companies can restructure by selling or buying plants or lines of business by altering reporting relationships, or by laying off employees. **Downsizing,** the planned elimination of positions or jobs, has had, and will continue to have, profound effects on organizations, managers at all levels, employees, labor markets, customers, and shareholders.[34] Based on the type of restructuring in question, one study examined restructuring's effects on profitability and stock returns of 500 representative companies listed on the New York Stock Exchange (Standard & Poor's 500) over an 18-year period (1982–2000). (Companies are included in the S&P 500 because of their size and financial contribution to the market.)

The study began by classifying the companies each year as stable employers, employment or asset downsizers, or employment or asset upsizers. Researchers observed the subsequent effects over the following three years.[35] In terms of profitability (return on assets) all categories of downsizers generated lower returns on assets than either stable employers or upsizers in the year prior to the announcement of the layoffs, in the year in which the layoffs occurred, and in the two subsequent years. This conclusion held up on an industry-adjusted basis, as well.

In terms of stock performance, on an industry-adjusted basis, only the asset upsizers yielded returns that were significantly higher than those of all other groups, including stable employers. The cumulative total return by the end of year two for a $1 investment was $1.69 for stable employers, $1.72 for both employment and asset downsizers, and $2.42 for asset upsizers.

Employment downsizers reduced their work forces by an average of 11%. Relative to their industries, they were able to attain a return on assets that was only 0.3% above their industry average by year two. The benefits of downsizing seem small when compared to the human cost. The message to employers is clear: Don't try to shrink your way to prosperity. Instead, the best way to prosper is by growing your business.

## Quality-Management Programs

One of the best known quality-management programs is **Six Sigma.**[36] Six Sigma originated at Motorola in 1986, and became a staple of corporate life in the 1990s after it was embraced by GE. Its goal is to reduce variability from a process (no more than 3.4 defects per million) in order to avoid errors (defects) and increase predictability. It is based on five steps: define, measure, analyze, improve, and control, or DMAIC (pronounced "dee-may-ic"). Originally invented as a way to improve quality, Six Sigma's main value to corporations today lies in its ability to save time and money. According to the American Society for Quality, 82 of the 100 largest companies in the United States—companies as varied as DuPont, Textron, Bank of America, and Sun Microsystems—have embraced Six Sigma. Yet there is an inherent tension between innovation and efficiency. Whereas process excellence demands precision, consistency, and repetition, innovation calls for variation, failure, and serendipity. As the emphasis shifts to today's idea-based, creative economy, Six Sigma may be less appropriate in companies like Google and 3M, which have the long-term strategy to dream up innovations.[37]

Unfortunately, quality-management programs have not been the final answer to customer satisfaction and productivity improvement. In many cases managers view quality as a quick fix and are disillusioned when results prove difficult to achieve. It generally takes three to five years before quality-management programs become institutionalized,[38] and some CEOs and managers are unwilling to make that kind of commitment. When such initiatives do work, however, it is often because managers have made major changes to their philosophies and HR programs. In fact, organizations known for the quality of their products and services strongly believe that employees are key to those results.[39]

## Reengineering

Some organizations have moved to a more comprehensive approach to redesigning business processes called reengineering. **Reengineering** is the fundamental rethinking and radical redesign of business processes to achieve dramatic improvements in cost, quality, and speed.[40] A **process** is a collection of activities (such as procurement, order fulfillment, product development, or credit issuance), that takes one or more kinds of input and creates an output that is of value to a customer. Customers may be internal or external. Consider credit issuance as an example. Instead of the separate jobs of credit checker and pricer, the two may be combined into one "deal structurer." Such integrated processes may cut response time and increase efficiency and productivity. Employees involved in the process are responsible for ensuring that customers' requirements are met on time and with no defects, and they are empowered to experiment in ways that will cut cycle time and reduce costs. Result: Less supervision is needed, while workers take on broader responsibilities and a wider purview of activities.

HR issues are central to the reengineering of business processes.[41] Reengineering requires that managers create an environment and an organizational culture that embraces, rather than resists, change. The effectiveness of such efforts depends on effective leadership and communication, both of which are people-related business processes. In fact, changes in job analyses, selection, training, performance management, career planning, compensation, and labor relations are all necessary in order to complement and support reengineering efforts.

## Flexibility

Almost 40 percent of employed U.S. adults don't take all of the vacation days they earn for the year, although more working Generation Xers (born between 1965 and 1978) than baby boomers (born between 1946 and 1964) do.[42] Time is employees' most precious commodity, and they want the flexibility to control their own time—where, when, and how they work. They want balance in their lives between work and leisure. Flexibility in schedules is the key, as organizations strive to retain talented workers.[43]

In practice, the concept of "flexibility" reflects a broad spectrum of possible work arrangements, as Table 1–3 makes clear. Unfortunately, flexibility is frequently viewed by managers and employees as an exception or employee accommodation, rather than as a new and effective way of working to achieve business results. A face-time culture, excessive workload, manager skepticism,

## Table 1–3

### IMPLEMENTING FLEXIBILITY: A SPECTRUM OF PRACTICE

**Individual Accommodations**
Special arrangements, or "deals," are granted on a case-by-case basis and are often kept secret.

**Policies and Programs in Place**
Policies and programs exist, but flexibility is used only in "pockets" across the organization.

**Flexibility's Many Faces**
Widespread use of formal and informal flexibility meets business and individual needs.

**New Ways of Working**
A results-driven culture, where flexible work practices are utilized as a management strategy to achieve business results, ensues.

*Source:* Corporate Voices for Working Families (2011, February). *Business Impacts of Flexibility: An Imperative for Expansion* (Updated, 2011), p. 16. Retrieved from *www.cvwf. org/publication-toolkits/business-impacts-flexibility-imperative-expansion-updated-2011* on September 29, 2011.

customer demands, and fear of negative career consequences are among the barriers that prevent employees from taking advantage of policies they might otherwise use—and that prevent companies from realizing the full benefits that flexibility might bestow.[44]

Three features are keys to making the business case for increased flexibility: talent management (specifically, attraction and retention); human capital outcomes (increased satisfaction and commitment, decreased stress); and financial, operational, and business outcomes. Consider the first of these, attraction and retention.

At IBM, responses to a recent global work-life survey from almost 42,000 IBM employees in 79 countries revealed that lack of work-life fit—of which flexibility is a significant component—is the second leading reason for potentially leaving IBM, behind compensation and benefits. In the Corporate Finance organization, for example, 94 percent of all managers reported positive impacts of flexible work options on the company's ability to retain talented professionals. In light of these findings showing the strong link between flexibility and retention, IBM actively promotes flexibility as a strategy for retaining key talent. In Case 1–1 at the end of this chapter, we will see how Best Buy takes this concept even further.

People make organizations go. How the people are selected, trained, and managed determines to a large extent how successful an organization will be. As you can certainly appreciate by now, the task of managing people in today's world of work is particularly challenging in light of the competitive realities we have discussed. To survive, let alone compete, firms need a strategy for managing talent. General Electric Company (GE) is legendary for doing that well. The HR Buzz box on pages 20 and 21 shows how GE does it.

# ETHICAL DILEMMA
## Conflict between American and Foreign Cultural Values

Each chapter of this book contains a brief scenario that illustrates a decision-making situation that could result in a breach of acceptable behavior. Such situations pose ethical dilemmas. To be ethical is to conform to moral standards or to conform to the standards of conduct of a given profession or group (e.g., medicine, auditing). **Ethical decisions about behavior** take account not only of one's own interests but also, equally, the interests of those affected by a decision. What would you recommend in response to the following situation?[a]

You are the director of HR for a large, southwestern teaching hospital. This hospital has a cooperative program with a major teaching hospital in Saudi Arabia. Each year several doctors from your hospital spend the year in Saudi Arabia teaching and doing research. The stay in Saudi Arabia is generally considered both lucrative and professionally rewarding.

This morning you had a visit from two of the doctors in the hospital who had been rejected for assignment to Saudi Arabia. They were very upset, as they are both very qualified and ambitious. You had carefully explained to them that although the selection committee was impressed with their abilities, the members had decided that because they were Jewish, it would be best if they were disqualified from consideration. In spite of vigorous protest from the two doctors, you had held your ground and supported the committee's decision. However, as you sit at home reading that evening, the situation replays itself in your mind, and you think about the decision and feel a little uncertain.

Is the director of HR correct in supporting the committee's decision? What criteria should the committee, and the director of HR, use to make a decision such as this? What would you recommend?

---

[a]Taylor, S., and Eder, R. W. (2000). U.S. expatriates and the Civil Rights Act of 1991: Dissolving boundaries. In M. Mendenhall and G. Oddou (Eds.), *Readings and Cases in International Human Resource Management* (3rd ed.). Cincinnati, OH: South-Western College Publishing, pp. 251–279.

## NURTURING LEADERS AT GENERAL ELECTRIC COMPANY[a]

On the eve of his retirement after 40 years with GE, the last 13 as head of HR, William J. Conaty, architect of GE's new vision of global leadership, shared seven secrets for nurturing leaders. Here they are.

**Dare to Differentiate.**   Conaty advises: Relentlessly assess and grade employees to build organizational vitality and to foster a true meritocracy. The knowledge that one is being measured against his or her peers helps boost performance. "We want to create angst in the system," he says.

**Constantly Raise the Bar.**   According to Conaty, leaders continually seek to improve performance, both their own and their team members'. "The one reason executives fail at GE is they stop learning. The job grows, accountability grows, and the people don't grow with it." GE employees think so highly of continuous learning that they consider training courses to be rewards.

**Don't Be Friends with the Boss.**   "The HR leader locks in with the CEO and the rest of the organization thinks the HR leader isn't trustworthy and can't be a confidant," Conaty explains. Although he deliberately socializes with other

---

[a]Brady, D. (2007, Apr. 9). Secrets of an HR superstar. *BusinessWeek*, pp. 66, 67.

colleagues at functions, Conaty is totally candid with leaders in private. CEO Jeff Immelt remarked, "I call Bill the 'first friend'—the guy that could walk in my office and kick my butt when it needed to be."

**Become Easy to Replace.**    Conaty believes that great leaders develop great succession plans and that insecure leaders are intimidated by them. So, at GE, leaders are judged by the strength of their teams and are rewarded for mentoring people throughout the organization. Conaty's own successor is someone he mentored through the HR department at GE, a fact he takes pride in.

**Be Inclusive.**    Conaty admits, within every organization there's a tendency to favor people you know. He believes that can undermine success. Take acquisitions, for example. GE has learned to rigorously assess the talent within companies before they are even acquired. Conaty elaborates, "We make special provisions to make 'top talent' feel financially welcome as well as emotionally welcome. Our GE people can't be the victors in these deals."

**Free up Others to Do Their Jobs.**    Conaty advises: Give people the tools and permission to work on their own terms. Take Sharon R. Daley, a senior HR executive who turned down a promotion to spend more time with her kids. GE worked with her, allowing her to work part time until she was ready to take on more responsibility. She eventually rose to company officer and top industry HR executive.

**Keep It Simple.**    Says Conaty, "You can't move 325,000 people with mixed messages and thousands of initiatives. Leaders succeed by being consistent and straightforward about a handful of core messages. And the best don't get derailed when times get tough. . . . Everyone experiences failure now and then. It's how you handle it that matters."

Each chapter of this book focuses on a different aspect of HRM and considers its impact on three important outcomes: productivity, quality of work life, and profits. In the next two sections we will examine the concepts of productivity and quality of work life. In the next chapter we will focus on the contribution of effective HRM to profits.

## PRODUCTIVITY: WHAT IS IT AND WHY IS IT IMPORTANT?

In general, **productivity** is a measure of the output of goods and services relative to the input of labor, capital, and equipment. The more productive an industry, the better its competitive position because its unit costs are lower. When productivity increases, businesses can pay higher wages without boosting inflation. As Figure 1–4 illustrates, nations vary significantly in terms of productivity, expressed as gross domestic product per person employed (in US$). Evidence indicates that innovative HR practices in manufacturing (e.g., production ideas drawn from nonmanagerial employees, job rotation, tying pay to performance) may account for as much as 89 percent of the growth in what economists call "multifactor" productivity—a measure of how businesses enhance production by combining workers and machines using technology, production processes, and managerial practices.[45]

Improving productivity is not working harder; it is working smarter. Today's world demands that we do more with less—fewer people, less money, less time, less space, and fewer resources in general. These ideas are shown graphically in Figure 1–5 and illustrated in the HR Buzz on page 23.

## Figure 1–4

Overall productivity, expressed as GDP per person employed, in US$, ranks 1–10 and 39–49.

(*Source:* Nation-Master.com, "PPP (most recent) by country," *http://www.nationmaster.com/graph/eco_ove_pro_ppp-economy-overall-productivity-ppp* accessed August 1, 2011. Permission granted by *IMD, World Competitiveness Yearbook 2011,* http://www.imd.org/wcc"www.imd.org/wcy.)

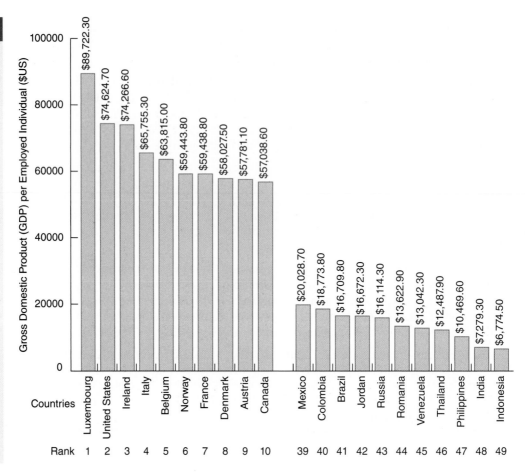

Gross Domestic Product (GDP) per Employed Individual ($US)

| Country | GDP | Rank |
|---|---|---|
| Luxembourg | $89,722.30 | 1 |
| United States | $74,624.70 | 2 |
| Ireland | $74,266.60 | 3 |
| Italy | $65,755.30 | 4 |
| Belgium | $63,815.00 | 5 |
| Norway | $59,443.80 | 6 |
| France | $59,438.80 | 7 |
| Denmark | $58,027.50 | 8 |
| Austria | $57,781.10 | 9 |
| Canada | $57,038.60 | 10 |
| Mexico | $20,028.70 | 39 |
| Colombia | $18,773.80 | 40 |
| Brazil | $16,709.80 | 41 |
| Jordan | $16,672.30 | 42 |
| Russia | $16,114.30 | 43 |
| Romania | $13,622.90 | 44 |
| Venezuela | $13,042.30 | 45 |
| Thailand | $12,487.90 | 46 |
| Philippines | $10,469.60 | 47 |
| India | $7,279.30 | 48 |
| Indonesia | $6,774.50 | 49 |

## Figure 1–5

More productive organizations get more goods and services out of a given amount of labor, capital, and equipment than do less productive organizations.

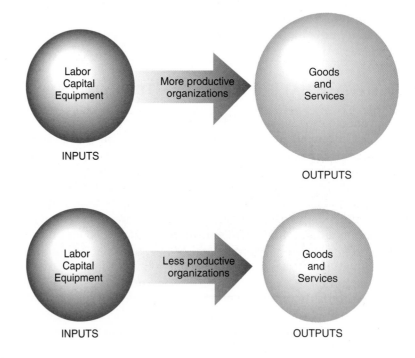

## ONE TRUCK A MINUTE AT FORD'S KANSAS CITY PLANT[a]

Ford's Kansas City automobile plant is one of the largest in the United States, turning out more than 490,000 F-150 pickup trucks, Ford Escapes, and Mazda Tributes each year. The plant is "flexible," meaning that with just a little tweaking it can produce any kind of car that Ford makes. Mostly it produces F-150s, the best-selling vehicle of any kind in the United States for the past 22 years. The new model has so many options, including a paint called Screaming Yellow, that there are more than one million possible combinations.

In a flexible plant, each vehicle is assigned a metal pallet on which it will be built. The pallet has a reprogrammable ID card that contains data on the vehicle-to-be. Parts arrive four to six hours before they're installed, in the sequence in which they will be used. Assembly is synchronized by computers down to the last rear-view mirror. As an example, consider the 11 people who attach suspensions to vehicle frames. Every task they do is listed on a computer printout posted at each workstation. They have 57.5 seconds to get their jobs done.

Ford is making a company-wide shift to flexible manufacturing. Doing so will enable it to save $2 billion over the next 10 years. When plant manager Dave Savchetz was asked what's changed over the years he replied: "We didn't have robots and computers 30 years ago." To a manager, the basic concepts haven't changed, so the magnitude of the operation still overwhelms Savchetz (the plant covers 18 acres). But what impresses him most, he says, is the way that auto-manufacturing facilities, such as the one in Kansas City, have made giant, often unnoticed leaps in productivity in order to stay competitive in the modern marketplace. How big a leap? The plant produces one truck a minute.

Automation has revolutionized automobile assembly.

[a]David, G. (2004, Apr. 5). One truck a minute: Ford's Kansas City factory builds more vehicles than any other assembly plant in the country. Here's how it gets done. *Fortune*, p. 255. From *Fortune* Magazine, April 5, 2004, © 2004 Time Inc. Used under license.

Greater productivity benefits organizations directly (i.e., it improves their competitive position relative to that of rivals), and it benefits workers indirectly (e.g., in higher pay and improved purchasing power). Many workers, however, want to see a tighter connection between working smarter and the tangible and psychological rewards they receive from doing their jobs well. They want to see significant improvements in their quality of work life.

## QUALITY OF WORK LIFE: WHAT IS IT?

There are two ways of looking at what **quality of work life (QWL)** means.[46] One way equates QWL with a set of objective organizational conditions and practices (e.g., promotion-from-within policies, democratic supervision, employee involvement, safe working conditions). The other way equates QWL with employees' perceptions that they are safe and relatively well satisfied, they have reasonable work-life balance, and they are able to grow and develop as human beings. This way relates QWL to the degree to which the full range of human needs is met.

In many cases, these two views merge: Workers who like their organizations and the ways their jobs are structured will feel that their work fulfills them. In such cases, either way of looking at one's quality of work life will lead to a common determination of whether a good QWL exists. However, because people differ and because the second view is quite subjective—it concedes, for example, that not everyone finds such things as democratic decision making and telework to be important components of a good QWL—we will define QWL in terms of employees' perceptions of their physical and mental well-being at work.

In theory, QWL is simple: It involves giving workers the opportunity to make decisions about the design of their jobs and workplaces, and what they need to make products or to deliver services most effectively. Of course, what workers want varies by country. It's competitive base pay in the United States, career opportunities in Brazil, chances to learn in China, challenging work in Japan, and work-life balance in Spain.[47]

Innovation, flexibility, individualism, flat organizational structures, and challenging roles for all are hallmarks of the new, creative economy. Success requires a willingness to share power, extensive training for workers and managers, and continuous experimentation with new ideas.[48]

None of this is simple or easily done, and it may take several years to become fully integrated into a business. Now that we understand the concepts of productivity and QWL, let's examine the impact of effective HRM on them as well as on the bottom line.

## BUSINESS TRENDS AND HR COMPETENCIES

Over the past decade, organizations have become more complex, dynamic, and fast-paced. As a result, senior managers recognize that attracting, retaining, and managing people effectively is more important than ever. In fact, the results of a recent study of more than 400 companies in North and South America, Europe, China, and Australia indicate that effective HR professionals play six key roles[49]:

1.  **Credible activists** deliver results with integrity, share information, build relationships of trust, take appropriate risks, provide candid observations,

## IMPACT OF EFFECTIVE HRM ON PRODUCTIVITY, QUALITY OF WORK LIFE, AND THE BOTTOM LINE

For most of the last two decades, downsizing set the tone for the modern employment contract. As companies frantically restructured to cope with slipping market share or heightened competition, they tore up old notions of paternalism. They told employees, "Don't expect to spend your life at one company anymore. You are responsible for your own career, so get all the skills you can and prepare to change jobs, employers, even industries. As for the implicit bond of loyalty that might have existed before, well, forget it. In these days of fierce global competition, loyalty is an unaffordable luxury."[a]

Today, faced with the retirements of large numbers of baby boomers, and impending labor shortages, employers have changed their tune. Now it's, "Don't leave. We need you. Work for us—you can build a career here." Employers are going to great lengths to persuade employees that they want them to stay for years. According to a recent survey, employees are less loyal to their companies, and they tend to put their own needs and interests above those of their employers. More often they are willing to trade off higher wages and benefits for flexibility and autonomy, job characteristics that allow them to balance their lives on and off the job. Almost 9 out of every 10 workers live with family members,

and nearly half care for dependents, including children, elderly parents, or ailing spouses.[b] Among employees who switched jobs in the last five years, pay and benefits rated in the bottom half of 20 possible reasons why they did so. Factors rated highest were "nature of work," "open communication," and "effect on personal/family life." What are the implications of these results? When companies fail to factor in quality-of-work-life issues and quality-of-life issues when introducing any of the popular schemes for improving productivity, the only thing they may gain is a view of the backs of their best people leaving for friendlier employers.[c]

---

[a]DeMeuse, K. P., and Dai, G. (In press.). Reducing costs and enhancing efficiency or damaging the company: Downsizing in today's global economy. In C. Cooper, A. Pandey, and J. C. Quick (Eds.). *Downsizing: Is Less Still More?* Cambridge, UK: Cambridge University Press.

[b]Galinsky, E., Aumann, K., and Bond, J. T. (2009). *Times Are Changing: Gender and Generation at Work and at Home.* New York, NY: Families and Work Institute. See also Lawler, E. E. III, and O'Toole, J. (2006). *The New American Workplace.* New York: Palgrave Macmillan.

[c]Spector, P. E., Cooper, C. L., Poelmans, S., Allen, T. D., O'Driscoll, M., Sanchez, J. I., Siu, O. L. et al. (2004). A cross-national comparative study of work/family stressors, working hours, and well-being. China and Latin America versus the Anglo world. *Personnel Psychology,* 57, pp. 119–142.

---

and influence others. They are admired and listened to, take positions, and challenge assumptions. This is the heart of what it takes to be an effective HR leader.

2. **Cultural stewards** recognize, articulate, and help shape company culture by facilitating change, helping employees find meaning in their work, managing work-life effectiveness, and encouraging innovation.

3. **Talent managers/organizational designers** ensure today's and tomorrow's talent, shape the organization, foster communication, and design reward systems. They do this by mastering theory, research, and practice in these areas.

4. **Strategy architects** know how to make the right changes happen. They execute changes in strategy, and energize others to accept and embrace the changes.

## IMPLICATIONS FOR MANAGEMENT PRACTICE

The trends we have reviewed in this chapter suggest that the old approaches to managing people may no longer be appropriate responses to economic or social reality. A willingness to experiment is healthy. To the extent that the newer approaches do enhance productivity, QWL, and profits, everybody wins. Competitive issues cannot simply be willed away, and because of this we may see even more radical experiments in organizations. The traditional role of the manager may be blurred further as workers take a greater and greater part in planning and controlling work, not simply doing what managers tell them to do. Take accounting firm Jefferson Wells, International (now owned by Manpower, Inc.).[a] Of its 2,000 employees, 10 percent work a flexible schedule, with benefits. A further 20 percent work even fewer hours, project by project, without benefits. The remaining 70 percent are full-time but still have a lot more control over their lives than is typical of the Big Four firms many come from, where travel schedules are often grueling. How does the firm do it? It is structured on a local-office model. Even when staff members are stationed in their clients' offices, the offices are usually within driving distance of home. The company relies on its commitment to work-life fit in order to attract top-caliber candidates to its auditing practice, and it will not hire anyone with fewer than seven years' experience. Programs such as these suggest that human resource management, an essential part of the jobs of all managers, will play an even more crucial role in the future world of work.

[a]Byrnes, N. (2005, Oct. 10). Treating part-timers like royalty. *BusinessWeek*, p. 78.

5. **Business allies** contribute to success by knowing how their businesses make money, who the customers are, and why customers buy the company's products and services. They are "business literate," for they understand the business and how it works, the financials, and the strategic issues.
6. **Operational executors** administer the day-to-day work of managing people by implementing workplace policies and advancing HR technology.

*Human Resource Management in Action: Conclusion*

## THE 21ST-CENTURY CORPORATION

Management systems that produce profits through people seem to share seven dimensions in common. Let's briefly examine each one.

1. **Employment security.** Such security is fundamental to most other high-performance management practices. The reason is that innovations in work practices or other forms of worker-management cooperation or productivity improvement are not likely to be sustained over time when workers fear that by increasing productivity they will work themselves out of a job. In addition, if the goal is to avoid layoffs, organizations will be motivated to hire sparingly in order to keep their labor forces smaller and more productive.
2. **Selective hiring.** This dimension has several prerequisites, the first of which is having a large applicant pool from which to select. Second, the organization

needs to be clear about the most critical skills and attributes in the applicant pool. At Southwest Airlines, for example, applicants for flight attendant positions are evaluated in interviews on the basis of initiative, judgment, adaptability, and ability to learn. Third, the skills and abilities sought should be consistent with particular job requirements and the organization's approach to the market (e.g., exceptional customer service). Fourth, interviewers screen for attributes that are difficult to change through training. For example, technical skills are easier to acquire than teamwork and a service attitude.

3. **Self-managed teams and decentralization are basic elements of organization design.** Teams substitute peer-based control for hierarchical control of work. They also make all of the people in a firm feel accountable and responsible for the operation and success of the enterprise, not just a few people in senior management. This increased sense of responsibility stimulates more initiative and effort on the part of everyone involved. By substituting peer for hierarchical control, teams permit removal of layers of hierarchy and the absorption of tasks previously performed by administrative specialists. The tremendously successful natural-foods grocery-store chain Whole Foods Markets is organized on the basis of teams. It attributes much of its success to that arrangement.

4. **Comparatively high compensation contingent on organizational performance.** It is simply not true that only certain industries can or should pay high wages. The extremely successful and profitable company SAS is the world's largest privately held software business and is ranked the #1 Best Company to Work For on Fortune magazine's 2010 and 2011 lists, SAS, the world's largest privately held software business and ranked the #1 best employer on *Fortune* magazine's 2010 and 2011 lists, yet it pays industry-average compensation plus profit sharing, in addition to offering eye-popping benefits to employees. Actually, compensation and benefits are only one part of a broader philosophy and culture that incorporates other practices such as training, information sharing, and delegation of responsibility. Perhaps that is why employee turnover at SAS is less than 4 percent, year after year.

5. **Extensive training.** Training is an essential component of high-performance work systems because these systems rely on front-line employee skills and initiative to identify and resolve problems, to initiate changes in work methods, and to take responsibility for quality. Firms such as the Men's Wearhouse (an off-price specialty retailer of men's tailored business attire and accessories) and Google use training as a source of competitive advantage. Google offers 100 hours of professional training per year to its employees. It is simply part and parcel of the overall management process of these firms.

6. **Reduced differences in status.** The fundamental premise of high-performance management systems is that organizations perform at a higher level when they are able to tap the ideas, skills, and efforts of all of their people. Reducing the status distinctions that separate individuals and groups—distinctions that cause some to feel less valued—helps make all members of an organization feel important and committed. Sam Walton, founder of Walmart, was one of the most underpaid CEOs in the United States. He wasn't poor, for he owned stock in his company. He also encouraged stock ownership for his employees. Having his fortune rise and fall along with those of other employees produces a sense of common fate and reduces status differences.

7. **Sharing of information.** The sharing of information on such things as financial performance, strategy, and operational measures conveys to an organization's people that they are trusted. Even motivated and trained people cannot contribute to enhancing organizational performance if they don't have information on important dimensions of performance and training on how to use and interpret that information. John Mackey, CEO of Whole Foods Markets, states, "If you're trying to create a high-trust organization . . . an organization where people are all-for-one and one-for-all, you can't have secrets."

It may appear easy to create a high-performance organization, but if that were so, then all firms would be as successful as the ones mentioned here. Do not be fooled. Implementing these ideas in a systematic, consistent fashion is tough, and it remains rare enough to be an important source of competitive advantage for firms in a number of industries. The bottom line is that management is a human art—and is becoming more so as information technology takes over routine tasks. Progressive managers understand that they will provide competitive advantage by tapping employees' most essential humanity, their ability to create, judge, imagine, and build relationships. As you can see from this case, managing 21st-century organizations is fast-paced, exciting, and full of people-related business challenges.

## SUMMARY

People are a major component of any business, and the management of people (or human resource management, HRM) is a major part of every manager's job. It is also the specialized responsibility of the HR department. In fact, we use the term "strategic HRM" to refer to the wisest possible use of people with respect to the strategic focus of the organization. HRM involves five major areas: staffing, retention, development, adjustment, and managing change. Together they compose the HRM system, for they describe a network of interrelated components. The HRM function is responsible for maximizing productivity, quality of work life, and profits through better management of people.

The competitive business environment of the 21st century reflects factors such as an aging and changing workforce in a high-tech workplace that demands and rewards ever-increasing skill, and increasing global competition in almost every sector of the economy. In response, new organization forms, such as the virtual corporation, the virtual workplace, and the modular corporation, are appearing. The new forms imply a redistribution of power, greater participation by workers, and more teamwork. Firms are also restructuring, reengineering, implementing quality-improvement programs, and building flexibility into work schedules in order to support their competitive strategies. The challenge of attracting, retaining, and motivating people has never been greater.

One of the most pressing demands we face today is for productivity improvement—getting more out of what is put in; doing better with what we have; and working smarter, not harder. Nevertheless, increased productivity does not preclude a high quality of work life (QWL). QWL refers to employees' perceptions of their physical and psychological well-being at work. It involves giving workers the opportunity to make decisions about their jobs, the design of their workplaces, and ensuring work-life fit. Its focus is on employees and managers operating a business together. HR professionals can help by serving as credible activists, cultural stewards, talent managers, strategy architects, business allies, and operational executors.

## KEY TERMS

| | |
|---|---|
| staffing | virtual workplace |
| retention | restructuring |
| development | downsizing |
| adjustment | Six Sigma |
| managing change | reengineering |
| HRM system | process |
| authority | ethical decisions about behavior |
| globalization | productivity |
| human resources information system | quality of work life |
| virtual organization | |

## DISCUSSION QUESTIONS

**1–1.** What are the HRM implications of globalization, technology, and e-commerce?

**1–2.** How will demographic changes and increasing diversity in the workplace affect the ways that organizations manage their people?

**1–3.** Considering everything we have discussed in this chapter, describe management styles and practices that will be effective for your country's businesses in the next decade.

**1–4.** What difficulties do you see in shifting from a hierarchical, departmentalized organization to a leaner, flatter one in which power is shared between workers and managers?

**1–5.** How can effective HRM contribute to improvements in productivity and quality of work life?

## APPLYING YOUR KNOWLEDGE

*Smashing the Clock\**                                                      *Case 1–1*

**No schedules. No mandatory meetings.**
**Inside Best Buy's radical reshaping of the workplace.**
One afternoon last year, Chap Achen, who oversees online orders at Best Buy Co., shut down his computer, stood up from his desk, and announced that he was leaving for the day.

*\*Sources: Conlin, M. (2006, Dec. 11). Smashing the clock. *BusinessWeek,* pp. 60–68. Fox, A. (2009, Sept.). Gap Outlet: Second retailer adopts results-only work environment strategy. Retrieved from *www.shrm.org/hrdisciplines/orgempdev/articles/Pages/GapOutletROWE.aspx* on May 20, 2011. See also Conlin, M. (2009, Sept. 17). Gap to employees: work wherever, whenever you want. Retrieved from *http://www.businessweek.com/careers/managementiq/archives/2009/09/gap_to_employee.html.*

It was around 2 p.m., and most of Achen's staff were slumped over their keyboards, deep in a post-lunch, LCD-lit trance. "See you tomorrow," said Achen. "I'm going to a matinee."

Under normal circumstances, an early-afternoon departure would have been totally un-Achen. After all, this was a 37-year-old corporate comer whose wife laughs in his face when he utters the words "work-life balance." But at Best Buy's Minneapolis headquarters, similar incidents of strangeness were breaking out all over the ultramodern campus. In employee relations, Steve Hance had suddenly started going hunting on workdays, a Remington 12-gauge in one hand, a Verizon LG in the other. In the retail training department, e-learning specialist Mark Wells was spending his days traveling around the country following rocker Dave Matthews. Single mother Kelly McDevitt, an online promotions manager, started leaving at 2:30 p.m. to pick up her 11-year-old son, Calvin, from school. Scott Jauman, a Six Sigma black belt, began spending a third of his time at his Northwoods cabin.

At most companies, going AWOL during daylight hours would be grounds for a pink slip. Not at Best Buy. The nation's leading electronics retailer has embarked on a radical—if risky—experiment to transform a culture once known for killer hours and herd-riding bosses. The endeavor, called ROWE, for "results-only work environment," seeks to demolish decades-old business dogma that equates physical presence with productivity. The goal at Best Buy is to judge performance on output instead of hours.

Hence workers pulling into the company's amenity-packed headquarters at 2 p.m. aren't considered late. Nor are those pulling out at 2 p.m. seen as leaving early. There are no schedules. No mandatory meetings. No impression-management hustles. Work is no longer a place where you go, but something you do. It's OK to take conference calls while you hunt, collaborate from your lakeside cabin, or log on after dinner so you can spend the afternoon with your kid.

Best Buy did not invent the post-geographic office. Tech companies have been going bedouin for several years. At IBM, 40 percent of the workforce has no official office; at AT&T, a third of managers are untethered. Sun Microsystems Inc. calculates that it has saved $400 million over six years in real estate costs by allowing nearly half of all employees to work anywhere they want. And this trend seems to have legs. A recent Boston Consulting Group study found that 85 percent of executives expect a big rise in the number of unleashed workers over the next five years. In fact, at many companies the most innovative new product may be the structure of the workplace itself.

But, arguably, no big business has smashed the clock quite so resolutely as Best Buy. The official policy for this post–face-time, location-agnostic way of working is that people are free to work wherever they want, whenever they want, as long as they get their work done. "This is like TiVo for your work," says the program's co-founder, Jody Thompson. By the end of 2007, all 4,000 staffers working at corporate will be on ROWE. Starting in February, the new work environment will become an official part of Best Buy's recruiting pitch as well as its orientation for new hires. And the company plans to take its clockless campaign to its stores—a high-stakes challenge that no company has tried before in a retail environment.

Another thing about this experiment: It wasn't imposed from the top down. It began as a covert guerrilla action that spread virally and eventually became a revolution. So secret was the operation that Chief Executive Brad Anderson only learned the details two years after it began transforming his company. Such bottom-up, stealth innovation is exactly the kind of thing Anderson encourages. The Best Buy chief aims to keep innovating even when something is ostensibly working. "ROWE was an idea born and nurtured by a handful of passionate employees," he says. "It wasn't created as the result of some edict."

So bullish are Anderson and his team on the idea that they have formed a subsidiary called CultureRx, set up to help other companies go clockless. CultureRx expects to sign up at least one large client in the coming months.

The CEO may have bought in, but there has been plenty of opposition inside the company. Many execs wondered if the program was simply flextime in a prettier bottle.

Others felt that working off-site would lead to longer hours and destroy forever the demarcation between work and personal time. Cynics thought it was all a PR stunt dreamed up by Machiavellian operatives in human resources. And as ROWE infected one department after the other, its supporters ran into old-guard saboteurs, who continue to plot an overthrow and spread warnings of an imminent paradise for slackers.

Then again, the new work structure's proponents say it's helping Best Buy overcome challenges. And thanks to early successes, some of the program's harshest critics have become true believers. With gross margins on electronics under pressure, and Walmart Stores Inc. and Target Corporation shouldering into Best Buy territory, the company has been moving into services, including its Geek Squad and "customer centricity" program in which salespeople act as technology counselors. But Best Buy was afflicted by stress, burnout, and high turnover. The hope was that ROWE, by freeing employees to make their own work-life decisions, could boost morale and productivity and keep the service initiative on track.

It seems to be working. Since the program's implementation, average voluntary turnover has fallen drastically, CultureRx says. Meanwhile, Best Buy notes that productivity is up an average 35 percent in departments that have switched to ROWE. Employee engagement, which measures employee satisfaction and is often a barometer for retention, is way up too, according to the Gallup Organization, which audits corporate cultures.

ROWE may also help the company pay for the customer-centricity campaign. The endeavor is hugely expensive because it involves tailoring stores to local markets and training employees to turn customer feedback into new business ideas. By letting people work off-campus, Best Buy figures it can reduce the need for corporate office space, perhaps rent out the empty cubicles to other companies, and plow the millions of dollars in savings into its services initiative.

Phyllis Moen, a University of Minnesota sociology professor who researches work-life issues, is studying the Best Buy experiment in a project sponsored by the National Institutes of Health. She says most companies are stuck in the 1930s when it comes to employees' and managers' relationships to time and work. "Our whole notion of paid work was developed within an assembly-line culture," Moen says. "Showing up was work. Best Buy is recognizing that sitting in a chair is no longer working."

## One Giant Wireless Kibbutz

Jody Thompson and Cali Ressler are two HR people you actually don't hate. They groan over cultish corporate slogans like "Build Superior Organizational Capability." They disdain Outlook junkies who double-book and showboating PowerPointers. But it's flextime, or Big Business's answer to overwork, long commutes, and lack of work–family balance, that elicits the harshest verdict. "A con game," says Thompson. "A total joke," adds Ressler.

Flexible work schedules, they say, heap needless bureaucracy on managers instead of addressing the real issue: how to work more efficiently in an era of transcontinental teams and multiple time zones. They add that flextime also stigmatizes those who use it (the reason so few do) and keeps companies acting like the military (fixated on schedules) when they should behave more like MySpace (social networks where real-time innovation can flourish). Besides, they say, if people can virtually carry their office around in their pockets or pocketbooks, why should it matter where and when they work if they are crushing their goals?

Thompson, 49, and Ressler, 29, met three years ago. The boomer and the Gen Xer got each other right away. When they talk about their meeting, it sounds like something out of *Plato for HR,* or two like minds making a whole. At the time, Best Buy was still a ferociously face-time place. Workers arriving after 8 a.m. on sub-zero mornings stashed their parkas in their cars to foil detection as late arrivals. Early escapees crept down back stairwells.

Cube-side, the living was equally uneasy. One manager required his MBAs to sign out for lunch and to list their restaurant locations and ETAs. Another insisted his team track its work—every 15 minutes. As at many companies, the last one to turn out the lights won.

Outside the office, Thompson and Ressler couldn't help noticing how wireless broadband was turning the world into one giant work kibbutz. They talked about how managers were mired in analog-age inertia, often judging performance on how much they saw you versus how much you did. Ressler and Thompson recognized the dangerous, life-wrecking cocktail in the making: The always-on worker also had to be always in.

The culture, not exactly Minnesota-nice, was threatening Best Buy's massive expansion plans. But Ressler and Thompson knew their solution was too radical to simply trot up to CEO Anderson. Nor, in the beginning, did they feel they could lobby their executive supervisors for official approval. Besides, they knew the usual corporate route of imposing something from the top down would bomb. So they met in private, stealthily strategizing about how to protect ROWE and then dribble it out under the radar in tiny pilot trials. Ressler and Thompson waited patiently for the right opportunity.

It came in 2003. Two managers—one in the properties division, the other in communications—were desperate. Top performers were complaining of unsustainable levels of stress, threatening business continuity just when Best Buy was rolling out its customer-centricity campaign in hundreds of stores. They also knew from employee engagement data that workers were suffering from the classic work-life hex: jobs with high demands (always-on, transcontinental availability) and low control (always on-site, no personal life).

Ressler and Thompson saw their opening in these two vanguard managers. Would they be willing to partake in a private management experiment? The two outlined their vision. They explained how in the world of ROWE, there would be no mandatory meetings. No times when you had to physically be at work. Performance would be based on output, not hours. Managers would base assessments on data and evidence, not feelings and anecdotes. The executives liked what they heard and agreed.

The experiment quickly gained social networking heat. Waiting in line at Best Buy's on-site Caribou Coffee, in e-mails, and during drive-bys at friends' desks, employees in other parts of the company started hearing about this seeming antidote to megahour agita. A curious culture of haves and have-nots emerged on the Best Buy campus, with those in ROWE sporting special stickers on their laptops as though they were part of some cabal. Hance, the hunter, started taking conference calls in tree stands and exchanging e-mails from his fishing boat. When Wells wasn't following around Dave Matthews, chances were he was biking around Minneapolis' network of urban lakes, and digging into work only after night had fallen. Hourly workers were still putting in a full 40, but they began doing so wherever and whenever they wanted.

At first, participants were loath to share anything about ROWE with higher-ups for fear the perk would be taken away or reversed. But by 2004, loftier and loftier levels of management began hearing about the experiment at about the same time that opposition to it grew more intense. Critics feared executives would lose control and coworkers would forfeit the collaboration born of proximity. If you can work anywhere, they asked, won't you always be working? Won't overbearing bosses start calling you in the middle of the night? Won't coasters see ROWE as a way to shirk work and force more dedicated colleagues to pick up the slack? And there were generational conflicts: Some boomers felt they'd been forced to choose between work and life during their careers. So everyone else should, too.

Shari Ballard, Best Buy's executive vice-president for human capital and leadership (an analog title if ever there was one), was originally skeptical, although she eventually bought in. At first she couldn't figure out why managers needed a new methodology to help solve the work-life conundrum. "It wasn't hugs and smiles," she says of Ressler's and Thompson's campaign. "Managers in the old mental model were totally irritated." In the e-learning division, many of Wells's older coworkers (read 40-year-olds; the average age at Best Buy is 36) expressed resentment over the change, insisting that work relationships are better face-to-face, not screen-to-screen. "We have people in our group who are like, 'I'm not going to do it,'" says Wells, who likes to sleep in and doesn't own an alarm clock. "I'm like, 'That's fine, but I'm outta here.'" In enemy circles, Ressler and Thompson are known to this day as "those two" and "the subversives."

Yet ROWE continues to spread through the company. If intrigued nonparticipants work for progressive superiors, they usually talk up the program and get their bosses to agree to trials. If they toil under clock-watchers, they form underground networks and quietly lobby for outside support until there is usually no choice but for their boss to switch. It was only this past summer that CEO Anderson got a full briefing, and total understanding, about what was happening. "We purposely waited until the tipping point before we took it to him," says Thompson. Until then he wasn't well-versed on the 13 ROWE commandments. No. 1: People at all levels stop doing any activity that is a waste of their time, the customer's time, or the company's money. No. 7: Nobody talks about how many hours they work. No. 9: It's OK to take a nap on a Tuesday afternoon, grocery shop on Wednesday morning, or catch a movie on Thursday afternoon.

That's the commandment Achen was following when he took off that day to see *Star Wars Episode III: Revenge of the Sith.* Doing so felt abnormal and uncomfortable. Achen felt guilty. But Ressler and Thompson had told him to "model the behavior." So he did. It helped that Achen saw in ROWE the potential to solve a couple of nagging business problems. As the head of the unit that monitors everything that happens after someone places an order at BestBuy.com, including manually reviewing orders and flagging them for possible fraud, Achen wanted to expand the hours of operation without mandating that people show up in the office at 6 a.m. He had another issue. One of his top-performing managers lived in St. Cloud, Minnesota, and commuted two and a half hours each way to work. He and Achen had a gentleman's agreement that he could work from home on Fridays. But the rest of the staff didn't appreciate the favoritism. "It was creating a lot of tension on my team," says Achen.

## Record Job Satisfaction

Ressler and Thompson had convinced Achen that ROWE would work. Now Achen would have to convince the general manager of BestBuy.com, senior vice-president John "J. T." Thompson. That wasn't going to be easy. Thompson, a former General Electric Company guy, was as old school as they come with his starched shirt, booming voice, and ramrod-straight posture. He came of age believing there were three 8-hour days in every 24 hours. He loved working in his office on weekends. At first, he pushed back hard. "I was not supportive," says Thompson, who was privately terrified about the loss of control. "He didn't want anything to do with it," says Achen. "He was all about measurement, and he kept asking me, 'How are you going to measure this so you know you're getting the same productivity out of people?'"

That's where Achen's performance metrics came in handy. He could measure how many orders per hour his team was processing no matter where they were. He told Thompson he'd reel everyone back to campus the minute he noticed a dip. Within a month, Achen could see that not only was his team's productivity up, but engagement scores, or measuring job satisfaction and retention, were the highest in the dot-com division's history.

For years, engagement had been a sore spot for Thompson. "I showed J. T. these scores, and his eyes lit up," says Achen. Thompson rushed to roll out ROWE to his entire department. Voluntary turnover among men dropped from 16.11 percent to 0. "For years I had been focused on the wrong currency," says Thompson. "I was always looking to see if people were here. I should have been looking at what they were getting done."

Today, Achen's commuting employee usually comes in once a week. Nearly three-quarters of his staff spend most of their time out of the office. Doesn't he worry that he loses some of the interoffice magic when they don't gather together all day, every day? What about the value in riffing on one another's ideas? What about teamwork and camaraderie? "You absolutely lose some of that," he says. "But what we get back far outweighs anything we've lost."

Achen says he would never go back. Orders processed by people who are not working in the office are up 13 percent to 18 percent over those who are. ROWE'ers are posting higher metrics for quality, too. Achen says he believes that's due to the new office paradox: Given the constant distractions, it sometimes feels impossible to get any work done at work.

Ressler and Thompson say all the Best Buy groups that have switched to the freer structure report similar results. Meanwhile, the two have other big plans for the company. Last month they launched a new pilot called Cube-Free. Ressler and Thompson believe offices encourage the wrong kinds of habits, keeping people wrapped up in a paper, prewireless mentality as opposed to pushing employees to use technology in the efficiency-enhancing way it was intended. Offices also waste space and time in an age when workers are becoming more and more place-neutral. "This also sets up Best Buy to be able to completely operate if disaster hits," says Thompson. Work groups that go cube-free will be able to redesign their spaces to better accommodate collaboration instead of working alone.

Next year Ressler and Thompson plan to pilot their boldest move yet, testing ROWE in retail stores among both managers and workers. How exactly they will do this in an environment where salespeople presumably need to put in regular hours, they won't say. And they acknowledge it won't be easy. Still, they are eager to try just about anything to help the company slash its 65 percent turnover rates in stores, where disgruntlement is common and workers form groups on MySpace with names like "Best Buy Losers Club!"

Best Buy has transformed its workplace culture in a remarkably short time. Isn't it also true that ROWE could unravel just as quickly? What happens if the company hits a speed bump? Competition isn't getting any less intense, after all. Best Buy sells a lot of extended warranties, an area where both Walmart and Target are eager to undercut the electronics retailer on price. What's more, the current boom in flat-panel, digital TVs will peak in a few years.

If Best Buy's business goes south, human nature dictates that the people who always believed the clockless office was a flaky New Age idea will see an opportunity to try to force a hasty retreat. Some at the company complain that productivity is up only because many Best Buyers are now working longer hours. And some die-hard ROWE opponents still privately roll their eyes when they see Ressler and Thompson in the hallway.

But it's worth remembering that most big companies fail to grow at the rate of inflation. That's true in part because the bigger the company gets, the harder it is to get the best out of each and every employee. ROWE is one of Best Buy's answers to avoiding that fate. "The old way of managing and looking at work isn't going to work anymore," says Ressler. "We want to revolutionize the way work gets done." Admit it, you're rooting for them, too.

Ressler and Thompson have since left Best Buy and set up their own consulting shop called CultureRx. The firm helps other companies migrate to ROWE. One of those is the headquarters staff at the Gap Outlet. A post-pilot assessment conducted in early 2009 revealed that productivity increased 21 percent and quality improved 15 percent among the pilot group. Turnover plummeted 18 percent, down to 5 percent in 2008 over the year prior. Engagement scores spiked from 67 percent in 2007 to 86 percent in 2008, and work–life balance scores rose significantly from 72 percent to 82 percent. Said Chief HR Officer Eva Sage-Gavin, " "If I were speaking to another CHRO, I would say that in this economic environment, it is critical to look into ROWE. Check your culture, look at your demographics and if all those are green, then what's the risk in trying it? Go slow, pilot it and check the results."

---

### Questions

1. Are there trade-offs in implementing a ROWE culture?
2. Can ROWE work with managers?
3. Is ROWE all or nothing? Might there be other options?
4. What types of employees might find ROWE most/least appealing?

# REFERENCES

1. Campbell, J. P., Dunnette, M. D., Lawler, E. E. III, *and* Weick, K. E., Jr. (1970). *Managerial Behavior, Performance, and Effectiveness.* NY: McGraw-Hill. *See also* Welch, J., and S. Welch. (2006, July 17). So many CEOs get this wrong. *Bloomberg Businessweek,* p. 92.

2. Welch, J. (with Welch, S.) (2005). *Winning.* New York: Harper Business.

3. Economist Intelligence Unit (2006, Jan.). *CEO Briefing: Corporate Priorities for 2006 and Beyond.* Retrieved from *http://www.eiu.com* on February 24, 2006.

4. Wright, P. M., and Stewart, M. (2011). *From Bunker to Building: Results from the 2010 Chief Human Resource Officer Survey. Ithaca, NY:* Cornell Center for Advanced Human Resource Studies, p. 13.

5. Cascio, W. F. (2007a ). The costs—and benefits—of human resources. *International Review of Industrial and Organizational Psychology* 22, pp. 71–109.

6. Crook, T. R., Todd, S. Y., Combs, J. G., Woehr, D. J., *and* Ketchen, D. J., Jr. (2011). Does human capital matter? A meta-analysis of the relationship between human capital and firm performance. *Journal of Applied Psychology* 96, pp. 443–456. *See also* Huselid, M. A. (1995). The impact of human resource management practices on turnover, productivity, and corporate financial performance. *Academy of Management Journal* 38, pp. 635–672.

7. Berrgren, E., and Strezo, M. (2011, May). How companies leverage business-execution software to drive excess shareholder return. SuccessFactors White Paper, San Mateo, CA. See also Frauenheim, E. (2011, May 31). SuccessFactors research ties performance management to stock market success. *Workforce Management.* Retrieved from *www.workforce.com* on June 2, 2011.

8. Boselie, P., Dietz, G., *and* Boon, C. (2005). Commonalities and contradictions in HRM and performance research. *Human Resource Management Journal* 15, pp. 67–94. See also Pfeffer, J., *and* Veiga, J. F. (1999). Putting people first for organizational success. *Academy Executive* 13(2), pp. 37–49.

9. *CNN Money. Top companies: Biggest performers. (2010).* Retrieved from *http://money.cnn.com/magazines/fortune/global500/2010/performers/companies/biggest/* on May 17, 2011.

10. Myers, R. (2011, May 11). The risk of globalization. *The Wall Street Journal,* pp. C10, C11. *See also* Walker, M. (2007, Jan. 25). Just how good is globalization? *The Wall Street Journal,* p. A10. See also Dapice, D. (2006, Feb. 6). Why so many oppose globalization. *The South China Morning Post,* p. A13.

11. Bloomberg Businessweek: Year in Review (2011, Jan. 2). *Bloomberg Businessweek: Year in Review,* p. 9.

12. Ramsey, M., *and* Moffett, S. (2011, March 24). Japan parts shortage hits auto makers. *The Wall Street Journal,* pp. B1, B2.

13. World Economic Forum and Boston Consulting Group. (2011). Global talent risk—Seven responses. Cologny/Geneva, Switzerland: Author. *See also* Woodyard, C. (2007, Mar. 22). Which is more American? *USA Today,* pp. 1B, 2B. *See also* Clark, D. (2004, Apr. 12). Another lure of outsourcing: Job expertise. *The Wall Street Journal,* pp. B1, B3. See also Reich, R. B. (1990, Jan.–Feb.). Who is us? *Harvard Business Review,* pp. 53–64.

14. Lublin, J. S. (2011, April 11). Hunt is on for fresh executive talent: Cultural flexibility in demand. *The Wall Street Journal,* pp. B1, B9. See also Economist Intelligence Unit. (2010). *Global Firms in 2020: The Next Decade of Change for Organizations and Workers.* Alexandria, VA: SHRM, *See also* Garten, J. (2004, June 21). Offshoring: You ain't seen nothing yet. *BusinessWeek,* p. 28. See also Colvin, G. (2004, Apr. 19). Stop blaming Bangalore for *our* jobs problem. *Fortune,* p. 68.

15. Kan, M. (2011, April 25). China approaches 900 million mobile phone users. Retrieved from *http://www.cio.com/article/680318/China_Approaches_900_Million_Mobile_Phone_Users* on May 18, 2011. *See also* Schweyer, A. (2006, Oct. 17). Managing

the virtual global workforce. *Human Resources* (Australia). Retrieved from *http://www.humanresourcesmagazine.com.au* on April 12, 2007.

16. Kessler, A. (2011, Feb. 17). Is your job an endangered species? *The Wall Street Journal,* p. A19.

17. Friedman, T. L. (2005). *The World Is Flat.* New York: Farrar, Straus *and* Giroux.

18. Kaplan, D. A. (2010, Jan. 22). SAS: A new *no.* 1 best employer. Retrieved from *http://money.cnn.com/2010/01/21/technology/sas_best_companies.fortune/index.htm* on August 23, 2010. *See also* Economist Intelligence Unit (2010), op. cit. *See also* Coy, P. (2000, Aug. 28). The creative economy. *BusinessWeek,* pp. 76–82.

19. Cascio, W. F., & Welle, B. (2010). Using HR data to make smarter organizational decisions. Pre-conference workshop (AM and PM). Annual conference of the Society for Industrial and Organizational Psychology, Atlanta, April 2010. *See also* Geutal, H. G., *and* Stone, D. L. (Eds.). (2005). *The Brave New World of eHR.* San Francisco: Jossey-Bass.

20. Hamel, G., *and* Sampler, J. (1998, Dec. 7). The *e*-corporation. *Fortune,* pp. 80–92.

21. Electronic commerce. *Wikipedia.* Retrieved from *http://en.wikipedia.org/wiki/E-commerce* on May 19, 2011.

22. White, D. S. (2010, Aug. 20). U.S. e-commerce growth 2000–2009. Retrieved from *http://dstevenwhite.com/2010/08/20/u-s-e-commerce-growth-2000–2009* on May 19, 2011.

23. Mitra S. (2011, Jan. 11). Top ten online advertising trends of the decade. Retrieved from *www.sramanamitra.com/2011/01/11/top-10-online-advertising-trends-of-the-decade/* on May 19, 2011.

24. Mullaney, T. J. (2004, May 10). E-biz strikes again! *BusinessWeek,* pp. 80–88.

25. Greene, K. (2005, Sept. 26). When we're all 64. *The Wall Street Journal,* pp. R1, R4.

26. Byrne, J. A. (1993, Feb. 8). The virtual corporation. *BusinessWeek,* pp. 98–103.

27. Mantell, R. (2011, May 17). Companies tie more of workers' pay to performance. Retrieved from *http://www.marketwatch.com/story/companies-tie-more-of-workers-pay-to-performance-2011-05-17* on May 19, 2011. *See also* The Associated Press (2011, April 6). Service sector growth continues expansion in March, but at slower pace. *The Denver Post,* p. 6B. *See also* Lee, L. (2011, May 16). Streamlining HR: Let somebody else do it. *The Wall Street Journal,* p. R6. *See also (2010, Sept. 19).* New priorities for employers. Bloomberg *Businessweek,* p. 54.

28. Haid, M. (2011). The workplace revolution: Six steps to build a successful virtual workplace. Retrieved from *http://www.shrmindia.org/workplace-revolution-six-steps-build-successful-virtual-workforce* on May 18, 2011. *See also* Snow, C. C., Lipnack, J., *and* Stamps, J. (1999). The virtual organization: Promises and payoffs, large and small. In C. L. Cooper and D. M. Rousseau (Eds.), *Trends in Organizational Behavior, Volume 6: The Virtual Organization.* New York: Wiley, pp. 15–30.

29. Raghuram, S., Tuertscher, P., *and* Garud, R. (2010, Dec.). Mapping the field of virtual work. *Information Systems Research,* pp. 983–999. *See also* Schweyer, op. cit. See also Furst, S. A., Reeves, M., Rosen, B., *and* Blackburn, R. S. (2004). Managing the life cycle of virtual teams. *Academy of Management Executive* 18(2), pp. 6–20. *See also* Cascio, W. F. (2000). Managing a virtual workplace. *Academy Executive* 13(3), pp. 81–90.

30. Lee, 2011, op. cit. *See also* Norman, T. J. (2010, Aug.). Human resource outsourcing: Measuring the hidden costs. Paper presented at the annual conference of the Academy of Management, Montreal, Canada. *See also* Sanders, P. (2009, July 2). Boeing tightens its grip on Dreamliner production. *The Wall Street Journal,* p. B1. *See also* Esen, E. (2004, July). *Human Resource Outsourcing.* Alexandria, VA: Society for Human Resource Management.

31. Ibid.

32. Economist Intelligence Unit, 2010, op. cit. *See also* Foulkes, F. K., Vachani, S., *and* Zaslow, J. (2006). Global sourcing of talent: Implications for the U.S. workforce. In

E. E. Lawler III *and* J. O'Toole (Eds.), *America at Work: Choices and Challenges.* New York: Palgrave Macmillan, pp. 257–273. See also Schweyer, op. cit.

33. Wessel, D. (2011, April 19). Big U.S. firms shift hiring abroad: Data show work forces shrinking at home, sharpening debate on the impact of globalization. *The Wall Street Journal.* Retrieved from *www.online.wsj.com* on April 28, 2011.

34. Cascio, W. F. (2010). *Employment Downsizing and Its Alternatives: Strategies for Long-Term Success.* Alexandria, VA: Society for Human Resource Management Foundation. *See also* DeMeuse, K. P., Marks, M. L., *and* Dai, G. (2011). Organizational downsizing, mergers and acquisitions, and strategic alliances: Using theory and research to enhance practice. In S. Zedeck (Ed.), *Handbook of Industrial and Organizational Psychology.* Washington, DC: APA Books, pp. 729–768.

35. Cascio, W. F., *and* Young, C. E. (2003). Financial consequences of employment-change decisions in major U.S. corporations, 1982–2000. In K. P. DeMeause *and* M. L. Marks (Eds.), *Resizing the Organization.* San Francisco: Jossey-Bass, pp. 131–156.

36. Arthur, J. (2007). *Lean Six Sigma Demystified.* New York: McGraw-Hill.

37. Hindo, B. (2007, June 4). At 3M, a struggle between efficiency and creativity. *BusinessWeek,* pp. 8–14.

38. Walton, M. (1986). *The Deming Management Method.* New York: Perigee.

39. Colvin, G. (2010, March 9). What makes most admired companies different? *Fortune.* Retrieved from *http://money.cnn.com* on April 17, 2010.

40. Hammer, M., *and* Champy, J. (2003). *Reengineering the Corporation: A Manifesto for Business Revolution* (Rev. ed.). New York: Harper Business.

41. Ibid. See also White, J. B. (1996, Nov. 26). Next big thing: Re-engineering gurus take steps to remodel their stalling vehicles. *The Wall Street Journal,* pp. A1, A10.

42. Aumann K., and Galinsky, E. (2009). *The State of Health in the American Workforce: Does Having an Effective Workplace Matter?* New York, NY: Families *and* Work Institute. See also Athavaley, A. (2007, Aug. 15). Vacation deflation: Breaks get shorter. *The Wall Street Journal,* pp. D1, D3.

43. Galinsky, E., Matos, K., *and* Backon, L. (In press). The future of work-life fit. *Organizational Dynamics.* See also *Society for Human Resource Management. (2009). Workplace Flexibility in the 21st Century.* Alexandria, VA: *SHRM.*

44. Corporate Voices for Working Families. (2011). *Business Impacts of Flexibility: An Imperative for Expansion.* Retrieved from *http://www.cvwf.org/publication-toolkits/business-impacts-flexibility-imperative-expansion-updated-2011* on August 3, 2011.

45. Mehring, J. (2004, May 24). What's lifting productivity. *BusinessWeek,* p. 32.

46. Kossek, E. E. (2006). Work and family in America: Growing tensions between employment policy and a transformed workforce. In E. E. Lawler III and J. O'Toole (Eds.), *America at Work: Choices and Challenges.* New York: Palgrave Macmillan, pp. 53–71.

47. Coy, P. (2007, Aug. 20, 27). Cog or co-worker? *BusinessWeek,* pp. 58, 60.

48. Schumpeter blog (2011, April 16). Fail often, fail well: Companies have a great deal to learn from failure, provided they manage it successfully. *The Economist,* p. 74.

49. Grossman, R. J. (2007, June). New competencies for HR. *HR Magazine,* pp. 58–62.

# 2

# THE FINANCIAL IMPACT OF HUMAN RESOURCE MANAGEMENT ACTIVITIES

*Questions This Chapter Will Help Managers Answer*

1. How can HR measures improve talent-related decisions in organizations?
2. If I want to know how much money employee turnover is costing us each year, what factors should I consider?
3. How do employees' attitudes relate to their engagement at work, customer satisfaction, and employee retention?
4. What's the business case for work-life programs?

## LINKING WORKER BELIEFS TO INCREASED PRODUCTIVITY AND PROFITABILITY*

Management is interested in employees' attitudes, such as employee job satisfaction, commitment, and engagement, principally because of the relationship between attitudes and behavior. Other things being equal, it is reasonable to assume that employees who are dissatisfied with their jobs and who are not engaged at work or committed strongly to their employers will tend to be absent or late for work, to quit more often, and to place less emphasis on customer satisfaction than those whose attitudes are positive. In short, poor job attitudes should lead to lower productivity and organizational performance. Evidence indicates that this is, in fact, the case, and that management's concerns are well placed.

From an economic perspective, the important questions are as follows: What is the financial impact of the behavioral outcomes associated with job attitudes, and can we measure the costs associated with different levels of those attitudes? An in-depth study by The Gallup Organization, the Princeton, New Jersey–based polling and research firm, identified 12 worker beliefs (measures of employee satisfaction-engagement) that play the biggest role in triggering a profitable, productive workplace. Its multiyear study was based on an analysis of data from more than 100,000 employees in 12 industries. A subsequent meta-analysis (quantitative summary of research results across studies) included data from almost 8,000 business units in 36 companies.

Analysis showed a consistent, reliable relationship between the 12 beliefs and outcomes such as profits, productivity, employee retention, and customer loyalty. For example, work groups that have these positive attitudes are 50 percent more likely to achieve customer loyalty and 44 percent more likely to produce above-average profitability.

Gallup analyzed employee data to determine how well the respondents' organizations supported the 12 employee statements. Organizations whose support of the statements ranked in the top 25 percent averaged 24 percent higher profitability, 29 percent higher revenue, and 10 percent lower employee turnover than those that scored lowest on the statements.

Although it might be tempting to conclude that employee attitudes cause higher profits, productivity, employee retention, and customer loyalty, it is also possible that more profitable organizations, for example, are particularly appealing places to work and to shop as customers. Without longitudinal data on both employee attitudes and organizational performance at multiple points in time, it is not possible to draw meaningful inferences about causal relationships. However, using a massive, longitudinal database that included 2,178 business units in 10 large organizations, a more recent meta-analysis of the Gallup data found evidence that supports the causal impact of work-related attitudes on bottom-line financial measures. Financial measures included business-unit sales (revenues) and profit margins. Because revenues and profit margins are highly correlated, the researchers used an equally weighted composite of sales and profits as their measure of financial performance.

*Sources:* Harter, J. K., Schmidt, F. L., Asplund, J. W., Killham, E. A., and Agrawal, S. (2010). Causal impact of employee work perceptions on the bottom line of organizations. *Perspectives on Psychological Science* 5(4), pp. 378–389. Harter, J. K., Schmidt, F. L., & Hayes, T. L. (2002). Business-unit-level relationship between employee satisfaction, employee engagement, and business outcomes: A meta-analysis. *Journal of Applied Psychology, 87,* 268–279. Cascio, W. F. and Boudreau, J. W. (2011). Investing in people (2nd ed.). Upper Saddle River, NJ: Pearson/Financial Times Publishing.

Evidence to support the reverse causality of bottom-line financial measures on work-related attitudes did exist, but it was weaker. In short, positive employee attitudes fuel better financial performance, and, to a lesser extent, better financial performance fuels positive employee attitudes. Evidence like this helps to resolve a long-standing debate about the direction of causality and has direct implications for managers.

For instance, consider employees' beliefs about the extent to which they receive recognition or praise for doing good work. Although it requires long-term commitment, managers can deliver on this—at very little cost. Providing regular information to employees about their progress at work is even less time consuming. Interestingly, researchers found significant variances between work groups or operating units within the same company. "What becomes clear from this investigation is that while we tend to celebrate great companies, in reality there are only great managers," said Gallup executive Curt Coffman.[a] In fact, it is on the front line that the hard work of building a stronger workplace gets done. Gallup has studied thousands of great managers and has identified the key behaviors that the best managers seem to share in helping to trigger these beliefs. In the conclusion to this chapter-opening vignette, we will consider what these key behaviors might be.

### Challenges

1. What kinds of organizational policies might help to support these beliefs?
2. What can a manager do in his or her everyday behavior to encourage these beliefs?
3. Why is it that work groups that hold these beliefs are 50 percent more likely to achieve customer loyalty? What might be the link?

---

[a]Micco, L. (1998, Sept.). Gallup study links worker beliefs, increased productivity. *HR News*, p. 16.

---

In business settings, it is hard to be convincing without data. If the data are developed systematically and comprehensively and are analyzed in terms of their strategic implications for the business or business unit, they are more convincing. The chapter-opening vignette demonstrates how the beliefs of workers on 12 issues affect important outcomes involving employees, customers, and company financial results. All of the material in this chapter is based on a simple principle, namely, that HR measurement is valuable to the extent that it improves vital decisions about talent and how it is organized. To have genuine strategic impact, HR measures must be embedded within logical frameworks that drive sound strategic decisions about talent. *Talent* refers to the potential and realized capacities of individuals and groups and how they are organized, including those within the organization and those who might join the organization.[1] We will begin the chapter by presenting a broad framework for enhancing talent-related decisions, and then consider the costs and benefits of HR activities in five key areas: employee attitudes, absenteeism, turnover, work-life programs, and training.

## ORIENTATION

As emphasized earlier, the focus of this book is *not* on training HR specialists. Rather, it is on training line managers who must, by the very nature of their jobs, manage people and work with them to accomplish organizational objectives.

Consequently, the purpose of this chapter is not to show how to measure the effectiveness of the HR department; the purpose is to show how to assess the costs and benefits of some people-related business activities and how to use the results of those analyses to drive strategic organizational change. The methods can and should be used in cooperation with the HR department, but they are not the exclusive domain of that department. They are general enough to be used by any manager in any department to measure the costs and benefits of employee behavior.

This is not to imply that dollars are the only barometer of the effectiveness of HR activities. The payoffs from some activities, such as managing diversity and providing child care, must be viewed in a broader social context. Furthermore, the firm's strategy and goals must guide the work of each business unit and of that unit's HR management activities. For example, to emphasize its outreach efforts to the disadvantaged, a firm might adopt a conscious strategy of *training* workers for entry-level jobs, while *hiring* workers from the outside who already have the skills to perform higher-level jobs. To make the most effective use of the information that follows, keep these points in mind. Let's begin by addressing a fundamental question: How can we make HR measures more strategic?

## THE LAMP MODEL: FOUNDATION FOR WORKFORCE MEASUREMENT*

The letters in **LAMP** stand for *logic, analytics, measures,* and *process,* four critical components of a measurement system that drives strategic change and organizational effectiveness. Measures represent only one component of this system. Although they are essential, without the other three components, the measures and data are destined to remain isolated from the true purpose of HR measurement systems. The model is shown graphically in Figure 2–1. Figure 2–1 shows that

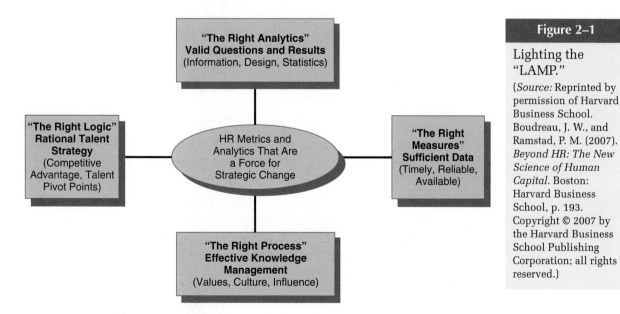

**Figure 2–1**

Lighting the "LAMP."

(*Source:* Reprinted by permission of Harvard Business School. Boudreau, J. W., and Ramstad, P. M. (2007). *Beyond HR: The New Science of Human Capital.* Boston: Harvard Business School, p. 193. Copyright © 2007 by the Harvard Business School Publishing Corporation; all rights reserved.)

* Material in this section is drawn from Cascio, W. F., and Boudreau, J. W. (2011). *Investing in people: Financial impact of human resource initiatives* (2nd ed.). Upper Saddle River, NJ: Pearson Education.

HR measurement systems are only as valuable as the decisions they improve and the organizational effectiveness to which they contribute. That is, such systems are valuable to the extent that they are a force for strategic change. Let's examine how the four components of the LAMP framework define a more complete measurement system. A brief description of each of these elements follows.

## Logic: The "Story" That Connects Numbers and Outcomes

Without a compelling *logic,* it's just not clear where to look for insights about what the numbers (HR measurement data) mean. Conversely, with well-grounded logic, it is easier to help leaders outside of HR to understand and use the measurement systems to enhance the talent-related decisions they make. Consider one such logical framework, the "service-value-profit" framework. It calls attention to the connections between HR and management practices, which, in turn, affect employee attitudes, engagement, and turnover; which, in turn, affect the experiences of customers. The experiences of customers, in turn, affect their buying behavior, which, in turn, affects sales, which, in turn, affects profits.

Can you appreciate the value of this approach, as opposed to a simple linkage between management practices and profits? Making the linkages explicit allows managers to understand more fully the intermediate connections and how investments in them might enhance profits.

## Analytics: Drawing Appropriate Conclusions from Data

*Analytics* transforms HR logic and measures into rigorous, relevant insights. While statistics and research design are analytical strategies for drawing correct conclusions from data, measures comprise the numbers that populate the statistical formulas. Yet it is easy to be misled. To illustrate, assume that a researcher observes a positive correlation between employee attitudes and customer attitudes. The correlation by itself does not prove that one causes the other, nor does it prove that improving one will improve the other. Such a correlation also happens when customer attitudes actually *cause* employee attitudes. This can happen because stores with more loyal and committed customers are more pleasant places to work. The correlation could, however, also result from a third, unmeasured factor. Perhaps stores in certain locations attract customers who buy more merchandise or services and are more enthusiastic. Employees in those locations like working with such customers and are more satisfied. Store location turns out to cause *both* store performance and employee satisfaction. The point is that a high correlation between employee attitudes and customer purchases could be due to any or all of these effects. Sound analytics can reveal which way the causal arrow actually is pointing.

## Measures: Getting the Numbers Right

The *measures* part of the LAMP model has received enormous attention in HR. In fact, if you type "HR measurement" into a search engine you will get more than 37 million results! Scorecards, summits, dashboards, data mines, data warehouses, and audits abound. Indeed, the array of HR measurement technologies is daunting. Consider the measurement of employee turnover. There is much debate about the appropriate formulas to use in estimating turnover and its costs, or the precision and frequency with which employee turnover should be calculated. Today's turnover-reporting systems can calculate turnover rates for virtually any employee group and business unit.

Armed with such systems, managers "slice and dice" the data in a wide variety of ways (ethnicity, skills, performance, and so on), with each manager pursuing his or her own pet theory about employee turnover and why it matters. Are their theories any good? If not, better measures, or more precise ones, won't help. That is why the logic component of the LAMP model is so vital to sound measurement; it tells a story about potential causes and consequences, and it identifies measures that are most appropriate.

In fact, the logic guiding the measurement of turnover is straightforward. It begins with the assumption that employee turnover is not equally important everywhere. Where turnover costs are very high, or where turnover represents a significant risk to the revenues or critical resources of the organization (such as when departing employees take clients with them or when they possess unique knowledge that cannot be recreated easily), it makes sense to track turnover very closely and with greater precision. However, this does not mean simply reporting turnover rates more frequently. It means that the turnover measurements in these situations should focus precisely on what matters. Lacking a common logic about how turnover affects business or strategic success, well-meaning managers might well draw conclusions that are misguided or dangerous. Conversely, they can make strategically sound decisions when a logical framework in which the measures are embedded guides them. When they do that, they get the numbers "right."

## Process: Creating Actionable Insights

*Process* is the final element of the LAMP framework. It refers to the process of using data to influence key decision makers. That influence process begins by convincing managers that the analysis of people-related business processes is possible as well as informative. The way to make that happen is not necessarily to present the most sophisticated analysis. The best approach may be to present relatively simple measures and analyses that match the mental models that managers already use. For example, calculating the costs of employee turnover can reveal millions of dollars that can be saved by reducing turnover. For many leaders outside of HR, a turnover-cost analysis may be their first realization that talent and organization decisions have tangible effects on the economic and accounting processes with which they are familiar. Certainly it is valuable for leaders to see that the same analytical logic used for financial, technological, and marketing investments can apply to human resources. Then, the door is open to more sophisticated analyses beyond the costs.

Education is also a core element of any change process. Application of the LAMP process reveals that it is a powerful tool for educating leaders outside of HR, and for embedding HR measures in their mental frameworks. When that happens, meaningful data provide the basis for people-related business decisions.[2]

In summary, we began this section by asking how we might make HR measures more strategic. As Figure 2–1 shows, the answer is by embedding the measures into a broader framework of logic, analytics, and process that will enable the measures to serve as a force for strategic change. In other words, the LAMP framework can help make measures matter. We will use it to illustrate the costs and benefits of several important areas within HR in the remainder of this chapter. Before we do that, however, it is necessary to define some important terms.

## Some Definitions

The measurement methods described below are based on several definitions and a few necessary assumptions. To begin with, there are, as in any costing situation, both controllable and uncontrollable costs, and there are direct and indirect measures of these costs.

**Direct measures** refer to actual costs, such as the accumulated, direct cost of recruiting.

**Indirect measures** do not deal directly with cost; they are usually expressed in terms of time, quantity, or quality.[3] In many cases indirect measures can be converted to direct measures. For example, if we know the length of time per pre-employment interview plus the interviewer's hourly pay, it is a simple matter to convert time per interview into cost per interview.

Indirect measures have value in and of themselves, and they also supply part of the data needed to develop a direct measure. As a further example, consider the direct and indirect costs associated with mismanaged organizational stress, as shown in Table 2–1.[4] The direct costs listed in the left column of Table 2–1 can all be expressed in terms of dollars. To understand this concept, consider just two items: the costs associated with work accidents and with grievances. Figure 2–2 represents just some of the direct costs associated with accidents; it is not meant to be exhaustive, and it does not include such

| *Table 2–1* | |
|---|---|
| **DIRECT AND INDIRECT COSTS ASSOCIATED WITH MISMANAGED STRESS** | |
| **Direct costs** | **Indirect costs** |
| Participation and membership:<br>    Absenteeism<br>    Tardiness<br>    Strikes and work stoppages | Loss of vitality:<br>    Low motivation<br>    Dissatisfaction |
| | Communication breakdowns:<br>    Decline in frequency of contact<br>    Distortions of messages |
| Performance on the job:<br>    Quality of productivity<br>    Quantity of productivity<br>    Grievances<br>    Accidents<br>    Unscheduled machine downtime<br>        and repair<br>    Material and supply<br>        overutilization<br>    Inventory shrinkages | Faulty decision making<br><br>Quality of work relations:<br>    Distrust<br>    Disrespect<br>    Animosity |
| Compensation awards | Opportunity costs |

*Source:* Macy, B. A., and Mirvis, P. H., *Evaluation Review* 6 (3), Figure 4–5. Copyright © 1982 by Sage Publications, Inc. Reprinted by permission.

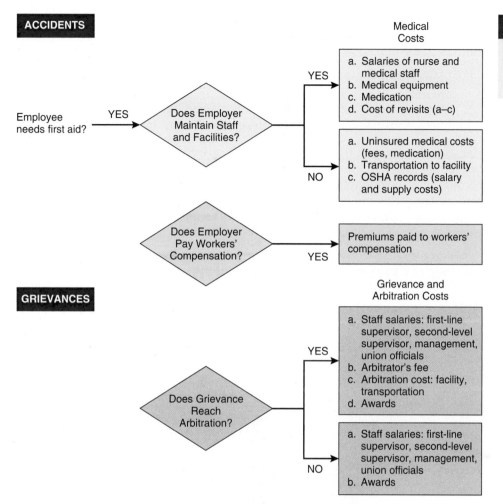

**Figure 2–2**

The costs of accidents and grievances.

items as lost time, replacement costs, institution of "work-to-rule" by coworkers if they feel the firm is responsible, the cost of the safety committee's investigation, and the costs associated with changing technology or job design to prevent future accidents. The items shown in the right column of Table 2–1 cannot be expressed as easily in dollar terms, but they are no less important, and the cost of these indirect items may in fact be far larger than the direct costs. Both direct and indirect costs, as well as benefits, must be considered to apply HR measurement methods properly.

## Controllable versus Uncontrollable Costs

In any area of **behavior costing,** some types of costs are controllable through prudent HR decisions, while other costs are simply beyond the control of the organization. Consider employee turnover as an example. To the extent that people leave for reasons of "better salary," "more opportunity for promotion and career development," or "greater job challenge," the costs associated with turnover are somewhat **controllable.** That is, the firm can alter its HR management practices to reduce the voluntary turnover. However, if the turnover is due to such factors as death, poor health, or spouse transfer, the costs are **uncontrollable.**

The point is that in assessing the costs of employee behaviors, the objective is not simply to *measure* those costs but also to *reduce* them by devoting resources to the more controllable factors. To do this, we must do two things well:

1. Identify, for each HR decision, which costs are controllable and which are not.
2. Measure these costs at Time 1 (prior to some intervention designed to reduce controllable costs) and then again at Time 2 (after the intervention).

Hence the real payoff from determining the costs of employee behaviors lies in being able to demonstrate a financial gain from the wise application of human resource management methods. After we present the definitions of some important concepts, we will present both hypothetical and actual company examples of such measurement in the areas of employee attitudes, absenteeism, turnover, work-life programs, and training.

## FINANCIAL EFFECTS OF EMPLOYEE ATTITUDES

**Attitudes** are internal states that focus on particular aspects of or objects in the environment. They include three elements: *cognition*, the knowledge an individual has about the focal object of the attitude; the *emotion* an individual feels toward the focal object; and an *action* tendency, a readiness to respond in a predetermined manner to the focal object.[5]

For example, **job satisfaction** is a multidimensional attitude; it is made up of attitudes toward pay, promotions, coworkers, supervision, the work itself, and so on.[6] Another attitude is **organizational commitment,** a bond or linking of an individual to the organization that makes it difficult to leave.[7] It is the emotional

Positive job attitudes drive a variety of desirable job behaviors.

engagement that people feel toward an organization. Commitment can be to the job or to the firm, and can be a commitment to contribute, to stay, or both.

The concept of employee engagement is closely related to commitment. It can be defined as a positive, fulfilling, work-related state of mind that is characterized by vigor, dedication, and absorption.[8] Engagement behaviors operate at the individual, team, and organizational levels.[9] Engagement fuels discretionary efforts and concern for quality. It is what prompts employees to identify with the success of their companies, to recommend them to others as good places to work, and to follow through to make sure problems get identified and solved.

Managers are interested in employees' attitudes principally because of the relationship between attitudes and behavior. They assume that employees who are dissatisfied with their jobs and disengaged at work, and who are not committed strongly to their organizations will tend to be absent or late for work, to quit more often, and to place less emphasis on customer satisfaction than those whose attitudes are positive. Poor job attitudes therefore lead to lowered productivity and organizational performance. Evidence indicates that this is, in fact, the case, and that management's concern is well placed.[10]

## Behavior Costing and Employee Attitudes

The behavior-costing approach to employee attitude valuation is based on the assumption that measures of attitudes are indicators of subsequent employee behaviors.[11] These behaviors can be assessed using cost-accounting procedures, and they have economic implications for organizations. Sysco Corporation, the largest food marketer and distributor in North America, applied behavior-costing methodology to study the relationship between employee attitudes, customer behavior, and profits. Its approach shows how all of the elements of the LAMP model come together. Sysco began with a logical framework that describes how it creates value from its human capital (see Figure 2–3). The framework is based on the service-profit chain model described earlier.[12]

## Logic: Linking Management Practices to Financial Outcomes

As Figure 2–3 shows, effective management practices drive employee satisfaction (and engagement). A satisfied and engaged workforce, in turn, enables a company to pursue excellence in innovation and execution. The logical proposition is that higher employee satisfaction-engagement drives innovation and execution,

**Sysco Practices:**
- Leadership Support
- Front-Line Supervisor
- Rewards
- Quality of Life
- Diversity/Engagement
- Customer Focus

**Figure 2–3**

Sysco's value-profit chain.
(*Source:* Society for Human Resource Management. (2004). *HR in Alignment: the Link to Business Results.* Alexandria, VA: Society for Human Resource Management.)

which, in turn, enhances customer satisfaction, customer purchasing behavior, and, eventually, long-term profitability and growth. Certainly, management needs to put in place systems, people, technology, and processes that will initiate and sustain innovation and execution—the principal components of an effective value-profit chain. Technology and processes are easily copied by competitors, but a highly skilled, committed, and fully engaged workforce is difficult to imitate.

## Analytics: Connecting the Model to Management Behaviors

Sysco's basic management model—the set of practices that describe how the company seeks to engage the hearts and minds of employees with its employer brand—has been termed the 5-STAR management model.[13] Its focus is on taking care of people: extending the same respect to employees as managers do to their external customers.

The framework is general enough to apply to any type of company structure or business model, and it gives businesses wide discretion in actual implementation. As Figure 2–3 shows, the five principles of the STAR model ("Management Practices" in Figure 2–3) are as follows:

- Ensuring that leaders offer direction and support.
- Strengthening front-line supervisors.
- Rewarding performance.
- Addressing employees' quality of life.
- Including employees by engaging them and leveraging diversity.

Employee attitudes are integral components of the STAR model because, as a set, those attitudes reflect employee satisfaction-engagement, a key component of the value-profit chain. At a broader level, Figure 2–3 shows how Sysco creates value from its human capital. It shows clearly the intermediate linkages between employee attitudes and financial performance. Indeed, the logic of the model is so compelling that it is taught to every manager and employee from the first day on the job.

## Measures

To measure the attitudes of its employees, Sysco developed a work climate/employee engagement survey built around each of the 5-STAR principles. All members of each Sysco operating company participate in a comprehensive annual self-assessment as well as impromptu and informal assessments on an as-needed basis.[14] The total survey comprises 61 items, but Sysco found that just 14 of them differentiated the top-performing 25 percent of its operating companies from the bottom 25 percent. Here are some examples:

- I know what is expected of me at work.
- Upper management spends time talking with employees about our business direction.
- My supervisor treats me with dignity and respect.
- I have received constructive feedback on my performance within the last six months.
- I am proud to work for Sysco.

Consider an additional item in the survey: "My supervisor removes obstacles so I can do my job better." A multiyear study of hundreds of knowledge workers in a variety of industries that tracked their day-to-day activities, emotions, and motivations through 120,000 journal entries strongly supports this driver of engagement. The study found that "workers reported feeling most engaged on days when they made headway or received support to overcome obstacles in their jobs."[15] They reported feeling least engaged when they hit brick walls. In short, small dents in work were as meaningful as large achievements.

## Analytics Combined with Process: The Sysco Web Portal

Sysco has a decentralized organizational structure comprised of 147 autonomous operating companies. It employs an organization-wide rewards system to encourage managers of the autonomous operating companies to share information with each other and to transfer best practices within the organization. Sysco built a "best business practices" Web portal on its intranet to provide a platform for organizationwide improvement. The Web architecture offered a framework for managers to do two things: (1) to share information on their own operating company's successful practices, and (2) to learn from the best practices of other Sysco operating companies. This is important because the company's in-house research showed that operating companies with the most satisfied employees consistently receive the highest scores from their customers and have higher retention of marketing associates and drivers. Table 2–2 shows these results.

The data in Table 2–2 are tantalizing, but it is important to emphasize that causes and effects are not clear. Are customers more loyal because employees are more satisfied and engaged? Or are employees more satisfied and engaged in their work in operating companies with loyal customers who make their work more rewarding? The data in Table 2–2 cannot tell us that. What they do suggest is that continued improvements in logic, analytics, measures, and process are vital, even in advanced systems like Sysco's.

## Monetary Payoffs

Table 2–2 does not include cost savings associated with improvements in the retention of marketing associates and drivers, but those cost savings were

### Table 2–2

**SATISFIED EMPLOYEES DELIVER BETTER RESULTS**

| | High | | | Low | |
|---|---|---|---|---|---|
| Associate satisfaction | 4.00–5.00 | 3.90–3.99 | 3.75–3.89 | 3.55–3.74 | <3.55 |
| Customer loyalty score | 4.55 | 4.40 | 4.25 | 4.15 | 4.05 |
| Retention marketing associates | 88% | 85% | 81% | 75% | 76% |
| Retention, drivers | 87% | 81% | 81% | 75% | 76% |

*Source:* Carrig, K., and Wright P. M. (2006). *Building Profit through Building People.* Alexandria, VA: Society for Human Resource Management Foundation.

significant. They reflect the economic impact of positive attitudes about staying at the company. In 2000, retention rates for marketing associates and drivers were 75 percent and 65 percent, respectively. By 2005, those retention rates improved to 88 percent and 87 percent, respectively. Sysco then estimated the replacement and training costs of these three groups of employees as $50,000 per marketing associate and $35,000 per driver.

Assuming 100 employees per business unit, from 2000 to 2005, each business unit saved (in terms of costs that were not incurred) $650,000 among marketing associates and $770,000 among drivers, for a total savings of $1.42 million ($1.65 million in 2011 dollars). Corporate-wide savings in retention over all categories of employees from 2000 to 2005, assuming 10,000 employees, totaled $156.5 million ($181.5 million in 2011 dollars).[16] Such savings contributed to the firm's long-term profitability and growth.

### Integrating the Value-Profit Chain into Organizational Systems

Today top executives at Sysco meet on a quarterly basis to review the metrics. What led Sysco executives to pay attention to the human capital indices? HR researchers found a high multiple correlation ($R^2 = 0.46$) between work climate/employee engagement scores, productivity, retention, and pretax earnings. This means that 46 percent of the variation in pretax earnings was associated with variation in the combination of the three remaining employee-related variables.

Sysco leaders began to pay attention when they realized that the human capital indices served as indicators of financial results that the executives could see in their own operating companies. The relationship is lagged about six months, and although exact cause–effect relationships have not been determined, the business model that the company uses assumes that employee satisfaction-engagement drives customer satisfaction, which drives long-term profitability and growth. In short, Sysco has been able to determine not only what practices and processes are helping to drive the human capital indices, but also how those, in fact, influence the financial metrics over time. Such powerful insights have focused and improved the overall management process.

### COSTING EMPLOYEE ABSENTEEISM

In any human resource costing application, it is important first to define exactly what is being measured. From a business standpoint, **absenteeism** is any failure of an employee to report for or to remain at work as scheduled, regardless of reason. The term "as scheduled" is very significant, for it automatically excludes vacations, holidays, jury duty, and the like. It also eliminates the problem of determining whether an absence is "excusable" or not. Medically verified illness is a good example. From a business perspective, the employee is absent and is simply not available to perform his or her job; that absence will cost money. How much money? According to a 2008 Mercer survey of 465 companies, if one excludes planned absences (vacations, holidays), the total direct and indirect costs consume 9 percent of payroll.[17] Direct costs include actual benefits paid to employees (such as sick leave and short- and long-term disability), while indirect costs reflect reduced productivity (delays, reduced morale of coworkers, and lower productivity of replacement employees).

Thus, a 1,000-employee company that averages $50,000 in salary per employee would have an annual payroll of $50 million. Nine percent of that is $4.5 million, or about $4,500 per employee when direct and indirect costs are both considered. Figures like that get management's attention.

Why are employees absent? In the United States, the five leading causes are personal illness (34 percent), family-related issues (22 percent), personal needs (18 percent), entitlement mentality (13 percent), and stress (13 percent).[18]

In costing absenteeism, an important qualification is necessary. Specifically, if workers can vary their work time to fit their personal schedules, if they need not "report" to a central location, and if they are accountable only in terms of results, then the concept of "absenteeism" may not have meaning. Teleworkers often fit this description. Building on this idea, we begin by presenting the logic of employee absenteeism, that is, how absenteeism creates costs (Figure 2–4).

In this figure, "pivotal" jobs refer to those where a change in the availability or quality of talent have the greatest impact on the success of an organization, such as mechanics at an airline, or new-product designers at a company that thrives on

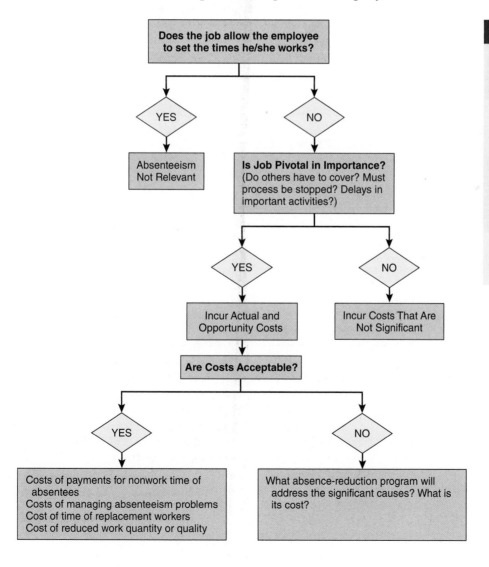

**Figure 2–4**

The logic of employee absenteeism: How absenteeism creates costs.
(*Source:* Cascio, W. F., and Boudreau, J. W. (2011). *Investing in People: Financial Impact of Human Resource Initiatives* (2nd ed.). © 2011, p. 57. Reprinted by permission of Pearson Education, Inc., Upper Saddle River, NJ.)

innovation. "Opportunity costs" refer to "opportunities foregone" that might have been realized if the absent employees were at work. These might include increased productivity or sales, for example. Figure 2–4 may serve as a "mental map" for decision makers, to help them understand the logic of employee absenteeism.

## Analytics and Measures for Employee Absenteeism

In the context of absenteeism, *analytics* refers to formulas (for instance, those for absence rate, total pay, supervisory time) and to comparisons to industry averages and adjustments for seasonality. Analytics also includes various methodologies, for example, surveys and interviews with employees and supervisors, used to identify the causes of absenteeism and to estimate variation in absenteeism across different segments of employees. Measures, on the other hand, focus on specific numbers (for example, finding employee pay-and-benefit numbers, time sampling to determine the lost time associated with managing absenteeism problems). Figure 2–5 is a flowchart that shows how to estimate the total cost of employee absenteeism over any period. Free online software that performs all of the calculations necessary to estimate absenteeism costs is available at *www.shrm.org/publications/books,* under "Investing in People."

**Figure 2–5**

Total estimated cost of employee absenteeism.
(*Source:* Cascio, W. F., and Boudreau, J. W. (2011). *Investing in People: Financial Impact of Human Resource Initiatives* (2nd ed.). © 2011, p. 59. Reprinted by permission of Pearson Education, Inc., Upper Saddle River, NJ.)

1. Compute total employee hours lost to absenteeism for the period.
2. Compute weighted average wage or salary/hour/absent employee.
3. Compute cost of employee benefits/hour/employee.

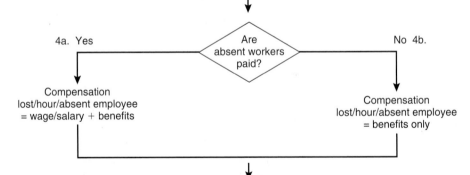

4a. Yes

Are absent workers paid?

No 4b.

Compensation lost/hour/absent employee = wage/salary + benefits

Compensation lost/hour/absent employee = benefits only

5. Compute total compensation lost to absent employees (1 × 4a or 4b, as applicable).
6. Estimate total supervisory hours lost to employee absenteeism.
7. Compare average hourly supervisory salary + benefits.
8. Estimate total supervisory salaries lost to managing absenteeism problems (6 × 7).
9. Estimate all other costs incidental to absenteeism.
10. Estimate total costs of absenteeism ($\Sigma$5, 8, 9).
11. Estimate total cost of absenteeism/employee (10 ÷ total no. employees).

## Process: Interpreting the Costs of Absenteeism

Remember, the purpose of the process component of the LAMP model is to make the insights gained as a result of costing employee absenteeism actionable. The first step in doing that is to interpret absenteeism costs in a meaningful manner. Indeed, one of the first questions management will ask upon seeing absenteeism-cost figures are, "What do they mean? Are we average, above average, below average?" Unfortunately, there are no industry-specific figures on the costs of employee absenteeism. Certainly, these costs will vary depending on the type of firm, the industry, and the level of employee that is absent (unskilled versus skilled or professional workers). As a benchmark, however, consider that the average employee in the United States misses 2.3 percent of scheduled work time, or an average of 5.5 unscheduled absences per year (slightly more than one workweek).[19] In comparison, the average European employee misses an average of 10 days per year, or two workweeks.[20]

It is also important to note that the dollar figure just determined (we will call it the "Time 1" figure) becomes meaningful as a baseline from which to measure the financial gains realized as a result of a strategy to reduce absenteeism. At some later time (we will call this "Time 2"), the total cost of absenteeism should be measured again. The difference between the Time 2 figure and the Time 1 figure, minus the cost of implementing the strategy to reduce absenteeism, represents net gain.

Another question that often arises at this point is, "Are these dollars real? Since supervisors are drawing their salaries anyway, what difference does it make if they have to manage absenteeism problems?" To be sure, many calculations in HR measurement other than absenteeism involve an assessment of the value of employees' time (for example, those involving exit interviews, attendance at training classes, or the time taken to screen job applications). One way to account for that time, in financial terms, is in terms of total pay to the employee. The idea is to use the value of what employees earn (salaries, benefits, and overhead costs) as a proxy for the value of their time.

Total pay, however, is generally not synonymous with the fixed costs, variable costs (e.g., those that vary with employee productivity, such as sales commissions), or opportunity costs of employee time. It is a convenient proxy, but must be used with great caution. In most situations, the costs of employee time simply don't change as a result of their allocation of time. They are paid no matter what they do, as long as it is a legitimate part of their jobs.

The more correct concept is the opportunity cost of the lost value that employees would have been creating if they had not been using their time to manage absenteeism problems. That cost is obviously not necessarily equal to the cost of their wages, benefits, and overhead. That said, it is so difficult to estimate the opportunity cost of employees' time that it is very common for accounting processes just to recommend multiplying the time by the value of total pay. The important thing to realize is the limits of such calculations, even if they provide a useful proxy.[21]

## COSTING EMPLOYEE TURNOVER

Organizations need a practical procedure for measuring and analyzing the costs of employee turnover, especially because top managers view the costs of hiring, training, and developing employees as investments that must be evaluated just like other corporate resources. The objective in costing human resources is not just to measure the relevant costs, but also to develop methods and programs to reduce the costs of human resources by managing the more controllable aspects of those costs.

Earlier we discussed the logic of turnover, namely, that it is not equally important everywhere in an organization, and that in talent pools where turnover costs are very high, or where turnover represents a significant risk to the revenues or critical resources of the organization (such as when departing employees take clients with them or when they possess unique knowledge that cannot be re-created easily), it makes sense to track turnover very closely and with greater precision. Even a very rigorous logic with good measures can flounder, however, if the analysis is incorrect.

**Turnover** occurs when an employee leaves an organization permanently. Not included as turnover within this definition, therefore, are transfers within an organization and temporary layoffs. The rate of turnover in percent over any period can be calculated by the following formula:

$$\frac{\text{Number of turnover incidents per period}}{\text{Average workforce size}} \times 100\%$$

In the United States, for example, monthly turnover rates vary considerably across industries (e.g., utilities versus hospitality) and economic conditions. Fewer people left their jobs during the global economic downturn than before it. In retail, for example, 25 percent of employees quit during the recession versus 40 percent before it.[22] However, these figures most likely represent both controllable turnover (controllable by the organization) and uncontrollable turnover. Controllable turnover is "voluntary" on the part of the employee, while uncontrollable turnover is "involuntary" (e.g., due to retirement, death, or spouse transfer). Furthermore, turnover may be *functional,* where the employee's departure produces a benefit for the organization, or *dysfunctional,* where the departing employee is someone the organization would like to retain.

High performers who are difficult to replace represent dysfunctional turnovers; low performers who are easy to replace represent functional turnovers. The crucial issues in analyzing turnover, therefore, are not how many employees leave but rather the performance and replaceability of those who leave versus those who stay, and the criticality of their skills.[23]

In costing employee turnover, first determine the total cost of all turnover and then estimate the percentage of that amount that represents controllable, dysfunctional turnover-resignations that represent a net loss to the firm and that the firm could have prevented. Thus, if total turnover costs $1 million and 50 percent is controllable and dysfunctional, $500,000 is the Time 1 baseline measure. To determine the net financial gain associated with the strategy adopted prior to Time 2, compare the total gain at Time 2 (say, $700,000) minus the cost of implementing the strategy to reduce turnover (say, $50,000) with the cost of turnover at Time 1 ($500,000). In this example, the net gain to the firm is $150,000. Now let's see how the total cost figure is derived.

## Analytics: The Components of Turnover Costs

There are three broad categories of costs in the basic turnover costing model: separation costs, replacement costs, and training costs. This section presents only the cost elements that make up each of these three broad categories. Those who wish to investigate the subject more deeply may seek information on the more detailed formulas that are available.[24]

## Separation Costs

Following are four cost elements in separation costs:

1. *Exit interview,* including the cost of the interviewer's time and the cost of the terminating employee's time.
2. *Administrative functions related to termination,* for example, removal of the employee from the payroll, termination of benefits, and turn-in of company equipment.
3. *Separation pay,* if applicable.
4. *Increased unemployment tax.* This is a relevant concern for firms doing business in the United States. Such an increase may come from either or both of two sources. First, in states that base unemployment tax rates on each company's turnover rate, high turnover will lead to a higher unemployment tax rate. Suppose a company with a 10 percent annual turnover rate was paying unemployment tax at a rate of 5 percent on the first $7,000 of each employee's wages in 2010. But in 2011, because its turnover rate jumped to 15 percent, the company's unemployment tax rate may increase to 5.5 percent. Second, replacements for those who leave will result in extra unemployment tax being paid. Thus a 500-employee firm with no turnover during the year will pay the tax on the first $7,000 (or whatever the state maximum is) of each employee's wages. The same firm with a 20 percent annual turnover rate will pay the tax on the first $7,000 of the wages of 600 employees.

The sum of these four cost elements represents the total separation costs for the firm.

## Replacement Costs

The eight cost elements associated with replacing employees who leave are the following:

1. *Communicating job availability.*
2. *Pre-employment administrative functions,* for example, accepting applications and checking references.
3. *Entrance interview,* or perhaps multiple interviews.
4. *Testing* and/or other types of assessment procedures.
5. *Staff meetings,* if applicable, to determine if replacements are needed, to recheck job analyses and job specifications, to pool information on candidates, and to reach final hiring decisions.
6. *Travel and moving expenses,* for example, travel for all applicants and travel plus moving expenses for all new hires.
7. *Postemployment acquisition and dissemination of information,* for example, all the activities associated with in-processing new employees.
8. *Medical examinations,* if applicable, either performed in-house or contracted out.

The sum of these eight cost elements represents the total cost of replacing those who leave.

## Training Costs

This third component of turnover costs includes four elements:

1.  *Informational literature,* for example, an employee handbook.
2.  *New-employee orientation* (sometimes called "on-boarding").
3.  *Instruction in a formal training program.*
4.  *Instruction by employee assignment,* for example, on-the-job training.

The sum of these four cost elements represents the total cost of training replacements for those who leave.

Note that a major cost associated with employee turnover, *reduced productivity during the learning period,* is generally not included along with the cost elements *instruction in a formal training program* and *instruction by employee assignment.* The reason for this is that formal work-measurement programs are not often found in employment situations. Thus, it is not possible to calculate accurately the dollar value of the loss in productivity during the learning period. If such a program does exist, then by all means include this cost. For example, a major brokerage firm did a formal work-measurement study of this problem and reported the results shown in Table 2–3. The bottom line is that we want to be conservative in our turnover-cost figures so that we can defend every number we generate.

### The Costs of Lost Productivity and Lost Business

By all means include the costs of lost productivity and lost business in the fully loaded cost of employee turnover, if your organization can tally those costs accurately. Such costs are not easily estimated in many jobs, and that is why they are not routinely included in the cost of turnover. Seven additional cost elements might be included:[25]

- The cost of additional overtime to cover the vacancy (Wages × Number of hours of overtime).
- The cost of additional temporary help (Wages + Benefits) × (Hours paid).

### Table 2–3

**PRODUCTIVITY LOSS OVER EACH THIRD OF THE LEARNING PERIOD FOR FOUR JOB CLASSIFICATIONS**

| Classification | Weeks in learning period | Productivity loss during each third of the learning period | | |
| --- | --- | --- | --- | --- |
| | | 1 | 2 | 3 |
| Management and partners | 24 | 75% | 40% | 15% |
| Professional and technicians | 16 | 70 | 40 | 15 |
| Office and clerical workers | 10 | 60 | 40 | 15 |
| Broker trainees | 104 | 85 | 75 | 50 |

*Note:* The learning period for the average broker trainee is two years, although the cost to the firm is generally incurred only in the first year. It is not until the end of the second year that the average broker trainee is fully productive.

- Wages and benefits saved due to the vacancy (these are subtracted from the overall tally of turnover costs).
- The cost of reduced productivity while the new employee is learning the job (Wages + Benefits) × (Length of the learning period × Percentage reduction in productivity).
- The cost of lost productive time due to low morale of remaining employees (estimated as aggregate time lost per day of the work group × (Wages + Benefits of a single employee) × Number of days).
- The cost of lost customers, sales, and profits due to the departure (Estimated number of customers × Gross profit lost per customer × Profit margin in percent).
- Cost of additional (related) employee departures. (If one additional employee leaves, the cost equals the total per-person cost of turnover.)

## The Total Cost of Turnover

The sum of the three component costs—separation, replacement, and training—represents the total cost of employee turnover for the period in question. Other factors could also be included in the tally, such as the uncompensated performance differential between leavers and their replacements, but that is beyond the scope of this book.[26]

Remember, *the purpose of measuring turnover costs is to improve management decision-making.* Once turnover figures are known, particularly among segments of the workforce deemed "pivotal," managers have a sound basis for choosing between current turnover costs and instituting some type of turnover-reduction strategy. These might include actions such as the following: anticipate who might leave, taking into account the criticality of his or her skill set, and take action to prevent the departure;[27] provide realistic job previews, hold managers and supervisors accountable for retention,[28] conduct and follow up on employee surveys; and institute merit-based rewards to retain high performers.[29]

Consider the impact of a simple, nonfinancial strategy to improve retention. Managers at Bank of America realized that voluntary turnover rates among back-office workers were much higher than those in the rest of the bank. After instituting a one-on-one communications program, the bank reduced voluntary turnover by 25 percent. How? By having line managers come in at off-hours (e.g., 1 a.m.) to meet with night-shift employees and thoroughly explain benefits of which the employees were unaware. The managers were trained to communicate with workers in a problem-solving manner—not "tell and sell"—and their efforts paid off.[30]

Think about the fully loaded cost of turnover. It includes not just separation and replacement costs, but also an exiting employee's lost leads and contacts, the new employee's depressed productivity while he or she is learning, and the time coworkers spend guiding him or her. The combined effect of those factors can easily cost 150 percent or more of the departing person's salary.[31] At Ernst & Young, this is the cost to fill a position vacated by a young auditor.[32] In fact, Merck & Company, the pharmaceutical giant, found that, depending on the job, turnover costs were 1.5 to 2.5 times the annual salary paid.[33]

In terms of process, there are opportunities in this area for enterprising managers to make significant bottom-line contributions to their organizations. Organizational budgeting practices sometimes provide a natural opportunity to use the costs of employee turnover as part of a broader framework to demonstrate tangible economic payoffs from effective management practices. Thus, when line managers complain that they cannot keep positions filled or that they cannot get enough people to join as new hires, that is a prime opportunity to elevate the conversation. How? By tying the fully loaded turnover costs among pivotal employees to the ability of the organization to achieve its long-term strategic objectives.

## FINANCIAL EFFECTS OF WORK-LIFE PROGRAMS

Although originally termed "work-family" programs, this book uses the term "work-life" programs to reflect a broader perspective of this issue. "Work-life" recognizes the fact that employees at every level in an organization, whether parents or nonparents, face personal or family issues that can affect their performance on the job. A **work-life program** includes any employer-sponsored benefit or working condition that helps an employee to balance work and nonwork demands.[34] At a general level, such programs span five broad areas:[35]

1. *Child and dependent care benefits* (e.g., onsite or near-site child or elder care programs, summer and weekend programs for dependents).
2. *Flexible working conditions* (e.g., flextime, job sharing, teleworking, part-time work, compressed work weeks).
3. *Leave options* (e.g., maternity, paternity, adoption leaves, sabbaticals, phased reentry, or retirement schemes).
4. *Information services and HR policies* (e.g., cafeteria benefits; life-skill educational programs such as parenting skills, health issues, financial management, retirement, exercise facilities, professional and personal counseling).
5. *Organizational cultural issues* (e.g., an organizational culture that is supportive with respect to the nonwork issues of employees, coworkers, and supervisors who are sensitive to family issues).

### The Logic of Work-Life Programs

There are consequences, both behavioral and financial, to decisions to offer, or not to offer, one or more work-life programs. If an organization chooses not to offer such programs, there may be negative consequences with respect to job performance. Some of these potential impacts include heightened stress, more burnout, a higher likelihood of mistakes, and more refusals of promotions by employees already feeling the strain of pressures for balance between their work and nonwork lives.

Assuming an organization does offer one or more work-life programs, Figure 2–6 shows that the financial and nonfinancial effects of those programs depend on several factors. These include the range, scope, cost, and quality of the programs; support for the programs from managers and supervisors; and the extent and quality of communications about them to employees. If those conditions are met, it is reasonable to expect improvements in talent management (reductions in withdrawal behaviors and voluntary turnover, and improvements in the ability to attract top talent); human-capital outcomes (increased satisfaction, commitment, and motivation to perform well); and financial, operational, and business outcomes.

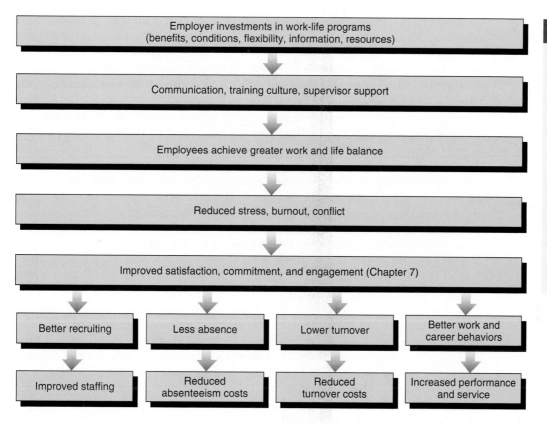

**Figure 2–6**

The logic of work-life programs. (*Source:* Adapted from Cascio, W. F., and Boudreau, J. W. (2011), © 2011, p. 173. Reprinted by permission of Pearson Education, Inc., Upper Saddle River, NJ.)

## Analytics and Measures: Connecting Work-Life Programs and Outcomes

For purposes of illustration, we will consider the financial effects of only two of the many possible work-life interventions: child care and flexible work arrangements. Then we will examine stock-market reactions to work-life initiatives.

### Child Care

U.S. employers lose an estimated $4 billion annually to absenteeism related to child care.[36] Several studies have examined the impact of child-care programs on absenteeism, retention, and return on investment. For example, Citigroup owns or participates in 12 child-care centers in the United States. Employees pay about half the cost to use Citigroup facilities managed by Bright Horizons Family Solutions or at non-Citigroup back-up centers. In two follow-up studies, Citigroup found the following:[37]

- A 51 percent reduction in turnover among center users compared to non-center users.
- An 18 percent reduction in absenteeism.
- A 98 percent retention rate of top performers.

Finally, a study of the **return on investment** (ROI) of backup child care (i.e., child care used in emergencies or when regular child care is unavailable) at JPMorgan Chase revealed the following. Child-care breakdowns were the cause of 6,900 days of potentially missed work by parents. Because backup child care was available, these lost days were not incurred. When multiplied by the average daily salary of the employee in question (expressed in 2011 dollars), gross savings were $2,440,875. The annual cost of the backup child-care center was $1,153,793 for a net savings of $1,287,082, and an ROI (economic gains divided by program costs) of better than 110 percent.[38]

It is important to emphasize that simply offering child care is no guarantee of results like those we have described. Employers considering offering such a benefit should understand child-care service delivery, the cost of care and its availability, what is available in the local market, and any challenges it presents. In addition, employers need to consider the business case for offering child care.[39] Depending on the nature of the business, the goal may be to improve recruitment and retention, support the advancement of women, reduce absenteeism, retain high performers, or be an employer of choice. Then measure what matters, considering key drivers of the business and the goals established for the program.

### Flexible Work Arrangements

Consider this quote from a recent study of flexible work arrangements in 29 American firms. "Flexibility is frequently viewed by managers and employees as an exception or employee accommodation, rather than as a new and effective way of working to achieve business results. A face-time culture, excessive workload, manager skepticism, customer demands, and fear of negative career consequences are among the barriers that prevent employees from taking advantage of policies they might otherwise use—and that prevent companies from realizing the full benefits that flexibility might bestow."[40]

To help inform the debate about flexible work arrangements, consider the financial and nonfinancial effects that have been reported for these key

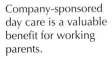

Company-sponsored day care is a valuable benefit for working parents.

outcomes: *talent management* (specifically, better recruiting and lower turn-over) and *human-capital outcomes* (increased satisfaction and commitment, decreased stress), which affect cost and performance, leading to *financial, operational,* and *business outcomes.* Here are some very brief findings in each of these areas from the same study of 29 American firms.

## Talent Management

IBM's global work-life survey demonstrated that flexibility is an important aspect of employees' decisions to stay with the company. Responses from almost 42,000 IBM employees in 79 countries revealed that work-life balance—of which flexibility is a significant component—is the second leading reason for potentially leaving IBM, behind compensation and benefits. Conversely, employees with higher work-life balance scores (and therefore also higher flexibility scores) reported significantly greater job satisfaction and were much more likely to agree with the statement "I would not leave IBM."

In the Corporate Finance organization, 94 percent of all managers reported positive impacts of flexible work options on the company's "ability to retain talented professionals." In light of these findings showing the strong link between flexibility and retention, IBM actively promotes flexibility as a strategy for retaining key talent.

## Human-Capital Outcomes—Employee Commitment

At Deloitte & Touche, one employee-survey item asked whether employees agreed with the statement "My manager grants me enough flexibility to meet my personal/family responsibilities." Those who agreed that they have access to flexibility scored 32 percent higher in commitment than those who believed they did not have access to flexibility. Likewise, AstraZeneca found that commitment scores were 28 percent higher for employees who said they had the flexibility they needed, compared to employees who did not have the flexibility they needed.

## Financial Performance, Operational and Business Outcomes—Client Service

Concern for quality and continuity of client or customer service is often one of the concerns raised about whether flexibility can work in a customer-focused organization. To be sure that compressed workweeks did not erode traditionally high levels of customer service, the Consumer Healthcare Division of GlaxoSmithKline surveyed customers as part of the evaluation of its flexibility pilot program. Fully 89 percent of customers said they had not seen any disruption in service, 98 percent said their inquiries had been answered in a timely manner, and 87 percent said they would not have any issues with the program becoming a permanent work schedule.

Studies such as these make it possible to reframe the discussion and to position flexibility not as a "perk," employee-friendly benefit, or advocacy cause, but as a powerful business tool that can enhance talent management, improve important human capital outcomes, and boost financial and operational performance.[41]

## Stock Market Reactions to Work-Life Initiatives

A recent study examined stock market effects of 130 announcements among *Fortune* 500 companies of work-life initiatives in *The Wall Street Journal*.[42] The study examined changes in share prices the day before, the day of, and the day after such announcements. The average share-price reaction over the three-day window was +0.39 percent, and the average dollar value of such changes was approximately $60 million per firm. Apparently investors anticipate that firms will have access to more resources (e.g., higher-quality talent) following the adoption of a work-life initiative. There is a difference, however, between announcements and actual implementation. Only firms that do what they say are likely to reap the benefits of work-life initiatives.

In another study, researchers used data from 1995 to 2002 to compare the financial and stock market performance of the "100 Best" companies for working mothers, as published each year by *Working Mother* magazine, to that of benchmark indexes of the performance of U.S. equities, the Standard & Poor's 500, and the Russell 3000.[43] In terms of financial performance, expressed as revenue productivity (sales per employee) and asset productivity (ROA), the study found no evidence that *Working Mother* "100 Best" companies were consistently more profitable or consistently more productive than their counterparts in S&P 500 companies.

At the same time, however, the total returns on common stock among *Working Mother* "100 Best" companies consistently outperformed the broader market benchmarks in each of the eight years of the study. Although the researchers found no evidence to indicate that "100 Best" companies are handicapped in the marketplace by offering generous work-life benefits, it may be the case that companies with superior stock returns have a lower cost of capital and therefore can afford to invest in such benefits. The results reflect *associations,* not *causation,* between firms that adopt family friendly work practices and financial and stock market outcomes.

Nonetheless, the results suggest the possibility that at least some of the association is due to the effects of family friendly investments on market outcomes.

## Cautions in Making the Business Case for Work-Life Programs

While the results of the studies just presented may seem compelling, remember that senior leaders have to buy in to the logic and analyses that underlie the adoption of work-life programs. At a general level, here is a three-pronged strategy to consider in securing that kind of buy-in:[44]

1. Make the business case for work-life initiatives through data, research, and anecdotal evidence.
2. Offer to train managers on how to use flexible management approaches— to understand that, for a variety of reasons, some people want to work long hours, way beyond the norm, but that's not for everybody. The objective is to train managers to understand that individual solutions will work better in the future than a one-size-fits-all approach.
3. Use surveys and focus groups to demonstrate the importance of work-life fit in retaining talent.

Beyond that, recognize that no one set of facts and figures will make the case for all firms. It depends on the strategic priorities of the organization in question. Figure 2–6 provides a diagnostic logic for conversations about this. One might start by discussing whether the organization's likely payoff will be primarily through talent management, human-capital outcomes (improved employee satisfaction, commitment, and engagement), business operations, or the costs of alternative programs. Start by finding out what your organization and its employees care about right now, what the workforce is going to look like in three to five years, and therefore, what they are going to need to care about in the future.[45]

Second, don't rely on isolated facts to make the business case. Considered by itself, any single study or fact is only one piece of the total picture. Think in terms of a multipronged approach:

- External data that describe trends in your organization's own industry.
- Internal data that outline what employees want and how they describe their needs.[46]
- Internal data, perhaps based on pilot studies, that examine the financial and nonfinancial effects of work-life programs. As one executive noted, "Nothing beats a within-firm story."[47]

Finally, recognize that some decision makers may well be skeptical even after all the facts and costs have been presented to them. That suggests that more deeply rooted attitudes and beliefs may underlie the skepticism—such as a belief that addressing personal concerns may erode service to clients or customers or that people will take unfair advantage of the benefits or that work-life issues are just women's issues. To inform that debate, HR leaders need to address attitudes and values, as well as data, on costs and benefits of work-life programs. As one set of authors noted, "Every workplace, small or large, can undertake efforts to treat employees with respect, to give them some autonomy over how they do their jobs, to help supervisors support employees to succeed on their jobs, and to help supervisors and coworkers promote work-life fit."[48]

Ultimately, a system of work-life programs, coupled with an organizational culture that supports that system, will help an organization create and sustain competitive advantage through its people.

## COSTING THE EFFECTS OF TRAINING ACTIVITIES

We will have more to say about the logic of training and development activities in Chapter 8. In this section, we place primary emphasis on analytics and measures, with the caution that sound design and effective implementation of training efforts are necessary, but not sufficient by themselves to ensure that what is learned in training actually is applied on the job.[49] For that to occur, managers must provide a work environment that actively supports the efforts of trainees to apply in practice what they learned in training. Then managers need to reward them for doing that.

From a measurement perspective, the task of evaluation is counting—counting clients, counting errors, counting dollars, counting hours, and so forth. The most difficult tasks of evaluation are deciding which things should be counted and developing routine methods for counting them. Managers should count the things that are most directly related to important strategic outcomes.

Training valuation (in financial terms) is not easy, but the technology to do it is available and well developed.[50] Evidence indicates that managers prefer to receive information about the financial results of training programs, rather than anecdotal information, regardless of the overall impact of such programs (low, average, or high).[51] Such information may be derived in two types of situations: one in which only indirect measures of dollar outcomes are available and one in which direct measures of dollar outcomes are available.

## Indirect Measures of Training Outcomes

**Indirect measures of training outcomes** are more common than direct measures. That is, many studies of training outcomes report improvements in job performance or decreases in errors, scrap, and waste. Relatively few studies report training outcomes directly in terms of dollars gained or saved. Indirect measures can often be converted into estimates of the dollar impact of training, however, by using a method known as utility analysis. Although the technical details of the method are beyond the scope of this chapter, following is a summary of one such study.[52]

A large, U.S.-based, multinational firm conducted a four-year investigation of the effect and utility of its corporate managerial and sales/technical training functions. The study is noteworthy because it adopted a strategic focus by comparing the payoffs from different types of training in order to assist decision makers in allocating training budgets and specifying the types of employees to be trained.[53]

### Project History

The CEO, a former research scientist, requested a report on the dollar value of training. He indicated that training should be evaluated experimentally, strategically aligned with the business goals of the organization, and thus demonstrated to be a worthwhile investment for the company. Thus, the impetus for this large-scale study came from the top of the organization.

### Methodological Issues

In a project of this scope and complexity, it is necessary to address several important methodological issues. The first concerns the outcomes or **criteria** to use in judging each program's effectiveness. Training courses that attempt to influence the supervisory style of managers may affect a large percentage of the tasks that comprise that job. Conversely, a course designed to affect sales of a specific product may only influence a few of the tasks in the sales representative's job. The researchers corrected for this issue to ensure that the estimate of economic payoff for each training program only represented the value of performance on specific job elements.

A second issue that must be considered when assessing the effectiveness of alternative training programs is the **transfer of trained skills** from the training to the job. For the training to have value, skills must be generalized to the job (i.e., exhibited on the job), and such transfer must be maintained for some period of time. To address the issue of transfer, the measure of performance on all training programs was behavioral performance on the job. Performance was assessed by means of a survey completed by each trainee's supervisor (for most courses), peers (i.e., hazardous energy control), or subordinates (i.e., team building) before and after training.

Because it was not possible to assess the length of training's effects in this study, decision makers assumed that training's effect (and economic utility) was maintained without decay or growth for precisely one year. In addition, the researchers calculated **break-even values,** which indicate the length of time the observed effect would need to be maintained in order to recover the cost of the training program.[54]

### Training Programs Evaluated

A sample of 18 high-use or high-cost courses was selected based on the recommendation of the training departments throughout the organization. Managerial training courses were defined as courses developed for individuals with managerial or supervisory duties. Sales training courses were defined as programs designed to enhance the performance of sales representatives by affecting sales performance or support of their own sales. Technical training courses (e.g., hazardous energy control, in-house time management) were defined as courses not specifically designed for sales or supervisory personnel.

Of the 18 programs, 8 evaluation studies used a **control-group design** in which training was provided to one group and not provided to a second group similar to the trained group in terms of relevant characteristics. The remaining 10 training program evaluations relied on a **pretest–posttest only design,** in which a control group was not used and the performance of the trained group alone was evaluated before and after the training program.

***Results.***     Over all 18 programs, assuming a normal distribution of performance on the job, the average improvement was about 17 percent (0.54 of a standard deviation, or SD). However, for technical/sales training it was higher (0.64 SD), and for managerial training it was lower (0.31 SD). Thus, training in general was effective.

The mean ROI was 45 percent for the managerial training programs, and 418 percent for the sales/technical training programs. However, one inexpensive time-management program developed in-house had an ROI of nearly 2,000 percent. When the economic utility of that program is removed, the overall average ROI of the remaining training programs was 84 percent and the ROI of sales/technical training was 156 percent.

***Time to Break-Even Values.***     There was considerable variability in these values. Break-even periods ranged from a few weeks (e.g., time management, written communications) to several years (supervisory skills, leadership skills). Several programs were found to have little positive or even slightly negative effects, and thus would never yield a financial gain.

### Conclusions

This study compared the effectiveness and economic utility of different types of training across sales, technical, and managerial jobs. The estimated cost of the four-year project, including the fully loaded cost of rater time, as well as the cost of consulting, travel, and materials, was approximately $790,000 (in 2011 dollars). This number may seem large. However, over the same time period, the organization spent more than $375 million on training. Thus the cost of the training program evaluation was approximately 0.2 percent of the training budget during the same period. Given budgets of this magnitude, some sort of accountability is prudent.

Despite the overall positive effects and utility of the training, there were some exceptions. The important lesson to be learned is that it is necessary to evaluate the effect and utility of each training program before drawing overall conclusions about the impact of training. It would be simplistic to claim that "training is a good investment" or that "training is a waste of time and money."[55]

## Direct Measures of Training Outcomes

When **direct measures of training outcomes** are available, standard valuation methods are appropriate. The following study valued the results of a behavior-modeling training program (described more fully below) for sales representatives in relation to the program's effects on sales performance.[56]

### Study Design

A large retailer conducted a behavior-modeling program in two departments, large appliances and radio/TV, within 14 of its stores in one large metropolitan area. The 14 stores were matched into seven pairs in terms of size, location, and market characteristics. Stores with unusual characteristics that could affect their overall performance, such as declining sales or recent changes in management, were not included in the study.

The training program was then introduced in seven stores, one in each of the matched pairs, and not in the other seven stores. Other kinds of ongoing sales training programs were provided in the control-group stores, but the behavior-modeling approach was used only in the seven experimental-group stores. In the experimental-group stores, 58 sales associates received the training, and their job performance was compared with that of 64 sales associates in the same departments in the control-group stores.

As in most sales organizations, detailed sales records for each individual were kept on a continuous basis. These records included total sales as well as hours worked on the sales floor. Because all individuals received commissions on their sales and because the value of the various products sold varied greatly, it was possible to compute a job performance measure for each individual in terms of average commissions per hour worked.

There was considerable variation in the month-to-month sales performance of each individual, but sales performance over six-month periods was more stable. In fact, the average correlation between consecutive sales periods of six months each was about 0.80 (where 1.00 equals perfect agreement). Hence, the researchers decided to compare the sales records of participants for six months before the training program was introduced with the results achieved during the same six months the following year, after the training was concluded. All sales promotions and other programs in the stores were identical, since these were administered on an areawide basis.

### The Training Program Itself

The program focused on specific aspects of sales situations, such as "approaching the customer," "explaining features, advantages, and benefits," and "closing the sale." The training itself proceeded according to the following procedure. First the trainers presented guidelines (or "learning points") for handling each aspect of a sales interaction. Then the trainees viewed a videotaped situation in which a "model" sales associate followed the guidelines in carrying out that aspect of the sales interaction with a customer. The trainees then practiced the same situation in role-playing rehearsals. Their performance was reinforced and shaped by their supervisors, who had been trained as their instructors.

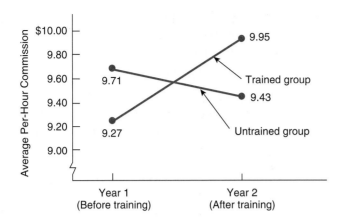

**Figure 2–7**

Changes in per-hour commissions before and after the behavior-modeling training program.

## Study Results

Of the original 58 trainees in the experimental group, 50 were still working as sales associates one year later. Of the remaining 8 associates, 4 had been promoted during the interim, and 4 others had left the company. In the control-group stores, only 49 of the original 64 were still working as sales associates one year later. Only 1 had been promoted, and 14 others had left the company. Thus, the behavior-modeling program may have had a substantial positive effect on turnover since only about 7 percent of the trained group left during the ensuing year, in comparison with 22 percent of those in the control group. (This result had not been predicted.)

Figure 2–7 presents the changes in average per-hour commissions for participants in both the trained and untrained groups from the six-month period before the training was conducted to the six-month period following the training. Note in Figure 2–7 that the trained and untrained groups did not have equal per-hour commissions at the start of the study. While the stores that members of the two groups worked in were matched at the start of the study, sales commissions were not. Sales associates in the trained group started at a lower point than did sales associates in the untrained group. Average per-hour commissions for the trained group increased over the year from $9.27 to $9.95 ($23.58 to $25.32 in 2011 dollars); average per-hour commissions for the untrained group declined over the year from $9.71 to $9.43 ($24.69 to $23.97 in 2011 dollars). In other words, the trained sales associates increased their average earnings by about 7 percent, whereas those who did not receive the behavior-modeling training experienced a 3 percent decline in average earnings. This difference was statistically significant. Other training outcomes (e.g., trainee attitudes, supervisory behaviors) were also assessed, but, for our purposes, the most important lesson was that the study provided objective evidence to indicate the dollar impact of the training on increased sales.

The program also had an important secondary effect on turnover. Because all sales associates are given considerable training (which represents an extensive investment of time and money), it appears that the behavior modeling contributed to *cost savings* in addition to *increased sales*. As noted in the previous discussion of turnover costs, an accurate estimate of these cost savings requires that the turnovers be separated into controllable and uncontrollable, because training can affect only controllable turnover.

Finally, the use of objective data as criterion measures in a study of this kind does entail some problems. As pointed out earlier, the researchers found that a six-month period was required to balance out the month-to-month variations in sales performance resulting from changing work schedules, sales promotions, and similar influences that affected individual results. It also took some vigilance to ensure that the records needed for the study were kept in a consistent and conscientious manner in each store. According to the researchers, however, these problems were not great in relation to the usefulness of the study results. "The evidence that the training program had a measurable effect on sales was certainly more convincing in demonstrating the value of the program than would be merely the opinions of participants that the training was worthwhile."[57]

## IMPACT OF HUMAN RESOURCE MANAGEMENT ACTIVITIES ON PRODUCTIVITY, QUALITY OF WORK LIFE, AND THE BOTTOM LINE

There is a growing consensus among managers in many industries that the future success of their firms may depend more on the skill with which human problems are handled than on the degree to which their firms maintain leadership in technical areas. For example, every year, *Fortune* magazine conducts an annual survey of the "100 Best Companies to Work For." If satisfied, engaged employees really do fuel corporate profits, one would expect "100 Best" employers to outperform broad indexes of firms that are publicly traded—and they do.[a]

In one well-controlled study, for example, researchers compared the organizational performance of *Fortune's* "100 Best Companies to Work For" with two sets of other companies, a matched group and the broad market of publicly traded firms, over a six-year period.[b] They found that organization-level employee attitudes of the 100 Best firms were both highly positive and stable over time. They also found that the return on assets and market-to-book value of the equity of publicly traded companies included on the 100 Best list were generally better than those of a matched comparison group. That finding established an important link between employee attitudes and organization-level financial performance.

As for stock returns, the same study found that the 100 Best companies outperformed the broad market when considering cumulative (longer-term) returns (82 percent versus 37 percent over a three-year period), although not consistently for annual returns. The authors concluded, "At the very least, our study finds no evidence that positive employee relations comes at the expense of financial performance. Firms can have both."[c]

[a]See, for example, Edmans, A. (2009, Aug. 12). Does the stock market fully value intangibles? Employee satisfaction and equity prices. Retrieved from *http://ssrn.com/abstract=985735* on May 28, 2010; Cappelli, P. (2008, June 26). The value of being a best employer. Retrieved from *http://www.hreonline.com* on June 26, 2008; Filbeck, G., and Preece, D. (2003). *Fortune's* Best 100 companies to work for in America: Do they work for shareholders? *Journal of Business Finance & Accounting* 30(5), pp. 771–797.

[b]Fulmer, I. S., Gerhart, B., and Scott, K. S. (2003). Are the 100 Best better? An empirical investigation of the relationship between being a "great place to work" and firm performance. *Personnel Psychology* 56, pp. 965–993.

[c]Ibid.

## LINKING WORKER BELIEFS TO INCREASED PRODUCTIVITY AND PROFITABILITY

*Human Resource Management in Action: Conclusion*

The very best managers seem to share four key behaviors that help to trigger the 12 worker beliefs that underlie a profitable, productive workplace.

1. **Select for talent.** Gallup defines talent in terms of patterns of thoughts, feelings, and behaviors that come naturally to an individual. The best managers identify talents that are needed for a particular position and then find people who fit the role. This means looking beyond a person's knowledge and skills to size up whether a job really "fits" him or her. To do that, one must take into account the broad range of factors—situational, contextual, strategic, and environmental—that may affect that person's performance.[58]
2. **Define the right outcomes.** Managers who do this best establish very clear objectives (so employees know exactly what they need to attain); they make sure that employees have the resources to do their jobs well (e.g., equipment, information, budget, staff); and then they allow employees to pave their own paths. The best managers don't define the steps for their employees or legislate style.
3. **Focus on strengths.** Rather than identifying workers' weaknesses and attempting to fix them, where the gains will be short-lived, managers focus on strengths. They identify and reinforce strengths, and then figure out where workers' strengths will serve the company best.[59]
4. **Find the right fit.** According to Gallup's Coffman, "Talent never becomes 'talented' without being given a role for it to shine." The best managers continually encourage their employees to look in the mirror and assess themselves in order to find the kind of work that will bring out their best talents.

## ETHICAL DILEMMA
### Survey Feedback: Nice or Necessary?

Is it unethical to ask employees for their opinions, attitudes, values, or beliefs on an attitude survey and then subsequently not give them any feedback about the results? We know that survey results that are not fed back to employees are unlikely to be translated into action strategies, and that it is poor management practice to fail to provide feedback.[a]

Is it unethical as well? (*Hint:* See the definition of ethical decision making in Chapter 1.)

[a]Wiley, J. W. (2010). *Strategic Employee Surveys: Evidenced-Based Guidelines for Driving Organizational Success.* San Francisco, CA: Jossey-Bass. See also Kraut, A. I. (1996). *Organizational Surveys.* San Francisco, CA: Jossey-Bass.

## IMPLICATIONS FOR MANAGEMENT PRACTICE

How can such substantial gains in productivity, quality, and profits as we have described in this chapter occur? They happen because high-performance management practices provide a number of sources for enhanced organizational performance:[a]

1. People work harder because of the increased involvement and commitment that comes from having more control and say in their work. Managers who adopt democratic leadership styles influence employees' perceptions of personal control over their work.

2. People work smarter because they are encouraged to build skills and competence. Managers have considerable influence over the opportunities for professional growth and development of their employees.

3. Finally, people work more responsibly because more responsibility is placed in the hands of employees farther down in the organization. Again, managers who delegate responsibility appropriately can foster such feelings of responsibility on the part of their subordinates. These practices work not because of some mystical process, but because they are grounded in sound social science principles that are supported by a great deal of evidence. Managers should use them to create win-win scenarios for themselves and for their people.

[a] Pfeffer, J., and Veiga, J. F. (1999). Putting people first for organizational success. *Academy of Management Excecutive* 13(2), pp. 37–48.

## SUMMARY

The overall theme of this chapter is that HR measurement is valuable to the extent that it improves vital decisions about talent and how it is organized. To have genuine strategic impact, HR measures must be embedded within logical frameworks that drive sound strategic decisions about talent. *Talent* refers to the potential and realized capacities of individuals and groups and how they are organized, including those within the organization and those who might join the organization.

As an organizing framework, we presented the LAMP model, where the letters LAMP stand for logic, analytics, measures, and process. *Logic* is the "story" that connects the numbers. *Analytics* transforms HR logic and measures into rigorous, relevant insights that enable researchers and managers to draw correct conclusions from data. Whereas statistics and research design are analytical strategies for drawing correct conclusions from data, *measures* comprise the numbers that populate the statistical formulas. *Process* is the final element of the LAMP framework. It calls attention to the fact that decisions and behavior unfold within a complex social system and that effective measurement systems must fit within a change-management process that begins by influencing key decision makers. The purpose of the process phase is to create actionable insights that lead to genuine strategic change.

Payoffs from determining the cost of employee behaviors lie in being able to demonstrate a financial gain from the wise application of human resource management methods. The remainder of the chapter used the LAMP framework to present both hypothetical and actual company examples of such measurement in the areas of employee attitudes, absenteeism, turnover, work-life programs, and training.

## KEY TERMS

LAMP

direct measures

indirect measures

behavior costing

controllable costs

uncontrollable costs

attitudes

job satisfaction

organizational commitment

absenteeism

turnover

work-life program

return on investment

indirect measures of training
  outcomes

criteria

transfer of trained skills

break-even values

control–group design

pretest–posttest only design

direct measures of training
  outcomes

## DISCUSSION QUESTIONS

**2–1.** What are the key elements of the LAMP model? What does each contribute?

**2–2.** Given the positive financial returns from high-performance work practices, why don't more firms implement them?

**2–3.** Why is management interested in the financial effects of employee attitudes?

**2–4.** Discuss three controllable and three uncontrollable costs associated with absenteeism.

**2–5.** Why should efforts to reduce turnover focus only on controllable costs?

**2–6.** In making the business case for work-life programs, what points would you emphasize?

## APPLYING YOUR KNOWLEDGE

### Absenteeism at ONO Inc.
*Case 2–1*

ONO Inc. is an auto-supply company with 11 employees. In addition, there are two supervisors and Fred Donofrio, the owner and general manager. Last year, ONO did $6 million in business and earned $305,000 in profits ($455,000 before taxes). The auto-supply business is extremely competitive, and owners must constantly be on the lookout for ways to reduce costs to remain profitable.

Employee salaries at ONO average $23.50 an hour, and benefits add another 33 percent to these labor costs. The two supervisors earn an average of $31.50 an hour, with a similar level (percentage) of benefits. Employees receive two weeks of vacation each year and 12 days of paid sick leave.

Over the last two years, Fred Donofrio has noted an increasing rate of absenteeism among his 11 employees. (There seems to be no similar problem with the two supervisors.) Last week, he asked Cal Jenson, his most senior supervisor, to go through the records from last year and determine how much absenteeism had cost ONO. Further, he asked Cal to make any recommendations to him that seemed appropriate depending on the magnitude of the problem.

Cal determined that ONO lost a total of 539 employee labor-hours (67.375 days) to absenteeism last year. (This figure did not, of course, include vacation time.) Further, he estimated that he and the other supervisor together averaged 1.5 hours in lost time whenever an employee was absent for a day. This time was spent dealing with the extra problems (rescheduling work, filling in for missing workers, etc.) that an absence created. On several occasions last year, ONO was so short of help that temporary workers had to be hired or present employees had to work overtime. Cal determined that the additional costs of overtime and outside help last year totaled $12,400. Cal is now in the process of preparing his report to Fred Donofrio.

---

### Questions

1. What figure will Cal Jenson report to Fred Donofrio for the amount that absenteeism cost ONO last year?
2. Is absenteeism a serious problem at ONO? Why or why not?
3. What recommendations for action could Cal Jenson make to Fred Donofrio?

---

## REFERENCES

1.  Cascio, W. F., and Boudreau, J. W. (2011). *Investing in People: Financial Impact of Human Resource Initiatives* (2nd ed.). Upper Saddle River, NJ: Pearson Education/ Financial Times Press.
2.  Herman, A. E., and Cascio, W. F. (2011, April). Learning in action: Leveraging data from the employee experience to drive performance. Paper presented at the annual conference of the Society for Industrial and Organizational Psychology, Chicago, IL.
3.  Huselid, M. A., Becker, B. E., and Beatty, R. W. (2005). *The Workforce Scorecard.* Boston: Harvard Business School Press. See also Fitz-enz, J. (1984). *How to Measure Human Resources Management.* New York: McGraw-Hill.
4.  For more on this issue see Jex, S. (2007). Stress, models and theories. In S. G. Rogelberg (Ed.), *Encyclopedia of Industrial and Organizational Psychology,* Vol. 2 Thousand Oaks, CA: Sage Publications, pp. 770–773. See also Sonnentag, S., and Frese, M. (2003). Stress in organizations. In W. C. Borman, D. R. Ilgen, and R. J. Klimoski. (Eds.), *Handbook of Psychology: Industrial and Organizational Psychology,* Vol. 12. Hoboken, NJ: Wiley, pp. 453–491. See also DeFrank, R. S., Konopaske, R., and Ivancevich, J. M. (2000). Executive travel stress: Perils of the road warrior. *Academy of Management Executive* 14(2), pp. 58–71.
5.  Beckler, S. J. (1984). Empirical validation of affect, behavior, and cognition as distinct components of attitude. *Journal of Personality and Social Psychology* 47, pp. 1191–1205.
6.  Hulin, C. L., and Judge, T. A. (2003). Job attitudes. In W. C. Borman, D. R. Ilgen, and R. J. Klimoski. (Eds.), *Handbook of Psychology: Industrial and Organizational Psychology,* Vol. 12. Hoboken, NJ: Wiley, pp. 255–276.
7.  Klein, H. J., Molloy, J. C., and Cooper, J. T. (2009). Conceptual foundations: Construct definitions and theoretical representations of workplace commitments. In H. J. Klein, T. E. Becker, and J. P. Meyer (Eds.), *Commitment in Organizations.* New York: Taylor

& Francis. See also Mathieu, J. E., and Zajac, D. M. (1990). A review and meta-analysis of the antecedents, correlates, and consequences of organizational commitment. *Psychological Bulletin* 108(2), pp. 171–194.

8.  Schaufeli, W. B., Bakker, A. B., and Salanova, M. (2006). The measurement of work engagement with a short questionnaire: A cross-national study. *Educational and Psychological Measurement,* 66, pp. 701–716.

9.  Macey, W. H., and Schneider, B. (2008). The meaning of employee engagement. *Industrial and Organizational Psychology: Perspectives on Science and Practice* 1, pp. 3–30.

10. Macey and Schneider, op. cit. See also Graen, G. (2008). Enriched engagement through assistance to systems change: A proposal. *Industrial and Organizational Psychology: Perspectives on Science and Practice,* 1, pp. 74–75. See also Ryan, A. M., Schmit, M. J., and Johnson, R. (1996). Attitudes and effectiveness: Examining relations at an organizational level. *Personnel Psychology* 49, pp. 853–883. See also Cohen, A. (1993). Organizational commitment and turnover: A meta-analysis. *Academy of Management Journal* 36, pp. 1140–1157. See also Ostroff, C. (1992). The relationship between satisfaction, attitudes, and performance: An organizational-level analysis. *Journal of Applied Psychology* 77, pp. 963–974.

11. Mirvis, P. H., and Lawler, E. E. III. (1977). Measuring the financial impact of employee attitudes. *Journal of Applied Psychology* 62, pp. 1–8.

12. Heskett, J. L., Jones, T. O., Loveman, G. W., Sasser, W. E., Jr., and Schlesinger, L. A. (1994, March/April). Putting the service-profit chain to work. Harvard Business Review 72, pp. 164–174.

13. Carrig, K., and Wright, P. M. (2006). *Building Profit through Building People: Making Your Workforce the Strongest Link in the Value-Profit Chain.* Alexandria, VA: Society for Human Resource Management.

14. Ibid.

15. Fox, A. (2010, May). Raising engagement. *HR Magazine* pp. 35–40.

16. Carrig and Wright, 2006, op. cit.

17. Society for Human Resource Management. (2009, June 15). Managing employee attendance. Retrieved from *www.shrm.org/Research/Articles/Articles/Pages/ManagingEmployeeAttendance* on May 11, 2010.

18. Society for Human Resource Management, 2009, op. cit.

19. Ibid.

20. On the job. (2006, Apr. 24). *BusinessWeek,* p. 13.

21. Cascio, W. F., and Boudreau, J. W. (2011). *Investing in People: Financial Impact of Human Resource Initiatives* (2nd Ed.). Upper Saddle River, NJ: Pearson Education.

22. United States Department of Labor, Bureau of Labor Statistics, Data Bases and Tables. Retrieved from *www.bls.gov/jlt/* on.

23. Cascio and Boudreau, 2011, op. cit.

24. Cascio, W. F., and Boudreau, J. W. (2011). *Investing in People: Financial impact of human Resource Initiatives* (2nd ed.). Upper Saddle River, NJ: Pearson Educational/Financial Times Press.

25. Dooney, J. (Nov. 2005). Cost of turnover. Retrieved from *www.shrm.org,* February 6, 2006.

26. For more on this subject, see Cascio, W. F., and Boudreau, J. W. (2008). *Investing in People: Financial Impact of Human Resource Initiatives.* Upper Saddle River, NJ: Pearson Educational/Financial Times Press.

27. Cossack, S. Guthridge, M., and Lawson, E. (2010, Aug.). Retaining key employees in times of change. *McKinsey Quarterly.* Retrieved from *http://www.mckinseyquarterly.com/Retaining_key_employees_in_times_of_change_2654* on December 30, 2010.

28. Allen, D. G. (2008). *Retaining Talent.* Alexandria, VA: SHRM Foundation.

29. For more on this, see Welch, J., and Welch, S. (2008, Jan. 28). Employee polls: A vote in favor. *BusinessWeek,* p. 90. See also Steel, R. P., Griffeth, R. W., and Hom, P. W. (2002). Practical retention policy for the practical manager. *Academy of Management Executive* 16(2), pp. 149–159. See also Griffeth, R. W., Hom, P. W., and Gaertner, S.

(2000). A meta-analysis of antecedents and correlates of employee turnover: Update, moderator tests, and research implications for the next millennium. *Journal of Management* 26, pp. 463–488.

30. Cascio, W. F., and Fogli, L. (2008, Apr.). Talent acquisition: New realities of attraction, selection, and retention . Workshop presented at the annual conference of the Society for Industrial and Organizational Psychology, Chicago.

31. Abbott, J., De Cieri, H., and Iverson, R. D. (1998). Costing turnover: Implications of work/family conflict at management level. *Asia Pacific Journal of Human Resources* 36(1), pp. 25–43. See also Branch, S. (1998, Nov. 9). You hired 'em. But can you keep 'em? *Fortune,* pp. 247–250.

32. Hewlett, S. A., and Luce, C. B. (2005, Mar.). Off-ramps and on-ramps: Keeping talented women on the road to success. *Harvard Business Review,* pp. 43–54.

33. Solomon, J. (1998, Dec. 29). Companies try measuring cost savings from new types of corporate benefits. *The Wall Street Journal,* p. B1.

34. Arthur, M. (2003). Share price reactions to work-family initiatives: An institutional perspective. *Academy of Management Journal* 46, 497–505. See also Edwards, J. R., and Rothbard, N. P. (2000). Mechanisms linking work and family: Clarifying the relationship between work and family constructs. *Academy of Management Review,* 25, pp. 178–199.

35. Bardoel, E. A., Tharenou, P., and Moss, S. A. (1998). Organizational predictors of work-family practices. *Asia Pacific Journal of Human Resources,* pp. 1–49.

36. Gurchiek, K., (2007, March 5). Child-care "investment" creates competitive advantage. *HR News.* Retrieved from *www.shrm.org* on May 25, 2010.

37. Ibid.

38. O'Connell, B. No baby sitter? Emergency child-care to the rescue, compensation & benefits forum. Retrieved from *www.shrm.org* May 25, 2010.

39. Gurchiek, 2007, op. cit.

40. Corporate Voices for Working Families. (2011, Feb.). Business impacts of flexibility: An imperative for expansion (p. 5). Retrieved from *http://www.cvwf.org/ publication-toolkits/business-impacts-flexibility-imperative-expansion-november-2005* on September 28, 2011.

41. Ibid.

42. Arthur, M. (2003). Share price reactions to work-family initiatives: an institutional perspective. *Academy of Management Journal* 46, pp. 497–505.

43. Cascio, W. F., and Young, C. (2005). Work-family balance: Does the market reward firms that respect it? In D. F. Halpern and S. E. Murphy (Eds.), *From Work-Family Balance to Work-Family Interaction: Changing the Metaphor.* Mahwah, NJ: Lawrence Erlbaum Associates, pp. 49–63.

44. Society for Human Resource Management. (2008, Sept. 26). Expert: Work/life initiatives start at the top. Retrieved from *http://www.shrm.org/Publications/HRNews/ Pages/InitiativesStartatTop.aspx* on May 25, 2010.

45. Pires, P. S. (2005). Sitting at the corporate table: How work-family policies are really made. In D. F. Halpern and S. E. Murphy (Eds.), *From Work-Family Balance to Work-Family Interaction: Changing the Metaphor.* Mahwah, NJ: Erlbaum, pp. 71–81.

46. Caminiti, S. (2004, Sept. 20). Reinventing the workplace. *Fortune,* pp. S12–S15.

47. Roberts, B. (2009 Oct.). Analyze This! *HR Magazine,* pp. 35–41.

48. Aumann, K., and Galinsky, E. (2009). *The 2008 National Study of the Changing Workforce: The State of Health of the American Workforce: Does Having an Effective Workplace Matter?* New York: Families and Work Institute.

49. Boudreau, J. W., and Ramstad, P. M. (2007). *Beyond HR: The New Science of Human Capital.* Boston: Harvard Business School Publishing.

50. Cascio and Boudreau, 2011, op. cit. See also Cascio, W. F. (1989). Using utility analysis to assess training outcomes. In I. L. Goldstein (Ed.), *Training and Development in Organizations* (2nd ed). San Francisco: Jossey-Bass, pp. 63–88.

51. Mattson, B. W. (2003). The effects of alternative reports of human resource development results on managerial support. *Human Resource Development Quarterly* 14(2), pp. 127–151.

52. Cascio, W. F., and Boudreau, J. W. (2011). Utility of selection systems: Supply-chain analysis applied to staffing decisions. In S. Zedeck (Ed.), *APA Handbook of Industrial and Organizational Psychology* (Vol. 2). Washington, D.C.: American Psychological Association, pp. 421–444. See also Boudreau, J. W., and Ramstad, P. M. (2003). Strategic industrial and organizational psychology and the role of utility analysis models. In W. C. Borman, D. R. Ilgen, and R. J. Klimoski (Eds.), *Handbook of Psychology: Industrial and Organizational Psychology,* Vol. 12. Hoboken, NJ: Wiley, pp. 193–221. For a contrarian view, see Skarlicki, D. P., Latham, G. P., and Whyte, G. (1996). Utility analysis: Its evolution and tenuous role in human resource management decision making. *Canadian Journal of Administrative Sciences* 13(1), pp. 13–21.

53. Morrow, C. C., Jarrett, M. Q., and Rupinski, M. T. (1997). An investigation of the effect and economic utility of corporate-wide training. *Personnel Psychology* 50, pp. 91–119.

54. For more on break-even analysis, see Cascio and Boudreau, 2011, op. cit., or Boudreau, J. W. (1984). Decision theory contributions to HRM research and practice. *Industrial Relations* 23, pp. 198–217.

55. Morrow, Jarrett, and Rupinski, 1997, op. cit.

56. Meyer, H. H., and Raich, J. S. (1983). An objective evaluation of a behavior modeling training program. *Personnel Psychology* 36, pp. 755–761.

57. Ibid., p. 761.

58. Cascio, W. F., and Aguinis, H. (2008). Staffing 21st-century organizations. *Academy of Management Annals* 2(1), pp. 133-165.

59. The founder and former chairman of SRI Gallup, Donald Clifton, co-authored three books on this very theme. Rath, T., and Clifton, D. O. (2004). *How Full Is Your Bucket? Positive Strategies for Work and Life.* Lincoln, NE: Gallup Press. Buckingham, M., and Clifton, D. O. (2001). *Now, Discover Your Strengths.* NY: Free Press. Clifton, D. O., and Nelson, P. (1992). *Soar with Your Strengths.* NY: Delacorte Press.

# 3

# THE LEGAL CONTEXT OF EMPLOYMENT DECISIONS

*Questions This Chapter Will Help Managers Answer*

1. How are employment practices affected by the civil rights laws and Supreme Court interpretations of those laws?
2. What should be the components of an effective policy to prevent sexual harassment?
3. What obligations does the Family and Medical Leave Act impose on employers? What rights does it grant to employees?
4. When a company is in the process of downsizing, what strategies can it use to avoid complaints of age discrimination?
5. What should senior management do to ensure that job applicants or employees with disabilities receive "reasonable accommodation"?

## RETALIATION: A NEW LEGAL STANDARD AND SOME PREVENTIVE MEASURES*

According to the U.S. Equal Employment Opportunity Commission (EEOC), an employer may not fire, demote, harass, or otherwise "retaliate" against an individual for filing a charge of discrimination, participating in a discrimination proceeding, or otherwise opposing discrimination. The same laws that prohibit discrimination based on race, color, sex, religion, national origin, age, and disability, as well as wage differences between men and women performing substantially equal work, also prohibit retaliation against individuals who oppose unlawful discrimination or participate in an employment discrimination proceeding.

Prior to a recent U.S. Supreme Court decision, case law had defined retaliation as largely meaning the loss of a job. The Court's ruling in *Burlington Northern & Santa Fe Railway Co. v. White* (126 S. Ct. 2405), however, expanded the definition of employer retaliation, making it easier for employees to file such claims. Specifically, the ruling allows workers to file retaliation suits even when an employment action does not diminish their pay, hours, or benefits, or cause them to suffer a monetary loss of any kind. Moreover, anti-retaliation law potentially extends to any employer conduct, even when it is not work-related.

First we will review the facts of the case, and then, in the conclusion at the end of the chapter, focus on its implications, as well as preventive actions by employers.

*The Facts of the Case.* In the Burlington Northern case, the Supreme Court grappled with a fundamental question: What kind of employer behavior constitutes retaliation under Title VII of the Civil Rights Act of 1964? The case centered on Sheila White, who worked in the railroad's Tennessee Yard and was assigned to operate a forklift—a cleaner, less onerous task than those performed by other yard workers.

White lost this plum assignment after making an internal sexual harassment complaint against her foreman, Bill Joiner. After an investigation, Joiner was disciplined. When Marvin Brown, the manager in charge, informed White of the investigation's results, he also told her she would no longer be operating the forklift because coworkers complained that she had received the cushier position despite having less seniority than some of her peers. As a result, White was assigned to perform the more arduous tasks performed by other yard workers. White reacted by filing a complaint with the EEOC, alleging sex discrimination and retaliation. She also filed a second discrimination charge with the EEOC for retaliation, alleging that Brown had placed her under surveillance.

Around the time of the second charge, White had a disagreement with her new foreman, Percy Sharkey. Sharkey reported the disagreement to Brown,

---

*\*Sources:* Janove, J. (2006, Oct.). Retaliation nation. *HRMagazine,* pp. 63–67. U.S. Equal Employment Opportunity Commission. Retaliation. n.d., Retrieved from *www.eeoc.gov/types/retaliation.html* on April 14, 2008. Payback of the week. (2006, July 10). *BusinessWeek,* p. 25. Brooks, B., Farb, G., and Ballard, M. (2011, Jan.). The future of retaliation claims. *HRMagazine* 56(1), pp. 69–71. Segal, J. A. (2009, Feb.). A warning about warnings. *HRMagazine* 54(2), pp. 67–70.

who decided that White's behavior constituted insubordination and that she should lose her job. Within three days of the second EEOC charge being mailed to Brown, he suspended White without pay. Under a company procedure, the suspension would convert to a discharge unless successfully challenged in grievance procedures.

White successfully challenged the suspension and was reinstated with full back pay and benefits. Nevertheless, she sued Burlington Northern in court for sex discrimination and retaliation. A jury found for the employer on the sex discrimination claim, but held that its behavior constituted unlawful retaliation. Appeals eventually led to the Supreme Court, which upheld the jury's verdict. The court held that White's removal from the forklift and her suspension constituted retaliation, even though her job status—including pay, hours, and benefits—did not change, and even though she did not suffer a monetary loss.

The fact that Burlington Northern reinstated White with back pay was immaterial as to whether it violated the law. The court ruled that the sweep of the antiretaliation law extends to any employer conduct, even when it is not work-related, that is severe enough to deter a reasonable employee from exercising her legal right to object to discrimination. For example, an employer can retaliate through actions taken outside the workplace, such as by filing false criminal charges against a former employee who complained about discrimination.

The court also ruled that whether such conduct reaches this threshold cannot be spelled out comprehensively. Rather, each case will have to be evaluated within its own context. For example, a supervisor's refusal to invite an employee to lunch is normally trivial, a petty slight. But suppose that same supervisor retaliates by excluding an employee from a weekly training lunch that contributes significantly to the employee's professional advancement? Such an action might well deter a reasonable employee from complaining about discrimination, and, consequently, might constitute illegal, retaliatory conduct, according to the court.

### Challenges

1. What effects do you think this decision has had on the number of retaliation charges filed with the EEOC?
2. What can an employer do to avoid liability for retaliation?
3. Following this ruling, what changes in company policies might be necessary?

## SOCIETAL OBJECTIVES

As a society, we espouse equality of opportunity, rather than equality of outcomes. That is, the broad goal is to provide for all Americans—regardless of race, age, gender, religion, national origin, or disability—an equal opportunity to compete for jobs for which they are qualified. The objective, therefore, is EEO (equal employment opportunity), not EE (equal employment, or equal numbers of employees from various subgroups).[1] For Americans with disabilities, the nation's goals are to ensure equality of opportunity, full participation, independent living, and economic self-sufficiency.

The U.S. population, as well as its workforce, is a diverse lot. Even among native-born English speakers, at least 22 different dialects of English are spoken in the United States! Whenever the members of such heterogeneous groups must work together, the possibility of unfair discrimination exists. Civil rights laws have been passed at the federal and state levels to provide remedies for job applicants or employees who feel they have been victims of unfair discrimination. From a managerial perspective, it is important to understand the rights as well as the obligations of employers, job candidates, and employees. Indeed, understanding these laws and their management implications is critical for all managers, not just for HR professionals. As we will see, ignorance in this area can turn out to be very expensive. Let's begin by considering the meaning of EEO and the forms of unfair discrimination.

## EEO AND UNFAIR DISCRIMINATION: WHAT ARE THEY?

Civil rights laws, judicial interpretations of the laws, and the many sets of guidelines issued by state and federal regulatory agencies have outlawed discrimination based on race, religion, national origin, age, sex, and physical disability. In short, they have attempted to frame national policy on **equal employment opportunity (EEO).** Although no law has ever attempted to define precisely the term **discrimination,** in the employment context it can be viewed broadly as the giving of an unfair advantage (or disadvantage) to the members of a particular group in comparison with the members of other groups.[2] The disadvantage usually results in a denial or restriction of employment opportunities or in an inequality in the terms or benefits of employment.

It is important to note that whenever there are more candidates than available positions, it is necessary to select some candidates in preference to others. Selection implies exclusion. And as long as the exclusion is based on what can be demonstrated to be job-related criteria, that kind of discrimination is entirely proper. It is only when candidates are excluded on a prohibited basis, one that is not related to the job (e.g., age, race, gender), that unlawful and unfair discrimination exists. In short, EEO implies at least two things:

1. *Evaluation of candidates for jobs in terms of characteristics that really do make a difference between success and failure* (e.g., in selection, promotion, performance appraisal, or layoff).
2. *Fair and equal treatment of employees on the job* (e.g., equal pay for equal work, equal benefits, freedom from sexual harassment).

Despite federal and state laws on these issues, they represent the basis of an enormous volume of court cases, indicating that stereotypes and prejudices do not die quickly or easily. Discrimination is a subtle and complex phenomenon that may assume two broad forms:

1. **Unequal** (disparate) **treatment** is based on an intention to discriminate, including the intention to retaliate against a person who opposes

discrimination, has brought charges, or has participated in an investigation or a hearing. There are three major subtheories of discrimination within the disparate treatment theory:

a. Cases that rely on **direct evidence** of the intention to discriminate. Such cases are proved with direct evidence of other pure bias based on an open expression of hatred, disrespect, or inequality, knowingly directed against members of a particular group; or blanket exclusionary policies, such as deliberate exclusion of an individual whose disability (an inability to walk) has nothing to do with the requirements of the job she is applying for (financial analyst).

b. Cases that are proved through **circumstantial evidence** of the intention to discriminate (see the *McDonnell Douglas v. Green* test, p. 83), including those that rely on statistical evidence as a method of circumstantially proving the intention to discriminate systematically against classes of individuals.

c. **Mixed-motive cases** (a hybrid theory) that often rely on both direct evidence of the intention to discriminate on some impermissible basis (e.g., gender, race, disability) and proof that the employer's stated legitimate basis for its employment decision is actually just a pretext for illegal discrimination.

2. **Adverse impact** (unintentional) **discrimination** occurs when identical standards or procedures are applied to everyone, despite the fact that they lead to a substantial difference in employment outcomes (e.g., selection, promotion, layoffs) for the members of a particular group, and they are unrelated to success on a job. For example, suppose that use of a minimum height requirement of 5 feet 8 inches for police cadets has an adverse impact on Asians, Hispanics, and women. The policy is neutral on its face but has an adverse impact. To use it, an employer would need to show that the height requirement is necessary to perform the job.

These two forms of illegal discrimination are illustrated graphically in Figure 3–1.

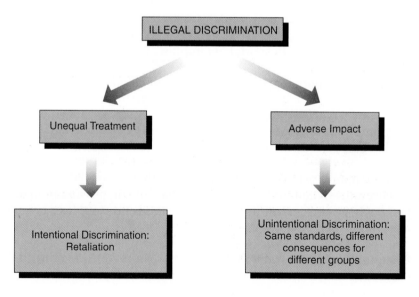

**Figure 3–1**

Major forms of illegal discrimination.

# THE LEGAL CONTEXT OF HUMAN RESOURCE DECISIONS

Now that we understand the forms that illegal discrimination can take, let's consider the major federal laws governing employment. Then we will consider the agencies that enforce the laws, as well as some important court cases that have interpreted them. The federal laws that we will discuss fall into two broad classes:

1. Laws of broad scope that prohibit unfair discrimination.
2. Laws of limited application, for example, those that require nondiscrimination as a condition for receiving federal funds (contracts, grants, revenue-sharing entitlements).

The particular laws that we shall discuss within each category are the following:

| Laws of broad scope | Laws of limited application |
| --- | --- |
| Thirteenth and Fourteenth Amendments to the U.S. Constitution | Executive Orders 11246, 11375, and 11478 |
| Civil Rights Acts of 1866 and 1871 | Rehabilitation Act of 1973 |
| Equal Pay Act of 1963 | Vietnam Era Veterans Readjustment Act of 1974 |
| Title VII of the Civil Rights Act of 1964 | Uniformed Services Employment and Reemployment Rights Act of 1994 |
| Civil Rights Act of 1991 | |
| Age Discrimination in Employment Act of 1967, as amended in 1986 | |
| Immigration Reform and Control Act of 1986 | |
| Americans with Disabilities Act of 1990, as amended in 2008 | |
| Family and Medical Leave Act of 1993 | |

## The Thirteenth and Fourteenth Amendments

The Thirteenth Amendment prohibits slavery and involuntary servitude. Any form of discrimination may be considered an incident of slavery or involuntary servitude and thus be liable to legal action under this amendment.[3] The Fourteenth Amendment guarantees equal protection of the law for all citizens. Both the Thirteenth and Fourteenth Amendments granted to Congress the constitutional power to enact legislation to enforce their provisions. It is from this source of constitutional power that all subsequent civil rights legislation originates.

## The Civil Rights Acts of 1866 and 1871

These laws were enacted on the basis of the provisions of the Thirteenth and Fourteenth Amendments. The Civil Rights Act of 1866 grants all citizens the right to make and enforce contracts for employment, and the Civil Rights Act of 1871 grants all citizens the right to sue in federal court if they feel they have been deprived of any rights or privileges guaranteed by the Constitution and other laws. It applies only to "persons within the jurisdiction of the United States," and does not extend to discriminatory conduct occurring overseas.[4]

Until recently, both of these civil rights acts were viewed narrowly as tools for solving Reconstruction-era racial problems. This is no longer so. In *Johnson v. Railway Express Agency Inc.*, the Supreme Court held that while the Civil Rights Act of 1866 on its face relates primarily to racial discrimination in the making and enforcement of contracts, it also provides a federal remedy against racial discrimination in private employment.[5] It is a powerful remedy. The Civil Rights Act of 1991 amended the Civil Rights Act of 1866 so that workers are protected from intentional discrimination in all aspects of employment, not just hiring and promotion. Thus, this civil rights law covers racial harassment. The Civil Rights Act of 1866 allows for jury trials and for compensatory and punitive damages* for victims of intentional racial and ethnic discrimination. It covers both large and small employers, even those with fewer than 15 employees, and in a 2008 decision, the Supreme Court ruled that employees also may sue for retaliation under this law.[6]

The 1866 law also has been used recently to broaden the definition of racial discrimination originally applied to African Americans. In a unanimous decision, the Supreme Court ruled that race was equated with ethnicity during the legislative debate after the Civil War, and therefore Arabs, Jews, and other ethnic groups thought of as "white" are not barred from suing under the 1866 act. The Court held that Congress intended to protect identifiable classes of persons who are subjected to intentional discrimination solely because of their ancestry or ethnic characteristics. Under the law, therefore, race involves more than just skin pigment.[7]

## The Equal Pay Act of 1963

This act was passed as an amendment to an earlier compensation-related law, the Fair Labor Standards Act of 1938. For those employees covered by the Fair Labor Standards Act, the Equal Pay Act requires that men and women working for the same establishment be paid the same rate of pay for work that is substantially equal in skill, effort, responsibility, and working conditions. Pay differentials are legal and appropriate if they are based on seniority, merit, systems that measure the quality or quantity of work, or any factor other than sex (e.g., shift differentials, completion of a job-related training program). Moreover, in correcting any inequity under the Equal Pay Act, employers must raise the rate of lower-paid employees, not lower the rate of higher-paid employees.[8]

Thousands of equal-pay suits have been filed (predominantly by women) since the law was passed. The EEOC receives about 1,000 equal-pay complaints per year.[9] For individual companies the price can be quite high. For example,

---

*Punitive damages are awarded in civil cases to punish or deter a defendant's conduct and are separate from compensatory damages, which are intended to reimburse a plaintiff for injuries or harm.

in 2011 Novartis Pharmaceutical Corporation settled a sex-discrimination lawsuit for $152.5 million.[10]

## Title VII of the Civil Rights Act of 1964

The Civil Rights Act of 1964 is divided into several sections, or titles, each dealing with a particular facet of discrimination (e.g., voting rights, public accommodations, public education). Title VII is most relevant to the employment context because it prohibits discrimination on the basis of race, color, religion, sex, or national origin in all aspects of employment (including apprenticeship programs). Title VII is the most important federal EEO law because it contains the broadest coverage, prohibitions, and remedies. Through it, the Equal Employment Opportunity Commission (EEOC) was created to ensure that employers, employment agencies, and labor organizations comply with Title VII.

Some may ask why we need such a law. As an expression of social policy, the law was passed to guarantee that people would be considered for jobs not on the basis of the color of their skin, their religion, their gender, or their national origin, but rather on the basis of the abilities and talents that are necessary to perform a job.

In 1972, the coverage of Title VII was expanded. It now includes almost all public and private employers with 15 or more employees, except (1) private clubs, (2) religious organizations (which are allowed to discriminate on the basis of religion in certain circumstances), and (3) places of employment connected with an Indian reservation. The 1972 amendments also prohibit the denial, termination, or suspension of government contracts (without a special hearing) if an employer has followed and is now following an affirmative action plan accepted by the federal government for the same facility within the past 12 months. **Affirmative action** refers to those actions appropriate to overcome the effects of past or present policies, practices, or other barriers to equal employment opportunity.[11]

Finally, back-pay awards in Title VII cases are limited to two years prior to the filing of a charge. For example, if a woman filed a Title VII claim in 2005, and the matter continued through investigation, conciliation, trial, and appeal until 2010, she might be entitled to as much as seven years' back pay, from 2003 (two years prior to the filing of the charge) until the matter was resolved in her favor. The two-year statute of limitations begins with the *filing* of a charge of discrimination.

The following are specifically exempted from Title VII coverage:

1.  *Bona fide occupational qualifications (BFOQs).* Discrimination is permissible when a prohibited factor (e.g., gender) is a **bona fide occupational qualification** for employment, that is, when it is considered "reasonably necessary to the operation of that particular business or enterprise." The burden of proof rests with the employer to demonstrate this. (According to one HR director, the only legitimate BFOQs that she could think of are sperm donor and wet nurse!) Both the EEOC and the courts interpret BFOQs quite narrowly.[12] Preferences of the employer, coworkers, or clients are irrelevant and do not constitute BFOQs. Moreover, BFOQ is not a viable defense to a Title VII race claim.

2.  *Seniority systems.* Although there are a number of legal questions associated with their use, Title VII explicitly permits bona fide seniority, merit,

or incentive systems "provided that such differences are not the result of an intention to discriminate."

3. *Pre-employment inquiries.* Inquiries regarding such matters as race, sex, or ethnic group are permissible as long as they can be shown to be job related. Even if not job related, some inquiries (e.g., regarding race or sex) are necessary to meet the reporting requirements of federal regulatory agencies. Applicants provide this information on a voluntary basis.

4. *Testing.* An employer may give or act upon any professionally developed ability test. If the results demonstrate adverse impact against a protected group, then the test itself must be shown to be job related (i.e., valid) for the position in question.

5. *Preferential treatment.* The Supreme Court has ruled that Title VII does not require the granting of preferential treatment to individuals or groups because of their race, sex, religion, or national origin on account of existing imbalances:

> The burden which shifts to the employer is merely that of proving that he based his employment decision on a legitimate consideration, and not an illegitimate one such as race. . . . Title VII forbids him from having as a goal a work force selected by any proscribed discriminatory practice, but it does not impose a duty to adopt a hiring procedure that maximizes hiring of minority employees.[13]

6. *National security.* Discrimination is permitted under Title VII when it is deemed necessary to protect the national security (e.g., against members of groups whose avowed aim is to overthrow the U.S. government).

Initially it appeared that these exemptions (summarized in Figure 3–2) would blunt the overall impact of the law significantly. However, it soon became clear that they would be interpreted very narrowly both by the EEOC and by the courts.

**Figure 3–2**

The six exemptions to Title VII coverage.

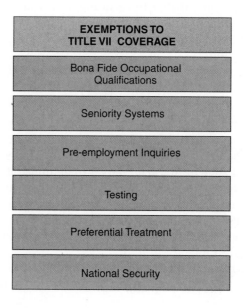

EXEMPTIONS TO
TITLE VII COVERAGE

Bona Fide Occupational Qualifications

Seniority Systems

Pre-employment Inquiries

Testing

Preferential Treatment

National Security

## Litigating Claims of Unfair Discrimination

If someone decides to bring suit under Title VII, the first step is to establish a **prima facie case** of discrimination (i.e., a body of facts presumed to be true until proved otherwise). However, the nature of prima facie evidence differs depending on the type of case brought before the court. If an individual alleges that a particular employment practice had an *adverse impact* on all members of a class that he or she represents, prima facie evidence is presented when adverse impact is shown to exist. Usually this is demonstrated by showing that the selection rate for the group in question is less than 80 percent of the rate of the dominant group (e.g., white males) and that the difference is statistically significant. If the individual alleges that he or she was treated differently from others in the context of some employment practice (i.e., *unequal-treatment discrimination*), a prima facie case is usually presented either through direct evidence of the intention to discriminate or by circumstantial evidence. The legal standard for circumstantial evidence is a four-part test first specified in the *McDonnell Douglas v. Green* case,[14] wherein a plaintiff must be able to demonstrate the following:

1. She or he has asserted a basis protected by Title VII, the Age Discrimination in Employment Act, or the Americans with Disabilities Act.
2. She or he was somehow harmed or disadvantaged (e.g., by not receiving a job offer or a promotion).
3. She or he was qualified to do the job or to perform the job in a satisfactory manner.
4. Either a similarly situated individual (or a group other than that of the plaintiff) was treated more favorably than the plaintiff, or the matter complained of involved an actual (rather than a nonexistent) employment opportunity.

Once the court accepts prima facie evidence, the burden of producing evidence shifts back and forth from plaintiff (the complaining party) to defendant (the employer). First, the employer is given the opportunity to articulate a legitimate, nondiscriminatory reason for the practice in question. Following that, in an unequal treatment case, the burden then shifts back to the plaintiff to show that the employer's reason is a pretext for illegal discrimination. In an adverse impact case, the plaintiff's burden is to show that a less discriminatory alternative practice exists and that the employer failed to use it. A similar process is followed in age discrimination cases.

## The Civil Rights Act of 1991[15]

This act overturned six Supreme Court decisions issued in 1989. Following are some key provisions that are likely to have the greatest impact in the context of employment.

### Monetary Damages and Jury Trials

A major effect of this act is to expand the remedies in discrimination cases. Individuals who feel they are the victims of intentional discrimination based on race, gender (including sexual harassment), religion, or disability can ask for compensatory damages for pain and suffering, as well as for punitive damages, and they may demand a jury trial. In the past, only plaintiffs in age discrimination cases had the right to demand a jury.

Compensatory and punitive damages are available only from nonpublic employers (public employers are still subject to compensatory damages up to $300,000) and not for adverse impact (unintentional discrimination) cases. Moreover, they may not be awarded in an Americans with Disabilities Act (ADA) case when an employer has engaged in good-faith efforts to provide a reasonable accommodation. Thus, the 1991 Civil Rights Act provides the sanctions for violations of the ADA. The total amount of damages that can be awarded depends on the size of the employer's workforce:

| Number of employees | Maximum combined damages per complaint |
|---|---|
| 15 to 100 | $ 50,000 |
| 101 to 200 | 100,000 |
| 201 to 500 | 200,000 |
| More than 500 | 300,000 |

In *Kolstad v. American Dental Association,* the U.S. Supreme Court held that the availability of punitive damages depends on the motive of the discriminator rather than on the nature of the conduct (the extent to which it is "egregious" or "outrageous"). Further, employers should not be assessed punitive damages if they implement, in good faith, sound antidiscrimination policies and practices. It is not enough simply to distribute a well-crafted policy. Supervisors must be trained to use it, and there should be consequences for failing to do so.[16]

### Adverse Impact (Unintentional Discrimination) Cases

The act clarifies each party's obligation in such cases. As we noted earlier, when an adverse impact charge is made, the plaintiff must identify a specific employment practice as the cause of discrimination. If the plaintiff is successful in demonstrating adverse impact, the burden of producing evidence shifts to the employer, who must prove that the challenged practice is "job-related for the position in question and consistent with business necessity."

### Protection in Foreign Countries

Protection from discrimination in employment, under Title VII of the 1964 Civil Rights Act, the Americans with Disabilities Act, and the Age Discrimination in Employment Act, is extended to U.S. citizens employed in a foreign facility owned or controlled by a U.S. company. However, the employer does not have to comply with U.S. discrimination law if to do so would violate the law of the foreign country. To be covered under this provision, the U.S. citizen must be employed overseas by a firm controlled by an American employer.[17]

### Racial Harassment

As we noted earlier, the act amended the Civil Rights Act of 1866 so that workers are protected from intentional discrimination in all aspects of employment, not just hiring and promotion.

## Challenges to Consent Decrees

Once a court order or consent decree is entered to resolve a lawsuit, nonparties to the original suit cannot challenge such enforcement actions.

## Mixed-Motive Cases

In a mixed-motive case, an employment decision was based on a combination of job-related factors as well as unlawful factors, such as race, gender, religion, or disability. Under the Civil Rights Act of 1991, an employer is guilty of discrimination if it can be shown that a prohibited consideration was a motivating factor in a decision, even though other factors, which are lawful, also were used. However, in a recent decision, *Gross v. FBL Financial Services Inc.,* the Supreme Court ruled that it is not enough for a plaintiff to prove that age was one of the motivating factors in a decision to terminate him. Instead, the plaintiff must prove that, but for his age, the adverse action would not have occurred.[18]

## Seniority Systems

The act provides that a seniority system that intentionally discriminates against the members of a protected group can be challenged (within 180 days) at any of three points: (1) when the system is adopted, (2) when an individual becomes subject to the system, or (3) when a person is injured by the system.

## "Race-Norming" and Affirmative Action

The act makes it unlawful "to adjust the scores of, use different cutoff scores for, or otherwise alter the results of employment-related tests on the basis of race, color, religion, sex, or national origin." Prior to the passage of this act, within-group percentile scoring (so-called race-norming) had been used extensively to adjust the test scores of minority candidates to make them more comparable to those of nonminority candidates. Under **race-norming**, each individual's percentile score on a selection test was computed relative only to others in his or her race/ethnic group and not relative to the scores of all persons who took the test. The percentile scores (high to low) were then merged into a single list, and the single list of percentiles was presented to those responsible for hiring decisions.

## Extension to U.S. Senate and Appointed Officials

The act extends protection from discrimination on the basis of race, color, religion, gender, national origin, age, and disability to employees of the U.S. Senate, political appointees of the president, and staff members employed by elected officials at the state level. Employees of the U.S. House of Representatives are covered by a House resolution adopted in 1988.

## The Age Discrimination in Employment Act of 1967 (ADEA)

As amended in 1986, this act prohibits discrimination in pay, benefits, or continued employment for employees age 40 and over, unless an employer can demonstrate that age is a BFOQ for the job in question. Like Title VII, this law is administered by the EEOC. A key objective of the law is to prevent financially troubled companies from singling out older employees when there are cutbacks. If a company claims that the layoffs were based on factors other than age, such as performance criteria or needed skills, the Supreme Court ruled in 2008 that the employer bears the burden of proving that its policy was, in fact, based on those non-age factors.[19] When there are cutbacks, however, older workers can waive their rights to sue under this law (e.g., in return for sweetened benefits for early retirement). Under the Older Workers Benefit Protection Act (OWBPA), an individual employee who does not have a pending claim has 21 days to consider such a waiver (45 days if terminated during a group reduction in force or if leaving voluntarily through a group incentive program), and 7 days after signing to revoke it.[20] Even after signing a waiver, employees age 40 and over can still sue for age discrimination if the employer did not comply with OWBPA requirements for obtaining a knowing and voluntary release.[21] On the other hand, courts have made clear that severance agreements will be upheld against challenges when agreements follow the rules and are written clearly and in a manner that will enable employees to understand what it is that they are agreeing to.[22]

### The Immigration Reform and Control Act of 1986 (IRCA)

This law applies to every employer in the United States, even to those with only one employee. It also applies to every employee—whether full time, part time, temporary, or seasonal—and it makes the enforcement of national immigration policy the job of every employer. While its provisions are complex, three basic features of the law are particularly relevant to employers:[23]

1. Employers may not hire or continue to employ "unauthorized aliens" (i.e., those not legally authorized to work in this country).
2. Employers must verify the identity and work authorization of every new employee. They may not require any particular form of documentation but must examine documents provided by job applicants (e.g., U.S. passports for U.S. citizens; "green cards" for resident aliens) showing identity and work authorization. Both employer and employee then sign a form (I-9), attesting under penalty of perjury that the employee is lawfully eligible to work in the United States. Experts advise firms to make copies of whatever documentation they accept for an individual's employment, such as a work visa or Social Security card. In addition, to show a good-faith effort to abide by the law, employers should do a self-audit of all I-9 forms, not just those of a particular ethnic group.[24]
3. Employers with 4 to 14 employees may not discriminate on the basis of citizenship or national origin. Those with 15 or more employees are already prohibited from national origin discrimination by Title VII. However, this prohibition is tempered by an exception that allows employers to select an applicant who is a U.S. citizen over an alien when the two applicants are equally qualified.

Penalties for noncompliance are severe. For example, for failure to comply with the verification rules, fines range from $100 to $1,100 for *each* employee whose identity and work authorization have not been verified. The act also provides for criminal sanctions for employers who engage in a pattern or practice of violations, and a 1996 executive order prohibits companies that knowingly hire illegal aliens from receiving federal contracts.[25] In fiscal year 2010, Immigration and Customs Enforcement removed more than 392,000 illegal workers, more than 195,000 of whom had been convicted of crimes.[26]

Qualified employees with disabilities can make important contributions to organizations.

## The Americans with Disabilities Act of 1990 (ADA)

Almost 13 percent of people ages 21 to 64 in the United States have at least one disability, a percentage that more than doubles to 30.2 percent for people ages 65 to 74. At the same time, the employment rate for working-age people with disabilities remains less than half that of those without disabilities (22 percent versus 70 percent).[27] Passed to protect people with disabilities from discrimination in employment, transportation, and public accommodation, Title I of the ADA, the employment section, protects approximately 86 percent of the American workforce.[28] It applies to all employers with 15 or more employees.

As a general rule, the ADA prohibits an employer from discriminating against a "qualified individual with a disability." A qualified individual is one who is able to perform the **essential** (i.e., primary) **functions** of a job with or without accommodation. **Disability** is a physical or mental impairment that substantially limits one or more major life activities, such as walking, talking, seeing, hearing, or learning. People are protected if they currently have an impairment and have a record of such impairment, or if the employer thinks they have an impairment (e.g., a person with diabetes under control).[29] Rehabilitated drug and alcohol abusers are protected, but current drug abusers may be fired. The alcoholic, in contrast, is covered and must be reasonably accommodated by being given a firm choice to rehabilitate himself or herself or face career-threatening consequences.[30] The law also protects people who have tested positive for HIV/AIDS.[31]

The ADA Amendments Act of 2008 overturned two Supreme Court decisions that interpreted ADA's definition of disability narrowly, and broadened the definition of a disability by expanding the term "major life activities." As a result, the focus for employers is less on what constitutes an ADA disability, and more on what constitutes reasonable accommodation.[32] However, companies do not have to lower work standards, tolerate misconduct, or give someone a make-work job.[33] Here are six major implications for employers:[34]

1. Any factory, office, retail store, bank, hotel, or other building open to the public will have to be made accessible to those with physical disabilities (e.g., by installing ramps, elevators, telephones with amplifiers). "Expensive" will be no excuse, unless such modifications will lead an employer to suffer an "undue hardship," considering the cost of the accommodation, the employer's size, financial resources, and the nature and structure of its operation.[35]

2. Employers must make "reasonable accommodations" for job applicants or employees with disabilities (e.g., by restructuring job and training programs, modifying work schedules, or purchasing new equipment that is "user friendly" to sight- or hearing-impaired people).[36] **Qualified job applicants** (i.e., individuals with disabilities who can perform the essential functions of a job with or without reasonable accommodation) must be considered for employment. Here are five strategies for improving employment opportunities for people with disabilities:[37]

   a. Partner with public and private disability agencies and community organizations.

   b. Provide information and outreach. For example, drugstore retailer Walgreens developed a Web site, *www.walgreensoutreach.com,* to provide information to potential employees with disabilities understand what work is like at its distribution centers.

   c. Mandate increased awareness and education. Giant Eagle Inc., a 223-store grocer in Pennsylvania with 36,000 employees, sponsors disability-awareness training for its HR managers every two years. In one exercise, for example, trainees maneuver through work activities in wheelchairs, going through doors, up and down ramps, or reaching for items on shelves.

   d. Use technology to redesign jobs. For example, Walgreens replaced keyboards with touch screens based on large pictures and icons, not words, making it easier for people with cognitive disabilities to learn and complete tasks.

   e. Establish pipelines to reach school-age recruits with disabilities. For example, Gap Inc., which operates Gap, Old Navy, and Banana Republic retail stores, partnered with nonprofit Abilities Inc. to develop a mock store where high-school students with disabilities who have expressed an interest in working with Gap upon graduation can learn real-world skills and gain practical experience.

3. Pre-employment physicals are now permissible only if all employees are subject to them, and they cannot be given until after a conditional offer of employment is made. That is, the employment offer is made conditional upon passing of the physical examination. Further, employers are not permitted to ask about past workers' compensation claims or disabilities in general. However, after describing essential job functions, an employer can ask whether the applicant can perform the job in question.[38] Here is an example of the difference between these two types of inquiries: "Do you have any back problems?" clearly violates the ADA because it is not

job specific. However, the employer could state the following: "This job involves lifting equipment weighing up to 50 pounds at least once every hour of an eight-hour shift. Can you do that?"

4. Medical information on employees must be kept separate from other personal or work-related information about them.

5. Drug-testing rules remain intact. An employer can still prohibit the use of alcohol and illegal drugs at the workplace and continue to give alcohol and drug tests.

6. Train supervisors, HR professionals, and anyone else who supervises employees, interviews candidates, and makes hiring decisions. Training should address who is covered under the ADA and its amendments, the process of interacting with someone who requests an accommodation, what accommodations are reasonable, and what is prohibited (harassment, retaliation). With respect to accommodations, keep the focus on performance or behavior without speculating or inquiring about the cause of a deficiency. Finally, identify HR or legal professionals who supervisors or higher-level managers can contact for advice.[39]

### Enforcement

The Equal Employment Opportunity Commission (EEOC) enforces the ADA.[40] In cases of intentional discrimination, the Supreme Court has ruled that individuals with disabilities may be awarded both compensatory and punitive damages up to $300,000 (depending on the size of the employer's workforce) if it can be shown that an employer engaged in discriminatory practices "with malice or with reckless indifference."[41]

## The Family and Medical Leave Act of 1993 (FMLA)

The FMLA covers all private-sector employers with 50 or more employees, including part timers who work 1,250 hours over a 12-month period (an average of 25 hours per week). The law gives workers up to 12 weeks' unpaid leave each year for birth, adoption, or foster care of a child within a year of the child's arrival; care for a spouse, parent, or child with a serious health condition; or the employee's own serious health condition if it prevents him or her from working. The employer is responsible for designating an absence or leave as FMLA leave, on the basis of information provided by the employee.[42] Employers can require workers to provide medical certification of such serious illnesses and can require a second medical opinion. Employers also can exempt from the FMLA key salaried employees who are among their highest-paid 10 percent. For leave takers, however, employers must maintain health insurance benefits and give the workers their previous jobs (or comparable positions) when their leaves are over.[43] Enforcement provisions of the FMLA are administered by the U.S. Department of Labor. The overall impact of this law was softened considerably by the exemption of some of its fiercest opponents—companies with fewer than 50 employees, or 95 percent of all businesses.[44]

The FMLA was amended and expanded to include military families in 2008. Businesses are required to offer up to 26 weeks of unpaid leave to employees who provide care to wounded U.S. military personnel. Employers also must provide 12 weeks of FMLA leave to immediate family members (spouses, children, or parents) of soldiers, reservists, and members of the National Guard who have a "qualifying exigency." While the measure does not define "qualifying exigency," examples could include overseas assignments, recalls to active duty, and troop mobilizations.[45]

Many employers already offer more than the law requires. In one large-scale survey, for example, 44 percent of responding companies said they offer job-protected leave for absences that are not covered under the law. The most common examples include substituting sick/vacation leave for FMLA leave, allowing more than 12 weeks for job-protected leave, and offering such leaves for employees with fewer than 12 months' service.[46]

This completes our discussion of "absolute prohibitions" against discrimination. The following sections discuss nondiscrimination as a basis for eligibility for federal funds.

## Executive Orders 11246, 11375, and 11478

Presidential executive orders in the realm of employment and discrimination are aimed specifically at federal agencies, contractors, and subcontractors. They have the force of law, even though they are issued unilaterally by the president without congressional approval, and they can be altered unilaterally as well. The requirements of these orders are parallel to those of Title VII.

In 1965, President Johnson issued Executive Order 11246, prohibiting discrimination on the basis of race, color, religion, or national origin as a condition of employment by federal agencies, contractors, and subcontractors with contracts of $10,000 or more. Those covered are required to establish and maintain a program of equal employment opportunity in every facility of 50 or more people. Such programs include employment, upgrading, demotion, transfer, recruitment or recruitment advertising, layoff or termination, pay rates, and selection for training.

In 1967, Executive Order 11375 prohibited discrimination in employment based on sex. Executive Order 11478, issued by President Nixon in 1969, went even further, for it prohibited discrimination in employment based on all the previous factors, plus political affiliation, marital status, or physical disability.

### Enforcement of Executive Orders

Executive Order 11246 provides considerable enforcement power, administered by the Department of Labor through its Office of Federal Contract Compliance Programs (OFCCP). Upon a finding by the OFCCP of noncompliance with the order, the Department of Justice may be advised to institute criminal proceedings, and the secretary of labor may cancel or suspend current contracts as well as the right to bid on future contracts. Needless to say, noncompliance can be *very* expensive.

## The Rehabilitation Act of 1973

This act requires federal contractors (those receiving more than $2,500 in federal contracts annually) and subcontractors to actively recruit qualified people with disabilities and to use their talents to the fullest extent possible. The legal requirements are similar to those of the Americans with Disabilities Act.

The purpose of this act is to eliminate *systemic discrimination,* that is, any business practice that results in the denial of equal employment opportunity.[47] Hence, the act emphasizes "screening in" applicants, not screening them out. It is enforced by the OFCCP.

## The Vietnam Era Veterans Readjustment Act of 1974

Federal contractors and subcontractors are required under this act to take affirmative action to ensure equal employment opportunity for Vietnam-era veterans (August 5, 1964, to May 7, 1975). The OFCCP enforces it.

## Uniformed Services Employment and Reemployment Rights Act of 1994

Regardless of the size of its organization, an employer may not deny a person initial employment, reemployment, promotion, or benefits on the basis of that person's membership or potential membership in the armed services. The Uniformed Services Employment and Reemployment Rights Act requires both public and private employers promptly to reemploy individuals returning from uniformed service (e.g., National Guard or activated reservists) in the position they would have occupied and with the seniority rights they would have enjoyed had they never left. Employers are also required to maintain health benefits for employees while they are away, but they are not required to make up the often significant difference between military and civilian pay.[48]

To be protected, the employee must provide advance notice, oral or written. Employers need not always rehire a returning service member (e.g., if the employee received a dishonorable discharge or if changed circumstances at the workplace make reemployment impossible or unreasonable), but the burden of proof will almost always be on the employer. The Veterans Employment and Training Service of the U.S. Department of Labor administers this law.[49]

## FEDERAL ENFORCEMENT AGENCIES: EEOC AND OFCCP

The Equal Employment Opportunity Commission (EEOC) is an independent regulatory agency whose five commissioners (one of whom is chairperson) are appointed by the president and confirmed by the Senate for terms of five years. No more than three of the commissioners may be from the same political party. Like the OFCCP, the EEOC sets policy and in individual cases determines whether there is "reasonable cause" to believe that unlawful discrimination has occurred. If the EEOC finds reasonable cause, it can sue either on its own behalf or on behalf of a claimant. As far as the employer is concerned, the simplest and least costly procedure is to establish a system to resolve complaints internally. However, if this system fails or if the employer does not make available an avenue for such complaints, an aggrieved individual (or group) can file a formal complaint with the EEOC. The process is shown graphically in Figure 3–3.

Once it receives a complaint of discrimination, the EEOC follows a three-step process: investigation, conciliation, and litigation.[50] As Figure 3–3 indicates, complaints must be filed within 180 days of an alleged violation (300 days if the same basis of discrimination is prohibited by either state or local laws). If that requirement is satisfied, the EEOC immediately refers the complaint to a state agency charged with enforcement of fair employment laws (if one exists) for resolution within 60 days. If the complaint cannot be resolved within that time, the state agency can file suit in a state district court and appeal any decision to a state appellate court, the state supreme court, or the U.S. Supreme Court. As an alternative to filing suit, the state agency may re-defer to the EEOC. Again, the EEOC seeks voluntary reconciliation, where the EEOC may serve as mediator. If mediation fails,

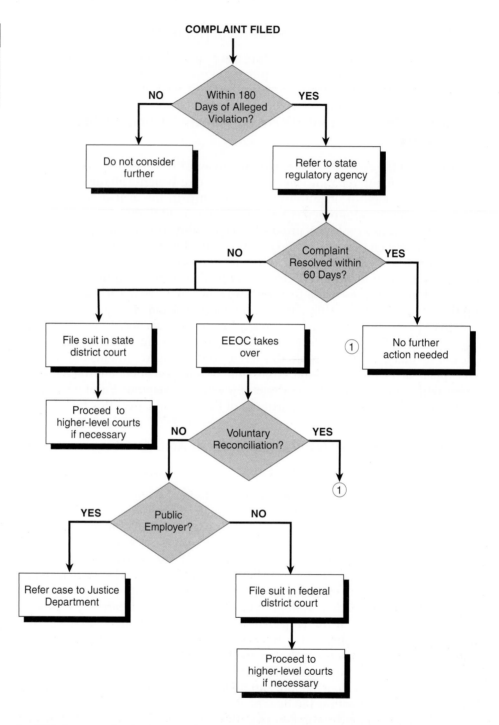

the EEOC may refer the case to the Justice Department (if the defendant is a public employer) or file suit in federal district court (if the defendant is a private employer). In 2010, for example, the EEOC filed 271 lawsuits against private employers and recovered $85.1 million in monetary benefits for aggrieved individuals.[51]

Like state-court decisions, federal-court decisions may be appealed to one of the 12 U.S. Courts of Appeal (corresponding to the geographical region, or circuit,

## Figure 3–4

The system of federal appellate courts in the United States.

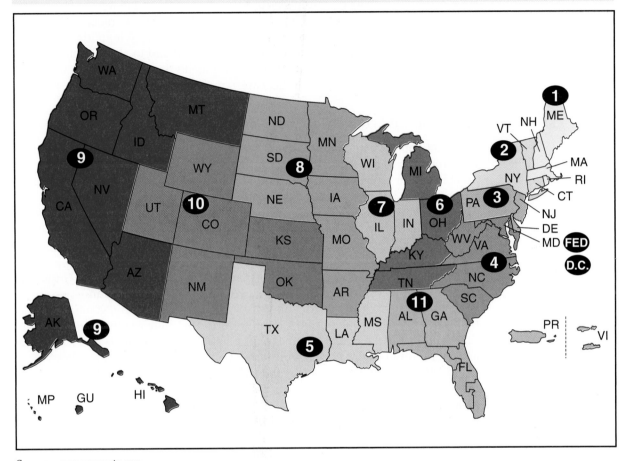

Source: www.uscourts.gov.

in which the case arose, see Figure 3–4). In turn, these decisions may be appealed to the U.S. Supreme Court, although very few cases are actually heard by the Supreme Court. Generally the Court will grant *certiorari* (discretionary review) when two or more circuit courts have reached different conclusions on the same point of law or when a major question of constitutional interpretation is involved. If the Supreme Court denies certiorari, the lower court's decision is binding.

## EEOC Guidelines

The EEOC has issued a number of guidelines for Title VII compliance.[52] Among these are guidelines on discrimination because of religion, national origin, gender, and pregnancy; guidelines on affirmative action programs; guidelines on employment tests and selection procedures; and a policy statement on pre-employment inquiries. These guidelines are not laws, although the Supreme Court has indicated that they are entitled to "great deference."[53]

### Information Gathering

Information gathering is another major EEOC function, for each organization in the United States with 100 or more employees must file an annual report (EEO-1) detailing the numbers of employees by job category (from laborers to executive/ senior-level officials and managers), and then by ethnicity, race, and gender. Through computerized analysis of the forms, the EEOC is able to identify broad patterns of discrimination **(systemic discrimination)** and to attack them through class actions. In any given year the EEOC typically receives about 95,000 complaints. In 2010, 38.3 percent of them were resolved within 180 days or fewer.[54]

## The Office of Federal Contract Compliance Programs

**Contract compliance** means that, in addition to quality, timeliness, and other requirements of federal contract work, contractors and subcontractors must meet EEO and affirmative action requirements. As we have seen, these requirements cover all aspects of employment.

Companies are willing to go to considerable lengths to avoid the loss of government contracts. Contractors and subcontractors with more than $50,000 in government business and with 50 or more employees must prepare and implement written affirmative action plans.[55]

In jobs where women and minorities are underrepresented in the workforce relative to their availability in the labor force, employers must establish goals and timetables for hiring and promotion. Theoretically, goals and timetables are distinguishable from rigid quotas in that they are flexible objectives that can be met in a realistic amount of time (Figure 3–5). Goals and timetables are not required under the Rehabilitation Act and Vietnam veterans law.

When a compliance review by the OFCCP does indicate problems that cannot be resolved easily, it tries to reach a conciliation agreement with the employer. Such an agreement might include back pay, seniority credit, special recruitment efforts, promotion, or other forms of relief for the victims of unlawful discrimination.

The conciliation agreement is the OFCCP's preferred route, but if such efforts are unsuccessful, formal enforcement action is necessary. Contractors may lose their government contracts, the government may withhold their payments, or they may be debarred from any government contract work. How has the agency

| Figure 3–5 | |
|---|---|
| The distinction between rigid quotas and goals and timetables. | 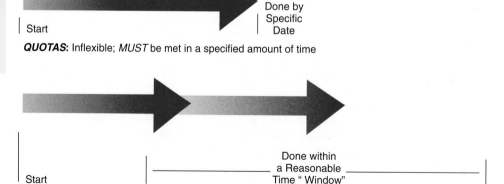 |

**QUOTAS:** Inflexible; *MUST* be met in a specified amount of time

**GOALS AND TIMETABLES:** Flexible; *MAY* be met in a realistic amount of time

done? In 2010, for example, OFCCP conducted 4,960 compliance reviews and recovered more than $9.7 million in back pay and other costs for 12,397 workers. The number of companies debarred varies each year, from none to about eight.[56]

### Affirmative Action Remedies

In three different cases, the Supreme Court found that Congress specifically endorsed the concept of non–victim-specific racial hiring goals to achieve compliance.[57] Further, the Court noted the benefits of flexible affirmative action rather than rigid application of a color-blind policy that would deprive employers of flexibility in administering human resources. We will have more to say about this in a following section.

## EMPLOYMENT CASE LAW: SOME GENERAL PRINCIPLES

Although Congress enacts laws, the courts interpret the laws and determine how they will be enforced. Such interpretations define what is called **case law,** which serves as a precedent to guide future legal decisions. And, of course, precedents are regularly subject to reinterpretation.

In the area of employment, a considerable body of case law has accumulated since 1964. Figure 3–6 illustrates areas in which case law is developed most extensively. Lawsuits affecting virtually every aspect of employment have been filed, and in the following sections we will consider some of the most significant decisions to date.

### Sex Discrimination

Suppose you run an organization that has 238 managerial positions—all filled by men. Only one promotional opportunity to a managerial position is available. Suppose that only a two-point difference in test scores separates the best-qualified man from the best-qualified woman. What do you do? Until a landmark Supreme Court decision (*Johnson v. Santa Clara Transportation Agency*[58]), if you promoted the woman you invited a lawsuit by the man. If you promoted the woman to correct past discrimination (thereby acknowledging past bias), you would invite discrimination suits by women. No longer. The Supreme Court ruled

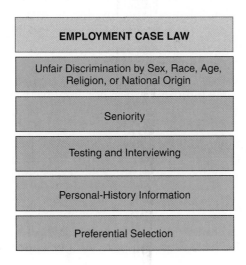

**Figure 3–6**

Areas making up the main body of employment case law.

unambiguously that in traditionally sex-segregated jobs, a qualified woman can be promoted over a marginally better qualified man to promote more balanced representation. The Court stressed the need for affirmative action plans to be flexible, gradual, and limited in their effect on whites and men. The Court also expressed disapproval of strict numerical quotas except where necessary (on a temporary basis) to remedy severe past discrimination.

Many employers are in similar positions. That is, they have not been proven guilty of past discrimination, but they have a significant underrepresentation of women or other protected groups in various job categories. This decision clearly put pressure on employers to institute voluntary affirmative action programs, but at the same time it also provided some welcome guidance on what they were permitted to do.

Sex-discrimination cases have been argued under both theories of unlawful discrimination: disparate treatment (e.g., sexual harassment) as well as adverse impact (e.g., physical ability tests). Many cases involve allegations of gender stereotyping (unwitting preferences by managers).[59] After reviewing a number of such cases, one attorney concluded that in some cases, gender stereotyping reflects hostility, and in others, ignorance and surprise. Some react differently to women in power, not because they dislike the idea of women having power, but because seeing women in power is relatively new to them. Of one thing we can be sure, however: gender stereotypes are not a thing of the past, and they will play important roles in future employment-law litigation.

## Pregnancy

The EEOC's interpretive guidelines for the Pregnancy Discrimination Act state:

> A written or unwritten employment policy or practice which excludes from employment applicants or employees because of pregnancy, childbirth, or related medical conditions is in prima facie violation of Title VII.[60]

Each year, the EEOC receives about 6,000 complaints related to pregnancy. In 2010, it resolved 6,293 of them and recovered $18 million in monetary benefits for the complaining parties, excluding benefits recovered through litigation.[61]

Under the law, an employer is never *required* to give pregnant employees special treatment. If an organization provides no disability benefits or sick leave to other employees, it is not required to provide them for pregnant employees.[62] The actual length of maternity leave, however, is an issue to be determined by the woman's and/or the company's physician.

Economic pressures on employers may make legal action unnecessary in the future. Evidence now indicates that many employers are doing their best to accommodate pregnant women through flexible work scheduling and generous maternity leave policies.[63] Given that about 75 percent of the 68 million working women in the United States will become pregnant (three-quarters of whom will return to work),[64] combined with the tight labor markets that employers face for many types of skills, there really is no other choice.

## Reproductive Hazards

Another way sex discrimination may be perpetuated is by barring women from competing for jobs that pose occupational health hazards to their reproductive systems. In a landmark decision *(UAW v. Johnson Controls Inc.),* the Supreme Court ruled on this issue.[65] It held that such "fetal protection" policies, which had been used by more than a dozen major companies, including General Motors, DuPont, Monsanto, Olin, Firestone, and B. F. Goodrich, are a form of illegal sex discrimination that is prohibited by Title VII. At issue was the policy of Johnson Controls Inc., a car battery manufacturer, that excluded women of childbearing age (unless sterile) from jobs involving exposure to lead.[66] The company argued that its policy was based on the BFOQ exception to Title VII, because it was essential to a safe workplace.

The Supreme Court disagreed, ruling that the BFOQ exception is a narrow one, limited to policies that are directly related to a worker's ability to do the job. "Women as capable of doing their jobs as their male counterparts may not be forced to choose between having a child and having a job. . . . Decisions about the welfare of future children must be left to the parents who conceive, bear, support, and raise them rather than to the employers who hire those parents," said the Court.[67]

What are businesses to do? Clearly, they will have to provide more complete information to inform and warn female (and male) workers about fetal health risks on the job. They may also urge women to consult their physicians before starting such assignments. However, the Supreme Court noted that it would be difficult to sue a company for negligence after it abandoned its fetal protection policy if (1) the employer fully informs women of the risk and (2) it has not acted negligently.[68] Mere exclusion of workers, both unions and managers agree, does not address chemicals remaining in the workplace to which other workers may be exposed, nor are women more sensitive to reproductive hazards than men. Changing the workplace, rather than the workforce, is a more enlightened policy.

## Sexual Harassment

Sexual harassment is not really about sex. It's about power—more to the point, the abuse of power.[69] In the vast majority of cases on this issue, females rather than males have suffered from sexual abuse at work. Such abuse may constitute illegal sex discrimination, a form of unequal treatment on the job. How prevalent is it? More than 29,000 complaints were filed with the EEOC in 2010, and $129.3 million was recovered for charging parties and other aggrieved individuals.[70] Fully 90 percent of *Fortune* 500 companies have dealt with sexual harassment complaints, and more than a third have been sued at least once. It is perilous self-deception for a manager to believe that sexual harassment does not exist in his or her own organization.

What is **sexual harassment?** According to the EEOC it is: "unwelcome sexual advances, requests for sexual favors, and other verbal or physical conduct of a sexual nature when submission to or rejection of this conduct explicitly or implicitly affects an individual's employment, unreasonably interferes with an individual's work performance, or creates an intimidating, hostile, or offensive work environment."[71]

Actually, the "no frills" definition can be put into one word: "unwelcome." According to the courts, for behavior to be treated as sexual harassment, the offender has to know that the behavior is unwelcome. If a person wants to file a grievance, therefore, it is important to be able to prove either that he or she told the perpetrator to back off or that the action was so offensive the harasser should have known it was unwelcome.

## ETHICAL DILEMMA
### Secret Taping of Supervisors: It May Be Legal, But Is It Ethical?

Employees who think a supervisor is out to get them have something new up their sleeves: hidden tape recorders. Secret tapings are on the rise, often by employees trying to protect their jobs, and aided by the availability of cheap, miniature recorders. Such taping, often done to support legal claims, outrages and exasperates employers. Defenders counter that secret recording sometimes is the only way to bring out the truth.

Federal law allows secret taping, as long as one of the people being recorded knows about it. However, in at least 11 other states, including California, the law requires that everyone being taped must know that he or she is being recorded (so-called "dual-consent" states).[a]

Most companies confronted with a tape quickly settle out of court. In one case, for example, a pregnant saleswoman's coworkers told her outright that they would force her off the job by making life hard on her at work. The workers were afraid the pregnancy would stop the woman from racking up sales, and they all would lose a bonus as a result. Once the woman sued for pregnancy discrimination, the coworkers lied about threatening her. They said, "We were all happy for her—we gave her a big hug when we found out she was pregnant." But the woman produced a secret tape she had made of the threats and won a $180,000 settlement.

What is a business to do? Issue a policy against covert recording. That way, employees who tape can be fired for breaking company rules. In states where secret taping is illegal, companies can turn the tables on employees by using the recordings against them. Employment lawyers also advise companies to hire experts to make sure the tapes are authentic and have not been edited. How about coworkers and managers? The cheapest and best protection of all is to avoid saying things you would be embarrassed to go into on a witness stand . . . or to see on the evening news.[b]

---

[a]Kesselman, D., and Williams, T. S. (2007, July). Speak, you're on candid recorder. *HRMagazine*, pp. 105–109.
[b]Ibid.

---

While many behaviors can constitute sexual harassment, there are two main types:

1. Quid pro quo (you give me this; I'll give you that).
2. Hostile work environment (an intimidating, hostile, or offensive atmosphere).

**Quid pro quo harassment** exists when the harassment is a condition of employment. For example, consider the case of *Barnes v. Costle:* The plaintiff rebuffed her director's repeated sexual overtures. She ignored his advice that sexual intimacy was the path she should take to improve her career opportunities. Subsequently the director abolished her job. The court of appeals found that sexual cooperation was a condition of her employment, a condition the director did not impose upon males. Therefore, sex discrimination occurred and the employer was liable.[72]

The U.S. Supreme Court has gone even further. In two key rulings, *Burlington Industries Inc. v. Ellerth*[73] and *Faragher v. City of Boca Raton,*[74] the Court held that employers always are potentially liable for a supervisor's sexual misconduct toward an employee, even if they knew nothing about that supervisor's conduct. However, in some cases an employer can defend itself by showing that it took reasonable steps to prevent harassment on the job.

**Hostile-environment harassment** was defined by the Supreme Court in the case of *Meritor Savings Bank v. Vinson.*[75] Vinson's boss had abused her verbally as well as sexually. However, because Vinson was making good career progress, the district court ruled that the relationship was a voluntary one having nothing to do with her continued employment or advancement. The Supreme Court disagreed, ruling that whether the relationship was "voluntary" is irrelevant. The key question was whether the sexual advances from the supervisor were "unwelcome." If so, and if they are "sufficiently severe or pervasive to be abusive,"[76] then they are illegal.

This case was groundbreaking because it expanded the definition of harassment to include verbal or physical conduct that creates an intimidating, hostile, or offensive work environment or interferes with an employee's job performance. Employers may also be liable for the harassing actions of nonemployees, such as customers, if they fail to take reasonable steps to stop the harassing behavior.[77] As we noted earlier, the Civil Rights Act of 1991 permits victims of sexual harassment—who previously could be awarded only missed wages—to collect a wide range of punitive damages and attorney's fees from employers who mishandle a complaint.

In a more recent case, *Pennsylvania State Police v. Suders,*[78] the Supreme Court emphasized that an employer has no defense when a supervisor harasses an employee and an adverse employment action results. In hostile-environment cases, however, the employer may avoid liability if it can prove that (1) it exercised reasonable care to prevent and promptly correct any sexually harassing behavior, and (2) the plaintiff failed to use any preventive or corrective methods provided by the employer. The key is to establish and follow a thorough antiharassment program in the workplace.[79] U.S. harassment laws are strict and specific, more so than in many other countries. As a result, foreign-based firms may be slower to react to harassment claims in the United States. To avoid potential problems, experts recommend that foreign-based firms design special orientation programs for newly arrived executives that focus on acceptable behavior in the United States.[80]

## Preventive Actions by Employers

What can an employer do to escape, or to at least limit, its liability for the sexually harassing acts of its managers or workers? An effective policy should include the following features:[81]

- A statement from the chief executive officer that states firmly that sexual harassment will not be tolerated.
- A workable definition of sexual harassment that is publicized via staff meetings, bulletin boards, handbooks, and in new-employee orientation programs. It should also include concrete examples of inappropriate behaviors (e.g., derogatory comments, demeaning jokes, visual messages, nicknames that refer to a person's membership in any protected group).
- Create an effective complaint procedure that includes multiple ways to file complaints (supervisor, high-level manager, senior manager, HR representative, or hotline), because the more choices employees have, the less reasonable will be their failure to complain. Every employee must sign a written acknowledgement of receipt of the policy.

- A clear statement of sanctions for violators and protection for those who make charges.
- Prompt, confidential investigation of every claim of harassment, no matter how trivial.
- Preservation of all investigative information, with records of all such complaints kept in a central location.
- Regular training of all managers and supervisors, including top managers, to model appropriate behavior and to recognize and respond to complaints. Give them written materials that outline their responsibilities and obligations when a complaint is made. Each person needs to sign a written acknowledgement of his or her participation in the training.
- Follow-up to determine if harassment has stopped.[82]

## Age Discrimination

The EEOC's guidelines on age discrimination emphasize that in order to defend an adverse employment action against employees age 40 and over, an employer must be able to demonstrate a "business necessity" for doing so. That is, it must be able to show that age is a factor directly related to the safe, efficient operation of a business. To establish a prima facie case of age discrimination with respect to termination, for example, an individual must show that[83]

1. She or he is within the protected age group (40 years of age and over).
2. She or he is doing satisfactory work.
3. She or he was discharged despite satisfactory work performance.
4. The position was filled by a person younger than the person replaced.

For example, an employee named Schwager had worked for Sun Oil Ltd. for 18 years, and his retirement benefits were to be vested (i.e., not contingent on future service) at 20 years. When the company reorganized and had to reduce the size of its workforce, the average age of those retained was 35 years, while the average age of those terminated was 45.7 years. The company was able to demonstrate, however, that economic considerations prompted the reorganization and that factors other than age were considered in Schwager's termination. The local manager had to let one person go, and he chose Schwager because he ranked lowest in overall job performance among salespeople in his district and did not measure up to their standards. Job performance, not age, was the reason for Schwager's termination. Employers can still fire unproductive workers, but the key is to base employment decisions on ability, not on age.[84] Aside from termination, age-discrimination complaints are likely to arise following reductions in force, or employment decisions that involve discipline, selection, or promotion. They can be brought under disparate treatment or adverse impact theories of discrimination.[85]

If a case gets to a jury, aggrieved employees have a 78 percent success rate at both state and local jury trials. In federal district courts, the median age-discrimination verdict is almost $300,000, the highest amount for all types of discrimination.[86]

## "Overqualified" Job Applicants

Employers sometimes hesitate to hire an individual who has a great deal of experience for a job that requires few qualifications and may be only an entry-level job. They assume that an overqualified individual will be bored in such a

## "ENGLISH-ONLY" RULES—NATIONAL ORIGIN DISCRIMINATION?

Rules that require employees to speak only English in the workplace have come under fire in recent years. Employees who speak a language other than English claim that such rules are not related to the ability to do a job and have a harsh impact on them because of their national origin. The EEOC and many courts agree that blanket English-only rules that lack business justification amount to unlawful national origin discrimination.[a]

Employers should be careful when instituting such a rule. While it is not necessarily illegal to make fluency in English a job requirement or to discipline an employee for violating an English-only rule, employers must be able to show there is a legitimate business need for it. For example, it's a safety issue when medical workers or firefighters do not understand or cannot make themselves understood.[b] Avoid requiring the use of English at all times and in all areas of the workplace. Inform employees in advance of the circumstances where speaking only in English is required and of the consequences of violating the rule. (Conversely, many employers would be delighted to have a worker who can speak the language of a non–English-speaking customer.) Otherwise, the employer may be subject to discrimination complaints on the basis of national origin.

[a] Society for Human Resource Management. (2007, April 18). Court upholds English-only rule. Retrieved from *http://www.shrm.org/LegalIssues/StateandLocalResources/Pages/CMS_021247.aspx* on June 15, 2011. See also Jordan, M. (2005, Nov. 8). Testing "English-only" rules. *The Wall Street Journal*, pp. B1, B13. See also Roffer, M. H., and Sanservino, Jr., N. J. (2000, Sept.). Holding employees' native tongues. *HRMagazine*, pp. 177–184.

[b] Holland, K. (2008, Jan. 27). When English is the rule at work. *The New York Times*. Retrieved from *http://nyti.ms/rbNHH0* on Aug. 24, 2008. See also Prengaman, P. (2003, Aug, 21). Language barrier a peril on fire lines. *The Denver Post*, p. 16A.

job or is using the job only to get a foot in the door so he or she can apply for another job at a later time. Beware of violating the Age Discrimination in Employment Act! An appeals court has ruled that rejection of an older worker because he or she is overqualified may be a pretext to mask the real reason for rejection—the employee's age.[87]

The key to success seems to be careful assessment prior to hire. Begin by defining overqualified. Is it too much experience? Is it being at the wrong level? Or is it salary expectations? How much is too much? Then ask if you can do something to position the job opportunity to take better advantage of this applicant's experience. Can you change or modify the job? Can the person be fast-tracked into a new position? With these strategies in mind, give applicants a realistic preview of what the job will be—the good, the bad, and the ugly. You want to note all the advantages, but also the things that might make the job less satisfying for an overqualified person. Doing so allows the candidate to make his or her own judgment. Finally ask, "Is there anything in this job that you feel wouldn't engage you?"[88]

### Seniority

*Seniority* is a term that connotes length of employment. A **seniority system** is a scheme that, alone or in tandem with "nonseniority" criteria, allots to employees ever-improving employment rights and benefits as their relative lengths of pertinent employment increase.[89]

Various features of seniority systems have been challenged in the courts for many years.[90] However, one of the most nettlesome issues is the impact of established seniority systems on programs designed to ensure equal employment opportunity. Employers often work hard to hire and promote members of protected groups. If layoffs become necessary, however, those individuals may be lost because of their low seniority. As a result, the employer takes a step backward in terms of workforce diversity. What is the employer to do when seniority conflicts with EEO?

The U.S. Supreme Court has been quite clear in its rulings on this issue in two landmark decisions: *Firefighters Local Union No. 1784 v. Stotts*[91] (decided under Title VII) and *Wygant v. Jackson Board of Education*[92] (decided under the equal protection clause of the Fourteenth Amendment). The Court ruled that an employer may not protect the jobs of recently hired African-American employees at the expense of whites who have more seniority.[93]

Voluntary modifications of seniority policies for affirmative action purposes remain proper, but where a collective bargaining agreement exists, courts have made it clear that the union must be a party to any decree that modifies a bona fide seniority system.[94] What about seniority and the ADA? In *US Airways v. Barnett*,[95] the Supreme Court ruled that that an employer is not required to grant an employee with a disability a job in place of an employee with more seniority—if a seniority system normally is used as a fundamental factor in such decisions. The Court emhasized that seniority does not always trump the ADA, and that such a question must be resolved on a case-by-case basis.[96]

Finally, the Uniformed Services Employment and Reemployment Rights Act (USERRA) provides that returning service members are re-employed in the job that they would have attained had they not been absent for military service with the same seniority, status, and pay, as well as other rights and benefits determined by seniority.  But what if some employees in that job have been laid off during the military service? If employees were selected for layoffs based on seniority, it should be relatively simple to determine whether the service member would have been laid off. If layoffs instead are based on performance, it can be more difficult to determine whether the employee would have been laid off or not.[97]

## Testing and Interviewing

Title VII clearly sanctions the use of "professionally developed" ability tests. Nevertheless, it took several landmark Supreme Court cases to clarify the proper role and use of tests. The first was *Griggs v. Duke Power Co.,* the most significant EEO case ever, which was decided in favor of Griggs.[98] Duke Power was prohibited from requiring a high school education or the passing of an intelligence test as a condition of employment or job transfer because it could not show that either standard was significantly related to job performance:

> What Congress has forbidden is giving these devices and mechanisms controlling force unless they are demonstrably a reasonable measure of job performance. . . . What Congress has commanded is that any tests used must measure the person for the job and not the person in the abstract.[99]

The ruling also included four other general principles:

1. The law prohibits not only open and deliberate discrimination but also practices that are fair in form but discriminatory in operation. That is, Title VII prohibits practices having an adverse impact on protected groups, unless they are job related. This is a landmark pronouncement because it officially established adverse impact as a category of illegal discrimination.

   For example, suppose an organization wants to use prior arrests as a basis for selection. In theory, arrests are a "neutral" practice because all persons are equally subject to arrest if they violate the law. However, if arrests cannot be shown to be job related, and, in addition, if a significantly higher proportion of African Americans than whites is arrested, the use of arrests as a basis for selection is discriminatory in operation.

2. The employer bears the burden of proof that any requirement for employment is related to job performance. As affirmed by the Civil Rights Act of 1991, when a charge of adverse impact is made, the plaintiff must identify a specific employment practice as the cause of the discrimination. If the plaintiff is successful, the burden shifts to the employer.

3. It is not necessary for the plaintiff to prove that the discrimination was intentional; intent is irrelevant. If the standards result in discrimination, they are unlawful.

4. Job-related tests and other employment selection procedures are legal and useful.

The confidentiality of individual test scores has also been addressed both by the profession[100] and by the courts. Thus, the Supreme Court affirmed the right of the Detroit Edison Company to refuse to hand over to a labor union copies of aptitude tests taken by job applicants and to refuse to disclose individual test scores without the written consent of employees.[101]

As is well known, interviews are commonly used as bases for employment decisions to hire or to promote certain candidates in preference to others. Must such "subjective" assessment procedures satisfy the same standards of job relatedness as more "objective" procedures, such as written tests? If they produce an adverse impact against a protected group, the answer is yes, according to the Supreme Court in *Watson v. Fort Worth Bank & Trust*.[102]

As in its *Griggs* ruling, the Court held that it is not necessary for the plaintiff to prove that the discrimination was intentional. If the interview ratings result in adverse impact, they are presumed to be unlawful, unless the employer can show some relationship between the content of the ratings and the requirements of a given job. This need not involve a formal validation study, although the Court agreed unanimously that it is possible to conduct such studies when subjective assessment devices are used.[103] The lesson for employers? Be sure that there is a legitimate, job-related reason for every question raised in an employment or promotional interview. Limit questioning to "need to know," rather than "nice to know," information, and monitor interview outcomes for adverse impact. Validate this selection method. It is unwise to wait until the selection system is challenged.

## Personal History

Frequently, job-qualification requirements involve personal background information. If the requirements have the effect of denying or restricting equal employment opportunity, they may violate Title VII. For example, in the *Griggs v. Duke Power Co.* case, a purportedly neutral practice (the high school education requirement that excluded a higher proportion of African Americans than whites from employment) was ruled unlawful because the company could not show that it was related to job performance. Other allegedly neutral practices that have been struck down by the courts on the basis of non-job relevance include

- Recruitment practices based on present employee referrals, where the work-force is nearly all white to begin with.[104]
- Height and weight requirements.[105]
- Arrest records, because they show only that a person has been accused of a crime, not that she or he was guilty of it; thus arrests may not be used as a basis for selection decisions,[106] except in certain sensitive and responsible positions (e.g., police officer, school principal).[107]
- Conviction records, unless the conviction is directly related to the work to be performed (e.g., a person convicted of embezzlement applying for a job as a bank teller).[108] In addition, employers should consider carefully the nature and gravity of the offense, the time that has passed since the conviction and/or completion of the sentence, and the nature of the job held or sought.[109]

Despite such decisions, personal history items are not unlawfully discriminatory per se, but to use them you must show that they are relevant to the job in question. Just as with employment interviews, collect this information on a "need to know," not on a "nice to know," basis.

## Preferential Selection

In an ideal world, selection and promotion decisions would be color blind. Thus, social policy as embodied in Title VII emphasizes that so-called **reverse discrimination** (discrimination against whites and in favor of members of protected groups) is just as unacceptable as is discrimination by whites against members of protected groups.[110] Indeed, this riddle has perplexed courts and the public since the dawn of affirmative action 40 years ago: How do you make things fair for oppressed groups while continuing to treat people as equal individuals?[111] Court cases, together with the Civil Rights Act of 1991, have clarified a number of issues in this area:

1. Courts may order, and employers voluntarily may establish, affirmative action plans, including goals and timetables, to address problems of underutilization of women and minorities. Individuals who were not parties to the original suit may not reopen court-approved affirmative action settlements.
2. The plans need not be directed solely to identified victims of discrimination but may include general, classwide relief.
3. While the courts will almost never approve a plan that would result in white people losing their jobs through layoffs, they may sanction plans that impose limited burdens on whites in hiring and promotions (i.e., plans that postpone hiring and promotion).

What about numerically based preferential programs? The U.S. Supreme Court issued two landmark rulings in 2003 that clarified this issue. Both cases

Cast a wide net to search for qualified talent, but make hiring/promotion decisions based on merit.

represented challenges to admissions policies at the University of Michigan, one involving undergraduate admissions *(Gratz v. Bollinger)* and one involving law-school admissions *(Grutter v. Bollinger).*[112] The undergraduate admissions policy was struck down because it was too mechanistic. It awarded 20 points of the 150 needed for admission (8 points more than is earned for a perfect SAT score) to any member of an officially recognized minority group. Such a disguised quota system denied other applicants the equal protection of the law guaranteed by the Fourteenth Amendment to the Constitution, and thus it was ruled illegal.

However, the Court also was mindful of arguments from leading businesses, educational institutions, and former military officials that a culturally diverse, well-educated workforce is vital to the competitiveness of the U.S. economy and that an integrated officer corps produced by diverse military academies and ROTC programs is vital to national security. The Court upheld the law school's approach to enrolling a "critical mass" of African Americans, Latinos, and Native Americans, under which the school considers each applicant individually and sets no explicit quota. To be consistent with the constitutional guarantee of equal treatment for all under the law, race-conscious admissions must be limited in time. Thus, the Court noted,

## IMPACT OF LEGAL FACTORS ON PRODUCTIVITY, QUALITY OF WORK LIFE, AND THE BOTTOM LINE

There are both direct and indirect costs associated with unlawful discrimination. For example, sexual harassment can create high levels of stress and anxiety for both the victim and the perpetrator. These psychological reactions can lead to outcomes that increase labor costs for employers. Job performance may suffer, and absenteeism, sick leave, and turnover may increase. Both internal discrimination against present employees and external discrimination against job applicants can lead to costly lawsuits. Litigation is a time-consuming, expensive exercise that no organization wants.[a] Yet organizations have been hit with lawsuits affecting virtually every aspect of the employment relationship, and many well-publicized awards to victims have reached millions of dollars.

Let's not view the legal and social aspects of the HR management process exclusively in negative terms. Most of the present civil rights laws and regulations were enacted as a result of gross violations of individual rights. In most instances, the flip side of unlawful discrimination is good HR practice. For example, it is good practice to use properly developed and validated employment-selection procedures and performance-appraisal systems. It is good HR practice to treat people as individuals and not to rely on stereotyped group membership characteristics (e.g., stereotypes about women, ethnic groups, older workers, workers with disabilities). Finally, it just makes good sense to pay people equally, regardless of gender, if they are equally qualified and are doing the same work. These kinds of HR practices can enhance productivity, provide a richer quality of work life, and contribute directly to the overall profitability of any enterprise.

---

[a]Grossman, R. J. (2009, May). Defusing discrimination claims. *HRMagazine* 54(5), pp. 47–51. See also Orey, M. (2007, Apr. 23). Fear of firing. *BusinessWeek,* pp. 52–62.

---

"We expect that 25 years from now the use of racial preferences will no longer be necessary."

The Court emphasized that diversity is a "compelling state interest" but that universities may not use quotas for members of racial or ethnic groups or put them on separate admissions tracks. The law school's admissions policy satisfied these principles by ensuring that applicants are evaluated individually. Under that approach, the Court noted, a nonminority student with a particularly interesting contribution to make to the law school's academic climate may sometimes be preferred over a minority student with better grades and test scores.

The net effect of the two rulings is to permit public and private universities to continue to use race as a "plus factor" in evaluating potential students—provided they take sufficient care to evaluate individually each applicant's ability to contribute to a diverse student body.[113] The Court made clear that its rationale for considering race was not to compensate for past discrimination, but to obtain educational benefits from a diverse student body. Corporate hiring policies also will have to reflect the Court's double message: Diversity efforts are acceptable, but quotas aren't.[114]

| RETALIATION: A NEW LEGAL STANDARD AND SOME PREVENTIVE MEASURES | *Human Resource Management in Action: Conclusion* |
|---|---|

Retaliation claims almost doubled between 1992 and 2003, from 11,096 to 22,690.[115] In fiscal year 2010, the EEOC received 36,258 charges of retaliation discrimination. Retaliation claims, which account for more than one of every three claims filed, have now surpassed racial discrimination as the most common type of claim made when a charge is filed with the EEOC. According to the EEOC, the vast majority of retaliation claims still generally involve actions such as discharge and suspension.

Perhaps the best way to avoid liability for retaliation is to prevent it from ever happening. Two management actions can help: (1) add an anti-retaliation policy (or update an existing one), and (2) provide specific training to supervisors on retaliation, using *BNSF v. White* to explain what might constitute retaliation.

Experts recommend that an antiretaliation policy include the following six elements:

1. Implement and follow a zero-tolerance anti-discrimination and anti-retaliation policy. Emphasize to employees at all levels that retaliatory acts will lead to discipline and/or discharge.
2. A brief illustration of types of conduct that might be prohibited by the policy.
3. A mechanism for reporting possible acts of retaliation, such as a toll-free telephone number.
4. A statement that complaints will be promptly investigated and resolved as appropriate.
5. A statement that complaints will be maintained as confidential to the extent practicable, given the need to investigate and resolve issues.
6. Follow up on discrimination and harassment complaints. Speak with complainants after the initial investigation to ensure they feel comfortable in the workplace and do not perceive retaliation.

With respect to training, an effective program will include the following:

1. A straightforward description of the company's antiharassment policy.
2. Examples and stories to explain what acts could be viewed as retaliatory, since retaliation might be even more difficult to define than harassment.
3. An explanation of the consequences of engaging in retaliation.
4. Practical steps and suggestions on how supervisors should vet possible actions toward protected employees with HR or legal counsel before acting.

Attorneys and HR professionals are well aware that it doesn't take a strong discrimination case to make a strong retaliation case. In fact, it's often the weak discrimination claim that produces the big-time retaliation lawsuit. Updated policies, effective training, and thoughtful attention to possible retaliatory actions by supervisors and higher-level managers can help safeguard an organization from potential legal liability.

## SUMMARY

Congress enacted the following laws to promote fair employment. They provide the basis for discrimination suits and subsequent judicial rulings:

- Thirteenth and Fourteenth Amendments to the U.S. Constitution.
- Civil Rights Acts of 1866 and 1871.
- Equal Pay Act of 1963.
- Title VII of the Civil Rights Act of 1964.
- Age Discrimination in Employment Act of 1967 (as amended in 1986).
- Immigration Reform and Control Act of 1986.
- Americans with Disabilities Act of 1990 (as amended in 2008).
- Civil Rights Act of 1991.
- Family and Medical Leave Act of 1993.
- Executive Orders 11246, 11375, and 11478.
- Rehabilitation Act of 1973.
- The Vietnam Era Veterans Readjustment Act of 1974.
- Uniformed Services Employment and Reemployment Rights Act of 1994.

The Equal Employment Opportunity Commission (EEOC) and the Office of Federal Contract Compliance Programs (OFCCP) are the two major federal regulatory agencies charged with enforcing these nondiscrimination laws. The EEOC is responsible both for private and public nonfederal employers, unions, and employment agencies. The OFCCP is responsible for ensuring compliance from government contractors and subcontractors.

A considerable body of case law has developed, affecting almost all aspects of the employment relationship. We discussed case law in the following areas:

- Sex discrimination, sexual harassment, reproductive hazards, and pregnancy.
- Age discrimination.
- National origin discrimination.
- Seniority.

## IMPLICATIONS FOR MANAGEMENT PRACTICE

A manager can easily feel swamped by the maze of laws, court rulings, and regulatory-agency pronouncements that organizations must navigate through. While it is true that in the foreseeable future there will continue to be legal pressure to avoid unlawful discrimination, as we saw in Chapter 1, there will be great economic pressure to find and retain top talent. Workforce diversity is a competitive necessity, and employers know it. Progressive managers recognize that now is the time to begin developing the kinds of corporate policies and interpersonal skills that will enable them to operate effectively in diverse, multicultural work environments.

- Testing and interviewing.
- Personal history (specifically, pre-employment inquiries).
- Preferential selection.

The bottom line in all these cases is that, as managers, we need to be very clear about job requirements and performance standards, we need to treat people as individuals, and we must evaluate each individual fairly relative to job requirements and performance standards.

## KEY TERMS

| | |
|---|---|
| equal employment opportunity | essential functions |
| discrimination | disability |
| unequal treatment | qualified job applicant |
| direct evidence | systemic discrimination |
| circumstantial evidence | contract compliance |
| mixed-motive cases | case law |
| adverse-impact discrimination | sexual harassment |
| affirmative action | quid pro quo harassment |
| bona fide occupational qualification | hostile-environment harassment |
| prima facie case | seniority system |
| race-norming | reverse discrimination |

## DISCUSSION QUESTIONS

**3–1.** If you were asked to advise a private employer (with no government contracts) of its equal employment opportunity responsibilities, what would you say?

**3–2.** As a manager, what steps can you take to deal with the organizational impact of the Family and Medical Leave Act?

**3–3.** Prepare a brief outline of an organizational policy on sexual harassment. Be sure to include complaint, investigation, and enforcement procedures.

**3–4.** What steps would you take as a manager to ensure fair treatment for older employees?

**3–5.** Collect two policies on EEO, sexual harassment, or family and medical leave from two different employers in your area. How are they similar (or different)? Which aspects of the policies support the appropriate law?

## APPLYING YOUR KNOWLEDGE

---

*A Case of Harassment?*                                                    *Case 3–1*

Erin Dempsey was working late trying to finish the analysis of the ticket report for her boss, Ron Hanson. The deadline was tomorrow, and she still had several hours of work to do before the analysis would be finished. Erin did not particularly enjoy working late, but she knew Ron would be expecting the report first thing in the morning. She had been working very hard recently, hoping that she would earn a promotion to senior travel agent at the large urban travel agency where she was employed. Getting the ticket report done on time would be absolutely essential for any promotion opportunities.

Matt Owens, a coworker at the travel agency, was also working late that evening. Suddenly, he appeared in her office uninvited and sat down in the side chair. "Got a big date tonight, eh, Erin?" Matt said with a touch of sarcasm in his voice.

"I'm working very hard on the ticket report tonight Matt, and I really could use a bit of privacy." Erin had sensed before that Matt was a pest, and she hoped that by being rather direct with him he would leave her alone.

"A cute chick like you shouldn't waste a perfectly good Wednesday evening working late."

"Please, Matt, I've got work to do."

"Oh come on, Erin. I've noticed the way you act when you walk by my office or when we pass in the halls. It's clear that you're dying to go out with me. Some things a guy can just sense. This is your big chance. I'll tell you what. Let's go to dinner at that new intimate French restaurant up on the hill. Afterwards we can stop by my place for some music, a fire in the fireplace, and a nightcap. I make a great Black Russian. What do you say?"

Erin was furious. "I say you're an egotistical, self-centered, obnoxious, dirty old man. If you don't get out of here right now, I'm going to call Ron Hanson at home and tell him that you're keeping me from finishing the ticket report."

"Oh my, you're even sexier when you're angry. I like that in a woman."

Erin could see that she was getting nowhere fast with this approach, so she decided to leave the room in hopes that Matt would get the hint and go home. As she stormed through the door, Matt mockingly held the door ajar, said "After you, sweet thing," and then patted Erin on the backside as she passed. Erin stopped in her tracks, turned to Matt, and said, "If you *ever* do that again, I'll . . ." She was so mad that she couldn't think of an appropriate threat. So instead she just stormed off down the hall and left the building.

The next morning, Erin was waiting in the office of Daryl Kolendich, the owner of the travel agency, when he arrived at work. Erin knew that Ron Hanson would probably be angry that she had gone over his head to the agency owner, but she was so furious with Matt Owens that she wanted immediate action. She described the incident to Daryl and demanded that some sort of disciplinary action be taken with Matt.

"Now calm down, Erin. Let's think through this problem a bit first. Isn't it possible that you can handle this sort of problem yourself? Is it possible that you may in fact have been encouraging Matt to act this way? Look, I understand that you're upset. I would be too, if I were in your shoes. But look at it this way. We've been hiring male travel agents for only the last few years now. Prior to that time there were only female agents, so problems like these never arose. Matt is from an older generation than yours. It takes time for men like him to get used to working on an equal basis with women. Can't you just try to make sure over the next few weeks that you give him no encouragement at all? If you do, I'm sure this problem will take care of itself."

Erin was not at all convinced. "But I *did* make it very clear I was not interested in him. It seemed to make him even more persistent. You're the owner and the boss here, and I'll do what you ask, but it seems to me that it's your responsibility to make sure this kind of sexual harassment doesn't take place in this agency."

"Erin, has your supervisor Ron Hanson ever suggested that your job opportunities here would be improved if you went out with him? Have I ever in any way intimated that a date with me could lead to a promotion for you?"

Erin was silent. It was true that none of the management staff at the agency had been guilty of sexual harassment. In fact, both Ron and Daryl had been highly supportive of her work ever since she arrived. Her annual pay raises had been higher than those of most other coworkers, both male and female.

Daryl broke the silence. "I guess my point is that we don't have a sexual harassment situation here. Please try what I've suggested and let me know in a couple of weeks if you feel it hasn't worked."

**Questions**

1.  What is sexual harassment in the workplace? Was Matt Owens guilty of sexual harassment?
2.  If you were Erin Dempsey, what would you do?
3.  What is an organization's responsibility with respect to sexual harassment among coworkers or supervisor-subordinate pairs? Do you think that Daryl Kolendich responded appropriately to the problem?
4.  Outline a brief policy that an organization could adopt to protect itself from sexual harassment lawsuits.

# REFERENCES

1.  Von Drehle, D. (2003, June 24). Court mirrors public opinion. *The Washington Post,* p. A1.
2.  Player, M. A. (2004). *Federal Law of Employment Discrimination in a Nutshell* (5th ed.). St. Paul, MN: West.
3.  Friedman, A. (1972). Attacking discrimination through the Thirteenth Amendment. *Cleveland State Law Review* 21, pp. 165–178.
4.  Peikes, L., and Mitchell, C. M. (2006, Aug.). 2nd Circuit: Employee working abroad has no remedy for extraterritorial discriminatory conduct. *HR News,* p. 1.
5.  *Johnson v. Railway Express Agency Inc.* (1975). 95 S. Ct. 1716.
6.  *CBOCS West Inc. v. Humphries.* (2008). 128 S. Ct. 1951.
7.  Civil rights statutes extended to Arabs, Jews. (1987, May 19). *Daily Labor Report,* pp. 1, 2, 6.
8.  Stites, J. (2005, May). Equal pay for the sexes. *HRMagazine,* pp. 64–69.
9.  Equal Employment Opportunity Commission. Charge statistics: FY 1997 through FY 2010. Retrieved from *http://www.eeoc.gov/eeoc/statistics/enforcement/charges.cfm* on June 13, 2011.
10. Society for Human Resources Management. (2011, Jan. 19). Novartis pays $152.5 million for bias. Retrieved from *www.shrm.org/LegalIssues/StateandLocalResources/ Pages/NovartisPays1525MillionforBias.aspx* on June 14, 2011. See also Wilson, D. (2010, May 17). Women win a bias suit against Novartis. *The New York Times.* Retrieved from *http://www.nytimes.com/2010/05/18/business/18novartis.html?scp=1 &sq=Women%20win%20a%20bias%20suit%20against%20Novartis&st=cse* on May 18, 2010.
11. Gamlem, C. (2007, Oct.). Affirmative action plans for federal contractors. Retrieved from *http://www.shrm.org/Research/Articles/Articles/Pages/CMS_000318.aspx* on April 16, 2008. See also *Bakke v. Regents of the University of California* (1978). 17 FEPC 1000.
12. Thompson, C. (2008, Mar.). Standard should not have been applied to hearing test. *HRMagazine,* p. 88.
13. *Furnco Construction Corp. v. Waters* (1978). 438 U.S. 567.
14. *McDonnell Douglas v. Green* (1973). 411 U.S. 972.
15. Civil Rights Act of 1991, Public Law No. 102–166, 105 Stat. 1071 (1991). Codified as amended at 42 U.S.C., Section 1981, 2000e *et seq.*
16. Valenza, G. (1999, Nov.–Dec.). The Supreme Court creates a safe harbor from liability for punitive damages. *Legal Report.* Washington, DC: Society for Human Resource Management, pp. 5–8.
17. Lau, S. (2008, Feb.). U.S. laws abroad. *HRMagazine,* p. 33.
18. *Gross v. FBL Financial Services Inc.* (2009). 129 S. Ct. 2343.
19. Biskupic, J. (2008, June 20). Court aids older workers alleging discrimination. *USAToday,* p. 5A.
20. Segal, J. A. (2008, July). Severance strategies. *HRMagazine* 53(7), pp. 95–98.
21. Ibid.

22. *Parsons v. Pioneer Hi-Bred Int'l Inc.* (2006, May 19). 8th Cir., No. 05–3496.

23. Chichoni, H. (2011, Feb.). I-9 compliance crackdowns. *HRMagazine* 56(2), pp. 63–68.

24. Ibid. See also Ladika, S. (2006, Oct.). Trouble on the hiring front. *HRMagazine,* pp. 56–61.

25. Lurie, D. (2005, Mar.). The I-9 form: everything HR professionals need to know about the I-9 employment-verification process. Retrieved from *www.shrm.org/hrresources/whitepapers_published/CMS_011693.asp* on April 15, 2008.

26. U.S. Immigration and Customs Enforcement. (2010, Oct. 8). DHS/ICE reveal highest immigration enforcement numbers on record in fiscal year 2010. Retrieved from *http://www.ice.gov/news/releases/1010/101008washingtondc.htm* on June 13, 2011. See also Krell, E. (2007, Dec.). Unmasking illegal workers. *HRMagazine,* pp. 49–52.

27. Hastings, R. R. (2010, July 9). Has the Americans with Disabilities Act made a difference? Retrieved from *http://www.shrm.org/hrdisciplines/Diversity/Articles/Pages/HastheADAMadeaDifference.aspx* on July 27, 2010.

28. Four years after the ADA. (1996, Nov–Dec.). *Working Age,* p. 2.

29. Equal Employment Opportunity Commission. Americans with Disabilities Act, questions and answers. Retrieved from *http://www.ada.gov/q&aeng02.htm* on June 14, 2011.

30. Ibid. See also Batiste, L. C. (2011). Accommodation and compliance series: Employees with drug addiction. Retrieved from *http://askjan.org/media/drugadd.html* on June 14, 2011.

31. Americans with Disabilities Act of 1990, Public Law No. 101–336, 104 Stat. 328 (1990). Codified at 42 U.S.C., Section 12101 *et seq.*

32. Segal, J. A. (2010, May). Presumed disability. *HRMagazine* 55(5), pp. 95–98.

33. EEOC, Americans with Disabilities Act, questions and answers, op. cit. See also Forster, J. (2000, Oct. 30). When workers just can't cope. *BusinessWeek,* pp. 100, 102.

34. Segal, J. A. (2010, June). ADA game changer. *HRMagazine* 55(6), pp. 121–126. See also Willman, S. K. (2003, Jan.–Feb.). Tips for minimizing abuses of the Americans with Disabilities Act. *Legal Report.* Alexandria, VA: Society for Human Resource Management, pp. 3–8. See also Janove, J. W. (2003, Mar.). Skating through the minefield. *HRMagazine,* pp. 107–113.

35. EEOC. The ADA: Your responsibilities as an employer. Retrieved from *www.eeoc.gov/facts/ada17.html* on June 14, 2011.

36. Mook, J. (2007, Jan.). Accommodation paradigm shifts. *HRMagazine,* pp. 115–120. See also Campbell, W. J., and Reilly, M. E. (2000). Accommodations for persons with disabilities. In J. F. Kehoe (Ed.), *Managing Selection in Changing Organizations.* San Francisco: Jossey-Bass, pp. 319–367.

37. Wells, S. J. (2008, Apr.). Counting on workers with disabilities. *HRMagazine,* pp. 44–49.

38. EEOC, The ADA: Your responsibilities as an employer, op. cit.

39. Zellers, V. (2009, Jan.). Make a resolution: ADA training. *HRMagazine* 54(1), 81–83.

40. Ibid.

41. *Kolstad v. American Dental Association.* (1999). 119 S. Ct. 2118.

42. Society for Human Resource Management. (2007). *FMLA: An Overview of the 2007 FMLA Survey.* Alexandria, VA: SHRM.

43. Cadrain, D. (2010, July). A leave law that just won't go away. *HRMagazine* 55(7), pp. 49–52. See also Davis, G. M. The Family and Medical Leave Act: 10 years later. Retrieved from *http://www.shrm.org/hrresources/lrpt_published/CMS_005127.asp* on August 22, 2003.

44. Most small businesses appear prepared to cope with new family-leave rules. (1993, Feb. 8). *The Wall Street Journal,* pp. B1, B2.

45. Leonard, B. (2008, Jan.). Bush signs military leave FMLA expansion into law. Retrieved from *http://www.shrm.org/hrnews_published/archives/CMS_024440.asp* on April 15, 2008.

46. Society for Human Resource Management. (2007). *FMLA: An overview of the 2007 FMLA survey.* Alexandria, VA: SHRM.

**47.** Gamlem, C. (2007, Oct.). Affirmative action plans for federal contractors. Retrieved from *http://www.shrm.org/Research/Articles/Articles/Pages/CMS_000318.aspx* on June 14, 2011. See also Jackson, D. J. (1978). Update on handicapped discrimination. *Personnel Journal* 57, pp. 488–491.

**48.** Thelen, J. (2006, Mar.–Apr.). Workplace rights for service members: The USERRA regulations deconstructed. *Legal Report,* pp. 1–8. See also *Carder v. Continental Airlines.* (2011, March 22). 5th Cir., No. 10-20105. See also Segal, J. A. (2006, Apr.). They go and come . . . and go. *HRMagazine,* pp. 127–133.

**49.** The Uniformed Services Employment and Reemployment Rights Act of 1994, Public Law 102–353 ; H. R. 995.

**50.** EEOC. Fiscal Year 2010 Performance and Accountability Report. Retrieved from *http://www.eeoc.gov/eeoc/plan/2010par_discussion.cfm* on June 14, 2011. See also EEOC. The charge-handling process. Retrieved from *http://www.eeoc.gov/employees/process.cfm* on June 14, 2011.

**51.** EEOC. EEOC litigation statistics, FY 1997 through FY 2010. Retrieved from *http://www.eeoc.gov/eeoc/statistics/enforcement/litigation.cfm* on June 14, 2011.

**52.** For more information, see EEOC. Laws and guidance. Retrieved from *http://www.eeoc.gov/policy/guidance.html* on June 14, 2011.

**53.** *Albemarle Paper Company v. Moody.* (1975). 442 U.S. 407.

**54.** EEOC. FY 2010 Performance and Accountability Report. Retrieved from *http://www.eeoc.gov/eeoc/plan/2010par_discussion.cfm* on June 14, 2011.

**55.** U.S. Department of Labor. New contractors' guide. Retrieved from *http://www.dol.gov/ofccp/TAguides/new_contractors_guide.htm* on June 14, 2011.

**56.** Healey, J. F., and O'Brien, E. (2007). *Race, Ethnicity, and Gender: Selected Readings* (2nd ed.). Thousand Oaks, CA: Pine Forge Press, an imprint of Sage Publications, Inc. See also Crosby, F. J., Iyer, A., Clayton, S., and Downing, R. A. (2003). Affirmative action: Psychological data and the policy debates. *American Psychologist* 58(2), pp. 93–115.

**57.** *Wygant v. Jackson Board of Education.* (1986). 106 S. Ct. 1842. See also *Local 28 Sheet MetalWorkers v. EEOC.* (1986). 106 S. Ct. 3019. See also *Local 93 Firefighters v. Cleveland.* (1986). 106 S. Ct. 3063.

**58.** *Johnson v. Santa Clara Transportation Agency.* (1987, Mar. 26). 107 S. Ct. 1442, 43 FEP Cases 411.

**59.** Fiske, S. T. (2010). Interpersonal stratification: Status, power, and subordination. In S. T. Fiske, D. T. Gilbert, and G. Lindzey (Eds.), *Handbook of Social Psychology* (5th ed.). New York: Wiley, pp. 941–982. See also Crosby, F. J., Stockdale, M. S., and Ropp, S. A. (Eds.). (2007). *Sex Discrimination in the Workplace.* Malden, MA: Blackwell. Gutek, B. A., and Stockdale, M. S. (2005). Sex discrimination in employment. In F. J. Landy. (Ed.), *Employment Discrimination Litigation.* San Francisco: Jossey-Bass, pp. 229–255. See also Copus, D. (2005). A lawyer's view: Avoiding junk science. In F. J. Landy. (Ed.), *Employment Discrimination Litigation.* San Francisco: Jossey-Bass, pp. 450–462. See also Parloff, R. (2007, Oct. 15). The war over unconscious bias. *Fortune,* pp. 90–102.

**60.** *Guidelines on discrimination because of sex,* 29CFR1604.10. Employment policies relating to pregnancy and childbirth (revised July 1, 2003).

**61.** EEOC. Pregnancy and discrimination charges: EEOC and FEPAs combined: FY 1997–FY 2010. Retrieved from *http://www.eeoc.gov/eeoc/statistics/enforcement/pregnancy.cfm* on June 14, 2011.

**62.** EEOC. Pregnancy discrimination. Retrieved from *http://www.eeoc.gov/laws/types/pregnancy.cfm* on June 14, 2011.

**63.** Galinsky, E., Sakai, K., and Wigton,T. (2011). *2011 Guide to Bold New Ideas for Making Work.* New York, NY: Families and Work Institute. See also Arthur, M. M. (2003). Share price reactions to work-family initiatives: An institutional perspective. *Academy of Management Journal* 46, pp. 497–505.

**64.** What to expect when you're expecting. (2008, May 26). *BusinessWeek,* p. 17.

**65.** *UAW v. Johnson Controls, Inc.* (1991). 499 U.S. 187.

66. Kilborn, P. (1990, Sept. 2). Manufacturer's policy, women's job rights clash. *Denver Post,* p. 2A.

67. Wermiel, S. (1991, Mar. 21). Justices bar "fetal protection" policies. *The Wall Street Journal,* pp. B1, B8. See also Epstein, A. (1991, Mar. 21). Ruling called women's rights victory. *Denver Post,* pp. 1A, 16A.

68. Noichl-Braun, C. (2000). Are fetal protection policies justified in view of employment discrimination? *Journal of Behavioral and Applied Management* 2(1), pp. 60–64. Retrieved from *http://www.ibam.com/pubs/jbam/articles/vol2/article_15.html* on October 10, 2011.

69. SHRM. (2010, April 16). Is workplace sexual harassment on the rise? SHRM poll. Retrieved from *http://www.shrm.org/Research/SurveyFindings/Articles/Pages/SexualHarassmentontheRise.aspx* on June 14, 2011. See also SHRM. (2011, April 5). Employer ordered to pay $451,000 for male-on-male sexual harassment. Retrieved from *http://www.shrm.org/LegalIssues/FederalResources/Pages/MaleonMaleSexual Harassment.aspx* on June 14, 2011. See also Fisher, A. B. (1993, Aug. 23). Sexual harassment: What to do. *Fortune,* pp. 84–88.

70. EEOC. Sex-based charges, FY 1997–FY 2010. Retrieved from *http://www.eeoc.gov/eeoc/statistics/enforcement/sex.cfm* on June 14, 2011.

71. EEOC. Guidelines on discrimination because of sex. Retrieved from *http://www.access.gpo.gov/nara/cfr/waisidx_06/29cfr1604_06.html* on June 14, 2011.

72. *Barnes v. Costle.* (1977). 561 F. 2d 983 (D. C. Cir.).

73. *Burlington Industries, Inc. v. Ellerth.* (1998, June 26). 118 S. Ct. 2257.

74. *Faragher v. City of Boca Raton.* (1998, June 26). 118 S. Ct. 2275.

75. *Meritor Savings Bank v. Vinson.* (1986). 477 U.S. 57.

76. Ibid.

77. France, A. H. (2011, Feb. 16). 10th Circuit: dismissal of claim of sexual harassment by non-employee reversed. Retrieved from *http://www.shrm.org/LegalIssues/Federal Resources/Pages/10thCircuitDismissal.aspx* on June 14, 2011.

78. *Pennsylvania State Police v. Suders.* 93 Fair Employment Practices Cases (BNA) 1473 (2004).

79. Jacobs, A. N. (2004, July 27). An instant message from the Supreme Court: Are you listening? *Employment Source Newsletter.* Retrieved from *www.epspros.com/NewsResources/Newsletters?find=14035* on October 10, 2011.

80. Lublin, J. S. (2006, May 15). Harassment law in U.S. is strict, foreigners find. *The Wall Street Journal,* pp. B1, B3. See also, Orey, M. (2006, May 22). Trouble at Toyota. *BusinessWeek,* pp. 46–48.

81. Ibid. See also SHRM. What guidelines should an employer follow when investigating allegations of sexual harassment? Retrieved from *http://www.shrm.org/Templates Tools/hrqa/Pages/investigatingharassment.aspx* on June 14, 2011. See also Segal, J. A. (1999, Nov.). Strategic planning for Troglodyte-free workplaces. *HRMagazine,* pp. 138–148.

82. For an example of an actual policy, see Sexual harassment policy #1. Retrieved from *http://www.shrm.org/TemplatesTools/Samples/Policies/Pages/CMS_000554.aspx* on October 10, 2011.

83. *Schwager v. Sun Oil Company of PA.* (1979). 591 F. 2d 58 (10th Cir.).

84. Danaher, M. G. (2009). Termination for obsolete skill set does not constitute age discrimination. *HRMagazine* 54(10), p. 73.

85. Sterns, H. L., Doverspike, D., and Lax, G. A. (2005). The Age Discrimination in Employment Act. In F. J. Landy. (Ed.), *Employment discrimination litigation.* San Francisco: Jossey-Bass, pp. 256–293. See also Bravin, J. (2005, Mar. 31). Court expands age-bias claims for work force. *The Wall Street Journal,* pp. B1–B3.

86. Grossman, R. J. (2003, Aug.). Are you ignoring older workers? *HRMagazine,* pp. 40–46.

87. Age discrimination—Overqualified. (1993, July). *Bulletin.* Denver: Mountain States Employers Council Inc., p. 2.

88. Hastings, R. R. (2008, Dec. 1). Overcoming the 'overqualified' label. Retrieved from *http://www.shrm.org/HRCareers/Pages/shrm_123107.aspx* on June 15, 2011. See also

Wells, S. J. (Oct. 2004). Too good to hire? *HRMagazine.* Retrieved from *http://www. shrm.org/hrmagazine/articles/1004/1004covstory.asp* on June 15, 2011.

89. What is seniority and how is it determined? (2009, May 7). Retrieved from *http:// www.shrm.org/TemplatesTools/hrqa/Pages/Whatisseniority.aspx* on June 15, 2011. See also *California Brewers Association v. Bryant.* (1982). 444 U.S. 598, p. 605.

90. See, for example, *Franks v. Bowman Transportation Co.* (1976). 424 U.S. 747; *International Brotherhood of Teamsters v. United States.* (1977). 432 U.S. 324; *American Tobacco Company v. Patterson.* (1982). 535 F. 2d 257 (CA-4). See also Gordon, M. E., and Johnson, W. A. (1982). Seniority: A review of its legal and scientific standing. *Personnel Psychology* 35, pp. 255–280.

91. *Firefighters Local Union No. 1784 v. Stotts.* (1984). 104 S. Ct. 2576.

92. *Wygant v. Jackson Board of Education.* (1986). 106 S. Ct. 1842.

93. Greenhouse, L. (1984, June 13). Seniority is held to outweigh race as a layoff guide. *The New York Times,* pp. A1, B12.

94. Britt, L. P., III (1984). Affirmative action: Is there life after Stotts? *Personnel Administrator* 29(9), pp. 96–100.

95. *US Airways, Inc. v. Barnett.* (00–1250) 535 U.S. 391 (2002) 228 F. 3d 1105.

96. Barrier, M. (2002, July). A line in the sand. Retrieved from *http://www.shrm.org/ hrmagazine/articles/0702/0702barrier.asp* on April 17, 2008.

97. Smith, A. (2010, March 23). USERRA rehiring obligation varies after layoffs. Retrieved from *http://www.shrm.org/LegalIssues/FederalResources/Pages/USERRA Rehire.aspx* on June 15, 2011.

98. *Griggs v. Duke Power Company.* (1971). 402 U.S. 424.

99. Ibid., p. 428.

100. Society for Industrial and Organization Psychology, Inc. (2003). *Principles for the Validation and Use of Personnel Selection Procedures* (4th ed.). Bowling Green, OH: Author. See also Committee on Psychological Tests and Assessment, American Psychological Association. (1996. June). Statement on the disclosure of test data. *American Psychologist* 51, pp. 644–648.

101. Justices uphold utility's stand on job testing. (1979, Mar. 6). *The Wall Street Journal,* p. 4.

102. *Watson v. Fort Worth Bank & Trust.* (1988). 108 S. Ct. 299.

103. McPhail, S. M. (Ed.). (2007). *Alternative Validation Strategies.* San Francisco: Jossey-Bass. See also Bersoff, D. N. (1988). Should subjective employment devices be scrutinized? *American Psychologist* 43, pp. 1016–1018.

104. *EEOC v. Radiator Specialty Company.* (1979). 610 F. 2d 178 (4th Cir.).

105. *Dothard v. Rawlinson.* (1977). 433 U.S. 321.

106. *Gregory v. Litton Systems Inc.* (1973). 472 F. 2d 631 (9th Cir.).

107. *Webster v. Redmond.* (1979). 599 F. 2d 793 (7th Cir.).

108. *Hyland v. Fukada.* (1978). 580 F. 2d 977 (9th Cir.).

109. Erlam, N. A. (2005). Walking the criminal records tightrope. Retrieved from *http:// www.shrm.org/ema/sm/articles/2005/octdec05Erlam.asp* on June 15, 2011.

110. *McDonald v. Santa Fe Transportation Co.* (1976). 427 U.S. 273.

111. Von Drehle, D. (2003, June 24). Court mirrors public opinion. *The Washington Post,* p. A1.

112. *Gratz v. Bollinger.* (2003, June 23). 539 U.S. 244. See also *Grutter v. Bollinger.* (2003). 539 U.S. 306.

113. Kronholz, J., Tomsho, R., Golden, D., and Greenberger, R. S. (2003, June 24). Court preserves affirmative action. (2003, June 24). *The Wall Street Journal,* pp. A1, A8. See also Lane, C. (2003, June 24). Affirmative action for diversity is upheld. *The Washington Post.* Retrieved from *http://www.washingtonpost.com.*

114. Kronholz, J., Tomsho, R., and Forelle, C. (2003). High court's ruling on race could affect business hiring. *The Wall Street Journal,* pp. A1, A6.

115. Zink, D. L., and Gutman, A. (2005). Statistical trends in private-sector employment discrimination suits. In F. J. Landy (Ed.), *Employment discrimination litigation: Behavioral, quantitative, and legal perspectives.* San Francisco: Jossey-Bass, pp. 101–131.

# 4

# DIVERSITY AT WORK

*Questions This Chapter Will Help Managers Answer*

1. Are there business reasons I should pay attention to "managing diversity"?
2. What are leading companies doing in this area?
3. What can I do to reverse the perception among many managers that the growing diversity of the workforce is a problem?
4. How can I maximize the potential of a racially and ethnically diverse workforce?
5. What can I do to accommodate women and older workers?

# MAKING THE BUSINESS CASE FOR DIVERSITY*

Diversity is more than just a passing blip on the corporate conscience. Over the past few years it has become a major competitive factor for many companies, and even something they are proud of. As an example, consider the *Fortune's* top 5 best companies to work for in 2011 and the percentage of women and minorities they employ, respectively: SAS (44%, 17%); Boston Consulting Group (45%, 27%); Wegmans Supermarkets (53%, 17%); Google (36%, 31%); and Net App (24%, 36%). Yet others remain to be convinced. They want the business justification for diversity to be sound and demonstrable. To do that, it's necessary to address five major issues. Here's how some companies responded:

1. *How does diversity help an organization expand into global markets?* "Our customers, suppliers, and strategic partners are increasingly global and multi-cultural. We must be positioned to relate to them" (Hewlett-Packard). "Our major growth opportunities will occur outside of our North American business. Our objectives for business growth for the next decade indicate that our international business will be as large as our domestic business. Diversity is a business imperative. There is no way to achieve our business strategy unless we develop and utilize diversity in the marketplace to achieve competitive advantage around the world. Just five years ago all of our operations were located at U.S. headquarters. Now four of our seven businesses are located outside of the United States in different regions of the globe" (Procter & Gamble).

2. *How can diversity help build brand equity, increase consumer purchasing, and grow the business?* As a result of hiring a multicultural staff, including Hispanics, for its previously homogeneous marketing department, Amtrak learned that a large percentage of the Latino population in the West relies not only on Spanish-language radio and newspapers for travel information, but also on Latino Catholic publications. At least partly as a result of advertising in those publications as well, ridership on Amtrak's West Coast routes has increased by 47 percent. Corporate America also purchases supplies from minority-owned suppliers. How much? In 2010 Microsoft alone purchased more than $1 billion in goods and services from minority- and women-owned businesses.[a]

3. *How does diversity support the organization's human asset/resource strategies?* "We are facing a tremendous threat to our ability to retain top talent. Our attrition rate for our technical managers exceeds 28 percent. The percentages are greater for our technical managers who are under the age of 30,

*Sources:* Hastings, R. R. (2010, Oct. 15). Business needs inform diversity strategies. Retrieved from *http://www.shrm.org/hrdisciplines/Diversity/Articles/Pages/BusinessNeedsInformDiversity Strategies.aspx* on June 20, 2011. See also SHRM Diversity Forum. What is the 'business case' for diversity? Retrieved from *http://shrm.org/diversity/library_published/nonIC/CMS_011965.asp* on June 20, 2011. See also Marquis, J. P., Lim, N., Scott, L. M., Harrell, M. C., and Kavanagh, J. (2008). *Managing Diversity in Corporate America.* Santa Monica, CA: Rand. See also 100 Best Companies to Work For 2011. Retrieved from *http://money.cnn.com/magazines/fortune/bestcompanies/2011.* See also Gunther, M. (2006, Dec. 11). Queer, Inc.: How corporate America fell in love with gays and lesbians. It's a movement. *Fortune,* pp. 94–110. See also Kochan, T., Bezrukova, K., Ely, R., Jackson, S., Joshi, A., Jehn, K., Leonard, J., Levine, D., and Thomas, D. (2003). The effects of diversity of business performance: Report of the diversity research network. *Human Resource Management,* 42(1), 3–21.

[a]Microsoft. Supplier diversity. Retrieved from *www.microsoft.com/about/companyinformation/ procurement/diversity/en/us/default.aspx* on June 20, 2011.

those with three to eight years' tenure, and across all race and gender categories. The dollar impact of losing this talent exceeds $15 million annually. The loss in intellectual capital is incalculable. The notion that our attrition is consistent with industry trends is totally unacceptable. We cannot hire talent fast enough to replace this brain drain. Diversity is a strategic imperative to retaining top talent and reducing our attrition rate by 50 percent in the next two years. We must identify the compelling factors that ensure we retain that talent for which we have invested so heavily" (*Fortune* 50 IT company, headquartered in the United States).

4. *How does diversity build our corporate image among our consumers?* Qualified and interested people are often attracted to employers who are able to show that they are committed to developing and promoting a wide array of people. Consider IBM, for example. Since 1995 the number of female executives worldwide has increased by 490 percent. The number of self-identified gay, lesbian, bisexual, and transgender (GLBT) employees has grown even faster—and the number of executives with disabilities has more than tripled. IBM buys $1.5 billion worth of goods and services from U.S. suppliers owned by women, minorities, or GLBT people and $745 million from these suppliers outside the U.S.[b] and it sells more than $500 million of goods and services by marketing to those groups.

5. *How does diversity enhance operational efficiency?* Employees from all groups now expect more from organizations—from nondiscriminatory, hostility-free workplaces to flexible schedules and benefits that include child-care assistance and work-life policies. A company's return on investment is reduced when commitment and productivity are lost because employees do not feel valued, time is wasted with conflicts and misunderstandings, and money is spent on legal fees and settlements. Conversely, an environment where employees feel valued and included yields greater commitment and motivation to succeed. It also means fewer resources spent on grievances, turnover, and replacement costs.

Of necessity, building the business case for diversity in any given company will vary, but in general it can be stated in two compelling arguments: (1) For both large and small companies these days, the neighborhood in which they sell is the entire world, so it is essential that their workforces look and think like the world, in all of its ethnic, racial, and behavioral variety. (2) The demographics of the United States are changing so dramatically that over the coming decades it will be impossible for employers to fill their ranks with members of the traditional workforce—white males. By 2040 an estimated 70 percent of American workers will be either women or members of what are now racial minorities.

While we can make a persuasive business case for diversity, a five-year research project in four large firms found few direct positive or negative effects of diversity on business performance. The researchers suggested that a more "nuanced" view of the business case for diversity may be more appropriate. In the concluding section of this case, we examine more closely that nuanced view and its implications for managers.

---

[b]IBM. Supply chain diversity. Retrieved from *www.ibm.com/ibm/responsibility/supply_diversity. shtml* on June 20, 2011.

Challenges

1. What is the objective of building and managing a diverse workforce?
2. Is there additional information beyond these five issues that you feel is necessary to make the business case for diversity?
3. What steps can you take as a manager to become more effective in a work environment that is more diverse than ever?

The United States workforce is diverse—and becoming more so every year.[1]

- More than half the U.S. workforce now consists of racial minorities (i.e., nonwhite), **ethnic minorities** (i.e., people classified according to common traits and customs), immigrants, and women.
- Women's share of the labor force was 46.5 percent in 2008; it will be 46.9 percent by 2018. Men's share is projected to decline slightly over the same time period, from 53.5 to 53.1 percent.
- White non-Hispanics accounted for 68.2 percent of the labor force in 2008. Their share of the labor force in 2018 will decrease modestly to 64 percent.
- The Asian, American Indian, Alaska Native, and Pacific Islanders' share of the labor force will increase from 7.1 to 8.5 percent, the Hispanic share will increase from 14.3 to 17.6 percent, and the African-American share will hold steady at about 12 percent between 2008 and 2018.
- The labor force will continue to age, with the 55-and-older group comprising 23.9 percent of the workforce in 2018, compared to 18.1 percent in 2008. Over the same time period, the percentage in the 25- to 54-year age group will shrink from 67.7 to 63.5 percent, and for the 16- to 24-year age group, it will shrink from 14.3 to 12.7 percent.

These demographic facts do not indicate that a diverse workforce is something a company ought to have. Rather, they tell us that all companies already do have—or soon will have—diverse workforces.

Unfortunately, attitudes and beliefs about the groups contributing to diversity change slowly. To some, workers and managers alike, workforce diversity is simply a problem that won't go away. Nothing can be gained with this perspective. To others, diversity represents an opportunity, an advantage that can be used to compete and win in the global marketplace, as we shall now see.

## WORKFORCE DIVERSITY: AN ESSENTIAL COMPONENT OF HR STRATEGY

To celebrate diversity is to appreciate and value individual differences. **Managing diversity** means *establishing a heterogeneous workforce (including white men) to perform to its potential in an equitable work environment where no member or group of members has an advantage or a disadvantage.*[2] This is a pragmatic business strategy that focuses on maximizing the productivity, creativity, and commitment of the workforce while meeting the needs of diverse consumer groups. Managing diversity is not the same thing as managing affirmative

## Table 4–1

### MAJOR DIFFERENCES BETWEEN EQUAL EMPLOYMENT OPPORTUNITY/ AFFIRMATIVE ACTION (EEO/AA) AND DIVERSITY

| EEO/AA | Diversity |
|---|---|
| Government initiated | Voluntary (company driven) |
| Legally driven | Productivity driven |
| Quantitative | Qualitative |
| Problem focused | Opportunity focused |
| Assumes assimilation | Assumes integration |
| Internally focused | Internally and externally focused |
| Reactive | Proactive |

*Sources:* The Diversity Training Group. Frequently asked questions. Retrieved from *www. diversitydtg.com* on April 21, 2008. See also SHRM. (2004, Aug. 5). How is a diversity initiative different from my organization's affirmative action plan? Retrieved from *www.shrm.org/diversity/* on April 21, 2008.

action. As we noted in Chapter 3, affirmative action refers to actions taken to overcome the effects of past or present practices, policies, or other barriers to equal employment opportunity.[3] It is a first step that gives managers the opportunity to correct imbalances, injustices, and past mistakes. Over the long term, however, the challenge is to create a work setting in which each person can perform to his or her full potential and therefore compete for promotions and other rewards on merit alone. Table 4–1 highlights some key differences between equal employment opportunity/affirmative action and diversity.

There are five reasons diversity has become a dominant activity in managing an organization's human resources (see Figure 4–1):

1. The shift from a manufacturing to a service economy.
2. Globalization of markets.
3. New business strategies that require more teamwork.
4. Mergers and alliances that require different corporate cultures to work together.
5. The changing labor market.[4]

### The Service Economy

Roughly 90 percent of U.S. employees work in service-based industries (see Table 4–2).[5] Manufacturing will maintain its share of total output, while productivity in this sector increases and the need for additional labor decreases. Virtually all of the growth in new jobs will come from service-producing industries. Service-industry jobs, such as in banking, financial services, health services, tourism, and retailing, imply lots of interaction with customers. Service employees need to be able to "read" their customers—to understand them, to anticipate and monitor their needs and expectations, and to respond sensitively and appropriately to those needs and expectations. In the service game, "customer literacy" is an essential skill. Considering that Hispanics, African

**Figure 4–1**

Increased diversity in the workforce meshes well with the evolving changes in organizations and markets.

Americans, Asians, people with disabilities, and gays/lesbians/bisexuals/transsexuals have a combined $1.5 trillion in buying power (equivalent to the GDP of France), why would any business want to ignore them?[6]

A growing number of companies now realize that their workforces should mirror their customers. Similarities in culture, dress, and language between service workers and customers creates more efficient interactions between them and better business for the firm. Bank of America in Baltimore discovered this when it studied the customer-retention records for its branches. The branches showing highest customer loyalty recruited locally to hire tellers, who could swap

## Table 4–2

### THE SHIFT FROM MANUFACTURING TO SERVICE JOBS, 1973–2011

| Year | Manufacturing jobs (%) | Service jobs (%) |
|------|------------------------|------------------|
| 1973 | 26.0 | 74 |
| 1983 | 20.0 | 80 |
| 1993 | 16.0 | 84 |
| 1998 | 13.0 | 87 |
| 2011 | 7.4 | 90 |

*Sources:* U.S. Bureau of Labor Statistics and Perry, M. J. (2011, Feb. 25). The truth about U.S. manufacturing. *The Wall Street Journal*, p. A13.

neighborhood gossip. The best of 20 branch managers worked in a distant suburb and was described as dressing "very blue collar. She doesn't look like a typical manager of people. But this woman is totally committed to her customers."[7]

When companies discover they can communicate better with their customers through employees who are similar to their customers, those companies then realize they have increased their internal diversity. And that means they have to manage and retain their new, diverse workforce. There is no going back; diversity breeds diversity. Managing it well is an essential part of HR strategy.

## The Globalization of Markets

As organizations around the world compete for customers, they offer customers choices unavailable to them domestically. With more options to choose from, customers have more power to insist that their needs and preferences be satisfied. To satisfy them, firms have to get closer and closer to their customers. Some firms have established a strong local presence (e.g., advertisements for Japanese-made cars that showcase local dealerships and satisfied American owners); others have forged strategic international alliances (e.g., Apple Inc. and Verizon). Either way, diversity must be managed—by working through domestic diversity (local presence) or by merging national as well as corporate cultures (international alliances). Successful global leaders measure success in this area of cultural learning as they measure other business factors.

For example, the CEO of Switzerland-based Novo Nordisk requires his managers to "buy" and "sell" three best practices to managers in other parts of the world each year on their corporate intranet. Doing so underscores three valuable lessons: (1) We must use technology to move information around the company. (2) We must learn from our colleagues around the globe and share information with them. (3) We must measure these "soft" skills as we measure "hard" business returns, and hold people accountable for them. In short, culture matters.[8]

## New Business Strategies That Require More Teamwork

To survive, to serve, and to succeed, organizations need to accomplish goals that are defined more broadly than ever before (e.g., world-class quality, reliability, and customer service), which means carrying out strategies that no one part of the organization can execute alone. For example, if a firm's business strategy emphasizes speed in every function (in developing new products, producing them, distributing them, and responding to feedback from customers), the firm needs to rely on teams of workers. Teams mean diverse workforces, whether as a result of drawing from the most talented or experienced staff or through deliberately structuring diversity to stimulate creativity.

Firms have found that only through work teams can they execute newly adopted strategies stressing better quality, innovation, cost control, or speed. Indeed, virtual teams—domestic or global—promise new kinds of management challenges. In a virtual team, members are dispersed geographically or organizationally. Their primary interaction is through some combination of electronic communication systems. They may never "meet" in the traditional sense. Further, team membership is often fluid, evolving according to changing task requirements. This has created a rich training agenda, as members from diverse backgrounds must learn to work productively together.[9]

Diversity is an inevitable byproduct of teamwork, especially when teams are drawn from a diverse base of employees. Young and old, male and female, American-born and non–American-born, better and less well educated—these are just some of the dimensions along which team members may differ. Coordinating team talents to develop new products, better customer service, or ways of working more efficiently is a difficult, yet essential, aspect of business strategy. As Ted Childs, former head of IBM Global Workforce Diversity, has noted: "When a company's vision includes the growing mix of the talent pool and the customer base, then the real argument for diversity is the business case."[10]

## Mergers and Strategic International Alliances

The managers who have worked out the results of all the mergers, acquisitions, and strategic international alliances occurring over the past 20 years know how important it is to knit together the new partners' financial, technological, production, and marketing resources.[11] However, the resources of the new enterprise also include people, and this means creating a partnership that spans different corporate cultures.

A key source of problems in mergers, acquisitions, and strategic international alliances is differences in corporate cultures.[12] According to two studies, integrating culture was the top challenge in mergers and acquisitions.[13] Corporate cultures may differ in many ways, such as the customs of conducting business, how people are expected to behave, and the kinds of behaviors that get rewarded.

When two foreign businesses attempt a long-distance marriage, the obstacles are national cultures as well as corporate cultures. Fifty percent of U.S. managers either resign or are fired within 18 months of a foreign takeover.[14] Many of the managers report a kind of "culture shock." As one manager put it, "You don't quite know their values, where they're coming from, or what they really have in mind for you."[16] Both workers and managers need to understand and capitalize on diversity as companies combine their efforts to offer products and services to customers in far-flung markets.

---

## A WORD ABOUT TERMINOLOGY

In recent years, few topics have sparked as much debate as "politically correct" language. Choosing the right words may take a bit more thought and effort, but it is imperative to do so in business communication. After all, it makes no sense to alienate employees and customers by using words that show a lack of respect or sensitivity.

Consider just two examples. Instead of referring to dark-skinned people (whose ethnic origins may be Hispanic or African) as black, it is more appropriate to refer to them as Hispanic Americans or African Americans. Instead of referring to people with physical or mental impairments as "the disabled" or "the handicapped" (terms that emphasize what a person cannot do rather than what he or she can do), it is more appropriate to refer to them as "people with disabilities." Showing respect and sensitivity to differences by means of the language we use in business is the first step toward building up the capabilities of a diverse workforce.

### The Changing Labor Market

You can be sure of this: Over the next 25 years the U.S. workforce will comprise more women, more immigrants, more people of color, and more older workers.[16] In fact, more than 500 million people, double the number today, will legally work outside their home countries in the next 20 years; why? Experts point to factors such as conflict, natural disasters, climate change, and economic opportunism.[17] Our workplaces will be characterized by more diversity in every respect. The first step to attaining the advantages of diversity is to teach all employees to understand and value different races, ethnic groups, cultures, languages, religions, sexual orientations, levels of physical ability, and family structures. Skeptical managers, supervisors, and policymakers need to understand that different does not mean deficient. Only when employees at every level truly believe this will the corporation they work for be able to build the trust that is essential among the members of high-performance work teams.[18] Such teams incorporate practices that provide their members with the information, skills, incentives, and responsibility to make decisions that are essential to innovate, to improve quality, and to respond rapidly to change.[19]

## DIVERSITY AT WORK—A PROBLEM FOR MANY ORGANIZATIONS

Reports of discrimination correlate with a tendency to feel "burned out," a reduced willingness to take initiative on the job, and a greater likelihood of planning to change jobs. Not surprisingly, therefore, a recent study of more than 475,000 professionals and managers from 20 large corporations found that minorities and women quit companies much more often than white males do, especially during the early period of employment, although over time, racial differences in quit rates disappear.[20] Such turnover represents millions of dollars in lost training and productivity.

### WHY IS A DIVERSITY PROGRAM SO DIFFICULT TO IMPLEMENT?

A recent survey by Boston-based Novations Group of more than 2,000 senior HR and training executives found both good news and bad news. The good news was that commitment to diversity was up about 60 percent from two years earlier, when the survey was last conducted. The bad news was that one-fourth of those polled were unsure about how to implement it, to make it work in practice, or to maximize its benefits in business terms. To a large extent that may be due to the attitudes of senior management. While about half of senior managers accept the business case for diversity and do what is necessary to leverage inclusion within their organizations, fully 28 percent either pay lip service to the ideas of diversity and inclusion, or are not convinced of the business case, but let HR pursue inclusion efforts. According to Novations CEO Mike Hyter, "inclusion is tough to make real when an organization's top people are confused or lukewarm. Any program is bound to be less effective if management isn't fully committed."[a]

[a]Hyter, quoted in Gurchiek, K. (2007, Aug. 27). Putting diversity into practice stymies many firms. *HR News*. Retrieved from *www.shrm.hrnews_published/articles/CMS_022806.asp* on September 7, 2007.

So how should you handle questions and concerns about diversity? Here are some suggestions: *inquire* ("What makes you say that?"), *show empathy* ("It is frustrating when you can't understand someone"), *educate* (debunk myths, provide facts, explain), *state your needs or expectations* ("Let's develop an approach we can both live with"), and *don't polarize people or groups* ("What might be other reasons for this behavior?"). Sometimes people respond differently to the same situation because of their culture. Culture is the foundation of group differences. In the following sections we will examine the concept of culture and then focus briefly on some key issues that characterize three racial/ethnic groups (African Americans, Hispanic Americans, and Asian Americans), women, and the four generations that make up the U.S. workforce. As in other chapters, we will present examples of companies that have provided progressive leadership in this area.

## Culture—The Foundation of Group Differences

**Culture** refers to the characteristic behavior of people in a country or region. Culture helps people make sense of their part of the world. It provides them with an identity—one they retain even when they emigrate.[21]

When we talk about culture, we include, for example, family patterns, customs, social classes, religions, political systems, clothing, music, food, literature, and laws.[22] Understanding the things that make up a person's culture helps diverse peoples to deal more constructively with one another. Conversely, misunderstandings among people of goodwill often cause unnecessary interpersonal problems and have undone countless business deals. We will examine the concept of culture more fully in our final chapter.

"Valuing diversity" means more than feeling comfortable with employees whose race, ethnicity, or gender differ from your own.[23] It means more than accepting their accents or language, their dress or food. It means learning to value and respect styles and ways of behaving that differ from yours. To manage diversity, there is no room for inflexibility and intolerance—displace them with adaptability and acceptance.

## African Americans in the Workforce

African Americans will make up about 12.1 percent of the U.S. civilian workforce by the year 2018.[24] Consider these facts:

- According to the U.S. Census Bureau, African Americans own 1.9 million businesses in the United States (38 percent of the owners are women), employ more than 921,000 people, and generate $137.5 billion in revenue.[25]
- Buying power of African-American consumers rose to $957 billion at the end of 2010, and is projected to reach $1.2 trillion by 2015.[26] (see Figure 4–2).
- Among the *Fortune* 500 largest firms, there were six African-American chief executive officers in 2011.[27]
- In financial services, for example, the top companies for African Americans in 2010 were American Express, Bank of America, Comerica, Fannie Mae, Freddie Mac, and Northern Trust.[28]

Despite these encouraging trends, sometimes progress only comes through the legal system. For example, in November 2000, Coca-Cola Company agreed

## Figure 4–2

African-American buying power in billions of dollars.
(Data from Fahmy, S. (2010, Nov 4.), Minority buying power report. Retrieved from *www.terry.uga.edu/news/releases/2010/minority-buying-power-report.html* on June 20, 2011.)

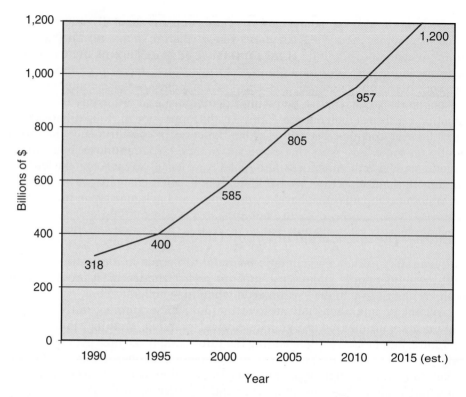

to a record $192.5 million settlement to a race discrimination lawsuit that alleged wide disparities in pay, promotions, and performance evaluations. The cost to Coke included $113 million in cash, $43.5 million to adjust salaries of African-American employees over the subsequent 10 years, and $36 million for implementation of various diversity initiatives and oversight by a seven-member panel of the company's employment practices.[29] Such settlements do lead to improvement, as Coca-Cola's own data show. By 2011, 20 percent of the company's U.S. workforce was comprised of African Americans, and 41 percent of the company was female. Even more impressive, the company ranked in the top 20 of DiversityInc's Top 50 Companies for Diversity® list for the eighth straight year.[30] Coca-Cola uses quarterly monitoring to ensure that individuals are being hired, retained, promoted, and rewarded on a fair and consistent basis. Continued monitoring is necessary, because, as has often been noted, "With diversity, there is no endgame."

Among companies that are committed to making diversity a competitive advantage, here are some other practices to consider:[31]

- Hire only those search firms with a solid track record for providing diverse slates of candidates for positions at all levels.
- Forge links with colleges and universities with significant numbers of minority students, and bring real jobs to the recruiting table.
- Start formal mentoring and succession programs to ensure that minorities are in the leadership pipeline.
- Include progress on diversity issues in management performance reviews and compensation.
- Set specific goals in critical areas, such as the percentages of minorities and women hired, promoted, and in the overall workforce. Also set goals for the

Employee networks can help ensure that products and services are relevant and culturally appropriate to various customer segments.

amount of business conducted with outside vendors owned by minorities and women.

- Provide all employees with confidential outlets to air and settle grievances, for example, telephone and e-mail hot lines.

## Hispanics in the Workforce

Hispanics, who will comprise 17.6 percent of the civilian labor force by the year 2018,[32] experience many of the same disadvantages as African Americans. However, the term *Hispanic* encompasses a large, diverse group of people who

### BOTTOM-LINE BENEFITS OF DIVERSITY AT PEPSICO*

**HR BUZZ**

In 2006 Indra Nooyi took the helm as CEO of PepsiCo, the largest U.S. company by market capitalization to put a woman in charge. Given Pepsi's culture, that is no surprise. It is well known that diversity programs cannot succeed without commitment from the organization's top executives. Nooyi's predecessor, CEO Steve Reinemund, was certainly committed. He enforced aggressive hiring and promotion rules. Half of all new hires at Pepsi have to be either women or ethnic minorities. And managers now earn their bonuses, in part, by how well they recruit and retain them. Today, 25 percent of Pepsi's managers are women, up from 22 percent four years ago, and six of its top 12 executives are now women or minorities.

The diversity push is part of Pepsi's game plan to understand better the disparate tastes of new consumers as it continues to expand globally. To do that, it needs to tap the creative, cultural, and creative skills of a variety of employees and to use those skills to improve company policies, products, and customer experiences. The Latino Employee Network at Frito-Lay, the snack-food division of PepsiCo, did just that. During the development of Doritos Guacamole-Flavored Tortilla Chips, members of the network provided feed-back on the taste and packaging to help ensure that the product would be regarded as authentic in the Latino community. Their insight helped make the guacamole-flavored Doritos one of the most successful new-product launches in the company's history, generating more than $100 million in sales in its first year alone.

* Yang, J. L. (2006, Sept. 4). Pepsi's diversity push pays off. *Fortune*, p. 32. See also Morris, B. (2008, Feb. 19). The Pepsi challenge. Retrieved from *money.cnn.com/2008/02/18/news/companies/ morris_nooyi.fortune/index.htm* on April 23, 2008. See also Rodriguez, 2006, op. cit.

come from distinctively different ethnic and racial backgrounds and who have achieved various economic and educational levels. For example, a third-generation, educated, white Cuban American has little in common with an uneducated Central American immigrant of mainly Native American ancestry who has fled civil upheaval and political persecution. Despite the fact that their differences far outweigh their similarities, both are classified as Hispanic. Why? Largely because of the language they speak (Spanish), their surnames, or their geographical origins.

Mexicans, Puerto Ricans, and Cubans constitute the three largest groups classified as Hispanic. They are concentrated in four geographic areas: Mexican Americans reside mostly in California and Texas, Puerto Ricans mostly in New York, and a majority of Cuban Americans in Florida. These four states account for 73 percent of the firms owned by Hispanics. Hispanics own a total of 1.6 million businesses in the United States (6 percent of all nonfarm businesses), generating $222 billion in revenue.[33] Labor-force participation rates for Hispanics (as a group) are growing rapidly, as Figure 4–3 shows.

Hispanics are also getting wealthier, as mean household income reached $37,913 in 2008..[34] Buying power among Hispanics—that is, the total personal income available after taxes for goods and services—is difficult to measure accurately, partly because of language and education differences, but is expected to soar from $1 trillion in 2010 to $1.5 trillion in 2015, accounting for nearly 11 percent of the nation's total buying power.[35]

To encourage greater diversity throughout its entire corporate structure, health-care benefits company Aetna is exemplary.

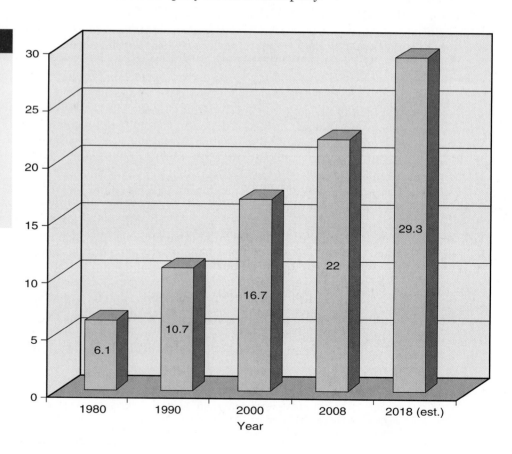

**Figure 4–3**

Growth of the civilian Hispanic labor force (in millions), 1980–2018 (est.).

(Source: Toossi, M. (2009, Nov.). Employment outlook: 2008-2018. *Monthly Labor Review,* pp. 30-51.)

## AETNA: EMBEDDING DIVERSITY INTO THE FABRIC OF THE BUSINESS*

Aetna is one of the nation's leading diversified healthcare-benefits companies, serving approximately 37.2 million people. Its healthcare network includes 4,919 hospitals, more than 843,000 healthcare professionals, and more than 490,000 primary-care doctors and specialists. More than 33,000 employees work for the company. Of those, 31 percent are people of color and 76 percent are women. People of color hold 16 percent of management/supervisory positions, and 15 percent of senior leaders are people of color. Women hold 62 percent of management/supervisory positions, and 26 percent of senior leaders are women.

Aetna employees live by a set of core values, known as the Aetna Way, which put the people who use the company's services at the core of everything it does. While business results are important, Aetna's senior managers believe that *how* the company achieves those results—how it makes a difference for the people it serves—is every bit as important. The four core values are: integrity, employee engagement, excellence and accountability, and quality service and value. Notice how they all revolve around Aetna's customers. Each value also describes how employees are expected to behave.

- **Integrity:** Do the right thing for the right reason, honor commitments, and behave ethically.
- **Employee engagement:** Lead people to success, value diversity, and build confidence and pride in our company.
- **Excellence and accountability:** Make a fair profit, innovate, anticipate the future—look, listen, and learn.
- **Quality service and value:** Make it easy. Eliminate hassles; make Aetna the standard by which others are judged; build trusting, valued relationships with all constituents.

### The "ICE" Strategy

Aetna's diversity strategy is a unique marriage of values and business strategy with roots from more than 35 years ago. Its core components are integration, communication, and education (ICE). *Integration* means that all diversity components are working together across the enterprise (marketing, HR, Aetna's philanthropic foundation, investments, procurement, sales, etc.), and that they are fully integrated into the short- and long-term business-planning process. *Communication* is the creation and dissemination of information to all employees and customers. Finally, *education* means deepening the understanding of what the diversity strategy is, including its components, the ways in which it is manifested in Aetna's business strategy, the people who are included, and the creation of development tools to increase individual and organizational competencies.

The outcome of this strategy is twofold: (1) to serve customers in current markets more effectively, while (2) identifying opportunities in new markets. It recognizes that Aetna's future success depends on a deep knowledge of all employee segments; clear and consistent communication to disseminate information to employees, customers, and other key constituents; and an increased

---

*Sources: Aetna. 2010 Diversity Annual Report. Retrieved from *www.aetna.com/diversityannual-report/pdf/2010_DiversityAR.pdf*. See also Aetna. 2010 annual report. Retrieved from *www.aetna.com/2010annualreport/* on June 21, 2011. See also Cascio, W. F. (2009). *Aetna: Investing in Diversity*. Alexandria, VA: Society for Human Resource Management.

focus on developing the cultural awareness and competency necessary to sustain its business success. To be sure, Aetna's ICE strategy extends well beyond diversity awareness to that of a strategic advantage.

## Payoffs from Aetna's Diversity Efforts

Aetna's business results are impressive. Its market value has zoomed from $3.3 billion in 2001 to almost $17 billion in 2011. Aetna's net income rose from a loss of $291.5 million in 2001 to $1.8 billion in 2010. Undoubtedly, much of the turnaround in business results can be traced to a more focused business strategy, but at the same time, the CEO made diversity a key business imperative. That aspect of Aetna's strategy has also paid off.

To begin to appreciate the broad range of recognition the company has received, consider just a few of its recent awards:

- Top 40 Companies for Diversity, *Black Enterprise* magazine.
- Readers' Choice, Best Diversity Company, *Engineering & Information Technology* magazine, diversity/careers category.
- Top 10 Companies for Executive Women, National Association for Female Executives.
- Top 50 Companies for Latinas, *Latina Style* magazine.
- Top employer for leadership and accomplishment in hiring and promoting people with disabilities, State of Connecticut Department of Social Services.
- 5-Star Employer Award, U.S. Department of Defense, Employer Support of the Guard and Reserve.
- Out and EqualWorkplace Advocates "Champion Award" presented to Aetna's CEO; it recognizes a non-lesbian, -gay, -bisexual, or -transgender (LGBT) person who has played a pivotal role in championing equal treatment of LGBT employees on the job and has demonstrated a significant commitment to LGBT workplace rights.
- America's Most Admired Companies, *Fortune* magazine, #1 in the health care insurance category.
- One of the 50 best places to launch a career, *Business Week*.

As these awards make clear, Aetna embraces diversity in its full breadth and richness—and it pays off handsomely.

## Asian Americans in the Workforce

The share of the workforce comprised by Asian Americans was 4.7 percent in 2008 and is expected to reach an estimated 5.6 percent by 2018, largely due to immigration.[36] Buying power among Asian Americans has increased from $269 billion in 2000 to $544 billion in 2010 to an estimated $775 billion in 2015. It is propelled by the fact that Asian Americans are better educated than the average American. Fully 50 percent of them ages 25 and over have a bachelor's degree or higher, compared with 28 percent of the total population. Thus, many hold top jobs, and the increasing number of successful Asian entrepreneurs also helps to increase the group's buying power.[37] Which are the best companies for Asian Americans to work for? Several notable ones are Applied Materials, Union Bank of California, Golden West Financial, Sempra Energy, and Schering-Plough. For example, at Applied Materials, a Santa Clara, California, maker of semiconductor equipment, Asians comprise 26.7 percent of the workforce. Minorities as a group comprise 39.4 percent of the workforce and 29.7 percent of officials and managers. The company focuses on diversity at the grassroots level, funding a San Jose charter school that seeks to get Latino students into college. At Union Bank of California, Asians comprise 25 percent of the workforce. Minorities as a group comprise 55.6 percent of the workforce, 38.6 percent of officials and managers, and 57 percent of new hires.

At United Parcel Service (UPS), diversity efforts have paid off handsomely. For example, Jennifer Kannar, a Hong Kong–raised product manager, proposed a bilingual support center to win the business of Korean-American entrepreneurs in Southern California. The company took several months to evaluate the proposal—to Kannar's frustration—but ultimately approved the center. Kannar is now expanding to include Vietnamese, Chinese, and Japanese businesses. Had UPS not consciously striven for a diverse workforce, it may well have missed the opportunity Kannar saw.[38]

## Women in the Workforce

Over the past 30 years, women have raised their expectations and levels of aspiration sharply higher, largely because of the women's movement, coupled with landmark civil rights legislation and well-publicized judgments against large companies for gender discrimination in hiring, promotion, and pay. In 1972, women questioned the possibility of having a family and holding a job at the same time. By the mid-1980s, they took it for granted that they could manage both, and by the mid-1990s, 89 percent of young women said they expected to have both a family and a job.[39] Today, about 62 percent of all working women are contributing half or more of their household income, and they hold about 40 percent of all managerial and professional positions. So much for the myth that women don't hold high-level business jobs because they supposedly don't aim high enough.[40] Five key forces account for these changes:

1. *Changes in the family.* Legalized abortion, contraception, divorce, and a declining birthrate have all contributed to a decrease in the number of years of their lives most women devote to rearing children. About 75 percent of the 68 million working women in the U.S. will become pregnant,"[41] and about 70 percent of mothers with school-age children work for pay outside the home, including 55 percent of mothers with children under one year old.[42] To lure new mothers back to work, employers like Bank of America, Accenture, and Boston Consulting Group are increasing maternity-leave pay, communicating benefits and support proactively, keeping in touch through maternity leave, offering meaningful jobs with reduced travel hours, and giving mothers fair access to bonuses and incentives.[43]

   The proportion of single-parent family groups with children under age 18 has increased dramatically, and today, single mothers are more likely than married mothers to be employed.[44] This is not surprising, since women head most single-parent families, and most working women have little choice except to work.

2. *Changes in education.* Since World War II, increasing numbers of women have been attending college. Women now earn almost 57 percent of all undergraduate degrees, 60 percent of all masters degrees, and 50 percent of all doctorates. Women also earn about 50 percent of all undergraduate business degrees and 55 percent of all MBAs.[45]

3. *Changes in self-perception.* Many women juggle work and family roles. This often causes personal conflict, and the higher they rise in an organization, the more that work demands of them in terms of time and commitment.[46] Many women executives pay a high personal price for their organizational status in the form of broken marriages or never marrying at all.[47] For example, according to a recent report by the Joint Economic Committee of Congress, female managers are less likely to be married than male managers, at rates of 59 percent versus 74 percent, respectively. The gap is even greater when it comes to children. Fully 63 percent of female managers are childless, compared with 57 percent of male managers. Of those managers who do have children, men on average have more children than their women counterparts.[48] Thus *a major goal of* **EEO for women** *is to raise the awareness of these issues among both women and men so that women can be given a fair chance to think about their interests and potential, to investigate other possibilities, to make an intelligent choice, and then to be considered for openings or promotions on an equal basis with men.*[49]

4. *Changes in technology.* Advances in technology, both in the home (e.g., frozen foods, microwave ovens) and in the workplace (e.g., robotics), have reduced the physical effort and time required to accomplish tasks. Through technology more women can now qualify for formerly all-male jobs, and, for some women and for some types of jobs, technology makes virtual work arrangements possible, thus helping the women to balance their work and personal lives.[50]

5. *Changes in the economy.* Although there has been an increasing shift away from goods production and toward service-related industries, there are increasing numbers of female employees in all types of industries. Here are some statistics characterizing these changes:[51]

   ■ Today, women make up 29 percent of U.S. business owners, generating $1.2 trillion in revenues.[52]

   ■ Women-owned businesses include the same types of industries as are in the *Fortune* 500.

   ■ Women comprise 46.8 percent of the total U.S. labor force and are projected to account for 46.9 percent of the labor force in 2018.

   ■ Where women work: 40 percent in management, professional, and related occupations; 32 percent in sales and office occupations; 21 percent in service occupations; 5 percent in production, transportation, and material moving occupations; and 1 percent in natural resources, construction, and maintenance occupations.

   ■ Almost 80 percent of couples are dual earners.

The statistics presented thus far imply that women have made considerable economic gains over the past three decades. However, there are also some disturbing facts that moderate any broad conclusions about women's social and economic progress:

■ Today, U.S. women who work full-time make about 77 cents for every dollar earned by men. At the current rate of increase, women will not reach wage parity with men until 2017. Asian-American women make the most, relative to men, while Hispanic women make the least.[53]

■ As a group, women who interrupt their careers for family reasons never again make as much money as women who stay on the job. How much? Women overall lose an average of 18 percent of their earning power when they take an off-ramp. In business, it's 28 percent. The longer the time out, the more severe the penalty. Three or more years out and women lose 37 percent of their earning power.[54] Working part-time accounts for about half the pay gap between the sexes, and outright discrimination against women accounts for about 10 percentage points of the pay gap, according to numerous studies.[55]

- Women in paid jobs still bear most of the responsibility for family care and housework.

### Conclusions Regarding Women in the Workforce

The clearest picture we need to see from the data reflecting all these changes is this: If all the working women in the United States were to quit their jobs tomorrow and stay at home to cook and clean, businesses would disintegrate. There is no going back to the way things were before women entered the workforce. What many people tend to think of as women's issues really are business and competitiveness issues. Examples: Companies that routinely don't offer child care and flexibility in work scheduling will suffer along with their deprived workers.[56] Women are not less committed employees; working mothers especially are not less committed to their work. Three-quarters of professional women who quit large companies did so because of lack of career progress; only 7 percent left to stay at home with their children.[57] Businesses should react to the kinds of issues reflected in these

---

## IBM—CHAMPION OF GLOBAL DIVERSITY AND FAMILY FRIENDLY POLICIES*

**HR BUZZ**

In 2010, DiversityInc named IBM the number one company for global diversity, and the company has made *Working Mother* magazine's list of 100 Best Companies for Working Mothers for more than 15 consecutive years, and is a member of the magazine's Hall of Fame. It continues to set lofty standards by researching new programs and policies, expanding and improving old ones, and extending such efforts worldwide. In keeping with its mission of becoming "the premier global employer for working mothers," IBM offers dependent care in 42 countries, and has spent $263 million on dependent care since 1983. Its Global Partnership for Workforce Flexibility sponsors pilot projects on alternative work arrangements and examines cultural barriers.

In the United States, no company can top IBM's leave for childbirth, which gives mothers six weeks of paid leave; mothers and fathers are both eligible for *three years* of unpaid, job-guaranteed time off with benefits. (However, if business needs require it, parents may be asked to come back part time after one year.) With a dependent-care fund of $8.3 million, IBM also ranks high on child care, supporting three on-site and 68 near-site centers—where employees' children have priority access—and more than 1,600 family child-care homes. If parents want to phase back gradually, they can reduce their work hours and take intermittent breaks during that three-year period. The company also offers a virtual support group for employees taking care of elderly parents.

*Source: Working Mother. 2010 Working Mother 100 Best Companies. Retrieved from *www.working mother.com/node/3836/list* on June 22, 2011. See also Diversity 3.0. Retrieved from *www-03.ibm.com/employment/us/diverse/* June 22, 2011.

examples based not on what is the right or wrong thing to do, but on what makes economic sense to do—which usually also is the right thing to do.

It is important that executives see that creative responses to work/family dilemmas are in the best interests of both employers and employees. Adjustments to work schedules (flextime), extended maternity and paternity leaves, and quality day care based near the job come a little closer to workable solutions. Chapter 10 will consider this issue in greater detail, but for now let's consider some practical steps that IBM is taking.

## Age-Based Diversity

At present, the U.S. workforce is populated by four different generations of workers, each with different, often conflicting values and attitudes.[58] Here is a brief sketch of each.

- The **silent generation** (born 1930–1945) was born in the middle of the Great Depression. Too young to have fought in World War II, they were heavily in demand. Many went to the best colleges, were courted by corporations, rose rapidly, and were paid more than any other group in history. In return they embraced their elders' values and became good "organization men" (i.e., they gave their hearts and souls to their employers and made whatever sacrifices were necessary to get ahead; in return, employers gave them increasing job responsibility, pay, and benefits). Many members of the silent generation have retired, but others hold positions of power (e.g., corporate leaders, members of Congress).
- The **baby-boom generation** (born 1946–1964) currently accounts for 78 million people and 54 percent of the workforce. The boomers believe in rights to privacy, due process, and freedom of speech in the workplace; that employees should not be fired without just cause; and that the best should be rewarded without regard to age, gender, race, position, or seniority. Downsizing (the planned elimination of positions or jobs) shocked and frustrated many boomers. They were frustrated over shrinking advancement opportunities for themselves and felt betrayed when many of them were fired or rushed into early retirement. Boomers represent a huge base of knowledge and talent in organizations. They bring years of management and leadership expertise that cannot be replaced easily.[59] Fortunately, they do not change jobs frequently. Median years of tenure on the job is only 3.1 for workers ages 25 to 34, but 10.0 for those aged 55 to 64.[60]
- **Generation X,** also known as "baby busters" (born 1965–1980), represent approximately 50 million Americans, or about one-third of the workforce. They have grown up in times of rapid change, both social and economic. Hurt more by parental divorce and having witnessed corporate downsizing first-hand, they tend to be independent and cynical and do not expect the security of long-term employment. On the other hand, they also tend to be practical, focused, and future oriented. They demand interesting work assignments, and thrive on open-ended projects that require sophisticated problem solving. This is a computer-literate generation. Five characteristics define the kinds of work environments that Gen Xers find most rewarding: (1) control over their own schedules, (2) opportunity to improve their marketable skills, (3) exposure to decision makers, (4) the chance to put their names on tangible results, and (5) clear areas of responsibility.[61]

- **Generation Y,** also known as "Millennials," (born 1981–1995) includes off-spring of the baby boomers as well as an influx of immigrants throughout the 1990s. With more than 73 million members, it will have a huge impact on future products, marketing, and management practices. Generation Y has grown up amid more sophisticated technologies and has been exposed to them earlier than members of Generation X ever were. This is a group that grew up texting and e-mailing. Multitasking is easy for them. As an example, consider the typical teenager doing homework on his or her computer: simultaneously using a word processor, surfing the Internet, chatting with friends via instant-messaging programs, downloading music, listening to a CD, and talking on the telephone, all while the television is turned on in the background! This implies both good news and bad news for employers. The good news is that Generation Y will be good at engaging in multiple tasks, filtering out distractions, and juggling numerous projects. The bad news: short attention spans, the constant need for stimulation/entertainment, and a blurring of the lines between work and leisure time while on the job.[62]

### Intergenerational Conflict

Evidence indicates that the incidence of intergenerational conflict is low, and that many myths exist about generational differences.[63] When it does occur, such conflict seems to stem from three primary causes: work ethic (different generations have different perceptions of what makes an employee dedicated), organizational hierarchy (some members of younger generations bypassing the chain of command; some members of older generations believing that seniority trumps qualifications), and managing change (some members of older generations are perceived as reluctant to change, while members of younger generations seem eager to try new ideas constantly).

In terms of solutions to intergenerational conflict, it appears that separating workers from different generations does not work. What does work is communicating information in multiple ways (oral and written, formal and informal) thereby addressing different generations' learning styles. Two other solutions are collaborative decision making ("co-creation") and training managers to handle generational differences. At the same time, it is important to recognize that all generations want to be treated with respect. They want leaders whom they can trust. Most people are uncomfortable with change, everyone wants to learn, and everyone likes feedback.[64]

## MANAGING DIVERSITY

As we have seen, racial and ethnic minorities, women, and immigrants will account for increasingly larger segments of the U.S. labor force over time. And there are other large and growing groups—older workers, workers with disabilities, gay/lesbian workers, members of Generations X and Y—that also affect the overall makeup of the workforce. Businesses that want to grow will have to rely on this diversity. Let us consider some practical steps that managers can take to prepare for these forthcoming changes.

### Racial and Ethnic Minorities

To derive maximum value from a diverse workforce—not merely to tolerate it—corporations now realize that it's not enough just to start a mentoring program or to put a woman on the board of directors. Rather, they have to undertake a host of programs—and not just inside the company. ChevronTexaco and Dow Chemical are building ties with minorities as early as high school. Rockwell Collins is building closer relationships with schools that have strong engineering programs as well as sizable minority populations. Cedar Rapids, Iowa–area employers have banded together with colleges and other organizations to promote diversity in the community.[65] More specifically, to attract and retain racial and ethnic minorities, consider taking the following steps:[66]

- *Focus* on bringing in the best talent, not on meeting numerical goals. At PepsiCo, for example, "diversity is no longer about counting heads; it's about making heads count."[67]
- *Establish* mentoring programs among employees of same and different races.
- *Hold* managers accountable for meeting diversity goals.
- *Develop* career plans for employees as part of performance reviews.
- *Promote* racial and ethnic minorities to decision-making positions, not just to staff jobs.
- *Diversify* the company's board of directors.

Diversity should be linked to every business strategy—for example, recruiting, selection, placement (after identifying high-visibility jobs that lead to other opportunities within the firm), succession planning, performance appraisal, and reward systems. Companies such as Four Seasons Hotels, Marriott, Qualcomm, Men's Wearhouse, and USAA do that extremely well.[68] Here are several other examples.

---

**HR BUZZ**

*Diverse by Design*[a]

## PEPSICO, BANK OF AMERICA, AND ABBOTT LABORATORIES

At PepsiCo each of the CEO's direct reports is responsible for the growth and development of a different group of employees. One executive partners with African-American employees, for example; one with women; yet another with Latinos; and one with gay, lesbian, bisexual, and transgender employees. They work to identify the key individuals in the groups, and often serve as their voice to the rest of the executive committee and the CEO. Every year all of the executives share with the rest of the committee the biggest concerns of their groups, identify the support the groups need, and articulate their plans to address the concerns faced by these diverse groups.

A 25-member executive diversity-advisory committee oversees Bank of America's 40 diversity councils across its national operations. That committee also ensures that top management, whose pay and incentives are tied to progress, sets targets to increase diversity in hiring. At Abbott Laboratories, the drug-maker has gone all out in its diversity efforts. Minorities now constitute 33 percent of new hires, 23 percent of the board of directors, and 20 percent of employees in career-tracking efforts as well as 11 of the 50 top-paid executives. New-employee affinity groups include separate ones for Chinese, Ibero Americans, and African Americans, among others.

What do these firms have in common? All are sending strong signals that they value workforce diversity, inclusion, and equal opportunities for people to succeed and to prosper.

---

[a] America's 50 best companies for minorities. *Fortune*. n.d., Retrieved from *www.fortune.com* on Nov. 6, 2004. See also Rodriguez, 2006, op. cit.

## Female Workers

Here are six ways that firms today provide women with opportunities not previously available to them:[69]

1.  *Alternative career paths.* This is especially popular in law, accounting, and consulting firms that have sanctioned part-time work for professionals. Booz Allen Hamilton and PricewaterhouseCoopers are champions of this approach.
2.  *Extended leave.* IBM, as we have seen, grants up to three years off with benefits and the guarantee of a comparable job on return. However, leave-takers must be on call for part-time work during two of the three years. At Russell Investment Group (Tacoma, Washington), associates receive eight weeks of paid time off after 10 years of service. It can be taken in one 8-week block or two 4-week blocks.
3.  *Flexible scheduling.* At NCNB, a bank based in North Carolina, employees create their own schedules and work at home. After six months' maternity leave, new mothers can increase their hours at work gradually. Most who choose to cut their hours work two-thirds time and receive two-thirds pay.
4.  *Flextime.* Through its Women's Interests Network, an 825-member task force with chapters in five states, American Express now has a universal framework for employees and their managers to implement flexible work arrangements at all of the company's 1,675 locations. Today, the best employers make access to flexibility a "conversational process" with all employees, not just to a favored few.[70]
5.  *Job sharing.* This is not for everyone, but it may work especially well with clerical positions where the need for coordination of the overall workload is minimal; that is, activities such as filing, word processing, and photocopying are relatively independent tasks that workers can share. In contrast, development of a new product or a new marketing campaign often requires a continuity of thought and coordinated action that cannot easily be assigned to different workers or managers. At Steelcase, the office-equipment manufacturer, for example, two employees can share a title, workload, salary, health benefits, and vacation.
6.  *Teleworking.* This is work carried out in a location that is remote from central offices or production facilities, where the worker has no personal contact with coworkers but is able to communicate with them using electronic means. It is a popular and rapidly growing alternative to the traditional, office-bound work style. At IBM, for example, efforts to create a flexible work environment have been so successful that 40 percent of its nearly 400,000 employees work from home, on the road, or at a client location on any given day. Survey results indicate that employees want more opportunities for telework and that their top priority is to gain the flexibility to control their own time.[71]

## Generations X and Y

Here are 11 suggestions for integrating Generations X and Y into the workforce:[72]

- Explain to them how their work contributes to the bottom line.
- Always provide full disclosure.
- Create customized career paths.
- Allow them to have input into decisions.
- Provide public praise.

Different generations
have much to learn from
each other.

- Treat them as sophisticated consumers.
- Encourage the use of mentors.
- Provide access to innovative technology. For example, IBM uses every imaginable technology—from blogs and podcasts to online brainstorming sessions called "jams"—to create a virtual network of peers, mentors, and senior staff.
- Consider new benefits and compensation strategies.
- Offer opportunities for community involvement.
- Emphasize "You can do it your way—in a collegial work environment."

In terms of compensation, it seems to be more more important to Gen Xers. In contrast, Gen Yers rate six types of rewards at least as important as compensation: high-quality colleagues, flexible work arrangements, prospects for advancement, recognition from one's company or boss, a steady rate of advancement and promotion, and access to new experiences and challenges.[73] With respect to community involvement, both generations have high rates of volunteerism. They will look for opportunities to continue this in the context of the workplace.

## Older Workers

In 1990, about 56 percent of persons aged 55–64 were in the U.S. labor force. By the end of 2008 that percentage had climbed to 64.5 percent, and it will rise to 68.1 by 2018[74]. By 2015, more than a third of all workers will be 50 and over, and 75 percent of them expect to work, at least part-time, during retirement.[75] To be sure, their experience, wisdom, and institutional memories (particularly about mission-critical procedures and processes) represent important assets to firms. As important elements of the diversity mix, progressive organizations will continue to develop and use these assets effectively. Here are six priorities to consider to maximize the use of older workers:[76]

1.  *Age/experience profile.* Executives should look at the age distribution across jobs, as compared with performance measures, to see what career paths for older workers might open in the future and what past performance

measures have indicated about the kinds of knowledge, skills, abilities, and other characteristics necessary to hold these positions. Why do this? Because it's important to identify types of jobs where older workers can use their experience and talents most effectively.

2. *Job-performance requirements.* Companies should then define more precisely the types of abilities and skills needed for various posts. While physical abilities decline with age, especially for heavy lifting, running, or sustained physical exertion (needed in jobs such as fire fighting and law enforcement), mental abilities generally remain stable well into a person's eighties. Clear job specifications must serve as the basis for improved staffing, job design, and performance-management systems. For example, jobs may be designed for self-pacing, may require periodic updating, or may require staffing by people with certain physical abilities.

3. *Performance management.* Not only must a firm analyze the requirements of jobs better, there must also be improved ways of managing the performance of workers in those jobs. For example, age biases may be reflected in managers' attitudes. This is known as **age grading:** subconscious expectations about what people can and cannot do at particular times of their lives. Contrary to common belief, most mature workers are still interested in self-improvement. Like other workers, they want feedback on how they could do their jobs better or extend their careers.

4. *Workforce-interest surveys.* Once management understands the abilities its older workers have, the next step is to determine what they want. Survey workers to determine their career goals so that the ones who are capable of achieving their goals won't stall. Not only must management decide that it wants to encourage some older workers to continue with the organization, it must also consider selectively encouraging turnover of workers it doesn't want to continue. And, of course, management must evaluate what effects different incentives will have on the workers it wants to continue and on the ones it doesn't.

5. *Training and counseling.* To meet the needs of the workforce remaining on the job, firms need to develop training programs to avoid **mid-career plateaus** (i.e., performance at an acceptable but not outstanding level, coupled with little or no effort to improve one's current performance), as well as training programs to reduce **obsolescence** (the tendency for knowledge or skills to become out of date). These programs must reflect the special needs of older workers, who can learn but need to be taught differently (e.g., by using self-paced programs instead of lectures).

6. *The structure of jobs.* To whatever degree management may consider changing older workers' work conditions, such as work pace or the length or timing of the workday, it should explore the proposed changes jointly with the workforce. After all, multiple generations are likely to be affected by the changes, and whether boomers, Gen Xers, or Gen Yers, all are more likely to support what they helped to create.

## Workers with Disabilities

A 30-year-old war veteran with a disability called a radio talk show recently to complain that prospective employers wouldn't consider him for jobs despite his outstanding credentials. "How many interviews have you had?" asked the talk-show host, who heads a nonprofit organization dedicated to placing people with disabilities in jobs. "Not one" he admitted. "As soon as I tell them I can't walk, type, and other things I can't do, they get off the telephone as quickly as possible."

"I'm not surprised," said the host. "Prospective employers want to know what job applicants can do for them, not what their limitations are. If you can show a prospective employer that you will bring in customers, design a new product, or do something else that makes a contribution, employers will hire you. Your disability won't matter if you can prove that you will contribute to the employer's bottom line."[77] In other words, organizations may not have jobs, but they always have problems. If you can show that you are a problem solver, then it won't matter if you are blue, green, or confined to a wheelchair.

The fact is that poll after poll of employers demonstrates that they regard most people with disabilities—roughly 22 million in the United States—as good workers, punctual, conscientious, and competent—if given reasonable accommodation. Despite this evidence, persons with disabilities are less likely to be working than any other demographic group under age 65. One survey found that two-thirds of persons with disabilities between the ages of 16 and 64 are unemployed. They also worked approximately one-third fewer hours than those without disabilities.[78]

Perhaps the biggest barrier is employers' lack of knowledge. For example, many are concerned about financial hardship because they assume it will be costly to make architectural changes to accommodate wheelchairs and add equipment to aid workers who are blind or deaf. In fact, according to the Job Accommodation Network, more than half of the accommodations needed by employees and job applicants with disabilities cost absolutely nothing. Of those accommodations that do come at a price, the typical expenditure is around $600, and there are tax incentives available to help businesses offset those costs.[79] Consider several possible modifications:[80]

- Placing a desk on blocks, lowering shelves, and using a carousel for files are all inexpensive accommodations that enable people in wheelchairs to be employed.
- Installing telephone amplifiers for hearing-impaired individuals or variable illumination for sight-impaired individuals is relatively easy. Much to their delight, employers have found that these systems helped them gain new customers with hearing or sight impairments.
- Flextime, job sharing, and other modifications to the work schedule that enable mothers with young children to continue to work are being used to help employees with AIDS, cancer, and other life-threatening diseases to continue to work.[81]

Actions like these enable persons with disabilities to work, gain self-esteem, and reach their full potential. That is a key objective of diversity at work.

## Gay/Lesbian/Bisexual/Transsexual Employees

Throughout this chapter we have emphasized that workforce diversity is a business issue: Either you attract, retain, and motivate the best talent or you lose business. Gay/lesbian/bisexual/transsexual (GLBT) employees, as a group, are highly educated; they comprise, by some estimates, 6 percent of the population (about 17 million people); and they have a buying power of $700 billion, which is growing by about 10 percent each year. GLBT consumers are very loyal to specific brands, wishing to support companies that support the gay community and also provide equal rights for GLBT workers.[82] Here's an example. Despite outside pressure not to do it, Walgreens made a $100,000 donation to support the 2006 Gay Games, a weeklong festival in Chicago that attracted 11,000 athletes. The company wanted to support its GLBT employees and to let gay and lesbian customers know that they are welcome at Walgreens. Today the company fills more prescriptions for AIDS-related drugs than any other pharmacy chain.

Raytheon, the $22 billion-a-year defense contractor, is a high-profile supporter of gay rights. Why? Not because gay people buy missiles or radar; rather it's because the competition to hire and retain engineers and other skilled workers is so brutal that Raytheon doesn't want to overlook anyone in the talent pool. This is one reason more than 75 percent of *Fortune* 1,000 firms have elected to add the words "sexual orientation" to their nondiscrimination policies and why 59 percent of *Fortune* 500 companies now offer health benefits to same-sex couples—up from 6 percent in 1996.[83] Well-known companies such as Apple Inc., REI, Nike, Google, IBM, Intel, Raytheon, and J. P. Morgan Chase are just a few examples of companies that offer such benefits.[84]

Among corporations, IBM is the number one financial supporter of gay-rights groups in the United States, and it also supports employee GLBT groups in 23 other countries, including Singapore, Slovakia, and Colombia. It even convened a group of gay college students at the Human Rights Campaign to form a national organization of gay students in science and technology.[85] American Airlines' "Rainbow Team" of gay employees brought in $192 million in revenue in one year by targeting the gay community. Efforts like these are surfacing some key lessons:

- Targeting diverse clients drives the need for a similarly diverse workforce.
- To drive the diversity initiative throughout the company, it must be integrated into business plans, with a requirement to measure specific results.
- Leaders of the efforts to acquire diverse clients must not only have client-acquisition expertise in that specific market segment, but also have strong project-management experience.

As we have seen, the workforce is now and will continue to be more and more diverse. A list of actions that managers can take to deal with these changes is presented in Figure 4–4.

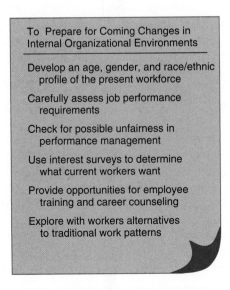

To Prepare for Coming Changes in Internal Organizational Environments

Develop an age, gender, and race/ethnic profile of the present workforce

Carefully assess job performance requirements

Check for possible unfairness in performance management

Use interest surveys to determine what current workers want

Provide opportunities for employee training and career counseling

Explore with workers alternatives to traditional work patterns

**Figure 4–4**

Priority listing of suggested actions to manage effectively the internal organizational environment of the future.

## ETHICAL DILEMMA
### Does Diversity Management Conflict with Maximizing Shareholder Value?

The main objective of profit-making businesses is to maximize overall returns to shareholders (increases in stock prices plus dividends). Because earnings affect this objective, management needs to determine the extent to which any new program—including any new workforce program—will affect the bottom line. There are sound business reasons why having a diverse workforce and managing it properly can increase shareholder value. However, companies generally tend to measure success in these programs by looking at indicators other than the bottom line. Affirmative action programs and some diversity-awareness programs have been criticized strongly for adding costs to firms but little or no financial benefits.[a] Given the costs involved, can diversity programs be justified over time purely on philosophical and moral grounds (i.e., it's the right thing to do)?

[a]Felton-O'Brien, M. (2008, March 26). Fatigued by diversity initiatives. Retrieved from *www.hreonline.com/HRE/story.jsp?storyId=83036993&sub=false* on March 26, 2011. See also Cavaleros, C., Vuuren, L. J., and Visser, D. (2002). The effectiveness of a diversity awareness training program. *SA Journal of Industrial Psychology* 28(3), pp. 50–61. See also Sharf, J. C., and Jones, D. P. (2000). Employment risk in management. In J. F. Kehoe (Ed.), *Managing Selection in Changing Organizations.* San Francisco: Jossey-Bass, pp. 271–318.

## IMPACT OF DIVERSITY ON PRODUCTIVITY, QUALITY OF WORK LIFE, AND THE BOTTOM LINE

All employees, no matter whom, no matter at what level, want to be treated with respect. They want to know that their employer values the work they do. That's the most basic thing you must do in managing diversity.[a] And when diversity is managed well—as at Du Pont, Procter & Gamble, Monsanto, and Ernst & Young—productivity and the quality of work life improve. So do stock prices. Researchers examined the effect on stock prices of announcements of U.S. Department of Labor awards for exemplary diversity programs and announcements of damage awards from the settlement of discrimination lawsuits. Announcements of awards were associated with significant, positive excess returns that represent the capitalization of positive information concerning improved business prospects. Conversely, damage awards were associated with significant negative stock-price changes, which represent the capitalization of negative economic implications associated with discriminatory corporate practices.[b] A company can easily spend $100,000 to get a meritless lawsuit alleging unfair discrimination tossed out before trial. And if a case goes to a jury, the fees skyrocket to $300,000, and often much higher.[c] As we noted earlier, diversity has evolved from being the correct thing to do to being the essential thing to do. It's a mistake, however, to think there is a cookie-cutter approach. Rather, the path to diversity success must take into account each organization's unique goals, resources, number of employees, business locations, product lines, and customer bases.[d]

[a]Retain talent, but develop it, Pepsi bottling chief says. (2008, Apr. 21). *USAToday,* p. 5B.

[b]Wright, P., Ferris, S. P., Hiller, J. S., and Kroll, M. (1995). Competitiveness through management of diversity: Effects on stock price valuation. *Academy of Management Journal* 38, pp. 273–287.

[c]Orey, M. (2007, Apr. 23). Fear of firing. BusinessWeek, pp. 52–62.

[d]Hastings, 2010, op. cit. See also Rand Corporation. (2008, Jan. 23). Path to diversity success varies according to company's history, culture, mission. Retrieved from *www.rand.org/news/press/2008/01/23.html* on March 10, 2008.

## IMPLICATIONS FOR MANAGEMENT PRACTICE

1.  Workforce diversity is here to stay. There is no going back to the demographic makeup of organizations 20 years ago. To be successful in this new environment, learn to value and respect cultural styles and ways of behaving that differ from your own.

2.  Recognize that there are tangible business reasons why managing workforce diversity effectively should be a high priority: (a) It is an opportunity to deepen understanding of the marketplace, the needs of various customers, and to penetrate new markets. (b) Demographic changes are coming so rapidly that employers will have to meet their hiring needs with a diverse labor force.

3.  To maximize the potential of all members of the workforce, link concerns for

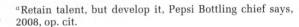

diversity to every business strategy: recruitment, staffing, placement, succession planning, performance management, and rewards.

4.  To retain talented women and minorities, follow the lead of Pepsi Bottling Group in developing long-term career plans that include stretch assignments—and don't be afraid to share the plan with the employees in question. As CEO Eric Foss noted, "Give them a lot of profit-and-loss responsibility, and show them that you care. If you do that, then most of your great people are going to stay."[a]

---

[a]Retain talent, but develop it, Pepsi Bottling chief says, 2008, op. cit.

## MAKING THE BUSINESS CASE FOR DIVERSITY

*Human Resource Management in Action: Conclusion*

In the course of their five-year research project on the effects of diversity on business performance, researchers studied four large firms (two in information processing, one in financial services, and one in retail).[86] Further, in an effort to develop a valid picture of the current state of practice in managing diversity in large organizations, they discussed the state of practice with more than 20 large, well-known firms. With appropriate caution, they offered the following implications for practice:

1.  **Modify the business case.** Start by recognizing that there is virtually no evidence to support the simple assertion that diversity is inevitably good or bad for business. Rather, focus on the conditions that can leverage the benefits from diversity, or at the very least, lessen its negative effects. Recognize that while diversity is a reality in labor markets and customer markets today, success in working with and gaining value from that diversity requires a sustained, systemic approach and long-term commitment. As one observer noted, "Diversity only endures when it is baked into the way the company does business every day."[87]

2.  **Look beyond the business case.** While there is no reason to believe that diversity will translate naturally into better or worse business results, it is both a labor-market imperative and a societal expectation and value. Managers should therefore focus on building an organizational culture,

HR practices, and the managerial and group-process skills needed to translate diversity into positive results at the level of the organization, the work group, and the individual.

3. **Adopt a more analytical approach.** If firms are unable to link HR practices to business performance, then their ability to learn how to manage diversity effectively will be limited, as will their claims for diversity as a strategic imperative that justifies financial investments. More sophisticated data collection and analyses are necessary to understand diversity's consequences and to monitor the effects of diversity on attitudes and performance. Questions such as the following will be most useful: Under what conditions do work units that are diverse (e.g., with respect to gender, ethnicity, and other characteristics) outperform or underperform work units that are more homogeneous? What conditions moderate the potential negative or positive effects of diversity?

4. **Experiment and evaluate.** Doing this requires that senior executives commit to learning and experimentation within their organizations. One of the reasons it is difficult to identify simple cause-and-effect relations between diversity and important business outcomes is that many other factors can affect those relationships. Examples include the nature of the task and the behavior of the leader, the degree of heterogeneity and the diversity characteristics of the work group, the extent of organizational support for diversity, and the effects of time. That is, some work groups function over long periods of time, while others work together for only short periods of time. Observers might draw different conclusions about the effects of diversity as a result of variations in these characteristics.

5. **Help managers and team members develop skills in conflict resolution and effective communications.** Training to develop group process and leadership skills like these is essential. Managers who attempt to make diversity a resource for learning, change, and renewal will inevitably confront challenges in these areas. Training alone, however, is not likely to be sufficient. Organizations also need to implement management practices and HR policies that promote cultures of mutual learning and cooperation.

## SUMMARY

More than half the U.S. workforce now consists of racial and ethnic minorities, immigrants, and women. White, native-born males, as a group, are still dominant in numbers over any other group, but today women comprise nearly half the entire workforce. The labor force will continue to age, with the annual growth rate of the 55-and-older group projected to be 1.0 percent from 2008 to 2018. By contrast, over the same time frame, the annual growth rate of the 25-to-54-year age group will be essentially flat, and that of the young age group consisting of 16-to-24-year-olds will actually be slightly negative (−0.8 percent).

Managing diversity means encouraging a heterogeneous workforce—which includes white men—to perform to its potential in an equitable work environment in which no one group enjoys an advantage or suffers a disadvantage. At least five factors account for the increasing attention companies are paying to diversity: (1) the shift from a manufacturing to a service economy, (2) the globalization of markets, (3) new business strategies that require more team-work, (4) mergers and alliances that require different corporate cultures to work together, and (5) the changing labor market. Each of these factors can represent opportunities for firms whose managers and employees understand what culture is and who appreciate cultural differences among other employees and managers, and especially the firm's market.

To attract and retain women, as well as persons with disabilities, compa-nies are making available to them alternative career paths, extended leaves, flexible scheduling, flextime, job sharing, and opportunities to telework. In addition, many companies now offer the same benefits to same-sex couples as to heterosexual couples.

A different aspect of diversity is generational diversity—important differ-ences in values, aspirations, and beliefs that characterize the silent generation, the baby-boom generation, Generation X, and Generation Y. To manage older workers effectively, managers should develop an age profile of the workforce, monitor job-performance requirements for the kinds of characteristics people need to do their jobs well, develop safeguards against age bias in performance management, conduct workforce-interest surveys, provide education and coun-seling, and consider modifying the structure of jobs.

Finally, to manage diversity effectively, do the following things well: focus on bringing in the best talent, not on meeting numerical goals; establish mentoring programs among employees of same and different races; hold man-agers accountable for meeting diversity goals; develop career plans for em-ployees as part of performance reviews; promote women and minorities to decision-making positions, not just to staff jobs; and diversify the company's board of directors.

## KEY TERMS

| | |
|---|---|
| ethnic minorities | extended leave |
| managing diversity | flexible scheduling |
| culture | flextime |
| EEO for women | job sharing |
| silent generation | teleworking |
| baby-boom generation | age grading |
| Generation X | mid-career plateaus |
| Generation Y | obsolescence |
| alternative career paths | |

## DISCUSSION QUESTIONS

**4–1.** In your opinion, what are some key business reasons for emphasizing the effec-tive management of a diverse workforce?

**4–2.** Why is there no simple relationship between diversity and business perfor-mance?

**4–3.** How would you respond to someone who has questions or concerns about diversity?

**4–4.** What would be the broad elements of a company policy to emphasize the management of diversity?

**4–5.** What are some possible sources of intergenerational friction? How might you deal with that?

**4–6.** Suppose you were asked to enter a debate in which your task was to argue against any special effort to manage workforce diversity. What would you say?

## APPLYING YOUR KNOWLEDGE

| | |
|---|---|
| **Case 4–1** | ### *The Challenge of Diversity\** |

Talk, talk, talk. As Ken Hartman, an African-American midlevel manager at Blahna Inc. recalls, that's all he got from the white men above him in top management—despite the fact that Blahna had long enjoyed a reputation as a socially responsible company. But that reputation didn't mean much to Hartman as he watched other African-American managers he thought were highly qualified get passed over for plum jobs and as his own career seemed stalled on a lonely plateau. Top management always mouthed diversity, Hartman said, "but in the end, they chose people they were comfortable with for key positions."

### Meeting the Challenge

Is this situation uncommon? Not at all. In the last decade, however, it has become increasingly apparent that appropriate management of a diverse workforce is critical for organizations that seek to improve and maintain their competitive advantage. Focusing on diversity and looking for more ways to be a truly inclusive organization—one that makes full use of the contributions of all employees—is not just a nice idea; it is good business sense that yields greater productivity and competitive advantage. Although Denny's Corporation had to experience and settle several costly discrimination cases to begin to see the value in managing diversity, today Denny's serves as an example of what other organizations should strive for in the way of diversity. Half of its Board of Directors as well as half of its senior-management team members are women or other minorities, along with 14 percent of African Americans and 33 percent of Hispanics among its 25,000 company employees. As of 2010, minorities made up 62 percent of the company's overall workforce, and 41 percent of management.[88] The company has won many awards and justifiable praise from numerous media outlets for its genuine efforts to make diversity a part of the very fabric of its business.

### The Strategy at Blahna Inc.

Ken Hartman's firm, Blahna Inc., has finally gotten the message. The company is now using diversity-management strategies to head off conflict and reduce turnover among employees it can ill afford to lose.

Several years ago, Blahna formed a 20-member Committee for Workplace Diversity, chaired by a vice president. The committee was chartered to consider why women and

---

*\*Sources:* Department of Defense. Crisis communication strategies, case study: Denny's class-action lawsuit. Retrieved from *www.ou.edu/deptcomm/dodjcc/groups/02C2/Denny's.htm* on June 22, 2011. Adamson, J. (2000). *The Denny's story: How a Company in Crisis Resurrected Its Good Name and Reputation.* NY: Wiley. See also White, E. (2006, March 20). Fostering diversity to aid business. *The Wall Street Journal,* p. B3.

minorities weren't better represented at all levels of the organization. Although the company had a good record of hiring women and minorities, the committee discovered that turnover was two to three times higher for these groups than it was for white males.

Sample exit interviews revealed that women and minorities left for culture-related reasons—for instance, because they didn't feel valued in their day-to-day work or in their communities, didn't have effective working relationships, or didn't sense that the work they were being given to do would lead to the fulfillment of their career goals. White males, on the other hand, left for business-related reasons, such as limited opportunities for future advancement.

As a result of this initial investigation, Blahna formed a 25-person diversity advisory committee. The committee developed a multipronged approach for dealing with diversity issues—including building bridges with the broader community outside of the company. Within the company itself, a key strategy involved training conducted by diversity consultants Hope & Associates.

To date, 60 percent of Blahna's 11,000 employees have gone through a two-day diversity seminar; 40 percent have gone through a more extensive six-day training program as well. "The premise of the training is that the more different you are, the more barriers there can be to working well together," explains Blahna's Chief Diversity Officer. Training sessions do not offer advice on how to get along with Asian Americans, women, or other specific groups. Rather, the emphasis is on learning skills that will make it easier to relate to and communicate with others.

A key part of the training offered by Hope & Associates is the implementation of a "consulting pairs" process. The consulting pairs approach is designed to help trainees take what they've learned in training and apply it on the job. When a conflict—which may or may not be related to diversity—first arises between two peers or between a manager and employee, a consulting pair is called in to facilitate discussion and problem solving. The unique feature of this approach is that the consulting pair is selected to match as closely as possible the backgrounds of the individuals who are involved in the conflict. Of course, all proceedings are strictly confidential.

The result? Ken Hartman is a happier guy these days. As president of one of Blahna's divisions, the 48-year-old executive is a step away from joining the ranks of senior management. Life has changed for him since Blahna "stopped talking about values like diversity and began behaving that way."

**Questions**

1. Why do many companies find increasing and managing diversity to be difficult challenges?
2. What were the key elements in Blahna's successful diversity strategy?
3. Under what circumstances might the consulting pairs approach be most useful?
4. What steps should management take to ensure that the consulting pairs approach is working?

## REFERENCES

1. Toossi, M. (2009, Nov.) Employment outlook: 2008–2018. *Monthly Labor Review,* pp. 30–51.
2. Society for Human Resource Management. Introduction to the human resources discipline of diversity. Retrieved from *http://www.shrm.org/hrdisciplines/Diversity/Pages/DiversityIntro.aspx* on June 20, 2011.

3. Society for Human Resource Management. (2004, Aug. 5). How is a diversity initiative different from my organization's affirmative action plan? Retrieved from *www.shrm.org/diversity* on August 5, 2004. See also Equal Employment Opportunity Commission (1979, Jan. 19). *Affirmative Action Guidelines.* Pub. no. 44 FR 4421. Washington, DC: U.S. Government Printing Office.

4. The diversity factor. (2003, Oct. 13). *Fortune,* pp. S1–S12. See also Jackson, S. E., and Alvarez, E. B. (1992). Working through diversity as a strategic imperative. In S. E. Jackson (Ed.), *Diversity in the Workplace.* New York: Guilford, pp. 13–35.

5. The data for Table 4–2 come from the U.S. Bureau of Labor Statistics, op. cit. See also Perry, M. J. (2011, Feb. 25). The truth about U. S. manufacturing. *The Wall Street Journal,* p. A13. See also Service sector growth continues. (2011, April 6). *The Denver Post,* p. 6B.

6. The diversity factor, op. cit. See also Newman, B. (2004, Apr. 28). Eastern influence. *The Wall Street Journal,* p. A1.

7. Sellers, P. (1990, June 4). What customers really want. *Fortune,* pp. 58–68.

8. Digh, P. (2000, Jan./Feb.). Diversity goes global. *Mosaics,* pp. 1, 4, 5.

9. Leonard, B. (2011, June). Managing virtual teams. *HR Magazine* 56(6), pp. 39–42. See also Malhotra, A., Majchrzak, A., and Rosen, B. (2007). Leading virtual teams. *Academy of Management Perspectives* 21(1), 60–70. See also Maznevski, M., Davison, S. C., and Jonsen, K. (2006), Global virtual team dynamics and effectiveness. In Stahl, G. K., & Björkman, I. (Eds.) (2006), *Handbook of Research in International Human Resource Management.* Northampton, MA: Edward Elgar, pp. 364–384.

10. Childs, quoted in The diversity factor, op. cit., p. S8.

11. Sherman, A. J. (2011). *Mergers and Acquisitions from A to Z* (3rd Ed.). NY: AMACOM. See also Schmidt, J. A. (2002). *Making Mergers Work: The Strategic Importance of People.* Alexandria, VA: Towers Perrin/Society for Human Resource Management Foundation.

12. Tepedino, L., and Watkins, M. (2010, June). Be a master of mergers and acquisitions. *HRMagazine* 55(6), 53-56. See also *Once the deal is done: Making mergers work.* (2010). Retrieved from *www.shrm.org/about/foundation/products/Pages/MakingMergersWork. aspx* on June 20, 2011. See also Serapio, M. G., Jr., and Cascio, W. F. (1996). End-games in international alliances. *Academy of Management Executive* 10(1), pp. 63–73.

13. Gitelson, G., Bing, J. W., and LaRoche, L. The Impact of culture on mergers and acquisitions. Retrieved from *www.itapintl.com/mergersandacquisitions.htm* on April 22, 2008.

14. Marks, M., and Mirvis, P. (2010). *Joining Forces: Making One Plus One Equals Three in Mergers, Acquisitions, and Alliances* (2nd ed.). San Francisco: Jossey-Bass. See also McWhirter, W. (1989, Oct. 9). I came, I saw, I blundered. *Time,* pp. 72, 77.

15. Ibid.

16. Toossi, op. cit.

17. Fox, A. (2010, Jan.). At work in 2020. *HR Magazine.* Retrieved from *www.shrm.org/ Publications/hrmagazine/EditorialContent/2010/0110/Pages/0110fox.aspx* on June 17, 2011.

18. Society for Human Resource Management Foundation. (2007). *Trust travels: The Starbucks story* (DVD). Alexandria, VA: SHRM Foundation. See also Jackson, S. E. (1992). Preview of the road to be traveled. In S. E. Jackson (Ed.), *Diversity in the Workplace.* New York: Guilford, pp. 4–12.

19. O'Toole, J., and Lawler, E. E. III. (2006). *The New American Workplace.* New York: Palgrave Macmillan.

20. Hom, P. W., Roberson, L., and Ellis, A. D. (2008). Challenging conventional wisdom about who quits: Revelations from corporate America. *Journal of Applied Psychology* 93, pp. 1–34.

21. Gelfand, M. J., Erez, M., and Aycan, Z. (2007). Cross-cultural organizational behavior. *Annual Review of Psychology* 58, pp. 479–514. See also Hofstede, G. (2001). *Culture's Consequences: Comparing Values, Behaviors, Institutions, and Organizations across Nations* (2nd ed.). Thousand Oaks, CA: Sage.

22. Moran, R. T., Harris, P. R., and Moran, S. V. (2011). *Managing Cultural Differences* (8th ed.). Oxford, UK: Elsevier.

23. Page, S. E. (2007). *The Difference: How the Power of Diversity Creates Better Groups, Firms, Schools, and Societies.* Princeton, NJ: Princeton University Press. See also Hewlett-Packard. (2002). *The Business Reasons: Diversity and Inclusion.* Palo Alto, CA: Author.

24. Toossi, op. cit.

25. Black-Owned Businesses Outpace Growth of Non-Minority-Owned Businesses. (2011, Feb. 8). Retrieved from *www.commerce.gov/blog/2011/02/08/black-owned-businesses-outpace-growth-non-minority-owned-businesses* on June 20, 2011.

26. Fahmy, S. (2010, Nov. 4). Minority buying power report. Retrieved from *www.terry.uga.edu/news/releases/2010/minority-buying-power-report.html* on June 20, 2011.

27. African American CEOs of Fortune 500 companies. Retrieved from *www.blackentrepreneurprofile.com/fortune-500-ceos/* on June 20, 2011.

28. 2010 40 best companies for diversity. Retrieved from *www.blackenterprise.com* on June 20, 2011.

29. McKay, B. (2000, Nov. 17). Coca-Cola agrees to settle bias suit for $192.5 million. *The Wall Street Journal,* pp. A3, A8.

30. The Coca-Cola Company. Our progress. Retrieved from *www.thecoca-colacompany.com/citizenship/our_progress.html* on June 20, 2011. Also see The DiversityInc 2011 top 50 companies for diversity. Retrieved *www.thecoca-colacompany.com/dynamic/press_center/2011/03/diversityinc-top-50.html* on June 20, 2011.

31. Hastings, R. R. (2010, Oct.). Business needs inform diversity strategies. Retrieved from *www.shrm.org/hrdisciplines/Diversity/Articles/Pages/BusinessNeedsInform-DiversityStrategies.aspx* on June 20, 2011. See also Rodriguez, R. (2006, Aug.). Diversity finds its place. *HR Magazine* 51(8), pp. 56–61. See also Babcock, P. (2004). Diversity down to the letter. *HR Magazine* 49(6), pp. 90–94.

32. Toossi, 2009, op. cit.

33. Matos, A. (2010, July 23). Hispanic-owned businesses on the rise, Census Bureau finds. Retrieved from *laprensa-sandiego.org/stories* on June 21, 2011. See also Marlantes, L. (2006, March 21). Hispanic-owned businesses booming. Retrieved from *www.abcnews.go.com/US/Story?id=1752325&page=1* on April 23, 2008.

34. U.S. Census Bureau. (2011). Income, expenditures, poverty, and wealth. *Statistical Abstract of the United States, 2011,* Table689.

35. Fahmy, 2010, op. cit. See also Porter, E. (2003, Apr. 18). Buying power of Hispanics is set to soar. *The Wall Street Journal,* pp. B1, B3.

36. Toossi, 2009, op. cit.

37. Fahmy, 2010, op cit. See also Asian Nation. 14 important statistics about Asian Americans. Retrieved from *www.asian-nation.org/14-statistics.shtml* on June 21, 2011.

38. Mehta, S. N. (2000, July 10). What minority employees really want. *Fortune,* pp. 181–186.

39. Shellenbarger, S. (1995, May 11). Women indicate satisfaction with role of big breadwinner. *The Wall Street Journal,* pp. B1, B2.

40. Rampell, C. (2010, Sept. 27). Still few women in management, report says. *The New York Times.* Retrieved from *www.nytimes.com/2010/09/28/business/28gender.html?sq=Still few women in management, report says&st=cse&adxnnl=1&scp=1&adxnnlx=1313174165-gBfQjo5cKOtEndpkVkeYAQ* on Oct. 27, 2010. See also Morris, B. (2005, Jan. 10). How corporate America is betraying women. *Fortune,* pp. 64–74.

41. What to expect when you're expecting. (2008, May 26). *BusinessWeek,* p. 17. See also Schwartz, F. N. (1992, Mar.–Apr.). Women as a business imperative. *Harvard Business Review,* pp. 105–113.

42. Galinsky, E., Aumann, K., and Bond, J. T. (2009). *The 2008 National Study of the Changing Workforce: Times Are Changing—Gender and Generation at Work and at Home.* New York: Families and Work Institute.

43. Tkaczyk, C. (2009, Sept. 28). Helping women get ahead. *Fortune*, p. 38. See also Shellenbarger, S. (2006, Sept. 28). The mommy drain: Employers beef up perks to lure new mothers back to work. *The Wall Street Journal*, p. D1.

44. Ibid. See also Pear, R. (2000, Nov. 5). Single moms working more. *The Denver Post*, p. J2.

45. Galinsky et al., 2009, op. cit. Women and work. (2006). *Workplace Visions* (No. 3). Alexandria, VA: Society for Human Resource Management.

46. Shipman, C. C., and Kay, K. (2009). *Womenomics: Write Your Own Rules for Success*. New York, NY: Harper Business.

47. Rampell, 2010, op. cit. Sellers, P. (1996, August 5). Women, sex, & power. *Fortune*, pp. 43–57.

48. Rampell, 2010, op. cit.

49. Boyle, M. B. (1975). Equal opportunity for women is smart business. *Harvard Business Review* 51, pp. 85–95.

50. Leonard, 2011, op. cit. Malhotra, Majchrzak, and Rosen, 2007, op. cit.

51. U.S. Department of Labor. Quick stats on women workers, 2009. Retrieved from *www.dol.gov/wb/stats/main.htm* on June 22, 2011. See also Galinsky et al., 2009, op. cit.

52. U.S. Census Bureau. (2010, Dec. 7). Retrieved from *www.census.gov/newsroom/releases/archives/business_ownership/cb10-184.html* on June 22, 2011.

53. Fitzpatrick, L. (2010, April 20). Why do women still earn less than men? *Time*. Retrieved from *www.time.com/time/nation/article/0,8599,1983185,00.html* on June 22, 2011. See also Milkovich, G. T., and Newman, J. M. (2011). *Compensation*. Burr Ridge, IL: McGraw-Hill/Irwin. See also Dey, J. G., and Hill, C. (2007). *Behind the Pay Gap*. Washington, D.C.: American Association of University Women Educational Foundation. See also Earnings gap. (2004, June 7). *BusinessWeek*, p. 13.

54. Hewlett, S. A., and Luce, C. B. (2005, Mar.). Off-ramps and on-ramps: Keeping talented women on the road to success. *Harvard Business Review*, pp. 43–54.

55. Bernstein, A. (2004, June 14). Women's pay: Why the gap remains a chasm. *BusinessWeek*, pp. 58–59.

56. Shellenbarger, S. (2007, Oct. 4). What makes a company a great place to work today. *The Wall Street Journal*, p. D1. See also The 2010 Working Mother 100 best companies. (2010). Retrieved from *www.workingmother.com/best-companies/2010-working-mother-100-best-companies-0* on June 22, 2011.

57. Deutsch, C. H. (2005, May 1). Behind the exodus of executive women: Boredom. *The New York Times*. Retrieved from *www.nytimes.com/2005/05/01/business/yourmoney/01women.html?scp=1&sq=Behind%20the%20exodus%20of%20executive%20women:%20Boredom&st=cse* on June 22, 2011.

58. The framework for this section was drawn from the following sources: Fox, A. (2011, May). Mixing it up. *HR Magazine* 56(5), pp. 22–27; Meister, J. C., and Willyerd, K. (2010, May). Mentoring millennials. *Harvard Business Review*. Retrieved from *epowerment.eqmentor.com/docs/Mentoring%20Millenials.pdf* on June 21, 2011; Generational differences: Myths and realities. (2007). *Workplace Visions* 2, pp. 1–8.

59. Anderson, R. (2007, Oct.). Baby boom retirement aftershock looms. *Worldlink* 4, pp. 4, 5.

60. Bureau of Labor Statistics, U. S. Dept. of Labor. Employee tenure in 2010. Retrieved from *www.bls.gov/news.release/pdf/tenure.pdf* on June 21, 2011.

61. Stephey, M. (2008, April 16). Gen-X: The ignored generation? Retrieved from *www.time.com/time/arts/article/0,8599,1731528,00.html* on June 4, 2011. See also Zaslow, J. (2007, Apr. 20). The most praised generation goes to work. *The Wall Street Journal*, pp. W1, W7.

62. Hira, N. A. (2007, May 28). You raised them, now manage them. *Fortune*, pp. 38–46.

63. Erickson, T. J. (2009, Feb.). Gen Y in the workforce. *Harvard Business Review*, Reprint R0902B. See also Deal, J. J. (2007). *Retiring the Generation Gap*. New York:

Wiley. See also Burke, M. E. (2004, Aug.). *Generational Differences Survey Report.* Alexandria, VA: Society for Human Resource Management.

64. Hastings, R. R. (2007, June). The myth of generational differences. Retrieved from *www.shrm.org/hrdisciplines/Diversity/Articles/Pages/CMS_021789.aspx* on June 21, 2011. See also Deal, 2007, op. cit.

65. White, E. (2006, March 20). Fostering diversity to aid business. *The Wall Street Journal,* p. B3.

66. Hastings, R. R., 2010, op.cit. See also Rodriguez, 2006, op. cit.

67. George, quoted in Rodriguez, 2006, op. cit., p. 59.

68. CNN Money. 100 best companies to work for, 2011: Most diverse. Retrieved from *money.cnn.com/magazines/fortune/bestcompanies/2011/minorities/* on June 21, 2011.

69. SHRM. *Workplace Flexibility in the 21st Century: Meeting the Needs of the Changing Workforce.* (2009). Alexandria, VA: Society for Human Resource Management. See also Thompson, H. A., and Fitzpatrick, B. A. (2007). Flexible work arrangements: A productivity triple play. Alexandria, VA: SHRM. See also Deutsch, 2005, op. cit.

70. Shellenbarger, 2007, op. cit. See also Conlin, M. (2007, Sept. 24). Netflix: Flex to the max. *Business Week,* 72, 74. See also Corporate Voices for Working Families. (2005, Nov.). Business impacts of flexibility: An imperative for expansion. Retrieved from *www.cvwf.org/publication-toolkits/business-impacts-flexibility-imperative-expansion-november-2005* on May 18, 2006.

71. Meinert, D. (2011, June). Make telecommuting pay off. *HR Magazine* 56(6), 32-37. See also Galinsky, E., and Matos, K. (In press). The future of work-life fit. *Organizational Dynamics.*

72. Ibid. See also Kadlec, D. (2007, Nov.). Don't trust anyone under thirty. *Money,* pp. 50, 52. See also Zaslow, op. cit. See also Leak, B. (2006, May 8). The draft picks get younger. *Business Week,* p. 96.

73. Hewlett, S. A., Sherbin, L., and Sumberg, K. (2009, July-August). How Gen Y and Boomers will reshape your agenda. *Harvard Business Review* 68, pp. 71–76.

74. Toossi, 2009, op. cit.

75. Greene, K. (2005, Sept. 26). When we're all 64. *The Wall Street Journal,* pp. R1, R4. See also Grossman, R. J. (2008). Keep pace with older workers. *HR Magazine* 53(5), pp. 39–46.

76. Ibid. See also Davidson, G., Lepeak, S., and Newman, E. (2007, Feb.). The impact of the aging workforce on public-sector organizations and mission. Retrieved from *unpan1.un.org/intradoc/groups/public/documents/IPMA-HR/UNPAN025894.pdf* on April 11, 2007. Few companies pursue strategies that would better utilize older workers. (2000, May/June). *Working Age,* pp. 2–3.

77. Just one break changes lives of disabled. (1994, Oct. 23). *The New York Times,* special supplement, The diversity challenge, p. 11.

78. Wells, S. J. (2008, April). Counting on workers with disabilities. *HR Magazine* 53(4). Retrieved from *www.shrm.org/Publications/hrmagazine/EditorialContent/Pages/4Wells-The%20Demographics%20of%20Disabilities.aspx* on June 21, 2011. See also Stapleton, D. C., and Burkhauser, R. V. (Eds.). (2003). *The Decline in Employment of People with Disabilities: A Policy Puzzle.* Kalamazoo, MI: Upjohn Institute. See also Bruyere, S. M. (2000, Nov./Dec.). Dealing effectively with disability accommodations. *Mosaics,* pp. 1, 4, 5.

79. Hastings, R. R. (2006, Apr.). Accommodations don't break the bank. Retrieved from *www.shrm.org/diversity/library_published/nonIC/CMS_016685.asp* on April 26, 2008. See also U.S. Department of Labor. Myths and facts about people with disabilities. Retrieved from *www.dol.gov/odep/pubs/fact/mythfact.htm* on June 21, 2011.

80. For much more information on this, consult the Job Accommodation Network at *www.jan.wvu.edu.*

81. See, for example, Stapleton and Burkhauser, 2003, op. cit. See also When workers just can't cope. (2000, Oct. 30). *BusinessWeek,* pp. 100, 102.

82. Hipps, J. (2008, Aug.). The power of gay—Buying power that is. Retrieved from *www.gayagenda.com* on June 21, 2011. See also Gay community–buying power. Retrieved from *en.wikipedia.org/wiki/Gay_community#Buying_Power,* June 21, 2011.

83. Human Rights Campaign. Domestic partner benefits. Retrieved from *www.hrc.org/issues/domestic_partner_benefits.htm* on June 21, 2011. See also Gunther, M. (2006, Dec. 11). Queer, Inc.: How corporate America fell in love with gays and lesbians. It's a movement. *Fortune,* 94–110.

84. Miller, S. (2010, July). Best-practice benefits for same-sex couples. Retrieved from *www.shrm.org/hrdisciplines/benefits/Articles/Pages/BestPracticeBenefits.aspx* on June 21, 2011. Tkaczyk, C. (2010, June 14). 100 Best Companies to Work For: REI. *Fortune,* p. 52. See also Gunther, 2006, op. cit.

85. IBM, Google among most gay-friendly firms: Survey. (2010, June 10). Retrieved from *www.torontosun.com/money/2010/06/10/14339156.html* on June 21, 2011. See also Gunther, 2006, op. cit.

86. Kochan, T., Bezrukova, K., Ely, R., Jackson, S., Joshi, A., Jehn, K., Leonard, J., Levine, D., and Thomas, D. (2003). The effects of diversity on business performance: Report of the diversity research network. *HR Management* 42(1), pp. 3–21.

87. Martinez, cited in Hastings, 2010, op. cit.

88. Denny's. 2010 Diversity Report. Retrieved from *www.dennysdiversity.com/report/DennysDiversityReport.pdf* on June 22, 2011.

# EMPLOYMENT

Now that you understand the competitive, legal, and social environments within which HR management activities take place, it is time to address three major aspects of the employment process: analyzing the work to be done, determining the types of skills needed to do the work, and hiring employees. Logically, before an organization can select employees, it must be able to specify the kind of work that needs to be done, how it should be done (in some cases), the number of people needed, and the personal characteristics required to do the work. Chapter 5 addresses these issues. Chapter 6 considers the planning, implementation, and evaluation of recruitment operations. Finally, Chapter 7 examines initial screening and employee selection—why they are important, how they are done, and how they can be evaluated.

# 5 PLANNING FOR PEOPLE

*Questions This Chapter Will Help Managers Answer*

1. How can business strategy be integrated with strategic workforce planning?

2. How might job-design principles and job analysis be useful to the practicing manager?

3. What is strategic workforce planning, and how should I begin that process?

4. How can organizations balance "make" versus "buy" decisions with respect to talent?

5. How should organizations manage leadership succession?

The death or illness of a chief executive is a crisis that most companies rarely face. McDonald's Corporation did so twice in just seven months in what was widely viewed as a model of **succession planning.** When James Cantalupo died of a heart attack in April, within hours the Board of Directors appointed his second-in-command, Charles Bell, who had been groomed for the job. And, when Bell resigned in late November after being diagnosed with colon cancer, the Board named Vice-Chairman James Skinner to the job. Leaving nothing to chance, it promoted U.S. operations chief Michael Roberts to president and chief operating officer, in line to succeed Skinner, 60.

Unfortunately McDonald's is the exception. Recent data indicate that only about half of public and private corporate boards have CEO-succession plans in place. This is the case even at giant global companies that have thousands of employees and spend millions each year to recruit and train talent. Thus, after a combined write-down of more than $15 billion at Citigroup and Merrill Lynch in late 2007, stemming from turmoil in the sub-prime mortgage market, the chief executives of both firms were forced out, and their respective boards of directors were left to scramble to find replacements. The same happened in 2009 when Bank of America CEO Ken Lewis resigned unexpectedly. Is this an anomaly? Hardly. Rather, these were just the latest examples of boards that failed to build solid leadership-succession plans, joining the boards at other firms who had made the same mistake in the past, such as Pfizer, Coca-Cola, Home Depot, AIG, and Hewlett-Packard. These companies stand in stark contrast to such firms as DuPont, ExxonMobil, Goldman Sachs, Johnson & Johnson, Kellogg, United Parcel Service, and PepsiCo, which benefited enormously from building strong teams of internal leaders, which, in turn, resulted in seamless transitions in executive leadership.

Why weren't the first set of boards grooming internal candidates for the leadership jobs? In part, because at the heart of succession lie personality, ego, power, and, most importantly, mortality. Said one expert, "Some CEOs find the prospect of succession downright depressing. For them it means failure or organizational death. They love the job; it is their identity. They think of building a cohort of potential leaders, not as the path to growth and prosperity, but as a sure route to lame-duck status." Moreover, some boards tend to look the other way on the succession question when the CEO makes the numbers and is singularly focused on pleasing Wall Street the next quarter, or when he or she purges talented subordinates rather than prepare them to take over. Here are several other, more concrete obstacles to leadership-succession planning: poor dynamics between the board and the CEO; the lack of a well-defined process; poorly defined ownership of succession-planning responsibilities; scarcity of internal, CEO-ready talent; inability to assess objectively any potential internal candidates.

*Sources:* Keller, J. J., and Carey, D. (2011, Q1). When finding the right CEO is job #1. *Korn/Ferry Briefings on Talent and Leadership,* pp. 50–57. See also Dutra, A., and Griesedieck, J. (2010, May). Succession success. *Leadership Excellence,* p. 14. See also Charan, R., and Colvin, G. (2010, Oct. 18). Directors: A harsh new reality. *Fortune,* pp. 97–100. See also Reingold, J. (2009, Dec. 7). The $79 billion handoff. *Fortune,* pp. 81–86. See also Fitzpatrick, D., Enrich, D., and Lublin, J. S. (2009, Oct. 2). BofA directors scramble to lay a succession plan. *The Wall Street Journal,* pp. C1, C3.

Are boards serving shareholders when they let these barriers get in the way of leadership-development and succession-planning efforts? Said one expert, "Not when global competition and technological change, in the context of an active market for corporate control, make the job of CEO about as tough as it has ever been. Companies need world-class efficiency, constant innovation, and a customer orientation. This requires a group of talented, dedicated people working as a team across business units and country boundaries."

Ideally, careful succession planning grooms people internally. Doing so maintains the intellectual capital of an organization, and also motivates senior-level executives to stay and to excel because they might get to lead the company someday. On the other hand, there are also sound reasons why a company might look to an outside successor. Boards that hire outsiders to be CEOs feel that change is more important than continuity, particularly so in situations where things have not been going well. As one observer noted in the context of the Citigroup and Merrill Lynch CEO searches, ". . . when there's a major failure in performance, then you don't want [to promote] the person you have groomed, even if you've done great succession planning. You want somebody with a fresh perspective." Another commented, "The best way to let people in the investment community know that you didn't like the way things were going is to get rid of everybody associated with the old approach. In that context, an internal successor has got no prayer of becoming CEO. It doesn't matter how wonderful the person is; he or she is tainted by their association with the previous regime. The directors feel a need to signal a change in direction, so pretty much anybody associated with the old regime can't be advanced."

In the conclusion to this case we will see how several leading-edge firms avoid a crisis in succession planning by institutionalizing their leadership-succession processes. We'll also offer some concrete steps that any board can take.

## Challenges

1. If planning for leadership succession is so important, why don't more organizations do it?
2. What sort of leadership-development process would you recommend?
3. As Board Chairperson, how might you overcome the resistance of a CEO to plan for succession?

---

To make intelligent decisions about HR strategy, the best ways to deploy and manage people, two types of information are essential: (1) a description of the strategy that a firm will use to compete for business in the marketplace, and (2) job design, including a description of the work to be done, the skills needed, and the training and experience required for various jobs. Once these are known, it makes sense to plan for the numbers and skills mix of people required at some future time period. We consider the first of these needs, business strategy, HR strategy, and job design, in the sections that follow. We consider strategic workforce planning in the latter part of the chapter.

# BUSINESS STRATEGY—FOUNDATION FOR ALL ORGANIZATIONAL DECISIONS

At the outset it is important to distinguish strategy formulation from strategy analysis.[1] Strategy formulation answers the basic question, "How will we compete?" It is a vital role of senior leaders within an organization, and it typically considers the external environment, customer trends, competitive positioning, and internal strengths and weaknesses. Strategy formulation may be quite formal and last over long periods, or it may be highly dynamic and adaptive. Strategy analysis defines the crucial (or pivotal) elements for the strategy's success. Analyzing the overall strategy to reveal implications of these pivotal elements focuses attention on the execution of the broader business strategy. With a common understanding of the strategy of a business, leaders at all levels can help ensure that all resources, including people, are deployed and managed in relation to their importance to strategic success and in a manner that allows an organization to sustain its competitive advantages. The final step in the process is strategy implementation (execution), in which firms take the necessary actions to implement their strategies. After all, decisions are of little use unless they are acted upon. Strategy implementation makes the intended strategy real.

How firms compete with each other and how they attain and sustain competitive advantage are the essence of what is known as strategic management.[2] Successful firms strive to develop bases for competitive advantage; that is, they try to do something that is valuable, rare, and difficult to imitate. For example, they may achieve competitive advantage through cost leadership or differentiation, or by focusing narrowly on a market segment. Consider differentiation as an example. It consists in creating differences in a firm's product or services by creating something that is perceived industrywide as unique and valued by customers, for example:

- Prestige (Ritz-Carlton hotels or BMW automobiles).
- Technology (Bose sound systems, Apple's iPad 2).
- Innovation (3M, Medtronic medical equipment, Intel).
- Customer service (Lexus, Nordstrom department stores).

FedEx CEO and founder, Fred Smith, claims that the key to his firm's success is innovation. He contends that his management team did not understand its real goal when the firm started operating in 1971: "We thought that we were selling the transportation of goods; in fact, we were selling peace of mind."[3] To that end, FedEx now provides each driver with a hand-held computer and a transmitting device that makes it possible for customers to track their packages right from their personal computers or from their mobile devices.

## Ensuring Coherence in Strategic Direction

Organizations are more likely to be successful if everyone from the mailroom to the boardroom is striving for common goals and objectives. From general to specific, stated goals form a hierarchy that includes vision, mission, and strategic objectives.

An organization's vision should be "massively inspiring, overarching, and long term."[4] Emotionally driven, it is a fundamental statement of an organization's values, aspirations, and goals. Here are some examples.[5]

- "To be the happiest place on earth" (Disneyland).
- "Restoring patients to full life" (Medtronic).
- "To be the world's best quick-service restaurant" (McDonald's).

A vision may or may not succeed. It depends on whether everything else happens according to a firm's strategy. In the case of McDonald's, the careful alignment of strategy formulation, analysis, and implementation led to its winning top honors in 2011 among the World's Most Admired Companies in three of nine categories: quality of management, wise use of corporate assets, and effectiveness in conducting its business globally.[6]

A mission statement differs from a vision statement in that it includes both the purpose of the company as well as the basis of competition and competitive advantage. Here is FedEx's: "To produce superior financial returns for our shareholders as we serve our customers with the highest-quality transportation, logistics, and e-commerce."[7]

The most important audience for a mission statement is employees, for it helps build a common understanding of an organization's purpose and the basis of its intended competitive advantage in the marketplace. Strategic objectives operationalize the mission statement. They may be financial or nonfinancial, but in both cases they need to provide guidance on how the organization can fulfill or move toward the higher-level goals: vision and mission. For example, Walgreen's set a strategic objective of operating 6,000 stores by 2010, up from 3,000 in the year 2000. Fortune Brands has the strategic objective of reducing corporate overhead costs by $30 million a year. These objectives are **SMART**—that is, they are *S*pecific, *M*easurable, *A*ppropriate (consistent with the vision and mission), *R*ealistic (challenging but doable), and *T*imely.

SMART objectives have several advantages. They help to channel the efforts of all employees toward common goals. They can motivate and inspire employees to higher levels of commitment and effort. Finally, they can provide a yardstick to measure performance, and thus the distribution of rewards and incentives.

Other objectives are even more specific. These are short-term objectives—essential components of action plans that are critical to implementing a firm's chosen strategy. We will have more to say about action plans later in the chapter as we discuss strategic workforce planning.

While planning business strategy clearly offers a number of benefits, there is also a potential downside in that it may lock companies into a particular vision of the future—one that may not come to pass. This poses a dilemma: how to plan for the future when the future changes so quickly. The answer is to make the planning process more democratic. Instead of relegating strategic planning to a separate staff—as in the past—it needs to include a wide range of people, from line managers to customers to suppliers. Top managers must listen and be prepared to shift plans in midstream, if conditions demand it. This is exactly the approach that Cisco Systems takes. It is not wedded to any particular technology, because it recognizes that customers are the arbiters of choice. It listens carefully to its customers and then offers solutions that customers want.

**Business strategy** provides an overall direction and focus for the organization as a whole, including for each functional area of the business. In this book our primary focus is on managing people, and overall business strategy, through an organization's hierarchy of goals—vision, mission, and strategic objectives—which provides helpful guidance about the type of talent that will be necessary to fulfill the organization's strategic objectives, and to move toward its mission and vision. **HR strategy** is much more specific with respect to the selection, deployment, and management of that talent. The next section addresses the relationship between HR and business strategy in more detail.

## RELATIONSHIP OF HR STRATEGY TO BUSINESS STRATEGY

Human resource (HR) strategy parallels and facilitates implementation of the strategic business plan. *HR strategy is the set of priorities a firm uses to align its resources, policies, and programs with its strategic business plan.* It requires a focus on planned major changes in the business and on critical issues such as the following: What are the HR implications of the proposed business strategies? What are the possible external constraints and requirements? What are the implications for management practices, management development, and management succession? What can be done in the short term to prepare for longer-term needs? In this approach to the strategic management of human resources, a firm's business strategy and its HR strategy are interdependent.[8]

Figure 5–1 is a model that shows the relationship of HR strategy to the broader business strategy.[9] Briefly, the model shows that planning proceeds top-down, while execution proceeds bottom-up. There are four links in the model, beginning with the fundamental question "How do we compete?" As we noted earlier, firms may compete on a number of nonindependent dimensions, such as innovation, quality, cost leadership, or speed. From that, it becomes possible to identify business or organizational processes that the firm must execute well in order to compete (e.g., speedy order fulfillment). When processes are executed well, the organization delights its internal and external customers through high performance. This may occur, for example, when an employee presents a timely, cost-effective solution to a customer's problem.

To manage and motivate employees to strive for high performance, the right competencies, incentives, and work practices must be in place. Execution proceeds bottom-up, as these appropriate competencies, challenging incentives, and work practices inspire high performance, which makes everyone happy. This, in turn, means that business processes are being executed efficiently, enabling the organization to compete successfully for business in the marketplace.

At a general level, high-performance work practices include such workplace features as the following:[10]

- Worker empowerment, participation, and autonomy.
- The use of self-managed and cross-functional teams.
- Commitment to superior product and service quality.
- Flat organizational structures.
- Use of contingent workers.

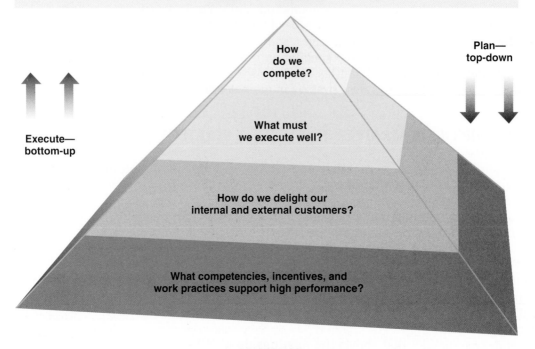

**Figure 5–1**

The relationship of HR strategy to the broader strategy of a business.

How do we compete?

Plan— top-down

What must we execute well?

Execute— bottom-up

How do we delight our internal and external customers?

What competencies, incentives, and work practices support high performance?

**HR METRICS**
What measures assess the key drivers of individual, team, and organizational performance?

*Source: HR in alignment.* (2004). DVD produced by the Society for Human Resource Management Foundation, Alexandria, VA. Retrieved from *http://www.shrm.org/about/foundation/products/Pages/HRinAlignmentDVD.aspx.*

- Flexible or enriched design of work that is defined by roles, processes, output requirements, and distal criteria (e.g., customer satisfaction), rather than (or in addition to) rigidly prescribed job-specific requirements.
- Rigorous staffing and performance management practices.
- Various worker- and family-friendly HR policies that reward employee development, continuous learning, and support work-life fit.

HR metrics serve as a kind of overlay to the model itself. HR metrics should reflect the key drivers of individual, team, and organizational performance. When they do, the organization is measuring what really matters.

## Strategic Workforce Plans

Strategic workforce plans parallel the plans for the business as a whole. They focus on questions such as these: What do the proposed business strategies imply with respect to human resources? What kinds of internal and external constraints will (or do) we face? For example, the projected retirements of large

## Figure 5–2

Impact of three levels of business planning on workforce planning.

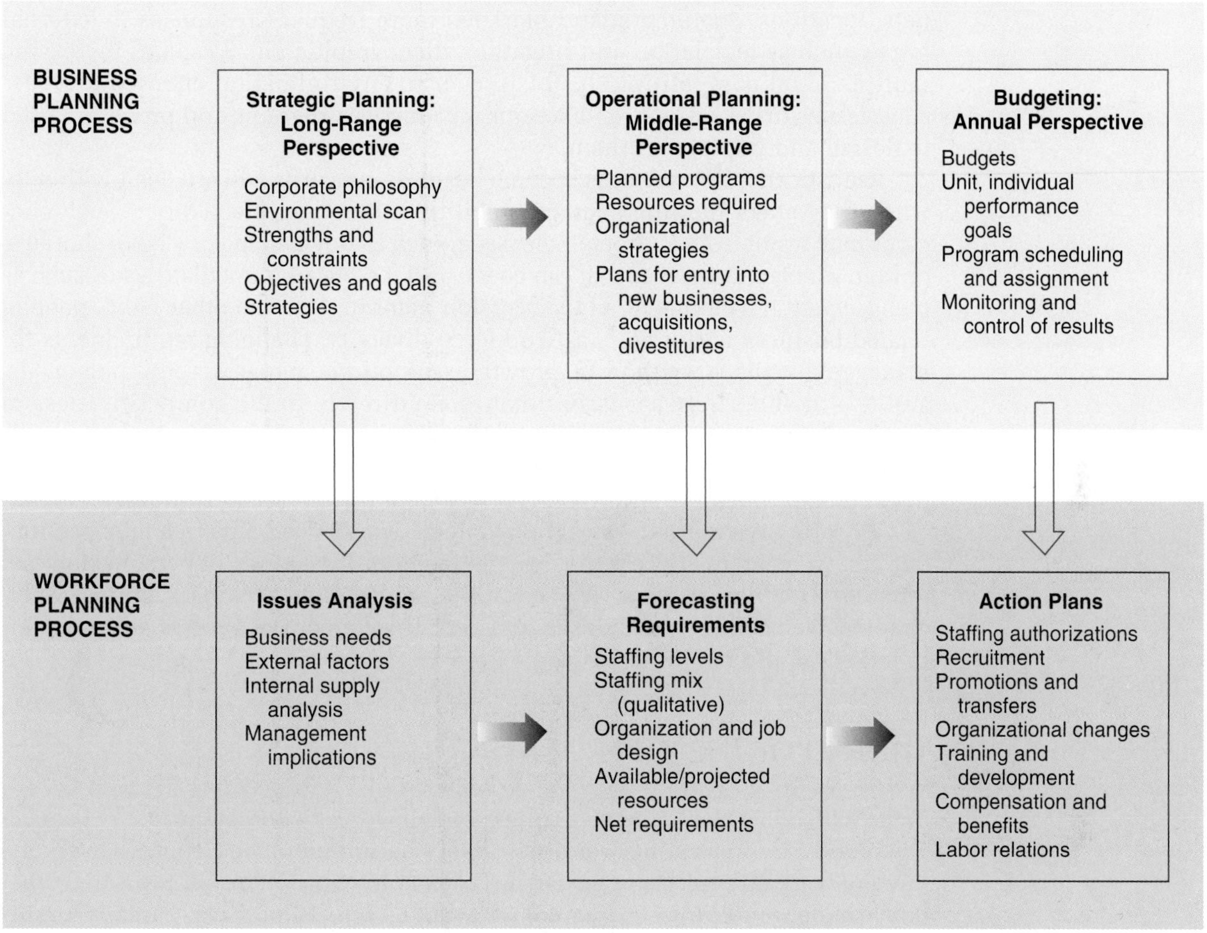

**BUSINESS PLANNING PROCESS**

**Strategic Planning: Long-Range Perspective**

Corporate philosophy
Environmental scan
Strengths and
  constraints
Objectives and goals
Strategies

**Operational Planning: Middle-Range Perspective**

Planned programs
Resources required
Organizational
  strategies
Plans for entry into
  new businesses,
  acquisitions,
  divestitures

**Budgeting: Annual Perspective**

Budgets
Unit, individual
  performance
  goals
Program scheduling
  and assignment
Monitoring and
  control of results

**WORKFORCE PLANNING PROCESS**

**Issues Analysis**

Business needs
External factors
Internal supply
  analysis
Management
  implications

**Forecasting Requirements**

Staffing levels
Staffing mix
  (qualitative)
Organization and job
  design
Available/projected
  resources
Net requirements

**Action Plans**

Staffing authorizations
Recruitment
Promotions and
  transfers
Organizational changes
Training and
  development
Compensation and
  benefits
Labor relations

numbers of older workers are an internal constraint on the ability of some firms to expand,[11] while a projected shortfall in the supply of college graduate electrical engineers (relative to the demand for them by employers) is an external constraint. What are the implications for staffing, compensation practices, training and development, and management succession? What can be done in the short run (tactically) to prepare for long-term (strategic) needs? Strategic workforce plans must be consistent with the broader HR strategy of an organization, which, in turn, must be consistent with the overall strategy of the business. Figure 5–2 shows the relationship between business planning—long-range, mid-range, and annual—and parallel processes that occur in strategic workforce planning.

As Figure 5–2 shows, strategic workforce plans focus on firm-level responses to people-related business issues over multiple time horizons. What are some examples of such issues, and how can managers identify them?

People-related business concerns, or issues, might include, "What types of skills must managers possess to run the business 3–5 years from now, and how do we make sure we'll have them?" At a broader level, issues include the impact of rapid technological change, more complex organizations (in terms of products, locations, customers, and markets) more frequent responses to external forces such as legislation and litigation, demographic changes, and increasing multinational competition. In this scenario, environmental changes drive issues, issues drive actions, and actions encompass programs and processes used to design and implement them.[12]

Realistically, HR concerns become business concerns and are dealt with only when they affect the line manager's ability to function effectively.[13] Such concerns may result from an immediate issue, such as downsizing or a labor shortage, or from a longer-term issue that can be felt as if it were an immediate issue, such as management development and succession planning. On the other hand, people-related business issues such as workforce diversity, changing requirements for managerial skills, growth or no-growth assumptions, mergers, retraining needs, and health and safety are issues that relate directly to the competitiveness of an organization and threaten its ability to survive. In short, progressive firms recognize that people-related business issues will have powerful impacts on their strategic business and workforce plans for the foreseeable future.

We will have more to say about strategic workforce plans in a later section, but first we need to address the design of jobs and the kinds of personal characteristics that they require. These are the subjects of the next sections of the chapter. We begin by considering whether the concept of a job is still relevant in today's world of work.

## THE END OF THE JOB?

In the mid-1990s books and magazines proclaimed "The End of the Job."[14] Post-job workers, so the reasoning went, will likely be self-employed contract workers, hired to work on projects or teams. Just look at Intel or Microsoft, firms that organize work around projects. People will work on 6 to 10 projects, perhaps for different employers at the same time. That may come to pass some day, but not yet.

A funny thing happened along the way—the Internet revolution. Go to any company's Web site, and discover that it invites applications—for jobs! True, employees may work on 6 to 10 projects at once, but only for one employer. This is not to imply that the concept of work is not changing. Sometimes the changes occur at a dizzying pace because fluid organizations fighting to stay competitive require their people to adapt constantly. Consider just two changes in "traditional" jobs:

1.  Librarians who used to recommend and shelve books and provide guidance for research projects now demonstrate how to run computerized searches to sort through an Internet world bursting with information.
2.  Automobile-assembly plants are replacing retiring workers who were hired right out of high school with people who are trained to operate computer-based machinery and who can also work well in teams.

Yet for all the changes, using a job as a way to organize and group tasks and responsibilities has not yet disappeared, especially in large organizations.[15]

**YOU DO WHAT? CORPORATE BANK ROBBER**                                                        HR BUZZ

Jim Stickley (CTO of TraceSecurity and author of *The Truth About Identity Theft*) has a fantasy job. He gets hired by banks to break through their security policies to steal information, and then to tell them how he did it and how to prevent such intrusions. To gain entrance, he may go in as a pest-control specialist, a health inspector, or a fire-safety official. Once inside, he uses ingenious methods to gain access to sensitive information. He says, "A good bank robber needs to know how to act under pressure and to talk his way out of anything."

*Source:* Mero, J. Corporate bank robber. *Fortune.* Retrieved from *http://money.cnn.com/magazines/fortune/fortune_archive/2006/05/15/8376898/index.htm* on October 30, 2011. From *Fortune* Magazine, May 15, 2006, © 2005 Time Inc. Used under license.

## ALTERNATIVE PERSPECTIVES ON JOBS

Jobs are frequently the subject of conversation: "I'm trying to get a job"; "I'm being promoted to a new job"; "I'd sure like to have my boss's job." Or, as Samuel Gompers, first president of the American Federation of Labor, once said, "A job's a job; if it doesn't pay enough, it's a lousy job."

Jobs are important to individuals: They help determine standards of living, places of residence, status (value ascribed to individuals because of their position), and even a personal sense of self-worth. Jobs are important to organizations because they are the vehicles through which work (and thus organizational objectives) are accomplished. Some jobs are highly unusual, as the example below illustrates.

Thinking about jobs and the organization of work suggests questions like the following:

- Who specifies the content of each job?
- Who decides how many jobs are necessary?
- How are the interrelationships among jobs determined and communicated?
- Has anyone looked at the number, design, and content of jobs from the perspective of the entire organization, the "big picture"?
- What are the minimum qualifications for each job?
- What should training programs stress?
- How should performance on each job be measured?
- How much is each job worth?

## Job Design

At the outset it is important to distinguish job analysis from job design. The term **job analysis** describes the process of obtaining information about jobs. Regardless of how it is collected, it usually includes information about the tasks to be done on the job, as well as the personal characteristics (education, experience, specialized training, personality) necessary to do the tasks. **Job design,** in contrast, focuses on the processes and outcomes of how work is structured, organized, experienced, and enacted.[16] If a job changes, then the process is referred to as job redesign. Job design should link closely to business strategy, because the strategy might require new and different tasks, for example, by incorporating new technology or different ways of performing the same tasks. Here is an HR example.

### TECHNOLOGY INNOVATION LEADS TO CHANGES IN JOB DESIGN

Sysco Corporation, of Houston, Texas, is the largest food marketer and distributor in North America. A major part of its operations involves delivering food to restaurants. To do that, the company receives orders from chefs, and fulfills those orders by loading relevant items from its warehouses onto trucks for delivery to the chefs. Accuracy in delivering exactly what was ordered is critical. Prior to the implementation of a computerized Enterprise Requirements Planning (ERP) system, warehouse clerks would check items manually to ensure a match between each item on an order sheet and the items actually loaded onto a delivery truck. Not surprisingly, this lead to an unacceptably high error rate, in terms of deliveries relative to orders. Errors increase costs, because separate trips are necessary to redeliver items.

After installation of the ERP system, the jobs of the warehouse clerks changed. They now wore "wrist computers" so that they could match electronically the bar code of each item on an order sheet (e.g., one case of 24-ounce cans of whole black olives) to that on a box of the same merchandise. An alarm sounded if there was a mismatch, so that the warehouse clerks could correct the problem before the wrong item was loaded onto a delivery truck. Result: better than 99 percent accuracy in deliveries! Note also how the design of the job of warehouse clerk changed in relation to an important strategic objective: to improve customer service by ensuring that deliveries match orders better than 99 percent of the time. Innovations in technology drove the change in the design of the job, which led directly to decreases in delivery costs.

As a general matter, jobs may vary from having a relatively narrow range of tasks (often simple, requiring little skill or training to perform them), to jobs that

A Sysco warehouse worker uses a wrist computer to match merchandise to a customer's order.

include a broad array of tasks that require multiple skills (e.g., a chief financial officer). Jobs designed with a narrow range of tasks generally focus on efficiency, while those designed with a broad range of tasks often seek to enhance innovation. There are a number of alternative theoretical perspectives to designing jobs, from industrial engineering,[a] to sociotechnical systems design that emphasizes teams and autonomous work groups,[b] to ergonomic and human-factors approaches that consider the physical and information-processing requirements of work,[c] to high-performance work systems and a job-characteristics approach that emphasizes motivation. Social information processing (how social cues affect job perceptions) and interdisciplinary models comprise others.[d] We will discuss just two of these to illustrate classic and contemporary approaches.

---

[a]F. Taylor. (1911). *The Principles of Scientific Management.* NY: Harper.

[b]Davis, L. E., and Trist, E. L. (1974). Improving the quality of work life: Sociotechnical case studies. In J. O'Toole (Ed.), *Work and the Quality of Life.* Cambridge, MA: MIT Press. pp. 111–145.

[c]Howell, W. C. (1991). Human factors in the workplace. In M. D. Dunnette and L. M. Hough (Eds.), *Handbook of Industrial and Organizational Psychology,* Vol. 2, 2nd Ed. Palo Alto, CA: Consulting Psychologists Press. pp. 209–269.

[d]Grant et al., 2011, op. cit.

## Scientific Management—"One Best Way"

Scientific management was the dominant approach to job design in the industrial society of the 20th century. Frederick W. Taylor was its prophet and the stopwatch was his bible.[17] Time-and-motion studies were key elements, for they could reveal the most efficient (that is, one best) way to perform work, by minimizing wasteful movements or unnecessary steps. Taylor believed that once the best way to perform work was identified, workers should be selected on the basis of their ability to do the job, they should be trained in the standard way to perform the job, and they should be offered monetary incentives to motivate them to do their best.

This approach to designing work is fully consistent with a cost-leadership business strategy. Design jobs so that they are simple to perform and easily learned. That way the firm can minimize the abilities required to perform the work, minimize training costs, and make turnover less costly. At the same time, however, jobs designed only to maximize efficiency lead to predictable psychological consequences, and these have been well documented.[18] Such jobs often lead to job dissatisfaction, surface attention to work, depersonalization and feelings of alienation (powerlessness, meaninglessness), and frustration for lack of personal growth and success. In the context of automobile assembly-line jobs in the early 1900s, Henry Ford lamented, "Why is it that I always get a whole person when what I really want is a pair of hands?"[19] In today's (and tomorrow's) world of work, characteristics of the whole person—cognitive as well as personality—are required to improve continuously the business processes that satisfy the needs of internal and external customers.

To counter some of the more unpleasant consequences of jobs designed solely to maximize efficiency, researchers turned to job rotation (moving employees from one relatively simple job to another after short time periods ranging from an hour to a day), job enlargement (increasing the number of tasks each employee performs), and job enrichment (increasing each worker's level of accountability and responsibility). While useful, none resolved all of the job-design problems that modern managers face or explained why failures could be expected to occur.[20] A more recent integrative approach, shown in Figure 5-3, offers a fuller explanation of the relationship of job characteristics to both proximal (near-term) and distal (longer-term) outcomes.

## Job Design Today

As we consider the changing nature of work in contemporary organizations, it is useful to begin by considering some important outcomes that organizations seek to achieve in the design of jobs and work, as Figure 5-3 shows. Those outcomes may be near-term (proximal), such as motivation, satisfaction, and learning; or they may be longer-term (distal), such as effective performance, minimizing withdrawal behaviors (e.g., absenteeism, turnover) and stress, or maximizing creativity and employee health and well being.

### Figure 5–3

An integrative model of job design.

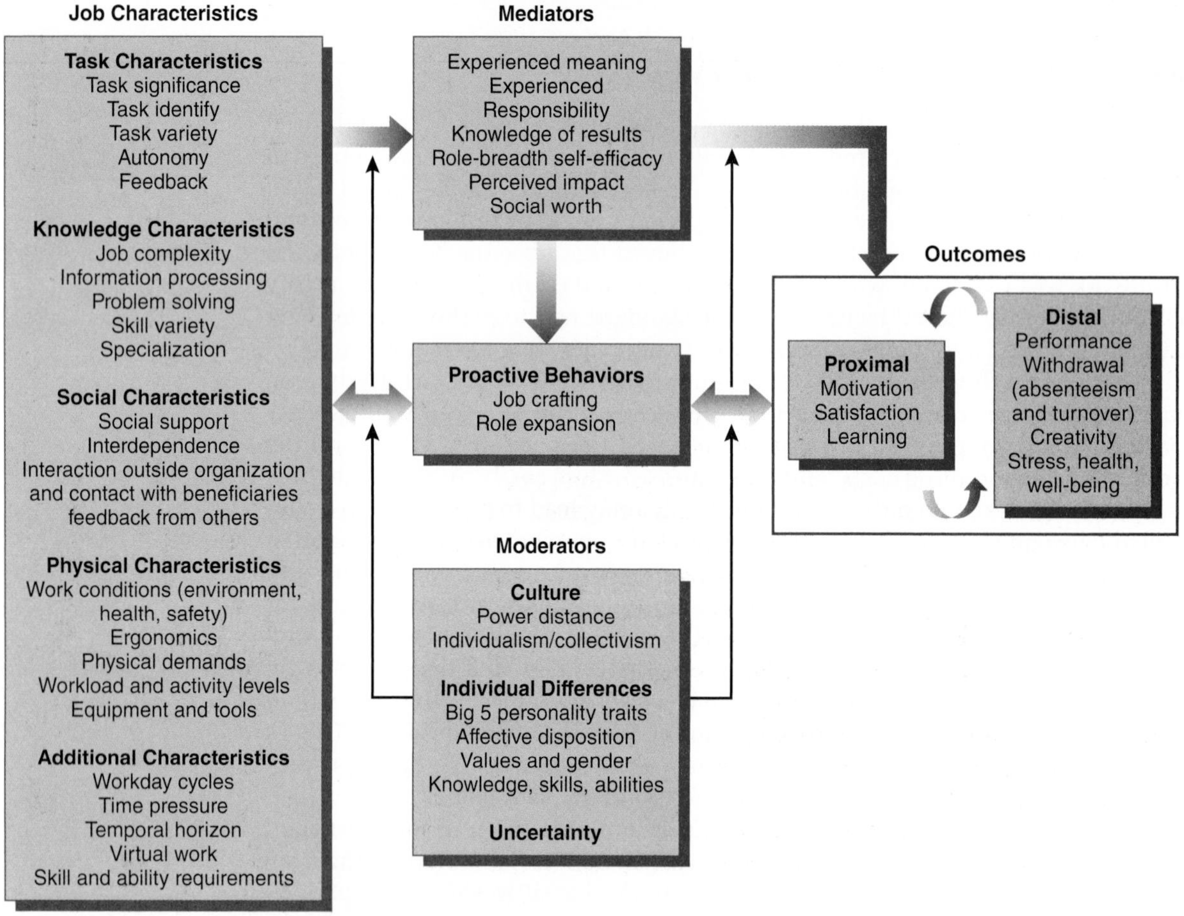

*Source:* Grant, A. M., Fried, Y., and Juillerat, T. (2011). Work matters: Job design in classic and contemporary perspectives. In S. Zedeck (Ed.), *APA Handbook of Industrial and Organizational Psychology,* Vol. 1. Washington, DC: American Psychological Association, p. 427.

To achieve those objectives, jobs and work must, of necessity, differ along a number of dimensions. For example, they differ in characteristics such as the nature of the tasks they require (e.g., in their significance, whether employees get to do a "whole" piece of work, how much variety and autonomy they permit, and the extent to which employees get feedback on their performance). Jobs and work also differ in the extent of their knowledge, social and physical characteristics, as well as in skill and ability requirements, time pressures, time horizons, workday cycles, and virtual versus co-located work. In any given situation, the Work Design Questionnaire can help assess the task, physical, knowledge, and social requirements of jobs.[21]

At the same time, not all individuals will experience work in the same way. Rather, the ability to achieve both proximal and distal outcomes will be affected by several important conditions. These include the extent to which each individual experiences meaningfulness and responsibility, and learns about the results of his or her work; whether roles are defined narrowly or broadly; each individual's confidence in the ability to perform a job well (self-efficacy); whether an individual can "grow" his or her own job and craft it to fit his or her style; and the perceived impact of the work.

Other important variables, such as culture, individual differences (personality, gender, disposition, values, knowledge, skills, and abilities) and work environments characterized by uncertainty are also likely to moderate the relationship of job characteristics to outcomes. As you can see, modern job-design research has come a long way from the "one best way" of scientific management. In the process, it has deepened our understanding and broadened our perspective on the relationship of job characteristics to important individual and organizational outcomes.

## Identifying the Work to Be Done and the Personal Characteristics Needed to Do the Work

The scientific-management approach to job design focused on the most efficient way to accomplish work tasks, while modern job-design approaches recognize a much wider variety of features of jobs that can influence near-term and longer-term outcomes. In order to implement either of those approaches, though, one must be able to specify the work to be done and the personal characteristics (knowledge, skills, abilities, personality characteristics) that are required to do the work. That is the purpose of job analysis.

One result of the process of job analysis is a **job description** (an overall written summary of task requirements). A second is a **job specification** (an overall written summary of worker requirements). In the past, such job definitions often tended to be quite narrow in scope. Today, however, some organizations are beginning to develop behavioral job descriptions or specifications of work-role requirements. They tend to be more stable, even as technologies and customer needs change.[22]

For example, instead of focusing on communication skills, such as writing, speaking, and making presentations, behavioral job descriptions incorporate broader behavioral statements, such as "actively listens, builds trust, and adapts his or her style and tactics to fit the audience." These behaviors will not change, even as the means of executing them evolve with technology. Instead of being responsible for simple procedures and predictable tasks, workers are now expected to draw inferences and render diagnoses, judgments, and decisions, often under severe time constraints.[23]

Job specifications should reflect *minimally* acceptable qualifications for job incumbents. Frequently they do not, reflecting instead a profile of the *ideal* job incumbent. How are job specifications set? Typically, they are set by consensus among experts—immediate supervisors, job incumbents, and job analysts.[24] Such a procedure is professionally acceptable, but care must be taken to distinguish between required and desirable qualifications. The term *required* denotes inflexibility; that is, it is assumed that without this qualification, an individual absolutely would be unable to do the job (e.g., certification or licensure). *Desirable* implies flexibility; it is "nice to have" this ability, but it is not a "need to have" (e.g., for some jobs, education or experience requirements). To be sure, required qualifications will exist in almost all jobs, but care must be exercised in establishing them, for such requirements must meet a higher standard.

---

**LEGALITIES**

## JOB ANALYSIS AND THE AMERICANS WITH DISABILITIES ACT (ADA) OF 1990

Job analyses are not legally required under the ADA, but sound professional practice suggests that they be done for three reasons:

1. The law makes it clear that job applicants must be able to understand what the essential functions of a job are before they can respond to the question "Can you perform the essential functions of the job for which you are applying?" Essential functions are those that require relatively more time and have serious consequences of error or nonperformance associated with them. A function may be essential because the reason the position exists at all is to perform that function (e.g., a baggage handler at an airport must be able to lift bags weighing up to 70 pounds repeatedly throughout an eight-hour shift). Alternatively, the function may be so highly specialized that it cannot be shifted to others (e.g., in a nuclear power plant, a nuclear engineer must perform inspections, often by crawling through tight spaces). Job analysis is a systematic procedure that can help to identify essential job functions.
2. Existing job analyses may need to be updated to reflect additional dimensions of jobs, namely, the physical demands, environmental demands, and mental abilities required to perform essential functions. Figure 5–4 shows a portion of a checklist of physical demands.
3. Once job analyses are updated as described, a summary of the results is normally prepared in writing in the form of a job description. What may work even better under the ADA, however, is a video job description, that provides concrete evidence to applicants of the physical, environmental (e.g., temperatures, noise level, working space), or mental (e.g., irate customers calling with complaints) demands of jobs. Candidates who are unable to perform a job because of a physical or mental disability may self-select out, thereby minimizing the likelihood of a legal challenge.

To ensure job relatedness, employers must be able to link required knowledge, skills, abilities, and other characteristics (measures of which candidates actually are assessed on) to essential job functions. Finally, recognize that under the ADA it is imperative to distinguish "essential" from "nonessential" functions *prior* to announcing a job or interviewing applicants.[a] If a candidate with a disability can perform the essential functions of a job and is hired, the employer must be willing

Use the symbols below to rate the following activities:

| | | |
|---|---|---|
| NP | Not present | Activity does not exist |
| O | Occasionally | Activity exists up to 1/3 of the time |
| F | Frequently | Activity exists from 1/3 to 2/3 of the time |
| C | Constantly | Activity exists 2/3 or more of the time |

1a. Strength (also enter the percentage of time spent in each activity)

_____ Standing  _____ percent

_____ Walking  _____ percent

_____ Sitting  _____ percent

1b. Also indicate the number of pounds that must be lifted, carried, pushed, or pulled.

_____ Lifting  _____ (weight)

_____ Carrying  _____ (weight)

_____ Pushing  _____ (weight)

_____ Pulling  _____ (weight)

2. Climbing _____

3. Balancing _____

4. Stooping _____

5. Kneeling _____

6. Crouching _____

7. Crawling _____

8. Reaching _____

9. Talking (Ordinary)_____(Other)_____

10. Hearing (Ordinary conversation)_____(Other)_____

**Figure 5–4**

Portion of a physical-abilities checklist.

to make "reasonable accommodations" to enable the person to work.[b] Here are some examples that the ADA defines as "reasonable" accommodation efforts:

- Restructuring a job so that someone else does the nonessential tasks a person with a disability cannot do.
- Modifying work hours or work schedules so that a person with a disability can commute during off-peak periods.
- Reassigning a worker who becomes disabled to a vacant position.
- Acquiring or modifying equipment or devices (e.g., a telecommunications device for the deaf).
- Adjusting or modifying examinations, training materials, or HR policies.
- Providing qualified readers or interpreters.

[a]U.S. EEOC. The ADA: Your responsibilities as an employer (addendum). Retrieved from *http://www.eeoc.gov/facts/ada17.html* on June 30, 2011.

[b]Ibid. See also Colella, A. J., and Bruyere, S. M. (2011). Disability and employment: New directions for industrial and organizational psychology. In S. Zedeck (Ed.), APA *Handbook of Industrial and Organizational Psychology,* Vol. 1. Washington, D.C.: American Psychological Association, pp. 473–503.

## Competency Models

**Competency models** attempt to identify variables related to overall organizational fit and to identify personality characteristics consistent with the organization's vision and mission (e.g., drive for results, persistence, innovation, flexibility).[25] As such, they are written in terms that operating managers can relate to.

Competency models are a form of job analysis that focuses on broader characteristics of individuals and on using these characteristics to inform HR practices. They focus on the full range of knowledge, skills, abilities, and other characteristics (e.g., motives, traits, attitudes, personality characteristics), so-called KSAOs, that are needed for effective performance on the job, and that characterize exceptional performers. Ideally, such a model consists of a set of **competencies** that have been identified as necessary for successful performance, with behavioral indicators associated with high performance on each competency specified.[26]

How does competency modeling differ from job analysis? A rigorous comparison concluded that competency approaches typically include a fairly substantial effort to understand an organization's business context and competitive strategy and to establish some direct line-of-sight between individual competency requirements and the broader goals of an organization. Job analyses, on the other hand, typically do not make this connection, but their level of rigor and documentation are more likely to enable them to withstand the close scrutiny of a legal challenge. As currently practiced, therefore, competency modeling is not a substitute or replacement for job analysis.

Neither job analysis nor competency modeling is a singular approach to studying work, and there is much variability in the ways they are implemented in actual practice.[27] Moreover, no single type of description of work content (competencies, KSAOs, work activities, performance standards) is appropriate for all purposes, and purpose is a key consideration in choosing any particular approach to the study of work.

## How Do We Study Job Requirements?

A number of methods are available to study jobs.[28] At the outset it is important to note that none of them alone is sufficient. Rather, it is important to use a combination of them to obtain a total picture of the task and the physical, mental, social, and environmental demands of a job. Here are five common methods of job analysis:

1.  *Job performance.* With this approach, an analyst actually performs the job under study to get firsthand exposure to what it demands.
2.  *Observation.* The analyst simply observes a worker or group of workers doing a job. Without interfering, the analyst records the what, why, and how of the various parts of the job. Usually this information is recorded in a standard format.
3.  *Interview.* In many jobs in which it is not possible for the analyst actually to perform the job (e.g., airline pilot) or where observation is impractical (e.g., architect), it is necessary to rely on workers' own descriptions of

what they do, why, and how. As with recordings of observations, use a standard format to collect input from all workers sampled to interview. In this way all questions and responses can be restricted to job-related topics. More importantly, standardization makes it possible to compare what different people are saying about the job in question.

4. *Critical incidents.* These are vignettes comprising brief actual reports that illustrate particularly effective or ineffective worker behaviors. For example:

   *On January 14, Mr. Vin, the restaurant's wine steward, was asked about an obscure bottle of wine. Without hesitation, he described the place of vintage and bottling, the meaning of the words on the label, and the characteristics of the grapes in the year of vintage.*

   After collecting many of these little incidents from knowledgeable individuals, it is possible to abstract and categorize them according to the general job area they describe. The end result is a fairly clear picture of actual job requirements.

5. *Structured questionnaires.* These questionnaires list tasks, behaviors (e.g., negotiating, coordinating, using both hands), or both. Tasks focus on *what* gets done. This is a job-oriented approach. Behaviors, on the other hand, focus on *how* a job is done. This is a worker-oriented, or ability-requirements, approach. Workers rate each task or behavior in terms of whether or not it is performed, and, if it is, they rate characteristics such as frequency, importance, level of difficulty, and relationship to overall performance. The ratings provide a basis for scoring the questionnaires and for developing a profile of actual job requirements.[29] The ability to represent job content in terms of numbers allows relatively precise comparisons across different jobs.[30] One of the most popular structured questionnaires is the position analysis questionnaire (PAQ).

   The PAQ is a behavior-oriented job-analysis questionnaire.[31] It consists of 187 items that fall into the following categories, plus 7 items that assess pay:

   - *Information input:* where and how the worker gets the information to do her or his job.
   - *Mental processes:* the reasoning, planning, and decision making involved in a job.
   - *Work output:* physical activities as well as the tools or devices used.
   - *Relationships with other persons.*
   - *Job context:* physical and social.
   - *Other job characteristics:* for example, apparel, work continuity, licensing, hours, and responsibility.

The items provide either for checking a job element if it applies or for rating it on a scale, such as in terms of importance, time, or possibility of occurrence. An example of some PAQ items is shown in Figure 5–5. Cumulative research indicates that the ratings are quite stable over time,[32] and evidence

**Figure 5–5**

Sample PAQ items.

| | | Code | *Importance to This Job* |
|---|---|---|---|
| | | DNA | Does not apply |
| | 5.3 Personal and Social Aspects | 1 | Very minor |
| | | 2 | Low |
| | This section includes various personal and social | 3 | Average |
| | aspects of jobs. Indicate by code the *importance* of | 4 | High |
| | these aspects as part of the job. | 5 | Extreme |

148 | I  Civic obligations (because of the job, the worker assumes, or is expected to assume, certain civil obligations or responsibilities)

149 | I  Frustrating situations (job situations in which attempts to deal with problems or achieve job objectives are obstructed or hindered, and may thus contribute to frustration on the part of the worker)

150 | I  Strained personal contacts (dealing with individuals or groups in "unpleasant" or "strained" situations, for example, certain aspects of police work, certain types of negotiations, handling certain mental patients)

indicates that PAQ dimension scores are related to compensation and worker-ability levels.[33]

While structured job-analysis questionnaires are growing in popularity, the newest applications are Web-based, and use company intranets and computer-generated graphics to help illustrate similarities and differences across jobs and organizational units. An additional benefit is that the products of the job analysis are available anytime, anywhere, to anyone who has access to the company's intranet.[34]

The preceding five methods of job analysis represent the popular ones in use today. Table 5–1 considers the pros and cons of each method. Regardless of the method used, the workers providing job information to the analyst must be experienced and knowledgeable about the jobs in question.[35] Trained analysts tend to provide the highest levels of agreement about the components of jobs,[36] although there seem to be no differences in the quality of information provided by members of different gender or race/ethnic subgroups,[37] or by high as opposed to low performers.[38] Incumbents, however, tend to provide higher ratings of abilities required in a job than do supervisors or trained job analysts.[39] In terms of the types of data actually collected, the most popular methods today are observation, interviews, and structured questionnaires.

## Job Analysis: Relating Method to Purpose

Given such a wide choice among available job-analysis methods, the combination of methods to use is the one that best fits the *purpose* of the job-analysis research (e.g., staffing, training design, performance appraisal). It is simply not true that a single type of job analysis can support any HR activity. Table 5–2 is a matrix that suggests some possible match-ups between job analysis methods and various purposes. For example, the job-performance method of job analysis is most appropriate for the development of tests and interviews, training design, and the design of performance appraisal systems.

## Table 5–1

### ADVANTAGES AND DISADVANTAGES OF FIVE POPULAR JOB-ANALYSIS METHODS

| Method | Advantages | Disadvantages |
|---|---|---|
| Job performance | With this method there is exposure to actual job tasks as well as to the physical, environmental, and social demands of the job. It is appropriate for jobs that can be learned in a relatively short period of time. | This method is inappropriate for jobs that require extensive training or are hazardous to perform. |
| Observation | Direct exposure to jobs can provide a richer, deeper understanding of job requirements than workers' descriptions of what they do. | If the work in question is primarily mental, observations alone may reveal little useful information. Critical, yet rare, job requirements (e.g., "copes with emergencies") simply may not be observed. |
| Interviews | This method can provide information about standard as well as nonstandard and mental work. Because the worker is also his or her own observer, he or she can report on activities that would not be observed often. In short, the worker can provide the analyst with information that might not be available from any other source. | Workers may be suspicious of interviewers and their motives; interviewers may ask ambiguous questions. Thus, distortion of information (either as a result of honest misunderstanding or as a result of purposeful misrepresentation) is a real possibility. For this reason, the interview should never be used as the sole job-analysis method. |
| Critical incidents | This method focuses directly on what people do in their jobs, and thus it provides insight into job dynamics. Because the behaviors in question are observable and measurable, information derived from this method can be used for most possible applications of job analysis. | It takes considerable time to gather, abstract, and categorize the incidents. Also, because by definition the incidents describe particularly effective or ineffective behavior, it may be difficult to develop a profile of average job behavior—our main objective in job analysis. |
| Structured questionnaires | This method is generally cheaper and quicker to administer than other methods. Questionnaires can be completed off the job, thus avoiding lost productive time. Web-based questionnaires allow analysts to survey large numbers of geographically dispersed job incumbents, in English as well as in other languages, thus providing a breadth of coverage and a speed of analysis and feedback that is impossible to obtain otherwise. | Questionnaires are often time consuming and expensive to develop. Rapport between analyst and respondent is not possible unless the analyst is present to explain items and clarify misunderstandings. Such an impersonal approach may have adverse effects on respondent cooperation and motivation. |

## Table 5–2

### JOB-ANALYSIS METHODS AND THE PURPOSES BEST SUITED TO EACH

| Method | Job descriptions | Development of tests | Development of interviews | Job evaluation | Training design | Performance appraisal design | Career path planning |
|---|---|---|---|---|---|---|---|
| Job performance | | X | X | | X | X | |
| Observation | X | X | X | | | | |
| Interviews | X | X | X | X | X | X | |
| Critical incidents | X | X | X | | X | X | |
| Questionnaires: | | | | | | | |
|   Task checklists | X | X | X | X | X | X | |
|   Behavior checklists | | | X | X | X | X | X |

## FROM JOB ANALYSIS TO STRATEGIC WORKFORCE PLANNING

Having identified the behavioral requirements of jobs, the organization is in a position to identify the numbers of employees and the skills required to do those jobs, at least in the short term. Further, an understanding of available competencies is necessary to allow the organization to plan for the changes to new jobs required by corporate goals. This process is known as **strategic workforce planning** (SWP)—the formal process that connects business strategy to human resource strategy and practices, and ensures that a company has the right people in the right place, at the right time, and at the right cost.[40] These are "buy-build-borrow-or-rent" decisions that have become more important in firms as a result of globalization, outsourcing, employee leasing, new technologies, organizational restructuring, and diversity in the workforce. All of these factors produce uncertainty—and because it's difficult to be efficient in an uncertain environment, firms develop business and workforce plans to reduce the impact of uncertainty. The plans may be short-term or long-term in nature, but to have a meaningful impact on future operations, it is important to link the business and workforce plans tightly to each other, as shown in Figure 5-6.

### Figure 5–6

Model of strategic workforce planning in action.
(*Source:* Reproduced with permission from The Conference Board, Inc. Young, Mary B. "Strategic Workforce Planning in Global Organizations" (2010). © 2010. The Conference Board, Inc.)

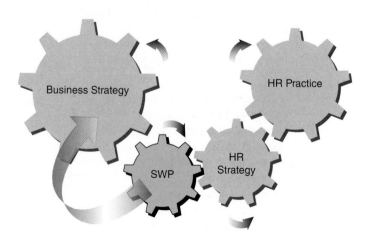

The arrows in Figure 5-6 show what happens as SWP matures and business leaders understand its value. No longer is SWP simply driven by business strategy. It also becomes an input to business strategy, providing data, analytics, and insights to inform, and sometimes challenge, executive decision making.[41]

In the course of its research with more than 25 organizations, The Conference Board has found that SWP is an iterative process that takes 3–5 years to reach its full potential. When itw does, business leaders grasp that it does not produce "just" HR data; it also delivers business intelligence. As a result, SWP becomes an input to business strategy.[42] In global organizations, SWP delivers value in four ways.[43]

1. *It uncovers significant differences among business units or locations,* such as which countries' workforces will grow or shrink, and by how much. It also reveals how the regional supply of talent compares to the demand, and where the company derives the highest return from its investments in human capital.

2. *It provides metrics and other tools to support business decisions.* For example, 3M uses productivity metrics to help determine which countries receive additional resources and which ones receive fewer. UBS used scenario planning—the anticipated future, a bear market, and a bull market—and financial indicators to signal when the bank needed to switch its workforce plans from one scenario to another.

3. *It enables leaders to compare the long-term implications of alternative business scenarios and HR options.* At UBS, for example, planners developed a cost model to illustrate the short-term trade-offs between various staffing options, and also the long-term costs of failing to develop a coherent, regional talent strategy.

4. *It supports different kinds of planning at different levels of the organization.* SWP does not simply retrieve information on demand. Rather, it raises the discussion from a tactical to a strategic level and incorporates long-term considerations such as labor supply, regulatory changes, infrastructure, and costs.

Now let's consider in more detail how SWPs actually work.

## Strategic Workforce-Planning Systems

Several specific, interrelated activities comprise a SWP system (see Figure 5–7). They include:

- A *talent inventory* to catalogue the skills, abilities, and potential of the current workforce.
- A *workforce forecast* to predict future people requirements based on an analysis of the future availability (supply) of labor and future labor requirements (demand), tempered by an analysis of external conditions (e.g., technologies, markets, competition).
- *Action plans* to enlarge the pool of people qualified to fill the projected vacancies through such actions as recruitment, selection, training, placement, transfer, promotion, development, and compensation.
- *Control and evaluation* to provide feedback on the overall effectiveness of the SWP system by monitoring the degree of attainment of HR objectives.

**Figure 5–7**

An integrated, strategic workforce planning system.

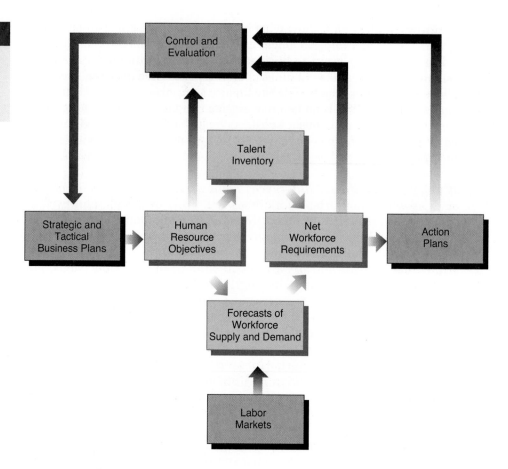

In practice, the 4-step process noted above is deceptively simple. Thus, when 3M began implementing its SWP model, it stumbled into a previously unseen reality, namely, that workforce plans should not be based on the long-term plans of each global business unit. Instead, it should begin at the country level, since that is where operational decisions (including staffing) are made.[44] Such unanticipated discoveries are not unusual. Keep that in mind as you read about each component of the 4-step model, beginning with a talent inventory.

## TALENT INVENTORY

A talent inventory is a fundamental requirement of an effective SWP system. It is an organized database of the existing skills, abilities, career interests, and experience of the current workforce. Prior to actual data collection, however, certain strategic questions must be addressed:

1. Who should be included in the inventory?
2. What specific information must be included for each individual?
3. How can this information best be obtained?
4. What is the most effective way to record such information?
5. How can inventory results be reported to decision makers?
6. How often must this information be updated?
7. How can the security of this information be protected?

Answers to these kinds of questions will provide both direction and scope for subsequent efforts. For example, IBM uses a technology-powered staff-deployment tool called "Workforce Management Initiative."[45] It's a sort of in-house version of Monster.com, the online job site. Built on a database of thousands of résumés, it lets managers search for employees with the precise skills they'll need for particular projects. The initiative has already saved IBM $500 million, and it has also improved productivity. For example, when a health-care client needed a consultant with a clinical background, the system almost instantly targeted Lynn Yarbrough, a former registered nurse. That search would have taken more than a week in the old days.

The Workforce Management Initiative's greatest impact, however, may be its ability to help managers analyze what skills staffers possess and how those talents match up to the business outlook. It's part of a broader SWP effort. When a talent inventory is linked to other databases, the set of such information enables an optimal workforce strategy and integrated supply chain for resource and talent management.[46]

Information such as the following is typically included in a profile developed for each employee:

- Current position information.
- Previous positions in the company.
- Other significant work experience (e.g., other companies, military).
- Education (including degrees, licenses, certifications).
- Language skills and relevant international experience.
- Training and development programs attended.
- Community or industry leadership responsibilities.
- Current and past performance appraisal data.
- Disciplinary actions.
- Awards received.

Information provided by individuals may also be included. At Schlumberger, for example, employees add their career goals, information about their families, past assignments, professional affiliations, publications, patents granted, and hobbies. IBM includes the individual's expressed preference for future assignments and locations, including interest in staff or line positions in other IBM locations and divisions.[47]

Although secondary uses of the talent-inventory data may emerge, it is important to specify the primary uses at the concept-development stage. Doing so provides direction and scope regarding who and what kinds of data should be included. Some common uses of a talent inventory include identification of candidates for promotion, succession planning, assignments to special projects, transfer, training, workforce-diversity planning and reporting, compensation planning, career planning, and organizational analysis.

Talent inventories and workforce forecasts must complement each other; an inventory of present talent is not particularly useful for planning purposes unless it can be analyzed in terms of future workforce requirements. On the other hand, a forecast of workforce requirements is useless unless it can be evaluated relative to the current and projected future supply of workers available internally. Only at that time, when we have a clear understanding of the projected surpluses or deficits of employees in terms of their numbers, their skills, and their experience, does it make sense to initiate action plans to rectify projected problems.

## WORKFORCE FORECASTS

The purpose of **workforce forecasting** is to estimate labor requirements at some future time period. Such forecasts are of two types: (1) the external and internal supply of labor and (2) the aggregate external and internal demand for labor. We consider each type separately because each rests on a different set of assumptions and depends on a different set of variables.[48]

Internal supply forecasts relate to conditions *inside* the organization, such as the age distribution of the workforce, terminations, retirements, and new hires within job classes. Both internal and external demand forecasts, on the other hand, depend primarily on the behavior of some business factor (e.g., projected number of retail outlets, projected sales, product volume) to which human resource needs can be related. Unlike internal and external supply forecasts, demand forecasts are subject to many uncertainties—in domestic or worldwide economic conditions, in technology, and in consumer behavior, to name just a few. The *Occupational Outlook Handbook,* published by the U.S. Department of Labor, focuses on macro forecasts of aggregate demand for various occupations. In terms of the percentage increase in demand between 2008 and 2018, here are the top 10 fast-growing occupations:[49]

- Biomedical engineers, 72 percent.
- Network systems analysts, 53 percent.
- Home health aides, 50 percent.
- Personal and home-care aides, 46 percent.
- Financial examiners, 41 percent.
- Medical scientists, 40 percent.
- Physician assistants, 39 percent.
- Skin-care specialists, 38 percent.
- Biochemists and biophysicists, 37 percent.
- Athletic trainers, 37 percent.

In the following sections we will consider several micro- or firm-level workforce forecasting techniques that have proven to be practical and useful.

### Forecasting External Workforce Supply

The recruiting and hiring of new employees are essential activities for virtually all firms, at least over the long run. Whether due to projected expansion of operations or normal workforce attrition, forays into the labor market are necessary.

Several agencies regularly make projections of external labor market conditions and estimates of the supply of labor to be available in general categories. These include the Bureau of Labor Statistics of the U.S. Department of Labor, the National Science Foundation, the Department of Education, and the Public Health Service of the Department of Health and Human Services. For new college and university graduates, the National Association of Colleges and Employers conducts a quarterly salary survey of starting salary offers to new college graduates at the bachelor's degree level (*www.naceweb.org*), and salary offers reflect supply/demand conditions in the external labor market. Organizations in industries as varied as oil and gas, nuclear power, digital-media advertising, construction, and heavy-equipment service are finding such projections of the external labor market to be helpful in preventing surpluses or deficits of employees.[50]

As an example, consider these facts. Several years ago some 47,000 jobs opened up worldwide in the field of computer animation, according to the Roncarelli Report, an industry survey. At the same time, only 14,000 animators graduated from art school. Such an imbalance between the demand for and the supply of new workers bids up starting salaries to the point where new hires may earn more than senior people at their companies! It's not just high-tech workers either. "Swiss-style" machinists, who specialize in the precision manufacturing of a wide range of products, from bone screws to roller balls for Bic pens, are also in short supply. Not surprisingly, therefore, these new hires are known as "gold-collar" workers. They are educated, smart, creative, computer literate, equipped with portable skills—and in demand.[51]

## Forecasting Internal Workforce Supply

A reasonable starting point for projecting a firm's future supply of labor is its current supply of labor. It's a form of risk management. Thus, when CNA Financial Corporation analyzed the demographics of the incumbents of various mission-critical jobs, it learned that 85 percent of its risk-control safety engineers, who inspect boilers and other machinery in buildings, were eligible for retirement. The company wanted to hold on to their specialized skills because they were so important to retaining current business. The forecast prompted the company to take action to ensure that projected deficits did not materialize.[52]

Perhaps the simplest type of internal-supply forecast is the **succession plan,** a concept that has been discussed in the planning literature for decades. Succession plans may be developed for management employees, nonmanagement employees, or both. In fact, an active succession-planning process is similar to an insurance policy; it should be there when you need it. When there is a crisis of leadership, for example, after a death or a departure, a robust succession-planning process provides needed assurance.

In a 2011 international study by the Conference Board of 704 senior executives, the top challenge identified was fueling business growth, with improving leadership development and growing talent internally viewed as key vehicles for implementing their business-growth strategies. Leadership-succession planning is a key element of that process.[53] As the chapter-opening vignette showed, there are some deep-seated reasons why some firms don't deal with succession issues: personality, ego, power, and, most importantly, mortality. Assuming that that barriers can be overcome, the actual mechanics for developing such a plan include steps such as the following: setting a planning horizon, assessing current performance and readiness for promotion, identifying replacement candidates for each key position, identifying career-development needs, and integrating the career goals of individuals with company goals. The overall objective, of course, is to ensure the availability of competent executive talent in the future or, in some cases, immediately.[54] In view of its importance, let's examine leadership-succession further in the next sections.

### Leadership-Succession Planning
This is the one activity that is pervasive, well accepted, and integrated with strategic business planning among firms that do SWP.[55] In fact, leadership-succession planning is considered by many firms to be the sum and substance of SWP. Here is an overview of how several companies do it.

Both GE and IBM have had similar processes in place for decades, and many other firms have modeled theirs on these two approaches. The stated objective of both programs is "to assure top quality and ready talent for all executive positions in the corporation worldwide." Responsibility for carrying out this process rests with line executives from division presidents up to the chief executive officer (CEO). Staff support is provided by an executive-resource staff located within the corporate HR function. Each responsible executive makes a formal presentation to a corporate policy committee consisting of the chairman, the vice chairman, and the president. The presentation usually consists of an overall assessment of the strengths and weaknesses of the unit's executive resources, the present performance and potential of key executives and potential replacements (supplemented with pictures of the individuals involved), and rankings of all incumbents of key positions in terms of present performance and expected potential.[56] Figure 5–8 is an abbreviated example of a succession-planning chart for an individual manager.

The policy committee reviews and critiques this information and often provides additional insights to line management on the strengths and weaknesses both of incumbents and their replacements. Sometimes the committee will even direct specific career-development actions to be accomplished before the next review.[57]

Leadership-succession processes are particularly well developed at 3M. With 2010 worldwide sales of $27 billion, 70 percent of which came from outside the United States, 3M sells 65,000 products in more than 200 countries, and it employs more than 70,000 people worldwide.[58] Figure 5–9 shows the overall process that 3M uses to align its HR practices with business strategy and leadership-succession planning. The following is a brief overview of each of the processes shown in Figure 5–9.

At the outset, it is important to note that a common set of leadership attributes links all management practices:

- Thinks from outside in.
- Drives innovation and growth.
- Develops, teaches, and engages others.
- Makes courageous decisions.
- Leads with energy, passion, and urgency.
- Lives 3M values.

| Figure 5–8 |
| --- |
| A typical chart used for leadership-succession planning. |

Name:
Title:
Months in position:

Photo

Performance (percentile)
Potential (high, medium, limited)

*Positive and negative attributes:*
+ Global thinker, great coach/mentor, solid technical background
− Still maturing as a leader
*Developmental needs:*
Needs experience in e-business
Attend company's senior leadership-development program

**Figure 5–9**

Alignment of HR processes at 3M. (*Source:* Society for Human Resource Management Foundation. (2008). *Seeing the Future: Leadership Succession and Development at 3M* (DVD). Alexandria, VA: SHRM Foundation. Used with permission.)

At a broad level, there are five objectives for the human-capital planning process. The most fundamental one is to align available knowledge, skills, abilities, and other characteristics with the strategy of the business. Beyond that, 3M seeks to identify talent and development needs early, and also to build depth in the organization; to leverage talent across businesses; to drive diversity throughout the organization as a business value; and to balance "make" (internal development) and "buy" (outside hiring). More specifically, the performance-appraisal process seeks to capture and document individual results, to recognize contributions, and to identify development needs.

The management team in a given area of business conducts consensus reviews. The objective is to use assessments of performance and leadership

## ETHICAL DILEMMA
### Should Leadership-Succession Plans Be Secret?

This is a thorny issue. If firms keep HR planning information about specific candidates secret, planning may have limited value. Thus, at a software company, a senior executive on her way out the door for a president's job at a competitor was told that the firm had expected her to be its next president. Her response? "If I'd known, I would have stayed."

A somewhat different course of events transpired at another firm whose policy was to talk openly about prospective candidates. There, employees learned what the company had in mind for them over the next three to five years. Subsequently, when they did not get the jobs they thought they were entitled to, employees felt betrayed. Some sued, others left. In your view, is it unethical to share planning information with employees and then not follow the plan? Conversely, do employees have a right to see such information?

attributes to build management consensus on each employee's contributions and development needs. The next process shown in Figure 5–9 is "tier" reviews. Each function (e.g., engineering, R&D, manufacturing, sales and marketing, information technology) engages in monthly as well as annual activities to assess and identify talent, both within a functional area and also across the six major businesses of the company. The resulting global talent pools are then used in succession planning and also in developing world-class leaders.

3M's leadership attributes underlie assessment, development, and succession. They describe what leaders need to know, what they need to do, and the personal qualities that leaders need to display. With respect to assessment, managers assess potential as part of the performance-appraisal process. All managers also receive 360-degree feedback as part of leadership classes. Executive hires at the leadership level all go through an extensive psychometric assessment. With respect to development, 3M's Leadership Development Institute focuses on "Leaders Teaching Leaders." It is delivered as a key development strategy in the formation of a global leadership pipeline. 3M also uses "action learning"—training that is focused on developing creative solutions to business-critical problems—as way to learn by doing. Participants present their final recommendations to senior-level executives. Finally, after follow-up coaching and individual-development plans, leaders are assessed in terms of the impact of their growth on the organization strategically.

Succession planning is the final step shown in Figure 5–9. Its objectives are three-fold: to identify top talent, that is, high-potential individuals, both within functions and corporate-wide; to develop pools of talent for critical positions; and to identify development plans for key leaders. 3M's Executive Resources Committee assures consistency both in policy and practice in global succession planning for key management and executive positions—including the process for identifying, developing, and tracking the progress of high-potential individuals.

### Lessons to Apply

Our brief review of leadership-succession processes at leading companies suggests five key lessons:

1. The CEO must drive the talent agenda. It all begins with commitment from the top.
2. Identify and communicate a common set of leadership attributes to serve as a "road map" for people in leadership positions, and for all other employees. This promotes a common set of expectations for everyone in the organization about what is expected of leaders.
3. Use candid, comprehensive performance reviews as the building block for assessment, development, and management consensus about performance and potential.
4. Keep to a regular schedule for performance reviews, broader talent reviews outside one's functional area, and the identification of talent pools for critical positions.
5. Link all decisions about talent to the strategy of the organization.

### Forecasting Workforce Demand

In contrast to supply forecasting, demand forecasting is beset with multiple uncertainties—changes in technology; consumer attitudes and patterns of

## SMALL BUSINESSES CONFRONT SUCCESSION PLANNING*

Thus far we have been discussing succession planning in large firms. But what about small firms, such as family-owned businesses? Only about 30 percent of family businesses outlive their founders, usually for lack of planning. Others were never designed for a long life. Depending on the opportunity that presents itself, it may be best for some family-owned businesses to start fast, grow quickly, and then be sold or merged with another. Not everyone truly wants to commit to the goal of a long and independent life. Yet, family-owned businesses come in all sorts of varieties. Some are simple and never expand beyond a single location. Others span the globe and have interests in a broad variety of fields. With respect to leadership succession, here are some of the ways families are trying to solve the problem:

- 25 percent plan to let the children compete and choose one or more successors with help from the board of directors.
- 35 percent plan to groom one child from an early age to take over.
- 15 percent plan to let the children compete and choose one or more successors, without input from a third party.
- 15 percent plan to form an "executive committee" of two or more children.
- 10 percent plan to let the children choose their own leader or leaders.

At the same time, this is no time for wishful thinking, hoping that an uninterested or incapable son or daughter will suddenly become full of passion and business skills. Evaluate each potential successor—including outsiders—on the following characteristics. Is the person available, capable, competent, committed to the firm, and motivated to stay over the long term? Sometimes family-owned firms look to outsiders, especially for new ideas and technology for the firm. Experts advise firms in that situation to start early, for it may take 3–5 years for the successor to become fully capable of assuming leadership for the company. During that time, careful mentorship of the successor is critical, since 80 percent of small businesses are substantially dependent on the historical competency of the business owner, and on the relationships he or she has formed over time. Finally, remember that the best successions are those that end with a clean and certain break. In other words, once the firm has a new leader in the driver's seat, the old leader should get off the bus.

*Sources: Hutcheson, J. O. (2007, Mar. 19). Building a family business to last. *BusinessWeek*. Retrieved from *http://www.businessweek.com/smallbiz/content/mar2007/sb20070319_688427.htm* on May 7, 2008. See also Klein, K. E. (2007, June 20). Succession planning without an heir. *BusinessWeek*. Retrieved from *http://www.businessweek.com/smallbiz/content/jun2007/sb20070620_135303.htm* on April 28, 2008. See also Brown, B. (1988, Aug. 4). Succession strategies for family firms. *The Wall Street Journal*, p. 23.

buying behavior; local, national, and international economies; number, size, and types of contracts won or lost; and government regulations that might open new markets or close off old ones, just to name a few. Consequently, forecasts of workforce demand are often more subjective than quantitative, although in practice a combination of the two is often used. Where should one begin?

### Identify Pivotal Talent

Begin the process by identifying pivotal jobs, those that drive strategy and revenue, and differentiate your organization in the marketplace.[59] For example, Valero Energy, a 23,000-employee oil refiner and gas retailer, began by defining 300 to 500 high-impact positions, and 3,000 to 4,000 mission-critical jobs, including engineers and welders employed at the company's 18 oil refineries. The company is able to link those specific positions directly to quantifiable revenues, business objectives, and business operations.[60]

### Assessing Future Workforce Demand

To develop a reasonable estimate of the numbers and skills mix of people needed over some future time period, for example, 2–3 years, it is important to tap into the collective wisdom of managers who are close to the scene of operations. Consider asking them questions such as the following:[61]

- What are our key business goals and objectives for the next two years?
- What are the top three priorities we must execute well in order to reach our goals over that time period?
- What are the most critical workforce issues we currently face?
- What are the 3–5 core capabilities we need to win in our markets?
- What are the required knowledge, skills, and abilities needed to execute the strategy?
- What types of positions will be required? What types will no longer be needed?
- Which types of skills should we have internally, versus buy or rent?
- What actions are necessary to align our resources with priorities?
- How will we know if we are effectively executing our workforce plan and staying on track?

### How Accurate Is Accurate?

Accuracy in forecasting the demand for labor varies considerably by firm and by industry type (e.g., utilities versus women's fashions), roughly from a 5 to 35 percent error factor. Certainly factors such as the duration of the planning period, the quality of the data on which forecasts are based (e.g., expected changes in the business factor and labor productivity), and the degree of integration of SWP with strategic business planning all affect accuracy. At the same time, SWP is not a static process. Evidence indicates that as it matures, four things happen. (1) Organizational boundaries disappear or become less important, so talent and skills can be utilized as a shared resource and managed more efficiently. (2) SWP gains broader support and ownership. (3) It incorporates tools from other functions and frameworks (e.g., finance, marketing, supply-chain management). (4) It becomes increasingly data driven, for example, modeling the feasibility and cost of executing alternative business scenarios.[62]

### Integrating Supply and Demand Forecasts

If forecasts are to prove genuinely useful to managers, they must result in an end product that is understandable and meaningful. Initial attempts at forecasting may result in voluminous printouts, but what is really required is a concise statement of projected staffing requirements that integrates supply and demand forecasts. In Figure 5–10, net workforce demand at the end of each year of a three-year forecast is compared with net workforce supply for the same year. This yields a "bottom line" figure that shows an increasing deficit each year during the three-year period. This is the kind of evidence senior managers need in order to make informed decisions regarding the future direction of HR initiatives.

## Make or Buy?

Assuming a firm has a choice, however, is it better to *select* workers who already have developed the skills necessary to perform competently or to select workers who do not have the skills immediately but who can be *trained* to perform competently? This is the same type of "make-or-buy" decision that managers often face in so many other areas of business. As a general principle, to avoid mismatched costs, balance "make" and "buy." Here are some guidelines for determining when "buying" is more effective than "making."[63]

- How accurate is your forecast of demand?
  If not accurate, do more buying.
- Do you have the "scale" to develop?
  If not, do more buying.
- Is there a job ladder to pull talent through?
  If not long, do more buying.
- How long will the talent be needed?
  If not long, do more buying.
- Do you want to change culture/direction?
  If yes, do more buying.

| | 2010 | 2011 | 2012 |
|---|---|---|---|
| **Demand** | | | |
| Beginning in position | 313 | 332 | 351 |
| Increases (decreases) | 19 | 19 | 19 |
| Total demand (year end) | 332 | 351 | 370 |
| **Supply (during year)** | | | |
| Beginning in position | 313 | 332 | 351 |
| Minus promotions | (38) | (41) | (41) |
| Minus terminations | (22) | (22) | (23) |
| Minus retirements | (16) | (16) | (16) |
| Minus transfers | (14) | (14) | (14) |
| **Subtotal** | 223 | 239 | 257 |
| Plus promotions in | 28 | 28 | 28 |
| Total supply (year end) | 251 | 267 | 285 |
| Surplus/deficit (year end) | (81) | (84) | (85) |

**Figure 5–10**

Integrated workforce supply-and-demand forecast.

## IMPACT OF STRATEGIC WORKFORCE PLANNING ON PRODUCTIVITY, QUALITY OF WORK LIFE, AND THE BOTTOM LINE

The design of jobs, and the kinds of personal characteristics needed to do those jobs, seems to be changing a lot these days. This is especially true of jobs at the bottom and at the top of today's organizations. Entry-level jobs now demand workers with new and different kinds of skills. Even simple clerical work now requires computer knowledge; bank tellers need more knowledge of financial transactions and sales techniques, and foreign competition means that assembly-line workers need more sophisticated understanding of mathematics and better reading and reasoning skills to cut costs and improve quality. At higher levels, executives need to be aware constantly of shifting competitive dynamics in their industries and of global trends that might alter those dynamics, and to be able to shift course rapidly, if necessary.[a] Such changes are likely to have implications for the numbers and skills mix of people needed to do the work, and for action plans to cope with projected HR needs in the future.

What are firms actually doing? Caterpillar Inc., the world's largest maker of construction and mining equipment, diesel and natural gas engines, and industrial gas turbines, is struggling to train enough service technicians. "We've got a global problem . . . and it's only going to get worse," says the company's HR director.[b] To deal with it, Caterpillar has established a network of vocational schools in six countries that teach a Caterpillar-approved curriculum, and students enter the program with a dealership already committed to hiring them. They will spend up to half their time in apprenticeships at Cat dealers, learning on the job. Caterpillar is just one of many companies in many countries that are facing such problems— problems that, if not addressed through SWP, can have dire effects on their bottom lines.

---

[a]Society for Human Resource Management. (2010). *The Post-recession Workplace: Competitive Strategies for Recovery and Beyond.* Alexandria, VA: Author. See also Reingold, 2009, op. cit.

[b]Coy and Ewing, 2007, op. cit., p. 28.

Recognize that, in today's fast-paced business environment, "deep benches" of candidates waiting for opportunity represent inventory. Inventory in talent often "walks" for jobs elsewhere, and that represents the biggest loss possible. In forecasting the demand for labor, therefore, it is often better to underestimate the numbers of people needed because overestimation is now too expensive. Use outside hiring to fill in gaps, but recognize that the other extreme (hiring *only* from the outside) can also be harmful. Why? Because doing so yields no unique skills and no unique culture.

## CONTROL AND EVALUATION OF SWP SYSTEMS

The purpose of control and evaluation is to guide SWP activities, identifying deviations from the plan and their causes. For this reason, we need yardsticks to measure performance. Qualitative and quantitative objectives can both play useful roles in SWP. Quantitative objectives make the control and evaluation process more objective and measure deviations from desired performance more precisely. Nevertheless, the nature of evaluation and control should always match the degree of development of the rest of the SWP process. In newly instituted SWP systems, for example, evaluation is likely to be more qualitative than quantitative, with little emphasis placed on control. This is because supply-and-demand forecasts are likely to be based more on "hunches" and subjective opinions than on hard data. Under these circumstances, workforce planners should attempt to assess the following:[64]

- The extent to which they are tuned in to workforce problems and opportunities, and the extent to which their priorities are sound.
- The quality of their working relationships with staff specialists and line managers who supply data and use SWP results. How closely do the planners work with these specialists and line managers on a day-to-day basis?
- The extent to which decision makers, from line managers who hire employees to top managers who develop business strategy, are making use of SWP forecasts, action plans, and recommendations.
- The perceived value of SWP among decision makers. Do they view the information provided by workforce planners as useful to them in their own jobs?

## IMPLICATIONS FOR MANAGEMENT PRACTICE

More and more, workforce issues are seen as people-related business issues. This suggests that as a manager you should do the following:

- Recognize that your company needs to compete just as fiercely in talent markets as it does in capital or customer markets. Consider a comment by the director of HR at Merck & Co.:

  Line managers are starting to address the needs of individual and organizational performance—for example, they know why every job exists in the organization, who the people in these jobs are, and how competent they are; and they know it is important to keep their skills updated. There is a saying at Merck: "Human resources are too important to be left to the HR department." Fully one-third of the performance evaluation of line managers is related to people management.[a]

- Plan for people in the context of managing the business strategically.
- Execute business as well as HR strategies. Tight linkage between the two, as at IBM, Canada Post, Starbucks, and Saudi Aramco, can lead to consistent levels of high performance. As one CEO noted: "We don't make financial, marketing, technical, or human resources decisions—we make business decisions [and] we routinely involve all the functions."[b]

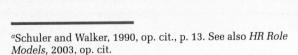

[a]Schuler and Walker, 1990, op. cit., p. 13. See also *HR Role Models,* 2003, op. cit.

[b]Buller, P. F. (1993). Successful partnership: HR and strategic planning at eight top firms. In R. S. Schuler (Ed.), *Strategic Human Resources Management.* NY: American Management Association, p. 23. See also Young, 2009 and 2010, op. cit.

In more established SWP systems, in which objectives and action plans are both underpinned by measured performance standards, key comparisons might include the following:[65]

- Actual staffing levels against forecast staffing requirements.
- Actual levels of labor productivity against anticipated levels of labor productivity.
- Action programs implemented against action programs planned (Were there more or fewer? Why?).
- The actual results of the action programs implemented against the expected results (e.g., improved applicant flows, lower quit rates, improved replacement ratios).
- Labor and action-program costs against budgets.
- Ratios of action-program benefits to action-program costs.

The advantage of quantitative information is that it highlights potential problem areas and can provide the basis for constructive discussion of the issues.

---

*Human Resource Management in Action: Conclusion*

## LEADERSHIP SUCCESSION—A KEY CHALLENGE FOR ALL ORGANIZATIONS

Research shows that planning for CEO succession should be part and parcel of the way a company is managed. Grooming potential leaders is a process that takes years. It's not an ad hoc event. In fact, developing leaders with strategic vision, and developing those who can implement strategy successfully, are two critical challenges for every chief executive. The best organizations are consciously strategic in their leadership planning. They tie HR development activities directly to the business strategy, and ask what business issue each developmental activity is designed to address. They view financial results as a lagging indicator of organizational success, while people development is a leading indicator. Consequently, people development is becoming an important part of the assessment of executive performance. PepsiCo is a good example. Historically it allocated one-third of incentive compensation to the development of people, with the remainder allocated to results. Now the company allocates equal amounts of incentive compensation for people development and results. To avoid a future crisis in leadership succession, here are some key steps to take.

1. *Ensure that the sitting CEO understands the importance of this task and makes it a priority.* At both G. E. and Procter & Gamble, managers at every rank are graded in performance reviews on whether they've retained and advanced their most talented employees.
2. *Focus on an organization's future needs, not past accomplishments.* In today's changing business landscape, companies need leaders with strengths and talents that differ from those of the previous CEO—no matter how successful he or she was.
3. *Encourage differences of opinion.* Give rising stars room to disagree with management decisions. Squelching those who challenge the status quo will drive out promising leaders and leave behind a crop of yes-men and -women who are unlikely to make good CEOs.

4. *Provide broad exposure.* Allow rising stars to rotate through jobs, changing responsibilities every 3–5 years. Be sure these managers are around long enough to see the results of their work (good or bad), but not so long that they will get stale. Let them shadow more-senior managers (e.g., for a week at a time) to see how decisions actually get made.

5. *Provide access to the Board.* Let up-and-comers make presentations to the Board of Directors. Managers get a sense of what matters to directors, and directors get to see the talent in the pipeline.

## SUMMARY

We are witnessing vast changes in the nature of work and competition, and in the types and numbers of jobs available. To reduce uncertainty and increase efficiency, careful attention needs to be paid to the linkages between strategic business planning, HR strategy, and strategic workforce planning. Business strategy provides an overall direction and focus for the organization as a whole, including for each functional area of the business. Human resource (HR) strategy parallels and facilitates implementation of the strategic business plan. HR strategy is the set of priorities a firm uses to align its resources, policies, and programs with its strategic business plan. Strategic workforce planning is the formal process that connects business strategy to HR strategy and practices.

Business strategy and job design provide a basic blueprint for the organization in terms of organizing work to accomplish important strategic objectives. Jobs can be designed to achieve several different objectives, for example, to maximize efficiency (scientific management), to facilitate the performance of teams (sociotechnical systems design), or to achieve near-term and longer-term objectives, such as increases in productivity or decreases in stress and turnover. In all cases, there is a need to identify the work to be done and the personal characteristics necessary to do the work. This is the purpose of job analysis.

A written summary of the task requirements for a particular job is called a job description, and a written summary of people requirements is called a job specification. Together they comprise a job analysis. A variety of methods are available to collect information about jobs and their requirements, such as job performance, observation, interviews, critical incidents, and structured questionnaires, and all have both advantages and disadvantages. Key considerations in the choice of methods are the method-purpose fit, cost, practicality, and an overall judgment of the appropriateness of the methods for the situation in question.

Competency models are a form of job analysis that focuses on broader characteristics of individuals and on using these characteristics to inform HR practices. They focus on the full range of knowledge, skills, abilities, and other characteristics (e.g., motives, traits, attitudes, personality characteristics), so-called KSAOs, that are needed for effective performance on the job and that characterize exceptional performers. As currently practiced, however, competency modeling is not a substitute or replacement for job analysis.

Information about jobs and business strategy are the key inputs to the SWP process. This perspective suggests several interrelated activities that together comprise an integrated SWP system. These include: (1) an inventory of talent currently on hand; (2) forecasts of labor supply and demand over short- and long-term periods; (3) action plans, such as hiring, training, or job transfer to meet forecasted HR needs; and (4) control and evaluation procedures.

## KEY TERMS

| | |
|---|---|
| succession planning | job description |
| SMART objectives | job specification |
| business strategy | competency models |
| HR strategy | competencies |
| job analysis | strategic workforce planning |
| job design | workforce forecasting |

## DISCUSSION QUESTIONS

**5–1.** How are workforce plans related to business and HR strategies?

**5–2.** Discuss the similarities and differences between job analysis and competency models.

**5–3.** For purposes of succession planning, what information would you want in order to evaluate potential?

**5–4.** Why are forecasts of workforce demand more uncertain than forecasts of workforce supply?

**5–5.** When is it more cost-effective to "buy" rather than to "make" competent employees?

**5–6.** Why should the output from forecasting models be tempered with the judgment of experienced line managers?

**5–7.** The chairperson of the board of directors at your firm asks for advice about SWP. What would you say?

## APPLYING YOUR KNOWLEDGE

---

*Case 5–1*        ***Leadership-Succession Planning—Successes and Failures****

Merrill Lynch, like many other financial companies, was caught in a bad situation. Subprime lending woes and a downwardly spiraling housing market resulted in enormous financial losses. Merrill Lynch benefitted from high returns for years, and showed little restraint in taking on enormous risks. Once the markets collapsed, Board members felt they had little recourse but to dismiss the CEO, Stan O'Neal, in order to placate angry investors. In addition, O'Neal reportedly had terminated any up-and-coming executives in an effort to protect his job from any hostile moves by the board. As a result, there was no talent capable of replacing the CEO. The board did not complain about O'Neal's practice, because O'Neal had appointed all of the Board members. Had there been any form of leadership-succession planning in place, a knowledgeable replacement would have

---

* Sources: Kimes, M. (2009, April 13). P&G's leadership machine. *Fortune*, p. 22. See also George, B. (2007, Nov. 29). An embarrassment of succession fiascoes. Retrieved from *http://www.businessweek.com/managing/content/nov2007/ca20071129_676015.htm* on April 28, 2008.

been available. Instead, the company risked going without a real leader for several months, at a time when tough decisions would likely determine how quickly it might recover from the credit crisis.

A similar scenario played out at Citigroup: huge financial losses due to risky lending and investing. Charles Prince, Citi's CEO, had been facing much scrutiny in the financial press long before the credit problems surfaced. Thus, the lack of leadership-succession planning was surprising. In both the Merrill Lynch and Citigroup cases, their respective boards went outside to find successors, perhaps to establish a clean break from the shoddy lending and investing practices that had grown over the years.

In contrast, Procter & Gamble prepared well for a leadership change. Its former CEO, A. G. Lafley, dedicated a portion of his time to working with senior managers in different divisions to identify promising talent and to report these candidates to the board. Board members, in turn, visited these individuals to become familiar with them and to let them know that they were being groomed as key players. As a result, board members were well versed on key successors, and the CEO shared information with these individuals to promote their continued growth, HR knew about these selections, and there were checks and balances in the entire process. A high level of trust existed among the CEO, successors, and board members. In late 2009, the board appointed Bob McDonald as P&G's next CEO.

A final example is Johnson & Johnson. Its Covenant of Corporate Governance includes a section on leadership-succession planning, which makes quite clear that the CEO is responsible for reviewing the succession plans of all key executives with the Nominating and Corporate Governing Committee of the Board of Directors. The Committee has oversight of the plan, and the CEO is responsible for presenting the plan to the board at least once a year. The board then evaluates all successors presented in the plan, and the annual review of the plan is an integral part of the performance review of the CEO.

---

**Questions**

1. What key differences seem to distinguish successful from unsuccessful leadership-succession processes?
2. If you were advising a firm on how to proceed in this area, what steps and priorities would you recommend?
3. If leadership succession is so important, why don't more companies do a better job of it?

---

## REFERENCES

1. Boudreau, J. W., and Ramstad, P. M. (2007). *Beyond HR: The New Science of Human Capital.* Boston: Harvard Business School Publishing.
2. Dess, G. D., Lumpkin, G. T., and Eisner, A. B. (2010). *Strategic Management* (5th Ed.). New York: McGraw-Hill/Irwin.
3. Rosenfeld, J. (2000, Apr.). Unit of one. *Fast Company,* p. 98.
4. Lipton, M. (1996). Demystifying the development of an organizational vision. *Sloan Management Review* 37(4), pp. 83–92.
5. Dess et al., 2010, op. cit.
6. Source: Colvin, G. (2011, March 21). The 50 all-stars: Asked to name the best of the best, 4,100 executives, directors, and analysts chose these businesses. *Fortune,* pp. 110–112.
7. Ibid.

8.  Becker, B. E., Huselid, M. A., and Ulrich, D. (2001). *The HR Scorecard: Linking People, Strategy, and Performance.* Boston: Harvard Business School Press. See also Huselid, M. A., Becker, B. E., and Beatty, R. W. (2005). *The Workforce Scorecard.* Boston: Harvard Business School Press.

9.  The model is based on the work of Boudreau, J. W., and Ramstad, P. M. (2003). Strategic industrial and organizational psychology and the role of utility analysis models. In W. C. Borman, D. R. Ilgen, and R. J. Klimoski (Eds.), *Handbook of Psychology: Industrial and Organizational Psychology*, Vol. 12. Hoboken, NJ: Wiley, pp. 193–221. See also Boudreau, J. W. (1998). Strategic human resource management measures: Key linkages and the PeopleVantage model. *Journal of Human Resource Costing and Accounting* 3(2), pp. 23–35.

10. Pearlman, K., and Sanchez, J. I. (2010). Work analysis. In Farr, J. L., and Tippins, N. T. (Eds.), *Handbook of Employee Selection.* New York, NY: Routledge Taylor & Francis Group, pp. 73–98.

11. Herbst, M. (2007, Dec. 13). Big oil's talent hunt. *BusinessWeek.* Retrieved from *http://www.businessweek.com/magazine/content/07_52/b4064062948731.htm* on January 27, 2008.

12. Dess et al., 2010, op. cit. See also Schuler, R. S., and Walker, J. W. (1990, Summer). Human resources strategy: Focusing on issues and actions. *Organizational Dynamics,* pp. 5–19.

13. Society for Human Resource Management Foundation. (2003) *HR Role Models* (DVD). Video retrieved from *http://www.shrm.org/about/foundation/products/Pages/HRRoleModelsDVD.aspx.*

14. Bridges, W. (1994a, Sept. 19). The end of the job. *Fortune,* pp. 62–64, 68, 72, 74. See also Bridges, W. (1994b). *Job Shift: How to Prosper in a World without Jobs.* Reading, MA: Addison-Wesley.

15. Milkovich, G. T., and Newman, J. M. (2011). *Compensation Management* (10th Ed.). New York: McGraw-Hill.

16. Grant, A. M., Fried, Y., and Juillerat, T. (2011). Work matters: Job design in classic and contemporary perspectives. In S. Zedeck (Ed.), *APA Handbook of Industrial and Organizational Psychology*, Vol. 1. Washington, DC: American Psychological Association, pp. 417–453.

17. Bell, D. (1972). Three technologies: Size, measurement, hierarchy. In L. E. Davis and J. C. Taylor (Eds.), *Design of Jobs.* London: Penguin, pp. 54–78.

18. *Work in America.* (1973). Report of a special task force to the Secretary of Health, Education, and Welfare. Cambridge, MA: MIT Press. See also Kornhauser, A. (1965). *Mental Health of the Industrial Worker.* NY: Wiley. See also Blauner, R. (1964) *Alienation and Freedom.* Chicago: University of Chicago Press.

19. Labich, K. (1994, Nov. 14). Why companies fail. *Fortune,* p. 64.

20. Grant et al., 2011, op. cit

21. Humphrey, S. E., Nahrgang, J. D., and Morgeson, F. P. (2007). Integrating motivational, social, and contextual work design features: A meta-analytic summary and theoretical extension of the work design literature. *Journal of Applied Psychology* 92, pp. 1332–1356. See also Morgeson, F. P., and Humphrey, S. E. (2006). The work design questionnaire (WDQ): Developing and validating a comprehensive measure for assessing job design and the nature of work. *Journal of Applied Psychology* 91, pp. 1321–1339.

22. Morgeson, F. P., and Dierdorff, E. C. (2011). Work analysis: From technique to theory. In S. Zedeck (Ed.), *APA Handbook of Industrial and Organizational Psychology*, Vol. 2. Washington, DC: American Psychological Association, pp. 3–41. Joinson, C. (2001). Refocusing job descriptions. *HRMagazine* 46(1), pp. 66–72.

23. Morgeson and Dierdorff, 2011, op. cit. See also Pearlman, K., and Sanchez, J. I. (2010). Work analysis. In Farr, J. L., and Tippins, N. T. (Eds.), *Handbook of Employee Selection,.* New York, NY: Routledge Taylor & Francis Group, pp. 73–98.

24.  A systematic procedure for developing minimum qualifications was presented by Levine, E. L., May, D. M., Ulm, R. A., and Gordon, T. R. (1997). A methodology for developing and validating minimum qualifications (MQs). *Personnel Psychology* 50, pp. 1009–1023.

25.  Pearlman and Sanchez, 2010, op. cit. Schippmann, J. S., Ash, R. A., Battista, M., Carr, L., Eyde, L. D., Hesketh, B., Kehoe, J., Pearlman, K., Prien, E. P., and Sanchez, J. I. (2000). The practice of competency modeling. *Personnel Psychology* 53, pp. 703–740.

26.  Goffin, R. D., and Woychesin, D. E. (2006). An empirical method of determining employee competencies/KSAOs from task-based job analysis. *Military Psychology* 18(2), pp. 121–130. See also Mihalevsky, M., Olson, K. S., and Maher, P. T. (2007). *Behavioral Competency Dictionary.* La Puente, CA: Bassett Unified School District. See also Sackett, P. R., and Laczo, R. M. (2003). Job and work analysis. In W. C. Borman, D. R. Ilgen, and R. J. Klimoski (Eds.), *Handbook of Psychology: Industrial and Organizational Psychology,* Vol. 12. Hoboken, NJ: Wiley. pp. 21–37.

27.  Morgeson and Dierdorff, 2011, op. cit. See also Pearlman and Sanchez, 2010, op. cit. Schmieder, R. A., and Frame, M. C. (2007). Competency modeling. In S. G. Rogelberg (Ed.), *Encyclopedia of Industrial and Organizational Psychology,* Vol. 1. Thousand Oaks, CA: Sage. pp. 85–87.

28.  Brannick, M. T., Levine, E. L., and Morgeson, F. P. (2007). *Job and Work Analysis: Methods, Research, and Applications for Human Resource Management.* Thousand Oaks, CA: Sage.

29.  Ibid. See also Fleishman, E. A., and Mumford, M. D. (1991). Evaluating classifications of job behavior: A construct validation of the ability requirements scales. *Personnel Psychology* 44, pp. 523–575.

30.  Harvey, R. J. (1991). Job analysis. In M. D. Dunnette and L. M. Hough (Eds.), *Handbook of Industrial and Organizational Psychology,* Vol. 2. Palo Alto, CA: Consulting Psychologists Press, pp. 71–163.

31.  McCormick, E. J., Jeanneret, P. R., and Mecham, R. C. (1972). A study of job characteristics and job dimensions as based on the Position Analysis Questionnaire (PAQ). *Journal of Applied Psychology* 56, pp. 347–368. See also PAQ Services, Inc. *http://www.paq2.com,* accessed June 30, 2011.

32.  Dierdorff, E. C., and Wilson, M. A. (2003). A meta-analysis of job analysis reliability. *Journal of Applied Psychology* 88, pp. 635–646. (The average intra-rater reliability of the PAQ in their meta-analysis was 0.82.)

33.  Morgeson, F. P. (2007). Job analysis methods. In S. G. Rogelberg (Ed.), *Encyclopedia of industrial and organizational psychology,* Vol. 1. Thousand Oaks, CA: Sage. pp. 380–383.

34.  Milkovich and Newman, 2011, op cit.

35.  Landy, F. J., and Vasey, J. (1991). Job analysis: The composition of SME samples. *Personnel Psychology* 44, pp. 27–50. See also DiNisi, A. S., Cornelius, E. T., III, and Blencoe, A. G. (1987). Further investigation of common knowledge effects on job analysis ratings. *Journal of Applied Psychology* 72, pp. 262–268. See also Friedman, L., and Harvey, R. J. (1986). Can raters with reduced job descriptive information provide accurate Position Analysis Questionnaire (PAQ) ratings? *Personnel Psychology* 39, pp. 779–789.

36.  Dierdorff and Wilson, 2003, op. cit.

37.  Schmitt, N., and Cohen, S. A. (1989). Internal analyses of task ratings by job incumbents. *Journal of Applied Psychology* 73, pp. 96–104.

38.  Conley, P. R., and Sackett, P. R. (1987). Effects of using high- versus low-performing job incumbents as sources of job-analysis information. *Journal of Applied Psychology* 72, pp. 434–437.

39.  Morgeson, F. P., Delaney-Klinger, K., Ferrara, P., Mayfield, M. S., and Campion, M. A. (2004). Self-presentation processes in job analysis: A field experiment investigating

inflation in abilities, tasks, and competencies. *Journal of Applied Psychology* 89, pp. 674–686.

40. Young, M. B. (2010, Feb.). *Strategic Workforce Planning in Global Organizations.* New York, NY: the Conference Board.

41. Young, M. B. (2009). *Implementing Strategic Workforce Planning.* New York, NY: The Conference Board.

42. Young, 2010, op. cit.

43. Ibid. See also Sutherland, D., and Wilkerson, B. (2010, Feb.). *Leading-Edge Workforce Planning Using Simulation and Optimization.* New York, NY: The Conference Board Council of Talent Management Executives.

44. Young, 2010, op. cit.

45. Boudreau, J. W. (2010). *IBM's Global Talent Management Strategy.* Alexandria, VA: Society for Human Resource Management. See also Byrnes, N. (2005, Oct. 10). Starsearch: How to recruit, train, and hold on to great people. What works, what doesn't. *BusinessWeek,* pp. 68–78.

46. Ibid. See also Young, 2009, op. cit. Davis, N. (2007, Oct. 7). Database is key to integrated talent management. *HR News.* Retrieved from *http://www.shrm.org/Publications/ HRNews/Pages/CMS_023319.aspx* on October 17, 2007.

47. Byrnes, 2005, op. cit.

48. Strack, R. (2011, May 25). Global talent risk, 7 responses. Presented at the World Economic Forum, Cologny/Geneva, Switzerland. See also Cappelli, P. (2008). *Talent on Demand: Managing Talent in an Age of Uncertainty.* Boston: Harvard Business School Press.

49. Lacey, T. A., and Wright, B. (2010, Dec. 22). Occupational employment projections to 2018. Retrieved from *http://www.bls.gov/opub/mlr/2009/11/art5full.pdf* on July 1, 2011.

50. Coy, P., and Ewing, J. (2007, Apr. 9). Where are all the workers? *BusinessWeek,* pp. 28–31. See also Aston, A. (2007, Jan. 22). Who will run the plants? *BusinessWeek,* p. 78. See also Herbst, 2007, op. cit. See also Vranica, S., and Steel, E. (2006, Oct. 23). Wanted: On-line media expertise. *The Wall Street Journal,* p. B4.

51. Carey, P. (2011, June 28). Select tech workers are in high demand. *San Jose Mercury News,* Retrieved from *http://www.standard.net/topics/business/2011/06/28/select-tech-workers-are-high-demand* on July 1, 2011. See also Aeppel, T. (2004, Aug. 17). Turn of the screw: In tepid job scene, certain workers are in hot demand. *The Wall Street Journal,* pp. A1, A4.

52. Hirschman, C. (2007, Mar.). Putting forecasting in focus. *HRMagazine* 52(3), pp. 44, 49.

53. Mitchell, C. (2011, April). *CEO challenge 2011: Fueling business growth with innovation and talent development.* New York, NY: The Conference Board, Report R-1474-11-RR.

54. Holstein, W. J. (2008, Jan. 10). McCormick's successful succession plan. *BusinessWeek.* Retrieved from *http://www.businessweek.com/managing/content/jan2008/ca20080110_ 155527.htm* on, April 28, 2008. See also Bower, J. L. (2008, Apr. 15). The leader within your company. *BusinessWeek.* Retrieved from *http://www.businessweek. com/managing/content/apr2008/ca20080415_746252.htm* on April 28, 2008. See also Bower, J. L. (2007, Nov.). Solve the succession crisis by growing inside-outside. *Harvard Business Review,* pp. 91–96.

55. Welch, J., and Byrne, J. A. (2001). *Jack: Straight from the Gut.* New York: Warner Books.

56. Conaty, W. J. (2007, Oct.). Leadership development at GE. Presented at Leadership Succession in a Changing World. Tampa, FL: Society for Human Resource Management Foundation.

57. Welch and Byrne, 2001, op. cit.

58. *3M Annual Report* (2010). Retrieved from *http://media.corporate-ir.net/media_ files/irol/80/80574/annualreport/2010_Annual_Report.pdf* on July 10, 2011.

59. Cascio, W. F., and Boudreau, J. W. (2011). *Investing in People: Financial Impact of Human Resource Initiatives* (2nd Ed.). Upper Saddle River, NJ: Pearson Education. Boudreau, J. W., and Ramstad, P. (2007). *Beyond HR: The New Science of Human Capital.* Boston: Harvard Business School Press.
60. Hale, quoted in Hirschman, 2007, op. cit., p. 48.
61. Hirschman, 2007, op. cit., p. 46.
62. Young, 2010, op. cit.
63. Cappelli, 2008a, op. cit.
64. Walker, J. W. (1980). *Human Resource Planning.* New York: McGraw-Hill.
65. Dyer, L., and Holder, G. W. (1988). A strategic perspective of human resource management. In L. Dyer and G. W. Holder (eds.), *Human Resource Management: Evolving Roles and Responsibilities.* Washington, DC: Bureau of National Affairs.

# 6

# RECRUITING

## Questions This Chapter Will Help Managers Answer

1. What factors are most important to consider in developing a recruitment policy?

2. Under what circumstances does it make sense to retain an executive search firm?

3. Do alternative recruitment sources yield differences in the quality of employees and in their "survival" rates on the job?

4. How can we communicate as realistic a picture as possible of a job and organization to prospective new employees? What kinds of issues are most crucial to them?

5. If I lose my current job, what's the most efficient strategy for finding a new one?

## THE PERILS AND PROMISE OF SOCIAL MEDIA*

Social media are here to stay. They facilitate the social relationships that we have with other people, and the use of Internet technologies makes those relationships easier to develop and maintain. Social media include at least four major types: (1) social-networking sites, such as Facebook, LinkedIn, Plaxo, and chat rooms; (2) blogs and microblogs, such as Twitter; (3) virtual worlds, such as Second Life; and (4) video-sharing Web sites, such as You-Tube. Facebook counts more than 800 million active users. Twitter, created in 2006, has more than 200 million registered users. Recruiters are using it to announce employment opportunities; job seekers can subscribe to their Twitter feeds to be notified when positions are available. At LinkedIn, more than 60 million members have logged on to create profiles, upload their employment histories, and build connections with people they know. Recruiters use personal and corporate pages on Facebook and LinkedIn to announce openings and to network with prospective clients.

The new imperative is to present your professional skills as attractively as possible, packing your profile with keywords (*marketing manager, global sourcing specialist*) that will send your name to the top of recruiters' searches. At the same time, you can connect your online professional interactions in one place, joining groups on the site (e.g., based on companies, schools, and affinities). Statistics show that 35 percent of adult Internet users have profiles on at least one social-networking site, 75 percent of recruiters use the Internet as part of the screening process, and 25 percent of those have eliminated candidates based on information found.

A big appeal of social media is that they appear to be able to solve business challenges without any associated costs. Why hire a search firm when you can tap your personal/contact list to find candidates without charge? Why hire consultants when one of your "friends" can give you free advice? Why hire a coach when you can get a volunteer mentor from your current executives? The end result is that personal relationships with outsiders can become just as important as those with fellow employees. Will the promise of social media really play out as described? Maybe, but only if organizations can find ways to manage the risks that they entail.

The top five social-media risks to business identified in a recent study include malware, brand hijacking, lack of content control, noncompliance with rules over recordkeeping, and unrealistic expectations of Internet performance. Here are seven more: sexual harassment, defamation, libel, disclosure of confidential information or trade secrets, disclosure of customer lists,

*Sources*: Lieber, L. (2011, June 30). Dangers of social media in the workplace: Managing liabilities. Webinar, *https://cc.readytalk.com/cc/s/meetingArchive?eventId=w010ho9mwpq1*. See also Efrati, A., and Ante, S. E. (2011, July 6). Twitter seeks $7 billion valuation. *The Wall Street Journal*, pp. B1, B2. See also Turner, B. (2011, May 14). Facebook banned by UK companies. *Tech Watch*. Retrieved from *http://www.techwatch.co.uk/2011/05/14/facebook-banned-by-uk-companies/* on May 16, 2011. See also Cappelli, P. (2010, May 24). The promise and limitations of social media. *Human Resource Executive Online*. Retrieved from *http://www.hreonline.com/HRE/story.jsp?storyId=432216581&query=social media* on May 27, 2010. See also Hempel, J. (2010, April 12). How LinkedIn will fire up your career. *Fortune*, pp. 74–82. Whitney, L. (2010, June 9). Study: social-media use puts companies at risk. Retrieved from *http://news.cnet.com/8301-1023_3-20007071-93.html?tag=mncol;1n* on June 9, 2010. See also Arnold, J. T. (2009, Dec.). Twittering and Facebooking while they work. *HRMagazine 54*(12), pp. 53–55.

**199**

tort law violations (negative comments about employers), and theft of employer time. After all, the use of social media is not free. It only appears to be so because companies do not account for the time employees spend using social media. Studies show that at least some employees spend up to three hours per day on social-networking Web sites!

What should organizations do? A recent study of United Kingdom companies found that nearly half have banned access to Facebook, and 63 percent of others discouraged their employees from using social media. Conversely, Vineet Nayar, CEO of HCL Technologies, says, "Facebook is such a popular application that is widely used for personal and business uses; it makes no sense to ban it. If companies do not address this, they could be at the mercy of corporate suicide." At the very least, companies should develop policies about the use of social media at work. At present, most do not have any. Thus one study found that 77 percent of employers had no policy about employees or supervisors providing references on LinkedIn. In the conclusion to this case we will consider what firms can do to avoid liability for their employees' use of social media, and also what sound social-media policies should contain.

Challenges

1. From your own perspective, what is the main appeal of social media in recruitment?
2. How can organizations manage the risks associated with social media?
3. How might a company measure the costs and benefits of social media in the workplace?

## RECRUITMENT AS A STRATEGIC IMPERATIVE

**Recruitment** is a form of business contest and it is fiercely competitive. Just as corporations strategize to develop, manufacture, and market the best product or service, so they must also vie to identify, attract, and hire the most qualified people. Recruitment is a business, and it is big business.[1] It demands serious attention from management because any business strategy will falter without the talent to execute it. According to former Apple CEO Steve Jobs (now deceased), "Recruiting is hard. It's finding the needles in the haystack. I've participated in the hiring of maybe 5,000-plus people in my life. I take it very seriously."[2]

Certainly the range of recruitment needs is broad. A small manufacturer in a well-populated rural area faces recruitment challenges that are far different from those of a high-technology firm operating in global markets. Both need talent—although different types of talent—to be successful in their respective markets. Regardless of the size of a firm, or what industry it is in, recruitment and selection of people with strategically relevant abilities is more important than ever. Let's begin by examining the big picture of the employee recruitment and selection process, along with some important legal issues. Then we'll focus specifically on the processes of planning, managing, and evaluating recruitment efforts. We will address the special issues associated with recruiting people for international assignments in Chapter 16.

# THE EMPLOYEE RECRUITMENT/SELECTION PROCESS

Recruitment is an important component of the staffing supply chain.[3] It begins, as Figure 6–1 indicates, by specifying human resource requirements (numbers, skills mix, levels, time frame). These requirements are typically the result of job analysis and strategic workforce planning (SWP) activities. Conceptually (and logically), job analysis precedes SWP in Figure 6–1 because, as we noted in Chapter 5, it is necessary to specify the work to be done and the personal characteristics necessary to do the work (competencies, knowledge, skills, abilities) before the numbers and types of people needed to do the work can be specified. Not shown in Figure 6–1—although critically important to the overall recruitment/selection process—are strategic business objectives. For example, recruitment and selection strategies for new employees are likely to differ considerably depending on whether a company's objective in hiring, say, new salespeople, is to identify candidates who are able to execute cold calls for new customers as opposed to servicing existing, long-term customers.

The step following recruitment is **initial screening,** which is basically a rapid, rough selection process. In the late nineteenth and early twentieth centuries, when line supervisors hired factory workers outside the gates of a plant, they simply looked over the candidates and then pointed to various people. "You, you, and you—the rest of you come back another day." That's an example of initial screening, and it was probably done only on the basis of physical characteristics. Today managers rely more on application forms, reference checks, and interviews at this stage. The **selection** process following initial screening is more rigorous. For example, physical characteristics alone do not provide many clues about a person's potential for management, or for any other kind of work, for that matter. What is needed, of course, are samples of behavior—revealed, for example, through tests and personal interviews—combined with the testimony of others about a candidate, for example, from references or background checks.

Past the selection stage, we are no longer dealing with job candidates, we are dealing with new employees. Typically, the first step in their introduction to company policies, practices, and benefits is an **orientation** program (sometimes called "on-boarding"). Orientation may take several hours or several weeks; it may be formal, informal, or some combination of the two. As we shall see in Chapter 8, orientation has more significant and lasting effects than most people might expect.

**Placement** occurs after orientation; placement is the assignment of individuals to jobs. In large firms, for example, individuals may be selected initially on the basis of their potential to succeed in general management. After they have been observed and assessed during an intensive management training program, however, the organization is in a much better position to assign them to specific jobs within broader job families, such as marketing, production, or sales. (There are instances in which employees are selected specifically to fill certain positions; these are so-called one-shot selection/placement programs.) The technical expertise and the resources necessary to implement optimal placement programs (select, orient, then place) are found mostly in very large organizations.

Once new employees are selected, oriented, and placed, they can be *trained* to achieve a competent level of job performance. As we shall see in Chapter 8, training is very big business.

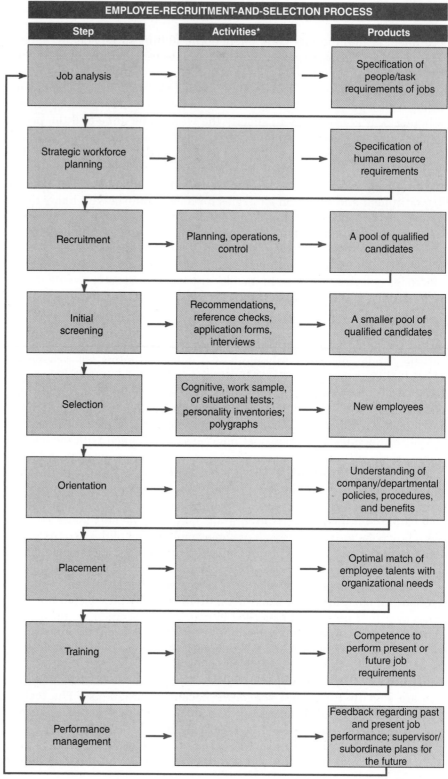

**Figure 6–1**

The employee-recruitment-and-selection process.

*For purposes of clarity and simplicity, relevant activities are shown only for recruitment, screening, and selection—the topics of this and the following chapter.

Finally, in the **performance-management** process, managers provide feedback to employees regarding their past and present job performance proficiency, as well as a basis for improving performance in the future. The first time a manager appraises a new employee's performance, it is like pushing the button that starts a continuous loop—more precisely, a continuous feedback loop encompassing the employee's performance, the manager's appraisal of it, and the communication between the two that comprises an ongoing performance-management system.

Of course, all the phases of recruiting and selecting employees are interrelated. But the final test of all phases comes with the appraisal of job performance. There is no point in reporting that, say, 150 possible candidates were recruited and screened, that 90 offers were extended, and that 65 candidates were hired and trained, if the first appraisal of their performance indicates that most were inept. Remember that, when you evaluate the performance of new hires, you are doing so within the context of a system, a network of human resource activities, and you are really appraising recruitment, selection, and training, among other HRM activities.

Recruitment policies ultimately depend on the structure and functioning of internal and external labor markets. Let us therefore discuss labor-market issues in some detail.

## Developing Recruitment Policies: Labor-Market Issues

A **labor market** is a geographical area within which the forces of supply (people looking for work) interact with the forces of demand (employers looking for people) and thereby determine the price of labor.[4] In a tight labor market, demand by employers exceeds the available supply of workers, which tends to exert upward pressure on wages. In a loose labor market, the reverse is true: The supply of workers exceeds employer demand, exerting downward pressure on wages. In recent years the labor markets for biomedical engineers, network systems and data communications analysts, financial examiners, and medical assistants have been fairly tight; wages for these jobs have been increasing steadily.[5] On the other hand, the labor markets for sewing machine operators, word processors, postal carriers, and telemarketers are projected to be extremely loose through 2018, thereby reducing pressure for wage increases for these workers.

Unfortunately, it is not possible to define the geographical boundaries of a labor market in any clear-cut manner.[6] Employers needing key employees will recruit far and wide if necessary. Indeed, for certain types of jobs and certain firms, the Internet has made recruitment from global labor markets a reality. In short, employers do not face a single, homogeneous market for labor but rather a series of discontinuous, segmented labor markets over which supply-and-demand conditions vary substantially.[7] Economists focus on this fact as the major explanation for wage differences among occupations and among geographical areas.

Of practical concern to managers, however, is a reasonably accurate definition of labor markets for planning purposes. Here are some factors that are important for defining the limits of a labor market:[8]

- Geography.
- Education and/or technical background required to perform a job.

# RECRUITMENT POLICIES

As a framework for setting recruitment policies, let us consider four different possible company postures:[a]

1. **Passive nondiscrimination** is a commitment to treat all races and both sexes equally in all decisions about hiring, promotion, and pay. No attempt is made to recruit actively among prospective minority applicants. This posture fails to recognize that discriminatory practices in the past may block prospective applicants from seeking present job opportunities.

2. **Pure diversity-based recruitment** is a concerted effort by the organization to actively expand the pool of applicants so that no one is excluded because of past or present discrimination. However, the decision to hire or to promote is based on the best-qualified individual, regardless of race or sex.

3. **Diversity-based recruitment with preferential hiring** goes further than pure diversity-based recruitment; it systematically favors women and minorities in hiring and promotion decisions. This is a "soft-quota" system.

4. **Hard quotas** represent a mandate to hire or promote specific numbers or proportions of women or minority group members.

Both private and government employers find hard quotas an unsavory strategy for rectifying the effects of past or present discrimination. Nevertheless, the courts have ordered temporary quotas in instances in which unfair discrimination has obviously taken place and where no other remedy is feasible.[b] Temporary quotas have bounds placed on them. For example, a judge might order an employer to hire two African-American employees for every white employee until the number of African-American employees reaches a certain percentage of the employer's workforce.

Passive nondiscrimination misses the mark. This became obvious as far back as 1968, when the secretary of labor publicly cited the Allen-Bradley Company of Milwaukee for failure to comply with Executive Order 11246 by not actively recruiting African Americans. The company was so well known in Milwaukee as a good place to work that it usually had a long waiting list of friends and relatives of current employees. As a matter of established business practice, the company preferred to hire referrals from current employees; almost no public recruiting was done for entry-level job openings. As a result, because almost all the present employees were white, so were almost all the referrals.[c]

As noted in Chapter 3's discussion of legal issues in employment, preferential selection is a sticky issue. However, in several landmark cases the Supreme Court established the following principle:[d] Staffing decisions must be made on a case-by-case basis; race or sex may be taken into account as one factor in an applicant's favor, but the overall decision to select or reject must be made on the basis of a combination of factors, such as entrance-test scores and previous performance. That leaves us with pure diversity-based recruitment as a recruitment and selection strategy. Indeed, in a free and open competitive labor market, that's the way it ought to be.

---

[a]Seligman, D. (1973, Mar.). How "equal opportunity" turned into employment quotas. *Fortune*, pp. 160–168.

[b]Replying in the affirmative (1987, Mar. 9). *Time*, p. 66.

[c]*Furnco Construction Corp. v. Waters*, 438 U.S. 567 (1978).

[d]*Gratz v. Bollinger*. (2003, June 23). 539 U.S. 244. See also *Grutter v. Bollinger*. (2003). 539 U.S. 306. See also Affirmative action upheld by high court as a remedy for past job discrimination (1986, July 3). *The New York Times*, pp. A1, B9.

- Industry.
- Licensing or certification requirements.
- Union membership.

Companies may use one or more of these factors to help define their labor markets. Thus, an agricultural-research firm that needs to hire four veterinarians cannot restrict its search to a local area since the market is national or international in scope. Union membership is not a concern in this market, but licensing and/or certification is. Typically a doctor of veterinary medicine degree is required along with state licensure to practice. Applicants are likely to be less concerned with where the job is located and more concerned with job design and career opportunities. On the other hand, suppose a brewery is trying to hire a master plumber. The brewery will be looking at a labor market defined primarily by geographic proximity and secondarily by people whose experience, technical background, and (possibly) willingness to join a union after employment qualify them for the job.

## Internal versus External Labor Markets

The discussion thus far has concerned the structure and function of external labor markets. Internal labor markets also affect recruitment policies (in many cases more directly) because firms often give preference to current employees in promotions, transfers, and other career-enhancing opportunities. Each employing unit is a separate market. At United Parcel Service (UPS), for example, virtually all jobs above the entry level are filled by internal promotion rather than by outside recruitment. UPS looks to its current employees as its source of labor supply, and workers look to this internal labor market to advance their careers. In the internal labor markets of most organizations, employees peddle their talents to available "buyers."[9] Three elements comprise the internal labor market:

- Formal and informal practices that determine how jobs are organized and described.
- Methods for choosing among candidates.
- Procedures and authorities through which potential candidates are generated by those responsible for filling open jobs.

In an open internal labor market, every available job is advertised throughout the organization and anyone can apply. Preference is given to internal candidates by withholding outside advertising until the job has been on the internal market for several days. Finally, each candidate for a job receives an interview.

## Recruitment Policies and Labor-Market Characteristics

A great deal of research suggests that employers change their policies in response to changes in market conditions.[10] For example, as labor becomes increasingly scarce, employers may change their policies in the following ways:

- Improving the characteristics of vacant positions, for example, by raising salaries or increasing training and educational benefits.
- Reducing hiring standards.
- Using more (and more expensive) recruiting methods.
- Extending searches over a wider geographical area.

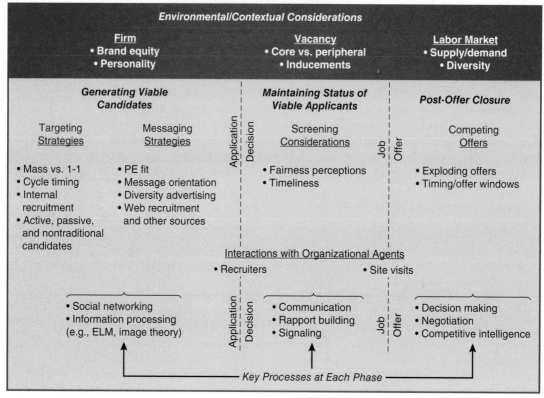

**Figure 6–2**

Framework of the recruitment process.*

*P-E = person-environment; ELM = elaboration likelihood model.

*Source:* Dineen, B. R., and Soltis, S. N. (2011). Recruitment: A review of research and emerging directions. In S. Zedeck (Ed.), *Handbook of Industrial and Organizational Psychology,* Vol. 2. Washington, D C: American Psychological Association, p. 46.

Before we address specific aspects of recruitment, let's consider an integrated model of the overall process.

## An Integrated Model of the Recruitment Process

Figure 6–2 serves as an overarching framework for many of the topics we will discuss in this chapter. It integrates earlier views of recruitment in terms of sequential stages, while also integrating contextual/environmental and "key-process" issues. As shown in Figure 6–2, two key decision points (application decision and job offer) separate these primary recruitment stages. Within each stage, the framework also identifies important subcategories.

Three contextual/environmental features affect all recruitment efforts, namely, characteristics of the firm (the value of its "brand" and its "personality"), characteristics of the vacancy itself (is it mission critical?), and characteristics of the labor markets in which an organization recruits. Likewise, three sequential stages characterize recruitment efforts: generating a pool of viable candidates, maintaining the status (or interest) of viable candidates, and "getting to yes" after making a job offer (post-offer closure).

Figure 6–2 also identifies key activities that affect each of these three stages. These include strategies for targeting potential candidates, and for communicating information to them ("messaging strategies"); issues related to screening viable candidates and to interactions with organizational agents (recruiters, managers, and employees encountered during site visits); and issues related to actual job offers (e.g., timing, "exploding" offers that disappear after specified periods of time). Finally, Figure 6–2 identifies some key processes that affect the outcomes of each stage of the recruitment process, for example, social networking and information processing (seen through the lens of the Elaboration Likelihood Model)[11] at the candidate-generation stage; communication, rapport-building, and signaling to maintain viable candidates; and negotiation, decision making, and competitive intelligence at the post–job-offer stage. Space constraints prevent us from discussing each of the issues, activities, and processes shown in Figure 11–1, but we present it here because it is rich in implications for advancing both the theory and practice of recruitment. Now let's begin by considering recruitment planning.

## RECRUITMENT PLANNING

Recruitment begins with a clear specification of (1) the number of people needed (e.g., through workforce forecasts and utilization analyses) and (2) when they are needed. Implicit in the latter is a time frame—the duration between the receipt of a résumé and the time a new hire starts work. This time frame is sometimes referred to as the recruitment pipeline. The flow of events through the pipeline is represented as in Table 6–1. The table shows that if an operating manager sends a requisition for a new hire to the HR department today, it will take almost a month and a half, 43 days on average, before an employee fulfilling that requisition actually starts work. Time to fill an open requisition is important in pivotal jobs, those that have a direct impact on firm success, but it can be misleading, especially if measures of the quality of new hires are ignored.[12] Here are simple examples: It is one thing to know that a firm's sales openings average 75 days to fill. It's another thing to know that the difference between filling them in 75 vs. 50 days costs the firm $30 million revenue, or that a 20% improvement in quality-of-hire will result in $18 million productivity improvement.[13]

### Table 6–1

#### AVERAGE TIME SPAN FOR EVENTS IN A RECRUITMENT PIPELINE

| Sequence of events | | |
| --- | --- | --- |
| From | To | Average number of days |
| Résumé | Invitation | 5 |
| Invitation | Interview | 6 |
| Interview | Offer | 4 |
| Offer | Acceptance | 7 |
| Acceptance | Report to work | <u>21</u> |
| Total length of the pipeline | | 43 |

One study of *Fortune* 500 firms found that the average firm cut about six days off its hiring cycle by posting jobs online instead of in newspapers, another four days by taking online applications instead of paper ones, and more than a week by screening and processing applications electronically.[14] A key assumption, however, is that intervals between events in the pipeline proceed as planned. In fact, longitudinal research indicates that delays in the timing of recruitment events are perceived very negatively by candidates, especially high-quality ones, and often cost job acceptances.[15]

## INTERNAL RECRUITMENT

In deciding where, when, and how to implement recruitment activities, initial consideration should be given to a company's current employees, especially for filling jobs above the entry level. If external recruitment efforts are undertaken without considering the desires, capabilities, and potential of present employees, a firm may incur both short- and long-run costs. In the short run, morale may degenerate; in the long run, firms with a reputation for consistent neglect of in-house talent may find it difficult to attract new employees and retain experienced ones. This is why soundly conceived action plans (that incorporate developmental and training needs) and leadership-succession plans are so important.

One of the thorniest issues confronting internal recruitment is the reluctance of managers to grant permission for their subordinates to be interviewed for potential transfer or promotion. To overcome this aversion, promotion-from-within policies must receive strong top-management support, coupled with a company philosophy that permits employees to consider available opportunities within the organization and incentives for managers to release them. At Dell, pay is now determined, in part, by how well a manager does at nurturing people. At 3M, monthly talent reviews by all managers in a particular function (e.g., manufacturing, R&D, sales) help ensure that high-potential employees get noticed.[16]

Among the channels available for internal recruitment, the most popular ones are succession plans (discussed in Chapter 5), job posting, employee referrals, and temporary worker pools.

### Job Posting

Advertising available jobs internally began in the early days of affirmative action, as a means of providing equal opportunity for women and minorities to compete. It served as a method of getting around the "old boy" network, where jobs sometimes were filled more by "who you knew" than by "what you knew." Today **job posting** is an established practice in many organizations, especially for filling jobs up to lower-executive levels.

Openings are published on company intranets, on bulletin boards, or in company newsletters. Interested employees must reply within a specified number of days, and they may or may not have to obtain the consent of their immediate supervisors.[17] Some job-posting systems apply only to the plant or office in which a job is located, while other companies will relocate employees.

Nortel Networks contracted with Monster.com to create its own job board, called Job Shop. Says the firm's director of internal mobility, "I want to make it drop-dead easy to find your next opportunity internally." The goal is to provide an internal version of what is available in the outside market, thereby redistributing talent within Nortel's growing businesses and preventing employees from leaving for competitors. Any employee can post a résumé on Job Shop without alerting his or her superior, and any manager can post a job opening. The system automatically alerts managers' superiors after openings are posted.[18]

While there are clear advantages to job posting, if no limits are placed on the bidding process, job-posting systems can impose substantial administrative costs. Thus, at some firms, employees cannot bid on a new job until at least one year after hire, and they must have accrued at least six months' tenure in their current jobs before becoming eligible to bid for new ones.[19]

Another problem might arise from poor communication. For example, if employees who unsuccessfully apply for open jobs do not receive feedback that might help them to be more competitive in the future, and if they have to find out through the grapevine that someone else got the job they applied for, a job-posting program cannot be successful. The lesson for managers is obvious: Regular communication and follow-up feedback are essential if job posting is to work properly.

Employee referrals can be an excellent source of new hires at all levels.

## Employee Referrals

Referral of job candidates by current employees has been and continues to be a major source of new hires at many levels, including professionals. It is an internal recruitment method; that is, internal rather than external sources are used to attract candidates. Typically such programs offer a cash or merchandise bonus when a current employee refers a successful candidate to fill a job opening. The logic behind employee referral is that "it takes one to know one." Interestingly, the rate of employee participation seems to remain unaffected by such efforts as higher cash bonuses, cars, or expense-paid trips.[20] This suggests that good employees will not refer potentially undesirable candidates even if the rewards are outstanding.

### What's New in Employee Referrals?[21]

When current employees recommend new hires, companies gain access to pools of talent they might not normally attract, particularly in the case of highly specialized positions that might be difficult to fill through conventional channels. That's because people tend to associate with others in their professions. The game-development division of Redmond, WA–based Nintendo is typical. Says Nintendo recruiting specialist Helen Fu, "Most of our hires are referred by other employees. It's a specialized skill set, a tight-knit community." Referrals work for many other jobs as well. Prudential considers its employees "talent ambassadors." They can earn between $500 and $2,500 for each successful referral, depending on the job level. Hiring managers are not required to hire a referral over a more qualified candidate—decisions are based on skills, experience, and qualifications—but they give serious consideration to those candidates who are referred by Prudential employees.

At Vistaprint, a print company focused on business cards and brochures, the company's "Everyone Here Is a Recruiter" program offers a $1,500 referral award for each successful hire, and a home-theater system for the employee with the most referrals hired. "At the end of that first year of the program, employee referrals jumped from 19% to 42%," said Kevin Murray, director of recruiting at the firm. Today it's more than 50 percent.

Another benefit of such a program is that it can provide the employer with a source of passive candidates—those workers who are not actively seeking new jobs. This not only expands the employer's pool of potential candidates but also tends to produce higher-quality candidates. Zynga, the popular social-gaming company, expects to double its 1,500-person workforce in one year. It uses software to match prospective hires with current employees who have worked with candidates previously, attended the same college, or share a similar interest, such as skiing. It then asks its employees to place an initial call to the target and talk about Zynga.

Be careful though. Some competing businesses may retaliate against your company for stealing their happily employed workers via employee-referral programs. To maintain good relations among companies that compete against each other, some companies have forged agreements not to make cold calls to employees that each company places on a do-not-call list. Many Silicon Valley companies, for example, both compete and cooperate with each other to jointly develop new products and services. A company may be less likely to collaborate on a project if it fears the partner company is intent on hiring away its best employees, thus undermining innovation. That may be so, but six leading technology companies—Apple, Google, Adobe, Pixar, Intuit, and Intel—recently reached an antitrust settlement with the Justice Department that increases the competition for sought-after technology workers. They agreed to abandon their arrangements not to cold-call each other's employees. The result? Expect even more competition for the best and the brightest.

Some firms have created online alumni networks to find and rehire former employees. From Dow Chemical to JPMorgan Chase, companies are urging former employees to maintain ties as members of the broader corporate team, almost like grads of the same alma mater, even if they end up moving to competing companies. Alumni networks follow an important principle of the knowledge economy: Personal connections transcend corporate boundaries. Throughout their careers, people in such networks can benefit from each other's knowledge, contacts, and referrals.[22]

Three factors seem to be instrumental in the prescreening process of referrals: the morale of present employees, the accuracy and detail of job information, and the closeness of the intermediary friend.[23] While employee referrals clearly have advantages, it is important to note that from an EEO perspective, employee referrals are fine as long as the workforce is diverse in gender, race, and ethnicity to begin with. A potential disadvantage, at least for some firms, is that employee referrals tend to perpetuate the perspective and belief systems of the current workforce. This may not be the best way to go for organizations that are trying to promote changes in strategy, outlook, or orientation.

## Temporary Worker Pools

Unlike workers supplied from temporary agencies, in-house "temporaries" work directly for the hiring organization and may receive benefits, depending on the number of scheduled hours worked per week. Temporary workers (e.g., in clerical jobs, accounting, and word processing) help meet fluctuating labor demands due to such factors as illness, vacations, terminations, and resignations. Companies save on commissions to outside agencies, which may be as high as 50 percent or more of a temporary employee's hourly wages.[24]

Long after the 2007–2009 economic recession ended, organizations increased temporary hires and avoided hiring full-time employees. To a large extent this was due to uncertainty surrounding the sustainability of an economic recovery. In a recent poll, however, the top reasons for hiring temporary workers are to work on specific projects (27 percent of respondents) and to provide extra staff during business or seasonal cycles (25 percent). A quarter of respondents reported that their organizations sometimes move temporary workers to full-time positions, but 64 percent of respondents rarely or never move a temporary worker into a full-time position.[25]

In-house temporary employees are generally protected by the same civil rights laws, worksite safety requirements, minimum wage and overtime provisions, and other labor and employment laws.[26] From a management perspective, it is especially important to survey customers (in-house departments that use temporary workers) periodically to ensure that they are meeting customer expectations. If not, then corrective action is necessary.

## EXTERNAL RECRUITMENT

To meet demands for talent brought about by business growth, a desire for fresh ideas, or to replace employees who leave, organizations periodically turn to the outside labor market. Keep in mind, however, that the recruitment practices of

## START-UP RED 5 STUDIOS LURES "PASSIVE" JOB CANDIDATES*

When a FedEx box landed on the desk of video-game designer Scott Youngblood, he was curious. Inside he found a glossy box nestled in thick foam. Inside that box was another, and, within that one, another. Eventually Mr. Youngblood opened five boxes, nested Russian-doll style, and discovered an IPod shuffle music player engraved with his name. He pressed "play," and heard the voice of Mark Kern, president and chef executive of Red 5 Studios, Inc., talking about Mr. Youngblood's past work on games and inviting him to a Web site to learn more about Red 5.

"I was blown away," says Mr. Youngblood. Within two weeks he interviewed at Red 5. About a month after that, he started a new job there—leaving his position at Sony Corp.'s Sony Computer Entertainment America, and moving more than 800 miles away.

Mr. Youngblood's package was one of 100 that Red 5 sent to its "dream hires," identified through a concerted recruiting campaign. While the project did draw the interest it hoped for, it was costly and time-consuming, and the firm does not plan to repeat it soon. It probably doesn't have to. Its résumé flow is about 10 times what it was before the campaign, it forged key relationships even with those who did not accept the firm's hiring offers, it boosted the firm's cachet within the industry, and it triggered a wave of blog postings from gamers, recruiters, and marketers.

*Source: Covel, S. (2007, June 4). Start-up lures talent with creative pitch. *The Wall Street Journal*, p. B4. Reprinted by permission of *The Wall Street Journal*, Copyright © (2007) Dow Jones & Company, Inc. All Rights Reserved Worldwide. License number 2781980968807.

large and small firms differ considerably. Larger firms tend to be more formal and bureaucratic than smaller firms. (See the Red 5 Studios HR Buzz example above.) In addition, many job seekers have distinct preferences regarding firm size, and they actively seek those types of employers to the exclusion of those who do not meet their preferences. It might be argued, therefore, that large and small firms comprise separate labor markets.[27] In this section we describe four of the most popular recruitment sources: university relations, executive search firms, employment agencies, and recruitment advertising. Because they are both time consuming and expensive, large employers are more likely to use university relations and executive search firms.

## University Relations

What used to be known as "college recruiting" is now considerably broader in many companies. Companies have targeted certain schools that best meet their needs and have broadened the scope of their interactions with them.[28] Such activities may now include—in addition to recruitment—gifts and grants to the institutions, summer employment and consulting projects for faculty, and invitations to placement officers to visit company plants and offices. In 2010, for example, the ExxonMobil Foundation provided $42.6 million in unrestricted grants to U.S. universities and colleges.[29]

PricewaterhouseCoopers (PwC) is an example of a company that works college campuses aggressively. It focuses on four main areas: early identification, team involvement, ongoing activities, and internships. PwC identifies promising students through involvement in campus clubs and participation in classrooms and presentations. At the same time, a senior member of the company—often a partner—coordinates PwC's recruiting/business efforts and meets regularly with faculty and deans. That person treats the university as a client and is supported by a recruiter. The company supports student activities but also builds relationships with faculty and deans. "Students are changing on a yearly basis," says the partner responsible for college recruiting in the United States, "but the faculty and deans are there for a long time. We have ongoing dialogues with them about what is happening in our business today, and what we're looking for."[30]

To enhance the yield from campus recruitment efforts, employers should consider the following research-based guidelines:[31]

1. Establish a "presence" on college campuses beyond just the on-campus interviewing period (as ExxonMobil has done).
2. Upgrade the content and specificity of recruiting materials. Many are far too general in nature. Instead, provide more detailed information about the characteristics of entry-level jobs, especially those that have had a significant positive effect on the decisions of prior applicants to join the organization. For example, consultants Booz Allen Hamilton launched a Web site featuring consultants as they work on projects for pro bono clients. Visitors to the site can follow consultants' progress and see how they deal with clients, team members, and their friends and families outside of work. The weekly episodes are edited video clips rather than live streaming video, and each one features interactive questions and answers plus detailed information about each of the project's consultants.[32]
3. Devote more time and resources to training on-campus interviewers to answer specific, job-related questions from applicants.
4. For those candidates who are invited for onsite company visits, provide itineraries and agendas prior to their arrival. Written materials should answer candidates' questions dealing with travel arrangements, expense reimbursements, and whom to contact at the company and how.
5. Ensure that the attributes of vacant positions are comparable to those of competitors. This is true for large and small organizations. Some of the key job attributes that influence the decisions of applicants are the opportunities for creativity or to exercise initiative, promotional opportunities, location of work, and company culture. Fully 46 percent of Generation Y is prepared to forego pay or promotion to work for an organization with a good reputation. That number rises to 48 percent for Gen X and to 53 percent for baby boomers.[33]

## Virtual Job Fairs

Driven in part by technology for popular video games that makes it possible to create ever more realistic scenarios, **virtual job fairs** now have the ability to use video, voice, and text to connect job seekers with recruiters, and to span time zones and continents in the process. At a virtual job fair, online visitors see a setup that is very similar to a physical one. They can listen to presentations, visit booths, leave résumés and business cards, participate in live chats, and get contact information from recruiters, HR managers, and even hiring managers. A third party—a college, a publication, or an association—that brings together companies runs most such job fairs.

For example, in the public-relations field, *PRWeek* magazine hosted a day-long virtual job fair attended by 13 companies and 1,000 job seekers. Each booth received an average of 563 visitors, and at the end of the event, recruiters received a report that tracked all visitors. The $4,700 that companies paid *PRWeek* covered the costs of the booth, the tracking report, and a 10-second pop-up ad. Recruiters liked the fact that they could span time zones and staff their booths with qualified representatives without having to pay travel or booth-construction costs. Candidates enjoyed visiting several companies without leaving their desks, along with the knowledge that they would not run into the HR manager from their company at the next booth.[34]

## Executive Search Firms

Executive search firms are typically retained to recruit for senior-level positions that command salaries that exceed $150,000. The reasons for doing so may include a need to maintain confidentiality from an incumbent or a competitor, a lack of local resources to recruit executive-level individuals, or insufficient time. To use an executive search consultant most effectively requires time and commitment from the hiring organization. It must allow the consultant to become a company "insider" and to develop knowledge and familiarity with the business, its strategic plans, and its key players.[35]

Although using an executive search firm has advantages, employers evaluating a search firm should carefully consider the following indications that the firms can do competent work:[36]

- The firm has defined its market position by industries rather than by disciplines or as a jack-of-all-trades.
- The firm understands how your organization functions within the industries served.
- The firm is performance oriented and compensates the search salesperson substantially on the basis of assignment completion.
- The firm combines the research and recruiting responsibilities into one function. Doing so allows the researcher/recruiter to make a more comprehensive and knowledgeable presentation to targeted candidates on behalf of the client.
- The firm is organized to function as a task force in the search for candidates, particularly where they are being recruited for multiple assignments or when placement speed is essential.
- The firm is a member of the Association of Executive Search Consultants (AESC) and subscribes to AESC's professional practice guidelines and code of ethics.
- The firm provides the client a full understanding of the services to be provided; the method of operation; any limitations that may affect the search; who is handling the assignment; and the totality of fees, expenses, and other expectations.

Compared with other recruitment sources, executive search firms are quite expensive. Total fees may reach 30 to 35 percent of the compensation package of the new hire, although more clients are now negotiating fixed-fee arrangements. Fees are often paid as follows: a retainer amounting to one-third the total fee as soon as the search is commissioned; one-third 60 days into the assignment; and a final third upon completion, plus expenses. If an organization hires a candidate on its own prior to the completion of the search, it still must pay all or some portion of the search firm's fee, unless it makes other arrangements.[37]

## Employment Agencies

Employment agencies are some of the most widely available and widely used outside sources. However, there is great variability in size and quality across agencies. To achieve the best results from this channel, cultivate a small number of firms and thoroughly describe the characteristics (e.g., education, training, experience) of candidates needed, the fee structure, and the method of resolving disputes. Be aware, however, that the Equal Employment Opportunity Commission's enforcement guidance is quite clear that there is no defense if a temporary staffing agency participates in a discriminatory staffing request from the client company.[38]

Most major temporary agencies act also as employment agencies, usually with the employer paying the fees. Manpower, Kelly, Office Mates, and Olsten (among many others) have direct-hire (fee paid by employer), or temporary-to-hire fee arrangements. With the latter, a temporary employee must either stay on the payroll for temporaries a certain number of weeks or the employer must pay a fee, depending on the salary range of the new hire.[39]

## Recruitment Advertising

Most people think of recruitment advertising as want ads in the local newspaper or trade magazine. Think again. This medium has become just as colorful, lively, and imaginative as consumer advertising. Today companies approach job candidates in much the same way as they approach prospective customers: Candidates are carefully identified and targeted, attracted to the company and its brand, and then sold on the job.

Corporate home pages on the Internet are often designed with potential recruits in mind, because they are frequently the first place job seekers look when they begin to evaluate companies. On their home pages, many companies highlight links to information about diversity, employee benefits, and balancing work and family. JPMorgan Chase, Electronic Arts, Accenture, and Enterprise Rent-a-Car are just some of the many companies that provide compelling materials on their Web sites about why people should work there.

---

### HELP WANTED                                                    HR BUZZ

It is no exaggeration to say that the Internet has revolutionized recruitment practice. For job seekers, there are more than 35,000 sites with literally millions of listings, as well as the ability to research employers and to network.[a] Fully 94 percent of the top 500 U.S. companies recruit via the Internet. Indeed, the only surprise may be that 6 percent aren't.[b] About a third of LinkedIn's revenue comes from corporate customers who buy rights for their recruiters to use LinkedIn's software as a service. At the same time, thousands of corporate recruiters are scouring Monster's database of more than 80 million employee profiles and résumés, 73 percent of which are from people who aren't actively seeking new jobs. In fact, corporate recruiters are increasingly acting like external search firms, hacking into the internal directories of competitors and raiding their employees.[c]

*Online Job Search*

In short, the Internet is where the action is in recruiting. Despite the allure of commercial job search sites, evidence indicates that nearly 60 percent of all Internet hires come from a company's own Web site.[d] The best ones make it simple for candidates to apply for jobs. They provide a wealth of information about the company, and leave candidates with a favorable impression.[e] Only about a third as many corporate job openings as were listed on corporate Web sites were posted on the three biggest job boards.[f] For senior executives who earn at least six figures, Forbes.com recommends the following sites: Netshare.com, Flipdog.com, Wetfeet.com, Spencerstuart.com, and Quintcareers.com.

Despite the reach and apparent ease that online searches offer, a surprisingly small proportion of jobs get filled that way. One study found that only 13 percent of external hires currently occur through any Internet site (excluding LinkedIn, which is categorized as "direct sourcing"), compared with 61 percent for networking with friends, family, or colleagues.[g] For that reason, online networking sites—such as LinkedIn, Facebook, Doostang, and Ryze—have become increasingly important to job seekers. Geared toward professional relationships, networking Web sites allow their members to build a web of social and business associates and to interact person-to-person with new contacts.[h] As an example, consider SilkRoad Technology's OpenHire 5.0. Once you've submitted your resume to a job site using OpenHire 5.0, you can view potential connections between the organization and your existing professional network. Aggregators such as Indeed.com and Simply-jobs.com go even farther. They examine thousands of job boards and employer sites free of charge. Both tell you what LinkedIn contacts you have at a company posting a job. That lets you follow up your job application with an e-mail to a colleague to request a referral or to set up an introduction to someone who can.[i]

---

[a]Cohen, J. (2001, May). Net a job. *Working Mother,* pp. 23–27.

[b]MacMillan, D. (2007, May 7). The art of the online résumé. *BusinessWeek,* p. 86.

[c]Ibid. See also Hempel, J. (2010, April 12). How LinkedIn will fire up your career. *Fortune,* pp. 74–82. See also Boyle, M. (2009, July 6). Enough to make Monster tremble. *Businessweek,* pp. 43–45.

[d]Forster, S. (2003, Sept. 15). The best way to recruit new workers and to find a job. *The Wall Street Journal,* p. R8.

[e]Frase-Blunt, M. (2004, Apr.). Make a good first impression. *HRMagazine* 49(4), 80–86.

[f]Steel, E. (2007), op. cit. See also Maher, K. (2003a, Jan. 14). Corporations cut middlemen and do their own recruiting. *The Wall Street Journal,* p. B10.

[g]Sixty percent of jobs are filled through referrals. (2011, May 10). Retrieved from *http://blog. resumebear.com/changing-careers/60-percent-of-jobs-are-filled-through-referrals/* on July 7, 2011. See also McGregor, J. (2010, June 14). Job sites: Are they worth it? *Fortune,* pp. 45, 46.

[h]Job sites: Reviews. (2008, Jan.). Retrieved from *http://www.consumersearch.com/www/internet/ job-sites* on May 22, 2008. See also Kadlec, D. (2007, Oct.). You oughta be in Facebook. *Money,* p. 44.

[i]Sixty percent of jobs, 2011, op. cit. See also McGregor, 2010, op. cit.

## Special Inducements—Relocation Aid, Help for the Trailing Spouse, and Sign-On Bonuses

Especially with higher-level jobs, newly recruited managers expect some form of relocation assistance. A basic package includes household-goods assistance; an allowance (usually equivalent to 2–4 weeks' salary) to cover incidental expenses; help with the sale of the relocating employee's home; covering the employee's loss, if any, on the sale of the home; and transportation costs for the final move to the new location, including hotels and meals during transit.[40] Fewer employers, however are offering temporary relocation benefits (28% in 2010 versus 43% in 2006) or location-visit assistance (20% in 2010 versus 40% in 2006). Moreover, about 80 percent of companies now have "tiered" mobility policies, offering different levels of mobility to senior-level and high-potential talent than they offer mid-level employees. Homeowner or renter status is a basis for placing employees in different mobility tiers that contain different housing subsidies.[41]

Prodded by the emergence of the dual-career family—75 percent of all families[42]—firms are finding that many managers and professionals, men and women alike, are reluctant to relocate unless the spouse will be able to find suitable employment in a new location. "If I can't work, I won't move." That is what more and more companies are hearing from the spouses of prospective transferees, and it is not music to their ears.[43] Spouse employment assistance typically includes job counseling, fees to placement agencies, contacts outside the company, and the costs of printing résumés.[44]

An increasingly common recruiting inducement, independent of any relocation assistance, is the sign-on bonus. Originally used in the sports world, signing bonuses are now common among executives, professionals (particularly in high-technology firms), and middle-level executives, as companies seek to buttress the eroding bonds between them and their employees. For example, to lure former stockbrokers who are willing to retrain to become financial advisers to wealthy clients, banking giant UBS offers signing bonuses equal to 100 percent of the revenue a broker produced in the previous 12 months.[45]

What's a company to do if things don't work out and the new person simply walks away with the cash? Firms such as General Electric and Owens-Corning require that the entire amount be repaid if the person leaves within one year, and 50 percent if he or she leaves within two years. After that, the repayment gradually drops to zero.[46]

## Summary of Findings Regarding Recruitment Sources

Now that we have examined some of the most popular sources for internal and external recruiting, it seems reasonable to ask, "Which sources are most popular with employers and job applicants?" Among employers, evidence indicates that

- Informal contacts are used widely and effectively at all occupational levels. In fact, word-of-mouse (informal, Web-based conversations about companies) is viewed as more credible and associated with higher organizational attractiveness than Web-based testimonials.[47]
- Use of public employment services declines as required skills levels increase.
- The internal market is a major recruitment source except for entry-level, unskilled, and semiskilled workers.
- Larger firms are the most frequent users of walk-ins, write-ins, and the internal market.[48]

In practice, most applicants use more than one recruitment source to learn about jobs. Hence, designation of *the* recruitment source they used is misleading and completely ignores the combined effect of multiple sources. In fact, the accumulated evidence on the relationship between recruitment sources, turn-over, and job performance suggests that such relationships are quite weak.[49] In light of these results, what may be more important than the source per se is how much support and information accompanies source usage, or the extent to which a source embeds prescreening on desired applicant characteristics.[50]

## DIVERSITY-ORIENTED RECRUITING

Special measures are called for in diversity-oriented recruiting. While it might appear obvious that employers should use women and members of underrepresented groups (1) in their HR offices as interviewers; (2) on recruiting trips to high schools, colleges, and job fairs; and (3) in employment advertisements, these are necessary, but not sufficient, steps. Diverse candidates consider broader factors in their decisions to apply or to remain with organizations. In fact, a recent WetFeet.com study found that although as many as 44 percent of African-American candidates said they eliminated a company from consideration because of a lack of gender or ethnic diversity, three other diversity-related attributes affected their decisions to apply or remain: the ready availability of training and career-development programs, the presence of a diverse upper management, and the presence of a diverse workforce.[51]

Employers need to establish contacts in the groups targeted for recruitment based on credibility between the employer and the contact, and credibility between the contact and the targeted groups. This is known as *relationship recruiting*. Allow plenty of lead time for the contacts in the targeted groups to notify prospective applicants and for the applicants to apply for available positions.

Various community or professional organizations might be contacted (e.g., Society of Mexican-American Engineers and Scientists, National Society of Black Engineers), and leaders of those organizations should be encouraged to visit the employer and talk with employees. Another source is *Finding Diversity*, a comprehensive listing of more than 300 diversity recruitment tools.[52] It includes Web sites, e-mail lists, newspapers, magazines, journals, career fairs, conferences, and other resources to help recruiters search for talent.

Finally, recognize two things: (1) It will take time to establish a credible, workable diversity-oriented recruitment program, and (2) there is no payoff from passive nondiscrimination. Progressive organizations gather data on who, when, and where they recruit, and how they fare with different groups. The goal is to create a consistent corporate image that will support recruiting efforts across the board.[53]

## MANAGING RECRUITMENT OPERATIONS

Administratively, recruitment is one of the easiest activities to foul up—with potentially long-term negative publicity for the firm. Traditionally, recruitment was intensively paper based. Today, however, the entire process has been reengineered so that it is computer based. Here is an example of one such system.

With Hiring Gateway from Yahoo! Resumix, automation replaces the entire manual process. Hiring Gateway is a Web-based recruiting and hiring process that takes companies from job requisitions through matching candidate qualifications to documented job requirements, then through the interviewing and hiring decision-and-offer process, to finally having new hires report on board. The software creates a self-service environment that allows hiring managers to create requisitions, permits candidates automatically to upload and edit their résumé information, and allows recruiters to use its "KnowledgeBase" technology to create statements of qualifications that are tied to each individual job as well as to apply screening questions and keyword searches, among other filters.

Hiring Gateway analytics allow recruiters to create many different kinds of reports, such as source effectiveness for different types of jobs and levels, measures of the performance of individual recruiters, measures of the performance of new hires, EEO reporting, and analysis of the database for volume and types of candidates. Figure 6–3 shows a typical screen from an applicant-tracking system. The job in question is "HR Generalist/Benefits Manager." In the Hiring Gateway system, KnowledgeBase software helps build the profile of required skills and competencies for any given job. The various column headings show status updates for each candidate. The radio buttons at the bottom of the screen make it easy to navigate to various screens, to show a candidate's history, or to update his or her status.

Developed over the past 15 years, KnowledgeBase search-and-extraction technology draws on more than 20,000 business competencies and 250,000 rules related to various job skills and qualifications. For example, it

- Recognizes the contextual meanings of words within the résumé. Thus, it can distinguish between John Harvard, a candidate; 140 Harvard Street, an address; Harvard University, a school; and Harvard, ID, a town. Simple

**Figure 6–3**

A typical applicant-tracking system.

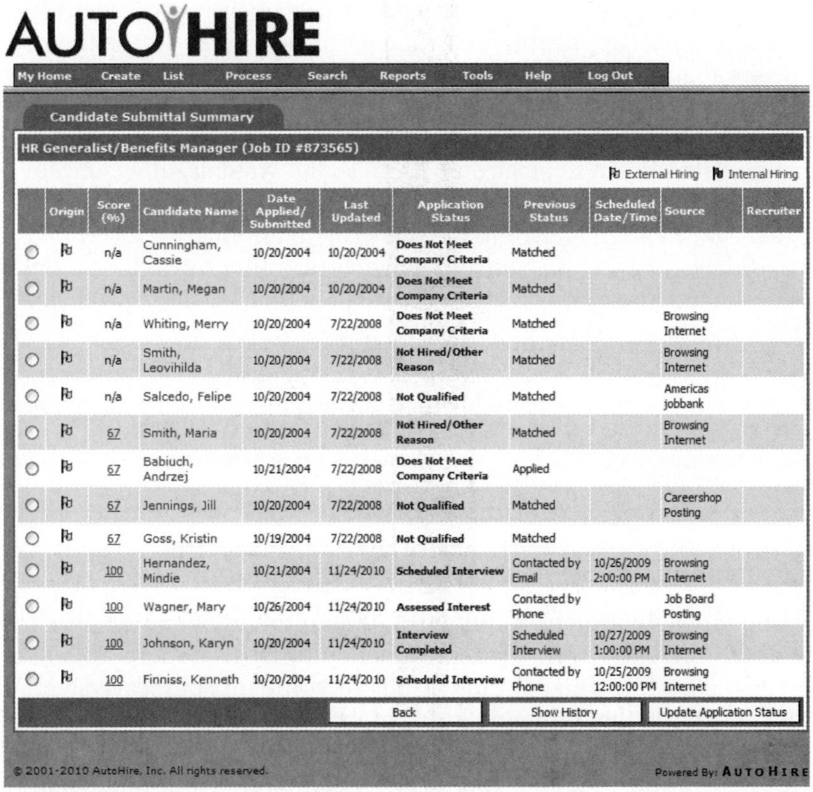


| | Origin | Score (%) | Candidate Name | Date Applied/ Submitted | Last Updated | Application Status | Previous Status | Scheduled Date/Time | Source | Recruiter |
|---|---|---|---|---|---|---|---|---|---|---|
| | | n/a | Cunningham, Cassie | 10/20/2004 | 10/20/2004 | Does Not Meet Company Criteria | Matched | | | |
| | | n/a | Martin, Megan | 10/20/2004 | 10/20/2004 | Does Not Meet Company Criteria | Matched | | | |
| | | n/a | Whiting, Merry | 10/20/2004 | 7/22/2008 | Does Not Meet Company Criteria | Matched | | Browsing Internet | |
| | | n/a | Smith, Leovihilda | 10/20/2004 | 7/22/2008 | Not Hired/Other Reason | Matched | | Browsing Internet | |
| | | n/a | Salcedo, Felipe | 10/20/2004 | 7/22/2008 | Not Qualified | Matched | | Americas jobbank | |
| | | 67 | Smith, Maria | 10/20/2004 | 7/22/2008 | Not Hired/Other Reason | Matched | | Browsing Internet | |
| | | 67 | Babiuch, Andrzej | 10/21/2004 | 7/22/2008 | Does Not Meet Company Criteria | Applied | | | |
| | | 67 | Jennings, Jill | 10/20/2004 | 7/22/2008 | Not Qualified | Matched | | Careershop Posting | |
| | | 67 | Goss, Kristin | 10/19/2004 | 7/22/2008 | Not Qualified | Matched | | | |
| | | 100 | Hernandez, Mindie | 10/21/2004 | 11/24/2010 | Scheduled Interview | Contacted by Email | 10/26/2009 2:00:00 PM | Browsing Internet | |
| | | 100 | Wagner, Mary | 10/26/2004 | 11/24/2010 | Assessed Interest | Contacted by Phone | | Job Board Posting | |
| | | 100 | Johnson, Karyn | 10/20/2004 | 11/24/2010 | Interview Completed | Scheduled Interview | 10/27/2009 1:00:00 PM | Browsing Internet | |
| | | 100 | Finniss, Kenneth | 10/20/2004 | 11/24/2010 | Scheduled Interview | Contacted by Phone | 10/25/2009 12:00:00 PM | Browsing Internet | |

*Source:* AutoHire. Retrieved from http://bit.ly/sGnUXi on November 17, 2011.

keyword-based systems are much less efficient because they will return all résumés containing the word "Harvard." Those resumes will then require subsequent analysis and classification.

- Distinguishes qualitative differences in experience, such as candidates who state that they *are* the manager versus those who state that they *report* to the manager.
- Knows when and how to draw logical inferences, such as using "experience managing a fast-growing team" as a proxy for "team-building skills."
- Understands different résumés that contain industry-specific terminology, syntax, and lingo.

Using integrated communication tools such as Yahoo! Instant Messenger, online scheduling, and automatic e-mail reminder alerts, Hiring Gateway enables recruiters, hiring managers, and interviewers to collaborate easily and intuitively in real time to pursue their top candidates.

How does the system work in practice? Firms such as Lockheed Martin, NASA, Citigroup, ChevronTexaco, and Allstate have found that Yahoo! Resumix has cut their cost-per-hire by up to 50 percent and shortened their hiring cycles by an average of 48 percent.[54] That's a competitive advantage! Hiring Gateway is a type of hiring management system. Here are others.

---

**HR BUZZ**

## MANAGEMENT SYSTEMS TO TRACK AND CONTACT APPLICANTS

Application service providers such as Kenexa 2x, Taleo, nowHire, and ICIMS enable companies to tap into sophisticated hiring management systems (HMSs). Such systems collect applications in a standardized format, screen them, determine where they came from (e.g., job boards or classified ads), monitor the progress of applications, and calculate how long it takes to fill various jobs (Kenexa 2x) or to get a new employee working productively (Taleo). All the application data remain in electronic form, so the systems allow employers to act quickly on the applications—checking references, getting comments from hiring managers, and making e-mail contact with applicants. JobApp even allows candidates to apply in multiple languages, either by Web or by phone.[a] Many large companies today use the latest-generation HMS software, and new software is available to help small companies as well.[b]

---

[a] JobApp Network. Hiring Management System. Retrieved from *www.jobappnetwork.com/hiring-management-system.aspx* on July 8, 2011. See also Cappelli, 2009, op. cit.

[b] Flandez, R. (2009, May 11). Resume overload: New software helps small companies keep up with the swarm of applicants. *The Wall Street Journal*, p. R5.

---

## Evaluation and Control of Recruitment Operations

The reason for evaluating past and current recruitment operations is simple: to improve the efficiency of future recruitment efforts. To do this, it is necessary to analyze the performance of the various recruitment sources systematically. Consider collecting the following kinds of information:[55]

- Cost of operations, that is, labor costs of company recruitment staff, operational costs (e.g., recruiting staff's travel and living expenses, agency fees, advertising expenses, brochures, supplies, and postage), and overhead expenses (e.g., rental of temporary facilities and equipment).

- Cost per hire, by source (firms vary considerably in the elements they use to compute this figure, but the four most common factors are advertising and event costs, online/Internet services, third-party agency contracts and fees, and recruiter fees).[56]
- Number and quality of résumés by source.
- Acceptance/offer ratio.
- Analysis of postvisit and rejection questionnaires.
- Salary offered—acceptances versus rejections.

These are operational measures of the recruitment function. Keep in mind though, that while any number of cost and quality analyses are possible, choose those that are strategically most relevant to your organization. In addition, strive to link staffing performance to business outcomes. To do that, metrics should express themselves in dollars. As we noted earlier, it is one thing to know that a firm's sales openings average 75 days to fill. It's another thing to know that the difference between filling them in 75 vs. 50 days costs the firm $30 million in revenue, or that a 20% improvement in quality-of-hire will result in $18 million productivity improvement.[57]

Several studies have examined the recruitment process from the perspective of applicants. They reveal, unfortunately, that many job applicants (1) have an incomplete and/or inaccurate understanding of what a job opening involves, (2) are not sure what they want from a position, (3) do not have a self-insight with regard to their knowledge, skills, and abilities, and (4) cannot accurately predict how they will react to the demands of a new position. What about applicants' reactions to recruiters?[58] Two theories have been proposed. One, the interview is an opportunity for recruiters to convey information about the organization, and warm, informative recruiters may do a better job of communicating with applicants. Two, the behavior of recruiters may signal unobserved characteristics of organizations. Thus recruiters who are warm are likely to have a friendly collegial culture. Those who are informative have a culture that respects employees' needs for information.[59]

What about a company's reputation? Evidence indicates that reputation provides firms with a competitive advantage by attracting more, and possibly higher-caliber, applicants.[60] Research findings also show that a company's reputation also affects applicants' willingness to pursue jobs because (1) they use reputation as a signal about the attributes of jobs (e.g., fun, challenging, lots of variety); (2) reputation affects the pride that individuals expect from joining the organization; and (3) applicants are willing to pay a premium in terms of lost wages to join firms with positive reputations.[61]

Other research has shown that job attributes (supervision, job challenge, location, salary, title) as well as recruitment activities (e.g., behavior during the interview) are important to applicants' reactions. The most important effects on interview outcomes, however, are candidates' perceived qualifications (e.g., ability to express ideas and demonstrated initiative).[62] In short, recruitment may be viewed as a market-exchange process in which employers attempt to differentiate their "products" (job opportunities) among "consumers" (job applicants) who vary in their levels of job-relevant knowledge, abilities, and skills.[63]

Timing issues in recruitment, particularly delays, are important factors in the job choice decisions of applicants.[64] Research indicates that (1) long delays between recruitment phases are not uncommon; (2) applicants react to such delays very negatively, often perceiving that "something is wrong" with the organization; and (3) regardless of their inferences, the most marketable candidates accept other offers if delays become extended. What are the implications of these findings? In a competitive marketplace, top talent disappears quickly. If you want to compete for it, streamline the decision-making process so that you can move fast.

## Realistic Job Previews

A conceptual framework that might help explain some of these research findings is that of the **realistic job preview** (RJP).[65] An RJP requires that, in addition to telling applicants about the nice things a job has to offer (e.g., pay, benefits, opportunities for advancement), recruiters must also tell applicants about the unpleasant aspects of the job. For example, "It's hot, dirty, and sometimes you'll have to work on weekends." Research in actual company settings has indicated consistent results.[66] That is, when the unrealistically positive expectations of job applicants are lowered to match the reality of the actual work setting prior to hire, job acceptance rates may be lower, but job performance, job satisfaction, and survival are higher for those who receive an RJP.[67] For example, after apartment-complex operator Aimco switched to realistic, "day-in-the-life-of" descriptions of customer-facing jobs, it found that only 3 percent of new hires left within 90 days, compared to 22 percent prior to the use of the RJP.[68] Over many studies, meta-analysis shows that RJPs improve retention rates, on average, by 9 percent.[69]

RJPs administered after hire also have positive effects. They help to reduce turnover, help new hires cope with work demands, and signal that the employer is concerned about the well being of its new hires.[70]

Longitudinal research shows that RJPs should be balanced in their orientation. That is, they should enhance overly pessimistic expectations and reduce overly optimistic expectations.[71] Applicants' overall evaluations of organizations, however, are influenced more by the *average* intensity of their immediate emotional reactions to an RJP, rather than by the relative balance of positive and negative information in the message. Thus one extremely positive aspect may offset multiple mildly negative aspects.[72]

A final recommendation is to develop RJPs even when there is no turnover problem (proactively rather than reactively). Use video and, where possible, show actual job incumbents.[73] Here are four research-based criteria for deciding what information to include in an RJP: (1) it is important to most recruits; (2) it is not widely known outside the organization; (3) it is a reason that leads newcomers to quit; and (4) it is related to successful job performance after being hired.[74]

Nevertheless, RJPs are not appropriate for all types of jobs. They seem to work best (1) when few applicants are actually hired (i.e., the selection ratio is low), (2) when used with entry-level positions (since those coming from outside to inside the organization tend to have more inflated expectations than those who make changes internally), and (3) when unemployment is low (since job candidates are more likely to have alternative jobs to choose from).[75]

## ETHICAL DILEMMA
### Online Résumés and Personal Privacy

Millions of people will transmit their résumés over the Internet this year. Is this a recruiting bonanza for employers? In one sense, yes, because they can scan online job boards using keywords to identify candidates with the educational background, training accomplishments, and workplace experience that they need. On the other hand, there are some very serious privacy concerns for job seekers and employee-relations concerns for employers, and they should be recognized.[a]

Résumés posted at one site can be traded or sold to other sites, they can be stolen by unscrupulous headhunters or duplicated and reposted by roving "spiders," and current employers can locate them as well. The Internet is so vast that many people think their résumés are safe there. Think again: A number of factors can wrest control from a job seeker. Here is one.

In the name of protecting company secrets, some corporations have begun to assign HR staff members to patrol cyberspace in search of wayward workers. Their objective is to reassign employees who are circulating their résumés online, and who therefore have one foot out the electronic door, off sensitive projects. Fair enough. But such a practice can also be viewed as an invasion of an employee's privacy and right to search for a job that might make better use of his or her skills. What do you think? Is it ethical for current employers to search the Internet in an effort to identify employees who have posted their résumés online?

---

[a]Ashford, K. (2006, Dec.). Is your résumé online? Watch out. *Money*, p. 36. See also Useem, J. (1999, May 24). Read this before you put a resume online. *Fortune*, pp. 290, 292.

## THE OTHER SIDE OF RECRUITMENT—JOB SEARCH

At some time or another, whether voluntarily or otherwise, almost everyone faces the difficult task of finding a job. How do they do it? Research shows that the most popular way that people land jobs is through personal contacts or networking rather than through employment agencies, Internet job sites, or other means.[76] This is especially true for executives, many of whom now make use of executive-networking sites such as LinkedIn, Execunet.com, and Netshare.com.[77] Keep this in mind as you read the following scenario.

### Scenario 1: Unemployed

This scenario has happened all too frequently over the last decade (as a result of mergers, restructurings, and downsizings), and it is expected to occur often this decade as economic conditions change.[78] You are a mid-level executive, well-regarded, well-paid, and seemingly well-established in your chosen field. Then—whammo!—a change in business strategy or a change in economic conditions results in your layoff from the firm you hoped to retire from. What do you do? How do you go about finding another job? According to management consultants and executive recruiters, the following are some of the key things not to do, followed by some suggestions for posting an Internet résumé.[79]

- *Don't panic.* A search takes time, even for well-qualified middle- and upper-level managers. Seven months to a year is not unusual. Be prepared to wait it out.
- *Don't be bitter.* Bitterness makes it harder to begin to search; it also turns off potential employers.
- *Don't kid yourself.* Do a thorough self-appraisal of your strengths and weaknesses, your likes and dislikes about jobs and organizations. Face up to what has happened, decide if you want to switch fields, figure out where you and your family want to live, and don't delay the search itself for long.
- *Don't drift.* Develop a plan, target companies, and go after them relentlessly. Realize that your job is to find a new job. Cast a wide net; consider industries (and countries) other than your own.
- *Don't be lazy.* The heart of a good job hunt is research. Use the Internet, public filings, and annual reports when drawing up a list of target companies. If negotiations get serious, talk to a range of insiders and knowledgeable outsiders to learn about politics and practices. You don't want to wind up in a worse fix than the one you left.
- *Don't be shy or overeager.* Because personal contacts are the most effective means to land a job, pull out all the stops to get the word out that you are available. At the same time, resist the temptation to accept the first job that comes along. Unless it's absolutely right for you, the chances of making a mistake are quite high.
- *Don't ignore your family.* Some executives are embarrassed and don't tell their families what's going on. A better approach, experts say, is to bring the family into the process and deal with issues honestly.
- *Don't lie.* Experts are unanimous on this point. Don't lie, and don't stretch a point—either on résumés or in interviews.[80] Be willing to address failures as well as strengths. Discuss openly and fully what went wrong at the old job, and what you learned from that experience. A recent study found that "reason for leaving last job" was the single most fibbed-about topic among executive job candidates. "Results and accomplishments" was a close second. Hmm. Coincidence?[81]
- *Don't jump the gun on salary.* Always let the potential employer bring this subject up first. But once it surfaces, thoroughly explore all aspects of your future compensation and benefits package. At the same time, a candid conversation with an outside recruiter about your present and desired salary is a good idea.[82]
- *Be careful when posting a résumé on the Internet.* Post a digital version on your own home page and place the word "résumé" in the Web site address to increase the chance of being noticed by Internet recruiters. These days knowing how to assemble a résumé for online consumption is a skill you will need for almost any job search. While it is important to use job-specific keywords, be careful! The latest recruiter-search tools, such as those from Trovix or VCG, can distinguish between a keyword inserted in a résumé at random, and one used to describe a person's work history. Use a keyword out of context and your résumé will be bumped to the bottom of the search results.[83]

Those who have been through the trauma of job loss and the challenge of finding a job often describe the entire process as a wrenching, stressful one. Avoiding the mistakes shown here can ensure that finding a new job need not take any longer than necessary.

## Scenario 2: Employed, But Searching for a New Job

People who are currently employed may decide to engage in job search for any one or more of the following reasons: to establish a network, to demonstrate their marketability to their current employers, or to develop other job choices to compare with their current positions. A study using currently employed managers found that they engaged in more job-search behavior the more agreeable (trusting, compliant, caring), neurotic (anxious, insecure, poorly emotionally adjusted), and open to experience (imaginative, nonconforming, autonomous) they were. In addition, managers higher in cognitive ability searched more actively, perhaps in an effort to ensure that their "hidden" abilities are recognized.[84] What are the implications of these results for organizations? Assuming the manager is someone you want to retain, communicate clearly that he or she is valued and that there are rich opportunities within the organization.

At the same time, employers know that top workers are often treated well, and may not be searching actively for a new job. These are so-called "passive prospects," and they are hot commodities. Locating them is easier now, given the availability of giant databases of employment data gleaned from publicly available sources like press releases, SEC filings, and articles in trade publications. Companies like ZoomInfo and Ziggs.com use this information to sift for high-quality passive prospects. More than a fifth of the Fortune 500, including blue-chip names like Pfizer, Sony, and Microsoft, use these outfits as part of their recruiting process.[85]

---

# IMPACT OF RECRUITMENT ON PRODUCTIVITY, QUALITY OF WORK LIFE, AND THE BOTTOM LINE

A close fit between individual strengths and interests and organizational and job characteristics almost guarantees a happy "marriage." On the other hand, because the bottom line of recruitment success lies in the number of successful placements made, the effects of ineffective recruitment may not appear for years. For this reason alone, a regular system for measuring and evaluating recruitment efforts is essential. Moreover, it's difficult to manage what you can't measure. Consider that the first-year turnover rate for new hires can be as high as 50 percent in some industries, such as fast-food restaurants.[a] To hire and retain 100 employees, therefore, the organization will need 200. However, if an RJP can boost retention by 50–59 percent, then the company will only need to hire 159 new people. For large fast-food chains that typically hire more than 100,000 newcomers corporation-wide at a cost of $300–$400 per hire, the savings in recruitment and hiring costs avoided may be in the tens of millions of dollars.

[a]Wanous, 2007, op. cit.

# IMPLICATIONS FOR MANAGEMENT PRACTICE

Talent is what makes firms go. Recruitment is therefore a strategic imperative and an important form of business competition. The following elements should be part of any successful recruitment program:

- Always view recruitment as a long-term strategy.
- Be responsive to employees' needs.
- Develop benefits that genuinely appeal to the employees being hired.
- Promote recruitment benefits to the target audience.
- Audit the recruitment programs in place.

Brands and reputations have always been important in product markets. Today they are just as important in labor markets. Companies with well-known brands and excellent reputations want to leverage them in their recruitment efforts. For example, consider firms that are named to various "Best Employer" lists. They strive to make those lists because they receive twice as many applications as firms that don't. In addition, they enjoy employee turnover levels that are less than half those of their competitors.[a] In short, people want to work at places where they are treated well, places that are doing well, and places where they are proud to work. Organizations with features like that will always be perceived as employers of choice.

[a]Cascio and Boudreau, 2011, op. cit.

---

**Human Resource Management in Action: Conclusion**

## THE PERILS AND PROMISE OF SOCIAL MEDIA

Here are seven steps that employers can take to avoid liability for their employees' use of social media:

1. Have a comprehensive, updated policy in writing.
2. Train all employees to know, understand, and use the policy.
3. Update all other related policies, such as those dealing with harassment, equal employment opportunity, confidentiality, code of conduct, information technology, references, violence in the workplace, and use of company equipment.
4. Instruct employees to respect professional boundaries.
5. Establish a clear procedure for making complaints.
6. Monitor compliance and enforce the social-media policy consistently.
7. Have a data-protection policy and procedure to thwart the unauthorized downloading of sensitive information.

The first item on this list is to establish a comprehensive policy about employees' use of social media. To do that, experts recommend the following steps.

- Make it specific to your business; don't simply adopt a "generic" policy.
- Coordinate it with other policies.
- Identify clearly who is covered and identify relevant media types.

- Explicitly reduce the expectations of employees about privacy at the workplace.
- Be specific about the consequences of violating the policy.
- Identify alternative ways to report violations of the policy.
- Identify appropriate contact persons by business unit or department.
- Distinguish the use of social media individually versus as an employee.
- Identify jobs that require the use of social media in the normal course of work (e.g., sales, recruitment).

## SUMMARY

Recruitment is a form of business contest, and it is fiercely competitive. It is an important component of the staffing supply chain. Recruitment begins with a clear statement of objectives, based on the number and types of knowledge, skills, abilities, and other characteristics that an organization needs to achieve its strategic business objectives. A recruitment policy must spell out clearly an organization's intention to evaluate and screen candidates without regard to factors such as race, gender, age, or disability (where these characteristics are unrelated to a person's ability to do a job successfully). The actual process of recruitment begins with a specification of workforce requirements—numbers, skills mix, levels, and the time frame within which such needs must be met.

Recruitment may involve internal or external labor markets, or both. Internal recruitment often relies on succession plans, job posting, employee referrals, or temporary worker pools. Many external recruitment sources are also available. In this chapter we discussed five such sources: university relations, virtual job fairs, executive search firms, employment agencies, and recruitment advertising, with special emphasis on online job searches. In managing and controlling recruitment operations, consider using a hiring management system that calculates the cost of operations, analyzes the performance of each source, and estimates payoffs of successful recruitment efforts. Why? Because the number of hires who actually perform their jobs successfully determines recruitment success.

## KEY TERMS

recruitment
initial screening
selection
orientation
placement
performance management process
passive nondiscrimination
pure diversity-based recruitment

diversity-based recruitment with preferential hiring
hard quotas
labor market
job posting
virtual job fair
realistic job preview

## DISCUSSION QUESTIONS

**6–1.** What special measures might be necessary for a successful diversity-oriented recruitment effort?

**6–2.** Discuss the conditions under which realistic job previews are and are not appropriate.

**6–3.** How would you advise a firm that wants to improve its unversity recruitment efforts?

**6–4.** Knowing that you have been studying the subject of recruitment, a friend asks you for advice on doing an online job search. What would you say?

**6–5.** Draft a recruitment ad for a trade journal to advertise a job opening at your company. Have a friend critique it, as well as—if possible—a knowledgeable HR professional from a local company. Summarize their suggestions for improvement and incorporate them into a final draft.

**6–6.** You have just lost your middle-management job. Outline a procedure to follow in trying to land a new one.

## APPLYING YOUR KNOWLEDGE

*Case 6–1*          ***Small Businesses Confront Recruiting Challenges[86]***

More and more executives from large corporations are being lured to small companies. In terms of recruitment tactics, it's clear that small companies can't compete with bigger rivals on compensation alone. Other motivators, however, can help attract talent, including greater responsibility, a more collegial corporate culture, the absence of bureaucracy, and the chance to build a business and to cash in if it eventually goes public. Often, the clincher in terms of closing the deal is the passion that a small-business CEO shows for his or her business. Take Dan Nye, for instance, the CEO of LinkedIn, the online networking service for business professionals. He tries to appeal to the desire of many large-company executives to make more of a mark than they can at their current employers. He says, "You have 20 to 25 years left in your career. Are you going to be the person who didn't take any risk and just lived a conservative, quiet life? But if you take this risk, even if it doesn't work out, you're going to feel great that you tried."

As another example, consider what happened less than a year after Tom Tiller retired as chief executive officer of snowmobile maker Polaris Industries. He was approached by a solar start-up about its top job. As he was mulling over the offer, a large crate arrived at his Minnesota home. Inside was a black solar panel with a message etched on its surface: "With your leadership we can change the way the world is powered." It was signed by the board and founding members of Abound Solar. "I was truly touched," recalls Tiller. "It helped me explain to my family and friends why I even considered packing up and moving to Colorado to become a CEO again."

**Questions**

1. Serious labor shortages exist in many places, but these are not the only reasons for the recruiting problems experienced by many small businesses. What are some others?

2. As a manager in such a small business, what sources might you use to find new workers?

3. What special advantages does a small business have over a large one? How can you incorporate these into the recruitment process?

# REFERENCES

1. Overman, S. (2008, Apr.). The CEO as recruiter. *HR Magazine,* pp. 81–84. See also Society for Human Resource Management (2007, Dec.). *2008 HR Trend Book.* Alexandria, VA: author. See also Griendling, H. (2008, May 2). *World-Class Recruiting.* Retrieved from *http://www.ere.net/articles/db/514928EADEF748CE98297A69348EEF16.asp* on July 6, 2011.

2. Jobs, S., cited in Morris, B. (2008, Mar. 17). What makes Apple golden. *Fortune,* p. 74.

3. Cascio, W. F., and Boudreau, J. W. (2011). Utility of selection systems: Supply-chain analysis applied to staffing decisions. In S. Zedeck (Ed.), *APA Handbook of Industrial and Organizational Psychology,* Vol. 2, pp. 421–444.

4. Ehrenberg, R. G., and Smith, R. S. (2011). *Modern Labor Economics* (11th Ed.). Upper Saddle River, NJ: Pearson Education. See also Cahuc, P., and Zilberberg, A. (2004). *Labor Economics.* Cambridge, MA: MIT Press.

5. U.S. Bureau of Labor Statistics. (2010). Fastest growing occupations, 2008 and projected 2018. Retrieved from *http://www.bls.gov/emp/ep_table_103.pdf* on July 6, 2011.

6. Milkovich, G. T., Newman, J. M., and Gerhart, B. (2011). *Compensation Management* (10th Ed.). Burr Ridge, IL: McGraw-Hill.

7. Ehrenberg and Smith, 2011, op. cit.

8. Milkovich and Newman, 2011, op. cit. See also Dineen, B. R., and Soltis, S. M. (2011). Recruitment: A review of research and emerging directions. In S. Zedeck (Ed.), *APA Handbook of Industrial and Organizational Psychology,* Vol. 2, pp. 43–66.

9. Ehrenberg and Smith, 2011, op. cit. See also Baron, J. N., Davis-Blake, A., and Bielby, W. T. (1986). The structure of opportunity: How promotion ladders vary within and among organizations. *Administrative Science Quarterly* 31, pp. 248–273. See also Stewman, S. (1986). Demographic models of internal labor markets. *Administrative Science Quarterly* 31, pp. 212–247.

10. For an excellent summary of this research, see Rynes, S. L., and Cable, D. M. (2003). Recruitment research in the twenty-first century. In W. C. Borman, D. R. Ilgen, and R. J. Klimoski (Eds.), *Handbook of Psychology: Industrial and Organizational Psychology,* Vol. 12. Hoboken, NJ: Wiley, pp. 55–76.

11. Jones, D. A., Shultz, J. W., and Chapman, D. S. (2006). Recruiting through job advertisements: The effects of cognitive elaboration on decision-making. *International Journal of Selection and Assessment* 11, pp. 167–179.

12. Welbourne, T. (In press.). Fast HR. *Organizational Dynamics.* See also Sullivan, J. (2008, May 19). Understanding why fast hiring is critical to recruitment success. Retrieved from *http://www.ere.net/articles/db/4EE49B909CC040D391C6275116-B111F8.asp* on May 21, 2008.

13. Griendling, 2008, op. cit.

14. Cappelli, P. (2001, Mar.). Making the most of on-line recruiting. *Harvard Business Review,* pp. 139–146.

15. Rynes and Cable, 2003, op. cit. See also Bretz, R. D., and Judge, T. A. (1998). Realistic job previews: A test of the adverse self-selection hypothesis. *Journal of Applied Psychology* 83, pp. 330–337. See also Rynes, S. L., Bretz, R. D., and Gerhart, B. (1991). The importance of recruitment in job choice: A different way of looking. *Personnel Psychology* 44, pp. 487–521.

16. Society for Human Resource Management. (2008, Aug.) *Seeing Forward: Succession Planning and Leadership Development at 3M* (DVD). Alexandria, VA: SHRM Foundation. See also, Byrnes, N. (2005, Oct. 10). Starsearch. *BusinessWeek,* pp. 68–78.

17. Gere, D., Scarborough, E. K., and Collison, J. (2002, Oct.). *SHRM/Recruitment Marketplace 2002 Recruiter Budget/Cost Survey.* Alexandria, VA: Society for Human Resource Management. See also Joinson, C. (2003, Winter). The real deal with sourcing. *Employment Management Today* 9(1). Retrieved from *http://www.shrm.org* on Aug. 24, 2004.

18. Cappelli, 2001, op. cit., p. 146.

19. Breaugh, J. A. (1992). *Recruitment: Science and Practice.* Boston: PWS-Kent.

20. Orgel, M. (2010, Feb. 10). It's who you know: Job seekers who don't network miss out on company referral programs. Retrieved from *http://www.marketwatch.com/story/job-seekers-aided-by-employee-referral-programs-2010-02-10* on July 7, 2011. Society for Human Resource Management. (2001). *SHRM 2001 Employee Referral Program Survey.* Alexandria, VA: Author.

21. Sources: Helyar, J., and MacMillan, D. (2011, March 13). In Tech, poaching is the sincerest form of flattery. *BusinessWeek,* pp. 17, 18. See also Lohr, S. (2010, Sept. 24). Six technology firms agree to more hiring competition. *The New York Times.* Retrieved from *http://www.nytimes.com/2010/09/25/technology/25hiring.html?scp=1&sq=Six%20technology%20firms%20agree%20to%20more%20hiring%20competition.%20&st=cse* on Sept. 27, 2010. See also Orgel, M., 2010, op. cit. See also Hakala, D. (2008, Aug. 12). The pros and cons of employee referral programs. *HR World.* Retrieved from *http://www.hrworld.com/features/employee-referral-pros-cons-081208/* on July 7, 2011.

22. Baker, S. (2009, May 4). You're fired—but stay in touch. *BusinessWeek,* pp. 54, 55.

23. Griffeth, R. W., Hom, P. W., Fink, L. S., and Cohen, D. J. (1997). Comparative tests of multivariate models of recruiting sources effects. *Journal of Management* 23, pp. 19–36. See also Kirnan, J. P., Farley, J. A., and Geisinger, K. F. (1989). The relationship between recruiting source, applicant quality, and hire performance: An analysis by sex, ethnicity, and age. *Personnel Psychology* 42, pp. 293–308.

24. Glube, N., Huxtable, J., and Stanard, A. (2002, June). Creating new temporary hire options through in-house agencies. SHRM White Paper. Retrieved from *http://www.shrm.org,* Aug. 24, 2004.

25. Few hiring changes in store for contract workers. (2011, May 16). Retrieved from *http://www.shrm.org/hrdisciplines/staffingmanagement/Articles/Pages/ContractWorkersPoll.aspx* on July 7, 2011. See also Zeidner, R. (2010, Feb.). Heady debate: Rely on temps or hire staff? *HR Magazine* 55(2), pp. 28–33.

26. Glube et al., 2002, op. cit.

27. Barber, A. E., Wesson, M. J., Roberson, Q. M., and Taylor, M. S. (1999). A tale of two job markets: Organizational size and its effect on hiring practices and job search behavior. *Personnel Psychology* 52, pp. 841–867.

28. Porter, J., and Lavelle, L. (2007, July 9). The professor is a headhunter. *BusinessWeek,* pp. 80–84. See also Joinson, C. (2001). Red hot college recruiting. *Employment Management Today* 7(1). Retrieved from *www.shrm.org/hrdisciplines/staffingmanagement/Articles/Pages/CMS_016148.aspx* on August 24, 2004. See also Poe, A. C. (2000, May). Face value: snag students by establishing a long-term, personal presence on campus. *HR Magazine,* pp. 60–68.

29. ExxonMobil. 2010 Community investments by focus area. Retrieved from *http://www.exxonmobil.com/Corporate/community_wwgiving.aspx* on July 7, 2011. See also Cohen, K. (2007, July 30). ExxonMobil plays by school rules. *BusinessWeek,* p. 18.

30. Joinson, 2001, op. cit.

31. Dineen and Soltis, 2011, op. cit. See also Kolenko, T. A. (1990). College recruiting: Models, myths, and management. In G. R. Ferris, K. M. Rowland, and M. R. Buckley (Eds.), *Human Resource Management: Perspectives and Issues* (2nd Ed.). Boston: Allyn & Bacon, pp. 109–121.

32. Silverman, R. E. (2000, Oct. 31). The jungle: What's news in recruitment and pay. *The Wall Street Journal,* p. B18.

33. Generation Y goes directly to source in job hunt. (2011, April 25). Retrieved from *http://www.shrm.org/Publications/HRNews/Pages/GenYGoesToSource.aspx* on July 7, 2011. See also Dineen and Soltis, 2011, op. cit. Social responsibility key to attracting top talent. (2009, Oct. 28). Retrieved from *http://www.smartmanager.us/eprise/main/web/us/hr_manager/document_center/kgwiglobalsocialrespon.pdf* on Oct. 31, 2010.

34. Agnvall, E. (2007, July). Job fairs go virtual. *HR Magazine,* pp. 85–87.

35. Columbia Consulting Group. (2000). *Executive Search Guidelines.* NY: Author.

36. Ibid. See also Association of Executive Search Consultants. (2010). Selecting an executive search firm. Retrieved from *https://members.aesc.org/eweb/upload/ 2011GuidelinesforSelectinganExecutiveSearchFirm.pdf* on July 7, 2011.

37. Wells, S. J. (2003). Slow times for executive recruiting. *HR Magazine* 48(4), pp. 60–68. See also Frase-Blunt, M. (2003). Traditional recruiting defined. *HRMagazine* 48(4), p. 72.

38. Schaible, S. R. (2002). Temporary staffing agencies and human resources: Compliance issues. SHRM White Paper. Retrieved from *http://www.shrm.org/hrdisciplines/ staffingmanagement/Articles/Pages/CMS_000329.aspx* on May 22, 2008.

39. Keefer, A. (2011). How does an employment agency work? Retrieved from *http:// www.ehow.com/how-does_4568145_employment-agency-work.html* on July 7, 2011. See also How much do employment agencies charge? (2011). Retrieved from *http://www.onlinebusinesscenterusa.com/jobs/how-much-do-employment-agencies- charge/* on July 7, 2011.

40. Woodward, N. H. (2007, Feb.). Surprise, surprise. *HR Magazine,* pp. 81–88.

41. Krell, E. (2011, March). Mobility officers on the move. *HR Magazine* 56(3), pp. 59–62. See also Krell, E. (2010, Aug.). Art of moving, by the numbers. *HR Magazine* 55(8), pp. 54–56.

42. Aumann, K., Galinsky, E., and Matos, K. (2011). *The New Male Mystique.* New York, NY: Families & Work Institute.

43. Peraud, P. (2001, June). Promoting a spouse's right to work. Retrieved from *www. erc.org/Mobility_online/current/0601perraud.shtml* on June 15, 2006. Article also accessed at *www.militaryhomefront.dod.mil/mhf_reports/QQoLR/QQoLR-8Of13.pdf* on October 11, 2011.

44. For current trends see *http://www.erc.org.* See also Krell, 2011, op. cit. See also Krell, 2010, op. cit.

45. Horowitz, J. (2004, Aug. 30). UBS aims to draw U.S. assets with acquisition, top brokers. *The Wall Street Journal,* p. C3.

46. Markels, A. (1996, Aug. 21). Signing bonuses rise to counter rich pay plans. *The Wall Street Journal,* pp. B1, B4.

47. Van Hoye, G., and Lievens, F. (2007). Investigating Web-based recruitment sources: Employee testimonials versus word-of-mouse. *International Journal of Selection and Assessment* 15, pp. 372–382.

48. Dineen and Soltis, 2011, op. cit. See also Breaugh, J. A. (2008). Employee recruitment: Current knowledge and important areas for future research. *Human Resource Management Review* 18, 103–118. See also Barber, A. E. (2007a). Recruitment sources. In S. G. Rogelberg (Ed.), *Encyclopedia of Industrial and Organizational Psychology,* Vol. 2. Thousand Oaks, CA: Sage, pp. 670–672. See also Barber, 1998, op. cit.

49. Ibid. See also Carlson, K. D., Connerly, M. L., and Mecham, R. L. (2002). Recruitment evaluation: the case for assessing the quality of applicants attracted. *Personnel Psychology* 55, pp. 461–490. See also Williams, C. R., Labig, C. E., Jr., and Stone, T. H. (1993). Recruitment sources and post-hire outcomes for job applicants and new hires: A test of two hypotheses. *Journal of Applied Psychology* 78, pp. 163–172.

50. Rynes and Cable, 2003, op. cit.

51. Gere et al., 2002, op. cit.

52. Ismail, L., and Kronemer, A. (2002). *Finding Diversity.* Alexandria, VA: Society for Human Resource Management.

53. Childs, J. T., Jr. (2010. April). Webcast: Six diversity and inclusion mega-trends. Retrieved from *http://www.shrm.org/multimedia/webcasts/Pages/0410childs.aspx* on July 8, 2011. See also Kilduff, C. (2007, Sept.). The diversity recruiting challenge goes on. SHRM White Paper. Retrieved from *http://www.shrm.org/hrresources/ whitepapers_published/CMS_023264.asp* on May 22, 2008.

54. For more information contact HiringGateway@yahoo-inc.com.

55. Cascio, W. F., and Aguinis, H. (2011). *Applied Psychology in Human Resource Management* (7th ed.). Upper Saddle River, NJ: Prentice-Hall.

56. Bowl, K., and Scanlan, F. (2002, July 23). SHRM, EMA investigate costs associated with recruiting and hiring. Retrieved from *www.shrm.org/Research/SurveyFindings/Documents/2002%20Staffing%20Metrics%20Survey%20Cost-per-Hire%20by%20SHRM%20and%20EMA.pdf* Aug. 30, 2004.

57. Cascio, W. F., and Boudreau, J. W. (2011). *Investing in People: Financial Impact of Human Resource Initiatives* (2nd Ed.). Upper Saddle River, NJ: Pearson Education. See also Griendling, 2008, op. cit.

58. Breaugh, J. A., Macan, T. H., and Grambow, D. M. (2008). Employee recruitment: Current knowledge and directions for future research. In G. P. Hodgkinson and J. K. Ford (Eds.), *International Review of Industrial and Organizational Psychology,* Vol. 23. Hoboken, NJ: Wiley, pp. 45–82. See also Rynes and Cable, 2003, op. cit.

59. Barber, A. E. (2007b). Recruitment. In S. G. Rogelberg (Ed.), *Encyclopedia of Industrial and Organizational Psychology,* Vol. 2. Thousand Oaks, CA: Sage, pp. 666–670.

60. Turban, D., and Cable, D. (2003). Firm reputation and applicant-pool characteristics. *Journal of Organizational Behavior* 24, pp. 733–751.

61. Social responsibility, 2009, op. cit. See also Cable, D., and Turban, D. (2003). The value of reputation in a recruitment context. *Journal of Applied Social Psychology* 33, pp. 2244–2266.

62. Graves, L. M., and Powell, G. N. (1995). The effect of sex similarity on recruiters' evaluations of actual applicants: A test of the similarity-attraction paradigm. *Personnel Psychology* 48, pp. 85–98.

63. Maurer, S. D., Howe, V., and Lee, T. W. (1992). Organizational recruiting as marketing management: An interdisciplinary study of engineering graduates. *Personnel Psychology* 45, pp. 807–833.

64. Dineen and Soltis, 2011, op. cit. Rynes et al., 1991, op. cit.

65. Wanous, J. P. (2007). Realistic job preview. In S. G. Rogelberg (Ed.), *Encyclopedia of Industrial and Organizational Psychology,* Vol. 2. Thousand Oaks, CA: Sage, pp. 663–666. Popovich, P., and Wanous, J. P. (1982). The realistic job preview as a persuasive communication. *Academy of Management Review* 7, pp. 570–578.

66. Hom, P. W. (2011). Organizational exit. In S. Zedeck (Ed.), *APA Handbook of Industrial and Organizational Psychology*, Vol. 2. Washington, D C: American Psychological Association, pp. 325–375. See also Breaugh, 2008, op. cit. See also Premack, S. L., and Wanous, J. P. (1985). A meta-analysis of realistic job preview experiments. *Journal of Applied Psychology* 70, pp. 706–719.

67. Phillips, J. M. (1998). Effects of realistic job previews on multiple organizational outcomes: A meta-analysis. *Academy of Management Journal* 41, pp. 673–690.

68. White, E. (2007, Mar. 12). Job ads loosen up, get real. *The Wall Street Journal,* p. B3.

69. Hom, P. W., Griffeth, R. W., Palich, L. E., and Bracker, J. S. (1998). An exploratory investigation into theoretical mechanisms underlying realistic job previews. *Personnel Psychology* 51, pp. 421–451. See also McEvoy, G. M., and Cascio, W. F. (1985). Strategies for reducing employee turnover. A meta-analysis. *Journal of Applied Psychology* 70, pp. 342–353.

70. Hom, P. W., Griffeth, R. W., Palich, L. E., and Bracker, J. S. (1999). Revisiting met expectations as a reason why realistic job previews work. *Personnel Psychology* 52, pp. 97–112.

71. Meglino, B. M., DeNisi, A. S., Youngblood, S. A., and Williams, K. J. (1988). Effects of realistic job previews: A comparison using an enhancement and a reduction preview. *Journal of Applied Psychology* 73, pp. 259–266.

72. Reeve, C., Highhouse, S., and Brooks, M. E. (2006). A closer look at reactions to realistic recruitment messages. *International Journal of Selection and Assessment* 14, pp. 1–15.

73. Wanous, J. P. (1989). Installing a realistic job preview: Ten tough choices. *Personnel Psychology* 42, pp. 117–134.

74. Wanous, 2007, op. cit.

75. Wanous, J. P. (1980). *Organizational Entry: Recruitment, Selection and Socialization of Newcomers.* Reading, MA: Addison-Wesley.

76. Berglas, L. (2010, April 12). How do I get a headhunter interested in me? *Fortune*, p. 40. See also Hempel, 2010, op. cit. See also McGrego, 2010, op. cit. See also Kadlec, 2007, op. cit. See also Wanberg, C. R., Kanfer, R., and Banas, J. T. (2000). Predictors and outcomes of networking intensity among unemployed job seekers. *Journal of Applied Psychology* 85, pp. 491–503. See also Granovetter, M. S. (1995). *Getting a Job* (2nd Ed.). Chicago: University of Chicago Press.

77. Hempel, 2010, op. cit. See also Needleman, S. E. (2007a, Sept. 9). Job seekers: Put your Web savvy to work. *The Wall Street Journal*, p. WSJ1.

78. Cascio, W. F. (2010). *Employment Downsizing and Its Alternatives*. Alexandria, VA: Society for Human Resource Management Foundation. See also Hallock, K. F. (2006). Layoffs in large U. S. firms from the perspective of senior management. *Personnel and Human Resources Management* 25, pp. 137–180. See also Cascio, W. F. (2002). *Responsible Restructuring: Creative and Profitable Alternatives to Layoffs*. San Francisco: Berrett-Kohler. See also Morris, J. R., Cascio, W. F., and Young, C. E. (1999, Winter). Downsizing after all these years. *Organizational Dynamics,* pp. 78–87.

79. Nishi, D. (2010, Oct. 17). Explain resume gaps. *The Wall Street Journal*, p. 3. See also Shellenbarger, S. (2010, Feb. 17). When getting the job is the easy part. *The Wall Street Journal*, Retrieved from *http://online.wsj.com* on February 19, 2010. See also MacMillan, 2007, op. cit. See also Needleman, S. E. (2007b, March 6). Why sneaky tactics may not help résumé. *The Wall Street Journal*, p. B8.

80. Soltis, C. (2006, March 21). Eagle-eyed employers scour résumés for little white lies. *The Wall Street Journal*, p. B7.

81. Fisher, A. (2004, July 12). Should you admit why you were fired? *Fortune*, p. 52. See also Coyne, T. (2001, Dec. 15). O'Leary's lies leave Irish eyes crying. *Rocky Mountain News*, p. C5.

82. Lublin, J. S. (2006, Jan. 31). When to disclose pay to a respective boss—and when to avoid it. *The Wall Street Journal,* p. B1.

83. MacMillan, 2007, op. cit. See also Needleman, 2007b, op. cit.

84. Boudreau, J. W., Boswell, W. R., Judge, T. A., and Bretz, R. D., Jr. (2001). Personality and cognitive ability as predictors of job search among employed managers. *Personnel Psychology* 54, pp. 25–50.

85. Lehoczky, E. (2005, Dec.). How to get a better job without really trying. *Money,* p. 56. See also Helyar and MacMillan, 2011, op. cit. See also Berglas, 2010, op. cit.

86. Martin, C. (2010, Oct. 17). Bringing good things to sunlight. *BusinessWeek*, pp. 54, 56. See also Barlyn, S. (2007, Aug. 20). Big fish, smaller ponds. *The Wall Street Journal*, p. R6.

# 7 STAFFING

*Questions This Chapter Will Help Managers Answer*

1. In what ways do business strategy and organizational culture affect staffing decisions?
2. What screening and selection methods are available, and which ones are most accurate?
3. What should be done to improve pre-employment interviews?
4. Can work-sample tests improve staffing decisions?
5. What are some advantages and potential problems to consider in using assessment centers to select managers?

## ORGANIZATIONAL CULTURE—KEY TO STAFFING "FIT"*

Is there a common denominator among the most admired companies? According to one study, the answer is yes. It's organizational culture—shared values, expectations, and behavior—that set the context of everything a company does. In the most admired companies, such as Apple, Google, Procter & Gamble, Amazon.com, Starbucks, Intel, FedEx, Netflix, and Southwest Airlines, the key priorities were teamwork, customer focus, fair treatment of employees, initiative, and innovation. In average companies, the top priorities were minimizing risk, respecting the chain of command, supporting the boss, and making budget. In addition, the most admired companies all have consensus at the top regarding cultural priorities. Rather than giving culture a few lines in the company handbook, the most admired companies live their cultures every day, and they go out of their way to communicate it both to current employees as well as to prospective new hires. Thus Intel works hard to retain the egalitarianism and cooperative spirit among employees that it started with. In practice that means that there are no reserved parking places, no executive dining rooms, no corner offices—and everyone gets stock options.

By contrast, it is all too common for average companies to say they value teamwork but then to award bonuses only on the basis of individual achievement. According to the Hay Group, the management consulting firm that conducted the study, the single best predictor of overall excellence was a company's ability to attract, retain, and motivate talented people. Organizational culture can either facilitate those activities or else inhibit them. It is a key to "fit" between employees and their organizations, and it is also the secret to enduring greatness among companies. New hires consider it in their decisions to accept or not to accept jobs. Not surprisingly, therefore, more and more companies are taking stock of what they stand for, what they are trying to achieve, and how they operate every day to achieve their goals. In the conclusion to this case, we will see what some of these companies are doing in this area.

### Challenges

1. What can a company do to communicate its culture to prospective new hires?
2. What might be the role of organizational culture in staffing decisions?
3. How might organizational culture affect the ways that employees deal with coworkers and customers?

---

*Sources:* The World's Most Admired Companies. (2011, March 21). *Fortune,* pp. 109–146. See also Copeland, M. V. (2010, Dec. 6). Reed Hastings: Leader of the pack. *Fortune,* pp. 121–130. See also Collins, J. (2008, May 5). The secret of enduring greatness. *Fortune,* pp. 73–76. See also Nocera, J. (2008, May 24). Parting words of an airline pioneer. *International Herald Tribune.* Retrieved from *www.redorbit.com,* May 27, 2008. See also Kelleher, H. I did it my way. *Fortune,* June 1, 2001. See also O'Reilly, C. A., III, and Pfeffer, J. (2000). Southwest Airlines: If success is so simple, why is it so hard to imitate? *Hidden value.* Boston: Harvard Business School Press, pp. 21–48.

The chapter-opening vignette describes the crucial role of organizational culture in attracting, retaining, and motivating employees to perform their best every day. As we shall see, the most progressive companies strive to convey their cultures to new hires as well as to current employees, and the degree of fit of a prospective new hire with the organizational culture plays a major role in staffing decisions. In addition to creating cultural fit, there is a constant need to align staffing decisions with business strategy. As we shall see in this chapter, a wide variety of tools for initial screening and selection decisions are available, and much is known about each one. We will examine the evidence of the relative effectiveness of the tools, so that decision makers can choose those that best fit their long- and short-range objectives. Let us begin by considering the role of business strategy in staffing decisions.

## ORGANIZATIONAL CONSIDERATIONS IN STAFFING DECISIONS

### Business Strategy

Clearly, there should be a fit between the intended strategy of an enterprise and the characteristics of the people who are expected to implement it. Unfortunately, very few firms actually link strategy and staffing decisions in a structured, logical way.[1] Nevertheless, we can learn how to effect such a fit by considering a two-dimensional model that relates an organization's strategy during the stages of its development to the style of its managers during each stage.[2]

For strategic reasons, it is important to consider the stage of development of a business because many characteristics of a business—such as its growth rate, product lines, market share, entry opportunity, and technology—change as the organization changes. One possible set of relationships between the development stage and the management selection strategies is shown in Figure 7–1. Although a model such as this is useful conceptually, in practice the stages might not be so clearly defined, and there are many exceptions.

Organizations that are just starting out are in the *embryonic* stage. They are characterized by high growth rates, basic product lines, heavy emphasis on product engineering, and little or no customer loyalty.

### Figure 7–1

The relationship between the development stage of an organization and the management selection strategy that best "fits" each stage.

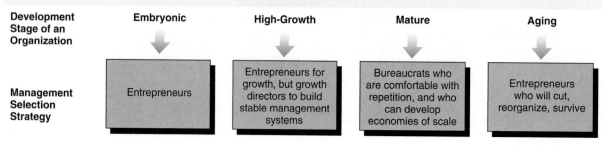

| Development Stage of an Organization | Embryonic | High-Growth | Mature | Aging |
|---|---|---|---|---|
| Management Selection Strategy | Entrepreneurs | Entrepreneurs for growth, but growth directors to build stable management systems | Bureaucrats who are comfortable with repetition, and who can develop economies of scale | Entrepreneurs who will cut, reorganize, survive |

Organizations in the *high-growth* stage are concerned with two things: fighting for market share and building excellence in their management teams. They focus on refining and extending product lines, and on building customer loyalty.

*Mature* organizations emphasize the maintenance of market share, cost reductions through economies of scale, more rigid management controls over workers' actions, and the generation of cash to develop new product lines. In contrast to the "freewheeling" style of an embryonic organization, there is much less flexibility and variability in a mature organization.

Finally, an *aging* organization struggles to hold market share in a declining market, and it demands extreme cost control obtained through consistency and centralized procedures. Economic survival becomes the primary motivation.

Different management styles seem to fit each of these development stages best. In the embryonic stage, there is a need for enterprising managers who can thrive in high-risk environments. These are known as entrepreneurs (Figure 7–1). They are decisive individuals who can respond rapidly to changing conditions.

During the high-growth stage, there is still a need for entrepreneurs, but it is also important to select the kinds of managers who can develop stable management systems to preserve the gains achieved during the embryonic stage. We might call these managers "growth directors."

As an organization matures, there is a need to select the kind of manager who does not need lots of variety in her or his work, who can oversee repetitive daily operations, and who can search continually for economies of scale. Individuals who fit best into mature organizations have a bureaucratic style of management.

Finally, an aging organization needs movers and shakers to invigorate it. Strategically, it becomes important to select (again) entrepreneurs capable of doing whatever is necessary to ensure the economic survival of the firm. This may involve divesting unprofitable operations, firing unproductive workers, or eliminating practices that are considered extravagant.

Admittedly, these characterizations are coarse, but they provide a starting point in the construction of an important link between the development stage of an organization and its staffing strategy. Such strategic concerns may be used to supplement job analyses as bases for staffing. This also suggests that job descriptions, which standardize and formalize behavior, should be broadened into role descriptions that reflect the broader and more changeable strategic requirements of an organization.

## Organizational Culture

Just as organizations choose people, people choose jobs and organizations that fit their personalities and career objectives and in which they can satisfy needs that are important to them.[3]

In the context of selection, it is important for an organization to describe the dimensions of its culture—the environment within which employment decisions are made and the environment within which employees work on a day-to-day basis. It has been described as the DNA of an organization—invisible to the naked eye, but critical in shaping the character of the workplace.[4] *Culture is the pattern of basic assumptions a given group has invented, discovered, or developed in learning to adapt both to its external and internal environments.* The pattern of assumptions has worked well enough to be considered valid and, therefore, to be taught to new members as the correct way to perceive, think, and feel in relation to those problems. **Organizational culture** is embedded and transmitted through mechanisms such as the following:[5]

1. Formal statements of organizational philosophy and materials used for recruitment, selection, and socialization of new employees.
2. Promotion criteria.
3. Stories, legends, and myths about key people and events.
4. What leaders pay attention to, measure, and control.
5. Implicit and possibly unconscious criteria that leaders use to determine who fits key slots in the organization.

Organizational culture has two implications for staffing decisions. First, cultures vary across organizations; individuals will consider this information if it is available to them in their job search process.[6] Companies such as IBM and Procter & Gamble have a strong marketing orientation, and their staffing decisions tend to reflect this value. Other companies, such as BMW and Hewlett-Packard, are oriented toward research and development and engineering, whereas still others, such as McDonald's, concentrate on consistency and efficiency. Recruiters assess person/job fit by focusing on specific knowledge, skills, and abilities. They assess person/organization fit by focusing more on values and personality characteristics.[7] By linking staffing decisions to cultural factors, companies try to ensure that their employees have internalized the strategic intent and core values of the enterprise. In this way they will be more likely to act in the interest of the company and as dedicated team members, regardless of their formal job duties.[8]

Second, other things being equal, individuals who choose jobs with organizations that are consistent with their own values, beliefs, and attitudes are more likely to be productive, satisfied employees. This was demonstrated in a study of 904 college graduates hired by six public accounting firms over a seven-year period. Those hired by firms that emphasized interpersonal relationship values (team orientation, respect for people) stayed an average of 45 months. Those hired by firms that emphasized work-task values (detail, stability, innovation) stayed with their firms an average of 31 months. This 14-month difference in survival rates translated into an opportunity loss of at least $10.5 million (in 2011 dollars) for each firm that emphasized work-task values.

Although the firms that emphasized the value of interpersonal relationships were uniformly more attractive to both strong and weak performers, strong performers stayed an average of 13 months longer in firms that emphasized work-task values (39 months versus 26 months for weak performers). The lesson for managers? Promote cultural values that are attractive to most new employees; don't just select individuals who fit a specific profile of cultural values.[9]

## The Logic of Personnel Selection

If variability in physical and psychological characteristics were not so prevalent, there would be little need for selection of people to fill various jobs. Without variability among individuals in abilities, aptitudes, interests, and personality traits, we would expect all job candidates to perform comparably. Research shows clearly that as jobs become more complex, individual differences in output also increase.[10] Likewise, if there were 10 job openings available and only 10 qualified candidates, selection again would not be a significant issue because all 10 candidates would have to be hired. Selection becomes a relevant concern only when there are more qualified candidates than there are positions to be filled: Selection implies choice and choice means exclusion.

Because practical considerations (safety, time, cost) make job tryouts for all candidates infeasible in most selection situations, it is necessary to predict the relative level of job performance of each candidate on the basis of available information. As we shall see, some methods for doing this are more accurate than others. However, before considering them, we need to focus on the fundamental technical requirements of all such methods—**reliability** and **validity.**

## Reliability of Measurement

The goal of any selection program is to identify applicants who score high on measures that purport to assess knowledge, skills, abilities, or other characteristics that are critical for job performance. Yet, we always run the risk of making errors in employee selection decisions. Selection errors are of two types: selecting someone who should be rejected (erroneous acceptance) and rejecting someone who should be accepted (erroneous rejection). These kinds of errors can be avoided by using measurement procedures that are reliable and valid.

*A measurement is considered to be reliable if it is consistent or stable,* for example,

- *Over time*—such as on a hearing test administered first on Monday morning and then again on Friday night.
- *Across different samples of items*—say, on form A and form B of a test of mathematical aptitude, or on a measure of vocational interests administered at the beginning of a student's sophomore year in college and then again at the end of her or his senior year.
- *Across different raters or judges working independently*—as in a gymnastics competition.

As you might suspect, inconsistency is present to some degree in all measurement situations. In employment settings, people generally are assessed only once. That is, organizations give them, for example, one test of their knowledge of a job, or one application form, or one interview. The procedures through which these assessments are made must be standardized in terms of content, administration, and scoring. Only then can the results of the assessments be compared meaningfully with one another. Those who desire more specific information about how reliability is actually estimated in quantitative terms should consult the technical appendix at the end of this chapter.

## Validity of Measurement

Reliability is certainly an important characteristic of any measurement procedure, but it is simply a means to an end, a step along the way to a goal. Unless a measure is reliable, it cannot be valid. This is so because unless a measure produces consistent, dependable, stable scores, we cannot begin to understand what implications high versus low scores have for later job performance and economic returns to the organization. Such understanding is the goal of the validation process. From a practical point of view, validity refers to the job relatedness of a measure—shown, for example, by assessing the strength of the relationship between scores from the measure and some indicator or rating of actual job performance.[11]

Although evidence of validity may be accumulated in many ways, validity always refers to the degree to which the evidence supports inferences that are drawn from scores or ratings on a selection procedure. It is the *inferences* regarding the specific use of a selection procedure that are validated, not the procedure itself.[12] Hence a user must first specify exactly why he or she intends to use a particular selection procedure (i.e., what inferences he or she intends to draw from it). Then the user can make an informed judgment about the adequacy of the available evidence of validity in support of that particular selection procedure when used for a particular purpose.

Scientific standards for validation are described in greater detail in *Principles for the Validation and Use of Personnel Selection Procedures*[13] and *Standards for Educational and Psychological Testing.*[14] Legal standards for validation are contained in the *Uniform Guidelines on Employee Selection Procedures.*[15] For those who desire an overview of the various strategies used to validate employee selection procedures, see the technical appendix at the end of the chapter.

Quantitative evidence of validity is often expressed in terms of a correlation coefficient (that may assume values between $-1$ and $+1$) between scores on a predictor of job performance (e.g., a test or an interview) and a criterion that reflects actual job performance (e.g., supervisory ratings, dollar volume of sales). In employment contexts, predictor validities typically vary between about 0.20 and 0.50. In the following sections we will consider some of the most commonly used methods for screening and selection decisions, together with validity evidence for each one.

## SCREENING AND SELECTION METHODS

### Employment Application Forms

Particularly when unemployment is high, organizations find themselves deluged with applications for employment for only a small number of available jobs. Many large companies, especially companies with solid reputations and strong company cultures, receive more than 1 million applications per year. Of course when applications are submitted electronically, it is possible to screen them for obvious mismatches by considering answers to questions such as "Are you willing to move?" and "When are you prepared to start work?" As we noted in Chapter 6, hiring-management systems using advanced software can help screen candidates on items such as background and experience, thereby streamlining the selection process considerably.

An important requirement of all employment application forms is that they ask only for information that is valid and fair with respect to the nature of the job. Organizations should regularly review employment application forms to be sure that the information they require complies with equal employment opportunity guidelines and case law. For example, under the Americans with Disabilities Act of 1990, an employer may not ask a general question about disabilities on an application form or whether an applicant has ever filed a workers' compensation claim. However, at a pre-employment interview, after describing the essential functions of a job, an employer may ask if there is any physical or mental reason the candidate cannot perform the essential functions. Here are some guidelines that will suggest which questions to delete:

- Any question that might lead to an adverse impact on the employment of members of groups protected under civil rights law.
- Any question that cannot be demonstrated to be job related or that does not concern a bona fide occupational qualification.
- Any question that could possibly constitute an invasion of privacy.

There is little consistency among state laws, not to mention cities and counties, for the use of criminal records in hiring. More than two dozen cities and counties, and at least five states, have narrowed questions on their job applications to cover only felony convictions. Both Massachusetts and Hawaii prohibit private-sector employers from asking any questions about criminal history on initial written applications. The laws and policies require employers to wait until later in the hiring process, when the hiring manager is ready to make an offer, to ask applicants about their criminal records.[16] At the same time, there is at least one question that employers should ask, namely, whether a candidate is subject to any post-termination agreements with a prior employer (e.g., an agreement not to work for a competitor for certain time period). Ignorance of such agreements does not protect the new employer from legal liability.[17]

## Recommendations, References, and Background Checks

Recommendations, along with reference and background checks, are used by 98 percent of employers to screen outside job applicants.[18] They can provide four kinds of information about a job applicant: (1) education and employment history, (2) character and interpersonal competence, (3) ability to perform the

---

**ETHICAL DILEMMA**
**Are Work History Omissions Unethical?**

Consider the following situation. A job applicant knowingly omits some previous work history on a company's application form, even though the form asks applicants to provide a complete list of previous jobs. However, the applicant is truthful about the dates of previous jobs he does report. He leaves it to the interviewer to discover and ask about the gaps in his work history. The interviewer fails to ask about the gaps. Is the job applicant's behavior unethical?

## VIDEO RÉSUMÉS?

Video résumés have been around for years, but their popularity has surged recently, with many postings on YouTube, contests on sites like New York-based Vault.com, and several new services such as WorkBlast.[a] Candidates can look their best, rehearse answers to questions, and, in general, present themselves in the "best possible light." Thus electronic boards CareerBuilder.com and Kforce.com allow applicants to submit audio/video clips of themselves for recruiters to use as screening tools.

These efforts, however, get mixed reviews from employers and recruiters, many of whom consider video résumés to be costly gimmicks that fail to provide as much useful information as an ordinary résumé. Here are some of their objections: Answers are shallow rather than in depth, the videos take considerable time to review, and they could cause legal problems for employers who reject candidates from protected groups. At the same time, they might appeal to small and mid-size companies that tend to attract few applicants through more traditional recruitment sources. Will video résumés catch on in a big way? Stay tuned.

---

[a] Ho, D. (2006, June 18). Resumes that are ready for a close-up. *The Denver Post*, p. 3C.

---

job, and (4) the willingness of the past or current employer to rehire the applicant. Many organizations are not aware of how deep a check must go to identify serious problems. A casual check may reveal only that a candidate has wonderful references, no criminal record, and no liens against him or her. A more extensive probe, however, could uncover the fact that a candidate sued every company he ever worked for, or that he mismanaged assets but his former employer decided not to prosecute.[19]

The $4 billion business of background checks is booming, with firms like ChoicePoint, USIS, First Advantage, and Kroll Background Screening handling most of it. Fully 96 percent of employers now conduct background checks on job candidates, and false accusations or wrong identities, infrequent though they may be, can ruin careers. To head off potential problems, some candidates are running background checks on themselves to learn if their personal or financial data are inaccurate or exposed to abuse.[20]

A recommendation or reference check will be meaningful, however, only if the person providing it (1) has had an adequate opportunity to observe the applicant in job-relevant situations, (2) is competent to evaluate the applicant's job performance, (3) can express such an evaluation in a way that is meaningful to the prospective employer, and (4) is completely candid.[21]

Unfortunately, evidence is beginning to show that there is little candor, and thus little value, in written recommendations and referrals, especially those that must, by law, be revealed to applicants if they petition to see them. Specifically, the Family Educational Rights and Privacy Act of 1974 gives students the legal right to see all letters of recommendation written about them. It also permits release of information about a student only to people approved by the student at the time of the request.

A meta-analysis of five studies found that the average inter-rater reliability for references is only 0.22. In fact, research indicates that there is more agreement between recommendations written by the same person for two different applicants than between two people writing recommendations for the same person![22] Other research suggests that if letters of recommendation are to be meaningful, they should contain the following information:[23]

1.  *Degree of writer familiarity with the candidate.* That is, time known, and time observed per week.
2.  *Degree of writer familiarity with the job in question.* To help the writer make this judgment, the reader should supply the writer with a description of the job in question.
3.  *Specific examples of performance.* That is, goals, task difficulty, work environment, and extent of cooperation from coworkers.
4.  *Individuals or groups to whom the candidate is compared.*

When seeking information about a candidate from references or in a background check, or when contacting individuals identified through professional networking sites like LinkedIn or Jobster, consider the following guidelines:[24]

■ Request job-related information only; put it in written form to prove that your hire or no-hire decision was based on relevant information.
■ The Fair Credit Reporting Act requires third-party investigators to secure the applicant's written consent prior to doing a background check. If a decision not to hire an applicant results from negative information found through a background check, an employer is obligated to provide the applicant with the results and an opportunity to dispute them.
■ When it comes to checking social-networking sites like Facebook, legal experts advise the following: (1) Prohibit managers from conducting such checks on their own. Have HR professionals do them like all other background checks. (2) Conduct such checks only after you have interviewed an individual and determined that he or she is a viable candidate. (3) Ensure that all candidates are subject to the same social-media checks at the same point in the hiring process (e.g., among finalists for a position). (4) If you reject a candidate based on a social-media site search, document what you discovered and relied on.[25]
■ Evaluate the credibility of the source of the reference material. Not everything available online is factual. Under most circumstances, an evaluation by a past immediate supervisor will be more credible than an evaluation by an HR representative.
■ Wherever possible, use public records to evaluate on-the-job behavior or personal conduct (e.g., records regarding criminal and civil litigation, driving, or bankruptcy).[26]

What kind of information will employers release and not release? Recent data indicate the following: 98 percent will verify dates of employment for current or former employees; 68 percent will not discuss work performance; 87 percent will not discuss a disciplinary action; and 82 percent will not discuss character or personality.[27] What should you do if you are asked to provide reference information? Here are some useful guidelines:[28]

- Develop a written policy outlining procedures for checking references, and then follow it.
- Restrict the employees who conduct reference checks to HR staff or hiring managers trained to ask appropriate questions.
- Ask each applicant to provide at least three professional references.
- Obtain the applicant's written consent to contact former employers.
- Try to contact at least two of the references via telephone, e-mail, or online survey.
- Document attempts to contact references, and note their responses.

Sweetening of résumés and previous work history is common. How common? One study of 2.6 million résumés found that 44 percent contained exaggerations or outright fabrications about work experience; 23 percent listed bogus credentials; and 41 percent boasted fictional degrees.[29] The lesson: Always verify key aspects of previous history.[30]

On the other hand, employers can be held liable for **negligent hiring** if they fail to check closely enough on a prospective employee who then commits a crime in the course of performing his or her job duties. The employer becomes liable if it knew, or should have known, about the applicant's unfitness to perform the job in question.[31] When courts receive negligent-hiring claims they consider the following: (1) Would the risk have been discovered through a thorough background check? (2) Did the nature of the job cause greater risk? (3) Did the employer have a greater responsibility to conduct a thorough background investigation because of the nature of the job? (4) Was the action intentional?[32]

Currently, an employer has no legal duty or obligation to provide information to prospective employers. However, if an employer's policy is to disclose reference information, providing false or speculative information could be grounds for a lawsuit.[33] Reference checking is not an infringement on privacy when fair reference checking practices are used. It is a sound evaluative tool that can provide objectivity for employers and fairness for job applicants. Figure 7–2 shows some current facts about reference and background checks.

## ASSESSMENT METHODS IN SELECTION

Evidence indicates that as the complexity of work increases, organizations use more selection methods and use selection methods that capture the applicant's capability to do the work.[34] For example, organizations frequently evaluate and select job candidates on the basis of the results of physical (e.g., drug testing) or psychological assessments (e.g., aptitude, work-sample, or personality tests). Tests are standardized measures of behavior. A great deal of published research is available on almost all of the assessments we describe. What follows is a brief description of available methods and techniques, together with a description of their track records to date.

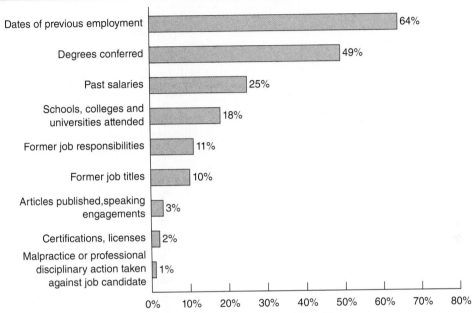

**Figure 7–2**

Inaccuracies uncovered by reference checks likely to block a job offer.

*Source:* Meinert, D. (2011, Feb.). Seeing behind the mask. *HR Magazine* 56(2), p. 37.

## Drug Screening

Drug-screening tests, which began in the military and spread to the sports world, are now becoming more common in employment. The math is simple. More than 75 percent of America's 14.8 million drug users have jobs. Drug users are almost four times as likely to be involved in a workplace accident as a sober worker, and five times as likely to file a workers' compensation claim. Drug users miss more days of work, show up late, and change jobs more often. Absenteeism and involuntary turnover are the outcomes that drug testing forecasts most accurately.[35] The cost of a drug test, meanwhile, is usually less than $50.[36] The number of job applicants and workers that test positive remains consistently about 4 percent, according to Quest Diagnostics, the largest testing company in the United States.[37]

Critics charge that such screening may not be cost effective, that it violates an individual's right to privacy, that it breaks the bonds of trust between employer and employees, and that employers should monitor work and performance—not drug use.[38] Employers counter that the widespread abuse of drugs is reason enough for wider testing.

Is such drug screening legal? The Supreme Court has upheld (1) the constitutionality of the government regulations that require railroad crews involved in accidents to submit to prompt urinalysis and blood tests and (2) urine tests for U.S. Customs Service employees seeking drug-enforcement posts. Indeed, more than 10 million civilian workers, mostly in law enforcement or in industries regulated by the U.S. Department of Transportation, are required by federal or state law to be tested.[39] After all, an employer has a legal right to ensure that employees perform their jobs competently and that no employee endangers the safety of other workers. So if illegal drug use either on or off the job may reduce job performance and endanger coworkers, the employer has adequate legal grounds for conducting drug tests.

To avoid legal challenge, consider instituting the following commonsense procedures:[40]

1. Inform all employees and job applicants, in writing, of the company's policy regarding drug use. Notify them 30–60 days before the drug-testing program takes effect.
2. Include the policy, and the possibility of testing, in all employment contracts.
3. Present the program in a medical and safety context. That is, state that drug screening will help improve the health of employees and will also help ensure a safer workplace.
4. Forbid employees from reporting to work or working while under the influence of alcohol or drugs.
5. Outline the procedures for taking the test. Tell employees who are taking prescription drugs to inform their supervisors. Notify employees that they may be required to provide a physician's release to work while using the medication.
6. If drug testing will be used with employees as well as job applicants, tell employees in advance that it will be a routine part of their employment.

**HR BUZZ**

## IMPAIRMENT TESTING—DOES IT WORK?*

Impairment testing is used to determine which workers in safety-sensitive jobs put themselves and others at risk by directly measuring the workers' current fitness for duty. Impairment may be due to a variety of sources, such as fatigue or illness, not just from illegal drug use. Drug screening, by contrast, attempts to determine which workers have used specific substances known to cause impairment in the relatively recent past. Drug screening may include urine tests, hair samples, or saliva samples. Impairment testing may involve a computer-based test of mental alertness, monitoring the ability of a worker's eyes to smoothly track an object moving horizontally, or monitoring his or her eyes' involuntary responses to light stimuli.

A recent study of almost every employer that has used impairment testing over the past 10 years (18 in total, and 14 participants in the study) showed that employers had used impairment-testing systems from five different manufacturers. Results indicated that 82 percent of the employers reported improvements in safety (reduced accidents) and no impact on productivity. Eighty-two percent of the employees in the study preferred impairment testing to urine testing, and 88 percent of employers expressed similar preferences. One drawback of impairment testing, however, is cost. It requires an initial investment both in hardware and software. After that, the variable cost is virtually zero. Drug screening, by contrast, requires no initial investment, but there is a variable cost per test that declines little with increasing quantity.

*Source: The National Workrights Institute. (2008). Impairment testing—Does it work? Retrieved from *www.workrights.org/issue_drugtest* on May 29, 2008.

7.  Employees who are more sensitive to job-safety issues are more likely to perceive drug screening as fair.[41]
8.  If drug testing is done, it should be uniform—that is, it should apply to managers as well as nonmanagers.

## Two Controversial Selection Techniques

### Graphology (Handwriting) Analysis

Graphology is the study of character or personality through handwriting. It is reportedly used as a hiring tool by 80 percent of French and Israeli companies.[42] Its use is not as widespread in the United States, although more than 150 multinational firms retain handwriting analysts as employment consultants. Such firms generally require job applicants to provide a one-page writing sample. Experts then examine it for 3 to 10 hours. They assess more than 300 personality traits, including enthusiasm, imagination, and ambition.[43] Are the analysts' predictions valid? In one study involving the prediction of sales success, 103 writers supplied two samples of their handwriting—one neutral in content, the second autobiographical. The data were then analyzed by 20 professional graphologists to predict supervisors' ratings of each salesperson's job performance, each salesperson's own ratings of his or her job performance, and sales productivity. The results indicated that the type of script sample did not make any difference. There was some evidence of inter-rater agreement, but there was no evidence for the validity of the graphologists' predictions.[44] Similar findings have been reported in other well-controlled studies and in meta-analyses (statistical cumulations) of such studies.[45] Validities vary from about 0.09 to 0.16, placing graphology at the lower end of the validity continuum, relative to other more commonly used staffing methods.[46] In short, there is little to recommend the use of handwriting analysis as a predictor of job performance.

### Polygraph Examinations

Advocates claim that polygraph (literally, "many pens") examinations are accurate in more than 90 percent of criminal and employment cases *if* interpreted by a competent examiner. Critics claim that the tests are accurate only two-thirds of the time and are far more likely to be unreliable for a subject who is telling the truth.[47] A quantitative analysis of 57 independent studies investigating the accuracy of the polygraph by the National Research Council concluded the following:[48]

- Polygraph accuracy for screening purposes is almost certainly lower than what can be achieved by specific-incident polygraph tests.
- The physiological indicators measured by the polygraph can be altered by conscious efforts through cognitive or physical means.
- Using the polygraph for security screening yields an unacceptable choice between too many loyal employees falsely judged deceptive and too many major security threats left undetected.

Prior to 1988, some 4 million polygraph tests were administered each year, 70 to 80 percent for pre-employment selection purposes.[49] However, a federal law passed in 1988, the Employee Polygraph Protection Act, severely restricts the use of polygraphs in the employment context (except in the case of firms providing security services and those manufacturing controlled substances). It permits polygraph examinations of current employees only under very restricted circumstances. Despite its problems, some agencies (e.g., U.S. Department of Energy) are using polygraph tests, given the security threats imposed by international terrorism.

## Integrity Tests

**Shrinkage**—an industry term for losses due to employee theft, shoplifting, vendor fraud, and administrative errors—is estimated to make up almost 2 percent of annual sales.[50] Employee theft alone is estimated to cause up to 30 percent of all business failures, it costs the nation's retailers $46 billion per year, and the average family of four an extra $440 a year in higher prices.[51] With statistics like these, it should come as no surprise that employers representing retail stores, nuclear plants, law enforcement agencies, and child-care facilities regularly use **integrity tests.** Most providers offer their tests online, and with volume pricing the cost per test can be under $10.[52] The integrity tests are of two types.[53] Overt integrity tests (clear-purpose tests) are designed to assess directly a person's attitudes toward dishonest behaviors. The second type, personality-based measures (disguised-purpose tests), aim to predict a broad range of counterproductive behaviors at work (disciplinary problems, violence on the job, excessive absenteeism, and drug abuse, in addition to theft).

Do they work? Yes—as a meta-analysis (a statistical cumulation of research results across studies) of 665 validity coefficients that used 576,460 test takers demonstrated. The average validity of the tests, when used to predict supervisory ratings of performance, was 0.41. The results for overt integrity and personality-based tests were similar. However, the average validity of overt tests for predicting theft per se was much lower, 0.13. For personality-based tests, there were no validity estimates available for the prediction of theft alone. Thus, theft appears to be less predictable than broadly counterproductive behaviors, at least by overt integrity tests.[54] The validity of integrity tests for predicting drug and alcohol abuse per se is about 0.30[55] and it is 0.25 for predicting absenteeism.[56] Finally, since there is no correlation between race and integrity test scores, such tests might well be used in combination with general mental-ability test scores to comprise a broader selection procedure.[57]

## Mental-Ability Tests

The major types of mental-ability tests used in business today include measures of general intelligence; verbal, nonverbal, and numerical skills; spatial relations ability (the ability to visualize the effects of manipulating or changing the position of objects); motor functions (speed, coordination); mechanical information, reasoning, and comprehension; clerical aptitudes (perceptual speed tests); and inductive reasoning (the ability to draw general conclusions on the basis of specific facts). When job analysis shows that the abilities or aptitudes measured by such tests are important for successful job performance, the tests are among the most valid predictors currently available (see Figure 7–3 and Table 7–1).[58] For administrative convenience and for

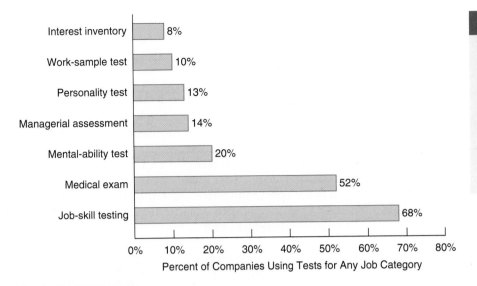

**Figure 7–3**

Most common tests and examinations used for selection.

(*Source:* American Management Association. (2001). *2001 AMA Survey on Workplace Testing.* New York: AMA, p. 2.)

## Table 7–1

### AVERAGE VALIDITIES OF ALTERNATIVE PREDICTORS OF JOB PERFORMANCE

| Measure | Validity* |
|---|---|
| General mental-ability tests | 0.51 |
| Work-sample tests | 0.54 |
| Integrity tests | 0.41 |
| Conscientiousness tests | 0.31 |
| Employment interviews (structured) | 0.51 |
| Employment interviews (unstructured) | 0.38 |
| Job-knowledge tests | 0.48 |
| Job-tryout procedure | 0.44 |
| Peer ratings | 0.49 |
| Ratings of training and experience | 0.45 |
| Reference checks | 0.26 |
| Job experience (years) | 0.18 |
| Biographical data | 0.35 |
| Assessment centers | 0.37 |
| Points assigned to training and experience | 0.11 |
| Years of education | 0.10 |
| Interests | 0.10 |
| Graphology | 0.02 |
| Age | −0.01 |

*Validity is based on cumulative findings that have been summarized using meta-analysis. Validity is expressed as a correlation coefficient that varies from −1 to +1.

*Source:* Adapted from Schmidt, F. L., and Hunter, J. E. (1998). The validity and utility of selection methods in personnel psychology: Practical and theoretical implications of 85 years of research findings. *Psychological Bulletin,* 24.

reasons of efficiency, many tests today are administered on personal computers, either at a dedicated physical location (such as a company office) or using Web-based assessments, available any time.[59] In high-stakes testing situations—for example, licensure, certification, and university admissions—there is general agreement that unproctored Internet testing is not acceptable, and that some cheating will occur.[60] Although job applicants tend to prefer multimedia, computer-based tests,[61] we do not know whether Internet selection affects the quantity and quality of the applicant pool and the performance of the people hired.[62]

With respect to the selection of managers, 70 years of research indicate that successful managers are forecast most accurately by tests of their cognitive ability, by their ability to draw conclusions from verbal or numerical information, and by their interests.[63] Cognitive ability is particularly effective in forecasting success in jobs with inconsistent tasks and unforeseen changes—as is often the case with managerial jobs.[64] Further research has found two other types of mental abilities that are related to successful performance as a manager: fluency with words and spatial relations ability.[65]

## Validity Generalization

A traditional belief of testing experts is that validity is situation specific. That is, a test with a demonstrated validity in one setting (e.g., selecting bus drivers in St. Louis) might not be valid in another, similar setting (e.g., selecting bus drivers in Atlanta), possibly as a result of differences in specific job tasks, duties, and behaviors. Thus, it would seem that the same test used to predict bus driver success in St. Louis and in Atlanta would have to be validated separately in each city.

Decades of research have cast serious doubt on this assumption.[66] In fact, it has been shown that the major reason for the variation in validity coefficients across settings is the size of the samples—they were too small. When the effect of sampling error is removed, the validities observed for similar test/job combinations across settings do not differ significantly. In short, the results of a validity study conducted in one situation can be generalized to other situations as long as it can be shown that jobs in the two situations are similar.

Because thousands of studies have been done on the prediction of job performance, **validity generalization** allows us to use this database to establish definite values for the average validity of most predictors. The average validities for predictors commonly in use are shown in Table 7–1.

## Personality Measures

**Personality** is the set of characteristics of a person that account for the consistent way he or she responds to situations. Five personality characteristics particularly relevant to performance at work are known as the "Big Five": neuroticism, extroversion, openness to experience, agreeableness, and conscientiousness.[67] **Neuroticism** concerns the degree to which an individual is insecure, anxious, depressed, and emotional versus calm, self-confident, and cool. **Extroversion** concerns the degree to which an individual is gregarious, assertive, and sociable versus reserved, timid, and quiet. **Openness to experience** concerns the degree to which an individual is creative, curious, and cultured versus practical with narrow interests. **Agreeableness** concerns the degree to which an individual is cooperative, warm, and agreeable versus cold, disagreeable, and antagonistic. **Conscientiousness** concerns the degree to which an individual is hard working, organized, dependable, and persevering versus lazy, disorganized, and unreliable. Research conducted over the past several decades shows that these are valid predictors of performance, but their validities differ depending on the nature of the job and the type of criteria. Conscientiousness has been shown to be the most generalizable predictor across jobs, with an average validity of 0.28. Validities tend to be highest when theory and job analysis information are used explicitly to select personality measures.[68]

Among employers, the most prevalent reasons for using personality tests is their contribution to improving employee fit, and to reducing turnover, while simultaneously increasing productivity.[69] According to one estimate, two-thirds of medium to large organizations use some type of psychological testing, including aptitude as well as personality, in screening job applicants.[70]

At this point you are probably asking yourself about the relationship of the Big Five to integrity tests. Integrity tests have been found to measure mostly conscientiousness but also some components of agreeableness and emotional stability.[71] That is why their validities tend to be higher than those of individual Big Five characteristics alone.

### The Issue of Faking

Can't applicants distort their responses in ways they believe will make a positive impression on the employer? The answer is yes.[72] Although *moderate* distortion may reduce predictive-related validities slightly, compared with validities obtained with job incumbents,[73] response distortion can have a dramatic effect on who is hired, even though it has no detectable effect on predictive validity.[74] On top of that, coaching can improve scores.[75] To control the effects of faking, one strategy is to perform statistical corrections, but they are not generally effective.[76] A more practical strategy is to warn job applicants in advance that distortion can and will be detected, that verification procedures exist, and that there will be a consequence for such distortion. Possible consequences might vary from elimination from the selection process to verification in a background check or oral interview. A review of eight studies that investigated the effects of such warnings found that, in all eight, warnings reduced the amount of intentional distortion in self-report instruments, relative to situations where no such warnings were given.[77]

### Measures of Emotional Intelligence

**Emotional intelligence** (EI) is the ability to perceive, appraise, and express emotion.[78] It is a well-established component of successful leadership. To appreciate the nature of EI, consider one instrument designed to measure it, the Emotional Competence Inventory—ECI 360. It is a 72-item, multirater assessment that includes input from self, manager, direct reports, peers, customers/clients, and others.[79] The ECI 360 measures personal competence (how people manage themselves) and social competence (how people manage relationships), and its purpose is to measure the key competencies that contribute to outstanding performance in the workplace.

Based on Goleman's Emotional Competence Framework, the ECI 360 is composed of four domains, each with associated competencies: (*personal competence*) (1) self-awareness (emotional self-awareness, accurate self-assessment, and self-confidence), (2) self-management (emotional self-control, transparency, adaptability, achievement, initiative, and optimism, i.e., *social competence*), (3) social awareness (empathy, organizational awareness, and service), and (4) relationship management (inspirational leadership, influence, developing others, change catalyst, conflict management, teamwork, and collaboration).

In recent years, EI has received considerable attention in practitioner as well as academic literature. Although some claims of its validity and ability to predict job performance over and above other, more traditional measures (cognitive ability, personality characteristics) have been viewed skeptically in the academic community,[80] at least one meta-analysis found an average validity of 0.23 with measures of performance.[81] It was criticized, however, for using outcome measures other than job performance, including only a small number of studies that used ability-based EI instruments, and a large number that used self-report data.[82] In short, the jury is still out regarding the incremental value of using EI as a basis for hiring or promotional decisions.

## Personal-History Data

Based on the assumption that one of the best predictors of what a person will do in the future is what he or she has done in the past, biographical information has been used widely and successfully as one basis for staffing decisions. Table 7–1 shows its average validity to be a very respectable 0.35. As with any other method, careful, competent research is necessary if biodata are to prove genuinely useful as predictors of job success.[83] For example, items that are more objective and verifiable are less likely to be faked,[84] although faking can be reduced by asking applicants to describe incidents to illustrate and support their answers.[85] The payoff is that biodata can add significant explanatory power over and above Big Five personality dimensions and also general mental ability.[86]

Google developed a biographical inventory to use in selecting job applicants by first asking its employees 300 questions and then correlating their responses to ratings of their job performance. Once it isolated items that predicted the performance of its current employees, Google asked applicants a smaller set of questions that ranged from the age at which the applicant first got excited about computers to whether the applicant ever turned a profit at his or her own side business.[87]

## Employment Interviews

Hands down, interviews are the most popular hiring tool across countries, jobs, and organizational levels. Yet employment interviewing is a difficult mental and social task. Managing a smooth social exchange while instantaneously processing information about a job candidate makes interviewing uniquely difficult

Personal interviews are a common feature of the hiring process in almost all organizations.

among all managerial tasks.[88] Well-designed interviews can be helpful because they allow examiners to gather information on characteristics not typically assessed via other means, such as empathy and personal initiative.[89] For example, a review of 388 characteristics that were rated in 47 actual interview studies revealed that personality traits (e.g., *responsibility, dependability,* and *persistence,* which are all related to conscientiousness) and applied social skills (e.g., *interpersonal relations, social skills, team focus,* and *ability to work with people*) are rated more often in employment interviews than any other type of construct.[90] In addition, interviews can contribute to the prediction of job performance over and above cognitive abilities and conscientiousness[91] as well as experience.[92] Reviews of the state-of-the-art of interviewing research and practice lead to the following recommendations:[93]

1. Base interview questions on a job analysis.
2. Ask the same general questions of each candidate. That is, use a structured interview.
3. Use detailed rating scales, with behavioral descriptions to illustrate scale points.
4. Take detailed notes that focus on behavioral information about candidates.[94]
5. Use multiple interviewers.
6. Provide extensive training on interviewing.
7. Do not discuss candidates or answers between interviews.
8. Use statistical weights for each dimension, as well as an overall judgment of suitability, to combine information.[95]

The validity of the pre-employment interview will be reduced to the extent that interviewers' decisions are overly influenced by such factors as first impressions, personal feelings about the kinds of characteristics that lead to success on the job, and contrast effects, among other nonobjective factors. **Contrast effects** describe a tendency among interviewers to evaluate a current candidate's interview performance relative to those that immediately preceded it. If a first candidate received a very positive evaluation and a second candidate is just average, interviewers tend to evaluate the second candidate more negatively than is deserved. The second candidate's performance is contrasted with that of the first.

Employers are likely to achieve nonbiased hiring decisions if they concentrate on shaping interviewer behavior.[96] One way to do that is to establish a specific system for conducting the employment interview. Building on the suggestions made earlier, here are some things to consider in setting up such a system:[97]

- To know what to look for in applicants, focus only on the competencies necessary for the job. Be sure to distinguish between entry-level and full-performance competencies.[98]
- Screen résumés and application forms by focusing on (1) key words that match job requirements, (2) quantifiers and qualifiers that show whether applicants have these requirements, and (3) skills that might transfer from previous jobs to the new job.
- Develop interview questions that are strictly based on the job analysis results; use open-ended questions (those that cannot be answered with a simple yes or no response); and use questions relevant to the individual's ability to perform, motivation to do a good job, and overall fit with the firm.
- Consider asking "What would you do if . . . ?" questions. Such questions comprise the situational interview, which is based on the assumption that a person's expressed behavioral intentions are related to subsequent behavior. In the situational interview, candidates are asked to describe how they think they would respond in certain job-related situations. Alternatively, in an experienced-based interview they are asked to provide detailed accounts of actual situations. For example, instead of asking "How would you reprimand an employee?" the interviewer might say, "Give me a specific example of a time you had to reprimand an employee. What action did you take, and what was the result?" Answers tend to be remarkably consistent with actual (subsequent) job behavior.[99] The empirically observed validities for both types of interviews, uncorrected for statistical artifacts, vary from about 0.22 to 0.28.[100]
- Conduct the interview in a relaxed physical setting. Begin by putting the applicant at ease with simple questions and general information about the organization and the position being filled. Throughout, note all nonverbal cues, such as lack of eye contact and facial expressions, as possible indicators of the candidate's interest in and ability to do the job.
- To evaluate applicants, develop a form containing a list of competencies weighted for overall importance to the job, and evaluate each applicant relative to each competency.

A systematic interview developed along these lines will minimize the uncertainty so inherent in decision making that is based predominantly on

### Table 7–2

**SOME EXAMPLES OF PROPER AND IMPROPER QUESTIONS IN EMPLOYMENT INTERVIEWS**

| Issue | Proper | Improper |
|---|---|---|
| Criminal history | Have you ever been convicted of a violation of a law? | Have you ever been arrested? |
| Marital status | None | Are you married? Do you prefer Ms., Miss, or Mrs.? What does your spouse do for a living? |
| National origin | None | Where were you born? Where were your parents born? |
| Disability | None | Do you have any disabilities or handicaps? Do you have any health problems? |
| Sexual orientation | None | With whom do you live? Do you ever intend to marry? |
| Citizenship status | Do you have a legal right to work in the United States? | Are you a U.S. citizen? Are you an alien? |
| Situational questions (Assumption: Job analysis has shown such questions to be job-related.) | How do you plan to keep up with current developments in your field? How do you measure your customers' satisfaction with your product or services? If you were a product, how would you position yourself? | |

"gut feeling." It also will contribute additional explanatory power over and above cognitive ability and measures of conscientiousness,[101] and it will reduce differences in evaluation scores among minorities and nonminorities. Does it matter if the interview is conducted face-to-face or via video-conference or by means of some other technology-mediated format (e.g. a telephone-based interview)? Evidence is beginning to accumulate that the increased efficiency of these approaches might be offset by less favorable reactions among those interviewed and the loss of potential applicants.[102] Table 7–2 shows some examples of proper and improper interview questions, along with several examples of situational-type questions.

## Work-Sample Tests

**Work-sample tests,** or situational tests, are standardized measures of behavior whose primary objective is to assess the ability *to do* rather than the ability *to know.* They may be motor-skills tests, involving physical manipulation of things (e.g., trade tests for carpenters, plumbers, electricians), or verbal-skills tests, involving problem situations that are primarily language- or people-oriented (e.g., situational tests for supervisory jobs).[103] Because work samples are miniature replicas of actual job requirements, they are difficult to fake, and they are unlikely to lead to charges of discrimination or invasion of privacy. They produce small minority/nonminority group differences in performance, a lack of bias by race or gender, and only modest losses in predictive validity, compared with traditional tests.[104] However, because the content of the test reflects the essential content of the job, the tests do have content-oriented evidence of validity.[105] Their use in one study of 263 applicants for city government jobs led to a reduction of turnover from 40 percent to less than 3 percent in the 9 to 26 months following their introduction.[106] Nevertheless, because each candidate must be tested individually, work-sample tests are probably not cost effective when large numbers of people must be evaluated.

Two types of situational tests are used to evaluate and select managers: group exercises, in which participants are placed in a situation where the successful completion of a task requires interaction among the participants, and individual exercises, in which participants complete a task independently. The context in which work-sample tests are administered is important, though. When used as stand-alone tests, work samples are designed to simulate actual job tasks. When used in the context of managerial selection, however, there is a de-emphasis on current knowledge and skill in a specific domain, and a strong focus on the assessment of future potential.[107] The following sections consider three of the most popular situational tests: the leaderless group discussion, the in-basket test, and the situational-judgment test.

## Leaderless Group Discussion

The **leaderless group discussion** (LGD) is simple and has been used for decades. A group of participants is given a job-related topic (e.g., which budget proposal to fund or which candidate to promote), and is asked simply to carry on a discussion about it for a period of time. No one is appointed leader, nor is anyone told where to sit. Instead of using a rectangular table (with a "head" at each end), a circular table is often used so that each position carries equal weight. Observers rate the performance of each participant.

In the course of the discussion, participants gravitate to roles in which they are comfortable. Usually someone will structure the meeting, someone will keep notes, some brainstorm well, some show skill at developing others' ideas, and some participate little. Assessors can see a whole range of competencies related to communication, influence, collaboration, resolving disagreements, problem solving, and relationship management.[108]

LGD ratings have forecast managerial performance accurately in virtually all the functional areas of business.[109] Previous LGD experience appears to have little effect on present LGD performance, although prior training clearly does.[110] Individuals in one study who received a 15-minute briefing on the history, development, rating instruments, and research relative to the LGD were rated significantly higher than untrained individuals. To control for this, all those with prior training in LGD should be put into the same groups.

## In-Basket Test

The **in-basket test** is a situational test designed to simulate important aspects of a position. The test assesses an individual's ability to work independently. In general, it takes the following form:

The test consists of letters, memoranda, notes of incoming telephone calls, and other materials that have supposedly collected in the in-basket of an administrative officer. The subject who takes the test is given appropriate background information concerning the school, business, military unit, or whatever institution is involved. She (or he) is told that she is the new incumbent of the administrative position and that she is to deal with the material in the in-basket. The background information is sufficiently detailed that the subject can reasonably be expected to take action on many of the problems presented by the in-basket documents. The subject is instructed that she is not to play a role, she is not to pretend to be someone else. She is to bring to the new job her own background of knowledge and experience, and her own personality, and she is to deal with the problems as though she were really the incumbent of the administrative position. She is not to say what she would do; she is actually to write letters and memoranda, prepare agenda for meetings, make notes and reminders for herself, as though she were actually on the job.[111] Some sample in-basket items are shown in Figure 7–4.

Although the situation is relatively unstructured, each candidate faces the same complex set of materials. Today, managers spend much less time than in the past handling memos in paper form, and a much greater amount of time in e-mail, voice-mail, and cell-phone communication. Thus, participants' work space for the in-basket test may include a computer, through which they can receive and send e-mails, and a phone/voice-mail system, through which they can communicate with others. The availability of such technology greatly increases the fidelity of the simulation, but it also greatly increases the workload on the assessors, who must keep track of such rapid communication via multimedia for several participants.[112]

The test is then scored by describing (if the purpose is development) or evaluating (if the purpose is selection for promotion) what the candidate did in terms of such dimensions as self-confidence; abilities to organize, plan, and set priorities; written communications; and decision making, risk taking, and coordinating with key resources. The dimensions to be evaluated are identified through job analysis prior to designing or selecting the exercise. The major advantages of the in-basket test, therefore, are its flexibility (it can be designed to fit many different types of situations), and the fact that it permits direct observation of individual behavior within the context of a job-relevant, standardized problem situation.

Decades of research on the in-basket test indicate that it validly forecasts subsequent job behavior and promotion.[113] Moreover, because performance on the LGD is not strongly related to performance on the in-basket test, in combination they are potentially powerful predictors of managerial success.

## The Situational-Judgment Test

Situational-judgment tests (SJTs) consist of a series of job-related situations presented in written, verbal, or visual form. In many SJTs, job applicants are asked to choose best and worst options among several choices available. Consider the following item from a SJT used for selecting retail associates:[114]

## Figure 7–4

### Sample in-basket items.

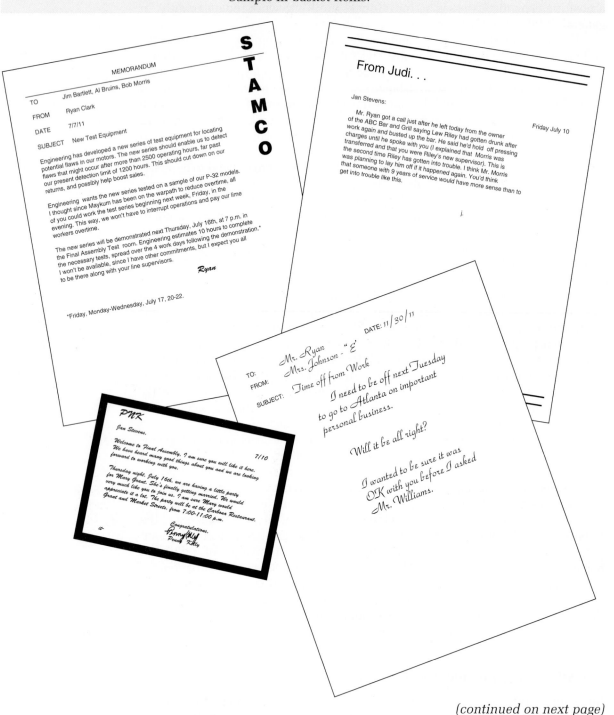

**S T A M C O**

MEMORANDUM

TO        Jim Bartlett, Al Bruins, Bob Morris

FROM      Ryan Clark

DATE      7/7/11

SUBJECT   New Test Equipment

Engineering has developed a new series of test equipment for locating potential flaws in our motors. The new series should enable us to detect flaws that might occur after more than 2500 operating hours, far past our present detection limit of 1200 hours. This should cut down on our returns, and possibly help boost sales.

Engineering wants the new series tested on a sample of our P-32 models. I thought since Maykum has been on the warpath to reduce overtime, all of you could work the test series beginning next week, Friday, in the evening. This way, we won't have to interrupt operations and pay our lime workers overtime.

The new series will be demonstrated next Thursday, July 16th, at 7 p.m. in the Final Assembly Test room. Engineering estimates 10 hours to complete the necessary tests, spread over the 4 work days following the demonstration.* I won't be available, since I have other commitments, but I expect you all to be there along with your line supervisors.

Ryan

*Friday, Monday-Wednesday, July 17, 20-22.

---

**From Judi. . .**

Jan Stevens:

Mr. Ryan got a call just after he left today from the owner of the ABC Bar and Grill saying Lew Riley had gotten drunk after work again and busted up the bar. He said he'd hold off pressing charges until he spoke with you (I explained that Morris was transferred and that you were Riley's new supervisor). This is the second time Riley has gotten into trouble. I think Mr. Morris was planning to lay him off if it happened again. You'd think that someone with 9 years of service would have more sense than to get into trouble like this.

Friday July 10

j.

---

**PNK**

Jan Stevens,

7/10

Welcome to Final Assembly. I am sure you will like it here. We have heard many good things about you and we are looking forward to working with you.

Thursday night, July 16th, we are having a little party for Mary Grant. She's finally getting married. We would very much like you to join us. I am sure Mary would appreciate it a lot. The party will be at the Carbona Restaurant, Grant and Market Streets, from 7:00-11:00 p.m.

Congratulations,
Penni Kelly

---

DATE: 11/30/11

TO:      Mr. Ryan

FROM:    Mrs. Johnson - "E"

SUBJECT:  Time off from Work

I need to be off next Tuesday to go to Atlanta on important personal business.

Will it be all right?

I wanted to be sure it was OK with you before I asked Mr. Williams.

---

(continued on next page)

**Figure 7–4**

(*continued*)

---

**DOWNTOWN KEY–WANIS CLUB**
Box 8003
Midville, Indiana

December 1, 2011

Mr. Sam Ryan, Superintendent
Midville Youth and Adult Development Center
Midville, Indiana

Dear Mr. Ryan:

We would like very much to have you speak at our luncheon meeting on Thursday, January 8th, at 12:30 p.m. at the Midville Hotel. Perhaps you could use the topic "The Extent of the Problem of Drug Abuse and Crime." The programs at our luncheon meetings usually run from 30-45 minutes.

We sincerely hope that you will be able to be with us on the 8th. Please let me know at the address shown above (or at telephone number 822-0136). If your schedule will not permit your accepting this invitation, perhaps one of your staff could present this program.

Yours truly,

*Jack Williams*

J.W. ("Jack") Williams
Program Chairman

---

2310 Lakewood Drive
Midville, Indiana
November 24, 2011

Mr. Sam Ryan
Midville Youth and Adult Development Center
Midville, Indiana

Dear Mr. Ryan:

The Youth Fellowship of Greenbriar Church would like to come to the Center and put on a Christmas Party for the people there. We would provide refreshments, presents for everybody, decorations, and all the rest.

Would you please let me know if this is possible? If it is, our committee will come out and talk to you about the plans. My phone number is 823-9322.

Sincerely,

*Cindy Fuller*

Cindy Fuller
President, Greenbriar
Youth Fellowship

*Bill—*
*How does this*
*sound to you?*
*S–R 11/25/11*

MR. RYAN-
THE LAST TIME WE HAD A
CHURCH GROUP PUT ON A PARTY
OUT HERE WAS BEFORE YOU
CAME. THINGS WERE OK
UNTIL THE HOUSEPARENTS
TOOK A COFFEE BREAK. WHILE
THEY WERE GONE, IT GOT
COMPLETELY OUT OF HAND.
WE COULD HAVE
PROBLEMS.
BILL 11/28/2011

---

**MIDVILLE APPLIANCE AND HARDWARE STORE**
149 Peabody Street
Midville, Indiana

November 28, 2011

Mr. Sam Ryan
Superintendent
Midville Youth and Adult
Development Center
Midville, Indiana

Dear Mr. Ryan:

As you know, my store is located between your rehabilitation center and Midville Vocational and Technical School. During the past several months we have had several cases of shoplifting from our store, and the police haven't been able to do anything about it. Also, your people have been observed acting funny, with a dazed look on their faces, as though they are on drugs.

I initially was a supporter of the rehabilitation center being in this neighborhood. However, I am about to change my mind, and I can assure you that my position on the zoning commission carries a lot of weight in this community.

I would appreciate hearing from you within the next week. Otherwise, I will be forced to take appropriate measures to ensure protection of my store and this community.

Sincerely,

*Arch Turkey*

Arch Turkey

---

memo

7/3/2011          from *Charlie Vernon*

*Bob:*

*We've had an 80% increase in rejects this week on our 38B model and most of them have been a result of poor armature wiring. Isn't that McGrady's operation? This doesn't help our production index, you know.*

A customer asks for a specific brand of merchandise the store doesn't carry. How would you respond to the customer?

1. Tell the customer which stores carry that brand, but point out that your brand is similar.

2. Ask the customer more questions so you can suggest something else.

3. Tell the customer that the store carries the highest-quality merchandise available.

4. Ask another associate to help.

5. Tell the customer which stores carry that brand.

*Questions for job applicants:*

- Which of the options above do you believe is the *best* under the circumstances?

- Which of the options above do you believe is the *worst* under the circumstances?

This illustration should remind you of the earlier discussion regarding the situational interview. In fact, situational interviews can be considered a special case of SJTs in which interviewers present the scenarios verbally and job applicants also respond verbally.

SJTs are inexpensive to develop, administer, and score compared with other types of work samples.[115] With respect to SJT validity, a recent meta-analysis, based on 134 validity coefficients and 28,494 individuals, found the following average levels of validity for various types of skills: teamwork (0.38), leadership (0.28), interpersonal skills (0.25), and job knowledge and skills (0.19). In each of these skill domains, video-based SJTs had stronger relationships with job performance than paper-and-pencil SJTs.[116] Perhaps more important, SJTs have been shown to make the prediction of job performance more accurate above and beyond job knowledge, cognitive ability, job experience, and conscientiousness, while showing less adverse impact based on ethnicity as compared with general cognitive ability tests.[117]

## Assessment Centers

The assessment-center approach was first used by German military psychologists during World War II to select officers. They felt that paper-and-pencil tests took too narrow a view of human nature; therefore, they chose to observe each candidate's behavior in a complex situation in order to develop a broader appraisal of his reactions. Borrowing from this work and that of the War Office Selection Board of the British army during the early 1940s, the U.S. Office of Strategic Services used this method to select spies during World War II. Each candidate had to develop a cover story that would hide her or his identity during the assessment. Testing for the ability to maintain cover was crucial, and ingenious situational tests were designed to seduce candidates into breaking cover.[118]

After World War II, many military psychologists and officers joined private companies, where they started small-scale assessment centers. In 1956, AT&T was the first to use the method as the basis of a large-scale study of managerial progress and career development. As a result of extensive research conducted over 25 years, AT&T found that managerial skills and abilities are best measured by the following procedures:[119]

1. *Administrative skills*—performance on the in-basket test.
2. *Interpersonal skills*—LGD, manufacturing problem.
3. *Intellectual ability*—paper-and-pencil ability tests.
4. *Stability of performance*—in-basket, LGD, manufacturing problem.
5. *Work-oriented motivation*—projective tests, interviews, simulations.
6. *Career orientation*—projective tests, interviews, personality inventories.
7. *Dependency on others*—projective tests.

Just four characteristics assessed with the original 1956 sample predicted management level attained 20 years later. Here are their validities: intellectual ability (0.64); ambition, measured by interviews and personality tests (0.62); interpersonal skills (0.60); and educational level (0.54).[120] Assessment centers do more than just test people. The **assessment-center method** is a process that evaluates a candidate's potential for management based on three sources: (1) multiple assessment techniques, such as situational tests, tests of mental abilities, and interest inventories; (2) standardized methods of making inferences from such techniques, because assessors are trained to distinguish between effective and ineffective behaviors by the candidates; and (3) pooled judgments from multiple assessors to rate each candidate's behavior.

Today assessment centers take many different forms, and they are used in a wide variety of settings and for a variety of purposes. Thousands of organizations in countries around the world are now using the assessment-center method, and more are doing so every year. In addition to evaluating and selecting managers, the method is being used to train and upgrade management skills, to encourage creativity among research and engineering professionals, to resolve interpersonal and interdepartmental conflicts, to assist individuals in career planning, to train managers in performance appraisal, and to provide information for workforce planning and organization design.

The assessment-center method offers great flexibility. The specific content and design of a center can be tailored to the characteristics of the job in question. For example, when used for management selection, the assessment-center method should be designed to predict how a person would behave in the next-higher-level management job. By relating each candidate's overall performance on the assessment-center exercises to such indicators as the management level subsequently achieved two (or more) years later or current salary, researchers have shown that the predictions for each candidate are very accurate. An accurate reading of each candidate's behavior before the promotion decision is made can help avoid potentially costly selection errors (erroneous acceptances as well as erroneous rejections).

As a specific example of the flexibility of the assessment-center method in using multiple assessment techniques, consider the following six types of exercises used to help select U.S. Army recruiters:[121]

■ *Structured interview.* Assessors ask a series of questions targeted at the subject's level of achievement motivation, potential for being a self-starter, and commitment to the Army.

- *Cold calls.* The subject has an opportunity to learn a little about three prospects and must phone each of them for the purpose of getting them to come into the office. Assessor role players have well-defined characters (prospects) to portray.
- *Interviews.* Two of the three cold-call prospects agree to come in for an interview. The subject's job is to follow up on what was learned in the cold-call conversations and to begin promoting Army enlistment to these people. A third walk-in prospect also appears for an interview with the subject.
- *Interview with concerned parent.* The subject is asked to prepare for and conduct an interview with the father of one of the prospects that he or she interviewed previously.
- *Five-minute speech about the Army.* The subject prepares a short talk about an Army career that she or he delivers to the rest of the group and to the assessors.
- *In-basket.* The subject is given an in-basket filled with notes, phone messages, and letters on which he or she must take some action.

A third feature of the assessment-center method is assessor training. Assessors are either line managers two or more levels above the candidates or professional psychologists. They are trained (from two days to several weeks, depending on the complexity of the center) in interviewing techniques, behavior observation, and in developing a common frame of reference with which to assess candidates.[122] In addition, assessors usually go through the exercises as participants before rating others.

This experience, plus the development of a consensus by assessors on effective versus ineffective responses by candidates to the situations presented, enables the assessors to standardize their interpretations of each candidate's behavior. Standardization ensures that each candidate will be assessed fairly, that is, in terms of the same "yardstick."[123]

Do managers or professional psychologists provide more valid assessments? Cumulative evidence across assessment-center studies indicates that professional psychologists who are trained to interpret behaviors in the assessment center relative to the requirements of specific jobs provide more valid assessment-center ratings than do managers.[124] Assessors seem to form an overall impression of participants' performance, and these overall impressions then drive more specific dimension ratings.[125]

To rate each candidate's behavior, organizations pool the judgments of multiple assessors. The advantage of pooling is that no candidate is subject to ratings from only one assessor. Because judgments from more than one source tend to be more reliable and valid, pooling enhances the overall accuracy of the judgments made. Each candidate is usually evaluated by a different assessor on each exercise. Although assessors make their judgments independently, the judgments must be combined into an overall rating on each dimension of interest. A summary report is then prepared and shared with each candidate.

These features of the assessment-center method—flexibility of form and content, the use of multiple assessment techniques, standardized methods of interpreting behavior, and pooled assessor judgments—account for the successful track record of this approach over the past five decades. It has consistently demonstrated high validity, with correlations between assessment-center performance and later job performance as a manager sometimes reaching the 0.50s and 0.60s.[126] Assessment-center ratings also predict long-term career success (i.e., corrected correlation of 0.39 between such ratings and average salary growth seven years later).[127] Both minorities and nonminorities and men and women acknowledge that the method provides them a fair opportunity to demonstrate what they are capable of doing in a management job.[128]

In terms of its bottom-line impact, two studies have shown that assessment centers are cost effective, even though the per-candidate cost may vary from as little as $100 to more than $4,000 (in 2011 dollars). Using the general utility equation (Equation 7–1 in the appendix to this chapter), both studies have demonstrated that the assessment-center method should not be measured against the cost of implementing it, but rather against the cost (in lost sales and declining productivity) of promoting the wrong person into a management job.[129] In a first-level management job, the gain in improved job performance as a result of promoting people via the assessment-center method is about $6,000 per year (in 2011 dollars). However, if the average tenure of first-level managers is, say, five years, the gain per person is about $31,000 (in 2011 dollars).

Despite its advantages, the method is not without potential problems, including the following:[130]

- Adoption of the assessment-center method without carefully analyzing the need for it and without adequate preparations to use it wisely.
- Blind acceptance of assessment data without considering other information on candidates, such as past and current performance.
- The tendency to rate only general exercise effectiveness, rather than performance relative to individual behavioral dimensions (e.g., by using a behavioral checklist), as the number of dimensions exceeds the ability of assessors to evaluate each dimension individually.
- Lack of control over the information generated during assessment; for example, "leaking" assessment ratings to operating managers.
- Failure to evaluate the utility of the program in terms of dollar benefits relative to costs.
- Inadequate feedback to participants.
- Not every competency can be simulated, especially those requiring long-term, cumulative actions, such as networking.[131]

Each of these problems can be overcome. Doing so will allow even more accurate prediction of each candidate's likely performance as a manager.

## HOW GOOGLE SEARCHES . . . FOR TALENT*

**HR BUZZ**

Google's mission is to organize the world's information. A complementary objective is to be just as innovative on the people side of the business as on the product side. In fact, it has to be innovative. After all, Google, the $167 billion company with more than 20,000 employees, receives more than 7,000 job applications per day, and is the ideal employer of almost one in five undergraduate students! The company sets very exacting hiring standards that may include an elaborate online survey that explores a job seeker's attitudes, behavior, personalty, and biographical details going back to high school, multiple interviews, even homework assignments (a personal statement plus a marketing plan for a future Google product). Executives take the hiring process very seriously—and devote an average of 5–8 hours a week on it. Even today, at least one of the co-founders reviews every job offer recommended by an internal hiring committee on a weekly basis, sometimes pushing back with questions about an individual's qualifications. The overall process has been described as "data-driven hiring."

Google uses "crowd sourcing"—based on the premise that any given group of people is always smarter than any given expert—in its hiring decisions. Here is how the process works. Google uses its applicant tracking system (ATS) to ask its current employees to weigh in on applicants who have submitted their résumés online. Information from the applications is parsed and stored in the ATS. The system then matches that information to data about existing Google employees, for example, based on the fact that they went to the same school.

Following the match, an e-mail automatically asks employees for internal references, which allows recruiters to tap employees who best understand the demands of the jobs and the nature of the culture in assessing the fit of potential hires. It allows current employees to build the community—even if they are not part of the formal interview process. This approach fits the Google culture perfectly because employees are being asked for their opinions.

To attract the hottest software programmers in South and Southeast Asia, the company hosts the Google India Code Jam. The fastest wins $6,900, and, more importantly, a coveted job at one of Google's R&D centers. About 14,000 contestants from all over South and Southeast Asia compete in the $3\frac{1}{2}$-hour event, and the top 50 are selected for the finals in Bangalore. Participants are tested on their problem-solving aptitude, on designing and writing code, and on testing peer-written work. Finalists are asked to create and test software for unique Web searches, and to get from Point A to B in a city with a minimum number of turns. The final challenge is to program a war-based board game, a task so complex that only a few contestants actually complete it.

The Code Jam is a shortcut through Google's hiring process. Another anomaly is to hire overqualified job applicants for HR jobs, as well as positions in other departments. Why? Because the company's brisk growth means that the scope of any job is expanding rapidly, and people may be promoted four, five, or even six times. Why are Google's hiring standards so demanding? Because the company believes that hiring the best talent will make it geometrically better than its competitors.

---

*Sources:* Wright, A. D. (2009). At Google, it takes a village to hire an employee. *SHRM's 2009 HR Trendbook* (Special supplement to *HR Magazine*), pp. 56–57. See also Bock, L. (2008, Apr. 8). People operations at Google. Presentation to IT Survey Group, Mountain View, CA. See also Delaney, K. J. (2006, Oct. 23). Google adjusts hiring process as needs grow. *The Wall Street Journal,* pp. B1, B8. See also Puliyenthuruthel, J. (2005, Apr. 11). How Google searches—for talent. *BusinessWeek,* p. 52.

## CHOOSING THE RIGHT PREDICTOR

In this chapter we have examined a number of possible predictors that might be used in the staffing process. Determining the right ones to use depends on considerations such as the following:

- *The nature of the job.*
- An estimate of the *validity of the predictor* in terms of the size of the correlation coefficient that summarizes the strength of the relationship between

applicants' scores on the predictor and their corresponding scores on some measure of performance.

- *The selection ratio,* or percentage of applicants selected.
- *The cost of the predictor.*

To the extent that job performance is multidimensional (as indicated in job analysis results), multiple predictors, each focused on critical competencies, might be used. Other things being equal, use predictors with the highest estimated validities; they will tend to minimize the number of erroneous acceptances and rejections, and they will tend to maximize workforce productivity. Look back at Table 7–1 for a summary of the accumulated validity evidence for a number of potential predictors.

It is important to take into account the **selection ratio** (the percentage of applicants hired) in evaluating the overall usefulness of any predictor, regardless of its validity. On the one hand, low selection ratios mean that more applicants must be evaluated; on the other hand, low selection ratios also mean that only the "cream" of the applicant crop will be selected. Hence, predictors with lower validity may be used when the selection ratio is low since it is necessary only to distinguish the very best qualified from everyone else.

Finally, the cost of selection is a consideration, but not a major one. Of course, if two predictors are roughly equal in estimated validity, then use the less costly procedure. However, the trade-off between cost and validity should almost always be resolved in favor of validity. Choose the more valid procedure because the major concern is not the cost of the procedure but rather the cost of a mistake if the wrong candidate is selected or promoted. In management jobs, such mistakes are likely to be particularly costly.[132]

---

## ORGANIZATIONAL CULTURE—KEY TO STAFFING "FIT"

*Human Resource Management in Action: Conclusion*

There is an old maxim about industry: It's a numbers game and a people business. The fundamental business proposition at Southwest Airlines is that its people come first. As cofounder Herb Kelleher commented,

> It used to be a business conundrum: Who comes first? The employees, customers, or shareholders? That's never been an issue to me. The employees come first. If they're happy, satisfied, dedicated, and energetic, they'll take real good care of the customers. When the customers are happy, they come back. And that makes the shareholders happy.

Southwest lets its best customers get involved in the pre-employment interviews for flight attendants. The entire process focuses on a positive attitude and teamwork. Peers play active roles in the hiring of peers; for example, pilots hire other pilots, baggage handlers other baggage handlers. In one case, Southwest pilots turned down a top pilot who worked for another major airline and did stunt work for movie studios. Even though he was a great pilot, he made the mistake of being rude to a Southwest receptionist. Teamwork also is critical. If applicants say "I" too much in the interview, they don't get hired. To be sure, Southwest's 34 consecutive years of profitable operations is not all due to the company's culture, but its culture is a major reason outsiders want to join the company and seasoned veterans want to remain.

The culture at Southwest has not changed, as Herb Kelleher noted upon stepping down as chairman after 37 years with the company. "We've never had layoffs. We could have made more money if we furloughed people. But we don't do that. And we honor them constantly. Our people know that if they are sick, we will take care of them. If there are occasions of grief or joy, we will be there with them. They know that we value them as people; they're not just cogs in a machine." On the day of Kelleher's final shareholders' meeting, Southwest pilots took out a full-page newspaper ad in *USA Today,* thanking Kelleher for all he had done.

Southwest's shareholders are also happy, because in 2010 it earned $0.74 per share, up from $0.19 per share in the prior year. It maintains a healthy balance sheet and has plenty of cash. Hmm, was Kelleher on to something when he put employees first? "There isn't any customer satisfaction without employee satisfaction," said Gordon Bethune, the former chief executive of Continental Airlines. In describing Kelleher, Bethune noted: "He recognized that good employee relations would affect the bottom line. He knew that having employees who wanted to do a good job would drive revenue and lower costs."

The best companies often create distinctive cultures. Thus from its first day in 1997, Netflix founder Reed Hastings focused on the start-up's culture, making it a place he enjoyed coming to every day, with people who pushed him intellectually, and a company of which he could be proud. When Hastings made public a 128-page PowerPoint presentation entitled, "Freedom and Responsibility Culture" in 2009, according to *Fortune* magazine, "the slide deck was inhaled by entrepreneurs across the Web."

At Netflix there is no vacation policy; employees take what they need as long as they get their jobs done. There are no strict compensation rules; workers choose their stock-to-cash ratios. There are few formal titles. Netflix employees come to the office, work extraordinarily hard, and go home. There are no beer bashes. Says one executive, "If you're looking for perks, this is the wrong place. The fun we have here is all about building products."

There is a simple lesson to learn from all of this. The ability to articulate a company's culture, to live it every day, and to make it real for applicants and for current employees, is a key feature of the decisions of successful applicants to join, and for seasoned veterans to stay and to compete for promotions.

## SUMMARY

In staffing an organization or an organizational unit, it is important to consider its developmental stage—embryonic, high growth, mature, or aging—in order to align staffing decisions with business strategy. It also is important to communicate an organization's culture, because research shows that applicants will consider this information to choose among jobs if it is available to them. To use selection techniques meaningfully, however, it is necessary to specify the kinds of competencies that are necessary for success.

Organizations commonly screen applicants through recommendations and reference checks, information on application forms, or employment interviews. In addition, some firms use written ability or integrity tests, work-sample tests, drug tests, or measures of emotional intelligence. In each case, it is important to pay careful attention to the reliability and validity of the information obtained. Reliability refers to the consistency or stability of scores over time, across different samples of items, or across different raters or judges. Validity refers to the job-relatedness of a measure—that is, the strength of the relationship between scores from the measure and some indicator or rating of actual job performance.

In the context of managerial selection, numerous techniques are available, but the research literature indicates that the most effective ones have been mental-ability tests, personality and interest inventories, peer assessments, personal-history data, and situational tests. The use of situational tests, such as the leaderless group discussion, the in-basket, and business simulations, lies at the heart of the assessment-center method. Key advantages of the method are its high validity, fair evaluation of each candidate's ability, and flexibility of form and content. Other features include the use of multiple assessment techniques, assessor training, and pooled assessor judgments in rating each candidate's behavior.

Recent research indicates, at least for ability tests, that a test that accurately forecasts performance on a particular job in one situation will also forecast performance on the same job in other situations. Hence it may not be necessary to

## IMPACT OF STAFFING DECISIONS ON PRODUCTIVITY, QUALITY OF WORK LIFE, AND THE BOTTOM LINE

Some companies avoid validating their screening and selection procedures because they think validation is too costly—and its benefits too elusive. Alternatively, scare tactics ("validate or else lose in court") have not encouraged widespread validation efforts either. However, a large body of research has shown that the economic gains in productivity associated with the use of valid selection and promotion procedures far outweigh the cost of those procedures.[a] Think about that. If people who score high on selection procedures also do well on their jobs, high scores suggest a close fit between individual capabilities and organizational needs. Low scores, on the other hand, suggest a poor fit. In both cases, productivity, quality of work life, and the bottom line stand to gain from the use of valid selection procedures.

Here's an example. T-Mobile used to be dead last in customer service among telecommunications companies. However, after the company changed its hiring practices to focus on characteristics that are critical to effective customer service—like empathy and quick thinking, along with a rigorous evaluation process for new hires, retraining for existing ones, and a new incentive plan called "Do More, Get More" that emphasizes courtesy and speed, results more than justified the effort. Two years later, absenteeism and turnover dropped 50 percent, and productivity tripled. And what do customers think? J. D. Power ranked T-Mobile #1 in customer service for two years running.

[a]Cascio & Fogli, 2010, op. cit.

conduct a new validity study each time a predictor is used. Research has also demonstrated that the economic benefits to an organization that uses valid selection procedures may be substantial. In choosing the right predictors for a given situation, pay careful attention to four factors: the nature of the job, the estimated validity of the predictor(s), the selection ratio, and the cost of the predictor(s). Doing so can pay handsome dividends to organizations and employees alike.

## KEY TERMS

| | |
|---|---|
| organizational culture | openness to experience |
| reliability | agreeableness |
| validity | conscientiousness |
| negligent hiring | emotional intelligence |
| shrinkage | contrast effects |
| integrity tests | work-sample tests |
| validity generalization | leaderless group discussion |
| personality | in-basket test |
| neuroticism | assessment-center method |
| extroversion | selection ratio |

## DISCUSSION QUESTIONS

7–1. Your boss asks you how she can improve the accuracy of pre-employment interviews. What would you tell her?

7–2. Why are reliability and validity key considerations for all assessment methods?

## IMPLICATIONS FOR MANAGEMENT PRACTICE

The research evidence is clear: Valid selection procedures can produce substantial economic gains for organizations. The implication for policy makers also is clear:

- Select the highest-caliber managers and lower-level employees, for they are most likely to profit from development programs.
- Do not assume that a large investment in training can transform marginally competent performers into innovative, motivated top performers.
- A wide variety of screening and selection procedures are available. It is your responsibility to ask "tough" questions of vendors and HR specialists about the reliability, job relatedness, and validity of each one proposed for use.
- Recognize that no one predictor is perfectly valid, and therefore that some mistakes in selection (erroneous acceptances or erroneous rejections) are inevitable. By consciously selecting managers and lower-level employees based on their fit with demonstrated job requirements, the strategic direction of a business, and organizational culture, you will minimize mistakes and make optimum choices.

**7–3.**  How does business strategy affect management selection?

**7–4.**  Discuss the dos and don'ts of effective reference checking.

**7–5.**  As jobs become more team oriented, assessment centers will be used more often for nonmanagement jobs. Do you agree or disagree?

**7–6.**  There are many possible staffing tools to help forecast later job performance. How do you decide which ones to use?

## APPLYING YOUR KNOWLEDGE

---

### *An In-Basket and an LGD for Selecting Managers*     *Exercise 7–1*

There are several means by which an organization can attempt to determine the right choices in the managerial selection process. An approach that is growing rapidly in popularity is to attempt to assess what a managerial candidate can do, rather than what he or she knows.

Various kinds of work samples or situational tests can be used to assess what a candidate can do. In this exercise, you will have an opportunity to see how two of the most valid managerial work samples operate—in-basket tests and leaderless group discussions (LGDs). An attractive feature of this combination of predictors is that although both are valid, the scores on each do not correlate highly with each other. This suggests that in-baskets and LGDs tap a different, but important, subset of the managerial performance domain.

#### Part A: In-Basket Exercise

An in-basket exercise is designed to assess a candidate's problem solving, decision making, and administrative skills. Further, because all responses are written ones, the exercise can also assess written communication ability.

An in-basket exercise consists of a set of letters, notes, memos, and telephone messages to which a candidate must respond. In practice, these items would typically be presented via e-mail or voice mail. To give you a sense of how an in-basket operates, however, here is a sample set of such items. The set is similar to the one in the text, except that for ease of administration, all items are stated in memorandum form.

#### Procedure

You are to assume that you have just been appointed director of human resources at Ace Manufacturing Company and that your name is George (or Georgina) Ryan. The president of the firm is Arnold ("Arnie") Ace. You were to replace the current HR director, John Armstrong, in two weeks, when he was scheduled to be transferred to Hong Kong. However, a family emergency in South Africa has required that John leave the country immediately, and you must fill in for him as best as you can. You have taken an alternate flight on an important business trip to Washington, DC, and have stopped over in Lompoc, where Ace's headquarters is located. It is Saturday morning, and no one else is available in the office. You must resume your flight to Washington, DC, within an hour.

Read through the items in your in-basket, decide what to do with each item, and record your decision on a separate sheet of paper. If any decisions require writing a letter or memo, you are to draft the response in the space provided. You are not to role-play how you think someone else might behave in this situation. Rather, you are to behave exactly as you yourself would in each situation.

---
### Item 1
---

MEMO TO:   John Armstrong, HR Director
FROM:        Jackie Williams, Downtown Business Club
SUBJECT:    Speaking engagement next week

Thanks again for your willingness to speak to our Business Club next week. As you know, this group represents a good cross section of the Lompoc business community as well as a number of Ace's best customers. We are all looking forward to what you have to say regarding the relationship between strategic planning and human resource information systems.

---
### Item 2
---

MEMO TO:   Mr. Ryan
FROM:        Judy [secretary to the director of human resources]
SUBJECT:    Tom Tipster's employment status

Just after Mr. Armstrong left yesterday, we received a call from the owner of Stockman's Bar and Grill saying that Tom Tipster had gotten drunk in the middle of the day again and busted up the bar. He said he'd hold off pressing charges until he talked to you (I explained that you were Mr. Armstrong's replacement). This is the third time that Mr. Tipster has gotten in trouble over his drinking problem. I think Mr. Armstrong was planning to fire him if he had another problem like this. You'd think that someone with 17 years of service at Ace would have more sense than to get into trouble like this especially with four kids at home to feed!

---
### Item 3
---

MEMO TO:   John
FROM:        Arnie
SUBJECT:    EEO Report

Where is that EEO report you promised me? There's no way I want to face the investigators from Denver Wednesday without it!

---
### Item 4
---

MEMO TO:   John Armstrong
FROM:        Lisa Buller, Administrator of Training Programs
SUBJECT:    Time off

I need to take next Thursday off to fly to San Francisco on important personal business. Will this be OK?

---
### Item 5
---

MEMO TO:   Mr. John Armstrong
FROM:        Arch Turkey
SUBJECT:    Thefts

As you know, my store is located between your downtown office extension and that of Deuce's. During the past several months we have had several cases of shoplifting from our store, and the police haven't been able to do anything about it. Further, several custodians from your facility have been observed acting funny (with dazed looks on their faces) and wandering around outside my store looking in. I think that your people may be responsible for the recent shoplifting losses I have suffered. I would appreciate hearing from you within the next week. Otherwise, I will be forced to take appropriate measures to ensure protection of my store.

---

### Item 6

MEMO TO:   John
FROM:         Alice Calmers, Director of Manufacturing
SUBJECT:   Thursday's training program

I finally got everything rearranged for that training program on Thursday. You can't imagine how difficult it is to try to rearrange the schedules of 15 very busy supervisors to attend anything at the same time. I certainly hope that Lisa's presentation is going to be worth all this juggling of schedules!

---

### Item 7

MEMO TO:   John Armstrong
FROM:         Ralph Herzberg, Manager of Customer Relations
SUBJECT:   New training program

We have a serious problem in the customer relations department. It is common for a large number of calls to come in all at once. When this happens, the customer-relations–contact employee is supposed to take the customer's phone number and get back to him or her within an hour. We've found in the past that this is a reasonable target since, after a big rush of calls, things usually settle down for a while. But when we check up on the contact employees, we find that they get back to the customer within an hour only about one-third of the time. Sometimes they don't get back to the customer until the next day! I sent a memo to all contact employees about a month ago reminding them of the importance of prompt responses on their parts, but it did very little good. We need a training program from your department to improve this critical performance area. Can we get together early next week?

## Responses

On a separate sheet of paper, provide your responses to the in-basket items.

Item 1: Speaking engagement next week.
Item 2: Tom Tipster's employment status.
Item 3: EEO report.
Item 4: Time off.
Item 5: Thefts.
Item 6: Thursday's training program.
Item 7: New training program.

## Part B: Leaderless Group Discussion (LGD)

Unlike the in-basket exercise, a leaderless group discussion exercise involves groups of managerial candidates working together on a job-related problem. The problem is usually designed to be as realistic as possible, and it is often tackled in groups of five or six candidates. No one in the group is appointed leader, nor is anyone told where to sit or how to act. Candidates are instructed simply to solve the problem to the best of their ability in the time allotted.

The LGD is used to assess such managerial traits and skills as aggressiveness, interpersonal skills, persuasive ability, oral communication skills, self-confidence, energy level, and resistance to stress.

### Procedure

The problem that follows is typical of those in an LGD. However, to conserve time, we have simplified it somewhat. Read the statement of the problem and then, working in groups of five or six students, arrive at a consensus regarding the solution to the problem. When finished, be prepared to discuss the kinds of management skills exhibited by students in your group.

### Bonus-Allocation Problem

Your organization has recently instituted an incentive bonus in an attempt to stimulate and reward key employee behaviors. The company has budgeted $95,000 for this purpose, to be spent every six months. You have been appointed to a committee charged with the responsibility of determining the allocation of bonus funds to deserving employees over the previous six-month period. A total of 25 employees were recommended by their supervisors. Decisions have already been made on 20 of them, and $70,000 of the original sum has been expended. Your task today is to decide on the size of the bonuses (if any) to be received by the remaining five employees. Summaries of the qualifications for the five employees are presented below:

### *Virginia Dewey*

Head custodian. 15 years with the firm. High school diploma. 22 years of relevant job experience. Manages a flawless custodial staff with low turnover and few union grievances. Present salary below average in most recent salary survey. Supports a family of six. Overlooked for salary increase last year.

### *Alfred Newman*

Accounting clerk. 3 years with the firm. 2-year college degree. 3 years of relevant work experience. Performs well under pressure of deadlines. Present salary is average in recent salary survey. Is known to be looking for other jobs.

### *Augusta Nie*

Manager of corporate data analysis. 7 years with the firm. Master's degree in computer science. 14 years of relevant work experience. Has developed the data analysis department into one of the most efficient in the company. Present salary is above average in recent salary survey. Has leadership potential and may be offered jobs from other firms. Difficult to replace good data processing personnel.

### *Barry Barngrover*

Machinist. 11 years with the firm. High school diploma. 11 years relevant job experience. Is the top performer in the milling machine department and exhibits a positive company attitude. Present salary is average in a recent salary survey. Is single and seems to have all the money he needs to support his chosen lifestyle.

*Harvey Slack*

Human resources staff. 1 year with the firm. College degree from prestigious Ivy League school. 3 years of relevant work experience. Very knowledgeable in subject matter but has trouble getting along with older coworkers. Present salary is above average in a recent salary survey. His mentor is the firm's vice president for human resources, who is said to be grooming Harvey for the VP position. Has received several offers from other firms recently.

---

## TECHNICAL APPENDIX

### The Estimation of Reliability

A quantitative estimate of the reliability of each measure used as a basis for employment decisions is important for two reasons: (1) If any measure is challenged legally, reliability estimates are important in establishing a defense, and (2) a measurement procedure cannot be any more valid (accurate) than it is reliable (consistent and stable). To estimate reliability, compute a coefficient of correlation (a measure of the degree of relationship between two variables) between two sets of scores obtained independently. As an example, consider the sets of scores shown in Table 7–3.

Table 7–3 shows two sets of scores obtained from two forms of the same test. The resulting correlation coefficient is called a parallel-forms reliability estimate. By the way, the correlation coefficient for the two sets of scores shown in Table 7–3 is 0.93, a very strong relationship. (The word "test" is used in the broad sense here to include any physical or psychological measurement instrument, technique, or procedure.) However, the scores in Table 7–3 could just as easily have been obtained from two administrations of the same test at two different times (test-retest reliability) or from independent ratings of the same test by two different scorers (inter-rater reliability).

Finally, in situations where it is not practical to use any of the preceding procedures and where a test can be administered only once, use a procedure known as split-half reliability. With this procedure, split a test statistically into two halves (e.g., odd items and even items) after it has been given, thereby generating two scores for each individual. In effect, therefore, two sets of scores (so-called parallel forms) are created from the same test for each individual. Then correlate scores on the two half-tests. However, because reliability increases as we sample larger and larger portions of a particular area of knowledge, skill, or ability, and because we have cut the length of the original test in half, the correlation between the two half tests underestimates the true reliability of the total test. Fortunately, formulas are available to correct such underestimates.

### Validation Strategies

Although a number of procedures are available for evaluating evidence of validity, three of the best-known strategies are construct oriented, content oriented, and criterion related. The three differ in terms of the conclusions and inferences that may be drawn, but they are interrelated logically and also in terms of the operations used to measure them.

## Table 7–3

### TWO SETS OF HYPOTHETICAL SCORES FOR THE SAME INDIVIDUALS ON FORM A AND FORM B OF A MATHEMATICAL APTITUDE TEST

| Person no. | Form A | Form B |
|:---:|:---:|:---:|
| 1 | 75 | 82 |
| 2 | 85 | 84 |
| 3 | 72 | 77 |
| 4 | 96 | 90 |
| 5 | 65 | 68 |
| 6 | 81 | 82 |
| 7 | 93 | 95 |
| 8 | 59 | 52 |
| 9 | 67 | 60 |
| 10 | 87 | 89 |

The coefficient of correlation between these sets of scores is 0.93. It is computed from the following formula:

$$r = \frac{\sum Z_x Z_y}{N}$$

where $r$ = the correlation coefficient

$\sum$ = sum of

$Z_x$ = the standard score on form A, where $Z = x$, each person's raw score on form A, minus $\bar{x}$, the mean score on form A, divided by the standard deviation of form A scores

$Z_y$ = the standard score on form B

$N$ = the number of persons in the sample (10 in this case)

Evaluation of *construct-oriented evidence of validity* begins by formulating hypotheses about the characteristics of those with high scores on a particular measurement procedure, in contrast to those with low scores. For example, we might hypothesize that sales managers will score significantly higher on the managerial interests scale of the California Psychological Inventory (CPI) than will pharmacy students (in fact, they do), and that they will also be more decisive and apt to take risks as well. The hypotheses form a tentative theory about the nature of the psychological construct, or trait, that the CPI is believed to be measuring. These hypotheses may then be used to predict how people at different score levels on the CPI will behave on other tests or in other situations during their careers. Construct validation is not accomplished in a single study. It requires that evidence be accumulated from different sources to determine the meaning of the test scores in terms of how people actually behave. It is a logical as well as an empirical process.

*Content-oriented evidence of validity* is also a judgmental, rational process. It requires an answer to the following question: Is the content of the measurement procedure a fair, representative sample of the content of the job it is supposed to represent? Such judgments can be made rather easily by job incumbents, supervisors, or other job experts when job knowledge or work-sample tests are used (e.g., typing tests and tests for electricians, plumbers, and computer programmers). However, content-oriented evidence becomes less appropriate as the behaviors in question become less observable and more abstract (e.g., the ability to draw conclusions from a written sample of material). In addition, because such judgments are not expressed in quantitative terms, it is difficult to justify ranking applicants in terms of predicted job-performance, and it is difficult to estimate directly the dollar benefits to the firm from using such a procedure. To overcome these problems, we need a criterion-related validity strategy.

The term *criterion-related evidence of validity* calls attention to the fact that the chief concern is with the relationship between predictor [the selection procedure(s) used] and criterion (job-performance) scores, not with predictor scores per se. Indeed, the content of the predictor measure is relatively unimportant, because it serves only as a vehicle to predict actual job performance.

There are two strategies of criterion-related validation: concurrent and predictive. A *concurrent strategy* is used to measure job incumbents. Job-performance (criterion) measures for this group are already available, so immediately after administering a selection measure to this group, it is possible to compute a correlation coefficient between predictor scores and criterion scores (over all individuals in the group). A procedure identical to that shown in Table 7–3 is used. If the selection measure is valid, those employees with the highest (or lowest) job performance scores should also score highest (or lowest) on the selection measure. In short, if the selection measure is valid, there should exist a systematic relationship between scores on that measure and job performance. The higher the test score, the better the job performance (and vice versa).

When a *predictive strategy* is used, the procedure is identical, except that we measure job candidates. We use the same methods that currently are used to select employees and simply add the new selection procedure to the overall process. However, we select candidates without using the results of the new procedure. At a later date (e.g., six months to a year), when it becomes possible to develop a meaningful measure of job performance for each new hire, scores on the new selection procedure are correlated with job performance scores. We then assess the strength of the predictor-criterion relationship in terms of the size of the correlation coefficient.

## Estimating the Economic Benefits of Selection Programs

If we assume that $n$ workers are hired during a given year and that the average job tenure of those workers is $t$ years, the dollar increase in productivity can be determined from Equation 7–1. Admittedly, this is a "cookbook recipe," but the formula was derived more than 60 years ago and is well established in applied psychology:[133]

$$\Delta U = ntr_{xy} SD_y \bar{Z}_x \qquad (7\text{–}1)$$

where $\Delta U$ = increase in productivity in dollars

$n$ = number of persons hired

$t$ = average job tenure in years of those hired

$r_{xy}$ = the validity coefficient representing the correlation between the predictor and job performance in the applicant population

$SD_y$ = the standard deviation of job performance in dollars (roughly 40 percent of annual wage)[134]

$\bar{Z}_x$ = the average predictor score of those selected in the applicant population, expressed in terms of standard scores

When Equation 7–1 was used to estimate the dollar gains in productivity associated with use of the programmer aptitude test (PAT) to select computer programmers for federal government jobs, given that an average of 618 programmers per year are selected, each with an average job tenure of 9.69 years, the payoff per selectee was $25,490 (in 2011 dollars) over his or her tenure on the job. This represents a per-year productivity gain of $2,630 for each new programmer.[135] Clearly, the dollar gains in increased productivity associated with the use of valid selection procedures (the estimated true validity of the PAT is 0.76) are not trivial, even after correcting them to account for corporate taxes and variable costs, and discounting future cash flows to express their present value. Indeed, in a globally competitive environment, businesses need to take advantage of every possible strategy for improving productivity. The widespread use of valid selection and promotion procedures should be a priority consideration in this effort.

Valid selection and promotion procedures also benefit applicants in several ways. One is that a more accurate matching of applicant knowledge, skills, ability, and other characteristics to job requirements helps enhance the likelihood of successful performance. This, in turn, helps workers feel better about their jobs and adjust to changes in them, as they are doing the kinds of things they do best. Moreover, because we know that there is a positive spillover effect between job satisfaction and life satisfaction, the accurate matching of people and jobs will also foster an improved quality of life, not just an improved quality of work life, for all concerned.

## REFERENCES

1. Cascio, W. F., and Aguinis, H. (2008). Staffing 21st-century organizations. In J. P. Walsh and A. P. Brief (Eds.), *Academy of Management Annals* 2(1), pp. 133–165.
2. Ployhart, R. E., and Weekley, J. A., (2010). Strategy, selection, and sustained competitive advantage. In Farr, J. L., and Tippins, N. T. (Eds.), *Handbook of Employee Selection*. New York, NY: Routledge, pp. 195–212. See also Heneman, H. G., III., Judge, T. and Kammeyer-Mueller, J. D. (2012). *Staffing Organizations* (7th Ed.). New York, NY: McGraw-Hill.
3. Kristof-Brown, A., and Guay, R. P. (2011). Person-environment fit. In S. Zedeck (Ed.), *APA Handbook of Industrial and Organizational Psychology*, Vol. 3. Washington, DC: American Psychological Association, pp. 3–50. See also Schneider, B., Smith, D. B., Taylor, S., and Fleenor, J. (1998). Personality and organizations: A test of the homogeneity of personality hypothesis. *Journal of Applied Psychology* 83, pp. 462–470. See also Schneider, B. (1987). The people make the place. *Personnel Psychology* 40, pp. 437–453.

4. Tetenbaum, T. (1999, Autumn). Beating the odds of merger and acquisition failure. *Organizational Dynamics,* pp. 22–36.

5. Schneider, B., Ehrhart, M. G., and Macey, W. H. (2011). Perspectives on organizational climate and culture. In S. Zedeck (Ed.), *APA Handbook of Industrial and Organizational Psychology*, Vol. 1. Washington, DC: American Psychological Association, pp. 373–414. Martin, J. (2002). *Organizational Culture: Mapping the Terrain.* Thousand Oaks, CA: Sage. See also Schein, E. H. (2004). *Organizational Culture and Leadership* (3rd Ed.). San Francisco: Jossey-Bass.

6. Kristof-Brown and Guay, 2011, op. cit. See also Power, D. J., and Aldag, R. J. (1985). Soelberg's job search and choice model: A clarification, review, and critique. *Academy of Management Review* 10, pp. 48–58.

7. Kristof-Brown and Guay, 2011, op. cit. See also Kristof-Brown, A. L. (2000). Perceived applicant fit: Distinguishing between recruiters' perceptions of person-job and person-organization fit. *Personnel Psychology* 53, pp. 643–671.

8. Snow, C. C., and Snell S. A. (1993). Staffing as strategy. In N. Schmitt and W.C. Borman (Eds.), *Personnel Selection in Organizations.* San Francisco: Jossey-Bass, pp. 448–478.

9. Sheridan, J. E. (1992). Organizational culture and employee retention. *Academy of Management Journal* 35, pp. 1036–1056. See also O'Reilly, C. A. III, and Pfeffer, J. (2000). *Hidden Value: How Great Companies Achieve Extraordinary Results with Ordinary People.* Boston: Harvard Business School Press.

10. Hunter, J. E., Schmidt, F. L., and Judiesch, M. K. (1990). Individual differences in output variability as a function of job complexity. *Journal of Applied Psychology* 75, pp. 28–42.

11. Schmitt, N. W., Arnold, J. D., and Nieminen, L. (2010). Validation strategies for primary studies. In Farr, J. L., and Tippins, N. T. (Eds.), *Handbook of Employee Selection.* New York, NY: Routledge, pp. 51–71.

12. Ibid. See also Cascio, W. F., and Aguinis, H. (2011). *Applied Psychology in Human Resource Management* (7th Ed.). Upper Saddle River, NJ: Prentice Hall.

13. Society for Industrial-Organizational Psychology. (2003). *Principles for the validation and use of personnel selection procedures* (4th Ed.). Bowling Green, OH: Society for Industrial-Organizational Psychology.

14. American Educational Research Association, American Psychological Association, National Council on Measurement in Education. (1999). *Standards for Educational and Psychological Testing.* Washington, DC: American Educational Research Association.

15. Uniform guidelines on employee selection procedures (1978). *Federal Register* 43, pp. 38290–38315.

16. Roberts, B. (2011, Feb.). Close-up on screening. *HR Magazine* 56(2), pp. 23–29.

17. Segal, J. A. (2011, July). Hiring days are here again. *HR Magazine* 56(7), pp. 58–60.

18. Meinert, D. (2011, Feb.). Seeing behind the mask. *HR Magazine* 56(2), pp. 31–37.

19. Kroll, J., and Turecek, P. (2003, Jan.). Why background checks on executives are critical. *Director's Monthly,* pp. 11, 12.

20. Terhune, C. (2008, June 9). The trouble with background checks. *BusinessWeek,* pp. 54–58. See also McQueen, M. P. (2007, Apr. 21). Why you should spy on yourself. *The Wall Street Journal,* pp. B1, B2.

21. Cascio and Aguinis, 2011, op cit.

22. Aamodt, M. G. (2007). Letters of recommendation. In S. G. Rogelberg (Ed.), *Encyclopedia of Industrial and Organizational Psychology,* Vol. 1. Thousand Oaks, CA: Sage, pp. 455, 456.

23. Knouse, S. B. (1987). An attribution theory approach to the letter of recommendation. *International Journal of Management* 4(1), pp. 5–13.

24. Wells, S. J. (2008, Feb.). Ground rules on background checks. *HR Magazine,* pp.47–54. See also Aamodt, 2007, op. cit. See also Maher, K. (2004, Jan. 20). Background checks stir up worries in many employees. *The Wall Street Journal,* p. B8. See also Babcock, P.

(2004, Mar.). It takes more than a reference check to weed out liars. Retrieved from *http://www.shrm.org/TemplatesTools/Samples/SupervisoryNewsletter/winter04/Pages/story3.aspx* on Aug. 31, 2004.

25. Segal, J. A. (2011, April). Dancing on the edge of a volcano. *HR Magazine* 56(4), pp. 83–86.

26. Athavaley, A. (2007, Sept. 27). Job references you can't control. *The Wall Street Journal,* pp. D1, D2. See also Zeidner, R. (2007, Oct.). How deep can you probe? *HR Magazine,* pp. 57–62.

27. Background checking: General background checks, SHRM Poll (2010, Jan. 22). Retrieved from *http://www.shrm.org/Research/SurveyFindings/Articles/Pages/BackgroundCheckingGeneral.aspx* on July 11, 2011.

28. Meinert, 2011, op. cit.

29. Meinert, 2011, op. cit. See also Soltis, C. (2006, Mar. 21). Eagle-eyed employers scour resumes for little white lies. *The Wall Street Journal,* p. B7. See also Fisher, A. (2003, May 26). How can we be sure we're not hiring a bunch of shady liars? *Fortune,* p. 180.

30. Zimmerman, A., and Stringer, K. (2004, Aug. 26). As background checks proliferate, excons face job lock. *The Wall Street Journal,* pp. B1, B3. See also Kroll and Turecek, 2003, op. cit.

31. Roberts, B. (2010, Dec.). Backgrounds to the foreground. *HR Magazine* 55(12), pp. 46–51. See also Ryan, A. M., and Lasek, M. (1991). Negligent hiring and defamation: Areas of liability related to pre-employment inquiries. *Personnel Psychology* 44, pp. 293–319.

32. Jackson, S., and Loftin, A. (2000, Jan.). Proactive practices avoid negligent hiring claims. *HR News, p.* 12.

33. Arnold, D. W. (1996, Feb.). Providing references. *HR News,* p. 16.

34. Sackett, P. R., and Lievens, F. (2008). Personnel selection. *Annual Review of Psychology* 59, pp. 419–450. See also Wilk, S. L., and Cappelli, P. (2003). Understanding the determinants of employer use of selection methods. *Personnel Psychology* 56, pp. 103–124.

35. Harris, M. M., and Heft, L. L. (1993). Pre-employment urinalysis drug testing: A critical review of psychometric and legal issues and effects on applicants. *Human Resource Management Review* 3, pp. 271–291.

36. Fahmy, D. (2007, May 10). Aiming for a drug-free workplace. *The New York Times,* p. C6.

37. Zeidner, 2007, op. cit. See also Gurchiek, K. (2007, Apr. 18). Employer testing credited for drop in worker drug use. *HR News.* Retrieved from *http://www.shrm.org/Publications/HRNews/Pages/CMS_021232.aspx* on May 28, 2008.

38. Blumberg, K. (2004). Critical components of workplace drug testing. *SHRM White Paper.* Retrieved from *http://www.shrm.org/Research/Articles/Articles/Pages/CMS_009212.aspx* on May 28, 2008.

39. Zeidner, R. (2010, Nov.). Putting drug screening to the test. *HR Magazine* 55(11), pp. 25–30.

40. Blumberg, 2004, op. cit. See also Fahmy, D. (2007, May 10). Legal advice is first step in setting up screening. *The New York Times,* p. 6. See also Bahls, J. E. (1998, March). Dealing with drugs: Keep it legal. *HR Magazine,* pp. 104–116.

41. Paronto, M. E., Truxillo, D. M., Bauer, T. N., and Leo, M. C. (2002). Drug testing, drug treatment, and marijuana use: A fairness perspective. *Journal of Applied Psychology* 87, pp. 1159–1166.

42. Simner, M. L., and Goffin, R. D. (2003). A position statement by the International Graphonomics Society on the use of graphology in personnel selection testing. *International Journal of Testing* 3(4), pp. 353–364.

43. Gorman, C. (1989, Jan. 23). Honestly, can we trust you? *Time,* p. 44. See also McCarthy, M. J. (1988, Aug. 25). Handwriting analysis as personnel tool. *The Wall Street Journal,* p. B1.

44. Rafaeli, A., and Klimoski, R. J. (1983). Predicting sales success through handwriting analysis: An evaluation of the effects of training and handwriting sample content. *Journal of Applied Psychology* 68, pp. 212–217.

45. Schmidt, F. L., and Hunter, J. E. (1998). The validity and utility of selection methods in personnel psychology: Practical and theoretical implications of 85 years of research findings. *Psychological Bulletin* 124, pp. 262–274. See also Dean, G. A. (1992). The bottom line: In B. L. Beyerstein and D. F. Beyerstein (Eds.), *The Write Stuff: Evaluations of Graphology—The Study of Handwriting Analysis.* Buffalo, NY: Prometheus. Neter, E., and Ben-Shakhar, G. (1989). The predictive validity of graphological inferences: A meta-analytic approach. *Personality and Individual Differences* 10, pp. 737–745. See also Ben-Shakhar, G., Bar-Hillel, M., Bilu, Y., Ben-Abba, E., and Flug, A. (1986). Can graphology predict occupational success? Two empirical studies and some methodological ruminations. *Journal of Applied Psychology* 71, pp. 645–653.

46. Simner and Goffin, 2003, op. cit.

47. Kleinmuntz, B. (1985, July–Aug.). Lie detectors fail the truth test. *Harvard Business Review* 63, pp. 36–42. See also Patrick, C. J., and Iacono, W. G. (1989). Psychopathy, threat, and polygraph test accuracy. *Journal of Applied Psychology* 74, pp. 347–355 See also Saxe, L., Dougherty, D., and Cross, T. (1985). The validity of polygraph testing. *American Psychologist* 40, pp. 355–356.

48. Committee to Review the Scientific Evidence on the Polygraph, National Research Council (2003). *The Polygraph and Lie Detection.* Washington, DC: National Academies Press.

49. Roberts, B. (2011, June). Your cheating heart. *HR Magazine* 56(6), pp. 55–60. Shaffer, D. J., and Schmidt, R. A. (1999, Sept.–Oct.). Personality testing in employment. *Legal Report,* pp. 1–5.

50. Waters, S. Top 4 sources of shrinkage. Retrieved from *http://retail.about.com/od/lossprevention/tp/shrink_sources.htm* on July 12, 2011. See also Ernst & Young (2003). Ernst & Young estimates retailers lose $46 billion annually to inventory shrinkage. Retrieved from *http://www.clear-vu.com/industrynews.cfm?newssel9* on May 21, 2006.

51. Ernst & Young, 2003, op. cit.

52. Roberts, 2011, op. cit.

53. Roberts, 2011, op. cit. Camara, W. J., and Schneider, D. L. (1994). Integrity tests: Facts and unresolved issues. *American Psychologist* 49(2), pp. 112–119. See also Sackett, P. R., Burris, L. R., and Callahan, C. (1989). Integrity testing for personnel selection: An update. *Personnel Psychology* 42, pp. 491–529.

54. Wanek, J. E. (1999). Integrity and honesty testing: What do we know? How do we use it? *International Journal of Selection and Assessment* 7, pp. 183–195. See also Schmidt and Hunter, 1998, op. cit. See also Ones, D. S., Viswesvaran, C., and Schmidt, F. L. (1993). Comprehensive meta-analysis of integrity test validities: Findings and implications for personnel selection and theories of job performance. *Journal of Applied Psychology* (monograph), 78, pp. 679–703.

55. Schmidt, F. L, Viswesvaran, V., and Ones, D. S. (1997). Validity of integrity tests for predicting drug and alcohol abuse: A meta-analysis. In Bukoski, W. J. (Ed.), *Meta-analysis of drug abuse prevention programs.* NIDA Research Monograph 170. Washington, DC: U.S. Department of Health and Human Services, pp. 69–95.

56. Rotundo, M., and Spector, P. E. (2010). Counterproductive work behavior and withdrawal. In J. Farr and N. T. Tippins (Eds.), *Handbook of Employee Selection.* New York, NY: Routledge, pp. 489–511. See also Ones, D. S., Viswesvaran, C., and Schmidt, F. L. (2003). Personality and absenteeism: A meta-analysis of integrity tests. *European Journal of Personality* 17, pp. S19–S38.

57. Roberts, 2011, op. cit. See also Schmidt and Hunter, 1998, op. cit.

58. Ones, D. S., Dilchert, S., Viswesvaran, C., and Salgado, J. (2010). Cognitive abilities. In J. Farr and N. T. Tippins (Eds.), *Handbook of Employee Selection.* New York,

NY: Routledge, pp. 255–275. See also Sackett and Lievens, 2008, op. cit. For an excellent discussion and summary of results across jobs, settings, jobs, and countries, see Ones, D. S., Viswesvaran, C., and Dilchert, S. (2004). Cognitive ability in selection decisions. In O. Wilhelm and R. W. Engle (Eds.), *Handbook of Understanding and Measuring Intelligence.* London: Sage, pp. 448–477.

**59.** Chapman, D. S., and Webster, J. (2003). The use of technologies in the recruiting, screening, and selection processes for job candidates. *International Journal of Selection and Assessment* 11, pp. 113–119. See also Jones, J. W., and Dages, K. D. (2003). Technology trends in staffing and assessment: A practice note. *International Journal of Selection and Assessment* 11, pp. 247–25.

**60.** Wunder, R. S., Thomas, L. L., and Luo, Z. (2010). Administering assessments and decision-making. In J. Farr and N. T. Tippins (Eds.), *Handbook of Employee Selection.* New York, NY: Routledge, pp. 377–398. Tippins, N. T., Beaty, J., Drasgow, F., Gibson, W. M., Pearlman, K., Segall, D. O., and Shepherd, W. (2006). Unproctored Internet testing in employment settings. *Personnel Psychology* 59, pp. 189–225.

**61.** Richman-Hirsch, W. L., Olson-Buchanan, J. B., and Drasgow, F. (2000). Examining the impact of administration medium on examinee perceptions and attitudes. *Journal of Applied Psychology* 85, pp. 880–887.

**62.** Sackett and Lievens, 2008, op. cit. See also Ployhart, R. E., Weekley, J. A., Holtz, B. C., and Kemp, C. (2003). Web-based and paper-and-pencil testing of applicants in a proctored setting: Are personality, biodata, and situational judgment tests comparable? *Personnel Psychology* 56, pp. 733–752. See also Donovan, M. A., Drasgow, F., and Probst, T. M. (2000). Does computerizing paper-and-pencil job attitude scales make a difference? New IRT analyses offer insight. *Journal of Applied Psychology* 85, pp. 305–313.

**63.** Goldstein, H. W., Yusko, K. P., Braverman, E. P., Smith, D. B., and Chung, B. (1998). The role of cognitive ability in the subgroup differences and incremental validity of assessment center exercises. *Personnel Psychology* 51, pp. 357–374. See also Ghiselli, E. E. (1973). The validity of aptitude tests in personnel selection. *Personnel Psychology* 26, pp. 461–467. See also Klimoski, R., and Brickner, M. (1987). Why do assessment centers work? The puzzle of assessment center validity. *Personnel Psychology* 40, pp. 243–260. See also Lord, R. G., DeVader, C. L., and Alliger, G. M. (1986). A meta-analysis of the relationship between personality traits and leadership perceptions: An application of validity generalization procedures. *Journal of Applied Psychology* 71, pp. 402–410.

**64.** Howard, A. (2010). The Management Progress Study and its legacy for selection. In J. Farr and N. T. Tippins (Eds.), *Handbook of Employee Selection.* New York, NY: Routledge, pp. 843–864. See also LePine, J. A. (2003). Team adaptation and post-change performance: Effects of team composition in terms of members' cognitive ability and personality. *Journal of Applied Psychology* 88, pp. 27–39. See also Farrell, J. N., and McDaniel, M. A. (2001). The stability of validity coefficients over time: Ackerman's (1988) model and the General Aptitude Test Battery. *Journal of Applied Psychology* 86, pp. 60–79.

**65.** Grimsley, G., and Jarrett, H. F. (1975). The relation of past managerial achievement to test measures obtained in the employment situation: Methodology and results—II. *Personnel Psychology* 28, pp. 215–231. See also Korman, A. K. (1968). The prediction of managerial performance: A review. *Personnel Psychology* 21, pp. 295–322. See also Kraut, A. I. (1969). Intellectual ability and promotional success among high-level managers. *Personnel Psychology* 22, pp. 281–290.

**66.** Kehoe, J., and Murphy, K. R. (2010). Current concepts of validity, validation, and generalizability. In J. Farr and N. T. Tippins (Eds.), *Handbook of Employee Selection.* New York, NY: Routledge, pp. 99–123. For a more skeptical view, see James, L. R., and McIntyre, H. (2010). Situational specificity and validity generalization. In

J. Farr and N. T. Tippins (Eds.), *Handbook of Employee Selection*. New York, NY: Routledge, pp. 909–920. See also Schmidt, F. L., and Hunter, J. (2003a). History, development, evolution, and impact of validity generalization and meta-analysis methods, 1975–2001. In K. R. Murphy (Ed.), *Validity Generalization: A Critical Review*. Mahwah, NJ: Lawrence Erlbaum, pp. 31–65.

67. Smith, D. B., Hanges, P. J., and Dickson, M. W. (2001). Personnel selection and the five-factor model: Reexamining the effects of applicant's frame of reference. *Journal of Applied Psychology* 86, pp. 304–315. See also Hough, L. M., and Schneider, R. J. (1996). Personality traits, taxonomies, and applications in organizations. In K. R. Murphy (Ed.), *Individual Differences and Behavior in Organizations*. San Francisco: Jossey-Bass, pp. 31–88. See also Salgado, J. F. (1997). The five-factor model of personality and job performance in the European Community. *Journal of Applied Psychology* 82, pp. 30–43.

68. Oswald, F., L., and Hough, L. M. (2011). Personality and its assessment in organizations: Theoretical and empirical developments. In S. Zedeck (Ed.), *APA Handbook of Industrial and Organizational Psychology*, Vol. 2. Washington, DC: American Psychological Association, pp. 153–184. See also Ones, D. S., Dilchert, S., Viswesvaran, C., and Judge, T. A. (2007). In support of personality assessment in organizational settings. *Personnel Psychology* 60, pp. 995–1027. See also Rothstein, M., and Goffin, R. D. (2006). The use of personality measures in personnel selection: What does current research support? *Human Resource Management Review* 16, pp. 155–180. See also Barrick, M. R., and Mount, M. K. (2003). Impact of meta-analysis methods on understanding personality-performance relations. In K. R. Murphy (Ed.), *Validity Generalization: A Critical Review*. Mahwah, NJ: Lawrence Erlbaum Associates, pp. 197–221.

69. Oswald and Hough, 2011, op. cit. See also Roberts, B. (2011, May). Hire intelligence. *HR Magazine* 56(5), pp. 63–67.

70. Rothstein and Goffin, 2006, op. cit. See also Bennet, J. (2005, Sept. 19). Do you have what it takes? *The Wall Street Journal,* p. R11.

71. Hogan, J., and Brinkmeyer, K. (1997). Bridging the gap between overt and personality based integrity tests. *Personnel Psychology* 50, pp. 587–599.

72. Oswald and Hough, 2011, op. cit. See also McFarland, L. A., and Ryan, A. M. (2000). Variance in faking across noncognitive measures. *Journal of Applied Psychology* 85, pp. 812–821. See also Rosse, J. G., Stecher, M. D., Miller, J. L., and Levin, R. A. (1998). The impact of response distortion on pre-employment personality testing and hiring decisions. *Journal of Applied Psychology* 83, pp. 634–644; Christiansen, N. D., Goffin, R. D., Johnston, N. G., and Rothstein, M. G. (1994). Correcting the 16PF for faking: Effects on criterion-related validity and individual hiring decisions. *Personnel Psychology* 47, pp. 847–860.

73. Hough, L. M. (1998). Effects of intentional distortion in personality measurement and evaluation of suggested palliatives. *Human Performance* 11, pp. 209–244. See also Hough, L. M. (1997). The millennium for personality psychology: New horizons or good old daze. *Applied Psychology: An International Review* 47, pp. 233–261. See also Hough, L. M., Eaton, N. K., Dunnette, M. D., Kamp, J. D., and McCloy, R. A. (1990). Criterion related validities of personality constructs and the effect of response distortion on those validities. *Journal of Applied Psychology Monograph* 71, pp. 581–595.

74. Mueller-Hanson, R., Heggestad, E. D., and Thornton, G. C. (2003). Faking and selection: Considering the use of personality from select-in and select-out perspectives. *Journal of Applied Psychology* 88, pp. 348–355. See also Rosse et al., 1998, op. cit.

75. Zickar, M. J., and Robie, C. (1999). Modeling faking good on personality items: An item-level analysis. *Journal of Applied Psychology* 84, pp. 551–563. See also Alliger, G. M., Lilienfeld, S. O., and Mitchell, K. E. (1996). The susceptibility of overt and covert integrity tests to coaching and faking. *Psychological Science* 11, pp. 32–39.

**76.** Sackett and Lievens, 2008, op. cit. See also Rothstein and Goffin, 2006, op. cit. See also Ellingson, J. E., Sackett, P. R., and Hough, L. M. (1999). Social desirability corrections in personality measurement: Issues of applicant comparison and construct validity. *Journal of Applied Psychology* 84, pp. 155–166. See also Rosse et al., 1998, op. cit.

**77.** Hough, 1998, op. cit.

**78.** Hughes, M., Patterson, L. B., and Terrell, J. B. (2005). *Emotional Intelligence in Action.* San Francisco, CA: Pfeiffer. See also Goleman, D. (1998). *Working with Emotional Intelligence.* New York: Bantam. See also Goleman, D. (1995). *Emotional Intelligence: Why It Can Matter More Than IQ.* New York: Bantam.

**79.** Goleman, D., Boyatzis, R., and McKee, A. (2002). *Primal Leadership: Realizing the Power of Emotional Intelligence.* Boston, MA: Harvard Business School Press.

**80.** Lievens, F., and Chan, D. (2010). Practical intelligence, emotional intelligence, and social intelligence. In J. Farr and N. T. Tippins (Eds.), *Handbook of Employee Selection.* New York, NY: Routledge, pp. 339–359. Mayer, J. D., Roberts, R. D., and Barsade, S. G. (2008). Emerging research in emotional intelligence. *Annual Review of Psychology* 59, pp. 501–536. See also Murphy, K. R. (2006). *A Critique of Emotional Intelligence: What Are the Problems and How Can They Be Fixed?* Mahwah, NJ: Erlbaum.

**81.** Van Rooy, D., L., and Viswesvaran, C. (2004). Emotional intelligence: A meta-analytic investigation of predictive validity and nomological net. *Journal of Vocational Behavior* 65, pp. 71–95.

**82.** Sackett and Lievens, 2008, op. cit.

**83.** Breaugh, J. A. (2009). The use of biodata for employee selection: Past research and future directions. *Human Resource Management Review*, 19, pp. 219–231. See also Carlson, K. D., Scullen, S. E., Schmidt, F. L., Rothstein, H., and Erwin, F. (1999). Generalizable biographical data validity can be achieved without multi-organizational development and keying. *Personnel Psychology* 52, pp. 731–75. See also Kluger, A. N., Reilly, R. R., and Russell, C. J. (1991). Faking biodata tests: Are option-keyed instruments more resistant? *Journal of Applied Psychology* 76, pp. 889–896.

**84.** Becker, T. E., and Colquitt, A. L. (1992). Potential versus actual faking of a biodata form: An analysis along several dimensions of item type. *Personnel Psychology* 45, pp. 389–406.

**85.** Sackett and Lievens, 2008, op. cit. See also Rothstein and Goffin, 2006, op. cit. See also Schmitt, N., and Kunce, C. (2002). The effects of required elaboration of answers to biodata questions. *Personnel Psychology* 55, pp. 569–587.

**86.** Mount, M. K., Witt, L. A., and Barrick, M. R. (2000). Incremental validity of empirically keyed biodata scales over GMA and the five-factor personality constructs. *Personnel Psychology* 53, pp. 299–323.

**87.** Hansell, S. (2007, Jan. 3). Google's answer to filling jobs is an algorithm. *The New York Times*, pp. A1, C9.

**88.** Burnett, J. R., and Motowidlo, S. J. (1998). Relations between different sources of information in the structured selection interview. *Personnel Psychology* 51, pp. 963–983. See also Hakel, M. D. (1989). Merit-based selection: Measuring the person for the job. In W. F. Cascio (Ed.), *Human Resource Planning, Employment, and Placement.* Washington, DC: Bureau of National Affairs, pp. 2–135 to 2–158.

**89.** Cliffordson, C. (2002). Interviewer agreement in the judgment of empathy in selection interviews. *International Journal of Selection & Assessment* 10, pp. 198–205. See also Fay, D., and Frese, M. (2001). The concept of personal initiative: An overview of validity studies. *Human Performance* 14, pp. 97–124.

**90.** Huffcutt, A. I., Conway, J. M., Roth, P. L., and Stone, N. J. (2001). Identification and meta-analytic assessment of psychological constructs measured in employment interviews. *Journal of Applied Psychology* 86, pp. 897–913.

91. Cortina, J. M., Goldstein, N. B., Payne, S. C., Davison, H. K., and Gilliland, S. W. (2000). The incremental validity of interview scores over and above cognitive ability and conscientiousness scores. *Personnel Psychology* 53, pp. 325–351.
92. Day, A. L., and Carroll, S. A. (2002). Situational and patterned behavior description interviews: A comparison of their validity, correlates, and perceived fairness. *Human Performance* 16, pp. 25–47.
93. Huffcutt, A. I., and Culbertson, S. S. (2011). Interviews. In S. Zedeck (Ed.), *APA Handbook of Industrial and Organizational Psychology*, Vol. 2. Washington, DC: American Psychological Association, pp. 185–203. See also Schmidt, F. L., and Zimmerman, R. D. (2004). A counter-intuitive hypothesis about employment-interview validity and some supporting evidence. *Journal of Applied Psychology* 89, pp. 553–561. See also Moscoso, S. (2000). Selection interviews: A review of validity evidence, adverse impact, and applicant reactions. *International Journal of Selection and Assessment* 8(4), pp. 237–247. See also Campion, M. A., Palmer, D. K., and Campion, J. E. (1997). A review of structure in the selection interview. *Personnel Psychology* 50, pp. 655–702. See also Conway, J. M., Jako, R. A., and Goodman, D. F. (1995). A meta-analysis of inter-rater and internal consistency reliability of selection interviews. *Journal of Applied Psychology* 80, pp. 565–579. See also McDaniel, M. A., Whetzel, D. L., Schmidt, F. L., and Maurer, S. (1994). The validity of employment interviews: A comprehensive review and meta-analysis. *Journal of Applied Psychology* 79, pp. 599–616.
94. Middendorf, C. H., and Macan, T. H. (2002). Note-taking in the employment interview: Effects on recall and judgments. *Journal of Applied Psychology* 87, pp. 293–303. See also Burnett, J. R., Fan, C., Motowidlo, S. J., and DeGroot, T. (1998). Interview notes and validity. *Personnel Psychology* 51, pp. 375–396.
95. Ganzach, Y., Kluger, A. N., and Klayman, N. (2000). Making decisions from an interview: Expert measurement and mechanical combination. *Personnel Psychology* 53, pp. 1–20. See also Westen, D. and Weinberger, J. (2004). When clinical description becomes statistical prediction. *American Psychologist* 59, pp. 595–613.
96. Posthuma, R. A, Morgeson, F. P., and Campion, M. A. (2002). Beyond employment interview validity: A comprehensive narrative review of recent research and trends over time. *Personnel Psychology* 55, pp. 1–81.
97. Cascio and Aguinis, 2011, op. cit. See also Campion et al., 1997, op. cit.
98. Shippmann, J. S., Ash, R. A., Battista, M., Carr, L., Eyde, L. D., Hesketh, B., Kehoe, J., Pearlman, K., Prien, E. P., and Sanchez, J. I. (2000). The practice of competency modeling. *Personnel Psychology* 53, pp. 703–740.
99. Dipboye, R. L., and Gaugler, B. B. (1993). Cognitive and behavioral processes in the selection interview. In N. Schmitt and W. C. Borman (Eds.), *Personnel Selection in Organizations*. San Francisco: Jossey-Bass, pp. 135–170. See also Weekley, J. A., and Gier, J. A. (1987). Reliability and validity of the situational interview for a sales position. *Journal of Applied Psychology* 72, pp. 484–487.
100. Motowidlo, S. J., Carter, G. W., Dunnette, M. D., Tippins, N., Werner, S., Burnett, J.R., and Vaughan, M. J. (1992). Studies of the structured behavioral interview. *Journal of Applied Psychology* 77, pp. 571–587.
101. Huffcutt and Culbertson, 2011, op. cit. See also Cortina et al., 2000, op. cit.
102. Reynolds, D. H., and Dickter, D. N. (2010). Technology and employee selection. In J. Farr and N. T. Tippins (Eds.), *Handbook of Employee Selection*. New York, NY: Routledge, pp. 171–193. See also Chapman, D. S, and Webster, J. (2003). The use of technologies in the recruiting, screening, and selection processes for job candidates. *International Journal of Selection and Assessment* 11, pp. 113–120.
103. Asher, J. J. and Sciarrino, J. A. (1974). Realistic work sample tests: A review. *Personnel Psychology* 27, pp. 519–533.
104. Roth, P. L., Bobko, P., and McFarland, L. A. (2005). A meta-analysis of work-sample test validity: Updating and integrating some classic literature. *Personnel Psychology*

58, pp. 1009–1037. See also Schmitt, N., and Mills, A. E. (2001). Traditional tests and job simulations: Minority and majority performance and test validities. *Journal of Applied Psychology* 86, pp. 451–458. See also Lance, C. E., Johnson, C. D., Douthitt, S. S., Bennett, W., and Harville, D. L. (2000). Good news: Work sample administrators' global performance judgments are (about) as valid as we've suspected. *Human Performance* 13, pp. 253–277.

105. Callinan, M., and Robertson, I. T. (2000). Work sample testing. *International Journal of Selection and Assessment* 8(4), pp. 248–260.

106. Cascio, W. F., and Phillips, N. (1979). Performance testing: A rose among thorns? *Personnel Psychology* 32, pp. 751–766.

107. Arthur, W., Jr., and Day, E. A. (2011). Assessment centers. In S. Zedeck (Ed.), *APA Handbook of Industrial and Organizational Psychology*, Vol. 2. Washington, DC: American Psychological Association, pp. 205–235.

108. Kello, J. (2007). Assessment center methods. In S. G. Rogelberg (Ed.), *Encyclopedia of Industrial and Organizational Psychology,* Vol. 1. Thousand Oaks, CA: Sage, pp. 34–37.

109. Ibid. See also Bass, B. M. (1954). The leaderless group discussion. *Psychological Bulletin* 51, pp. 465–492. See also Tziner, A., and Dolan, S. (1982.) Validity of an assessment center for identifying future female officers in the military. *Journal of Applied Psychology* 67, pp. 728–736.

110. Kurecka, P. M., Austin, J. M., Jr., Johnson, W., and Mendoza, J. L. (1982). Full anderrant coaching effects on assigned role leaderless group discussion performance. *Personnel Psychology* 35, pp. 805–812. See also Petty, M. M. (1974). A multivariate analysis of the effects of experience and training upon performance in a leaderless group discussion. *Personnel Psychology* 27, pp. 271–282.

111. Arthur and Day, 2011, op. cit. See also Fredericksen, N. (1962). Factors in in-basket performance. *Psychological Monographs* 76(22, whole no. 541), p. 1.

112. Kello, 2007, op. cit.

113. See, for example, Howard, A. (2010). The Management Progress Study and its legacy for selection. In J. Farr and N. T. Tippins (Eds.), *Handbook of Employee Selection*. New York, NY: Routledge, pp. 843–864. See also Brass, G. J., and Oldham, G. R. (1976). Validating an in-basket test using an alternative set of leadership scoring dimensions. *Journal of Applied Psychology* 61, pp. 652–657. See also Tziner, A., and Dolan, S. (1982). Validity of an assessment center for identifying future female officers in the military. *Journal of Applied Psychology* 67, pp. 728–736.

114. Weekley, J. A., and Jones, C. (1999). Further studies of situational tests. *Personnel Psychology* 52, pp. 679–700.

115. Clevenger, J., Pereira, G. M., Wiechmann, D., Schmitt, N., and Harvey, V. S. (2001). Incremental validity of situational judgment tests. *Journal of Applied Psychology* 86, pp. 410–417.

116. Christian, M. S., Edwards, B. D., and Bradley, J. C. (2010). Situational judgment tests: Constructs assessed and meta-analysis of their criterion-related validities. *Personnel Psychology* 63, pp. 83–117.

117. Clevenger et al., 2001, op. cit. See also McDaniel, M. A., and Nguyen, N. T. (2001). Situational judgment tests: A review of practice and constructs assessed. *International Journal of Selection and Assessment* 9, pp. 103–113.

118. Arthur and Day, 2011, op. cit. See also Howard, 2010, op. cit. See also McKinnon, D. W. (1975). Assessment centers then and now. *Assessment and Development* 2, pp. 8–9. See also Office of Strategic Services (OSS) Assessment Staff (1948). *Assessment of Men.* New York: Rinehart.

119. Howard, 2010, op. cit. See also Bray, D. W. (1976). The assessment center method. In R. L. Craig (Ed.), *Training and Development Handbook* (2nd Ed.). New York: McGraw-Hill, pp. 17–1 to 17–15.

120. Howard, 2010, op. cit.

121. Borman, W. C. (1982). Validity of behavioral assessment for predicting military re-cruiter performance. *Journal of Applied Psychology* 67, pp. 3–9. See also Pulakos, E. D., Borman, W. C., and Hough, L. M. (1988). Test validation for scientific understanding: Two demonstrations of an approach to studying predictor-criterion linkages. *Personnel Psychology* 41, pp. 703–716.

122. Arthur and Day, 2011, op. cit. See also Lievens, F. (2001). Assessor training strategies and their effects on accuracy, interrater reliability, and discriminant validity. *Journal of Applied Psychology* 86, pp. 255–264.

123. Schleicher, D. J., Day, D. V., Mayes, B. T., and Riggio, R. E. (2002). A new frame for frame-of-reference training: Enhancing the construct validity of assessment centers. *Journal of Applied Psychology* 87, pp. 735–746. See also Kolk, N. J., Born, M. P., vander Flier, H., and Olman, J. M. (2002). Assessment center procedures: Cognitive load during the observation phase. *International Journal of Selection & Assessment* 10, pp. 271–278.

124. Thornton, G. C., III, Hollenbeck, G. P., and Johnson, S. K. (2010). Selecting leaders: Executives and high potentials. In J. Farr and N. T. Tippins (Eds.), *Handbook of Employee Selection*. New York, NY: Routledge, pp. 823–840. See also Gaugler, B. B., Rosenthal, D. B., Thornton, G. C., III, and Bentson, C. (1987). Meta-analysis of assessment center validity. *Journal of Applied Psychology* 72, pp. 493–511.

125. Lance, C. E., Foster, M. R., Gentry, W. A., and Thoresen, J. D. (2004). Assessor cognitive processes in an operational assessment center. *Journal of Applied Psychology* 89, pp. 22–35.

126. Thornton, G. C., III, and Rupp, D. E. (2006). *Assessment Centers in Human Resource Management: Strategies for Prediction, Diagnosis, and Development.* Mahwah, NJ: Lawrence Erlbaum Associates. See also Arthur, W., Day, E. A., McNelly, T. L., and Edens, P. S. (2003). A meta-analysis of the criterion-related validity of assessment center dimensions. *Personnel Psychology* 56, pp. 125–154. See also Dayan, K., Kasten, R., and Fox, S. (2002). Entry-level police candidate assessment center: An efficient tool or a hammer to kill a fly? *Personnel Psychology* 55, pp. 827–849. See also Gaugler et al., 1987, op. cit. See also Howard, A. (1974). An assessment of assessment centers. *Academy of Management Journal* 17, pp. 115–134.

127. Jansen, P. G. W., and Stoop, B. A. M. (2001). The dynamics of assessment center validity: Results of a 7-year study. *Journal of Applied Psychology* 86, pp. 741–753.

128. Howard, 2010, op. cit. Hoffman, C. C., Thornton, G. C. (1997). Examining selection utility where competing predictors differ in adverse impact. *Personnel Psychology* 50, pp. 455–470. See also Thornton, G. C., III, and Byham, W. C. (1982). *Assessment Centers and Managerial Performance.* New York: Academic Press. See also Huck, J. R., and Bray, D. W. (1976). Management assessment center evaluations and subsequent job performance of white and black females. *Personnel Psychology* 29, pp. 13–30.

129. Cascio, W. F., and Ramos, R. A. (1986). Development and application of a new method for assessing job performance in behavioral/economic terms. *Journal of Applied Psychology* 71, pp. 20–28. See also Cascio, W. F., and Silbey, V. (1979). Utility of the assessment center as a selection device. *Journal of Applied Psychology* 64, pp. 107–118.

130. Lievens, F. (2002). Trying to understand the different pieces of the construct validity puzzle of assessment centers: An examination of assessor and assessee effects. *Journal of Applied Psychology* 87, pp. 675–686. See also Klimoski et al., 1987, op. cit. See also Gaugler, B. B., and Thornton, G. C., III (1989). Number of assessment center dimensions as a determinant of assessor accuracy. *Journal of Applied Psychology* 74, pp. 611–618. See also Reilly, R. R., Henry, S., and Smither, J. W. (1990). An examination of the effects of using behavior checklists on the construct validity of assessment center dimensions. *Journal of Applied Psychology* 43, pp. 71–84.

**131.** Howard, 2010, op. cit.

**132.** Cascio, W. F., and Fogli, L. (2010). The business value of employee selection. In J. Farr and N. T. Tippins (Eds.), *Handbook of Employee Selection*. New York, NY: Routledge, pp. 235–252. See also Cascio and Ramos, 1986, op. cit.

**133.** Cascio and Boudreau, 2011, op. cit. See also Boudreau and Ramstad, 2003, op. cit.

**134.** Hunter, J. E., and Schmidt, F. L. (1983). Quantifying the effects of psychological interventions on employee job performance and workforce productivity. *American Psychologist* 38, pp. 473–478.

**135.** Schmidt, F. L., Hunter, J. E., McKenzie, R., and Muldrow, T. (1979). The impact of valid selection procedures on workforce productivity. *Journal of Applied Psychology* 64, pp. 609–626. For other approaches to demonstrating the business value of selection, see Cascio and Fogli, 2010, op. cit.

# 3

## DEVELOPMENT

Once employees are "on board," their personal growth and development over time become a major concern. Change is a fact of organizational life, and to cope with it effectively, planned programs of employee training, development, and career management are essential. We address these issues in Chapters 8, 9, and 10. Chapter 8 examines what is known about training and developing management and nonmanagement employees. Chapter 9 is concerned with performance management—particularly with the design, implementation, and evaluation of such systems. Finally, Chapter 10 considers the many issues involved in managing careers—from the perspective of individuals at different career stages and from the perspective of organizational staffing decisions. The overall objective of Part 3 is to establish a framework for managing the development process of employees as their careers in organizations unfold.

# 8

# WORKPLACE TRAINING

*Questions This Chapter Will Help Managers Answer*

1. Why should firms expect to expand their training outlays and their menu of choices for employees at all levels?

2. What kind of evidence is necessary to justify investments in training programs?

3. What are the key issues that should be addressed in the design, conduct, and evaluation of training programs?

4. Why should we invest time and money on new-employee orientation? Is there a payoff?

5. How should new-employee orientation be managed for maximum positive impact?

# TECHNOLOGY-DELIVERED INSTRUCTION (TDI) CATCHES ON*

Whether training is Web-based or delivered on a single work station, on a PDA, or on an MP3 player, TDI is catching on. Canon Inc., for example, uses a video game to train copier technicians. The technicians must drag and drop parts into the right spot on a copier. As in the board game Operation, a light flashes and a buzzer sounds if the technician gets it wrong. According to Canon, workers who played the game showed a 58 percent improvement in their training scores compared with older training techniques, such as manuals. Canon uses 11 other training games as well. Corporate trainers are betting that the games' interactivity and fun will hook young, tech-savvy employees, and help them grasp and retain sales, technical, and management skills.

Before we go any further, let's take a moment to define our terms. TDI is the presentation of text, graphics, video, audio, or animation in digitized form for the purpose of building job-relevant knowledge and skill. TDI includes asynchronous (meaning it is not delivered to every user at the same time) text-based courses, job aids, educational games, and video and audio segments, as well as synchronous media, such as video-conferencing and chat rooms.

TDI is projected to boom in the next five years. What's driving the trend? Both demand and supply forces are operating. On the demand side, rapid obsolescence of knowledge and training makes learning and relearning essential if workers are to keep up with the latest developments in their fields. In addition, there is a growing demand for just-in-time training delivery, coupled with demand for cost-effective ways to meet the learning needs of a globally distributed workforce. Finally, there is demand for flexible access to lifelong learning.

On the supply side, Internet access is becoming standard at work and at home, and advances in digital technologies now enable training designers to create interactive, media-rich content. In addition, increasing bandwidth and better delivery platforms make TDI particularly attractive. Finally, there is a growing selection of high-quality products and services.

Features like these allow smaller companies, such as Arrow Electronics, to work with a vendor (BrandGames) to make a game that teaches customer-account managers customer-service skills and supply-chain management. They also led the Greater Seattle Chamber of Commerce to create an online learning center for its 2,200 members—most of whom employ fewer than 100 employees. Online learning also permits large firms, such as General Motors, to reach more than 175,000 employees at 7,500 dealerships in less than a week, using interactive distance learning (IDL) technology. IDL will let employees view a live course beamed in by satellite and ask questions of the instructor without leaving their dealerships, which slashes travel time and costs, and improves quality, because GM can select its best instructors to teach each course.

*Sources:* Sitzmann, T. (2011). A meta-analytic examination of the instructional effectiveness of computer-based simulation games. *Personnel Psychology* 64, pp. 489–528. See also Aguinis, H., and Kraiger, K. (2009). Benefits of training and development for individuals and teams, organizations, and society. *Annual Review of Psychology* 60, pp. 451–474. See also Gabriel, T. (2010, Nov. 5). Live vs. distance learning: Measuring the differences. *The New York Times*, p. A3. See also Jana, R. (2006, Mar. 27). On-the-job video gaming. *BusinessWeek*, p. 43. See also Brown, K. G., and Ford, J. K. (2002). Using computer technology in training: Building an infrastructure for active learning. In K. Kraiger (Ed.), *Creating, Implementing, and Managing Effective Training and Development*. San Francisco: Jossey-Bass, pp. 192–233. See also Brown, K. G. (2001). Using computers to deliver training: Which employees learn and why? *Personnel Psychology* 54, pp. 271–296.

Classroom courses are not going away (58 percent of training hours were delivered in face-to-face classrooms in 2010, down from 70 percent in 2005) and TDI does have its drawbacks, as we shall see in the conclusion to this case, but one thing is certain: TDI is changing corporate training forever.

## Challenges

1. What are some of the key advantages of TDI?
2. Are some types of material or course work better suited than others to TDI?
3. What disadvantages or opportunity costs can you identify with this approach?

Traditionally, lower-level employees were "trained," while higher-level employees were "developed." This distinction, focusing on the learning of hands-on skills versus interpersonal and decision-making skills, has become too blurry in practice to be useful. Throughout the remainder of this chapter, therefore, we will use the terms *training* and *development* interchangeably. Worldwide, training is big business, and the first half of this chapter examines some current issues in the design, conduct, and evaluation of training programs.

Change, growth, and sometimes displacement (e.g., through layoffs and restructuring) are facts of modern organizational life. Young people entering the workforce today can expect to be laid off several times by the time they reach age 50.[1] As those laid off find new jobs, they discover what all new employees do: You have to "relearn the ropes" in the new job setting. Orientation training, sometimes called "on-boarding," is the subject of the second part of this chapter. It can ease that transition considerably, with positive results both for the new employee and for the company. Trends such as leased employees, disposable managers, and free-agent workers will make orientation even more important in the future. Let's begin by defining training, and consider some emerging trends in this area.

## EMPLOYEE TRAINING

### What Is Training?

**Training** consists of planned programs designed to improve performance at the individual, group, and/or organizational levels. Improved performance, in turn, implies that there have been measurable changes in knowledge, skills, attitudes, and/or social behavior.

When we examine the training enterprise as a whole, it is clear that training issues can be addressed from at least two perspectives. At the structural level, we can examine issues such as the following, among others: the aggregate level of expenditures by the various providers of training (e.g., federal, state, and local governments, educational institutions, private-sector businesses), the degree of cooperation among the providers, incentives (or lack of incentives) for providing training, who gets training, and the economic impact of training.[2] These are macro-level concerns.

At the micro level, we may choose to examine issues such as the following: what types of training seem to yield positive outcomes for organizations and trainees (i.e., *what works*); how to identify if training is needed and, if so, what type of training best fits the needs that have been identified; how to structure the delivery of training programs; and how to evaluate the outcomes of training efforts.

Unfortunately, organizations sometimes place too much emphasis on the techniques and methods of training and not enough on first defining what the employee should learn in relation to desired job behaviors. In addition, fewer than half of all organizations even try to measure the value of training, and fewer still (just 5 percent) calculate the return in monetary terms.[3]

This is true even of sales training, which would seem easy to measure. Just 11 percent of companies attempt to assess the payoffs of training on sales.[4]

In this section, we will do two things: (1) discuss several structural issues at the macro level and (2) illustrate research-based findings that might lead to improvements in the design, delivery, and evaluation of training systems. Before we do so, however, let's consider some important training trends.

## Training Trends

Several trends suggest that the time and money budgeted for training will increase during the next decade. These include technology and e-commerce; continuing worker displacement as a function of mergers, acquisitions, and downsizing; and the ongoing shift from manufacturing to service jobs.[5] Here are some other major challenges that companies and institutions face:[6]

- *Hypercompetition.* There will be increased competition at both domestic and international levels, largely due to trade agreements and technology, most notably, the Internet. As a result, senior executives will be required to lead an almost constant reinvention of business strategies/models and organizational structures.
- *A power shift to the customer.* Using the Internet, customers can access databases that allow them to compare prices and examine product reviews; hence there is an ongoing necessity to meet the product and service needs of customers.
- *Collaboration across organizational and geographic boundaries.* In some cases suppliers are collocated with manufacturers and share access to inventory levels. Outsourcing, the geographical dispersion of work, and strategic international alliances often lead to new organizational forms that involve multinational teams. As a result, organizations must address cultural and language issues, along with new approaches to collaboration.[7]
- *The need to maintain high levels of talent.* Because products and services can be copied, the ability of a workforce to innovate, refine processes, solve problems, and form relationships becomes an organization's only sustainable advantage. Attracting, retaining, and developing people with critical competencies is necessary for success.
- *Changes in the workforce.* Shifting demographics suggest that many unskilled and undereducated youth will be needed for entry-level jobs, and currently underutilized groups of racial and ethnic minorities, women, and older workers will need training. At the same time, as the members of the baby boom generation retire, knowledge management, or the transfer of mission-critical knowledge to those who remain, will become a top priority.
- *Changes in technology* impose training and retraining requirements on the existing workforce.

- *Teams.* As more firms move to employee involvement and teams in the workplace, team members need to learn behaviors such as asking for ideas, offering help without being asked, listening and providing feedback, and recognizing and considering the ideas of others.[8]

Indeed, as the demands of the information age spread, companies are coming to regard training expenses as a no-less-critical part of their capital costs than plants and equipment. Over all industries, U.S. businesses spent $48.9 billion on training in 2010, or about $682 per learner.[9] At the level of the individual firm, Google, is exemplary. It offers each employee 100 hours of professional training per year.[10]

What's the bottom line in all of this? Organizations that provide superior opportunities for learning and growth have a distinct advantage when competing for talented employees.[11]

These trends suggest a dual responsibility: The organization is responsible for providing an atmosphere that will support and encourage change, and the individual is responsible for deriving maximum benefit from the learning opportunities provided. This may involve the acquisition of new information, skills, attitudes, or patterns of social behavior through training and development.

Retraining can pay off too. A study by the Work in America Institute found that retraining current workers for new jobs is more cost effective than firing them and hiring new ones—not to mention the difference that retraining makes to employee morale. Intel illustrates this approach nicely.

**HR BUZZ**

*Redeployment\**

## INTEL

Intel, the company that invented the microchip and whose average product life cycle is just 2.5 *years,* avoided major layoffs until 2007 through a strong in-house redeployment policy. Every employee receives a brochure, entitled "Owning Your Own Employability," and each is afforded tools and resources to take advantage of the redeployment option. A redeployment event occurs when there is a business downturn or lack of a need for a particular skill, but it does not replace performance management. To qualify, a fulltime employee must have two consecutive years of performance reviews that meet requirements.

Should an employee become eligible for redeployment, he or she is given options, tools, and resources. The company has five employee development centers offering self-assessment tools, career counseling, educational opportunities, and job listings within Intel. Job skills were redefined to encourage people to find new places within the company, and temporary assignments and internal training are provided to prepare them for new positions. Funds are also available for relocation. The company provides full pay and benefits for up to 8 weeks while a displaced employee searches for a new job within Intel or elsewhere. The entire process is managed through a system that provides centralized tracking and reporting of all redeployment activity.

The ranks of Intel employees are filled with those who have made successful transitions from shop floor to sales and public relations positions, or from obsolete technology divisions to high-margin technology centers within the

*\*Sources:* Frauenheim, E. (2008, Jan. 14). Restructuring 101. *Workforce Management,* p. 14. See also Cascio, W. F. (1995, May). *Guide to Responsible Restructuring.* Washington, DC: U.S. Department of Labor, Office of the American Workplace.

company. If none of this works, the company provides generous severance payments to affected employees. Redeployment is a continuing challenge at Intel because the company's competitive strategy is to stay ahead of its rivals by making its products obsolete!

Intel's redeployment program continues on a smaller scale today than in the 1990s, but a major shift in business strategy in 2007 made widespread layoffs necessary. That said, the redeployment policy is a strong deterrent to litigation based on allegations of wrongful discharge. It is a sound employee relations tool.

## Impact of Training on Individuals, Teams, Organizations, and Society

A recent review of the research literature on training and development identified 13 benefits, most of which have been demonstrated at the individual and team levels of analysis.[12]

1. *Meta-analyses (quantitative summaries of accumulated results across many studies) have demonstrated repeatedly that training has an overall positive effect on job-related behaviors or performance.*[13] The average effect size, or *d,* equals 0.62—that is, it is 0.62 standard deviations better than performance without training—but the effectiveness of training varies, depending on the delivery method and the skill or task being trained.

2. *Training may lead to greater innovation and tacit skills.* Tacit skills are behaviors acquired through informal learning that are useful for effective performance. They are useful to a physician who requires the right touch or feel when probing the body for abnormalities during a physical exam, to the carpenter hanging a door, or to the mechanic tuning an engine.

3. *Training can improve technical skills.* Generally this occurs through improvements in declarative knowledge (facts, meaning of terms) as well as procedural knowledge (how to perform skilled behavior).

4. *Training can improve strategic knowledge, that is, knowing when to apply a specific knowledge or skill.*

5. *Training, and especially practice, helps to maintain consistency in performance.* Think of a chef who must cook various items on a menu over and over in a consistent manner, or a professional athlete who must perform at a consistently high level to be successful.

6. *Performance consistency also results from enhancing the self-efficacy or self-management of trainees.* Self-efficacy is a personal belief that one can accomplish a task successfully. Self-management is a strategy that trainees adopt to help them to maintain desired behaviors (e.g., getting to work on time, staying out of trouble), or to recognize symptoms that indicate variance from a desired path (e.g., in substance-abuse relapse prevention).

7. *Management development programs show positive effects.* They seem to affect two types of outcomes: knowledge—principles, facts, and skills (average effect sizes range from 0.96 to 1.37)—and changes in on-the-job behavior (average effect sizes range from 0.35 to 1.01).[14]

8. *Cross-cultural training improves expatriate adjustment and performance.* One study of 29 conceptual reviews and 16 empirical studies concluded, however, that several important variables determine the actual effectivness of such training in any given situation. These include the timing of the

training (predeparture, postarrival, postassignment), the spouse's adjustment, attributes of the job (e.g., discretion), and the cultural "distance" between home and host countries.[15]

9.  *Leadership training seems to enhance the attitudes and performance of followers.* Specifically, it seems to have a positive effect on the motivation, values, and self-efficacy of followers.[16]

10. *Training in team communication and team effectiveness have positive effects on team performance and, in the case of airplane cockpit crews, safety.* They also seem to affect nontechnical skills (team building) as well as situation awareness and decision making. We will have more to say about this topic later in the chapter.

11. *There are many fewer studies documenting the effects of training at the level of the organization, but available data show positive effects on outcomes such as employee and customer satisfaction, owner/shareholder satisfaction, and productivity (e.g., sales per employee).* Unfortunately, the causal links between training and organizational outcomes tend to be weak. In other words, other variables might well explain the results that have been observed.[17]

12. *At the level of the organization, training is a key enabler of e-commerce, an important strategic priority for many firms, both large and small.*

13. *At the level of society, macroeconomic studies have concluded that training improves the quality of the labor force.* In turn, a high-quality labor force enhances a country's economic growth. This has led many countries around the world (e.g., members of the European Union, Singapore, Germany) to adopt national policies to encourage the design and delivery of training programs. One such country is India, as the international application below illustrates.

## INTERNATIONAL APPLICATION
### Infosys U.—The Taj Mahal of Training Centers

The $120 million Infosys facility in Mysore, India, about 90 miles from the company's Bangalore headquarters, is part Disney World, part Club Med, part American college campus. Its real mission, however, is teaching the Infosys Way to the 15,000 employees the fast-growing company hires per year—an average of 40 a day. According to Infosys co-founder Nandan Nilekani, "Companies haven't been investing enough in people. Rather than train them, they let them go. Our people are our capital. The more we invest in them, the more they can be effective."

While most of the training focuses on technical skills, new recruits spend a lot of time working on softer skills as well. These include team building, comportment, and improving interpersonal communication. In one class, for example, students listen intently as the instructor tells them to practice smiling in front of a mirror. In another, on corporate etiquette, the teacher emphasizes, "You are all brand ambassadors. That brand now attracts attention far beyond India's borders, for the company has offices in 18 countries."[a]

[a] Schlosser, J. (2006, Mar. 20). Infosys U. *Fortune*, pp. 41, 42 © 2006 Time Inc. Used under license.

## CHARACTERISTICS OF EFFECTIVE TRAINING PRACTICE

Despite the rosy picture painted earlier, keep in mind that if training is ill conceived, poorly planned, or inadequately executed, then it is likely to be ineffective and waste precious resources (time and money). Conversely, four characteristics seem to distinguish companies with the most effective training practices:[18]

- Top management is committed to training and development; training is part of the corporate culture. This is especially true of leading companies, such as Google, Disney, Marriott, and Cisco.
- Training is tied to business strategy and objectives and is linked to bottom-line results.
- Organizational environments are feedback rich; they stress continuous improvement, promote risk taking, offer one-on-one coaching, and afford opportunities to learn from the successes and failures of decisions.
- There is commitment to invest the necessary resources, to provide sufficient time and money for training.

### The Training Paradox

Some businesses, small and large, shy away from training because they think that by upgrading the skills of the workforce, their employees will be more marketable to competitors. That is true. However, there is also an interesting paradox that affects both employee and employer. That is, if an employee takes charge of her own employability by keeping her skills updated and varied so she can work for anyone, she also builds more security with her current employer—assuming the company values highly skilled, motivated employees.

As Hewlett-Packard's director of education noted, "What's going to entice them away? Money? Maybe you can buy them for a short time, but what keeps people excited is growing and learning." This is especially true in the great global talent race.[19]

At the same time, if a company provides a large number of training and learning opportunities, it is more likely to retain workers because it creates an interesting and challenging environment. As the general manager of London-based Marks & Spencer noted, "Train them to the point where you may lose them, and then you won't lose them."[20] This is the **training paradox:** Increasing an individual's employability outside the company simultaneously increases his or her job security and desire to stay with the current employer (assuming that employer creates challenging jobs and provides an exciting work environment).

### How Training Relates to Competitive Strategies

Competitive strategy refers to the decisions, processes, and choices that organizations make to position themselves for sustainable success.[21] HR strategy, in turn, refers to the decisions, processes, and choices organizations make about managing people. Training is an important aspect of HR strategy, and a key objective of any training program is to tie workplace training to the strategy of a business. 3M is especially adept at this. For instance, it will set a goal to reduce product-development cycle time (i.e., to increase speed), then create a course on how to do it. This is not learning for its own sake; rather all leadership-development courses are linked to business objectives.[22] Thus, if a company's strategy is to provide high-quality customer service, it is likely to emphasize, for example, training in problem solving, conflict resolution, negotiation, and team building. If its objective is innovation, then topics like technical training, effective communications, and—for managers—training in feedback and communication are more typical. While the potential returns from well-conducted training programs are hefty, considerable planning and evaluation are necessary to realize these returns. The remainder of this chapter examines some key issues that managers need to consider. Let us begin by examining the broad phases that comprise training systems.

## WHAT DETERMINES EFFECTIVE TRAINING?

Research shows that a number of factors affect training effectiveness.[23] For example, training success is determined not only by the quality of training but also by an individual's readiness for training and the degree of organizational support for the training. Characteristics of the individual as well as the work environment are important influences before training (by affecting the motivation to participate), during training (by affecting learning), and after training (by influencing the transfer of learning and skills from the training situation to the job situation).

Admittedly some individual characteristics, such as trainability (i.e., the ability to learn the content of the training) and personality are difficult, if not impossible, for organizations to influence through policies and practices. The organization clearly can influence others, however, in such areas as job or career attitudes, a person's belief that he or she can learn the content of the training successfully, the attractiveness of training outcomes, and the work environment itself.[24]

## ASSESSING TRAINING NEEDS AND DESIGNING TRAINING PROGRAMS

One way to keep in mind the phases of training is to portray them graphically, in the form of a model that illustrates the interaction among the phases. One such model is shown in Figure 8–1.

The **assessment** (or planning) **phase** serves as a foundation for the entire training effort. As Figure 8–1 shows, the **training and development phase** and the **evaluation phase** depend on inputs from assessment. The purpose of the assessment phase is to define what it is the employee should learn in relation to desired job behaviors. If this phase is not carefully done, the training program as a whole will have little chance of achieving what it is intended to do.

Assuming that managers specify the objectives of the training program carefully, the next task is to design the environment in which to achieve those objectives. This is the purpose of the training phase. Choose methods and techniques carefully and deliver them systematically in a supportive, encouraging environment, based on sound principles of learning. More on this later.

Finally, if both the assessment phase and the training and development phase have been done competently, evaluation should present few problems. Evaluation is a twofold process that involves (1) establishing indicators of success in training, as well as on the job, and (2) determining exactly what job-related changes have occurred as a result of the training. Evaluation must provide a continuous stream of feedback that can be used to reassess training needs, thereby creating input for the next stage of employee development.

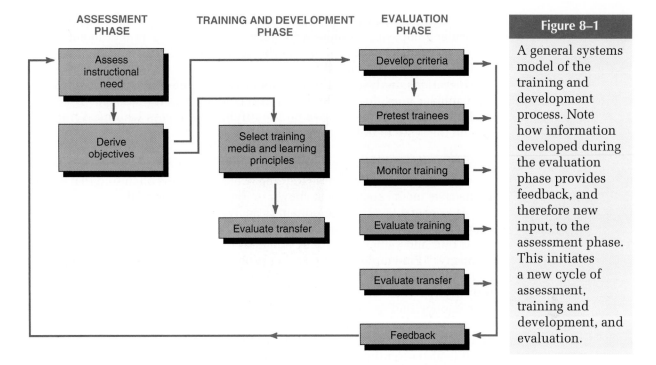

| ASSESSMENT PHASE | TRAINING AND DEVELOPMENT PHASE | EVALUATION PHASE |
| --- | --- | --- |

**Figure 8–1**

A general systems model of the training and development process. Note how information developed during the evaluation phase provides feedback, and therefore new input, to the assessment phase. This initiates a new cycle of assessment, training and development, and evaluation.

## An Alternative Approach: Rapid Prototyping

Admittedly, the model shown in Figure 8–1 is a bit ponderous. Over the past decade, the pressure to develop training (and other HR processes) more quickly has resulted in the development of alternative, more streamlined models, collectively known as "Fast HR."[25] One such model, rapid prototyping, is based on process models used in software development. It's a three-phase approach to training.[26] The first phase involves the assessment of needs and the determination of training objectives. The second phase involves constructing prototypes and testing them with users. The third phase involves implementing and refining the training. This approach relies on parallel work efforts, minimal commitments, and extensive user testing. Designers are expected to create and test training before the needs assessment is complete, and to modify it based on the results of user tests. If instruction can be created, tested, and modified quickly, then rapid prototyping might be appropriate. It is impractical in settings where instruction is costly to develop or when user testing is not feasible.

Now that we have a broad overview of the training process, let us consider the elements of Figure 8–1 in greater detail.

## Assessing Training Needs

The purpose of needs assessment is to determine if training is necessary. There are four levels of analysis for determining the needs that training can fulfill:[27]

- **Organization analysis** focuses on identifying whether training supports the company's strategic direction; whether managers, peers, and employees support training activity; and what training resources are available.

- **Demographic analysis** is helpful in determining the special needs of a particular group, such as older workers, women, or managers at different levels. Those needs may be specified at the organizational level, the business-unit level, or at the individual level.
- **Operations analysis** attempts to identify the content of training—what an employee must do in order to perform competently.
- **Individual analysis** focuses on identifying employees who need training, and the types of training they need.

Training needs might surface in any one of these four broad areas. But to ask productive questions regarding training needs, managers often find that a comprehensive model such as that shown in Figure 8–2 is helpful.

At a general level, it is important to analyze training needs against the backdrop of organizational objectives and strategies. Unless you do this, you may waste time and money on training programs that do not advance the cause of the company.[28] **Pre-employment training programs** (PETs) are prime examples of close alignment between organizational needs and training curricula. PETs are industry-specific, community-based coalitions. Member companies contribute time, money, and expertise to designing training, and they also contribute employees to teach courses. Such programs can be found in the aviation industry, in manufacturing technology in polymer chemistry, and in customer service.[29]

It is also essential to analyze the organization's external environment and internal climate. Trends in the strategic priorities of a business, judicial decisions, civil rights laws, union activity, productivity, accidents, turnover, absenteeism, and on-the-job employee behavior will provide relevant information at this level. The important question then becomes "Will training produce changes in employee behavior that will contribute to our organization's goals?"

In summary, the critical first step is to relate training needs to the achievement of key strategic business objectives. If you cannot make that connection, the training is probably unnecessary. However, if a training need does surface at the organizational level, a demographic analysis is the next step.

Demographic analysis provides information that may transcend particular jobs, even divisions, of an organization. With respect to managers, for example, level, function, and attitudes toward the usefulness of training all affect their self-reported training needs.[30] Taking this information into account lends additional perspective to the operations and person analyses to follow.

Operations analysis requires a careful examination of the work to be performed after training. It involves: (1) a systematic collection of information that describes how work is done; (2) determination of standards of performance for that work; (3) how tasks are to be performed to meet the standards; and (4) the competencies necessary for effective task performance. In fact, validated competency models can be very helpful in driving training curricula.[31] Job analyses, performance appraisals, interviews with subject-matter experts (jobholders, supervisors, higher-level managers, even knowledgeable customers and suppliers), and analyses of operating problems (quality control, downtime reports, and customer complaints) all provide important inputs to the analysis of training needs.

Finally, there is individual analysis. At this level, training needs may be defined in terms of the following general idea: The difference between desired performance and actual performance is the individual's training need. Performance standards, identified in the operations analysis phase, constitute desired

**Figure 8–2**

Training needs-assessment model.

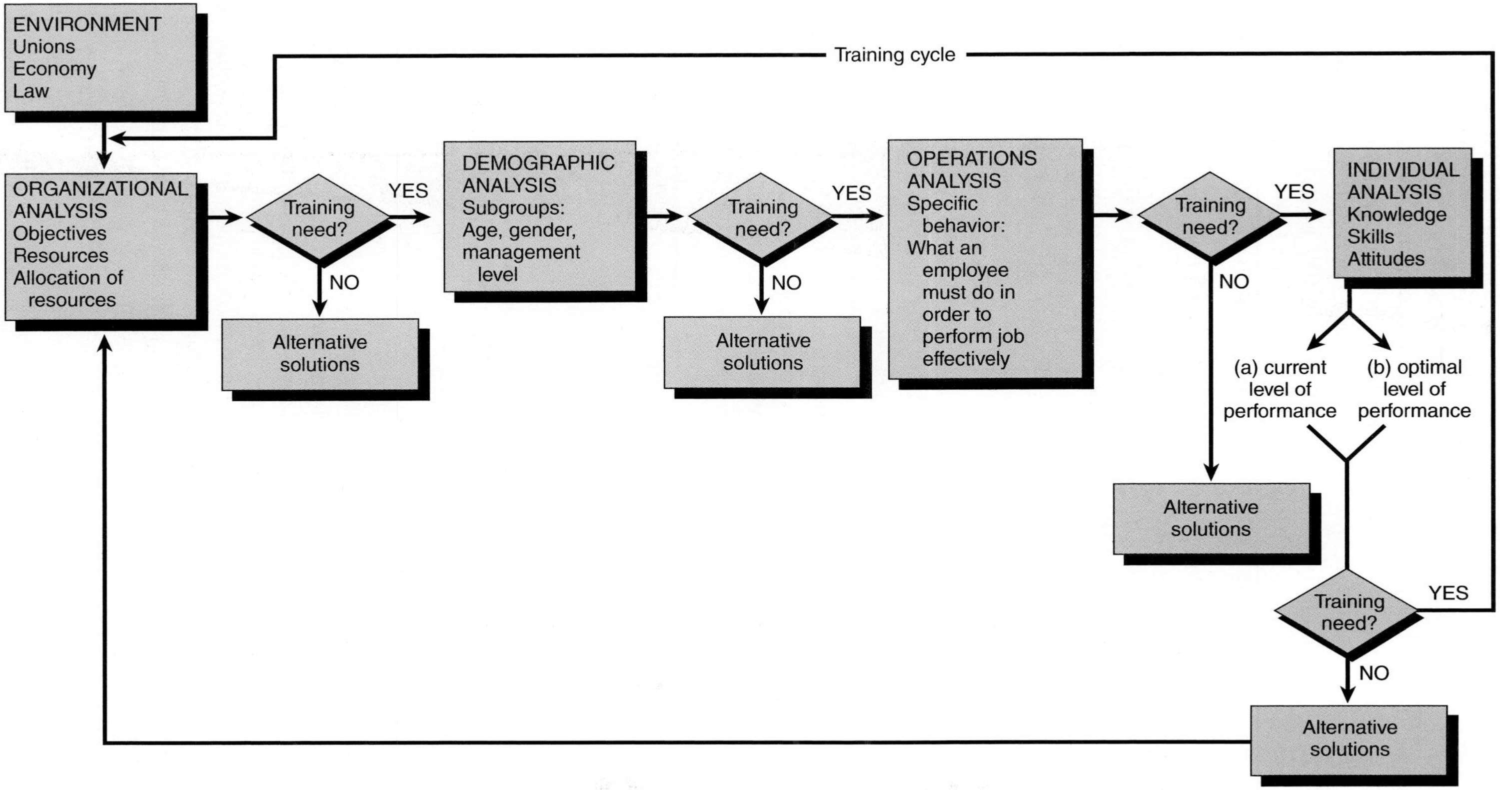

performance. Individual performance data; diagnostic ratings of employees by their supervisors, peers, or customers; records of performance kept by workers in diary form; and attitude surveys, interviews, or tests (job knowledge, work sample, or situational) can provide information on actual performance against which each employee can be compared with desired performance standards. A gap between actual and desired performance may be filled by training.

One especially fruitful approach to the identification of individual training needs is to combine behaviorally based performance-management systems with individual development plans (IDPs) derived from self-analysis. IDPs provide a blueprint for self-development, and should include:

1. *Statements of aims*—desired changes in knowledge, skills, attitudes, values, or relationships with others.
2. *Definitions*—descriptions of areas of study, search, reflection, or testing, including lists of activities, experiences, or questions that can help achieve these aims.
3. *Ideas about priorities*—feelings of preference or urgency about what should be learned first.

Individuals often construct their own IDPs, with assistance, in career planning workshops, through structured exercises, in the practice of management by objectives, or in assessment centers. They provide a blueprint for self-development.

As a result of needs assessment, it should be possible to determine what workers do, what behaviors are essential to do what they do effectively, what type of learning is necessary to acquire those behaviors, and what type of instructional content is most likely to accomplish that type of learning.[32] This information should guide all future choices about training methods and evaluation strategies.

---

**HR BUZZ**

### CLASSIC TRAINING DESIGN MEETS NEW TECHNOLOGY: BOEING'S 787 DREAMLINER*

Mechanics going through Boeing's 25-day training course for the 787 Dreamliner learn to fix all kinds of problems, from broken lights in the cabin to major malfunctions with flight controls. One thing they won't soon do: touch one of the planes. Instead, using laptop and desktop computers inside a classroom with huge diagrams, the mechanics train on a system that displays an interactive 787 cockpit, as well as a 3-D exterior of the plane. Using a mouse, the mechanics "walk" around the jet, open virtual maintenance access panels, and go inside the plane to repair and replace parts. At the end of the course, the mechanics get all training materials on a tiny memory stick. Once they are in the field staring up at an actual Dreamliner, they will also use laptop PCs to diagnose and solve real problems with the planes. Boeing has already established eight Dreamliner training suites, including some in London, Seattle, Shanghai, Singapore, and Tokyo.

As for pilots, they train on full-motion flight simulators (rather than actual airplanes). However, designers know that "trainee readiness" (basic skills plus the motivation to succeed) vary among trainees, and also are critical to successful training outcomes. So before getting into a simulator, the pilots receive initial

*Source:* Sanders, P. (2010, Sept. 2). Boeing 787 training takes virtual path. *The Wall Street Journal,* p. B8. Reprinted by permission of *The Wall Street Journal,* Copyright © (2010) Dow Jones & Company, Inc. All Rights Reserved Worldwide. License number 2871941076673.

training on a suite of computers and get hundreds of pages of training documentation on tablet PC devices. Then they move to a mocked-up cockpit with flat-panel monitors and touch-screen displays to learn the basics of handling the plane.

In the full-motion simulation, pilots practice emergency procedures in a replica cockpit that mimics a variety of locales and weather situations. At the end of the course the pilots receive a USB flash drive that contains all of the Dreamliner flying manuals and the students' own notes, jotted down during training with a stylus directly onto the pages of an electronic manual.

Yes, Dreamliner training does use the latest whiz-bang technology, but don't be fooled into thinking that's all there is. Undergirding all of those bells and whistles is extremely thorough, detailed training-needs analysis, coupled with careful consideration of alternative design and delivery options to optimize each trainee's learning. These classic tools have not changed appreciably in decades, and given the time and expense incurred in training mechanics and pilots, Boeing is using every one of them to maximize the return on its investment.

Once training needs have been identified, the next step is to structure the training environment for maximum learning. Careful attention to the fundamental principles of learning will enhance this process.

## PRINCIPLES THAT ENHANCE LEARNING

To promote efficient learning, long-term retention, and application of the skills or factual information learned in training to the job situation, training programs should incorporate principles of learning developed over the past century. Which principles should they consider? It depends on whether the trainees are learning skills (e.g., drafting) or factual material (e.g., principles of life insurance).[33]

To be most effective, *skill learning* should include four essential ingredients: (1) goal setting, (2) behavior modeling, (3) practice, and (4) feedback. However, when the focus is on *learning facts,* the sequence should change slightly: (1) goal setting, (2) meaningfulness of material, (3) practice, and (4) feedback. Let's consider each of these in greater detail.

### Motivating the Trainee: Goal Setting

A person who wants to develop herself or himself will do so; a person who wants to be developed rarely is. This statement illustrates the role that motivation plays in training—to learn, you must want to learn. While cognitive ability does predict training outcomes, so also does motivation. What determines motivation to succeed in training? Both personal and contextual factors are important. At the level of the individual, the personality characteristics of conscientiousness (striving for excellence, having high performance standards, setting challenging personal goals) and internal locus of control (belief that one controls his or her own fate) are important determinants of motivation to learn. At the level of the organization, the climate in which the trainee functions, coupled with the support he or she receives from supervisor and peers, is also critical.[34]

Perhaps the most effective way to raise a trainee's motivation is by setting goals. More than 500 studies have demonstrated goal setting's proven track record of success in improving employee performance in a variety of settings and cultures.[35] On average, goal setting leads to a 10 percent improvement in productivity, and it works best with tasks of low complexity.[36]

**Goal theory** is founded on the premise that an individual's conscious goals or intentions regulate her or his behavior.[37] Research indicates that once an individual accepts a goal and is committed to achieving it, difficult but attainable goals result in higher levels of performance than do easy goals or even a generalized goal such as "do your best."[38] These findings have three important implications for motivating trainees:

1. Make the objectives of the training program clear at the outset.
2. Set goals that are challenging and difficult enough that the trainees can derive personal satisfaction from achieving them, but not so difficult that they are perceived as impossible to reach.
3. Supplement the ultimate goal of finishing the program with subgoals during training, such as trainer evaluations, work-sample tests, and periodic quizzes. As trainees clear each hurdle successfully, their confidence about attaining the ultimate goal increases.

While goal setting clearly affects trainees' motivation, so also do the expectations of the trainer. In fact, expectations have a way of becoming self-fulfilling prophecies, so that the higher the expectations, the better the trainees perform. Conversely, the lower the expectations, the worse the trainees perform. This phenomenon of the self-fulfilling prophecy is known as the **Pygmalion effect.** Legend has it that Pygmalion, a king of Cyprus, sculpted an ivory statue of a maiden named Galatea. Pygmalion fell in love with the statue, and, at his prayer, Aphrodite, the goddess of love and beauty, gave it life. Pygmalion's fondest wish—his expectation—came true.

## Behavior Modeling

Much of what we learn is acquired by observing others. We will imitate other people's actions when they lead to desirable outcomes (e.g., promotions, increased sales, or more accurate tennis serves). The models' actions serve as a cue as to what constitutes appropriate behavior.[39] A model is someone who is seen as competent, powerful, and friendly and has high status within an organization. We try to identify with this model because her or his behavior is seen as desirable and appropriate. **Behavior modeling** tends to increase when the model is rewarded for behavior and when the rewards (e.g., influence, pay) are things the imitator would like to have. In the context of training (or coaching or teaching), we attempt to maximize trainees' identification with a model. To do this well, research suggests the following:

1. The model should be similar to the observer in age, gender, and race. If the observer sees little similarity between himself or herself and the model, it is unlikely that he or she will imitate the model's behaviors.
2. Portray the behaviors to be modeled clearly and in detail. To focus the trainees' attention on specific behaviors to imitate, provide them with a list of key behaviors to attend to when observing the model and allow them to express the behaviors in language that is most comfortable for them. For example, when one group of supervisors was being taught how to coach

## PYGMALION IN ACTION: MANAGERS GET THE KIND OF PERFORMANCE THEY EXPECT

To test the Pygmalion effect and to examine the impact of instructors' prior expectations about trainees on the instructors' subsequent style of leadership toward the trainees, a field experiment was conducted at a military training base.[a] In a 15-week combat-command course, 105 trainees were matched on aptitude and assigned randomly to one of three experimental groups. Each group corresponded to a particular level of expectation that was communicated to the instructors: high, average, or no prespecified level of expectation (due to insufficient information). Four days before the trainees arrived at the base, and prior to any acquaintance between instructors and trainees, the instructors were assembled and given a score (known as command potential, or CP) for each trainee that represented the trainee's potential to command others. The instructors were told that the CP score had been developed on the basis of psychological test scores, data from a previous course on leadership, and ratings by previous commanders. The instructors were also told that course grades predict CP in 95 percent of the cases. The instructors were then given a list of the trainees assigned to them, along with their CPs, and asked to copy each trainee's CP into his or her personal record. The instructors were also requested to learn their trainees' names and their CPs before the beginning of the course.

The Pygmalion hypothesis that the instructor's prior expectation influences the trainee's performance was confirmed. Trainees of whom instructors expected better performance scored significantly higher on objective achievement tests, exhibited more positive attitudes, and were perceived as better leaders. In fact, the prior expectations of the instructors explained 73 percent of the variability in the trainees' performance, 66 percent in their attitudes, and 28 percent in leadership. The lesson to be learned from these results is unmistakable: Trainers (and managers) get the kind of performance they expect. This is not an isolated instance. The Pygmalion effect has been confirmed in many studies, using both male and female trainees.[b]

---

[a]Eden, D., & Shani, A. B. (1982). Pygmalion goes to boot camp: Expectancy, leadership, and trainee performance. *Journal of Applied Psychology*, 67, pp. 194-199.

[b]Begley, S. (2003, Nov. 7). Expectations may alter outcomes far more than we realize. *The Wall Street Journal*, p. B1.

---

employees, the supervisors received a list of the following key behaviors:[40] (1) Focus on the problem, not on the person; (2) ask for the employees' suggestions, and get their ideas on how to solve the problem; (3) listen openly; (4) agree on the steps that each of you will take to solve the problem; and (5) plan a specific follow-up date.

3. Rank the behaviors to be modeled in a sequence from least to most difficult, and be sure the trainees observe lots of repetitions of the behaviors being modeled.

4. Finally, have several models portray the behaviors, not just one.[41]

Research continues to demonstrate the effectiveness of behavior modeling in learning facts and procedures, and also in changing behavior on the job.[42] It is particularly appropriate for teaching interpersonal and computer skills.[43] To a large extent, this is because behavior modeling overcomes one of the shortcomings of earlier approaches to training: telling instead of showing.

## Meaningfulness of the Material

It's easier to learn and remember factual material when it is meaningful. **Meaningfulness** refers to material that is rich in associations for the trainees and is therefore easily understood by them. To structure material to maximize its meaningfulness:

1. Provide trainees with an overview of the material to be presented during the training. Seeing the overall picture helps trainees understand how each unit of the program fits together and how it contributes to the overall training objectives.[44]

2. Present the material by using examples, terms, and concepts that are familiar to the trainees in order to clarify and reinforce key learning points. Show them how they can use the content of the training to do their jobs better.

3. As complex intellectual skills are invariably made up of simpler ones, teach the simpler skills before the complex ones.[45] This is true whether teaching accounting, computer programming, or X-ray technology.

## Practice (Makes Perfect)

Anyone learning a new skill or acquiring factual knowledge must have an opportunity to practice what he or she is learning.[46] Practice, the active use of training content, has three aspects: active practice, overlearning, and the length of the practice session. Let's consider each of these.

- *Active practice.* During the early stages of learning, the trainer should be available to oversee the trainee's practice directly. In contrast to traditional approaches that focus on teaching correct methods (and avoiding errors), a newer approach, known as error-management training, encourages employees to make errors, and then to engage in reflection to understand why they made them, and to develop strategies to avoid making them in the future.[47]

- *Overlearning.* When trainees are given the opportunity to practice far beyond the point where they have performed a task correctly several times, the task becomes second nature and is "overlearned." For some tasks, **overlearning** is critical.[48] This is true of any task that must be performed infrequently and under great stress: for example, performing CPR on a patient who is not breathing. It is less important in types of work where an individual practices his or her skills on a daily basis (e.g., auto mechanics, electronics technicians, assemblers).

- *Length of the practice session.* Suppose you have only one week to memorize the lines of a play, and during that week, you have only 12 hours available to practice. What practice schedule will produce the greatest improvement? Should you practice two hours a day for six days, should you practice for six hours each of the final two days before the deadline, or should you adopt some other schedule? The two extremes represent **distributed practice** (which implies rest intervals between sessions) and **massed practice** (in which the practice sessions are crowded together). Although there are exceptions, most of the research evidence on this question indicates that for the same amount of practice, learning is better when practice is distributed rather than massed.[49] This is especially true for learning simple motor tasks that involve very brief rest periods. It is less true for tasks of high complexity, such as those often

Constructive feedback facilitates learning and supports a trainee's desire to perform well.

found in organizational training settings. Under those circumstances, longer rest periods appear to be more beneficial for learning.[50]

## Feedback

This is a form of information about one's attempts to improve. **Feedback** is essential both for learning and for trainee motivation.[51] If trainees are to understand what leads to good as well as poor performance, however, the level of specificity of feedback should vary.[52] Increasing the specificity of feedback benefits the learning of responses for good performance, but it may be detrimental to the learning of responses for poor performance. For example, in learning to operate a piece of equipment, less specific feedback may cause trainees to make errors that lead to equipment problems, providing them with opportunities to learn which behaviors lead to problems, and how to fix those problems. It is also important to emphasize that feedback affects team, as well as individual, performance.[53] For example, application of performance-based feedback in a small fast-food store over a one-year period led to a 15 percent decrease in food costs and a 193 percent increase in profits.[54]

To have the greatest impact, provide feedback as soon as possible after the trainee demonstrates good performance, especially to novices.[55] It need not be instantaneous, but there should be no confusion regarding exactly what the trainee did and the trainer's reaction to it. Feedback need not always be positive, but keep in mind that the most powerful rewards are likely to be those provided by the trainee's immediate supervisor. In fact, if the supervisor does not reinforce what is learned in training, the training will be transferred ineffectively to the job—if at all.

## Transfer of Training

**Transfer of training** refers to the extent to which competencies learned in training can be applied on the job. Transfer may be positive (i.e., it enhances job performance), negative (i.e., it hampers job performance), or neutral. Long-term training or retraining probably includes segments that contain all three of these conditions. Training that results in negative transfer is costly in two ways—the cost of the training (which proved to be useless) and the cost of hampered performance. To maximize positive transfer, designers of training programs should consider doing the following before, during, and after training:[56]

1. Maximize the similarity between the training situation and the job situation. Use interactive activities during training to encourage participation.
2. Provide trainees as much experience as possible with the tasks, concepts, or skills being taught so that they can deal with situations that do not fit textbook examples exactly. This is adaptive expertise.[57]
3. Provide a strong link between training content and job content ("What you learn in training today, you'll use on the job tomorrow").
4. In the context of team-based training (e.g., in employee involvement), transfer is maximized when teams have open, unrestricted access to information, when the membership includes diverse job functions and administrative backgrounds, and when a team has more members to draw upon to accomplish its activities.[58]
5. Ensure that what is learned in training is used and rewarded on the job. Supervisors and peers are key gatekeepers in this process. If immediate supervisors or peers, by their words or by their example, do not support what was learned in training, don't expect the training to have much of an impact on job performance.[59]

**Action learning,** in which participants focus on real business problems in order to learn through experience and application, is an excellent vehicle for facilitating positive transfer from learning to doing.[60] It's not just for executives either, as the following example illustrates.

## Team Training

Up to this point, we have been discussing training and development as an individual enterprise. Yet today, as we have noted, there is an increasing emphasis on *team* performance, with 80 percent of U.S. corporations using teams of one sort or another.[61] For example, cross-functional teams, intact or virtual, are common features of many organizations. A **team** is a group of individuals who are working together, with shared responsibility, toward a common goal. It is this common goal that really defines a team, and if team members have opposite or conflicting goals, the efficiency of the total unit is likely to suffer. For example, consider the effects on a basketball team when one of the players *always* tries to score, regardless of the team's situation.

A systematic approach to team training should include four steps:[62]

1. *Conduct a team-training needs analysis.* Such an analysis has two objectives: (a) to identify interdependencies among team members and the skills required to master coordination of team tasks, and (b) to identify the cognitive skills and knowledge needed to interact as a team (e.g., knowledge of team-member roles and responsibilities).
2. *Develop training objectives that address both task-work and teamwork skills.* In general, a core set of skills characterizes effective teamwork.

## ACTION LEARNING AT UPS*

When UPS, affectionately known as "Big Brown," found that some 30 percent of its twentysomething driver candidates were flunking its traditional driver training, it had a serious problem on its hands: how to train Generation Y for a hard, blue-collar job. Gen Yers make up more than 60 percent of the part-time loader workforce, from which it draws the majority of new-driver hires. To address the issue head on, UPS created a whole new approach.

In late 2007, UPS opened its first full-service training center, in Landover, Maryland. The 11,500-square-foot facility known as Integrad is much like a movie set, and it's aimed directly at young, would-be drivers. It is fashioned around an approach known as "technology-enhanced, hands-on learning." More than 170 people, including UPS executives, professors and design students at Virginia Tech, a team at MIT, forecasters at the Institute for the Future, and animators at an Indian company called Brainvisa, helped develop the facility and curriculum. On top of that, UPS received a $1.8 million grant from the U.S. Department of Labor. Thus, much of the project's data, including research related to safety and generational differences, will be made available to the public. That information may help many companies in a variety of industries realize the impact of this new generation.

There are many aspects to the rigorous training that UPS provides, but consider just one of those, the transparent UPS "package car." The car is stocked with rows of (weighted) packages. It may look like a big toy, but its purpose is serious. Package selection is the most fundamental part of a UPS driver's job, and yet it can seem impossible when you are staring into the gaping back door

Odd-size packages and cramped space can make the UPS driver's job difficult.

*Source:* Levitz, J. (2010, April 6). UPS thinks outside the box on driver training. *The Wall Street Journal,* pp. B1, B2. See also Hira, N. A. (2007, Nov. 12). The making of a UPS driver. *Fortune,* pp. 118–130.

of a package car, scrambling to locate your five packages and trying to decide how you are going to get them out in the 65.5 seconds that the company's "human engineering" experts have allotted to you.

When learning package-selection techniques, demonstration in an actual package car is a lot more effective than a lecture: Watching an instructor deal with the same shelving system, odd-size packages, and cramped space that drivers have on the road—and then getting to try it yourself before your first trip out—proves invaluable.

New drivers also get to experience the slip-and-fall simulator. Such mishaps cost UPS significantly each year, and first-year drivers fall victim the most. After the simulator experience, novices quickly learn to adjust their gait to minimize the likelihood that they will take a tumble on the job. Actual driving at Integrad is done at a mini-town that has real street and stop signs, a toy house and toy stores, a UPS dropbox, and even a loading dock. Trainees spend time there each day of their 5-day training. Tasks increase in difficulty, and facilitators and fellow trainees stand in as customers to test the drivers on their customer service.

Driver candidates also play a videogame that places them in the driver's seat and has them identify obstacles. They progress from computer simulations to "Clarksville," an artificial village of miniature houses and businesses on the property where they drive a real truck and must successfully execute five deliveries in 19 minutes.

Driver training is critical for UPS, which employs 99,000 drivers and expects to hire 25,000 more over the next five years. Has its high-tech approach to training worked? Of the 1,629 trainees who have completed Integrad, only 10 percent have failed the training program, which takes a total of six weeks overall and includes 30 days driving a truck in the real world. Action learning virtually ensures high positive transfer to the job, and the reduction in the failure rate from 30% to 10% is a win-win for the company, its drivers, and the customers it serves.

These include adaptability, shared awareness of situations, performance monitoring and feedback, leadership/team management, interpersonal skills, coordination, communication, and decision-making skills. Attitudinal skills that characterize effective teamwork include beliefs about the importance of teamwork skills, belief in placing the team's goals above those of individual members, mutual trust, and shared vision.[63] Sequence the training so that trainees can master task-work skills before learning teamwork skills.

3. *Design exercises and training events based on the objectives from step 2.* As with individual training, opportunities for guided practice and constructive feedback are particularly important for team training. This may include, for example, **team-coordination training** (focusing on teamwork skills that facilitate information exchange, cooperation, and coordination of job-related behaviors); **cross-training** (providing exposure to and practice with other teammates' tasks, roles, and responsibilities in an effort to increase shared understanding and knowledge among team members); and **guided team self-correction** (providing guidance to team members in reviewing team events, identifying errors and exchanging feedback, and developing plans for the future).

4. *Design measures of team effectiveness based on the objectives from step 2, evaluate the effectiveness of the team training, and use this information to guide future team training.*

Other research has revealed two broad principles regarding the composition and management of teams. First, individual skills are a necessary, but not sufficient, condition for effective team performance.[64] Thus, individual training and development are still important. But individual training is only a partial solution because interactions among team members must also be addressed. This interaction is what makes team training unique—it always uses some form of simulation or real-life practice, and it always focuses on the interaction of team members, equipment, and work procedures.[65] To improve team communication and team effectiveness, and therefore aviation safety, among air crews for example, a popular intervention is Crew Resource Management (CRM) training, usually conducted using sophisticated flight simulators. Evidence across more than 50 studies shows positive benefits in terms of improved communication and performance.[66]

Second, managers of effective work groups tend to monitor the performance of their team members regularly, and they provide frequent feedback to them. This is as true of traditional teams as it is of virtual teams.[67] In fact, as much as 35 percent of the variability in team performance can be explained by the frequency of use of monitors and consequences. Incorporating these findings into the training of team members and their managers should lead to better overall team performance.

## Selecting Training Methods

New training methods appear every year. While some are well founded in learning theory or models of behavior change (e.g., behavior modeling), others result more from technological than theoretical developments (e.g., presentation software, use of animation and sound, computer-based business simulations).

Training methods, that is, tactics used in the training environment to stimulate learning, can be classified in three ways: information presentation, simulation methods, or on-the-job training.[68]

- *Information-presentation techniques* include lectures, conferences, correspondence courses, videos/compact discs (CDs), distance learning, interactive multimedia (CDs/DVDs), intranet and Internet, intelligent tutoring (software that models a learner's current state of knowledge and skill relative to an expert, then selects tactics to help the learner progress from novice to expert),[69] and **organization development**—systematic, long-range programs of organizational improvement.
- *Simulation methods* include the case method, role playing, behavior modeling, interactive simulations for virtual teams, virtual reality, the in-basket technique, and business simulations.
- *On-the-job training methods* include orientation training, apprenticeships, on-the-job training, near-the-job training (using identical equipment but away from the job itself), job rotation, committee assignments (or junior executive boards), understudy assignments, on-the-job coaching, and performance management.

In the context of developing interpersonal skills, training methods are typically chosen to achieve one or more of three objectives:

- Promoting self-insight and environmental awareness—that is, an understanding of how a person's actions affect others and how a person is viewed

---

## ETHICAL DILEMMA
### Anger Management: Whose Responsibility Is It?*

Workplace stress is high these days, given the fact that many employers have reduced the size of their workforces, instituted pay cuts, or imposed furloughs. Often, remaining employees are saddled with increased workloads. As one expert put it, "Anger comes in two flavors: hot and cold contempt. Hot contempt is what we traditionally think of as anger: red face and bulging veins. But 90 percent of workplace anger is cold contempt: gossip, back-stabbing, withdrawal, simmering resentment, and the desire to see others fail." Either type of anger can cost a company in terms of lost productivity and higher health premiums.

Should supervisors and higher-level managers be responsible for dealing with the anger issues of those who report to them? Some might argue that it is unreasonable to expect anyone other than a highly credentialed and experienced provider, schooled in clinical psychology, counseling, or medicine, to be able to deal effectively with issues like that. What do you think?

*Source:* Tyler, K. (2010, May). Helping employees cool it. *HRMagazine* 55(4), 53-55.

---

by others. For example, at Parfums Stern, employees act out customer/salesperson roles to better understand customers' emotions. Wendy's International videotapes customers with disabilities; in one video a blind person asks that change be counted out loud. Meridian Bancorp has workers walk with seeds in their shoes to simulate older customers' corns and calluses.[70]

- Improving the ability of managers and lower-level employees to make decisions and to solve job-related problems in a constructive fashion.
- Maximizing the desire to perform well.

To choose the training method (or combination of methods) that best fits a given situation, *first define carefully what you wish to teach*. That is the purpose of the needs-assessment phase. Only then can you choose a method that best fits these requirements. To be useful, the method should meet the minimal conditions needed for effective learning to take place; that is, the training method should

- Motivate the trainee to improve his or her performance.
- Clearly illustrate desired skills.
- Allow the trainee to participate actively.
- Provide an opportunity to practice.
- Provide timely feedback on the trainee's performance.
- Provide some means for reinforcement while the trainee learns.
- Be structured from simple to complex tasks.
- Be adaptable to specific problems.
- Encourage positive transfer from the training to the job.

## EVALUATING TRAINING PROGRAMS

To evaluate training, you must systematically document the outcomes of the training in terms of how trainees actually behave back on their jobs and the relevance of that behavior to the objectives of the organization.[71] To assess the utility or value of training, we seek answers to questions such as the following:

1. Have trainees achieved a specific level of skill, knowledge, or performance?
2. Did change occur?
3. Is the change due to training?
4. Is the change positively related to the achievement of organizational goals?
5. Will similar changes occur with new participants in the same training program?[72]

In evaluating training programs, it is important to distinguish targets of evaluation (training content and design, changes in learners, and organizational payoffs) from data-collection methods (e.g., with respect to organizational payoffs, cost-benefit analyses, ratings, and surveys). Figure 8–3 presents a model that illustrates these distinctions. Targets and methods are linked through the options available for measurement, that is, its focus (e.g., with respect to changes in learners, the focus might be cognitive, affective, or behavioral changes). Finally, targets, focus, and methods are linked to the purpose of the evaluation—feedback (to trainers or learners), decision making, and marketing.

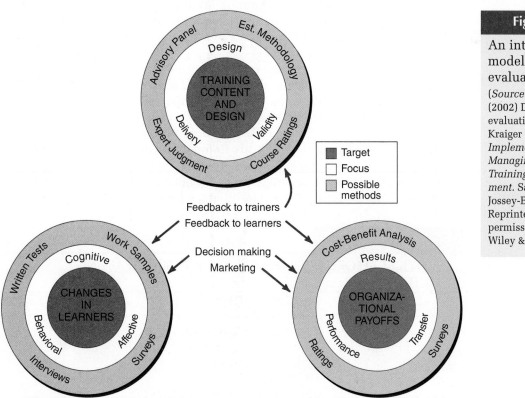

**Figure 8–3**

An integrative model of training evaluation.
(*Source:* Kraiger, K. (2002) Decision-based evaluation. In K. Kraiger (Ed.), *Creating, Implementing, and Managing Effective Training and Development.* San Francisco: Jossey-Bass, p. 343. Reprinted with permission of John Wiley & Sons Inc.)

Consider organizational payoffs, for example. The focus might be on transfer of training (e.g., transfer climate, opportunity to perform, on-the-job behavior change), on results (performance effectiveness or tangible outcomes to a work-group or organization), or on the financial impact of the training (e.g., through measures of return-on-investment or utility analysis).

## ADDITIONAL CONSIDERATIONS IN MEASURING THE OUTCOMES OF TRAINING

Regardless of the measures used, our goal is to be able to make meaningful inferences and to rule out alternative explanations for results (e.g., lengthened job experience, outside economic events, changes in supervision or performance incentives). To do so, it is important to administer the measures according to some logical plan or procedure (experimental design) (e.g., before and after training as well as to a comparable control group).

To rule out these rival explanations for the changes that occurred, it is essential to design a plan for evaluation that includes *before* and *after* measurement of the trained group's performance relative to that of one or more untrained control groups. (However, when it is relatively costly to bring participants to an evaluation and administration costs are particularly high, after-only measurement of trained and untrained groups is best.[73]) Match members of the untrained control group as closely as possible to those in the trained group. Table 8–1 shows a standard design for such a study. If the outcomes of the training are positive, the untrained control group at time 1 may become the trained group at a later time. It is important to note that the post-training appraisal of performance should not be done sooner than three months (or more) following the training so that the trainees have an opportunity to put into practice what they have learned.

Finally, the impact of training on organizational results is the most significant, but most difficult, effect to demonstrate. *Measures of results are the bottom line of training success.* Exciting developments in this area have come from recent research showing how the general utility equation (Equation 7–1 on page 275) can be modified to reflect the dollar value of improved job performance resulting from training.[74] Utility formulas are now available for evaluating the dollar value of a single training program compared to a control group, a training program re-administered periodically (e.g., annually), and a comparison between two or more different training programs.

## Table 8–1

**A TYPICAL BEFORE-AFTER DESIGN FOR ASSESSING TRAINING OUTCOMES**

|           | Trained group | Untrained group |
|-----------|---------------|-----------------|
| Pretest   | Yes           | Yes             |
| Training  | Yes           | No              |
| Post-test | Yes           | Yes             |

## EXECUTIVE COACHING

External coaches are often used to help talented executives who are in trouble because of behavioral or style deficiencies, or to help them lead critical transitions, such as having to lead a major change effort. Unfortunately, practice is far ahead of theory and research in this area, and there is a lack of consensus about definitions, methods, and techniques. In addition, there are no barriers to entry and no generally accepted standards for certification. In terms of coaching's effectiveness, it is difficult to identify causal connections between specific actions and outcomes like strategy execution and change management because the coaching process unfolds over a relatively long period of time, and feedback on outcomes is therefore a long-term process. Any immediate feedback is likely to be related to outcomes like leadership behaviors or individual performance.[a]

*Does It Pay Off?*

That said, executive coaching has the following characteristics. It is

- One-on-one.
- Relationship-based.
- Methodology-based (draws on specific tools and techniques as part of a relatively structured overall process).
- Provided by a professional coach.
- Scheduled in multiple sessions over time.
- Goal-oriented for both organizational and individual benefit.
- Customized to the person.
- Intended to enhance the person's ability to learn and develop independently.[b]

The best coaching is aligned with an organization's overall talent-management strategy. The organization has a clear understanding of its talent and development needs, the array of development tools that might be used (including coaching), and a method for matching the talent need with the appropriate solution.

Does coaching work? A review of four studies revealed an average return on investment (ROI) of five to seven times its cost. There is reason to be skeptical, however, since it is extremely difficult to estimate accurately the future financial value of any capabilities acquired through coaching. Another study found five main areas of improvement: people management, relationships with managers, goal setting and prioritization, personal productivity and engagement at work, and communications with colleagues.[c]

Beyond this evidence, there is the simple but compelling logic that executive coaching incorporates multiple techniques already shown to be effective in learning. These include goal setting; feedback; accountability; behavioral practice; communicating performance expectations; enhancing self-efficacy; reflection; and establishing a trusting, supportive relationship.[d]

In addition, evidence shows that coaching improves managers' use of 360-degree feedback by helping them set specific goals for improvement and solicit ideas for improvement. Those actions lead to improved performance.[e]

Remember, not all coaches are equally proficient in what they do, and not every executive is equally likely to change from coaching.[f] The best coaches are empathetic, supportive, practical, and self-confident, but do not appear to know all the answers or tell others what to do. To be receptive to coaching, employees need to be open-minded and interested, not defensive and close-minded. Both parties need to be coached to take risks in the relationship. To evaluate a prospective coach, consider asking questions such as the following. Experienced coaches should have good answers to each of them:

- With whom have you worked, in what types of organizations and jobs, and at what levels?
- What processes do you build in to ensure that you get results?
- What kind of assessment will we go through to focus on the right things for me?
- What is your approach to help me learn new things?
- How can we know we have achieved what we set out to achieve?
- Who would you turn down, and why?[g]

---

[a] Peterson, D. B. (2011). Executive coaching: A critical review and recommendations for advancing the practice. In S. Zedeck (Ed.), *Handbook of Industrial and Organizational Psychology*, Vol. 2. Washington, DC: American Psychological Association, pp. 527–566.

[b] Ibid.

[c] Kombarakaran, F. A., Yang, J. A., Baker, M. N., and Fernandes, P. B. (2008). *Executive coaching: It works! Consulting Psychology Journal: Practice and Research* 60, pp. 78–90.

[d] Peterson, 2011, op. cit.

[e] Smither, J. M., London, M., Flautt, R., Vargas, Y., & Kucine, L. (2003). Can working with an executive coach improve multisource ratings over time? A quasiexperimental field study. *Personnel Psychology* 56, pp. 23–44.

[f] Ibid.

[g] Tyler, K. (2000, June). Scoring big in the workplace. *HR Magazine*, pp. 96–106.

## NEW-EMPLOYEE ORIENTATION: THE ON-BOARDING PROCESS

An often neglected part of the training enterprise is the orientation of new employees to the company and its culture. Because most turnover occurs during the first few months on the job (at Marriott, 40 percent of the new employees who leave do so during the first three months[75]), failure to provide a thorough orientation can be a very expensive mistake.[76] Let's consider what progressive companies are doing in this area.

One definition of **orientation** is "familiarization with and adaptation to a situation or an environment." While 8 out of every 10 organizations in the United States that have more than 50 employees provide orientation, the time and effort devoted to its design, conduct, and evaluation are woefully inadequate. In practice, orientation is often just a superficial indoctrination into company philosophy, policies, and rules; sometimes it includes the presentation of an employee handbook and a quick tour of the office or plant. This can be costly. Here is why.

In one way, a displaced worker from the factory who is hired into another environment is similar to a new college graduate. Upon starting a new job, both will face a kind of culture shock. As they are exposed for the first time to a new organizational culture, both find that the new job is not quite what they imagined it to be. In fact, coming to work at a new company is not unlike visiting a foreign country. Either you are told about the local customs, or else you learn them on your own by a process of trial and error. An effective orientation program can help lessen the impact of this shock. But there must be more, such as a period of **socialization,** or learning to function as a contributing member of the corporate "family." A well-designed new-employee orientation will facilitate socialization. The payoff? Higher levels of job satisfaction and commitment, along with reduced levels of employee turnover, and a deeper understanding of a firm's goals, values, history, and people.[77]

The cost of hiring, training, and orienting a new person is far higher than most of us realize. For example, Merck & Co., the pharmaceutical giant, found that—depending on the job—turnover costs are 1.5 to 2.5 times the annual salary paid for the job.[78] Moreover, because the turnover rate among new college hires can be as great as 50 percent during the first 12 months, such costs can be considerable.

A new employee's experiences during the initial period with an organization can have a major impact on his or her career. A new hire stands on the boundary of the organization—certainly no longer an outsider but not yet embraced by those within. There is great stress. The new hire wants to reduce this stress by becoming incorporated into the "interior" as quickly as possible. Consequently, during this period an employee is more receptive to cues from the organizational environment than she or he is ever likely to be again. Such cues to proper behavior may come from a variety of sources, for example,

- Official literature of the organization.
- Examples set by senior people.
- Formal instructions given by senior people.
- Examples given by peers.
- Rewards and punishments that flow from the employee's efforts.
- Responses to the employee's ideas.
- Degree of challenge in the assignments the employee receives.

Special problems may arise for a young new employee whose life until now has been spent mainly in an educational setting. As she approaches her first job, the recent graduate may feel motivated entirely by personal creativity. She is information rich but experience poor, eager to apply her knowledge to new processes and problems. Unfortunately, there are conditions that may stifle this creative urge. During her undergraduate days, the new employee exercised direct control over her work. Now she faces regular hours, greater restrictions, possibly a less pleasant environment, and a need to work through other people—often finding that most of the work is mundane and unchallenging. In short, three typical problems face the new employee:

1. *Problems in entering a group.* The new employee asks herself whether she will (a) be acceptable to the other group members, (b) be liked, and (c) be safe—that is, free from physical and psychological harm. These issues must be resolved before she can feel comfortable and productive in the new situation.
2. *Naive expectations.* Organizations find it much easier to communicate factual information about pay and benefits, vacations, and company policies than information about employee norms (rules or guides to acceptable behavior), company attitudes, or "what it really takes to get ahead around here." Simple fairness suggests that employees ought to be told about these intangibles. The bonus is that being up front and honest with job candidates produces positive results. As we saw in Chapter 6, the research on realistic job previews (RJPs) indicates that job acceptance rates will likely be lower for those who receive an RJP, but job survival rates will be higher.[79]
3. *First-job environment.* Does the new environment help or hinder the new employee trying to climb aboard? Can peers be counted on to socialize the new employee to desired job standards? How and why was the first job assignment chosen? Is it clear to the new employee what she or he can expect to get out of it?

To appreciate the kinds of problems a new employee faces, consider how Dave Savchetz, plant manager of Ford Motor Company's Kansas City, Missouri, factory, describes his first day on the job 20 years ago:[80]

> It was a shock. To be honest, it was pretty traumatic. You got hired in this group of 30 people you've never met, and you sign a form, and the foreman comes in, and you walk out into this factory. And it's just the first time, you know? Things are moving, and you just look around, and you go, "What's going on here?" Quite frankly, the first day I got lost.

In fact, the first year with an organization is the critical period during which an employee will or will not learn to become a high performer. The careful matching of company and employee expectations during this period can result in positive job attitudes and high standards, which then can be reinforced in new and more demanding jobs.

## PLANNING, PACKAGING, AND EVALUATING AN ON-BOARDING PROGRAM

Typically some time will elapse between the acceptance of a job and the actual start date. Some companies use this time to begin the orientation process. One West Coast company mails correspondence to the new employee's home, indicating how happy it is that the new employee will be joining the company's team. It also sends the employee handbook, along with information about the geographical area, as well as major, ongoing projects in the department where the new employee will be working. The company then follows up with a personal phone call to answer any new or outstanding questions that the new employee may have. Lastly, it calls the new employee the day before he or she is scheduled to begin work. This all occurs *before* the employee actually reports![81] By this time, the new employee probably feels extremely welcome and will be quite comfortable during the first day on the job.

At a broad level, new employees need specific information in the following areas:[82]

- Company standards, expectations, goals, history, politics (information about formal and informal power structures), and language (knowledge of the organization's acronyms, slang, and jargon).
- Social behavior, such as approved conduct, the work climate, and getting to know fellow workers and supervisors.
- Technical aspects of the job so that they can become proficient and perform well.

Some employers now offer a rich online orientation experience. For example, IBM uses the Internet-based virtual-world platform Second Life to enable its interns and new hires from all over the world to learn about corporate culture and business processes by having their avatars attend meetings, view presentations, and interact with other avatars in a virtual IBM Community. Such an approach allows IBM to provide consistent information to employees in an interactive, engaging way and to set the tone with new employees.[83]

Houston-based ION Geophysical uses a simulation called RedCarpet to provide a consistent, personalized welcome message to new hires in the five countries in which it operates. Through the new-employee portal, the chief executive officer offers a welcome message via streaming video. New hires can view photos and profiles of members of their work team, get instructions on setting up voice mail, and access career-development information. Based on the new hire's location, he or she can also view information on local amenities, such as dry cleaners, fitness centers, banks, and restaurants. The system even accommodates multiple languages so international employees can receive information in their native tongues.[84]

Appealing though the gaming approach may be, there are also drawbacks. Research shows that when orientation is more individualized, newcomers are less likely to seek feedback and information, to build relationships, and to socialize.[85]

Be sure to avoid these approaches to orientation:[86]

- *An emphasis on paperwork.* After completing forms required by the HR department, manually, the new employee is given a cursory welcome. Then the employee is directed to his or her immediate supervisor. The likely result: The employee does not feel like part of the company. In contrast, one company reduced the number of times new hires had to sign their names, from 32 with a manual process to just twice with an online on-boarding system. That saving in time frees up the new employee to spend the first day meeting people and adjusting to the company's culture and work environment.[87]
- *A sketchy overview of the basics.* A quick, superficial orientation, and the new employee is immediately put to work—sink or swim.
- *Mickey Mouse assignments.* The new employee's first tasks are insignificant duties, supposedly intended to teach the job "from the ground up."
- *Suffocation.* Giving too much information too fast is a well-intentioned but disastrous approach, causing the new employee to feel overwhelmed and suffocated.

We know from other companies' mistakes what works and what does not. For example, consider how The Container Store handles new employee orientation.

---

## THE CONTAINER STORE

**HR BUZZ**

Listen as Barbara Anderson, of Dallas-based The Container Store, a perennial member of *Fortune* magazine's "100 Best Companies to Work for in America," describes Foundation Week: "Our orientation begins with the interview process. Full-time employees will have a minimum of three interviews with three different people, which is very unusual for retail," says Anderson. "But we want the right fit. We have a quirky culture, and spend a lot of time talking about how and why we do business the way we do."

*Foundation Week\**

Anderson says that her company went from doing absolutely nothing for orientation when the company started in 1978, to the structured Foundation Week that has been in place since 1996. "We started years ago with two hours of orientation, and then four, after which employees were given an apron and told to go to work," she says. "We lost a lot of good people that way—they couldn't learn by osmosis."

The Container Store today has a formatted approach to orientation that Anderson says layers information. "Each layer goes back to reinforce what the employee learned the day before. By the end of the week, the new employee has heard the most important things five different times from five different people."

---

*Source:* Joinson, C. (2001, Winter). Hit the floor running, start the cart . . . and other new ways to train new employees. *Employment Management Today* 6(1). Retrieved from *http://www.shrm.org* on Sept. 8, 2004.

Day One of Foundation Week begins with philosophy and time with the store manager. "This day usually blows people away—the fact that the manager spends most of the day talking to them," says Anderson. "Right away, they know they're in a different culture."

"Many companies spend the first day on where to park and benefits—boring!" says Anderson, who intersperses this kind of information in a crossword puzzle format. "Employees have a handbook and an assignment before they start, and we tell them to come prepared for discussion."

Day Two progresses to visual information. "This is very important," says Anderson. "We show them how we get the product into the store, how we put it on the shelves, how we make signs." Anderson says that during Foundation Week, new hires actually work as full-fledged store employees—without the apron. But because of the training they receive during this week, she says, "When they do put on their aprons and go out on the floor, right away they can be productive and have something to do."

On Day Three, employees spend time with salespeople, learning the different sections of the store and the various selling techniques for each section. Day Four teaches the employee different roles like that of host (greeter) and cashier, and how to provide customer service in these roles. The employee learns about inventory and back-room operations on Day Five, and gets a recap with the manager.

"Then we have a ceremony that cheers on the new employees," says Anderson. "And that is when they get their apron. The psychological effect of having to wait for that apron is incredible."

Although it's difficult to attribute retention to a single factor like a good orientation program, Anderson believes that starting employees out right certainly helps with her company's low turnover. According to the Washington, DC–based National Retail Federation, average turnover rates for store managers, full-time employees, and part-time employees in most businesses are 33.6, 73.6, and 124.3 percent, respectively. In comparison, Anderson says that The Container Store's turnover rate, which includes part-time and seasonal employees, is 25 to 30 percent.

Anderson believes the time in Foundation Week is well spent. "We have a productive employee much more quickly, rather than a warm body trying to sell." In the past, when The Container Store didn't do orientation this way, employees did not have the same self-confidence. She says: "Whenever we short this, we set the employee back about three months."

## Orientation Follow-Up

The worst mistake a company can make is to ignore the new employee after orientation. Almost as bad is an informal open-door policy: "Come see me sometime if you have any questions." Many new employees are simply not assertive enough to seek out the supervisor or HR representative—more than likely, they fear looking dumb. What is needed is formal and systematic orientation follow-up; for example, National Semiconductor uses focus groups of randomly selected new employees to find out what they like and don't like.[88] It found that many of the topics covered during orientation need to be explained briefly again—once the employee has had the opportunity to experience them firsthand. This is natural and understandable in view of the blizzard of information that often is communicated during orientation. One hospital asks new employees to complete a "six-week checkup" by answering questions such as, "How well do you know your supervisor?" "What do you like best (least) about your job?" "What additional training do you need?" and "How can we help you do your job better?"

## Evaluation of the Orientation Program

At least once a year, review the orientation program to determine if it is meeting its objectives and to identify future improvements. To improve orientation, you need candid, comprehensive feedback from everyone involved in the program. There are several ways to provide this kind of feedback: through roundtable discussions with new employees after their first year on the job, through in-depth interviews with randomly selected employees and supervisors, and through questionnaires for mass coverage of all recent hires. Now let's consider some important lessons that any company can use.

## LESSONS LEARNED

As a result of The Container Store's experience and the recent experiences of many other companies, we offer the following considerations to guide the process of orienting new employees. They apply to any type of organization, large or small, and to any function or level of job:[89]

1. The impressions formed by new employees within their first 60 to 90 days on a job are lasting.
2. Day one is crucial—new employees remember it for years. It must be managed well.
3. New employees are interested in learning about the total organization—and how they and their unit fit into the big picture. This is just as important as is specific information about the new employee's own job and department. For example, new employees at Corning go through an intranet scavenger hunt that requires them to use information learned during orientation and to demonstrate that they are comfortable with using the company's intranet system.
4. Give new employees major responsibility for their own orientation, through guided self-learning, but with direction and support.
5. Avoid information overload—provide it in reasonable amounts.
6. Recognize that community, social, and family adjustment is a critical aspect of orientation for new employees.
7. Make the immediate supervisor ultimately responsible for the success of the orientation process.
8. Thorough orientation is a "must" for productivity improvement. It is a vital part of the total management system—and therefore the foundation of any effort to improve employee productivity.

These lessons are exciting and provocative. They suggest that we should be at least as concerned with preparing the new employee for the social context of his or her job and for coping with the insecurities and frustrations of a new learning situation as with the development of the technical skills necessary to perform well.

## IMPACT OF TRAINING AND DEVELOPMENT ON PRODUCTIVITY, QUALITY OF WORK LIFE, AND THE BOTTOM LINE

Does training work? One investigation reported the following returns on investment (ROI) for various types of training: 5:1 (behavior modification), 4.8:1 (customer service), 13.7:1 (team training), 15:1 (role of the manager), and 21:1 (sales training).[a] At a more general level, the literature on training evaluation shows that while the potential returns from well-conducted training programs can be substantial, there is often considerable variability in the effectiveness with which any given training method or content area is implemented.[b] As we have seen, considerable planning (through needs analysis) and follow-up program-evaluation efforts are necessary in order to realize these returns. Given the pace of change in modern society and technology, retraining is imperative to enable individuals to compete for or retain their jobs and to enable organizations to compete in the marketplace. In recruiting and retaining a diverse workforce, for example, a WetFeet.com study reported that "opportunities for training and career development" was the number 1 feature that candidates demand.[c] Continual investments in training and learning are therefore essential, as they have such direct impacts on the productivity of organizations and on the quality of work life of those who work in them.

[a] Philips, J. J. (1996, Feb.). ROI: the search for best practices. *Training and Development,* p. 45. See also Arthur, Bennett, Edens, and Bell, (2003), op. cit.

[b] Aguinis and Kraiger, (2009), op. cit.

[c] Thaler-Carter, R. E. (2001, June). Diversify your recruitment advertising. *HR Magazine,* pp. 92–100.

*Human Resource Management in Action: Conclusion*

## TECHNOLOGY-DELIVERED INSTRUCTION (TDI) CATCHES ON

Simulation games are one popular type of TDI. They refer to instruction delivered via personal computer that immerses trainees in a decision-making exercise in an artificial environment in order to learn the consequences of their decisions. The games are intrinsically motivating, and people report a loss of time when playing their favorite ones. When used for training, they seem to pay off nicely. Meta-analysis results indicate that relative to a comparison group, post-training self-efficacy (belief that one can succeed) was 20 percent higher, knowledge of facts was 11 percent higher, skill-based knowledge was 14 percent higher, and retention was 9 percent higher for trainees taught with simulation games.

Trainees learned more when simulation games conveyed course material actively rather than passively, trainees could access the simulation game as many times as they desired, and the simulation game was a supplement to other instructional methods rather than stand-alone instruction. Trainees learned less, however, when the instruction the comparison group received as a substitute for the simulation game actively engaged them in the learning experience.

Here's an example. Cold Stone Creamery developed a simulation game to teach customer service and portion control in a virtual Cold Stone store. Players race against the clock to service customers in a timely fashion while maximizing the company's profit by avoiding wasting too much ice cream. The first week the simulation game was available, more than 8,000 employees—30 percent of the workforce— voluntarily downloaded the simulation game. Corporate trainers believe that the entertainment value will motivate employees to play the game continuously while simultaneously teaching them retail sales, technical, and managerial skills.

There are drawbacks, however. Computer-based simulation games are more expensive to develop than other forms of TDI, with complex simulation games costing between $5 and $20 million to create. Traditional online training takes an average of 220 hours to create each hour of instructional content, whereas online simulations require 750 to 1,500 hours to create each hour of instructional content. Needless to say, in order to maximize the utility of simulation games, designers need to focus on content reuse, using software that streamlines the game-development process, and offsetting development costs with savings in travel costs for training that used to be delivered via classroom instruction. Here is another consideration.

Although some people may relish the opportunity to squeeze in a little training via a computer or CD at home, on a plane, or in a hotel room, others may regard after-hours training as an unwarranted intrusion on their personal time. This raises an interesting question. If a company does not provide time for training during regular working hours, is it arbitrarily extending the workday? Some firms, such as GlaxoSmithKline, urge managers to provide time for training during the work day. Other employers provide tools to help employees carve training time out of their work days. Cisco Systems gives employees police tape to stretch across their cubicle doors. Others hand out signs saying "Learning in Progress." As learning becomes more a part of every job—and of day-to-day life—more companies will develop policies on these issues.

## IMPLICATIONS FOR MANAGEMENT PRACTICE

One of the greatest fears of managers and lower-level employees is obsolescence. Perhaps the **Paul principle** expresses this phenomenon most aptly: Over time, people become uneducated, and therefore incompetent, to perform at a level at which they once performed adequately.[a] Training is an important antidote to obsolescence, but it is important to be realistic about what training can and cannot accomplish.

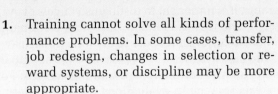

1. Training cannot solve all kinds of performance problems. In some cases, transfer, job redesign, changes in selection or reward systems, or discipline may be more appropriate.

2. Because productivity (the value of outputs per unit of labor) is a characteristic of a system, such as a firm or an industry, and not of an individual, changes in individual or team performance are only one possible cause of changes in productivity.[b]

3. As a manager, you need to ask yourself three key questions:
   - Do we have an actual or a potential performance problem for which training is the answer?
   - Have we defined what is to be learned and what the content of training should be before we choose a particular training method or technique?
   - What kind of evaluation procedure will we use to determine if the benefits of the training outweigh its costs?

[a] Armer, P. (1970). The individual: His privacy, self-image, and obsolescence. *Proceedings of the meeting of the panel on science and technology, 11th "Science and Astronautics."* Washington, DC: U.S. Government Printing Office.

[b] Campbell, J. P. (1988). Training design for performance improvement. In J. P. Campbell and R. J. Campbell (Eds.), *Productivity in organizations.* San Francisco: Jossey-Bass, pp. 177–215.

Suppose you are considering offering TDI to your employees. Experts say that it is critical to test drive each potential course from the vendor. Experience the course. See how easy it is to navigate the site, how fast it loads, and if it provides quality take-home information. Are all elements of the course integrated? Is technical support available 24/7? An online course won't be of much use if employees can't access it or can't get help with it anytime they want. Inadequate support equals frustrated learners. Finally, simulation games or any other type of TDI should not be used in training simply because the technology exists. Rather, determine training needs carefully, and identify the kinds of instructional features that should be included in order to maximize learning.

A final issue is this. Who profits most from e-learning? A recent study found considerable variability in the amount of time participants spent on each module and the time they spent practicing what was taught. Not surprisingly, employees who learned most from this type of learning environment were those who completed more of the practice opportunities made available and took more time to complete the experience.

## SUMMARY

The pace of change in our society is forcing employees at all levels continually to acquire new knowledge and skills. In most organizations, therefore, lifelong training is essential. To be maximally effective, training programs should follow a three-phase sequence: needs assessment, implementation, and evaluation. First define clearly what is to be learned before choosing a particular method or technique. To define what is to be learned, a continuous cycle of organization analysis, demographic analysis, operations analysis, and analysis of the training needs of employees is necessary.

Then, relate training needs to the achievement of broader organizational goals and ensure that they are consistent with management's perceptions of strategy and tactics. Beyond these fundamental concerns, principles of learning—goal setting, behavior modeling, meaningfulness of material, practice, feedback, and transfer of training—are essential considerations in the design of any training program. Choose a particular technique according to the degree to which it fits identified needs and incorporates the learning principles.

In evaluating training programs, it is important to distinguish targets of evaluation (training content and design, changes in learners, and organizational payoffs) from data-collection methods (e.g., with respect to organizational payoffs, cost-benefit analyses, ratings, and surveys). However, measures of the impact of training on organizational results are the bottom line of training success. Fortunately, advances in utility analysis now make evaluations possible in terms of economic benefits and economic costs.

One of the most neglected areas of training is new-employee orientation, also known as on-boarding. Clearly, a new employee's initial experience with a firm can have a major effect on his or her later career. To maximize the impact of orientation, it is important to recognize that new employees need specific information in three major areas: (1) company standards, expectations, goals, history, politics, and language; (2) social behavior; and (3) technical aspects of the job. While some aspects of orientation can be handled via computer (e.g., forms completion, history of the organization), the more socially rich areas should not. Rather, use a formal, social-based program to do that, and be sure to involve HR as well as non-HR executives and employees in the process. An orientation follow-up is essential (e.g., after one week and one month by the supervisor, and after one month and every few months thereafter by an HR representative) to ensure proper quality control plus continual improvement.

## KEY TERMS

| | |
|---|---|
| training | overlearning |
| training paradox | distributed practice |
| assessment phase | massed practice |
| training and development phase | feedback |
| evaluation phase | transfer of training |
| organization analysis | action learning |
| demographic analysis | team |
| operations analysis | team-coordination training |
| individual analysis | cross-training |
| pre-employment training programs | guided team self-correction |
| goal theory | organization development |
| Pygmalion effect | orientation |
| behavior modeling | socialization |
| meaningfulness (of material) | Paul principle |

## DISCUSSION QUESTIONS

**8–1.** Would you be able to recognize a sound training program if you saw one? What features would you look for?

**8–2.** How does goal-setting affect trainee learning and motivation?

**8–3.** Outline an evaluation procedure for a training program designed to teach sales principles and strategies.

**8–4.** Why do organizations so frequently overlook new-employee orientation?

**8–5.** Think back to your first day on the most recent job you have held. What could the organization have done to hasten your socialization and your adjustment to the job?

## APPLYING YOUR KNOWLEDGE

*Evaluating Training at Hutchinson Inc.*                                                      *Case 8–1*

Hutchinson Inc. is a large insurance brokerage firm operating out of Seattle, Washington. The company was founded in 1942 by John Hutchinson, Sr., great-grandfather of the current president. Hutchinson offers a complete line of insurance services for both individuals and business firms. As is true with other insurance companies, Hutchinson emphasizes sales. In fact, more than half of all corporate employees are involved in sales to some degree.

Because the sales activity is so important to Hutchinson, the company spends a considerable amount of time, effort, and money in sales training. Its training director, Tom Jordan, is constantly on the lookout for new training techniques that can improve sales and profits. He recently uncovered one that he had never heard of before, but which seemed to have some promise. He immediately scheduled a meeting with his boss, Cathy Archer, vice president for human resources at Hutchinson, to discuss the possibility of sending some salespeople to this new training course.

*Cathy:*  Come in, Tom. What's this I hear about a new sales-training course?

*Tom:*  Well, as you know, Cathy, I always try to keep up-to-date on the latest in training techniques so that we can remain competitive. I got a flyer yesterday in the mail announcing a new approach to sales training. The course is offered by a guy named Bagwan Shri Lansig. Apparently, the course involves flying trainees off to a secluded spot in the mountains of Oregon where they undergo a week of intensive training, personal-growth exercises, synchronized chanting, and transcendental meditation. The brochure is brimming with personal testimonials from "million-dollar" salespeople who claim to have been helped immeasurably by the training. I already have 10 people in mind to send to the training session next month, but before I speak with them, I thought I'd run it by you.

*Cathy:*  How much does it cost?

*Tom:*  It's not bad. Only $6,500 per person. And there's a 10 percent discount if we send more than five people.

*Cathy:*  I don't know, Tom. That sounds a little steep to me. Besides, John has been bugging me again about the results of our last training effort. He wants to know whether all the money we're spending on sales training is really paying off. As you know, sales and profits are down this quarter, and John is looking for places to cut corners. I'm afraid that if we can't demonstrate a payoff somehow for our training courses, he is going to pull the rug out from under us.

*Tom:*  But we evaluate all our training programs! The last one got rave reviews from all the participants. Remember how they said that they hardly had time to enjoy Hawaii because they were so busy learning about proper closing techniques?

*Cathy:*  That's true, Tom. But John wants more proof than just the reactions of the salespeople. He wants something more tangible. Now before we buy into any more sales-training programs, I want you to develop a plan for evaluation of the training effort.

---

### Questions

1. What is meant by the statement that training is extremely "faddish"?
2. How can Hutchinson Inc. avoid becoming a victim of a training fad?
3. Develop a detailed training-evaluation strategy that Tom can present to Cathy, which would provide evidence of the effectiveness of a particular training technique.

---

## REFERENCES

1. Cascio, W. F. (2002). *Responsible Restructuring: Creative and Profitable Alternatives to Layoffs.* San Francisco: Jossey-Bass. See also DeMeuse, K. P., Marks, M. L., and Dai, G. (2011). Organizational downsizing, mergers and acquisitions, and strategic alliances: Using theory and research to enhance practice. In S. Zedeck (Ed.), *Handbook of Industrial and Organizational Psychology,* Vol. 3. Washington, DC: American Psychological Association, pp. 729–768.
2. O'Leonard, K. (2011). *The Corporate Learning Factbook 2011.* Oakland, CA: Bersin & Associates.

3.  Swanson, R. A. (2001). *Assessing the Financial Benefits of Human Resource Development.* Cambridge, MA: Perseus.

4.  Stewart, T. A. (2001, Apr. 2). Mystified by training? Here are some clues. *Fortune,* p. 184.

5.  Cascio, W. F. (2010). The changing world of work. In A. Linley, S. Harrington, and N. Garcea (Eds.), *Oxford Handbook of Positive Psychology and Work.* Oxford, UK: Oxford University Press, pp. 13–23.

6.  World Economic Forum and Boston Consulting Group. (2011). Global talent risk: Seven responses. Geneva, Switzerland: Author. See also Economist Intelligence Unit. (2010). Global firms in 2020. Alexandria, VA: Society for Human Resource Management; CEO challenge 2011. (2011, April). New York: The Conference Board; Tannenbaum, S. (2002). A strategic view of organizational training and learning. In K. Kraiger (Ed.), *Creating, Implementing, and Managing Effective Training and Development.* San Francisco: Jossey-Bass, pp. 10–52; Noe, R. A. (2008). *Employee Training and Development* (4th Ed.). Burr Ridge, IL: Irwin McGraw-Hill.

7.  See also Boudreau, J. W. (2010). *Retooling HR.* Boston: Harvard Business School Press.

8.  Cannon-Bowers, J. A., and Bowers, C. (2011). Team development and functioning. In S. Zedeck (Ed.), *Handbook of Industrial and Organizational Psychology,* Vol. 1, pp. 597–650. Washington, DC: American Psychological Association.

9.  O'Leonard, 2011, op. cit.

10.  100 Best companies to work for. (2008, Feb. 4). *Fortune.* Retrieved from *http://money.cnn.com/magazines/fortune/bestcompanies/2008/snapshots/1.html* on March 14, 2008.

11.  Kane, Y. I., and Sherr, I. (2011, June 15). Retail secrets from Apple. *The Wall Street Journal*, pp. A11, A12. See also Levitz, J. (2010, April 6). UPS thinks outside the box on driver training. *The Wall Street Journal,* pp. B1, B2.

12.  Aguinis, H., and Kraiger, K. (2009). Benefits of training and development for individuals and teams, organizations, and society. *Annual Review of Psychology* 60, pp. 451–474.

13.  Arthur, W. J., Bennett, W. J., Edens, P., and Bell, S. T. (2003). Effectiveness of training in organizations: A meta-analysis of design and evaluation features. *Journal of Applied Psychology* 88, pp. 234–245. See also, Brown, K., and Stizmann, T. (2011). Training and employee development for improved performance. In S. Zedeck (Ed.), *Handbook of Industrial and Organizational Psychology*, Vol. 2. Washington, DC: American Psychological Association, pp. 469–503.

14.  Cullen, J., and Turnbull, S. (2005). A meta-review of the management development literature. *Human Resource Development Review* 4, pp. 335–355.

15.  Littrell, L. N., Salas, E., Hess, K. P., Paley, M., and Riedel, S. (2006). Expatriate preparation: A critical analysis of 25 years of cross-cultural training research. *Human Resource Development Review* 5, pp. 355–388.

16.  Dvir, T., Eden, D., Avolio, B. J., and Shamir, B. (2002). Impact of transformational leadership on follower development and performance: A field experiment. *Academy of Management Journal* 45, pp. 735–744.

17.  Tharenou, P., Saks, A. M., and Moore, C. (2007). A review and critique of research on training and organizational-level outcomes. *Human Resource Management Review* 17, pp. 251–273.

18.  Rifkin, G. (2011, 3rd Qtr.). Brains on fire: How Cisco does leadership development. *The Korn/Ferry Institute Briefings on Talent and Leadership,* pp. 27–34; 74. See also Colvin, G. (2009, Dec. 7). How to build great leaders. *Fortune,* pp. 70–72.

19.  World Economic Forum, 2011, op. cit. See also Hansen, F. (2006, Apr. 10). The great global talent race: One world, one workforce. *Workforce Management,* pp. 1, 20–23.

20.  General Manager, Marks & Spencer. (2000, Mar.). London Business School, Career Creativity Conference, London.

21.  Lawler, E. E. III, and Worley, C. G., with Creelman, D. (2011). *Management Reset: Organizing for Sustainable Effectiveness.* San Francisco: Jossey-Bass.

22. Society for Human Resource Management Foundation. (2008). *Seeing Forward: Succession Planning and Leadership Development at 3M* (DVD). Alexandria, VA: SHRM Foundation.

23. Noe, R. A., and Colquitt, J. A. (2002). Planning for training impact: Principles of training effectiveness. In K. Kraiger (Ed.), *Creating, Implementing, and Managing Effective Training and Development.* San Francisco: Jossey-Bass, pp. 53–79. See also Colquitt, J. A., LePine, J. A., and Noe, R. A. (2000). Toward an integrative theory of training motivation: A meta-analytic path analysis of 20 years of research. *Journal of Applied Psychology* 85, pp. 678–707.

24. Brown and Sitzmann, 2011, op. cit. See also Quinones, M. A. (1997). Contextual influences on training effectiveness. In M. A. Quinones and A. Ehrenstein (Eds.), *Training for a Rapidly Changing Workplace.* Washington, DC: American Psychological Association, pp. 177–200.

25. Welbourne, T. R. (In press). Fast HR—Enhancing service excellence. *Organizational Dynamics.*

26. For more on this approach, see Brown and Sitzmann, 2011, op. cit.

27. Noe, op. cit. See also Goldstein, I. L., and Ford, J. K. (2002). *Training in Organizations: Needs Assessment, Development, and Evaluation* (4th Ed.). Belmont, CA: Wadsworth.

28. Blanchard, P. N., and Thacker, J. W. (2010). *Effective Training: Systems, Strategies, and Practices* (4th Ed.). Upper Saddle River, NJ: Pearson Education. See also Brown and Sitzmann, 2011, op. cit. Moore, M. L., and Dutton, P. (1978). Training needs analysis: Review and critique. *Academy of Management Review* 3, pp. 532–454.

29. Overman, S. (2001, May). PET projects: Train before you hire. *HR Magazine,* pp. 66–74.

30. Ford, J. K., and Noe, R. A. (1987). Self-assessed training needs: The effects of attitudes toward training, managerial level, and function. *Personnel Psychology* 40, pp. 39–53.

31. Brannick, M. T., Levine, E. L., and Morgeson, F. P. (2007). *Job and Work Analysis: Methods, Research, and Applications for Human Resource Management.* Thousand Oaks, CA: Sage. See also Kraiger, K. (2003). Perspectives on training and development. In W. C. Borman, D. R. Ilgen, and R. J. Klimosky (Eds.), *Handbook of Psychology: Industrial and Organizational Psychology*, Vol. 12. Hoboken, NJ: Wiley, pp. 171–192.

32. Goldstein, I. L., and Ford, J. K. (2002). *Training in Organizations: Needs Assessment, Development, and Evaluation* (4th Ed.). Belmont, CA: Wadsworth. See also Blanchard and Thacker, 2010, op. cit.

33. Wexley, K. N., and Latham, G. P. (2000). *Developing and Training Human Resources in Organizations* (3rd Ed.). Upper Saddle River, NJ: Prentice Hall.

34. Colquitt, LePine, and Noe, op. cit.

35. Latham, G. P. (2009). *Becoming the Evidence-Based Manager: Making the Science of Management Work for You.* Boston: Davies-Black. See also Locke, E. A., and Latham, G. P. (2002). Building a practically useful theory of goal setting and task motivation. *American Psychologist* 57, pp. 705–717. See also Locke, E. A., and Latham, G. P. (1990). *A Theory of Goal Setting and Task Performance.* Englewood Cliffs, NJ: Prentice-Hall.

36. Wood, R. E., Mento, A. J., and Locke, E. A. (1987). Task complexity as a moderator of goal effects: A meta-analysis. *Journal of Applied Psychology* 72, pp. 416–425.

37. Locke, E. A. (1968). Toward a theory of task motivation and incentives. *Organizational Behavior and Human Performance* 3, pp. 157–189.

38. Klein, H. J., Wesson, M. J., Hollenbeck, J. R., and Alge, B. J. (1999). Goal commitment and the goal-setting process: Conceptual clarification and empirical synthesis. *Journal of Applied Psychology* 84, pp. 885–896. See also Locke, E. A., Latham, G. P., and Erez, M. (1988). The determinants of goal commitment. *Academy of Management Review* 13, pp. 23–39.

39. Bandura, A. (1986). *Social Foundations of Thought and Action: A Social Cognitive Theory.* Englewood Cliffs, NJ: Prentice Hall.

40. Hogan, P. M., Hakel, M. D., and Decker, P. J. (1986). Effects of trainee-generated versus trainer-provided rule codes on generalization in behavior-modeling training. *Journal of Applied Psychology* 71, pp. 469–473.

41. Goldstein, A. P., and Sorcher, M. (1974). *Changing Supervisor Behavior.* New York: Pergamon Press. See also Latham, G. P., and Saari, L. M. (1979). The application of social learning theory to training supervisors through behavior modeling. *Journal of Applied Psychology* 64, pp. 239–246.

42. Taylor, P. J., Russ-Eft, D. F., and Chan, D. W. L. (2005). A meta-analytic review of behavior-modeling training. *Journal of Applied Psychology* 90, pp. 692–709.

43. Davis, F. D., and Yi, M. Y. (2004). Improving computer-skill training: Behavior modeling, symbolic mental rehearsal, and the role of knowledge structures. *Journal of Applied Psychology* 89, pp. 509–523.

44. Wexley, K. N., and Latham, G. P. (2000). *Developing and Training Human Resources in Organizations* (3rd Ed.). Upper Saddle River, NJ: Prentice Hall.

45. Gist, M. E. (1997). Training design and pedagogy: Implications for skill acquisition, maintenance, and generalization. In M. A. Quinones and A. Ehrenstein (Eds.), *Training for a Rapidly Changing Workplace.* Washington, DC: American Psychological Association, pp. 201–222. See also Gagné, R. M. (1977). *The Conditions of Learning.* New York: Holt, Rinehart, & Winston.

46. Ehrenstein, A., Walker, B. N., Czerwinski, M., and Feldman, E. M. (1997). Some fundamentals of training and transfer: Practice benefits are not automatic. In M. A. Quinones and A. Ehrenstein (Eds.), *Training for a Rapidly Changing Workplace.* Washington, DC: American Psychological Association, pp. 119–147.

47. Keith, N., and Frese, M. (2008). Effectiveness of error-management training: A meta-analysis. *Journal of Applied Psychology* 93, pp. 59–69.

48. Driskell, J. E., Willis, R. P., and Copper, C. (1992). Effect of overlearning on retention. *Journal of Applied Psychology* 77, pp. 615–622.

49. Goldstein and Ford, op. cit. See also Tyler, K. (2000, May). Hold on to what you've learned. *HR Magazine,* pp. 94–102.

50. Donovan, J. J., and Radosevich, D. J. (1999). A meta-analytic review of the distribution of practice effect: Now you see it, now you don't. *Journal of Applied Psychology* 84, pp. 795–805.

51. Stajkovic, A. D., and Luthans, F. (2003). Behavioral management and task performance in organizations: Conceptual background, meta-analysis, and test of alternative models. *Personnel Psychology* 56, pp. 155–194. See also Martocchio, J. J., and Webster, J. (1992). Effects of feedback and cognitive playfulness on performance in microcomputer software training. *Personnel Psychology* 45, pp. 553–578.

52. Goodman, J. S., and Wood, R. E. (2004). Feedback specificity, learning opportunities, and learning. *Journal of Applied Psychology* 89, pp. 809–821.

53. Cannon-Bowers and Bowers, 2011, op. cit. See also Pritchard, R. D., Jones, S. D., Roth, P. L., Steubing, K. K., and Ekeberg, S. E. (1988). Effects of group feedback, goal setting, and incentives on organizational productivity. *Journal of Applied Psychology* 73, pp. 337–358.

54. Florin-Thuma, B. C., and Boudreau, J. W. (1987). Performance feedback utility in a small organization: Effects on organizational outcomes and managerial decision processes. *Personnel Psychology* 40, pp. 693–713.

55. Cascio, W. F., and Aguinis, H. (2011). *Applied Psychology in Human Resource Management* (7th Ed.). Upper Saddle River, NJ: Prentice Hall. See also Brown, K. G., and Ford, J. K. (2002). Using computer technology in training: Building an infrastructure for active learning. In K. Kraiger (Ed.), *Creating, Implementing, and Managing Effective Training and Development.* San Francisco: Jossey-Bass, pp. 192–233.

56. Brown and Sitzmann, 2011, op. cit. See also Burke, L. A., and Hutchins, H. M. (2008). A study of best practices in training transfer and a proposed model of transfer. *Human Resource Development Quarterly* 19, pp. 107–128. See also Machin, M. A.

(2002). Planning, managing, and optimizing transfer of training. In K. Kraiger (Ed.), *Creating, Implementing, and Managing Effective Training and Development.* San Francisco: Jossey-Bass, pp. 263–301.

57. Baldwin, T. T., Ford, J. K., and Blume, B. D. (2009). Transfer of training 1988–2008: An updated review and agenda for future research. *International Review of Industrial and Organizational Psychology* 24, pp. 41–70. Hoboken, NJ: Wiley.

58. Magjuka, R. J., and Baldwin, T. T. (1991). Team-based employee involvement programs: Effects of design and administration. *Personnel Psychology* 44, pp. 793–812.

59. Chiaburu, D. S., and Marinova, S. V. (2005). What predicts skill transfer? An exploratory study of goal orientation, training self-efficacy, and organizational supports. *International Journal of Training and Development* 9, pp. 110–123. See also Pidd, K. (2004). The impact of workplace support and identity on training transfer: A case study of drug and alcohol safety training in Australia. *International Journal of Training and Development* 8, pp. 274–288.

60. Johnson, C. (2008). *Succession Planning at 3M* (DVD). Alexandria, VA: Society for Human Resource Management Foundation.

61. Vella, M. (2008, Apr. 28). White-collar workers shoulder together–Like it or not. *BusinessWeek,* p. 58.

62. Cannon-Bowers and Bowers, 2011, op. cit. See also Salas, E., Burke, C. S., and Cannon-Bowers, J. A. (2002). What we know about designing and delivering team training: Tips and guidelines. In K. Kraiger (Ed.), *Creating, Implementing, and Managing Effective Training and Development.* San Francisco: Jossey-Bass, pp. 234–259. See also Salas, E., and Cannon-Bowers, J. A. (2000). Designing training systems systematically. In E. A. Locke (Ed.), *The Blackwell Handbook of Principles of Organizational Behavior.* Malden, MA: Blackwell, pp. 43–59.

63. Collins, J. (2009, May 25). How the mighty fall. *BusinessWeek*, pp. 26–38. See also Cannon-Bowers, J. A., Tannenbaum, S. I., Salas, E., and Volpe, C. E. (1995). Defining competencies and establishing team training requirements. In R. A. Guzzo and E. Salas (Eds.), *Team Effectiveness and Decision Making in Organizations.* San Francisco: Jossey-Bass, pp. 333–380.

64. Cannon-Bowers and Bowers, 2011, op. cit. See also Ganster, D. C., Williams, S., and Poppler, P. (1991). Does training in problem solving improve the quality of group decisions? *Journal of Applied Psychology* 76, pp. 479–483.

65. Salas and Cannon-Bowers, 2000, op. cit. See also Bass, B. M. (1980). Team productivity and individual member competence. *Small Group Behavior* 11, pp. 431–504. See also Colvin, G. (2006, June 12). Why dream teams fail. *Fortune,* pp. 87–92.

66. Aguinis and Kraiger, 2009, op. cit.

67. Walvoord, A., Redden, E., Elliott, L., and Coovert, M. (2008). Empowering followers in virtual teams: Guiding principles from theory and practice. *Computers in Human Behavior* 24, pp. 1884–1906. See also Komaki, J. L., Desselles, J. L., and Bowman, E. D. (1989). Definitely not a breeze: Extending an operant model of supervision to teams. *Journal of Applied Psychology* 74, pp. 522–529.

68. Campbell, J. P., Dunnette, M. D., Lawler, E. E., and Weick, K. E. (1970). *Managerial Behavior, Performance, and Effectiveness.* New York: McGraw-Hill.

69. Salas, E., and Rosen, M. A. (2010). Experts at work: Principles for developing expertise in organizations. In S. W. J. Kozlowski and E. Salas (Eds.), *Learning, Training, and Development in Organizations.* New York, NY: Routledge, pp. 99–134. See also Steele-Johnson, D., and Hyde, B. G. (1997). Advanced technologies in training: Intelligent tutoring systems and virtual reality. In M. A. Quinones and A. Ehrenstein (Eds.), *Training for a Rapidly Changing Workplace.* Washington, DC: American Psychological Association, pp. 225–248.

70. Labor letter (1990, May 8). *The Wall Street Journal,* p. A1.

71. Noe, op. cit. See also Kraiger, K. (2002). Decision-based evaluation. In K. Kraiger (Ed.), *Creating, Implementing, and Managing Effective Training and Development.* San Francisco: Jossey-Bass, pp. 331–375.

72. Brown and Sitzmann, 2011, op. cit. See also Ford, J. K., Kraiger, K., and Merritt, S. (2010). An updated review of the multi-dimensionality of training outcomes: New directions for training-evaluation research. In S. W. J. Kozlowski, and E. Salas (Eds.), *Learning, Training, and Development in Organizations*. New York, NY: Routledge, pp. 135–165. See also Sackett, P. R., and Mullen, E. J. (1993). Beyond formal experimental design: Towards an expanded view of the training evaluation process. *Personnel Psychology* 46, pp. 613–627. See also Goldstein and Ford, 2002, op. cit.

73. Kraiger, K., McLinden, D., and Casper, W. J. (2004). Collaborative planning for training impact. *Human Resource Management* 43, pp. 337–351. See also Arvey, R. D., Maxwell, S. E., and Salas, E. (1992). The relative power of training evaluation designs under different cost configurations. *Journal of Applied Psychology* 77, pp. 155–160.

74. Cascio, W. F., and Boudreau, J. W. (2011). *Investing in People: Financial Impact of Human Resource Initiatives* (2nd Ed.). Upper Saddle River, NJ: Pearson. See also Swanson, R. A. (2001). *Assessing the Financial Benefits of Human Resource Development*. Cambridge, MA: Perseus. See also Cascio, W. F. (1989). Using utility analysis to assess training outcomes. In I. L. Goldstein (Ed.), *Training and Development in Organizations*. San Francisco: Jossey-Bass, pp. 63–88.

75. Klein, H. J., and Weaver, N. A. (2000). The effectiveness of an organizational-level orientation training program in the socialization of new hires. *Personnel Psychology* 53, pp. 47–66.

76. Bauer, T., and Erdogan, B. (2011). Organizational socialization: The effective onboarding of new employees. In S. Zedeck (Ed.), *Handbook of Industrial and Organizational Psychology*, Vol. 3. Washington, DC: American Psychological Association, pp. 51–64. See also Arnold, J. T. (2010, May). Ramping up onboarding. *HR Magazine* 55(5), pp. 75–78.

77. Bauer and Erdogan, 2011, op. cit.

78. Cascio, W. F., and Boudreau, J. W. (2011). *Investing in People: Financial Impact of Human Resource Initiatives* (2nd Ed.). Upper Saddle River, NJ: Pearson Education. See also Solomon, J. (1988, Dec. 29). Companies try measuring cost savings from new types of corporate benefits. *The Wall Street Journal*, p. B1.

79. Hom, P. W. (2011). Organizational exit. In S. Zedeck (Ed.), *Handbook of Industrial and Organizational Psychology*, Vol. 2. Washington, DC: American Psychological Association, pp. 325–375. See also Phillips, J. M. (1998). Effects of realistic job previews on multiple organizational outcomes: A meta-analysis. *Academy of Management Journal* 41, pp. 673–690.

80. Savchetz, D., quoted in David, G. (2004, Apr. 5). One truck a minute. *Fortune*, p. 258.

81. Lindo, D. K. (1999, Aug.). New employee orientation is your job! *Supervision* 60(8), pp. 6–10.

82. Wesson, M. J., and Gogus, C. I. (2005). Shaking hands with a computer: An examination of two methods of organizational newcomer orientation. *Journal of Applied Psychology* 90, pp. 1018–1026.

83. Arnold, J. T. (2009). Gaming technology used to orient new hires. *HR Trend Book*, A special supplement to *HR Magazine,* pp. 36–38.

84. Arnold, J. T. (2010, May). Ramping up onboarding. *HR Magazine* 55(5), pp. 75–.

85. Bauer and Erdogan, 2011, op. cit. See also Gruman, J. A., Saks, A. M., and Zweig, D. I. (2006). Organizational socialization tactics and newcomer proactive behaviors: An integrative study. *Journal of Vocational Behavior* 69, pp. 90–104.

86. St. John, W. D. (1980, May). The complete employee orientation program. *Personnel Journal,* pp. 373–378.

87. Arnold, 2010, op. cit.

88. Starcke, A. M. (1996). Building a better orientation program. *HR Magazine* 41(11), pp. 108–114.

89. Bauer and Erdogan, 2011, op. cit. See also Watkins, M. (2003). *The First 90 Days: Critical Success Strategies for Leaders at All Levels*. Boston, MA: Harvard Business School Publishing.

# 9 PERFORMANCE MANAGEMENT

*Questions This Chapter Will Help Managers Answer*

1. What steps can I, as a manager, take to make the performance-management process more relevant and acceptable to those who will be affected by it?

2. How can we best fit our approach to performance management with the strategic direction of our department and business?

3. Should managers and nonmanagers be appraised from multiple perspectives, for example, by those above, by those below, by coequals, and by customers?

4. What strategy should we use to train raters at all levels in the mechanics of performance management and in the art of giving feedback?

5. What would an effective performance-management process look like?

## PERFORMANCE REVIEWS: THE DILEMMA OF FORCED RANKING*

In companies across the country, from General Electric to Hewlett-Packard, forced-ranking systems (also known as forced distributions or "rank and yank")—in which all employees are ranked against one another and grades are distributed along some sort of bell-shaped curve—are creating a firestorm of controversy. In recent years employees have filed class-action lawsuits against Microsoft and Conoco as well as Ford, claiming that the companies discriminate in assigning grades. In each case a different group of disaffected employees brought the charges: older workers at Ford, African Americans and women at Microsoft, U.S. citizens at Conoco. When the American Association of Retired Persons (AARP) sued Goodyear for age discrimination, the company immediately abandoned its forced-ranking system.

Companies implement forced ranking in various ways. General Electric offers its curve, comprised of top (20 percent), middle (70 percent), and bottom (10 percent) categories, as a set of guidelines. Hewlett-Packard uses a 1-to-5 scale, with 15 percent of employees getting a 5 (the top grade) and 5 percent getting a 1. The percentage of employees getting 2, 3, and 4 varies. At AIG, 10 percent of employees receive the top ranking of 1, 20 percent are ranked 2, 50 percent are ranked 3, and the bottom 20 percent are ranked 4. Yahoo! compares each employee to a standard rather than to peers, and has eliminated category labels altogether. The purpose is to improve the dialogue between employees and managers by not focusing on which performance grade they were assigned.

Such systems have been around for decades, but thanks to a global economic recession and an increased focus on pay for performance, 20 percent of the *Fortune* 1,000 (by one estimate) have instituted such forced rankings or gotten tougher with their existing systems. For example, at Hewlett-Packard a full 5 percent of its workforce now receive HP's lowest grade, rather than the fuzzy 0 to 5 percent of years past.

Of course, one reason that employees are up in arms about forced rankings is that they suspect—often correctly—that managers game the system and that the rankings are a way for companies to rationalize firings more easily. Evidence indicates that doing so actually reduces the effectiveness of a performance-management system. In fact, former General Electric CEO Jack Welch noted an important caution against implementing a forced distribution in *any* company:

> *I wouldn't want to inject a vitality curve [i.e., a forced distribution] cold-turkey into an organization without a performance culture already in place. Differentiation is hard stuff. Our curve works because we spent over a decade with candor and openness at every level.*

In the conclusion to this case we will examine some of the arguments for and against the use of forced rankings, and explain the dilemma they pose, but in the meantime, what do you think?

---

*Sources: Ng, S, and Lublin, J. S. (2010, Feb. 11). AIG pay plan: Rank and rile. *The Wall Street Journal*, pp. C1, C4. See also Knowledge@Wharton. (2010, Aug. 18). Ranking employees: Why comparing workers to their peers can often backfire. Retrieved from *http://knowledge.wharton.upenn.edu/article.cfm? articleid=2567* on July 20, 2011. See also Murphy, K. R. (2008). Explaining the weak relationship between job performance and ratings of job performance. *Industrial and Organizational Psychology* 1, pp. 148–160. See also McGregor, J. (2006, Jan. 9). The struggle to measure performance. *BusinessWeek*, pp. 26–28. See also Welch, J., & Welch, S. (2006, Oct. 2). The case for 20-70-10. *BusinessWeek*, p. 108.

Challenges

1. Do you support the use of forced rankings or not?
2. If the criteria used to determine an employee's rank are more qualitative than quantitative, does this undermine the forced-ranking system?
3. Suppose all of the members of a team are superstars. Can forced ranking deal with that situation?

The chapter-opening vignette reveals just how complex performance management can be because it includes both developmental (feedback) and administrative (pay, promotions) issues, as well as both technical aspects (design of an appraisal system) and interpersonal aspects (appraisal interviews). This chapter's objective is to present a balanced view of the performance-management process, considering both its technical and its interpersonal aspects. Let's begin by examining the nature of this process.

## MANAGING FOR MAXIMUM PERFORMANCE[1]

Consider the following situations:

- The athlete searching for a coach who really understands her.
- The student scheduled to see his guidance counselor at school.
- The worker who has just begun working for a new boss.
- A self-managing work team and a supervisor about to meet to discuss objectives for the next quarter.

What do these situations all have in common? The need to manage performance effectively—either at the level of the individual or of the work team. Think of **performance management** as a kind of compass, one that indicates a person's actual direction as well as a person's desired direction. Like a compass, the job of the manager (or athletic coach or school guidance counselor) is to indicate where that person is now, and to help focus attention and effort on the desired direction.

Unfortunately, the concept of performance management means something very specific, and much too narrow, to many managers. They tend to equate it with **performance appraisal** an administrative exercise they typically do once a year to identify and discuss job-relevant strengths and weaknesses of individuals or work teams. This is a mistake! Would it surprise you to learn that in a recent poll of 750 HR executives, 58 percent of them graded their own performance-management systems a C or below? Many were frustrated that managers do not have the courage to give constructive feedback to employees. Indeed, only 30 percent of respondents agreed that employees have a sense of trust in their performance-management systems. Although HR professionals often devise the systems and follow up at the end, they cannot control how effectively managers execute reviews. Clearly there is lots of room for improvement.[2]

On the other hand, there are solid organizational payoffs for implementing strong performance-management systems, as a recent study found. Organizations with such systems are 51 percent more likely to outperform their competitors on financial measures, and 41 percent more likely to outperform their competitors on nonfinancial measures (e.g., customer satisfaction, employee retention, quality of products or services).[3]

Obviously if performance management were easy to do, more firms would do it. One of the reasons it is difficult to execute well throughout an entire organization is that performance management demands daily, not annual, attention from every manager. It is part of a continuous process of improvement over time.

So what is the role of performance appraisal in the overall performance-management process? Performance appraisal is a necessary, but far from sufficient, part of performance management. Managers who are committed to moving from a performance-appraisal orientation to one of performance management tell us that the first step is probably the hardest, for it involves a break with tradition. Typically, appraisal is done annually, or in some firms, quarterly. *Performance management requires willingness and a commitment to focus on improving performance at the level of the individual or team every day.* A compass provides instantaneous, real-time information that describes the difference between one's current and desired course. To practice sound performance management, managers must do the same thing—provide timely feedback about performance, while constantly focusing everyone's attention on the ultimate objective (e.g., world-class customer service).

At a general level, the broad process of performance management requires that you do three things well:

1. Define performance.
2. Facilitate performance.
3. Encourage performance.

Let's explore each of these ideas briefly.

## Define Performance

A manager who defines performance ensures that individual employees or teams know what is expected of them, and that they stay focused on effective performance.[4] How does the manager do this? By paying careful attention to three key elements: *goals, measures,* and *assessment.*

*Goal setting* has a proven track record of success in improving performance in a variety of settings and cultures.[5] How does it improve performance? Studies show that goals direct attention to the specific performance in question (e.g., percentage of satisfied customers), they mobilize efforts to accomplish higher levels of performance, and they foster persistence for higher levels of performance.[6] The practical implications of this work are clear: Set specific, challenging goals, for this clarifies precisely what is expected and leads to high levels of performance.[7] Several important qualifications are in order, though. One, some jobs are too fluid and unpredictable for objectives to be practical. Says the Director of IT operations at Netflix, "I've been here three years, and so far my job and responsibilities have changed every six months." Two, individual objectives do not work well when work is team based or when results depend on factors outside an employee's control.[8] When individual goal setting is appropriate, however, on average, studies show that you can expect to improve productivity 10 percent by using goal setting.[9]

The mere presence of goals is not sufficient. Managers must also be able to *measure* the extent to which goals have been accomplished. Goals such as "make the company successful" are too vague to be useful. Measures such as the number of defective parts produced per million or the average time to respond to a customer's inquiry are much more tangible.

In defining performance, the third requirement is *assessment*. Here is where performance appraisal comes in. Regular assessment of progress toward goals focuses the attention and efforts of an employee or a team. If a manager takes the time to identify measurable goals but then fails to assess progress toward them, he's asking for trouble. To define performance properly, therefore, you must do three things well: set goals, decide how to measure accomplishment, and provide regular assessments of progress. Doing so will leave no doubt in the minds of your people what is expected of them, how it will be measured, and where they stand at any given point in time. There should be no surprises in the performance-management process—and regular appraisals help ensure that there won't be.

## Facilitate Performance

Managers who are committed to managing for maximum performance recognize that one of their major responsibilities is to eliminate roadblocks to successful performance.[10] Another is to provide adequate resources to get a job done right and on time, and a third is to pay careful attention to selecting employees, all of which are part of **performance facilitation.**

What are some examples of *obstacles* that can inhibit maximum performance? Consider just a few: outdated or poorly maintained equipment, delays in receiving supplies, inefficient design of work spaces, and ineffective work methods. Employees are well aware of these, and they are only too willing to identify them—if managers will only ask for their input. Then it's the manager's job to eliminate these obstacles.

Having eliminated roadblocks to successful performance, the next step is to *provide adequate resources*—capital resources, material resources, or human resources. After all, if employees lack the tools to reach the challenging goals they have set, they will become frustrated and disenchanted. Indeed, one observer has gone so far as to say "It's immoral not to give people tools to meet tough goals."[11] Conversely, employees really appreciate it when their employer provides everything they need to perform well. Not surprisingly, they usually do perform well under those circumstances.

A final aspect of performance facilitation is the *careful selection of employees*. After all, the last thing any manager wants is to have people who are ill-suited to their jobs (e.g., by temperament or training) because this often leads to overstaffing, excessive labor costs, and reduced productivity. In leading companies like Apple and Google, even top managers are expected to get actively involved in selecting new employees. Both companies typically require even experienced software developers to go through five or six hours of intense interviews.[12] If you're truly committed to managing for maximum performance, you pay attention to all of the details—all of the factors that might affect performance—and leave nothing to chance. That doesn't mean that you are constantly looking over everyone's shoulder. On the contrary, it implies greater self-management, more autonomy, and lots of opportunities to experiment, take risks, and be entrepreneurial.

## Encourage Performance

The last area of management responsibility in a coordinated approach to performance management is **performance encouragement.** To encourage performance, especially repeated good performance, it's important to do three more things well: (1) *provide a sufficient number of rewards that employees really value,* (2) *in a timely fashion, and* (3) *in a fair manner.*

Don't bother offering rewards that nobody cares about, like a gift certificate to see a fortune teller. On the contrary, *begin by asking your people what's most important to them*—for example, pay, benefits, free time, merchandise, or special privileges. Then consider tailoring your awards program so that employees or teams can choose from a menu of similarly valued options.

Next, *provide rewards in a timely manner,* soon after major accomplishments. If there is an excessive delay between effective performance and receipt of the reward, then the reward loses its potential to motivate subsequent high performance.

Finally, provide rewards in a manner that employees consider *fair.* Fairness is a subjective concept, but it can be enhanced by adhering to four important practices:[13]

1. Voice—collect employee input through surveys or interviews.
2. Consistency—ensure that all employees are treated consistently when seeking input and communicating about the process for administering rewards.
3. Relevance—as noted earlier, include rewards that employees really care about.
4. Communication—explain clearly the rules and logic of the rewards process.

In practice, there is much room for improvement. Thus, in a recent survey of 10,000 managers and employees, only 46 percent of the managers and 29 percent of the employees agreed with the statement, "My last raise was based on performance."

In summary, managing for maximum performance requires that you do three things well: define performance, facilitate performance, and encourage performance. Like a compass, the role of the manager is to provide orientation, direction, and feedback. These ideas are shown graphically in Figure 9–1.

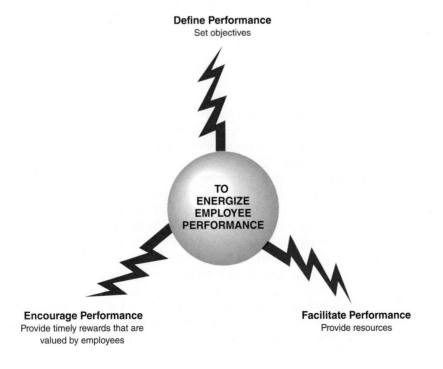

**Define Performance**
Set objectives

**TO ENERGIZE EMPLOYEE PERFORMANCE**

**Encourage Performance**
Provide timely rewards that are valued by employees

**Facilitate Performance**
Provide resources

**Figure 9–1**

Elements of a performance-management system.

## Performance Management in Practice

A study by RainmakerThinking of more than 500 managers in 40 different organizations found, unfortunately, that few managers consistently provide their direct reports with what Rainmaker calls the five management basics: clear statements of what's expected of each employee, explicit and measurable goals and deadlines, detailed evaluation of each person's work, clear feedback, and rewards distributed fairly. Can you see the similarity with the "Define, Facilitate, Encourage Performance" approach shown in Figure 9–1? Only 10 percent of managers provide all five of the basics at least once a week. Only 25 percent do so once a month. About a third fail to provide them even once a year![14] Even more worrisome are the results of a 2009 poll of 700 business leaders in which 92 percent said they recognize superior talent as providing a competitive advantage, but only 7 percent of managers and 10 percent of senior executives are held accountable for developing their direct reports through performance-management processes.[15] Clearly there is much room for improvement.

## PURPOSES OF PERFORMANCE-APPRAISAL SYSTEMS

As we have seen, performance appraisal plays an important part in the overall process of performance management. Hence, it is important that we examine it in some detail. Performance appraisal has many facets. It is an exercise in observation and judgment, it is a feedback process, and it is an organizational intervention. It is a measurement process as well as an intensely emotional process. Above all, it is an inexact, human process. Not surprisingly, therefore, more than 60 percent of workers say reviews don't do anything to help their future performance.[16] In view of such widespread dissatisfaction, why do appraisals continue to be used? What purposes do they serve?

In general, appraisal serves a twofold purpose: (1) to improve employees' work performance by helping them realize and use their full potential in carrying out their firms' missions, and (2) to provide information to employees and managers for use in making work-related decisions. More specifically, appraisals serve the following purposes:

1. *Appraisals provide legal and formal organizational justification for employment decisions* to promote outstanding performers; to weed out marginal or low performers; to train, transfer, or discipline others; to justify merit increases (or no increases); and as one basis for reducing the size of the workforce. In short, appraisal serves as a key input for administering a formal organizational reward and punishment system.
2. *Appraisals are used as criteria in test validation.* That is, test results are correlated with appraisal results to evaluate the hypothesis that test scores predict job performance.[17] However, if appraisals are not done carefully, or if considerations other than performance influence appraisal results, the appraisals cannot be used legitimately for any purpose.
3. *Appraisals provide feedback to employees* and thereby serve as vehicles for personal and career development.
4. *Appraisals can help to identify developmental needs of employees* and also to *establish objectives for training programs.*

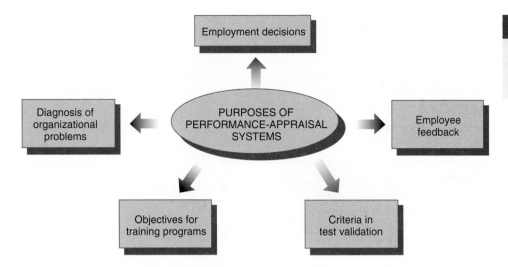

**Figure 9–2**

Purposes of performance-appraisal systems.

5. *Appraisals can help diagnose organizational problems* by identifying training needs and the personal characteristics to consider in hiring, and they also provide a basis for distinguishing between effective and ineffective performers. Appraisal therefore represents the beginning of a process, rather than an end product. These ideas are shown graphically in Figure 9–2.

Despite their shortcomings, appraisals continue to be used widely, especially as a basis for tying pay to performance.[18] To attempt to avoid these shortcomings by doing away with appraisals is no solution, for whenever people interact in organized settings, appraisals will be made—formally or informally. The real challenge, then, is to identify appraisal techniques and practices that (1) are most likely to achieve a particular objective, and (2) are least vulnerable to the obstacles listed above. Let us begin by considering some of the fundamental requirements that determine whether a performance-appraisal system will succeed or fail.

## Requirements of Effective Appraisal Systems

Legally and scientifically, the key requirements of any appraisal system are relevance, sensitivity, and reliability. In the context of ongoing operations, the key requirements are acceptability and practicality.[19] Let's consider each of these.

### Relevance
**Relevance** implies that there are clear links between the performance standards for a particular job and organizational objectives and between the critical job elements identified through a job analysis and the dimensions to be rated on an appraisal form. In short, relevance is determined by answering the question "What really makes the difference between success and failure on a particular job, and according to whom?" The answer to the latter question is simple: the customer. Customers may be internal (e.g., your immediate boss, workers in another department) or external (those who buy your company's products or services). In all cases, it is important to pay attention to the things that the customer believes are important (e.g., on-time delivery, zero defects, information to solve business problems).

## ETHICAL DILEMMA
### Performance-Appraisal Decisions

Performance appraisal actually encompasses two distinct processes: observation and judgment. Managers must observe performance, certainly a representative sample of an employee's performance, if they are to be competent to judge its effectiveness.[a] Yet some managers assign performance ratings on the basis of small (and perhaps unrepresentative) samples of their subordinates' work. Others assign ratings based only on the subordinate's most recent work. Is this ethical? And further, is it ethical to assign performance ratings (either good or bad) that differ from what a manager knows a subordinate deserves?

[a] Aguinis, H. (2009). *Performance Management* (2nd Ed.). Upper Saddle River, NJ: Pearson Prentice Hall. See also Moser, K., Schuler, H., and Funke, U. (1999). The moderating effect of raters' opportunities to observe rates' job performance on the validity of an assessment center. *International Journal of Selection and Assessment* 7(3), pp. 355–367.

**Performance standards** translate job requirements into levels of acceptable or unacceptable employee behavior. They play a critical role in the job analysis-performance appraisal linkage, as Figure 9–3 indicates. Job analysis identifies *what* is to be done. Performance standards specify *how well* work is to be done. Such standards may be quantitative (e.g., time, errors) or qualitative (e.g., quality of work, ability to analyze market research data or a machine malfunction).

Relevance also implies the periodic maintenance and updating of job analyses, performance standards, and appraisal systems. Should the system be challenged in court, relevance will be a fundamental consideration in the arguments presented by both sides.

### Sensitivity

**Sensitivity** implies that a performance-appraisal system is capable of distinguishing effective from ineffective performers. If it is not, and the best employees are rated no differently from the worst employees, then the appraisal system cannot be used for any administrative purpose. It certainly will not help employees to develop, and it will undermine the motivation of both supervisors ("pointless paperwork") and subordinates.

A major concern here is the purpose of the rating. One study found that raters process identical sets of performance-appraisal information differently,

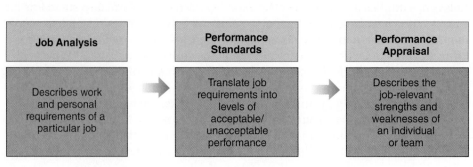

**Figure 9–3**

Relationship of performance standards to job analysis and performance appraisal.

depending on whether a merit pay raise, a recommendation for further development, or the retention of a probationary employee is involved.[20] These results highlight the conflict between appraisals made for administrative purposes and those made for employee development. Appraisal systems designed for administrative purposes demand performance information about differences *between* individuals, while systems designed to promote employee growth demand information about differences *within* individuals. The two different types of information are not interchangeable in terms of purposes, and that is why performance-management systems designed to meet both purposes are more complex and costly.

## Reliability

A third requirement of sound appraisal systems is **reliability.** In this context it refers to consistency of judgment. For any given employee, appraisals made by raters working independently of one another should agree closely. In practice, ratings made by supervisors tend to be more reliable than those made by peers.[21] Certainly raters with different perspectives (e.g., supervisors, peers, subordinates) may see the same individual's job performance very differently, and this can actually make the feedback less useful and more problematic.[22] To provide reliable data, each rater must have an adequate opportunity to observe what the employee has done and the conditions under which he or she has done it; otherwise, unreliability may be confused with unfamiliarity.

Note that throughout this discussion there has been no mention of the validity or accuracy of appraisal judgments. This is because we really do not know what "truth" is in performance appraisal. However, by making appraisal systems relevant, sensitive, and reliable—by satisfying the scientific and legal requirements for workable appraisal systems—we can assume that the resulting judgments are valid, as well.

## Acceptability

In practice, **acceptability** is the most important requirement of all. HR programs must have the support of those who will use them, or human ingenuity will be used to thwart them. Unfortunately, many organizations have not put much effort into garnering the front-end support and participation of those who will use the appraisal system. We know this in theory, but practice is another matter. On the other hand, evidence indicates that appraisal systems that are acceptable to those who will be affected by them lead to more favorable reactions to the process, increased motivation to improve performance, and increased trust for top management.[23]

Smart managers enlist the active support and cooperation of subordinates or teams by making explicit exactly what aspects of job performance they will be evaluated on. As we have seen, performance definition is the first step in performance management. Only after managers and subordinates or team members define performance clearly can we hope for the kind of acceptability and commitment that is so sorely needed in performance appraisal.

## Practicality

**Practicality** implies that appraisal instruments are easy for managers and employees to understand and use. Those that are not, or that impose inordinate time demands on all parties, simply are not practical, and managers will resist using them. As we have seen, managers need as much encouragement and organizational support as possible if thoughtful performance management is to take place.

In a broader context, we are concerned with developing employment-decision systems. From this perspective, relevance, sensitivity, and reliability are simply technical components of a system designed to make decisions about employees. As we have seen, just as much attention needs to be paid to ensuring the acceptability and practicality of appraisal systems. These are the five basic requirements of performance-appraisal systems, and none of them can be ignored. However, because some degree of error is inevitable in all employment decisions, the crucial question to be answered in regard to each appraisal system is whether its use results in less human, social, and organizational cost than is currently paid for these errors. Answers to that question will result in a wiser, fuller use of talent.

---

**LEGALITIES**

## PERFORMANCE APPRAISAL

There is a rich body of case law on performance appraisal, and multiple reviews of it reached similar conclusions.[24] To avoid legal difficulties, consider taking the following steps:

1. Conduct a job analysis to determine the characteristics necessary for successful job performance.
2. Incorporate these characteristics into a rating instrument. This may be done by tying rating instruments to specific job behaviors (e.g., *Behaviorally Anchored Rating Scales,* as described later in this chapter), but the courts routinely accept less sophisticated approaches, such as simple graphic rating scales. Regardless of the method used, provide written standards to all raters.
3. Provide written instructions and train supervisors to use the rating instrument properly, including how to apply performance standards when making judgments. The uniform application of standards is very important. The vast majority of cases lost by organizations have involved evidence that subjective standards were applied unevenly to members of protected groups versus all other employees.
4. Establish a system to detect potentially discriminatory effects or abuses of the appraisal process.
5. Include formal appeal mechanisms, coupled with higher-level review of appraisals.
6. Document the appraisals and the reason for any termination decisions. This information may prove decisive in court, as long as it was not generated after the supervisor made the decision to terminate. Credibility is enhanced by documented appraisal ratings that describe specific examples of poor performance based on personal knowledge.[25]
7. Provide some form of performance counseling or corrective guidance to assist poor performers.

Here is a good example of step 6. In *Stone v. Xerox,* the organization had a fairly elaborate procedure for assisting poor performers.[26] Stone was employed as a sales representative and in fewer than six months had been given several written reprimands concerning customer complaints about his selling methods and failure to develop adequate written selling proposals. As a result, he was placed on a one-month performance-improvement program designed to correct these deficiencies. This program was extended 30 days at Stone's request. When his performance still did not improve, he was placed on probation and told that failure to improve substantially would result in termination. Stone's performance continued to be substandard, and he was discharged at the end of the probationary period. When he sued Xerox, he lost.

Certainly, the type of evidence required to defend performance ratings is linked to the *purposes* for which the ratings are made. For example, if appraisal of past performance is to be used as a predictor of future performance (i.e., promotions), evidence must show (1) that the ratings of past performance are, in fact, valid, and (2) that the ratings of past performance are statistically related to *future* performance in another job.[27] At the very least, this latter step should include job analysis results indicating the extent to which the requirements of the lower- and higher-level jobs overlap. Finally, to assess adverse impact, organizations should keep accurate records of who is eligible for and interested in promotion. These two factors, *eligibility* and *interest,* define the **applicant group.**

In summary, it is not difficult to offer prescriptions for scientifically sound, court-proof appraisal systems, but as we have seen, implementing them requires diligent attention by organizations plus a commitment to make them work. In developing a performance-appraisal system, the most basic requirement is to determine what you want the system to accomplish. This requires a strategy for the management of performance.

## The Strategic Dimension of Performance Appraisal

In the study of work motivation, a fairly well-established principle is that the things that get rewarded get done. At least one author has termed this "The greatest management principle in the world."[28] A fundamental issue for managers, then, is "What kind of behavior do I want to encourage in my subordinates?" If employees are rewarded for generating short-term results, they will generate short-term results. If they are rewarded (e.g., through progressively higher commissions or bonuses) for generating repeat business or for reaching quality standards over long periods of time, then they will do those things.

Managers, therefore, have choices. They can emphasize short- or long-term objectives in the performance-management process, or some combination of the two. Short-term objectives emphasize such things as bottom-line results for the current quarter. Long-term objectives emphasize such things as increasing market share and securing repeat business from customers. To be most useful, however, the strategic management of performance must be linked to the strategies an organization (or strategic business unit) uses to gain competitive advantage—for example, innovation, speed, quality enhancement, or cost control.[29] As one manager observed, "If you can't find hard measures of why something's strategically important, you let it go."[30]

Some appraisal systems that are popular in the United States, such as management by objectives (MBO), are less popular in other parts of the world, such as Japan and France. MBO focuses primarily on results, rather than on how the results were accomplished. Typically it has a short-term focus, although this need not always be the case.

In Japan, greater emphasis is placed on the psychological and behavioral sides of performance appraisal than on objective outcomes. Thus, an employee will be rated in terms of the effort he or she puts into a job; on integrity, loyalty, and cooperative spirit; and on how well he or she serves the customer. Short-term results tend to be much less important than long-term personal development, the establishment and maintenance of long-term relationships with customers (i.e., behaviors), and increasing market share.[31]

Once managers decide what they want the appraisal system to accomplish, their next questions are "What's the best method of performance appraisal? Which technique should I use?" As in so many other areas of HR management, there is no simple answer. The following section considers some alternative methods, along with their strengths and weaknesses. Because readers of this book are more likely to be users than developers of appraisal systems, the following will focus most on describing and illustrating them. For more detailed information, consult the references cited.

## ALTERNATIVE METHODS OF APPRAISING EMPLOYEE PERFORMANCE

Many regard rating methods or formats as the central issue in performance appraisal; this, however, is not the case.[32] Broader issues must also be considered—such as *trust* in the appraisal system; the *attitudes* of managers and employees; the *purpose, frequency,* and *source* of appraisal data; and rater *training*. Viewed in this light, rating formats play only a supporting role in the overall appraisal process.

**Behavior-oriented rating methods** focus on employee behaviors, either by comparing the performance of employees to that of other employees (so-called **relative rating systems**) or by evaluating each employee in terms of performance standards without reference to others (so-called **absolute rating systems**). **Results-oriented rating methods** place primary emphasis on what an employee produces; dollar volume of sales, number of units produced, and number of wins during a baseball season are examples. Management by objectives (MBO) and work planning and review use this results-oriented approach.

Evidence indicates that ratings (i.e., judgments about performance) are not strongly related to results.[33] Why? Ratings depend heavily on the mental processes of the rater. Because these processes are complex, there may be errors of judgment in the ratings. Conversely, results depend heavily on conditions that may be outside the control of the individual worker, such as the availability of supplies or the contributions of others. Thus, most measures of results provide only partial coverage of the overall domain of job performance. With these considerations in mind, let's examine the behavior- and results-oriented systems more fully.

## Behavior-Oriented Rating Methods

### Narrative Essay

The simplest type of absolute rating system is the **narrative essay,** in which a rater describes, in writing, an employee's strengths, weaknesses, and potential, together with suggestions for improvement. This approach assumes that a candid statement from a rater who is knowledgeable about an employee's performance is just as valid as more formal and more complicated rating methods.

If essays are done well, they can provide detailed feedback to subordinates regarding their performance. On the other hand, comparisons across individuals, groups, or departments are almost impossible since different essays touch on different aspects of each subordinate's performance. This makes it difficult to use essay information for employment decisions because subordinates are not compared objectively and ranked relative to one another. Methods that compare employees to one another are more useful for this purpose.

### Ranking

**Simple ranking** requires only that a rater order all employees from highest to lowest, from "best" employee to "worst" employee. **Alternation ranking** requires that a rater initially list all employees on a sheet of paper. From this list he or she first chooses the best employee (No. 1), then the worst employee (No. $n$ ), then the second best (No. 2), then the second worst (No. $n - 1$), and so forth, alternating from the top to the bottom of the list until all employees have been ranked.

### Paired Comparisons

Use of **paired comparisons** is a more systematic method for comparing employees to one another. Here each employee is compared with every other employee, usually in terms of an overall category such as "present value to the organization." The number of pairs of ratees to be compared may be calculated from the formula $[n(n - 1)]/2$. Hence if 10 individuals were being compared, $[10(9)]/2$ or 45 comparisons would be required. The rater's task is simply to choose the "better" of each pair, and each employee's rank is determined by counting the number of times she or he was rated superior. As you can see, the number of comparisons becomes quite large as the number of employees increases. On the other hand, ranking methods that compare employees to one another are useful for generating initial rankings for purposes of employment decisions.

### Forced Distribution

**Forced distribution** is another method of comparing employees to one another. As the chapter-opening vignette noted, the overall distribution of ratings is forced into a normal, or bell-shaped, curve under the assumption that a relatively small portion of employees is truly outstanding, a relatively small portion is unsatisfactory, and everybody else falls in between. Figure 9–4 illustrates this method, assuming that five rating categories are used.

Forced distribution does eliminate clustering almost all employees at the top of the distribution (rater **leniency**), at the bottom of the distribution (rater **severity**), or in the middle (**central tendency**). Who tends to be most lenient? One study found that individuals who score high in agreeableness (trustful, sympathetic, cooperative, and polite) tend to be most lenient, while those who score high in conscientiousness (strive for excellence, high performance standards, set difficult goals) tend to be least lenient.[34]

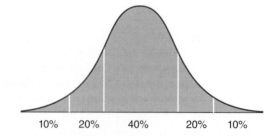

Forced distribution can foster a great deal of employee resentment, however, if an entire group of employees *as a group* is either superior or substandard. In general, such systems are seen as less fair than absolute rating systems.[35] They are most useful when a large number of employees must be rated and there is more than one rater.

### Behavioral Checklist

Here the rater is provided with a series of statements that describe job-related behavior. His or her task is simply to check which of the statements, or the extent to which each statement, describes the employee. In this approach raters are not so much evaluators as reporters whose task is to describe job behavior. Moreover, descriptive ratings are likely to be more reliable than evaluative (good–bad) ratings,[36] and they reduce the cognitive demands placed on raters.[37] One such method, the **Likert method of summed ratings,** presents a declarative statement (e.g., "She or he follows up on customer complaints") followed by several response categories, such as "always," "very often," "fairly often," "occasionally," and "never." The rater checks the response category that he or she thinks describes the employee best. Each category is weighted, for example, from 5 ("always") to 1 ("never") if the statement describes desirable behavior. To derive an overall numerical rating (or score) for each employee, the weights of the responses that were checked for each item are summed. Figure 9–5 shows a portion of a summed rating scale for appraising teacher performance.

**Figure 9–5**

A portion of a summed rating scale. The rater simply checks the response category that best describes the teacher's behavior. Response categories vary in scale value from 5 points (strongly agree) to 1 point (strongly disagree). A total score is computed by summing the points associated with each item.

| | Strongly agree | Agree | Neutral | Disagree | Strongly disagree |
|---|---|---|---|---|---|
| The teacher was well prepared. | | | | | |
| The teacher used understandable language. | | | | | |
| The teacher made me think. | | | | | |
| The teacher's feedback on students' work aided learning. | | | | | |
| The teacher knew his or her field well. | | | | | |

## Critical Incidents

**Critical incidents** are brief anecdotal reports by supervisors of things employees do that are particularly effective or ineffective in accomplishing parts of their jobs. They focus on behaviors, not traits. For example, a store manager in a retail computer store observed Mr. Wang, a salesperson, doing the following:

> Mr. Wang encouraged the customer to try our latest word-processing package by having the customer sit down at the computer and write a letter. The finished product was full of grammatical and spelling errors, each of which was highlighted for the customer when Mr. Wang applied a "spelling checker" and "grammar examiner" to the written material. As a result, Mr. Wang sold the customer the word-processing program plus a typing tutor.

Such anecdotes force attention onto the ways in which situations determine job behavior and also on ways of doing the job successfully that may be unique to the person described. Hence they can provide the basis for training programs. Critical incidents also lend themselves nicely to appraisal interviews because supervisors can focus on actual job behaviors rather than on vaguely defined traits. They are judging performance, not personality. On the other hand, supervisors may find that recording incidents for their subordinates on a daily, or even a weekly, basis is burdensome. Moreover, incidents alone do not permit comparisons across individuals or departments. Graphic rating scales may overcome this problem.

## Graphic Rating Scales

Many organizations use **graphic rating scales.**[38] Figure 9–6 shows a portion of one such scale. Many different forms of graphic rating scales exist. In terms of the amount of structure provided, the scales differ in three ways:

1. The degree to which the meaning of the response categories is defined (in Figure 9–6, what does "conditional" mean?).

**Figure 9–6**

A portion of a graphic rating scale.

| Rating factors | Level of performance | | | | |
|---|---|---|---|---|---|
| | Unsatisfactory | Conditional | Satisfactory | Above satisfactory | Outstanding |
| Attendance | | | | | |
| Appearance | | | | | |
| Dependability | | | | | |
| Quality of work | | | | | |
| Quantity of work | | | | | |
| Relationship with people | | | | | |
| Job knowledge | | | | | |

2. The degree to which the individual who is interpreting the ratings (e.g., a higher-level reviewing official) can tell clearly what response was intended.

3. The degree to which the performance dimensions are defined for the rater (in Figure 9–6, what does "dependability" mean?).

Graphic rating scales may not yield the depth of essays or critical incidents, but they are less time-consuming to develop and administer. They also allow results to be expressed in quantitative terms; they consider more than one performance dimension; and, because the scales are standardized, they facilitate comparisons across employees. Graphic rating scales have come under frequent attack, but when compared with more sophisticated forced-choice scales, the graphic scales have proven just as reliable and valid and are more acceptable to raters.[39]

### Behaviorally Anchored Rating Scales

Graphic rating scales that use critical incidents to anchor various points along the scale are known as **behaviorally anchored rating scales (BARS).** Their major advantage is that they define the dimensions to be rated in behavioral terms and use critical incidents to describe various levels of performance. BARS therefore provide a common frame of reference for raters. An example of the job-knowledge portion of a BARS for police patrol officers is shown in Figure 9–7. BARS require considerable effort to develop,[40] yet there is little research evidence to support the superiority of BARS over other types of rating systems.[41] Nevertheless, the participative process required to develop them

**Figure 9–7**

A behaviorally anchored rating scale to assess the job knowledge of police patrol officers.

**JOB KNOWLEDGE** (Awareness of procedures, laws, and court rulings and changes in them)

**High**
**(7, 8, or 9)**

Always follows correct procedures for evidence preservation at the scene of a crime

Is fully aware of recent court rulings and conducts himself or herself accordingly

Searches a citizen's vehicle with probable cause, thereby discovering smuggled narcotics

**Average**
**(4, 5, or 6)**

Arrests a suspect at 11:00 p.m. on a warrant only after ensuring that the warrant had been cleared for night service

Distinguishes between civil matters and police matters

Seldom has to ask others about points of law

**Low**
**(1, 2, or 3)**

Is consistently unaware of general orders and/or departmental policy

Arrests a suspect for a misdemeanor not committed in his or her presence

Misinforms the public on legal matters through lack of knowledge

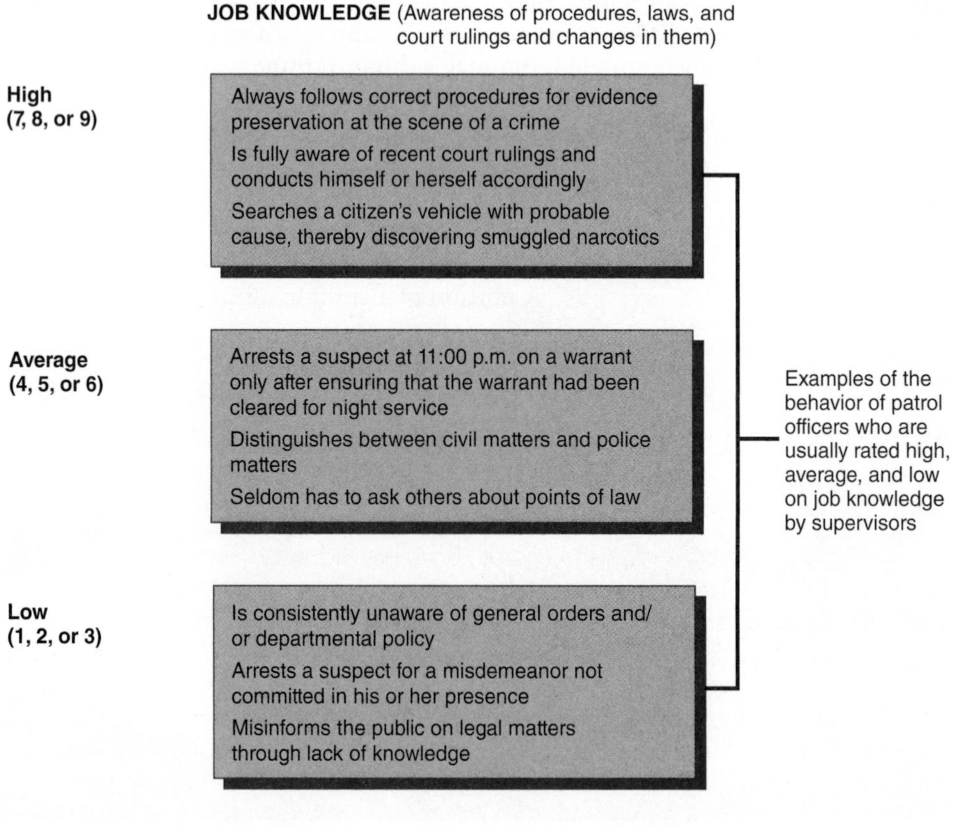

Examples of the behavior of patrol officers who are usually rated high, average, and low on job knowledge by supervisors

provides information that is useful for other organizational purposes, such as communicating clearly to employees exactly what good performance means in the context of their jobs.

## Results-Oriented Rating Methods

### Management by Objectives

**Management by objectives (MBO)** is a well-known process of managing that relies on goal setting to establish objectives for the organization as a whole, for each department, for each manager within each department, and for each employee. MBO is not a measure of employee behavior. Rather, it is a measure of each employee's contribution to the success of the organization.[42]

To establish objectives, the key people involved should do three things: (1) meet to *agree on the major objectives* for a given period of time (e.g., every year, every six months, or quarterly), (2) *develop plans* for how and when the objectives will be accomplished, and (3) *agree on the measurement tools* for determining whether the objectives have been met. Progress reviews are held regularly until the end of the period for which the objectives were established. At that time, those who established objectives at each level in the organization meet to evaluate the results and to agree on the objectives for the next period.[43]

To some, MBO is a complete system of planning and control and a complete philosophy of management.[44] In theory, MBO promotes success in each employee because, as each employee succeeds, so do that employee's manager, the department, and the organization. But this is true only to the extent that the individual, departmental, and organizational goals are compatible.[45] That is typically not the case.[46]

Beyond that, in light of the corporate scandals that characterized the early part of the 21st century, progressive firms such as Lockheed Martin and 3M do not focus only on results achieved. Rather, they also focus on *how* those results were achieved. That approach is known as "full-spectrum leadership."[47] Consistent with this approach, Scripps Health, a community health-care system in San Diego, evaluates each of its 12,000 employees on results as well as behaviors. The latter include three core values at Scripps: respect, quality, and efficiency.[48]

### Work Planning and Review

**Work planning and review** is similar to MBO; however, it places greater emphasis on the periodic review of work plans by both supervisor and subordinate in order to identify goals attained, problems encountered, and the need for training.[49] This approach has long been used by Corning Inc. Table 9–1 presents a summary of the appraisal methods we have just discussed.

## When Should Each Technique Be Used?

You have just read about a number of alternative appraisal formats, each with its own advantages and disadvantages. At this point you are probably asking yourself "What's the bottom line? I know that no method is perfect, but what should I do?" First, remember that the rating format is not as important as the relevance and acceptability of the rating system. Second, here is some advice based on systematic comparisons among the various methods.

An extensive review of the research literature that relates the various rating methods to indicators of performance appraisal effectiveness found no clear

| Table 9–1 |
| --- |

### A SNAPSHOT OF THE ADVANTAGES AND DISADVANTAGES OF ALTERNATIVE APPRAISAL METHODS

**Behavior-oriented methods**

*Narrative essay.* Good for individual feedback and development, but difficult to make comparisons across employees.

*Ranking and paired comparisons.* Good for making comparisons across employees, but provides little basis for individual feedback and development.

*Forced distribution.* Forces raters to make distinctions among employees, but may be unfair and inaccurate if a group of employees, as a group, is either very effective or ineffective.

*Behavioral checklist.* Easy to use, provides a direct link between job analysis and performance appraisal, can be numerically scored, and facilitates comparisons across employees. However, the meaning of response categories may be interpreted differently by different raters.

*Critical incidents.* Focuses directly on job behaviors, emphasizes what employees did that was effective or ineffective, but can be very time consuming to develop.

*Graphic rating scales (including BARS).* Easy to use, very helpful for providing feedback for individual development and facilitating comparisons across employees. BARS are very time consuming to develop, but dimensions and scale points are defined clearly. Graphic rating scales often do not define dimensions or scale points clearly.

**Results-oriented systems**

*Management by objectives.* Focuses on results and on identifying each employee's contribution to the success of the unit or organization. However, MBO is generally short-term oriented, provides few insights into employee behavior, and does not facilitate comparison across employees.

*Work planning and review.* In contrast to MBO, emphasizes process over outcomes. Requires frequent supervisor/subordinate review of work plans. Is time consuming to implement properly, and does not facilitate comparisons across employees.

"winner, and researchers generally agree that the type of rating scale per se does not lead to better ratings"[50] However, the researchers were able to provide several "if . . . then" propositions and general statements based on their study, including the following:

- If the objective is to compare employees across raters for important employment decisions (e.g., promotion, merit pay), then don't use MBO or work planning and review. They are not based on a standardized rating scheme for all employees.
- If you use a BARS, then also make diary keeping a part of the process. This will improve the accuracy of the ratings, and it also will help supervisors distinguish between effective and ineffective employees.
- If objective performance data are available, then MBO is the best strategy to use. Work planning and review is not as effective as MBO under these

circumstances. Remember though, that *how* an employee or manager achieves results is also important.

- In general, appraisal methods that are best in a broad, organizational sense— BARS and MBO—are the most difficult to use and maintain. No rating method is foolproof.
- Methods that focus on describing, rather than evaluating, behavior (e.g., BARS, summed rating scales) produce results that are the most interpretable across raters. They help remove the effects of individual differences in raters.[51]
- No rating method has been an unqualified success when used as a basis for merit pay or promotional decisions.
- When certain statistical corrections are made, the correlations between scores on alternative rating formats are very high. Hence all the formats measure essentially the same thing.

Which techniques are most popular? One survey of performance-management systems and practices in 278 organizations (two-thirds of which were multinational enterprises) from 15 different countries revealed three important findings:

1. Managers rely on a balance of subjective (66 percent) and objective (71 percent) data in performance reviews.
2. Over the past five years forced rankings have become more common (34 percent of organizations use them), but few managers find them to be effective.
3. Only 20 percent of organizations use online or software-based performance-management systems, but another third plan to introduce them.[52]

## WHO SHOULD EVALUATE PERFORMANCE?

The most fundamental requirement for any rater is that he or she has an adequate opportunity to observe the ratee's job performance over a reasonable period of time (e.g., six months). This suggests several possible raters.

***The Immediate Supervisor.*** Among the nearly 80 percent of firms that conduct performance appraisals, this person is the most common rater.[53] She or he is probably most familiar with the individual's performance and, in most jobs, has had the best opportunity to observe actual job performance. Furthermore, the immediate supervisor is probably best able to relate the individual's performance to what the department and organization are trying to accomplish, and to distinguish among various dimensions of performance.[54] Because she or he also is responsible for reward (and punishment) decisions, and for managing the overall performance-management process,[55] it is not surprising that feedback from supervisors is more highly related to performance than that from any other source.[56]

***Peers.*** In some jobs, such as outside sales, the immediate supervisor may observe a subordinate's actual job performance only rarely (and indirectly, through written reports). In other environments, such as self-managed work teams, there is no supervisor. Sometimes objective indicators, such as number of units sold, can provide useful performance-related information, but in other circumstances the judgment of peers is even better. Peers can provide a perspective on performance that is different from that of immediate supervisors.

Thus, a member of a cross-functional team may be in a better position to rate another team member than that team member's immediate supervisor. However, to reduce potential friendship bias while simultaneously increasing the feedback value of the information provided, it is important to specify exactly what the peers are to evaluate[57]—for example, "the quality of her help on technical problems." Even then, however, it is important to be aware of *context effects*. That is, ratings might differ, depending on the context in which the technical problems occurred—in a crisis versus a less stressful context.[58] Peer ratings can provide useful information, but in light of the potential problems associated with them, friendship bias and context effects, it is wise not to rely on them as the sole source of information about performance.

***Subordinates.***   Appraisal by subordinates can be a useful input to the immediate supervisor's development,[59] and the ratings are of significantly higher quality when used for that purpose.[60] Subordinates know firsthand the extent to which the supervisor *actually* delegates, how well he or she communicates, the type of leadership style he or she is most comfortable with, and the extent to which he or she plans and organizes. Longitudinal research shows that managers who met with their direct reports to discuss their upward feedback improved more than other managers. Further, managers improved more in years when they discussed the previous year's feedback with their direct reports than in years when they did not. This is important because it demonstrates that what managers do with upward feedback is related to its benefits.[61]

Should subordinate ratings be anonymous? Managers want to know who said what, but subordinates prefer to remain anonymous to avoid retribution. To address these concerns, collect and combine the ratings in such a manner that a manager's overall rating is not distorted by an extremely divergent opinion.[62] Like peer assessments, they provide only one piece of the appraisal puzzle, although evidence indicates that ratings provided by peers and subordinates are comparable, for they reflect the same underlying dimensions.[63]

***Self-Appraisal.***   There are several arguments to recommend wider use of self-appraisals. The opportunity to participate in the performance-appraisal process, particularly if appraisal is combined with goal setting, improves the ratee's motivation and reduces her or his defensiveness during the appraisal interview.[64] On the other hand, self-appraisals tend to be more lenient, less variable, more biased, and to show less agreement with the judgments of others.[65] Thus a recent study of 3,850 managers of Walgreens drugstores who were in the same store and had the same boss for two straight years found a correlation of of only 0.40 between self- and boss-ratings.[66] Moreover, because U.S. employees tend to give themselves higher marks than their supervisors do (conflicting findings have been found with mainland Chinese and Taiwanese employees),[67] self-appraisals are probably more appropriate for counseling and development than for employment decisions.

***Customers Served.***   In some situations the consumers of an individual's or organization's services can provide a unique perspective on job performance. Examples abound: subscribers to a cable-television service, bank customers, clients of a brokerage house, and citizens of a local police- or fire-protection district. Although the customers' objectives cannot be expected to correspond completely with the organization's objectives, the information that customers

Customers are often able to rate important aspects of the performance of employees in front-line customer-contact positions.

provide can serve as useful input for employment decisions, such as those regarding promotion, transfer, and need for training. It can also be used to assess the impact of training or as a basis for self-development. At General Electric, for example, the customers of senior managers are interviewed formally and regularly as part of the managers' appraisal process. Their evaluations are important in appraisal, but at the same time they also build commitment, because customers are giving time and information to help GE.[68]

***Computers.*** As noted earlier, employees spend a lot of time unsupervised by their bosses. Now technology has made continuous supervision possible—and very real for millions of workers. What sort of technology? Computer software that monitors employee performance.

Not everyone views monitoring as a modern-day version of *Modern Times,* the Charlie Chaplin movie in which the hapless hero was tyrannized by automation. At the Third National Bank of Nashville, for example, encoding clerks can earn up to 25 percent more than their base pay if their output is high—and they like that system.

To be sure, monitoring itself is neither good nor bad; how managers use it determines its acceptance in the workplace. Practices such as giving employees access to data collected on them, establishing procedures for challenging erroneous records, and training supervisors to base actions and decisions on actual observation of employees, not just on computer-generated records, can alleviate the fears of employees.[b] At American Express, for example, monitored employees are given feedback about their performance every two weeks.

Managers who impose monitoring standards without asking employees what is reasonable may be surprised at the responses of employees. Tactics can include workstation operators who pound the space bar or hold down the underlining bar while chatting, and telephone operators who hang up on customers with complicated problems. The lesson, perhaps, is that even the most sophisticated technology can be thwarted by human beings who feel they are being pushed beyond acceptable limits.[c]

---

[a] Alge, B. J. (2001). Effects of computer surveillance on perceptions of privacy and procedural justice. *Journal of Applied Psychology* 86, pp. 797–804. See also Piller, C. (1993, July). Privacy in peril. *Macworld,* pp. 124–130. See also Brophy, B. (1986, Sept. 29). New technology, high anxiety. *U.S. News & World Report,* pp. 54, 55.

[b] Alge, 2001, op. cit. See also Nebeker, D. M., and Tatum, C. B. (1993). The effects of computer monitoring, standards, and rewards on work performance and stress. *Journal of Applied Psychology* 28, pp. 508–534. See also Chalykoff, J., and Kochan, T. A. (1989). Computer-aided monitoring: Its influence on employee job satisfaction and turnover. *Personnel Psychology* 42, pp. 807–834.

[c] Brophy, 1986, op. cit.

### Are Supervisors' Ratings Affected by Other Sources of Information about Performance?

Thus far we have assumed that each source of performance information, be it the supervisor, peer, subordinate, self, or client, makes his or her judgment individually and independently from other individuals. In practice, however, appraising performance is not strictly an individual task. Thus Toronto software firm Rypple lets people post Twitter-length questions about their performance in exchange for anonymous feedback. Two-thirds of the questions come from managers.[69] In other words, supervisors often use information from outside sources in making their own judgments about performance. Furthermore, supervisors may change their ratings, particularly when a ratee's peers provide information perceived as useful.[70] Indirect information is perceived to be most useful when it agrees with the rater's direct observation of the employee's performance.[71] In sum, although direct observation is the main influence on ratings, the presence of indirect information also is likely to affect them.[72] Beyond that, supervisors are not simply passive measurement instruments, trying their best to provide accurate assessments of the performance of their subordinates. In fact, they may distort their ratings to accomplish goals that they value (e.g., motivating subordinates), or to avoid negative repercussions from assigning ratings that their subordinates or their superiors will find objectionable.[73] Now let's consider a more formal procedure for incorporating multiple sources of performance information.

## Multirater or 360-Degree Feedback

Many organizations now use input from managers, subordinates, peers, and customers to provide a perspective on performance from all angles (360 degrees). There are at least four reasons such an approach is potentially valuable:[74]

1. It includes observations from different perspectives, and perhaps includes different aspects of performance that capture the complexities of an individual's performance in multiple roles.
2. Feedback from multiple sources may reinforce feedback from the boss, thereby making it harder to discount the viewpoint of that single person.
3. Discrepancies between self-ratings and those received from others may create an awareness of a person's needs for development, and motivate individuals to improve their performance in order to reduce or eliminate such discrepancies.
4. At least some senior managers believe that if they can improve leadership among their organization's leaders, ultimately that will benefit the bottom line.

What does the research literature on **360-degree feedback** tell us? Evidence indicates that ratings from these different sources generally do not agree closely with each other. Thus, one study found that the correlations among ratings made by self, peer, supervisor, and subordinate raters ranged from a high of 0.79 (supervisor–peer) to a low of 0.14 (subordinate–self).[75] However, evidence also indicates that ratings from the different sources are comparable, for they reflect the same underlying dimensions of performance.[76]

What about the effectiveness of feedback from such systems? Does it improve subsequent job performance? A comprehensive review found that the effects of multi-source feedback have been mixed at best.[77] Perhaps the biggest problem is that conflicting feedback information often generated from 360-degree appraisal systems can actually make the feedback less useful and even problematic. This finding has led many practitioners to become quite negative about these systems, even though they had been quite positive when the systems were first introduced.[78]

To overcome these potential problems, decision-makers need to be aware of the personal biases of raters and attempt to control their effects. To do this, consider taking the following steps:[79]

- Make sure appraisal has a single, clear purpose—development.
- Train all raters to understand the overall process as well as how to complete forms and avoid common rating errors. UPS, for example, explains the 360-degree feedback process and discusses how data will be used. Recognize, however, that no amount of training is going to be of any help if the organizational climate is politically charged and trust is low.[80]
- Seek a variety of types of information about performance, and make raters accountable to upper-level review. Allowing employees to nominate raters

who will provide information about their performance (typically 6 to 12 raters) increases acceptance of the results.[81]

- Help employees interpret and react to the ratings, perhaps with the help of a personal coach.[82] Longitudinal research demonstrates convincingly that a key ingredient in producing positive changes in the ratee's behavior is organizational support that facilitates both the feedback and development process.[83]
- Link 360-degree feedback to other HR systems (e.g., training, rewards), and take the time to evaluate their effectiveness.[84] Today, many organizations administer 360-degree feedback via the Internet in order to minimize paperwork and to reduce the time involved in collecting, organizing, and summarizing the data. Termed "talent-management" systems, they allow organizations to manage data about employees in a systematic and coordinated way.[85]

Finally, the written report should contain the following elements: a summary that integrates the main themes from the scores (assuming quantitative results are part of the process) and a detailed summary of ratings from each source.[86] Careful attention to these action steps is an integral component of performance management. Another important consideration is the timing and frequency of performance appraisal.

## WHEN AND HOW OFTEN SHOULD APPRAISAL BE DONE?

Traditionally, formal appraisal is done once, or at best twice, a year. Research, however, has indicated that once or twice a year is far too infrequent.[87] Unless he or she keeps a diary, considerable difficulties face a rater who is asked to remember what several employees did over the previous 6 or 12 months. This is why firms such as Hamilton Standard, Southern California Gas, and Synygy add frequent, informal "progress" reviews between the annual ones.[88]

Research indicates that if a rater is asked to assess an employee's performance over a 6- to 12-month period, biased ratings may result, especially if information has been stored in the rater's memory according to irrelevant, oversimplistic, or otherwise faulty categories.[89] Unfortunately, faulty categorization seems to be the rule more often than the exception.

For example, consider the impact of prior expectations on ratings.[90] Supervisors of tellers at a large West Coast bank provided predictions about the future job performance of their new tellers. Six months later they rated the job performance of each teller. The result? Inconsistencies between prior expectations and later performance clearly affected the judgments of the raters. Thus, when a teller's actual performance disappointed or exceeded a supervisor's prior expectations about that performance, ratings were lower than warranted by actual performance. The lesson to be learned is that it is unwise to assume that raters are faulty, but motivationally neutral, observers of on-the-job behavior.

More and more companies are realizing that once-a-year reviews don't work very well. There should be no surprises in appraisals, and one way to ensure this is to do them frequently. We noted earlier that social-networking–style systems developed by Accenture and Rypple now let employees post

Twitter-length questions, such as "How can I run meetings better?" in exchange for anonymous feedback. This enables them to get job-related feedback as often as they want. At the very least, says former GE chief executive Jack Welch, "it's reasonable to expect two candid performance appraisals a year that make it absolutely clear how you're doing relative to your peers and ambitions. . . . No boss is doing his job properly if he's not letting each of his people know where they stand in constructive detail."[91]

## EVALUATING THE PERFORMANCE OF TEAMS

Our discussion so far has focused on the assessment and improvement of *individual* performance. However, numerous organizations (80 percent of U.S. corporations) are structured around teams.[92] Team-based organizations do not necessarily outperform organizations that are not structured around teams,[93] but there seems to be an increased interest in organizing how work is done around teams.[94] Therefore, given the popularity of teams, it makes sense for performance-management systems to target not only individual performance, but also an individual's contribution to the performance of his or her team(s)— as well as the performance of teams as a whole.

The assessment of team performance does not imply that individual contributions should be ignored. On the contrary, if individual performance is not assessed and recognized, social loafing may occur.[95] Even worse, when other team members see there is a "free rider," they are likely to withdraw their effort in support of team performance.[96] Assessing team performance, therefore, should be seen as complementary to the assessment and recognition of (1) individual performance (as we have discussed so far), and (2) individuals' behaviors and skills that contribute to team performance (e.g., self-management, communication, decision making, collaboration).[97]

Not all teams are created equal, however. Different types of teams require different emphasis on performance measurement at the individual and team levels. Depending on the complexity of the task (from routine to nonroutine) and membership configuration (from static to dynamic), we can identify three different types of teams:[98]

- *Work or service teams*. Intact teams engaged on routine tasks (e.g., manufacturing or service tasks).
- *Project teams*. Teams assembled for a specific purpose and expected to disband once their task is completed. Their tasks are outside the core production or service of the organization and therefore less routine than those of work or service teams.
- *Network teams*. Teams that include membership not constrained by time or space and membership is not limited by organizational boundaries (i.e., they are typically geographically dispersed and stay in touch via telecommunications technology). Their work is extremely nonroutine.

Table 9–2 shows a summary of recommended measurement methods for each of the three types of teams.

For example, regarding project teams, end-of-project outcome measures may not benefit the team's development because the team is likely to disband once the

## Table 9–2

### APPRAISAL METHODS FOR DIFFERENT TYPES OF TEAMS

| Team type | Who is being rated? | Who provides rating? | What is rated? | | | How is the rating used? | | |
|---|---|---|---|---|---|---|---|---|
| | | | Outcome | Behavior | Competency | Development | Evaluation | Self regulation |
| Work or service team | Team member | Manager | ✓ | ✓ | ✓ | ✓ | ✓ | |
| | | Other team members | | ✓ | ✓ | ✓ | | |
| | | Customers | | ✓ | | ✓ | | |
| | | Self | ✓ | ✓ | ✓ | ✓ | | ✓ |
| | Entire team | Manager | ✓ | ✓ | ✓ | ✓ | ✓ | |
| | | Other teams | | ✓ | | | | |
| | | Customers | | ✓ | | | | |
| | | Self | ✓ | ✓ | ✓ | ✓ | | ✓ |
| Project team | Team member | Manager | ✓ | | ✓ | ✓ | ✓ | |
| | | Project leaders | | ✓ | ✓ | ✓ | | |
| | | Other team members | | ✓ | ✓ | ✓ | | |
| | | Customers | | ✓ | | | | |
| | | Self | ✓ | ✓ | ✓ | ✓ | | ✓ |
| | Entire team | Customers | ✓ | ✓ | | | ✓ | |
| | | Self | ✓ | ✓ | ✓ | ✓ | | ✓ |
| Network team | Team member | Manager | | ✓ | ✓ | ✓ | ✓ | |
| | | Team leaders | | ✓ | ✓ | ✓ | | |
| | | Coworkers | | ✓ | ✓ | ✓ | | |
| | | Other team members | | ✓ | ✓ | ✓ | | |
| | | Customers | | ✓ | ✓ | ✓ | | |
| | | Self | ✓ | ✓ | ✓ | ✓ | | ✓ |
| | Entire team | Customers | ✓ | | | | ✓ | |

*Source:* Scott, S. G., and Einstein, W. O. (2001, May). Strategic performance appraisal in team-based organizations: One size does not fit all. *Academy of Management Executive* 15, p. 111. Reprinted by permission of the Academy of Management Executive.

project is over. Instead, measurements taken during the project can be implemented so that corrective action can be taken if necessary before the project is over. This is what Hewlett-Packard uses with its product-development teams.[99]

Regardless of whether performance is measured at the individual level or at the individual and team levels, raters are likely to make intentional or unintentional mistakes in assigning performance scores.[100] The good news, however, is that raters can be trained to minimize such biases. We address this topic next.

## INTERNATIONAL APPLICATION
### The Impact of National Culture on Performance Management

It is one thing to institute a performance management system with a home-country manager on an international assignment. It is quite another to do so with a local manager or local employees whose customs and culture differ from one's own. Western expatriate managers are often surprised to learn that their management practices have unintended consequences when applied in non-Western cultures. For example, we know that concepts such as individual rewards for individual performance and making explicit distinctions in performance among employees are not universally accepted. Indeed, where the prevailing view is that it takes contributions from everyone to achieve continuous improvement (that is, the concept of kaizen in Japanese enterprises), the practice of singling out one employee's contribution may actually cause that employee to "lose face" among his or her fellow work-group members. In other cultures, where nepotism is common and extended family members work together, the primary objective is to preserve working relationships. That objective may cause host-country managers to overlook results that more objective observers might judge to be inadequate.[a]

As a general conclusion, managers will need to modify the performance management process that is familiar to them when working with cultures other than their own. Doing so shows respect and recognizes the importance of groups as well as individuals in the organization.[b]

---

[a]Cascio, W. F. (2011). The puzzle of performance management in the multinational enterprise. *Industrial and Organizational Psychology* 4, pp. 190–193. See also McEvoy, G. M., and Cascio, W. F. (1990). The United States and Taiwan: Two different cultures look at performance appraisal. *Research in Personnel and Human Resources Management* (Suppl. 2), pp. 201–219.
[b]For more on this see Cascio (In press), op. cit.

## APPRAISAL ERRORS AND RATER-TRAINING STRATEGIES

The use of ratings assumes that the human observer is reasonably objective and accurate. As we have seen, raters' memories are quite fallible, and raters subscribe to their own sets of likes, dislikes, and expectations about people, expectations that may or may not be valid.[101] These biases produce rating errors, or deviations between the true rating an employee deserves and the actual rating assigned.[102] We discussed some of the most common types of rating errors previously: leniency, severity, and central tendency. Three other types are halo, contrast, and recency errors.

1.  **Halo error** is not as common as is commonly believed.[103] Raters who commit this error assign their ratings on the basis of global (good or bad) impressions of ratees. An employee is rated either high or low on many aspects of job performance because the rater knows (or thinks she or he knows) that the employee is high or low on some specific aspect. In practice, halo is probably due to situational factors or to the interaction of a rater and a situation (e.g., a supervisor who has limited opportunity to observe her subordinates because they are in the field dealing with customers).[104] Thus, halo is probably a better indicator of how raters process cognitive information than it is as a measure of rating validity or accuracy.[105]

2. **Contrast error** results when a rater compares several employees to one another rather than to an objective standard of performance.[106] If, say, the first two workers are unsatisfactory while the third is average, the third worker may well be rated outstanding because, in contrast to the first two, her or his average level of job performance is magnified. Likewise, average performance could be downgraded unfairly if the first few workers are outstanding. In both cases, the average worker receives a biased rating.

3. **Recency error** results when a rater assigns his or her ratings on the basis of the employee's most recent performance. It is most likely to occur when appraisals are done only after long periods. Here is how one manager described the dilemma of the recency error: "Many of us have trouble rating for the entire year. If one of my people has a stellar three months prior to the review . . . [I] don't want to do anything that impedes that person's momentum and progress."[107] Of course, if the subordinate's performance peaks three months prior to appraisal *every year*, that suggests a different problem!

Recent survey data indicate that training for managers (55 percent) and nonmanagers (28 percent) has doubled in the past 10 years but that fewer than 40 percent of firms hold managers accountable for the effectiveness of the performance-management system.[108] Implementing a performance-management system without training all parties in how to use it as designed is a waste of time and money. Training managers, but then not holding them accountable for implementing what they have been trained on, is just as bad. What can be done? Begin by identifying some key topics to address with respect to performance-management training. These include the following:[109]

- Philosophy and uses of the system.
- Description of the rating process.
- Roles and responsibilities of employees and managers.
- How to define performance, and how to set expectations and goals.
- How to provide accurate assessments of performance, minimizing rating errors and rating inflation.
- The importance of ongoing, constructive feedback in behavioral terms.
- How to give feedback in a manner that minimizes defensiveness and maintains the self-esteem of the receiver.
- How to react to and act on feedback in a constructive manner.
- How to seek feedback from others effectively.
- How to identify and address needs for training and development.

Of the many types of rater training programs available today, meta-analytic evidence has demonstrated reliably that **frame-of-reference (FOR) training**[110] is most effective at improving the accuracy of performance appraisals.[111] Moreover, the addition of other types of training in combination with FOR training does not seem to improve rating accuracy beyond the effects of FOR training alone.[112] Such FOR training proceeds as follows:[113]

1. Participants are told that they will evaluate the performance of three ratees on three separate performance dimensions.
2. They are given rating scales and instructed to read them as the trainer reads the dimension definitions and scale anchors aloud.
3. The trainer then discusses ratee behaviors that illustrate different performance levels for each scale. The goal is to create a common performance theory

(frame of reference) among raters such that they will agree on the appropriate performance dimension and effectiveness level for different behaviors.

4. Participants are shown a videotape of a practice vignette and are asked to evaluate the manager using the scales provided.

5. Ratings are then written on a blackboard and discussed by the group of participants. The trainer seeks to identify which behaviors participants used to decide on their assigned ratings, and to clarify any discrepancies among the ratings.

6. The trainer provides feedback to participants, explaining why the ratee should receive a certain rating (target score) on a given dimension.

FOR training provides trainees with a *theory of performance* that allows them to understand the various performance dimensions, how to match these performance dimensions to rate behaviors, how to judge the effectiveness of various ratee behaviors, and how to integrate their judgments into an overall rating of performance.[114] Rater training is clearly worth the effort, and research indicates that the kind of approach advocated here is especially effective in improving the meaningfulness and usefulness of the performance-management process.[115]

## SECRETS OF EFFECTIVE PERFORMANCE-FEEDBACK INTERVIEWS

The use of performance feedback, at least in terms of company policies on the subject, is widespread. Most companies require that appraisal results be discussed with employees.[116] As is well known, however, the existence of a policy

---

### IMPACT OF PERFORMANCE MANAGEMENT ON PRODUCTIVITY, QUALITY OF WORK LIFE, AND THE BOTTOM LINE

Performance management is fundamentally a feedback process, and research indicates that feedback may result in increases in performance varying from 10 to 30 percent, although it is not uniformly effective.[a] Feedback is a fairly inexpensive way to improve productivity, but, to work effectively, feedback programs require sustained commitment. The challenge for managers, then, is to establish clear goals, and then to provide feedback regularly to all their employees.

From an employee's perspective, lack of regular feedback about performance detracts from his or her quality of work life. Most people want to improve their performance on the job, to receive constructive suggestions regarding areas they need to work on, and to be commended for

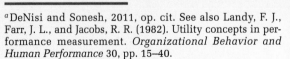

things that they do well. The cost of failure to provide such feedback may result in the loss of key professional employees, the continued poor performance of employees who are not meeting performance standards, and a loss of commitment by all employees. In sum, the myth that employees know how they are doing without adequate feedback from management can be an expensive fantasy.[b]

---

[a]DeNisi and Sonesh, 2011, op. cit. See also Landy, F. J., Farr, J. L., and Jacobs, R. R. (1982). Utility concepts in performance measurement. *Organizational Behavior and Human Performance* 30, pp. 15–40.
[b]Hymowitz, C. (2007, Mar. 19). Managers lose talent when they neglect to coach their staffs. *The Wall Street Journal*, p. B1. See also Joinson, C. (1996, Aug.). Re-creating the indifferent employee. *HR Magazine*, pp. 77–80.

is no guarantee that it will be implemented, or implemented effectively. Consider just two examples. First, we know that feedback is most effective when it is given immediately following the behavior in question.[117] How effective can feedback be if it is given only once a year during an appraisal interview?

Second, we have known for decades that when managers use a problem-solving approach, subordinates express a stronger motivation to improve performance than when other approaches are used.[118] Yet evidence indicates that most organizations still use a "tell-and-sell" approach in which a manager completes an appraisal independently, shows it to the subordinate, justifies the rating, discusses what must be done to improve performance, and then asks for the subordinate's reaction and sign-off on the appraisal.[119] Are the negative reactions of subordinates really that surprising?

If organizations really are serious about fostering improved job performance as a result of performance-feedback interviews, the kinds of activities shown in Table 9–3 are essential before, during, and after the interview. Let's briefly examine each of these important activities.

***Communicate Frequently.*** Research on the appraisal interview at General Electric indicated clearly that once-a-year performance appraisals are of questionable value and that coaching should be a day-to-day activity—particularly with poor performers or new employees.[120] Feedback has maximum impact when it is given as close as possible to the action. If a subordinate behaves effectively

| *Table 9–3* | |
|---|---|
| **SUPERVISORY ACTIVITIES BEFORE, DURING, AND AFTER PERFORMANCE-FEEDBACK INTERVIEWS** | |
| **Before:** | |
| Communicate frequently with subordinates about their performance. Get training in performance appraisal interviewing. Plan to use a problem-solving approach rather than "tell-and-sell." Encourage subordinates to prepare for performance-feedback interviews. | |
| **During:** | |
| Encourage subordinates to participate. Judge performance, not personality and mannerisms. Be specific. Be an active listener. Set mutually agreeable goals for future improvements. Avoid destructive criticism. | |
| **After:** | |
| Communicate frequently with subordinates about their performance. Periodically assess progress toward goals. Make organizational rewards contingent on performance. | |

(ineffectively), tell him or her immediately. Don't file incidents away so that they can be discussed in six to nine months.

Research strongly supports this view. Thus, one study found that communication of performance feedback in an interview is most effective when the subordinate already has relatively accurate perceptions of her or his performance before the session.[121]

***Get Training in Performance Feedback and Appraisal Interviewing.***   As we noted earlier, raters should be trained to observe behavior accurately and fairly. Focus on managerial characteristics that are difficult to rate and on characteristics that people think are easy to rate but that generally result in disagreements. Such factors include risk taking and development of subordinates.[122] Use a problem-solving, rather than a "tell-and-sell," approach, as noted earlier.

***Encourage Subordinates to Prepare.***   Research conducted across a variety of organizations has yielded consistent results. Subordinates who spend more time prior to performance-feedback interviews analyzing their job responsibilities and duties, problems they encounter on the job, and the quality of their performance are more likely to be satisfied with the performance-management process, more likely to be motivated to improve their performance, and more likely actually to improve.[123]

***Encourage Participation.***   A perception of ownership—a feeling by the subordinate that his or her ideas are genuinely welcomed by the manager—is related strongly to subordinates' satisfaction with the appraisal interview, the appraisal system, motivation to improve performance, and the perceived fairness of the system.[124] Participation provides an opportunity for employee voice in performance appraisal. It encourages the belief that the interview was a fair process, that it was a constructive activity, that some current job problems were cleared up, and that future goals were set.[125]

***Judge Performance, Not Personality.***   In addition to the potential legal liability of dwelling on personality rather than on job performance, supervisors are far less likely to change a subordinate's personality than they are his or her job performance. Maintain the problem-solving, job-related focus established earlier because evidence indicates that supervisory support enhances employees' motivation to improve.[126] Conversely, an emphasis on the employee as a person or his or her self-concept, as opposed to the task and task performance only, is likely to lead to lower levels of future performance.[127]

***Be Specific, and Be an Active Listener.***   Maximize information relating to performance improvements and minimize information concerning the relative performance of other employees.[128] By being candid and specific, the supervisor offers clear feedback to the subordinate concerning past actions. She or he also demonstrates knowledge of the subordinate's level of performance and job duties. By being an active listener, the supervisor demonstrates genuine interest in the subordinate's ideas. **Active listening** requires that you do five things well:

1.  Take the time to listen—hold all phone calls and do not allow interruptions.
2.  Communicate verbally and nonverbally (e.g., by maintaining eye contact) that you genuinely want to help.

3. As the subordinate begins to tell his or her side of the story, do not interrupt and do not argue.
4. Watch for verbal as well as nonverbal cues regarding the subordinate's agreement or disagreement with your message.
5. Summarize what was said and what was agreed to.

Specific feedback and active listening are essential to subordinates' perceptions of the fairness and accuracy of the process.[129]

***Avoid Destructive Criticism.***   **Destructive criticism** is general in nature, is frequently delivered in a biting, sarcastic tone, and often attributes poor performance to internal causes (e.g., lack of motivation or ability). It leads to three predictable consequences:

1. It produces negative feelings among recipients and can initiate or intensify conflict.
2. It reduces the preference of individuals for handling future disagreements with the giver of the feedback in a conciliatory manner (e.g., compromise, collaboration).
3. It has negative effects on self-set goals and on feelings of self-confidence.[130]

Needless to say, this is one type of communication to avoid.

***Set Mutually Agreeable Goals.***   How does goal setting work to improve performance? Studies demonstrate that goals direct attention to the specific performance in question, that they mobilize effort to accomplish higher levels of performance, and that they foster persistence for higher levels of performance.[131] The practical implications of this work are clear: Set specific, challenging goals, because this clarifies for the subordinate precisely what is expected and leads to high levels of performance. We cannot change the past, but interviews that include goal setting and specific feedback can affect future job performance.

***Continue to Communicate, and Assess Progress toward Goals Regularly.***   Periodic tracking of progress toward goals has three advantages:

1. It helps keep behavior on target.
2. It provides a better understanding of the reasons behind a given level of performance.
3. It enhances the subordinate's commitment to perform effectively.

All of this helps to improve supervisor/subordinate work relationships. Improving supervisor/subordinate work relationships, in turn, has positive effects on performance.[132]

***Make Organizational Rewards Contingent on Performance.***   Research results are clear-cut on this point. If subordinates see a link between appraisal results and employment decisions regarding issues such as merit pay and promotion, they are more likely to prepare for performance-feedback interviews, to participate actively in them, and to be satisfied with the overall performance-management system.[133] At Netflix for example, CEO Reed Hastings rewards managers who unleash talent and generate high performance from their staffs.[134]

## IMPLICATIONS FOR MANAGEMENT PRACTICE

Throughout this chapter we have emphasized the difficulty of implementing and sustaining performance-management systems. A basic issue for every manager is "What's in it for me?" If organizations are serious about improving the performance-management process, top management must consider the following policy changes:

- Make *quality of performance feedback to subordinates* and *development of subordinates* integral parts of every manager's job description.
- Tie rewards to effective performance in these areas.
- Recognize that performance management and appraisal is a dialogue involving people and data; both political and interpersonal issues are involved. No method is perfect, but with management commitment and employee buy-in, performance management can be a very useful and powerful tool.

## PERFORMANCE REVIEWS: THE DILEMMA OF FORCED RANKING

*Human Resource Management in Action: Conclusion*

Here's the dilemma: Forced distributions do differentiate employees from one another and they eliminate rater leniency, but evidence indicates that they tend to be associated with lower effectiveness of performance-management systems, particularly when appraisal results are tied to termination. Proponents of forced rankings argue that they facilitate budgeting and guard against spineless managers who are too afraid to jettison poor performers. Forced rankings, the thinking goes, force managers to be honest with workers about how they are doing. Like any such system, forced rankings can also be undermined, as by managers who avoid having to assign the lowest grades to any of their people by trading employees beforehand with supervisors of other teams.

Critics say forced rankings compel managers to penalize a good, but not great, employee who is part of a superstar team. Conversely, a mediocre employee on a struggling unit can come out looking great. Most companies guard against this problem by refraining from rigidly applying the distribution to smaller teams—but this means the spread has to be made up somewhere else. The result: Different managers spend hours haggling with one another to meet the overall distribution requirements. According to one middle manager at Microsoft, this horse-trading process can be frustrating and time consuming. While the company says it does not require managers to assign a certain percentage of employees to each level, the middle manager says there is unspoken pressure to do so.

Another area of contention is the ranking criteria. In contrast to objective criteria, such as sales revenue generated or error-free products produced, many organizations use fuzzy, qualitative criteria to evaluate employees. While there is no doubt that teamwork and communication skills are vital, they are tough to measure. After all, one manager's team player is another's yes-person. Indeed a senior manager at one large firm admits that the company's ranking criteria are "very subjective," adding, "There aren't easy labels for what type of person someone is."

After a string of age-discrimination suits, fewer companies seem to be adopting forced-distribution systems. A major problem seems to be that they simply don't work well in company cultures that value teamwork, collaboration, and risk taking. Moreover, they mask differences in performance across divisions and workgroups. That is, it is likely that some workgroups are more effective than others, but with forced-distribution ratings it is impossible to distinguish groups that are performing well from those that are performing poorly.

## SUMMARY

Performance management requires the willingness and commitment to focus on improving performance at the level of the individual or team *every day*. Like a compass, an ongoing performance-management system provides instantaneous, real-time information that describes the difference between the current and the desired course. To practice sound performance management, managers must do the same thing—provide timely feedback about performance, while constantly focusing everyone's attention on the ultimate objective (e.g., world-class customer service).

At a general level, the broad process of performance management requires that you do three things well: define performance (through goals, measures, and assessments), facilitate performance (by identifying obstacles to good performance and providing resources to accomplish objectives), and encourage performance (by providing fair and timely rewards that people care about in a sufficient amount).

Performance appraisal (the systematic description of the job-relevant strengths and weaknesses of an individual or a team) is a necessary, but not sufficient, part of the performance-management process. It serves two major purposes in organizations: (1) to improve the job performance of employees, and (2) to provide information to employees and managers for use in making decisions. In practice, many performance-appraisal systems fail because they do not satisfy one or more of the following requirements: relevance, sensitivity, reliability, acceptability, and practicality. The failure is frequently accompanied by legal challenge to the system based on its adverse impact against one or more protected groups.

Performance appraisal is done once or twice a year in most organizations, but research indicates that this is far too infrequent. It should happen upon the completion of projects or upon the achievement of important milestones. The specific rating method used depends on the purpose for which the appraisal is intended. Thus, comparisons among employees are most appropriate for generating rankings for salary-administration purposes, while MBO, work planning and review, and narrative essays are least appropriate for this purpose. For purposes of employee development, critical incidents or behaviorally anchored rating scales are most appropriate. Finally, rating methods that focus on describing rather than evaluating behavior (e.g., BARS, behavioral checklists) are the most interpretable across raters.

Performance management and appraisal may be done at the level of the individual or the team. Because different types of teams exist, such as work or service teams, project teams, and network teams, different appraisal methods are most appropriate for each team type (see Table 9–2). Recognize, however, that rater judgments are subject to various types of biases: leniency; severity; central tendency; and halo, contrast, and recency effects. To improve the reliability and validity of ratings, use frame-of-reference training to help raters observe behavior more accurately. To improve the value of performance-feedback interviews, communicate frequently with subordinates; encourage them to prepare and to participate in the process; judge performance, not personality; be specific; avoid destructive criticism; set goals; assess progress toward goals regularly; and make rewards contingent on performance.

## KEY TERMS

| | |
|---|---|
| performance management | paired comparisons |
| performance appraisal | forced distribution |
| performance facilitation | leniency |
| performance encouragement | severity |
| relevance | central tendency |
| performance standards | Likert method of summed ratings |
| sensitivity | critical incidents |
| reliability | graphic rating scales |
| acceptability | behaviorally anchored rating scales (BARS) |
| practicality | management by objectives (MBO) |
| applicant group | work planning and review |
| behavior-oriented rating methods | 360-degree feedback |
| relative rating systems | halo error |
| absolute rating systems | contrast error |
| results-oriented rating methods | recency error |
| narrative essay | frame-of-reference (FOR) training |
| simple ranking | active listening |
| alternation ranking | destructive criticism |

## DISCUSSION QUESTIONS

**9–1.** What would an effective performance-management system look like?

**9–2.** What is the difference between performance management and performance appraisal?

**9–3.** You have been asked to design a rater-training program. What types of elements would you build into the process?

**9–4.** Working in small groups, develop a performance-management system for a cashier in a neighborhood grocery with little technology but lots of personal touch.

**9–5.** The chief counsel for a large corporation comes to you for advice. She wants to know what makes a firm's appraisal system legally vulnerable. What would you tell her?

**9–6.** How is performance appraisal for teams different from performance appraisal for individuals?

**9-7.** How can we overcome employee defensiveness in performance-feedback interviews?

**9-8.** Should discussions of employee job performance be separated from salary considerations?

# APPLYING YOUR KNOWLEDGE

*Case 9-1*    **Problems in Appraisal at Peak Power**

Peak Power, a medium-size hydroelectric power plant near Seattle, Washington, has been having difficulty with its performance-appraisal system. The plant's present appraisal system has been in existence for about 10 years and was designed by the head of administrative operations, a clerk who had been promoted into the position without any professional training in human resource management. Presently, all operating employees are evaluated once a year by their supervisors, using the following form:

## PEAK POWER PERFORMANCE-APPRAISAL FORM

*General Instructions:* Complete the following form either by typing your responses or printing them in ink, and then make three copies. After the employee's performance has been evaluated by the supervisor and reviewed by higher-level supervision, the employee will be informed of his or her performance rating and will sign all copies of the form indicating that he or she has been so informed. The employee's signature does not necessarily indicate that he or she agrees with the ratings given. Send one completed form to the human resources office, and allow the employee to keep a copy for his or her files. The other copy is the supervisor's.

Complete the form by marking an "X" in the appropriate locations below.

| Performance dimension | Excellent | Above average | Average | Below average | Poor |
|---|---|---|---|---|---|
| Quantity of work | | | | | |
| Quality of work | | | | | |
| Dependability | | | | | |
| Initiative | | | | | |
| Cooperativeness | | | | | |
| Leadership potential | | | | | |

"Excellent" is worth 5 points, "Above average" is worth 4 points, "Average" is worth 3 points, "Below average" is worth 2 points, and "Poor" is worth 1 point. Determine the employee's overall evaluation by summing the appropriate number of points from each of the six dimension scores above, and place the total here _____.
Supervisor's signature _____
Employee's signature _____
Reviewed by _____

Ratings from each year are maintained in employee files in the HR department. If promotions come up, the cumulative ratings are considered at that time. Further, ratings are supposed to be used as a check when raises are given. In practice, little use is made of the ratings, either for determination of promotions or for salary decisions. Employee feelings about the appraisal system range from indifference to outright hostility. A small, informal survey two years ago determined that supervisors spent on average about 3 minutes filling out the form and less than 10 minutes discussing it with employees.

Recent problems in other areas of HR management at the plant and the fear of potential lawsuits led Peak's president to consider hiring an experienced HR professional to upgrade all HR systems. You are being interviewed for the job, and have just been presented with the preceding information.

---

**Questions**

1. The president asks you for your general evaluation of this appraisal system. What is your response?
2. The president asks you for some suggestions for ways in which the present system can be improved. What would you say?
3. If you should be selected for this position, outline some steps you would take to ensure that a new performance-management system will be accepted by its users.

---

# REFERENCES

1. O'Leary, R. S., and Pulakos, E. D. (2011). Managing performance through the manager-employee relationship. *Industrial and Organizational Psychology* 4, pp. 208–214. See also Cascio, W. F. (1996, Sept.). Managing for maximum performance. *HRMonthly* (Australia), pp. 10–13.
2. Light, J. (2010, Nov. 8). Human-resources executives say reviews are off the mark. *The Wall Street Journal*, p. B8.
3. Bernthal, P. R., Rogers, R. W., and Smith, A. B. (2003, Apr.). *Managing Performance: Building Accountability for Organizational Success.* Pittsburgh, PA: Development Dimensions International.
4. Bernardin, H. J., Hagan, C. M., Kane, J. S., and Villanova, P. (1998). Effective performance management. In J. W. Smither (Ed.), *Performance Appraisal: State of the Art in Practice.* San Francisco: Jossey-Bass, pp. 3–48.
5. Latham, G. P. (2009). *Becoming the Evidence-Based Manager: Making the Science of Management Work for You.* Boston, MA: Davies-Black. See also Locke, E. A., and Latham, G. P. (2002). Building a practically useful theory of goal setting and task motivation. *American Psychologist* 57, pp. 705–717. See also Locke, E. A., and Latham, G. P. (1990). *A Theory of Goal Setting and Task Performance.* Englewood Cliffs, NJ: Prentice-Hall.
6. Tubbs, M. E. (1986). Goal setting: A meta-analytic examination of the empirical evidence. *Journal of Applied Psychology* 71, pp. 474–483.
7. Knight, D., Durham, C. C., and Locke, E. A. (2001). The relationship of team goals, incentives, and efficacy to strategic risk, tactical implementation, and performance. *Academy of Management Journal* 44, pp. 326–338.
8. Pulakos, E. D., and O'Leary, R. S. (2011). Why is performance management broken? *Industrial and Organizational Psychology* 4, pp, 146–164. See also Stokes, W., quoted in Grossman, R. J. (2010, April). Tough love at Netflix. *HR Magazine* 55(4), p. 40.

**9.** Wood, R. E., Mento, A. J., and Locke, E. A. (1987). Task complexity as a moderator of goal effects: A meta-analysis. *Journal of Applied Psychology* 72, pp. 416–425.

**10.** Kaiser, R. B., Hogan, R., and Craig, S. B. (2008). Leadership and the fate of organizations. *American Psychologist* 63, pp. 96–110.

**11.** Kerr, S. In Sherman, S. (1995, Nov. 13). Stretch goals: The dark side of asking for miracles. *Fortune*, p. 31. See also McGregor, J. (2009, July 6). Straight talk in a slump. *BusinessWeek*, p. 52.

**12.** Delaney, K. J. (2006, Oct. 23). Google adjusts hiring process as needs grow. *The Wall Street Journal*, pp. B1, B8. See also Morris, B. (2008, March 3). What makes Apple golden. *Fortune*. Retrieved from *money.cnn.com/2008/02/29/news/companies/amac_apple.fortune/index.htm* on September 2, 2011.

**13.** Greenberg, J. (2011). Organizational justice: The dynamics of fairness in the workplace. In S. Zedeck (Ed.), *APA Handbook of Industrial and Organizational Psychology,* Vol. 3. Washington, DC: American Psychological Association, pp. 271–327. See also Kanovsky, M. (2000). Understanding procedural justice and its impact on business organizations. *Journal of Management* 26, pp. 489–511. See also Gilliland, S. W., and Langdon, J. C. (1998). Creating performance management systems that promote perceptions of fairness. In J. W. Smither (Ed.), *Performance Appraisal: State of the Art in Practice.* San Francisco: Jossey-Bass, pp. 209–243.

**14.** Tulgan, B. (2004, June 28). The under-management epidemic. Retrieved from *www.rainmakerthinking.com/backwttw/2004/june30.htm* on September 13, 2004. See also Pfeffer, J. (2009, Aug. 3). Low grades for performance reviews. *BusinessWeek*, p. 68.

**15.** Wells, S. J. (2009, June). Prescription for a turnaround. *HR Magazine* 54(6), pp. 88–94.

**16.** Fox, A. (2009, Jan.). Curing what ails performance reviews. *HR Magazine* 54(1), pp. 52–56. See also Light, 2010, op. cit. See also Culbert, S. A. (2008). Get rid of the performance review! *The Wall Street Journal,* p. R4. See also Sandberg, J. (2007, Nov. 20). Performance reviews need some work, don't meet potential. *The Wall Street Journal,* p. B1.

**17.** Cascio, W. F., and Aguinis, H. (2011). *Applied Psychology in Human Resource Management* (7th Ed.). Upper Saddle River, NJ: Prentice-Hall. See also Murphy, K. R. (2008). Explaining the weak relationship between job performance and ratings of job performance. *Industrial and Organizational Psychology* 1, pp. 148–160.

**18.** Reasons for raises. (2006, May 29). *BusinessWeek,* p. 11. See also Lawler, E. E. III. (2003). Reward practices and performance management system effectiveness. *Organizational Dynamics* 32(4), pp. 396–404. See also Arvey, R. D., and Murphy, K. R. (1998). Performance evaluation in work settings. *Annual Review of Psychology* 49, pp. 141–168.

**19.** Woehr, D. J. (2008). On the relationship between job performance and ratings of job performance. What do we really know? *Industrial and Organizational Psychology* 1, pp. 161–166. See also Cascio, W. F. (1982). Scientific, legal, and operational imperatives of workable performance appraisal systems. *Public Personnel Management* 11, pp. 367–375.

**20.** Zedeck, S., and Cascio, W. F. (1982). Performance appraisal decisions as a function of rater training and purpose of the appraisal. *Journal of Applied Psychology* 67, pp. 752–758. See also Murphy, 2008, op. cit.

**21.** Ones, D. S., Viswesvaran, C., and Schmidt, F. L. (2008). No new terrain: Reliability and construct validity of job performance ratings. *Industrial and Organizational Psychology* 1, pp. 174–179. See also Viswesvaran, C., Ones, D. S., and Schmidt, F. L. (1996). Comparative analysis of the reliability of job performance ratings. *Journal of Applied Psychology* 81, pp. 557–574.

22. DeNisi, A. S., and Sonesh, S. (2011). The appraisal and management of performance at work. In S. Zedeck (Ed.), *APA Handbook of Industrial and Organizational Psychology,* Vol. 2. Washington, DC: American Psychological Association, pp. 255–279.

23. Mayer, R. C., and Davis, J. H. (1999). The effect of the performance appraisal system on trust for management: A field quasi-experiment. *Journal of Applied Psychology* 84, pp. 123–136. See also Cawley, B. D., Keeping, L. M., and Levy, P. E. (1998). Participation in the performance appraisal process and employee reactions: A meta-analytic review of field investigations. *Journal of Applied Psychology* 83, pp. 615–633. See also Taylor, M. S., Masterson, S. S., Renard, M. K., and Tracy, K. B. (1998). Managers' reactions to procedurally just performance management systems. *Academy of Management Journal* 41, pp. 568–579.

24. Segal, J. A. (2010, Nov.). Performance management blunders. *HR Magazine* 55(11), pp. 75–78. See also Malos, S. B. (1998). Current legal issues in performance appraisal. In J. W. Smither (Ed.), *Performance Appraisal: State of the Art in Practice.* San Francisco: Jossey-Bass, pp. 49–94.

25. *Paquin v. Federal National Mortgage Association* (1996, July 31). Civil Action No. 94-1261 SSH.

26. *Stone v. Xerox* (1982). 685 F. 2d 1387 (11th Cir.).

27. *United States v. City of Chicago* (1978). 573 F. 2d 416 (7th Cir.).

28. LeBoeuf, M. (1987). *The Greatest Management Principle in the World.* New York: Berkley Publishing Co. See also Luthans, F. (2010). *Organizational Behavior* (12th Ed.). Burr Ridge, IL: McGraw-Hill-Irwin.

29. See also Milkovich, G. T., Newman, J. M., and Gerhart, B. (2011). *Compensation* (10th ed.). New York, NY: McGraw-Hill. See also Aguinis, 2009, op. cit.

30. Buzachero, V., quoted in Wells, S. J. (2009, June). Prescription for a turnaround. *HR Magazine* 54(6), p. 94.

31. Cascio, W. F. (In press). Global performance management systems. In I. Bjorkman, G. Stahl, and S. Morris (Eds.), *Handbook of Research in International Human Resource Management* (2nd Ed.). London, UK: Edward Elgar. See also Engle, A. D., Sr., Dowling, P. J., and Festing, M. (2008). State of origin: Research in global performance management, a proposed research domain and emerging implications. *European Journal of International Management* 2, pp. 153–169.

32. Fox, 2009, op. cit. See also Murphy, 2008, op. cit. See also Woehr, 2008, op. cit. See also Smither, J. W. (Ed.). (1998). *Performance Appraisal: State of the Art in Practice.* San Francisco: Jossey-Bass.

33. DeNisi and Sonesh, 2011, op. cit. See also Bommer, W. H., Johnson, J. L., Rich, G. A., Podsakoff, P. M., and Mackenzie, S. B. (1995). On the interchangeability of objective and subjective measures of employee performance: A meta-analysis. *Personnel Psychology* 48, pp. 587–605. See also Heneman, R. L. (1986). The relationship between supervisory ratings and results-oriented measures of performance: A meta-analysis. *Personnel Psychology* 39, pp. 811–826.

34. Bernardin, H. J., Cooke, D. K., and Villanova, P. (2000). Conscientiousness and agreeableness as predictors of rating leniency. *Journal of Applied Psychology* 85, pp. 232–234.

35. Roch, S. G., Sturnburgh, A. M., and Caputo, P. M. (2007). Absolute vs. relative rating formats: Implications for fairness and organizational justice. *International Journal of Selection and Assessment* 15, pp. 302–316.

36. DeNisi and Sonesh, 2011, op. cit. See also Stockford, L., and Bissell, H. W. (1949). Factors involved in establishing a merit rating scale. *Personnel* 26, pp. 94–116.

37. Hennessy, J., Mabey, B., and Warr, P. (1998). Assessment centre observation procedures: An experimental comparison of traditional, checklist and coding methods. *International Journal of Selection and Assessment* 6, pp. 222–231.

38. Aguinis, 2009, op. cit. See also Murphy, 2008, op. cit. See also Landy, F. J., and Rastegary, H. (1988). Criteria for selection. In M. Smith and I. Robertson (Eds.), *Advances in Personnel Selection and Assessment.* New York: Wiley, pp. 68–115.

39. Cascio and Aguinis, 2011, op. cit.

40. Bernardin, H. J., and Smith, P. C. (1981). A clarification of some issues regarding the development and use of behaviorally anchored rating scales. *Journal of Applied Psychology* 66, pp. 458–463.

41. Cascio and Aguinis, 2011, op. cit. See also Borman, op. cit.

42. Campbell, J. P., Dunnette, M. D., Lawler, E. E., and Weick, K. E. (1970). *Managerial Behavior, Performance, and Effectiveness.* New York: McGraw-Hill.

43. McConkie, M. L. (1979). A clarification of the goal-setting and appraisal process in MBO. *Academy of Management Review* 4, pp. 29–40.

44. Albrecht, K. (1978). *Successful Management by Objectives: An Action Manual.* Englewood Cliffs, NJ: Prentice-Hall. See also Odiorne, G. S. (1965). *Management by Objectives: A System of Managerial Leadership.* Belmont, CA: Fearon.

45. Pulakos and O'Leary, 2011, op. cit. See also Barton, R. F. (1981). An MCDM approach for resolving goal conflict in MBO. *Academy of Management Review* 6, pp. 231–241.

46. Pulakos and O'Leary, 2011, op. cit. See also Kondrasuk, J. N. (1981). Studies in MBO effectiveness. *Academy of Management Review* 6, pp. 419–430.

47. Society for Human Resource Management Foundation. (2008). *Seeing Forward: Succession Planning at 3M* (DVD). Alexandria, VA: Author. Society for Human Resource Management Foundation. (2006). *Ethics: The Fabric of Business* (DVD). Alexandria, VA: Author.

48. Wells, 2009, op. cit.

49. Meyer, H. H., Kay, E., and French, J. R. P. (1965). Split roles in performance appraisal. *Harvard Business Review* 43, pp. 123–129.

50. Bernardin, H. J., and Beatty, R. W. (1984). *Performance Appraisal: An Organizational Perspective.* Boston: Allyn & Bacon. See also Murphy, 2008, op. cit. and Woehr, 2008, op. cit.

51. Hartel, C. E. J. (1993). Rating format research revisited: Format effectiveness and acceptability depend on rater characteristics. *Journal of Applied Psychology* 78, pp. 212–217.

52. Bernthal et al., 2003, op. cit.

53. Fox, 2009, op. cit.

54. Greguras, G. J. (2005). Managerial experience and the measurement equivalence of performance ratings. *Journal of Business and Psychology* 19, pp. 383–397.

55. Ghorpade, J., and Chen, M. M. (1995). Creating quality-driven performance appraisal systems. *Academy of Management Executive* 9(1), pp. 32–39.

56. Becker, T. E., and Klimoski, R. J. (1989). A field study of the relationship between the organizational feedback environment and performance. *Personnel Psychology* 42, pp. 353–358.

57. McEvoy, G. M., and Buller, P. F. (1987). User acceptance of peer appraisals in an industrial setting. *Personnel Psychology* 40, pp. 785–787.

58. Dierdorff, E. C., and Surface, E. A. (2007). Placing peer ratings in context: Systematic influences beyond ratee performance. *Personnel Psychology* 60, pp. 93–126.

59. Wells, 2009, op. cit. See also Reilly, R. R., Smither, J. W., and Vasilopoulos, N. L. (1996). A longitudinal study of upward feedback. *Personnel Psychology* 49, pp. 599–612. See also Smither, J. W., London, M., Vasilopoulos, N. L., Reilly, R. R., Millsap, R., and Salvemini, N. (1995). An examination of the effects of an upward feedback program over time. *Personnel Psychology* 48, pp. 1–34.

60. Greguras, G. J., Robie, C., Schleicher, D. J., and Goff, M. (2003). A field study of the effects of rating purpose on the quality of multisource ratings. *Personnel Psychology* 56, pp. 1–21.

61. Walker, A. G., and Smither, J. W. (1999). A five-year study of upward feedback: What managers do with their results matters. *Personnel Psychology* 52, pp. 393–423.

62. Antonioni, D. (1994). The effects of feedback accountability on upward appraisal ratings. *Personnel Psychology* 47, pp. 249–256.

63. Maurer, T. J., Raju, N. S., and Collins, W. C. (1998). Peer and subordinate performance appraisal measurement equivalence. *Journal of Applied Psychology* 83, pp. 693–702.

64. Campbell, D. J., and Lee, C. (1988). Self-appraisal in performance evaluation: Development versus evaluation. *Academy of Management Review* 13, pp. 302–314.

65. van Hooft, E. A. J., van der Flier, H., and Minne, M. R. (2006). Construct validity of multi-source performance ratings: An examination of the relationship of self-, supervisor-, and peer-ratings with cognitive and personality measures. *International Journal of Selection and Assessment* 14, pp. 67–81. See also Atkins, P. W. B., and Wood, R. E. (2002). Self- versus others' ratings as predictors of assessment center ratings: Validation evidence for 360-degree feedback programs. *Personnel Psychology* 55, pp. 871–904. See also Cheung, G. W. (1999). Multifaceted conceptions of self-other ratings disagreement. *Personnel Psychology* 52, pp. 1–36. See also Harris, M., and Schaubroeck, J. (1988). A meta-analysis of self-supervisory, self-peer, and peer-supervisory ratings. *Personnel Psychology* 41, pp. 43–62.

66. King, J. F. (2008). How managers think: Why the mediated model makes sense. *Industrial and Organizational Psychology* 1, pp. 180–182.

67. Barron, L. G., and Sackett, P. R. (2008). Asian variability in performance-rating modesty and leniency bias. *Human Performance* 21, pp. 277–290. See also Yu, J., and Murphy, K. R. (1993). Modesty bias in self-ratings of performance: A test of the cultural relativity hypothesis. *Personnel Psychology* 46, pp. 357–363. But see also Farh, J. L., Dobbins, G. H., and Cheng, B. S. (1991). Cultural relativity in action: A comparison of self-ratings made by Chinese and U.S. workers. *Personnel Psychology* 44, pp. 129–147.

68. Ulrich, D. (1989, Summer). Tie the corporate knot: Gaining complete customer commitment. *Sloan Management Review* 10(4), pp. 19–27, 63.

69. McGregor, J. (2009, March 30). Job review in 140 keystrokes. *BusinessWeek*, p. 58.

70. Makiney, J. D., and Levy, P. E. (1998). The influence of self-ratings versus peer ratings on supervisors' performance judgments. *Organizational Behavior & Human Decision Processes* 74, pp. 212–222.

71. Uggerslev, K. L., and Sulsky, L. M. (2002). Presentation modality and indirect performance information: Effects on ratings, reactions, and memory. *Journal of Applied Psychology* 87, pp. 940–950.

72. Ibid. See also Martell, R. F., and Leavitt, K. N. (2002). Reducing the performance-cue bias in work behavior ratings: Can groups help? *Journal of Applied Psychology* 87, pp. 1032–1041.

73. Murphy, K. R. (2008a). Perspectives on the relationship between job performance and ratings of job performance. *Industrial and Organizational Psychology* 1, pp. 197–205. See also Harris, M. M., Ispas, D., and Schmidt, G. F. (2008). Inaccurate performance ratings are a reflection of larger organizational issues. *Industrial and Organizational Psychology* 1, pp. 190–193.

74. Waldman, D., and Atwater, L. E. (1998). *The Power of 360-Degree Feedback: How to Leverage Performance Evaluations for Top Productivity.* Houston: Gulf Publishing. See also Borman, W. C. (1997). 360-degree ratings: An analysis of assumptions and a research agenda for assessing their validity. *Human Resource Management Review* 7, pp. 299–315.

75. Conway, J. M., and Huffcutt, A. I. (1997). Psychometric properties of multisource performance ratings: A meta-analysis of subordinate, supervisor, peer, and self-ratings. *Human Performance* 10, pp. 331–360.

76. Ones et al., 2008, op. cit. See also Facteua, J. D., and Craig, S. B. (2001). Are performance appraisal ratings from different rating sources comparable? *Journal of Applied Psychology* 86, pp. 215–227.

77. Smither, J. W., London, M., and Reilly, R. R. (2005). Does performance improve following multisource feedback? A theoretical model, meta-analysis, and review of empirical findings. *Personnel Psychology* 58, pp. 33–66.

78. DeNisi and Sonesh, 2011, op. cit. See also DeNisi, A. S., and Kluger, A. N. (2000). Feedback effectiveness: Can 360-degree appraisals be improved? *Academy of Management Executive* 14(1), pp. 129–139.

79. Toegel, G., and Conger, J. A. (2003). 360-degree assessment: Time for reinvention. *Academy of Management Learning & Education* 2, pp. 297–311.

80. Ghorpade, J. (2000). Managing the five paradoxes of 360-degree feedback. *Academy of Management Executive* 14(1), pp. 140–150. See also Waldman, D. A., Atwater, L. E., and Antonioni, D. (1998). Has a 360-degree feedback gone amok? *Academy of Management Executive* 12(2), pp. 86–94.

81. Becton, J. B., and Schraeder, M. (2004). Participant input into rater selection: Potential effects on the quality and acceptance of ratings in the context of 360-degree feedback. *Public Personnel Management* 33, pp. 23–32.

82. Luthans, F., and Peterson, S. J. (2003). 360-degree feedback with systematic coaching: Empirical analysis suggests a winning combination. *Human Resource Management* 42, pp. 243–256.

83. Bailey, C., and Austin, M. (2006). 360-degree feedback and developmental outcomes: The role of feedback characteristics, self-efficacy and importance of feedback dimensions to focal managers' current role. *International Journal of Selection and Assessment* 14, pp. 51–66.

84. Morgan, A., Cannan, K., and Cullinane, J. (2005). 360-degree feedback: A critical enquiry. *Personnel Review* 34, pp. 663–680. See also Kozlowski, S. W. J., Chao, G. T., and Morrison, R. F. (1998). Games raters play. In J. W. Smither (Ed.), *Performance Appraisal: State of the Art in Practice*. San Francisco: Jossey-Bass, pp. 163–205. See also Mount, M. K., Judge, T. A., Scullen, S. E., Sytsma, M. R., and Hezlett, S. A. (1998). Trait, rater, and level effects in 360-degree performance ratings. *Personnel Psychology* 51, pp. 557–576.

85. Davis, S., and Nosal, D. (2010, Aug. 6). Companies reinvent their workforce, talent management systems. Retrieved from *www.shrm.org/hrdisciplines/orgempdev/articles/Pages/ReinventTheWorkforce.aspx* on July 21, 2011.

86. Bailey and Austin, 2006, op. cit.

87. Aguinis, 2009, op. cit. See also Meyer et al., 1965, op. cit.

88. Aguinis, 2009, op. cit.

89. DeNisi and Sonesh, 2011, op. cit. See also Fisher, C. D. (2008). What if we took within-person performance variability seriously? *Industrial and Organizational Psychology* 1, pp. 185–189. See also Mount, M. K., and Thompson, D. E. (1987). Cognitive categorization and quality of performance ratings. *Journal of Applied Psychology* 72, pp. 240–246.

90. Hogan, E. A. (1987). Effects of prior expectations on performance ratings: A longitudinal study. *Academy of Management Journal* 30, pp. 354–368.

91. McGregor, 2009, op. cit. Welch, J., and Welch. S. (2009, March 16). An employee bill of rights. *BusinessWeek*, p. 72.

92. White-collar workers shoulder together—Like it or not. (2008, Apr. 28). *BusinessWeek,* p. 58. See also LaFasto, F. M., and Larson, EC. E. (2001). *When Teams Work Best: 6,000 Team Members and Leaders Tell What It Takes to Succeed.* Thousand Oaks, CA: Sage.

93. Hackman, J. R. (1998). Why teams don't work. In R. S. Tindale and L. Heath (Eds.), *Theory and Research on Small Groups*. New York: Plenum Press, pp. 245–267.

94. Useem, J. (2006, June 12). What's that spell? Teamwork! *Fortune,* pp. 65, 66. See also Hochman, P. (2006, June 12). Pack mentality. *Fortune,* pp. 145–151. See also Naquin, C. E., and Tynan, R. O. (2003). The team halo effect: Why teams are not blamed for their failures. *Journal of Applied Psychology* 88, pp. 332–340.

95. Scott, S. G., and Einstein, W. O. (2001). Strategic performance appraisal in team-based organizations: One size does not fit all. *Academy of Management Executive* 15, pp. 107–116.

96. Fox, A. (2010, Dec.). Taking up slack. *HR Magazine* 55(12), pp. 26–31. See also Heneman, R. L., and von Hippel, C. (1995). Balancing individual and group rewards: Rewarding individual contributions to the team. *Compensation and Benefits Review* 27, pp. 745–759.

97. Cannon-Bowers, J. A., and Bowers, C. (2011). Team development and functioning. In S. Zedeck (Ed.), *APA Handbook of Industrial and Organizational Psychology,* Vol. 1. Washington, DC: American Psychological Association, pp. 597–650. See also Reilly, R. R., and McGourty, J. (1998). Performance appraisal in team settings. In J. W. Smither (Ed.), *Performance Appraisal: State of the Art in Practice.* San Francisco: Jossey-Bass, pp. 244–277.

98. Scott and Einstein, 2001, op. cit.

99. Ibid.

100. DeNisi and Sonesh, 2011, op. cit. See also Naquin and Tynan, 2003, op. cit.

101. Murphy, 2008a, op. cit. See also Varma, A., DeNisi, A. S., and Peters, L. M. (1996). Interpersonal affect and performance appraisal: A field study. *Personnel Psychology* 49, pp. 341–360.

102. Ones et al., 2008, op. cit. See also Guion, R. M. (1998). *Assessment, Measurement, and Prediction for Personnel Decisions.* Mahwah, NJ: Lawrence Erlbaum.

103. Murphy, K. R., Jako, R. A., and Anhalt, R. L. (1993). Nature and consequences of halo error: A critical analysis. *Journal of Applied Psychology* 78, pp. 218–225.

104. Murphy, K. R., and Anhalt, R. L. (1992). Is halo error a property of the rater, ratees, or the specific behavior observed? *Journal of Applied Psychology* 77, pp. 494–500.

105. Cascio and Aguinis, 2011, op. cit. See also Balzer, W. K., and Sulsky, L. M. (1992). Halo and performance appraisal research: A critical examination. *Journal of Applied Psychology* 77, pp. 975–985.

106. Sumer, H. C., and Knight, P. A. (1996). Assimilation and contrast effects in performance ratings: Effects of rating the previous performance on rating subsequent performance. *Journal of Applied Psychology* 81, pp. 436–442. See also Maurer, T. J., Palmer, J. K., and Ashe, D. K. (1993). Diaries, checklists, evaluations, and contrast effects in the measurement of behavior. *Journal of Applied Psychology* 78, pp. 226–231.

107. Longenecker, C. O., and Gioia, D. A. (1994, Winter). Delving into the dark side: The politics of executive appraisal. *Organizational Dynamics,* pp. 47–58. See also Fox, 2009, op. cit.

108. Bernthal et al., 2003, op. cit.

109. Pulakos, E. D. (2004). *Effective Practice Guidelines for Performance Management.* Unpublished manuscript. Alexandria, VA: Society for Human Resource Management Foundation.

110. Bernardin, H. J., and Buckley, M. R. (1981). A consideration of strategies in rater training. *Academy of Management Review* 6, pp. 205–212.

111. Dierdorff, E. C., Surface, E. A., and Brown, K. G. (2010). Frame-of-reference training effectiveness: Effects of goal orientation and self-efficacy on affective, cognitive, skill-based, and transfer outcomes. *Journal of Applied Psychology* 95, pp. 1181–1191. See also Woehr, D. J., and Huffcutt, A. I. (1994). Rater training for performance appraisal: A quantitative review. *Journal of Occupational and Organizational Psychology* 67, pp. 189–205.

**112.** Noonan, L. E., and Sulsky, L. M. (2001). Impact of frame-of-reference and behavioral observation training on alternative training effectiveness criteria in a Canadian military sample. *Human Performance* 14, pp. 3–26.

**113.** Pulakos, E. D. (1984). A comparison of rater training programs: Error training and accuracy training. *Journal of Applied Psychology* 69, pp. 581–588. See also Pulakos, E. D. (1986). The development of training programs to increase accuracy with different rating tasks. *Organizational Behavior and Human Decision Processes* 38, pp. 76–91.

**114.** Fox, 2009, op. cit. See also King, 2008, op. cit. See also Sulsky, L. M., and Day, D. V. (1992). Frame-of-reference training and cognitive categorization: An empirical investigation of rater memory issues. *Journal of Applied Psychology* 77, pp. 501–510.

**115.** Sanchez, J. I., and DeLaTorre, P. (1996). A second look at the relationship between rating and behavioral accuracy in performance appraisal. *Journal of Applied Psychology* 81, pp. 3–10. See also Day, D. V., and Sulsky, L. M. (1995). Effects of frame-of-reference training and information configuration on memory organization and rating accuracy. *Journal of Applied Psychology* 80, pp. 159–167.

**116.** Fox, 2009, op. cit. See also London, M. (2003). *Job Feedback: Giving, Seeking, and Using Feedback for Performance Improvement* (2nd Ed.). Mahwah, NJ: Lawrence Erlbaum.

**117.** Murphy, K. R., and Cleveland, J. N. (1995). *Understanding Performance Appraisal: Social, Organizational, and Goal-Based Perspectives.* Thousand Oaks, CA: Sage.

**118.** Wexley, K. N., Singh, V. P., and Yukl, G. A. (1973). Subordinate participation in three types of appraisal interviews. *Journal of Applied Psychology* 58, pp. 54–57.

**119.** Fox, 2009, op. cit. See also Sandberg, 2007, op. cit. See also Schellhardt, T. D. (1996, Nov. 19). Annual agony: It's time to evaluate your work and all involved are groaning. *The Wall Street Journal,* pp. A1, A5.

**120.** Pulakos and O'Leary, 2011, op. cit. See also Sulkowicz, 2007, op. cit. See also McGregor, 2006, op. cit. See also Meyer, H. H. (1991). A solution to the performance appraisal feedback enigma. *Academy of Management Executive* 5(1), pp. 68–76. See also Cederblom, D. (1982). The performance appraisal interview: A review, implications, and suggestions. *Academy of Management Review* 7, pp. 219–227.

**121.** Ilgen, D. R., Mitchell, T. R., and Frederickson, J. W. (1981). Poor performers: Supervisors' and subordinates' responses. *Organizational Behavior and Human Performance* 27, pp. 386–410.

**122.** Wohlers, A. J., and London, M. (1989). Ratings of managerial characteristics: Evaluation, difficulty, co-worker agreement, and self-awareness. *Personnel Psychology* 42, pp. 235–261.

**123.** Cawley et al., 1998, op. cit.

**124.** Ibid.

**125.** Dulebohn, J. H., and Ferris, G. R. (1999). The role of influence tactics in perceptions of performance evaluations' fairness. *Academy of Management Journal* 42, pp. 288–303. See also Nathan, B. R., Mohrman, A. M., Jr., and Milliman, J. (1991). Interpersonal relations as a context for the effects of appraisal interviews on performance and satisfaction: A longitudinal study. *Academy of Management Journal* 34(2), pp. 352–369.

**126.** Dorfman, P. W., Stephan, W. G., and Loveland, J. (1986). Performance appraisal behaviors: Supervisor perceptions and subordinate reactions. *Personnel Psychology* 39, pp. 579–597.

**127.** DeNisi, A. S., and Kluger, A. N. (2000). Feedback effectiveness: Can 360-degree appraisals be improved? *Academy of Management Executive* 14, pp. 129–139.

**128.** Ibid.

129. Latham, 2009, op. cit. Landy, F. J., Barnes-Farrell, J., and Cleveland, J. N. (1980). Perceived fairness and accuracy of performance evaluation: A follow-up. *Journal of Applied Psychology* 65, pp. 355–356.

130. Sulkowicz, 2007, op. cit. See also Baron, R. A. (1988). Negative effects of destructive criticism: Impact on conflict, self-efficacy, and task performance. *Journal of Applied Psychology* 73, pp. 199–207.

131. Latham, 2009, op. cit. See also Locke and Latham, 2002, op. cit. See also Locke and Latham, 1990, op. cit.

132. O'Leary and Pulakos, 2011, op. cit. See also Hymowitz, 2007, op. cit. See also Judge, T. A., and Ferris, G. R. (1993). Social context of performance evaluation decisions. *Academy of Management Journal* 36, pp. 80–105.

133. Latham, 2009, op. cit. See also Lawler, 2003, op. cit. See also Burke, R. S., Wertzel, W., and Weir, T. (1978). Characteristics of effective employee performance review and development interviews: Replication and extension. *Personnel Psychology* 31, pp. 903–919.

134. Grossman, 2010, op. cit.

# 10

# MANAGING CAREERS

## Questions This Chapter Will Help Managers Answer

1.  What strategies might employees use to self-manage their careers?
2.  What can supervisors do to improve their management of dual-career couples?
3.  Why are the characteristics and environment of an employee's first job so important?
4.  What strategies are available for dealing with plateaued workers?
5.  What steps can managers take to do a better job of responding to the special needs of workers in their early, middle, and late career stages?

# SELF-RELIANCE: KEY TO CAREER MANAGEMENT*

Consider this stark fact: In today's corporate environment, you are ever more likely to crash into the ranks of the unemployed with no safety net, and it could happen over and over again. Moreover, candor about career issues is in short supply at many companies these days. Bottom line: Career survival is up to you—not the company. Consider yourself to be self-employed, responsible for your own career development, CEO of You Inc. This new approach is based on an underlying assumption that would have been considered heresy 10 or 20 years ago in the paternalistic "We'll take care of you" environments of many companies—self-reliance is now *the key* to career management.

This does not mean that everyone will be working as self-employed contractors, enhancing their marketability by changing jobs frequently, learning cutting-edge skills, and working as a roving gun-for-hire. According to recruiters, such a pattern of employment over a long time can actually be a detriment because it does not show any pattern of loyalty or any kind of stability—precisely the characteristics employers are looking for in today's workers.

In the past, many companies assumed responsibility for the career paths and growth of their employees. The company determined to what position, and at what speed, people would advance. That approach worked reasonably well in the corporate climate of the latter 20th century. However, the corporate disruptions of the last decade have rendered this approach to employee career development largely unworkable.

Acquisitions, divestitures, rapid growth, and massive downsizing of 8.5 million jobs in the United States, many of which are gone for good, have left many companies unable to deliver on the implicit career promises made to their employees. Organizations find themselves in the painful position of having to renege on career mobility opportunities their employees had come to expect. In extreme cases, employees who expected career growth no longer even have jobs! At the same time, attitudes about women's and men's work and family roles have changed significantly, such that both women and men recognize that work isn't everything. As a result, people in every industry are passing up opportunities for promotions so that they can have a life.

Increasingly, corporations have come to realize that they cannot win if they take total responsibility for the career development of their employees. No matter what happens, employees often blame top management or "the company" for their lack of career growth, and those who want to be top contributors at their current level often feel pressured to move up. That's a potentially lose–lose proposition for organizations and their employees.

---

*Source: For more information on the new approach to career self-management, see Feldman, A. (2010, March 8). The road to reinvention. *BusinessWeek,* pp. 68–70. See also Gurchiek, K. (2010, March 17). Recession alters relationship between employers, workers. *HR News,* Retrieved from *www.shrm.org/Publications/HRNews/Pages/RecessionAlters.aspx* on March 24, 2010. See also Galinsky, E., Aumann, K., and Bond, J. T. (2009). *Times Are Changing: Gender and Generation at Work and at Home.* New York, NY: Families & Work Institute. See also Guest, D., and Sturges, J. (2007). Living to work—working to live. In H. Gunz and M. Peiperl (Eds.), *Handbook of Career Studies.* Thousand Oaks, CA: Sage, pp. 310–326. See also Weber, J. (2007, May 14). Please don't promote me. *BusinessWeek,* p. 13.

## Characteristics of the New Approach

Although the primary and final responsibility for career development rests with each employee, the company has complementary responsibilities. The company is responsible for communicating to employees where it wants to go and how it plans to get there (the corporate strategy), providing employees with as much information about the business as possible, and responding to the career initiatives of employees with candid, complete information. One of the most important contributions a company can make to each employee's development is to provide him or her with honest performance feedback about current job performance. Employees, in turn, are responsible for knowing what their skills and capabilities are and what assistance they need from their employers, asking for that assistance, and preparing themselves to assume new responsibilities—if that is what they want. If not, then employees are responsible for communicating their intentions to their bosses. Career self-reliance, or career resilience, as we noted earlier, does not mean free agency. Rather, each individual needs to become an *informed opportunist,* combining accurate information with a flexible, opportunistic approach to his or her career.

This approach to career management can be summed up as follows: assign employees the responsibility for managing their own careers, then provide the support they need to do it. This support takes different forms in different companies but usually contains several core components—as we will see in the conclusion to this vignette.

### Challenges

1. Should employees be responsible for their own career development?
2. Is the new approach to corporate career management likely to be a passing fad, or is it here to stay?
3. What kinds of support mechanisms are necessary to make career self-management work?

As this chapter-opening vignette demonstrates, corporate career management has come a long way in the last several decades. This chapter presents a number of topics that have sparked this re-evaluation. We will consider the impact of mergers, acquisitions, and downsizing on corporate loyalty; the impact of dual-career couples on the career-management process; and the major issues that workers and managers must deal with during the early-, middle-, and late- career stages of the adult life cycle. Finally we will examine alternative patterns of career change: promotions, demotions, lateral transfers, relocations, layoffs, and retirements. Career management has many facets, both for the individual and for the organization. The chapter-opening vignette emphasized that in the new concept of career management the company and the employee are partners in career development. This chapter carries that theme. Let's begin by attempting to define the word *career.*

## TOWARD A DEFINITION OF *CAREER*

In everyday parlance, the word *career* is used in a number of different ways. People speak of "pursuing a career"; career planning workshops are common; colleges and universities hold "career days" during which they publicize jobs in different fields and assist individuals through "career counseling." A person may be characterized as a "career" woman or man who shops in a store that specializes in "career clothing." Likewise, a person may be characterized as a "career military officer." We may overhear a person say, "That movie made his career" (i.e., it enhanced his reputation) or in a derogatory tone, after a subordinate has insulted the CEO, "She can kiss her career good-bye" (i.e., she has tarnished her reputation). Finally, an angry supervisor may remark to her dawdling subordinate, "Watney, are you going to make a career out of finishing that project?"

As these examples illustrate, the word **career** can be viewed from a number of different perspectives. From one perspective, *a career is a sequence of positions occupied by a person during the course of a lifetime.* This is the *objective* career. From another perspective, though, *a career consists of a sense of where a person is going in his or her work life.* This is the *subjective* career, and it is held together by a self-concept that consists of (1) perceived talents and abilities, (2) basic values, and (3) career motives and needs.[1] Both of these perspectives, objective and subjective, focus on the individual. Both assume that people have some degree of control over their destinies and that they can manipulate opportunities in order to maximize the success and satisfaction derived from their careers.[2] They assume further that HR activities should recognize career stages and assist employees with the development tasks they face at each stage. Career planning is important because the consequences of career success or failure are linked closely to each individual's self-concept, identity, and satisfaction with career and life.

Given the downsizing mentality that has characterized most large organizations over the past decade, some firms have de-emphasized career development and planning as employees wondered if they would even have jobs, much less careers. Companies that ignore career issues are mistaken if they think those issues will somehow go away. They won't. Here are some reasons why:[3]

1. Rising concerns for quality of work life and for personal life planning.
2. Pressures to expand workforce diversity throughout all levels of an organization.
3. Growing needs of firms to retain workers at all levels.
4. Slow economic growth and reduced opportunities for advancement.

## PROACTIVE CAREER MANAGEMENT

A career is not something that should be left to chance; instead, in the evolving world of work, it should be shaped and managed more by the individual than by the organization.[4] Traditionally, careers tended to evolve in the context of one or two firms and to progress in linear stages, as workers moved upward through the hierarchy of positions in an organization. Today, given the disruptions caused by downsizing, restructuring, technological advancements, and global competition, careers span multiple organizations and they are distinctly nonlinear. They are *boundaryless* and tend to be characterized by features such as the following:[5]

- Portable knowledge, skills, and abilities across multiple firms.
- Personal identification with meaningful work.
- Massive downsizing from 2007 to 2010 that eroded employees' loyalty to employers.

- Distinct differences in the work patterns of men and women. Career goals tend to be the primary concerns of men. Women, on the other hand, tend to evaluate each career action in light of the impact such a decision may have on their relationships with others—children, spouses, aging parents, coworkers, and friends. Theirs are kaleidoscope careers in which they rotate different aspects of their lives to arrange their roles and relationships in new ways.
- Development of multiple networks of associates and peer-learning relationships.
- Responsibility for managing your own career.

The concept of a boundaryless career raises an interesting question, namely, what is the meaning of "career success"?

## Toward a Definition of *Career Success*

The tradition-oriented "organization man" of the 1950s had a clear definition of success and a stable model for achieving it. However, massive changes in the business environment have forced employees at all levels to explore alternative models of **career success,** and they are confronted with a variety of possibilities.[6] Is it occupational success? Job satisfaction? Growth and development of skills? Successful movement through various life stages? Traditionally, career development and success have been defined in terms of occupational advancement, which is clear and easy to measure. Today, however, it seems appropriate to consider a new model as more careers tend to be cyclical in nature. That is, they involve periodic cycles of skill apprenticeship, mastery, and reskilling. Lateral, rather than upward, movement often constitutes career development, and cross-functional experience is essential to multiskilling and continued employability. Late careers increasingly are defined in terms of phased retirement.[7] In this new world, the ultimate goal is *psychological success,* the feeling of pride and personal accomplishment that comes from achieving your most important goals in life, be they career achievement, family happiness, inner peace, or something else.[8] The following section examines career management in more detail; by way of background to this, let's consider the adult life-cycle stages.

## Adult Life-Cycle Stages

For years, researchers have attempted to identify the major developmental tasks that employees face during their working lives and to organize these tasks into broader career stages (such as early, middle, and late career).[9] Although a number of models have been proposed, very little research has tested their accuracy. Moreover, there is little, if any, agreement about whether career stages are linked to age or not. Most theorists give age ranges for each stage, but these vary widely. Rather than a linear life path of "I went to school, got a job, and then retired," experts find that today people tend to go back and forth. They go to school, they work, they go back to school, retire, and decide to go back to school and go back into the workforce again.[10]

Such a *blended life course* allows for differences in the number of distinct stages through which individuals may pass, the overlapping tasks and issues they may face at each stage, and the role of transition periods between stages. The lesson for managers is that all models of adult life-cycle stages should be viewed as broad guidelines rather than as exact representations of reality.

## MERGERS, ACQUISITIONS, RESTRUCTURINGS, AND THE DEMISE OF CORPORATE LOYALTY

Every year there are thousands of mergers and acquisitions, totaling trillions of dollars worldwide.[a] While deals are typically done for financial reasons (assets, portfolios, business synergies), they often fail because of a lack of "human due diligence"—understanding the culture of an organization, the roles that individuals play, and the capabilities and attitudes of its people.[b] The restructuring that frequently follows, including downsizing, regularly leads to diminished loyalty from employees. In the wave of takeovers, mergers, downsizings, and layoffs, thousands of workers have discovered that years of service mean little to a struggling management or a new corporate parent. This leads to a rise in stress and a decrease in satisfaction, commitment, intentions to stay, and perceptions of an organization's trustworthiness, honesty, and caring about its employees.[c]

Companies counter that today's competitive business environment makes it difficult to protect workers. Understandably, organizations are streamlining in order to become more competitive by cutting labor costs and to become more flexible in their response to the demands of the marketplace. But the rising disaffection of workers at all levels has profound implications for employers.

Every year U.S. companies create and destroy more than 20 percent of their jobs.[d] Median years of tenure on the job is only 3.1 for workers ages 25 to 34, but 10.4 for those ages 55 to 64.[e] Furthermore, employee turnover is expensive. Merck found that it costs as much as 1.5 to 2.5 times a worker's annual salary, when separation, replacement, and training costs are considered.[f] The average worker goes through about nine jobs by age 32, and 10 percent of the American workforce actually switches occupations every year![g] Yet there is hope, as companies such as Southwest Airlines, Aflac Insurance, and Cisco Systems recognize an opportunity to create value in the midst of such turmoil. How? By understanding that they can only retain loyal customers with a base of loyal employees.[h] Decreasing defection rates of customers, employees, and investors can lead to substantial growth, profits, and lasting value. That's a win–win for all concerned.

---

[a]Cascio, W. F. (2010, Oct.). Done deal: Now manage the postmerger integration. *HR Magazine* 55(10), pp. 42–46. See also Marks, M. L., and Mirvis, P. H. (2010). *Joining Forces* (2nd ed.). San Francisco: Jossey-Bass.

[b]Ibid. See also Harding, D., and Rouse, T. (2007, Oct. 2). Human due diligence. *The Wall Street Journal,* p. A16.

[c]Cascio, W. F. (2010). Employment downsizing and its alternatives: Strategies for long-term success. Alexandria, VA: Society for Human Resource Management Foundation. See also Cascio, W. F. (2009). Downsizing and redundancy. In A. Wilkinson, N. Bacon, T. Redman, and S. Snell (Eds.), *Sage Handbook of Human Resource Management.* London, UK: Sage, pp. 336–348. See also Cascio, W. F. (2002). *Responsible Restructuring: Creative and Profitable Alternatives to Layoffs.* San Francisco: Jossey-Bass.

[d]The myth of job security. (2005, Sept. 12). *Infoworld,* p. 64.

[e]Bureau of Labor Statistics. Median years of tenure with current employer for employed wage and salary workers by age and sex, selected years, 1996–2010. Retrieved from *www.bls.gov/news.release/tenure.t01.htm* on July 28, 2011.

[f]For more on this, see Cascio, W. F., and Boudreau, J. W. (2011). *Investing in People: Impact of Human Resource Initiatives* (2nd Ed.). Upper Saddle River, NJ: Pearson.

[g]Daniels, C., and Vinzant, C. (2000, Feb. 7). The joy of quitting. *Fortune,* pp. 199–02. See also Henkoff, R. (1996, Jan. 15). So, you want to change your job. *Fortune,* pp. 52–56.

[h]Gerdes, L. (2009, Sept. 14). The best places to launch a career. *BusinessWeek,* pp. 32–41. See also White, J. B., and Lublin, J. S. (1996, Sept. 27). Some companies try to rebuild loyalty. *The Wall Street Journal,* pp. B1, B2.

## CAREER MANAGEMENT: INDIVIDUALS FOCUSING ON THEMSELVES

In thinking about career management, it is important to emphasize the increasingly *temporary* relationships between individuals and organizations. Said a victim of three corporate downsizings in four years: "A job is just an opportunity to learn new skills that you can then peddle elsewhere in the marketplace."[11] While such a view might appear cynical to some, the fact is that responsibility for career development ultimately belongs to each individual. Unfortunately, few individuals are technically prepared—and willing—to handle this assignment. This is not surprising, for very few college programs specifically address the problems of managing one's own career. However, as long as it remains difficult for organizations to match the career expectations of their employees (a following section shows actual corporate examples of this), one option for employees will be to switch organizations. Guidelines for doing this fall into the following three major categories.[12]

### Selecting a Field of Employment and an Employer

1. You cannot manage your career unless you have a macro, long-range objective. The first step, therefore, is to think in terms of where you ultimately want to be, recognizing, of course, that your career goals will change over time.
2. View every potential employer and position in terms of your long-range career goal. That is, how well does this job serve to position me in terms of my ultimate objective? For example, if you aspire to reach senior management by the year 2017, consider the extent to which your current job helps you practice critical thinking, develop public-speaking skills, practice the "bring out the best in people" leadership style, and demonstrate collaboration and team-building skills. These are now, and will continue to be, key requirements for such senior positions.[13]
3. Accept short-term trade-offs for long-term benefits. Certain lateral moves or low-paying jobs can provide extremely valuable training opportunities or career contacts.
4. Consider carefully whether to accept highly specialized jobs or isolated job assignments that might restrict or impede your visibility and career development.

### Knowing Where You Are

1. Always be aware of opportunities available to you in your current position—for example, training programs that might further your career development.
2. Carefully and honestly assess your current performance. How do you see yourself, and how do you think higher management sees your performance? Ask yourself, "Am I in the right job? Are my skills of real value to my organization, and does this organization help me fulfill my life's goals and values? What other positions might fit my needs and skills well?"[14]
3. Try to recognize when you and your organization have outlived your utility for each other. This is not an admission of failure, but rather an honest reflection of the fact that there is little more the organization can do for you and, in turn, that your contribution to the organization has reached a point of diminishing returns.

Here are five important symptoms: Your job ranks low on a "joy and meaning" scale; requests for advancement or new opportunities are ignored consistently or only half met; the job doesn't adequately meet your needs in areas you care about, such as work-life fit, work location, and compensation; your standing in the office has been diminished—for example, key clients or vendors no longer deal with you; or you are not fulfilling your dreams.[15]

### Planning Your Exit

1. Try to leave at your convenience, not the organization's. To do this, you must do two things well: (a) know when it is time to leave (as before), and (b) since downsizing can come at any time, establish networking relationships while you still have a job.[16]
2. Leave your current organization on good terms and not under questionable circumstances.
3. Don't leave your current job until you've landed another one; it's easier to find a new job when you're currently employed. Like bank loans, jobs often go to people who don't seem to need them.

### The Role of the Organization

Up to this point it may sound as though managing your career is all one-sided. This is not true; the organization should be a proactive force in this process. To do so, organizations must think and plan in terms of shorter employment relationships. This can be done, for example, at the time of hire, by granting all employees stock that they earn over time (e.g., 25 percent per year).

A second strategy for organizations is to invest adequate time and energy in job design and equipment. Given that mobility among workers is expected to increase, careful attention to these elements will make it easier to make replacements fully productive as soon as possible. Perhaps the most persuasive reason for helping employees manage their own careers is the need to remain competitive. Although it might seem like a contradiction, such efforts can enhance a company's stability by developing more purposeful, self-assured employees. As noted earlier, today's employees are more difficult to manage. Companies that recognize the need to provide employees with satisfying opportunities will have the decided advantage of a loyal and industrious workforce.

### Dual-Career Couples: Problems and Opportunities

One of the most challenging career management problems organizations face today is that of the dual-career couple. Let's examine this issue in detail.

Today, families in which both parents are working comprise 79 percent of married couples with children.[17] In fact, dual-career couples now comprise 47.8 percent of the workforce,[18] and they face the problems of managing work and family responsibilities. Furthermore, it appears that there may be an interaction effect that compounds the problems and stresses of each separate career.[19] This implies that, by itself, career planning and development may be meaningless unless an employee's role as a family member also is considered, particularly when this role conflicts with work activities. What can be done?

Research indicates that if dual-career couples are to manage their family responsibilities successfully, they (and their managers) must be flexible; they must be mutually committed to both careers; and they must develop the competencies to manage their careers through planning, goal setting, and problem solving.[20]

From an organizational perspective, successful management of the dual-career couple includes flexible work schedules and company-supported child care. It also includes customized career paths that include elements such as the ability to turn down advancement and be offered it again in the future, the ability to move laterally for development, the ability to turn down relocation and be asked again in the future, and the ability to specialize in one area of the organization.[21] Evidence across a wide array of industries indicates that some firms are more responsive to work-family issues than others. Firms are more likely to offer such benefits when work and family issues are prominent and important to senior HR executives and the executives believe that failure to offer the benefits will detract from the ability of the organization to perform well in the marketplace.[22]

---

**HR BUZZ**

## BOTTOM-LINE BENEFITS FOR FAMILY-FRIENDLY COMPANIES*

Companies that truly "get it" actually go farther and integrate family-support mechanisms into the business itself. Thus, Hewlett-Packard requires that every business unit identify work-family issues and propose an action plan as part of its annual business review. Lost Arrow Corporation, the Ventura, California, maker of Patagonia apparel and sporting goods, opened its onsite facility for employees' children in 1984. Today it spends about $530,000 a year on familyfriendly benefits. In return, it captures more than $190,000 in federal and state tax breaks, and it saves an estimated $350,000 in costs associated with recruiting, training, and productivity because its family-friendly approach helps hold turnover below the average for apparel manufacturers. Citigroup owns or participates in 12 child-care centers in the United States. Employees pay about half the cost to use Citigroup facilities managed by Bright Horizons Family Solutions or at non-Citigroup back-up centers. In two follow-up studies, Citigroup found the following:

- A 51 percent reduction in turnover among center users compared to non-center users.
- An 18 percent reduction in absenteeism.
- A 98 percent retention rate of top performers.

Finally, Canadian financial services giant CIBC offers onsite back-up child care in 14 Canadian cities. Employees can take advantage of the program for up to 20 days per year at no cost to them. The company's net savings total more than 6,800 employee days since the first facility opened in 2002. Just as important, however, the program is a big winner with CIBC's workers. Bottom line: Work-family strategies haven't just hit the corporate mainstream—they've become a competitive advantage.

---

\**Sources:* Cascio, W. F., and Boudreau, J. W. (2011). *Investing in People* (2nd Ed.). Upper Saddle River, NJ: Pearson. See also O'Connell, B. (2005, May). No baby sitter? Emergency child care to the rescue. *Compensation & Benefits Forum.* Retrieved from *www.shrm.org/hrdisciplines/benefits/Articles/Pages/ CMS_012518.aspx* on July 7, 2008. See also Demby, E. R. (2004, Jan.). Do your family-friendly programs make sense? *HR Magazine,* pp. 75–78. See also Perry-Smith, J. E., and Blum, T. C. (2000). Work-family human resource bundles and perceived organizational performance. *Academy of Management Journal* 43, pp. 1107–1117.

For all the talk about family-friendly policies, however, only 11 percent of companies that operate during daytime hours provide child care, while another 20 percent offer resources and referrals. However, less than 1 percent of companies offer child care for parents working outside regular hours.[23] Yet demand for the service has never been greater. In 36 states, the cost of center-based care for an infant exceeds 10 percent of median income for a married couple, and in 40 states the average annual cost for an infant in center-based care is higher than a year's tuition and fees at a four-year public college.[24] Here are some reasons employer-supported child care will continue to grow:

- Dual-career couples now comprise a preponderance of the workforce.
- There has been a significant rise in the number of single parents, more than half of whom use child-care facilities.[25]
- More and more, career-oriented women are arranging their lives to include motherhood *and* professional goals. After all, about 75 percent of the 68 million working women in the U.S. will become pregnant, with three-quarters of those returning to work.[26]

Employer-sponsored dependent care is no longer limited just to onsite or near-site child-care centers, however. The concept has expanded to include elder care, intergenerational care, sick-child care, and programs for school-age children (before and after school, as well as holiday programs). Other variations include centers located in office and industrial parks for use by all tenants and centers sponsored by networks of businesses.[27]

Data from a national random sample indicate that *providing family benefits promotes a dedicated, loyal workforce among people who benefit directly from the policies, as well as from those who do not.*[28] However, the lesson from two other studies is clear: Don't expect that a day-care center or a flexible schedule will keep women managers from leaving corporations. They may be quite willing to throw corporate loyalty to the wind if they aren't getting adequate opportunities for career growth and job satisfaction.[29]

Managing dual-career couples, from an individual as well as from an organizational perspective, is difficult. But if current conditions are any indication of long-term trends, we can be quite sure of one thing: This "problem" is not going to go away.

## CAREER MANAGEMENT: ORGANIZATIONS FOCUSING ON INDIVIDUALS

In this section we examine current organizational practices used to manage workers at various stages of their careers. Let's begin by considering organizational entry.

### Organizational Entry

Once a person has entered the workforce, the next stage is to enter a specific organization, to settle down, and to begin establishing a career there. **Organizational entry** refers to the process of "moving inside," or becoming more involved in a particular organization.[30] To do this well, a longitudinal process known as socialization or on-boarding (see Chapter 8) is essential. **Socialization** helps a newcomer to transition from an outsider to an effective and integrated insider. Learning organizational policies, norms, traditions, and values is an important part of the process. Getting to know your peers, supervisor, and subordinates is, also. All of this enhances the newcomer's commitment, job satisfaction, job performance, and desire for personal control.[31] Because most turnover occurs early in a person's tenure with an organization, programs that accelerate socialization will tend also to reduce early turnover (i.e., at entry) and therefore reduce a company's overall turnover rate. At Cisco Systems, for example, when young hires come onboard, they get to choose which department they'll join and which manager they'll work for. After a weeklong overview of the company and a week of presentations from managers at more than 30 business units, the Cisco Choice program kicks in. Then the new hires spend a final week meeting with the managers and employees in each of their five favorite business units. Each employee then selects his or her top three managers and awaits placement. Since its inception in 2006, more than 2,500 new hires, mostly engineering grads, have completed Cisco Choice. Of these, 98 percent were still with the company after two years. That's an astonishing retention rate for Gen Yers in their first jobs.[32]

## Mentoring

A **mentor** is a teacher, an advisor, a sponsor, and a confidant.[33] He or she should be bright and well-seasoned enough to understand the dynamics of power and politics in the organization and also be willing to share this knowledge with one or more new hires. Indeed, to overcome the potential problems associated with one-on-one, male-female mentoring relationships, some firms have established "quad squads" that consist of a mentor plus three new hires: a male, a female, and one other member of a protected group. Bank of America is typical. It assigns mentors to three or four promising young executives for a year at a time. There are also benefits for the mentor. For example, just being chosen as a mentor, according to one 35-year-old female branch bank manager, boosted her self-esteem. Another was deeply touched when a fledgling coworker left the following note on her desk: "I will carry your lessons with me throughout my life."

Does mentoring pay off? A recent study at Sun Microsystems (now part of Oracle) found that mentors were promoted six times more often, and protégés were promoted five times more often than those not in the program.[34]

Mentors matter. Evidence indicates that a new employee's satisfaction with the mentoring relationship has a greater impact on job and career attitudes than whether the mentoring was formal or informal.[35] Conversely, bad mentoring may be destructive and worse than no mentoring at all.[36]

The mentor's role is to be a culture carrier, to teach new hires the ropes, to provide candid feedback on how they are being perceived by others, and to serve as a confidential sounding board for dealing with work-related problems. If successful, mentor relationships can help reduce the inflated expectations that newcomers often have about organizations, can relieve the stress experienced by all new hires, and, best of all, can improve the newcomer's chances for survival and growth in the organization.[37]

Companies like General Electric and employment agency Randstad USA use **reverse mentoring,** in which older managers meet with younger subordinates to learn about new technology and electronic commerce. It's a win–win

## ETHICAL DILEMMA
### Bringing Mentors and Protégés Together

Research has revealed that informal mentorships (spontaneous relationships that occur without involvement from the organization) lead to more positive career outcomes than do formal mentorships (programs that are managed and sanctioned by the organization).[a] Random assignment of protégés to mentors is like a blind date—there is only a small chance that the match will be successful. On the other hand, not all new hires are willing or able actively to seek out opportunities to work with a mentor. For those who do not, is it ethically acceptable to assign them randomly to mentors, or to let them sink or

swim, perhaps by finding their way to networks of like-minded professionals?[b] How would you advise an organization faced with this dilemma to proceed?

[a]Eby, 2011, op. cit. See also Ragins, B. R., and Cotton, J. L. (1999). Mentor functions and outcomes: A comparison of men and women in formal and informal mentoring relationships. *Journal of Psychology* 84, pp. 529–550. See also Chao, G. T., Walz, P. M., and Gardner, P. D. (1992). Formal and informal mentorships: A comparison of mentoring functions and contrast with non-mentored counterparts. *Personnel Psychology* 45, pp. 619–636.

[b]Brady, D., and McGregor, J. (2007, June 18). What works in women's networks. *BusinessWeek,* pp. 58, 59.

for both parties, and both are expected to teach each other. One 27-year-old mentor said the sessions made her more comfortable in dealing with her 54-year-old boss. "I can teach him things. . . . I know things he doesn't know." At the same time, she gets to observe first-hand the skills a manager needs to run a big operation, such as the ability to communicate with lots of different people.[38]

Thus far we have assumed that a mentor is a single individual. Yet forces such as rapidly changing technology, shifting organizational structures, and global marketplace dynamics have transformed mentoring into a process that often extends beyond the services of a single mentor. Group mentoring through peer-to-peer sharing, anonymous mentoring, and mentoring with microfeedback (limited to 140 characters) are some recent variations of traditional mentoring.[39] The lesson: Actively strive to build a diverse portfolio of mentors.

### Early Career: The Impact of the First Job

Many studies of early careers focus on the first jobs to which new employees are assigned. The positive impact of initial job challenge upon later career success and retention has been found many times in a wide variety of settings. Among engineers, challenging early work assignments were related to strong initial performance as well as to the maintenance of competence and performance throughout the engineer's career.[40] In other words, challenging initial job assignments are an antidote to career obsolescence.

The characteristics of the first supervisor are also critical. He or she must be personally secure; unthreatened by the new subordinate's training, ambition, and energy; and able to communicate company norms and values.[41] Beyond that, the supervisor ideally should be able to play the roles of coach, feedback provider, trainer, role model, and protector in an accepting, esteem-building manner.

**HR BUZZ**

## IMPACT OF THE FIRST JOB ON LATER CAREER SUCCESS

Traditionally researchers tended to accept the view that unless an individual has a challenging first job and receives quick, early promotions, the entire career will suffer. This is a *tournament model* of upward mobility. It assumes that everyone has an equal chance in the early contests but that the losers are not eligible for later contests, at least not those of the major tournament. An alternative model is called *signaling theory.* It suggests three cues (signals) that those responsible for promotion may use: (1) prior history of promotions (a signal of ability), (2) functional-area background, and (3) number of different jobs held.

A study of the patterns of early upward mobility for 180 employees of an oil company over an 11-year period are enlightening.[a] The company's very detailed job classification systems and actual salary grades served as measures of career attainment. The results generally did not support the tournament model of career mobility, because the losers—those passed over in the early periods—were later able to move up quickly. Rather, the results were more analogous to a horse race: Position out of the gate had relatively little effect in comparison to position entering the home stretch.

Different mobility patterns for administration and technical personnel helped to explain why the pattern of the early years did not always persist. Those who started early in administrative positions began to move up early but also plateaued early. A technical background meant a longer wait before upward movement, followed by relatively rapid promotion. The number of different positions held also predicted higher attainment.

In summary, past position, functional background, and number of different jobs all seem to act as signals to those making decisions about promotions. All were related strongly to career attainment. Together they accounted for more than 60 percent of the variability in promotions.

[a]Forbes, J. B. (1987). Early intraorganizational mobility: Patterns and influences. *Academy of Management Journal* 30, pp. 110–125.

One other variable affects the likelihood of obtaining a high-level job later in one's career: *initial aspirations.* Encourage employees to aim high because, in general, higher aspirations lead to higher performance.[42] Parents, teachers, employers, and friends should therefore avoid discouraging so-called impractical aspirations.

### Managing Men and Women in Midcareer

To a large extent, middle age is still a mystery. Myths about psychological landmarks of midlife, such as the "empty-nest syndrome," the "midlife crisis," and the menopausal "change of life" have little scientific basis.[43] Nevertheless, the following issues may arise for women as well as for men at some point during the ages of 35 to 55:[44]

- An awareness of advancing age and an awareness of death.
- An awareness of bodily changes related to aging.
- Knowing how many career goals have been or will be attained.
- A search for new life goals.
- A marked change in family relationships.

- A change in work relationships (now more of a coach than a novice or rookie).
- A growing sense of obsolescence at work (as the saying goes, "Never look back; someone may be gaining on you").
- A feeling of decreased job mobility and increased concern for job security.[45]

Everyone experiences career transitions, but such transitions need not morph into full-blown crises. The key is to recognize the warning signs, such as depression, a stagnant marriage, an unsatisfying career, or heavy emotional baggage from years past. Curbing impulsive behavior is crucial to limiting the human damage a midlife crisis can do. Evidence also indicates that there are distinct differences between men and women as they search for meaning across the courses of their lives, and that more women than men now report turbulent midlife transitions: 36.1 percent versus 34 percent, respectively. Whereas male midlife crises are more likely to be driven by work or career issues, women's are more likely to begin with family events or problems, such as a divorce, a parent's death, or an extramarital affair.[46]

The midlife turmoil is manifesting itself in a number of ways. While the number of extramarital affairs among women (nearly one in six) is approaching that of men (about one in five), organized religion is also drawing significant support from midlife women's quest for meaning. Many women are changing careers to pursue work that is more altruistic or fulfilling. Others are returning to higher education to pursue new interests, or engaging in adventurous sports (e.g., wall-climbing, kayaking, wilderness camping). Interviews with older women in their 60s and 70s who had experienced midlife crises more than a decade ago revealed, without exception, that if given the chance to do it all again, they would embrace new undertakings even more enthusiastically.[47]

From a career perspective, the fact is that for many, if not most, midcareer employees, promotions tend to slow down markedly as managers are put into holding patterns. While career success traditionally has been defined in terms of upward mobility, more and more leading corporations are trying to convince employees that *plateauing* is a fact of life, not a measure of personal failure, and that lateral mobility can also lead to rewards and fulfillment. Does such a move make sense? Yes, if it puts a **plateaued worker** into a core business, gives that person closer contact with customers, or teaches new skills that will increase marketability (both inside and outside one's present company) in case the person is fired.[48]

What can a middle-aged man or woman do? The rapid growth of technology and the accelerating development of new knowledge require that a person in midlife make some sort of *change* for her or his own survival. A 30-year-old might make the statement "I can afford to change jobs or careers a couple of more times before I have to settle down." But a 50-year-old faces the possibility that there is only one chance left for change, and now may be the time to take it.[49]

Not everyone who goes through this period in life is destined to experience problems, but everyone does go through the transition, and some are better equipped to cope than are others. Evidence now indicates that the older people are, the more control they feel in their work, finances, and marriages, but the less control they feel over health, children, and sex.[50] Life planning and career-planning exercises are available that encourage employees to face up to feelings of restlessness and insecurity, to reexamine their values and life goals, and to set new ones or to recommit themselves to old ones.

One strategy is to *train midcareer employees to develop younger employees* (i.e., to serve as coaches or mentors). Both parties can win under such an arrangement. The midcareer employee keeps himself or herself fresh, energetic, and

**HR BUZZ**

### STRATEGIES FOR COPING WITH PLATEAUED WORKERS*

Here are three signs that your career is stalled: others hired about the same time as you, at the same level, have been promoted or have moved on to better jobs; you've been in your job twice as long as anyone else in the same position; and you know exactly what you're going to do every day. To change things up a bit, firms like Chevron, General Motors, and First Banks Inc. are encouraging employees to move across departmental lines on a horizontal basis since flatter organizations have made vertical promotions less frequent. In banking, for example, someone from auditing might switch to commercial training; someone from systems research and development might move into international development. The inflexible HRM policies of the past are rapidly fading to accommodate new realities. Another strategy is to create dual technical/management ladders. New "technical executive" positions are equal to management jobs in title and dollars. For example, First Banks has created senior lending positions and positions for accounting and systems specialists that are equivalent to senior managerial posts in those departments.

An alternative way to placate people who do not move up is to pay them more for jobs well done. For years, companies that rely heavily for growth on creative people—scientists, engineers, writers, artists—have provided incentives for them to stay on. Companies are now offering such incentives to a broader spectrum. For example, at Monsanto, favored scientists can now climb a universitylike track of associate fellow, fellow, senior fellow, distinguished fellow.

Prudential Life Insurance Company rotates managers to improve their performance. At General Electric, employees who are plateaued (either organizationally, through a lack of available promotions, or personally, through lack of ability or desire) are sometimes assigned to task forces or study teams. These employees have not been promoted in a technical sense, but at least they have gotten a new assignment, a fresh perspective, and a change in their daily work.

*Sources:* Rosato, D. (2005, Apr.). 21 ways to jump-start your career. *Money*, pp. 161–166. See also London, M. (1996). Redeployment and continuous learning in the 21st century: Hard lessons and positive examples from the downsizing era. *Academy of Management Executive* 10(4), pp. 67–79. See also Fierman, J. (1993, Sept. 6). Beating the midlife career crisis. *Fortune*, pp. 52–60. See also Ference, T. P., Stoner, J. A., and Warren, E. K. (1977). Managing the career plateau. *Academy of Management Review* 2, pp. 602–612.

up to date, while the younger employee learns to see the big picture and to profit from the experience of the older employee. An important psychological need at midcareer is to build something lasting, something that will be a permanent contribution to the organization or profession. The development of a future generation of leaders could be a significant, lasting, and highly satisfying contribution.

Another strategy for coping with midcareer problems is to *deal with or prevent obsolescence*. To deal with the problem, some firms send their employees to seminars, workshops, university courses, and other forms of retooling. But a better solution is to prevent obsolescence from occurring in the first place. One way to do this is by asking questions such as the following:

- Can you suggest new ways to do things that we haven't done before?
- What specific things do you want to do in the next year here that you haven't had a chance to do before?

■ What skills are you willing to invest time in developing so you can stay ahead of the curve in your profession?[51]

Furthermore, three personal characteristics tend to be associated with low obsolescence: high intellectual ability, high self-motivation, and personal flexibility (lack of rigidity).

Of course, those who are unwilling to wait for promotions in large corporations may become entrepreneurs and start their own businesses.[52] Others may simply accept the status quo; readjust their life and career goals; and attempt to satisfy their needs for achievement, recognition, and personal growth off the job. Research at AT&T supports this proposition. By the time managers were interviewed after 20 years on the job, most had long ago given up their early dreams, and many could not even remember how high they had aspired in the first place. At least on the surface, most had accepted their career plateaus and adjusted to them. Midlife was indeed a crisis to some of the managers, but not to the majority.[53]

It is possible to move through the middle years of life without reevaluation of one's goals and life. But it is probably healthier to develop a new or revised game plan during this period.

## Managing the Older Worker

"Work is life" is a phrase philosophers throughout the ages have emphasized. Today, advances in health and medicine make it possible for people in developed

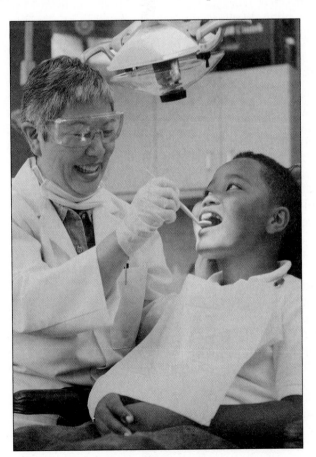

Many older workers have valuable skills that contribute significantly to organizations and society.

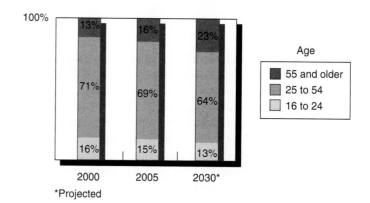

**Figure 10–1**

Age Distribution of U.S. Labor Force: 2000, 2005, and 2030.

(*Source:* Bureau of Labor Statistics; and M. Toossi, *Monthly Labor Review* (November 2006).

countries to live 77–82 years, on average, although there is great variability, particularly among the poor and the wealthy.[54] The result: an army of healthy, older workers. Legally, the elimination of mandatory retirement at any age has made this issue even more significant. As managers, what can we expect in terms of demographic trends?

In a nutshell, we can expect fewer younger workers and more older workers. As Figure 10-1 shows, the percentage of the U.S. labor force age 55 and older will increase from 13 percent in 2000 to 23 percent in 2030. At the same time, the percentage of workers age 25–54 will shrink from 71 percent in 2000 to 64 percent in 2030. In short, the baby boom of the postwar period will become the "rocking-chair boom" of the early 21st century.

### Myths versus Facts about Older Workers

Age stereotypes are an unfortunate impediment to the continued growth and development of workers over the age of 50. A U.S.-based survey by the Association of Executive Search Consultants found that more than 60 percent of respondents reported that age discrimination was apparent between age 50 and 55.[55] A broader survey of G7 nations (Canada, France, Germany, Italy, Japan, the United Kingdom, and the United States) reported that 60 percent of employees over 50 see age discrimination as the primary barrier to finding new jobs, while only 38 percent view their employers as welcoming toward older workers.[56] Here are some common myths about age, along with the facts:

*Myth.* Older workers are less productive than younger workers.

*Fact.* Cumulative research evidence across three large-scale meta-analyses indicates that in both professional and nonprofessional jobs, age and performance on core job tasks are generally unrelated.[57] Nor is there any systematic relationship between age and scientific productivity.[58] The relationship of aging to the ability to function, and the implication of aging for job performance, is complex. Overwhelming evidence contradicts simple notions that rate of decline is tied in some linear or direct fashion to chronological age. Rather, the effects of aging on performance can be characterized by stability and growth, as well as decline, with large individual differences in the timing and amount of change in the ability to function.[59]

*Myth.* It costs more to prepare older workers for a job.

*Fact.* Studies show that mental abilities, such as verbal, numerical, and reasoning skills, remain stable into a person's seventies.[60]

*Myth.* Older workers are absent more often because of age-related infirmities and above-average rates of illness.

*Fact.* Large-scale, cumulative research has found that, considering all causes for absence, older workers tend to be absent less frequently than younger workers (meta-correlation = −0.26). With respect to absence due to sickness, however, there is a very weak (0.02) but positive relationship with age. Hence the duration of the sickness-related absences that do take place tends to be longer.[61]

*Myth.* Older workers have an unacceptably high rate of accidents on the job.

*Fact.* The same large-scale, cumulative research found that age was related positively (0.10) to self-rated compliance with safety rules and procedures, and it was related negatively to the frequency of work injuries (−0.08).[62] It could be argued that this is because older workers have more experience on a job, and that those who have had many accidents are no longer there. Regardless of length of experience, however, the younger the employee, the higher the accident rate (see Chapter 15).

*Myth.* Older workers do not get along well with other employees.

*Fact.* A pattern of empirical findings supports the conclusion that older adults display higher levels of emotional intelligence, and they show less workplace aggression, on-the-job substance abuse, and tardiness. Thus the stereotype of older workers as difficult colleagues is largely unfounded. In fact, the over-50 worker's sense of responsibility and consistent job performance provide a positive role model for younger workers.[63]

*Myth.* The cost of health-care benefits outweighs any other possible benefits from hiring older workers.

*Fact.* True, when older people get sick, the illness is often chronic and requires repeated doctor's visits and hospitalization, and the growth rate in costs per capita for acute care does increase by age.[64] However, the costs of health-care for an older worker are lower than those for a younger, married worker with several children.[65]

*Myth.* Older people are less creative than younger ones.

*Fact.* Two recent meta-analyses reported that age was not related to employee creativity, either as rated by supervisors or by employees themselves. One might argue, however, that regardless of age, poor performers are weeded out over time, so that there are no major differences in task performance or creativity among those who remain.[66]

*Myth.* You can't train older workers.

*Fact.* Across many studies, age shows a weak (−0.04) negative relationship with performance in training programs. That is, older workers' training performance is slightly lower than that of younger workers.[67] Particularly with older workers, it is important to provide a nonthreatening training environment that does not emphasize speed and does not expose the older learner to unfavorable comparisons with younger learners. Encourage self-confidence by allowing the older worker to master a skill-development task, by observing similarly aged models who are performing well, and by offering verbal assurances, ample time, and privacy.[68]

***Myth.*** Older people do not function well if constantly interrupted.

***Fact.*** Neither do younger people.

### Implications of the Aging Workforce for HRM

Certainly not all older workers are model employees, just as not all older workers fit traditional stereotypes. What are the implications of this growing group of able-bodied individuals for human resource management?

We know what the future labor market will look like in general terms: Both the demand for and the supply of older workers will continue to expand, as more older workers delay retirement. To capitalize on these trends, one approach is to recruit workers from those individuals who would otherwise retire. Make the job more attractive than retirement, and keep the employee who would otherwise need replacing.[69] As the following example illustrates, some companies are doing exactly this.

---

**HR BUZZ**

### UNRETIREES

Baptist Health South Florida is one of a growing number of organizations that are finding their own retirees to be a valuable source of experienced, dependable, and motivated help. In fact, workers who leave and return within five years are "bridged," retaining seniority and salary level.[a] At Travelers, retirees meet seasonal or sporadic employment needs for the company, and the company gets a tax break. The retirees fill a variety of jobs, including data-entry operators, systems analysts, underwriters, and accountants. Working a maximum of 40 hours per month, retirees are paid at the midpoint of the salary range for their job classifications. If they work more than half a standard workweek, they risk losing their pension benefits. Nevertheless, retirees generally like the program because it keeps them in better physical, mental, and financial shape than full-time retirement does.[b]

With a smaller cohort of young workers entering the workforce, other companies are also seeking workers who once would have been considered "over the hill." Deloitte Consulting launched a Senior Leaders Program to allow high-talent executives to redesign their jobs rather than lose them to early retirement. Both Monsanto and Prudential use retirees as temporary workers to do everything from sophisticated technical jobs to answering phones. When Richmond-based Bon Secours Virginia Health System systematically examined why older workers leave, it found that the lack of workplace flexibility was the cause for nearly all concerns. Fully 40 percent of its employees are age 50 or older.[c]

---

[a]Grossman, 2008a, op. cit.

[b]Feldman, 2007, op. cit. See also Wang, P. (2000, Nov.) Is this retirement? *Money,* pp. 101–108.

[c]Krell, E. (2010, Oct.). Ways to phase retirement. *HR Magazine* 55(10), p. 96.

A second approach is to survey the needs of older workers and, where feasible, adjust HRM practices and policies to accommodate these needs:[70]

1. Keep records on why employees retire and on why they continue to work.
2. Implement flexible work patterns and options, whether time based or location based, or using phased retirement.
3. Where possible, redesign jobs to match the physical capabilities of the aging worker, including those that do not require overtime or being on call.
4. Provide opportunities for retraining in technical and managerial skills. Fully two-thirds of older workers want more training and leadership-development opportunities. Unfortunately, two-thirds of HR executives say their firms don't offer such training for older workers as an incentive to upgrade their skills.[71]
5. Manage the organization's culture to implement incentives to debunk stereotypes, empower innovative thinking, and create clear performance expectations. To avoid age-discrimination suits, be able to provide documented evidence of ineffective job performance.
6. Despite the encouraging findings presented earlier, in the section "Myths versus Facts about Older Workers," research has indicated no overall improvement in attitudes toward older workers.[72] Characteristics employers consider most desirable in employees—flexibility, adaptability to change, capacity and willingness to exercise independent judgment—are not commonly associated with older workers.[73]

For their part, older workers say their biggest problem is discrimination by would-be employers who underestimate their skills. They say they must convince supervisors and coworkers, not to mention some customers, that they're not stubborn, persnickety, or feeble.[74] To change this trend, workers and managers alike need to know the facts about older workers, so that they do not continue to espouse myths.

## CAREER MANAGEMENT: ORGANIZATIONS FOCUSING ON THEIR OWN MAINTENANCE AND GROWTH

Ultimately, it is top management's responsibility to develop and implement a cost-effective career-management program. The program must fit the nature of the business, its competitive employment practices, and the current (or desired) organizational structure. This process is complex because career management combines areas that previously have been regarded as individual issues: performance management, development, transfer, and promotion. Before coaching and counseling take place, however, it is important to identify characteristic career paths that employees tend to follow.

**Career paths** represent logical and possible sequences of positions that could be held, based on an analysis of what people actually do in an organization.[75] Career paths should

- Represent real progression possibilities, whether lateral or upward, without implied "normal" rates of progress or forced specialization in a technical area.
- Be tentative and responsive to changes in job content, work priorities, organizational patterns, and management needs.

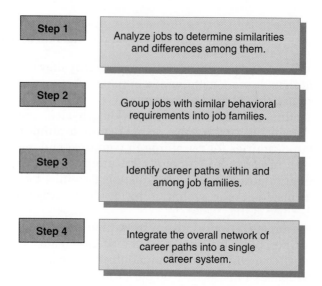

**Figure 10–2**

Development of a career system composed of individual career paths.

**Step 1** — Analyze jobs to determine similarities and differences among them.

**Step 2** — Group jobs with similar behavioral requirements into job families.

**Step 3** — Identify career paths within and among job families.

**Step 4** — Integrate the overall network of career paths into a single career system.

- Be flexible, taking into consideration the compensating qualities of a particular employee, managers, subordinates, or others who influence the way that work is performed.
- Specify the skills, knowledge, and other attributes required to perform effectively at each position along the paths and specify how they can be acquired. (If specifications are limited to educational credentials, age, and experience, some capable performers may be excluded from career opportunities.)

Behaviorally based job analyses (see Chapter 5) that can be expressed in quantitative terms are well suited to this task because they focus directly on what people must do effectively in each job. Clusters or families of jobs requiring similar patterns of behavior can then be identified. Once this is done, the next task is to identify career paths within and among the job families and to integrate the overall network of these paths into a single career system. The process is shown graphically in Figure 10–2.

DISH Network, the satellite-TV service, uses a career-path program to help retain call-center agents. The program followed the steps outlined in Figure 10–2. The company asks agents to identify their career goals, and supervisors help create plans to achieve them. Agents can win rapid promotions within call centers, or to other jobs with the company, by meeting skills and training requirements, with company help. Company executives say the program is working: The average call-center agent now stays for 19 months, up from 9 months two years ago.[76]

In practice, career-management systems sometimes fail for the following reasons: (1) Employees believe that supervisors do not care about their career development, (2) neither the employee nor the organization is fully aware of the employee's needs and organizational constraints, and (3) career plans are developed without regard for the support systems necessary to fulfill the plans.[77] The following section gives examples of several companies that avoided these pitfalls.

## Internal Staffing Decisions: Patterns of Career Change

From the organization's point of view, there are four broad types of internal moves: up, down, over, and out (Figure 10–3). These moves correspond to promotions (up);

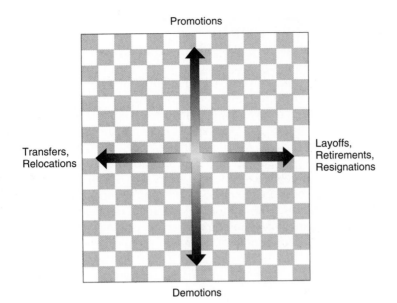

Promotions

Transfers, Relocations

Layoffs, Retirements, Resignations

Demotions

**Figure 10–3**

As in chess, people can make a variety of internal moves in an organization.

demotions (down); transfers and relocations (over); and layoffs, retirements, and resignations (out). Technically, dismissals also fall into the last category, but we will consider them in Chapter 14, in the context of disciplinary actions and procedural justice. Briefly, let's consider each of these patterns of movement.

### Promotions

Promoted employees usually assume greater responsibility and authority in return for higher pay, benefits, and privileges. Psychologically, promotions help satisfy employees' needs for security, belonging, and personal growth. **Promotions** are important organizational decisions that should receive the same careful attention as any other employment decision. They are more likely to be successful to the extent that firms

1. Conduct an extensive search for candidates.
2. Make standardized, clearly understandable information available on all candidates.[78]

Organizations must continue to live with those who are bypassed for promotion. Research indicates that these individuals often feel they have not been treated fairly, their commitment decreases, and their absenteeism increases. Conversely, promoted individuals tend to increase their commitment.[79] To minimize defensive behavior, it is critical that the procedures used for promotion decisions (e.g., assessment centers plus performance appraisals) be acceptable, valid, and fair to the unsuccessful candidates. Further, emphasize the greater merits of the promoted candidates, relative to those who were not promoted.

For many people, promotions can be stressful events. In fact, in a recent survey of 785 business leaders, nearly one in five ranked getting a promotion as their most challenging life event. A big reason for that, the survey also showed, is that 40 percent of managers get little or no support as they enter their new jobs. In addition, along with the gain, promotions also involve losses, for example, losing the comfort of a familiar role and the relationships that went with that. It's also not unusual for the newly promoted to worry that they cannot handle the responsibilities of their new jobs. These issues are important to address because,

## PROFESSIONAL SERVICE FIRMS

Professional service firms (PSFs) are involved in a variety of activities, from consulting, law, civil engineering, and architecture to software production. They trade mainly on the knowledge of their human capital—employees and producer–owners—to develop and deliver solutions to client problems. The usual ownership form of the PSF is the partnership, and a key decision for the existing owners is promotion to partner. This has implications for the reputation of the firm, as well as for its future direction.

Conventionally, PSFs use up-or-out promotion policies, excluding from permanent tenure all except those offered partnership. If employees fail to obtain promotion within a certain time period, they are expected to quit or are dismissed. The attraction of up-or-out for the owners of the firm is that it creates a strong incentive for aspiring juniors to perform, reducing supervision or monitoring costs. It also leaves career paths inside the firm relatively clear by exiting those not elected to the top jobs, thereby helping to attract ambitious entrants who do not want to be stuck in a promotion logjam. However, up-or-out also involves losing talented and knowledgeable staff in whom the firm will have invested not only formal training (and possibly signing bonuses) but also the time and effort associated with mentoring and developing them.

In general, the more that firms value their knowledge base and see it as a source of competitive advantage, or where the knowledge loss represents a competitive threat, the greater the costs of losing the knowledge that exiting unsuccessful candidates take with them through up-or-out. In such cases, firms may adapt by creating permanent career positions. There are costs to this strategy as well, in the form of the need for higher-powered incentives linked to the performance of the firm for those in permanent career positions below the level of partner (to reduce the risk of shirking or loafing), and higher compensation to attract and retain good quality staff. What's the bottom line in all of this? Where firms perceive their knowledge base as distinctive and a source of competitive advantage, a promotion system like up-or-out may be less appropriate. Where the knowledge is codified and publicly available (as in public accounting firms), firms are more likely to retain up-or-out.

*\*Sources:* Morris, T. (2000). Promotion policies and knowledge bases in the professional service firm. In M. Peiperl, M. Arthur, R. Coffee, and T. Morris (Eds.), *Career Frontiers*. Oxford, U.K.: Oxford University Press, pp. 138–152. By permission of Oxford University Press.

as many baby boomers retire, they will leave an even bigger mentoring void for upwardly mobile executives.[80]

A further issue concerns promotion from within versus outside the organization. In organizations where the top executive team has served together for a long time, there is a much greater tendency to promote from within.[81] Other firms, such as Southwest Airlines, have strict promotion-from-within policies. However, there are situations in which high-level jobs or newly created jobs require talents that are just not available in-house. Under these circumstances, even the most rigid promotion-from-within policy must yield to a search for outside candidates.

### Demotions

Employee **demotions** within a firm usually involve a cut in pay, status, privilege, or opportunity. They occur infrequently because they tend to be accompanied by problems of employee apathy, depression, and inefficiency that can undermine the morale of a work group. For these reasons, many managers prefer to discharge or to move employees laterally rather than demote them. In either case, careful planning, documentation, and concern for the employee should precede such moves.

What causes demotion? It could be a disciplinary action, inability of an employee to handle the requirements of a higher-level job, health problems, or changing interests (e.g., a desire to move from production to sales). Demotions also may result from structural changes, as one-time managers are recast into project leaders, technical specialists, or internal consultants by companies in the throes of reorganization. In many cases, demotion is mutually satisfactory to the organization and to the affected employee.[82]

What about dismissals for cause? In the case of chief executive officers, empirical evidence indicates that unethical behavior and low ability to handle the CEO's job both trigger early CEO dismissal. Two other explanations were not supported, however: shareholder pressure and personality clashes or disagreements over strategic direction.[83]

## Transfers and Relocations

Who is most likely to be transferred? A survey by the Employee Relocation Council found that the prototypical transferee is a married 37-year-old male with children. Female workers are less likely to be transferred, although this situation is changing.[84] Reduced mobility, like leaves of absence, tends to retard women's salary progression relative to that of similarly situated men.[85]

With respect to relocations, senior management sometimes faces resistance from employees for family reasons, although in 2009 the main reason was because of the depressed housing market.[86] The effect of a move on a family can be profound.[87] For the employee, relocation often means increased prestige and income. However, the costs of moving and the complications resulting from upsetting routines, loss of friends, and changing schools and jobs are borne by the family. Uprooted families often suffer from loss of credentials as well. They do not enjoy the built-in status that awaits the employee at the new job; they must start from scratch. Wives may become more dependent on their husbands for social contacts (or vice versa, depending on who is transferred).

Currently, about a third of transferees are female, and one in four trailing spouses is male. Do such moves work out? In an early study, Exxon Mobil Corporation found that a man generally would follow his wife only if she earned at least 25 percent to 40 percent a year more than he did.[88] Today, about one in four wives makes more than her husband. That's up from 16 percent 25 years ago.[89] There is one bright side to all of this, however. Research has shown that transfers produce little short-term impact on the mental or physical health of children.[90]

Transferred employees who are promoted estimate that it will take them a full nine months to get up to speed in their new posts. Lateral transfers take an average of 7.8 months. However, the actual time taken to reach competency varies with (1) the degree of similarity between the old and new jobs, and (2) the amount of support from peers and superiors at the new job.[91]

As an overall strategy on relocation, some companies have developed frequency standards whereby no manager can be relocated more than once in 2 years or three times in 10 years. Another firm has set up one-stop rotational programs at its larger facilities to replace what used to be four stints of six months each at different plants over a two-year training period.

The financial implications of relocation are another major consideration. As we noted in Chapter 6, a top-tier, complete relocation package for executives includes ongoing cost-of-living differentials; mortgage interest differentials; home-disposal and home-finding expenses; expenses to help defray losses on home sales; real estate commissions; home-purchase expenses; home-maintenance, -repair, and -refurbishing costs; equity loans; and, for renters, lease-breaking expenses. Employees on temporary assignments often receive home property management expenses. All of this adds up. The average cost of relocating a home-owning employee within the United States now exceeds $76,000, but the costs for renters and home-owning new hires are much lower.[92]

Organizations are well aware of these social and financial problems, and, in many cases, they are responding by providing improved support systems to make the process easier. These include special online relocation programs, intranets, "house-hunting" on the Internet, and electronic data interchange (EDI) that lets relocation professionals keep track of every detail of every move.[93] MasterCard Worldwide is typical. It provides a lump-sum payment for home-finding and temporary housing. Transferees appreciate having immediate access to funds, which eases cash-flow concerns, eliminates the need to do expense reports, and gives the transferee discretion in allocating funds.[94]

### Layoffs, Retirements, and Resignations
These all involve employees moving *out* of the organization.

***Layoffs.*** How safe is my job? For many people, that is the issue of the early 21st century. It's becoming clear that corporate cutbacks were not an oddity of the 1990s but rather are likely to persist through this decade as well.[95]

Involuntary layoffs are never pleasant, and management policies must consider the impacts on those who leave, on those who stay, on the local community, and on the company. For laid-off workers, efforts should be directed toward a rapid, successful, and orderly career transition.[96] Emphasize outplacement programs that help laid-off employees deal with the psychological stages of career transition (anger, grief, depression, family stress), assess individual strengths and weaknesses, and develop support networks.[97]

How long does it take on average to find a new job? While it depends a great deal on the state of the economy and on the amount of effort put into the job search, a recent survey of 35- to 60-year-old job seekers showed that the older they were, the fewer interviews they got, and the longer it took them to find a job. How much longer? Compared to a 35- to 40-year-old job seeker, it took almost 25 percent longer for a 46- to 50-year-old, and 65 percent longer for a 50- to 60-year-old.[98] Some members of that older group may never find comparable work, even if they are willing to take a big cut in pay.[99]

Termination is a traumatic experience. Egos are shattered, and employees may become bitter and angry. Family problems may also occur because of the added emotional and financial strain.[100] For those who remain, it is important that they retain the highest level of loyalty, trust, teamwork, motivation, and productivity possible. This doesn't just happen—and unless there is a good deal of face-to-face, candid, open communication between senior management and "survivors," it probably won't.[101] Within the community, layoff policies should consider the company's reputation and image in addition to the impact of the layoff on the local economy and social services agencies. Although layoffs are intended to reduce costs, some costs may in fact increase, including those in the following table.

## DIRECT AND INDIRECT COSTS OF DOWNSIZING

| Direct costs | Indirect costs |
|---|---|
| ■ Severance pay, pay in lieu of notice. | ■ Recruiting and employment cost of new hires. |
| ■ Accrued vacation and sick pay. | ■ Low morale, risk-averse survivors. |
| ■ Supplemental unemployment benefits. | ■ Decreased productivity among survivors. |
| ■ Outplacement. | ■ Increase in unemployment tax rate. |
| ■ Pension and benefit payoffs. | ■ Lack of staff when economy rebounds. |
| ■ Administrative processing costs. | ■ Start-up costs (recruiting, training, staffing). |
| ■ Costs of rehiring former employees. | ■ Voluntary terminations of those who remain. |
| | ■ Opportunity costs of lost sales. |
| | ■ Potential lawsuits from aggrieved employees. |
| | ■ Potential strikes by unions in some countries. |
| | ■ Loss of institutional memory and trust in management. |
| | ■ Brand equity costs—damage to the company's brand as an employer of choice. |

*Source:* Cascio, W. F. (2010). *Employment Downsizing and Its Alternatives.* Alexandria, VA: Society for Human Resource Management Foundation, p. 12.

Many organizations, unfortunately, often use employment downsizing as a first resort, before trying any other options. Of course, if the expected downturn in business is expected to be permanent, then the only alternative to layoffs is to retrain employees to develop new lines of business. In many cases, however, there are other options. Figure 10-4 presents 14 of them, but these are by no means exhaustive. Ultimately the decision to try one or more alternatives to downsizing comes down to a single question: "Do the benefits of retaining employees, preserving morale, and maintaining the capacity to respond to increases in demand when the economy recovers outweigh the costs of reducing the workforce through downsizing?"

■ Cut temporary staff.
■ Eliminate overtime.
■ Offer voluntary retirement.
■ Freeze salaries.
■ Cut salaries.
■ Delay raises.
■ Freeze hiring.
■ Reduce work hours.
■ Use temporary layoffs (furloughs).
■ Use furloughs with incentives.
■ Cancel business trips and costly perquisites.
■ Reduce or suspend matching contributions to company-sponsored savings plans.
■ Raises employee contributions to benefits plans.
■ Postpone or eliminate bonuses.

### Figure 10–4

Alternatives to Employment Downsizing for Temporary Downturns.

(*Source:* Cascio, W. F. (2010). *Employment Downsizing and Its Alternatives.* Alexandria, VA: Society for Human Resource Management Foundation, p. 13.)

***Retirements.***   For some employees, early retirement is a possible alternative to being laid off. Early retirement programs are intended to provide incentives to terminate; they are not intended to replace regular retirement benefits. Research indicates that lump-sum bonuses are relatively ineffective in persuading older workers to retire early, that poor performers are more likely to accept early retirement incentives than good performers, and that it is difficult to estimate accurately how many older workers will accept such offers.[102] At General Motors, for example, 19,000 workers (out of 74,000 offered) left the company with voluntary buyout packages in 2008.[103]

What about the effects on those who remain? With respect to layoffs, generous benefits provided to victims tend to be associated with *lower* intentions to quit on the part of survivors. With an early retirement program, however, perceptions of overly generous benefits to early retirees tends to be associated with *higher* intentions to quit on the part of ineligible employees who remain.[104] That is not the only risk associated with voluntary severance and early retirement programs. Both Kodak and IBM lost skilled, senior-level employees in past cutbacks. To overcome that problem, the firms targeted subsequent programs to specific groups of employees, such as those in manufacturing and in some administrative jobs.[105] The keys to success are to *identify, before the incentives are offered, exactly which jobs are targeted for attrition and to understand the needs of the employees targeted to leave.*[106]

Because mandatory retirement at a specified age can no longer be required legally (in the United States), most employees will choose their own times to retire. A typical man now retires at 63, and a typical woman at 62, although those ages are likely to increase, given the drop in the percentage of companies

## IMPACT OF CAREER MANAGEMENT ON PRODUCTIVITY, QUALITY OF WORK LIFE, AND THE BOTTOM LINE

From first-job effects through midcareer transition to preretirement counseling, career management has a direct bearing on productivity, quality of work life, and the bottom line. It is precisely because organizations are sensitive to these concerns that career management activities have become as popular as they are. The saying "Organizations have many jobs, but individuals have only one career" is as true today as it ever was. While organizations find themselves in global competition, most individuals are striving for achievement, recognition, personal growth, variety, and inspiration of colleagues.[a] In a world that is becoming flatter, more interconnected, and boundaryless, attempting to seek balance, equilibrium, and stability may be counterproductive. Leave behind the notion that the amount of time and energy devoted to "work" needs to balance the time and energy devoted to "life." Instead, focus on enriching your overall quality of life. Reframing the issues in this way changes the focus from *work* to *life* and from *balance* to *quality.*[b] The payoff is obvious for individuals and their organizations.

[a]Hewlett, S. A., Sherbin, L., and Sumberg, K. (2009, Aug.). How Gen Y & boomers will reshape your agenda. *Harvard Business Review,* pp. 3–9, Reprint #R0907G. See also The new workforce: Generation Y. (2001). *Workplace Visions* 2, pp. 1–7; Daniels, C. Where the next generation wants to work. (1999, Oct. 11). *Fortune,* p. 322.

[b]Galinsky et al., 2009, op. cit. See also Collard, B., and Gelatt, H. B. (2000). Beyond balance to life quality. In J. M. Kummerow (Ed.), *New Directions in Career Planning and the Workplace.* Palo Alto, CA: Davies-Black, pp. 197–225.

## IMPLICATIONS FOR MANAGEMENT PRACTICE

To profit from current workforce trends, consider taking the following steps:

- Develop explicit policies to attract and retain dual-career couples.
- Consider mentoring and reverse-mentoring programs to promote two-way learning and growth.
- Plan to use plateaued workers more effectively, as well as those who are in midcareer transitions.

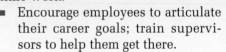

- Educate other managers and workers in the facts about older workers; where possible, hire older workers, including retirees, for full-time or part-time work.
- Encourage employees to articulate their career goals; train supervisors to help them get there.

providing coverage for retiree healthcare (25 percent in 2011 versus 35 percent in 2007) and traditional pensions (22 percent in 2011 versus 40 percent in 2007).[107]

Research indicates that both personal and situational factors affect retirement decisions. Personally, individuals with Type A behavior patterns (hard-driving, aggressive, impatient) are less likely to prefer to retire, while those with obsolete job skills, chronic health problems, and sufficient financial resources are more likely to retire. Situationally, employees are more likely to retire to the extent that they have reached their occupational goals, that their jobs have undesirable characteristics, that home life is seen as preferable to work life, and that there are attractive alternative (leisure) activities.[108]

While retirement is certainly attractive to some, among baby boomers, 80 percent say they plan to do at least some work after they "retire"; specifically, they plan to work part-time for interest or enjoyment (30 percent), work part-time for income (25 percent), start their own business (15 percent), work full-time in a new job or career (7 percent), and pursue other interests (3 percent).[109] Others need the money, and they need health benefits to compensate for those they have lost. Many want in retirement what they don't currently have: *balance*. They want what aging experts now call a **blended life course**—an ongoing mix of work, leisure, and education.[110]

*Resignations.*    Different motives underlie voluntary resignation.[111] **Impulsive quitters** resign "on the spot" (as a result of sharp negative emotions) without any advance planning. **Comparison quitters,** in contrast, rationally evaluate alternative jobs and are relatively free of strong negative emotions toward their former employers. **Preplanned quitters** plan in advance to quit at a specific time in the future (e.g., upon reaching age 60). This type is least avoidable and therefore least preventable by management. Finally, **conditional quitters** hold the view "I will quit as soon as I get another job offer that meets certain conditions."

While the motives for voluntary resignation may vary, the rules for how to do it have not. Experts generally agree that the fastest way to derail a promising career is to tell your boss "to take this job and shove it." Instead, leave gracefully and responsibly, stressing the value of your experience in the company. In addition, give plenty of notice (at least two weeks), work hard to complete all of your outstanding obligations, and even consider sending your former boss a thank-you note, focusing on the positive aspects of your work there. After all, the working world is smaller than you think.[112]

---

## SELF-RELIANCE: KEY TO CAREER MANAGEMENT

Corporate career management programs often include one or more of the following support mechanisms:

1. **Self-assessment.** The goal of **self-assessment** is to help employees focus on appropriate career goals. For example, Leadership Architect, formerly known as Career Architect, is a deck of 67 skills cards that each employee sorts into three piles: greatest strengths, strengths, and weaknesses. The system, also available in software form, helps employees walk themselves through the difficult and sometimes emotional process of assessing their own skills—for example, dealing with new technology or working in teams. It is a process of identifying and calibrating your professional aptitudes and capabilities and of identifying improvements that will enhance your career growth.[113] Alternatively, employees may complete an interest inventory, such as iStartStrong, to help identify the kinds of activities that they are most interested in. As a rule, people are happiest doing things that fit their interests and skills, and they tend to avoid jobs or activities in which they are uninterested or for which they lack necessary skills.[114]

2. **Career planning.** Verizon uses the results of Leadership Architect to chart the skills the company most needs for future business and to forge career development plans for its high-potential managers. Royal Insurance created a series of success profiles for important jobs using the cards.[115] The companies then teach employees how to plan their career growth once they have determined where they want to go. Employees learn what they need as well as how to "read" the corporate environment and to become "savvy" about how to get ahead in their own companies.

3. **Supervisory training.** Employees frequently turn first to their immediate supervisors for help with career management. At Sikorsky Aircraft, for example, supervisors are taught how to provide relevant information and to question the logic of each employee's career plans, but not to give specific career advice. Giving advice relieves the employee of responsibility for managing his or her own career.

4. **Succession planning.** Simply designating replacements for key managers and executives is no guarantee that those replacements will be ready when needed. Enlightened companies such as K. Hovnanian Enterprises, a $2.6 billion homebuilder in Red Bank, New Jersey, are adopting an approach to succession planning that is consistent with the concept of career self-management. They develop their employees broadly to prepare them for any of several positions that may become available. As business needs change, broadly developed people can be moved into positions that are critical to the success of the business.[116]

While the concept of career self-management is appealing, research has revealed some significant cautions. First, don't make the programs mandatory. Second, don't offer the programs as a one-time opportunity that will not be repeated in the future. Integrate it into the performance management process. And finally, provide opportunities for employees to practice their career self-management behaviors in the workplace. This may require new HR policies and new roles for supervisors.

The practice of making career self-management part of the corporate culture has spread rapidly over the past several years. Companies are using this approach to build a significant competitive advantage. Given today's turbulent—sometimes convulsive—corporate environments, plus workers who seek greater control over their own destinies, it may be the only approach that can succeed over the long term.

## SUMMARY

A career is a sequence of positions occupied by a person during the course of a lifetime. Career planning is important because the consequences of career success or failure are closely linked to an individual's self-concept and identity, as well as with career and life satisfaction. This chapter has addressed career management from three perspectives. The first was that of individuals focusing on themselves: self-management of a person's own career, establishment of career objectives, and dual-career couples. The second perspective was that of organizations focusing on individuals: that is, managing individuals during early career (organizational entry, impact of the first job); midcareer, including strategies for coping with midlife transitions and plateaued workers; and late career (age 50 and over) stages. We considered the implications of each of these stages for human resource management in both large- and small-business settings. Finally, a third perspective was that of organizations focusing on their own maintenance and growth. This requires the development of career management systems based on career paths defined in terms of employee behaviors. It involves the management of patterns of career movement up, down, over, and out.

## KEY TERMS

| | |
|---|---|
| career | promotions |
| career success | demotions |
| organizational entry | blended life course |
| socialization | impulsive quitters |
| mentor | comparison quitters |
| reverse mentoring | preplanned quitters |
| plateaued worker | conditional quitters |
| career paths | self-assessment |

## DISCUSSION QUESTIONS

**10–1.** Why is the design of one's first permanent job so important?
**10–2.** What practical steps can you suggest to minimize midcareer crises?
**10–3.** How can an organization make the best possible use of older workers?

**10–4.** Discuss the special problems faced by dual-career couples.

**10–5.** A friend of yours is considering accepting a new job offer but can't figure out how to tell his current boss he's leaving, or what steps to take. What advice would you give him?

**10–6.** What does the concept of loyalty mean in today's world of work?

**10–7.** Identify some tell-tale signs that it's time to quit your current job.

**10–8.** Working in small groups, develop a corporate policy that specifies how career management relates to training, performance management, and reward systems.

## APPLYING YOUR KNOWLEDGE

*Exercise 10–1*        *Self-Assessment and Career Planning*

Awareness of both the job market and your own strengths, weaknesses, needs, and desires is required to make an effective career choice. This exercise focuses on the second part of the equation: personal traits, interests, needs, and aspirations as they relate to the choice of a career. Professionally developed interest inventories and personality tests can help in this diagnosis. They are usually available through college placement offices.

Following are three exercises designed to help you discover how your personal characteristics relate to your career choices. A sample self-assessment exercise is followed by an exercise providing guidelines for discussing and evaluating answers to the self-assessment questions. The final exercise provides additional ways to examine self-perceptions and interests.

### A. Self-Assessment

An approach that has proved useful is that of answering a series of probing questions. A list of typical questions is provided below. Answer them as honestly as you can.

1. List five words that describe my personality best (not roles such as student, husband, daughter).
2. Who am I? List five statements that answer this question.
3. My best childhood memory is:
4. The single achievement in my life of which I am most proud is:
5. The type of people I like best are:
6. When I have 15 minutes to do anything I want, I most enjoy:
7. When I think about making changes, I feel:
8. My overriding goal in life is to:
9. My greatest strengths in the following work-related areas are (list specific strengths):
   a. Intellectual abilities
   b. Social skills
   c. Leadership skills
   d. Communication skills
10. My greatest weaknesses in the following work-related areas are (list specific weaknesses):
    a. Intellectual abilities
    b. Social skills
    c. Leadership skills
    d. Communication skills
11. Ranking values. Rank the following 16 values in terms of their importance to you (1 is most important, 2 is second most important, etc.).
    a. Family security
    b. A world at peace

    c.   Social recognition
    d.   Self-respect
    e.   Salvation
    f.   True friendship
    g.   An exciting life
    h.   Happiness
    i.   A world of beauty
    j.   Equality
    k.   Inner harmony
    l.   Wisdom
    m.   Mature love
    n.   Freedom
    o.   Accomplishment
    p.   Pleasure

12. Ranking job outcomes. Rank the following 14 job outcomes in terms of their importance to you (1 is most important, 2 is second most important, etc.).
    a.   Status
    b.   Travel
    c.   Money
    d.   Respect
    e.   Security
    f.   Flexible hours
    g.   Variety
    h.   Working conditions
    i.   Independence
    j.   Socially important work
    k.   Power
    l.   Self-actualization
    m.   Challenge
    n.   Achievement

13. Life line. Draw a line representing your life. Use peaks and valleys to represent positive and negative periods or events in your life. Mark an "X" where you are now; then project your life line out to the end. At the end of your life line, write the epitaph that you think will best summarize your life's work.

## B. Discussion and Career Planning

The class should now divide into groups of two (dyads). Each individual in turn should explain to the other what insights were gained about himself or herself from answering the questions in part A. Then the dyads should discuss appropriate career options based on the answers. Finally, using the insights and information gained from the responses to the questions and from the discussions, each student should answer the following questions individually.

1. What are my three major career strengths?
2. What characteristics of jobs are most important to me?
3. What occupations, jobs, and types of organizations seem most suitable for me?
4. What career goals should I set for myself, both long term and short term?
5. What steps should I take, and by when should I take them, to accomplish these goals?

## C. Further Exploration of Self-Perceptions and Interests

1. It is frequently helpful in career planning to get others' perspectives on you to compare with your self-perceptions. One way to do this involves interviewing one or two people who know you very well, such as a parent, spouse, or best friend. Ask them the same questions you asked yourself in part A of this exercise. Then compare

their responses with your own. What are the similarities and differences? What explains the differences?

2. Another way to get a different perspective beyond your own is to take an interest inventory. Such questionnaires typically assess your career interests according to some underlying model of careers and compare your responses with those of individuals in a variety of career fields. Your career development office on campus should be able to administer an instrument such as the Strong Interest Inventory or the Kuder Preference Scale.

3. It is also sometimes useful to keep a 24-hour diary. For one full school day, keep track of how you spend your time. Then repeat the process for a weekend day or some other day when you do no schoolwork. What did you learn about how you like to spend your time? What does this indicate about your interests?

## REFERENCES

1. Baruch, Y., and Bozionelos, N. (2011). Career issues. In S. Zedeck (Ed.), *APA Handbook of Industrial and Organizational Psychology*, Vol. 2. Washington, DC: American Psychological Association, pp. 67–113. See also Khapova, S. N., Arthur, M. B., and Wilderom, C. P. M. (2007). The subjective career in the knowledge economy. In H. Gunz and M. Peiperl (Eds.), *Handbook of Career Studies*. Thousand Oaks, CA: Sage, pp. 114–130.

2. Greenhaus, J. H. (1987). *Career Management.* Chicago: Dryden.

3. Baruch and Bozionelos, 2011, op. cit. See also Badal, J. (2006, July 24). "Career path" programs help retain workers. *The Wall Street Journal,* pp. B1, B4. See also Hymowitz, C., and Dunham, K. J. (2004, Mar. 29). How to get unstuck. *The Wall Street Journal,* pp. R1–R8. See also Sullivan, S. E. (1999). The changing nature of careers: A review and research agenda. *Journal of Management* 25, pp. 457–484.

4. Grove, A. (1999, Mar. 29). Andy Grove on navigating your career. *Fortune,* pp. 187–192. See also Hall, D. T., and Mirvis, P. H. (1995). Careers as lifelong learning. In A. Howard (Ed.), *The Changing Nature of Work.* San Francisco: Jossey-Bass, pp. 323–361.

5. Wang, S. S. (2011, June 21). A healthy dose of loyalty. *The Wall Street* Journal, pp. D1, D2. See also Gurchiek, K. (2010, March 17). Recession alters relationship between employers, workers. *HR News.* Retrieved from *www.shrm.org/Publications/HRNews/Pages/RecessionAlters.aspx* on March 24, 2010. See also Greenhaus, J. H., Callanan, G. A., and DiRenzo, M. (2008). A boundaryless perspective on careers. In J. Barling and C. L. Cooper (Eds.), *The Sage Handbook of Organizational Behavior,* Vol. 1. London, UK: Sage, pp. 277–299. See also Mainiero, L. A., and Sullivan, S. E. (2005). Kaleidoscope careers: An alternate explanation for the "opt-out" revolution. *Academy of Management Executive 19,* pp. 106–123.

6. Baruch and Bozionelos, 2011, op. cit. See also Anders, G. (2006, Sept. 18). What is success, anyway? *The Wall Street Journal,* p. R10. See also Rousseau, D. M., and Wade-Benzoni, K. A. (1995). Changing individual-organizational attachments. In A. Howard (Ed.), *The Changing Nature of Work.* San Francisco: Jossey-Bass, pp. 290–322.

7. Krell, E. (2010, Oct.). Ways to phase retirement. *HR Magazine* 55(10), pp. 89–96. See also Allen, S. G. (2004, May). The value of phased retirement. NBER working Paper No. W10531. Cambridge, MA: National Bureau of Economic Research.

8. Briscoe, J. P., and Hall, D. T. (2006). The interplay of boundaryless and protean careers: Combinations and implications. *Journal of Vocational Behavior* 69, pp. 4–18. See also Hall, D. T. (1996). Protean careers of the 21st century. *Academy of Management Executive* 10(4), pp. 8–16.

9. Sullivan, S. E., and Crocitto, M. (2007). The developmental theories: A critical examination of their continuing impact on careers research. In H. Gunz and M. Peiperl (Eds.), *Handbook of Career Studies.* Thousand Oaks, CA: Sage, pp. 283–309.

10. Baruch and Bozionelos, 2011, op. cit.  See also Jayson, S. (2007, June 13). No age limit on stages of life. *USA Today,* pp. 1D, 2D. See also More, C., Gunz, H., and Peiperl, M. (2007). Tracing the historical roots of career theory in management and organization studies. In H. Gunz and M. Peiperl (Eds.), *Handbook of Career Studies.* Thousand Oaks, CA: Sage, pp. 13–38.

11. Working scared (1992, Apr. 17). *NBC News.*

12. Bolles, R. N. (2011). *What Color Is Your Parachute? 2011: A Practical Manual for Job-Hunters and Career-Changers.* New York, NY: Ten-Speed Press. See also Lublin, J. S. (2010, June 1). Greasing the inside track to a job. *The Wall Street Journal,* p. D4. See also Yang, J. L. (2009, April 13). How to get a job. *Fortune,* pp. 49–56.

13. Pofeldt, E. (2011, May). Put some punch into your career. *Money,* pp. 23, 24. Barrett, A., and Beeson, J. (2004). *Developing Business Leaders for 2010.* NY: The Conference Board.

14. Waterman, J. A. (2000). Informed opportunism: Career and life planning for the new millennium. In J. M. Kummerow (Ed.), *New Directions in Career Planning and the Workplace.* Palo Alto, CA: Davies-Black, pp. 163–196.

15. Fisher, A. (2006, Aug. 21). Have you outgrown your job? *Fortune,* pp. 46–56. See also Welch, J., and Welch, S. (2007, May 28). Which job is the right job? *BusinessWeek,* p. 110. See also Helyar, J. (2005, May 16). 50 and fired. *Fortune,* pp. 78–90.

16. Porter, W. (2010, Dec. 14). You're fired. *The Denver Post,* pp. 1D, 5D. See also Tyler, K. (2010, Feb.). Leaving with style. *HR Magazine* 55(2), pp. 55–57. See also Rosato, D. (2009, April). Networking for people who hate to network. *Money,* pp. 25, 26. See also Fisher, A. (2005, Apr. 4). How to network—and enjoy it. *Fortune,* p. 38.

17. Galinsky, E., Aumann, K., and Bond, J. T. (2009). *Times Are Changing: Gender and Generation at Work and at Home.* New York, NY: Families & Work Institute.

18. Bureau of Labor Statistics. (2011, March 24). Employment characteristics of families summary. Retrieved from *www.bls.gov/news.release/famee.nr0.htm* on July 28, 2011.

19. Greenhaus, J. H., and Foley, S. (2007). The intersection of work and family lives. In H. Gunz and M. Peiperl (Eds.), *Handbook of Career Studies.* Thousand Oaks, CA: Sage, pp. 131–152.

20. Shellenbarger, S. (2010, July 14). When your co-worker is your spouse. *The Wall Street Journal,* pp. B1, B4. See also Halpern, D. F., and Murphy, S. E. (2005). *From Work-Family Balance to Work-Family Interaction: Changing the Cetaphor.* Mahwah, NJ: Erlbaum.

21. Hube, K. (2004, Mar. 29). Thanks, but no thanks. *The Wall Street Journal,* pp. R4, R7. See also Lublin, J. S. (2000, May 30). Working dads find family involvements can help out careers. *The Wall Street Journal,* p. B1.

22. Murphy, S. E., and Zagorski, D. A. (2005). Enhancing work-family and work-life interaction: The role of management. In D. F. Halpern and S. E. Murphy (Eds.), *From Work-Family Balance to Work-Family Interaction: Changing the Metaphor.* Mahwah, NJ: Erlbaum, pp. 27–47.

23. Demby, E. R. (2004, Jan. 1). Do your family-friendly programs make cents? *HRMagazine,* 49(1), Retrieved from *www.shrm.org/Publications/hrmagazine/EditorialContent/Pages/0104demby.aspx* on October 25, 2011. See also *SHRM 2004 benefits survey report.* (2004, June). Alexandria, VA: Society for Human Resource Management.

24. Belkin, L. (2010, Aug. 9). Child care costs more than college. Retrieved from *parenting. blogs.nytimes.com/2010/08/09/child-care-costs-more-than-college/?scp=1&sq= Child%20care%20costs%20more%20than%20college&st=cse* on July 28, 2011.

25. Galinsky et al., 2009, op. cit.

26. Coplan, J. H. (2008, May 26). What to expect when you're expecting. *BusinessWeek,* p. 17. See also Shellenbarger, S. (2008, June 11). Downsizing maternity leave: Employers cut pay, time off. *The Wall Street Journal,* p. D1.

27. Childcare options: Pros, cons, and costs. (2011, July). Retrieved from *www.babycenter. com/childcare-options* on July 28, 2011.

28. Grover, S. L., and Crooker, K. J. (1995). Who appreciates family-responsive human resource policies: The impact of family-friendly policies on the organizational attachments of parents and non-parents. *Personnel Psychology* 48, pp. 271–288. See also Demby, 2004, op. cit.

29. Galinsky et al., 2009, op. cit. See also Mainiero, L., and Sullivan, S. (2006). *The Opt-out Revolt: Why People Are Leaving Companies to Create Kaleidoscope Careers.* Mountain View, CA: Davies-Black.

30. Breaugh, J. A. (1992). *Recruitment: Science and Practice.* Boston: PWS-Kent.

31. Bauer, T., and Erdogan, B. (2011). Organizational socialization: The effective onboarding of new employees. In S. Zedeck (Ed.), *Handbook of Industrial and Organizational Psychology*, Vol. 3. Washington, DC: American Psychological Association, pp. 51–64. See also Cooper-Thomas, H. D., and Anderson, N. (2007). Organizational socialization. In S. G. Rogelberg (Ed.), *Encyclopedia of Industrial and Organizational Psychology.* Vol. 2. Thousand Oaks, CA: Sage, pp. 581–583. See also Wannberg, C. R., and Kammeyer-Mueller, J. D. (2000). Predictors and outcomes of proactivity in the socialization process. *Journal of Applied Psychology 85,* pp. 373–385.

32. Gerdes, 2009, op. cit.

33. Eby, L. T. (2011). Mentoring. In S. Zedeck (Ed.), *Handbook of Industrial and Organizational Psychology*, Vol. 2. Washington, DC: American Psychological Association, pp. 505–525. See also Meister, J. C., and Willyerd, K. (2010, May). Mentoring millennials. *Harvard Business Review,* pp. 1–4, Reprint R1005D. See also Pease, D. C. (2009, May). Make mentoring memorable. *HR Magazine* 54(5), pp. 63–65. See also Morris, A. (2007, Apr. 3). Leaving your mentor, the right way. *The Wall Street Journal,* p. B6. See also Janasz, S. C., Sullivan, S. E., and Whiting, V. (2003). Mentor networks and career success: Lessons for turbulent times. *Academy of Management Executive* 17(4), pp. 78–91.

34. Wells, S. J. (2009, May). Tending talent. *HR Magazine* 54(5), pp. 53–57. See also Geltzeiler, E. (2005, July 18). Not all senior workers are created equal. *BusinessWeek,* p. 18.

35. Ragins, B. R., Cotton, J. L., and Miller, J. S. (2000). Marginal mentoring: The effects of type of mentor, quality of relationship, and program design on work and career attitudes. *Academy of Management Journal* 43, pp. 1177–1194. See also Young, A. M., and Perrewe, P. L. (2000). What did you expect? An examination of career-related support and social support among mentors and proteges. *Journal of Management* 26, pp. 611–632.

36. Eby, 2011, op. cit. Dunham, K. J. (2003, Sept. 23). Mentors may not help. *The Wall Street Journal*, p. B8. See also Scandura, T. A. (1998). Dysfunctional mentoring relationships and outcomes. *Journal of Management* 24, pp. 449–467.

37. Chandler, D. E., and Kram, K. E. (2007). Mentoring and developmental networks in the new career context. In H. Gunz and M. Peiperl (Eds.), *Handbook of Career Studies.* Thousand Oaks, CA: Sage, pp. 241–267. See also Murray, M. (2000, Feb. 15). GE mentoring program turns underlings into teachers of the web. *The Wall Street Journal,* pp. B1, B18.

38. Meister and Willyerd, 2010, op. cit. See also Berfield, S. (2007, Sept. 17). Bridging the generation gap. *BusinessWeek,* pp. 60, 61.

39. Meister and Willyerd, 2010, op. cit. See also Spors, K. K. (2008, June 3). Web sites offer access to mentors. *The Wall Street Journal,* p. B7.

40. Gerdes, 2009, op. cit. See also Northrup, H. R., and Malin, M. E. (1986). *Personnel Policies for Engineers and Scientists.* Philadelphia: Industrial Research Unit, The Wharton School, University of Pennsylvania.

41. Eby, 2011, op. cit. See also Schein, E. H. (1978). *Career Dynamics: Matching Individual and Organizational Needs.* Reading, MA: Addison-Wesley.

42. Latham, G. P. (2009). *Becoming the Evidence-Based Manager: Making the Science of Management Work for You.* Boston, MA: Davies-Black. See also Locke, E. A.,

and Latham, G. P. (2002). Building a practically useful theory of goal setting and task motivation. *American Psychologist* 57, pp. 705–717.

**43.** Baruch and Bozionelos, 2011, op. cit. See also Lachman, M. E. (2004). Development in midlife. *Annual Review of Psychology* 55, pp. 305–331.

**44.** Shellenbarger, S. (2003, Aug. 14). Mom, please, no bungee-jumping: The lows (and highs) of a midlife crisis. *The Wall Street Journal,* p. D8.

**45.** Gurchiek, 2010, op. cit. See also Regnier, P. (2009, Sept.). Oh, to be young again (for real). *Money,* p. 124. See also Helyar, 2005, op. cit. See also Fisher, A. (2004, Feb. 9). Older, wiser, job hunting. *Fortune,* p. 46.

**46.** Shellenbarger, S. (2005). *The Breaking Point: How Female Midlife Crisis is Transforming Today's Women.* New York: Henry Holt. See also Helyar, 2005, op. cit.

**47.** Shellenbarger, 2005, op. cit.

**48.** Gurchiek, K. (2010, March 17). Recession alters relationship between employers, workers. Retrieved from *www.shrm.org/Publications/HRNews/Pages/RecessionAlters.aspx* on April 20, 2010. See also Murray, M. (2003, Nov. 18). To get out of a slump, get ready to make a change in your work. *The Wall Street Journal,* p. B1. See also Lublin, J. S. (1993, Aug. 4). Strategic sliding: Lateral moves aren't always a mistake. *The Wall Street Journal,* p. B1.

**49.** Cappelli, P., and Novelli, B. (2010). *Managing the Older Worker: How to Prepare for the New Organizational Order.* Boston, MA: Harvard Business Press. See also Helyar, 2005, op. cit. See also Fisher, 2004, op. cit.

**50.** Grossman, R. J. (2008a, May). Keep pace with older workers. *HR Magazine* 53(5), pp. 39–46.

**51.** Grensing-Pophal, L. (2009, March). Holding pattern. *HR Magazine* 54(3), pp. 64–67.

**52.** Elmer, V. (2011, Feb. 7). The invisible promotion. *Fortune,* pp. 31, 32. See also Gurchiek, 2010, op. cit. See also Needleman, S. E. (2009, May 6). Negotiating the freelance economy. *The Wall Street Journal.* Retrieved from *http://finance.yahoo.com/focus-retirement/article/107055/Negotiating-the-Freelance-Economy?mod=fidelity-changingjobs* on May 8, 2009.

**53.** Howard, A., and Bray, D. W. (1982, Mar. 21). AT&T: The hopes of middle managers. *The New York Times,* p. F1.

**54.** Rosenberg, M. World life expectancy chart. Retrieved from *geography.about.com/library/weekly/aa042000b.htm* on July 29, 2011.

**55.** Cappelli and Novelli, 2010, op. cit.

**56.** Byrne, J. (2007, Oct.). AARP: G7 nations must end age bias to meet workforce needs. *Global HR News.* Retrieved from *www.shrm.org/global/news_published/CMS_023238.asp* on July 8, 2008.

**57.** Ng, T., and Feldman, D. C. (2008). The relationship of age to ten dimensions of job performance. *Journal of Applied Psychology* 93, pp. 392–423. See also Sturman, M. C. (2003). Searching for the inverted U-shaped relationship between time and performance: Meta-analyses of the experience/performance, tenure/performance, and age/performance relationships. *Journal of Management* 29, pp. 609–640. See also McEvoy, G. M., and Cascio, W. F. (1989). Cumulative evidence of the relationship between employee age and job performance. *Journal of Applied Psychology* 74, pp. 11–20.

**58.** Stroebe, W. (2010, Oct.). The graying of academia: Will it reduce scientific productivity? *American Psychologist* 65(7), pp. 660–673.

**59.** Cappelli and Novelli, 2010, op. cit. See also Grossman, 2008a, op. cit. See also Czaja, S. J. (1995, Spring). Aging and work performance. *Review of Public Personnel Administration,* pp. 46–61. See also Sterns, H. L., and Miklos, S. M. (1995). The aging worker in a changing environment: Organizational and individual issues. *Journal of Vocational Behavior* 47, pp. 248–268.

**60.** Grossman, R. J. (2008b, May). Use it or lose it. *HR Magazine* 53(5), pp. 44–45. See also Feldman, D. C. (2007). Late-career and retirement issues. In H. Gunz and M. Peiperl

(Eds.), *Handbook of Career Studies*. Thousand Oaks, CA: Sage, pp. 153–168. See also Wellner, A. S. (2002). Tapping a silver mine. *HR Magazine* 47(3), pp. 26–32. See also Berkowitz, M. (1988). Functioning ability and job performance as workers age. In M. E. Borus, H. S. Parnes, S. H. Sandell, and B. Seidman (Eds.), *The Older Worker*. Madison, WI: Industrial Relations Research Association, pp. 87–114.

61. Ng and Feldman, 2008, op. cit. See also Martocchio, J. J. (1989). Age-related differences in employee absenteeism: A meta-analysis. *Psychology and Aging 4*, pp. 401–414.

62. Ng and Feldman, 2008, op. cit.

63. Cappelli and Novelli, 2010, op. cit. See also Grossman, 2008a, op. cit. See also Ng and Feldman, 2008, op. cit. See also Chapman, B. P., and Hayslip, B. (2006). Emotional intelligence in young and middle adulthood: Cross-sectional analysis of latent structure and means. *Psychology and Aging* 21, pp. 411–418. See also Grossman, R. J. (2003). Are you ignoring older workers? *HR Magazine* 48(8), pp. 40–46.

64. Cappelli and Novelli, 2010, op. cit. See also Polder, J. J., Bonneaux, L., Meerding, W. J., and Van Der Maas, P. J. (2002). Age-specific increases in health care costs. *European Journal of Public Health* 12, pp. 57–62.

65. Grossman, R. J. (2008c, May). Mature workers: Myths and realities. *HR Magazine* 53(5), pp. 40, 41. See also New study cracks myth about the costs of older workers. (1995). *Working Age* 11(4), pp. 2–3.

66. Stroebe, 2010, op. cit. See also Ng and Feldman, 2008, op. cit. See also Kanfer, R., Crosby, J. V., and Brandt, D. M. (1988). Investigating behavioral antecedents of turnover at three job levels. *Journal of Applied Psychology* 73, pp. 331–335.

67. Ng and Feldman, 2008, op. cit.

68. Cappelli and Novelli, 2010, op. cit. See also Grossman, 2008a, 2008c, op. cit. See also Maurer, T. J. (2001). Career-relevant learning and development, worker age, and beliefs about self-efficacy for development. *Journal of Management 27*, pp. 123–140.

69. Grensing-Pophal, 2009, op. cit. See also Cappelli and Novelli, 2010, op. cit.

70. Ibid. See also Byrne, 2007, op. cit. See also Paul, R. J., and Townsend, J. B. (1993) Managing the older worker—Don't just rinse away the gray. *Academy of Management Executive* 7(3), pp. 67–74.

71. Grossman, 2008a, 2003, op. cit.

72. Cappelli and Novelli, 2010, op. cit. See also Feldman, 2007, op. cit. See also Fisher, 2004, op. cit. See also Too many gray hairs. (2002, Oct. 21). *BusinessWeek,* p. 16. See also Bird, C. P., and Fisher, T. D. (1986). Thirty years later: Attitudes toward the employment of older workers. *Journal of Applied Psychology* 71, pp. 315–317.

73. Grossman, 2008a, op. cit. New study cracks myth about the costs of older workers, 1995, op. cit.

74. Byron, E. (2009, Sept. 14). Seeing store shelves through senior eyes. *The Wall Street Journal,* pp. B1, B2. See also Fisher, A. (2002, Nov. 11). What you call old age, I call a lifetime of experience. *Fortune,* p. 46. See also Leger, D. E. (2000, May 29). Help! I'm the new boss. *Fortune,* pp. 281–284.

75. Young, M. B. (2009). *Strategic Workforce Planning in Global Organizations*. New York, NY: The Conference Board. See also Walker, J. W. (1992). *Human Resource Strategy.* New York: McGraw-Hill.

76. Badal, J. (2006, July 24). "Career path" programs help retain workers. *The Wall Street Journal,* pp. B1, B4.

77. Bates, S. (2004). Getting engaged. *HR Magazine* 49(2), pp. 44–51.

78. Stumpf, S. A., and London, M. (1981). Management promotions: Individual and organizational factors influencing the decision process. *Academy of Management Review* 6, pp. 539–549.

79. Avery, D. R. (2011). Why the playing field remains uneven: Impediments to promotions in organizations. In S. Zedeck (Ed.), *APA Handbook of Industrial and Organizational Psychology*, Vol. 3. Washington, DC: American Psychological Association, pp. 577–613. See also Schwarzwald, J., Koslowsky, M., and Shalit, B.

(1992). A field study of employees' attitudes and behaviors after promotion decisions. *Journal of Applied Psychology* 77, pp. 511–514.

80. Delayed departures. (2010). 2010 HR Trendbook. *Special Supplement to HR Magazine* 54(12), pp. 9, 10. See also Weber, 2007, op. cit. See also Sulkowicz, K. (2007, May 21). Stressed for success. *BusinessWeek,* p. 18.

81. Feldman, 2007, op. cit.

82. Feldman, 2007, op. cit. See also Lancaster, H. (1996, Nov. 19). A demotion does not have to mean the end of a fulfilling career. *The Wall Street Journal,* p. B1.

83. Ertugul, M., and Krishnan, K. (2011). Can CEO dismissals be proactive? *Journal of Corporate Finance* 17, *pp. 134–151.*

84. Auerbach, J. (1996, Apr. 5). Executive relocations—and hassles—increase. *The Wall Street Journal,* p. B8.

85. Judiesch, M. K., and Lyness, K. S. (1999). Left behind? The impact of leaves of absence on managers' career success. *Academy of Management Journal* 42, pp. 641–651. See also Stroh, L. K., Brett, J. M., and Reilly, A. H. (1992). All the right stuff: A comparison of female and male managers' career progression. *Journal of Applied Psychology* 77, pp. 251–260.

86. Roberts, B. (2009, Aug.). Lowdown on relo. *HR Magazine* 54(8), pp. 49–51.

87. Grensing-Pophal, L. (2000, May). Think about the children. *HR Magazine,* pp. 133–142.

88. Lubin, J. S. (1993, Apr. 13). Husbands in limbo. *The Wall Street Journal,* pp. A1, A8.

89. Kadlec, D. (2007, Mar.). Reversal of fortune: When she makes more. *Money,* pp. 36, 38.

90. Labor letter (1989, Nov. 17). *The Wall Street Journal,* p. A1.

91. Pinder, C. C., and Schroeder, K. G. (1987). Time to proficiency following job transfers. *Academy of Management Journal* 30, pp. 336–353.

92. Krell, E. (2010a, Aug.). The business of relocation: Not good. *HR Magazine* 55(8), pp. 47–52.

93. Krell, E. (2010b). Art of moving, by the numbers. *HR Magazine* 55(8), pp. 54–56. See also Mumma, J. S. (1996, Oct.). New technologies speed relocation process. *HR Magazine,* pp. 55–60.

94. Krell, 2010a, op. cit. See also Grensing-Pophal, L. (2004, Feb.). *Retrieved from www.shrm.org/Publications/hrmagazine/EditorialContent/Pages/0204pophal.aspx* on March 25, 2004. A sum for all reasons. *HR Magazine* 49(2). Retrieved from *www.shrm.org/Publications/hrmagazine/EditorialContent/Pages/0204pophal.aspx* on March 25, 2004.

95. De Meuse, K. P., Marks, M. L., and Dai, G. (2011). Organizational downsizing, mergers and acquisitions, and strategic alliances: Using theory and research to enhance practice. In S. Zedeck (Ed.), *Handbook of Industrial and Organizational Psychology,* Vol. 3. Washington, DC: American Psychological Association, pp. 729–768. See also Uchitelle, L. (2007). *The Disposable American.* New York, NY: Vintage.

96. Granatstein, S., and Young, N. (Producers). (2009, Jan. 25). The winter of our hardship. *60 Minutes* (CBS). Retrieved from *www.cbsnews.com/video/watch/?id=4752 321n&tag=related;photovideo.* See also Cascio, W. F. (2010). *Employment Downsizing and Its Alternatives.* Alexandria, VA: Society for Human Resource Management. See also Bragg, R. (1996, Mar. 5). Big holes where the dignity used to be. *The New York Times,* pp. 1, 8–10.

97. De Meuse et al., 2011, op. cit. See also Pfeffer, J. (2010, Feb. 5). Lay off the layoffs. *Newsweek.* Retrieved from *www.thedailybeast.com/newsweek/2010/02/04/lay-off-the-layoffs.html* on February 10, 2010. See also Cascio, W. F. (2004). Downsizing and outplacement. In S. Zedeck (Ed.), *Encyclopedia of Applied Psychology,* Vol. 1. London, UK: Elsevier, pp. 621–626. See also Leana, C. R., Feldman, D. C., and Tan, G. Y. (1998). Predictors of coping behavior after a lay-off. *Journal of Organizational Behavior* 19(1), pp. 85–97. See also Leana, C. R., and Feldman, D. C. (1992). *Coping with Job Loss: How Individuals, Organizations, and Communities Respond to Layoffs.* New York: Macmillan/Lexington Books.

**98.** Regnier, 2009, op. cit. See also The job-huntin' blues. (1998, Dec. 14). *BusinessWeek,* p. 8.

**99.** Cascio, W. F. (In press). How does downsizing come about? In Cooper, C. L., Quick, J. C., and Pandey, A. (Eds.), *Downsizing: Is Less Still More?* Cambridge, UK: Cambridge University Press. See also Helyar, 2005, op. cit.

**100.** Cascio, 2010, op. cit. See also Uchitelle, 2007, op. cit. See also Leana, C. R. (1996, Apr. 14). Why downsizing won't work. *Chicago Tribune Magazine,* pp. 15–18.

**101.** Kimes, M. (2009, March 2). Does your team have PLSD (Post-Layoff Survivor Disorder)? *Fortune,* p. 24. See also Kiviat, B. (2009, Feb. 1). After layoffs there's survivor's guilt. *Time.* Retrieved from *www.time.com/time/business/article/0,8599,1874592,00.html* on September 8, 2011. See also Devine, K., Reay, T., Stainton, L., and Collins-Nakai, R. (2003). Downsizing outcomes: Better a victim than a survivor? *Human Resource Management* 42(2), pp. 109–124.

**102.** Feldman, 2007, op. cit. See also Bates, S. (2003). A model retirement. *HR Magazine,* pp. 71–73. See also Bland, T. S. (2000). New EEOC guidance on discrimination in employee benefits. SHRM White Paper. Retrieved from *www.shrm.org/Templates-Tools/Toolkits/Pages/CMS_000018.aspx* on September 22, 2004.

**103.** Strieber, M. (2008, May 30). GM sheds 19,000 workers in voluntary buyout. Retrieved from *wot.motortrend.com/6248470/auto-news/gm-sheds-19000-workers-in-voluntary-buyout/index.html* on July 9, 2008.

**104.** Mollica, K. A., and DeWitt, R. L. (2000). When others retire early: What about me? *Academy of Management Journal* 43, pp. 1068–1075.

**105.** Snip, snip, oops! (2001, Oct. 13). *The Economist,* pp. 59, 60. See also Take the money and run—or take your chances. (1993, Aug. 16). *BusinessWeek,* pp. 28, 29.

**106.** Hymowitz, C. (2001, July 24). Using layoffs to battle downturns often costs more than it saves. *The Wall Street Journal,* p. B1.

**107.** Brandon, E. (2011, July 22). 21 workplace benefits that are rapidly disappearing. *US News & World Report.* Retrieved from *money.usnews.com/money/retirement/articles/2011/07/22/21-workplace-benefits-that-are-rapidly-disappearing* on July 30, 2011.

**108.** Feldman, 2007, op. cit. See also Kim, S., and Feldman, D. C. (1998). Healthy, wealthy, or wise: Predicting actual acceptances of early retirement incentives at three points in time. *Personnel Psychology* 51, pp. 623–642.

**109.** Porter, 2010, op. cit. See also Farrell, C. (2004, July 26). No need to hit the panic button. *BusinessWeek,* pp. 77–80. See also Just what kind of retiree will you be? (2002, June 17). *BusinessWeek,* p. 10.

**110.** Morris, B. (1996, Aug. 19). The future of retirement. *Fortune,* pp. 86–94.

**111.** Maertz, C. P., Jr., and Campion, M. A. (2004). Profiles in quitting: Integrating process and content turnover theory. *Academy of Management Journal* 47, pp. 566–582.

**112.** Porter, 2010, op. cit. See also MacDonald, J. Going out on the right note. Retrieved from *www.bankrate.com/brm/news/advice/20030113a.asp* on September 22, 2004.

**113.** Available at *store.lominger.com/store/lominger/en_US/DisplayCategoryProduct ListPage/categoryID.19947700/parentCategoryID.19946100.*

**114.** For more on this, see *www.discoveryourpersonality.com/strongandmbticareer.html.* See also Kummerow, J. M. (2000). Using the Strong Interest Inventory® and the Meyers Briggs Type Indicator together: The whole is greater than the sum of its parts. In J. M. Kummerow (Ed.), *New Directions in Career Planning and the Workplace.* Palo Alto, CA: Davies-Black, pp. 310–350.

**115.** Lancaster, H. (1995, Aug. 29). Professionals try new way to assess and develop skills. *The Wall Street Journal,* p. B1.

**116.** Wells, S. (2003, Nov.). Who's next? *HR Magazine,* pp. 44–50.

# 4

# COMPENSATION

Compensation is a critical component of the employment relationship. It includes direct cash payments, indirect payments in the form of employee benefits, and incentives to motivate employees to strive for higher levels of productivity. Compensation is affected by forces as diverse as labor-market factors, collective bargaining, government legislation, and top management's philosophy regarding pay and benefits. This is a dynamic area, and Chapters 11 and 12 present the latest developments in compensation theory and examples of company practices. Chapter 11 is a nontechnical introduction to the subject of pay and incentive systems, while Chapter 12 focuses on employee benefits. You will find that the material in each chapter has direct implications for sound management practice.

# 11 | PAY AND INCENTIVE SYSTEMS

*Questions This Chapter Will Help Managers Answer*

1. How can we tie compensation strategy to general business strategy?
2. What economic and legal factors should we consider in establishing pay levels for different jobs?
3. What is the best way to develop pay systems that are understandable, workable, and acceptable to employees at all levels?
4. How can we tie incentives to individual, team, or organizationwide performance?
5. In implementing a pay-for-performance system, what key traps must we avoid to make the system work as planned?

## THE TRUST GAP*

Over the years, few topics have generated as much controversy as executive compensation. CEOs say, "We're a team; we're all in this together." But employees look at the difference between their pay and the CEO's. They see top management's perks—oak dining rooms and heated garages—versus cafeterias for lower-level workers and parking spaces a half mile from the plant. And they wonder, "Is this togetherness?" As the disparity in pay widens, the wonder grows. Thus the median value of total direct compensation for CEOs of Standard & Poor's (S&P) 500 companies was $8.4 million in 2010. Their total compensation in 2010 averaged $11.4 million. Hourly workers and supervisors indeed agree that "we're all in this together," but what we're in turns out to be a frame of mind that mistrusts senior management's intentions, doubts its competence, and resents its self-congratulatory pay. What's at stake, in short, is nothing less than the public trust essential to a thriving free-market economy.

Study after study, involving hundreds of companies and thousands of workers, has found evidence of a **trust gap**—and it is growing. Indeed, the attitudes of middle managers and professionals toward the workplace are becoming more like those of hourly workers, historically the most disaffected group.

According to the Economic Policy Institute, executive pay rose about 300 percent from 1992 to 2007. This compares with growth in the same period of about 14 percent in the inflation-adjusted real wages of college graduates. The gap persists because bonuses, typically tied to profits, are routinely awarded to top managers but not to other employees.

What about shareholder pressure to limit CEO pay? The 2010 Dodd-Frank Wall Street Reform and Consumer Protection Act grants shareholders a "say on pay" vote on executive compensation. In the year after the law was passed, however, shareholders rejected pay plans at only 39 out of 2,502 companies (1.5 percent).

To be sure, much of the trust gap can be traced to inconsistencies between what management says and what it does—between saying "People are our most important asset" and in the next breath ordering layoffs, or between sloganeering about quality while continuing to evaluate workers by how many pieces they push out the door.

There are other causes as well: lack of penalties to executives who caused the global financial crisis and the meltdown in financial services, together with pay systems that rewarded financial engineering and greed rather than prudent risk management and value creation. Moreover, financial-services leaders and board members failed to say, "Here's what went wrong. Here's how faulty incentives contributed to the problem; here's how we are going to fix it."

---

*Sources: Davidoff, S. M. (2011, July 13). Efforts to rein in executive pay meet with little success. *The New York Times.* Retrieved from *http://nyti.ms/uwMaNt* on July 31, 2011. See also ABC News. (2011, April 22). CEO pay averaged $11.4 million at largest companies in 2010. Retrieved from *abcnews.go.com/Business/ceo-pay-increased-23-percent-2010/story?id=13420978* on April 22, 2011. See also George, B. (2010, Sept. 19). executive pay: Rebuilding trust in an era of rage. *BusinessWeek,* p. 56. See also Heineman, B. (2009, Feb. 16). Executive compensation: The leadership failure that led to pay caps. Retrieved from *blogs.hbr.org/hbr/hbreditors/2009/02/reaping_the_exec_comp_whirlwin.html* on February 20, 2009. See also Colvin, G. (2008, Jan. 21). AmEx gets CEO pay right. *Fortune,* pp. 22, 24. See also Kaplan, S. N. (2008). Are U. S. CEOs overpaid? *Academy of Management Perspectives* 22, pp. 5–20. See also Lublin, J. S. (2007 Apr. 9). Ten ways to restore investor confidence in compensation. *The Wall Street Journal,* pp. R1, R3. See also Farnham, A. (1989, Dec. 4). The trust gap, *Fortune,* pp. 56–78.

The result is a world in which top management thinks it's sending crucial messages but employees never hear a word. Thus, a recent survey found that 82 percent of *Fortune* 500 executives believe their corporate strategy is understood by everyone who needs to know. Unfortunately, less than a third of employees in the same companies say management provides clear goals and direction.

Confidence in top management's competence is collapsing. The days when top management could say, "Trust us; this is for your own good," are over. Employees have seen that if the company embarks on a new strategic tack and it doesn't work, employees are the ones who lose their jobs—not management.

While competence may be hard to judge, pay is known, and to the penny. The rate of increase in CEOs' pay split from workers' in 1979 and has rocketed upward ever since. CEOs who make 350 times the average hourly worker's pay are no longer rare. What is rare are policies like those of Whole Foods Market that prevent any executive from earning more than 14 times what the average worker makes. Said one observer, "The gap is widening beyond what the guy at the bottom can even understand. There's very little common ground left in terms of the experience of the average worker and the CEO."

While most U.S. workers are willing to accept substantial differentials in pay between corporate highs and lows and acknowledge that the highs should receive their just rewards, more and more of the lows—and the middles—are asking, "Just how just is just?"

### Challenges

1. To many people, a deep-seated sense of unfairness lies at the heart of the trust gap. How might perceptions of unfairness develop?
2. What are some of the predictable consequences of a trust gap?
3. Can you suggest alternative strategies for reducing the trust gap?

---

The chapter-opening vignette illustrates important changes in the current thinking about pay: Levels of pay will always be evaluated by employees in terms of fairness, and unless pay systems are acceptable to those affected by them, they will breed mistrust and lack of commitment. Pay policies and practices are critically important because they affect every single employee, from the janitor to the CEO. This chapter begins by exploring four major questions: (1) What economic and legal factors determine pay levels within a firm? (2) How do firms tie compensation strategy to general business strategy? (3) How do firms develop systematic pay structures that reflect different levels of pay for different jobs? (4) What key policy issues in pay planning and administration must managers address? These challenges are shown graphically in Figure 11–1.

We will then consider what is known about incentives at the individual, team, and organizationwide levels. As an educated worker or manager, it is important that you become knowledgeable about these important issues. This chapter will help you develop that knowledge base.

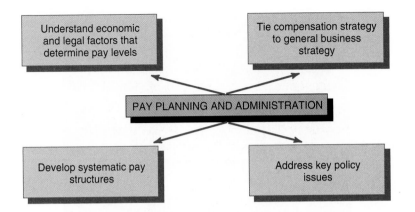

**Figure 11–1**

Four key challenges in planning and administering a pay system.

## CHANGING PHILOSOPHIES REGARDING PAY SYSTEMS

Today there is a continuing move away from policies of salary entitlement, in which inflation or seniority, not performance, were the driving forces behind pay increases. Pay-for-performance is the new mantra.[1] Managers are asking, "What have you done for me lately?" Current performance is what counts, and every year performance standards are raised. In this atmosphere, we are seeing three major changes in company philosophies concerning pay and benefits:

1. Increased willingness to reduce the size of the workforce; to outsource jobs overseas; and to restrict pay to control the costs of wages, salaries, and benefits.
2. Less concern with pay position relative to that of competitors and more concern with what the company can afford.
3. Implementation of programs to encourage and reward performance—thereby making pay more variable. In fact, a recent study revealed that this is one of the most critical compensation issues facing large companies today.[2]

We will consider each of these changes, as well as other material in this and the following chapter, from the perspective of the line manager, not from that of the technical compensation specialist.

### Cost-Containment Actions

Given that wage and salary payments may account for more than 50 percent of total costs, employers have an obvious interest in controlling them.[3] To do so, they are attempting to contain staff sizes, payrolls, and benefits costs. Some of the cutbacks are only temporary, such as pay freezes and postponements of raises.[4] Other changes are meant to be permanent: firing executives or offering them early retirement; asking employees to work longer hours, to take fewer days off, and to shorten their vacations; reducing the coverage of medical plans or asking employees to pay part of the cost; and trimming expense accounts, with bans on first-class travel and restrictions on phone calls and entertainment. If such a strategy is to work, however, CEOs will first need to demonstrate to employees at all levels, by means of tangible actions, that they are serious about closing the trust gap (see chapter-opening vignette).

Robert Iger, President and CEO of The Walt Disney Company, has been richly rewarded for his stellar leadership of the diversified worldwide entertainment company.

## Paying What the Company Can Afford

To cover its labor costs and other expenses, a company must earn sufficient revenues through the sales of its products or services. It follows, then, that an employer's ability to pay is constrained by its ability to compete. The nature of the product or service markets affects a firm's external competitiveness and the pay level it sets.[5]

Key factors in the product and service markets are the degree of competition among producers (e.g., fast-food outlets) and the level of demand for the products or services (e.g., the number of customers in a given area). Both of these affect the ability of a firm to change the prices of its products or services. If an employer cannot change prices without suffering a loss of revenues due to decreased sales, that employer's ability to raise the level of pay is constrained. If the employer does pay more, it has two options: try to pass the increased costs on to consumers or hold prices fixed and allocate a greater portion of revenues to cover labor costs.[6]

## Programs That Encourage and Reward Performance

Firms are continuing to relocate to areas where organized labor is weak and pay rates are low. They are developing pay plans that channel more dollars into incentive awards and fewer into fixed salaries. Entrepreneurs in startup, high-risk organizations, salespeople, piecework factory workers, and rock stars have long lived with erratic incomes.[7] People in other jobs are used to fairly fixed paychecks that grow a bit every year. It is a bedrock of the U.S. compensation system, but it is gradually being nudged aside by programs that put more pay at risk. In 2010, for example, base pay comprised only 10 percent of CEO compensation.[8] These programs are being linked to profit and productivity gains—usually a moving, ever-rising target.

At lower levels, such variable-pay systems almost guarantee cost control. In many new plans, any productivity gains are shared 25 percent by the employees and 75 percent by the company. If business takes off, more pay goes to workers. If it doesn't, the company is not locked into high fixed costs of labor. In the United States, 90 percent of large and medium-sized companies now offer some kind of variable pay—such as profit-sharing and bonus awards—up from 47 percent in 1990 (see Figure 11–2). Globally, that figure is about 80 percent.[9]

## INTERNATIONAL APPLICATION
### Tying Pay to Performance in the United States, Europe, and Japan[a]

In an effort to hold down labor costs, thousands of U.S. companies are changing the way they increase workers' pay. Instead of the traditional annual increase, millions of workers in industries as diverse as supermarkets and aircraft manufacturing are receiving cash bonuses. For most workers, the plans mean less money. The bonuses take many names: "profit sharing" at Abbott Laboratories and Hewlett-Packard, "gain sharing" at Mack Trucks and Panhandle Energy, and "lump-sum payments" at Boeing. All have two elements in common: (1) They can vary with the company's fortunes, and (2) they are not permanent. Because the bonuses are not folded into base pay (as merit increases are), there is no compounding effect over time. They are simply provided on top of a constant base level of pay. This means that both wages and benefits rise more slowly than they would have if the base level of pay was rising each year. The result: a flattening of wages nationally.

*Flexible pay*—tied mostly to profitability and promising better job security, but not guaranteeing it—is at the heart of the evolving bonus system. Employees are being asked to share the risks of the new global marketplace.

How large must the rewards be? While hard data on this question are scarce, most experts agree that employees don't begin to notice incentive payouts unless they are at least 10 percent, with 15 to 20 percent more likely to evoke the desired response.[b] In the United States and most European Union countries, bonus payments have been averaging about 11 percent of a worker's base pay annually.[c] Conversely, the Japanese currently pay many workers a bonus that represents about 25 percent of base pay. For workers in all nations, a significant amount of their pay is at risk.

Have such plans generated greater productivity in the U.S. manufacturing sector in recent years? Maybe, but an equally plausible explanation is that the gains were due to automation; to company efforts to give workers more of a say in how they do their jobs; and to workers' fear that if they did not improve their productivity, their plants would become uncompetitive and be closed. In short, the jury is still out on the productivity impact of bonus systems, but evidence does indicate that bonus satisfaction is a separate and distinct component of overall pay satisfaction.[d]

---

[a]Mantell, R. (2011, May 17). Companies tie more of workers' pay to performance. *http://online.wsj.com/article/BT-CO-20110517-706252.html* on May 18, 2011. See also Nelson, E. (1995, Sept. 29). Gas company's gain-sharing plan turns employees into cost-cutting vigilantes. *The Wall Street Journal*, pp. B1, B4. See also Uchitelle, L. (1987, June 26). Bonuses replace wage raises and workers are the losers. *The New York Times*, pp. A1, D3.

[b]Milkovich, G. T., Newman, J. M., and Gerhart, B. (2011). *Compensation* (10th ed.). New York: McGraw-Hill.

[c]Miller, 2010, op. cit. See also Hall, K. (2009). CEO pay: Don't look to Japan for answers. *BusinessWeek*, p. 60.

[d]Sturman, M. C., and Short, J. C. (2000). Lump-sum bonus satisfaction: Testing the construct validity of a new pay satisfaction dimension. *Personnel Psychology* 53, pp. 673–700.

---

Later in this chapter we will discuss pay-for-performance more fully and how it can be put into effect.

This international example focused on the *outcomes* of bonus decisions. However, the *process* is also important. To a large extent, the relative emphasis managers place on performance versus relationships varies with cultural factors. Thus, when making bonus decisions, Chinese managers tend to place less emphasis on employees' work performance than do American managers. However, when making decisions about nonmonetary recognition of employees, Chinese managers tend to place

**Figure 11–2**

Percent of companies offering some form of variable pay, 1990–2008.

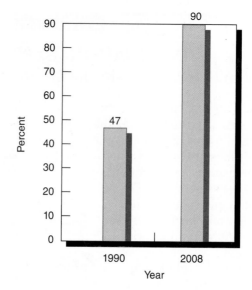

more emphasis on employees' relationships with coworkers and managers than do their American counterparts. Finally, Chinese managers tend to give larger bonuses to employees with greater personal needs, while American managers tend not to take personal needs into consideration when making bonus decisions.[10]

## COMPONENTS AND OBJECTIVES OF ORGANIZATIONAL REWARD SYSTEMS

At a broad level, an **organizational reward system** includes anything an employee values and desires that an employer is able and willing to offer in exchange for employee contributions. More specifically, such **compensation** includes both financial and nonfinancial rewards. **Financial rewards** include direct payments (e.g., salary) plus indirect payments in the form of employee benefits (see Chapter 12). **Nonfinancial rewards** include everything in a work environment that enhances a worker's sense of self-respect and esteem by others (e.g., work environments that are physically, socially, and mentally healthy; opportunities for training and personal development; effective supervision; recognition). These ideas are shown graphically in Figure 11–3.

While money is obviously a powerful tool used to capture the minds and hearts of workers and to maximize their productivity, don't underestimate the impact of nonfinancial rewards. In an improved economy, one way companies are trying to keep their employees satisfied is by offering perks—gyms, flexible hours, and other amenities. As an example, consider goodmortgage.com, a 56-employee business in Charlotte, North Carolina. Employees gather in the morning to follow exercise videos on a large flat-screen TV in the full gym and to eat breakfast cooked for them by management. After one employee won a $500 gas card in one of the company's ongoing sales contests, she remarked, "I have a lot of friends in the mortgage industry and a lot of people have tried to recruit me, but no one treats their employees like we're treated here."[11]

Companies are doing these things because they don't have much choice. Giving their workers more ease and freedom is simply enlightened self-interest. As one executive noted, "In yesteryear you worked 9 to 5 and that was work-life balance. Today, people look for more flexibility." Flexibility is just one part of

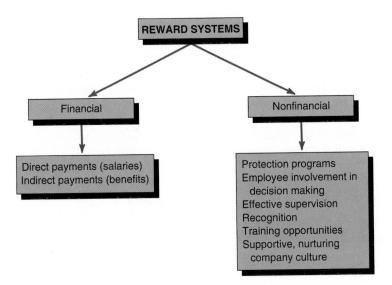

**Figure 11–3**

Organizational reward systems include financial as well as nonfinancial components.

a total rewards system. Employers are rethinking each aspect of it, especially in light of findings from a 2011 Manpower Group survey in which 75 percent of employers reported involuntarily losing some of their highest-performing employees, despite a lagging job market.[12]

Rewards bridge the gap between organizational objectives and individual expectations and aspirations. To be effective, organizational reward systems should provide four things: (1) a sufficient level of rewards to fulfill basic needs, (2) equity with the external labor market, (3) equity within the organization, and (4) treatment of each member of the organization in terms of his or her individual needs.[13] More broadly, pay systems are designed to attract, retain, and motivate employees. This is the ARM concept. Indeed, much of the design of compensation systems involves working out tradeoffs among more or less seriously conflicting objectives.[14]

Perhaps the most important objective of any pay system is fairness, or equity. Equity can be assessed on at least three dimensions:

1. **Internal equity.** Are pay rates fair in terms of the relative worth of individual jobs to an organization?
2. **External equity.** Are the wages paid by an organization fair in terms of competitive market rates outside the organization?
3. **Individual equity.** Is each individual's pay fair relative to that of other individuals doing the same or similar jobs?

Researchers have proposed several bases for determining equitable payment for work.[15] They have three points in common:

1. Each assumes that employees perceive a fair return for what they contribute to their jobs.
2. All include the concept of social comparison, whereby employees determine what their equitable return should be after comparing their inputs (e.g., skills, education, effort) and outcomes (e.g., pay, promotion, job status) with those of their peers or coworkers (comparison persons).
3. The theories assume that employees who perceive themselves to be in an inequitable situation will seek to reduce that inequity. They may do so by mentally distorting their inputs or outcomes, by directly altering their inputs or outcomes, or by leaving the organization.

Reviews of both laboratory and field tests of equity theory are quite consistent: Individuals tend to follow the equity norm and to use it as a basis for distributing rewards. They report inequitable conditions as distressing, although there may be individual differences in sensitivity to equity.[16]

A final objective is **balance**—the relative size of pay differentials among different segments of the workforce. If pay systems are to accomplish the objectives set for them, ultimately they must be perceived as adequate and equitable. For example, there should be a balance in pay relationships between supervisors and the highest paid subordinates reporting to them. This differential typically varies from 5 to 30 percent.[17] As the chapter-opening vignette illustrated, ratios of 350 to 1 (or greater) between the highest- and lowest-paid employees are generally regarded as out of balance.

## STRATEGIC INTEGRATION OF COMPENSATION PLANS AND BUSINESS PLANS

Unfortunately, the rationale behind many compensation programs is "Two-thirds of our competitors do it" or "That's corporate policy." Compensation plans need to be tied to an organization's strategic mission and should take their direction from that mission. They must support the general business strategy,

---

### ETHICAL DILEMMA
### Does Being Ethical Pay?*

Social responsibility has become big business for many corporations. Companies spend billions of dollars doing good works—everything from boosting diversity in their ranks to developing eco-friendly technology— and then trumpeting those efforts to the public. Do those efforts pay off?

In a series of experiments, consumers were shown the same products—coffee and T-shirts. One group was told that the items were made using high ethical standards, another was told that the items were made using low ethical standards, and a third group (the control group) received no information. In the case of coffee, consumers were willing to pay $9.71 for a pound produced using high ethical standards, $5.89 for a pound produced using unethical standards, and $8.31 when given no information about the ethical standards used in coffee production. Results for T-shirts were similar. The researchers concluded that consumers are willing to pay a small premium for goods produced ethically, but they will punish a product made unethically even more harshly, by buying it only at a steep discount.

The implication of this research is that companies should segment their overall markets, and make special efforts to reach out to buyers with high ethical standards. Those are the customers who can deliver the biggest potential profits on ethically produced goods.

In an effort to attract, retain, and motivate top talent, do you believe that companies should also trumpet their ethical standards? Is there a payoff? What specific actions would you recommend with respect to developing a strategy to recruit new employees and to retain and motivate existing ones?

*Source: Trudel, R., and Cotte, J. (2008, May 12). Does being ethical pay? *The Wall Street Journal*, p. R4.

for example, differentiation (setting yourself apart from the competition) or cost leadership.[18] Further, evidence now shows that inferior performance by a firm is associated with a lack of fit between its pay policy and its business strategy.[19] From a managerial perspective, therefore, the most fundamental question is "What do you want your pay system to accomplish?"

As an example, consider IBM's strategic and cultural transformation. The company describes its current strategy as having a "focus on the high-growth, high-value segments of the IT industry." It notes, for example, that it "has exited commoditizing businesses like personal computers and hard disk drives." IBM describes its current global capabilities as including "services, software, hardware, fundamental research, and financing," and that this "broad mix of businesses and capabilities are combined to provide business insight and solutions for the company's clients."[20] A new business strategy meant a new compensation strategy. To do that, IBM cut layers of management, redesigned jobs to build in more flexibility, increased incentive pay to differentiate performance more clearly, and aggressively cut costs. The company changed its pay strategy and pay system to support its changed business strategy.

This approach to managing compensation and business strategies dictates that actual levels of compensation should not be strictly a matter of what is being paid in the marketplace. Instead, compensation levels derive from an assessment of what must be paid to attract and retain the right people, what the organization can afford, and what will be required to meet the organization's strategic goals. The idea is to align the interests of managers and employees.

When compensation is viewed from a strategic perspective, therefore, firms do the following:

1. They recognize compensation as a pivotal control and incentive mechanism that can be used flexibly by management to attain business objectives.
2. They make the pay system an integral part of strategy formulation.
3. They integrate pay considerations into strategic decision-making processes, such as those that involve planning and control.
4. They view the firm's performance as the ultimate criterion of the success of strategic pay decisions and operational compensation programs.[21]

## DETERMINANTS OF PAY STRUCTURE AND LEVEL

Marginal revenue theory in labor economics holds that unless an employee can produce a value equal to the value received in wages, it will not be worthwhile to hire that worker.[22] In practice, a number of factors interact to determine wage levels. Some of the most influential of these are labor-market conditions, legislation, collective bargaining, management attitudes, and an organization's ability to pay. Let us examine each of these.

### Labor Market Conditions

As noted in Chapter 6, whether a labor market is "tight" or "loose" has a major impact on wage structures and levels. Thus, if the demand for certain skills is high while the supply is low (a tight market), there tends to be an increase in the price paid for these skills. Conversely, if the supply of labor is plentiful, relative to the demand for it, wages tend to decrease. As an example, consider Jordan Machine Company.

## JORDAN MACHINE COMPANY

Jordan Machine Company of Birmingham, Alabama, has never worked so hard to find so few employees. "We've turned over barrels and drums and searched just about everywhere we can think," says Jerry Edwards, chief executive officer. The company needs skilled machinists to help manufacture molds for everything from fishing lures to submarine hatch covers.[a]

Despite his efforts—including offers of high pay, full health benefits, and a company-sponsored savings program—Edwards estimated that his company lost more than half a million dollars last year, simply because it couldn't find enough workers to meet the demand for new orders.

Jordan Machine Company is not alone. Companies, high-tech and low-tech alike, simply cannot find workers when labor markets are tight. In tight labor markets, labor shortages are the number 1 headache for many employers. In some cases it has curbed growth and expansion possibilities, and in others it has forced operators to shut down early for lack of staff.[b] Such tight labor markets have predictable effects on wages. Consider auto-repair technicians, long stereotyped as low-paid grease monkeys. With increasing computerization and complex diagnostics in autos, many older mechanics are choosing to change careers rather than go back for more training. The scarcity is forcing some dealers to poach other shops, and it has driven up auto-repair costs as well as the wages of repair technicians. Their average wages exceeded $41,000 in 2010, up 25 percent in the past decade, and demand for them is projected to grow 5 percent from 2008 to 2018.[c]

[a]Jaffe, G. (1997, Jan. 15). South's growth rate hits speed bump. *The Wall Street Journal,* p. A2. See also World Economic Forum, in collaboration with the Boston Consulting Group. (2011). *Global Talent Risk—Seven Responses.* Geneva, Switzerland: World Economic Forum.

[b]Morse, D. (2000, Aug. 22). Labor shortage has franchisees hustling for workers. *The Wall Street Journal,* p. B2.

[c]Bureau of Labor Statistics. Automotive service technicians and mechanics. *Operational Outlook Handbook, 2010–2011 Edition.* Retrieved from *www.bls.gov/oco/ocos181.htm* on August 1, 2011. See also Where the money is. (2010, Sept. 19), *BusinessWeek,* pp. 76, 77. See also Higgins, M. (2004, Sept. 23). Latest car-repair problem: Finding a mechanic. *The Wall Street Journal,* p. D6.

Another labor market phenomenon that causes substantial differences in pay rates, even among people who work in the same field and are of similar age and education, is the payment of wage premiums by some employers to attract the best talent available and to enhance productivity in order to offset any increase in labor costs. This is known as the *efficiency wage hypothesis* in labor economics, and it has received some support among economic researchers.[23] The forces discussed thus far affect pay levels to a considerable extent. So also does government legislation.

### Legislation

As in other areas, legislation related to pay plays a vital role in determining internal organization practices. Although we cannot analyze all the relevant laws here, Table 11–1 presents a summary of the coverage, major provisions, and federal agencies charged with administering four major federal laws that affect compensation.

## Table 11–1

### FOUR MAJOR FEDERAL WAGE-HOUR LAWS

| | Scope of coverage | Major provisions | Administrative agency |
|---|---|---|---|
| Fair Labor Standards Act (FLSA) of 1938 (as amended) | Employers involved in interstate commerce or in the production of goods for interstate commerce. Exemption from overtime provisions for managers, supervisors, executives, outside salespersons, and professional workers. | Minimum wage of $7.25 per hour for covered employees as of July, 2009; time-and-a-half pay for more than 40 hours per week; restrictions by occupation or industry on the employment of persons under 18; prohibition of wage differentials based exclusively on sex—equal pay for equal work. No extra pay required for weekends, vacations, holidays, or severance. | Wage and Hour Division of the Employment Standards Administration, U.S. Department of Labor |
| Equal Pay Act (1963) | Equal Pay required for men and women doing "substantially similar" work in terms of skill, effort, responsibility, and working conditions. | Equal Employment Opportunity Commission | |
| Sarbanes-Oxley Act (SOX, 2002) | Executives (CEOs and CFOs) cannot retain bonuses or profits from selling company stock if they mislead the public about the financial health of the company. | Public Company Accounting Oversight Board, Securities and Exchange Commission | |
| Title VII of the American Recovery and Reinvestment Act (ARRA, 2009) | Top executives in companies receiving government support are subject to "clawbacks." That is, companies can seek repayment for bonuses, retention awards, or incentives paid to the top five senior executive officers or the next 20 most highly compensated employees based on statements of earnings, revenues, gains, or other criteria later found to be materially inaccurate. | Securities and Exchange Commission | |

Of the four laws shown in Table 11–1, the Fair Labor Standards Act (FLSA) affects almost every organization in the United States. It is the source of the terms *exempt employees* (exempt from the overtime provisions of the law) and *nonexempt employees.* It established the first national minimum wage (25 cents an hour) in 1938; subsequent changes in the minimum wage and in national policy on equal pay for equal work for both sexes (the Equal Pay Act of 1963) were passed as amendments to this law. About 115 million employees—86 percent of the U.S. workforce—are covered by federal over-time rules, and those rules apply to salaried and hourly workers alike.[24] At the same time, many of today's employees no longer fit into the law's outdated categories (see Figure 11–4).

There are many loopholes in FLSA minimum-wage coverage.[25] Certain work-ers, including casual babysitters and most farm workers, are excluded, as are employees of small businesses and firms not engaged in interstate commerce. State minimum-wage laws are intended to cover these workers. At the same time, if a state's minimum is higher than the federal minimum, the state mini-mum applies. For example, while the federal minimum wage is $7.25, more than 17 states have higher minimums. For example, the state of Washington's is $8.55, and it is $8 in California and Massachusetts.[26] More than 70 cities and counties pay their workers or contractors a *living wage*, which is tailored to living costs in an area and may be more than double the federal or state minimums. While

| Figure 11–4 |
| :---: |

## Who must be paid overtime?

### THE RULES REFLECT OLD ASSUMPTIONS . . .
When Congress passed a law in 1938 mandating overtime pay, it also created a series of exemptions listing various types of workers who weren't entitled to it

**EXECUTIVE:**
The boss, of course, is not en-titled to overtime. An executive is defined as a manager who supervises at least two em-ployees, with authority to hire, fire, and promote.

**PROFESSIONALS AND CREATIVES:**
Overtime is also denied to those whose job requires ad-vanced training, a professional degree, or artistic imagination.

**ADMINISTRATIVE:**
Nor are many white-collar worker bees able to collect overtime. This exemption cov-ers people who primarily do office work and exercise "inde-pendent judgment."

**OUTSIDE SALESPEOPLE:**
Think Willy Loman. No over-time for salespeople who are regularly away from the em-ployer's place of business.

### . . . THAT DON'T ALWAYS APPLY IN TODAY'S WORKPLACE
A big reason that wage and hour litigation is exploding is because so many employees no longer fit into the law's outdated categories

**STARBUCKS STORE MANAGER:**
The company claims they are executives, but store managers may spend more time serving than supervising. The company settled a case in California, where state law says you have to spend more than 50% of your time actually managing, but is fighting a case in Florida under more flexible federal rules.

**MERCK SALES REPRESENTATIVE:**
Drug company reps don't actually sell anything. They merely attempt to influ-ence doctors' prescribing, so the sales exemption may be invalid. And the ad-ministrative exemption requires exercise of discretion, but the pitches to physi-cians are tightly scripted. Cases have been filed against every major drug man-ufacturer, and the legal status of these workers is unclear.

**ERNST & YOUNG ACCOUNTANT:**
If someone with an accounting degree is actually exercising his judgment as a CPA, the professional exemption applies. But a worker who simply gathers audit data and enters it in a spreadsheet can't—licensed or not—be classified as a professional. Litigation pending against Ernst & Young makes overtime claims on behalf of E&Y staff, including some with professional degrees.

*Source:* Orey, M. (2007, Oct. 1). Wage wars. *BusinessWeek,* p. 58.

opponents argue that such laws will force some businesses to close, at least some academic research suggests that living wage laws do more good than harm. They have imposed little—if any—cost to the cities that have passed them, they have led to few job losses, and they have lifted many families out of poverty.[27]

An important feature of the FLSA is its provision regarding the employment of young workers. On school days, 14- and 15-year-olds are allowed to work no more than 3 hours (no more than 8 hours on nonschool days), or a total of 18 hours a week when school is in session. They may work 40-hour weeks during the summer and during school vacations, but they may not work outside the hours of 7 a.m. to 7 p.m. (or 9 p.m. June 1 to Labor Day). Both federal and state laws allow 16- and 17-year-olds to work any hours but forbid them to work in hazardous occupations, such as driving or working with power-driven meat slicers.

Of the remaining three laws shown in Table 11–1, the Equal Pay Act was passed as an amendment to the FLSA. SOX and ARRA apply only to senior-level executives.

## Collective Bargaining

Another major influence on wages in unionized as well as nonunionized firms is collective bargaining. Nonunionized firms are affected by collective bargaining agreements made elsewhere since they must compete with unionized firms for the services and loyalties of workers. Collective bargaining affects two key factors: (1) the level of wages and (2) the behavior of workers in relevant labor markets. In an open, competitive market, workers tend to gravitate toward higher-paying jobs. To the extent that nonunionized firms fail to match the wages of unionized firms, they may have difficulty attracting and keeping workers. Furthermore, benefits negotiated under union agreements have had the effect of increasing the package of benefits in firms that have attempted to avoid unionization. In addition to wages and benefits, collective bargaining is also used to negotiate procedures for administering pay, procedures for resolving grievances regarding compensation decisions, and methods used to determine the relative worth of jobs.[28]

## Managerial Attitudes and an Organization's Ability to Pay

These factors have a major impact on wage structures and levels. Earlier we noted that an organization's ability to pay depends, to a large extent, on the competitive dynamics it faces in its product or service markets. Therefore, regardless of its espoused competitive position on wages, an organization's ability to pay ultimately will be a key factor that limits actual wages.

This is not to downplay the role of management philosophy and attitudes on pay. On the contrary, management's desire to maintain or improve morale, attract high-caliber employees, reduce turnover, and improve employees' standards of living also affect wages, as does the relative importance of a given position to a firm.[29] A safety engineer is more important to a chemical company than to a bank. Wage structures tend to vary across firms to the extent that managers view any given position as more or less critical to their firms. Thus, compensation administration reflects management judgment to a considerable degree. Ultimately, top management renders judgments regarding the overall competitive pay position of the firm (above-market, at-market, or below-market rates), factors to be considered in determining job worth, and the relative weight to be given seniority and performance in pay decisions. Such judgments are key determinants of the structure and level of wages.[30]

## AN OVERVIEW OF PAY-SYSTEM MECHANICS

The procedures described in this section for developing pay systems help those involved in the development process to apply their judgments in a systematic manner. The hallmarks of success in compensation management, as in other areas, are understandability, workability, and acceptability. The broad objective in developing pay systems is to assign a monetary value to each job in the organization (a base rate) and an orderly procedure for increasing the base rate (e.g., based on merit, inflation, experience, or some combination of these). To develop such a system, we need four basic tools:

1. Updated job descriptions.
2. A job-evaluation method (i.e., one that will rank jobs in terms of their overall worth to the organization).
3. Pay surveys.
4. A pay structure.

Figure 11–5 presents an overview of this process.

Job descriptions are key tools in the design of pay systems, and they serve two purposes:

1. They identify important characteristics of each job so that the relative worth of jobs can be determined.
2. From them we can identify, define, and weight **compensable factors** (common job characteristics that an organization is willing to pay for, such as skill, effort, responsibility, and working conditions).

| **Figure 11–5** |
| --- |

Traditional job-based compensation model.

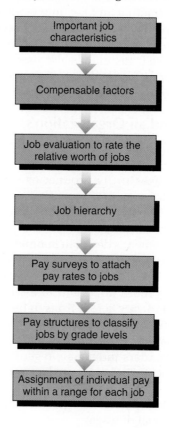

- Important job characteristics
- Compensable factors
- Job evaluation to rate the relative worth of jobs
- Job hierarchy
- Pay surveys to attach pay rates to jobs
- Pay structures to classify jobs by grade levels
- Assignment of individual pay within a range for each job

Once this has been done, the next step is to rate the worth of all jobs using a predetermined system.

A number of **job-evaluation** methods are available. Their purpose is to provide a work-related and business-related logic to support decisions about pay. All of the methods also have the same final objective: to rank jobs in terms of their relative worth to the organization so that an equitable rate of pay can be determined for each job. However, different job-evaluation methods yield different rank-orders of jobs, and therefore different pay structures.[31] In short, method matters.

As an illustration, consider the point method of job evaluation, the approach most commonly used in the United States and Europe.[32] Each job is analyzed and defined in terms of the compensable factors an organization has agreed to adopt. Points are assigned to each level (or degree) of a compensable factor, such as responsibility. The total points assigned to each job across each compensable factor are then summed. A hierarchy of job worth is therefore defined when jobs are rank-ordered from highest point total to lowest point total.

While job evaluation provides a business-related order and logic that supports pay differences among jobs, not all firms use it. One reason is that several policy issues must be resolved first, including[33]

- Does management perceive meaningful differences among jobs?
- Is it possible to identify and operationalize meaningful criteria for distinguishing among jobs?
- Will job evaluation result in meaningful distinctions in the eyes of employees?
- Are jobs stable, and will they remain stable in the future?
- Is job evaluation consistent with the organization's goals and strategies? For example, if the goal is to ensure maximum flexibility among job assignments, a knowledge- or skill-based pay system may be most appropriate. We will address that topic more fully in a later section.

## Linking Internal Pay Relationships to Market Data

In the point-factor method of job evaluation, the next task is to translate the point totals into a pay structure. Two key components of this process are identifying and surveying pay rates in relevant labor markets. This can often be a complex task because employers must pay attention not only to labor markets but also to product markets (e.g., level of demand and degree of competition).[34] Pay practices must be designed not only to attract and retain employees but also to ensure that labor costs (as part of the overall costs of production) do not become excessive in relation to those of competing employers.

The definition of relevant labor markets requires two key decisions: which jobs to survey and which markets are relevant for each job. Jobs selected for a survey are generally characterized by stable tasks and stable job specifications (e.g., computer programmers, purchasing managers). Jobs with these characteristics are known as *key* or **benchmark jobs.** Jobs that do not meet these criteria but that are characterized by high turnover or are difficult to fill should also be included.

As we noted earlier, the definition of **relevant labor markets** should consider geographical boundaries (local, regional, national, or international) as well as product-market competitors (e.g., banks compared to banks, auto dealers to auto dealers). Such an approach might begin with product-market competitors as the initial market, followed by adjustments downward (e.g., from national to regional markets) on the basis of geographical considerations.

Once target populations and relevant markets have been identified, the next task is to obtain survey data. Surveys are available from a variety of sources, including the federal government (Bureau of Labor Statistics), employers' associations, trade and professional associations, users of a given job-evaluation system (e.g., the Hay Group's point-factor system), and compensation consulting firms.[35]

---

**HR BUZZ**

*What Are
You Worth?*

## SALARY-COMPARISON SOURCES

In a world where information is power, salary negotiations have long been greatly imbalanced. The Internet, however, is leveling the playing field, as a growing number of Web sites offer salary surveys, job listings with specified pay levels, and even customized compensation analyses.[a] For example, America's Career InfoNet (*www. acinet.org*) provides access to wage data compiled by the Bureau of Labor Statistics. However, Salary.com is arguably the most popular provider of salary comparisons, for it provides detailed geographic information and matching job descriptions for more than 3,000 benchmark jobs. The primary tool used by Salary.com is the Salary Wizard, which allows users to enter a job title and zip code and receive a median salary number as well as a range from 25 percent through 75 percent of the median.

The Salary Wizard is based on Salary.com's analysis of data supplied predominately by compensation-consulting firms, which the company's team of compensation specialists aggregates into a database and then uses to power the Wizard. If you prefer to see data presented by industry, try cafepharma.com, Vault.com/Salary, dice.com, healthcaresalary.com, or business.com. Go to these sites and compare the kinds of information presented in each one. Do they provide information on which employers are included and which are not? Where do their data come from? Answering questions like these can help to judge the credibility of the data. Credible data, in turn, can help you do a better job of negotiating compensation in a new job—or trying to improve your pay at your current one. How much more should you expect when switching jobs? Before the global financial crisis, the average was about 12 to 14 percent more than you were currently making, but if a company really wanted you, and the hiring manager knew you were in demand elsewhere, you could reasonably expect an offer of 20 percent more than your current salary. Today, to land a candidate with high-demand skills, the best that one can expect is for a firm to offer a starting salary within 10 percent of the ceiling for a position. What's the moral of this story? The better the fit, the more wiggle room you have.[b]

---

[a]Coleman, B. (2004). How HR pros can use online compensation data. Retrieved from *www. salary.com/advice/layouthtmls/advl_display_Cat14_Ser65_Par145.html* on September 28, 2004. See also Geary, L. H., and Kirwan, R. (2000, Sept.). Get paid more! *Money*, pp. 111–118.

[b]Sammer, J. (2009, Sept.). Money matters in the hiring process. *HR Magazine* 54(9), pp. 93–96.

---

Managers should be aware of two potential problems with pay-survey data.[36] The most serious is the assurance of an accurate job match. If only a "thumbnail sketch" (i.e., a very brief description) is used to characterize a job, there is always the possibility of legitimate misunderstanding among survey respondents. To deal with this, some surveys ask respondents if their salary data for a job are direct matches or somewhat higher or lower than those described (and therefore worthy of more or less pay).

A second problem has resulted from the explosion of *at-risk* forms of pay, some of which are based on individual performance and some on the profitability of an organization. As we noted earlier, base pay is becoming a smaller part of the total compensation package for a broad range of employees. This makes it difficult to determine the actual pay of job incumbents and can make survey results difficult to interpret. For example, how do we compare salary figures that include only base pay or direct cash payouts with at-risk pay that may take the form of a lump-sum bonus, additional time off with pay, or an employee stock-ownership plan? Despite these potential problems, all indications are that pay surveys will continue to be used widely.

The end result is often a chart, as in Figure 11–6, that relates current wage rates to the total points assigned to each job. For each point total, a trend line is fitted to indicate the average relationship between points assigned to the bench-mark jobs and the hourly wages paid for those jobs. Once a midpoint trend line is fitted, two others are also drawn: (1) a trend line that represents the minimum rate of pay for each point total and (2) a trend line that represents the maximum rate of pay for each point total.[37]

## Developing a Pay Structure

The final step in attaching dollar values to jobs using the point method is to estab-lish pay grades, or ranges, characterized by a point spread from minimum to max-imum for each grade. Starting wages are given by the trend line that represents the

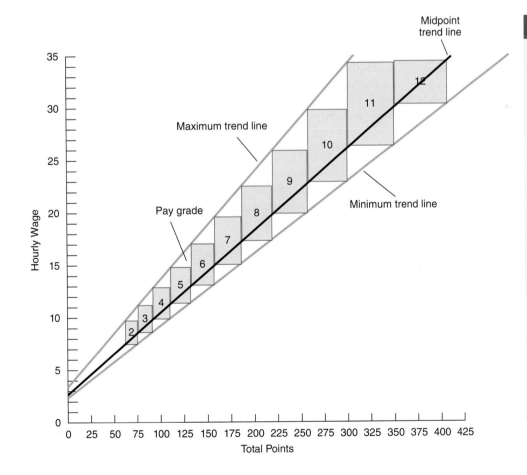

**Figure 11–6**

Chart relating hourly wage rates to the total points assigned to each job. Three trend lines are shown— minimum, midpoint, and maximum—as well as 11 pay grades. Within each pay grade there is a 30 percent spread from minimum to maximum and a 50 percent overlap from one pay grade to the next.

## Table 11–2

**ILLUSTRATIVE PAY STRUCTURE SHOWING PAY GRADES, THE SPREAD OF POINTS WITHIN GRADES, THE MIDPOINT OF EACH PAY GRADE, AND THE MINIMUM AND MAXIMUM RATES OF PAY PER GRADE**

| Grade | Point spread | Midpoint | Minimum rate of pay | Maximum rate of pay |
|---|---|---|---|---|
| 2 | 62–75 | 68 | $ 7.50 | $ 9.75 |
| 3 | 76–91 | 83 | 8.63 | 11.21 |
| 4 | 92–110 | 101 | 9.92 | 12.90 |
| 5 | 111–132 | 121 | 11.41 | 14.83 |
| 6 | 133–157 | 145 | 13.12 | 17.06 |
| 7 | 158–186 | 172 | 15.09 | 19.62 |
| 8 | 187–219 | 203 | 17.35 | 22.56 |
| 9 | 220–257 | 238 | 19.95 | 25.94 |
| 10 | 258–300 | 279 | 22.95 | 29.83 |
| 11 | 301–350 | 325 | 26.39 | 34.31 |
| 12 | 351–407 | 379 | 30.35 | 34.45 |

minimum rate of pay for each pay grade, while the highest wages that can be earned within a grade are given by the trend line that represents the maximum rate of pay. The pay structure is described numerically in Table 11–2.

For example, consider the job of administrative clerk. Let's assume that the job evaluation committee arrived at a total allocation of 142 points across all compensable factors. The job therefore falls into pay grade 6. Starting pay is $13.12 per hour, with a maximum pay rate of $17.06 per hour.

The actual development of a pay structure is a complex process, but there are certain rules of thumb to follow:

- Jobs of the same general value should be clustered into the same pay grade.
- Jobs that clearly differ in value should be in different pay grades.
- There should be a smooth progression of point groupings.
- The new system should fit realistically into the existing allocation of pay within a company.
- The pay grades should conform reasonably well to pay patterns in the relevant labor markets.[38]

Once such a pay structure is in place, the determination of each individual's pay (based on experience, seniority, and performance) becomes a more systematic, orderly procedure. A compensation-planning worksheet, such as that shown in Figure 11–7, can be very useful to managers confronted with these weighty decisions.

### Alternatives to Pay Systems Based on Job Evaluation

There are at least two alternatives to pay systems based on job evaluation: market-based pay and skill- or knowledge-based pay, also referred to as competency-based pay.

**Figure 11–7**

Sample annual compensation-planning worksheet.

**ANNUAL COMPENSATION-PLANNING WORKSHEET**

ORG. UNIT _____

MGR. OR SUPV. _____

| EMPLOYEE NAME | JOB TITLE | LAST SALARY ADJUSTMENT | | | | CURRENT SALARY | RANGE MINIMUM | RANGE MIDPOINT | RANGE MAXIMUM | PERFORMANCE APPRAISAL | FORECAST SALARY ADJUSTMENT (If Any) | | | | |
|---|---|---|---|---|---|---|---|---|---|---|---|---|---|---|---|
| | | Amt. | % | Date | Type* | | | | | | Amt. | % | Date | New Salary | Inter-val |
| | | | | | | | | | | | | | | | |
| | | | | | | | | | | | | | | | |
| | | | | | | | | | | | | | | | |
| | | | | | | | | | | | | | | | |
| | | | | | | | | | | | | | | | |
| | | | | | | | | | | | | | | | |
| | | | | | | | | | | | | | | | |
| | | | | | | | | | | | | | | | |
| | | | | | | | | | | | | | | | |
| | | | | | | | | | | | | | | | |
| | | | | | | | | | | | | | | | |

*Code for "Type"
1—Promotion
2—Merit

PREPARED BY _____

## Market-Based Pay

The **market-based pay system** uses a direct market-pricing approach for all of a firm's jobs. This type of pay structure is feasible if all jobs are benchmark jobs and direct matches can be found in the market (e.g., senior-executive positions). Pay surveys can then be used to determine the market prices of the jobs in question. If competitors' pay decisions determine a company's pay structure though, then the level of pay or the mix of pay forms is no longer a source of potential competitive advantage. It is neither unique nor difficult to imitate. As a result, many firms are questioning the use of peer-group surveys to set compensation. Instead they are looking at the relationship of pay to company performance and to aligning pay structures more closely with the business strategy.[39]

## Competency-Based Pay

Under a **competency-based pay system,** workers are paid not on the basis of the job they currently are doing, but rather on the basis of their skills or on their depth of knowledge, both of which are termed "competencies." Skill-based plans are usually applied to so-called blue-collar work and competencies to so-called white-collar work. The distinctions are not hard and fast. They can focus on depth (specialists in corporate law, finance, or welding and hydraulic maintenance), breadth (generalists with knowledge in all phases of operations including marketing, manufacturing, finance, and HR), or self-management (gaining skills that might previously have been reserved for higher levels in the organization, such as planning, training, or budgeting).[40] In a world of slimmed-down big companies and agile small ones, the last thing any manager wants to hear from an employee is "It's not my job." To see how such systems might work in practice, let's consider General Mills and 3M.

---

**HR BUZZ**

*Skill- and Competency-Based Pay\**

### GENERAL MILLS AND 3M

Skill-based plans rely on very specific information on every aspect of the production process. For example, food-products manufacturer General Mills uses four skill categories corresponding to the steps in the production process: materials handling, mixing, filling, and packaging. Each skill category has three blocks: entry level, accomplished, and advanced. A new employee could therefore start at entry level in materials handling and, after being certified in all skills included at that level, can begin training for skills either at the accomplished level within materials handling or else at the entry level in mixing.

3M has developed a set of six leadership competencies for all executives. They are: thinks from outside in; drives innovation and growth; develops, teaches, and engages others; makes courageous decisions; leads with energy, passion, and urgency; and lives 3M values. Behavioral anchors are used to rate an executive on each of these competencies. The ratings are then used to assess and develop executives worldwide. Because 3M relies so heavily on promotion from within, competency ratings help to develop executive talent for succession planning. While the link to development is clear, the link to pay is less clear.

---

*\*Sources:* Society for Human Resource Management Foundation. (2008). Seeing forward: Succession planning at 3M (DVD). Alexandria, VA: Society for Human Resource Management Foundation. See also Allredge, M. E., and Nilan, K. J. (2000, Summer/Fall). 3M's leadership competency model: An internally developed solution. *Human Resource Management* 39, pp. 133–145. See also Shaw, J. D., Gupta, N., Mitra, A., and Ledford, G. E., Jr. (2005). Success and survival of skill-based pay plans. *Journal of Management* 31, pp. 28–49.

---

In such learning environments, the more workers learn, the more they earn. Companies view skill- and competency-based pay plans as a way to develop the critical behaviors and abilities employees need to achieve specific business results. By linking compensation directly to individual contributions that make a difference to the organization, a company can maintain the highest caliber of workers, regardless of their particular specialties or roles. Such plans also provide a mechanism for cross-training employees to ensure that people in different functional areas have the behavioral or technical skills to take on additional responsibilities as needed.[41]

On the other hand, both skill- and competency-based plans become increasingly expensive as the majority of employees become certified at the highest pay levels. As a result, the employer may have an average wage higher than competitors who use conventional job evaluation. Unless the increased flexibility permits leaner staffing, the employer may also experience higher labor costs. This is what caused Motorola and TRW to abandon their plans after just a few years.[42]

Research at nine manufacturing plants concluded that the number of managers in plants using skill-based pay was as much as 50 percent lower, compared to traditional plants. Of course, this is also likely to dampen managers' enthusiasm for using skill-based pay![43] Is there any impact on productivity, quality, or labor costs?

A 37-month study in a component-assembly plant found a 58 percent improvement in productivity, a 16 percent reduction in the cost of labor per part, and an 82 percent reduction in scrap, compared to a similar facility that did not use skill-based pay.[44] Another study linked the ease of communication and understanding of skill-based plans to employees' general perceptions of being treated fairly by the employer.[45] A final study analyzed the relationship between competencies and performance among managers. Managers' competencies were related to their performance ratings, but there was no relationship to unit-level performance.[46] The lesson from these studies is that each organization must weigh the advantages and disadvantages of such plans, relative to its own context and strategy. Currently, only 7 percent of U.S. organizations use skill- or competency-based pay plans.[47]

In summary, if compensation systems are to be used strategically, it is important that management (1) understand clearly what types of behavior it wants the compensation system to reinforce, (2) recognize that compensation systems are integral components of planning and control, and (3) view the firm's performance as the ultimate criterion of the success of strategic pay decisions and operational compensation programs.

Now let us consider some key policy issues.

## POLICY ISSUES IN PAY PLANNING AND ADMINISTRATION

### Pay Secrecy

Do workers know what the person in the next office makes? The answer: Not really. Pay secrecy is a difficult policy to maintain, particularly as so much pay-related information is now available on the Web. Anyone with access to the Internet can find out fairly easily what a position is worth in the job market. At Glassdoor.com, which relies on anonymous posting of salary information, they can find out what a position pays at a given company. What about discussing salaries within a particular firm, say, your own employer? As a general matter, salary discussions among employees are protected under the National Labor Relations Act, which protects the right of employees to discuss their wages, hours, and other terms and conditions of their employment.[48]

In the UK, the Equality Act of 2010 bans "gag orders" that forbid employees from discussing their pay and bonuses with colleagues. The Act does not prohibit pay secrecy clauses. Instead, it makes them "unenforceable" against employees who make or solicit a "relevant pay disclosure"—that is, one designed to uncover inequality in the pay scale based on protected characteristics, such as race or gender.[49]

Openness versus secrecy is not an either/or phenomenon. Rather, it is a matter of degree. For example, organizations may choose to disclose one or more of the following: (1) the work- and business-related rationale on which the system is based, (2) pay ranges, (3) pay-increase schedules, and (4) the availability of pay-related data from the compensation department.[50] Posting salary ranges, experts contend, is a public show of trust in employees. It demonstrates that the employer values them and will help them to advance.[51] However, there are also disadvantages to **pay openness:**

1. It forces managers to defend their pay decisions and practices publicly. Because the process is inherently subjective, there is no guarantee that satisfactory answers will ever be found that can please all concerned parties.

2. The cost of a mistaken pay decision escalates because all the system's inconsistencies and weaknesses become visible once the cloak of secrecy is lifted.

3. Open pay might induce some managers to reduce differences in pay among subordinates in order to avoid conflict and the need to explain such differences to disappointed employees.[52]

In general, open-pay systems tend to work best under the following circumstances: Individual or team performance can be measured objectively, performance measures can be developed for all the important aspects of a job, and effort and performance are related closely over a relatively short timespan.

## The Effect of Inflation

All organizations must make some allowance for inflation in their salary programs. Given an inflation rate of 4 percent, for example, the firm that fails to increase its salary ranges at all over a two-year period will be 8 percent behind its competitors. Needless to say, it becomes difficult to recruit new employees under these circumstances, and it becomes difficult to motivate present employees to remain and, if they do remain, to produce.

How do firms cope? Average increases for salaried employees were 1.5 percent in 2009, for example, while consumer prices rose an average of 2.7 percent. The result: a slight decline in real wages for the average employee.[53] To offset that loss, many companies are granting more time off to employees, and implementing flexible schedules (51 percent of companies).[54] Companies such as Sprint, WD-40, Corning, DuPont, and Merck are tying pay more to performance in an attempt to make the costs of labor more variable and less fixed. More and more companies, large and small, feel the same way.

## Pay Compression

**Pay compression** is related to the general problem of inflation. It is a narrowing of the ratios of pay between jobs or pay grades in a firm's pay structure.[55] Pay compression exists in many forms, including (1) higher starting salaries for new hires, which lead long-term employees to see only a slight difference between their current pay and that of new hires; (2) hourly pay increases for unionized employees that exceed those of salaried and nonunion employees; (3) recruitment of new college graduates for management or professional jobs at salaries above those of current jobholders; and (4) excessive overtime payments to some employees or payment of different overtime rates (e.g., time and a half for some, double time for others). Failure of organizations to address compression issues may cause long-serving employees to rethink their commitment to a company they think does not value or reward loyalty. Their frustration also can show up in the form of lower productivity, reluctance to work overtime, and unwillingness to cooperate with higher-paid new recruits.[56] However, first-line supervisors, unlike middle managers, may actually benefit from pay inflation among nonmanagement employees since companies generally maintain a differential between the supervisors' pay and that of their highest paid subordinates.[57]

One solution to the problem of pay compression is to institute equity adjustments; that is, give increases in pay to employees to maintain differences in job worth between their jobs and those of others. Of course this increases an organization's overall wage bill, especially relative to competitors. Another approach is to grant sign-on bonuses to new hires in order to offer a competitive total compensation package, especially to those with scarce skills. Because bonuses do not increase base salaries, the structure of differences in pay between new hires and experienced employees does not change. A third approach is to provide benefits that increase gradually to more senior employees. Thus, although the difference between the direct pay of this group and that of their shorter-service coworkers may be slim, senior employees have a distinct advantage when the entire compensation package is considered.

Overtime as a cause of compression can be dealt with in two ways. First, it can be rotated among employees so that all share overtime equally. However, in situations where this kind of arrangement is not feasible, firms might consider establishing an overtime pay policy for management employees; for example, a supervisor may be paid an overtime rate after he or she works a minimum number of overtime hours. Such a practice does not violate the Fair Labor Standards Act; under the law, overtime pay is not required for exempt jobs, although organizations may adopt it voluntarily.[58]

Pay compression is certainly a difficult problem—but not so difficult that it cannot be managed. Indeed, it must be managed if companies are to achieve their goal of providing pay that is perceived as fair.

## Pay Raises

Coping with inflation is the biggest hurdle to overcome in a pay-for-performance plan. On the other hand, the only measure of a raise is how much it exceeds the increase in the cost of living. In 2011, wages in Vietnam rose an average of 12 percent. Unfortunately that trailed the annual inflation rate, so real wages actually dropped. Said one worker, "The price of everything—food, gas, electricity—has gone up by more than my pay raise."[59]

The simplest, most effective method for dealing with inflation in a merit-pay system is to increase salary ranges. By raising salary ranges (e.g., based on a survey of average increases in starting salaries for the coming year) without giving general increases, a firm can maintain competitive hiring rates and at the same time maintain the merit concept surrounding salary increases.

The size of the merit increase for a given level of performance should decrease as the employee moves farther up the salary range. Merit guide charts provide a means for doing this. Guide charts identify (1) an employee's current performance rating, and (2) his or her location in a pay grade. The intersection of these two dimensions identifies a percentage of pay increase based on the performance level and location of the employee in the pay grade. Figure 11–8 shows an example of such a chart. The rationale for the merit-guide-chart approach is that a person at the top of the range is already making more than the going rate for that job. Hence she or he should have to demonstrate more than satisfactory performance in order to continue moving farther above the going rate. Performance incentives, one-time awards that must be re-earned each year, allow employees to supplement their income. Let's turn now to this topic.

**Figure 11–8**

Sample merit
guide chart.

| EMPLOYEE PERFORMANCE | PERCENT INCREASE | | | | |
|---|---|---|---|---|---|
| Distinguished | 12% | 10% | 9% | 8% | 7% |
| Commendable | 9% | 8% | 7% | 6% | Ceiling |
| Competent | 7% | 6% | 5% | Ceiling | |
| Adequate | 4% | 0 | Ceiling | | |
| Provisional | 0 | Ceiling | | | |
| Salary (as % of midpoint) is: | 80% → 88% → 96% → 104% → 112% → 120% | | | | |

## PERFORMANCE INCENTIVES

"Using strong incentives opens up the possibility of obtaining substantial performance gains, but it also increases the possibility of something going terribly wrong."[60] To illustrate something going terribly wrong, consider the 2008–2009 global financial crisis.

Experts generally agree that the origination and distribution of subprime mortgages was a key cause (but not the only one) of the crisis. The entire process was riddled with perverse incentives that induced key employees of financial firms to take excessive risks during economic upswings. One key ingredient was the packaging of subprime mortgages into marketable securities. This made it possible to rain down fee income throughout the system—to mortgage brokers who sold the loans, investment bankers who packaged the loans into securities, banks and specialist institutions who serviced the securities, ratings agencies who gave them their seal of approval, and insurance companies that guaranteed holders of such securities against loss through the use of credit default swaps. Since the fees did not have to be returned if the securities later suffered large losses, everyone involved had strong incentives to maximize the flow of loans through the system—whether or not they were sound. The rise in systemic risk fed by these incentives throughout the "perfect calm" helped cause the global financial crisis.[61]

This is not to suggest that companies abandon financial incentives. Indeed, there is a wealth of evidence demonstrating that they can motivate higher levels of performance and productivity.[62] It is important, though, to be attentive to possible unintended consequences, for under certain circumstances, financial incentives may lead to *unethical behavior, fuel employee turnover, and foster envy and discontent.*[63]

Today, incentives comprise almost 12 percent of payroll, up from only 4 percent in 1990.[64] Evidence indicates that they work. A quantitative review of 39 studies containing 47 relationships revealed that financial incentives were not related to performance quality, but were related fairly strongly (correlation of 0.34) to performance quantity.[65]

When it comes to performance incentives, the possibilities are endless. Because each has different consequences, each needs special treatment. One way to classify them is according to the level of performance targeted—individual, team, or total organization. Within these broad categories, literally hundreds of different approaches for relating pay to performance exist. This chapter considers the three categories described earlier, beginning with merit pay for individuals—both executives and lower-level workers. First, however, let's consider some fundamental requirements of all incentive programs.

## REQUIREMENTS OF EFFECTIVE INCENTIVE SYSTEMS

At the outset it is important to distinguish merit systems from incentive systems. Both are designed to motivate employees to improve their job performance. Most commonly, merit systems are applied to exempt employees in the form of permanent increases to their base pay. The goal is to tie pay increases to each employee's level of job performance. **Incentives** (e.g., sales commissions, bonuses, profit sharing) are one-time supplements to base pay. They are also awarded on the basis of performance (individual, team, organization, or some combination of those), and are applied to broader segments of the labor force, including nonexempt and unionized employees.

Properly designed incentive programs work because they are based on two well-accepted psychological principles: (1) increased motivation improves performance and (2) recognition is a major factor in motivation.[66] Unfortunately, however, many incentive programs are improperly designed, and they do not work. They violate one or more of the following rules (shown graphically in Figure 11–9):

1.  *Be simple.* The rules of the system should be brief, clear, and understandable.
2.  *Be specific.* It is not sufficient to say "Produce more" or "Stop accidents." Employees need to know precisely what they are expected to do.
3.  *Be attainable.* Every employee should have a reasonable chance to gain something.

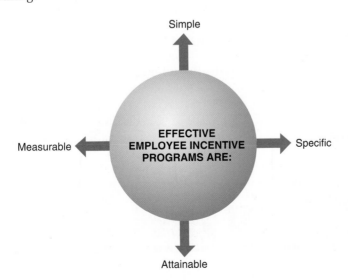

Simple

Measurable ← **EFFECTIVE EMPLOYEE INCENTIVE PROGRAMS ARE:** → Specific

Attainable

**Figure 11–9**

Requirements of effective incentive systems.

4.  *Be measurable.* Measurable objectives are the foundation on which incentive plans are built. Program dollars will be wasted (and program evaluation hampered) if specific accomplishments cannot be related to dollars spent.

## MERIT-PAY SYSTEMS

Surveys show that about 90 percent of U.S. employers use **merit-pay systems.**[67] Unfortunately, many of the plans don't work. Here are some reasons:[68]

1.  *The incentive value of the reward offered is too low.* Give someone a $5,000 raise and she keeps $250 a month after taxes. The stakes, after taxes, are nominal.
2.  *The link between performance and rewards is weak.* In one survey of 10,000 U.S. workers, only 35 percent believed that performance, not seniority, determines pay at their workplaces.[69] Another by Towers Watson reported that fewer than 40 percent of top-performing employees believe that they receive "moderately or significantly better pay raises, annual bonuses, or total pay than do employees with average performance."[70]
3.  *Supervisors often resist performance appraisal.* Few supervisors are trained in the art of giving feedback accurately, comfortably, and with a minimum likelihood of creating other problems (see Chapter 8). As a result, many are afraid to make distinctions among workers—and they do not.[71] When the best performers receive rewards that are no higher than the worst performers, motivation plummets.
4.  *Union contracts influence pay-for-performance decisions within and between organizations.* Failure to match union wages over a three- or four-year period (especially during periods of high inflation) invites dissension and turnover among nonunion employees.
5.  *The "annuity" problem.* As past merit payments are incorporated into an individual's base salary, the payments form an annuity (a sum of money received at regular intervals) and allow formerly productive individuals to slack off for several years and still earn high pay—an effect called the **annuity problem.** The annuity feature also leads to another problem: topping out. After a long period in a job, individuals often reach the top of the pay range for their jobs. As a result, pay no longer serves as a motivator because it cannot increase as a result of performance.

These reasons are shown graphically in Figure 11–10.

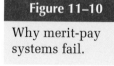

**Figure 11–10**

Why merit-pay systems fail.

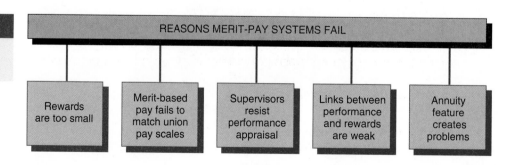

REASONS MERIT-PAY SYSTEMS FAIL

| Rewards are too small | Merit-based pay fails to match union pay scales | Supervisors resist performance appraisal | Links between performance and rewards are weak | Annuity feature creates problems |

## Barriers Can Be Overcome

Lincoln Electric, a Cleveland-based manufacturer of welding machines and motors, boasts a productivity rate more than double that of other manufacturers in its industry. It follows two cardinal rules:

1. Pay employees for productivity, and only for productivity.
2. Promote employees for productivity, and only for productivity.[72]

Furthermore, research on the effect of merit-pay practices on performance in white-collar jobs indicates that not all such reward systems are equal. Companies providing variable pay to their best workers are 68 percent more likely than other firms to report outstanding financial performance.[73] This may be due a **sorting effect,** that is, those who do not want to have their pay tied to their performance don't accept jobs at such companies, or else they leave when pay for performance is implemented. This leaves a residual workforce that is more productive and more responsive to merit rewards.[74]

## GUIDELINES FOR EFFECTIVE MERIT-PAY SYSTEMS

Those affected by the merit-pay system must support it if it is to work as designed. This is in addition to the requirements for incentive programs shown in Figure 11–9. From the very inception of a merit-pay system, it is important that employees feel a sense of ownership of the system. Involve them in the design process, if possible. Here are five other steps to follow:

1. *Establish high standards of performance.* Low expectations tend to be self-fulfilling prophecies. In the world of sports, successful coaches such as Lombardi, Wooden, and Shula have demanded excellence. Excellence rarely results from expectations of mediocrity.
2. *Develop and implement sound performance management systems.* As we noted in Chapter 9, such systems include clear definitions of what good performance looks like, elimination of roadblocks that might impede performance, regular coaching and feedback, and timely rewards that encourage good performance.
3. *Train supervisors in the mechanics of performance appraisal and in the art of giving feedback to subordinates.* Train them to manage ineffective performance constructively.
4. *Tie rewards closely to performance.* For example, use quarterly or semi-annual performance reviews as bases for merit increases (or no increases). One review found that 40 of 42 studies looking at merit pay reported increases in performance when pay was tied closely to performance.[75]
5. *Use a wide range of increases.* Make pay increases meaningful.

Merit-pay systems can work, but they need to follow these guidelines if they are to work effectively. Figure 11–11 depicts these guidelines graphically.

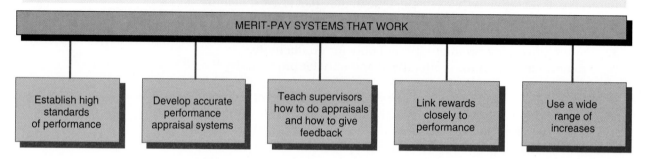

**Figure 11–11**

Guidelines for effective merit-pay systems.

| MERIT-PAY SYSTEMS THAT WORK | | | | |
|---|---|---|---|---|
| Establish high standards of performance | Develop accurate performance appraisal systems | Teach supervisors how to do appraisals and how to give feedback | Link rewards closely to performance | Use a wide range of increases |

## INCENTIVES FOR EXECUTIVES

"It took me a long while to learn that people do what you pay them to do, not what you ask them to do," says Hicks Waldron, former chairman and CEO of Avon Products Inc.[76]

Companies with a history of outperforming their rivals, regardless of industry or economic climate, have two common characteristics: (1) a long-term, strategic view of their executives and (2) stability in their executive groups.[77] It makes sense, therefore, to develop integrated plans for total executive compensation so that rewards are based on achieving the company's long-term strategic goals. This may require a rebalancing of the elements of executive reward systems: base salary, annual (short-term) incentives, long-term incentives, employee benefits, and perquisites.[78]

Regardless of the exact form of rebalancing, base salaries (considerably more than $1 million a year for CEOs of the largest American corporations[79]) will continue to be a focal point of executive compensation. This is because they generally serve as an index for benefit values. For example, objectives for short-term incentives frequently are defined as a percentage of base salary. A typical allocation of direct compensation is salary, 18 percent; short-term bonus, 24 percent; and long-term incentives, 58 percent. Why place such emphasis on long-term incentives?[80]

1.  Annual, or short-term, incentive plans encourage the efficient use of existing assets. They are usually based on indicators of corporate performance, such as net income, expenses, or customer-loyalty measures. In light of the salary freezes and pay cuts that many companies implemented during the Great Recession, firms such as Home Depot, Cisco, and Xerox started awarding twice-a-year bonuses. Despite their clear focus on achieving short-term objectives, advocates argue that they boost morale, improve retention, and allow boards to raise goals quickly if economic conditions improve.[81]

2.  Long-term plans encourage the development of new processes, plants, and products that open new markets and restore old ones. Hence long-term performance encompasses qualitative progress as well as quantitative accomplishments. Long-term incentive plans are designed to reward strategic gains rather than short-term contributions to profits. A small but growing number of companies, such as PepsiCo and Lincoln National Corp., let top executives choose how their long-term compensation is paid.[82] The choices include, in addition to stock options, **restricted stock** (common stock that

vests after a specified period); **restricted stock units** (shares awarded over time to defer taxes); **performance shares** (essentially stock grants awarded for meeting goals); and **performance-accelerated shares** (stock that vests sooner if the executive meets goals ahead of schedule). This is the kind of view we should be encouraging among executives, for it relates consistently to company success.

In the face of widespread criticism of executive pay practices, some firms are rethinking the way they reward top executives.[83] Take stock options, for example. Prior to 2004, they did not have to be disclosed as expenses on financial statements. Since that time, however, according to Financial Accounting Standards Board Statement 123R, the value of all employee stock options must be expensed at estimates of fair value on financial statements (thereby reducing earnings). This has made them less attractive, as firms shift to restricted stock or performance shares, for example. Moreover, even enthusiasts can't prove that options motivate executives to perform better. Critics contend that stock options reward executives not just for their own performance but for a booming stock market. To a large extent, they are right; as much as 70 percent of the change in a company's stock price depends only on changes in the overall market.[84] In response, some firms link payoffs from options to outperforming the stock of competitors or to a market index.[85] Others now grant stock options not at the market price but at some higher price. These are known as **premium-price options.**[86] Thus, executives will profit only after the stock has risen substantially. Take Monsanto, for example.

---

**MONSANTO**    HR BUZZ

At Monsanto, the CEO and 31 other executives receive options to purchase stock at prices that *ascend* over time. Before their options are "in the money" they must increase the stock price by 50 percent over a five-year period. Because all of these executives have to pay for their options, they must raise the share price even higher (an average of 10.5 percent per year) before they can start cashing in. The company allowed them to plow as much as half their salaries into options over the first two years of the plan. All elected to participate. Monsanto is now being run as though its managers have a stake in it, because they really do. If the CEO and his top executives are right about the company's future prospects, they will be richly rewarded. If not, and the market drops and stays depressed, their options will be underwater and the company will have to find some other way to motivate them to stay on.[a]

*Premium-Price Options*

---

[a]Silverman, R. E. (2001, Apr. 12). Breathing underwater: Companies look for ways to help workers stuck with worthless stock options. *The Wall Street Journal*, p. R8. See also Simon, R., and Dugan, I. J. (2001, June 4). Options overdose. *The Wall Street Journal*, pp. C1, C17.

## INCENTIVES FOR LOWER-LEVEL EMPLOYEES

As noted earlier in this chapter, a common practice is to supplement employees' pay with increments related to improvements in job performance. One example is a **lump-sum bonus,** in which employees receive an end-of-year bonus (based on employee or company performance) that does not build into base pay. Their purpose is to create shock waves in an entitlement culture. By giving lump-sum bonuses for several years, a company is essentially freezing base pay and repositioning itself relative to competitors.[87] Another is the **spot bonus.** Thus, if an employee's performance has been exceptional—such as filling in for a sick colleague or working nights and weekends to complete a project—the employer may reward the worker with a one-time bonus of $50, $100, or $500 shortly after the noteworthy actions. Fully 55 percent of companies now offer such programs.[88]

Individual incentive plans have a *baseline,* or normal, performance standard; productivity above this standard is rewarded. The baseline should be high enough so that employees are not given extra rewards for what is really just a normal day's work. On the other hand, the baseline should not be so high that it is impossible to earn additional pay.

It is more difficult to specify performance standards in some jobs than in others. At the top-management level, for instance, what constitutes a normal day's output? As one moves down the organizational hierarchy, however, jobs can be defined more clearly, and shorter-run goals and targets can be established.

## Setting Performance Standards

All incentive systems depend on **performance standards.** The standards provide a relatively objective definition of the job, they give employees targets to shoot for, and they make it easier for supervisors to assign work equitably. Make no mistake about it, though, effective performance is often hard to define. For example, when a Corning group set up a trial program to reward workers for improving their efficiency, a team in one business unit struggled to figure out "What's a meaningful thing to measure? What's reasonable?" The measures finally settled on included safety, quality, shipping efficiency, and forecast accuracy.[89] Once performance standards are set, employees have an opportunity to earn more than their base salaries, sometimes as much as 20 to 25 percent more. In short, they have an incentive to work both harder and smarter.

In setting performance standards for production work, the ideal job (ideal only in terms of the ability to measure performance, not in terms of improving work motivation or job satisfaction) should (1) be highly repetitive, (2) have a short job cycle, and (3) produce a clear, measurable output. The standards themselves will vary, of course, according to the *type* of product or service (e.g., a hospital, a factory, a cable television company); the *method of service delivery;* the degree to which service can be *quantified;* and *organizational needs,* including legal and social pressures. In fact, the many different forms of incentive plans for lower-level employees really differ only along two dimensions:

1.  How premium rates are determined.
2.  How the extra payments are made.

To be sure, incentives oriented toward individuals are becoming less popular as work increasingly becomes interdependent in nature. Nevertheless, individual incentives remain popular in some industries, particularly manufacturing. Lincoln Electric is a prime example.

**HR BUZZ**

## LINCOLN ELECTRIC*

Founded in 1895, Lincoln Electric Company of Cleveland, Ohio, has charted a unique path in worker-management relations, featuring high wages, guaranteed employment, few supervisors, a lucrative bonus-incentive system, and piecework compensation. The company is the world's largest maker of arc-welding equipment.

With 40 percent of its revenues from outside the U.S., Lincoln has 9,500 employees in 20 countries and a network of distributors and sales offices in 160 countries. Among the innovative management practices that set Lincoln apart are these:

*Individual Incentives*

- Guaranteed employment for all full-time workers with more than two years' service, and no mandatory retirement. No worker has been laid off since 1948, and turnover is less than 4 percent for those with more than 180 days on the job.
- High wages, including a substantial annual bonus (up to 100 percent of base pay) based on the company's profits. Wages at Lincoln are roughly equivalent to wages for similar work elsewhere in the Cleveland area, but the bonuses the company pays make its compensation substantially higher. Lincoln has never had a strike and has not missed a bonus payment since the system was instituted in 1934. Individual bonuses are set by a formula that judges workers on five dimensions: quality, output, dependability, ideas, and cooperation. The ratings determine how much of the total corporate bonus pool each worker will get, on top of his or her hourly wage.
- Piecework—more than half of Lincoln's workers are paid according to what they produce, rather than an hourly or weekly wage. If a worker is sick, he or she does not get paid.
- Promotion is almost exclusively from within, according to merit, not seniority.
- Few supervisors, with a supervisor-to-worker ratio of 1 to 100, far lower than in much of the industry. Each employee is supposed to be a self-managing entrepreneur, and each is accountable for the quality of his or her own work.
- No break periods, and mandatory overtime. Workers must work overtime, if ordered to, during peak production periods and must agree to change jobs to meet production schedules or to maintain the company's guaranteed employment program.

While the company insists on individual initiative—and pays according to individual effort—it works diligently to foster the notion of teamwork. And it did so long before the Japanese became known for emphasizing such concepts. If a worker is overly competitive with fellow employees, he or she is rated poorly in terms of cooperation and team play on his or her semiannual rating reports. Thus, that worker's bonus will be smaller. Says one company official: "This is not an easy style to manage; it takes a lot of time and a willingness to work with people."

---

*\*Sources:* Lincoln Electric Company, Annual Report, 2010. Retrieved from *www.lincolnelectric.com/en-us/company/Documents/annualreport2010.pdf* on August 5, 2011. See also Koller, 2010, op. cit. See also Wiley, C. (1993, Aug.). Incentive plan pushes production, *Personnel Journal,* pp. 86–91. See also Serrin, W. (1984, Jan. 15). The way that works at Lincoln. *The New York Times,* p. D1.

## Union Attitudes

A unionized employer may establish an incentive system, but it will be subject to negotiation through collective bargaining. Unions may also wish to participate in the day-to-day management of the incentive system, and management ought to consider that demand seriously. Employees often fear that management will manipulate the system to the disadvantage of employees. Joint participation helps reassure employees that the plan is fair.

Union attitudes toward incentives vary with the type of incentive offered. Unions tend to oppose individual piece-rate systems because they pit worker against worker and can create unfavorable intergroup conflict. However, unions tend to support organizationwide systems, such as profit sharing, because of the extra earnings they provide to their members.[90] In one experiment, for example, an electric utility instituted a division-level incentive plan in one division but not in others. The incentive payout was based on equal percentage shares based on salary. Relative to a control division, the one operating under the incentive plan performed significantly better in reducing unit cost, budget performance, and on 9 of 10 other objective indicators. Nevertheless, union employees helped kill the plan for two reasons: (1) negative reactions from union members in other divisions who did not operate under the incentive plan and (2) a preference for equal dollar shares, rather than equal percentage shares, because the earnings of bargaining-unit employees were lower, on average, than those of managers and staff employees.[91]

## TEAM INCENTIVES

To provide broader motivation than is furnished by incentive plans geared to individual employees, several other approaches have been tried. Their aim is twofold: increase productivity and improve morale by giving employees a feeling of participation in and identification with the company. Team or work-group incentives are one such plan.

Team incentives provide an opportunity for each team member to receive a bonus based on the output of the team as a whole. Teams may be as small as 4 to 7 employees or as large as 35 to 40 employees. Team incentives are most appropriate when jobs are highly interrelated. In fact, highly interrelated jobs are the wave of the future and, in many cases, the wave of the present. In the past, relatively few firms used team incentives. In the future, they will need to be more creative in using team performance management and team incentives.[92] Here's an example of one firm's efforts to do so.

---

**HR BUZZ**

*Team Incentives that Fit the Organization's Culture\**

### Nucor Corporation

Nucor, the largest steel producer in the United States, lives and dies by the spirit of teamwork. That is evident in its organizational design, management philosophy, and incentive plans. Every one of its 11,700 employees participates in one of four incentive plans. The purest team-based compensation plan, however, is the one aimed at groups of 12 to 20 production employees, including maintenance workers and supervisors.

Perhaps the most striking feature of the plan is its simplicity: quality tons out the door and pay weekly. Nucor's plan is a true incentive because workers can gain from good performance (bonuses average 170 to 180 percent of weekly base salaries), or lose money for poor performance. That happens when the tonnage of sub-par products is subtracted from total output—in increasing multiples the farther bad products travel from the source. If a team catches inferior goods in its work area, the tonnage is simply subtracted. If it reaches the next internal customer or the

---

*Sources:* Motley Fool Staff. (2011, Jan. 10). Q-and-A with Nucor CEO Dan DiMicco. Retrieved from *www.fool.com/investing/general/2011/01/10/q-and-a-with-nucor-ceo-dan-dimicco.aspx* on August 5, 2011. See also Bolch, M. (2007, Feb.). Rewarding the team. *HR Magazine*, pp. 91–93.

shipping department, the amount of bad product subtracted is doubled. If it reaches a customer, the bad tonnage is tripled, and then subtracted from total output.

With bonuses included, the typical Nucor steel mill worker makes $72,000 a year, and participates in a profit-sharing plan that paid out an additional $20,000 per employee per year from 2004 to 2008. On any given day, nearly every production worker can tell you within a tenth of a percent what his or her weekly bonus will be. Says the company's manager of HR and organizational development: "It's truly remarkable how much information the employees know. It's a beautiful thing to see." Since Nucor adopted its incentive plan in 1966, the company has been profitable every quarter and not a single employee has been laid off. Case 11–1 describes Nucor in more detail.

Team incentives have the following advantages:

1. They make it possible to reward workers who provide essential services to line workers (so-called indirect labor), yet who are paid only their regular base pay. These employees do things like transport supplies and materials, maintain equipment, or inspect work output.
2. They encourage cooperation, not competition, among workers.

On the other hand, team incentives also have disadvantages:

1. Competition between teams.
2. Inability of workers to see their individual contributions to the output of the team. If they do not see the link between their individual effort and increased rewards, they will not be motivated to produce more.
3. Top performers grow disenchanted with having to carry "free riders" (those who don't carry their share of the load).

Recent large-scale research with work groups has revealed the critical relationship between employees' understanding of the work-group incentive plan and their perceptions of the fairness of that plan. Managers should ensure that all members of work groups understand how pay-plan goals are established, what the goals and performance standards themselves are, how the plan goals are evaluated, and how the payouts are determined.[93] To overcome some of the first two disadvantages of team incentives, many firms have introduced organizationwide incentives.

## ORGANIZATIONWIDE INCENTIVES

In this final section, we consider three broad classes of organizationwide incentives: profit sharing, gain sharing, and employee stock-ownership plans. As we shall see, each is different in its objectives and implementation.

### Profit Sharing

**Profit-sharing** plans pay out if a firm meets its profitability target (e.g., return on assets or net income). Profit-sharing can be either deferred (i.e., to fund retirement) or paid in cash, while payouts may be either formula-based (e.g., a fixed percentage of net income) or discretionary. Firms use it for one or more of the following reasons: (1) to provide a group incentive for increased productivity, (2) to provide retirement income for their employees, (3) to institute a flexible reward structure that reflects a company's actual economic position, (4) to enhance employees' security and identification with the company, (5) to attract and retain workers more easily, and/or (6) to educate individuals about the factors that underlie business success and the capitalistic system.[94]

On the downside, most employees don't feel that their jobs have a direct impact on profits, or at least they can't see that link. Why? Because profits depend on numerous factors in addition to operating efficiency—such as the strength of consumer demand, global competition, and accounting practices.

In most plans, employees receive a bonus that is normally based on some percentage (e.g., 10 to 30 percent) of the company's profits beyond some minimum level. Does profit sharing improve productivity? One review of 27 econometric studies found that profit-sharing was positively related to productivity in better than 9 of every 10 instances. Productivity was generally 3 to 5 percent higher in firms with profit-sharing plans than in those without plans.[95]

Offsetting those encouraging results, however, are research findings that profit sharing seems to be associated with higher overall labor costs (because workers require a compensating differential for accepting the risk involved in such a variable-compensation program). Moreover, despite profit sharing's demonstrated relationship with productivity, it is not clear that one of these *causes* increases in the other. Finally, the potential to make labor costs variable in relation to profitability will be realized only if profit- sharing plans survive years when no payouts are made.[96] While profit sharing can stimulate innovation and creativity, the actual success of such plans depends on the stability and security of the overall work environment, the company's overall HR management policy, and the state of labor-management relations.[97] This is even more true of gain-sharing plans.

## Gain Sharing

Gain sharing is a results-based program that generally links pay to performance at the facility level.[98] In contrast to profit sharing, where many employees cannot see the link between what they do and company profits, **gain sharing** focuses on achieving savings in areas over which employees do have control—for example, reduced scrap or lower labor or utility costs. As the name suggests, employees share in the gains achieved. Gain sharing is a reward system that has existed in a variety of forms for decades. At present, about 12 percent of firms, mostly in manufacturing, have gain-sharing plans. Sometimes known as the Scanlon plan, the Rucker plan, or Improshare (improved productivity through sharing), gain sharing comprises three elements:[99]

1. A philosophy of cooperation.
2. An involvement system.
3. A financial bonus.

The philosophy of cooperation refers to an organizational climate characterized by high levels of trust, two-way communication, participation, and harmonious industrial relations. The involvement system refers to the structure and process for improving organizational productivity. Typically, it is a broadly based suggestion system implemented by an employee-staffed committee structure that usually reaches all areas of the organization. Sometimes this structure involves work teams, but usually it is simply an employee-based suggestion system. The employees involved develop and implement ideas related to productivity. The third component, the financial bonus, is determined by a calculation that measures the difference between expected and actual costs during a bonus period.

The three components mutually reinforce one another. High levels of cooperation lead to information sharing, which in turn leads to employee involvement, which leads to new behaviors, such as offering suggestions to improve organizational productivity. This increase in productivity then results in a financial bonus (based on the amount of the productivity increase), which rewards and reinforces the philosophy of cooperation.

Gain sharing differs from profit sharing in three important ways:[100]

1.  Gain sharing is based on a measure of productivity. Profit sharing is based on a global profitability measure.
2.  Gain sharing, productivity measurement, and bonus payments are frequent events, distributed monthly or quarterly, in contrast to the annual measures and rewards of profit-sharing plans.
3.  Gain-sharing plans are current-distribution plans, in contrast to most profit-sharing plans, which have deferred payments. Hence gain-sharing plans are true incentive plans rather than employee benefits. As such, they are more directly related to individual behavior and therefore can motivate worker productivity.

When gain-sharing plans work, they work well, with improvements in sales, customer satisfaction, and profits in the 4 to 5 percent range.[101] Nevertheless, in the 50 years since the inception of gain sharing, it has been abandoned by firms about as often as it has been retained. Here are some reasons:

1.  Generally, it does not work well in piecework operations.
2.  The returns from gain-sharing programs appear to dwindle with increasing plan size.
3.  Some firms are uncomfortable with bringing unions into business planning.
4.  Some managers may feel they are giving up their prerogatives.[102]

Some features of gain-sharing plans clearly favor success, though. Employee (and union) participation in the design of the plan, positive managerial attitudes, the number of years a company has had such a plan, favorable and realistic employee attitudes, and involvement by a high-level executive are strongly related to the success of gain-sharing plans.[103] To develop an organizationwide incentive plan that has a chance to survive, let alone succeed, careful, in-depth planning must precede implementation. It is true of all incentive plans, though, that *none will work well except in a climate of trustworthy labor-management relations and sound human resource management practices.*

## Employee Stock-Ownership Plans

**Employee stock-ownership plans** (ESOPs) have become popular in both large and small companies in the United States (e.g., PepsiCo, Lincoln Electric,

DuPont, Procter & Gamble) as well as in western Europe, some countries in central Europe, and China.[104] The typical ESOP company is a closely held, small-to-midsize firm, with a few hundred employees. In the United States there were 11,400 ESOPs in 2009, with 13 million participants holding more than $600 billion in assets. The goal is to increase employee involvement in decision making, and hopefully this will build the business. Recent evidence indicates that ESOPs do just that. During the 2007–2009 recession, for example, revenue at ESOP firms grew an average of 15.1 percent, compared to a decline of 3.4 percent for all private-industry revenue. ESOP firms also showed employment growth, faster wage growth, and higher average wages during 2008, compared to declines in those same metrics at other firms.[105]

Generally, ESOPs are established for any of the following reasons:

- As a means of tax-favored, company-financed transfer of ownership from a departing owner to a firm's employees. This is often done in small firms with closely held stock.[106]
- As a way of borrowing money relatively inexpensively. A firm borrows money from a bank using its stock as collateral, and places the stock in an employee stock-ownership trust. As the loan is repaid, the trust distributes the stock at no cost to employees. Companies can deduct the principal

## IMPACT OF PAY AND INCENTIVES ON PRODUCTIVITY, QUALITY OF WORK LIFE, AND THE BOTTOM LINE

High salary levels alone do not ensure a productive, motivated workforce. It is not *how much* a company pays its workers but, more importantly, *how the pay system is designed, communicated, and managed.*[a] Excessively high labor costs can bankrupt a company.[b] This is especially likely if, to cover its labor costs, the company cannot price its products competitively. If that happens, productivity and profits both suffer directly, and the quality of work life suffers indirectly. Conversely, when the interests of employees and their organizations are aligned, then employees are likely to engage in behavior that goes above and beyond the call of duty (such as helping others accomplish their goals), is not recognized by the formal reward system, and contributes to organizational effectiveness.[c] This improves both quality of work life and productivity. What's the bottom line? When sensible policies on pay and incentives are established using the principles discussed in this chapter, everybody wins: the company, the employees, and employees' families.

---

[a]Jackson, 2010, op. cit.

[b]Martocchio, J. J. (2011). Strategic reward and compensation plans. In S. Zedeck (Ed.), *APA Handbook of Industrial and Organizational Psychology*, Vol. 1. Washington, DC: American Psychological Association, pp. 343–372. See also Stajkovic, A. D., and Luthans, F. (2001). Differential effects of incentive motivators on work performance. *Academy of Management Journal* 44(3), pp. 580–590.

[c]Taub, S. (2004, Sept. 30). Airlines wage pay-cut war. Retrieved from *www.cfo.com/article.cfm/3242603?f=search* on September 30, 2004.

as well as interest on the amount borrowed, and lenders pay taxes on only 50 percent of their income from ESOP loans.

- To fulfill a philosophical belief in employee ownership. Says Barbara Gabel, retiring cofounder of Zachary's Chicago Pizza, "Our community has a great affinity for the mom-and-pop small businesses, and they love it that a company they respect is employee owned. It enhances our hard-earned goodwill. . . . Currently our employees own about 75 percent of the company, and are on the brink of owning 100 percent. It will be with a sweet sense of joy and pride that we sit on the sidelines and watch them create their own destinies."[107]
- As an additional employee benefit.

Do ESOPs improve employee motivation and satisfaction? Longitudinal research spanning 45 case studies found that stock ownership alone does not make employees work harder or enjoy their day-to-day work more.[108] At the same time, however,

1. ESOP satisfaction tends to be highest in companies where (a) the company makes relatively large annual contributions to the plan; (b) management is committed to employee ownership and is willing to share power and decision-making authority with employees; and (c) there are extensive company communications about the ESOP, the company's current performance, and its future plans.[109]

2. Employees tend to be most satisfied with stock ownership when the company established its ESOP for employee-centered reasons (management was committed to employee ownership) rather than for strategic or financial reasons (e.g., as an anti-takeover device or to gain tax savings).

How does employee stock ownership affect economic performance? In the largest study of its kind to date, researchers matched 234 pairs of ESOP and non-ESOP companies on size, industry, and region and then examined sales and employment data from three years prior to the adoption of the ESOP and three years after its adoption. ESOPs appear to increase sales, employment, and sales per employee by about 2.3 to 2.4 percent per year over what would have been expected absent an ESOP. ESOP companies are also somewhat more likely to still be in business several years later. Surprisingly, ESOP companies are considerably more likely to offer other kinds of retirement plans [e.g., 33 percent of ESOP companies offered 401(k) savings plans, while only 6 percent of non-ESOP companies did]. A general assumption had been that ESOPs must be a trade-off for other wages or benefits. While this may be true in some ESOP companies, this study shows that in the benefits area, they are an overall net addition to, not a substitute for, retirement plans.[110] All ESOPs are not created equally, though, for a recent review found a declining pattern of economic returns by firm size.[111]

While such data do not prove that employee stock ownership causes success (it may be that successful firms are more likely to make employees part owners), they do suggest that if implemented properly, such plans can improve employee attitudes and economic productivity. Nevertheless, ESOPs are not risk-free to employees. ESOPs are not insured, and if a company goes bankrupt, its stock may be worthless.

# IMPLICATIONS FOR MANAGEMENT PRACTICE

In thinking about pay and incentives, expect to see three trends continue:

1. The movement to performance-based pay plans, in which workers put more of their pay at risk in return for potentially higher rewards. Recognize, however, that organizations facing higher risks place less emphasis on short-term incentives than do other organizations. To compensate for such uncertainty, they tend to rely more on higher base pay.[a]
2. The movement toward the use of teamwide or organizationwide incentive plans at all levels.
3. Use of a wide range of pay increases, in an effort to make distinctions in performance as meaningful as possible.

In the wave of restructurings and reengineerings that continue to unfold, research has found that the jobs of employees who remain may well impose greater demands on them in the form of know-how, problem solving, and accountability.[b] Be prepared to reevaluate those jobs, and, if justified, to adjust compensation accordingly.

---

[a]Tuna, C. (2008, July 7). Pay, your own way: Firm lets workers pick salary. *The Wall Street Journal,* p. B6. See also Bloom, M., and Milkovich, G. T. (1998). Relationships among risk, incentive pay, and organizational performance. *Academy of Management Journal* 41, pp. 283–297.

[b]Elmer, V. (2011, Feb. 1). How to deal with an invisible promotion. *Fortune.* Retrieved from *management.fortune.cnn.com/2011/02/01/how-to-deal-with-an-invisiblepromotion* on August 5, 2011. See also Tullar, W. L. (1998). Compensation consequences of reengineering. *Journal of Applied Psychology* 83, pp. 975–980.

---

**Human Resource Management in Action: Conclusion**

## THE TRUST GAP

What steps can companies take to sew corporate top and bottom back together? Here are seven suggestions:

1. **Start with the obvious.** Forge a closer link between CEO compensation and company performance. At American Express, CEO Ken Chenault received a huge grant of stock options in 2007, but to get any of them, he has to beat several stretch goals by 2013. AmEx's earnings per share must grow by an average of 15 percent a year, revenues must grow by at least 10 percent a year, return on equity must average at least 36 percent per year, and total return to shareholders must beat the S&P 500 average by at least 2.5 percent per year. Chenault can receive a fraction of the grant for lesser performance, but below certain limits, which are still high, he gets nothing.
2. **Consider instituting profit sharing, gain sharing, or some other program** that lets employees profit from their efforts. At Aflac, the insurer based in Columbus, Georgia, all of the company's 4,500 employees, from those in the call center to top executives, receive a percentage of their annual salaries in the form of profit-sharing bonuses.
3. **Rethink perquisites.** Now that proxy-disclosure rules require that all perks of the top five officers who exceed $10,000 be revealed, they just don't have the same appeal to executives as they used to. Yet they still have at least the same downside with the rank and file.

4. **Make sure the Board's pay consultants don't work for management.** Adopt a written policy that outlaws such an obvious conflict of interest.
5. **Make sure your door is really open.** If that means meeting with employees at unorthodox times, such as when their shifts end, then do it. Not a single one of the CEOs interviewed by *Fortune* could recall employees ever abusing an open-door policy. The lesson is clear for managers at all levels: Employees don't walk through your door unless they have to.
6. **If you don't survey employee attitudes now, start.** What you find can help identify problems before they become crises. Share findings, and be sure employees know how subsequent decisions may be related to them. Don't worry about raising expectations too high. As one executive commented, "Employees by and large are reasonable people. They understand you can't do everything they want. As long as they know their views are being considered and they get some feedback from you to that effect, you will be meeting their expectations."
7. **Explain things—personally.** While one study found that 97 percent of CEOs believe that communicating with employees has a positive impact on job satisfaction and 79 percent think it benefits the bottom line, only 22 percent do it weekly or more often.

There is no doubt that these seven steps can help close the trust gap that exists in so many U.S. organizations today. On the other hand, virtually all experts cite one important qualification: It is suicidal to start down this road unless you are absolutely sincere.

## SUMMARY

Contemporary pay systems (outside the entertainment and professional sports fields) are characterized by cost containment, pay and benefit levels commensurate with what a company can afford, and programs that encourage and reward performance.

Generally speaking, pay systems are designed to attract, retain, and motivate employees; achieve internal, external, and individual equity; and maintain a balance in relationships between direct and indirect forms of compensation and between the pay rates of supervisory and nonsupervisory employees. Pay systems need to be tied to the strategic mission of an organization, and they should take their direction from that strategic mission. However, actual wage levels depend on labor market conditions, legislation, collective bargaining, management attitudes, and an organization's ability to pay. Our broad objective in developing pay systems is to assign a monetary value to each job or skill set in the organization (a base rate) and to establish an orderly procedure for increasing the base rate. To develop a job-based system, we need four basic tools: job analyses and job descriptions, a job-evaluation plan, pay surveys, and a pay structure. In addition, the following pay policy issues are important: pay secrecy versus openness, the effect of inflation on pay systems, pay compression, and pay raises.

In terms of incentive plans, the most effective ones are simple, specific, attainable, and measurable. Consider merit pay, for example. Merit pay works best when these guidelines are followed: (1) Establish high standards of performance; (2) develop sound performance management systems; (3) train supervisors in the mechanics of performance appraisal and in the art of giving constructive feedback; (4) tie rewards closely to performance; and (5) provide a wide range of possible pay increases.

Long-term incentives, in the form of stock options, restricted stock, or performance shares, are becoming a larger proportion of executive pay packages. Finally, there is a wide variety of individual, group, and organizationwide incentive plans (e.g., profit sharing, gain sharing, employee stock-ownership plans) with different impacts on employee motivation and economic outcomes. Blending fixed versus variable pay in a manner that is understandable and acceptable to employees will present a management challenge for years to come.

## KEY TERMS

| | |
|---|---|
| trust gap | pay compression |
| organizational reward system | incentives |
| compensation | merit-pay systems |
| financial rewards | annuity problem |
| nonfinancial rewards | sorting effect |
| internal equity | restricted stock |
| external equity | restricted stock units |
| individual equity | performance shares |
| balance | performance-accelerated shares |
| compensable factors | premium-price options |
| job evaluation | lump-sum bonus |
| benchmark jobs | spot bonus |
| relevant labor markets | performance standards |
| market-based pay system | profit sharing |
| competency-based pay system | gain sharing |
| pay openness | employee stock-ownership plans |

## DISCUSSION QUESTIONS

11–1.　What steps can a company take to align its compensation system with its general business strategy?

11–2.　What can companies do to ensure internal, external, and individual equity for all employees?

11–3.　Discuss the advantages and disadvantages of competency- or skill-based pay systems.

11–4.　What cautions would you advise in interpreting data from pay surveys?

11–5.　How has strategic thinking affected executive incentives?

11–6.　Distinguish profit sharing from gain sharing.

11–7.　If you were implementing an employee stock-ownership plan, what key factors would you consider?

## APPLYING YOUR KNOWLEDGE

*Nucor: The Art of Motivation*                                                    *Case 11–1*

### Forging a Winning Workforce

**Nucor's egalitarian culture places a premium on teamwork and idea-sharing between frontline workers and management. Result: A highly profitable partnership.**

**Pay for Performance**
On average, *two-thirds of a Nucor steelworker's pay is based on a production bonus*, with profit-sharing layered on top of that. It can be a lucrative formula, but the risks are real. In 2005 the typical worker received $91,293; three years earlier a steel slump left workers with $58,931. CEO and executive pay is similarly tied to performance targets.

**Listen to the Front Line**
Execs say almost all of *the best ideas come from the factory floor*—and the newest workers often come up with them. In the wake of its recent acquisitions, Nucor is sending new workers to existing plants to hunt for improvement opportunities and having older workers see what they can learn from newly acquired plants.

**Push-Down Authority**
To minimize layers of management, Nucor has pushed work that used to be done by supervisors, such as ordering parts, down to line workers, and pushed the duties of plant managers down to supervisors. CEO DiMicco says his *executive vice-presidents are like "mini CEOs, and I'm their board."*

**Protect Your Culture**
As Nucor grows, protecting its egalitarian philosophy and team spirit is more of a challenge. A decentralized structure helps, but management makes *cultural compatibility a big focus of its acquisition research.* In visits to potential acquisitions, careful attention is paid to how plant workers and managers interact.

**Try Unproven Technologies**
Forays into new technologies haven't always paid off for Nucor, but it realizes *the importance of taking risks.* One project to make wire from steel failed miserably, and a $200 million attempt to build up a supply of raw materials in the Caribbean had to be scrapped. But successes such as thin slab casting of sheet metal have made Nucor an industry leader.

*Source:* Nucor, the art of motivation: What you can learn from a company that treats workers like owners. Inside the surprising performance culture of steelmaker Nucor. (2006, May 1). *BusinessWeek,* p. 59.

### Questions
1. What does Nucor's approach to managing its people require of managers?
2. Suggest several ways that a company might encourage its more experienced workers to listen to ideas from newer employees.
3. What might an organization do to preserve its culture among newly hired employees and those who arrive through acquisition?
4. Guaranteed pay at Nucor is considerably lower than that of the industry. Yet Nucor workers earn much more in total compensation than comparable workers in their industry. Why?

## REFERENCES

1. Krell, E. (2011, Jan.). All for incentives, incentives for all. *HR Magazine* 56(1), pp. 35–38. See also White, E. (2006, Jan. 30). The best vs. the rest: Companies eschew across-the-board increases to give top performers a bigger slice of the raise pie. *The Wall Street Journal,* pp. B1, B3.

2. Bates, S. (2003a). Top pay for best performance. *HR Magazine* 48(1), pp. 31–38.

3. Milkovich, G. T., Newman, J. M., and Gerhart, B. (2011). *Compensation* (10th Ed.). Burr Ridge, IL: McGraw-Hill/Irwin.

4. See, for example, WorldatWork. (2010, Jan. 18). Pay cuts not as prevalent as pay freezes in 2009. Retrieved from *www.worldatwork.org/waw/adimComment?id=36151* on January 21, 2010.

5. Milkovich et al., 2011, op. cit.

6. Ibid.

7. Stroh, L. K., Brett, J. M., Baumann, J. P., and Reilly, A. H. (1996). Agency theory and variable pay compensation strategies. *Academy of Management Journal* 39, pp. 751–767.

8. 2011 executive paywatch. Retrieved from *www.aflcio.org/paywatch* on July 31, 2011. See also Show you the money? It's with variable pay. (2000, Nov. 16). *BusinessWeek,* p. 8. See also Koretz, G. (1999, Dec. 13). A safety valve for wages? Variable pay's rewards—and risks. *BusinessWeek,* p. 32.

9. Miller, S. (2010, March 1). Companies worldwide rewarding performance with variable pay. Retrieved from *www.shrm.org/hrdisciplines/compensation/Articles/Pages/VariableWorld.aspx* on July 31, 2011. Hewitt Study Finds That While Salary Increases Were Lowest in 33 Years, Variable Pay Awards Reached an All Time High in 2009. Retrieved from *www.interbiznet.com/ern/archives/090812.html* on July 14, 2010.

10. Zhou, J., and Martocchio, J. J. (2001). Chinese and American managers' compensation-award decisions: A comparative policy-capturing study. *Personnel Psychology* 54, pp. 115–145.

11. Kucera, D. (2010, July 25). Companies ramp up perks to keep workers as economy improves. Retrieved from *www.wopular.com/companies-ramp-perks-keep-workers-economy-improves* on July 26, 2010.

12. Ibid. See also Most companies lose top talent. (2011, July 26). Retrieved from *www.bizjournals.com/dayton/news/2011/07/26/companies-lose-top-talent-in-past-year.html* on July 27, 2011.

13. Milkovich et al., 2011, op. cit. See also Martocchio, J. J. (2011). *Strategic compensation* (6th Ed.). Upper Saddle River, NJ: Pearson/Prentice Hall. See also Lawler, E. E. III. (2000). *Rewarding excellence: Pay strategies for the new economy.* San Francisco: Jossey-Bass.

14. Garvey, C. (2005, Jan.). Philosophizing compensation. *HRMagazine.* Retrieved from *www.shrm.org* on July 14, 2008.

15. Trevor, C. O., and Wazeter, D. L. (2006). A contingent view of reactions to objective pay conditions: Interdependence among pay structure characteristics and pay relative to internal and external referents. *Journal of Applied Psychology* 91, pp. 1260–1275. See also Gerhart, B., and Rynes, S. (2003). *Compensation: Theory, Evidence, and Strategic Implications.* Thousand Oaks, CA: Sage.

16. Greenberg, J. (2011). Organizational justice: The dynamics of fairness in the workplace. *APA Handbook of Industrial and Organizational Psychology*, Vol. 3, pp. 271–327. See also Huseman, R. C., Hatfield, J. D., and Miles, E. W. (1987). A new perspective on equity theory: The equity sensitivity construct. *Academy of Management Review* 12, pp. 222–234.

17. Milkovich et al., 2011, op. cit.

18. Ibid. See also Martocchio, 2011, op. cit. See also Grossman, W., and Hoskisson, R. E. (1998). CEO pay at the crossroads of Wall Street and Main: Toward the strategic design of executive compensation. *Academy of Management Executive* 12(1), pp. 43–57.

**19.** Grossman and Hoskisson, 1998, op. cit. See also Montemayor, E. (1996). Congruence between pay policy and competitive strategy in high-performing firms. *Journal of Management* 22, pp. 889–908.

**20.** IBM. Our strategy. Retrieved from *www.ibm.com/investor/strategy/* on August 1, 2011.

**21.** Milkovich et al., 2011, op. cit. See also Gerhart and Rynes, 2003, op. cit.

**22.** Milkovich et al., 2011, op. cit.

**23.** Lazear, E. P. (1998). *Personnel Economics*. NY: Wiley. See also Klaas, B. S., and Ullman, J. C. (1995). Sticky wages revisited: Organizational responses to a declining market-clearing wage. *Academy of Management Review* 20, pp. 281–310. See also Cappelli, P., and Chauvin, K. (1991). An interplant test of the efficiency wage hypothesis. *Quarterly Journal of Economics* 106, pp. 769–794.

**24.** Orey, M. (2007, Oct. 1). Wage wars. *BusinessWeek,* pp. 50–60.

**25.** Orey, 2007, op. cit. See also Ormiston, K. A. (1988, May 10). States know best what labor's worth. *The Wall Street Journal,* p. 38.

**26.** Department of Labor. Minimum wage laws in the states—January 1, 2011. Retrieved from *www.dol.gov/whd/minwage/america.htm* on August 1, 2011.

**27.** Living wage facts at a glance. *Economic Policy Institute.* Retrieved from *http://houstonhs.scsk12.org/~mrobinson/Mr._Robinsons_Web_Site_at_Houston_High_School/Contemporary_Issues_Resource_Page_files/Living%20wage-%20Facts%20at%20a%20Glance.pdf* on August 1, 2011. See also, Gertner, J. (2006, Jan. 15). What is a living wage? *New York Times Magazine.* Retrieved from *www.nytimes.com/2006/01/15/magazine/15wage.html?pagewanted=all* on July 15, 2008.

**28.** Budd, J. W. (2010). *Labor Relations: Striking a Balance* (3rd Ed.). Burr Ridge, IL: Irwin/McGraw-Hill. See also Fossum, J. A. (2012). *Labor Relations: Development, Structure, Process* (11th Ed.). Burr Ridge, IL: Irwin/McGraw-Hill.

**29.** Milkovich et al., 2011, op. cit. See also Pfeffer, J., and Davis-Blake, A. (1987). Understanding organizational wage structures: A resource dependence approach. *Academy of Management Journal* 30, pp. 437–455.

**30.** Lawler, E. E. III, and Worley, C. G., with Creelman, D. (2011). *Management Reset: Organizing for Sustainable Effectiveness.* San Francisco: Jossey-Bass. See also Klaas, B. (1999). Containing compensation costs: Why firms differ in their willingness to reduce pay. *Journal of Management* 25, pp. 829–850.

**31.** Van Sliedregt, T., Voskiujl, O. F., and Thierry, H. (2001). Job evaluation systems and pay-grade structures: Do they match? *International Journal of Human Resource Management* 12(8), pp. 1313–1324. See also Collins, J. M., and Muchinsky, P. M. (1993). An assessment of the construct validity of three job evaluation methods: A field experiment. *Academy of Management Journal* 36(4), pp. 895–904. See also Madigan, R. M., and Hoover, D. J. (1986). Effects of alternative job evaluation methods on decisions involving pay equity. *Academy of Management Journal* 29(1), pp. 84–100.

**32.** Milkovich et al., 2011, op. cit.

**33.** Ibid. See also Gerhart and Rynes, 2003, op. cit.

**34.** Trevor, C., and Graham, M. E. (2000). Deriving the market wage derivatives: Three decision areas in the compensation survey process. *WorldatWork Journal* 9(4), pp. 69–77. See also Klaas, B., and McClendon, J. A. (1996). To lead, lag, or match: Estimating the financial impact of pay level policies. *Personnel Psychology* 49, pp. 121–140. See also Rynes, S. L., and Milkovich, G. T. (1986). Wage surveys: Dispelling some myths about the "market wage." *Personnel Psychology* 39, pp. 71–90.

**35.** See, for example, *http://www.aon.com/human-capital-consulting/default.jsp, www.haygrouppaynet.com,* or *www.mercer.com.*

**36.** Milkovich et al., 2011, op. cit.

**37.** Ibid. See also Martocchio, 2011, op. cit.

**38.** Sibson, R. E. (1991). *Compensation* (5th Ed.). New York: American Management Association.

**39.** Winter, C. (2011, May 1). General Electric: Adjusting the boss's pay. *BusinessWeek,* p. 29. See also Ceron, G. F. (2004, Apr. 12). The company we keep. *The Wall Street Journal,* pp. R4, R5.

**40.** Ledford, G. E., Jr., and Heneman, H. G. III. (2011, June). *Skill-Based Pay.* Society for Industrial & Organizational Psychology, Inc. "SIOP Science" Series. Alexandria, VA: Society for Human Resource Management.

**41.** Grib, G., and O'Donnell, S. (1995, July). Pay plans that reward employee achievement. *HR Magazine,* pp. 49, 50. See also Leonard, B. (1995, Feb.). Creating opportunities to excel. *HR Magazine,* pp. 47–51.

**42.** Southall, D., and Newman, J. (2000). *Skill-Based Pay Development.* Buffalo, NY: HR Foundations Inc.

**43.** Ledford, G. (2008, 1st Qtr.). Factors affecting the long-term success of skill-based pay. *WorldatWork Journal,* pp. 6–18. See also Canavan, J. (2008, 1st Qtr.). Overcoming the challenge of aligning skill-based pay levels to the external market. *WorldatWork Journal,* pp. 18–24. See also Batt, R. (2004). Who benefits from teams? Comparing workers, supervisors, and managers. *Industrial Relations* 43, pp. 183–212.

**44.** Murray, B., and Gerhart, B. (1998). An empirical analysis of a skill-based pay program and plant performance outcomes. *Academy of Management Journal* 41, pp. 68–78.

**45.** Lee, C., Law, K. S., and Bobko, P. (1999). The importance of justice perceptions on pay effectiveness: A two-year study of a skill-based pay plan. *Journal of Management* 25(6), pp. 851–873.

**46.** Levenson, A. R., Van der Stede, W. A., and Cohen, S. G. (2006). Measuring the relationship between managerial competencies and performance. *Journal of Management* 32, pp. 360–380.

**47.** Dovey, C. (2006, Jan.). *Compensation trends.* SHRM White Paper. Retrieved from *www.shrm.org/hrdisciplines/compensation/Articles/Pages/CMS_011730.aspx* on July 15, 2008.

**48.** Lee, A. (2007, Sept. 13). Communication rules in the workplace: Secret salaries? Retrieved from *blogs.payscale.com/ask_dr_salary/2007/09/communication-r.html* on July 15, 2008. See also Hindo, B. (2007, June 18). Mind if I peek at your paycheck? *BusinessWeek,* pp. 40, 42.

**49.** Leonard, P. (2010, 22 July). Pay secrecy policies need close scrutiny as the Equality Act 2010 comes into force. *HR Magazine* (UK). Retrieved from *www.hrmagazine.co.uk/hro/features/1018162/pay-secrecy-policies-close-scrutiny-equality-act-2010-comes-force* on August 2, 2011.

**50.** Milkovich et al., 2011, op. cit.

**51.** Belkin, L. (2008, Aug. 21). Psst! Your salary is showing. *The New York Times.* Retrieved from *www.nytimes.com/2008/08/21/fashion/21Work.html?sq=Psst! Your salary is showing&st=nyt&adxnnl=1&scp=1&adxnnlx=1315923403-2/gUT+IYSX/rQFsAJEl64w* on October 24, 2009. See also Rouzer, P. A. (2000, Aug.). Adding salary ranges to internal postings. *HR Magazine,* pp. 107–114.

**52.** Belkin, op. cit. See also Markels, A., and Berton, L. (1996, Apr. 11). Something to talk about. *The Wall Street Journal Supplement,* p. R10.

**53.** Miller, S. (2010, Feb. 15). US salary-increase budgets barely matching inflation. Retrieved from *www.shrm.org/hrdisciplines/compensation/Articles/Pages/PayBudgets.aspx* on March 12, 2010.

**54.** Miller, S. (2008, July). More time off, flex schedules, in lieu of higher pay. Retrieved from *www.shrm.org* on July 15, 2008. See also Barnett, R. (2010, July 5). I deserve a raise. Do I dare ask for one? *Fortune,* p. 36.

**55.** Milkovich et al., 2011, op. cit.

**56.** Miller, 2010, op. cit. See also Dreazen, Y. (2000, July 25). Morale problem: When recruits earn more. *The Wall Street Journal,* pp. B1, B10.

**57.** Sanders, P. (2006, Oct. 5). Steve Wynn betters the odds for bosses at Las Vegas casino. Dealers must now share tips with their supervisors, who earn less money. *The Wall Street Journal,* pp. A1, A7.

**58.** Orey, 2007, op. cit. See also Bates, S. (2004, Apr. 5). Beyond the rules: Market pressures influence who gets overtime pay. Retrieved from *www.shrm.org* on Sept. 28, 2004. See also Revenge of the "managers." (2001, Mar. 12). *BusinessWeek,* pp. 60, 62.

**59.** Ha, O., and Pham, D. N. (2011, July 3). The cheap China gets a lot more volatile. *BusinessWeek,* p. 15.

**60.** Gerhart and Rynes, 2003, op. cit., p. 176.

**61.** Crotty, J. (2008, Aug. 28). *Structural Causes of the Global Financial Crisis: A Critical Assessment of the "New Financial Architecture."* University of Massachusetts—Amherst, Economics Department, Working Paper 16. Retrieved from *scholarworks. umass.edu/econ_workingpaper/16* on August 3, 2011.

**62.** Sturman, M. C., Trevor, C. O., Boudreau, J. W., and Gerhart, B. (2003). Is it worth it to win the talent war? Evaluating the utility of performance-based pay. *Personnel Psychology* 56, pp. 997–1035. See also Stajkovic, A. D., and Luthans, F. (2001). Differential effects of incentive motivators on work performance. *Academy of Management Journal* 44, pp. 580–590. See also Banker, R. D., Lee, S. Y., Potter, G., and Srinivasan, D. (1996). Contextual analysis of performance impacts of outcome-based incentive compensation. *Academy of Management Journal* 39, pp. 920–948.

**63.** Knowledge@Wharton. (2011, March 30). The problem with financial incentives—and what to do about it. Retrieved from *knowledge.wharton.upenn.edu/article. cfm?articleid=2741* on March 31, 2011. See also Cascio, W. F., and Cappelli, P. (2009, Jan.). Lessons from the financial services crisis. *HR Magazine* 54(1), pp. 47–50. See also Kerr, S. The best laid incentive plans. (2003, Jan.). *Harvard Business Review,* pp. 27–37.

**64.** Mantell, 2011, op. cit. See also Hewitt study, 2007, op. cit. See also Perking up the workforce. (2003, Sept. 29). *Fortune,* pp. S1–S10.

**65.** Jenkins, G. D., Jr., Mitra, A., Gupta, N., and Shaw, J. D. (1998). Are financial incentives related to performance? A meta-analytic review of empirical research. *Journal of Applied Psychology* 83, pp. 777–787.

**66.** Latham, G. P. (2009). *Becoming the Evidence-Based Manager: Making the Science of Management Work for You.* Boston, MA: Davies-Black. See also Bolger, B. (2004, Spring). Ten steps to designing an effective incentive program. *Employment Relations Today,* pp. 25–33. See also Heneman, R. L. (2002). *Strategic Reward Management: Design, Implementation, and Evaluation.* Greenwich, CT: Information Age Publishing. See also Dunham, K. J. (2002, Nov. 19). Amid sinking workplace morale, employers turn to recognition. *The Wall Street Journal,* p. B8.

**67.** Gerhart, B., Rynes, S. L., and Fulmer, I. S. (2009). Pay and performance: Individuals, groups, and executives. *Academy of Management Annals* 3, pp. 251–315. See also Bennett, A. (1991, Sept. 10). Paying workers to meet goals spreads, but gauging performance proves tough. *The Wall Street Journal,* pp. B1, B2.

**68.** Wallace, C. (2008, Feb. 13). How to make great teachers. *Time.* Retrieved from *www. time.com/time/magazine/article/0,9171,1713473-1,00.html* on March 18, 2008. See also Waldman, S., and Roberts, B. (1988, Nov. 14). Grading "merit pay." *Newsweek,* pp. 45, 46.

**69.** The stat. (2005, July 4). *BusinessWeek,* p. 12.

**70.** Bates, 2003a, op. cit.

**71.** Light, J. (2010, Nov. 8). Human-resources executives say reviews are off the mark. *The Wall Street Journal*, p. B8.

**72.** Koller, F. (2010). *Spark: How Old-Fashioned Values Drive a Twenty-First-Century Corporation.* New York, NY: Perseus. See also Wiley, C. (1993, Aug.). Incentive plan pushes production. *Personnel Journal,* pp. 86–91.

**73.** Bates, 2003a, op. cit.

**74.** Rynes, S. L., Gerhart, B., and Parks, L. (2005). Personnel psychology: Performance evaluation and pay for performance. *Annual Review of Psychology* 56, pp. 571–600.

**75.** Lawler, E. E. III. (2003). Reward practices and performance management system effectiveness. *Organizational Dynamics* 32(4), pp. 396–404. See also Heneman, R. L. (2002). A survey of merit pay-plan effectiveness: End of the line for merit pay or hope for improvement? In R. L. Heneman (Ed.), *Strategic Reward Management.* Greenwich, CT: Information Age Publishing, pp. 167–192.

**76.** Bennett, A. (1991, Apr. 17). The hot seat: Talking to the people responsible for setting pay. *The Wall Street Journal,* p. R3.

**77.** Collins, J. (2009). *How the Mighty Fall: And Why Some Companies Never Give In.* New York, NY: Harper Collins. See also Collins, J. (2001). *Good to Great.* New York, NY: HarperCollins.

**78.** Grossman, R. J. (2009). Executive pay: Perception and reality. *HR Magazine,* 54(4), pp. 26–32. See also Ellig, B. (2002). *The Complete Guide to Executive Compensation.* NY: McGraw-Hill.

**79.** Kim, S. (2011, April 22). CEO pay averaged $11.4 million at largest companies in 2010. Retrieved from *abcnews.go.com/Business/ceo-pay-increased-23-percent-2010/story?id=13420978* on April 22, 2011.

**80.** Grossman, 2009, op. cit. See also Hilzenrath, D. (2007, July 16). How thick are their wallets? *The Washington Post,* pp. D1, D5.

**81.** Lublin, J. S. (2010, March 15). Semiannual bonuses gain traction. *The Wall Street Journal.* Retrieved from *online.wsj.com/article/SB100014240527487034471045751 17583294022358.html?KEYWORDS=Semiannual+bonuses+gain+traction* on March 15, 2010.

**82.** Bernard, T. S. (2004, Apr. 12). It's your choice. *The Wall Street Journal,* p. R3.

**83.** Grossman, 2009, op. cit. See also Tully, S. (2006, July 10). Five commandments for paying the boss. *Fortune,* pp. 89–92. See also Lavelle, L. (2005, Apr. 18). A payday for performance. *BusinessWeek,* pp. 78–80.

**84.** Bennett, A. (1992, Mar. 11). Taking stock: Big firms rely more on options but fail to end pay criticism. *The Wall Street Journal,* pp. A1, A8.

**85.** Winter, C., 2011, op. cit.

**86.** Lublin, J. S. (2004, Apr. 12). Here comes politically correct pay. *The Wall Street Journal,* pp. R1, R4. See also Tully, S. (1998, June 8). Raising the bar. *Fortune,* pp. 272–278.

**87.** Milkovich et al., 2011, op. cit.

**88.** Taylor, C. (2004). On-the-spot incentives. *HR Magazine* 49(5), pp. 80–84.

**89.** Bates, S. (2003b). Goalsharing at Corning. *HR Magazine* 48(1), p. 33. See also Bennett, 1992, op. cit.

**90.** Smith, M., Director of Hose Manufacturing, and Cecil, T., Manufacturing Supervisor, Gates Rubber Company, Denver. Interview by the author, December 1996.

**91.** Petty, M. M., Singleton, B., and Connell, D. W. (1992). An experimental evaluation of an organizational incentive plan in the electric utility industry. *Journal of Applied Psychology* 77, pp. 427–436.

**92.** Gerhart et al., 2009, op. cit. See also Cadrain, D. (2003). Put success in sight. *HR Magazine* 48(5), pp. 84–92. See also Rowland, M. (1992, Feb. 9). Pay for quality, by the group. *The New York Times,* p. D6.

**93.** Ibid. See also Dulebohn, J. H., and Martocchio, J. J. (1998). Employee perceptions of the fairness of work-group incentive plans. *Journal of Management* 24, pp. 469–488.

**94.** Gerhart et al. 2009, op. cit. See also Schroeder, M. (1988, Nov. 7). Watching the bottom line instead of the clock. *BusinessWeek,* pp. 134, 136. See also Florkowski, G. W. (1987). The organizational impact of profit sharing. *Academy of Management Review* 12, pp. 622–636.

**95.** Kruse, D. L. (1993). *Profit Sharing: Does It Make a Difference?* Kalamazoo, MI: Upjohn Institute for Employment Research. See also Banerjee, N. (1994, Apr. 12). Rebounding earnings stir old debate on productivity's tie to profit sharing. *The Wall Street Journal,* pp. A2, A12.

**96.** Gerhart et al., 2009, op. cit.

**97.** Colvin, G. (1998, Aug. 17). What money makes you do. *Fortune,* pp. 213, 214.

**98.** Gerhart et al., 2009, op. cit.

**99.** Collins, D., Hatcher, L., and Ross, T. L. (1993). The decision to implement gain-sharing: Role of work climate, expected outcomes, and union status. *Personnel Psychology* 46, pp. 77–104. See also Graham-Moore, B., and Ross, T. L. (1990). Understanding gainsharing. In B. Graham-Moore and T. L. Ross (Eds.), *Gainsharing.* Washington, DC: Bureau of National Affairs, pp. 3–18.

**100.** Hammer, T. H. (1988). New developments in profit sharing, gainsharing, and employee ownership. In J. P. Campbell and R. J. Campbell (Eds.), *Productivity in Organizations.* San Francisco: Jossey-Bass, pp. 328–366.

**101.** Milkovich et al., 2011, op. cit. See also Shives, G. K., and Scott, K. D. (2003, First Quarter). Gainsharing and EVA: The U.S. Postal experience. *WorldatWork Journal,* pp. 1–30.

**102.** Gerhart et al., 2009, op. cit. See also Masternak, R. (1997, Sept.–Oct.). How to make gainsharing successful: The collective experience of 17 facilities. *Compensation and Benefits Review,* pp. 43–52. See also Tyler, L. S., and Fisher, B. (1983). The Scanlon concept: A philosophy as much as a system. *Personnel Administrator* 29(7), pp. 33–37.

**103.** Kim, D. (1999). Determinants of the survival of gainsharing programs. *Industrial and Labor Relations Review* 53(1), pp. 21–42. See also White, J. K. (1979). The Scanlon plan: Causes and consequences of success. *Academy of Management Journal* 22, pp. 292–312.

**104.** Society for Human Resource Management. (2008). *2008 Employee Benefits.* Alexandria, VA: Author. See also Sammer, J. (2007, Aug.). Taking ownership. *HR Magazine,* pp. 73–78. See also National Center for Employee Ownership. (2006). Data show widespread employee ownership in U.S. Retrieved from *www.nceo.org/main/article.php/id/10/* on July 17, 2008.

**105.** Jackson, N. M. (2010, June 17). ESOP plans let founders cash out and employees cash in. *Money.* Retrieved from *money.cnn.com/2010/06/03/smallbusiness/esop_plans/index.htm* on August 5, 2011.

**106.** Klein, K. E. (2010, March 26). ESOPs on the rise among small businesses. *BusinessWeek.* Retrieved from *www.businessweek.com/smallbiz/content/mar2010/sb20100325_591132.htm* on August 5, 2011. See also Sammer, 2007, op. cit.

**107.** Organ, D. W., Podsakoff, P. M., and Podsakoff, N. P. (2011). Expanding the criterion domain to include organizational citizenship behavior: Implications for employee selection. In S. Zedeck (Ed.), *APA Handbook of Industrial and Organizational Psychology,* Vol. 2. Washington, DC: American Psychological Association, pp. 281–323. See also Deckop, J. R., Mangel, R., and Cirka, C. (1999). Getting more than you pay for: Organizational citizenship behavior and pay-for-performance plans. *Academy of Management Journal* 42, pp. 420–428.

**108.** Klein, K. J., and Hall, R. J. (1988). Correlates of employee satisfaction with stock ownership: Who likes an ESOP most? *Journal of Applied Psychology* 73, pp. 630–638. See also Klein, K. J. (1987). Employee stock ownership and employee attitudes: A test of three models. *Journal of Applied Psychology* 72, pp. 319–332. See also Rosen, C., Klein, K. J., and Young, K. M. (1986). When employees share the profits. *Psychology Today* 20, pp. 30–36.

**109.** Gerhart et al., 2009, op. cit. See also An ESOP to the workers. (2007, April 14). *The Economist,* pp. 26–28. See also Sammer, 2007, op. cit. See also Labich, K. (1996, Oct. 14). When workers really count. *Fortune,* pp. 212–214.

**110.** Kruse, D., and Blasi, J. (2002). Largest study yet shows ESOPs improve performance and employee benefits. Retrieved from *www.nceo.org/main/article.php/id/25/* on September 30, 2004.

**111.** Gerhart et al, 2009, op. cit. Elmer, V. (2011, Feb. 1). How to deal with an invisible promotion. *Fortune.* Retrieved from *management.fortune.cnn.com/2011/02/01/how-to-deal-with-an-invisible-promotion* on August 5, 2011. See also Tullar, W. L. (1998). Compensation consequences of reengineering. *Journal of Applied Psychology* 83, pp. 975–980.

# 12

# INDIRECT COMPENSATION: EMPLOYEE BENEFIT PLANS

## *Questions This Chapter Will Help Managers Answer*

1. What strategic considerations should guide the design of benefits programs?

2. What options are available to help a business control the rapid escalation of health-care costs?

3. What are some of the key trends in benefits offered and strategies to pay for them?

4. What cost-effective benefits options are available to a small business?

5. In view of the considerable sums of money that are spent each year on employee benefits, what is the best way to communicate this information to employees?

# THE NEW WORLD OF EMPLOYEE BENEFITS*

We are witnessing the globalization of business and benefits. Thus a senior executive of a large American multinational firm recently commented, "Less than half our workforce is now in the United States—but 95 percent of our health-care costs are." Workforce growth in firms like these is coming largely from outside the United States, not from within it. As a result, total compensation costs and tax/social benefit structures outside the United States play an increasingly dominant role in the benefits that American workers receive.

It wasn't always this way. In the past, major corporations offered their employees a wide array of company-paid insurance and retirement benefits. Corporations decided what was best for their employees. Now, in no small measure due to rising expenses, a struggling economy, and global competition, most employers are not only changing the range of benefit choices they offer, but also changing the basic structure of their benefits. Take retiree health benefits, for example. In 2007, 35 percent of companies offered them. In 2011, that number shrank to just 25 percent.

Firms such as IBM, Delta Air Lines, and Coca-Cola Enterprises have not eliminated retiree health benefits entirely, but each company has capped the amount it will pay in premiums—leaving retirees to shoulder the impact of rising health-care costs. The lesson? A new era of shrinking benefits has arrived. Says an HR executive at restaurant chain Ruby Tuesday, "We're trying to delicately balance our responsibilities to the shareholders to conserve expenses in the slower sales environment at the same time we're trying to provide a rewarding work environment."

Economics and demographics are driving these changes. Economically, most employers realize that the traditional blanket approach to benefits—total coverage for everyone—would subject them to unbearable expense. Benefits are no longer the "fringe" of compensation. The growth in the cost of providing health benefits to U.S. workers continues to run 50 percent higher than growth in workers' earnings, and is double the rate of overall inflation. Employers warn that this rate is not sustainable. Increasing life expectancy has made pensions more costly as well. And the combination of increased longevity, rising health-care costs, and an accounting standard that requires firms to report the cost of future retiree health-care benefits on their balance sheets—thereby reducing profits—has led employers to rethink their entire approach to employee benefits dramatically.

Demographically, the United States now has a much more diverse workforce than it has had in the past. As a result, the "one-size-fits-all" approach to employee benefits doesn't work. Employees who have working spouses covered by health insurance have different insurance needs from those who are sole breadwinners. Single parents and childless couples place very different priorities on child care benefits. So rather than attempt to fashion a single approach that suits all of these

*Sources: Miller, S. (2011, June 27). Employee benefits 2011: Fewer guarantees. Retrieved from *www.shrm.org/hrdisciplines/benefits/Articles/Pages/Benefits2011.aspx* on August 5, 2011. See also Brandon, E. (2011, July 22). 21 workplace benefits that are rapidly disappearing. *US News & World Report.* Retrieved from *money.usnews.com/money/retirement/articles/2011/07/22/21-workplace-benefits-that-are-rapidly-disappearing* on July 30, 2011. See also Banham, R. (2009, April 2). Employee benefits: Tough responsibilities in a tough era. *The Wall Street Journal,* pp. A9, A10. See also Society for Human Resource Management. (2009). Small and medium-sized businesses and the recession. *Workplace Visions* 3, pp. 1–6. Fuhrmans, V., and Francis, T. (2008, July 16). Retiree benefits take another hit. *The Wall Street Journal,* pp. D1, D3. See also Salisbury, D. L. (2008, Apr. 22). Benefit trends: Change is now constant. *The Wall Street Journal,* pp. A11, A12. See also McQueen, M. P. (2007, Jan. 16). The shifting calculus of employee benefits. *The Wall Street Journal,* pp. D1, D2.

interests, many employers determine a sum they'll spend on each employee, establish a menu of benefits, and then let each employee choose the benefits he or she wants or needs. At the same time such plans allow employers to trim benefits merely by raising the prices of the various options on the benefits menu.

These changes reflect more than demographic diversity, however. A fundamental change in philosophy is taking place as employees are forced to take more responsibility. Part of this is a movement toward employee self-management. Indeed, the new approach might well be described as one of "sharing costs, sharing risks." The conclusion to this case will showcase four major areas that change has affected most profoundly.

Challenges

1. Do you think companies should provide a broader menu of benefits (e.g., child care, veterinary care, financial counseling) or improve the menu of core benefits (e.g., health care, insurance, pensions)? Why?
2. How might your preference for various benefits change as you grow older or as your family situation changes?
3. What role do benefits play, in your opinion, in attracting and retaining workers? Might that role be different for different generations or for employees at different stages of their careers?

In 2011 U.S. organizations spent an average of 38 percent of payroll on employee benefits: 19 percent on mandatory benefits and 19 percent on voluntary benefits.[1] Here are some reasons benefits have grown:

- The imposition of wage ceilings during World War II forced organizations to offer more benefits in place of wage increases to attract, retain, and motivate employees.
- The interest by unions in bargaining over benefits has grown, particularly because employers are pushing for more cost-sharing by employees.[2]
- The tax treatment of benefits makes them preferable to wages. Many benefits remain nontaxable to the employee and are deductible by the employer. With other benefits, taxes are deferred. Hence employees' disposable income increases because they are receiving benefits and services that they would otherwise have to purchase with after-tax dollars.
- Granting benefits (in a nonunionized firm) or bargaining over them (in a unionized firm) confers an aura of social responsibility on employers; they are "taking care" of their employees.[3]

## STRATEGIC CONSIDERATIONS IN THE DESIGN OF BENEFITS PROGRAMS

As is the case with compensation systems in general, managers need to think carefully about what they wish to accomplish by means of their benefits programs. After all, for every dollar that an employee earns in direct compensation, he or she earns almost 40 cents more in benefits. Employers spent $1.5 trillion on major voluntary and mandatory employee benefit programs in 2009, including $764.2 billion for retirement programs, $648.3 billion for health benefit programs, and $117.9 billion for other benefit programs.[4] It is no exaggeration to say that for most firms, benefits represent substantial annual expenditures. To leverage their impact, managers should be prepared to answer questions such as the following:

- Are the type and level of our benefits coverage consistent with our long-term strategic business plans?
- Given the characteristics of our workforce, are we meeting the needs of our employees?
- What legal requirements must we satisfy in the benefits we offer?
- Are our benefits competitive in cost, structure, and value to employees and their dependents?
- Is our benefits package consistent with the key objectives of our total compensation strategy, namely, adequacy, equity, cost control, and balance?

In the following sections, we discuss each of these points.

## Long-Term Strategic Business Plans

Such plans outline the basic directions in which an organization wishes to move in the next three to five years. One strategic issue that should influence the design of benefits is an organization's stage of development. For example, a startup venture probably will offer low base pay and benefits but high incentives; a mature firm with well-established products and substantial market share will probably offer much more generous pay and benefits combined with moderate incentives.

Other strategic considerations include the projected rate of employment growth or downsizing, geographic redeployment, acquisitions, and expected changes in profitability. Each of these conditions suggests a change in the optimum mix of benefits in order to be most consistent with an organization's business plans.

---

### McKINSEY & COMPANY

HR BUZZ

Despite their high cost, CEOs, senior executives, and board members strongly believe that investing in employee benefits is worthwhile, even crucial. In a recent McKinsey survey, an overwhelming majority—89 percent—said that providing benefits is either "somewhat important" or "extremely important" to their company's ability to win the competition for talented workers. On the other hand, most of these same individuals have not taken steps to learn what employees want from benefit offerings or to assess explicitly the performance of their benefit strategy.

Just 13 percent said their companies understand employee benefit preferences "extremely well"; 43 percent said their companies understand the benefit-related preferences of employees only "somewhat" or "not at all." Further, the vast majority don't measure performance against benefit objectives.

This situation is unfortunate. McKinsey's data suggest that when executives understand their employees' benefit preferences better, they are more likely to say that their company receives an adequate return on its investments in benefits. Among respondents who claimed to understand their employees' benefit preferences "well" or "extremely well," 68 percent said they received an adequate return on investment. In contrast, only 38 percent of those who admitted to understand-

*An Executive Perspective on Employee Benefits**

---

*Sources:* McKinsey & Co. (2006, June). An executive perspective on employee benefits: A McKinsey survey. Retrieved from *www.mckinseyquarterly.com/Organizational/Talent/An_executive_ perspective_on_employee_benefits_A_McKinsey_Survey_1776* on June 15, 2006. See also Atkinson, W. (2009, Nov.). Filling in around the edges. *HR Magazine 54*(11), pp. 55–58.

ing their employees' preferences less well considered the return on investment to be adequate. There also seems to be a spillover effect between satisfaction with benefits and satisfaction with one's job. A recent MetLife survey, for example, revealed that 73 percent of employees who are highly satisfied with their benefits are also satisfied with their jobs. Only 22 percent of employees who are not satisfied with their benefits are satisfied with their jobs.[a]

[a]Atkinson, W. (2009, Nov.). Filling in around the edges. *HR Magazine* 54(11), pp. 55–58.

### Diversity in the Workforce Means Diversity in Benefits Preferences

Young employees who are just starting out are likely to be more concerned with direct pay (e.g., for a house purchase) than with a generous pension program. Older workers may desire the reverse. Unionized workers may prefer a uniform benefits package, while single parents, older workers, or workers with disabilities may place heavy emphasis on flexible work schedules. Employers that hire large numbers of temporary or part-time workers may offer entirely different benefits to these groups. Evidence indicates that the perceived value of benefits rises when employers introduce choice through a flexible benefits package. Next to job security, employees value benefits more than any other factor in determining their overall job satisfaction.[5]

### Legal Requirements

The government plays a central role in the design of any benefits package. While controlling the cost of benefits is a major concern of employers, the social and economic welfare of citizens is the major concern of government.[6] As examples of such concern, consider the four income-maintenance laws shown in Table 12–1.

## Table 12–1

### FOUR MAJOR INCOME-MAINTENANCE LAWS

| Law | Scope of coverage | Funding | Benefits | Administrative agency |
|-----|-------------------|---------|----------|------------------------|
| Social Security Act (1935) | Full coverage for retirees, dependent survivors, and disabled persons insured by 40 quarters of payroll taxes on their past earnings or earnings of heads of households. Federal government employees | For 2011, payroll tax of 5.65% for employees and 7.65% for employers on the first $106,800 in earnings. Self-employed persons pay 13.3% of this wage base. Payroll taxes include 1.45% for Medicare (2.9% for Medicare if self-employed). The Omnibus Budget | *Full retirement* payments after age 67 (for those born in 1960 or later), or at reduced rates after 62, to worker and spouse. Size of payment depends on past earnings. *Survivor benefits* for the family of a deceased worker or retiree. At full retirement age a widow or widower receives the full pension granted to the deceased. A widow or widower of any age with dependent children under 16, and | Social Security Administration |

## Table 12–1 (cont.)

### FOUR MAJOR INCOME-MAINTENANCE LAWS

| Law | Scope of coverage | Funding | Benefits | Administrative agency |
|---|---|---|---|---|
| | hired prior to January 1, 1984, and railroad workers are excluded. | Reconciliation Act of 1993 extended the 1.45% Medicare payroll tax to all wages and self-employment income. | each unmarried child under 18, receives a 75% benefit check. *Disability benefits* to totally disabled workers, after a 5-month waiting period, as well as to their spouses and children. *Health insurance* for persons over 65 (Medicare). All benefits are adjusted upward whenever the consumer price index (CPI) increases more than 3% in a calendar year and trust funds are at a specified level. Otherwise the adjustment is based on the lower of the CPI increase or the increase in average national wages (1983 amendments). | |
| Federal Unemployment Tax Act (1935) | All employees except some state and local government workers, domestic and farm workers, railroad workers, and some nonprofit employees. | Payroll tax of 6.2% of first $7,000 of earnings paid by employer. (Employees also taxed in Alaska, Alabama, and New Jersey.) States may raise both the percentage and base earnings taxed through legislation. Employer contributions may be reduced if state experience ratings for them are low. | Benefits are based on a percentage of average weekly earnings and are available for up to 26 weeks (up to 99 weeks through the end of 2011). Those eligible for benefits have been employed for some specified minimum period and have lost their jobs through no fault of their own. Most states exclude strikers. During periods of high unemployment, benefits may be extended for an additional 13–26 weeks; varies by state. | U.S. Department of Labor, Employment and Training Administration, and the several state employment security commissions |
| Workers' compensation (state laws) | Generally, employees of nonagricultural, private-sector firms are entitled to benefits for | One of the following options, depending on state law: self-insurance, insurance through a private carrier, or payroll-based | Benefits average about two-thirds of an employee's weekly wage and continue for the term of the disability. Supplemental payments are made for medical | Various state commissions |

(*continued*)

## Table 12–1 (cont.)

### FOUR MAJOR INCOME-MAINTENANCE LAWS

| Law | Scope of coverage | Funding | Benefits | Administrative agency |
|---|---|---|---|---|
| | work-related accidents and illnesses leading to temporary or permanent disabilities. | payments to a state insurance system. Premiums depend on the riskiness of the occupation and the experience rating of the insured. | care and rehabilitative services. In case of a fatal accident, survivor benefits are payable. | |
| Employee Retirement Income Security Act (ERISA) (1974) | Private-sector employees over age 21 enrolled in noncontributory (100% employer-paid) retirement plans who have one year's service. | Employer contributions. | Under the Pension Protection Act of 2006, employer contributions made after 2006 to a defined-contribution plan must become vested at 100% after three years or under a second- to sixth-year gradual-vesting schedule (20% per year beginning with the second year of service, i.e., 100% after six years). Different rules apply with respect to employer contributions made before 2007. Employee contributions are always 100% **vested.** Once an employee is vested, receipt of the pension is not contingent on future service. Authorizes tax-free transfer of vested benefits to another employer or to an individual retirement account ("portability") if a vested employee changes jobs and if the present employer agrees. Employers must fund plans on an actuarially sound basis. Pension trustees ("fiduciaries") must make prudent investments. Employers may insure vested benefits through the federal Pension Benefit Guaranty Corporation. | Department of Labor, Internal Revenue Service, Pension Benefit Guaranty Corporation |

Income-maintenance laws were enacted to provide employees and their families with income security in case of death, disability, unemployment, or retirement. At a broad level, government tax policy has had, and will continue to have, a major impact on the design of benefits programs. Two principles have had the greatest impact on benefits.[7] One is the **doctrine of constructive receipt,** which holds that an individual must pay taxes on benefits that have monetary value when the individual receives them. The other principle is the **anti-discrimination rule,** which holds that employers can obtain tax advantages only for those benefits that do not discriminate in favor of highly compensated employees.

These two tax-policy principles define the conditions for the preferential tax treatment of benefits. Together they hold that if benefits discriminate in favor of highly paid or key employees, both the employer and the employee receiving those benefits may have to pay taxes on the benefits when they are transferred.

## Competitiveness of the Benefits Offered

The issue of benefits-program competitiveness is much more complicated than that of salary competitiveness.[8] In the case of salary, both employees and management focus on the same item: direct pay (fixed plus variable). However, in determining the competitiveness of benefits, senior management tends to focus mainly on cost, while employees are more interested in value. The two may conflict. Thus, employees' perceptions of the value of their benefits as competitive may lead to excessive costs, in the view of top management. On the other hand, achieving cost competitiveness provides no assurance that employees will perceive the benefits program as valuable to them.

## Total Compensation Strategy

The broad objective of the design of compensation programs (i.e., direct as well as indirect compensation) is to integrate salary and benefits into a package that

---

### NIKE

To attract and retain skilled workers, Nike enlisted current employees to help enrich its benefits offerings. It started by probing workers' fears, needs, and desires in focus groups and surveys, in which employees often expressed worries about not being able to buy a house, send their children to college, or care for elderly parents. Then Nike asked employee teams to design new benefits packages that offer more choices without raising costs. Some of the choices the teams came up with include company-matching funds for college tuition, subsidies for child care or elder care, paid time off for family leave, group discounts on auto or home insurance, discounted mortgages, legal services, and financial planning advice.

*Matching People with Benefits**

Many of the new offerings were relatively cheap for the company. To contain costs further, Nike gives employees incentives to make health benefits trade-offs, such as pledging to stop smoking or using company-chosen physician networks. By tailoring its benefits to those that employees really need and care deeply about, Nike is maximizing the return on its "benefits bucks."

---

*\*Sources:* Shellenbarger, S. (1993, Dec. 17). Firms try to match people with benefits. *The Wall Street Journal,* p. B1. Reprinted by permission of The Wall Street Journal, Copyright © (1993) Dow Jones & Company, Inc. All Rights Reserved Worldwide. License number 2781950393417.

will encourage the achievement of an organization's goals. For example, while a generous pension plan may help retain employees, it probably does little to motivate them to perform on a day-to-day basis. This is because the length of time between performance and reward is too great. On the other hand, a generous severance package offered to targeted segments of the employee population may facilitate an organization's objective of downsizing to a specified staffing level. In all cases, considerations of adequacy, equity, cost control, and balance should guide decision-making in the context of a total compensation strategy.

With these considerations in mind, let us now examine some key components of the benefits package.

## COMPONENTS OF THE BENEFITS PACKAGE

There are many ways to classify benefits, but we will follow the classification scheme used by the U.S. Chamber of Commerce. According to this system, benefits fall into three categories: security and health, payments for time not worked, and employee services. Within each of these categories there is a bewildering array of options. The following discussions consider only the most popular options and cover only those that have not been mentioned previously.

### Cost

How much do benefits cost? In its 2011 benefits survey, the Society for Human Resource Management found that across organizations of all sizes in a variety of industries, the average percentage of salary reflecting the cost of mandatory benefits (e.g., Social Security, unemployment insurance) was 19 percent, and voluntary benefits (e.g., health care, retirement) was also 19 percent. As one might expect, companies with more than 500 employees spent more than smaller companies on voluntary benefits.[9] Thus, for a company that pays an average salary of $45,000 per year, its average cost of benefits *per employee* exceeds $17,000.

### Security and Health Benefits

These include the following:

- Life insurance.
- Workers' compensation.
- Disability insurance.
- Hospitalization, surgical, and maternity coverage.
- Health maintenance organizations (HMOs).
- Other medical coverage.
- Sick leave.
- Pension plans.
- Social Security.
- Unemployment insurance.
- Supplemental unemployment insurance.
- Severance pay.

Insurance is the basic building block of almost all benefits packages, because it protects employees against income loss caused by death, accident, or ill health. Most organizations provide group coverage for their employees. The plans may be **contributory** (in which employees share in the cost of the premiums) or **non-contributory** (in which the employer pays the full cost of the premiums).

It used to be that when a worker switched jobs, he or she lost health-insurance coverage. The worker had to "go naked" for months until coverage began at a new employer. No longer. Under the Consolidated Omnibus Budget Reconciliation Act (COBRA) of 1986, companies with at least 20 employees must make medical coverage available at group insurance rates (100 percent premium plus a 2 percent administration fee) for as long as 18 months after the employee leaves—whether the worker left voluntarily, retired, or was dismissed. The law also provides that, following a worker's death or divorce, the employee's family has the right to buy group-rate health insurance for as long as three years. The rising costs of health-insurance premiums cause serious financing problems for the unemployed, with only one of every four workers who get laid off being able to afford continued health insurance through COBRA.[10]

However, because some corporate medical plans do not cover preexisting conditions, some employees have found that when they changed jobs (and health plans), their benefits were reduced sharply. To alleviate that problem, Congress passed the Health Insurance Portability and Accountability Act (HIPAA) in 1996. HIPAA was enacted to make health insurance more "portable" from one employer to another by (1) lessening an employer's ability to deny coverage for a preexisting condition, and (2) by prohibiting discrimination on the basis of health-related status.

Perhaps the most significant element of HIPAA is its strict privacy provisions.[11] An individual or group health plan that provides or pays the cost of medical care may not use or disclose **protected health information** (medical information that contains any of a number of patient identifiers, such as name or social security number), except with the consent or authorization of the individual in question.[12] With this in mind, let us consider the major forms of security and health benefits commonly provided to employees.

## Group Life Insurance

This type of insurance is usually **yearly renewable term insurance**—that is, each employee is insured one year at a time. The actual amounts of coverage vary, but typical group-term life insurance coverage is one to two times the employee's annual salary. This amount provides a reasonable financial cushion to the surviving spouse during the difficult transition to a different way of life. Thus, a manager making $75,000 per year may have a group-term life policy with a face value of $150,000. Keep in mind, however, that the more expenses and dependents you have, the more life insurance you will need.[13] About 85 percent of companies offer this benefit.[14] To discourage turnover, almost all of them cancel it if an employee terminates.

Life insurance has been heavily affected by **flexible-benefits** programs. Typically such programs provide a core of basic life coverage (e.g., $25,000) and then permit employees to choose greater coverage (e.g., in increments of $10,000 to $25,000) as part of their optional package. Employees purchase the additional insurance through payroll deductions.

## Workers' Compensation

**Workers' compensation programs** cover 128 million workers in the United States. They provide payments to workers who are injured on the job or who contract a work-related illness. The payments cover three areas: payments to replace lost wages, medical treatment and rehabilitation costs, and retraining to perform a different type of work (if necessary). As shown in Table 12–1, these payments vary by state, and the differences in costs may be substantial. So also are benefits paid to injured workers. Nationally, the average weekly benefit payment per covered worker is $432, but payments per covered worker vary from $190 in Arkansas to $1,034 in West Virginia.[15] Disability benefits in some states have been extended to cover stress-related claims, but employees must be able to demonstrate some bodily injury manifestation of stress—that is, mental, physical, or where some specific and defined event occurred.[16] Employers spend $55 billion a year to provide health care and cash payments to disabled workers and their families. Of this total, $26.5 billion is for medical care and the remainder is paid out as cash benefits.[17]

A state's industrial structure also plays a big part in setting disability insurance rates. Thus, serious injuries are more common and costly among Oregon loggers and Michigan machinists than among assembly-line workers in a Texas semiconductor plant. Sometimes the costs can get out of hand, as they did in California. In 2010, employers paid $2.36 in premiums per $100 of payroll costs, compared with a record high of $6.44 in 2003 before the state legislature approved a landmark overhaul of the multibillion-dollar system.[18]

---

**HR BUZZ**

*Controlling the Costs*

## WORKERS' COMPENSATION

As we have seen, workers' compensation is a major cost of doing business. Some of the driving forces behind these costs are higher medical costs, the increasing involvement of attorneys, and widespread fraud. According to *The New York Times,* as much as 20 percent or more of claims may involve cheating.[a] What are states and companies doing to control costs?

California set up a fund, financed by employers, that pays for special teams to go after fraud. Job injury claims declined to 8.4 per 100 workers, from nearly 10 two years earlier. Connecticut no longer awards disability benefits for mental or psychological disorders unless they are the result of an injury. It has eliminated cost-of-living adjustments on disability benefits, and has cut some benefits by a third. Insurance premiums in the state have fallen 24 percent in the last two years.

Finally, workers' compensation insurers are forming alliances with managed care providers in order to take advantage of case-management methods and volume discounting. At Coca-Cola Bottling Company in New York, the company paid an average of $3,164 in workers' compensation claims when it turned to managed care and addressed long-standing safety issues in its plants. Six years later its average claim was $1,257—a 60 percent reduction.[b]

Is there an underlying theme in these approaches? Yes, and it's simple: Aggressive management of workplace safety issues pays dividends for workers and for their employers as well.

---

[a]Treaster, J. B. (2003, June 23). Cost of insurance for work injuries soars across U.S. *The New York Times.* Retrieved from *http://nyti.ms/v6m0ef* on July 21, 2008. See also Kerr, P. (1991, Dec. 29). Vast amount of fraud discovered in workers' compensation system. *The New York Times,* pp. 1, 14.

[b]First aid for workers comp. (1996, March 18). *BusinessWeek,* p. 106. See also Quint, M. (1995, Mar. 16). Crackdown on job-injury costs: New workers' compensation rules have double edge. The *New York Times,* pp. D1, D7. See also Evangelista-Uhl, G. A. (1995, June). Avoid the workers' comp crunch. *HR Magazine,* pp. 95–99.

At present, all 50 states have workers' compensation laws. While specific terms and levels of coverage vary by state, all state laws share the following features:[19]

- All job-related injuries and illnesses are covered.
- Coverage is provided regardless of who caused the injury or illness (i.e., regardless of who was "at fault").
- Payments are usually made through an insurance program financed by employer-paid premiums.
- A worker's loss is usually not covered fully by the insurance program. Most cash payments are at least two-thirds of the worker's weekly wage, but, together with disability benefits from Social Security, the payments may not exceed 80 percent of the worker's weekly wage.
- Workers' compensation programs protect employees, dependents, and survivors against income loss resulting from total disability, partial disability, or death; medical expenses; and rehabilitation expenses.

## Disability Insurance

An illness or accident will keep one in five employees out of work for at least a year before the age of 65.[20] Disability coverage provides a supplemental, one-time payment when death is accidental, and it provides a range of benefits when employees become disabled—that is, when they can't perform the main functions of their occupations.[21] **Long-term disability** (LTD) plans (offered by 76 percent of employers in 2011) and **short-term disability** plans (offered by 66 percent of employers in 2011) provide income replacement for employees whose illness or injury causes a longer absence from work. Short-term disability usually starts after a one- to two-week absence, and LTD usually goes into effect after six weeks to three months.[22]

---

### CANADIAN IMPERIAL BANK OF COMMERCE

HR BUZZ

To control disability-leave costs, Canadian Imperial Bank of Commerce (CIBC) turned to **disability-management** programs that emphasize a partnership among the physician, the employee, the manager, and the HR representative, known as a *facilitator*. The physician's role is to specify what the employee can and cannot do. Ongoing discussions between the employee and manager, assisted by the facilitator, determine what tasks an employee is actually capable of doing—the opposite of traditional disability management, which focuses on what the employee cannot do. This approach balances flexibility in meeting individual needs with consistency and fairness.

*Controlling Disability Costs\**

Does disability management work? At CIBC, the average duration for short-term disability dropped by 32 percent in the first nine months of the program. In addition, the firm's long-term disability (LTD) insurance carrier reported that employees on LTD were back to work 38 percent faster than the average for LTD claimants in general.

---

*\*Sources:* Lawrence, L. (2000, Dec.). Disability management partnerships save time, money. *HR News*, pp. 11, 17. See also Tobenkin, D. (2010, May). Keeping disability payments in check. *HR Magazine* 55(5), pp. 81–85. See also Quick, E. (2011, March 25). Integrated disability management in a challenging economy. Retrieved from *www.shrm.org/hrdisciplines/benefits/Articles/Pages/DisabilityManagement.aspx* on August 11, 2011.

## Figure 12–1

Cumulative changes in workers' contribution to premiums, inflation, and workers' earnings, 1999–2010.

(*Source:* Kaiser Family Foundation and Health Research and Educational Trust Annual Survey of Employer-Sponsored Health Benefits, 2011. (2011, Sept.). Menlo Park, CA: The Henry J. Kaiser Family Foundation and HRET.)

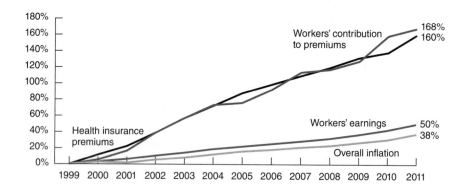

While paid sick leave usually covers an employee's entire salary, short- and long-term disability benefits may cover only a portion of that salary. For example, LTD recipients typically receive no more than 60 percent of their base pay, until they begin receiving pension benefits. In the aggregate, disability leaves cost companies between 8 and 20 percent of payroll annually.[23] The following company example shows what progressive firms are doing to control these costs.

Although disability benefits traditionally were divided into salary continuation, short-term disability, and long-term disability, combined disability-management programs now merge all three. Doing so allows for a single claim-application process and uniform case management. An employee whose short-term illness turns into a lengthy disability doesn't have to reapply for benefits or start over with a new case manager; the process is uniform and seamless, regardless of the length of the disability.

Another developing trend is toward outsourcing disability management as part of a broader effort to manage employee absences. Doing so may create common reporting systems for all absences, including those related to workers' compensation.[24]

## Hospitalization, Surgical, and Maternity Coverage

Hospitalization, surgical, and maternity coverage are essential benefits for most working Americans. Self-insurance is out of the question because the costs incurred by one serious, prolonged illness could easily wipe out a lifetime of savings and assets and place a family in debt for years to come. The U.S. health-insurance system is based primarily on group coverage provided by employers. More than 7 out of every 10 workers has health insurance through an employer, a number than has been unchanged for more than a decade.[25]

Yet there is widespread anxiety about the reliability of the system.[26] Indeed, if current trends continue, health care spending will be a quarter of the economy in 2035. Consider those trends. Between 1999 and 2010, the cost to employers of providing health benefits to workers increased 138 percent, while workers' wages and overall inflation increased only 42 and 31 percent, respectively. Workers also are paying much more for health benefits today than they were in 1999. Since that time, workers' contributions to health-care coverage has increased 159 percent, and that has depressed wage increases they otherwise would have received. Figure 12–1 shows these trends graphically. Figure 12–2 shows that from 1999 to 2010 large employers were much more likely than small employers to offer health-care coverage.

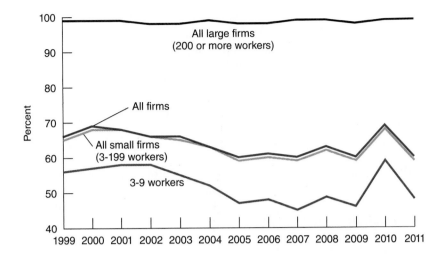

**Figure 12–2**

Percentage of firms offering health-care benefits, by firm size, 1999 to 2010. (*Source:* Kaiser Family Foundation and Health Research and Educational Trust Annual Survey of Employer-Sponsored Health Benefits, 2011. (2011, Sept.). Menlo Park, CA: The Henry J. Kaiser Family Foundation and HRET.)

Because employers pay most of the nation's health-care premiums (about 79 percent),[27] over time such increases may make them less competitive in global markets. In fact, Australia, Britain, Canada, Germany, the Netherlands, and New Zealand (all of whom provide universal health-care coverage for their citizens) spend half as much of their gross domestic product on health care as the U.S. does. In an effort to reform the U.S. health-care system, Congress passed the Patient Protection and Affordable Care Act in March 2010. While many of the law's implementation details remain unanswered, here are some of its major provisions.[28]

## Mandated Benefits
By the end of 2010, all existing health insurance plans were required to:

- Prohibit lifetime limits of insurance coverage.
- Prohibit exclusions of coverage for preexisting conditions.
- Restrict annual limits of insurance coverage.
- Include a requirement to provide coverage for nondependent children up to age 26; before 2014, this requirement is limited to nondependent children who do not have coverage by an employer.
- Beginning in 2014, group health plans must prohibit annual limits.

## Health Care Exchanges
The law requires states to create and maintain health care "exchanges" in which health insurance providers compete for customers on equal terms. The exchanges will be open to anyone without employer-provided coverage who wants to purchase a health insurance plan. If a state does not create an exchange, the federal government will create one for it.

## Employer Penalties
The law has a number of implications for employers, including penalties for noncompliance.

***For Not Offering Coverage:*** The law does not require employers to offer health insurance; however, beginning in 2014, employers with more than 50 full-time employees, including full-time–equivalent employees, who do not offer health-care coverage and who have at least one employee receiving a tax credit for health-coverage premiums will have to pay a penalty of $2,000 per year for each for full-time employee. The first 30 employees are excluded from that headcount.

***For Unaffordable Coverage:***   If an employee opts out of an employer plan because coverage is "unaffordable"—that is, if the premium exceeds 9.5 percent of family income—the employer must pay a $3,000 penalty for each full-time employee who receives a government subsidy and purchases coverage through an exchange.

***No Penalty for Waiting Periods:***   Employers will not be required to pay a penalty for employees during a waiting period that is required before an employee can enroll in an employer-provided health insurance plan. Beginning in 2014, however, a waiting period cannot exceed 90 days.

***Automatic Enrollment Procedure:***   The law will require employers with more than 200 employees to enroll employees automatically into health insurance plans offered by the employer beginning in 2014.

***Restrictions on Cafeteria Plans:***   The law caps flexible spending account (FSA) contributions at $2,500 and excludes over-the-counter medications without a doctor's prescription as reimbursable expenses.

***Incentives for Wellness:***   Starting in 2014, the law allows employers to adopt wellness initiatives that offer an employee incentive of up to 30 percent of the cost of employee-only coverage (up from the current 20 percent incentive). Further, with the approval of various federal agencies, wellness incentives could reach 50 percent of the cost of employee-only coverage.

***Tax on High-Value ("Cadillac") Plans:***   Beginning in 2018, there will be a 40 percent excise tax on insurance companies and plan administrators for group health coverage that exceeds a threshold of $10,200 for single coverage and $27,500 for families, not counting stand-alone dental and vision plans. For retirees over age 55 and for plans that cover employees in high-risk professions, the thresholds are $11,850 for single coverage and $30,950 for families. The tax applies to the amount of the premium that exceeds the threshold. Beginning in 2019, the thresholds will be indexed to the rate of general inflation plus 1 percentage point.

***Required W-2 Reporting:***   Since 2011, employers have been required to report the value of employees' health benefits on W-2 forms.

***Long-Term–Care Enrollment Procedures:***   The law creates a national social insurance program that provides limited long-term–care coverage for active employees through the workplace. All premium costs can be charged to employees. Since 2011, employers must use automatic enrollment procedures that allow workers to opt out or to initiate enrollment.

***Breaks for Nursing Mothers:***   A provision in the law amends the Fair Labor Standards Act to require employers, with some exceptions, to furnish "reasonable break time for an employee to express breast milk for her nursing child" for one year after the child's birth. It requires employers to provide a place, other than a bathroom, that is shielded from view and free from intrusion from coworkers and the public, where an employee can express breast milk.

Why is this happening? What's driving these increases in the cost of health care? In addition to an aging population, an increase in obesity (one-third of the American adult population, double the rate in 1990), general inflation, and excess medical inflation (including administrative costs that add millions to the country's health-care spending), other factors are mergers among local hospitals, costly new drugs and rising prescription volumes, plus the cost of new technology.[29]

When it comes to health-care technology, the United States relies far more heavily on it than do other advanced nations. On a per-capita basis, for example, the United States has four times as many diagnostic imaging machines (magnetic resonance imaging) as Germany and eight times as many as Canada. As one expert noted: "There's no way to shut it off. The doctors crave it, it's reassuring, and patients crave it."[30] On top of that, hospitals often push to buy the latest machines in order to retain their competitive status as full-service, modern health-care centers.

## Cost-Containment Strategies

Strategies to contain the high costs of health care are taking center stage in the boardroom as well as in the health-care industry itself. Here are some measures that firms have taken to gain tighter management control over the cost of health care:

1. *Band together with other companies to form a "purchasing coalition" to negotiate better rates with insurers.* Such coalitions have become key cost-control devices for small businesses, but Rochester, NY, took it further. Six big companies, such as Xerox, Kodak, and Bausch & Lomb, set up a health and fitness program for all of the metropolitan area's 1.04 million people. They also had their own efficiency experts help three hospitals streamline their operations free of charge, and they contributed $685,000 toward establishing a regional electronic health records system. As a result, Rochester's health costs have dropped from 5% below the national average in 2005 to 15% below in 2009.[31]

2. *Deal with hospitals and insurers as with any other suppliers.* Begin by providing benefits information online. Companies are using the Internet and their intranet sites to give employees access to medical-treatment information, as well as sophisticated comparisons of benefit-plan options. For example, health insurer Cigna is using claims information and new national databases to sort out how much hospitals and doctors' practices are charging, and to find out about the quality of care. Cigna customers can go online to find out whether a specialist practice ranks as especially cheap or especially good. Employees pay a lower coinsurance rate when they choose a provider who scores well.[32] While such steps are helpful in enabling employees to gain some control and in reducing administrative costs, there are limits. Most experts agree that the idea that people will be able to shop the medical marketplace, fully informed, the way they shop for computers or airlines, is just not realistic.[33]

3. *Encourage the use of generic drugs.* Fully 96 percent of companies offer prescription-drug program coverage.[34] Express Scripts, which provides pharmacy-benefit management services, says its clients save $1.4 billion per year through the increased use of generic drugs and lower-cost brands.[35]

4.  *Audit the eligibility of dependents under company health plans.* The goal is to remove ineligible people from the benefits rolls, and companies such as Boeing, General Motors, and American Airlines have been asking workers to send in marriage licenses, birth certificates, and tax returns to prove that their dependents should be covered. To be sure, changing family dynamics—high divorce rates and blended families—have helped to lead to more ineligible dependents. Audits are finding that 3 to 8 percent of enrolled employees' dependents are ineligible. Depending on company size the and the complexity of the health plans, consultants typically charge fees ranging from $10,000 to as high as $150,00. Sound like a lot? Assuming an average annual cost to the employer of $1,900 per dependent, plans with 3 percent ineligibility per 10,000 dependents would save $570,000. Those with 8 percent ineligibility might net a return of about $1.5 million.[36]

5.  *Use a managed-care approach.* **Managed care** relies on a *gatekeeper* system of cost controls. The **gatekeeper** is a primary-care physician who monitors the medical history and care of each employee and his or her family. The doctor orders testing, makes referrals to specialists, and recommends hospitalization, surgery, or outpatient care, as appropriate. Managed care may take a variety of forms. Table 12–2 presents a summary of alternative

## Table 12–2

### THE ABCs OF MANAGED CARE

| Plan | How it works | What you pay | Benefits |
|------|--------------|--------------|----------|
| **Health maintenance organization (HMO)** | A specified group of doctors and hospitals provide the care. A gatekeeper must approve all services before they are performed. | There is no deductible. The nominal fees generally range from $5 to $30 per visit depending on the service performed. | Virtually all services are covered, including preventive care. Out-of-pocket costs tend to be lower than for any other managed-care plan. |
| **Preferred provider organization (PPO)** | In-network care comes from a specified group of physicians and hospitals. Patients can pay extra to get care from outside the network. There generally is no gatekeeper. | The typical yearly family deductible is $500. The plan pays 80 to 100% for what is done within the network, but only 50 to 70% for services rendered outside it. | Preventive services may be covered. There are lower deductibles and copayments for in-network care than for out-of-network care. |
| **Point-of-service (POS) plan** | POSs combine the features of HMOs and PPOs. Patients can get care in or out of the network, but there is an in-network gatekeeper who must approve all services. | In addition to a deductible, there is a flat $5 to $30 fee for in-network care, and patients pay 20 to 60% of the bills for care they get outside the network. | Preventive services are generally covered. And there are low out-of-pocket costs for the care patients get in the network. |

types of managed-care plans: health maintenance organizations (HMOs), preferred provider organizations (PPOs), and point-of-service (POS) plans. Evidence indicates that when given a choice, employees are moving away from the more stringent HMO and POS plans toward preferred-provider organizations (PPOs), even though PPOs are more expensive. In 2010, for example, 58 percent of covered workers were enrolled in PPOs, 19 percent in HMOs, and 8 percent in POS plans. Another 13 percent were enrolled in high-deductible health plans with a savings option (see below).[37]

6.   *Adopt a **consumer-driven health plan (CDHP)**.* Such plans involve a high-deductible insurance plan combined with a health-care spending account from which unreimbursed health-care costs are paid. One type of CDHP is the health savings account (HSA). HSAs allow qualified workers to put aside a limited amount of pretax dollars every year. Contributions and the account's earnings must be used to pay for qualified health-care costs. The money grows tax-free, and workers can keep their accounts if they switch jobs. To open an HSA, the employer must provide a high-deductible health-insurance plan, which typically has a lower premium, and the employee cannot be enrolled in Medicare or another traditional plan, such as an HMO. GE adopted such a plan with three tiers of costs. The company funds up to $1,000 for two of the three tiers. While GE's plans offer free preventive care, it now makes smokers pay an extra $625 per year.[38] High-deductible plans are attractive for many people, especially young, healthy workers who are less likely to generate big health-care bills, making the higher deductible less of a concern, and lowering their monthly premiums.[39]

## Toward the Future

A variety of trends are helping to shape the future in health-care coverage. Here are a few of them:[40]

- Expect to see more experimentation with health-care designs as electronic medical records are introduced, more research is conducted on medical effectiveness, and results are built into treatment and payment structures.
- Fewer companies will provide health-care coverage for retirees; that means the government and individuals will pay in the decades ahead, although large employers may facilitate value purchasing.
- Expect to see ongoing refinements with respect to payments for wellness and preventive care, chronic disease, and prescription drugs. The good news is that a 2011 survey revealed that 73 percent of American workers would enroll in employer wellness programs to improve personal health if offered an incentive. At Johnson & Johnson, employees who enroll in such programs get a $500 discount on their insurance premiums. About 85 percent of them participate.[41]
- As for consumer-driven health care, it will continue to grow—unless the plans fail to show proven savings, or if workers find themselves stuck only with the higher bills and none of the new information and control that are supposed to be part of the package.
- Finally, as individuals, we are entering a new era of health care, in which each of us will increasingly be expected to check up on prices and to shop around before undergoing surgery or popping a pill. Many will not like this, but they must learn to manage the new system, for it could either earn them or cost them thousands of dollars. Beyond that, it could mean a lot to their health!

## Other Medical Coverage

Medical coverage in areas such as employee assistance programs and mental illness is offered by about 75 percent and 82 percent of large companies, respectively.[42] As for dental care, dental HMOs, PPOs, and indemnity (traditional fee-for-service plans) are growing fast. As with medical HMOs, a dental plan is usually paid a set annual fee per employee (usually about 10 to 15 percent of the amounts paid for medical benefits). Dental coverage is a standard inclusion for 94 percent of U.S. employers. Fully 76 percent offer their employees some form of vision-care insurance as well.[43]

## Sick-Leave Programs

Sick-leave programs provide short-term insurance to workers against loss of wages due to short-term illness. In 2011, 37 percent of U.S. firms offered paid sick-leave benefits.[44] However, in many firms such well-intentioned programs have often *added* to labor costs because of abuse by employees and because of the widespread perception that sick leave is a right and that if it is not used, it will be lost ("use it or lose it"). From the employer's perspective, such unscheduled absences cost between 8 and 20 percent of payroll annually. To control these costs, 48 percent of firms are turning to paid time-off (PTO) plans that combine sick leave, vacation, and personal days into one plan.[45] The number of PTO days that employees receive varies across employers. For example, at Pinnacol Assurance, employees receive 20 days of PTO at the start of employment, 25 after five years, and 30 after nine years. Employees manage their own sick and vacation time and are free to take a day off without having to offer an explanation. If an employee uses up all of this time before the end of the year and needs a day off, that time is unpaid.

What about unused sick time? "Buy–back" programs allow employees to convert unused time to vacation or to accrue time and be paid for a portion of it. Employers rate PTO plans as the most effective of all absence-control programs.[46]

## Pensions

A **pension** is a sum of money paid at regular intervals to an employee (or to his or her dependents) who has retired from a company and is eligible to receive such benefits. For much of the 20th century, there were no standards and little regulation, which led to abuses in funding many pension plans and to the denial of pension benefits to employees who had worked many years. Perhaps the most notorious example of this occurred in 1963, when Studebaker closed its South Bend, Indiana, car factory and stopped payments to the seriously underfunded plan that covered the workers. Only those already retired or on the verge of retirement received the pension benefits they expected. Others got only a fraction—or nothing.[47]

Incidents like these led to the passage of the Employee Retirement Income Security Act (ERISA; see Table 12–1) in 1974. ERISA does not require employers to establish pension plans or to provide a minimum level of benefits. Instead, it regulates the operation of a pension plan once it has been established. ERISA sets minimum standards for pension plans in private industry. It was enacted to protect the interests of employee-benefit-plan participants and their beneficiaries by requiring the disclosure to them of financial and other information concerning the plan; by establishing standards of conduct for plan fiduciaries (someone who acts on behalf of another in circumstances that assume a relationship of trust and confidence); and by providing for appropriate remedies and access to the federal courts.[48]

Money set aside by employers to cover pension obligations has become the nation's largest source of capital, with total assets (private employers plus local, state, and federal government pensions) of $15.3 trillion.[49] This is an enormous force in the nation's (and the world's) capital markets.

The "perfect storm" of falling stock prices and low interest rates that characterized the Great Recession, together with practices such as using pension assets to pay for the costs of laying off workers and retiree health benefits, caused many pension plans to become underfunded (i.e., their assets fell to less than 85 percent of their projected benefits obligations).[50] By 2011, for example, U.S. public pension systems were underfunded by at least $1 trillion.[51] Although ERISA does not address public pensions, to ensure that covered private-sector workers will receive their accrued benefits even if their companies fail, ERISA created the Pension Benefit Guaranty Corporation (PBGC). This agency acts as an insurance company, collecting annual premiums from companies with defined-benefit plans ($19 per participant in most plans) that spell out specific payments upon retirement.[52] A company can still walk away from its obligation to pay pension benefits to employees entitled to receive them, but it must then hand over up to 30 percent of its net worth to the PBGC for distribution to the affected employees.

The PBGC insures 27,500 pension plans that cover 44 million workers and retirees. In 2010 the PBGC paid about $5.6 billion in benefits owed to retirees and their surviving beneficiaries because their pension plans could not.[53] If a company terminates its pension plan, the PBGC guarantees the payment of vested benefits to employees up to a maximum amount set by law. In 2011, that maximum amount for a worker at full retirement age was $54,000.[54]

Despite these protections, the consequences of pension plan termination can still be devastating to some pensioners. Executives whose accrued benefits are bigger than the PBGC's guaranteed limits can see their monthly checks shrivel. Employees who haven't worked at a company long enough (typically five years[55]) to be vested—that is, when their receipt of pension benefits does not depend on future service—aren't entitled to any benefits. So they wind up having to get by with less to support them than they had planned. Nevertheless, as a matter of social policy, it is important that, as retirees, most workers end up getting nearly all that is promised to them—and they do.

## How Pension Plans Work

Contributions to pension funds are typically managed by trustees or outside financial institutions, frequently insurance companies. As an incentive for employers to begin and maintain such plans, the government defers taxes on the pension contributions and their earnings. Retirees pay taxes on the money as they receive it.

Traditionally, most big corporate plans have been **defined-benefit plans,** under which an employer promises to pay a retiree a stated pension, often expressed as a percentage of preretirement pay. In 2011, 22 percent of companies offered them (down from 33 percent in 2008).[56] The most common formula is 1.5 percent of average salary over the last five years prior to retirement ("final average pay") times the number of years employed. In determining final average pay, the company may use base pay alone or base pay plus bonuses and other compensation. An example of a monthly pension for a worker earning a final average pay of $75,000 a year, as a function of years of service, is shown in Figure 12–3. When combined with Social Security benefits, that percentage

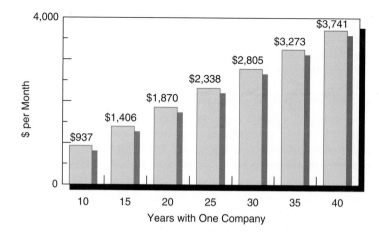

**Figure 12–3**

Monthly pension for a worker whose final average pay is $75,000 per year.

is often about 50 percent of final average pay.[57] The company then pays into the fund each year whatever is needed to cover expected benefit payments.

A second type of pension plan, popular either as a support to an existing defined-benefit plan or as a stand-alone retirement-savings vehicle, is called a **defined-contribution plan.** Fully 93 percent of U.S. employers offered some form of such a plan in 2011.[58] Examples include stock bonuses, savings plans, profit sharing, and various kinds of employee stock-ownership plans. Brief descriptions of five types of such plans are shown in Table 12–3.

Defined-contribution plans fix a rate for employer contributions to the fund. Future benefits depend on how fast the fund grows. Such plans therefore favor

## Table 12–3

### FIVE TYPES OF DEFINED-CONTRIBUTION PENSION PLANS

- **Profit-sharing plan.** The company puts a designated amount of its profits into each employee's account and then invests the money. ESOPs are a form of profit-sharing.
- **ESOP.** An employee stock-ownership plan pays off in company stock. Each employee gets shares of company stock that are deposited into a retirement account. Dividends from the stock are then added to the account.
- **401(k) plan.** A program in which an employee can deduct up to $16,500 of his or her income (in 2011, $22,000 for workers over 50) from taxable income and place the money into a personal retirement account. Many employers add matching funds, and the combined contributions grow tax-free until they are withdrawn, usually at retirement.
- **Money-purchase plan.** The employer contributes a set percentage of each employee's salary, up to 25 percent of net income, or $49,000 (whichever is less), to each employee's account. Employees must be vested to be eligible to receive funds. Withdrawals after age 59 1/2 are taxed at ordinary income tax rates.
- **Simplified employee pension (SEP).** Under SEP, a small-business employer can contribute up to the lesser of 100 percent of an employee's salary or $49,000. The employee is vested immediately for the amount paid into the account. The employee cannot withdraw any funds before age 59 1/2 without penalty.

*Sources:* IRS. Retirement plans FAQs regarding SEPs. Retrieved from *www.irs.gov/retirement/article/0,,id=111419,00.html#contributions* on August 10, 2011. See also Geary, L. H., and Feldman, J. (2001, Aug. 1). What the tax cut means to you. *Money,* pp. 90–96.

young employees who are just beginning their careers (because they contribute for many years). Defined-benefit plans favor older, long-service workers—and they are on their way out as more employers freeze or terminate them. Among workers under age 35, only 16 percent in a recent survey said that a traditional (defined benefit) plan was of high importance to them in choosing an employer; 64 percent said it was of little or no importance.[59]

Defined-contribution plans have great appeal for employers because a company will never owe more than what was contributed. However, because the amount of benefits received depends on the investment performance of the monies contributed, employees cannot be sure of the size of their retirement checks. In fact, regardless of whether a plan is a defined-benefit or defined contribution plan, employees will not know what the purchasing power of their pension checks will be, because the inflation rate is variable.

A third type of pension plan is known as a **cash-balance plan,** offered by 8 percent of large employers.[60] Under it, everyone gets the same, steady annual credit toward an eventual pension, adding to his or her pension account "cash balance." Employers contribute a percentage of an employee's pay, typically 4 percent. The balance earns an interest credit, usually around 5 percent. It is portable when the employee leaves, but cash-balance plans do not vest any sooner than traditional pension plans. One big advantage, however, is that cash-balance plans provide insulation from stock market swings that can whipsaw 401(k) accounts.[61]

For the young, 4 percent of pay each year is more than what they were accruing under a defined-benefit plan. But for those nearing retirement the amount is far less. So an older employee who is switched into a cash-balance system can find his or her eventual pension reduced by 20 to 50 percent, and in rare cases,

---

### THE SUPER 401(k)

HR BUZZ

Devon Energy of Oklahoma City, Oklahoma, like 34 percent of other employers, is automatically enrolling workers in its 401(k) plan at a 3 percent contribution level. What is different, though, is that rather than rely on employees to take the initiative to save, Devon plans to save for them—by making annual contributions to these accounts in line with what it would have spent to provide a traditional pension benefit.

*Retirement Benefits and Small Business\**

Depending on an employee's tenure, the company will put 8 to 16 percent of annual compensation into the 401(k)—regardless of whether the employee kicks in a dime. For those who put money into the plan, the company will also match it dollar for dollar up to 6 percent of salary. Add it all up, and Devon workers who divert 6 percent of their pay into the super 401(k) could receive as much as 22 percent per year from the company.

Why is the company being so generous? Sure, it wants to decrease the pension liabilities on its books, but beyond that, amid boom times for the oil and gas industry, the company is facing a labor shortage that is expected to become more acute over the next decade, as 57 percent of its U.S. workforce becomes eligible to retire. HR executives are betting that the super 401(k) will be attractive to younger workers, who prefer such plans, in part because they can take the money with them if they change jobs.

---

\**Sources:* Tergesen, A. (2007, Dec. 10). Redrawing the route to retirement. *BusinessWeek,* pp. 78–82.

even more.[62] A 2006 ruling by the 7th Circuit Court of Appeals upheld as nondiscriminatory against older workers IBM's decision to end its defined-benefit pension plan in favor of a cash-balance plan. That provided welcome guidance to other organizations that had been considering such conversions.[63]

At a broader level, empirical research shows that employees differ in their preferences for various features of defined-benefit, defined-contribution, and cash-balance plans. Allowing employees to choose plans that are consistent with their personal characteristics and needs should lead to greater satisfaction with the plans and also serve as an effective tool in attracting and retaining employees.[64]

### The Pension Protection Act (PPA) of 2006

This law made extensive changes to the Employee Retirement Income Security Act (ERISA) of 1974 that governs employer-sponsored, qualified (for tax deferral) retirement-benefit plans.[65] For example, it extended provisions of an earlier act that specified conditions such as the following:

- Higher limits on the annual amount of compensation that can be taken into account for retirement-plan benefits.
- Higher limits on the annual amount of permissible benefit and employer contributions.
- Ability of individuals age 50 and older to make "catch-up" salary-deferral contributions.

In addition, the PPA specifies that ERISA preempts any state wage-withholding law that would prevent an employee's participation in a 401(k) plan under an automatic-enrollment provision. It also permits employers to adopt new cash-balance plans and to convert existing defined-benefit plans into cash-balance plans, if the latter satisfy specific requirements.

Finally, the PPA also provides "safe harbor" protection for employers from complex and costly compliance regulations and from liability for breach of fiduciary duty with respect to the performance of default investments if employers do the following:

- Automatically enroll workers in the company plan at a default savings-contribution rate.
- Establish default investments, for example, those that automatically invest a worker's 401(k) contributions in an age-appropriate "life-cycle" diversified fund (larger equity exposure for younger participants; greater fixed income for older ones).
- Automatically escalate workers' contributions to their 401(k) accounts on a periodic basis.

Under the PPA, 401(k) participants can still exercise individual control over their investments if they want to, but the law encourages sponsors to set up such plans in a manner that helps workers to help themselves simply by doing nothing. By 2011, 41 percent of employers adopted automatic enrollment.[66]

### Social Security

Table 12–1 outlined provisions for this program. Social Security is an income-maintenance program, not a pension program. It is the nation's best defense

## Table 12–4

### AVERAGE 2011 SOCIAL SECURITY BENEFITS—MONTHLY

| | |
|---|---|
| Retired worker | $1,177 |
| Retired couple | 1,907 |
| Disabled worker | 1,067 |
| Disabled worker with a spouse and child | 1,813 |
| Widow or widower | 1,133 |
| Young widow or widower with two children | 2,409 |

against poverty for the elderly, and it has worked well. Without it, according to one study, the poverty rate among the elderly would have jumped from about 15 to 50 percent.[67] Table 12–4 shows average Social Security benefits for 2011.[68]

Current Social Security beneficiaries are benefiting from the massive surplus accumulated in the first decade of the 21st century, as baby boomers hit their peak earning potential. In 2010, that surplus was $2.5 trillion. It is projected to increase with the help of interest income through 2022 and allow full payment of scheduled benefits on a timely basis until 2036. After that benefits would need to be reduced by more than 20 percent to match revenue.[69] Remember, Social Security is a pay-as-you-go system. Payroll taxes earned by current workers are distributed to pay benefits for those who are already retired. Right now there are about 3 workers for every retiree in our society, but by 2015 there will only be 2.7, and by 2030 there will only be about 2 workers per retiree.[70] In addition, people are living substantially longer—by 2020 the life expectancy for 65-year-old men and women will be 81.5 and 85 years, respectively.

To meet such long-term funding needs, the system will have to be reformed soon—by raising payroll taxes or retirement ages, cutting benefits, or by investing a portion of the current surplus in the stock market.[71]

Keep in mind, however, that Social Security was never intended to cover 100 percent of retirement expenses. For a worker earning $60,000 a year, for example, experts estimate that he or she will need about 75 percent of that in retirement. Social Security will replace about 40 percent of preretirement income; pensions and personal savings will have to make up the rest. How does this compare to the actual distribution of retirees' income?

Figure 12–4 shows the distribution of retirees' income, on average. Note that 59.5 percent comes from Social Security plus pensions; the rest comes primarily

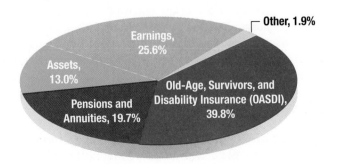

### Figure 12–4

Where retirees get their income.

(*Source:* McDonnell, K. (2010, June). Income of the elderly population age 65 and over, 2008. *EBRI Notes* 31(6), p. 3.)

## INTERNATIONAL APPLICATION
### Social Security in Other Countries

An ever-increasing number of countries are publicizing their social security programs on the World Wide Web. For a listing of them, see *www.ssa.gov/international/links.html.* Here is a brief sample of countries that have adopted pension programs that combine social security with private retirement accounts.

In Britain, workers can opt out of part of the state pension system by applying up to 44 percent of their social security tax to their own private individual investment accounts. Japan, Finland, Sweden, France, and Switzerland have similar programs. In these countries, the social-security component of the pension system remains on a pay-as-you-go basis in which current tax receipts are used to pay for both current benefits and other government programs.

In contrast, Chile's retirement system is 100 percent privatized, with a mandatory 10 percent of employees' pay going into individual accounts. Australia is moving to a privatization plan that calls for 9 percent of workers' pay to go into private retirement accounts, up from 6 percent previously. The employer chooses a menu of investment options that employees can use to allocate their retirement savings.

Singapore uses a payroll tax to fund retirement through a mandatory savings scheme that works like a private pension system. Employees must contribute about 20 percent of their salaries to their individually owned accounts, with employers contributing another 13 percent. At full retirement age (62), a worker gets a lump-sum payment equal to the total worker and employer contributions, plus at least 2.5 percent in compound interest. At age 55, however, workers must put about $42,000 in a retirement account to ensure income after age 62.

Employees can withdraw money from their retirement funds to purchase housing (or to pay for a child's education or for medical expenses), and, as a result, 80 percent of Singapore's citizens own their own residences. If an employee is dissatisfied with the return earned by the public fund, he or she can transfer the account to investments in the Singapore stock market or other approved vehicles. The asset balance in a Singaporean's retirement fund passes to his or her beneficiaries upon death. Among the countries that have systems similar to Singapore's are India, Kenya, Malaysia, Zambia, and Indonesia.[a]

[a]Lev, M. A. (2005, Mar. 2). Singapore's plan for retirees offers lessons for U.S. *Chicago Tribune,* p. 3. See also Riley, B. (1996, Oct. 29). All work and no pension. *Financial Times,* p. 12.

from personal savings and current earnings in retirement. By contrast, the percentage of final salary that Social Security replaces depends on the actual final salary of the retiree. For a worker whose final salary is $50,000, Social Security replaces 45 percent in the United States, 75 percent in Italy, 74 percent in Portugal, 63 percent in Spain, 51 percent in France, 43 percent in Germany, 31 percent in the Netherlands, 21 percent in Ireland, and just 14 percent in the United Kingdom.[72]

### Unemployment Insurance

Although 97 percent of the workforce is covered by federal and state unemployment insurance laws, each worker must meet eligibility requirements in order to receive benefits. That is, an unemployed worker must (1) be able and available to work and be actively seeking work, (2) not have refused suitable employment, (3) not be unemployed because of a labor dispute (except in Rhode Island and New York), (4) not have left a job voluntarily, (5) not have been terminated for gross misconduct, and (6) have been employed previously in a covered industry or occupation, earning a designated minimum amount for a minimum amount of time. Many claims are disallowed for failure to satisfy one or more of these requirements.

The unemployment insurance system is a financial partnership between the federal and state governments. It is intended to be counter-cyclical, that is, to accumulate and hold significant funds during good economic times, pay out benefits during bad ones, and stimulate stagnant economies (because unemployed workers tend to spend most or all of their unemployment checks quickly).[73]

Every unemployed worker's benefits are charged against one or more companies. The more money paid out on behalf of a firm, the higher is the unemployment insurance rate for that firm. The tax in most states amounts to 6.2 percent of the first $7,000 earned by each worker. The state receives 5.4 percent of this 6.2 percent, and the remainder goes to the federal government. However, the tax rate may fall to 0 percent in some states for employers who have had no recent claims by former employees, and it may rise to 10 percent for organizations with large numbers of layoffs.

Benefits ordinarily last 26 weeks in most states. However, faced with the Great Recession, Congress passed a series of federal extensions that gave people up to 99 weeks of benefits, nearly two years' worth. Benefits are subject to federal income taxes and must be reported on workers' federal income tax returns. In general, benefits are based on a percentage of a worker's earnings over a recent 52-week period, up to a state maximum amount. In 2010 the average was $310 per week.[74]

Unemployment insurance benefits provide a "safety net" for individuals who qualify. Other agencies, like this one, help them prepare for new jobs.

## Severance Pay

Such pay is not legally required, and, because of unemployment compensation, many firms do not offer it. However, severance pay has been used extensively by some firms that are downsizing in order to provide a smooth outflow of employees.[75] This is a good example of the strategic use of compensation. For example, General Motors offered workers at bankrupt parts-maker Delphi severance payments up to $140,000.[76] In Germany, as part of a restructuring effort, Volkswagen offered severance packages of as much as €249,480, or about $385,000 each, to 85,000 workers at factories in western Germany.[77] In general, however, as a 28-country study recently found, employees laid off in the United States earn the least amount of severance pay worldwide, no matter what level of employee or amount of tenure with the organization.[78]

While length of service, organization level, size of the organization, and the cause of the termination are key factors that affect the amount of severance pay, those amounts have been declining. For example, the typical manager now gets just 12.5 weeks of severance pay, down from 22 weeks at the height of the tech boom in 1999.[79] Chief executive officers with management contracts may receive two to three years' salary in the event of a takeover.[80]

## Payments for Time Not Worked

Included in this category are such benefits as the following:

| | |
|---|---|
| Vacations | Personal excused absences |
| Holidays | Grievances and negotiations |
| Reporting time | Sabbatical leaves |

Suppose you could take as much vacation time as you like. Sound crazy? Think about your own experience. On your last vacation did you do no work at all? Or did you listen to your voice mail, check your e-mail, and spend further time responding to messages and maybe participating in one or two phone meetings? According to a survey by travel-booking company Expedia.com, only 38 percent of U.S. employees use all their allotted vacation time. The average worker takes only 14 of 18 days permitted.[81] More than a third take fewer than seven days of vacation a year.[82] Suppose instead that you had no allotted vacation time. When you go on vacation is up to you, something to be worked out with your goals and your coworkers in mind. At Netflix, the emphasis is on what people get done, not on how many hours or days they work. Might people abuse this freedom? Or would they recognize that they are responsible for most decisions that affect their job performance and that decisions about vacation time fall into that general category? What do you think?

---

**HR BUZZ**

## INTEL, McDONALD'S, AND MORNINGSTAR

Company policies vary from quite liberal to restricted. Chip-maker Intel grants all full-time employees a paid, eight-week sabbatical on every anniversary divisible by seven, along with their usual 3–4 weeks of vacation. Some 4,350 workers, or nearly one in 20 at Intel, take sabbaticals in a given year. Fast-food giant McDonald's gives every salaried employee an 8-week paid

leave for every ten years of employment—executives through managers of its company-owned restaurants in the U.S. That's thousands of leaves every year. To attract and retain new employees, McDonald's adds an in-between breather: an extra week off for every anniversary that ends in a five. Mutual-fund researcher Morningstar allows all employees a six-week, paid sabbatical every four years to do whatever they choose. Evidence indicates that most employees return more committed and more energized. In fact, sabbaticals are so alluring that companies report that it is almost impossible for competitors to poach anyone within a few years of his or her bonus vacation.

*Sabbatical Leaves\**

About 15 percent of large employers in the United States currently offer unpaid sabbaticals, and another 4 percent offer paid sabbaticals.[a] They are most popular at law firms, computer firms, and consulting companies, where burnout is often a problem. Beyond that, HR managers argue, since sabbaticals encourage people to stick around, they don't have to spend as much on recruitment and training.

*Sources: Arndt, M. (2006, Jan. 9). Nice work if you can get it. BusinessWeek, pp. 56, 57. See also White, E., and Trachtenberg, J. A. (2005, Aug. 2). Sabbaticals: the pause that refreshes. The Wall Street Journal, pp. B1, B4.
[a] SHRM, 2011, op. cit.

## Employee Services

A broad group of benefits falls into the employee-services category. Employees qualify for them purely by virtue of their membership in the organization, and not because of merit. Some examples include the following:

| | |
|---|---|
| Tuition aid[83] | Thrift and short-term savings plans |
| Credit unions | Stock-purchase plans |
| Auto insurance | Fitness and wellness programs |
| Food service | Moving and transfer allowances |
| Company car | Transportation and parking[85] |
| Career clothing | Merchandise purchasing |
| Financial planning[84] | Professional-association memberships |
| Legal services | Christmas bonuses |
| Counseling | Service and seniority awards |
| Child adoption | Umbrella liability coverage |
| Child care | Social activities |
| Elder care | Referral awards |
| Gift matching | Purchase of used equipment |
| Charter flights | Family leaves |
| Domestic-partner benefits | Flexible work arrangements |

National survey data now indicate that people are more attached and committed to organizations that offer work-life benefits, regardless of the extent to which they benefit personally from them.[86] Such benefits include onsite child care,

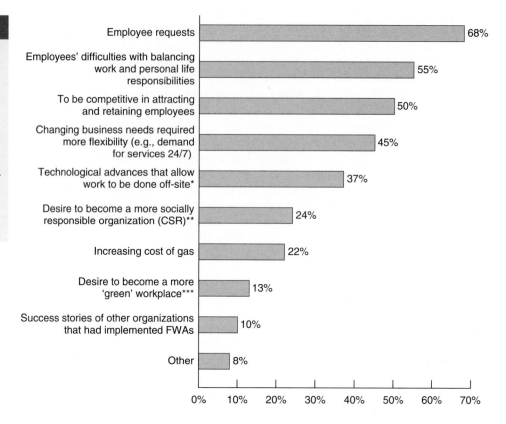

**Figure 12–5**

Reasons that prompted organizations to offer formal flexible work arrangements.

(*Source:* Society for Human Resource Management. (2009). *Workplace Flexibility in the 21st Century.* Alexandria, VA: SHRM, p. 7.)

subsidized child care onsite and offsite, child adoption, elder care, flexible work schedules (flex-time and flex-place), and the ability to convert sick days into personal days that employees can use to care for a sick child or family member. Figure 12–5 shows the reasons that prompted organizations to offer flexible work arrangements.

Once viewed as an expense with little return, such policies are now endorsed by a growing number of executives as an investment that pays dividends in morale, productivity, and ability to attract and retain top-notch talent. Pharmaceutical giant Merck & Co. found that it cost approximately $50,000 to replace the "average" employee, but only $38,000 to give the employee a six-month parental leave of absence with partial pay and benefits. Merck provides employees with benefits and full pay for up to eight weeks following the birth or adoption of a child. After eight weeks and up to six months, employees on parental leave do not get paid but keep their benefits and are guaranteed reinstatement. From 6 to 18 months, they retain their benefits but are not guaranteed job reinstatement, although they have access to in-house job postings.[87]

Domestic-partner benefits are voluntarily offered by employers to an employee's unmarried partner, whether of the same or opposite sex. Firms such as General Motors, Ford, Chrysler, Boeing, Citigroup, General Mills, Goldman Sachs, and Texas Instruments offer such benefits, as do about 35 percent of U.S. firms.[88] They do so to be fair to all employees, regardless of their sexual

## ETHICAL DILEMMA
### What to Do with Bad News?*

Consider this situation. You are the Chief HR Officer (CHRO) of a company whose stock is publicly traded. A supervisor tells you about an impending penalty from a federal regulatory agency, a penalty large enough to make headlines and to slam the company's stock price. The supervisor wants the CHRO to convince the CEO to begin making 401(k) matches with cash instead of company stock and to advise employees to move their company stock in the 401(k) plan into one of the other fund selections.

The CHRO is a member of the company's executive committee, but is not a member of the committee that oversees the 401(k) plan. Administration of the plan is outsourced to a company that provides general financial education to all employees on saving for retirement in the 401(k) plan but that offers no third-party advice on how the funds should be invested. What should the CHRO do? Would doing something about it constitute insider trading?

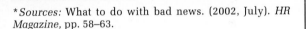

---

*Sources:* What to do with bad news. (2002, July). *HR Magazine*, pp. 58–63.

---

orientation and marital status, and because of the competition and diversity that characterize today's labor markets.

## BENEFITS ADMINISTRATION

### Benefits and Equal Employment Opportunity

Equal-employment-opportunity requirements also affect the administration of benefits. Consider as examples health-care coverage and pensions. The Age Discrimination in Employment Act has eliminated mandatory retirement at any age. It also requires employers to continue the same group health-insurance coverage offered to younger employees to employees over the age of 70. Medicare payments are limited to what Medicare would have paid for in the absence of a group health plan and to the actual charge for the services. This is another example of government **cost shifting** to the private sector.

With regard to pensions, the IRS considers a plan *discriminatory* unless the employer's contribution for the benefit of lower-paid employees covered by the plan is comparable to contributions for the benefit of higher-paid employees. An example of this is the 401(k) salary-reduction plan described briefly in Table 12–3. The plan permits significant savings out of pretax compensation, produces higher take-home pay, and results in lower Social Security taxes. The catch: *The plan has to be available to everyone in any company that implements it.* Maximum employee contributions each year ($16,500 in 2011 for workers under 50; $22,000 for those over 50) are based on average company participation. Thus, poor participation by lower-paid employees curbs the ability of the higher-paid to make full use of the 401(k).[89]

## Costing Benefits

Despite the high cost of benefits, many employees take them for granted. A major reason for this is that employers have failed to do in-depth cost analyses of their benefit programs and thus have not communicated the value of such programs to employees. Four approaches are used widely to express the costs of employee benefits and services. Although each has value individually, a combination of all four often enhances their impact on employees. The four methods are:[90]

- *Annual cost of benefits for all employees.* Valuable for developing budgets and for describing the total cost of the benefits program.
- *Cost per employee per year.* The total annual cost of each benefits program divided by the number of employees participating in it.
- *Percentage of payroll.* The total annual cost divided by total annual payroll (this figure is valuable in comparing benefits costs across organizations).
- *Cents per hour.* The total annual cost of benefits divided by the total number of hours worked by all employees during the year.

Table 12–5 presents a company example of actual benefits costs for a fictitious firm named Sun Inc. The table includes all four methods of costing benefits. Can you find an example of each?

### Table 12–5

**EMPLOYEE BENEFITS: THE FORGOTTEN EXTRAS**

Listed below are the benefits for the average full-time employee of Sun Inc. (annual salary $60,000*).

| Benefit | Who pays | Sun's annual cost | Percentage of base earnings | What the employee receives |
|---|---|---|---|---|
| Health, dental, and life insurance | Sun and employee | $4,860 | 8.01 | Comprehensive health and dental plus life insurance equivalent to the employee's salary |
| Holidays | Sun | 3,000 | 5.00 | 13 paid holidays |
| Annual leave (vacation) | Sun | 2,310 | 3.85 | 10 days of vacation per year (additional days starting with sixth year of service) |
| Sick days | Sun | 2,766 | 4.61 | 12 days annually |
| Company retirement | Sun | 5,328 | 8.88 | Vested after 5 years of service |
| Social Security | Sun and employee | 4,590 | 7.65 | Retirement and disability benefits as provided by law |
| Workers' compensation and unemployment insurance | Sun | 600 | 1.00 | Compensation if injured on duty and if eligible; income while seeking employment |
| Total | | $23,454 or $11.28 per hour | 39.00 | |

*The dollar amount and percentages will differ slightly depending upon the employee's salary. If an employee's annual salary is less than $60,000, the percentage of base pay will be greater. If the employee's salary is greater than $60,000, the percentage will be less but the dollar amount will be greater. Benefit costs to Sun Inc. on behalf of 5,480 employees are more than $128 million per year.

## Cafeteria, or Flexible, Benefits

The theory underlying the **cafeteria-benefits** approach is simple: Instead of all workers at a company getting the same benefits, each worker can pick and choose among alternative options cafeteria style. Thus, the elderly bachelor might pass up maternity coverage for additional pension contributions. The mother whose children are covered under her husband's health insurance may choose legal and auto insurance instead.

The typical plan works like this: Workers are offered a package of benefits that includes basic and optional items. Basics might include modest medical coverage, life insurance equal to a year's salary, vacation time based on length of service, and some retirement pay. Then employees can use flexible credits to choose among such additional benefits as full medical coverage, dental and eye care, more vacation time, additional disability income, and higher company payments to the retirement fund. Nationwide, 32 percent of firms offered full flexible-benefit plans in 2011.[91] Two studies examined employees' satisfaction with their benefits and understanding of them both before and after the introduction of a flexible-benefits plan. Both found substantial improvements in satisfaction and understanding after the plan was implemented.[92]

There are advantages for employers as well. Under conventional plans, employers risked alienating employees if they cut benefits, regardless of increases in the costs of coverage. Flexible plans allow them to pass some of the increases on to workers more easily. Instead of providing employees a set package of benefits, the employer says, "Based on your $60,000 annual salary, I promise you $23,400 to spend any way you want." If health-care costs soar, the employee—not the employer—decides whether to pay more or to take less coverage.

There's help for employees even under these circumstances if they work for firms that sponsor **flexible-spending accounts** (almost three out of four large firms). Employees can save for expenses such as additional health

## IMPACT OF BENEFITS ON PRODUCTIVITY, QUALITY OF WORK LIFE, AND THE BOTTOM LINE

Generally speaking, employee benefits do not enhance productivity. Rather, they are powerful tools for attracting and retaining talent, and for improving the quality of life of employees and their dependents.[a] Today there is widespread recognition among employers and employees that benefits are an important component of total compensation. As long as employees perceive that their total compensation is equitable and that their benefit options are priced fairly, benefits programs can achieve the strategic objectives set for them. The challenge for executives will be to maintain control over the costs of benefits while providing genuine value to employees in the benefits offered. If they can do this, everybody wins.

[a]MetLife, 2011, op. cit. See also Kucera, D. (2010, July 25). Companies ramp up perks to keep workers as economy improves. *The Charlotte Observer*. Retrieved from *www.wopular.com/companies-ramp-perks-keep-workers-economy-improves* on July 28, 2010. See also Atkinson, 2009, op. cit.

insurance or day care with pretax dollars, up to a specified amount (e.g., in a dependent-care spending account, up to $5,000 for child or elder care). As a result, it's a win-win situation for both employer and employee.[93]

To realize these potential advantages, major communications efforts are needed to help employees understand their benefits fully. Because employees have more choices, they often experience anxiety about making the right choices. In addition, they need benefits information on a continuing basis to ensure that their choices continue to support their changing needs. Careful attention to communication can enhance recruitment efforts, help cut turnover, and make employees more aware of their total package of benefits.

## Communicating the Benefits

Try to make a list of good reasons a company should *not* make a deliberate effort to market its benefits package effectively. It will be a short list. Generally speaking, there are four broad objectives in communicating benefits:

1. To make employees *aware* of them. This can be done by reminding them of their coverages periodically and of how to apply for benefits when needed.
2. To help employees *understand* the benefits information they receive in order to take full advantage of the plans.
3. To make employees confident that they can *trust* the information they receive.
4. To show employees how their benefits will meet their needs and help them reach their personal goals. After all, it's their "hidden paycheck."[94]

A growing number of companies are giving employees direct access to information about their total rewards—direct as well as indirect compensation. Aircraft manufacturer Boeing takes such an approach with its 137,000 employees through its "Pay & Benefits Profile," accessed through the company's intranet portal. The software, hosted by benefits provider Aon Corp., extracts data from about 30 different sources at Boeing and its service providers. The profile includes salary and bonuses as well as special services that Boeing offers its employees, such as travel and child-care referral services, wellness programs from the Mayo Clinic, and elder-care services.

The key to the site is personalization. Employees can see every component of their overall rewards rolled into a total-compensation statement, and they can see what those benefits cost the company. In addition, employees also have access to interactive tools they can use for financial planning.[95]

Companies are trying to engage employees more actively, for example, by placing online interactive tools outside company intranet firewalls so employees and spouses can access them from home. Perhaps the most important change is that the tools help employees to learn what's right for them.[96] IBM is a good example of this approach. Its employees use an interactive question-and-answer tool called "Plan Finder" on the company's intranet to weigh the merits of different benefits and criteria, such as cost, coverage, customer service, or performance. The tool sorts through dozens of different health plans offered by the company, uses data and choices supplied by the employee, and then returns views of preferred plans, ranked and graphed. "Plan Finder" allows employees to model the information that is most important to them in order to make better benefits selections. It's no surprise that 80 percent of employees now enroll via the intranet system, saving IBM $1 million per year in costs associated with the delivery of benefits information.

---

## THE NEW WORLD OF EMPLOYEE BENEFITS

Evidence indicates a strong link between employee satisfaction with benefits programs and overall employee satisfaction and retention. Among those who are highly satisfied, 85 percent expect to be working for their employers 18 months hence, versus only 50 percent of those who are not satisfied with their benefits. Here are four areas that affect employee satisfaction profoundly: health insurance, programs to promote healthy lifestyles, retirement programs, and employee savings programs.

- **Health insurance.** No more blank checks. Employers and insurers are both taking an aggressive role in managing chronic diseases. About 160 companies now use disease-management programs to help patients with costly chronic diseases such as asthma, diabetes, and heart disease manage their illnesses better so they don't progress and become costlier to treat.[97] These patients, some 90 million people, account for an astounding 75 percent of the nation's health-care bill. Disease managers, usually nurses, operate from call centers. They check in regularly with patients by phone to encourage them to get all the necessary tests and treatments for their diseases. Does it work? Early results say yes. American Healthways saved Blue Cross and Blue Shield of Minnesota $40 million in a single year, shaving three percentage points off its overall cost increase.[98]

- **Keeping employees healthier.** One of the most important themes in employee benefits is now prevention: limiting health-care claims by keeping employees and their families healthier. The Travelers Insurance Companies thoroughly studied its own programs in this area and found that the funds it spent on health promotion helped it save $7.8 million in employee benefits costs. That's a savings of $3.40 for every dollar spent. The biggest payoffs came from education programs, including efforts to discourage smoking and drinking and to encourage healthier diets.

  Some companies have added new benefits, even as they eliminated others. Johnson & Johnson and Hewlett-Packard began paying for routine checkups and tests for infants, while AT&T launched a prenatal care program.

- **Retirement programs—sharing the risk.** In 2008, IBM moved all of its employees to enhanced 401(k) plans for all future service.[99] IBM is not alone: 9 out of 10 companies that offer 401(k)s provide a partial matching (up to $5,000 a year or more) of employees' savings. Such plans provide a true incentive to save because they are easily funded through payroll deductions. The old final-average-pay, life-annuity, employer-paid pension is pretty much gone as a model for the private sector.

- **Expanding the 401(k) concept.** To many observers, the kind of sharing and choice embodied in 401(k) plans is the wave of the future in employee benefits. The Pension Protection Act of 2006 addressed several important issues by exempting employers from costly and complex compliance regulations if they implement "the automatics" in their 401(k) plans: automatic enrollment of workers in their plans; automatic enrollment in a qualified (for tax deferment) diversified fund; and automatic escalation of 401(k) contributions on a periodic basis. The automatic-escalation feature alone is likely to increase overall 401(k) contributions between 11 and 28 percent for participants in the lowest-income group, and between 5 and 12 percent for those in the highest-income group.[100]

The upshot of all of these changes is that workers who are fortunate enough to be offered health and retirement coverage through their jobs can expect to be more involved in decision-making about their benefits and to share more of the costs of those benefits in the future.

## SUMMARY

Managers need to think carefully about what they wish to accomplish by means of their benefits programs. At an average cost of 38 percent of base pay for every employee on the payroll, benefits represent substantial annual expenditures. Factors such as the following are important strategic considerations in the design of benefits programs: the long-term plans of a business, its stage of development, its projected rate of growth or downsizing, characteristics of its workforce, legal requirements, the competitiveness of its overall benefits package, and its total compensation strategy.

## IMPLICATIONS FOR MANAGEMENT PRACTICE

As you think about the design and implementation of employee benefit plans, consider three practical issues:

1. What are you trying to accomplish with your benefits package? Conduct a comprehensive strategic review of your benefits plan and its ability to meet diverse employee needs and to achieve business goals.

2. Perform a detailed audit of your workforce to assess the value of enhancing demographically targeted programs, voluntary benefits, and wellness programs as a means of differentiating your plan.[a]

3. Develop an effective strategy for communicating benefits regularly to all employees.

[a]Wells, 2010, op. cit. See also MetLife, 2011, op. cit.

There are three major components of the benefits package: security and health, payments for time not worked, and employee services. Despite the high cost of benefits, many employees take them for granted. A major reason for this is that employers have not done in-depth cost analyses or communicated the value of their benefits programs. This is a multimillion-dollar oversight. Certainly the counseling that must accompany the wide array of offerings on the benefits menu, coupled with the use of computer-based expert systems and decision-support systems, can do much to alleviate this problem.

## KEY TERMS

| | |
|---|---|
| vesting | gatekeeper |
| doctrine of constructive receipt | health maintenance organization (HMO) |
| anti-discrimination rule | preferred provider organization (PPO) |
| contributory plans | point-of-service plan (POS) |
| noncontributory plans | consumer-driven health plan (CDHP) |
| protected health information | pension |
| yearly renewable term insurance | defined-benefit plan |
| flexible benefits | defined-contribution plan |
| workers' compensation programs | cash-balance plan |
| long-term disability | cost shifting |
| short-term disability | cafeteria benefits |
| disability management | flexible-spending accounts |
| managed care | |

## DISCUSSION QUESTIONS

12–1.  What should a company do over the short and long term to maximize the use and value of its benefits choices to employees?

12–2.  The new world of employee benefits is best described as "sharing costs, sharing risks." Discuss the impact of that philosophy on the broad areas of health care and pensions.

12–3.  In terms of the "attract-retain-motivate" philosophy, how do benefits affect employee behavior?

12–4.  What can large firms do to control health-care costs? What about small firms?

12–5.  Your company has just developed a new, company-sponsored savings plan for employees. Develop a strategy to publicize the program and to encourage employees to participate in it.

## APPLYING YOUR KNOWLEDGE

---

*Reducing Health-Care Costs*                                                   *Case 12–1*

In the spring of 2009, Ron McGee, vice president of group insurance and labor relations at Polson Corporation, delivered the bad news to top management. Medical-insurance premiums for the following fiscal year were expected to increase approximately 20 percent, up dramatically from the 8 percent increase of the previous year—and future cost projections were equally grim. It was estimated that by 2013, the company's $647 million annual health-care bill would increase to a staggering $997 million.

Polson is a large, high-technology, automotive and electronics products company that employs about 70,000 people in the United States. The company decided not to tinker with traditional remedies to escalating health-care costs, such as increasing deductibles and shifting larger copayments to employees. Instead, it turned to managed health care. It did so by contracting with Whitefish Corporation, a large employee-benefits company specializing in such managed health-care plans.

A task force was formed in 2009 under the direction of McGee. The task force included HR executives from the corporate office of Polson in Morristown, New Jersey. This group was given the challenge of developing a custom-designed program that would hold down health-care premium costs to a reasonable level. The group decided that the new program would be built on the following foundation:

1. The insurance carrier, Whitefish Corporation, would be a partner in the program and would carry a financial risk, not merely be an administrator that paid the bills as they came in.
2. The insurance carrier would use its buying power to establish a network of highly qualified primary-care physicians and specialists throughout the United States, coinciding with the company's primary locations.
3. The insurance carrier would guarantee a high level of quality care to be provided to Polson's employees.
4. Unlike other health maintenance organization (HMO) plans, under the new Polson plan, employees would be able to switch from managed care to a traditional indemnity plan at will, but they would pay extra for exercising this option.

"We sought to change the way health care was delivered to our employees," says Al Gesler, corporate director of HR for Polson. "The net result was a hybrid program, taking into account the best features of HMOs and indemnity plans and combining that with a partnership arrangement between Whitefish, Polson, and its employees." Whitefish was chosen because it was a large and experienced insurance carrier and had a health-care network in place across the United States that pretty well coincided with major locations where Polson had operations.

In March 2009, Polson signed a three-year agreement with Whitefish for a managed-care program that was called "The Health Care Connection." This plan covered medical, dental, vision, and hearing care, as well as prescription medications. It also included a well-care program covering such items as an annual physical exam and prenatal care. An important feature of the plan was that Whitefish guaranteed annual premium increases of less than 10 percent during each of the three contract years on the managed-care side of the program. No similar guarantee was provided on the indemnity side. The actual figure would depend on the number of employees using the indemnity portion of the program.

"We wanted a very strong gatekeeper system," says McGee. "For our employees to take advantage of the extremely comprehensive benefits found on the in-network side of The Health Care Connection program, as well as the modest $30 copayment feature, they had to agree to choose a primary-care physician from within the closed panel and visit specialists in hospitals only when referred by their primary-care physicians. That was the trade-off." Where employees stayed in the network, the costs were very modest: a $30 copayment per office visit and $25 per prescription (generic drug) and 35 percent of the cost of a brand-name drug. If employees chose to go outside the network, they could switch to the indemnity side of the plan at any time for any particular illness or injury with no restrictions. Those who did, however, paid an annual deductible equal to 1 percent of their annual salaries and then were subject to an 80/20 copayment split (in other words, employees paid 20 percent of the medical care costs after the deductible was met).

"The basic concept behind managed care is just that, managing it," says McGee. "By staying in the network, everyone saves money. We felt this was a major effort aimed at limiting unnecessary care."

For its part, Whitefish is responsible for guaranteeing the quality of the managed-care side of the network. It is responsible for using its buying power to ensure that hospitals in the plan attract an adequate supply of high-quality physicians. It also means continual monitoring of employee usage of different types of medical care through utilization studies.

---

Questions

1. How should Polson communicate its new health-benefits plan to employees?
2. What results in terms of cost reduction do you anticipate Polson will achieve through the implementation of its new health-care program?
3. What additional follow-up should the benefits-administration people at Polson take now that the program has been in effect for several years?
4. To what extent do you believe health-care plans such as those at Polson are the wave of the future for health-benefits plans in major American corporations?

---

# REFERENCES

1. Miller, S. (2011, June 27). Employee benefits 2011: Fewer guarantees. Retrieved from *www.shrm.org/hrdisciplines/benefits/Articles/Pages/Benefits2011.aspx* on August 5, 2011.
2. Benziger, G. (2011, Aug. 8). Unions walk out at Verizon. *The Wall Street Journal,* pp. B1, B2. See also Smith, A. (2007, Oct. 5). GM-UAW deal shows benefits' central role in labor negotiations. Retrieved from *www.shrm.org/LegalIssues/ FederalResources/FederalLegalNews/Pages/XMS_023245.aspx* on October 12, 2007.
3. Shellenbarger, S. (2009, March 18). Perking up: Some companies offer surprising new benefits. *The Wall Street Journal,* pp. B1, B2. See also Byrnes, N. (2004, July 19). The benefits trap. *BusinessWeek,* pp. 64–72.
4. Employee Benefit Research Institute. (2010, Nov.). *Finances of employee benefits.* Retrieved from *www.ebri.org/pdf/publications/books/databook/DB.Chapter%2002. pdf* on August 8, 2011.
5. Small and medium-sized businesses and the recession. (2009). *Workplace Visions 3,* pp. 1–6. See also Cable, D. M., and Judge, T. A. (1994). Pay preferences and job search decisions: A person-organization fit perspective. *Personnel Psychology 47,* pp. 317–348.
6. Ledvinka, J., and Scarpello, V. G. (1991). *Federal regulation of personnel and human resource management* (2nd Ed.). Boston: PWS-Kent.
7. Ibid.
8. Milkovich, G. T., Newman, J. M., and Gerhart, B. (2011). *Compensation* (10th Ed.). Burr Ridge, IL: Irwin/McGraw-Hill.
9. Society for Human Resource Management. (2011, June). *2011 Benefits Survey.* Alexandria, VA: Author.
10. Milkovich et al., 2011, op. cit.

11. You can view the HIPAA Privacy Rules on the Department of Health and Human Services Web site at *www.hhs.gov/ocr/hipaa/privacy.html.* A HIPAA toolkit is also available on the SHRM site at *www.shrm.org/hrtools/toolkits/hipaatoolkit.asp.*

12. U.S. Department of Health & Human Services. Health information privacy. Retrieved from *www.hhs.gov/ocr/privacy* on August 8, 2011.

13. For a calculator to determine how much life insurance you need, go to *www.bankrate.com/calculators/insurance/life-insurance-calculator.aspx.* See also *www.smartmoney.com/personal-finance/insurance/how-much-life-insurance-do-you-need-12949*

14. SHRM, 2011, op. cit.

15. Keating, M. (2008, Nov. 1). The cost variations. Retrieved from *www.riskandinsurance.com/story.jsp?storyId=141402198* on August 8, 2011.

16. Atkinson, W. (2000, July). Is workers' comp changing? *HR Magazine,* pp. 50–61.

17. Milkovich et al., 2011, op. cit.

18. Lifsher, M. (2010, Nov. 20). Proposed 28% increase in workers' comp rates blasted. Retrieved from *http://articles.latimes.com/2010/nov/20/business/la-fi-workers-comp-rates-20101120* on August 8, 2011.

19. Kilgour, J. G. (2007, Aug.) A primer on workers' compensation laws and programs. SHRM white paper. Retrieved from *www.shrm.org/hrdisciplines/compensation/Articles/Pages/CMS_000039.aspx* on July 21, 2008.

20. Andrews, M. (2011, June). 5 things you need to know about disability insurance. *Money,* p. 55.

21. Young, L. (2009, Feb. 9). Weaving that safety net. *BusinessWeek,* p. 62. Clark, M. M., and Bates, S. (2003, Dec.). A torn safety net? *HR Magazine.* Retrieved from *www.shrm.org/Publications/hrmagazine/EditorialContent/Pages/1103clark.aspx* on July 21, 2008.

22. SHRM, 2011, op. cit.

23. The young and the disabled. (2001, June 4). *BusinessWeek,* p. 30. See also King, D. (1996, Oct.). A comprehensive approach to disability management. *HR Magazine,* pp. 97–102.

24. Sammer, J. (2006, Oct.). Outsourcing disability management. Retrieved from *www.shrm.org/hrdisciplines/Pages/CMS_018708.aspx* on August 8, 2011.

25. Fronstin, P., and Blakely, S. (2008, Apr. 22). Is the tipping point in health benefits near? *The Wall Street Journal,* p. A16.

26. Wells, S. J. (2009). Rebalancing health costs. *HR Magazine* 54(9), pp. 43–48. See also Fronstin and Blakely, 2008, op. cit. See also America's angry patients. (2007, Nov. 12). *BusinessWeek,* p. 40. See also Fuhrmans, V. (2004, July 13). Attacking rise in health costs, big company meets resistance. *The Wall Street Journal,* pp. A1, A10.

27. Kaiser Family Foundation. (2011). *Employer health benefits 2011.* Menlo Park, CA: Author.

28. Health care reform: Employer requirements at a glance. (2010, April 7). Retrieved from *www.shrm.org/Publications/HRNews/Pages/ReformAtGlance.aspx* on August 9, 2011. See also Gengler, A. (2011, March). The future of your health care. *Money,* pp. 98–106. Wells, S. J. (2011, June). Health care reform: Big changes considered. *HR Magazine* 56(6), pp. 63–66. See also Klein, K. E. The health-care bill. (2010, May 2). *BusinessWeek,* p. 74. See also Tyler, K. (2010, Sept.). Health care reform now: First things first. *HR Magazine* 55(9), pp.41–54. See also Kushner, G. B. (2010, June). Now it's employers' turn. *HR Magazine* 55(6), pp. 35–39.

29. Miller, S. (2011, April 20). Declining health of U.S. workers is driving up employer costs. Retrieved from *www.shrm.org/hrdisciplines/benefits/Articles/Pages/DecliningHealth.aspx* on April 26, 2011. See also Dalrymple, T. (2010, May 2). Our big problem. *The Wall Street Journal,* pp. W1, W2. See also Colvin, G.

(2010, March 1). C-Suite strategies: The Cleveland Clinic's Delos Cosgrove. *Fortune,* pp. 38–45.

30. Fuhrmans, 2004, op. cit. See also A crisis of medical success. (1993, Mar. 15). *BusinessWeek,* pp. 78–80. See also Pollack, A. (1991, Apr. 29). Medical technology "arms race" adds billions to the nation's bills. *The New York Times,* pp. A1, B8–B10.

31. Arnst, C. (2009, Nov. 23). 10 ways to cut health-care costs now. *BusinessWeek,* pp. 34–39.

32. Gengler, 2011, op. cit.

33. Gengler, A., and Mangla, I. S. (2008, Apr.). Take charge of your health care. *Money,* pp. 87–92.

34. SHRM, 2011, op. cit.

35. Miller, S. (2010, May 4). Individuals' behavior costs billions annually in pharmacy costs. Retrieved from *www.shrm.org/hrdisciplines/benefits/Articles/Pages/PharmacyCosts.aspx* on May 11, 2011.

36. Wells, S. J. (2010, July). Overseeing audits of your health plans. *HR Magazine* 55(7), pp. 34–39. See also Epstein, K., and McGregor, J. (2007, Nov. 26). You've got dependents? Prove it. *BusinessWeek,* pp. 91–93.

37. Kaiser Family Foundation, 2011, op. cit.

38. McGregor, J. (2009, Nov. 30). Health care: GE gets radical. *BusinessWeek,* p. 30.

39. Miller, S. (2010, Dec.).Unexpected boost for consumer-directed health plans. *HR Magazine* 55(12), pp. 33, 34. See also Gengler and Mangla, 2008, op. cit.

40. Gengler, 2011, op. cit. See also Lear, S. (2010, Oct.). What to expect at open enrollment. *Money,* p. 16. See also Salisbury, D. L. (2008, Apr. 22). Benefit trends: Change is now constant. *The Wall Street Journal,* pp. A11, A12.

41. Miller, 2011, April 20, op. cit. See also Arnst, 2009, op. cit.

42. SHRM, 2011, op. cit.

43. SHRM, 2011, op. cit.

44. SHRM, 2011, op. cit. See also Warren, J. (2010, June 13). Cough if you need sick leave. *BusinessWeek,* p. 33.

45. SHRM, 2011, op. cit.

46. Frase, M. (2010, March). Taking time off to the bank. *HR Magazine* 55(3), pp. 41–46.

47. Colvin, G. (1982, Oct. 4). How sick companies are endangering the pension system. *Fortune,* pp. 72–78.

48. U.S. Department of Labor. Employee Retirement Income Security Act. Retrieved from *www.dol.gov/compliance/laws/comp-erisa.htm* on August 10, 2011.

49. TowersWatson. (2011, Feb.). Global pension asset study 2011. Retrieved from *www.towerswatson.com/assets/pdf/3761/Global-Pensions-Asset-Study-2011.pdf* on August 10, 2011.

50. Jones, S. D., and Mattioli, D. (2010, Oct. 23). Companies pump up pension plans. *The Wall Street Journal,* pp. B1, B3. See also Colvin, G. (2006, June 26). The end of a dream. *Fortune,* pp. 85–92. See also Schultz, E. E. (2003, July 10). Coming up short: Firms had a hand in pension plight they now bemoan. *The Wall Street Journal,* pp. A1, A6.

51. Lowenstein, R. (2011, April 10). How did benefits for public workers get to be public enemy No. 1? *BusinessWeek,* pp. 78–83.

52. Bater, J. (2003, Jan. 31). U.S. pension insurer posts gap of $3.64 billion, after surplus. *The Wall Street Journal,* p. B8.

53. Pension Benefit Guaranty Corporation. *2010 annual report.* Retrieved from *www.pbgc.gov/Documents/2010_annual_report.pdf* on August 10, 2011.

54. Pension Benefit Guaranty Corporation. PBGC maximum monthly guarantees for 2011. Retrieved from *www.pbgc.gov/wr/benefits/guaranteed-benefits/maximum-guarantee.html#2011* on August 10, 2011.

55. U.S. Department of Labor. What you should know about your retirement plan. Retrieved from *www.dol.gov/ebsa/publications/wyskapr.html* on August 10, 2011.

56. SHRM, 2011, op. cit.

57. Schultz, E. E. (2001, June 20). Big send-off: As firms pare pensions for most, they boost those for executives. *The Wall Street Journal,* pp. A1, A8.

58. SHRM, 2011, op. cit.

59. Colvin, 2006, op. cit. See also Greene, K. (2011, June 14). Retirement plans make comeback, with limits. *The Wall Street Journal,* pp. A1, A2.

60. SHRM, 2011, op. cit. See also Sammer, J. (2009, May). Rescuing pension plans. *HR Magazine* 54(5), pp. 38–43.

61. Ibid.

62. Fitch, A. (2006, Dec.). Is my new pension plan worth less? *Money,* p. 50. See also Schultz, E. E., and Francis, T. (2006, Aug. 8). IBM ruling paves way for changes to pensions. *The Wall Street Journal,* p. A3.

63. Ibid. See also Feldman, A. (2009, July 20). Why IBM's 401(k) is the leader of the pack. *BusinessWeek,* pp. 58–61.

64. Metropolitan Life Insurance Company. (2011). *The 9th Annual MetLife Study of Employee Benefits Trends.* (2011). New York, NY: Author. See also Dulebohn, J. H., Murray, B., and Sun, M. (2000). Selection among employer-sponsored pension plans: The role of individual differences. *Personnel Psychology* 53, pp. 405–432.

65. VanDerhei, J. (2008, Apr. 22.). The Pension Protection Act and 401(k)s. *The Wall Street Journal,* p. A12. See also Pilzner, A. M. (2006, Nov.). *Pension Protection Act of 2006: Mandates and Options for Retirement Plans.* Alexandria, VA: Society for Human Resource Management.

66. SHRM, 2011, op. cit. See also Young, L. (2009, Jan. 12). Supersizing the 401(k). *BusinessWeek,* pp. 38, 39. See also Laise, E. (2009, Oct. 18). Employers begin driving your 401(k). *The Wall Street Journal,* pp. B1, B2.

67. Social Security is more secure. (2000, June 26). *BusinessWeek,* p. 34.

68. Social Security Online. (2011, Aug.). *Understanding the benefits* (SSA Publication No. 05-10024). Retrieved from *www.socialsecurity.gov/pubs/10024.html* on August 10, 2011.

69. Geithner, T. F., Solis, H. L., Sebelius, K., et al. (2011). The 2011 annual report of the board of trustees of the federal old-age and survivors insurance and federal disability insurance trust funds. Retrieved from *www.ssa.gov/oact/TR/2011/tr2011.pdf* on August 10, 2011.

70. Orszag, P. (2010, Nov. 4). Safer Social Security. *The New York* Times. Retrieved from *www.nytimes.com/2010/11/15/opinion/15orszag.html?ref=peterorszag* on August 10, 2011. See also Sloan, A. (2009, Aug. 17). The next great bailout. *Fortune,* pp. 71–78. See also Wolf, R. (2007, Oct. 9). Social Security hits first wave of boomers. *USA Today,* pp. A1, A2.

71. Orszag, 2010, op. cit. See also Sloan, 2009, op. cit. See also Wolf, 2007, op. cit.

72. Winestock, G. (2000, Oct. 30). Social Security reform rocks the world. *The Wall Street Journal,* p. A21, A24.

73. Murray, S. (2010, July 6). Long recession ignites debate on jobless benefits. *The Wall Street Journal.* Retrieved from *online.wsj.com/article/SB100014240527487 04334604575338691913994892.html?KEYWORDS=Long+recession+ignites+ debate+on+jobless+benefits* on July 10, 2010. See also Wells, S. J. (2009, July). Unemployment insurance: How much more will it cost? *HR Magazine 54*(7), pp. 35–38.

74. Murray, 2010, op. cit. See also Coy, P., and Hunt, A. (2010, Dec. 19). Jobless benefits: Corrupting or compassionate? *BusinessWeek,* pp. 11, 12.

75. De Meuse, K. P., Marks, M. L., and Dai, G. (2011). Organizational downsizing, mergers and acquisitions, and strategic alliances: Using theory and research to

enhance practice. In S. Zedeck (Ed.), *Handbook of Industrial and Organizational Psychology* (Vol. 3). Washington, DC: APA Books, pp. 729–768. See also Cascio, W. F. (2010). Downsizing and redundancy. In A. Wilkinson, N. Bacon, T. Redman, and S. Snell (Eds.), *Sage Handbook of Human Resource Management.* Thousand Oaks, CA: Sage, pp. 336–348.

76. Maurer, H. (2006, June 26). Shelling out in Detroit. *BusinessWeek,* p. 32.

77. VW seeks return to longer work week in Germany. (2006, June 13). *The Wall Street Journal,* p. A11.

78. Miller, S. (2008, Dec.). U.S. employees earn least amount of severance. Retrieved from *www.shrm.org/hrdisciplines/compensation/Articles/Pages/USEmployeesEarn LeastAmountofSeverance.aspx* on July 8, 2010.

79. Pilon, M. (2009, Nov. 10). Life on severance: Comfort, then crisis. *The Wall Street Journal.* Retrieved from *online.wsj.com/article/SB125780714976639687. html?KEYWORDS=Life+on+severance%3A+Comfort+then+crisis* on May 13, 2010.

80. Grossman, R. J. (2009, April). Executive pay: Perception and reality. *HR Magazine* 54(4), pp. 26–32.

81. Shellenbarger, S. (2011, July 20). Unlimited vacation, but can you take it? *The Wall Street Journal,* p. D3.

82. Rushin, S. (2008, July). One nation, in need of a vacation. *Encompass,* p. 54. See also Conlin, M. (2007, May 21). Do us a favor, take a vacation. *BusinessWeek,* pp. 88, 89.

83. Offered by 58 percent of firms. The maximum reimbursement allowed is, on average, $4,563 (SHRM, 2011, op. cit.). See also White, E. (2007, May 21). Corporate tuition aid appears to keep workers loyal. *The Wall Street Journal,* p. B4.

84. Atkinson, W. (2009, Nov.). Filling in around the edges. *HR Magazine* 54(11), pp. 55–58. See also Lorenzetti, J. P. (2002). Financial planning services on the rise. *HR Magazine* 47(4), pp. 85–89.

85. See, for example, Hirschman, C. (2004). Commuter connections. *HR Magazine,* pp. 99–102.

86. Galinsky, E., and Matos, K. (In press.). The future of work-life fit. *Organizational Dynamics.* See also Galinsky, E., Bond, J. T., and Sakai, K. (2008, June). *2008 National Study of Employers.* NY: Families and Work Institute. See also Demby, E. R. (2004). Do your family-friendly programs make cents? *HR Magazine* 49(1), pp. 74–79. See also Grover, S. L., and Crooker, K. J. (1995). Who appreciates family responsive human resource policies: The impact of family-friendly policies on the organizational attachment of parents and non-parents. *Personnel Psychology* 48, pp. 271–288.

87. Demby, 2004, op. cit.

88. SHRM, 2011, op. cit.

89. Grensing-Pophal, L. (2009, Jan. 2). Benefits communication: Is it working? Retrieved from *www.shrm.org/hrdisciplines/benefits/Articles/Pages/BenefitsCommunication IsItWorking.aspx* on August 11, 2011.

90. McCaffery, R. M. (1992). *Employee Benefit Programs: A Total Compensation Perspective* (2nd Ed.). Boston: PWS-Kent.

91. SHRM, 2011, op. cit.

92. Sturman, M. C., Hannon, J. M., and Milkovich, G. T. (1996). Computerized decision aids for flexible-benefits decisions: The effects of an expert system and decision-support system on employee intentions and satisfaction with benefits. *Personnel Psychology* 49, pp. 883–908. See also Barber, A. E., Dunham, R. B., and Formisano, R. A. (1992). The impact of flexible benefits on employee satisfaction: A field study. *Personnel Psychology 45,* pp. 55–75.

93. Health Care Reform: FSA, HRA, HSA, Archer MSA Plan Changes: What is the impact of the PPACA on FSAs, HSAs, Archer MSAs and HRAs? (2010, April 14). Retrieved

from *www.shrm.org/TemplatesTools/hrqa/Pages/FSAHRAHSAMSAChanges.aspx* on August 11, 2011.

94. Robb, D. (2011, May). Benefits choices: Educating the consumer. *HR Magazine* 56(3), pp. 29–34. See also Heuring, L. (2003). Laying out enrollment options. *HR Magazine* 47(8), pp. 65–70.

95. Robb, D. (2007, Aug.). A total view of employee rewards. *HR Magazine,* pp. 93–95.

96. Robb, 2011, op. cit.

97. Ruffenach, G. (2004, Aug. 9). Miracle cure? *The Wall Street Journal,* pp. R5, R6.

98. Stires, D. (2003, May 3). Rx for investors. *Fortune,* pp. 158–172.

99. Feldman, 2009, op. cit.

100. Van Derhei, J. (2008, Apr. 22). The Pension Protection Act and 401(k)s. *The Wall Street Journal,* p. A12.

PART

5

# LABOR-MANAGEMENT ACCOMMODATION

Harmonious working relations between labor and management are critical to organizations. Traditionally, both parties have assumed a win–lose, adversarial posture toward each other. This must change if U.S. firms are to remain competitive in the international marketplace. Part 5 is entitled "Labor-Management Accommodation" to emphasize a general theme: To achieve long-term success, labor and management must learn to accommodate each other's needs, rather than repudiate them. By doing so, management and labor can achieve two goals at once: increase productivity and improve the quality of work life. In the current climate of wants and needs, there is no other alternative.

The focus of Chapter 13 is on union representation and collective bargaining. Chapter 14 focuses on procedural justice, ethics, and concerns for privacy in employee relations. These are currently some of the most dominant issues in this field. As managers, you must develop and implement sound practices with respect to them. Chapters 13 and 14 will help you do that.

# CHAPTER

# 13

# UNION REPRESENTATION AND COLLECTIVE BARGAINING

*Questions This Chapter Will Help Managers Answer*

1. How have changes in product and service markets affected the way labor and management relate to each other?
2. How should management respond to a union organizing campaign?
3. To what extent should labor-management cooperative efforts be encouraged?
4. What kinds of dispute-resolution mechanisms should be established in order to guarantee due process for all employees?

# RESTRUCTURING THROUGH UNION-MANAGEMENT COLLABORATION*

The forces of globalization and technology that began pounding labor's manufacturing strongholds in the 1970s have intensified in recent years as the global financial crisis and a prolonged recession ensued. In everything from retailing and services to health care and steel, deregulation, heightened global competition, and cheap immigrant labor have forced employers into an endless struggle to keep costs down, including wages and benefits.

With more employees and retirees losing company-paid health coverage, and worker anxiety heightened by high unemployment and the shift of white-collar jobs overseas, it is clear that the old, adversarial "us-versus-them" approach to labor-management relations has long passed its "sell-by" date. Concerns about all of those issues have led to unprecedented levels of union-management cooperation in recent years.

The 2007–2011 agreements between auto makers Ford, General Motors, Chrysler, and the United Auto Workers, for example, froze union members' base pay for four years, shifted retiree health-care obligations to a union-run trust, and paid new workers lower wages for the same work as veterans. Why did the union agree to those concessions? Because, in return, the auto makers agreed to invest billions of dollars in U.S. plants and to keep factories open. That means a lot to economically depressed communities in states like Ohio, Michigan, and Pennsylvania. For the workers and their families, it's all about job security, steady wages, and health coverage. As the new contract talks began, Ford, GM, and Chrysler sought to be free of fixed wage increases that were part of past union contracts. Instead they offered profit sharing and performance bonuses that allow workers to share in the companies' prosperity. They also sought more cost shifting to workers for health-care coverage.

Consider two related industries, steel and rubber (tire makers). Both had been sliding toward extinction until union leaders stepped forward to work with management in the development of innovative agreements that keep these industries profitable and competitive through higher worker productivity.

Thus, when the leaders of the United Steelworkers (USW) union sat down with Goodyear Tire & Rubber Company to negotiate a new labor agreement, they knew they were headed for trouble. The nation's largest tire maker had lost $1 billion the previous year as rivals selling cheap tires made in low-wage countries sliced its market share by three full percentage points, to 19.5 percent. Just as bad, a revolving door of executives had racked up a crushing $5 million in debt as new acquisitions and tire products did not succeed. The union's options? Allow Goodyear to replace some of its 14 U.S. plants with ones in Asia, or fight the company with a strike that could force it into bankruptcy.

---

*Sources:* Dolan, M. (2011, July 25). For UAW, jobs trump pay. *The Wall Street Journal*, pp. B1, B11. See also Ramsey, M. (2011, May 23). VW chops labor costs in U.S. *The Wall Street Journal*, pp. B1, B2. See also Goodyear. (2009, Sept.19). Goodyear's innovative USW contract improves efficiency, cuts costs. Retrieved from *www.goodyear.com/investor/pdf/8k/2009/20090929122201079663078.PDF* on August 17, 2011. See also Spector, M., McCracken, J., and Stoll, J. D. (2007, Oct. 10). How less pay, more risk, "sells itself". *The Wall Street Journal*, pp. B1, B11. See also Maher, K. (2007, Jan. 22). Are unions relevant? *The Wall Street Journal*, p. R5. See also Michelin, S. A. (2004, Aug. 30). BF Goodrich workers approve about 20% cut in labor costs. *The Wall Street Journal*, p. B6. See also Welch, D. (2003, Oct. 20). What Goodyear got from its union. *BusinessWeek*, pp. 148, 149.

Instead, the USW came up with a third choice. The union hired a boutique Wall Street firm to devise a long-term strategic plan for the company. The goal: to make Goodyear globally competitive in a way that would preserve as many of the union's 19,000 jobs as possible. In the conclusion to this case we will see what happened, but one thing is clear: Both sides would have to agree to major changes in the way the business is run if there was to be any hope of keeping this old-line manufacturing industry competitive—and keeping it in the United States.

## Challenges

1. What are some key obstacles that stand in the way of true cooperation by labor and management?
2. Is labor-management cooperation just a short-term solution to economic problems, or can it become institutionalized into the very culture of an organization?
3. Will widespread labor-management cooperation lead to a loss of union power?

## WHY DO EMPLOYEES JOIN UNIONS?

Visualize this scenario: It's 7:30 on a cool December evening in Las Vegas, and 105 off-duty hotel maids, cooks, and bellhops are waiting for their monthly union meeting to start. It has been a long day working in the big casino hotels, but still the room buzzes with energy. One by one, a dozen or so members recount their success in recruiting 2,700 new colleagues at the MGM Grand, the world's largest hotel. After a three-year campaign of street demonstrations, mass arrests, and attacks on the company's HR practices that helped oust a stridently anti-labor CEO, MGM Grand recognized the union a year later without an election. Another group reports on the victory at New York, New York, a new hotel that agreed to the unionization of 900 workers.

This is the essence of a **labor union**: a group of workers who join together to influence the nature of their employment. Perhaps they are seeking improved wages and benefits, protection against arbitrary treatment and discharge, or a greater voice in workplace decision making. For employers, in contrast, labor relations are about managing relationships with employees and unions in ways that promote organizational goals such as profitability (in the private sector) or cost-effective service delivery (in the public sector). Nonunion employers typically pursue these goals by trying to remain union free—either through aggressive antiunion tactics or through progressive HR management tactics that seek to make unions unnecessary.[1]

To be sure, the attitudes of workers toward unions are not based simply on expected economic gains; much deeper values are at stake.[2] As one union leader recently noted: "Our union has never seen itself as just a collective-bargaining agent, but as an agent for social change."[3] Indeed,

> If one talks to any worker long enough, and candidly enough, one discovers that his loyalty to the union is not simply economic. One may even be able to show him that, on a strictly cost-benefit analysis, measuring income lost from strikes, and jobs

lost as a result of contract terms, the cumulative economic benefits are delusions. It won't matter. In the end, he will tell you, the union is the only institution that ensures and protects his "dignity" as a worker, that prevents him from losing his personal identity, and from being transformed into an infinitesimal unit in one huge and abstract "factor of production."[4]

Managers who fail to treat workers with respect, or companies that view workers only as costs to be cut rather than as assets to be developed, *invite* collective action by employees to remedy these conditions.[5] Among employees who see management as unwilling to share power, more than 70 percent say they would vote for a union.[6] However, unions are not without sin either, and workers will vote against them to the extent that the unions are seen as unsympathetic to a company's need to remain viable, or if they feel unions abuse their power by calling strikes or have fat-cat leaders who selfishly promote their own interests at the expense of the members' interests.[7]

## UNION MEMBERSHIP IN THE UNITED STATES

Union membership has shrunk from a high of 35 percent of the workforce in 1945 to 22 percent in 1980 to 11.9 percent in 2010. Unions still represent 14.7 million workers, but that's just about one in every 10 employees. Excluding public-sector membership, unions represented just 6.9 percent of private-sector employees in 2010.[8] Figure 13–1 shows the percentage of nonfarm employees represented by unions between 1930 and 2010.

Several economic and demographic forces favor a resurgence of unions. The same trends toward globalization, technology, and corporate downsizing that have sharply cut union membership have also created a new receptiveness for union organizers among surviving employees, who find themselves overworked and under excessive stress. In the public sector, several states have attempted to curb collective-bargaining rights for workers, but public sentiment is against this approach by nearly a two-to-one margin.[9] And it is not just blue-collar workers who are organizing. In fact, many of the fastest-growing unions in the United

**Figure 13–1**

Percentage of nonfarm employees represented by unions between 1930 and 2010.

(*Sources:* Bureau of the Census, *Historical statistics of the United States, colonial times to 1970;* Bureau of Labor Statistics, *Handbook of labor statistics* Bulletin 2070, Dec. 1980; Bureau of Labor Statistics, *Employment and earnings,* Jan., various years, 1983–2010. Originally prepared by the AFL-CIO.) *Note:* Bureau of Labor Statistics information before 1981 was compiled on a different basis from the present series and it is not necessarily comparable; data for 1981 and 1982 were imputed.

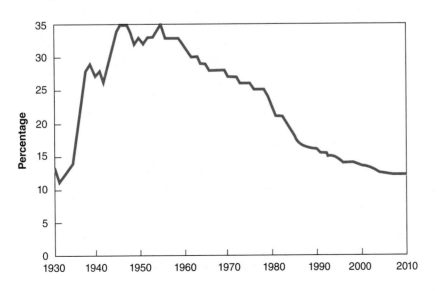

States represent white-collar professionals (more than 51 percent of all union members), including physicians, nuclear engineers, psychologists, and judges.[10]

Finally, women, immigrants, and other minority-group members, who are expected to continue entering the workforce at a high rate, tend to favor unions. Evidence indicates that women's participation is likely to be enhanced to the extent that there is greater representation of women in local union offices.[11]

Despite these factors, a large-scale resurgence of unions seems unlikely. Organized labor complains that U.S. labor laws favor employers,[12] but what complicates organizing efforts is that many in this new generation are white-collar workers—in fields as diverse as insurance, information technology, and electronics. Their goals and desires are different from those of labor's traditional blue-collar stalwarts, who seemed to want little more than high wages and steady work. As one expert noted, ". . . people want something that looks more like a voice in the workplace—and less like collective bargaining and conflict with management." And because so many young workers are highly mobile (average job tenure for workers ages 25 to 34 was just 3.1 years in 2010[13]), they may not be willing to support a six-month unionization drive that could culminate in a strike to win a first contract. Finally, many young workers are taking jobs in the rapidly growing service sector—banking, computer programming, and financial services—92 percent of which remains unorganized.[14]

The very nature of high-tech industry also hampers organizing efforts. Many software designers and biotechnical engineers work for small, start-up companies that unions find difficult and expensive to organize. Many are focused on earning stock options and other rewards for performance instead of wage increases and health insurance that unions typically seek[15]

Despite the drop-off in membership, unions are powerful social, political, and organizational forces. Strategies used by the United Steelworkers are typical. Rather than simply pounding the table for higher pay or threatening strikes, it is blocking takeovers, taking sides in bidding wars, and fighting for board seats.[16] In the unionized firm, managers must deal with the union rather than directly with employees on many issues. Indeed, the "rules of the game" regarding wages, hours, and conditions of employment are described in a collective-bargaining agreement (or contract) between management and labor. Although it need not always be so, and is not productive over the long run, adversarial "us" and "them" feelings are frequently an unfortunate by-product of this process.

Economic and working conditions in unionized firms directly affect those in nonunionized firms, as managers strive to provide competitive working conditions for their employees. Yet the nature of the internal and external environments of most U.S. firms has changed dramatically relative to that of earlier periods. This difference has led to fundamental changes in labor-management relations, as we will see in the next section.

## THE CHANGING NATURE OF INDUSTRIAL RELATIONS IN THE UNITED STATES

Fundamentally, labor-management relations are about power—who has it and how they use it. As the chapter-opening vignette illustrated, both parties are finding that they achieve the best results when they share power rather than revert to a win–lose orientation.[17] In recent years, unions have lost power as a result of six interrelated factors: global competition, nonunion domestic competition, deregulation, the growth of service industries, corporate downsizing (which has depleted the membership of many unions), and the willingness of firms to move operations overseas. In today's world, firms face more competitive pressures than ever before. That competition arises from abroad (e.g., Toyota, Nissan, Hyundai, Sanyo, Pohang, and steelmakers from developing countries); from domestic, nonunion operators (e.g., Nucor in steel); and from nonregulated new entities (e.g., dozens of new telecommunications companies).

The deregulation of many product markets created two key challenges to existing union relationships. First, it made market entry much easier, for example, in over-the-road trucking, airlines, and telecommunications. Second, under regulation, management had little incentive to cut labor costs because high labor costs could be passed on to consumers; conversely, labor-cost savings could not be used to gain a competitive advantage in the product market. Under deregulation, however, even major airlines (which are almost entirely organized) found that low costs translated into low fares and a competitive advantage. As a result, all carriers need to match the lowest costs of their competitors by matching their labor contracts.[18]

These competitive pressures have forced business to develop the ability to shift rapidly, to cut costs, to innovate, to enter new markets, and to devise a flexible labor force strategy. As managers seek to make the most cost-effective use of their human resources, and as companies move forward into a more integrated, globalized world economy, they need to understand the legal and employment implications of different systems that underly the infrastructure and operations of unions in nations where they do business.[19]

Traditionally, the power of unions to set industrywide wage levels and to relate these in "patterns" was based on the market power of strong domestic producers or industries sheltered by regulation. As employers lost their market power in the 1970s and 1980s, union wage dominance shrank and fragmented. One union segment had to compete with another and with nonunion labor both in the United States and abroad. Management's objective was (and is) to get labor costs per unit of output to a point below that of the competition at the product-line level. Out of this approach have come wage-level differences and, with them, the breakdown of pattern bargaining. As a result, even under union bargaining pressures, wages are now far more responsive to economic conditions at the industry and firm levels, and even at the product-line level, than they traditionally have been.[20]

The labor relations system that evolved during the 1940s and lasted until the early 1980s was institutionalized around the market power of the firm and around those unions that had come to represent large proportions, if not nearly all, of an industry's domestic workforce. The driving force for change in the new millennium has been business conditions in the firm. Those conditions have changed for good—and so must the U.S. industrial relations system. To put that system into better perspective, let us consider some of its fundamental features.

## FUNDAMENTAL FEATURES OF THE U.S. INDUSTRIAL RELATIONS SYSTEM

Six distinctive features of the U.S. system, compared with those in other countries, are as follows:[21]

1.  *Exclusive representation.* One and only one union in a given job territory (**exclusive representation**), selected by majority vote. However, multiple unions may represent different groups of employees who work for the same

employer (e.g., pilots, flight attendants, and machinists at an airline). This situation is in contrast to that existing in continental Europe, where affiliations by religious and ideological attachment exist in the same job territory.

2. *Collective agreements that embody a sharp distinction between negotiation of and interpretation of an agreement.* Most agreements are of fixed duration, often two or three years (sometimes shorter in uncertain economic times),[22] and they result from legitimate, overt conflict that is confined to a negotiations period. They incorporate nostrike (by employees) and no-lockout (by employer) provisions during the term of the agreement, as well as interpretation of the agreement by private arbitrators or umpires. In contrast, the British system features open-ended, nonenforceable agreements.

3. *Decentralized collective bargaining,* largely due to the size of the United States, the diversity of its economic activity, and the historic role of product markets in shaping the contours of collective bargaining. By contrast, in Sweden, the government establishes wage rates, and in Australia, some wages are set by arbitration councils and others by bargaining at the enterprise level.[23]

4. *Relatively high union dues and large union staffs* to negotiate and administer private, decentralized agreements, including grievance arbitration to organize against massive employer opposition and to lobby before legislative and administrative tribunals.

---

## INTERNATIONAL APPLICATION
## Comparing Industrial Relations Systems around the World

Direct comparisons among industrial relations (IR) systems are almost impossible. Here are three reasons:[a]

1. *The same concept may be interpreted differently in different industrial relations contexts.* For example, consider the concept of collective bargaining. In the United States, it is understood to mean negotiations between a labor union local and management. In Sweden and Germany, however, the term refers to negotiation between an employers' organization and a trade union at the industry level.[b]

2. *The objectives of the bargaining process may differ in different countries.* For example, European unions view collective bargaining as a form of class struggle, but in the United States, collective bargaining is viewed mainly in economic terms.

3. *No IR system can be understood without an appreciation of its historical origins.* Such historical differences may be due to managerial strategies for labor relations in large companies, ideological divisions within the trade-union movement, the influence of religious organizations on the development of trade unions, methods of union regulation by governments, or the mode of technology and industrial organization at critical stages of union development.[c]

[a]Evans, P., Pucik, V., and Bjorkman, I. (2011). *The Global Challenge: International Human Resource Management* (2nd Ed.). New York, NY: McGraw-Hill. See also Dowling, P. J., Festing, M., and Engle, A. D., Sr. (2009). *International Human Resource Management* (5th Ed.). Mason, OH: Thomson South-Western.

[b]Katz et al., 2008, op. cit. See also Budd, 2010, op. cit.

[c]Fossum, 2012, op. cit. See also Poole, M. (1986). *Industrial Relations: Origins and Patterns of National Diversity.* London: Routledge & Kegan Paul.

5. *Opposition by both large and small employers to union organization,* in contrast to countries such as France and Germany. Such opposition has been modified in terms of the constraints placed on management only slightly by more than 65 years of legislation.

6. *The role of government* in the U.S. industrial relations system, as compared with other systems, such as those of Mexico and Australia. The U.S. government has been relatively passive in dispute resolution and highly legalistic, both in administrative procedures and in the courts.[24] In the U.S., the traditional view is that the role of government is not to establish labor standards, only to promote competition.[25]

Before we examine the U.S. system in greater detail, let's briefly consider its historical origins.

## A BRIEF HISTORY OF U.S. LABOR RELATIONS

The labor movement has had a long, colorful, and turbulent history in the United States. It began with the Industrial Revolution of the 19th century. Economically, the Industrial Revolution was a great boon to productive output and to capital accumulation by business owners. Not so for the average worker. Wages were generally low and working conditions were often hazardous. Labor was considered a commodity to be bought and sold, and the prevailing political philosophy of *laissez faire* (leave things alone) resulted in little action by governments to protect the lot of workers.[26] Against this backdrop, it was inevitable that workers would organize collectively to improve their wages and working conditions.

The first overt union activity in the United States took place in 1794 when the Philadelphia shoemakers attempted to raise their wages, in reaction to a wage cut by their employers. The employers sued the union, arguing that the combination of workers to raise their wages constituted an illegal conspiracy in restraint of trade. In 1806 a federal court ruled in favor of the employers and fined the employees involved. Until this **conspiracy doctrine** was overturned in 1842 in the case of *Commonwealth of Massachusetts v. Hunt,* workers were discouraged from forming unions. In that case, the court ruled that labor unions were not criminal per se, for they could have honorable as well as destructive objectives. In short, a union's conduct will determine whether it is legal or illegal.[27]

### Emergence of the American Federation of Labor (AFL)

The AFL was organized in 1886 as a group of national craft unions. Some of these unions were the Metal Workers, Carpenters, Cigar Makers, Iron Molders, Miners, Granite Cutters, Bakers, Furniture Workers, Tailors, and Typographers. It espoused no particular political philosophy or set of broad social goals because its objectives were more pragmatic. It sought immediate benefits for its members in the companies where they were employed. In the words of Samuel Gompers, the AFL's first president, the goals of the AFL were "More, more, more; now, now, now."[28]

## Emergence of the Congress of Industrial Organizations (CIO)

A combination of factors in the 1930s made industrial unionism attractive:

1. The Great Depression, which engendered such general gloom and pessimism in the entire economic system that it inevitably increased the propensity of workers to join unions.
2. Passage of federal labor laws that made it easier to organize workers.
3. The emergence of rebel leaders within the AFL who wanted to organize unskilled workers into industrial unions.

In 1935 the rebels formed their own Congress of Industrial Organizations (CIO) and intended to work within the AFL. However, the issue of craft versus industrial unionism, together with power rivalries within the AFL, led to an open break. The CIO's strategy was to organize *all* the workers in a given plant or company rather than to focus on certain crafts. It was quite successful, principally through the use of the **sit-down strike,** in which workers refused to leave the premises until employers met their demands for recognition. Even before the formal AFL-CIO break in 1937, membership in CIO unions had reached 3.7 million, exceeding AFL membership by 300,000 workers.[29]

## Merger of the AFL-CIO

By the early 1950s, both the AFL and CIO realized they were sacrificing power and efficiency by fighting on two fronts simultaneously: against employers and against each other. In 1955 they merged into the AFL-CIO under the leadership of George Meany, new president of the AFL, and Walter Reuther, former head of the United Auto Workers and new president of the CIO. In 1967, however, Meany and Reuther became bitter enemies when Reuther withdrew his United Auto Workers from the federation in a policy dispute. Meany became the first president of the AFL-CIO.

Integrity was Meany's hallmark, and he vigorously fought union corruption, most notably by expelling Jimmy Hoffa's Teamsters union from the AFL-CIO in 1957. Throughout his career, Meany said that the wages and working conditions of the laborer, not economic philosophy, were his primary concerns. But he elevated the labor movement beyond wages and hours to unprecedented standing in Washington, particularly with Democratic presidents. In fact, Meany played the game of power politics so well that by 1979, when he retired, organized labor, in the words of a noted labor lawyer, "became a middle-class movement of people earning $25,000, $30,000 a year [roughly $65,000 to $75,000 in 2011 dollars], supplemented by federal benefits."[30] Things certainly were different when Meany first appeared on the national scene in 1934. Then there was no Social Security to provide for aging workers, no National Labor Relations Act, public employee unions were unheard of, and the first national minimum wage—25 cents per hour for a 48-hour work week—was still four years away.

## Breaking Away from the AFL-CIO

On its 50th anniversary, the AFL-CIO experienced a dramatic turn of events. Several union leaders from within the federation were frustrated over the continued decline in membership, and they pressed the AFL-CIO to change its priorities, from spending on political activities (lobbying and get-out-the-vote drives) to organizing activities (campaigns to unionize nonunion workplaces). As a result of this disagreement, several unions left the AFL-CIO in 2005 and formed their own federation—**Change to Win.** The new federation includes only four unions, but they represent 5.5 million workers, more than 60 percent of the AFL-CIO's total membership. The member unions are the Service Employees, the Teamsters, the United Food and Commercial Workers, and the Farm Workers.[31]

Change to Win is all about action, as fully 75 percent of its budget goes to field organizing. Will the split from the AFL-CIO strengthen or sap the labor movement? Only time will tell, but what we do know now is that more resources are being put into organizing, political action, and cooperation with labor organizations and governments in other countries than has been the case for the last half century.[32]

Unionizing nonunion workplaces is a top priority for the labor movement. Our next section describes how this process works under current labor law.

## THE UNIONIZATION PROCESS

### The Legal Basis

The Wagner Act, or *National Labor Relations Act,* of 1935 affirmed the right of all employees to engage in union activities, to organize, and to bargain collectively without interference or coercion from management. It also created the National Labor Relations Board (NLRB) to supervise representation elections and to investigate charges of unfair labor practices by management. The *Taft-Hartley Act* of 1947 reaffirmed those rights and, in addition, specified unfair labor practices for both management and unions. The unfair labor practices are shown in Table 13–1. The act was later amended (by the *Landrum Griffin Act* of 1959) to add the **secondary boycott** as an unfair labor practice.

A secondary boycott occurs when a union appeals to firms or other unions to stop doing business with an employer who sells or handles a struck product.

A so-called **free-speech clause** in the act specifies that management has the right to express its opinion about unions or unionism to employees, provided that it does not threaten or promise favors to employees to obtain antiunion actions. The Taft-Hartley Act covers most private-sector employers and nonmanagerial employees, except railroad and airline employees (they are covered under the *Railway Labor Act* of 1926). Federal-government employees are covered by the *Civil Service Reform Act* of 1978. That act affirmed their right to organize and to bargain collectively over working conditions, established unfair labor practices for both management and unions, established the Federal Labor Relations Authority to administer the act, authorized the Federal Services Impasse Panel to take whatever action is necessary to resolve impasses in collective bargaining, and prohibited strikes in the public sector.

## Table 13–1

### UNFAIR LABOR PRACTICES FOR MANAGEMENT AND UNIONS UNDER THE TAFT-HARTLEY ACT OF 1947

#### Management

1.   Interference with, coercion of, or restraint of employees in their right to organize.
2.   Domination of, interference with, or illegal assistance of a labor organization.
3.   Discrimination in employment because of union activities.
4.   Discrimination because the employee has filed charges or given testimony under the act.
5.   Refusal to bargain in good faith.
6.   "Hot cargo" agreements: refusals to handle another employer's products because of that employer's relationship with the union.

#### Union

1.   Restraint or coercion of employees who do not want to participate in union activities.
2.   Any attempt to influence an employer to discriminate against an employee.
3.   Refusal to bargain in good faith.
4.   Excessive, discriminatory membership fees.
5.   Make-work or featherbedding provisions in labor contracts that require employers to pay for services that are not performed.
6.   Use of pickets to force an organization to bargain with a union, when the organization already has a lawfully recognized union.
7.   "Hot cargo" agreements: that is, refusals to handle, use, sell, transport, or otherwise deal in another employer's products.

## ETHICAL DILEMMA
### Are Unfair Practices Unethical?

Are the unfair labor practices shown in Table 13–1 also unethical? Are there circumstances under which activities  might be legal (e.g., cutting off health-care benefits for striking workers) but at the same time also be unethical?

## WHEN IS REFUSAL TO HIRE A UNION SYMPATHIZER UNLAWFUL?

Note unfair labor practice no. 3 for management in Table 13–1. It is unlawful for management to discriminate in employment because of union activities. In 1995 the Supreme Court decided in *NLRB v. Town & Country Electric Inc.* that paid union organizers, despite their employment relationship with the union, are nonetheless "employees" and therefore are protected against discrimination in hiring based on their union affiliation. Once hired, however, they are subject to the same work rules and performance standards as are other employees. More recently, in *Masiongale Electrical-Mechanical Inc. v. NLRB* the 7th Circuit Court of Appeals provided the following four-part test in order to establish a discriminatory refusal to hire:

1. The employer was hiring, or had concrete plans to hire, at the time of the alleged unlawful conduct.
2. The applicants had experience or training relevant to the announced or generally known requirements of the positions.
3. The employer did not adhere uniformly to such requirements, or the requirements themselves were a pretext for discrimination.
4. Antiunion bias contributed to the decision not to hire the applicants.

At the same time, the sympathizers must also have a genuine interest in working for the employer.[a] Once this is established, the burden shifts to the employer to show that it would not have hired the applicants even in the absence of their union activity or affiliation.[b]

---

[a] *Toering Electric Company,* 351 NLRB No. 18 (2007).

[b] Clark, M. M. (2003, Oct.). When the union knocks . . . on the recruiter's door: Legal rules on the hiring of union "salts." *Legal Report,* pp. 7–8.

---

## The Organizing Drive

There are three ways to kick off an organizing campaign: (1) Employees themselves may begin it; (2) employees may request that a union begin one for them; or (3) in some instances, national and international unions may contact employees in organizations that have been targeted for organizing. In all three cases, employees are asked to sign **authorization cards** that designate the union as the employees' exclusive representative in bargaining with management.

Well-defined rules govern organizing activities:

1. Employee organizers may solicit fellow employees to sign authorization cards on company premises but not during working time. This includes e-mail solicitation. In fact, some have argued that because of the sheer importance of e-mail for daily communication, employees should be allowed to use it for union-related activities unless a company can show a valid business reason for restricting it.[33]

2. Outside organizers may not solicit on premises if a company has an existing policy of prohibiting all forms of solicitation and if that policy has been enforced consistently.[34]

3. Management representatives may express their views about unions through speeches to employees on company premises. However, they are legally prohibited from interfering with an employee's freedom of choice concerning union membership.

The organizing drive usually continues until the union obtains signed authorization cards from 30 percent of the employees. At that point it can petition the NLRB for a representation election. If the union secures authorization cards from more than 50 percent of the employees, however, it may ask management directly for the right to exclusive representation. This is known as a **card check** (referring to the index-card-sized slips of paper that workers sign). Its goal is to circumvent management's power to influence an election. In its 2007 *Dana Corporation* decision, however, the NLRB diminished the effectiveness of these agreements by allowing employees and rival unions to challenge voluntary recognition agreements reached between employers and unions. As a result, voluntary agreements are no longer the "easy" road for a union seeking to organize a group of employees.[35]

## The Bargaining Unit

When the petition for election is received, the NLRB conducts a hearing to determine the appropriate (collective) **bargaining unit,** that is, the group of employees eligible to vote in the representation election. Sometimes labor and management agree jointly on the appropriate bargaining unit. When they do not, the NLRB must determine the unit. The NLRB is guided in its decision, especially if there is no previous history of bargaining between the parties, by a concept called **community of interest.** That is, the NLRB will define a unit that reflects the shared interests of the employees involved. Such elements include similar wages, hours, and working conditions; the physical proximity of employees to one another; common supervision; the amount of interchange of employees within the proposed unit; and the degree of integration of the employer's production process or operation.[36] Under the Taft-Hartley Act, however, professional employees cannot be forced into a bargaining unit with nonprofessionals without their majority consent.

The *size* of the bargaining unit is critical for both the union and the employer because it is strongly related to the outcome of the representation election. The larger the bargaining unit, the more difficult it is for the union to win. In fact, if a bargaining unit contains several hundred employees, the unit is almost invulnerable.[37]

## The Election Campaign

Emotions on both sides run high during a representation election campaign. However, management typically is unaware that a union campaign is under way until most or all of the cards have been signed. At that point, management has some tactical advantages over the union. It can use company time and premises to stress the positive aspects of the current situation, and it can emphasize the costs of unionization and the loss of individual freedom that may result from collective representation. Supervisors may hold information meetings to emphasize these antiunion themes. However, certain practices by management are prohibited by law, such as

1.  Physical interference, threats, or violent behavior toward union organizers.
2.  Interference with employees involved with the organizing drive.
3.  Discipline or discharge of employees for pro-union activities.
4.  Promises to provide or withhold future benefits depending on the outcome of the representation election.

These illegal activities are *TIPS*—that is, management may not *T*hreaten, *I*nterrogate, *P*romise, or *S*py.[38] To illustrate, expressions of distaste for union organizing efforts by the president of Griffin Electric, one of the largest nonunion electrical contractors in the northeastern United States, were interpreted by the 4th U.S. Circuit Court of Appeals as threats. The president's remarks that the company would "never be union" and that employees who signed union cards would be "stabbing him in the back" were interpreted as threats because of his direct involvement with employee discipline and promotional opportunities.[39]

Unions are also prohibited from unfair labor practices (see Table 13–1), such as coercing or threatening employees if they fail to join the union. In addition, the union can picket the employer *only* if (1) the employer is not currently unionized, (2) the petition for election has been filed with the NLRB in the past 30 days, and (3) a representation election has not been held during the previous year. Unions tend to emphasize three themes during organizing campaigns:

■  The union's ability to help employees satisfy their economic and personal needs.
■  The union's ability to ensure that workers are treated fairly.
■  The union's ability to improve working conditions.[40]

The campaign tactics of management and the union are monitored by the NLRB. If the NLRB finds that either party engaged in unfair labor practices during the campaign, the election results may be invalidated and a new election conducted. However, a federal appeals court has ruled that the NLRB cannot force a company to bargain with a union that is not recognized by a majority of the workers, even if the company has made "outrageous" attempts to thwart unionization.[41] For example, firing union activists—as companies do in fully one-quarter of such campaigns, according to studies of NLRB cases—is difficult to prove, takes years to work through the courts, and takes place long after an organizing drive has lost steam.[42]

## The Representation Election and Certification

If management and the union jointly agree on the size and composition of the bargaining unit, a representation election occurs shortly thereafter. However, if management does not agree, a long delay may ensue. Since such delays, sometimes as long as five years, often erode rank-and-file union support, they work to management's advantage. In fact, roughly 45 percent of newly formed unions fail to negotiate a first contract with an employer within two years.[43] Not surprisingly, therefore, few employers agree with unions on the size and composition of the bargaining unit.

When a date for the representation election is finally established, the NLRB conducts a **secret-ballot election.** If the union receives a majority of the ballots *cast* (not a majority of votes from members of the bargaining unit), the union becomes certified as the **exclusive bargaining representative** of all employees in the unit. Once a representation election is held, regardless of the outcome, no further elections can be held in that bargaining unit for one year. The entire process is shown graphically in Figure 13–2.

### Figure 13–2

Steps involved and decisions to be made in a union organizing campaign.

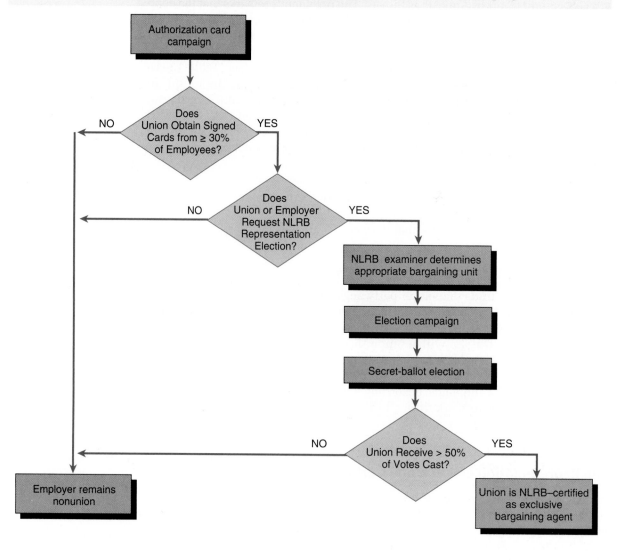

The records of elections won and lost by unions and management have changed since the 1950s. In the 1950s, unions won more than 70 percent of representation elections. More recently, however, a five-year study of more than 22,000 petitions for certification elections filed with the NLRB found that only 8,100 resulted in union election victories, and only 4,600 resulted in signed contracts within a year of victory.[44] In other words, unions need to file five petitions to gain one new bargaining unit with a signed contract.

## The Decertification of a Union

If a representation election results in union certification, the first thing many employers want to know is when and how they can *decertify* the union. Under federal law, a union has 12 months as an exclusive representative to reach a contract for the newly organized workers. After that, it risks facing decertification campaigns or challenges from rival unions. Under NLRB rules, an incumbent union can be decertified if a majority of employees within the bargaining unit vote to rescind the union's status as their collective-bargaining agent in another representation election conducted by the NLRB. Unions lose about two-thirds of decertification elections, but such elections may not be held while a contract is in effect.[45]

Because **decertification** is most likely to occur the first year or so after certification, unions will often insist on multiyear contracts. Once both parties agree to the terms and duration of the labor contract, the employer is obligated to recognize the union and to follow the provisions of the contract for the specified contract period.

In an important ruling in 2001, the NLRB held that an employer need only demonstrate a "reasonable, good faith uncertainty" that union representation is still preferred by the majority of bargaining-unit employees in order to call for a decertification election. Evidence such as the following is necessary:[46]

- Unverified statements about other employees' views of union representation.
- Employee statements expressing dissatisfaction with the union's performance.
- A majority of employees did not support the union during a strike.
- The union has become less and less active as a representative of employees.
- There was substantial turnover among employees subsequent to certification.
- The union has admitted a lack of majority support.

In 2006, for example, the Communications Workers of America won first contracts for a group of cable-industry workers after a five-year struggle. Initially the union was certified to represent 1,000 workers in 10 bargaining units. By the time the contract was finally signed, however, only 400 workers in five units remained. The others had voted the union out or else dwindled through attrition.[47] As with certification elections, the outcome of a decertification election is determined by a majority of the votes cast. Following such an election, a full year must elapse before another representation election can take place.

Once a union is legally certified as the exclusive bargaining agent for workers, the next task is to negotiate a contract that is mutually acceptable to management and labor. We examine this process in more detail next.

## COLLECTIVE BARGAINING: CORNERSTONE OF AMERICAN LABOR RELATIONS

### The Art of Negotiation

Negotiation is a two-party transaction whereby both parties intend to resolve a conflict.[48] What constitutes a good settlement of a negotiation? To be sure, the best outcome occurs when both parties win. Sometimes negotiations fall short of this ideal. A really bad bargain is one in which both parties lose, yet this is a risk that is inherent in the process. Despite its limitations, abuses, and hazards, negotiation has become an indispensable process in free societies in general and in the U.S. labor movement in particular. The fact is that negotiation is the most effective device thus far invented for realizing common interests while compromising on conflicting interests.[49] Any practice that threatens the process of collective bargaining will be resisted vigorously by organized labor.

In general, there are two postures that the parties involved in bargaining might assume: win–lose and win–win. In win–lose, or **distributive bargaining,** the goals of the parties initially are irreconcilable—or at least they appear that way. Central to the conflict is the belief that there is a limited, controlled amount of key resources available—a "fixed-pie" situation. Both parties may want to be the winner; both may want more than half of what is available.[50]

Evidence indicates that when one party adopts a distributive, contentious posture, the other party tends to reciprocate with contentious communications. To break the spiral of conflict, use mixed communications, that is, use both contentious and cooperative problem-solving communications in one speaking turn. For example, a negotiator might threaten, "If you persist in these demands we'd prefer to see you in court, where we expect the judge to find in our favor." The other party might respond with the following mixed communication: "We are prepared to let a judge decide, but we think that we will both be better off if we reach an agreement based on interests. Tell me again what your software needs are."[51]

In contrast, in win–win, or **integrative bargaining,** the goals of the parties are not mutually exclusive. If one side pursues its goals, this does not prohibit the other side from achieving its own goals. One party's gain is not necessarily at the other party's expense. The fundamental structure of an integrative bargaining situation is that it is possible for both sides to achieve their objectives.[52] While the conflict initially may appear to be win–lose to the parties, discussion and mutual exploration usually will suggest win–win alternatives.

In practice, distributive and integrative bargaining styles contrast sharply with each other. To do well in a distributive-bargaining situation, negotiators typically find it valuable to, among other things, overstate demands, withhold information, and project a stern, tough image. Effective integrative bargaining, on the other hand, involves first identifying, and then solving, problems. Effective tactics include the open exchange and sharing of information, and airing multiple voices. The problem is that it is difficult to be effective at both distributive and integrative bargaining in the same negotiations. One side might move into distributive mode, just at the moment when the other side is ready for integrative problem solving. Confronted with hard, distributive tactics, the other side might become discouraged about the possibility of integrative bargaining, making it difficult for such bargaining ever to occur.[53]

To be sure, there is no shortage of advice on negotiation tactics. Consider just four lessons from skilled negotiators:[54]

- The single biggest tool in any negotiation is the willingness to get up and walk away from the table without a deal.
- Many people listen, but few actually hear. You can't learn anything if you are doing all of the talking.
- In the long run, instincts are no match for information.
- The very best negotiators debrief themselves after every negotiation. They keep notes on their own performance as well as that of their opponents. You never know when that information may be gold.

As you should be able to appreciate by now, negotiations are full of strategy and at least a little bit of drama and gamesmanship. Thus far we have assumed that negotiation takes place face-to-face. Suppose, however, that virtual teams negotiate online. One study found that relative to face-to-face negotiations, those conducted online yielded lower levels of interpersonal trust *both* before and after negotiations. Online negotiators also were less satisfied with their outcomes and less confident in the quality of their performance, despite the absence of differences in the quality of economic outcomes relative to face-to-face negotiations. These results suggest that the greatest problems for online negotiations are associated with creating positive relationships and feelings rather than with the creation of low-quality agreements.[55]

There is one important qualifier in any discussion of negotiation strategies: national culture. Evidence indicates that managers from the United States, Japan, and Germany use different strategies to negotiate conflict. Americans value individualism, egalitarianism, and multitasking. They try to integrate their interests with those of the other party. Germans value explicit contracting, which leads them to rely on independent, objective standards as a basis for resolving conflict. Finally, the Japanese value collectivism and hierarchy and tend to resolve conflict by emphasizing status differences between the parties.[56] What is the bottom line in all this? If you want to become a win–win negotiator, be aware of the behaviors to imitate and those to avoid and make an effort to understand the cultural norms that influence the behavior of the other party.[57]

Successful collective bargaining results in an agreement that is mutually acceptable both to labor and management. Table 13–2 shows some of the major sections of a typical agreement.

Unfortunately, contract negotiations sometimes fail because the parties are not able to reach a timely and mutually acceptable settlement of the issues—economic, noneconomic, or a combination of both. When this happens, the union may strike, management may shut down operations (a lockout), or both parties may appeal for third-party involvement. Let's examine these processes in some detail.

## Table 13–2

**MAJOR SECTIONS OF A TYPICAL COLLECTIVE-BARGAINING AGREEMENT IN THE U.S.**

**Compensation:** wages, benefits, vacations, holidays, shift premiums, profit sharing.

**Employment policies and procedures:** layoff, promotion, and transfer policies; overtime and vacation rules.

**Employee rights and responsibilities:** seniority rights, job standards, workplace rules.

**Employer rights and responsibilities:** management rights, just-cause discipline and discharge, subcontracting, safety standards.

**Dispute resolution and ongoing decision making:** grievance procedures, committees, consultation, renegotiation procedures.

*Source:* Adapted from Budd, J. W. (2010). *Labor Relations: Striking a Balance* (3rd Ed.). New York, NY: McGraw-Hill, pp. 229, 230.

## BARGAINING IMPASSES: STRIKES, LOCKOUTS, OR THIRD-PARTY INVOLVEMENT

### Strikes

In every labor negotiation there exists the possibility of a strike. The right of employees to strike in support of their bargaining demands is protected by the Landrum-Griffin Act. However, there is no unqualified right to strike. A work stoppage by employees must be the result of a lawful labor dispute and not in violation of an existing agreement between management and the union. Strikers engaged in activities protected by law may not be discharged, but they may be replaced during the strike. Strikers engaged in activities that are not protected by law need not be rehired after the strike.[58]

#### Types of Strikes

As you might suspect by now, there are several different types of strikes. Let's consider the major types:

***Unfair Labor Practice Strikes.*** Unfair labor practices of the employer cause or prolong **unfair labor practice strikes.** Employees engaged in this type of strike are afforded the highest degree of protection under the act, and under most circumstances they are entitled to reinstatement once the strike ends. Management must exercise great caution in handling unfair labor practice strikes because the NLRB will become involved and company liability can be substantial.

***Economic Strikes.*** Actions by the union of withdrawing its labor in support of bargaining demands, including those for recognition or organization, are **economic strikes.** Economic strikers have limited rights to reinstatement.

***Unprotected Strikes.*** These include all remaining types of work stoppages, both lawful and unlawful, such as sit-down strikes, strikes in violation of federal laws (e.g., the prohibition of strikes by employees of the federal government), slowdowns, wildcat strikes that occur while a contract is in force, and partial walkouts. Participants in **unprotected strikes** may be discharged by their employers.

Union members have a legal right to strike in support of their bargaining demands after their collective-bargaining contract expires.

***Sympathy Strikes.*** Strikes in support of other workers on strike (e.g., when more than one union is functioning in an organization) are **sympathy strikes.** Although the NLRB and the courts have recognized the right of the sympathy striker to stand in the shoes of the primary striker, the facts of any particular situation ultimately will determine the legal status of a sympathy strike.[59]

During a strike, certain rules of conduct apply to both parties; these are summarized in Table 13–3. In addition, certain special rules apply to management. *Management must not*

- Offer extra rewards to nonstrikers or attempt to withhold the "extras" from strikers once the strike has ended and some or all strikers are reinstated.

*(continued on p. 529)*

## Table 13–3

### RULES OF CONDUCT DURING A STRIKE

- People working in or having any business with the organization have a right to pass freely in and out.
- Pickets must not block a door, passageway, driveway, crosswalk, or other entrance or exit.
- Profanity on streets and sidewalks may be a violation of state law or local ordinances.
- Company officials, with the assistance of local law-enforcement agents, should make every effort to permit individuals and vehicles to move in and out of the facility in a normal manner.
- Union officials or pickets have a right to talk to people going in or out. Intimidation, threats, and coercion are not permitted, either by verbal remarks or by physical action.
- The use of sound trucks may be regulated by state law or local ordinance with respect to noise level, location, and permit requirements.
- If acts of violence or trespassing occur on the premises, officials should file complaints or seek injunctions. If you are the object of violence, sign a warrant for the arrest of the person or persons causing the violence.
- Fighting, assault, battery, violence, threats, and intimidation are not permissible under the law. The carrying of knives, firearms, clubs, and other dangerous weapons may be prohibited by state law or local ordinance.

HR BUZZ

## WHY THERE ARE FEWER STRIKES IN THE UNITED STATES*

The number of strikes involving 1,000 workers or more has been declining for more than 50 years (see Figure 13–3). Today they occur only in about 5 percent of all labor-management negotiations. To a large extent this is due to some major economic and social changes that are prompting both companies and union leaders to reassess their tactics. Here are two of them:

1. Companies have proven their willingness to hire replacement workers and wait out strikers. With only 6.9 percent of private-sector Americans belonging to a union, strikes don't carry the same resonance with the public as they did in the past. Members of the public who are most likely to support a strike support unions in general, and believe that the contract offered to the strikers was unfair. At the same time, many companies have little desire to provoke a fight, especially during times of economic weakness and pressure on profits. While that may appear to give unions an advantage at the bargaining table, unions also recognize the reality that companies may need concessions to prosper. In short, tough demands are being made on both sides.

2. Technology and global markets make it easier than ever for big companies to displace highly paid but low-skilled workers—either through outsourcing or by relocating plants to cheaper, foreign sites, such as Mexico. If U.S. workers do go on strike, employers use replacement workers, thereby blunting the overall effectiveness of a strike. One reason for the drop in membership at the United Auto Workers, from a peak of 1.5 million in the mid-1970s to 376,000 at the end of 2010, is that much of the work traditionally done in automakers' own factories has been outsourced to suppliers' plants, which tend to be non-union. Any labor disruption would affect not only the union members, but thousands more hourly workers in the factories that supply the manufacturers.

*Sources: Katz et al., 2008, op. cit. See also Kelloway, E. K., Francis, L., Catano, V. M., and Dupre, K. E. (2008). Third-party support for strike action. *Journal of Applied Psychology* 93, pp. 806–817. See also Kiley, D. (2007, Dec. 24). Labor's new roll of the dice. *BusinessWeek,* p. 37. See also Tejada, C. (2003, Aug. 22). Labor talks turn into marathons: Wary of economic climate, unions, businesses strive to avoid strikes, lockouts. *The Wall Street Journal,* pp. A3, A10.

### Figure 13–3

Number of work stoppages involving 1,000 employees or more.

(*Source:* Bureau of Labor Statistics. Work stoppages involving 1,000 or more workers, 1947–2010. Retrieved from *www.bls.gov/news. release/wkstp.t01.htm* on August 18, 2011.)

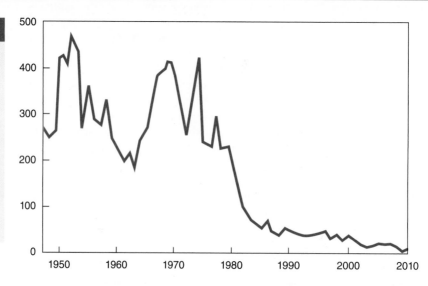

- Threaten nonstrikers or strikers.
- Promise benefits to strikers in an attempt to end the strike or to undermine the union.
- Threaten employees with discharge for taking part in a lawful strike.
- Discharge nonstrikers who refuse to take over a striker's job.

## When the Strike Is Over

The period of time immediately after a strike is critical, because an organization's problems are not over when the strike is settled. There is the problem of conflict between strikers and their replacements (if replacements were hired) and the re-accommodation of strikers to the workplace. After an economic strike is settled, the method of reinstatement is best protected by a written memorandum of agreement with the union that outlines the intended procedure. A key point of consideration in any strike aftermath is misconduct by some strikers. To refuse reinstatement for such strikers following an economic strike, management must be able to present evidence (e.g., photographs) to prove the misconduct.

The most important human aspect at the end of the strike is the restoration of harmonious working relations as soon as possible so that full operations can be resumed. A letter, a video, or a speech to employees welcoming them back to work can help this process along, as can meetings with supervisors indicating that no resentment or ill-will is to be shown toward returning strikers. In practice, this may be difficult to do. However, keep these points in mind:

- Nothing is gained by allowing vindictiveness of any type in any echelon of management.
- The burden of maintaining healthy labor-management relations now lies with the organization.
- There is always another negotiation ahead, and rancor has no place at any bargaining table.[60]

## Lockouts

A **lockout** may occur when a collective-bargaining agreement has expired. If the parties cannot agree on a contract, an employer may legally *lock out* its employees in order to put economic pressure on a union to settle a contract on terms favorable to the employer. Lockouts are legitimate employer tactics to decrease union power in situations where the lockout is done to avoid economic loss or to preserve customer goodwill.[61] This is what the National Football League's owners did when the collective-bargaining agreement with the players expired in 2011.[62] The lockout lasted 159 days, with both sides making concessions in order to reach a 10-year collective-bargaining agreement. The lockout put heavy pressure on both sides, but especially on the players because their playing lives average just 3.6 years. Missing a year of competition and salary has huge consequences on lifetime earnings.[63]

It is legal for a company to replace the locked-out workers with temporary replacements in order to continue operations during the lockout. However, the use of permanent replacements (without first consulting the union) is not permissible, according to the National Labor Relations Board, because such an action would completely destroy the bargaining unit and represent an unlawful withdrawal of recognition of a duly designated union.[64]

## Third-Party Involvement

A **bargaining impasse** occurs when the parties are unable to move further toward settlement. However, because there is no clear formula to determine if or when an impasse in negotiations has been reached, litigation often ensues, and a judge must decide the issue.[65] In an effort to resolve the impasse, a neutral third party may become involved. In most private-sector negotiations, the parties have to agree voluntarily before any third-party involvement can be imposed on them. Because employees in the public sector are prohibited by law from striking, the use of third parties is more prevalent there.[66]

Three general types of third-party involvement are common: mediation, fact-finding, and interest arbitration. Each becomes progressively more constraining on the freedom of the parties.

### Mediation

**Mediation** is a process by which a neutral third party attempts to help the parties in dispute to reach a settlement of the issues that divide them. The neutral third party does not act as a judge to decide the resolution of the dispute (a process referred to as *arbitration*).[67] Rather, mediation involves persuading, opening communications, allowing readjustment and reassessment of bargaining stances, and making procedural suggestions (e.g., scheduling, conducting, and controlling meetings; establishing or extending deadlines).

Mediators have two restrictions on their power: (1) They are involved by invitation only, and (2) their advice lacks even so much as the umpire's option of throwing someone out of the game. However, mediation has some important advantages. It is a face-saving procedure in that each side can make concessions to the other without appearing weak. Disputants often see mediation procedures as fair, and this helps account for its 60 to 80 percent settlement rate.[68] Settlement rates tend to be higher when mediators are perceived by disputants as having high expertise,[69] and when both parties trust the mediator.[70] Hostility between the parties substantially reduces the possibility of an agreement.

### Fact-Finding

**Fact-finding** is a dispute-resolution mechanism that is commonly used in the public sector at the state and local government levels to help resolve an impasse in negotiation. In a fact-finding procedure, each party submits whatever information it believes is relevant to a resolution of the dispute. A neutral fact-finder then examines the evidence and prepares a report on the facts. The assumption is that a neutral report will bring sufficient pressure on the parties to induce them to accept the recommendations of the fact finder or to use the fact-finder's report as a basis for a negotiated settlement.[71]

Actually, the term *fact-finding* is a misnomer because fact-finders often proceed, with statutory authority, to render a public recommendation of a reasonable settlement. In this respect, fact-finding is similar to mediation. However, neither fact-finding nor mediation necessarily results in a contract between management and labor. Consequently, the parties often resort to arbitration of a dispute, either as a matter of law (*compulsory arbitration*) or by mutual agreement between union and management (*interest arbitration*).

## Interest Arbitration

Like fact-finding, **interest arbitration** is used primarily in the public sector. However, arbitration differs considerably from mediation and fact-finding. As one author noted: "While mediation assists the parties to reach their own settlement, arbitration hears the positions of both and decides on binding settlement terms. While fact-finding would recommend a settlement, arbitration dictates it."[72]

Interest arbitration is controversial because imposition of a settlement eliminates the need for the parties to negotiate on their own. If they reach an impasse, settlement by an outsider is certain.[73] While the use of interest arbitration in the public sector has reduced the probability of strikes more than fact-finding, there is little evidence of excessive use of interest arbitration. Even in systems that have been followed for as long as 30 years, the rate of cases going to interest arbitration rarely has exceeded 25 percent. The overall effect of interest arbitration on wage levels appears to be modest—5 to 10 percent higher than wages in jurisdictions where arbitration is not available.[74]

---

## DOES THE ADA OVERRIDE SENIORITY RIGHTS?

LEGALITIES

Does the requirement in the Americans with Disabilities Act for "reasonable accommodation" supersede collectively bargained seniority rights? A federal appeals court ruled on this issue in a case that involved an employee of Consolidated Rail Corporation who was diagnosed with epilepsy. Medical restrictions prevented him from returning to his night-time shift. So he sought to invoke a provision in the collective-bargaining agreement that permitted an employee with a disability, upon written agreement of the employer and the union, to "bump" a more senior employee or to occupy a more senior position and be immune from bumping by more senior employees. When the union refused to sign the agreement, the employee brought suit under the ADA.

The court rejected the employee's argument, finding that "collective-bargaining seniority rights have a preexisting special status in the law and that Congress to date has shown no intent to alter this status by the duties created by the ADA." in fact, the majority of courts have held that the employer need not violate a seniority clause in a collective-bargaining agreement in order to give a light-duty job to a worker with a disability, as opposed to the most senior worker.[a]

---

[a]Postol, L. P. (2008, Dec. 22). January 2009: ADAAA will result in renewed emphasis on reasonable accommodations. *Society for Human Resource Management*. Retrieved from *www.shrm.org/Publications/LegalReport/Pages/ADAAAOverview.aspx* on August 18, 2011. See also Union contracts and the ADA (1996, Nov./Dec.). *Mountain States Employers Council Bulletin*, p. 2.

---

## ADMINISTRATION OF THE COLLECTIVE-BARGAINING AGREEMENT

To many union and management officials, the real test of effective labor relations comes after the agreement is signed, that is, in its day-to-day administration. At that point, the major concern of the union is to obtain in practice the employee rights that management has granted on paper. The major concern of management is to establish its right to manage the business and to keep operations

## Table 13–4

**FORMS OF UNION SECURITY AND THEIR LEGAL STATUS IN RIGHT-TO-WORK STATES**

|  | Legal | Illegal |
|---|:---:|:---:|
| **Closed shop.** An individual must join the union that represents employees in order to be considered for employment. |  | X |
| **Union shop.** As a condition of continued employment, an individual must join the union that represents employees after a probationary period (typically a minimum of 30 days). |  | X |
| **Preferential shop.** Union members are given preference in hiring. |  | X |
| **Agency shop.** Employees need not join the union that represents them, but, in lieu of dues, they must pay a service charge for representation. |  | X |
| **Maintenance of membership.** An employee must remain a member of the union once he or she joins. |  | X |
| **Checkoff.** An employee may request that union dues be deducted from his or her pay and be sent directly to the union. | X |  |

running.[75] A key consideration for both is the form of union security that governs conditions of employment.

### Union-Security Clauses

Section 14b of the Taft-Hartley Act enables states to enact **right-to-work laws** that prohibit compulsory union membership (after a probationary period) as a condition of continued employment. Table 13–4 illustrates the forms that such **union-security clauses** can take and indicates that most of them are illegal in the 22 states that have passed right-to-work laws. In the remaining 28 non–right-to-work states, unions are allowed to negotiate union- or agency-shop provisions into their contracts with employers.[76]

### Grievance Procedures in the Unionized Firm

Occasionally during the life of a contract, disputes arise about the interpretation, application, or enforcement of the collective-bargaining agreement. Under these circumstances, an aggrieved party may file a grievance. A **grievance** is an alleged violation of the rights of workers on the job.[77] A formal process known as a **grievance procedure** is then invoked to help the parties resolve the dispute. Grievance procedures are the keystone of labor-management relations because of their ability to resolve disputed issues while work continues without litigation, strikes, or other radical dispute-resolution strategies.[78]

In addition to providing a formal mechanism for resolving disputes, the grievance procedure defines and narrows the nature of the complaint. Thus, each grievance must be expressed in writing. The written grievance identifies the grievant, when the incident leading to the grievance occurred (it could, of course, be ongoing), and where the incident happened. The written statement

**Figure 13–4**

Example of a formal grievance procedure in a unionized firm.

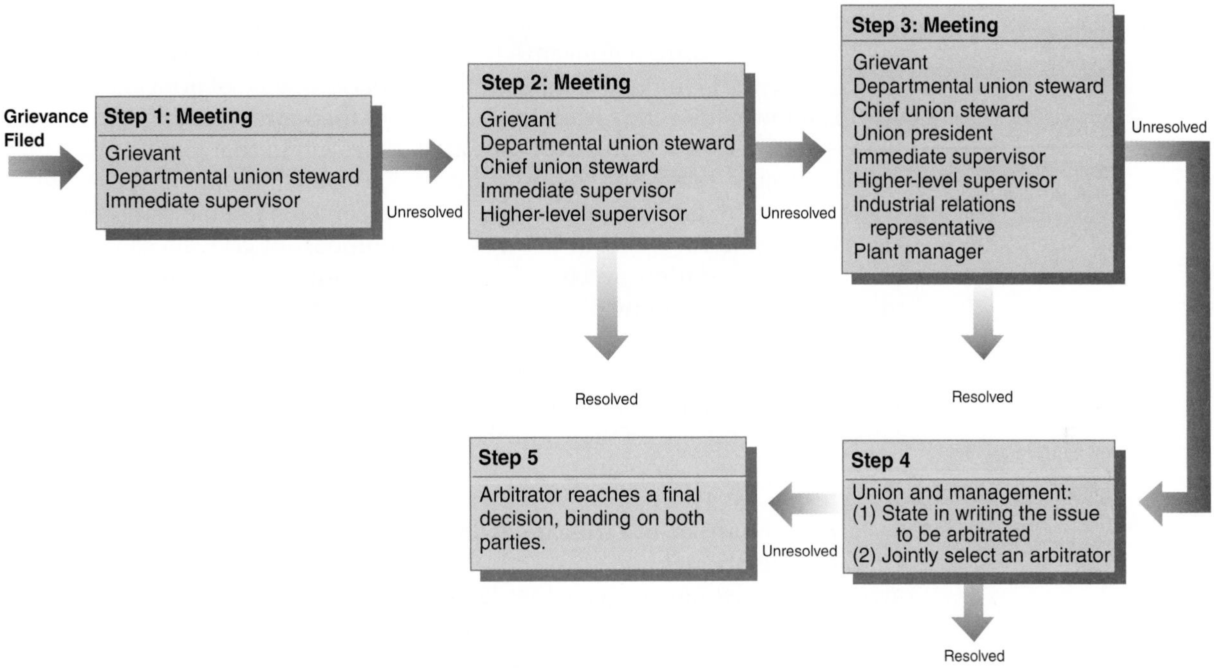

also indicates why the complaint is considered a grievance and what the grievant thinks should be done about the matter.[79] A typical grievance procedure in a unionized firm works as shown in Figure 13–4. As the figure indicates, unresolved grievances proceed progressively to higher and higher levels of management and union representation and culminate in voluntary, binding arbitration. Specific time limits for management's decision and the union's approval are normally imposed at each step, for example, 3 days for each party at step 1, 5 days for each party at steps 2 and 3, and 10 days for each party at step 4.

Typical grievance rates in unionized employers are about 10 per 100 employees per year. The vast majority of those are resolved without resorting to arbitration. In fact, for every 100 grievances, only about 2 percent require arbitration to resolve them—and that takes time. How much time? One study found for example, that the average length of time between the request for an arbitrator and the award being issued was 401 days.[80] Grievance-administration can be expensive as well. Thus the American Postal Workers Union allocates fully 20 percent of its members' dues to the costs of processing grievances.[81]

### Resolving Grievances

Unions and management each win about half the time. However, unions tend to win more grievances related to such issues as the denial of sick benefits, termination, transfer, suspension, and disciplinary memoranda. Ordinarily, the burden of proof in a grievance proceeding is on the union. Because fewer issues of interpretation are involved in the areas that unions usually win, this pattern of grievance resolution is not surprising.[82]

In summary, there are two key advantages to the grievance procedure. First, it ensures that the complaints and problems of workers can be heard, rather than simply allowed to fester. Second, grievance procedures provide formal mechanisms to ensure due process for all parties. Research indicates that employees who have access to such a system are more willing to continue working for their organizations after filing a grievance than are employees who do not have access to such a system.[83] On the other hand, the job performance of grievance filers is likely to be lower after they learn the outcome of their grievances.[84]

The process is not completely objective, however, in that factors other than merit sometimes determine the outcome of a grievance. Some of these factors include the cost of granting a grievance, the perceived need for management to placate disgruntled workers or to settle large numbers of grievances in order to expedite the negotiation process,[85] and the grievant's work history (good performance, long tenure, few disciplinary incidents).[86]

What is the role of the line manager in all this? It is to know and understand the collective-bargaining contract, as well as federal and state labor laws. Above all, whether you agree or disagree with the terms of the contract, it is legally binding on both labor and management. Respect its provisions, and manage according to the spirit as well as the letter of the contract.

### Does a High Number of Grievances Indicate Poor Labor Relations?

Conventional wisdom suggests that large numbers of grievances signal an unhealthy organizational climate. This is often the case, as indicated by the number of grievances pending at the U.S. Postal Service: an average of 27.5 per 100 workers over a six-year period. Postal workers file grievances to protest issues such as the elimination of paid wash-up time, the installation of monitoring equipment that tracks their movements, or changes to different work shifts. They also file grievances because they have few other ways to air their gripes. The massive number of grievances stifles productivity and innovation, and it is terribly expensive. Just keeping the grievance system going takes an army of 300 outside arbitrators and costs about $200 million a year.[87]

On the other hand, a six-year longitudinal study of grievances filed at a utility company in the western United States reached a different conclusion, namely, that a large number of grievances signals the presence of a friendly system that is easily accessible and time efficient. At a minimum, it seems that high grievance rates do not invariably indicate poor labor relations.[88]

### Grievance Arbitration

**Grievance arbitration** is used widely by management and labor to settle disputes arising out of and during the term of a labor contract.[89] Figure 13–4 shows that compulsory, binding arbitration is the final stage of the grievance process. It is also used as an alternative to a work stoppage, and it is used to ensure labor peace for the duration of a labor contract. Arbitrators may be chosen from a list of qualified people supplied by the American Arbitration Association or the Federal Mediation and Conciliation Service.

Arbitration hearings are quasi-judicial proceedings. Both parties may file prehearing briefs, along with lists of witnesses to be called. Witnesses are cross-examined, and documentary evidence may be introduced. However, arbitrators are not bound by the formal rules of evidence, as they would be in a court of law.

Following the hearing, the parties may each submit briefs to reiterate their positions, evidence supporting them, and proposed decisions. The arbitrator considers the evidence, the contract clause in dispute, and the powers granted the arbitrator under the labor agreement. The arbitrator then issues a decision. In the rare instances where a losing party refuses to honor the arbitrator's decision, the decision can be enforced by taking that party to federal court.[90]

Generally an arbitration award cannot be appealed in court simply because one party believes the arbitrator made a mistake in interpreting an agreement. Courts have held that arbitrator awards are extensions of labor contracts, and court deference is the rule.[91]

We noted earlier that only 11.9 percent of U.S. workers belong to unions. To put this issue into perspective, let us examine rates of union membership in other countries.

## UNION MEMBERSHIP IN COUNTRIES OTHER THAN THE UNITED STATES

Figure 13–5 shows current union membership as a percentage of the workforce in 12 countries. Union membership is highest in Sweden and Finland and then drops off considerably in Western European countries: 23.5 percent in the United Kingdom, 20 percent in Germany, 16 percent in Spain, and 8 percent in France. Among Asian countries, unions represent 18.5 percent of

### Figure 13–5

Percentage of union members in 12 countries.

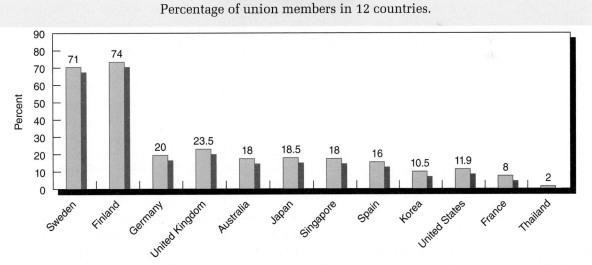

*Sources:* Fulton, L. (2011). Worker representation in Europe. Labour Research Department and ETUI. Retrieved from *www. worker-participation.eu/National-Industrial-Relations/Countries* on August 19, 2011. See also Australian Bureau of Statstics. (2011, May 25). Employee earnings, benefits and trade union membership, Australia, Aug.2010. Retrieved from *www.abs.gov.au/ ausstats/abs@.nsf/mf/6310.0* on August 19, 2011. See also Yoshikane, A. (2009, Dec. 23). Uptick in Japan's union members mirrors U.S. trend. Retrieved from *www.inthesetimes.com/working/entry/5351/uptick_in_japans_union_members_mirrors_u.s._ trend/* on August 19, 2011. See also Korea International Labour Foundation. (2009, Nov. 24). Union density and membership. Retrieved from *www.koilaf.org/KFeng/engStatistics/bbs_read_dis.php?board_no=212&page=1&keyField=&keyWord=* on August 19, 2011. Yearbook of statistics in Singapore, 2011. Retrieved from *www.singstat.gov.sg/pubn/reference/yos11/yos2011. pdf* on August 19, 2011.

the workforce in Japan, 18 percent in Singapore, 10.5 percent in Korea, and just 2 percent in Thailand. In Australia, 18 percent of the workforce belongs to unions. Unions remain powerful forces in wage-determination processes, largely because of wage premiums in unionized firms and the spillover effect on nonunion employers. Our next section explores these issues in more detail.

## UNION WAGE PREMIUMS AND THE SPILLOVER EFFECT

In the United States, workers represented by unions are estimated to earn wages that are approximately 15 percent higher than comparable nonunion workers.[92] For example, unionized aircraft assembly workers in Washington State earn an average of $26 an hour. Their nonunion counterparts in South Carolina make $15 an hour. This disparity made South Carolina more attractive to Boeing as it built a second assembly line for the 787 Dreamliner.[93] Of course, these wage differentials reflect a variety of influences, in addition to coverage by a collective-bargaining agreement, such as occupation, firm size, geographical region, and industry. For example, some of the traditional union strongholds, such as construction and trucking, enjoy much larger union–nonunion differentials than do less unionized segments such as services and utilities.[94]

What about the gap between worker wages and what their managers are paid in union and nonunion firms? Recent evidence suggests that the gap between these two groups is 23 percent smaller in unionized firms.[95] Interestingly, the narrowing does not occur at the expense of lower or even constant wages for managers, combined with higher union wages. Rather, managers in union firms receive higher wages than do those in nonunion firms, perhaps in an effort to maintain internal equity. Apparently the gap narrows because workers' wages increase faster than managers' wages in unionized firms.[96]

The impact of unions in general would be understated if we did not account for what is called the **spillover effect;** that is, employers seek to avoid unionization by offering workers the wages, benefits, and working conditions that rival unionized firms do. The nonunion employer continues to stay that way, and workers receive the spillover of rewards already obtained by their unionized counterparts. Another aspect of spillover occurs when U.S. unions attempt to increase their influence on U.S.-based multinational corporations by assisting foreign unions in organizing the corporations' offshore employees, particularly in low-wage, developing economies.[97]

| *Human Resource Management in Action: Conclusion* | *RESTRUCTURING THROUGH UNION-MANAGEMENT COLLABORATION* |
| --- | --- |

Make no mistake about it: The recent popularity of cooperation stems largely from the sweeping changes in the economic environment that have occurred. Another reason is new technology—the Internet, factory automation, robotics, and more modern production systems. Cooperation offers a pragmatic approach to problems that threaten the survival of companies, the jobs and income security of their employees, and the institutional future of their unions. Progressive unions such as the United Auto workers (UAW), Service Employees International Union

# IMPACT OF POOR LABOR RELATIONS ON PRODUCTIVITY, QUALITY OF WORK LIFE, AND THE BOTTOM LINE

Do workers exert more effort and due diligence if they feel they are treated fairly, and with dignity and respect? Conversely, does a poor labor relations climate affect product quality? Both economic and psychological research suggests that the answer is yes.[a] Unfortunately, the consequences may be deadly, as indicated in an analysis by two Princeton University economists of Bridgestone/Firestone tire production at the firm's Decatur, Illinois, plant when labor and management were battling.[b]

When a previous contract expired on April 1, 1994, employees worked for three months without a contract before going on strike. In negotiations, Bridgestone/Firestone broke with its industry by moving from an 8-hour to a 12-hour shift that would rotate between days and nights, as well as cutting pay for new hires by 30 percent, cutting wages for most job classifications by $5.34 per hour (to about $12 per hour), reducing incentive pay for piecework, cutting two weeks of vacation for senior workers, and requiring hourly workers to contribute to their health care costs. It is noteworthy that the company insisted on such large concessions during a period when the overall economy was growing.

Using replacements, the company imposed 12-hour shifts and kept production going. The union workers surrendered in May 1995, returning under the terms originally demanded by Bridgestone/Firestone. Although the strike officially ended in May 1995, the labor dispute continued until a final settlement was reached in December 1996. For nearly three years, therefore, from April 1994 to December 1996, union workers at the Decatur plant either were on strike or working without a contract. During this period tires were produced by 1,048 replacement workers, union members who crossed the picket line, management, and recalled strikers.

The Princeton analysis is compelling because three different sets of data all point the same way: (1) Firestone tires made in Decatur during the labor strike were 376 percent more likely to prompt a complaint to the National Highway Transportation Safety Administration than tires made at two comparison plants. In times of labor peace, Decatur tires were 14 percent *less* likely to prompt a complaint. (2) Customers with tires made in Decatur during the dispute were more than 250 percent as likely to seek compensation from Firestone for property damage or injury blamed on faulty tires than were customers of tires made there during more peaceful times. (3) Tires made in Decatur during the labor dispute did worse on laboratory stress tests that Firestone conducted than those made at other times or at other plants. The consequences were lethal, for the report concluded that more than 40 lives were lost as a result of the excessive number of problem tires produced in Decatur during the labor dispute.

Is there a lesson to be learned in all of this? According to one observer, ". . . squeezing workers, even in an age of weakened unions, can be bad management, especially when employers abruptly change the rules. A company can shut a plant and successfully hire lower-paid workers elsewhere. And if management convinces workers that the alternative to wage cuts is unemployment, workers may go along. But brute force can backfire, and the consequences can be severe."[c]

[a] Greenberg, J. (2011). Organizational justice: The dynamics of fairness in the workplace. In S. Zedeck (Ed.), *APA Handbook of Industrial and Organizational Psychology,* Vol. 3. Washington, DC: American Psychological Association, pp. 271–327. See also Fehr, F., and Gächter, S. (2000). Fairness and retaliation. *Journal of Economic Perspectives* 14(3), pp. 159–182.

[b] Krueger, A. B., and Mas, A. (2002, Jan.). Strikes, scabs, and tread separations: Labor strife and the production of defective Bridgestone/Firestone tires. Retrieved from *www.irs.princeton.edu/pubs/pdfs/461a.pdf* on January 11, 2002.

[c] Wessel, D. (2002, Jan. 10). The hidden cost of labor strife. *The Wall Street Journal,* p. A1.

## IMPLICATIONS FOR MANAGEMENT PRACTICE

In a globalized, technology-based world, a distributive (win–lose) orientation toward labor is simply inefficient. Worker demographics, along with the growing importance of labor disputes and alliances across the globe, help shape the interactions between unions and employers. Multinational companies that add operations in major offshoring destinations are being affected by unionization trends and labor disputes in those countries. The lesson? Whether you are managing people in Boston, Budapest, or Beijing, view your employees as a source of potential competitive advantage. Treat them with dignity and respect, and they will respond in kind. As a cover of *Fast Company* magazine noted, "The best leaders know where all great companies start. (It's the people, stupid!)"[a]

[a]Cited in Hitt, M. (2001, Aug.). The human capital advantage in the new millennium. Paper presented at the Society for Human Resource Management Foundation, Thought Leaders Conference, Washington, DC.

(SEIU), and the United Steelworkers (USW) are at the forefront of a revolutionary change in the way unions view cooperation with management.

That was exactly the case with the USW-Goodyear agreements in 2006 and 2009, of which the latter runs through 2013. The USW offered to slash labor costs by $555 million over three years and to cut staffing levels at five plants. In exchange, Goodyear promised to keep—and invest in—all but two of its U.S. factories and to limit imports from its factories in Brazil and Asia. The company also promised to go along with a more aggressive debt-restructuring timetable that the USW's Wall Street advisers recommended as a way to rein in management. In return, Goodyear agreed to institute profit sharing and to invest $600 million over the next four years in its USW facilities to make them more efficient and productive.

In this new era of collaboration, here are five tips from former SEIU president Andy Stern on how labor and management can work together more effectively:

1. *Relationships are not a matter of chance; they are a matter of choice.* We don't see our employers as enemies. We need to build successful employers—to understand markets, competition, and where we can be helpful in increasing creativity, innovation, and entrepreneurial activity. To do that, everyone needs to be involved, to have a voice, and to share in the employers' success.
2. *Approach partnerships by making "finding a solution" a higher priority than placing blame.*
3. *Learn to disagree without being disagreeable.*
4. *Offer incentives that encourage others to take prudent risks.*
5. *Keep an open mind, rather than an open mouth, be willing to change, and stay focused on shared goals.*

As we have seen, the business world has changed dramatically, largely due to changes in technology and global competition. If U.S. labor leaders let today's opportunities for labor-management cooperation slip by, they may not get another chance to be part of the solution to the continuing challenge to improve productivity, quality of work life, and profits.

## SUMMARY

At a general level, the goal of unions is to improve economic and other conditions of employment. Although unions have been successful over the years in achieving these goals, more recently they have been confronted with challenges that have led to membership losses. Unions are trying to reverse that decline by organizing workers in different industries (e.g., casinos, museums, services), many of whom are white-collar workers (e.g., physicians, nuclear engineers, psychologists, immigration judges).

Six features characterize the U.S. industrial relations system: exclusive representation, collective agreements that embody a sharp distinction between negotiation and interpretation of an agreement, decentralized collective bargaining, relatively high union dues and large union staffs, opposition by both large and small employers to union organization, and a government role that is relatively passive in dispute resolution and highly legalistic in administrative proceedings and in the courts.

The National Labor Relations Board, created by the Wagner Act, supervises union organizing campaigns and representation elections. If the union wins, it becomes the sole bargaining agent for employees. Collective bargaining is the cornerstone of the U.S. labor movement, and anything that threatens its continued viability will be resisted vigorously by organized labor.

Unfortunately, bargaining sometimes reaches an impasse, at which point the parties may resort to a strike (workers) or a lockout (management). Alternatively, the parties may request third-party intervention in the form of mediation, fact-finding, or interest arbitration. In the public sector, such intervention is usually required.

Occasionally during the life of a contract, disputes arise about the interpretation of the collective-bargaining agreement. Under these circumstances, an aggrieved party may file a grievance. A grievance is an alleged violation of the rights of workers on the job. A formal process known as a grievance procedure is then invoked to help the parties resolve the dispute. Compulsory, binding arbitration is the final stage of the grievance process. It is also used as an alternative to a work stoppage, and it is used to ensure labor peace for the duration of a labor contract.

Unionized workers still enjoy a wage premium over their nonunion counterparts, but factors other than union status per se may account for the difference. A spillover effect occurs when nonunion employers raise compensation in an effort to maintain their nonunion status, or when U.S. unions attempt to increase their influence on U.S.-based multinational corporations by assisting foreign unions in organizing the corporations' offshore employees. Finally, as the chapter-opening vignette illustrated, labor and management are cooperating more often in an effort to enhance the productivity and overall competitiveness of their enterprises. In the current climate of global competition and the migration of technology and capital across borders, this seems more appropriate than the old adversarial win–lose approach.

## KEY TERMS

| | |
|---|---|
| labor union | unfair labor practice strike |
| exclusive representation | economic strike |
| conspiracy doctrine | unprotected strike |
| sit-down strike | sympathy strike |
| Change to Win | lockout |
| secondary boycott | bargaining impasse |
| free-speech clause | mediation |
| authorization cards | fact-finding |
| card check | interest arbitration |
| bargaining unit | right-to-work laws |
| community of interest | union-security clauses |
| secret-ballot election | grievance |
| exclusive bargaining representative | grievance procedure |
| decertification | grievance arbitration |
| distributive bargaining | spillover effect |
| integrative bargaining | |

## DISCUSSION QUESTIONS

**13–1.** Are the roles of labor and management inherently adversarial?

**13–2.** Discuss the rights and obligations of unions and management during a union-organizing drive.

**13–3.** Why is it so difficult to be effective at both distributive and integrative bargaining in the course of the same negotiations?

**13–4.** What are the key features of the U.S. industrial relations system?

**13–5.** Compare and contrast mediation, interest arbitration, and grievance arbitration.

**13–6.** Why is it in the best interests of management and labor to work together? Or is it?

## APPLYING YOUR KNOWLEDGE

---

*Exercise 13–1*     ***Contract Negotiations at Moulton Machine Shop***

Collective bargaining is the cornerstone of American labor relations. Face-to-face negotiations involving give-and-take on the part of both management and labor representatives are an inherent part of our present system. It is through these negotiations that both sides attempt to understand the positions of the other and attempt to persuade the other side of the fairness of their own demands.

The purpose of this exercise is for you to experience the collective-bargaining process and to gain an awareness of the nature and complexity of labor negotiations.

### Background Information

Moulton Machine Shop is a 60-year-old shop located near Lake Erie in Pennsylvania. The company manufactures a wide variety of made-to-order products, but its primary business is the repair of mechanical airplane parts and components, a business that it conducts on an international basis. The firm has developed a reputation for quality and timely work on difficult machining projects. The mostly blue-collar workforce at Moulton consists of about 200 workers who were organized 40 years ago by the International Machinists Union (IMU). The labor-relations climate at Moulton has been fairly good over the past 20 years (after a rather stormy beginning), with no strikes in the last 9 years. In the past two years, however, the number of grievances has increased substantially.

Recent economic conditions have been difficult for Moulton. Over the past five years, increased competition from lower-priced, foreign-based machine shops has pruned Moulton's profit margins. Overall, sales are down about 10 percent compared with projections made earlier in the year. Moulton's management believes that competition will intensify in the near future, creating even more problems for the firm. The union is aware of the financial situation at Moulton and is sympathetic, but it has been very clear in its overtures to management that it intends to fight for an improved contract for its members because they have fallen behind equivalent workers in recent years.

## CURRENT CONTRACT PROVISIONS

| Clause | Current contract |
| --- | --- |
| Wages | Average hourly wage is $20.66. |
| Benefits | Company-paid life insurance and a $100-deductible medical insurance plan. |
| Overtime | Time and a half. |
| Layoffs | A 2-week notice is required to lay off any union member who has been at Moulton more than 2 months. |
| Vacations | 2 weeks for all employees except those with over 20 years' service, who receive 3 weeks. |
| Holidays | 9 paid per year. |
| Sick leave | 4 paid days per year unless verified by doctor, in which case, can be up to 10 days. |
| Length of contract | 2 years. |

## Additional Information

1. Hourly wage rates for union members doing similar work elsewhere in the local vicinity average $22.73.
2. A $100-deductible dental insurance plan would cost about $75 per employee.
3. Overtime averaged 185 hours per employee last year.
4. Among competitors, the most frequent vacation, holiday, and sick-leave schedules are as follows: (1) two weeks' vacation for starters, three weeks after 10 years of service, and four weeks after 25 years; (b) 10 paid holidays per year; and (c) six paid sick-leave days per year (although there is a wide variation here, with a few firms having no paid sick leave at all).
5. Contract length at similar firms varies from one to three years.

## Procedure

Divide the class into groups of three. Each group consists of a union negotiator, a management negotiator, and an observer. The instructor will provide a role statement for each negotiator. These role statements should not be shared with the other negotiator or with the observer. Each group's task is to negotiate a contract between Moulton Machine Shop and the IMU. Your instructor will tell you how much time you have available for this task. It is important that you settle this contract in the limited time available so that you can avert a costly strike.

As the negotiations proceed, observers should record significant events. (Use the sample observation form shown below.) When the negotiations end, observers will be asked to report the final agreed-upon contract provisions to the rest of the class and to describe the process by which the negotiations took place in each group.

---

### CONTRACT NEGOTIATIONS OBSERVATION FORM

| Clause | Final settlement |
| --- | --- |
| Wages | _____ |
| Benefits | _____ |
| Overtime | _____ |
| Layoffs | _____ |
| Vacations | _____ |
| Holidays | _____ |
| Sick leave | _____ |
| Length of contract | _____ |
| Other provisions | _____ |

---

### Questions

1. How do the negotiations begin? Which side talks the most in the beginning? Does each side have a clear understanding of the purpose of the negotiations?
2. What behaviors of the negotiators seem either to bring the parties closer together or to drive them farther apart?
3. How does the climate of the negotiations change over time? Which side talks the most as the negotiations wear on? Do the parties agree more or less as time passes?
4. How do the negotiations end? Are the parties friendly with each other? Do they both seem committed to the final solution? Are future union-management relations likely to get better or worse as a result of this agreement?

## REFERENCES

1. Budd, J. W. (2010). *Labor Relations* (3rd Ed.). New York, NY: McGraw-Hill.
2. Daniels, C. (2004 , May 17). Up against the Walmart. *Fortune,* pp. 112–120.
3. Bunn, E., quoted in Whitford, D. (2007, Sept. 17). UAW's latest gamble. *BusinessWeek,* p. 27.
4. Kristol, I. (1978, Oct. 23). Understanding trade unionism. *The Wall Street Journal,* p. 28.
5. Kirkland, R. (2006, Oct. 16). The new face of labor. *Fortune,* pp. 122–132. See also Fiorito, J. (2001). Human resource management practices and worker desires for union representation. *Journal of Labor Research* 22(2), pp. 35–54.

6. Freeman, R. B., and Rogers, J. (1999). *What Workers Want.* Ithaca, NY: ILR Press.

7. Bernstein, A. (2005). Big labor's day of reckoning. *BusinessWeek,* pp. 65, 66. See also Whitford, D. (2001, July 23). Carpenter gives AFL-CIO labor pains. *Fortune,* pp. 44, 46. See also Kochan, T. A. (1979). How American workers view labor unions. *Monthly Labor Review* 103(4), pp. 23–31.

8. Bureau of Labor Statistics. (2011, Jan. 21). Union members—2010. Retrieved from *www.bls.gov/news.release/pdf/union2.pdf* on August 17, 2011.

9. Hananel, S. (2011, March 3). AFL-CIO president sees possible union resurgence growing out of clash in Wisconsin. *Decatur Daily.* Retrieved from *www.decaturdaily.com/stories/AFL-CIO-president-sees-possible-union-resurgence-growing-out-of-clash-in-Wisconsin,76043?content_source=&category_id=&search_filter=AFL-CIO+president+sees+possible+union+resurgence+growing+out+of+clash+in+Wisconsin* on August 17, 2011.

10. Maher, K. (2005, Sept. 27). The new union worker. *The Wall Street Journal,* pp. B1, B11.

11. Schmitt, J., and Warner, K. (2009, Nov.). *The Changing Face of Labor, 1983–2008.* Washington, DC: Center for Economic and Policy Research. See also Mellor, S. (1995). Gender composition and gender representation in local unions: Relationships between women's participation in local office and women's participation in local activities. *Journal of Applied Psychology* 80, pp. 706–720.

12. Maher, K. (2007, Jan. 22). Are unions relevant? *The Wall Street Journal,* p. R5. See also Greenhouse, S. (2000, Oct. 24). Labor law hinders unions, leaders say. *The Denver Post,* p. 20A.

13. Bureau of Labor Statistics. Employee tenure in 2010. Retrieved from *www.bls.gov/news.release/pdf/tenure.pdf* on August 17, 2011.

14. Fields, G., Aeppel, T., Maher, K., and Adamy, J. (2005, July 27). Reinventing the union. *The Wall Street Journal,* pp. B1, B2.

15. Fields et al., 2005, op. cit.

16. Wysocki, B., Jr., Maher, K., and Glader, P. (2007, May 9). A labor union's power: Blocking takeover bids. *The Wall Street Journal,* pp. A1, A12.

17. Goodyear, 2009, op. cit. See also Kirkland, 2006, op. cit. See also Arndt, M. (2003, Feb. 3). Salvation from the shop floor. *BusinessWeek,* pp. 100, 101. See also The UAW: Using trade-offs to gain traction. (2003, Sept. 8). *BusinessWeek,* pp. 80–82.

18. Carey, S., and McCartney, S. (2003, Feb. 25). United's bid to cut labor costs could force rivals to follow. *The Wall Street Journal,* pp. A1, A6. See also Tully, S. (2003, Feb. 17). Straighten up and fly right. *Fortune,* pp. 66–70. See also Brooker, K. (2001, May 28). The chairman of the board looks back. *Fortune,* pp. 63–76.

19. Fossum, J. A. (2012). *Labor Relations: Development, Structure, Process* (11th Ed.). Burr Ridge, IL: McGraw-Hill/Irwin.

20. Frasch, K. B. (2011, Aug. 17). As unions decline, so do wages. *Human Resource Executive Online.* Retrieved from *www.hreonline.com/HRE/story.jsp?storyId=533340603* on August 17, 2011.

21. Budd, 2010, op. cit. See also Katz, H. C., Kochan, T. A., and Colvin, A. J. S. (2008). *An Introduction to Collective Bargaining and Industrial Relations* (4th Ed.). Burr Ridge, IL: McGraw-Hill/Irwin. See also Dunlop, J. T. (1988, May). Have the 1980s changed U.S. industrial relations? *Monthly Labor Review,* pp. 29–34.

22. Buckley, B., and Rubin, D. K. (2011, June 27). Hard times draw the line for bargaining. *ENR 2Q Cost Report,* pp. 16–19. Retrieved from *enr.construction.com/engineering/pdf/quarterly_cost_reports/2011-2Q_Cost_Report.pdf* on August 17, 2011.

23. Davis, E. (2003). Industrial relations in Australia. In CCH Australia, Macquarie Graduate School of Management, and Baker & McKenzie, *Australian Master Human Resources Guide.* Sydney: CCH Australia, pp. 349–381. See also Dabscheck, B. (2001). "A felt need for increased efficiency": Industrial relations at the end of the millennium. *Asia Pacific Journal of Human Resources* 39(2), pp. 4–30.

24. Budd, 2010, op. cit. See also White House lends an ear to airlines in labor woes: Settlements between Delta, Northwest, and unions followed aggressive lobbying. (2001, Apr. 24). *The Wall Street Journal,* p. A26.

25. Epstein, R. A. (1995). *Simple Rules for a Complex World.* Cambridge, MA: Harvard University Press.

26. Dulles, F. R. (1960). *Labor in America: A History* (2nd rev. Ed.). New York: Crowell.

27. Commons, J. R., and Filmore, E. A. (Eds.). (1958). *Labor Conspiracy Cases, 1806–1842,* Vol. 3: *A Documentary History of American Industrial Society.* New York: Russell & Russell.

28. Dulles, 1960, op. cit.

29. Ibid.

30. Meany's legacy. (1980, Jan. 13). *The Miami Herald,* p. 5E.

31. Change to Win. About us. Retrieved from *www.changetowin.org/about* on August 17, 2011.

32. Budd, 2010, op. cit. See also Fossum, 2012, op. cit. See also Rosenkrantz, H. (2010, April 25). What Andy Stern leaves behind. *BusinessWeek,* p. 23. One big union? (2008, June 9). *BusinessWeek,* p. 6.

33. Hirsch, J. M. (2008). The silicon bullet: Will the Internet kill the NLRA? *George Washington Law Review* 76, pp. 262–304. See also Olson, C. A., and Rybick, M. J. (2002, May–June). Spotlight on union organizing: "No-solicitation, no distribution," and related rules in the age of email and the Internet. *Legal Report,* pp. 5–7.

34. *NLRB v. Babcock & Wilcox* (1956). 105 U.S. 351.

35. Morgan Lewis. NLRB diminishes effectiveness of cardcheck recognition agreements. (2007, October 5). Retrieved from *www.morganlewis.com/pubs/LEPG_NLRBDiminshes_LF_05oct07.pdf* on August 17, 2011.

36. Budd, 2010, op. cit. See also Fossum, 2012, op. cit.

37. Farber, H. S. (2001). Union success in representation elections: Why does unit size matter? *Industrial and Labor Relations Review* 54, pp. 329–348. See also Demsetz, R. S. (1993). Voting behavior in union representation elections: The influence of skill homogeneity and skill-group size. *Industrial and Labor Relations Review* 47, pp. 99–113.

38. For more on the tactics both sides use, see Budd, 2010, op. cit.; Fossum, 2012, op. cit.; Daniels (2004), op. cit.; Kirkland, 2006, op. cit.

39. *Wayne J. Griffin Electric v. NLRB and IBEW* (2002, June 7). 4th Cir., Nos. 01-2258 and 01-2423. See also Loose lips: Anti-union remarks amount to unlawful threats. (2002, Aug.). *HR News,* p. 8.

40. Fossum, 2012, op. cit. See also Kirkland, 2006, op. cit.

41. Wermiel, S. (1983, Nov. 16). NLRB can't force companies to bargain with minority unions, U.S. court rules. *The Wall Street Journal,* p. 12.

42. Zellner, W. (2002, Oct. 28). How Wal-Mart keeps unions at bay. *BusinessWeek,* pp. 94–96.

43. Maher, K. (2006, July 5). Unions set pacts at slower pace as clout wanes, employers resist. *The Wall Street Journal,* p. A2.

44. Ferguson, J. P. (2008). The eyes of the needles: A sequential model of union organizing drives, 1999–2004. *Industrial and Labor Relations Review* 62, pp. 3–21.

45. Budd, 2010, op. cit. See also Maher, 2006, op. cit. See also McGolrick, S. (2001, May). NLRB revises standards for employers to withdraw union recognition. *HR News,* pp. 7, 22.

46. McGolrick, 2001, op. cit.

47. Maher, 2006, op. cit.

48. Fisher, R., Ury, W., and Patton, B. (1991). Getting to Yes (2nd Ed.). New York: Penguin.

49. Ibid.

50. Lewicki, R. J., Barry, B., and Saunders, D. M. (2011). *Essentials of Negotiation* (5th Ed.). Burr Ridge, IL: Irwin/McGraw-Hill. See also Tinsley, C. H., O'Connor, K. M., and Sullivan, B. A. (2002). Tough guys finish last: The perils of a distributive reputation. *Organizational Behavior & Human Decision Processes* 88, pp. 621–642.

51. Brett, J. M., Shapiro, D. L., and Lytle, A. L. (1998). Breaking the bonds of reciprocity in negotiations. *Academy of Management Journal* 41, pp. 410–424.

52. Ibid. See also Walton, R. E., and McKersie, R. B. (1965). *A Behavioral Theory of Labor Negotiations.* New York: McGraw-Hill.

53. Katz et al., 2008, op. cit.

54. Mackay, H. (2006, July 8). 24 tips to improve negotiating expertise. *The Rocky Mountain News,* p. 4C.

55. Naquin, C. E., and Paulson, G. D. (2003). Online bargaining and interpersonal trust. *Journal of Applied Psychology* 88, pp. 113–120.

56. Rudd, J. E., and Lawson, D. R. (2007). *Communicating in Global Business Negotiations.* Thousand Oaks, CA: Sage. See also Tinsley, C. H. (2001). How negotiators get to yes: Predicting the constellation of strategies used across cultures to negotiate conflict. *Journal of Applied Psychology* 86, pp. 583–593.

57. Gelfand, M. J., Fulmer, C. A., and Severance, L. (2011). The psychology of negotiation and mediation. In S. Zedeck (Ed.), *APA Handbook of Industrial and Organizational Psychology,* Vol. 3. Washington, DC: American Psychological Association, pp. 495–554. See also Gelfand, M. J., Higgins, M., Nishii, L. H., Raver, J. L., Dominguez, A., Murakami, F., Yamaguchi, S., and Toyama, M. (2002). Culture and egocentric perceptions of fairness in conflict and negotiation. *Journal of Applied Psychology* 87, pp. 833–845. See also Adair, W. L., Okumura, T., and Brett, J. M. (2001). Negotiation behaviors when cultures collide: The United States and Japan. *Journal of Applied Psychology* 86, pp. 371–385. See also Brett, J. M., and Okumura, T. (1998). Inter- and intra-cultural negotiation: U.S. and Japanese negotiators. *Academy of Management Journal* 41, pp. 495–510.

58. Budd, 2010, op. cit. See also Fossum, 2012, op. cit. See also Katz et al., 2008, op. cit.

59. Budd, 2010, op. cit.

60. Grossman, R. J. (1998, Sept.). Trying to heal the wounds. *HR Magazine,* pp. 85–92.

61. Budd, 2010, op. cit.

62. Peralta, E. (2011, July 25). Football is back: Players, owners strike deal to end NFL lockout. Retrieved from *www.npr.org/blogs/thetwo-way/2011/07/25/138671825/reports-nfl-owners-players-agree-to-new-deal-ending-lockout* on July 26, 2011.

63. Iyer, V., and Brown, C. (2011, July 25). NFL lockout ends as owners, player reps agree to 10-year CBA. *Sporting News.* Retrieved from *aol.sportingnews.com/nfl/feed/2010-09/nfl-labor-talks/story/nfl-lockout-ends-owners-nflpa-10-year-deal-2011-season-cba-labor-agreement* on July 26, 2011.

64. Brown, E. (2002, Oct. 28). Fallout. *Fortune,* p. 32. See also A labor-management standoff of two years nears an end. (2001, Aug. 1). *The Wall Street Journal,* p. A1.

65. Oviatt, C. R., Jr. (1995, Oct.). Case shows difficulty of declaring negotiating impasse. *HR News,* pp. 13, 16.

66. Budd, 2010, op. cit. See also Fossum, 2012, op. cit.

67. Hirschman, C. (2001, July). Order in the hearing! *HR Magazine,* pp. 58–64. See also Ross, W. H., and Conlon, D. E. (2000). Hybrid forms of third-party dispute resolution: Theoretical implications of combining mediation and arbitration. *Academy of Management Review* 25, pp. 416–427.

68. Ibid.

69. Arnold, J. A., and O'Connor, K. M. (1999). Ombudspersons or peers? The effect of third-party expertise and recommendations on negotiation. *Journal of Applied Psychology* 84, pp. 776–785.

70. Goldberg, S. B. (2005). The secrets of successful mediators. *Negotiation Journal* 21, pp. 365–376.

71. Katz et al., 2008, op. cit.

72. Fossum, 2012, op. cit., p. 402.

73. Katz et al., 2008, op. cit.

74. Ibid.

75. Fossum, 2012, op. cit.

76. Budd, 2010, op. cit.

77. Ibid.

78. De Dreu, C. K. (2011). Conflict at work: Basic principles and applied issues. In S. Zedeck (Ed.), *APA Handbook of Industrial and Organizational Psychology,* Vol. 3. Washington, DC: American Psychological Association, pp. 461–493. See also Colvin, A. J. S. (2001). The relationship between employment arbitration and workplace dispute-resolution procedures. *Ohio State Journal on Dispute Resolution* 16, pp. 643–668. See also Labig, C. E., and Greer, C. R. (1988). Grievance initiation: A literature survey and directions for future research. *Journal of Labor Research* 9, pp. 1–27.

79. Fossum, 2012, op. cit.

80. Fossum, 2012, op. cit. See also Katz et al., 2008, op. cit.

81. Leonard, D. (2011, June 5). The end of mail. *BusinessWeek,* pp. 59–65. See also Brooks, R. (2001, June 28). Mail disorder: Blizzard of grievances joins a sack of woes at U.S. Postal Service. *The Wall Street Journal,* pp. A1, A4.

82. Mesch, D. J., and Dalton, D. R. (1992). Unexpected consequences of improving workplace justice: A six-year time series assessment. *Academy of Management Journal* 35, pp. 1099–1114. See also Dalton, D. R., and Todor, W. D. (1985). Gender and workplace justice: A field assessment. *Personnel Psychology* 38, pp. 133–151.

83. Aryee, S., and Chay, Y. W. (2001). Workplace justice, citizenship behavior, and turnover intentions in a union context: Examining the mediating role of perceived union support and union instrumentality. *Journal of Applied Psychology* 86, pp. 154–160.

84. Olson-Buchanan, J. B. (1996). Voicing discontent: What happens to the grievance filer after the grievance? *Journal of Applied Psychology* 81, pp. 52–63.

85. Meyer, D., and Cooke, W. (1988). Economic and political factors in the resolution of formal grievances. *Industrial Relations* 27, pp. 318–335.

86. Klaas, B. S. (1989). Managerial decision-making about employee grievances: The impact of the grievant's work history. *Personnel Psychology* 42, pp. 53–68. See also Dalton, D. R., Todor, W. D., and Owen, C. L. (1987). Sex effects in workplace justice outcomes: A field assessment. *Journal of Applied Psychology* 72, pp. 156–159. See also Dalton and Todor, 1985, op. cit.

87. U.S. Postal Service, Office of the Inspector General. (2005, Sept. 30). White paper on the nature of grievances and the initiatives taken to reduce and prevent them (Report Number HM-OT-05-001). Retrieved from *www.uspsoig.gov/foia_files/HM-OT-05-001. pdf* on August 19, 2011. See also Brooks, 2001, op. cit.

88. Mesch and Dalton, 1994, op. cit.

89. Budd, 2010, op. cit. See also Katz et al., 2008, op. cit.

90. Carbonneau, T. E. (2009). *Arbitration in a Nutshell* (2nd Ed.). St. Paul, MN: Thomson/ West. See also Loughran, C. S. (2006). *How to Prepare and Present a Labor Arbitration Case: Strategy and Tactics for Advocates* (2nd ed.). Washington, DC: Bureau of National Affairs.

91. Budd, 2010, op. cit. See also Petersen, D. J., and Boller, H. R. (2004, Jan). Applying the public-policy exception to labor arbitration awards. *Dispute Resolution Journal.* Retrieved from *findarticles.com/p/articles/mi_qa3923/is_200311/ai_n9463726* on July 31, 2008.

92. Budd, 2010, op. cit.
93. Foust, D., and Bachman, J. (2009, Nov. 16). Boeing's flight from union labor. *BusinessWeek,* p. 34.
94. Pratsberg, B., and Ragan, J., Jr. (2002). Changes in the union wage premium by industry. *Industrial and Labor Relations Review* 56(1), pp. 65–83.
95. Colvin, A. J. S., Batt, R., and Katz, H. C. (2001). How high-performance human resource practices and workforce unionization affect managerial pay. *Personnel Psychology* 54(4), pp. 903–927.
96. Ibid.
97. Dolan, M., and Boudette, A. N. (2011, March 23). UAW to send activists abroad. *The Wall Street Journal,* p. B2. See also Fong, M., and Maher, K. (2007, June 22). U.S. labor leader aided China's Wal-Mart coup. *The Wall Street Journal,* pp. A1, A4.

CHAPTER

# 14

# PROCEDURAL JUSTICE AND ETHICS IN EMPLOYEE RELATIONS

*Questions This Chapter Will Help Managers Answer*

1. How can I ensure procedural justice in the resolution of conflicts between employees and managers?
2. How can I administer discipline without simultaneously engendering resentment toward me or my company?
3. How do I fire people legally and humanely?
4. What should be the components of a fair information practice policy?
5. What is ethical decision making in employee relations? What steps or considerations are involved?

## ALTERNATIVE DISPUTE RESOLUTION: GOOD FOR THE COMPANY, GOOD FOR EMPLOYEES?*

At the McGraw-Hill Companies, word came down from the chief executive officer: It was time to supplement the open-door policy with a formal, in-house **alternative dispute resolution (ADR) program.** He told attorneys in the legal department to develop something that settled disputes quickly, something good for morale.

After six months of work with consultants and meetings with employees and managers, as well as executives from JPMorgan Chase Bank, Cigna, JCPenney, and the KBR construction company—all of whom have ADR programs—McGraw-Hill unveiled its Fast and Impartial Resolution (FAIR) ADR program. The three-step program is voluntary and starts with bringing in a supervisor or HR representative to resolve a dispute. If that doesn't work, it moves to mediation with a third party. If mediation is fruitless, the third step is binding arbitration with a written decision. The company pays the costs of mediation and arbitration.

The FAIR program is typical of the programs many organizations are developing. Others incorporate multilevel, internal appeals procedures or waivers of jury trials. Such programs save employers time and money. According to JAMS/Endispute, based in Irvine, California, it takes up to six weeks from the time that company is contacted to the time mediation actually begins. The parties spend an average of 12.5 hours in the process, and problems are resolved in up to 90 percent of cases. Says David Gage, a professional mediator, "Mediation is really a teaching experience for people in the workplace. We sit down and we actually listen. We give everybody a chance to talk. We try to identify problems, and then we brainstorm for alternative solutions." The Equal Employment Opportunity Commission has been promoting voluntary mediation of employment discrimination claims for years, and with good reason. Charges that go to mediation are disposed of in an average of 86 days—about half the time required for charges that are not mediated. In addition, the cost of settling an EEOC charge has increased by almost 79 percent since the early 1990s.

Houston-based Brown & Root has had about 1,100 ADR cases, with 17 going to arbitration. Roughly 75 percent of the cases are resolved within two months, as opposed to several years in the courts. In Irvine, California, American Savings Bank's four-step program is enjoying similar success, reducing legal costs by more than 60 percent. The American Arbitration Association (AAA), whose ADR programs cover more than 7 million U.S. employees, has found that 80 percent of disputes are resolved at the first step, just by people sitting down and talking to each other. Of those that aren't, about 1,100 move to the next step, mediation, where a mediator helps both sides to agree. Only about 300 result in binding arbitration, but even in those cases, each side has veto power over the choice of arbitrator. To control the

*Sources:* Smith, A. (2011, April 13). ADR is underused tool for resolving disputes. Retrieved from *www.shrm.org/LegalIssues/FederalResources/Pages/ADRIsUnderusedTool.aspx* on August 22, 2011. See also Posthuma, R. A. (2010). *Workplace Dispute Resolution.* Alexandria, VA: Society for Human Resource Management. See also Slate, W. K. II. (2007, May 21). The positive side of arbitration. *BusinessWeek,* p. 22. See also Salvatore, P., & Garber, R. (2006, Feb.). Mediation and arbitration of employment law claims. SHRM White Paper, Retrieved from *www.shrm.org,* August 4, 2008. See also Orey, M. (2007, April 30). The vanishing trial. *BusinessWeek,* pp. 38, 39. See also Phillips, F. P. (2004, Sept.). Ten ways to sabotage dispute management. *HRMagazine,* pp. 163–168. See also Fisher, A. (2003, Nov. 24). I'm suspicious, not litigious—Should I sign my rights away? *Fortune,* p. 254.

costs of such cases, AAA offers the parties several options: limiting the number of arbitrators presiding on a case, offering expedited procedures, and even allowing for the entire process to be conducted over the Internet (to reduce travel costs).

On the other hand, compulsory arbitration agreements—in which employees sign agreements to arbitrate rather than litigate future disputes over alleged violations of employment law—are the subject of intense debate. While arbitration offers significant benefits with respect to speed, cost, and the specialized expertise of arbitrators, some fear that it may unfairly favor employers. In the conclusion to this case, we will examine what a fair ADR program looks like.

Challenges

1. What do you see as some key advantages and disadvantages of ADR programs?
2. Should an employee's agreement to binding arbitration be a condition of employment or a condition of continuing employment?
3. Working in small groups, identify characteristics that would make an ADR program fair both for employees and employers.

The chapter-opening vignette illustrates another facet of labor-management accommodation: the use of workplace due process to resolve disputes. It is another attempt to enhance the productivity and quality of life of employees. Indeed, the broad theme of this chapter is "justice on the job." We will consider alternative methods for resolving disputes, such as nonunion grievance and arbitration procedures. We also examine discipline and termination in the employment context. Finally, we will examine the growing concern for employee privacy and ethical issues in these three areas: fair information practice in the Internet age, the assessment of job applicants and employees, and whistle-blowing. Let us begin by defining some important terms.

## SOME DEFINITIONS

In this chapter we are concerned with three broad issues in the context of employee relations: (1) procedural justice, (2) due process, and (3) ethical decisions about behavior.

**Employee relations** includes all the practices that implement the philosophy and policy of an organization with respect to employment.[1]

**Justice** refers to the maintenance or administration of what is just, especially by the impartial adjustment of conflicting claims or the assignment of merited rewards or punishments.[2] It is one of the fundamental bases of cooperative action in organizations.[3]

**Procedural justice** focuses on the fairness of the procedures used to make decisions. Procedures are fair to the extent that they are consistent across persons and over time, free from bias, based on accurate information, correctable, and based on prevailing moral and ethical standards.[4]

**Distributive justice** focuses on the fairness of the outcomes of decisions, for example, in the allocation of bonuses or merit pay, or in making reasonable accommodations for employees with disabilities.[5]

**Due process** in legal proceedings provides individuals with rights such as the following: prior notice of prohibited conduct; timely procedures adhered to at each step of the procedure; notice of the charges or issues prior to a hearing; impartial judges or hearing officers; representation by counsel; opportunity to confront and to cross-examine adverse witnesses and evidence, as well as to present proof in one's own defense; notice of decision; and protection from retaliation for using a complaint procedure in a legitimate manner. These are **constitutional due-process rights.** They protect individual rights with respect to state, municipal, and federal government processes. However, they normally do not apply to work situations. Hence, employee rights to due process are based on a collective bargaining agreement, legislative protections, or procedures provided unilaterally by an employer.[6]

**Ethical decisions about behavior** concern conformity to moral standards or to the standards of conduct of a given profession or group. Ethical decisions about behavior take account not only of a person's own interests but also equally of the interests of those affected by the decision.[7]

## WHY ADDRESS PROCEDURAL JUSTICE?

In the wake of decisions that affect them, such as those involving pay, promotions, or assignments, employees often ask, "Was that fair?" Judgments about the fairness or equity of procedures used to make decisions, that is, procedural justice, are rooted in the perceptions of employees. Strong research evidence indicates that such perceptions lead to important consequences, such as employee behavior and attitudes, as well as business outcomes, such as customer satisfaction ratings.[8] In short, the judgments of employees about procedural justice matter. Perceptions of fairness are especially important in the context of HR management, for example, in the hiring process, in performance management, and in compensation.

Procedurally fair treatment has been demonstrated to result in reduced stress[9] and increased performance, job satisfaction, commitment to an organization, trust, and **organizational citizenship behaviors** (OCBs). OCBs are discretionary behaviors performed outside of one's formal role that help other employees perform their jobs or that show support for and conscientiousness toward the organization).[10] They account for 15 to 30 percent of business outcomes, and as much as 40 percent of the outcomes in customer-service settings.[11] OCBs include behaviors such as the following:

- Altruism (e.g., helping out when a coworker is not feeling well).
- Conscientiousness (e.g., staying late to finish a project).
- Civic virtue (e.g., volunteering for a community program to represent the firm).
- Sportsmanship (e.g., sharing the failure of a team project that would have been successful if the team had followed your advice).
- Courtesy (e.g., being understanding and empathetic, even when provoked).[12]

Procedural justice affects citizenship behaviors by influencing employees' perceptions of **organizational support,** the extent to which the organization values employees' general contributions and cares for their well being. In turn, this prompts employees to reciprocate with organizational citizenship behaviors.[13] These effects have been demonstrated to occur at the level of the work group as well as at the level of the individual.[14] In general, perceptions of procedural justice are most relevant and important to employees during times of significant organizational change. When employees experience change, their perceptions of fairness become especially potent factors that determine their attitudes and their behavior.[15] Because the only constant in organizations is change, considerations of procedural justice will always be relevant.

### Components of Procedural Justice

Although there is disagreement in the professional literature about the number of components of the broad topic of organizational justice,[16] we consider procedural justice to have three components. The first of these is **employee voice,** illustrated by organizational policies and rules that provide lots of opportunities for employee input to decisions. We will have more to say about employee voice later.

**Interactional justice** is a second component. It refers to the quality of interpersonal treatment that employees receive in their everyday work. Treating others with dignity and respect is the positive side of interactional justice. Derogatory judgments, deception, invasion of privacy, inconsiderate or abusive actions, public criticism, and coercion represent the negative side of interactional justice.[17] Violating any of these elements of interactional justice leads to decreased perceptions of fair treatment. Evidence indicates that employee perceptions of interactional justice that stem from the quality of their relationships with their supervisors are positively related to their performance, citizenship behaviors directed toward their supervisors, and job satisfaction.[18]

**Informational justice** is the third component of procedural justice. It is expressed in terms of providing explanations or accounts for decisions made. Consider layoffs, for example. Evidence indicates that layoff survivors who were provided explanations for the layoffs, or who received advance notice of them, had more positive reactions to layoffs and higher commitment to the organization.[19] Survivors had the most negative reactions to layoffs when they identified with the victims and when they perceived the layoffs to be unfair.[20]

In practice, when employees observe an example of organization-level unfairness, they tend to take into account the organization's justice track record. When they observe managerial unfairness, they consider the supervisor's justice record.[21] Think about your own experiences in times of change. Was the fairness of procedures important to you? Did your perceptions affect your attitudes toward your employer and your behavior at work? Did you wish you had more say in decisions that might affect you? This is the role of employee-voice systems, and we consider them further in the next section.

## PROCEDURAL JUSTICE IN ACTION: EMPLOYEE VOICE SYSTEMS

For most organizations, the most important thing they can do to ensure procedural justice is to provide individuals and groups the capacity to be heard, a way to communicate their interests upward—a voice system. Voice systems serve four important functions:

1. They ensure fair treatment to employees.
2. They provide a context in which unfair treatment can be appealed.

**3.** They help to improve the effectiveness of an organization.

**4.** They sustain employee loyalty and commitment.[22]

Here are some examples of voice systems that are commonly used:

- Grievance or internal complaint procedures, by which an employee can seek a formal, impartial review of an action that affects him or her.[23]
- Ombudspersons, who may investigate claims of unfair treatment or act as intermediaries between an employee and senior management and recommend possible courses of action to the parties.[24]
- Open-door policies by which employees can approach senior managers with problems that they may not be willing to take to their immediate supervisors. A related mechanism, particularly appropriate when the immediate supervisor is the problem, is a **skip-level policy,** whereby an employee may proceed directly to the next higher level of management above his or her supervisor.
- Participative management systems that encourage employee involvement in all aspects of organizational strategy and decision making.
- Committees or meetings that poll employee input on key problems and decisions.
- Senior-management visits, where employees can meet with senior company officials and openly ask questions about company strategy, policies, and practices or raise concerns about unfair treatment.
- Question/answer newsletters, in which employee questions and concerns are submitted to a newsletter editor and investigated by that office, and then answered and openly reported to the organizational community.[25]
- Toll-free telephone numbers that employees can use anonymously to report waste, fraud, or abuse.
- E-mail communication between remote workers, as well as online bulletin boards.[26]

## Characteristics of Effective Voice Systems

A thorough review of the literature on voice systems revealed five "core" characteristics of the most effective ones. These are shown in Table 14–1.

The first criterion is *elegance.* That is, the system should be simple to understand, it should apply to a broad range of issues, it should use an effective diagnostic framework, and finally, those who manage the system should be able to respond definitively to the issues raised.

The second criterion is *accessibility.* Effective voice systems are easy-to-use, well-advertised, comprehensible, open processes. Information is publicized on how to file a complaint. Indeed, research has found that employees view this feature as a key attribute of an effective dispute-handling system.[27]

The third criterion of effective voice systems is *correctness*—that is, the system should provide the right answer to problems by being unbiased, thorough, and effective. The more correct a system, the more likely it is that (1) the complainant can provide relevant input about the problem, (2) the organization can investigate and call for more information if it needs it, (3) a system exists for classifying and coding information in order to determine the nature of the problem, (4) employees can appeal lower-level decisions, and (5) both procedures and outcomes make good sense to most employees.[28]

| Table 14–1 | |
|---|---|
| **CORE CHARACTERISTICS OF EFFECTIVE VOICE SYSTEMS** | |

**Elegance**—simple procedures, broad application, vested authority, good diagnostic system

**Accessibility**—easy to use, advertised, comprehensive, open process

**Correctness**—administered well, includes follow-up, self-redesigning, correctable outcomes

**Responsiveness**—timely, culturally viable, tangible results, management commitment

**Nonpunitiveness**—appeal system, anonymity, no retaliation for using the system

*Source:* Sheppard, B. H., Lewicki, R. J., and Minton, J. W. (1992). *Organizational Justice: The Search for Fairness in the Workplace.* New York: Lexington Books, p. 149.

A fourth criterion is *responsiveness.* At the most basic level, responsive systems let individuals know that their input has been received. Thus, IBM's "Speak-Up" program requires the manager of the function in question to prepare a written response to the employee within three days or face severe sanctions. Responsive systems provide timely responses, are backed by management commitment, are designed to fit an organization's culture, provide tangible results, involve participants in the decision-making process, and give those who manage the system sufficient clout to ensure that it works effectively.

Finally, effective voice systems are *nonpunitive.* This is essential if employees are to trust the system. Individuals must be able to present problems, identify concerns, and challenge the organization in such a way that they are not punished for providing this input, even if the issues raised are sensitive and highly politicized. If the input concerns wrongdoing or malfeasance, the individual's identity must be protected so that direct or indirect retribution cannot occur. Employees as well as managers must be protected.[29]

Now that we have discussed the theory of procedural justice, let's examine how it can be applied in a number of areas of employee relations. We begin by examining nonunion grievance procedures.

## GRIEVANCE PROCEDURES IN NONUNION COMPANIES: WORKPLACE DUE PROCESS

Conflicts in which employees feel unfairly treated, harassed, overlooked in promotions, or deserving of a raise may arise in any workplace, union or nonunion. Methods for resolving such conflicts are needed. Grievance procedures serve that purpose because they introduce justice systems into the workplace. Today they are found in almost all workplaces of 100 or more employees, and they serve the following purposes:[30]

1. Increase organizational commitment and performance by treating employees fairly and by identifying problem areas.

2. Avoid costly lawsuits.
3. Prevent unionization.

Nonunion grievance procedures can take several forms. The simplest is an **open-door policy,** in which employees are invited to bring their concerns to a manager, who will attempt to resolve it. A second form is a **peer-review panel,** which uses fellow employees as decision makers, and a third is **nonunion arbitration,** which relies on third-party neutral arbitrators to settle disputes. Other dispute-resolution mechanisms include internal or external **mediation** and **ombudspersons.** An ombudsperson counsels employees on how to resolve issues themselves, conducts formal or informal investigations of disputes, or simply serves as a support system for employees to defuse negative emotions, animosity, and hostility.[31]

Figure 14–1 illustrates how such a procedure works in one company. This procedure emphasizes the supervisor as a key figure in the resolution of grievances. If this is inappropriate, then the employee should feel free to contact the director of human resources or any officer of the company. Employees are always encouraged to follow their chain of command. If the employee is not satisfied with the response of the appropriate officer of the corporation, the employee may bring the matter to the president's attention by filing a written copy of the request and the response or action taken.[32]

Note that this process lacks several elements of due process. Specifically, employees generally lack representation or assistance in presenting their grievances (as is the case with formal union grievance procedures), and management is the ultimate decision maker. For genuine due process to operate, a procedure must include an objective investigator and decision maker who has the power to make a binding decision on both employee and employer.[33] To

---

### Figure 14–1

Example of a nonunion grievance procedure. This diagram indicates the possible routes a grievant may take to resolve a complaint. The regular procedural route is designed to resolve the grievance at the lowest possible level—the supervisor. However, if the grievant feels uncomfortable approaching the supervisor, the grievance may be presented directly to the supervisor's supervisor, to the director of HR, or to any officer of the company, with a final appeal to the company president.

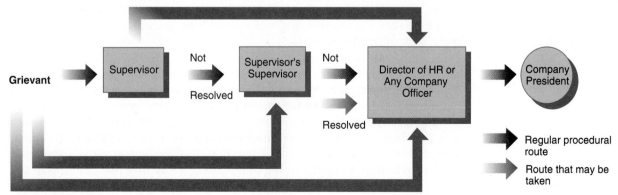

*Source:* Adapted from Posthuma, R. A. (2010). *Workplace Dispute Resolution.* Alexandria, VA: Society for Human Resource Management, p. 32.

## INTERNATIONAL APPLICATION
### Perceptions of Procedural Justice across Cultures

Research seems to indicate that perceptions of procedural justice are similar across cultures and that employee-voice systems in particular are associated with judgments of fairness in different cultures. These findings are consistent across cultures as diverse as Argentina, the Dominican Republic, Mexico, Great Britain, the Netherlands, and United States.[a] What about distributing rewards in the workplace (distributive justice)? Here, research indicates that different norms seem to be preferred in different nations. While Americans prefer the equity norm (rewards distributed based on individual contributions), the Dutch favor equal distributions, and people from India favor distributions that are sensitive to fulfilling the needs of others.[b]

Individualism and collectivism also seem to influence judgments of procedural justice. Specifically, people in individualistic cultures such as the United States prefer to have higher levels of control over the processes used to make decisions than do people in more collectivistic cultures, such as Ecuador. This may be due to the more confrontational orientation of people in individualistic cultures, in contrast to the orientation toward harmony in collectivistic cultures.[c]

Reviews of the literature in this area indicate that there is a growing body of research on culture and justice in intercultural contexts. Shared perceptions of justice are critical for the effectiveness of intercultural alliances, especially when cultural distance between the parties is high. Yet intercultural settings are precisely where there may be conflict due to differences in perceptions of justice.[d]

---

[a]Kim, T. Y., and Leung, K. (2007). Forming and reacting to overall fairness: A cross-cultural comparison. *Organizational Behavior and Human Decision Processes* 104, pp. 83–95. See also Cropanzano, R., Aguinis, H., Schminke, M., and Denham, D. L. (1999). Disputant reactions to managerial conflict resolution tactics: A comparison among Argentina, the Dominican Republic, Mexico, and the United States. *Group and Organization Management* 24, pp. 124–154.

[b]Greenberg, 2011, op. cit.

[c]Erez, M. (2011). Cross-cultural and global issues in organizational psychology. In S. Zedeck (Ed.), *APA Handbook of Industrial and Organizational Psychology*, Vol. 3. Washington, DC: American Psychological Association, pp. 807–854.

[d]Erez, 2011, op. cit. See also Greenberg, 2011, op. cit. See also Gelfand, M. J., Erez, M., and Aycan, Z. (2007). Cross-cultural organizational behavior. *Annual Review of Psychology* 58, pp. 479–514. See also Luo, Y. (2005). How important are shared perceptions of procedural justice in cooperative alliances? *Academy of Management Journal* 48, pp. 695–709.

---

address potential shortcomings of the process, one or more elements are often added to the basic nonunion grievance procedure: ombudspersons, peer-review panels, and arbitration.

As we noted earlier, an ombudsperson is a neutral facilitator between employees and managers; he or she assists them in resolving workplace disputes. That is, the ombudsperson is much more of a mediator than an arbitrator or fact finder.[34]

Peer-review panels sometimes comprise the appeal process in a nonunion grievance procedure. In this system, grievances can be appealed to a review panel in which employees (not managers) comprise a majority of the panel members (hence the name *peer*-review panel). Peer-review panels are established to counter perceptions of unfairness in dispute-resolution systems where managers make the final decisions.[35] For example, FedEx Corporation's "guaranteed fair-treatment process" lets employees appeal problems to a peer-review board chosen by the worker involved and that also includes several members of management. The board rules for employees about half the time. Bosses cannot appeal decisions, but employees can appeal to a panel of top executives up to and including the chairman of the board.[36]

In some, but by no means all instances, arbitration is the final step of a nonunion workplace dispute-resolution system. Nonunion arbitration of grievances might provide less due process to employees than unionized grievance arbitration if there are limitations on discovery (how much information the grievant can collect from the company), if the use of outside advocates such as attorneys is restricted, or if arbitrators favor management to increase their chances of being selected for future cases.[37]

Workplace due process is a growing trend. To work effectively, however, such a procedure should meet four basic requirements:[38]

1. *All employees must know about the procedure and understand exactly how it operates.* Describe the system in the employee handbook and publicize it widely. GlaxoSmithKline goes even further. Periodically, it features its internal complaint procedure on closed-circuit television for all company employees to see.
2. *Employees must believe that there will be no reprisals taken against them for using it.*
3. *Management must respond quickly and thoroughly to all grievances.* Use trained investigators to gather facts in a timely manner. The investigator should then discuss possible actions with the manager who has the power to make a final decision, and the manager should subsequently share the decision with the complainant.
4. *Provide employees with an appeal process.*

The trend toward workplace due process represents an effort by companies to broaden employees' rights in disciplinary matters. As one observer noted: "It is inherently difficult for the management power structure to concede to a system that allows review of its decision making. . . . But any concept of employee justice is incomplete without the presence of some mechanism to challenge the power system."[39] Due-process mechanisms build an open, trusting atmosphere, enhance employee commitment, and stem the growth of costly lawsuits alleging wrongful discharge and discrimination.

## Discipline

Make no mistake about it: Most employees want to conduct themselves in a manner acceptable to the company and to their fellow employees. Occasionally, problems of absenteeism, poor work performance, or rule violations arise. When informal conversations or coaching sessions fail to resolve these problems, formal disciplinary action is called for.

In a unionized firm, the *management rights* clause of the collective bargaining agreement typically retains for management the authority to impose reasonable rules for workplace conduct and to discipline employees for **just cause.** The concept of just cause requires an employer not only to produce persuasive evidence of an employee's liability or negligence, but also to provide the employee a fair hearing and to impose a penalty appropriate to the proven offense.[40] Unions rarely object to employee discipline, provided that (1) it is applied consistently, (2) the rules are publicized clearly, and (3) the rules are considered reasonable.

Discipline is indispensable to management control. Ideally, it should serve as a corrective mechanism to create and maintain a productive, responsive workforce.[41] Unfortunately, some managers go to great lengths to avoid using discipline. To some extent this is understandable, because discipline is one of the hardest management actions to take. Managers may avoid imposing discipline because of (1) ignorance of organizational rules, (2) fear of formal grievances, or (3) fear of losing the friendship of employees.[42] Yet failure to administer discipline can result in implied acceptance or approval of the offense. Thereafter, problems may become more frequent or severe, and discipline becomes that much more difficult to administer.[43]

In fact, evidence indicates that discipline (i.e., punishment) may be beneficial.[44] Consider that

- Discipline may alert the marginal employee to his or her low performance and result in a change in behavior.
- Discipline may send a signal to other employees regarding expected levels of performance and standards of behavior.
- If the discipline is perceived as legitimate by other employees, it may increase motivation, morale, and performance.

Department managers in a retail store chain who used informal warnings, formal warnings, and dismissals more frequently than their peers had higher departmental performance ratings (in terms of annual cost and sales data and ratings by higher-level managers). This relationship held even when length of service was taken into account. More frequent use of sanctions was associated with improved performance. Why is this so?

The answer may lie in **social learning theory**.[45] According to that theory, individuals in groups look to others to learn appropriate behaviors and attitudes. They learn them by modeling the behavior of others, adopting standard operating procedures, and following group norms. Individuals whose attitudes or behaviors violate these norms may cause problems. Tolerance of such behavior by the supervisor may threaten the group by causing feelings of uncertainty and unfairness. On the other hand, management actions that are seen as maintaining legitimate group standards may instill feelings of fairness and result in improved performance. Failure to invoke sanctions may lead to a loss of management control and unproductive employee behavior.[46] Finally, do not underestimate the *symbolic* value of disciplinary actions, especially since punitive behavior tends to make a lasting impression on employees.[47]

## Progressive Discipline

Many firms, both unionized and nonunionized, follow a procedure of **progressive discipline** that proceeds from an oral warning to a written warning to a suspension to dismissal. If progressive discipline is to be effective, however, employers need to follow four rules. Specifically, the employee needs to (1) know what the problem is, (2) know what he or she must do to fix the problem, (3) have a reasonable period of time to fix the problem, and (4) understand the consequences of inaction.[48]

At the same time, there are downsides to progressive discipline. It can be frustrating for managers and employees to tolerate poor behavior and performance while they "wait out" the progressive-discipline process. It is time-consuming and it requires proper documentation. On balance, however, progressive discipline is the policy of choice for most employers. By giving employees a second or third chance to change their inappropriate behavior to conform to the company's standards of conduct, such a policy is employee friendly and less susceptible to challenge in litigation than alternative approaches without progressive steps.[49]

At a broader level, is it possible to administer discipline without simultaneously engendering resentment by the disciplined employee? The answer is yes, if managers follow what Douglas McGregor called the **red-hot-stove rule.** Discipline should be

- *Immediate.* Just like touching a hot stove, where feedback is immediate, there should be no misunderstanding about why discipline was imposed. People are disciplined not because of who they are (personality), but because of what they did (behavior).
- *With warning.* Small children know that if they touch a hot stove, they will be burned. Likewise, employees must know very clearly what the consequences of undesirable work behavior will be. They must be given adequate warning.
- *Consistent.* Every time a person touches a red-hot stove, he or she gets burned. Likewise, if discipline is to be perceived as fair, it must be administered consistently, given similar circumstances surrounding the undesirable behavior. Consistency among individual managers across the organization is essential, but evidence indicates that line managers vary considerably in their attitudes about discipline,[50] and that they tend to be less concerned with consistency than with satisfying immediate needs within their work units.[51]
- *Impersonal.* A hot stove is blind to who touches it. So also, managers cannot play favorites by disciplining subordinates they do not like while allowing the same behavior to go unpunished for those they do like.

A recent review of arbitration cases and case law suggests two other characteristics of a legally defensible progressive discipline system: (1) *allow an employee the opportunity to respond,* and (2) *allow employees a reasonable period of time to improve their performance.*[52]

## Documenting Performance-Related Incidents

Documentation is a fact of organizational life for most managers. While such paperwork is never pleasant, it should conform to the following guidelines:

- Describe what led up to the incident—the problem and the setting. Is this a first offense or part of a pattern?
- Describe what actually happened and be specific—that is, include names, dates, times, witnesses, and other pertinent facts.
- Describe what must be done to correct the situation and by when.
- State the consequences of further violations.

| Figure 14–2 | |
|---|---|
| Sample written warning of disciplinary action. | DATE: August 14, 2011 <br><br> TO: J. Hartwig <br> FROM: D. Curtis <br> SUBJECT: Written Warning <br><br> Today you were 30 minutes late to work with no justification for your tardiness. A similar offense occurred last Friday. At that time you were told that failure to report for work on schedule will not be condoned. I now find it necessary to tell you in writing that you must report to work on time. Failure to do so will result in your dismissal from employment. Please sign below that you have read and that you understand this warning. <br><br><br> [Name]                               [Date] |

Can you see the parallel with the four rules of progressive discipline described earlier? Conclude the warning by obtaining the employee's signature that he or she has read and understands the warning. A sample written warning is shown in Figure 14–2. Note how it includes each of the ingredients just described.

## The Disciplinary Interview

Generally, disciplinary interviews are held for one of two reasons: (1) over issues of *workplace conduct*, such as attendance or punctuality, or (2) over issues of *job performance*, such as low productivity. They tend to be very legalistic. As an example, consider the following scenario.

You are a first-line supervisor at a unionized facility. You suspect that one of your subordinates, Steve Fox, has been distorting his time reports to misrepresent his daily starting time. While some of the evidence is sketchy, you know that Fox's time reports are false. Accompanied by an industrial-relations representative, you decide to confront Fox directly in a disciplinary interview. However, before you can begin the meeting, Fox announces, "I'd appreciate it if a coworker of mine could be present during this meeting. If a coworker cannot be present, I refuse to participate." Your reaction to this startling request is to

**A.** Ask Fox which coworker he desires and reconvene the meeting once the employee is present.

**B.** Deny his request and order him to participate or face immediate discipline for insubordination.

**C.** Terminate the meeting with no further discussion.

**D.** Ignore the request and proceed with the meeting, hoping that Fox will participate anyway.

**E.** Inform Fox that, as his supervisor, you are a coworker and attempt to proceed with the meeting.

Unless your reaction was A or C, you have probably committed a violation of the National Labor Relations Act.

In *NLRB v. J. Weingarten Inc.,* the Supreme Court ruled that a *union* employee has the right to demand that a union representative be present at an investigatory interview that the employee reasonably believes may result in disciplinary action.[53] Currently however, nonunion employees do not enjoy the same right, but employers are not prohibited from extending Weingarten rights to these employees if they choose to do so.[54] To summarize the Weingarten mandate,

1. The employee must *request* representation; the employer has no obligation to offer it voluntarily. If such a request is made, the union representative may meet with the employee privately before the investigatory interview takes place.[55]
2. The employee must reasonably believe that the investigation may result in disciplinary action taken against him or her.
3. The employer is not obligated to carry on the interview or to justify its refusal to do so. The employer may simply cancel the interview and thus effectively disallow union or coworker representation.
4. The employer has no duty to bargain with any union representative during the interview, and the union representative may not limit the employer's questioning.[56]

If the National Labor Relations Board determines that these rights were violated and that an employee subsequently was disciplined for conduct that was the subject of the unlawful interview, the board will issue a "make-whole" remedy. This may include (1) restitution of back pay, (2) an order expunging from the employee's personnel records any notation of related discipline, or (3) a cease-and-desist order. To avoid these kinds of problems, top management must decide what company policy will be in such cases, communicate that policy to first-line supervisors, and give them clear, concise instructions regarding their responsibilities should an employee who is a union member request representation at an investigatory interview.[57]

Having satisfied their legal burden, how should supervisors actually conduct the disciplinary interview? They must do *nine* things well:

1. Come to the interview with as many facts as possible. Check the employee's employment file for previous offenses as well as for evidence of exemplary behavior and performance.
2. Conduct the interview in a quiet, private place. "Praise in public, discipline in private" is a good rule to remember. Whether the employee's attitude is truculent or contrite, recognize that he or she will be apprehensive. In contrast to other interviews, where your first objective is to dispel any fears and help the person relax, a "light touch" is inappropriate here.
3. Avoid aggressive accusations. State the facts in a simple, straightforward way. Be sure that any fact you use is accurate, and never rely on hearsay, rumor, or unconfirmed guesswork.
4. Be sure that the employee understands the rule in question and the reason it exists.
5. Allow the employee to make a full defense, even if you think he or she has none. If any point the employee makes has merit, tell him or her so and take it into consideration in your final decision.

6.  Stay cool and calm treat the subordinate as an adult. Never use foul language or touch the subordinate. Such behaviors may be misinterpreted or grossly distorted at a later date.
7.  If you made a mistake, be big enough to admit it.
8.  Consider extenuating circumstances, and allow for honest mistakes on the part of the subordinate.
9.  Even when corrective discipline is required, try to express confidence in the subordinate's worth as a person and ability to perform acceptably in the future. Rather than dwelling on the past, which you cannot change, focus on the future, which you can.

## Employment at Will

For U.S. workers who are not covered by a collective-bargaining agreement or an individual employment contract, dismissal is an ever-present possibility.[58] The doctrine of **"employment at will"** or "at-will employment" refers to an employment relationship between an employer and an employee, under which either party can terminate the relationship without notice, at any time

---

**HR BUZZ**

*The "Facebook Firing" Case*

### Social-Media Policies and "At-Will" Employment*

American Medical Response (AMR), a Connecticut ambulance-service company, terminated an employee after she posted negative comments about her employer and her supervisor on her Facebook page. The comments were derogatory and included profanity. AMR's policy on this issue stated, "Employees are prohibited from making disparaging, discriminatory, or defamatory comments when discussing the Company or the employee's superiors, co-workers, or competitors." Following an investigation, the National Labor Relations Board issued a complaint against AMR, claiming that the discharge violated the National Labor Relations Act and its protection of the right to discuss the terms and conditions of one's employment. The case settled the day before a scheduled hearing, but subsequently it has become known as the "Facebook firing" case.

According to labor-law experts, under current law, an employer could face a charge of unfair labor practices from the NLRB *even* if the employer is non-union, *and even* if no disciplinary action is taken. Employers certainly have a legitimate interest in protecting against disclosure of trade secrets and trade-marked, copyrighted, and other private information. At the same time, however, they are not permitted to restrict employees' use of social media (Facebook, Skype, Yahoo! Twitter, blogs, chat forums, etc.) and the Internet to unionize, bargain collectively, and in general, to discuss the terms and conditions of their employment. Any social-media policy should therefore remind employees that they are prohibited from disclosing the employer's confidential information or its customers' private information. Employees should also be transparent about their role at their companies in all posts related to company matters.

*Sources: Johnson, M. B., and Murphy, M. R. (2011, Feb.). Social media policies after the NLRB "Facebook firing" case settles: What are employers to do? DrinkerBiddle Labor & Employment Alert. Retrieved from www.drinkerbiddle.com/files/Publication/1254e85a-d4ef-456f-8bb5-fba88c14458f/ Presentation/PublicationAttachment/864b2565-616a-44e6-af29-54b9b5d2d1a6/NLRB% 20Social%20Media.pdf on May 7, 2011. See also Conlin, M., and MacMillen, D. (2009, June 1). Managing the Tweets. BusinessWeek, pp. 20, 21.*

and for any reason not prohibited by law.[59] Under certain situations, however, successful victims of unjust dismissal can collect sizable punitive and compensatory damages from their former employers.

In recent years, several important exceptions to the "at-will" doctrine have emerged. These exceptions provide important protections for workers. The first—and most important—is legislative. Federal laws limit an employer's right to terminate at-will employees for such reasons as age, race, sex, religion, national origin, union activity, reporting of unsafe working conditions, or disability.[60] However, employment at will is primarily a matter of state law.[61]

State courts have carved out three judicial exceptions. The first is a **public policy exception.** That is, an employee may not be fired because he or she refuses to commit an illegal act, such as perjury or price fixing. Second, when an employer has promised not to terminate an employee except for unsatisfactory job performance or other good cause, the courts will insist that the employer carry out that promise. This includes **implied promises** (such as oral promises and implied covenants of good faith and fair dealing) as well as explicit ones.[62] In addition, courts in 34 states have found that informal assurances of job security can sometimes amount to an enforceable contract.[63]

The third exception allows employees to seek damages for outrageous acts related to termination, including character defamation (see earlier Company Example). This includes so-called **retaliatory discharge** cases, where a worker is fired for actions ranging from filing a workers' compensation claim to reporting safety violations to government agencies. The Supreme Court has ruled that where state law permits (as it does in 34 states), union as well as nonunion employees have the right to sue over their dismissals, even if they are covered by a collective bargaining contract that provides a grievance procedure and remedies.[64]

It might thus appear that the "at-will" doctrine has been severely restricted. Think again. For example, age discrimination is still permissible for workers under age 40, and many other areas remain untouched by employment law. In what is known as **lifestyle discrimination,** workers have been fired for refusing to quit smoking, for living with someone without being married, drinking a competitor's product, motorcycling, and other legal activities outside of work.[65] To avoid potential charges of unjust dismissal, managers should scrutinize each facet of the HR management system. They should look, for example, at the following:

- *Recruitment.* Beware of creating implicit or explicit contracts in recruitment advertisements. Ensure that no job duration is implied and that employment is not guaranteed or "permanent."
- *Interviewing.* Phrases intended to entice a candidate into accepting a position, such as "employment security," "lifelong relationship" with the company, "permanent" hiring, and so forth, can create future problems.
- *Employment applications.* Include a statement that describes the rights of the at-will employee, as well as those of the employer. However, do not be so strident that you scare off applicants.
- *Handbooks and manuals.* A major source of company policy statements regarding "permanent" employment and discharge for "just cause" is the employee handbook. According to a growing number of state laws, such handbook language constitutes an implied contract for employment. Courts have upheld an employer's prerogative to refrain from making any promises to employees regarding how a termination will be conducted or the conditions under which

they may be fired. However, if an employer does make such a promise of job security, whether implied verbally or in writing in an employment document or employee handbook, the employer is bound by that promise.[66]

- *Performance appraisals.* Include training and written instructions for all raters, and use systems that minimize subjectivity to the greatest extent possible. Give employees the right to read and comment on their appraisals, and require them to sign an acknowledgment that they have done so whether or not they agree with the contents of the appraisal.[67] Encourage managers to give honest appraisals if an employee is not meeting minimum standards of performance—"tell it like it is" rather than leading the employee to believe that his or her performance is satisfactory. Document employee misconduct and poor performance, and provide a progressive disciplinary policy, thereby building a record establishing just cause.[68]

## Employment Contracts

Earlier we noted that employees with contracts (bargained collectively or individually) are not at-will employees. In fact, where a collective-bargaining contract does exist, employers cannot enter into separate employment agreements with employees covered by that contract.[69] However, more and more executives, professionals, and even middle managers are demanding contracts. While getting a contract can be a wise career move, when is the proper time to ask for one—and how?

You should consider asking for a contract in any business where the competition for talent is intense, where ideas are at a premium, or when the conditions of your employment differ in unusual ways from a company's standard practices. A contract assures you of a job and a minimum salary for some period of time, usually two to three years, during which you agree not to quit. Other typical provisions include your title, compensation (salary, procedures for salary increases, bonuses), benefits, stock options, length of vacation, the circumstances under which you can be fired, and severance pay. However, with all these perks come a handful of restrictive covenants, or clauses, that basically limit your ability to work elsewhere. For example,[70]

- A *nonsolicitation* clause prohibits you from recruiting key clients or employees away from your former employer for a year or two.
- *Payback* clauses require that you not take another job until you have repaid the company any expenses incurred in your relocation and recruitment.
- Less common is a clause that mandates that the company must have an opportunity to *match* any employment offer that you get. If the employer matches a competing offer, you must remain.
- A *non disclosure* clause prohibits you from divulging trade secrets or other proprietary information to outsiders during your employment at a company or after you leave.
- A *non compete* clause bars you from working for a competitor for six months up to five years.[71] As a practical matter, however, a New York State court found that a non compete clause that restricted an employee from working for a competitor for 12 months was "too long" in the Internet business.[72] The clause is valid whether you are fired, your job is eliminated, or you leave voluntarily.

**Non compete agreements** are most common in such highly competitive industries as computers, pharmaceuticals, toys, biotechnology, and electronics. Since information is what gives businesses their competitive edge, more of them are using non compete agreements to make sure that inside information about products or services does not leak out to competitors. Such agreements now attempt to prevent people in industries as varied as tax preparers, advertising executives, car salespeople, event planners, hairdressers, flower arrangers, exterminators, and even housecleaners from jumping to rival companies.[73] In a 2010 case involving taxpreparers, the 11th Circuit Court of Appeals ruled that a non compete agreement is valid if it is reasonable and balanced with respect to three issues: duration, geographic territory, and scope of activity.[74]

Whether or not a contract has been signed, however, executives are still required to maintain all trade secrets with which their employers have entrusted them. This obligation, often called a **fiduciary duty of loyalty,** cannot keep the executive out of the job market, but it does provide the former employer with legal recourse if an executive joins a competitor and tells all. Indeed, this is precisely what Campbell Soup claimed when it succeeded in muzzling a former key executive.

---

## CAMPBELL SOUP

HR BUZZ

*Protecting Trade Secrets*

A high-profile dispute recently played out in front of a national audience when a key executive of Campbell Soup, who had signed a non compete agreement, "jumped ship" to go to work for Campbell's main rival, H. J. Heinz Company. After weeks of acrimonious litigation, a settlement finally was reached. It included an agreement that the departing Campbell's executive would not be allowed to begin working for Heinz for several months, would keep a log of all contacts he had with Heinz employees once he did start working there, and would forfeit pension and other benefits from Campbell's. For its part, Heinz agreed to permit certain of its facilities to be inspected regularly to assure Campbell's that none of its trade secrets were being used.

This case is unusual only for its high profile. While it grabbed headlines, the fact is that every day, in courtrooms all over the country, companies, their employees, and their competitors are suing each other, seeking to enforce, limit, or get out from under non compete agreements. More often than not, the parties resolve their disputes by coming to some sort of an agreement among themselves. The lesson? Companies are now playing hardball when it comes to the disclosure of trade secrets. For all parties, the stakes are high.

---

Companies say they need non compete agreements now that growing numbers of acquisitions, bankruptcies, mergers, and layoffs regularly set loose employees with access to trade secrets and other sensitive information. Sometimes, however, judges find that the agreements go too far in restraining employees. As we have seen, however, in such cases, they will limit their provisions substantially.[75]

From the company's perspective, it is important to recognize that employment agreements are governed by state law.[76] California, for example, does not allow no-compete agreements.[77] To avoid having to deal with multiple interpretations of the same agreement in different states, firms generally include a **choice-of-law provision,** which designates that the laws of a particular state will be used to interpret the contract. Where feasible, companies are choosing states that tend to uphold such restrictions. Finally, a contract should state that it reflects the entire agreement of the parties and can only be amended in writing, signed by both parties. Doing so prevents employee claims that the employer made oral promises or agreements that expanded his or her rights.[78]

Now back to the negotiation process for employment contracts. In dealing with a prospective employer, do not raise the issue of a contract until you have been offered a job and have thoroughly discussed the terms of your employment. How do you broach the subject? Calmly. Say, for example, "I'd appreciate a letter confirming these arrangements." If the employer asks why, you might point out that both of you are used to putting business agreements on paper and that it's to your mutual benefit to keep all these details straight.[79] Here are some tips on how to negotiate an employment contract:

1. Keep the tone upbeat. Don't use the words "I" and "you"; talk about "we"—as though you're already aboard.
2. Decide beforehand on three or four "make or break" issues (e.g., salary, job assignment, location). These are your "need-to-haves." Also make a list of secondary issues, so-called "nice-to-haves" (e.g., company car, sign-on bonus).
3. Negotiate the entire package at one time. Don't keep coming back to nit-pick.
4. Be flexible (except on your "make-or-break" issues); let the company win on some things.

Once you receive the proposed contract, have an attorney review it before you sign. Remember: Employment contracts are legally enforceable documents.

## Termination

We discussed layoffs in Chapter 10. The focus here is on how to terminate employees for cause, typically for disciplinary reasons or for poor performance. Termination is one of the most difficult tasks a manager has to perform. For those fired, the perception of inequity, or procedural injustice, is often what drives them to court.

Courts expect employers to provide a full course of progressive discipline (including written and final written warnings) for employees whose job performance does not meet standards. When it comes to inappropriate workplace conduct, however, such as theft, physical violence, or gross misconduct, the courts are much more lenient. As a manager, even if you choose not to terminate for inappropriate workplace conduct on the first offense, you may issue a final written warning, such as the following:[80]

> If you *ever again* engage in behavior that could be construed as hostile or intimidating, or if you violate any other company standards of performance and conduct, then you will be dismissed immediately.

Termination for cause is not an infrequent occurrence; some 2 million workers in the United States are fired every year, and that doesn't include large-scale layoffs.[81] With respect to layoffs, while the Worker Adjustment and Retraining Notification (WARN) Act requires employers of more than 100 workers to grant 60 days' written notice before closing a plant or before laying off more than one-third of a workforce in excess of 150 people, few firms provide any training to supervisors on how to conduct terminations.[82]

While termination may be traumatic for the employee, it is often no less so for the boss. Faced with saying the words "Your services are no longer required," even the strongest person can get the shakes, sleepless nights, and sweaty palms. So how should termination be handled? Certainly not the way it was at one company that sent an email to its employees around lunchtime, with instructions to call a toll-free number. When they did, they heard a voice recording saying that the company, a small technology firm, was closing its doors and all employees needed to leave right away. Is this procedural justice? Certainly not. In fact, assuming an organization is not going out of business, insensitive firings can tarnish its reputation among business partners, vendors, and customers, as well as make it difficult to recruit and retain talent.[83]

As an alternative, more humane procedure, companies should familiarize all supervisors with company policies and provide a termination checklist to use when conducting dismissals. One such checklist is shown in Figure 14–3.

Before deciding to dismiss an employee, managers should conduct a detailed review of all relevant facts, including the employee's side of the story. To

<table>
<tr><td colspan="2">Employee Information</td></tr>
<tr><td>Employee Name</td><td>Employee Number     Term Date</td></tr>
</table>

**Employee Information**

| Employee Name | Employee Number | Term Date |
|---|---|---|
|  |  |  |

**If termination is involuntary**

[ ] Documentation of performance issues and disciplinary action is in employee file

**Before employee's last day of employment**

| **Human Resources** | **Accounting / Finance** |
|---|---|
| [ ] Prepare COBRA letter<br>[ ] Schedule exit interview<br>[ ] Cancel stock options | [ ] Final paycheck is being prepared<br>[ ] Check for final balances on corporate credit card and cancel card<br>[ ] Final expense reports submitted<br>[ ] Final expense reports paid |

**Office Coordinator / Facilities**
[ ] Cancel voice mail account effective employee's last day
[ ] Request to have employee's network access closed effective employee's last day

**Last day of employment**

| | |
|---|---|
| [ ] Provide COBRA letter & explain<br>- 60 days to elect coverage<br>- 45 days to send in premium for<br>all months since coverage ceased<br>- premium due 1st of the month<br>[ ] Nondisclosure Agreement<br>- Provide copy<br>- Explain Noncompete<br>- Retrieve any confidential information<br>[ ] Vested stock options<br>- 90 days submit the form to exercise<br>[ ] Last paycheck (please check one)<br>   [ ] Provided at exit interview<br>OR<br>   [ ] Mailed after termination date | [ ] Provide 401(k) withdrawl form<br>[ ] Address changes verified<br>[ ] Collect or verify computer system(s) or equipment<br>[ ] Collect security card<br>[ ] Collect cell phone<br>[ ] Collect phone card<br>[ ] Collect corporate credit card<br>[ ] Exit interview questionnaire<br>[ ] Departure is communicated to staff<br>[ ] Eligible for rehire?<br>Yes_____ No_____<br>[ ] Terminate status in the HRIS system |

**After the employee's last day**

[ ] Check for any additional amounts owed for commissions, expense reports, etc.
[ ] Mail final pay stub to former employee, if necessary
[ ] Complete and submit benefit forms to stop coverage with insurance providers
[ ] If former employee submits a request for COBRA coverage, re-enroll using insurance-enrollment forms (Refer to COBRA process document)

**Figure 14–3**

The termination checklist.
(*Source:* Society for Human Resource Management. Retrieved from *www.shrm.org/ TemplatesTools/ Samples/HRForms/ Articles/Pages/ CMS_002039.aspx* on August 24, 2011.)

ensure consistent treatment, the supervisor should also examine how similar cases have been handled in the past. Once the decision to terminate has been made, the termination interview should minimize the trauma for the affected employee. Prior to conducting such an interview, the supervisor should be prepared to answer four basic questions: Who? When? Where? How?[84]

- *Who?* Typically, the employee's direct supervisor and a human resources representative will attend a termination meeting. This helps avoid a situation where it is one person's word against another's as to what occurred during the meeting.
- *When?* There is no "right" day of the week or time of day for every discharge. Termination at the end of the day may make sense if the employer has reason to believe the employee may be disruptive or threatening. Termination mid-day may allow the employee time to say good-bye to coworkers and clean out his or her office. A termination first thing in the morning may relieve managers from worrying about the meeting all day long, but it may leave the employee feeling like the employer wasted his or her time by making the employee come to work unnecessarily.
- *Where?* In private. The firing manager should arrange a neutral location and select seats that minimize the risk that an angry or violent employee will be able to block the exit.
- *How?* Employers should be prepared in advance to block computer-system access; change pass codes; remove the employee's name as a signatory to bank accounts or post-office boxes; collect keys, identification badges, and company property; and obtain adequate personal security if the situation becomes hostile.

Following these activities, the firing manager should follow five rules for the termination interview:[85]

1. *Present the situation in a clear, concise, and final manner.* Don't confuse the message to be delivered, and don't drag it out. "Tom, as you know, theft of company property is a serious offense, and the facts show clearly that you have done that on multiple occasions." Remember: Spend only a few minutes, don't make excuses, don't bargain, and don't compromise. Get to the point quickly and succinctly.
2. *Avoid debates or a rehash of the past.* Every employee has some redeeming features, so emphasize something positive about the employee, along with any deficiencies that may have contributed to the termination decision. Arguments about past performance may only compound bad feelings that already exist.
3. *Never talk down to the individual.* Be considerate and supportive, and allow the employee to maintain his or her dignity. Your objective should be to remove as much of the emotion and trauma as possible. Emphasize that it's a situation that isn't working and that the decision is made. It's a business decision—don't make excuses or apologies.
4. *Be empathetic but not compromising.* "I'm sorry that this has to happen, but the decision has been made."
5. *What's the next step?* "I'm going to give you this letter outlining remaining pay and benefit arrangements. If you have questions about any of these issues, there is a phone number listed in the letter, where you can receive further information from HR."

Be prepared for a variety of reactions from disbelief to silent acceptance to rage. The key is to remain calm and focus on helping the employee confront the reality of the situation. Maintain your distance and composure. It does no good to argue or cry along with the employee.

How do you handle the firing of people who just don't fit in—their work is passable but they just aren't suitable for the job, for reasons ranging from personal chemistry to mismatched skills? First, be sure that as the manager, you have explained what the job requires and what you expect. At Banco Popular North America, for example, managers are instructed to tell employees who are not fitting in exactly where they are not meeting expectations and to offer training to fix the problem before considering dismissal. Those are important steps, since many jobs at the bank have changed in recent years as a result of acquisitions and changes in marketing strategy.

If an employee must be fired, be honest, give as much notice as possible, and perhaps offer outplacement counseling or provide severance pay. "That way they walk out with their dignity and respect," says the bank's head of HR. Remember, employees who are not fitting in well are often unhappy themselves. They may agree that they would be better off elsewhere.[86] Having examined a very public issue, termination, let us now turn our attention to a related issue, employee privacy.

## EMPLOYEE PRIVACY AND ETHICAL ISSUES

In an 1890 *Harvard Law Review* article, former U.S. Supreme Court Justice Louis Brandeis defined **privacy** as the "right to be left alone."[87] It is the interest employees have in controlling the use of their personal information and in being able to engage in behavior free from regulation or surveillance.[88] Attention centers on three main issues: the kind of information collected and retained about individuals, how that information is used, and the extent to which it can be disclosed to

Organizations have the right to monitor the use of their computers by employees.

others. These issues often lead to **ethical dilemmas** for managers, that is, situations that have the potential to result in a breach of acceptable behavior.

But what is acceptable behavior? The difficulty lies in maintaining a proper balance between the common good and personal freedom, between the legitimate business needs of an organization and a worker's feelings of dignity and worth.[89] Although we cannot prescribe the *content* of ethical behavior across all conceivable situations, we can prescribe *processes* that may lead to an acceptable (and temporary) consensus among interested parties regarding an ethical course of action. In the remainder of this chapter, we will examine several areas that pose potential ethical dilemmas for employers and privacy concerns for employees or job applicants. Let us begin by considering fair-information-practice policies.

### Fair Information Practices in the Internet Age

Let's begin by discussing individual privacy outside of work settings. Every time you use the Web, companies can learn about you; thus 80 percent of major sites tracked user behavior in 2009, versus 40 percent in 2005. Many of them skirt privacy rules by sharing data with sister firms so that they can target ads to your demographic characteristics and interests. Chances are you are also revealing more than you know on social-media sites. Fully 73 percent of social-media profiles can be found through a public search engine, and 77 percent of social-network users do not restrict access to their photo albums. The risk? Losing out on jobs, among others. As of 2011, 58 percent of employers use social-networking sites to research job candidates, and 33 percent of those have found information that caused them not to hire a candidate.[90]

European regulators have established privacy guidelines for social-networking sites. Here are four key ones:[91]

- Sites should offer privacy-friendly default settings.
- Users should be advised that pictures should only be uploaded with the individual's consent.
- Sites must set maximum periods to retain data on inactive users. Abandoned accounts must be deleted.
- Users should be allowed to adopt a pseudonym.

In 2011 Facebook seized the initiative and rolled out new controls for sharing personal information, giving its more than 800 million users new tools to manage who can see information about them. It moved a number of privacy controls—which previously required navigating to a separate settings page—to users' home pages and profile pages, next to where they view and post content. The result? Facebook is now competing on privacy.[92]

On a company's intranet in the workplace, it is important to emphasize that, as a general matter, no absolute privacy exists, even for bosses.[93] They may view employees on video monitors; tap their phones, e-mail, and network communications; and rummage through their computer files with or without employee knowledge or consent, 24 hours a day. In some cases, however, courts are finding that unless employers explicitly tell employees that they will monitor e-mail, they do not have the legal right to do it—even if the e-mail in question was a personal one using a work account, rather than a personal address.[94]

What about instant messaging (IM), the immensely popular computer programs that let users exchange short text messages with online buddies in real time? Companies can pull up message logs stored locally on employees' computers, search logs stored remotely on a corporate or Web-hosted server, and even establish policies to block IMs containing certain words from being sent at all.[95]

Among major U.S. companies, about 78 percent do some form of electronic monitoring of employees. Some 74 percent monitor Internet connections, 72 percent e-mail, 31 percent IMs, and 40 percent phone conversations.[96]

Why do employers monitor their employees? They are mostly worried about two things: their legal liability for employee abuse of company information systems and employees' productivity.[97] Companies monitor e-mail and Internet activity to minimize their exposure to defamation, trade-secret, and breach-of-contract lawsuits. They also worry about copyright-infringement suits based on material employees download, including pictures, music files, and software. Their biggest concern, however, has to do with sexually explicit, racist, or other potentially offensive material that could lead to charges of a hostile work environment, as defined by harassment and discrimination laws. As an employee, how do you stay out of trouble? Consider adhering to the following practices in your personal conduct at work:

- Know your company's written policy. Ask your boss what constitutes "unreasonable" or "inappropriate" use.
- If you have any doubt about what personal Internet use your company allows, total abstinence is the best bet.
- Use your own e-mail account instead of your company's for personal correspondence at work.
- Limit personal surfing and e-mail to times clearly outside office hours.
- When composing e-mail or downloading Internet information, ask yourself if you would be willing to post it on your office door. If the answer is no, then don't proceed further.
- Remember this: When it comes to privacy in the workplace, it's best to assume that you don't have any.[98]

Safeguards to protect personal privacy are more important than ever. What should managers do? To establish a fair-information-practice policy, here are some general recommendations:

1. Set up guidelines and policies to protect information in the organization: types of data to be sought, methods of obtaining the data, retention and dissemination of information, employee or third-party access to information, release of information about former employees, and mishandling of information.
2. If you store, develop, or process data on a vendor's server running on the Internet, or "in the cloud," it is critical to perform due diligence to minimize the risks of compromised data, and to ensure that the service provider can meet regulatory requirements.[99]
3. Inform employees of these information-handling policies.
4. Become thoroughly familiar with state and federal laws regarding privacy.
5. Establish a policy that states specifically that employees and prospective employees cannot waive their rights to privacy.

---

## ETHICAL DILEMMA
### When a Soon-to-Be-Laid-Off Employee Asks for Advice*

You are a manager of a division targeted for lay-offs. You've seen the list of employees to be cut, but you've been asked to keep the information secret for two weeks. An employee on the list asks you whether he should be putting a down payment on his first home.

If you don't tell him, then he could be heading into a financial nightmare. If you do tell, you obviously break confidence with your company.

Word may spread, panicking enough employees that you end up with a stampede to the exit door. The problem deepens if yours is a public company implementing layoffs because of a pending merger or acquisition that has yet to be announced. If the employee you tell acts on the information or passes it on to others who do, you might incur legal problems because of violated securities regulations. What would you do?

*Source: Seglin, J. (2001, July 23). When an employee about to be axed asks for advice . . . *Fortune*, p. 268.

---

6. Establish a policy that any manager or nonmanager who violates these privacy principles will be subject to discipline or termination.
7. Allow employees to authorize disclosure of personal information and to maintain personal information within the organization.[100] Research has shown that an individual's perceived control over the uses of information after its disclosure is the single most important variable affecting perceptions of invasion of privacy.[101]

Next, managers should articulate, communicate, and carry out fair-information-practice policies by taking the following actions:[102]

1. Avoid fraudulent, secretive, or unfair means of collecting data. When possible, collect data directly from the individual concerned.
2. Do not maintain secret files on individuals. Inform them of what information is stored on them, the purpose for which it was collected, how it will be used, and how long it will be kept.
3. Collect only job-related information that is relevant for specific decisions.
4. Maintain records of individuals or organizations who have regular access or who request information on a need-to-know basis.
5. Periodically allow employees the right to inspect and update information stored on them.
6. Gain assurance that any information released to outside parties will be used only for the purposes set forth prior to its release.

Particularly since the corporate wrongdoings of Enron, Arthur Andersen, Adelphia, Tyco, WorldCom, and other organizations, the public in general, as well as peers and subordinates, tend to give executives low marks for honesty and ethical behavior.[103] Companies that have taken the kinds of measures just described, such as IBM, Bank of America, AT&T, Cummins Engine, Avis, and USAA, report that they have not been overly costly, produced burdensome traffic in access demands, or reduced the general quality of their HR decisions. Furthermore, they receive strong employee approval for their policies when they ask about them on company attitude surveys. By matching words with deeds, companies such as these are weaving their concerns for employee privacy into the very fabric of their corporate cultures.

## Assessment of Job Applicants and Employees

Decisions to hire, promote, train, or transfer are major events in individuals' careers. Frequently, such decisions are made with the aid of tests, interviews, situational exercises, performance appraisals, and other assessment techniques. Developers and users of these instruments must be concerned with questions of fairness, propriety, and individual rights, as well as with other ethical issues.

Developers, if they are members of professional associations such as the American Psychological Association, the Society for Human Resource Management, or the Academy of Management, are bound by the ethical standards put forth by those bodies.[104] Managers who use assessment instruments are subject to other ethical principles, beyond the general concerns for accuracy and equality of opportunity, including the following:[105]

- Guarding against invasion of privacy (e.g., with respect to biodata items, four areas seem to generate the greatest concern: self-incriminating items, those that require applicants to recall traumatic events, intimacy, and religion).[106]
- Guaranteeing confidentiality (treating information provided with the expectation that it will not be disclosed to others).
- Obtaining informed consent from employees and applicants before assessing them.
- Respecting employees' rights to know (e.g., regarding test content and the meaning, interpretation, and intended use of scores).
- Imposing time limitations on data (i.e., removing information that has not been used for HR decisions, especially if it has been updated).
- Using the most valid procedures available, thereby minimizing erroneous acceptances and erroneous rejections.
- Treating applicants and employees with respect and consideration (i.e., by standardizing procedures for all candidates).

What can applicants do when confronted by a question they believe is irrelevant or an invasion of privacy? Some may choose not to respond. However, research indicates that employers tend to view such nonresponse as an attempt to conceal facts that would reflect poorly on an applicant. Hence applicants (especially those who have nothing to hide) are ill advised not to respond.[107] Clearly, it is the employer's responsibility to (1) know the kinds of questions that are being asked of candidates and (2) to review the appropriateness and job relatedness of all such questions.

## Whistle-Blowing

Like a referee on a playing field who can blow the whistle to stop action, **whistle-blowing** refers to disclosure by former or current organization members of illegal, immoral, or illegitimate practices under the control of their employers to persons or organizations that may be able to do something about it.[108] Research indicates that individuals can be conditioned to behave unethically (if they are rewarded for it), especially under increased competition,[109] but that the threat of punishment has a counterbalancing influence.[110] More importantly, when a formal or informal organizational policy is present that favors ethical behavior, ethical behavior tends to increase.[111]

What are organizations actually doing? A 2011 poll of 390 organizations revealed that the top two methods that organizations use to let their employees know how to report unethical and/or illegal behavior are the employee handbook/company intranet (85 percent) and new-employee orientation (70 percent). As for reporting such behavior, most organizations (85 percent) encourage employees to contact HR. The next two most frequently offered channels are contacting the reporting employee's direct supervisor (65 percent) and contacting other senior managers (53 percent). About two out of five organizations (41 percent) offer an ethics hotline, but most employees would rather report wrongdoing directly to somebody they know than to a hotline. As for investigations themselves, the largest percentage of respondents indicated that HR investigates reported unethical behavior (89 percent) and illegal activity (86 percent). The next most often-cited source that conducts investigations is senior management (53 percent).[112]

After the wave of accounting scandals in the early 2000s, Congress passed whistle-blower protections in the 2002 Sarbanes-Oxley corporate reform law.[113] The act

- Makes it unlawful to discharge, demote, suspend, threaten, harass, or in any manner discriminate against a whistle-blower.
- Establishes criminal penalties of up to 10 years in jail for executives who retaliate against whistle-blowers.
- Requires board audit committees to establish procedures for hearing whistle-blower complaints.
- Allows the Secretary of Labor to order a company to rehire a terminated whistle-blower with no court hearings whatsoever.
- Gives a whistle-blower a right to a jury trial, bypassing months or years of cumbersome administrative hearings.

More recently, Congress passed the 2010 Dodd-Frank Wall Street Reform and Consumer Protection Act, which contains powerful new incentives for whistle-blowers as well as enhanced antiretaliation protections. These whistle-blower protections reach well beyond the financial-services industry and are not limited to public companies. The Act creates a substantial financial incentive for whistle-blowers who voluntarily report "original information" directly to the Securities and Exchange Commission (SEC) or to the Commodity Futures Trading Commission (CFTC) that leads to successful enforcement and the recovery of more than $1 million in monetary sanctions. Those who qualify may be awarded 10 to 30 percent of the collected monetary sanctions, with the specific amount determined by the SEC or CFTC.

To encourage employees to use internal compliance programs, SEC regulations provide that an employee will be treated as a whistle-blower as of the date the employee provides the information internally as long as the employee provides the same information to the SEC within 90 days. In addition, the SEC

# IMPACT OF PROCEDURAL JUSTICE AND ETHICS ON PRODUCTIVITY, QUALITY OF WORK LIFE, AND THE BOTTOM LINE

As we have seen throughout this chapter, employees and former employees are very sensitive to the general issue of "justice on the job." On a broad range of issues, they expect to be treated justly, fairly, and with due process. Doing so certainly contributes to improved productivity and quality of work life, because grievances are both time consuming and costly. On the other hand, organizations that disregard employee rights can expect two things: (1) to be hit with lawsuits, and (2) to find courts and juries to be sympathetic to tales of employer wrongdoing. Whistle-blower cases illustrate this trend clearly. The monetary consequences can be substantial as well. After whistle-blowers uncovered massive fraud at Cendant Corporation, the firm's market capitalization dropped a breathtaking $20 billion.[a] Conversely, a study of 2,481 firms subject to Sarbanes-Oxley corporate-governance compliance found that those with strong internal controls in place enjoyed market-beating gains in their share prices, while those with weak internal controls under-performed the market.[b] As in so many other areas of employee relations, careful attention to procedural justice and ethical decision making yields direct as well as indirect benefits. The old adage "An ounce of prevention is worth a pound of cure" says it all.

---

[a]Nelson, E., and Lublin, J. S. (1999, Aug. 13). Buy the numbers? How whistle-blowers set off a fraud probe that crushed Cendant. *The Wall Street Journal*, pp. A1, A8.

[b]Reilly, D. (2006, May 8). Checks on internal controls pay off. *The Wall Street Journal*, p. C3.

will "consider higher percentage awards for whistleblowers who first report violations through their company's internal compliance programs." Finally, The Dodd-Frank Act amends SOX to lengthen the statute of limitations for a SOX retaliation claim from 90 days to 180 days and to clarify that employees are entitled to have SOX retaliation claims tried before a jury.[114]

Despite retaliation, financial loss, and high emotional and physical stress,[115] whistle-blowers continue to come forward, and they are likely to continue to do so. In a recent study of 230 corporate fraud cases, almost 20 percent of them came to light as a result of employee disclosure, more often than the media, industry regulators, analysts, auditors, or the Securities and Exchange Commission. Yet 82 percent of the employees who uncovered the frauds said they were penalized—ostracized, demoted, or pressured to quit, for instance.[116] Are they social misfits? On the contrary, research indicates that most of them are well-adjusted individuals who have strong personal values that they live by.[117]

In the case of federal contractors, disclosure of fraud, waste, and abuse can lead to substantial financial gains by whistle-blowers. Thus under the federal False Claims Act of 1863, as amended, private citizens may sue a contractor for fraud on the government's behalf and share up to 30 percent of whatever financial recovery the government makes as a result of the charges.[118] In addition, the Dodd-Frank Act established a three-year statute of limitations for a retaliation claim under that Act. For example, when TAP Pharmaceutical Products paid an $875 million fine for conspiring with doctors to cheat the government,

## IMPLICATIONS FOR MANAGEMENT PRACTICE

Managers who fail to address employee concerns for ethics and procedural justice do so at their peril. In 2009, fully 63 percent of American workers who observed misconduct reported it, usually to an internal company authority.[a] Ethics programs are control systems whose objectives are to standardize employee behavior within the domains of ethics and legal compliance. Evidence now indicates that management, and especially top-management, commitment to an ethics program affects both its scope and control orientation. Programs of broad scope include multiple elements, dedicated staff, and extensive employee involvement. Control may be *compliance oriented,* emphasizing adherence to rules, monitoring employee behavior, and disciplining misconduct, or it may be *values oriented,* emphasizing commitment to shared values and encouraging ethical aspirations. Some programs strive for both, so that organizational values are not perceived as empty rhetoric.[b] Remember that employees' perceptions influence their judgments about procedural justice. In fact, multiple **meta-analyses** (quantitative cumulations of research studies) of studies of organizational justice have confirmed the beneficial effects on employee attitudes and performance of procedural-justice safeguards.[c] Provide explicit procedures for resolving conflicts and be sure that all employees know how to use them. Treat all people with dignity and respect, and they will respond with high levels of performance and commitment.

---

[a] Ethics Resource Center. (2010, Dec.) Blowing the whistle on workplace misconduct. Retrieved from *www.ethics.org/files/u5/WhistleblowerWP.pdf* on August 25, 2011.

[b] Weaver, G. R., Trevino, L. K., and Cochran, P. L. (1999). Corporate ethics programs as control systems: Influences of executive commitment and environmental factors. *Academy of Management Journal* 42, pp. 41–57.

[c] Greenberg, 2011, op. cit.

whistle-blower Doug Durand received $77 million for his efforts in the six-year investigation to expose the massive fraud.[119]

Whistle-blowing is likely to be effective to the extent that (1) the whistle-blower is credible and relatively powerful, (2) the reported information is clearly illegal and unambiguous, (3) the evidence is convincing, and (4) the organization itself encourages whistle-blowing and discourages retaliation against whistle-blowers.[120] If you have a tale to tell, begin by asking yourself four important questions:[121]

1. *Is this the only way?* Don't blow the whistle unless you have tried to correct the problem by reporting up the normal chain of command and gotten no results. Make sure your allegations are not minor complaints.
2. *Do I have the goods?* Gather documentary evidence that proves your case, and keep it in a safe place. Keep detailed notes, perhaps even a daily diary. Make sure you are seeing fraud, not merely incompetence or sloppiness.
3. *Why am I doing this?* Examine your motives. Don't act out of frustration or because you feel underappreciated or mistreated. Do not embellish your case, and do not violate any confidentiality agreements you may have.
4. *Am I ready?* Think through the impact on your family. Be prepared for unemployment and the possibility of being blacklisted in your profession. Last but not least, consult a lawyer.

## Conclusion

Ethical behavior is not governed by hard-and-fast rules. Rather, it adapts and changes in response to social norms. This is nowhere more obvious than in human resource management. What was considered ethical in the 1950s and 1960s (deep-probing selection interviews; management prescriptions of standards of dress, ideology, and lifestyle; refusal to let employees examine their own employment files) would be considered improper today. Indeed, as we have seen, growing concern for employee rights has placed organizational decision-making policies in the public domain. The beneficial effect of this, of course, is that it is sensitizing both employers and employees to new concerns.

To be sure, ethical choices are rarely easy. The challenge in managing human resources lies not in the mechanical application of moral prescriptions, but rather in the process of creating and maintaining genuine relationships from which to address ethical dilemmas that cannot be covered by prescription.[122]

---

### *ALTERNATIVE DISPUTE RESOLUTION: GOOD FOR THE COMPANY, GOOD FOR EMPLOYEES?*

*Human Resource Management in Action: Conclusion*

In a 2001 decision (*Circuit City Stores Inc. v. Adams*), the U.S. Supreme Court ruled that an employer can enforce a signed agreement that obligates an employee to take all employment-related disputes to arbitration rather than to court. While job applicants can be required to sign an agreement to arbitrate employment disputes as the exclusive remedy for claims against the company, current employees may require different treatment. The employer may encourage—but not require—current employees to sign such an agreement with some "additional consideration." Such consideration often takes the form of a one-time payment or bonus or some form of time off. Now that there is no question about enforceability of such agreements, opponents might point to flaws in the procedural fairness of the process as a basis for a petition to a court to nullify an agreement.

This raises another issue, namely, what does a fair ADR program look like? According to attorneys and HR professionals, a fair ADR program is neutral, confidential, provides due process to the employee, and does not limit the remedies available to the employee. Moreover, it imposes fees (if any) that are no higher than what it would cost an employee to file a claim in court. In addition to these features, sound ADR programs incorporate the following principles:

- **Don't argue needlessly.** Employers with well-managed programs often use internal appeals procedures with multiple levels. The employee first discusses his or her problem with the immediate supervisor. If not resolved, the employee appeals to a higher level of management or a committee composed of management, employees, or a combination of the two.
- **Top management emphasizes that the program is not voluntary.** Everyone is expected to work to make it a success.
- **Involve all stakeholders in the design of the program.** Seek their input and support.
- **Identify metrics to measure the program's progress.** Compare your system with those of other companies.

- **Train employees and managers to address and resolve conflicts early and at the lowest possible level.**
- **Listen to any dissatisfied user of the program and make appropriate adjustments.**
- **Market the program internally to ensure trust and use, and externally to publicize your company's strength.** It is an employee benefit that distinguishes your company as an open-minded, fair employer and a good place to work.

Like other HR initiatives, ADR programs have both negative and positive features. On the one hand, ADR procedures may increase the number of employee claims, and unfavorable arbitration decisions are almost impossible to overturn. On the other hand, employees can pursue the same claims in arbitration that they could in court, and claims can be resolved much more quickly. Arbitrators can award damages in the same fashion that a judge or jury can. On balance, therefore, programs that incorporate features that are designed to ensure procedural justice are good for employers *and* good for employees. They will likely encourage both sides to make greater use of ADR in the future.

## SUMMARY

The broad theme of this chapter is "justice on the job." This includes procedural justice, due process, and ethical decision making. Each of these processes should guide the formulation of policy in matters involving dispute resolution (e.g., through grievance procedures), arbitration, discipline, employment contracts, and termination for disciplinary or economic reasons. Indeed, such concerns for procedural justice and due process form the basis for many challenges to the employment-at-will doctrine.

Two of the most important employment issues of our time are employee privacy and ethical decision making. Three areas that involve employee privacy are receiving considerable emphasis: fair information practices in the Internet age, the assessment of job applicants and employees, and whistle-blowing. Although it is not possible to prescribe the content of ethical behavior in each of these areas, processes that incorporate procedural justice can lead to an acceptable (and temporary) consensus among interested parties regarding an ethical course of action.

## KEY TERMS

| | |
|---|---|
| alternative dispute resolution (ADR) program | organizational citizenship behaviors |
| employee relations | organizational support |
| justice | employee voice |
| procedural justice | interactional justice |
| distributive justice | informational justice |
| due process | skip-level policy |
| constitutional due-process rights | open-door policy |
| ethical decisions about behavior | peer-review panel |

nonunion arbitration

mediation

ombudspersons

just cause

social learning theory

progressive discipline

red-hot-stove rule

employment at will

public policy exception

implied promises

retaliatory discharge

lifestyle discrimination

noncompete agreements

fiduciary duty of loyalty

choice-of-law provision

privacy

ethical dilemma

whistle-blowing

meta-analysis

## DISCUSSION QUESTIONS

**14–1.** Discuss the similarities and differences in these concepts: procedural justice, workplace due process, and ethical decisions about behavior.

**14–2.** What advice would you give to an executive who is about to negotiate an employment contract?

**14–3.** Is it ethical to record a conversation with your boss without his or her knowledge?

**14–4.** How can a firm avoid lawsuits for employment at will?

**14–5.** What are some guidelines to follow in determining a reasonable compromise between a company's need to run its business and employee rights to privacy?

**14–6.** In the course of your job, you learn that someone is "cooking the books." Discuss the steps you would take to resolve the issue.

## APPLYING YOUR KNOWLEDGE

*Blowing the Whistle*                                                              *Case 14–1*

Consider four well-known whistle-blowing incidents and their consequences.

■ **Cynthia Cooper, WorldCom.** In 2002, Cooper, the telecommunications firm's internal auditor, and others, uncovered what was then the biggest accounting scandal in U.S. history. Working after hours, Cooper's team found $3.8 billion in phantom expenses and dicey balance-sheet entries. After they reported their findings to the company's board of directors, chief financial officer Scott Sullivan was fired and later pleaded guilty to securities fraud and other crimes. Four other WorldCom executives went to jail, but justice came down hardest on the company's founder, Bernard J. Ebbers, who was sentenced to 25 years of hard time.

■ **Coleen Rowley, FBI.** After the September 11, 2001, attacks, attorney and Special Agent Rowley wrote a paper for FBI Director Robert Mueller documenting how the FBI's internal organization and mishandling of information related to the September 11, 2001, attacks may have left the U.S. vulnerable. Rowley was one of many agents frustrated by the events that led up to the attacks. She also testified in front of the Senate and for the 9/11 Commission about these matters. Mueller and Iowa senator Chuck Grassley pushed for and got a major reorganization, focused on creation of the new Office of Intelligence at the FBI. Rowley retired from the FBI in 2004 after 24 years with the agency.

■ **Christoph Meili, UBS.** The UBS night guard discovered that the Swiss financial-services giant was destroying Holocaust-era asset records of deceased Jews whose heirs could not be found, among other illegal activities. He turned some of the remaining documents over to a Zurich-based Jewish organization, leading to a civil suit by heirs of Holocaust victims against Swiss banks that was settled for $1.25 billion in 1998. For his troubles, Meili was fired from his job, received death threats, and was investigated by Swiss prosecutors for violating banking-secrecy laws. He was granted political asylum in the United States in 1997, but returned to Switzerland in 2009.

■ **Sherron Watkins, Vice President of Corporate Development, Enron.** When she wrote to then-chairman Kenneth Lay in 2001, "I am incredibly nervous that we will implode in a wave of accounting scandals," Lay paid little mind, and was rewarded by becoming the poster boy for corporate malfeasance when those practices exploded into a national scandal soon after. For her efforts, Sherron Watkins was selected as one of three "Persons of the Year 2002" by *Time magazine.* The two whistleblowers who joined her were Cynthia Cooper of WorldCom and Coleen Rowley of the FBI.

### Questions

1. What kinds of circumstances might drive employees to blow the whistle?
2. Why might some employees observe wrongdoing and come forward, while others do not?
3. As a manager, what procedures or processes might you suggest to encourage more employees to blow the whistle when necessary?
4. Use the four-part framework presented earlier (namely, is this the only way, do I have the goods, why am I doing this, am I ready to accept the consequences?) to analyze each whistle-blower's actions. What additional information do you need to answer the four questions?

## REFERENCES

1. Fossum, J. A. (2012). *Labor Relations: Development, Structure, Process.* (11th Ed.). Burr Ridge, IL: McGraw-Hill/Irwin.
2. *Merriam-Webster's Collegiate Dictionary.* (11th ed.) (2003). Springfield, MA: Merriam-Webster.
3. Greenberg, J. (2011). Organizational justice: The dynamics of fairness in the workplace. In S. Zedeck (Ed.), *APA Handbook of Industrial and Organizational Psychology,* Vol. 3. Washington, DC: American Psychological Association, pp. 271–327.
4. Ibid. See also Colquitt, J. A., Conlon, D. E., Wesson, M. J., Porter, C. O. L. H., and Ng, K. Y. (2001). Justice at the millennium: A meta-analytic review of 25 years of organizational justice research. *Journal of Applied Psychology* 86, pp. 425–445.
5. Greenberg, 2011, op. cit. See also Colella, A. (2001). Coworker distributive fairness judgments of the workplace accommodation of employees with disabilities. *Academy of Management Review* 26, pp. 100–116.
6. Wesman, E. C., and Eischen, D. E. (1990). Due process. In J. A. Fossum (Ed.), *Employee and Labor Relations.* Washington, DC: Bureau of National Affairs, pp. 4–82 to 4–133.
7. MacKinnon, B. (2011). *Ethics: Theory and Contemporary Issues.* Belmont, CA: Wadsworth. See also Lefkowitz , J. (2006). The constancy of ethics amidst the changing world of work. *Human Resource Management Review* 16, pp. 245–268. See also Nielsen, R. P. (1989). Changing unethical organizational behavior. *Academy of Management Executive* 3(2), pp. 123–130.

**8.** Greenberg, 2011, op. cit. See also Simons, T., and Roberson, Q. (2003). Why managers should care about fairness: The effects of aggregate justice perceptions on organizational outcomes. *Journal of Applied Psychology* 88, pp. 432–443. See also Kanovsky, M. (2000). Understanding procedural justice and its impact on business organizations. *Journal of Management* 26, pp. 489–511.

**9.** Greenberg, J. (2010). Organizational injustice as an occupational health risk. *Academy of Management Annals* 4, pp. 205–243. See also Elovainio, M., Kivimaki, M., and Helkama, K. (2001). Organizational justice evaluations, job control, and occupational strain. *Journal of Applied Psychology* 86, pp. 418–424.

**10.** Organ, D. W. Podsakoff, P. M., and Podsakoff, N. P. (2011). Expanding the criterion domain to include organizational citizenship behavior: Implications for employee selection. In S. Zedeck (Ed.), *APA Handbook of Industrial and Organizational Psychology,* Vol. 2. Washington, DC: American Psychological Association, pp. 281–323.

**11.** Ehrhart, M. (2004). Leadership and procedural justice climate as antecedents of unit-level organizational citizenship behavior. *Personnel Psychology* 57, pp. 61–94.

**12.** Organ, D. W., and Ryan, K. (1995). A meta-analytic review of attitudinal and dispositional predictors of organizational citizenship behavior. *Personnel Psychology* 48, pp. 775–802. See also Allen, T. D., and Rush, M. C. (1998). The effects of organizational citizenship behavior on performance judgments: A field study and a laboratory experiment. *Journal of Applied Psychology* 83, pp. 247–260.

**13.** Organ et al., 2011, op. cit. See also Moorman, R. H., Blakely, G. L., and Niehoff, B. P. (1998). Does perceived organizational support mediate the relationship between procedural justice and organizational citizenship behavior? *Academy of Management Journal* 41, pp. 351–357.

**14.** Organ et al., 2011, op. cit. See also Liao, H., and Rupp, D. E. (2005). The impact of justice climate and justice orientation on work outcomes: A cross-level multifoci framework. *Journal of Applied Psychology* 90, pp. 242–256. See also Naumann, S. E., and Bennett, N. (2000). A case for procedural justice climate: Development and test of a multilevel model. *Academy of Management Journal* 43, pp. 881–889.

**15.** Kanovsky, 2000, op. cit.

**16.** Colquitt, J. A. (2001). On the dimensionality of organizational justice: A construct validation of a measure. *Journal of Applied Psychology* 86, pp. 386–400.

**17.** Greenberg, 2011, op. cit. See also Leung, K., Tong, K. K., and Ho, S. S. Y. (2004). Effects of interactional justice on egocentric bias in resource allocation decisions. *Journal of Applied Psychology* 89, pp. 405–415. See also Bies, R. J. (2001). Interactional (in)justice: The sacred and the profane. In J. Greenberg and R. Cropanzano (Eds.), *Advances in Organizational Justice.* Lexington, MA: Lexington Press.

**18.** Choi, J. (2008). Event justice perceptions and employees' reactions: Perceptions of social entity justice as a moderator. *Journal of Applied Psychology* 93, pp. 513–528. See also Masterson, S. S., Lewis, K., Goldman, B. M., and Taylor, M. S. (2000). Integrating justice and social exchange: The differing effects of fair procedures and treatment on work relationships. *Academy of Management Journal* 4, pp. 738–748.

**19.** Brockner, J. (2010). *A Contemporary Look at Organizational Justice: Multiplying Insult Times Injury.* New York, NY: Routledge. See also Gopinath, C., and Becker, T. E. (2000). Communication, procedural justice, and employee attitudes: Relationships under conditions of divestiture. *Journal of Management* 26, pp. 63–83.

**20.** Mishra, A. K., and Spreitzer, G. M. (1998). Explaining how survivors respond to downsizing: The roles of trust, empowerment, justice, and work redesign. *Academy of Management Journal* 23, pp. 567–588. See also Brockner, J., and Wiesenfeld, B. M. (1996). An integrative framework for explaining reactions to decisions: Interactive effects of outcomes and procedures. *Psychological Bulletin* 120, pp. 189–208.

**21.** Choi, 2008, op. cit.

**22.** Sheppard, B. H., Lewicki, R. J., and Minton, J. W. (1992). *Organizational Justice: The Search for Fairness in the Workplace.* New York: Lexington.

23. De Dreu, C. K. (2011). Conflict at work: Basic principles and applied issues. In S. Zedeck (Ed.), *APA Handbook of Industrial and Organizational Psychology,* Vol. 3. Washington, DC: American Psychological Association, pp. 461–493. See also Budd, J. W. (2010). *Labor Relations: Striking a Balance* (2nd Ed.). Burr Ridge, IL: McGraw-Hill/Irwin.

24. Hirschman, C. (2003). Someone to listen. *HR Magazine* 48(1), pp. 46–51. See also Arnold, J. A., and O'Connor, K. M. (1999). Ombudspersons or peers? The effect of third-party expertise and recommendations on negotiation. *Journal of Applied Psychology* 84, pp. 776–785.

25. Sheppard et al., 1992, op. cit.

26. Budd, 2010, op. cit.

27. De Dreu, 2011, op. cit. Sheppard et al., 1992, op. cit.

28. Tyler, T. R., and Bies, R. J. (1990). Beyond formal procedures: The interpersonal context of procedural justice. In J. S. Carroll (Ed.), *Applied Psychology and Organizational Settings.* Hillsdale, NJ: Erlbaum, pp. 77–98.

29. Brockner, 2010, op. cit. See also Society for Human Resource Management Foundation. (2006). *Ethics, the Fabric of Business* (DVD). Alexandria, VA: SHRM Foundation.

30. Schwalje, M. K. (2010, March 12). Under-the-radar ADR decision. *HR News.* Retrieved from *www.shrm.org/Publications/LegalReport/Pages/March2010Under-the-RadarADRDecision.aspx* on August 22, 2011. See also Olson-Buchanan, J. B., and Boswell, W. R. (2008). Organizational dispute-resolution systems. In C. K. W. De Dreu and M. J. Gelfand (Eds.), *The Psychology of Conflict and Conflict Management in Organizations.* New York, NY: Erlbaum, pp. 321–352. See also Katz, H. C., Kochan, T. A., and Colvin, A. J. S. (2008). *An Introduction to Collective Bargaining and Industrial Relations* (4th Ed.). Burr Ridge, IL: McGraw-Hill/Irwin. See also Colvin, A. J. S. (2003). Institutional pressures, human resource strategies, and the rise of nonunion dispute-resolution procedures. *Industrial and Labor Relations Review* 56, pp. 375–392.

31. De Dreu, 2011, op. cit. See also Katz et al., 2008, op. cit.

32. Posthuma, R. A. (2010). *Workplace Dispute Resolution.* Alexandria, VA: Society for Human Resource Management.

33. Fossum, 2012, op. cit. See also Katz et al., 2008, op. cit.

34. Katz et al., 2008, op. cit. See also Hirschman, 2003, op. cit.

35. Budd, 2010, op. cit.

36. FedEx attributes success to people-first philosophy. Retrieved from *www.fedex.com/ma/about/overview/philosophy.html* on August 23, 2011. See also Ewing, J. B. (1989, Oct. 23). Corporate due process lowers legal costs. *The Wall Street Journal,* p. A14.

37. Budd, 2010, op. cit.

38. Smith, A. (2011, April 13). ADR is underused tool for resolving disputes. *HR News.* Retrieved from *www.shrm.org/LegalIssues/FederalResources/Pages/ADRIsUnderusedTool.aspx* on August 22, 2011. See also Hendriks, E. S. (2000, June). Do more than open doors. *HR Magazine,* pp. 171–181.

39. Seeley, R. S. (1992, July). Corporate due process. *HR Magazine,* pp. 46–49.

40. Katz et al., 2008, op. cit. See also Budd, 2010, op. cit. See also Wesman and Eischen, 1990, op. cit.

41. Welch, J., and Welch, S. (2006, Nov. 13). Send the jerks packing. *BusinessWeek,* p. 136. See also Cottringer, W. (2003, April). The abc's of employee discipline. *Supervision* 64(4), pp. 5, 7. See also Falcone, P. (1997, Feb.). Fundamentals of progressive discipline. *HR Magazine,* pp. 90–94.

42. Hymowitz, C. (1998, July 28). Managers struggle to find a way to let someone go. *The Wall Street Journal,* p. B1.

43. Andrews, L. W. (2004, Dec.). Hard-core offenders. *HR Magazine,* pp. 43–48.

44. Fossum, 2012, op. cit. See also Cottringer, 2003, op. cit. See also O'Reilly, C. A. III, and Weitz, B. A. (1980). Managing marginal employees: The use of warnings and dismissals. *Administrative Science Quarterly* 25, pp. 467–484.

45. Bandura, A. (1986). *Social Foundations of Thought and Action: A Social Cognitive Theory.* Englewood Cliffs, NJ: Prentice-Hall.

46. Trevino, L. K. (1992). The social effects of punishments in organizations: A justice perspective. *Academy of Management Review* 17, pp. 647–676.

47. Salvo, T. (2004, July). Practical tips for successful progressive discipline. Retrieved from *www.shrm.org/Research/Articles/Articles/Pages/CMS_009030.aspx,* on August 23, 2011. See also O'Reilly, C. A. III, and Puffer, S. M. (1989). The impact of rewards and punishments in a social context: A laboratory and field experiment. *Journal of Occupational Psychology* 62, pp. 41–53.

48. Salvo, 2004, op. cit. See also Cottringer, 2003, op. cit.

49. Hastings, R. R. (2010, Jan. 9). Is progressive discipline a thing of the past? *HR News.* Retrieved from *www.shrm.org/hrdisciplines/employeerelations/articles/Pages/IsProgressiveDisciplineaThing.aspx* on August 23, 2011.

50. Klaas, B. S., and Feldman, D. C. (1994). The impact of appeal system structure on disciplinary decisions. *Personnel Psychology* 47, pp. 91–108. See also Klaas, B. S., and Dell'omo, G. G. (1991). The determinants of disciplinary decisions: The case of employee drug use. *Personnel Psychology* 44, pp. 813–835.

51. Klaas, B. S., and Wheeler, H. N. (1990). Managerial decision making about employee discipline: A policy-capturing approach. *Personnel Psychology* 43, pp. 117–134.

52. Katz et al., 2008, op. cit.

53. *NLRB v. J. Weingarten* (1975). 420 U.S. 251, 95 S. Ct. 959.

54. Budd, 2010, op. cit. See also Discipline: I've heard non-union employees can no longer appeal to Weingarten rights. Is this true? (2008, Feb. 25). *HR News.* Retrieved from *www.shrm.org/TemplatesTools/hrqa/Pages/weingartenrights.aspx* on August 23, 2011.

55. Weingarten rights include prior consultation (1992, Aug.). *Mountain States Employers Council Bulletin,* p. 4.

56. Employee's "Weingarten" rights limited by NLRB. (1993, Jan.). *Mountain States Employers Council Bulletin,* p. 4.

57. Budd, 2010, op. cit.

58. Siegel, M. (1998, Oct. 26). Yes, they *can* fire you. *Fortune,* p. 301.

59. Involuntary termination of employment in the United States. (2008, Dec. 8). *SHRM Online.* Retrieved from *www.shrm.org/Research/Articles/Articles/Pages/InvoluntaryTerminationofEmploymentintheUnitedStates.aspx* on August 23, 2011.

60. Budd, 2010, op. cit. See also Mitchell, B. (1999, Jan. 25). "At-will" employment isn't safe harbor for companies. *The Denver Post,* p. 5L.

61. Koys, D. J., Briggs, S., and Grenig, J. (1987). State court disparity on employment-at-will. *Personnel Psychology* 40, pp. 565–577.

62. Falcone, P. (2002, May). Fire my assistant now! *HR Magazine,* pp. 105–111. See also Click, J. (1999, July). Handbook created contract employer can't unilaterally alter. *HR News,* p. 8. See also Heshizer, B. (1984). The implied contract exception to at-will employment. *Labor Law Journal* 35, pp. 131–141.

63. Siegel, 1998, op. cit.

64. Wermiel, S. (1988, June 7). Justices expand union workers' right to sue. *The Wall Street Journal,* p. 4.

65. Rives, A. L. (2006). You're not the boss of me: A call for federal lifestyle discrimination legislation. *George Washington Law Review* 74, pp. 553–568. See also Safer, M. (2006, July 16). Whose life is it anyway? *60 Minutes,* CBS News.

66. Click, 1999, op. cit. See also Handbooks. (1994, Jan.). *Mountain States Employers Council Bulletin,* p. 2. See also Fulmer, W. E., and Casey, A. W. (1990). Employment at will: Options for managers. *Academy of Management Executive* 4(2), pp. 102–107.

67. Involuntary termination of employment in the United States, 2008, op. cit.

68. Katz et al., 2008, op. cit. See also Engel, P. G. (1985, Mar. 18). Preserving the right to fire. *Industry Week,* pp. 39–40.

69. Obdyke, L. K. (2002, Aug). Written employment contracts—When? Why? How? Retrieved from *www.shrm.org/Publications/LegalReport/Pages/CMS_000959.aspx* on October 19, 2004.

70. Baig, E. C. (1997, Mar. 17). Beware the ties that bind. *Fortune,* pp. 120–121.

71. Armstrong, D. (2004, June 14). What does a non-compete pact truly bar? Nasty row sorts it out. *The Wall Street Journal,* pp. A1, A8.

72. Wirtz, D. M. (2002, Nov.). Tip the scales on non-compete agreements. *HR Magazine,* pp. 107–115.

73. Arbery, C. (2010, June 4). 11th Circuit: Noncompete valid if it is reasonable and balanced. *SHRM Legal Report.* Retrieved from *www.shrm.org/LegalIssues/Federal Resources/Pages/11thNoncompete.aspx* on August 18, 2010.

74. Sandler, D. R. (1998, Winter). Non-compete agreements: Considering ties that bind. *SHRM Legal Report,* pp. 5–8.

75. Nadel, D. E., and Freimann, M. A. (2007, Aug. 27). Colorado court clarifies parameters of permissible noncompete agreements. Retrieved from *www.shrm.org* on July 27, 2007. See also Delaney, K. J., and Guth, R. A. (2005, Sept. 14). Ruling lets Lee go to work at Google. *The Wall Street Journal,* p. B2.

76. Deschenaux, J. (2007, Aug. 28). Enforceability of noncompete agreements differs from state to state. *SHRM Legal Report.* Retrieved from *www.shrm.org/LegalIssues/ EmploymentLawAreas/Pages/CMS_022828.aspx* on August 23, 2011.

77. Jamgotchian, R. (2006, Sept.). Noncompete agreements have no place in Calif. employment contracts. Retrieved from *www.shrm.org/LegalIssues/StateandLocalResources/ Pages/CMS_018480.aspx* on Sept. 26, 2007.

78. Orey, M. (Ed). (2007, Aug. 27). How you mop could be a trade secret. *BusinessWeek,* p. 76. See also Obdyke, L. K. (1998, Spring). Written employment contracts—When? Why? How? *SHRM Legal Report,* pp. 1–4.

79. Written employment contracts: Pros and cons. Retrieved from *www.nolo.com/legal-encyclopedia/written-employment-contracts-pros-cons-30193.html* on August 23, 2011. See also Stickney, J. (1984, Dec.). Settling the terms of employment. *Money,* pp. 127–128, 132.

80. Falcone, 2002, op. cit.

81. Geyelin, M. (1989, Sept. 7). Fired managers winning more lawsuits. *The Wall Street Journal,* p. B13.

82. Warner, M. (2001, Jan. 22). Pity the poor dot-commer (a little bit). *Fortune,* p. 40.

83. Needleman, S. (2008, July 8). Bad firings can hurt firm's reputation. *The Wall Street Journal,* p. D4. See also Bliss, W., and Thornton, G. R. (2006). *Employment Termination Sourcebook.* Alexandria, VA: Society for Human Resource Management. See also Bing, S. (1997, Feb. 3). Stepping up to the firing line. *Fortune,* pp. 51–52.

84. Involuntary termination of employment in the United States, 2008, op. cit. See also Needleman, 2008, op. cit. See also Kane, K. (2004). Best practices for employee termination. Retrieved from *www.recruitersnetwork.com/articles/article.cfm?ID=1152,* on October 19, 2004.

85. Coleman, F. T. (2006, July). Cardinal rules of termination. Retrieved from *www.shrm. org/Publications/LegalReport/Pages/CMS_000943.aspx* on August 5, 2008. See also Coleman, F. T. (2001). *Ending the Employment Relationship without Ending up in Court.* Alexandria, VA: Society for Human Resource Management.

86. Dvorak, P. (2006, May 1). Firing good workers who are a bad fit. *The Wall Street Journal,* p. B5.

87. Zeidner, R. (2008, Aug.). Out of the breach. *HR Magazine* 53(8). Retrieved from *www.shrm.org/Publications/hrmagazine/EditorialContent/Pages/0808zeidner. aspx* on August 5, 2008.

88. Piller, C. (1993, July). Privacy in peril. *Macworld,* pp. 124–130.

89. Searcey, D. (2009, Nov. 19). Some courts raise bar on reading employee email. *The Wall Street Journal,* p. A17. See also Leaving "friendprints": How online social

networks are redefining privacy and personal security. (2009, June 10). *Knowledge@ Wharton,* pp. 1–3. See also Privacy. (1999, Apr. 5). *BusinessWeek,* pp. 84–90.

90. Mangla, I. S. (2011, May). The cost of losing your online privacy. *Money,* p. 16.

91. Dalton, M. (2009, June 24). EU lays out web privacy rules. *The Wall Street Journal,* p. B8.

92. Fowler, G. A., and Efrati, A. (2011, Aug. 24). Facebook revamps privacy controls. *The Wall Street Journal,* p. B6.

93. E-mail may be hazardous to your career. (2007, May 14). *Fortune,* pp. 24–25. See also Leonard, D. C., and France, A. H. (2006, Dec.). Workplace monitoring: Balancing business interests with employee privacy rights. *SHRM Legal Report,* pp. 3–7.

94. Searcey, 2009, op. cit.

95. Sharma, A., and Vascellaro, J. E. (2006, Oct. 4). Those IMs aren't as private as you think. *The Wall Street Journal,* pp. D1, D2.

96. Zeidner, 2008, op. cit. See also Leonard and France, 2006, op. cit.

97. Searcey, 2009, op. cit. See also Richmond, R. (2004, Jan. 12). It's 10 A.M. Do you know where your workers are? *The Wall Street Journal,* pp. R1, R4.

98. Sandberg, J. (2005, May 18). Monitoring of workers is boss's right, but why not include top brass? *The Wall Street Journal,* pp. B1, B4. See also Maher, K. (2003, Nov. 4). Big employer is watching. *The Wall Street Journal,* pp. B1, B6. See also Segal, J. A. (2002). Security vs. privacy. *HR Magazine* 47(2), pp. 93–96.

99. Wright, A. D. (2011, Aug. 15). Cloud computing and security: How safe is HR data in the cloud? SHRM Online. Retrieved from *www.shrm.org/hrdisciplines/technology/Articles/Pages/CloudSecurity.aspx* on August 23, 2011.

100. Roberts, B. (2008, May). Protecting employee data globally. *HR Magazine* 53(5), pp. 83–86. See also Eddy, E. R., Stone, D. L., and Stone-Romero, E. F. (1999). The effects of information management policies on reactions to human resource information systems: An integration of privacy and procedural justice perspectives. *Personnel Psychology* 52, pp. 335–358.

101. Fusilier, M. R., and Hoyer, W. D. (1980). Variables affecting perceptions of invasion of privacy in a personnel selection situation. *Journal of Applied Psychology* 65, pp. 623–626.

102. Leonard and France, 2006, op. cit. See also Borrus, A. (2000, July 17). Web privacy: That's one small step. *BusinessWeek,* p. 50. See also Cook, S. H. (1987). Privacy rights: Whose life is it anyway? *Personnel Administrator* 32(4), pp. 58–65.

103. Wulfhorst, E. (2009, Feb. 27). Wall Street rates poorly for ethics, honesty. Retrieved from *www.reuters.com/article/2009/02/27/us-usa-ethics-idUSTRE51Q02T20090227* on August 24, 2011. See also Saad, L. (2008, Nov. 24). Nurses shine, bankers slump in ethics ratings. Retrieved from *www.gallup.com/poll/112264/Nurses-Shine-While-Bankers-Slump-Ethics-Ratings.aspx* on August 24, 2011. See also Alsop, R. (2004, Feb. 19). Corporate scandals hit home. *The Wall Street Journal.* Retrieved from *www.reputationinstitute.com/press/WSJ_19Feb2004.pdf* on October 20, 2004.

104. See, for example, Academy of Management. (2005, Dec.). The Academy of Management code of ethics. Retrieved from *www.aomonline.org/GovernanceAndEthics/AOMCodeOfEthics.pdf* on August 25, 2011. See also American Psychological Association. (2002). Ethical principles of psychologists and code of conduct. *American Psychologist* 57, pp. 1060–1073. See also Society for Industrial and Organization Psychology Inc. (2003). *Principles for the Validation and Use of Personnel Selection Procedures* (4th Ed.). Bowling Green, OH: Author. See also Society for Human Resource Management. (2007, Nov. 16). SHRM code of ethical and professional standards in human resource management. Retrieved from *www.shrm.org/ethics/code-of-ethics.asp* on August 25, 2011.

105. Cascio, W. F., and Aguinis, H. (2011). *Applied Psychology in Human Resource Management* (7th Ed.). Upper Saddle River, NJ: Prentice-Hall.

106. Mael, F. A., Connerley, M., and Morath, R. A. (1996). None of your business: Parameters of biodata invasiveness. *Personnel Psychology* 49, pp. 614–650.

107. Stone, D. L., and Stone, E. F. (1987). Effects of missing application-blank information on personnel selection decisions: Do privacy-protection strategies bias the outcome? *Journal of Applied Psychology* 72, pp. 452–456.

108. Miceli, M. P., and Near, J. P. (1992). *Blowing the Whistle.* New York: Lexington.

109. Craig, G. (2008, May 11). Fraud trial raises issues over purse strings at Kodak. Retrieved from *www.democratandchronicle.com* on May 12, 2008. See also A whistle-blower rocks an industry. (2002, June 24). *BusinessWeek,* pp. 126–130.

110. Lunsford, J. L. (2006, June 13). Piloting Boeing's new course. *The Wall Street Journal,* pp. B1, B3. See also Jansen, E., and Von Glinow, M. A. (1985). Ethical ambivalence and organizational reward systems. *Academy of Management Review* 10, pp. 815–822.

111. Bates, S. (2011, Jan. 12). View of senior management critical to whistle-blowers, research finds. *SHRM Online.* Retrieved from *www.shrm.org/hrdisciplines/ethics/ articles/Pages/CultureAndWhistleblowers.aspx* on August 25, 2011. See also White, E. (2006, June 12). What would you do? Ethics courses get context. *The Wall Street Journal,* p. B3. See also Hegarty, W. H., and Sims, H. P., Jr. (1979). Organizational philosophy, policies, and objectives related to unethical decision behavior: A laboratory experiment. *Journal of Applied Psychology* 64, pp. 331–338.

112. Society for Human Resource Management. (2011, Mar. 25). *Organizational whistle blowing—Reporting unethical and illegal behavior in the workplace.* (2011, March 25). Alexandria, VA: Society for Human Resource Management. See also Ethics Resource Center. (2010, Dec.). Blowing the whistle on workplace misconduct. Retrieved from *www.ethics.org/files/u5/WhistleblowerWP.pdf* on August 25, 2011.

113. Salvatore, P., and Leonard, L. S. (2006, Dec.). *The Sarbanes-Oxley Act of 2002: New federal protection for whistleblowers.* Retrieved from *www.shrm.org/Publications/ LegalReport/Pages/CMS_001022.aspx* on August 6, 2008.

114. Lawrence-Hardy, A. J., and Peiffer, L. A. (2011, July 25). SEC's whistle-blower rules effective soon: What employers need to know now. *SHRM Legal Report.* Retrieved from *www.shrm.org/LegalIssues/EmploymentLawAreas/Pages/SECWhistleBlowerRules. aspx* on August 25, 2011. See also Petrulakis, K. J., and Parsons, A. S. (2011, March 30). April 2011: New traps—Whistle-blower protections in the Dodd-Frank Act. *SHRM Legal Report.* Retrieved from *www.shrm.org/Publications/LegalReport/ Pages/NewTrapsWhistleBlowerProtections.aspx* on August 25, 2011.

115. Kesselheim, A. S., Studdert, D. M., and Mello, M. (2010). Whistle-blowers' experiences in fraud litigation against pharmaceutical companies. *New England Journal of Medicine* 362, pp. 1832–1839. See also Ethics Resource Center, 2010, op. cit.

116. Levisohn, B. (2008, Jan. 28). Getting more workers to whistle. *BusinessWeek,* p. 18. See also Bates, 2011, op. cit.

117. A whistleblower rocks an industry, 2002, op. cit. See also Gomes, L. (1998, April 27). A whistle-blower finds jackpot at the end of his quest. *The Wall Street Journal,* pp. B1, B6. See also Miceli, M. P., and Near, J. P. (1988). Individual and situational correlates of whistle-blowing. *Personnel Psychology* 41, pp. 267–281.

118. Petrulakis and Parsons, 2011, op. cit. See also Berkowitz, P. M. (2005, July–Aug.). Sarbanes-Oxley whistleblower claims: The meaning of "fraud against shareholders." *SHRM Legal Report,* pp. 1–8.

119. A whistleblower rocks an industry, 2002, op. cit.

120. Bates, 2011, op. cit. See also Near, J. P., and Miceli, M. P. (1995). Effective whistleblowing. *Academy of Management Review* 20, pp. 679–708.

121. Moore, B. (2011, March 21). See wrongdoing on the job? Here's what you need to know. *The New York Post.* Retrieved from *www.nypost.com/p/news/business/jobs/ telling_tales_mFyTtQpfqrHMVmJk0T9kcN* on August 25, 2011.

122. Cascio and Aguinis, 2011, op. cit.

# SUPPORT AND INTERNATIONAL IMPLICATIONS

This capstone section deals with two broad themes: organizational support for employees and the international implications of human resource management activities. Chapter 15 examines key issues involved in employee safety and health, both mental and physical. Chapter 16 considers key issues in international human resource management. Given the rapid growth of multinational corporations, it is perhaps in this area more than any other that employees and their families need special social and financial support from their firms.

# 15

# SAFETY, HEALTH, AND EMPLOYEE ASSISTANCE PROGRAMS

*Questions This Chapter Will Help Managers Answer*

1. What is the cost–benefit trade-off of adopting measures to enhance workplace safety and health?
2. Which approaches to job safety and health really work?
3. What should an informed, progressive HIV/AIDS policy look like?
4. What are some key issues to consider in establishing and monitoring an employee assistance program?
5. Does it make sound business sense to institute a worksite wellness program? If so, how should it be implemented and what should it include?

Experts estimate that 5 to 10 percent of employees in any company have a substance-abuse problem (alcohol or drugs) serious enough to merit treatment. The situation may be even worse. Over a two-year period, unbeknown to employees and job applicants, ChevronTexaco Corp. carried out anonymous drug testing. About 30 percent of all applicants and 20 percent of all employees tested positive for illegal drug use.

What is an appropriate policy for managers to adopt in these circumstances? Zero-tolerance policies in the workplace drive the problem underground, which does not make it go away but does reduce significantly the number of employees willing to come forward for treatment. Firing workers who test positive in random drug tests without offering any treatment or rehabilitation is not only the most expensive approach—especially when the cost of replacing a worker is compared with the cost of treatment—but this approach also passes the worker on to the next employer in no better shape than before.

Another approach is simply to demote people who have been in treatment. As one professional in the field says, "[Companies] won't have a written policy, but they'll guide that person into a position of no strategic importance. If asked, the companies won't acknowledge it. They don't want the bad publicity of being a mean guy."

Buoying these hard-liners are some very public drug- and alcohol-related accidents, of which the Exxon Valdez oil spill into Prince William Sound, Alaska, is probably the best known.[a] When the tanker ran aground, it spilled 11 million gallons of oil, damaged 1,300 miles of shoreline, disrupted the lives and livelihoods of people in the region, and killed hundreds of thousands of birds and marine animals. It occurred after the ship's captain, an alcoholic, left the bridge at a crucial moment. According to witnesses, he had downed five double vodkas on the night of the disaster. In a 2007 incident, the harbor pilot of a container ship that slammed into the San Francisco-Oakland Bay Bridge, causing a huge oil spill, had a drunken driving conviction, a history of alcohol abuse, and took numerous prescription drugs that might have impaired him. Pilots have been arrested and convicted of operating commercial airliners while intoxicated. What should firms do? While dismissal and demotion are two obvious policy choices, rehabilitation is a third.

Among companies that endorse rehabilitation, however, there is considerable debate about whether employees should be returned to their jobs if they

*Sources:* Intoxicated pilot arrested minutes before take-off. (2010, Sept. 15). *The Telegraph.* Retrieved from *www.telegraph.co.uk/news/worldnews/europe/netherlands/8004440/Intoxicated-pilot-arrested-minutes-before-take-off.html* on August 26, 2011. See also 'Drunk' pilot sparks revolt on flight to New York. (2009, Feb. 4). *The Times.* Retrieved from *www.foxnews.com/story/0,2933,487665,00.html* on August 26, 2011. See also Liptak, A. (2008, June 26). Damages cut against Exxon in Valdez case. *The New York Times.* Retrieved from *www.nytimes.com/2008/06/26/washington/26punitive.html?scp= 1&sq=Damages%20cut%20against%20Exxon%20in%20Valdez%20case&st=cse,* on August 11, 2008. See also Oil-spill pilot's record indicated problems. (2008, Apr. 10). *The New York Times,* p. A17. See also Ex-pilots guilty of operating airliner while intoxicated. (2005, June 9). *USA Today,* p. 4A. See also Franze, L. M., & Burns, M. B. (2005, Nov.). See also Firms debate hard line on alcoholics. (1989, Apr. 13). *The Wall Street Journal,* p. B1.

[a]The spill occurred in 1989. Over the next 19 years, a flood of litigation followed. It was finally resolved in 2008. See Gold, R., and Gleason, S. (2011, July 3). Exxon seeks to overturn $1.5 billion verdict. *The Wall Street Journal,* p. B3.

are successfully rehabilitated. Standard industry practice is to return people to their jobs after treatment, a policy that is consistent with the provisions of the Americans With Disabilities Act, which protects past substance abusers from discrimination. ExxonMobil, however, bucked the industry trend following the wreck of its oil tanker Exxon Valdez. The ship's captain had previously been treated for alcoholism and returned to work. After the accident, ExxonMobil took bold steps to prevent future accidents. It decided that these individuals posed too much of a risk to hold jobs that were both safety-sensitive and performed without much supervision—like the job of a ship captain. For this small group of jobs only, ExxonMobil instituted a blanket exclusion of individuals with a history of substance abuse, although they will be given other jobs. In short order, the new policy embroiled the company in litigation with the EEOC that lasted many years and finally ended up in the 5th Circuit Court of Appeals. We will consider the Court's ruling and its implications in the conclusion to this case.

Those who favor returning people to work after rehabilitation argue that it is not only more humane but also more effective. Refusing to return people to work—even in safety-sensitive positions—would be ". . . shortsighted. It will make sure that no one who's an alcoholic ever gets help," according to the medical director of United Airlines (which regularly returns pilots to their jobs after treatment). Those who take a more hard-line attitude toward drug and alcohol abuse point out that many companies are reexamining their policies, in light of the high-profile incidents described earlier.

### Challenges

1. What are some arguments for and against each of these policies: dismissal, demotion, return to the same job following rehabilitation, return to a different job following rehabilitation?
2. Should follow-up be required after rehabilitation? If so, how long should it last and what form should it take?

As the chapter-opening vignette shows, managers face tough policy issues in the area of workplace health and safety. As we shall see, a combination of external factors (e.g., the spiraling cost of health care) and internal factors (e.g., new technology) are making these issues impossible to ignore. This chapter begins by examining how social and legal policies on the federal and state levels have evolved on this issue, beginning with workers' compensation laws and culminating with the passage of the Occupational Safety and Health Act. The chapter then considers enforcement of the act, with special emphasis on the rights and obligations of management. It also examines prevailing approaches to job safety and health in other countries. Finally, it considers the problems of HIV/AIDS and business, employee assistance programs, and corporate "wellness" programs. Underlying all these efforts is a conviction on the part of many firms that it is morally right to improve job safety and health—and that doing so will enhance the productivity and quality of work life of employees at all levels.

# THE EXTENT AND COST OF SAFETY AND HEALTH PROBLEMS

Consider these startling facts about U.S. workplaces:[1]

- About 13 workers die on the job each day;[2] in general, this number has been declining over the past 10 years.
- More than 3.3 million workers (roughly 3.6 of every 100) either get sick or are injured because of their jobs each year. A 2008 study by Microsoft found that 68 percent of office workers develop work-related ergonomics injuries, such as repetitive-stress injuries (RSIs). RSIs are classified as illnesses because of their long-term nature.[3] In the U.S. they cost $45 to $54 billion in medical expenses and lost productivity.[4]
- Being hit by an object is the most common workplace injury, followed by sprains, strains, slips, and falls. Falls account for 14 percent of fatal work injuries.[5]
- Low-back injuries account for one-fourth of all workers' compensation claims and cost an average of $13,250 (in 2011 dollars), more than twice the average workplace claim.[6]
- 35 million workdays are lost each year because of workplace injuries.

Commercial fishing and logging are the most dangerous occupations. Although workplace fatalities and injuries have been trending downward for several years, it is difficult to tell how much of the improvement is the result of jobs lost to the recession versus genuine improvements in workplace safety. Accidents remain expensive, however. At the level of the individual firm, a DuPont safety engineer determined that a disabling injury costs an average of roughly $40,000 (in 2011 dollars). A company with 1,000 employees could expect to have 27 lost-workday injuries per year. With a 4.5 percent profit margin, the company would need almost $24 million of sales to offset that cost.[7] At Southern California Edison, over an eight-year period, the average cost of an injury (disabling or not) was about $10,000 (in 2011 dollars). Of this cost, 41.2 percent represented lost productivity, 30 percent medical, and 28.8 percent comprised direct, nonmedical costs.[8]

Regardless of your perspective, social or economic, these are disturbing figures. In response, public policy has focused on two types of actions: *monetary compensation* for job-related injuries and *preventive measures* to enhance job safety and health. State-run workers' compensation programs and the federal Occupational Safety and Health Administration (OSHA) are responsible for implementing public policy in these areas. Because we discussed workers' compensation in some detail in Chapter 12, we focus here on job safety and health, beginning with the Occupational Safety and Health Act of 1970.

# THE OCCUPATIONAL SAFETY AND HEALTH ACT

## Purpose and Coverage

The purpose of the Occupational Safety and Health Act is an ambitious one: to prevent work-related injuries, illnesses, and deaths.[9] Its coverage is equally ambitious, because the law extends to any business (regardless of size) that *affects* interstate commerce. Because almost any business affects interstate commerce, about 8.9 million U.S. workplaces and 135 million workers are included.[10] Federal, state, and local government workers are excluded, although the Act does require federal agencies to comply with standards consistent with those for private-sector employers. OSHA also conducts inspections in response to complaints from government workers or their managers.

## Administration

The 1970 act established three government agencies to administer and enforce the law:

- The *Occupational Safety and Health Administration (OSHA)* to establish and enforce the necessary safety and health standards. However, a 1998 law prohibits OSHA from evaluating compliance officers and their supervisors on the basis of enforcement activities, such as the number of citations issued or penalties assessed.[11] Today OSHA emphasizes three overarching goals: 1) strong, fair, and effective enforcement; 2) outreach, education, and compliance assistance; and 3) partnerships and cooperative programs.
- The *Occupational Safety and Health Review Commission* (a three-member board appointed by the president) to rule on the appropriateness of OSHA's enforcement actions when they are contested by employers, employees, or unions.
- The *National Institute for Occupational Safety and Health (NIOSH)* to conduct research on the causes and prevention of occupational injury and illness, to recommend new standards (based on this research) to the secretary of labor, and to develop educational programs.

## Safety and Health Standards

Under the law, each employer has a "general duty" to provide a place of employment "free from recognized hazards." Employers also have the "special duty" to comply with all standards of safety and health established under the act.

OSHA has issued a large number of detailed standards covering numerous environmental hazards. These include power tools, machine guards, compressed gas, materials handling and storage, and toxic substances, such as asbestos, cotton dust, silica, lead, and carbon monoxide.

As an example, consider OSHA's blood-borne pathogen standard. Workers exposed to blood and bodily fluids (e.g., health-care providers, first-aid providers) are covered by the rule, but it does not apply to workers who give first aid as "good Samaritans." It requires facilities to develop exposure-control plans, implement engineering controls and worker training to reduce the incidence of needle sticks, provide personal protective equipment and hepatitis B vaccinations, and communicate hazards to workers.[12]

To date, NIOSH has identified more than 15,000 toxic substances based on its research, but the transition from research findings to workplace standards is often a long, contentious process. Currently, it takes 38 to 46 months to set a standard. For example, consider the group of injuries and illnesses that affect the musculoskeletal system—so-called ergonomic injuries (for which there is no single diagnosis). When OSHA proposed ergonomics rules, the process dragged on for years. As a result OSHA is developing guidelines (rather than rules) for employers in specific industries to follow.[13]

## Figure 15–1

OSHA Form 300, log and summary of occupational injuries and illnesses.

OSHA's Form 300 (Rev. 01/2004)

### Log of Work-Related Injuries and Illnesses

**Attention:** This form contains information relating to employee health and must be used in a manner that protects the confidentiality of employees to the extent possible while the information is being used for occupational safety and health purposes.

Year 20___

**U.S. Department of Labor**
Occupational Safety and Health Administration

Form approved OMB no. 1218-0176

You must record information about every work-related death and about every work-related injury or illness that involves loss of consciousness, restricted work activity or job transfer, days away from work, or medical treatment beyond first aid. You must also record significant work-related injuries and illnesses that are diagnosed by a physician or licensed health care professional. You must also record work-related injuries and illnesses that meet any of the specific recording criteria listed in 29 CFR Part 1904.8 through 1904.12. Feel free to use two lines for a single case if you need to. You must complete an Injury and Illness Incident Report (OSHA Form 301) or equivalent form for each injury or illness recorded on this form. If you're not sure whether a case is recordable, call your local OSHA office for help.

Establishment name _____

City _____   State _____

| Identify the person | | | Describe the case | | | | Classify the case | | | | | | | | | | |
|---|---|---|---|---|---|---|---|---|---|---|---|---|---|---|---|---|---|---|

Public reporting burden for this collection of information is estimated to average 14 minutes per response, including time to review the instructions, search and gather the data needed, and complete and review the collection of information. Persons are not required to respond to the collection of information unless it displays a currently valid OMB control number. If you have any comments about these estimates or any other aspects of this data collection, contact: US Department of Labor, OSHA Office of Statistical Analysis, Room N-3644, 200 Constitution Avenue, NW, Washington, DC 20210. Do not send the completed forms to this office.

Page totals ▶

Be sure to transfer these totals to the Summary page (Form 300A) before you post it.

Page ___ of ___

## Record-Keeping Requirements

A good deal of paperwork is required of employers under the act. Specifically,

- Log of work-related injuries and illnesses (OSHA Form 300) (see Figure 15–1).
- Injury and illness reporting form (OSHA Form 301).
- Summary of work-related injuries and illnesses (OSHA Form 300A).

Employees are guaranteed access, on request, to Form 300 at their workplaces, and the records must be retained for five years following the calendar year they cover. The purpose of these reports is to identify where safety and health problems have been occurring (if at all). Such information helps call management's attention to the problems, as well as that of an OSHA inspector, should one visit the workplace. The annual summary must be sent to OSHA directly, to help the agency determine which workplaces should receive priority for inspection.

## OSHA Enforcement

In administering the act, OSHA inspectors have the right to enter a workplace (but not the home office of a teleworking employee) and to conduct a compliance inspection.[14] However, in its *Marshall v. Barlow's Inc.* decision, the Supreme Court ruled that employers could require a search warrant before allowing the inspector onto company premises.[15] In practice, only about 3 percent of employers go that far, perhaps because the resulting inspection is likely then to be an especially close one.[16] Employers are prohibited from discriminating against employees who file complaints, and an employee representative is entitled to accompany the OSHA representative during the inspection.

Because it is impossible for the 1,100 agency inspectors (most of whom are either safety engineers or industrial hygienists) to visit the nation's 8.9 million workplaces, a system of priorities has been established. OSHA assigns top priority to reports of imminent dangers—accidents about to happen. Second are fatalities or accidents serious enough to send three or more workers to the hospital. Third are employee complaints. Referrals from other government agencies are fourth, and special-emphasis programs are fifth. These involve hazardous work such as trenching or equipment such as mechanical power presses.[17]

At the worksite, inspectors concentrate more on dangerous hazards than on technical infractions. For example, OSHA fined industrial laundry giant Cintas Corp. $2.8 million for the death of an employee who fell from a conveyor belt into a large dryer. According to police, he was trapped for 20 minutes in temperatures reaching 300 degrees. The company said he wasn't following safety rules and appealed the fine. OSHA's investigators found that employees were not trained in how to shut off equipment properly, and produced videotape taken over several weeks prior to the accident at the same plant showing workers engaging in activities similar to what led to their coworker's death.[18]

Considerable emphasis has been given to OSHA's role of *enforcement,* but not much to its role of *consultation.* For example, OSHA offers an extensive Web site at *www.osha.gov* that includes a special section devoted to small businesses, as well as interactive e-Tools to help employers and employees address specific hazards and prevent injuries. In any given year, about 80 million visitors log on to OSHA's Web site.[19]

Employers who want help in recognizing and correcting safety and health hazards can get it from a free, onsite consultation service funded by OSHA. State governments or private-sector contractors provide this service using well-trained safety and/or health professionals (e.g., industrial hygienists). Primarily targeting small and medium-sized businesses, this program is penalty free and completely separate from the OSHA inspection effort. An employer's only obligation is a commitment to correct serious job safety and health hazards. In 2010, OSHA's On-site Consultation Program conducted over 30,000 visits to small-business worksites.[20]

## Penalties

Fines are mandatory where serious violations are found. For each **willful violation** (one in which an employer either knew that what was being done constituted a violation of federal regulations or was aware that a hazardous condition existed and made no reasonable effort to eliminate it), an employer can be assessed a civil penalty of up to $70,000 for each violation. An employer that fails to correct a violation (within the allowed time limit) for which a citation has been issued can be fined up to $7,000 for each day the violation continues. Finally, a willful first violation involving the death of a worker can carry a criminal penalty as high as $70,000 and six months in prison. A second such conviction can mean up to $140,000 and a full year behind bars.[21]

Executives can also receive criminal penalties. Calling their conduct everything from assault and battery to reckless homicide, prosecutors have sought hard time for employers who ignore warnings to improve safety on the job. One plant owner was sentenced to nearly 20 years after 25 workers died in a fire at his food-processing plant. Investigators found that the high death count had been the result of illegally locked plant doors and the absence of a sprinkler system.[22] Other examples:

- Owners of a plumbing company pled guilty to criminal charges of willfully violating OSHA trenching safety standards after two employees were killed in a trench collapse.
- An employee fell to his death while laying steel decking at a construction site. The company had a history of OSHA violations, and had been warned about its failure to buy protection against falls. The company owner pled guilty to a willful violation and was sentenced to four months in prison.
- An employee was killed when he fell while retrieving equipment from a tower. The owners attempted to avoid disclosing that the employee was not wearing proper safety equipment. The owners pled guilty and were sentenced to three months in prison.[23]

### Appeals

Employers can appeal citations, proposed penalties, and corrections they have been ordered to make through multiple levels of the agency, culminating with the Occupational Safety and Health Review Commission. The commission presumes the employer to be free of violations and puts the burden of proof on OSHA.[24] Further appeals can be pursued through the federal court system.

### The Role of the States

Although OSHA is a federally run program, the act allows states to develop and administer their own programs if they are approved by the secretary of labor. There are many criteria for approval, but the most important is that the state program must be judged "at least as effective" as the federal program. Currently, 27 states and territories have approved plans in operation. In 2010 OSHA inspected 38,335 workplaces and levied more than $107 million in fines. The 27 states running their own OSHA programs conducted an additional 57,124 inspections and levied more than $61 million in fines.[25]

### Workers' Rights to Health and Safety

Both unionized and nonunionized workers have walked off the job when subjected to unsafe working conditions.[26] In unionized firms, walkouts have occurred during the term of valid collective bargaining agreements that contained no-strike and grievance and/or arbitration clauses.[27] Are such walkouts legal? Yes, the Supreme Court has ruled, as long as objective evidence is presented to support the claim that abnormally dangerous working conditions exist. Under those circumstances:[28]

- A walkout is legal regardless of the existence of a no-strike or arbitration clause.
- It is an unfair labor practice for an employer to interfere with a walkout under such circumstances. This is true whether a firm is unionized or nonunionized.

- Expert testimony (e.g., by an industrial hygienist) is critically important in establishing the presence of abnormally dangerous working conditions.
- If a good-faith belief is not supported by objective evidence, employees who walk off the job are subject to disciplinary action.

## OSHA's Impact

From its inception, OSHA has been both cussed and discussed, and its effectiveness in improving workplace safety and health has been questioned by the very firms it regulates. Employers complain of excessively detailed and costly regulations that, they believe, ignore workplace realities. However, even critics acknowledge that the agency has made the workplace safer. Since its inception in 1971, OSHA has helped cut workplace fatalities by more than 60 percent and occupational injury and illness rates by 40 percent. At the same time, U.S. employment has increased from 56 million workers at 3.5 million worksites to more than 135 million workers at 8.9 million worksites.[29] On the other hand, OSHA has also been accused of overreaching, as when it issued proposed ergonomics standards that would be extremely costly to implement and when it issued a letter applying its rules to home workplaces. Both of those actions were greeted with howls of protest, and both were withdrawn.[30] On the other hand, employers sometimes try to improve their competitiveness at the expense of safety. Here's an example.

---

**HR BUZZ**

*The Language of Training*

### PRODUCTIVITY VERSUS SAFETY IN A SMALL BUSINESS

Preoccupied with staying in business, many small businesses skimp on safety information and worker training. That can be especially risky because such companies rely more heavily than do big companies on workers who are young or who speak little English.[a] As an example, consider the case of Everardo Rangel-Jasso.

Rangel-Jasso was crushed to death at Denton Plastics Inc. in Portland, Oregon. The 17-year-old was backing up a forklift, with a box high on its fork, when he cut the rear wheels sharply and the vehicle tipped over. A posted sign, in English, warned forklift drivers to wear seat belts—but the Mexican youth didn't speak English. According to an OSHA investigator, a seat belt might have saved his life.

Employees told OSHA that Hispanic workers learned their jobs through "hand signals and body gestures." Rangel-Jasso hadn't received any forklift training and lacked a driver's license and a juvenile's work permit. Federal and state officials levied more than $150,000 in fines against the company, and two senior managers faced criminal indictments. This is not an isolated incident. Hispanic workers have a 21 percent higher fatality rate than other workers in the United States. As of 2010, OSHA required employers to provide training in a language and vocabulary that employees can understand.[b]

---

[a]New challenges for health and safety in the workplace. *Workplace Visions* 3, pp. 5, 6.

[b]Occupational Safety and Health Administration (2010, June 11). Where to find OSHA training requirements and how they apply to Spanish-speaking employees. Retrieved from *www.osha.gov/dcsp/compliance_assistance/quickstarts/hispanic/hispanic_step4.html* on October 4, 2011.

---

Management's willingness to correct hazards and to improve such vital environmental conditions as ventilation, noise levels, and machine safety is much greater now than it was before OSHA. Moreover, because of OSHA and the National Institute for Occupational Safety and Health, we now know far more about such dangerous substances as vinyl chloride, PCBs, asbestos, cotton dust, and a host of other carcinogens. As a result, management has taken at least the initial actions needed to protect workers from them.

Finally, any analysis of OSHA's impact must consider the fundamental issue of the *causes* of workplace accidents. OSHA standards govern potentially unsafe *work conditions* that employees may be exposed to. There are no standards that govern potentially unsafe *employee behaviors*. And while employers may be penalized for failure to comply with safety and health standards, employees are subject to no such threat. Research suggests that the enforcement of OSHA standards, directed as it is to environmental accidents and illnesses, can hope *at best* to affect 25 percent of on-the-job accidents.[31] The remaining 75 percent require *behavioral* rather than *technical* modifications.

## ASSESSING THE COSTS AND BENEFITS OF OCCUPATIONAL SAFETY AND HEALTH PROGRAMS

Let's face it: Accidents are expensive. Aside from workers' compensation (*direct*) costs, consider the **indirect costs of an accident:**

1. Cost of wages paid for time lost.
2. Cost of damage to material or equipment.
3. Cost of overtime work by others required by the accident.
4. Cost of wages paid to supervisors while their time is required for activities resulting from the accident.
5. Costs of decreased output of the injured worker after she or he returns to work.
6. Costs associated with the time it takes for a new worker to learn the job.
7. Uninsured medical costs borne by the company.
8. Cost of time spent by higher management and clerical workers to investigate or to process workers' compensation forms.[32]

On the other hand, safety pays, as the following examples illustrate.

---

### DUPONT AND THE AVIATION INDUSTRY

HR BUZZ

At DuPont Corp., safety experts provide feedback while engineers observe workers and then redesign valves and install key locks to deter accident-causing behavior. When injuries do happen, the company reports them quickly to workers to provide a sense of immediacy, trying to show the behavior that caused the accident without naming the offender. It also fosters peer pressure to work safely by giving units common goals—that way workers are working together instead of independently. DuPont offers carrots, too. Its directors regularly give safety awards, and workers win $15 to $20 prizes if their divisions are accident free for six to nine months. The company's incentive for doing this is not altogether altruistic—it estimates its annual cost savings to be $150 million. Says the president of DuPont safety resources; "When a business culture focuses on safety, it makes a public proclamation of its commitment to

*Safety Pays*

caring about the welfare of its people. A workplace noted for safe practices builds both trust and faith across the board."[a]

The aviation industry, in particular, has focused intensely on analyzing accidents to learn how human error, mechanical failures, and unforeseen circumstances impact a catastrophe. To address those issues, it adopted crew-resource management (CRM) training to help workers approach their jobs as part of a team rather than as individuals. Perhaps the most famous example of the efficacy of CRM occurred on January 15, 2009, when US Airways flight 1549, piloted by Capt. Chesley B. Sullenberger, made an emergency landing on the Hudson River in New York City. Not a single passenger was injured, and all reports indicate that the crew practiced the key elements of CRM: teamwork, planning and organizing, listening, leadership, problem solving and decision-making, and safety awareness.[b] At a broader level, according to the Liberty Mutual Research Institute for Safety, for every $1 invested in workplace safety, there is between a $3 and $6 savings.[c]

---

[a]Forsman, J. (2003). New challenges for health and safety in the workplace. *Workplace Visions* 3, p. 6.

[b]NTSB issues report on US Airways Flight 1549 Hudson River ditching. (2010, May 5). Retrieved from *www.examiner.com* on Aug. 27, 2011. See also Capt. Sullenberger details drama of emergency Hudson River landing. (2009, June 10). *Los Angeles Times*. Retrieved from *http://articles. latimes.com* on Aug. 27, 2011.

[c]Colford, 2005, op. cit. See also Cadrain, 2002, op. cit.

Like many other problems of the marketplace, safety and health programs involve what economists call **externalities**—the fact that not all the social costs of production are necessarily included on a firm's profit and loss statement. The employer does not suffer from the worker's injury or disease and therefore lacks the full incentive to reduce it. As long as the outlays required for preventive measures are less than the social costs of disability among workers, higher fatality rates, and the diversion of medical resources, the enforcement of safety and health standards is well worth it and society will benefit.

## ORGANIZATIONAL SAFETY AND HEALTH PROGRAMS

As noted earlier, accidents result from two broad causes: *unsafe work conditions* (physical and environmental) and *unsafe work behaviors.* Unsafe physical conditions include defective equipment, inadequate machine guards, and lack of protective equipment. Examples of unsafe environmental conditions are noise, radiation, dust, fumes, and stress. In one study of work injuries, 50 percent resulted from unsafe work conditions, 45 percent resulted from unsafe work behaviors, and 5 percent were of indeterminate origin.[33] However, accidents often result from an *interaction* of unsafe conditions and unsafe acts. Thus, if a particular operation forces a worker to lift a heavy part and twist around to set it on a bench, the operation itself forces the worker to perform an unsafe act. Telling the worker not to lift and twist at the same time will not solve the problem. The *unsafe condition itself* must be corrected, either by redesigning the flow of material or by providing the worker with a mechanical device for lifting.

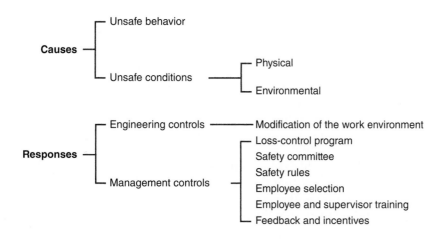

**Figure 15–2**

Causes of and responses to workplace accidents.

To eliminate, or at least reduce, the number and severity of workplace accidents, a combination of management and engineering controls is essential. These are shown in Figure 15–2. **Engineering controls** attempt to eliminate unsafe work conditions and to neutralize unsafe worker behaviors. They involve some modification of the work environment: for example, installing a metal cover over the blades of a lawn mower to make it almost impossible for a member of a grounds crew to catch his or her foot in the blades. **Management controls** attempt to increase safe behaviors. The following sections examine each of the elements shown in Figure 15–2.

## Loss Control

Management's first duty is to formulate a safety policy. Its second duty is to implement and sustain this policy through a **loss-control program.** Such a program has four components: a safety budget, safety records, management's personal concern, and management's good example.[34]

To reduce the frequency of accidents, management must be willing to spend money and to budget for safety. Unfortunately, it sometimes takes a tragic accident before this occurs. After the 2010 explosion of the Deepwater Horizon drilling rig in the Gulf of Mexico that left 11 workers dead and resulted in the worst oil spill is U.S. history, BP took serious steps to change its business culture to emphasize safety. It established a safety division, and, in the fourth quarter of 2010, it based 100 percent of managers' incentive pay on four criteria: safety, compliance, operational risk management, and whether they exhibit and reinforce behaviors consistent with these goals.[35]

Detailed analysis of accident reports, as well as management's personal concern (e.g., meeting with department heads over safety issues; onsite visits by top executives to discuss the need for safety, as practiced at Alcoa; and publication of the company's accident record), keeps employees aware constantly of the need for safety. Understanding the economic losses your organization has sustained in the past is a good indication of the extent of safety problems. Identifying the problems is the first step toward developing training or other approaches to correcting them.[36]

*Study after study has shown the crucial role that management plays in effective safety programs.*[37] Such concern is manifest in a number of ways: appointment of a high-level safety officer, rewards to supervisors on the basis of their subordinates' safety records, and comparison of safety results against preset objectives. Evidence indicates that employees who perceive their organizations as supporting safety initiatives and those who have high-quality relationships with their leaders are more likely to feel free to raise safety-related concerns. Such safety-related communication, in turn, is related to safety commitment, and, ultimately, to the frequency of accidents.[38]

Management's good example completes a loss-control program. If hard hats are required at a particular operation, then executives should wear hard hats even if they are in business suits. If employees see executives disregarding safety rules or treating hazardous situations lightly by not conforming with regulations, they will feel that they, too, have the right to violate the rules. In short, organizations show their concern for loss control by establishing a clear safety policy and by assuming the responsibility for its implementation.

### The Role of the Safety Committee

Representation of employees, managers, and safety specialists on the safety committee and frequent meetings of the committee (especially for highly hazardous work environments) can lead to a much higher commitment to safety than might otherwise be the case.[39] Indeed, merely establishing the committee indicates management's concern. Beyond that, however, the committee has important work to do:

- Recommend (or critique) safety policies issued by top management.
- Develop in-house safety standards and ensure compliance with OSHA standards.
- Provide safety training for employees and supervisors.
- Conduct safety inspections.
- Continually promote the theme of job safety through the elimination of unsafe conditions and unsafe behaviors.

As an example of recommendations that such a committee might make, consider some possible policies to reduce the incidence of **repetitive-motion injuries** (more broadly, musculoskeletal disorders, or MSDs). Such injuries afflict not only meatpackers and pianists but also telephone and computer operators and supermarket checkout clerks who repeatedly slide customers' purchases over price scanners.

---

**HR BUZZ**

*Best Practices in Reducing Repetitive-Stress Injuries*

### AETNA LIFE & CASUALTY, GROCERY STORES, AND 3M

Aetna Life & Casualty Co. (now owned by Travelers Insurance Group) installed ergonomically designed chairs with lower-back supports, adjustable seats, and armrests.[a] Grocery stores rotate checkout clerks who use scanners. At 3M, when workers complained about discomfort on a packaging line, an ergonomics team analyzed the entire process. The workers were packing an epoxy product that included two different size pails, gloves, and a stir stick. The team's solution was to go to a separate sealed pouch, eliminating the need for the pails and stir stick. Getting rid of the pails decreased the need for warehouse space and cut costs because the plastic pouches were cheaper. It also decreased reaching motions by the workers, made the product easier for the customer to use, and saved $370,000 per year (in 2011 dollars).

---

[a]Kuntz, 2000, op. cit. See also Repetitive stress: The pain has just begun. (1992, July 13). *BusinessWeek*, pp. 142, 143. See also Crippled by computers. (1992, Oct. 12). *Time*, pp. 70, 71.

These two approaches, modifying equipment and analyzing the way work is done, are the two most common preventive actions by employers. Best practices also include upper-management support, employee participation, an early reporting system, and proactive evaluation of hazards.[b] With ergonomics injuries accounting for as much as 40 percent of workers' compensation costs, that's smart business.[c]

---

[b]Krucoff, C., and Krucoff, M. (2001, Jan.). Wear and tear: Preventing repetitive stress injury in the workplace. *American Fitness.* Retrieved from *findarticles.com/p/articles/mi_m0675/is_1_19/ai_69651754/?tag=content;col1* on August 13, 2008. See also Grossman, R. J. (2000, Apr.). Make ergonomics go. *HR Magazine,* pp. 36–42.

[c]Cadrain, 2002, op. cit.

## Safety Rules

Safety rules are important refinements of the general safety policies issued by top management. To be effective, they should make clear the consequences of not following the rules, for example, progressive discipline. Evidence indicates, unfortunately, that in many cases the rules are not obeyed. Take protective equipment, for example.

OSHA standards require that employers *furnish* and employees *use* suitable protective equipment (e.g., hard hats, goggles, face shields, earplugs, respirators) where there is a "reasonable probability" that injuries can be prevented by such equipment. Companies often find that it is in their own best interests to do so as well. A five-year study of 36,000 Home Depot Inc. employees found that back-support devices reduced low-back injuries by about a third. The study compared the incidence of such injuries before and after the company made corsets mandatory for all store employees.[40]

As the following account shows, however, "You can lead a horse to water, but you can't make it drink."[42] Over an 18-month period, 11 fatal accidents among construction workers on the Las Vegas Strip prompted a strike by 6,000 workers and investigations by various authorities. The workers involved were crushed under concrete, severed by heavy machinery, or plummeted to their deaths at a number of different work sites. In one incident, for example, a man working on a high-rise building without an attached harness fell to his death. Experts agree that the man should have been wearing a harness, but they also note that the employer should have provided safety netting to break his fall. Some attribute the accidents to an emphasis on speed over safety, but they also note that mistakes are more likely to happen if supervisors fail to enforce or encourage safety practices.

It is possible that rules are not being obeyed because they are not being enforced. But it is also possible that they are not being obeyed because of flaws in employee-selection practices, because of inadequate training, or because there is simply no incentive for doing so.

## Employee Selection

To the extent that keen vision, dexterity, hearing, balance, and other physical or psychological characteristics make a critical difference between success and failure on a job, they should be used to screen applicants. However, there are two other factors that also relate strongly to accident rates among workers: *age* and *length of service.*[42] Regardless of length of service, the younger the employee, the higher the accident rate. In fact, accident rates are substantially higher during the first month of employment than in all subsequent time periods, regardless of age. And when workers of the same age are studied, accident rates decrease as length of service increases. One large-scale study found that workers over age 55 are a third less likely than their younger colleagues to be injured at work seriously enough to lose work time. The injuries they do report, however, are two to three times more costly than those for younger workers.[43] This is true in industries as diverse as mining, retail trade, transportation, public utilities, and services. The lesson for managers is clear: *New worker equals high risk!*

## Training for Employees and Supervisors

*Accidents often occur because workers lack one vital tool to protect themselves: information.*[44] Consider the following data collected by the Bureau of Labor Statistics:

- Nearly one out of every five workers injured while operating power saws received no safety training on the equipment.
- Of 724 workers hurt while using scaffolds, 27 percent had received no information on safety requirements for installing the kind of scaffold on which they were injured.
- Of 554 workers hurt while servicing equipment, 61 percent were not told about lockout procedures that prevent the equipment from being turned on inadvertently while it is being serviced.

In general, research indicates that safety training should focus on four general areas: using personal protective equipment, engaging in work practices to reduce risk, communicating health and safety information, and exercising employee rights and responsibilities.[45] Non–English-speaking workers who do not comprehend training information, however, are unable to apply lessons they have not learned. To address that issue, OSHA's 2010 Training Standards Policy Statement requires employers to provide instruction in a language and vocabulary that employees can understand.[46]

On the other hand, evidence indicates that training by itself is not the answer. Rather, employers need to pay more attention to the design of jobs—specifically, to reduce employees' exposure to physical hazards and heavy workloads and to increase autonomy and task variety. Supervisors also need to learn about and look for signs of substance abuse on the job because it relates strongly to the incidence of work injuries. Evidence indicates that these three factors—employee training, job design, and employer monitoring—can contribute to safer workplaces.[47] So also can "right-to-know" rules, which affect workers exposed to high levels of chemicals or other possible causes of disease.

The notification rules come under OSHA's hazard-communication standard, also known as the Right-to-Know Law.[48] It is designed to ensure that information about workplace hazards and protective measures is made available to employees, and it requires every workplace in the United States to identify and list hazardous chemicals being used ("from bleach to bowl cleaner").[49] The Right-to-Know Law requires all chemical manufacturers and importers to make available to their customers a material safety data sheet (MSDS) for products containing hazardous chemicals. Employers that use such products, in turn, must make the information available to employees.

MSDSs inform employees of the ingredients and hazards of dangerous materials, safe handling, use and storage, and first-aid steps to take in the event of exposure.[50] The availability of such information in today's workplaces makes it less likely that situations such as the following will occur.

---

## THE CHEMICAL INDUSTRY

HR BUZZ

Cathy Zimmerman, a 26-year-old lab technician at Hercules Inc. in Wilmington, Delaware, was pouring chemicals last year when she noticed that the bottles were labeled "mutagen" and "teratogen." She went to her dictionary, which said that a mutagen can alter chromosomes and a teratogen can cause malformations in fetuses. "I said, 'Oh, my God!'" she recalls. "When I saw that, I talked to my boss and told him I was scared. I didn't want to take a chance." Right-to-know rules had not yet taken effect.

*Right-to-Know Rules*

Zimmerman, who is expecting her first child, has since been transferred to Hercules' flavoring division, where she works with less hazardous materials. OSHA's right-to-know training program will eliminate such surprises. "With right-to-know, we'd have gone over it first, before it came into the lab," she says. "We didn't have that before."[a]

Indeed, with more than 30 million workers potentially exposed to one or more chemical hazards and an estimated 650,000 existing hazardous chemical products, with hundreds of new ones being introduced annually, "right-to-know" training is more important than ever.[b]

---

[a]Hays, L. (1986, July 8). New rules on workplace hazards prompt intensified on-the-job training programs. *The Wall Street Journal,* p. 31.

[b]OSHA. Hazard Communication: OSHA Standards. Retrieved from *www.osha.gov/dsg/hazcom/standards.html* on October 5, 2011.

---

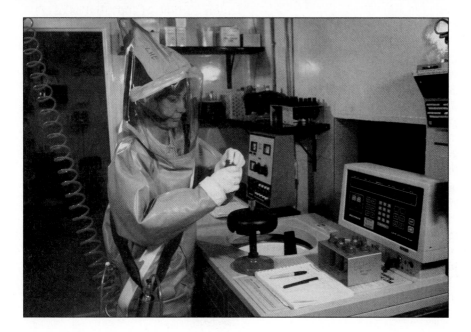

"Right-to-know" rules inform employees about workplace hazards as well as protective measures to ensure their safety.

Lack of information and training is unfortunate, but a problem that is just as serious occurs when safety practices that are taught in training are not reinforced on the job. Regular feedback and incentives for compliance are essential.

### Feedback and Incentives

Previous chapters have underscored the positive impact on the motivation of employees when they are given feedback and incentives to improve productivity. The same principles can also be used to improve safe behavior.[51] Thus, in one study of a wholesale bakery that was experiencing a sharp increase in work accidents, researchers developed a detailed coding sheet for observing safe and unsafe behaviors. Observers then used the sheets to record systematically both safe and unsafe employee behaviors over a 25-week period before, during, and after a safety-training program. Slides were used to illustrate both safe and unsafe behaviors. Trainees were also shown data on the percentage of safe behaviors in their departments, and a goal of 90 percent safe behaviors was established. Following all of this, the actual percentage of safe behaviors was posted in each department. Supervisors were trained to use positive reinforcement (praise) when they observed safe behaviors. In comparison to departments that received no training,

---

## INTERNATIONAL APPLICATION
## Health and Safety—The Response by Governments and Multinational Firms in Less-Developed Countries

In 1984, 45 tons of lethal gas leaked from the Union Carbide (India) Ltd. pesticide plant in the central Indian city of Bhopal, killing more than 3,800 people (25,000 by 2010) and causing more than 100,000 to suffer from chronic illnesses in history's worst industrial disaster. Subsequently, the Indian Supreme Court ordered Union Carbide to pay $470 million in damages to victims of the disaster (although dissatisfied survivors could still file claims in the United States as well);[a] and an Indian judge ordered the seizure of all of Carbide's Indian assets as part of continuing criminal proceedings against the company.[b] In 2010, more than 25 years after the accident, a district court in Bhopal found seven former company officials guilty of causing death by negligence.[c]

These events produced important consequences. U.S. multinational firms found out that liability for any Bhopal-like disaster could be decided in U.S. courts under the Alien Torts Claims Act. Such claims have led to endless litigation.[d] Successor firms also may incur legal liabilities and political pressure. Dow Chemical bought Union Carbide in 2001, but as of 2008, protesters in India were pushing Dow to remove toxic waste from Bhopal and to provide clean water to area residents, and pressuring their government to take legal action against Dow. Large Dow Chemical shareholders in the U.S. want

---

[a]McMurray, S. (1991, Oct. 4). India's high court upholds settlement paid by Carbide in Bhopal gas leak. *The Wall Street Journal*, p. B3. See also Damages for a deadly cloud. (1989, Feb. 27). *Time*, p. 53.

[b]McMurray, S., and Harlan, C. (1992, May 1). Indian judge orders seizure of Carbide assets in country. *The Wall Street Journal*, p. B5.

[c]Lahiri, T. (2010, June 8). Court convicts seven in Bhopal gas leak. *The Wall Street Journal*, p. A11.

[d]Kripalani, M. (2008, June 9). Dow Chemical: Liable for Bhopal? *BusinessWeek*, pp. 61, 62. See also One CEO's nightmare: Bhopal ghosts (still) haunt Union Carbide. (2000, April 3). *Fortune*, pp. 44, 46.

the company to disclose fully its potential liabilities related to Bhopal. This, more than pressure from governments of developing countries, has forced companies to tighten safety procedures, upgrade plants, supervise maintenance more closely, and educate workers and communities in their far-flung empires.[e]

In Mexico, a gas explosion at Pemex, the state-owned oil monopoly, killed at least 500 people and wounded thousands of others at about the same time as the Bhopal disaster. One year later, little had been done to improve the conditions that caused the explosion. After years of neglect and rampant pollution at Pemex facilities, the government was loath to clamp down because that would focus attention on the main culprit: the Mexican government itself.[f]

Neither the Bhopal nor the Pemex incident had any noticeable effect on multinational investment in Mexico. In fact, all the developing countries in one survey seem to rely on the multinationals, rather than on draconian new regulations, to prevent a repeat of Bhopal. This is true in South Korea, China, Taiwan, Egypt, and Thailand, for example. In Thailand, a fire at a toy factory killed more than 240 workers. There were no fire escapes, fire alarms, sprinkler systems, or other safety features. Experts say such negligence is common throughout the region, where labor unions are weak, there is lax enforcement of labor laws, and corruption is often endemic.[g] As these few examples make clear, in many of the less-developed countries around the world, foreign investment is a political and economic issue, not a safety issue.

This may be changing. The rapid globalization of business now links manufacturers, investors, and consumers everywhere. Take Taiwan-based Foxconn, also known as Hon Hai Precision Industry, which employs 920,000 Chinese workers to feed the world's hunger for hi-tech gadgets and toys from electronics heavyweights such as Apple, Dell, Hewlett-Packard, Nintendo, and Sony. After a dozen workers committed suicide in 2010, many of these clients announced inquiries. What they found was a tough culture to work in. Conversation on the production line was forbidden, bathroom breaks were kept to 10 minutes every two hours, workers routinely put in overtime in excess of the 36 hours a month permitted under Chinese law, and they got yelled at frequently. Said one worker, "I do the same thing every day. I have no future." In response, Foxconn more than doubled wages in coastal Shenzen, instituted a program it calls "Care-Love," and moved some of its production inland, where wages are 30 percent cheaper. The lesson is that economic pressure from multinational customers may force firms to become as much trendsetters in labor as they are in the hi-tech products they manufacture.[h]

---

[e] Kripilani, 2008, op. cit. See also Foreign firms feel the impact of Bhopal most. (1985, Nov. 26). *The Wall Street Journal*, p. 24.

[f] Ibid.

[g] Barboza, D. (2008, Jan. 5). In Chinese factories, lost fingers and low pay. The New York Times. Retrieved from *www.nytimes.com/2008/01/05/business/worldbusiness/05sweatshop.html?scp=1&sq=%20In%20Chinese%20factories,%20lost%20fingers%20and%20low%20pay.%20&st=cse* on January 7, 2008. See also A crusader for industry's casualties. (2000, Dec. 18). *BusinessWeek*, p. 188. See also Thailand fire shows region cuts corners on safety to boost profits (1993, May 13). *The Wall Street Journal*, p. A13.

[h] How to beat the high cost of happy workers. (2011, May 15). *BusinessWeek*, pp. 39, 40. See also Inside Foxconn. (2010, Sept. 19). *BusinessWeek*, pp. 58–69. See also Suicides at Foxconn: A series of deaths expose a big computer-maker to unaccustomed scrutiny. (2010, May 29). *The Economist*, p. 67. See also Life and death at the iPad factory. (2010, June 13). *BusinessWeek*, pp. 35, 36.

---

workers in the trained departments averaged almost 24 percent more safe behaviors. Not only did employees react favorably to the program, but the company was able to maintain it. One year prior to the program, the number of lost-time injuries per million hours worked was 53.8. Even in highly hazardous industries, this figure rarely exceeds 35. One year after the program, it was less than 10.[52]

Newport News Shipbuilding cut its injury rate in half by using a similar behavioral approach to safety management. The company's bottom-up approach empowers employees to correct others' unsafe behavior and take it upon themselves to fix unsafe things they observe.[53] The results of these studies suggest that training, goal setting, and feedback provide useful alternatives to disciplinary sanctions to encourage compliance with the rules. As one safety consultant noted: "It's better to recognize a guy for success than to beat him up for failure."[54]

As we have seen, in the United States there is considerable pressure to improve plant safety. We considered the situation in other countries on pp. 604 and 605.

## HEALTH HAZARDS AT WORK

### The Need for Safeguards

The National Institute of Occupational Safety and Health has identified more than 15,000 toxic substances, of which some 500 might require regulation as carcinogens (cancer-causing substances). The list of harmful chemical, physical, and biological hazards is a long one. It includes carbon monoxide, vinyl chloride, dusts, particulates, gases and vapors, radiation, excessive noise and vibration, and extreme temperatures. When present in high concentrations, these agents can lead to respiratory, kidney, liver, skin, neurological, and other disorders. Scary, isn't it?

There have been some well-publicized lawsuits against employers for causing occupational illnesses as a result of lack of proper safeguards or technical controls.[55] The U.S. Supreme Court has ruled that the states can prosecute company officials under criminal statutes for endangering the health of employees, even if such hazards are also regulated by OSHA.[56] Nevertheless, some of the criticism against employers is not fair. To prove negligence, it must be shown that management *knew* of the connection between exposure to the hazards and negative health consequences and that management *chose* to do nothing to reduce worker exposure. Yet few such connections were made until recent years. Even now, alternative explanations for the causes of disease or illness cannot be ruled out in many cases.[57] This has led to ethical dilemmas such as the chemical-testing discussion in the box below.

The primary emphasis to date has been on installing engineering controls that *prevent* exposure to harmful substances, for example, by installing improved

---

## ETHICAL DILEMMA
### To Wait or Not to Wait for Chemical Testing?

According to experts, there are 100,000 commercial chemicals in use in the United States. Of that number, perhaps 500—certainly fewer than 1,000—have ever really been studied. Your business has the opportunity to introduce a cutting-edge semiconductor chip, but you know that the list of chemical dangers associated with making such chips is alarmingly long. Do you wait for years of chemical testing before you begin to manufacture the chip? Or do you move forward now? While not waiting might seem reasonable from a business perspective, it is also dangerous, some might say frightening, from a public-health perspective.[a] What do you do?

[a] Varchaver, 2003, op. cit.

ventilation systems.[58] Thus, after OSHA established or toughened workplace exposure limits for 376 toxic chemicals, compliance cost employers $1.7 billion a year (in 2011 dollars). While this figure might sound steep, consider that an estimated $67 billion (in 2011 dollars) is spent annually just to treat preventable cancer. The benefits? According to OSHA, the new limits should save nearly 700 lives a year and reduce work-related illnesses, such as cancer, liver and kidney impairments, and respiratory and cardiovascular illnesses by about 55,000 cases a year.[59] But is cost–benefit analysis appropriate when lives are literally at stake?

The Supreme Court recognized this problem in its 1981 "cotton dust" decision. It held that OSHA need not balance the costs of implementing standards against the benefits expected. OSHA has to show only that it is *economically feasible* to implement the standards. The decision held that Congress had already decided the balance between costs and benefits in favor of the worker when it passed the law.[60] On one issue all parties agree: The nature of cancer itself makes it virtually impossible for workers to protect themselves from exposure to cancer-causing substances. In recent years, another health hazard has entered the workplace. While its origins lie outside the workplace, businesses cannot ignore either its costs or its consequences. That health hazard is HIV/AIDS.

## HIV/AIDS and Business

AIDS (acquired immune deficiency syndrome) is a medical time bomb. With about 7,000 newly diagnosed cases of HIV/AIDS worldwide each day, employers are having to deal with increasing numbers of people with HIV in the workplace. Unlike other life-threatening illnesses, such as Alzheimer's or heart disease, the vast majority of those dying from AIDS are of working age—between 25 and 44. It's a bottom-line business issue.[61] Consider these facts and prognoses about the disease:

- As of 2011, more than 34 million people worldwide were estimated to be infected with HIV. Worse yet, 95 percent of those infected with HIV may not know that they have it—and could spread the virus unknowingly. Yet AIDS, a killer, can itself be killed through education and the adoption of safe behaviors.[62]
- By 2011, the disease had already killed 30 million people worldwide, and it had orphaned more than 14 million children.[63]
- The average HIV patient in America takes a combination of drugs that add up to around $14,000 a year.[64] However, the total cost of treating the disease will escalate over time as people with HIV live longer—largely due to better drugs to fight the disease and the growing availability of HIV-related health care. While the death rate from HIV/AIDS has dropped by about half as a result of the combination drug, or "cocktail" therapy, the average time period from infection with HIV to the development of AIDS is 8 to 11 years.[65] More than 18,000 people with AIDS still die each year in the U.S.[66]
- The cumulative costs of long-term disability payments to people with HIV/AIDS are expected to exceed $2 billion.
- Direct costs to companies will escalate in three ways: through (1) increased medical premiums to cover their employees with HIV/AIDS, (2) increased medical premiums to cover HIV/AIDS victims without insurance, and (3) an increased Medicaid burden.
- Indirect costs will also affect the bottom line in at least three ways: (1) Lost work time of HIV/AIDS patients is dramatic. Because the Americans with Disabilities

Act protects the jobs held by HIV/AIDS-affected persons (as well as job applicants who have the disease), others have to do their work while they are out, and they may be less productive. (2) Productivity may suffer if coworkers refuse to work with an HIV-infected employee. (3) Recruitment costs will increase as HIV-infected employees can no longer work and those employees (or coworkers who quit rather than work with an HIV-infected employee) must be replaced.

Progressive firms are taking action. Thus, the Global Business Coalition on HIV/AIDS is an alliance of 200 companies doing business in 138 countries dedicated to combating the epidemic. Based in New York City, it includes such well-known names as Coca-Cola, American Express, Royal Dutch Shell, Ford, Intel, and Unilever, just to name a few.[67] In terms of specific actions, Volkswagen established an HIV/AIDS-care program in Brazil that installed condom machines in company bathrooms and provided HIV-positive workers with medical care. Four years later the company found that hospitalizations were down 90 percent and HIV costs were down 40 percent.[68] Here's how Anglo American is tackling the issue.

---

**HR BUZZ**

*Financial and Nonfinancial Payoffs*

## THE BUSINESS OF FIGHTING AIDS

Anglo American is one of the world's largest mining companies, focusing on platinum, diamonds, copper, nickel, iron ore, and coal. Anglo is South Africa's largest private-sector employer, and HIV affects 12,000 of its employees—or 16 percent of its 70,000-strong permanent staff.

The implications are enormous. Chief Medical Officer Brian Brink recalls the sense of panic when the scale of the challenge became clear. "There was a time when investors were getting on the phone and asking whether the disease was going to bring down the organization. We were training two people for the same role in case one died on the job. It was that bad."

South Africa is at the center of Anglo's global empire, producing about 51 percent of group operating profit and generating 48 percent of revenue. So what happens there matters more than anywhere else. More than 300,000 people die from AIDS each year in South Africa, and 6 million people in a population of 50 million are living with HIV. Not so long ago, Brink battled to get the South African government to do more to combat the disease. Things are different today under the presidency of Jacob Zuma. Zuma is behind an initiative to make life-prolonging anti-retroviral drugs available to more people with HIV. Male circumcision programs (which significantly reduce the risk of men contracting HIV) also are being used more widely.

Zuma's approach is very different from that of his predecessor, Thabo Mbeki, who questioned the link between HIV and AIDS. The new programs are long overdue. In some regions, 40 percent of pregnant women are diagnosed with HIV, and women between the ages of 18 and 24 are eight times more likely to get the virus than men.

At Anglo, a turning point came in August 2002 when the company offered free HIV tests to all its employees, and free treatment for sufferers and their dependents. The rate of voluntary HIV testing at Anglo clinics or hospitals near its mines is about 94 percent. Free anti-retroviral therapy (ART) has helped morale among Anglo's workers and improved relations with trade unions. The company views its outlay of $10 million a year, providing staff with support and drugs, as a sound investment.

The cost of treatment is $126 per HIV-positive employee—but people on ART are able to work, and absenteeism declines by 1.9 days per employee per month. The use of in-house healthcare services also declines, as does staff turnover. At the individual level, the total savings of $219 per patient per month amounts to about 174 percent of the cost of providing treatment. Pay-offs go way beyond financial outcomes alone. According to Brian Brink, "There is hope here, where once there was very little."[a]

[a]Wachman, R. (2011, Nov. 3). The business of fighting AIDS. *The Guardian.* Retrieved from *www. guardian.co.uk/business/2011/nov/03/anglo-american-medical-officer-brian-brink-interview* on November 23, 2011. Copyright Guardian News & Media Ltd. 2011.

## EMPLOYEE ASSISTANCE PROGRAMS

Another (brighter) side of the employee health issue is reflected in **employee assistance programs** (EAPs). Such programs represent an expansion of traditional work in occupational alcoholism-treatment programs. From a handful of programs begun in the 1940s (led by DuPont), today 75 percent of companies offer EAPs.[69] About 2,400 EAPs serve roughly 90 percent of the North American market, but just six large ones account for 80 percent of the market.[70]

By its very title, "employee assistance program" signals a change both in application and in technique from the traditional occupational alcoholism-treatment program. Modern EAPs are comprehensive management tools that address behavioral risks in the workplace by extending professional counseling and medical services to all "troubled" employees.[71] A **troubled employee** is an individual who is confronted by unresolved personal or work-related problems. Such problems run the gamut from alcoholism, drug abuse, and high stress to marital, family, and financial problems. While some of these may originate outside the work context, they most certainly will have spillover effects to the work context.

### Do Employee Assistance Programs Work?

At the outset it is important to distinguish in-house or worksite programs from out-of-house or network programs. Worksite programs are onsite and hire their own professionals to work in the program. Network programs are separate EAP service providers that are not affiliated with a company, and they may have multiple locations to make it easy for clients to access. As such, they are especially convenient to small employers who do not have the resources to provide internal services. On the other hand, a comparison of the two models found that worksite EAPs received 500 percent more referrals from supervisors and 300 percent more employee cases. Perhaps this is because most employees do not seek assistance on their own. They get help only when referred by their supervisors.[72]

Employer involvement makes a huge difference in outcomes. According to one expert: "You're looking at a 13 percent to 15 percent cure rate without employer involvement. The success rate is 75 percent to 80 percent when the employer plays a role."[73] By offering assistance to troubled employees, the companies promote positive employee-relations climates; contribute to their employees' well-being; and enhance their ability to function productively at work, at home, and in the community.[74]

From a business perspective, well-run programs seem to pay off handsomely. In well-run programs, management at various levels expresses support for the program; educates employees about the program and provides necessary training on its use; makes the program accessible to employees; and ensures that it operates in a confidential, credible, and neutral manner.[75] Here are two examples of well-run programs.

General Motors Corp., whose EAP counsels more than 6,500 employees with alcohol problems each year, reports a 65 to 75 percent success rate and estimates that it gains $3 for every $1 spent on care. In addition, blue-collar workers who resolve their alcohol and drug-abuse problems through an EAP file only half as many grievances as they did before treatment. With respect to referrals for substance abuse and other problems, Chevron determined that its *annual* savings from referrals to the EAP were approximately $10 million. In addition, employees treated for substance abuse had no more on- or off-the-job lost-time accidents than the broader employee population.[76]

On the other hand, not all programs are equally effective. *Beware of making strong statements about a program's impact at least until repeated evaluations have demonstrated the same findings for different groups of employees.*[77] It is also important to emphasize that findings do not generalize across studies unless the EAP is implemented in the same way. For example, as we noted earlier, in some companies, counselors are available onsite. In others, it is only possible to access an EAP counselor through a toll-free telephone number. Evidence indicates that when counselors are available onsite, as opposed to being accessible through a toll-free number, the programs are more effective.[78]

### How Employee Assistance Programs Work

There are five steps involved in starting an EAP:[79]

1.  *Develop a written statement* that confirms the company's desire to offer help to employees with behavioral or medical problems, and emphasize that such help will be offered on a personal and confidential basis.
2.  *Teach managers, supervisors, and union representatives what to do*—and what not to do—when they confront the troubled employee and when they use the program to resolve job-performance problems. Both the supervisor and the steward need to be trained to recognize that they are helping, not hurting, the employee by referring her or him to the EAP.
3.  *Establish procedures for referral* of the troubled employee to an in-house or outside professional who can take the time to assess what is wrong and arrange for treatment.
4.  *Establish a planned program of communications* to employees to announce (and periodically to remind them) that the service is available, that it is confidential, and that other employees are using it.
5.  *Continually evaluate* the program in terms of its stated objectives.

EAP costs vary considerably, from a minimum of $9.00 per employee to as much as $83.00.[80] This is because programs are tailored to fit each organization, and organizations vary so much in terms of their cultures, work environments, and needs.

### More on the Role of the Supervisor

In the traditional alcoholism-treatment program, the supervisor had to look for symptoms of alcoholism and then diagnose the problem. Under an EAP, however, the supervisor is responsible only for identifying declining work performance. If normal corrective measures do not work, the supervisor confronts the employee with evidence of his or her poor performance and offers the EAP. Recognize, however, that classic warning signs, such as chronic tardiness and absenteeism, are not always evident at companies where some employees telework or where workers may be geographically separated from their supervisors. Nevertheless, here are some recommendations on how to proceed:[81]

1. Once you suspect a problem, begin documenting instances in which job performance has fallen short. Absenteeism (leaving early, arriving late for work, taking more days off than allowed by policy), accidents, errors, a slackened commitment to completing tasks, and a rise in conflicts with other employees (due to changes in mood swings) may become evident.

2. Having assembled the facts, set up a meeting. Keep the discussion focused on performance, and don't try to make a diagnosis. Outline the employee's shortcomings, insist on improvement, and then say, "I need to bring you to the medical department, something isn't right here. . . . I'm taking you to the experts."

3. Often managers are scared of potential liability and scared to be wrong. They worry "Can the person sue me?" As long as the discussion focuses on declining job performance, legal experts say that a defamation claim is highly unlikely. Besides, confrontation without focusing on job performance is usually ineffective anyway.

This approach leaves the diagnosis and treatment recommendations to trained counselors. Beware of making referral to an EAP *formal,* as opposed to voluntary, where the employee self-refers. In extreme cases where a formal referral may be warranted, be sure that the employee has a job-performance problem in addition to appearing to be hostile, depressed, or suicidal. Recent case law shows that formal referrals have created burdens on employers under the Americans with Disabilities Act (ADA). The ADA protects individuals who either have or are perceived to have a disability. Mandatory EAP referral suggests that the employer did indeed *perceive* that the employee has a disability. That could be problematic if the employer subsequently decides to take some adverse action (such as termination) against the employee.[82]

Now that we understand what EAPs are, their effects, and how they work, let us examine three of today's most pressing workplace problems. These are alcoholism, drug abuse, and violence.

## Alcoholism

Management's concern over the issue is understandable, for alcohol misuse by employees is costly in terms of productivity, time lost from work, and treatment. According to the National Institute on Alcohol Abuse and Alcoholism (NIAAA), **harmful patterns of drinking** are defined as drinking *too much, too fast* (more than 4 drinks in two hours for men, and more than 3 in two hours for women) or *too much, too often* (more than 14 drinks per week for men, and more than 7 for women).[83] How prevalent is alcoholism, and how costly is it?[84]

■ About 10 percent of full-time employees have a serious drinking problem. This percentage has remained constant for the past 15 years. That's about 14 million Americans.[85]

- Annual deaths due to alcohol number about 105,000.
- Of all hospitalized patients, about 25 percent have alcohol-related problems.
- Alcohol results in about 500 million lost workdays annually, and it is involved in 40 percent of industrial fatalities and 47 percent of industrial accidents.
- Fully half of all auto fatalities involve alcohol.
- Alcohol abusers drain resources and reduce productivity. They use more sick days, show up late more often, and stay in jobs for shorter amounts of time. They are 3.5 times more likely to cause accidents at work and in transit, and their health costs are double their peers'.[86]

Alcoholism affects employees at every level, but it is costliest at the top. Experts estimate that it afflicts at least 10 percent of senior executives. As an example, consider an executive who makes $150,000 per year, is unproductive, and files large health claims. That cost is certainly far higher than a $15,000 treatment program.[87]

A study done for McDonnell Douglas Corp. (now part of Boeing) shows how expensive it is to ignore substance-abuse problems in the workplace. The company found that in the previous five years, each worker with an alcohol (or drug) problem was absent 113 more days than the average employee and filed $30,000 more in medical claims (in 2011 dollars). Their dependents also filed some $48,000 more in claims than the average family. Intervention works, as long as it includes ongoing case management and post-treatment monitoring.[88] Recovered alcoholics frequently credit such programs with literally saving their lives. Companies win, too—by reclaiming employees whose gratitude and restored abilities can result in years of productive service.

## Drug Abuse

Drug abuse is no less insidious. Of the 17.4 million illicit drug users ages 18 or older in 2007, 13 million (75 percent) were employed either full or part time.[89] Drug abuse cuts across all job levels and types of organizations and, together with employee alcohol abuse, costs U.S. businesses $640 for every worker, regardless if they are substance abusers.[90]

Evidence clearly shows that drug abuse affects on-the-job behaviors.[91] Here is a profile of the typical drug user in today's workforce. He or she

- Is late three times as often as fellow employees.
- Requests early dismissal or time off during work 2.2 times as often.
- Has three times as many absences of eight days or more.
- Uses three times the normal level of sick benefits.
- Is four times more likely to be involved in a workplace accident.
- Is five times as likely to file a workers' compensation claim.
- Is one-third less productive than fellow workers.

A longitudinal study of 5,465 applicants for jobs with the U.S. Postal Service found that after an average of 1.3 years of employment, employees who had tested positive for illicit drugs (typically about 5 percent) had an absenteeism rate 59.3 percent higher than employees who had tested negative. Those who had tested positive also had a 47 percent higher rate of involuntary turnover than those who had tested negative. However, there was no relationship between drug test results and measures of injury and accident occurrence.[92] At a national level, 80 percent of drug abusers steal from their employers to support their illegal drug use, and drug abuse is the third leading cause of workplace violence.[93]

Remember, the ADA protects rehabilitated alcohol and drug abusers from discrimination in employment. However, anyone who is currently using drugs illegally is not protected by the ADA and may be denied employment or fired on the basis of such use.[94] The law explicitly allows employers to hold alcoholic or drug-abusing employees to the same standards of performance and conduct that are set for other employees. The key requirement is documented evidence of decreased job performance.

## Violence at Work

What do Xerox, NASA, and the U.S. Postal Service have in common? They have employees who died violently while at work. In 2010, for example, 506 Americans died as a result of workplace violence, a rate that has declined by more than 50 percent since 1994.[95] It is important to emphasize, however, that a large majority of workplace homicides do *not* involve murderous assaults between coworkers in an organization. Rather they occur in connection with robberies and related crimes.[96] Those most at risk are taxi drivers, police officers, retail workers, people who work with money or valuables, and people who work alone or at night.

Violence disrupts productivity, causes untold damage to those exposed to the trauma, is related to workplace abuse of drugs or alcohol and absenteeism, and costs employers billions of dollars.[97] In a stressed-out, downsized business environment, people are searching for someone to blame for their problems. With the loss of a job or other event the employee perceives as unfair, the employer may become the focus of a disgruntled individual's fear and frustration. Under these circumstances, some form of **workplace aggression**—that is, efforts by individuals to harm others with whom they work, or have worked, or their organization itself—is likely.[98]

What can organizations do? Although many American employers have a formal anti-violence policy, among those that do not the key obstacle seems to be a widespread assumption that violence is more or less random—that there is no way to predict when a troubled worker will suddenly snap. Yet according to a former FBI agent, "People don't suddenly 'just go crazy.' Workplace violence is one of the few types of violent behavior that follows a clear pattern."[99] To be sure, fair treatment (procedural justice) on the job, adequate compensation, a climate of honesty by leaders, communicating a policy about counterproductive behavior, consistently punishing unacceptable behavior, and taking steps to reduce job stress can reduce the likelihood of workplace violence and aggression.[100] In addition, both employees and supervisors should be alert to warning signs, such as[101]

- *Verbal threats.* Take seriously remarks from an employee about what he or she may do. Experts say that individuals who make such statements usually have been mentally committed to the act for a long period of time. It may take very little provocation to trigger the violence.
- *Physical actions.* Employees who demonstrate threatening physical actions at work are dangerous. The employer, working with experts trained to assess a

possibly violent situation, needs to investigate and intervene. Failure to do so may be interpreted as permission to do further or more serious damage.

- *Behaviors.* Watch for changes such as irritability and a short temper. Is the employee showing a low tolerance to work stress or frustrations?[102]

Here are some additional preventive steps:[103]

- *Consult specialists*—professionals in the area of facility security, violence assessment, EAP counseling, community support services, and local law enforcement—to formulate a plan for identifying, defusing, and recovering from a violent event.
- *Create and communicate to all employees a written policy* that explains the organization's position on intimidating, threatening, or violent behavior and establishes a procedure for investigating any potentially violent talk or action.
- *Establish a crisis-management team* with the authority to make decisions quickly. This group should meet regularly to share information, evaluate problems, and develop plans for selecting intervention techniques and coordinating follow-up activities, such as counseling for victims and dealing with the media.
- *Offer training and employee orientation.* Train supervisors and managers in how to recognize aggressive behavior, identify the warning signs of violence, be effective communicators, and resolve conflict. (Untrained supervisors often escalate violent situations.) Orient all employees on facility-security procedures and on how to recognize and report threats of violence in the workplace.
- *Help employees adjust to change*—for example, in the event of a downsizing, a merger, or an acquisition, give employees advance notice to keep them informed about impending changes. Providing additional benefits, such as severance pay or EAP stress-management counseling, can help employees adjust to the change.

## IMPACT OF SAFETY, HEALTH, AND EAPs ON PRODUCTIVITY, QUALITY OF WORK LIFE, AND THE BOTTOM LINE

We know that the technology is available to make workplaces safe and healthy for the nation's men and women. We also know that legislation can never substitute for managerial commitment to safe, healthy workplaces based on demonstrated economic and social benefits. We noted earlier that the return on investment of investments in job safety and health is typically 3:1, according to the Liberty Mutual Research Institute for Safety. After BP's 2010 disaster in the Gulf of Mexico, one observer noted, "As top safety officer, chief executives must communicate throughout their organizations this core cultural value: Sticking to rigorous safety systems and procedures won't cost money; it will save lives and make money. Acting otherwise is unacceptable."[a]

On balance, commitment to job safety, health, and EAPs is a win–win situation for employees and their companies. Productivity, quality of work life, and the bottom line all stand to gain.

[a]Krause, T. R. (2010, Sept. 20). Oil CEOs must all be chief safety officers now. *Forbes.* Retrieved from *www.forbes.com/ 2010/09/20/chief-safety-officer-oil-companies-leadership- citizenship-ceos.html* on August 30, 2011.

■ *Be aware of potential risks and respond appropriately.* Remarks such as "I'll kill you" or "I'd like to put out a contract on him" should not be taken lightly. Experts say that in many cases an individual who becomes violent has given multiple clues of potentially violent behavior to a number of people within the organization. However, these warnings were overlooked or dismissed. Be proactive; don't assume the employee doesn't mean it, because when employees feel powerless, there is a greater likelihood of violence. Report the incident to management for investigation.[104]

## CORPORATE HEALTH PROMOTION: THE CONCEPT OF "WELLNESS"

Consider these sobering facts about the U.S. population:

■ Employees with chronic diseases such as asthma, diabetes, and congestive heart failure, all of which can be managed, account for 60 percent of the typical employer's total medical costs.[105]

■ Nearly two-thirds of U.S. adults are overweight or obese.[106] Medical expenses for those employees are 42 percent higher than those for employees with healthy weights.[107] Common backaches alone account for about 25 percent of all workdays lost per year, for a total cost of $15 to $20 billion in lost productivity, disability payments, and lawsuits.[108] For employees who miss time due to back problems, the median time away from the job is six to seven days.[109]

■ About 25 percent of the population still smokes. According to the 2006 Surgeon General's report, smokers die, on average, 13 to 14 years before nonsmokers. Tobacco use is responsible for one in five U.S. deaths, excess medical costs and productivity losses cost employers more than $193 billion a year, and for individual employers, a smoker is 18 percent more expensive than a nonsmoker.[110]

■ 29 percent have high blood pressure (one-third are unaware of it).

■ A majority don't exercise regularly.

■ 50 percent don't wear seatbelts.

■ 200,000 employees ages 45 to 65 are killed or disabled by heart disease each year, at an average lifetime cost among survivors that exceeds $767,000 per case.[111]

Keep in mind that health plans do not promise good health. They simply pay for the cost of ill health and the associated rehabilitation. Because 8 of the 10 leading causes of death are largely preventable, however, employers are beginning to look to health promotion and disease management as one way to reduce health-care spending. **Disease management** is a combination of strategies developed to reduce the costs of chronic conditions that require significant changes in behavior. Its goals are to reduce episodes of acute illness, avoid repeated hospitalizations, and lower mortality risks. To do that, it is necessary to do three things well: (1) Identify the condition in its early stages, (2) provide appropriate levels of care (treatment matched to the severity of the problem), and (3) deliver intensive follow-up to reinforce compliance.[112]

Is it possible that health care costs can be tamed through on-the-job exercise programs and health-promotion efforts? Apparently most U.S. employers think so, since 75 percent provide wellness resources and information, and 60 percent offer wellness programs, according to a large-scale 2011 survey.[113]

Do such programs work? In a moment we will consider that question, but first let's define our terms and look at the overall concept.

The process of corporate health promotion begins by promoting health awareness, that is, knowledge of the present and future consequences of behaviors and lifestyles and the risks they may present. The objective of **wellness programs** is not to eliminate symptoms and disease; it is to help employees build lifestyles that will enable them to achieve their full physical and mental potential. Wellness programs differ from EAPs in that wellness focuses on prevention, while EAPs focus on rehabilitation. **Health promotion** is a four-step process:[114]

1.  Educating emplyees about health-risk factors—life habits or body characteristics that may increase the chances of developing a serious illness. For heart disease (the leading cause of death), some of these risk factors are high blood pressure, cigarette smoking, high cholesterol levels, diabetes, a sedentary lifestyle, and obesity. Some factors, such as smoking, physical inactivity, stress, and poor nutrition, are associated with many diseases.[115]
2.  Identifying the health-risk factors that each employee faces.
3.  Helping employees eliminate or reduce these risks through healthier lifestyles and habits.
4.  Helping employees maintain their new, healthier lifestyles through self-monitoring and evaluation. The central theme of health promotion is "No one takes better care of you than you do."

To date, the most popular programs are smoking cessation, blood-pressure control, cholesterol reduction, weight control and fitness, and stress management. In well-designed programs that offer incentives, 60 to 70 percent of employees can be expected to participate.[116] However, it's the 10 percent to 20 percent of high-risk employees who account for up to 80 percent of all claims that are the most difficult to reach.[117] Here is why it is important to try.

### Linking Unhealthy Lifestyles to Health-Care Costs

A four-year study of 15,000 Ceridian Corporation employees showed dramatic relationships between employees' health habits and insurance-claim costs. For example, people whose weekly exercise was equivalent to climbing fewer than five flights of stairs or walking less than half a mile spent 114 percent more on health claims than those who climbed at least 15 flights of stairs or walked 1.5 miles weekly. Health-care costs for obese people were 11 percent higher than those for thin ones. And workers who routinely failed to use seat belts spent 54 percent more days in the hospital than those who usually buckled up. Finally, people who smoked an average of one or more packs of cigarettes a day had 118 percent higher medical expenses than nonsmokers.[118] Similar results were found in another longitudinal study that appeared at about the same time.[119] Rockford Products Corp., which makes metal parts used in items from Caterpillar earth movers to yo-yos, combed through 15 years of records and found that 31 of 32 workers who had heart attacks or required major heart surgery—including two who keeled over in the factory—were smokers.[120] Results like these may form the basis for incentive programs to (1) improve workers' health habits and (2) reduce employees' contributions to health insurance costs or increase their benefits. Here's what two companies are doing.

---

**IBM AND SCOTTS MIRACLE-GRO**

**HR BUZZ**

**Reaching "High-Risk" Employees**

In 2010 IBM added an incentive dubbed the "Personal Vitality Rebate" to encourage lifestyle changes to build energy, better health, and vitality through personal well-being. The program joined four similar healthy-living rebates promoting physical activity and nutrition, preventive care, children's' health, and new-hire healthy living. Each offers $150 cash incentives available to all 120,000 full-time U. S. employees. Employees choosing to participate in any two programs receive up to $300 cash per year. The payoff? Over a three-year period, IBM invested $79 million in wellness programs, and saved about $191 million in lower health-care costs for participants, as compared to nonparticipants.[a]

At Scotts Miracle-Gro, if workers and spouses agree to get their weight, blood pressure, and cholesterol checked regularly, they can reduce their health-care premiums by $60 a month. The company also refuses to hire smokers. While that policy upsets some employees, the company's health premiums have risen at about half the U. S. average since it implemented the smoker-hiring ban four years earlier.[b]

---

[a]Wechsler, P. (2011, July 10). And you thought cigarettes were pricey. *BusinessWeek*, pp. 24–26.
[b]Ibid.

---

## Evaluation: Do Wellness Programs Work?

Wellness programs are especially difficult to evaluate, for at least six reasons:[121]

1. Health-related costs that actually decrease are hard to identify.
2. Program sponsors use different methods to measure and report costs and benefits.
3. Program effects may vary depending on *when* they are measured (immediate versus lagged effects), and on *how long* they are measured.
4. Potential biases exist as a result of self-selection and exclusion of drop-outs.
5. Few studies use control groups.
6. Data on effectiveness are limited in the choice of variables, estimation of the economic value of indirect costs and benefits, estimation of the timing and duration of program effects, and estimation of the present value of future benefits.

Although a growing number of studies report favorable cost–benefit results, it is difficult to evaluate and compare them because different authors use different assumptions in their estimates of wellness-intervention costs and dollar benefits, and small changes in assumptions can have large effects on the interpretation of results. Meta-analyses (that is, quantitative cumulations of research results across studies) and single studies that are based on very large sample sizes can deal with many of these methodological difficulties.[122]

## ETHICAL DILEMMA
### Should Employees Be Punished for Unhealthy Lifestyles?*

Johnson & Johnson Health Care Systems Inc., which sells wellness programs to companies, estimates that 15 to 25 percent of corporate health-care costs stem from employees' unhealthy lifestyle conditions. As a result, individuals may not be hired, might even be fired, and could wind up paying a monthly penalty based on their after-hours activities. Here are some examples:

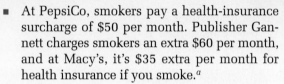

- At PepsiCo, smokers pay a health-insurance surcharge of $50 per month. Publisher Gannett charges smokers an extra $60 per month, and at Macy's, it's $35 extra per month for health insurance if you smoke.[a]
- Turner Broadcasting won't hire smokers.
- Multi-Developers won't hire anyone who engages in what the company views as high-risk activities: skydiving, piloting a private aircraft, mountain climbing, or motorcycling.

Federal civil rights laws generally don't protect against **lifestyle discrimination** because smokers and skydivers aren't named as protected classes. However, about 30 states and the District of Columbia have passed laws that protect employees and job applicants from any adverse employment actions if their use of a lawful product (such as tobacco) occurs outside of work.[c] Should employers be able to implement "lifestyle policies"?

---

*\*Source:* Hirschman, C. (2003, Feb.). Off duty, out of work. *HR Magazine* 48(2), pp. 50–56.

[a]Wechsler, 2011, op. cit. See also Deschenaux, J. (2011, July). Is a "smoker-free" workplace right for you? *HR Magazine* 56(7), pp. 43–45.

[c]Overman, S. (2010, March). Prescribing wellness. *HR Magazine* 55(3), pp. 49–54.

Typical annual costs of running a wellness program are $30 to $140 per participant, with most programs in the range of $60 to $100.[123] The return on investment (ROI) for wellness programs has been reported anywhere from $1.41 (SAS Institute) to $6 (grocery retailer H-E-B) per dollar invested. H-E-B found that annual health-care claims are about $1,500 higher among nonparticipants in its wellness program than among participants with a high-risk health status. Moving just 10 percent of high- and medium-risk employees to low-risk status yields an ROI of 6 to 1.[124]

Peer-reviewed evaluations and meta-analyses show that ROI is achieved through improved worker health, reduced benefit expense, and enhanced productivity.[125] A review of 72 articles concluded that health-promotion programs achieve an average ROI of $3.48 per $1 invested when considering health-care costs alone, $5.82 when considering absenteeism, and $4.30 when both are considered.[126] In a separate investigation, researchers conducted a 38-month case study of 23,000 participants in Citibank N.A.'s health-management program. They reported that within a two-year period Citibank enjoyed an ROI of between $4.56 and $4.73. A follow-up study found improvements in the risk profiles of participants, with the high-risk group improving more than the "usual-care" group as a result of more intensive programs.[127]

A later meta-analysis suggested that individualized risk reduction for high-risk employees within the context of a comprehensive health-promotion program is the critical element in achieving positive cost outcomes in worksite interventions.[128] This takes time, and studies show that a positive impact on medical costs generally requires three to five years of program participation.[129]

Based on the research reviewed, it is clear that wellness programs can yield significant payoffs to organizations that adopt them. It also is clear, however, that the programs do not work under all circumstances and that the problems associated with assessing relative costs and benefits may be complex. The most successful programs have six essential pillars: engaged leadership at multiple levels; strategic alignment with the organization's identity and aspirations; programs that are broad in scope and high in relevance and quality; broad accessibility; internal and external partnerships; and effective communication.[130] If wellness programs then apply these lessons, and if they are successful in attracting at-risk employees into the programs, then the programs will flourish, even in an era of limited resources.

## Wellness Programs and the Americans with Disabilities Act

Employers violate the ADA if they *require* employees to submit to wellness initiatives, such as health-risk appraisals (questionnaires about one's health history and current lifestyle) and assessments (physical and biomedical tests that screen for specific health conditions). This is because the act forbids employers from conducting mandatory medical exams once an employee is hired, unless the inquiry is "job-related and consistent with business necessity."

Employers also must be careful when tying financial incentives or disincentives (e.g., cash bonuses, lower health-insurance contributions) to test results. The employer can offer an incentive only upon verification that the employee went for the test. The incentive cannot be tied to the test results. Under the ADA, employers cannot discriminate in pay or benefits based on a legally protected disability. In addition, any test results from wellness screening must be kept confidential.

What types of wellness programs do not violate the ADA? Companies such as American Honda, AstraZeneca, and Cal-Neva Resort, Spa & Casino encourage employees to use health-monitoring kiosks in cafeterias and employee break rooms that measure users' blood pressure, heart rate, and weight noninvasively. Using touch screens, employees answer questions about their lifestyles and health choices (e.g., level of exercise, smoking habits). Based on their answers, the computer generates a personalized health-risk appraisal that places users in government-defined health-risk categories. Use of the kiosks is completely up to the employee. In keeping with medical-information-privacy law, neither employers nor the vendor can access employee-specific information in the kiosks. Employers can get aggregate data, however, to see what employee populations are using the monitoring stations and what their health concerns are. Employers can then use those data to develop health programs to address issues that employees have identified.[131] By helping employees to take an interest in their future health, employers should ultimately be able to keep at least a loose lid on claims and major expenses.

| *Human Resource Management in Action: Conclusion* | **SUBSTANCE ABUSE ON THE JOB PRODUCES TOUGH POLICY CHOICES FOR MANAGERS** |

In *EEOC v. Exxon USA Inc.,* the 5th Circuit Court of Appeals ruled in favor of Exxon. An employer can justify a general safety requirement—applied to all employees in a given job classification—by showing that the requirement is job-related and consistent with business necessity. There was no further review by the Supreme Court. The ruling emphasized that, ordinarily, it is not the role of the courts to question or interfere with an employer's business objectives. The practical implications of this decision for employers are clear. A review of safety-related job qualifications under a simple standard of job-relatedness will allow employers to exclude individuals with impairments based on considerations of safety, even if there is a possibility that the impairments are ADA disabilities.

Not all employers will adopt such a policy. In fact, given the amounts of time and money invested in employees, especially highly skilled knowledge workers, many firms try to rehabilitate those with substance-abuse problems. But how do firms get problem employees into rehabilitation programs? The most popular approaches are self-referral and referral by family, friends, or co-workers. Among pilots who have gone through the airline industry's alcohol-rehabilitation program, in effect since 1973, 85 percent were initially turned in by family, friends, or coworkers.

According to the Air Line Pilots Association, one of the hallmarks of the industry's program is a willingness of people to turn in an alcoholic pilot. That willingness, in turn, depends on knowing that the pilot can return to work. If people know that by turning in a pilot they will also be taking away his or her livelihood, they may not do it.

The key to returning to work, in the opinion of most professionals in the field of substance abuse, is follow-up, because substance abuse is a recurring disease.[132]

---

## IMPLICATIONS FOR MANAGEMENT PRACTICE

In the coming years, we can expect to see three developments in occupational safety and health:

1. Increased emphasis on prevention programs—including multilingual safety training, health promotion, and formal policies on counter-productive behaviors that involve substance abuse or violence at work.
2. Promotion of OSHA's consultative role, particularly as small businesses recognize that this is a no-cost, no-penalty option available to them.
3. Broadening of the target group for EAPs and wellness programs to include dependents and retirees.

The high costs of disabling injuries and occupational diseases, together with these three trends, suggest that the commitment of resources to enhance job safety and health makes good business sense over and above concerns for corporate social responsibility.

Under United's program, rehabilitated pilots are monitored for at least two years. During this time, the pilot is required to meet monthly with a committee comprising counselors and representatives of both union and management in a kind of group-therapy session with other recovering pilots. They may also be required to undergo periodic surprise alcohol or drug tests. United has never had an alcohol-related accident.

Companies with the best success rates in rehabilitating employees with alcohol or drug problems have the most heavily structured follow-up programs. Chevron, Shell, DuPont, American Airlines, and others have demonstrated that a 75 percent success rate is attainable, provided there are mechanisms in place to monitor and reinforce the recovery process.

## SUMMARY

Public policy regarding occupational safety and health has focused on state-run workers' compensation programs for job-related injuries and federally mandated preventive measures to enhance job safety and health. OSHA enforces the provisions of the 1970 Occupational Safety and Health Act, under which employers have a "general duty" to provide a place of employment "free from recognized hazards." Employers also have the special duty to comply with all standards of safety and health established under the act. OSHA's effectiveness has been debated for decades, but it is important to note that workplace accidents can result either from *unsafe work conditions* or from *unsafe work behaviors.* OSHA can affect only unsafe work conditions. There are no standards that govern potentially unsafe employee behaviors.

A major concern of employers today is with the possible health hazards associated with high-technology products, such as semiconductors, with diseases related to radiation or carcinogenic substances that may have long latency periods, and with HIV/AIDS. In response, OSHA has established or toughened workplace exposure limits for many carcinogenic substances. Management's first duty in this area is to develop a safety and health policy. Management's second duty is to establish controls that include a loss-control program, a safety committee, safety rules, careful selection of employees, extensive training, and feedback and incentives for maintaining a safe work environment.

Employee assistance programs represent a brighter side of the health issue. Such programs offer assistance to all "troubled" employees. Under an EAP, supervisors need be concerned only with identifying declining work performance, not with involving themselves in employee problems. Treatment is left to professionals. Finally, health promotion, or "wellness," programs differ from EAPs in that their primary focus is on prevention, not rehabilitation. Both EAPs and wellness programs hold considerable promise for improving productivity, quality of work life, and profits.

## KEY TERMS

willful violation

indirect costs of an accident

externalities

engineering controls

management controls

loss-control program

repetitive-motion injuries

employee assistance program

troubled employee

harmful patterns of drinking

workplace aggression

disease management

wellness programs

health promotion

lifestyle discrimination

## DISCUSSION QUESTIONS

**15–1.** Should OSHA's enforcement activities be expanded? Why or why not?

**15–2.** What can firms do to encourage all employees to behave safely on the job?

**15–3.** Discuss the relative effectiveness of engineering versus management controls to improve job safety and health.

**15–4.** Explain how a disease-management program might be used to address substance-abuse problems.

**15–5.** If the benefits of EAPs cannot be demonstrated to exceed their costs, should EAPs be discontinued?

**15–6.** You observe a coworker threatening another employee. What should you do?

**15–7.** Should organizations be willing to invest more money in employee wellness? Why or why not?

## APPLYING YOUR KNOWLEDGE

*Case 15–1*          *Skyline Machine Shop*

Skyline Machine Shop is a medium-sized firm located in San Jose, California. It employs almost 1,000 workers when business is good. Skyline specializes in doing precision machining on a subcontract basis for several large aerospace companies. Skilled machinists are always in short supply, and therefore command high salaries and generous benefit packages.

Recently, one of the plant foremen, Len Fulkner, paid a visit to Skyline's HR manager, Jamie Trenton, to discuss a problem at work.

*Fulkner:*   You know, Jamie, I've been around the barn a time or two. I've seen all kinds of people-type problems over the years. But I guess maybe I'm over the hill—53 is no spring chicken, you know! The other day I ran into a situation like I've never seen before, and I need your help.

*Trenton:*   What happened Len?

*Fulkner:*   Well, last Thursday one of my best machinists, Harry Boecker, began acting really weird. He seemed to be in a daze, couldn't seem to concentrate on the part he was milling, and began dropping tools and engineering drawings all over. At first I thought he'd been drinking. But I smelled his breath and couldn't smell anything. When I asked him what was wrong, he mumbled something about "coke."

*Trenton:*  What did you do?

*Fulkner:*  I called a taxi and sent him home for the rest of the day. I didn't know what else to do, but I knew he was a danger to himself and to others, so I had to get him out of the plant. I hope I did the right thing. I'm really worried about the guy, Jamie. I'd hate to lose a good machinist like that, but I don't know the first thing about drugs or how to handle workers who have been taking them. Can you help me?

The next day, Trenton had a meeting scheduled with the president of Skyline. She had been thinking for some time about recommending an employee assistance program (EAP) to the president, and her conversation with Fulkner convinced her that now was the appropriate time. Quite a few other firms in the San Jose area had instituted EAPs— seemingly with some success. However, Trenton knew that Skyline's president was skeptical of "follow-the-leader" approaches to employee benefits.

## Questions

1. Did Len Fulkner handle the situation with Harry Boecker correctly? Why or why not?
2. Prepare an outline of a cost–benefit analysis that Jamie Trenton could use in presenting her EAP proposal to Skyline's president. In particular, what categories of benefits might be quantifiable?
3. If Trenton's proposal is accepted, what key steps would you recommend to her in implementing a new EAP at Skyline Machine Shop?

## REFERENCES

1. OSHA. Facts. Retrieved from *www.bls.gov/news.release/cfoi.nr0.htm* on August 26, 2011.
2. Bureau of Labor Statistics. National census of fatal occupational injuries in 2010. Retrieved from *www.bls.gov/news.release/cfoi.nr0.htm* on August 26, 2011.
3. Kuntz, P. (2000, Sept. 18). What a pain: Proposed OSHA rules for workplace injuries make companies ache. *The Wall Street Journal,* pp. A1, A14.
4. Two thirds of office staff suffer from repetitive strain injury. (2008, June 4). *Daily Mail Online.* Retrieved from *www.dailymail.co.uk/health/article-1024097/Two-thirds-office-staff-suffer-repetitive-strain-injury.html* on August 26, 2011. See also Cadrain, D. (2002, Oct.). Workplace safety's ergonomic twist. *HR Magazine,* pp. 43–47.
5. Bureau of Labor Statistics, 2010, op. cit.
6. University of Minnesota, Environmental and Health Sciences. (2004). Back injuries in the workplace. Retrieved from *enhs.umn.edu/2004injuryprevent/back/backinjury.html* on August 11, 2008. See also Rundle, B. (1996, Oct. 9). Back corsets receive support in UCLA study. *The Wall Street Journal,* pp. B1, B2.
7. Labor letter. (1987, Apr. 14). *The Wall Street Journal,* p. 1.

8. Dieterly, D. (1994). Industrial injury cost analysis by occupation in an electric utility. Occupational Research Division, Southern California Edison Co.

9. OSHA. Frequently asked questions. Retrieved from *www.osha.gov/html/comp-links-faq.html* on August 26, 2011.

10. All about OSHA. Retrieved from *www.osha.gov/Publications/about-osha/3302-06N-2006-English.html* on August 26, 2011. See also OSHA facts. Retrieved from *www.osha-safety.org/osha_facts.asp* on August 11, 2008.

11. OSH Act is changed to emphasize cooperation. (1998, Sept.). *HR News,* p. 14.

12. Occupational exposure to blood-borne pathogens: Explanation of the standard. Retrieved from *www.osha.gov/pls/oshaweb/owadisp.show_document?p_id=811&p_table=PREAMBLES* on August 26, 2011.

13. OSHA. Ergonomics: Enforcement. Retrieved from *www.osha.gov/SLTC/ergonomics/faqs.html* on August 26, 2011. See also Karr, A. R. (2003, Sept. 8). Business groups sound ergonomics alarm. *The Wall Street Journal,* p. A4.

14. OSHA kept out of homes. (2000, Feb. 28). *The Denver Post,* p. 4A.

15. *Marshall v. Barlow's Inc.* (1978). 1978 OSHD, Sn. 22,735. Chicago: Commerce Clearing House.

16. Etter, I. B. (1993, Sept.). You can't hide from an OSHA inspector. *Safety & Health,* p. 3.

17. OSHA. OSHA fact sheet: OSHA inspections. Retrieved from *www.osha.gov/OshDoc/data_General_Facts/factsheet-inspections.pdf* on Aug. 26, 2011.

18. Bandler, J., and Maher, K. (2008, Apr. 23). House panel to examine Cintas plants' safety record. *The Wall Street Journal,* pp. B1, B2. See also Maher, K. (2007, Dec. 5). Safety issues beset industrial laundries. *The Wall Street Journal,* p. A14.

19. OSHA, Facts, op. cit.

20. OSHA. On-site consultation. Retrieved from *www.osha.gov/dcsp/smallbusiness/consult.html* on August 27, 2011.

21. Powell, D. D. (2010, Oct. 6). Client alert: OSHA penalties triple. *Brownstein Client Alert.* See also OSHA, Facts, op. cit.

22. Davis, A. (1997, Feb. 26). Treating on-the-job injuries as true crimes. *The Wall Street Journal,* pp. B1, B6. See also Gibbons, C. (2011, Aug. 6). Grain firm fined in death. *The Denver Post,* pp. 1B, 4B.

23. Hilder, P. H. (2011). Criminal prosecution for safety violations is no accident. Retrieved from *www.docstoc.com/docs/86307999/CRIMINAL-PROSECUTION-FOR-SAFETY-VIOLATION-IS-NO-ACCIDENT* on August 27, 2011. See also Fischer, H. (2010, April 17). Corporations on hook for employee deaths. *East Valley Tribune.* Retrieved from *www.eastvalleytribune.com/local/article_be482066-061f-5691-b5ab-eed1154991e1.html* on August 19, 2010.

24. The Occupational Safety and Health Review Commission. About OSHRC. Retrieved from *www.oshrc.gov/about/how-oshrc.html* on August 27, 2011.

25. WFL. OSHA citation results for fiscal 2010. *www.wfl-stl.com/RM-CitationResults.aspx* on August 27, 2011. See also In compliance: OSHA direction for 2012. (2011, March 10). Retrieved from pmanewsline.com/2011/03/10/in-compliance-osha-direction-for-2012/ on August 27, 2011. See also OSHA. FY 2010 State plan inspections by state. Retrieved from *www.osha.gov/dcsp/osp/inspections_2010_bystate.html* on August 27, 2011.

26. *NLRB v. Jasper Seating Co.* (1988). CA 7, 129 LRRM 2337. See also *Whirlpool Corporation v. Marshall* (1981, Feb. 26). *Daily Labor Report,* Washington, DC: Bureau of National Affairs, pp. D3–D10.

27. Audi, T. (2008, June 10). Worker deaths at Las Vegas site spur safety debate. *The Wall Street Journal,* pp. B1, B3. *See also Gateway Coal Co. v. United Mine Workers of America* (1974). 1974 OSHD, Sn. 17,085. Chicago: Commerce Clearing House.

28. Ledvinka, J., and Scarpello, V. G. (1991). *Federal Regulation of Personnel and Human Resource Management* (2nd Ed.). Boston: PWS-Kent, p. 619.

**29.** OSHA, Facts, op. cit.

**30.** Ergonomics: Enforcement, op. cit. See also Karr, 2003, op. cit. See also Kuntz, 2000, op. cit.

**31.** Cook, W. N., and Gautschi, F. H. (1981). OSHA plant safety programs and injury reduction. *Industrial Relations* 20(3), pp. 245–257.

**32.** Colford, J. (2005, Sept. 12). The ROI of safety. *BusinessWeek,* pp. 68–74. See also Adams, S. (2003, Jan.). Costs drive safety-training needs. *HR Magazine,* pp. 63–66.

**33.** Liberty Mutual. 2010 Liberty Mutual workplace safety index. Retrieved from *www.libertymutualgroup.com/omapps/ContentServer?c=cms_document&pagename= LMGResearchInstitute%2Fcms_document%2FShowDoc&cid=1138365240689* on August 27, 2011. See also Follmann, J. F., Jr. (1978). *The Economics of Industrial Health.* New York: AMACOM.

**34.** Elkind, P., and Whitford, D. (2011, Feb. 7). An accident waiting to happen. *Fortune,* pp. 105–132. See also Roughton, J. (2011). Management's role in developing an effective safety culture. Retrieved from *ezinearticles.com/? Managements-Role-in-Developing-an-Effective-Safety-Culture&id=1285414* on August 27, 2011. See also Krause, T. R. (2010, Sept. 20). Oil CEOs must all be chief safety officers now. *Forbes.* Retrieved from *www.forbes.com/2010/09/20/ chief-safety-officer-oil-companies-leadership-citizenship-ceos.html* on September 22, 2010.

**35.** Chazan, G, Faucon, B., and Casselman, B. (2010, June 30). Safety and cost drives clashed as CEO Hayward remade BP. *The Wall Street Journal,* pp. A1, A8. See also Katz, J. (2010, Oct. 21). Could BP's safety incentives backfire? *Industry Week.* Retrieved from *www.industryweek.com/articles/could_bps_safety_incentives_back-fire_23073.aspx?ShowAll=1* on August 27, 2011.

**36.** Ciccarelli, M. C. (2011, March). BP's bubbling cauldron. *Human Resource Executive,* pp. 1, 18–21. See also Elkind and Whitford, 2011, op. cit.

**37.** Christian, M. S., Bradley, J. C., Wallace, J. C., and Burke, M. J. (2009). Antecedents of occupational safety performance and outcomes: A meta-analysis. *Journal of Applied Psychology* 94, pp. 1103–1127. See also Chazan et al., 2010, op. cit. See also Krause, 2010, op. cit. See also Newnam, S., Griffin, M. A., and Mason, C. (2008). Safety in work vehicles: A multilevel study linking safety values and individual predictors to work-related driving crashes. *Journal of Applied Psychology* 93, pp. 632–644. See also Zohar, D., and Luria, G. (2005). A multilevel model of safety climate: Cross-level relationships between organization and group-level climates. *Journal of Applied Psychology* 90, pp. 616–628. See also Hofmann, D. A., and Morgeson, F. P. (1999). Safety-related behavior as a social exchange: The role of perceived organizational support and leader-member exchange. *Journal of Applied Psychology* 84, pp. 286–296.

**38.** Kaplan, S., and Tetrick, L. E. (2011). Workplace safety and accidents: An industrial and organizational psychology perspective. In S. Zedeck (Ed.), *APA Handbook of Industrial and Organizational Psychology,* Vol. 1. Washington, DC: American Psychological Association, pp. 455–472. See also Newnam et al., 2008, op. cit. See also Zohar, D., and Luria, G. (2004). Climate as a social-cognitive construction of supervisory safety practices: Scripts as proxy of behavior patterns. *Journal of Applied Psychology* 89, pp. 322–333. See also Hofmann, D. A., and Stetzer, A. (1998). The role of safety climate and communication in accident interpretation: Implications of learning from negative events. *Academy of Management Journal* 41, pp. 644–657.

**39.** Christian et al., 2009, op. cit. See also Cadrain, 2002, op. cit.

**40.** Burke, M. J., Sarpy, S. A., Tesluk, P. E., and Smith-Crowe, K. (2002). General safety performance: A test of a grounded theoretical model. *Personnel Psychology* 55, pp. 429–457. See also Rundle, 1996, op. cit.

41. Audi, T. (2008, June 10). Worker deaths at Las Vegas site spur safety debate. *The Wall Street Journal,* pp. B1, B3.

42. Kaplan and Tetrick, 2011, op. cit. See also Breslin, F. C., Tompa, E., Mustard, C., Zhao, R., Smith, P., and Hogg-Johnson, S. (2007). Association between the decline in workers' compensation claims and workforce composition. *American Journal of Public Health* 97, pp. 453–455. See also Liao, H., Arvey, R. D., and Butler, R. J. (2001). Correlates of work injury frequency and duration among firefighters. *Journal of Occupational Health Psychology* 6(3), pp. 229–242. See also Graham, S. (1996, Jan.). Debunk the myths about older workers. *Safety & Health,* pp. 38–41. See also Siskind, F. (1982). Another look at the link between work injuries and job experience. *Monthly Labor Review* 105(2), pp. 38–41. See also Root, N. (1981). Injuries at work are fewer among older employees. *Monthly Labor Review* 104(3), pp. 30–34.

43. Maurer, R. (2009, July 7). The future of work: Safety and health issues of an aging workforce. *SHRM Online.* Retrieved from *www.shrm.org/hrdisciplines/safetysecurity/ articles/Pages/SafetyAgingWorkforce.aspx* on July 14, 2009.

44. Burke, M. J., Sarpy, S. A., Smith-Crowe, K., Chan-Serafin, S., Salvador, R. O., and Islam, G. (2006). Relative effectiveness of worker safety and health training methods. *American Journal of Public Health* 96, pp. 315–324.

45. Kaplan and Tetrick, 2011, op. cit. Burke et al., 2002, op. cit.

46. Michaels, D. (2010, April 28). OSHA training standards policy statement. Retrieved from *www.osha.gov/dep/standards-policy-statement-memo-04-28-10.html* on October 5, 2010.

47. Kaplan and Tetrick, 2011, op. cit. See also Barling, J., Kelloway, E. K., and Iverson, R. D. (2003). High-quality work, job satisfaction, and occupational injuries. *Journal of Applied Psychology* 88, pp. 276–283. See also Frone, M. R. (1998). Predictors of work injuries among employed adolescents. *Journal of Applied Psychology* 8, pp. 565–576.

48. OSHA Hazard Communication Standard. (2010, July 1). 29 CFR 1910.1200.

49. Jacobs, S. L. (1988, Nov. 22). Small business slowly wakes to OSHA hazard rule. *The Wall Street Journal,* p. B2.

50. Understanding OSHA right-to-know regulations. Retrieved from *safety.hubpages. com/hub/OSHA-Right-To-Know* on August 28, 2011.

51. Kaplan and Tetrick, 2011, op. cit. See also Barling, J., and Frone, M. R. (Eds.). (2004). *The Psychology of Workplace Safety.* Washington, DC: American Psychological Association. See also Zohar, D. (2002). Modifying supervisory practices to improve subunit safety: A leadership-based intervention model. *Journal of Applied Psychology* 87, pp. 156–163.

52. Komaki, J., Barwick, K. D., and Scott, L. R. (1978). A behavioral approach to occupational safety: Pinpointing and reinforcing safe performance in a food manufacturing plant. *Journal of Applied Psychology* 63, pp. 434–445. See also Zohar, D., and Luria, G. (2004). Climate as a social-cognitive construction of supervisory safety practices: Scripts as proxy of behavior patterns. *Journal of Applied Psychology* 89, pp. 322–333.

53. Yandrick, R. M. (1996, Feb.). Behavioral safety helps shipbuilder cut accident rates. *HR News,* pp. 3, 11. See also Neal, A., and Griffin, M. A. (2006). A study of the lagged relationships among safety climate, safety motivation, safety behavior, and accidents at the individual and group levels. *Journal of Applied Psychology* 91, pp. 946–953. See also Reber, R. A., and Walli, J. A. (1984). The effects of training, goal setting, and knowledge of results on safe behavior: A component analysis. *Academy of Management Journal* 27, pp. 544–560.

54. Milbank, D. (1991, Mar. 29). Companies turn to peer pressure to cut injuries as psychologists join the battle. *The Wall Street Journal,* pp. B1, B3.

55. See, for example, Parloff, R. (2005, June 13). Diagnosing for dollars. *Fortune,* pp. 95–110. See also Robbins, M. A. (2005, July 12). Silica order could affect future mass tort litigation. Retrieved from *www.law.com/jsp/tx/PubArticleTX.*

*jsp?id=900005544349&slreturn=1* on August 13, 2008. See also Varchaver, N. (2003, Dec. 8). What really happened in IBM's clean room? *Fortune,* pp. 91–100. See also *Illinois v. Chicago Magnet Wire Corp.* (1990, Oct. 24). 126 Ill. 2d 356, 534 N.E., 2d 962, 128 Ill. See also Energy Employees Occupational Illness Compensation Program Act, Public Law 106-398, Title XXXVI, § 3601.

56. Wermiel, S. (1989, Oct. 3). Justices let states prosecute executives for job hazards covered by U.S. law. *The Wall Street Journal,* p. A11.

57. Parloff, 2005, op. cit. Robbins, 2005, op. cit. Varchaver, 2003, op. cit.

58. Grossman, R. J. (2000, Oct.). Out with the bad air. *HR Magazine,* pp. 36–45.

59. Karr, A. R. (1989, Jan. 16). OSHA sets or toughens exposure limits on 376 toxic chemicals in workplace. *The Wall Street Journal,* p. C16.

60. Stead, W. E., and Stead, J. G. (1983, Jan.). OSHA's cancer-prevention policy: Where did it come from and where is it going? *Personnel Journal,* pp. 54–60.

61. 7,000 people a day still catching AIDS: U.N. (2011, June 5). *The International Herald Tribune,* p. 1. UNAIDS global facts and figures, 2009. Retrieved from *www.unaids. org/en/media/unaids/contentassets/dataimport/pub/factsheet/2009/20091124_fs_ global_en.pdf* on August 28, 2011.

62. UNAIDS. 2009 AIDS epidemic update. Retrieved from *www.unaids.org/en/media/ unaids/contentassets/dataimport/pub/report/2009/jc1700_epi_update_2009_en.pdf* on August 28, 2011. Turning the tide. (2004, July 26). *Fortune,* pp. S1–S5.

63. Until There's a Cure. Vital statistics. Retrieved from *www.until.org/statistics.shtml* on August 28, 2011. See also Turning the tide, 2004, op. cit.

64. Wessner, D. (2010, Oct. 26). What does HIV/AIDS cost? Retrieved from *the-aids-pandemic.blogspot.com* on August 28, 2011.

65. Disabled World. (2010). HIV and AIDS, symptoms, information, and treatment. Retrieved from *www.disabled-world.com/health/aids/* on August 28, 2011.

66. Until There's a Cure, 2011, op. cit.

67. Turning the tide, 2004, op. cit.

68. Taking stock of the devastation. (2000, July 17). *BusinessWeek,* pp. 84, 85.

69. Society for Human Resource Management. (2011). *2011 Employee Benefits.* Alexandria, VA: Author.

70. Grossman, R. J. (2010, Nov.). What to do about substance abuse. HR Magazine 55(11), pp. 32–38. See also Lockwood, N. R. (2004a). Employee assistance programs: HR tool to address top issues in today's workplace. Retrieved from *www. shrm.org/Research/Articles/Articles/Pages/EAP_20Series_20Part_20I_20-_20EAP %27s__20HR_20Tool_20to_20Address_20Top_20Issues_20in_20Today%27s_20W orkplace.aspx* on October 27, 2009.

71. National Business Group on Health. (2009, March 4). An employer's guide to employee assistance programs. Retrieved from *www.businessgrouphealth.org/ pdfs/FINAL%20NBGH%20Guide%20to%20EAPs%204%2030%2008.pdf* on August 29, 2011.

72. Grossman, 2010, op. cit. See also Prochaska, S. (2003, May). Employee assistance programs: What does HR need to know? Retrieved from *www.shrm.org/hrdisci-plines/benefits/Articles/Pages/WL-EAPs.aspx* on October 20, 2010.

73. Sonnenstuhl, W., quoted in Grossman, 2010, op. cit., p. 37.

74. Stone, D. L., and Kotch, D. A. (1989). Individuals' attitudes toward organizational drug-testing policies and practices. *Journal of Applied Psychology* 74, pp. 518–521.

75. National Business Group on Health, 2009, op. cit. See also Milne, S. H., Blum, T. C., and Roman, P. M. (1994). Factors influencing employees' propensity to use an employee assistance program. *Personnel Psychology* 47, pp. 123–145.

76. Collins, K. R. (2003, Jan.). Identifying and treating employee substance abuse problems. Retrieved from *www.shrm.org/Research/Articles/Articles/Pages/ CMS_000187.aspx* on October 27, 2004.

77. Cascio, W. F., and Boudreau, J. W. (2011). *Investing in People: Financial Impact of Human Resource Initiatives* (2nd Ed.). Upper Saddle River, NJ: Pearson. See also Foote, A., and Erfurt, J. (1981, Sept.–Oct.). Evaluating an employee assistance program. *EAP Digest,* pp. 14–25.

78. Collins, 2003, op. cit. See also Collins, K. (2001b, Apr.). HR must find new ways to battle substance abuse in the workplace. *HR News,* pp. 11, 16.

79. National Business Group on Health, 2009, op. cit. See also Gurchiek, K. (2007a, July 20). Tips, resources for dealing with addiction in the workplace. *HR News.* Retrieved from *www.shrm.org/Publications/HRNews/Pages/CMS_022376.aspx* on July 25, 2007. See also Trieber, E. (2005, Apr.). Employee assistance programs: Getting your money's worth. Retrieved from *www.shrm.org/hrdisciplines/benefits/Articles/Pages/CMS_011907.aspx* on August 14, 2008.

80. Lockwood, 2004a, op. cit.

81. Falcone, P. (2003, May). Dealing with employees in crisis. *HR Magazine,* pp. 117–121. See also How to confront—and help—an alcoholic employee (1991, Mar. 25). *BusinessWeek,* p. 78.

82. Falcone, 2003, op. cit.

83. Beck, M. (2008, Jan. 8). Are you an alcoholic? *The Wall Street Journal,* pp. D1, D2.

84. Grossman, 2010, op. cit. See also National Institute on Alcohol Abuse and Alcoholism. (2011). FAQs for the general public. Retrieved from *www.niaaa.nih.gov/FAQs/General-English/Pages/default.aspx* on August 29, 2011. See also Gurchiek, K. (2007b, July 20). Few organizations deal proactively with substance abuse. *HR News.* Retrieved from *www.shrm.org/Publications/HRNews/Pages/CMS_022375.aspx* on August 29, 2011. See also Collins, 2003, op. cit.. See also Is business bungling its battle with booze? (1991, Mar. 25). *BusinessWeek,* pp. 76–78.

85. Grossman, 2010, op. cit. See also Frone, M. R. (2006). Prevalence and distribution of alcohol use and impairment in the workplace: A U.S. national survey. *Journal of Studies of Alcohol* 76, pp. 147–56.

86. Grossman, 2010, op. cit. See also Lockwood, N. R. (2004b, Sept.). Employee assistance programs: Targeting substance and alcohol abuse. Retrieved from *www.shrm.org/Research/Articles/Articles/Pages/EAP_20Series_20Part_20II_20_20EAP%27s__20Targeting_20Substance_20and_20Alcohol_20Abuse.aspx* on October 27, 2009.

87. How much does drug rehab cost? Retrieved from *www.sober-solutions.com/how-much-does-drug-rehab-cost/* on August 14, 2010. See also Pollock, E. J. (1996, Sept. 9). In leaner, meaner workplace, bosses get tough on addiction. *The Wall Street Journal,* pp. B1, B2.

88. Grossman, 2010, op. cit. See also Collins, 2003, op. cit.

89. U.S. Department of Labor. (2009). Substance use and abuse in America, 2007. Retrieved from *www.dol.gov* on August 30, 2011.

90. National Drug-Free Workplace Alliance. (2005, Sept.). Drug-free workplace statistics. Retrieved from *www.ndfwa.org/Editor/assets/statistics.pdf* on August 14, 2008. See also Collins, 2003, op. cit.

91. Drug Free Idaho. (2010). How drug use affects the workplace: Statistics. Retrieved from *www.drugfreeidaho.org/?s=How+drug+use+affects+the+workplace&x=0&y=0* on August 30, 2011. National Drug-Free Workplace Alliance, 2005, op. cit. See also Lockwood, 2004a, op. cit. See also Lehman, W. E. K., and Simpson, D. D. (1992). Employee substance abuse and on-the-job behaviors. *Journal of Applied Psychology* 77, pp. 309–321.

92. Drug tests keep paying off, but continued gains are tougher. (1998, May 5). *The Wall Street Journal,* p. A1. See also Normand, J., Salyards, S. D., and Mahoney, J. J. (1990). An evaluation of pre-employment drug testing. *Journal of Applied Psychology* 75, pp. 629–639.

93. Drug Free Idaho, 2010, op. cit. See also National Drug-Free Workplace Alliance, 2005, op. cit.

94. Equal Employment Opportunity Commission. (2011). The ADA: Your responsibilities as an employer. Retrieved from *www.eeoc.gov/eeoc/publications/ada17.cfm* on August 30, 2011. See also Grossman, 2010, op. cit.

95. Bureau of Labor Statistics (2011). Census of fatal occupational injuries: Current and revised data. Retrieved from *www.bls.gov/iif/oshcfoi1.htm* on August 30, 2011.

96. Romano, S. J., Levi-Minzi, M. E., Rugala, E. A., and Van Hasselt, V. B. (2011, Jan.). Workplace violence prevention. *FBI Law Enforcement Bulletin.* Retrieved from *www.fbi.gov/stats-services/publications/law-enforcement-bulletin/january2011/ workplace_violence_prevention* on August 30, 2011. See also Neuman, J. H., and Baron, R. A. (1998). Workplace violence and workplace aggression: Evidence concerning specific forms, potential causes, and preferred targets. *Journal of Management* 24, pp. 391–419.

97. Romano et al., 2011, op. cit. See also Fisher, A. (2005, Feb. 21). How to prevent violence at work. *Fortune,* p. 42. See also After the shooting stops. (2001, Mar. 12). *BusinessWeek,* pp. 98–100.

98. Romano et al., 2011, op. cit. See also Dewan, S., and Hubbell, J. M. (2008, Aug. 15). Arkansas suspect quit job on day of killing. *The New York Times.* Retrieved from *www.nytimes.com/2008/08/15/us/15arkansas.html?scp=1&sq=Arkansas% 20suspect%20quit%20job%20on%20day%20of%20killing&st=cse* on August 15, 2008. See also Madkour, R. (2007, Apr. 22). Job review spurred shooting. *The Denver Post,* p. 2A.

99. Romano et al., 2011, op. cit. See also Kane, D., quoted in Fisher, 2005, op. cit., p. 42.

100. Greenberg, J. (2010). Organizational injustice as an occupational health risk. *Academy of Management Annals* 4, pp. 205–243.

101. Romano et al., 2011, op. cit. See also Thelen, J. B. (2009, Dec.). Is that a threat? *HR Magazine* 54(12), pp. 61–63. Neuman and Baron, 1998, op. cit.

102. Romano et al., 2011, op. cit. See also Fisher, 2005, op. cit.

103. Romano et al., 2011, op. cit. See also Bush, D. F. (2002, Aug.). Workplace violence: Shift focus to prevention. *HR News,* p. 22.

104. Romano et al., 2011, op. cit. See also Thelen, 2009, op. cit. See also Bush, 2002, op. cit.

105. Britt, J. (2004, May 27). Expert: Disease management programs cut health care costs. Retrieved from *www.selfconnect.org/Assets/Files/Dr%20Thomas%20 Barela%20on%20the%20need%20for%20Wellness%20Programs.pdf* on October 28, 2004.

106. Aumann, K., and Galinsky, E. (2009). *The State of Health in the American Workforce: Does Having an Effective Workplace Matter?* New York, NY: Families & Work Institute. See also Holland, K. (2008, June 22). Waistlines expand into a workplace issue. *The New York Times.* Retrieved from *www.nytimes.com/2008/06/22/ jobs/22mgmt.html?scp=1&sq=Waistlines%20expand%20into%20a%20work-place%20issue&st=cse* on August 15, 2008.

107. Holland, 2008, op. cit. See also Pudgeball nation. (2001, July 23). *BusinessWeek,* p. 16.

108. Rundle, 1996, op. cit. See also Hollenbeck, J. R., Ilgen, D. R., and Crampton, S. M. (1992). Lower back disability in occupational settings: A review of the literature from a human resource management view. *Personnel Psychology* 45, pp. 247–278.

109. Grossman, R. J. (2001, Aug.). Back with a vengeance. *HR Magazine,* pp. 36–46.

110. Centers for Disease Control and Prevention. (2011, March 21). Fact sheet: Health effects of cigarette smoking. Downloaded from *www.cdc.gov/tobacco/data_ statistics/fact_sheets/health_effects/effects_cig_smoking/index.htm* on August 30,

2011. See also Wechsler, P. (2011, July 10). And you thought cigarettes were pricey. *BusinessWeek,* pp. 24, 25. See also U.S. Department of Health and Human Services. (2006). The health consequences of involuntary exposure to tobacco smoke: A report of the surgeon general—executive summary, 2006. Retrieved from *www.surgeongeneral.gov/library/secondhandsmoke/report/executivesummary.pdf* on October 5, 2011.

111. National Business Group on Health. (2011). Costs of heart disease. Retrieved from *www.wbgh.org/healthtopics/womenheartdiseasearticle.cfm* on November 30, 2011.

112. Britt, 2004, op. cit.

113. Society for Human Resource Management, 2011, op. cit. See also Mincer, J. (2010, Oct. 31). Firms push wellness. *The Wall Street Journal,* pp. B1, B2.

114. Terborg, J. (1998). Health psychology in the United States: A critique and selected review. *Applied Psychology: An International Review* 47(2), pp. 199–217. See also Epstein, S. S. (1989). *A Note on Health Promotion in the Workplace.* Boston: Harvard Business School.

115. Centers for Disease Control and Prevention, 2011, op. cit. See also U.S. Department of Health and Human Services, 2006, op. cit.

116. Berry, L. L., Mirabito, A. M., and Baun, W. B. (2010, Dec.). What's the hard return on employee wellness programs? *Harvard Business Review,* pp. 104–112. See also Wells, S. J. (2010, Feb.). Getting paid for staying well. *HR Magazine* 55(2), pp. 59–62.

117. Aeppel, T. (2003, June 17). Ill will: Skyrocketing health costs start to pit worker vs. worker. *The Wall Street Journal,* pp. A1, A6. See also Schlosser, J. (2003, Feb. 3). Uphill battle. *Fortune,* p. 64.

118. Jose, W. S., Anderson, D. R., and Haight, S. A. (1987). The StayWell strategy for health-care cost containment. In J. P. Opatz (Ed.), *Health Promotion Evaluation: Measuring the Organizational Impact.* Stevens Point, WI: National Wellness Institute, pp. 15–34.

119. Parkes, K. R. (1987). Relative weight, smoking, and mental health as predictors of sickness and absence from work. *Journal of Applied Psychology* 72, pp. 275–286.

120. Aeppel, 2003, op. cit.

121. Cascio and Boudreau, 2011, op. cit.

122. Schmidt, F. L. (2008). Meta-analysis: A constantly evolving research-integration tool. *Organizational Research Methods* 11, pp. 96–113. See also Hunter, J. S., and Schmidt, F. L. (2004). *Methods of Meta-analysis: Correcting Error and Bias in Research Findings* (2nd Ed.) Thousand Oaks, CA: Sage.

123. Wells, S. J. (2011, March). Navigating the expanding wellness industry. *HR Magazine* 56(3), pp. 45–50.

124. Berry et al., 2010, op. cit.

125. Zank, D., and Friedsam, D. (2005, Sept.). Employee health-promotion programs: What is the return on investment? *Wisconsin Public Health and Health Policy Institute Issue Brief.* Retrieved from *uwphi.pophealth.wisc.edu/publications/issueBriefs/issueBriefv06n05.pdf* on February 15, 2008.

126. Aldana, S. G. (2001). Financial impact of health-promotion programs: A comprehensive review of the literature. *American Journal of Health Promotion* 15(5), pp. 295–320.

127. Ozminkowski, R. J., Goetzel, R. W., Smith, M. W., Cantor, R. I., Shaughnessy, A., and Harrison, M. (2000). The impact of the Citibank N.A. health management program on changes in employee health risks over time. *Journal of Occupational and Environmental Medicine* 42(5), pp. 502–511.

128. Pelletier, K. R. (2001). A review and analysis of the clinical and cost-effectiveness studies of comprehensive health-promotion and disease-management programs at the worksite: 1998–2000 update. *American Journal of Health Promotion* 16(2), pp. 107–116.

**129.** Ibid. See also Edington, M. D., Karjalainen, T., Hirschland, D. and Edington, D. W. (2002). The UAW-GM health-promotion program: Successful outcomes. *AAOHN Journal* 50(1), pp. 25–31.

**130.** Berry et al., 2010, op. cit.

**131.** Overman, 2010, op. cit. See also Onley, D. (2005, Jan.). Doc in a box. *HR Magazine,* pp. 83–85.

**132.** Witkiewitz, K., and Marlatt, A. (2004). Relapse prevention for alcohol and drug problems. *American Psychologist* 59, pp. 224–235.

# 16 INTERNATIONAL DIMENSIONS OF HUMAN RESOURCE MANAGEMENT

*Questions This Chapter Will Help Managers Answer*

1. What factors should I consider in evaluating managers, employees, and customers from a different culture?
2. What should be the components of expatriate recruitment, selection, orientation, and training strategies?
3. How should an expatriate compensation package be structured?
4. What kinds of career management issues should a manager consider before deciding to work for a foreign-owned firm in the United States?
5. What special issues deserve attention in the repatriation of overseas employees?

## WHAT'S IT LIKE TO BE A GLOBAL MANAGER?*

My first day on the job is turning into a nightmare. I am about to meet with a promising young manager who has just botched a new assignment, and in just a few hours, I'm scheduled to make a strategy presentation to my new boss. But the phone won't stop ringing, and I'm being deluged with e-mail.

It's a good thing this isn't really happening. I'm at a makeshift office in suburban London taking part in a workplace-simulation exercise. It's just like the one that hundreds of Motorola Inc. executives around the world will go through in the coming months as part of a wide-ranging effort at the company to identify and evaluate tomorrow's top international managers.

Like many multinationals, Motorola is pressing to find talented leaders to run its increasingly complicated global business. As companies cross borders to make acquisitions and expand operations, the demand for employees with international management skills is growing exponentially. The consequences can be dire for firms that fail to build up a cadre of competent global managers. Poor decisions can lead to multibillion-dollar flubs, as products flop and marketing campaigns go awry.

Motorola's Internet-based test, developed with Aon Consulting Worldwide (now Aon Hewitt), can be administered remotely any place in the world. As Aon Hewitt executives explained to me how the simulation would work, I imagined myself enduring several hours of awkward play-acting. In practice, the experience is startlingly lifelike.

My role is Chris Jefferson, regional manager in the finance unit of a fictitious conglomerate, Globalcom. My laptop computer has been specially set up so that I can send and receive e-mail, look up information about my employer, and consult my calendar—where several meetings have already been scheduled. An Aon Hewitt psychologist will play several roles, phoning me from an adjacent office and popping in at the end in the role of Jean Dubois, my boss.

As soon as I settle in to my windowless, brick-walled office, the telephone calls begin, and unexpected visitors arrive. Urgent tasks come so fast and furiously that I quickly forget it is all a game. Several calls and e-mails concern a promising middle manager who has let several details of a critical new assignment fall through the cracks.

Another Aon Hewitt psychologist is playing the role of the manager, and he enters my office for our meeting. I try teasing out of him information about what's going wrong. We talk for several minutes before a voice in the back of my brain reminds me that it's all only make-believe.

The meeting is over and I have less than two hours to get my presentation ready. I hurry to prepare, scouring my computer for information about Globalcom. I find things like market research, news reports, results of an employee survey, and corporate press releases, but just like one of those bad dreams, I keep getting sidetracked by a steady stream of telephone calls. An irate customer rails shrilly at me about poor service and threatens to bolt to the competition. E-mails, some of them demanding immediate attention, keep popping up on my computer screen.

---

Challenges

1.  Can you identify any differences between managing domestically versus internationally?
2.  How accurate are such workplace simulations? In what form might results show up?
3.  Do simulations like Motorola's "travel well"? That is, do you think they will work in different cultures?

Increasingly, the world is becoming a "global village" as multinational investment continues to grow. All the HR management issues that we have discussed to this point are interrelated conceptually and operationally and are particularly relevant in the international context: strategic workforce planning, recruitment, selection, orientation, training and development, career management, compensation, and labor relations. In examining all these issues, as well as considering the special problems of repatriation (the process of reentering one's native culture after being absent from it), this chapter thus provides a capstone to the book.

## THE GLOBAL CORPORATION: A FACT OF MODERN ORGANIZATIONAL LIFE

The demise of communism, the fall of trade barriers, and the rise of networked information have unleashed a revolution in business. Market capitalism guides every major country on earth. Goods and services flow across borders more freely than ever; vast information networks instantly link nations, companies, and people; and foreign direct investment is expected to reach nearly $2 trillion in 2012 with approximately 57 percent coming from and going to developed countries. The result—21st-century capitalism.[1] To begin to appreciate the magnitude of this trend, consider a snapshot of the 2011 *Fortune* Global 500 (the largest 500 firms in the world). The aggregate revenues of the top 10 firms exceeded $3.3 trillion, with profits of 118.5 billion and the top 10 largest employers provided jobs for 9.7 million of the world's people.[2]

### Signs of Globalization

Globalization is the dominant driving force in the world economy, reshaping societies and politics as it changes lives. Moreover, an expanding high-tech, information-based economy increasingly defines globalization and shapes the business cycles within it. Much of the flow of capital, labor, services, and goods among Asia, America, and Europe are technology based. Without chips, screens, and software help from Asia, the U.S. economy would grind to a halt.[3] Many factors are driving change, but none is more important than the rise of Internet technologies.[4] The Internet, as it continues to develop, has certainly changed the ways that people live and work. Indeed, in some industries, such as music and e-commerce, it has completely revolutionized the rules of the game.

At the same time, mass collaboration through file-sharing, blogs, and social-networking services is making leaps in creativity possible, and it is changing the way companies in a variety of industries do business.[5] Here are some examples.

- *Research and Development* (R&D). Procter & Gamble makes use of outside scientific networks to generate 35 percent of new products from outside the company, up from 20 percent three years ago. That has helped boost sales per R&D person by 40 percent.
- *Software Development.* By coordinating their efforts online, programmers worldwide volunteer on more than 100,000 open-source projects, such as Linux, thereby challenging traditional software.
- *Telecommunications.* More than 41 million people use Skype software to share computer-processing power and bandwidth, allowing them to call each other free over the Internet. That has cut revenues sharply at traditional telecom providers.
- *Retail.* With 61 million active members, eBay has created a self-sustaining alternative to retail stores.

The Net gives everyone in the organization, at any level and in every functional area, the ability to access a mind-boggling array of information—instantaneously from anywhere. Instead of seeping out over months or years, ideas can be zapped around the globe in the blink of an eye. As just one example, consider Apple's iPhone. It lets you control a universe of information with a swipe. Facebook is another example. It counts more than 800 million active users, 70 percent of whom are outside of the United States.[6] Indeed, a global marketplace has been created by factors such as the following:

- Global telecommunications enhanced by fiber optics, satellites, and computer technology.
- E-commerce that makes firms global from the moment their Web sites are up and running, as customers from around the world log on.
- Giant multinational corporations such as AstraZeneca, Unilever, and Nestlé, which have begun to lose their national identities as they integrate and coordinate product design, manufacturing, sales, and services on a worldwide basis. For example, Coca-Cola Company currently generates 75 percent of its sales outside the United States.[7]
- Growing free trade among nations (e.g., the European Union; the North American Free Trade Agreement among Mexico, the United States, and Canada; and the Association of Southeast Asian Nations).
- Financial markets are now open 24 hours a day around the world.
- Cost pressures (that prod firms to move where labor and other resources are cheapest), coupled with a search for new markets (as firms and consumers around the world seek foreign goods and services).
- The integration of cultures and values through international travel, as well as the spread of goods such as music, food, and clothing. In combination, these have led to common consumer demands around the world.[8]
- The emergence of global standards and regulations for trade, commerce, finance, products, and services.[9]

## The Backlash against Globalization

Open borders have allowed new ideas and technology to flow freely around the globe, accelerating productivity growth and allowing companies to be more competitive than they have been in decades. Yet there is a growing fear on the part of many people that globalization benefits big companies instead of average citizens. Several factors are driving this backlash:

- *Insecurity.* As companies restructure and adapt to market forces, they are churning their workforces.[10] Many operations are being sent overseas, as both blue- and white-collar workers watch their jobs migrate to India, the Philippines, Mexico, Canada, China, Ireland, and elsewhere. U.S. companies cut their work forces in the U.S. by 2.9 million during the 2000s, while increasing employment overseas by 2.4 million. That's a big switch from the 1990s, when they added jobs everywhere: 4.4 million in the U.S. and 2.7 million abroad.[11]
- *Mistrust.* Big, multilateral institutions such as the International Monetary Fund (IMF), the World Bank, and the World Trade Organization are losing their credibility. Their secret decisions made behind closed doors are not acceptable to citizens accustomed to transparent, democratic institutions.
- *Managing global supply networks.* Boeing learned this the hard way as it sourced 70 percent of components for its new 787 Dreamliner aircraft. Managing such an extended network of relationships requires more transparency, better communication, greater trust, and genuine reciprocity, as client-service-provider relationships shift from adversarial to collaborative, from procurement to partnership.[12]
- *Priorities.* Whether business likes it or not, the environment and also labor standards overseas are genuine issues with growing support among high-tech workers, students, and the young in America. These are new issues on the global agenda, and they won't go away.[13]
- *Technophobia.* The battle against genetically modified food is just one indicator of the growing reaction against the high-tech world. In the United States, and especially in Europe, science and innovation are seen by many as threats, not solutions. Preservation of traditional, national values is most important.[14] Globalization is the enemy.

In the public eye, multinational corporations are synonymous with globalization. In all of their far-flung operations, therefore, they bear responsibility to be good corporate citizens, to preserve the environment, to uphold labor standards, to provide decent working conditions and competitive wages, to treat their employees fairly, and to contribute to the communities in which they operate. Some have done so admirably. Levi Strauss & Co. has ethical manufacturing standards for its overseas operations. Home Depot Inc. has adopted an eco-friendly lumber-supply program with the Rainforest Action Network. Starbucks is working with Conservation International to buy coffee from farmers preserving forests.[15] Actions like these make a strong case for continued globalization.

An estimated 82,000 **multinational enterprises** (MNEs), with 80 million employees and US$18 trillion in sales, are currently operating in countries around the globe.[16] Before proceeding further, let's define some terms that we will use throughout the chapter:

- A **global corporation** is one that has become an "insider" in any market or nation where it operates and is thus competitive with domestic firms operating in local markets.[17] Unlike domestic firms, however, the global corporation has a global strategic perspective and claims its legitimacy from its effective use of assets to serve its far-flung customers.

- An **expatriate** or *foreign-service employee* is a generic term applied to anyone working outside her or his home country with a planned return to that or a third country.
- **Home country** is the expatriate's country of residence.
- **Host country** is the country in which the expatriate is working.
- A **third-country national** is an expatriate who has transferred to an additional country while working abroad. A German working for a U.S. firm in Spain is a third-country national.

Expatriates staff many, if not most, overseas operations of multinational firms, and the costs can be astronomical.

## The Costs of Overseas Executives

One of the first lessons global corporations learn is that it is far cheaper to hire competent host-country nationals (if they are available) than to send their own executives overseas. Foreign-service employees typically cost at least twice the salary of a comparable domestic employee, and often many more times the salary of a local national employee in the assignment country (see Table 16–1).[18] An employee with a $75,000 to $100,000 base salary will cost his or her firm an average of $1 million during a three-year assignment.[19] While the exact number of U.S. expatriates is not known, the State Department estimates it at about 3.5 to 4 million, and the number is growing. Indeed, a recent study by consulting firm PriceWaterhouse Coopers found that assignee levels increased by 25 percent over the last decade, and that the average MNE had assignees in 22 countries in 2010. The same study predicts a further 50 percent growth in assignments by 2020. There will be more assignees, more business travel, more virtual tools, and especially more quick, short- term, and commuter assignments. Moreover, the millennial generation will view overseas assignments as a rite of passage.[20]

Comparing prices on 200 items, including food, clothing, and housing, in 214 cities, Mercer HR Consulting reported in its 2011 cost-of-living survey that the 10 most expensive cities in the world for expatriates were Luanda (Angola), Tokyo, Ndjamena (Chad), Moscow, Geneva, Osaka, Libreville (Gabon), Hong Kong, Zurich, and Copenhagen. Karachi (Pakistan) is the world's least expensive city.[21]

Of course, costs fluctuate with international exchange rates relative to the U.S. dollar. In view of these high costs, firms are working hard to reduce these costs, for example, through the use of **efficient-purchaser indexes** for established expatriates. Such indexes assume that a person is not completely new to a situation and has learned about some local brands and outlets and therefore pays prices that are lower than someone who is not familiar with the location.[22] Firms also are working hard to reduce the failure rate among their expatriates, where failure is defined as a return home before the period of assignment is completed or as unmet business objectives. That rate is about 5 to 10 percent of expatriate assignments, but may be as high as 20 percent.[23] For companies, the costs of mistaken expatriation include the costs of initial recruitment, relocation expenses, premium compensation, repatriation costs (i.e., costs associated with resettling the expatriate), replacement costs, and the tangible costs of poor job performance. When an overseas assignment does not work out, it still costs a company, on average, twice the employee's base salary. For employees, the costs are more personal: diminished self-esteem, impaired relationships, and interrupted careers.[24]

## Table 16-1

**SAMPLE PROJECTION FOR AN EXPATRIATE COMPENSATION PACKAGE**

Resource Cost Projection Summary
Doe, Jane
Projection Name:
From 1/1/2010 To 12/31/2012

Home Country:                         Host Country: AVG Cost
Home State:                           Host State: N/A
Report Currency: US dollar           Inflation Rate: 0

| | 12/31/2010 | 12/31/2011 | 12/31/2012 | 12/31/2013 | Total |
|---|---|---|---|---|---|
| Base salary | $100,000 | $100,000 | $100,000 | 0 | $300,000 |
| **Total base payroll** | 100,000 | 100,000 | 100,000 | 0 | 300,000 |
| Goods & service differential | $ 60,000 | $ 60,000 | $ 60,000 | 0 | $180,000 |
| Housing differential | 57,479 | 57,479 | 57,479 | 0 | 172,437 |
| **Total assignment allowances (paid per period)** | $117,479 | $117,479 | $117,479 | 0 | $352,437 |
| Education allowance | $ 10,000 | $ 10,000 | $ 10,000 | 0 | $ 30,000 |
| Assignee home leave | 0 | 1,800 | 1,800 | 0 | 3,600 |
| Family home leave | 0 | 3,600 | 3,600 | 0 | 7,200 |
| Property management cost | 2,000 | 2,000 | 2,000 | 0 | 6,000 |
| Tax preparation fees | 3,000 | 3,000 | 3,000 | 0 | 9,000 |
| **Total other assignment allowances** | $ 15,000 | $ 20,400 | $ 20,400 | 0 | $ 55,800 |
| Storage: annual | $ 3,000 | $ 3,000 | $ 3,000 | 0 | $ 9,000 |
| Airfares: moving in/moving out | 2,790 | 0 | 2,790 | 0 | 5,580 |
| Shipment: in/out | 10,000 | 0 | 12,000 | 0 | 22,000 |
| Temporary lodging: in/out | 4,070 | 0 | 3,070 | 0 | 7,140 |
| Temporary meals & incidentals: in/out | 3,530 | 0 | 1,810 | 0 | 5,340 |
| Destination services | 5,000 | 0 | 0 | 0 | 5,000 |
| Premove/househunting airfare | 3,600 | 0 | 0 | 0 | 3,600 |
| Premove/househunting lodging | 1,008 | 0 | 0 | 0 | 1,008 |
| Premove/househunting per diem | 1,848 | 0 | 0 | 0 | 1,848 |
| Lump sum relocation allowance: in/out | 8,333 | 0 | 8,333 | 0 | 16,666 |
| Language class allowance | 5,000 | 0 | 0 | 0 | 5,000 |
| Cultural orientation | 3,900 | 0 | 0 | 0 | 3,900 |
| Home auto loss reimbursement | 3,000 | 0 | 0 | 0 | 3,000 |
| **Total relocation expenses** | $ 56,079 | $ 3,000 | $ 31,003 | 0 | $ 89,082 |
| **Net compensation** | $287,558 | $240,879 | $268,882 | 0 | $797,319 |
| **Tax costs:** | | | | | |
| Host-country tax cost | $ 57,299 | $ 75,142 | $ 65,149 | $ 8,254 | $203,844 |
| Home-country tax cost | 13,034 | 14,306 | 15,686 | 9,942 | 52,969 |
| Hypothetical tax* | (20,738) | (20,738) | (20,738) | 0 | (62,214) |
| **Total excess tax costs** | $ 48,595 | $ 68,710 | $ 60,099 | $16,195 | $194,598 |
| **Total assignment costs including salary** | $337,153 | $309,589 | $328,981 | $16,195 | $991,917 |

Source: Provided By Eileen Mullaney, Principal, PricewaterhouseCoopers LLP. Used with permission.

*Hypothetical tax is the tax that the expatriate would pay if he or she never left home.

Although the costs of expatriates are considerable, there are also compensating benefits to multinational firms. In particular, overseas postings allow managers to develop international experience outside their home countries—the kind of experience needed to compete successfully in the global economy that we now live in.

Nevertheless, it is senseless to send people abroad who do not know what they are doing overseas and cannot be effective in the foreign culture. More specifically, companies need to consider the impact of culture on international HR management. But what is culture? **Culture** refers to characteristic ways of doing things and behaving that people in a given country or region have evolved over time. It helps people to make sense of their part of the world and provides them with an identity. It is rooted in fundamental values and beliefs.

## THE ROLE OF CULTURAL UNDERSTANDING IN INTERNATIONAL MANAGEMENT PRACTICE

Managers who have no appreciation for cultural differences have a **local perspective.** They believe in the inherent superiority of their own group and culture, and they tend to look down on those considered "foreign." Rather than accepting differences as legitimate, they view and measure alien cultures in terms of their own.

By contrast, managers with a **cosmopolitan perspective** are sensitive to cultural differences, respect the distinctive practices of others, and make allowances for such factors when communicating with representatives of different cultural groups. Recognizing that culture and behavior are relative, they are more tentative and less absolute in their interactions with others.[25]

Such cultural understanding can minimize "culture shock" and allow managers to be more effective with both employees and customers. The first step in this process is an increase in general awareness of differences across cultures, because such differences deeply affect human resource management practices.

## HUMAN RESOURCE MANAGEMENT PRACTICES AS A CULTURAL VARIABLE

Particularly when business does not go well, Americans returning from overseas assignments tend to blame the local people, calling them irresponsible, unmotivated, or downright dishonest. Such judgments are pointless, for many of the problems are a matter of fundamental cultural differences that profoundly affect how different people view the world and operate in business. This section presents a systematic framework of 10 broad classifications that will help managers assess any culture and examine its people systematically. It does not consider every aspect of culture, and by no means is it the only way to analyze culture. Rather, it is a useful beginning for cultural understanding. The framework is comprised of the following 10 factors:[26]

- Sense of self and space.
- Dress and appearance.
- Food and feeding habits.
- Communication and language.
- Time and time consciousness.
- Relationships.

- Values and norms.
- Beliefs and attitudes.
- Work motivation and practices.
- Mental processes and learning.

### Sense of Self and Space

Self-identity may be manifested by a humble bearing in some places, by macho behavior in others. Some countries (e.g., the United States) may promote independence and creativity, while others (e.g., Japan) emphasize group cooperation and conformity. Americans have a sense of space that requires more distance between people, while Latins and Vietnamese prefer to get much closer. Each culture has its own unique ways of doing things.

### Dress and Appearance

Dress includes outward garments as well as body decorations. Many cultures wear distinctive clothing—the Japanese kimono, the Indian turban, the Polynesian sarong, the "organization-man or -woman" look of business, and uniforms that distinguish wearers from everybody else. Cosmetics are more popular and accepted in some cultures than in others, as is cologne or after-shave lotion for men.

### Food and Feeding Habits

The manner in which food is selected, prepared, presented, and eaten often differs by culture. Most major cities have restaurants that specialize in the distinctive cuisine of various cultures—everything from Afghan to Zambian. Feeding habits also differ, ranging from bare hands to chopsticks to full sets of cutlery. Subcultures exist as well, from the executive's dining room, to the soldier's mess hall, to the worker's submarine sandwich shop, to the ladies' tea room. Knowledge of food and eating habits often provides insights into customs and culture.

### Communication and Language

The axiom "Words mean different things to different people" is especially true in cross-cultural communication. When an American says she is "tabling" a proposition, it is generally accepted that it will be put off. In England, "tabling" means to discuss something now. Translations from one language to another can generate even more confusion as a result of differences in style and context. Coca-Cola found this out when it began marketing its soft-drink products in China in the 1920s.

The traditional Coca-Cola trademark took on an unintended translation when shopkeepers added their own calligraphy to the company name. "Coca-Cola," pronounced "ke kou ke la" in one Chinese dialect, translates as "bite the wax tadpole." Reshuffling the pronunciation to "ko kou ko le" roughly translates to "may the mouth rejoice."[27]

In many cultures, directness and openness are not appreciated. An open person may be seen as weak and untrustworthy, and directness can be interpreted as abrupt, hostile behavior. Providing specific details may be seen as insulting to one's intelligence. Insisting on a written contract may suggest that a person's word is not good.

Nonverbal cues may also mean different things. In the United States, one who does not look someone in the eye arouses suspicion and is called "shifty-eyed." In some other countries, however, looking someone in the eye is perceived as aggression. Just as communication skills are key ingredients for success in U.S. business, such skills are basic to success in international business. There is no compromise on this issue; ignorance of local customs and communications protocol is disrespectful.[28]

## Time and Time Consciousness

To Americans, time is money. We live by schedules, deadlines, and agendas; we hate to be kept waiting, and we like to "get down to business" quickly. In many countries, however, people simply will not be rushed. They arrive late for appointments, and business is preceded by hours of social rapport. People in a rush are thought to be arrogant and untrustworthy.

In the United States, the most important issues are generally discussed first when making a business deal. In Ethiopia, however, the most important things are taken up last. While being late seems to be the norm for business meetings in Latin America, the reverse is true in Switzerland, Sweden, and Germany, where prompt efficiency is the watchword.[29] The lesson for Americans doing business overseas is clear: *Be flexible about time and realistic about what can be accomplished.* Adapt to the process of doing business in any particular country.

## Relationships

Cultures fix human and organizational relationships by age, gender, status, and family relationships, as well as by wealth, power, and wisdom. Relationships between and among people vary by category—in some cultures the elderly are honored; in others they are ignored. In some cultures women must wear veils and act deferentially; in others the female is considered the equal, if not the superior, of the male.

In some cultures (e.g., France, Japan, Korea, and to some extent the United States and Great Britain), where a person went to school may affect his or her status.[30] Often, lifelong relationships are established among individuals who attended the same school. Finally, the issue of nepotism is viewed very differently in different parts of the world. While most U.S. firms frown upon the practice of hiring or contracting work directly with family members, in Latin America or Arab countries, it only makes sense to hire someone you can trust.[31]

## Values and Norms

Values reflect what is important in a society. For example, in Arab culture, dignity, honor, and reputation are considered to be paramount virtues. America is a country in the midst of a values revolution, as the children of the Depression give way to the children of affluence, who are concerned with quality of life, self-fulfillment, and meaning in experiences.[32]

From its value system, a culture sets **norms of behavior,** or what some call "local customs." One such norm is that in Eastern countries businesspeople strive for successful business outcomes after personal relationships have been established, while Westerners develop social relationships after business interests have been addressed. International managers ignore such norms at their peril.[33] For example, consider the impact of values and norms on management styles and HR practices in the European Union. See International Application on page 643.

## Beliefs and Attitudes

To some degree, religion expresses the philosophy of a people about important facets in life. While Western culture is largely influenced by Judeo-Christian traditions and Middle Eastern culture by Islam, Oriental and Indian cultures are dominated by Buddhism, Confucianism, Taoism, and Hinduism. In cultures where a religious view of work still prevails, work is viewed as an act of service to God and people and is expressed in a moral commitment to the job or quality of effort. In Japan, the cultural loyalty to family is transferred to the work organization. It is expressed in work-group participation, communication, and consensus.[34]

T. Fujisawa, cofounder of Honda Motor Co., once remarked: "Japanese and American management is 95 percent the same, and differs in all important respects." In other words, while organizations are becoming more similar in terms of structure and technology, people's emotions, attitudes, and behavior within those organizations continue to reveal culturally based differences.[35]

## Work Motivation and Practices

Knowledge of what motivates workers in a given culture, combined with (or based on) a knowledge of what they think matters in life, is critical to the success of the international manager. Europeans pay particular attention to power and status, which results in more formal management and operating styles in comparison to the informality found in the United States. In the United States individual initiative and achievement are rewarded, but in Japan managers are encouraged to seek consensus before acting, and employees work as teams. Reward systems, job designs, decision-making and goal-setting processes, quality-improvement programs, and other management practices that are consistent with the dominant values of a culture are most likely to motivate employees to perform well. Practices that are not consistent with the dominant values of a culture are less likely to have positive effects on employees' performance and behavior.[36]

## Mental Processes and Learning

Linguists, anthropologists, and other experts who have studied mental processes and learning have found vast differences in the ways people think and learn in different cultures. While some cultures favor abstract thinking and conceptualization, others prefer rote memory and learning. The Chinese, Japanese, and Korean written languages are based on ideograms, or "word pictures." On the other hand, English is based on precise expression using words. Western cultures stress linear thinking and logic—that is, A, then B, then C, then D. Among Arabic and Oriental cultures, however, nonlinear thinking prevails—that is, A may be followed by C, then back to B and on to D. This has direct implications for negotiation processes. Such an approach, in which issues

# INTERNATIONAL APPLICATION
## Human Resource Management in the European Union

The European Union (EU) comprises 27 countries. The 15 older members are Austria, Belgium, Denmark, Finland, France, Germany, Ireland, Italy, Greece, Luxembourg, Netherlands, Portugal, Spain, Sweden, and the United Kingdom. The 12 newer members include Bulgaria, Cyprus, Czech Republic, Estonia, Hungary, Latvia, Lithuania, Malta, Poland, Romania, Slovakia, and Slovenia. With its new members, the EU represents a consumer market of 502 million people, with an annual GDP that exceeds US$16 trillion.[a] A central EU theme is respect for differences that we live with; we do not fight about them.

The EU represents the economic and political unification of Europe—the free movement of capital, goods, and people and the harmonization of EU legislation. Does this mean that multinationals operating in Europe can deal with people in the various EU countries on a regional basis and in a universal manner? Is there such a thing as "European HRM"? An analysis of 12,965 articles published over a 24-year period from 26 HR journals in the original nine languages of 10 EU countries indicates that the answer is no.[b] Indeed, a 2011 EU survey of HR executives revealed that for the first time, a majority of HR executives did not hold positive perceptions of the impact of the EU on their country's economy, on their company's performance, or on their own lives.[c]

In spite of the economic, political, and social unification of Europe as a result of the EU, there is no harmonized manner in which HR services are delivered across or within the various European countries. Rather, Euro-HRM is a mosaic of practices that differ primarily on the basis of the size of the company, and the different national, cultural, legal, and geographic contexts. Outsiders should know eight key things about HRM in the EU countries:[d]

1. Each country has a unique set of intricate laws that govern employment and labor relations.
2. Each country has a unique culture that impacts management styles and the corporate cultures of companies.
3. Within some EU countries there are different subcultures that influence HRM.
4. The power of the labor unions is decreasing, but labor-relations issues remain very important.
5. Each country has developed a set of institutions that reflects its traditions and influences the way HR is practiced.
6. Distinct underlying social models have an impact on the way HR is practiced in each country. For example, the Dutch social-justice model emphasizes the widespread belief that the government should play an active, interventionist role to provide social justice in areas such as occupational health, safety, and terminations. In contrast, the Italian social model is a mixture of Christian and Marxist values. It emphasizes the individual's need for protection and solidarity and is less meritocratic and competitive than Protestant cultures.
7. There are formal consultation processes in place that allow for greater involvement of employees and trade unions in the decision-making processes of companies.
8. Importing HR practices from abroad without attempting to localize them to the specific culture, laws, and languages of the country provides little chance of successful implementation.

---

[a]Eurostat. Key facts and figures about Europe and the Europeans. Retrieved from *epp.eurostat.ec.europa.eu* on September 5, 2011. See also CIA World Factbook. Retrieved from *www.cia.gov/library/publications/the-world-factbook/index.html* on September 5, 2011.

[b]Claus, L. (2001). *Euro-HRM.* Monterey, CA: Monterey Institute of International Studies.

[c]Aon Hewitt and European Club for Human Resources. (2011, Sept.). 6th European HR barometer: Trends and perspectives on the human resources function in Europe. Retrieved from *www.aon.com/human-capital-consulting/thought-leadership/leadership/article_EuropeanHRBarometer.jsp* on October 10, 2011.

[d]Briscoe et al., 2009, op. cit. See also Falcone, P. (2004, Feb.). Learning from our overseas counterparts. *HR Magazine,* pp. 113–116.

are treated as independent and not linked by sequence, can be confusing and frustrating to Westerners because it does not appear logical. What can we conclude from this? What seems to be universal is that each culture has a reasoning process, but each manifests the process in its own distinctive way.[37] Managers who do not understand or appreciate such differences may conclude (erroneously and to their detriment) that certain cultures are "inscrutable."

---

**HR BUZZ**

*Cultural Differences among Workers Worldwide*

**IBM**

Geert Hofstede, a Dutch researcher, identified five dimensions of cultural variation in values in more than 50 countries and three regions (East Africa, West Africa, and Arab countries). Initially, he relied on a database of surveys covering, among other things, the values of employees of subsidiaries of IBM in 72 countries.[a] He analyzed 116,000 questionnaires, completed in 20 languages, matching respondents by occupation, gender, and age at different time periods (1968 and 1972). Over the next several decades, he collected additional data from other populations, unrelated to IBM but matched across countries. Hofstede's five dimensions reflect basic problems that any society has to cope with but for which solutions differ: power distance, uncertainty avoidance, individualism, masculinity, and long-term versus short-term orientation. Other researchers generally have confirmed these dimensions.[b]

**Power distance** refers to the extent that members of an organization accept inequality and whether they perceive much distance between those with power (e.g., top management) and those with little power (e.g., rank-and-file workers). Hofstede found the top power-distance countries to be Malaysia, Guatemala, and the Philippines; the bottom ones were Austria, Israel, and Denmark.

**Uncertainty avoidance** is the extent to which a culture programs its members to feel either comfortable or uncomfortable in unstructured situations (novel, unknown, surprising, different from usual). Countries that score high on this dimension (e.g., Greece, Portugal, Belgium, Japan) tend to rely more on rules and rituals to make the future more predictable. Those that score low (e.g., Singapore, Denmark, Sweden, and Hong Kong) tend to be more pragmatic. The United States scores low on this dimension.

**Individualism** reflects the extent to which people emphasize personal or group goals. If they live in nuclear families that allow them to "do their own thing," individualism flourishes. However, if they live with extended families or tribes that control their behavior, collectivism—the essence of which is giving

---

[a]Hofstede, G. (2001). *Culture's Consequences: Comparing Values, Behaviors, Institutions, and Organizations across Nations* (2nd Ed.). Thousand Oaks, CA: Sage.

[b]Erez, M. (2011). Cross-cultural and global issues in organizational psychology. In S. Zedeck (Ed.), *APA Handbook of Industrial and Organizational Psychology*, Vol. 3. Washington, DC: American Psychological Association, pp. 807–854. See also Kirkman, B. L., Lowe, K. B., and Gibson, C. B. (2006). A quarter century of *Culture's Consequences:* A review of empirical research incorporating Hofstede's cultural values framework. *Journal of International Business Studies* 37, pp. 285–320. See also Gerhart, B., and Fang, M. (2005). National culture and human resource management: Assumptions and evidence. *International Journal of Human Resource Management* 16(6), pp. 971–986. See also Triandis, H. C. (2004). The many dimensions of culture. *Academy of Management Executive* 18(1), pp. 88–93.

preference to in-group over individual goals—is more likely.[c] The most individualistic countries are the United States and the other English-speaking countries. The most collectivist countries are Guatemala, Ecuador, and Panama.

Hofstede's fourth dimension, **masculinity,** is found in societies that differentiate very strongly by gender. Femininity is characteristic of cultures where sex-role distinctions are minimal. Whereas masculine cultures tend to emphasize ego goals—the centrality of work, careers, and money—feminine cultures tend to emphasize social goals—quality of life, helping others, and relationships. Hofstede found the most masculine cultures to be Japan, Austria, and Venezuela, while the most feminine were Sweden, Norway, and the Netherlands.

Finally, **long-term versus short-term orientation** refers to the extent to which a culture programs its members to accept delayed gratification of their material, social, and emotional needs. Countries scoring highest in long-term orientation include China, Hong Kong, and Taiwan; Pakistan, Nigeria, and the Philippines score at the opposite end. Americans tend to be relatively short-term oriented.

In a 2010 meta-analysis of almost 600 studies based on Hofstede's cultural-value dimensions (except for long-term versus short-term orientation, for which there were too few studies), representing more than 200,000 individuals, researchers drew the following conclusions. Cultural values predict country-level differences best (average meta-correlation of 0.35), and individual-level differences less well (average meta-correlation of 0.18). Second, the predictive power of the cultural values was significantly lower for personality traits and demographic characteristics for certain outcomes (job performance, absenteeism, turnover), but it was significantly higher for others (organizational commitment, citizenship behavior, team-related attitudes, and feedback seeking). Cultural values were more strongly related to outcomes for managers than students, and for older, male, and more educated respondents. Finally, the effects of cultural values were much stronger in culturally tighter countries (those with strong social norms and close systems of monitoring and sanctioning behavior), rather than culturally looser ones.[d]

This work is valuable because it provides a set of benchmarks against which other studies can be organized conceptually. It also helps us to understand and place into perspective current theories of motivation, leadership, and organizational behavior.

[c]Gelfand et al., 2007. See also Triandis, H. C. (1998). Vertical and horizontal individualism and collectivism: Theory and research implications for international comparative management. In J. L. Cheng and R. B. Peterson (Eds.), *Advances in International and Comparative Management.* Greenwich, CT: JAI Press, pp. 7–35.

[d]Taras, V., Kirkman, B. L., and Steel, P. (2010). Examining the impact of *Culture's Consequences:* A three-decade, multilevel, meta-analytic review of Hofstede's cultural value dimensions. *Journal of Applied Psychology* Monograph 95, pp. 405–439.

## Lessons Regarding Cross-Cultural Differences

There are three important lessons to be learned from this brief overview of cross-cultural differences:

1. *Do not export headquarters-country bias.* As we have seen, the HR management approach that works well in the headquarters country might be totally out of step in another country. Managers who bear responsibility

As companies become more global in their operations, cross-cultural interaction becomes more common.

for international operations need to understand the cultural differences inherent in the management systems of the countries in which their firms do business.

2. *Think in global terms.* We live in a world in which a worldwide allocation of physical and human resources is necessary for continued survival.

3. *Recognize that no country has all the answers.* Flexible work hours, quality circles, and various innovative approaches to productivity have arisen outside the United States. Effective multinational managers must not only think in global terms, but also be able to synthesize the best management approaches to deal with complex problems.

---

**HR BUZZ**

## SHOULD YOU WORK FOR A FOREIGN-OWNED FIRM IN THE UNITED STATES?

Increasing numbers of American managers are joining foreign-based companies that are doing business in the U.S. market. However, working for such a company can be difficult. Its offices typically are managed by expatriates, who are most comfortable with the culture, language, and customs of their mother country and are likely to import international management styles into the U.S. workplace. For their U.S. subordinates, that could mean fewer opportunities for advancement and a wide range of other cultural differences. Such problems arise frequently when a U.S. firm merges with or is acquired by a foreign one, such as Germany's Daimler and the American company, Chrysler. From the beginning of the formal relationship, in late 1998, until the company was sold to U.S. private-equity firm Cerberus in 2007, issues that should have been handled easily, like labor relations or differences in emission-control policies, got bogged down in turf battles. Instead of trying to blend the best of each company's culture, in the words of one senior executive, "it became a question of comparing the styles of the two and picking one." This had led to serious integration problems.

Does it help to know the language of the foreign firm? Yes, but even if people are linguistically capable, say experts, learning how to praise or criticize someone from a different culture is a difficult skill. Asking a Swiss or German boss for a performance appraisal would probably lead to a very specific answer, while a Japanese, Korean, or Chinese boss would tend to be more vague.

Depending on the corporate culture, the staffing of the U.S. office, and the nationality of the company, it is possible to work for a foreign firm and barely notice cultural differences. Such is the case at Ebel U.S.A. Inc., a U.S. sales agent of a Swiss watch company, or at the Los Angeles office of the National Bank of Canada. Other companies have become so international that they're essentially melting pots. Schlumberger Ltd., for example, was founded by two French brothers, is incorporated in the Netherlands Antilles, has executive offices in New York and Paris, and does business in more than 100 countries. Says one manager: "When you join Schlumberger, you put your passport away."

Despite these difficulties, there will be healthy payoffs for those who can cross cultural boundaries. Many foreign-owned companies doing business in the United States offer competitive salaries and assignments abroad. In addition, working for a foreign company can promote empathy for other cultures and a skill at working with people from around the world. Those are attractive characteristics in a global job market.[a]

---

[a]Welch, D., Kiley, D., and Ihiwan, M. (2008, Mar. 6). My way or the highway at Hyundai. *BusinessWeek.* Retrieved from *www.businessweek.com/magazine/content/08_11/b4075048450463.htm* on August 19, 2008. See also Associated Press. (2007, May 14). Chrysler Group to be sold for $7.4 billion. Retrieved from *www.msnbc.msn.com/id/18645179/ns/business-autos/t/chrysler-group-be-sold-billion/#.TpMP4OyyiWE* on September 5, 2011. See also Lessons from a casualty of the culture wars. (1999, Nov. 29). *BusinessWeek,* p. 198. See also Lancaster, H. (1996, June 4). How you can learn to feel at home in a foreign-based firm. *The Wall Street Journal,* p. B1.

## HUMAN RESOURCE MANAGEMENT ACTIVITIES OF GLOBAL CORPORATIONS

Before we consider recruitment, selection, training, and other international HR management issues, it is important that we address a fundamental question: Is this subject worthy of study in its own right? The answer is yes, for two reasons—scope and risk exposure.[38] In terms of *scope,* there are at least four important differences between domestic and international operations. International operations have

1. More HR activities, such as taxation, coordination of dependents, and co-ordination of multiple-salary currencies.
2. More involvement in employees' personal lives, such as housing, health, education, and recreation.
3. Different approaches to management, coupled with complex equity issues, as the workforce mix of expatriates and locals varies.
4. Broader external influences, such as from societies and governments.

Heightened *risk exposure* is a second distinguishing characteristic of international HR management. A variety of legal issues confront companies in each country, and the human and financial consequences of a mistake in the international arena are much more severe. For example, the cost of a failed international assignment can be as high as $1 million (U.S. dollars).[39] On top of that, terrorism is now an ever-present risk for executives overseas, and it clearly affects how they assess international assignments.[40] The annual worldwide cost of kidnapping totals $500 million, and there were 8,000 kidnappings in 2010, a 100 percent increase worldwide in the last six years.[41]

All of this has had an important effect on how people are prepared for and moved to and from international assignment locations. In light of these considerations, it seems reasonable to ask, "Why do people accept overseas assignments?" Why *do* they go? As companies' global ambitions grow, fasttrack executives at companies such as General Mills, Procter & Gamble, Gillette, General Electric, and ExxonMobil see foreign tours as necessary for career advancement.[42] Evidence indicates that U.S.-based multinationals actually do perform better when they have CEOs with international-assignment experience.[43]

## Organizational Structure

Traditionally, businesses tended to evolve from domestic (exporters) to international (manufacturing and some technology resources allocated outside the home country) to multinational (allocating resources among national or regional areas) to global (treating the entire world as one large company) organizations.[44] Today, a new form is evolving among high-technology companies—call them **transnational corporations.** What makes them different is that even the executive suite is virtual. They use geo-diversity to great advantage, placing their top executives and core corporate functions in different countries to gain a competitive edge through the availability of talent or capital, low costs, or proximity to their most important customers. Of course, it is all made possible by the Internet, as improved communication facilitates an integrated global network of operations.[45]

Consider Lenovo. It was a Chinese computer maker until it bought IBM's personal computer business in 2005. Initially it planned to move its corporate headquarters to New York from Beijing, but the executive team decided that having a central base slowed the company down. Today Lenovo is incorporated in Hong Kong, where its stock is listed, but its top managers and corporate functions are scattered across the globe. Its chief executive is based in Singapore, and its chairman in Raleigh, North Carolina. The chief financial officer is in Hong Kong and the chief HR officer is in Seattle. Worldwide marketing is coordinated in India, and the company's top 20 leaders meet monthly in a different place.[46]

The development of transnationals has led to a fundamental rethinking about the nature of a multinational company. Does it have a home country? What does headquarters mean? Is it possible to fragment corporate functions globally? To be sure, organizational structure directly affects all HR functions from recruitment through retirement because, to be effective, HR management must be integrated into the overall strategy of the organization. Indeed, from the perspective of strategic management, the fundamental problem is to keep the strategy, structure, and HR dimensions of the organization in direct alignment.[47]

## Workforce Planning

This issue is particularly critical for firms doing business overseas. They need to analyze the local *and* the international external labor markets as well as their own internal labor markets in order to estimate the supply of people with the skills that will be required at some time in the future, relative to the demand for them. Unfortunately, the seemingly inexhaustible pools of cheap labor from China, India, and elsewhere are drying up as demand outstrips the supply of people with the needed skills. Indeed, a 2011 report from the World Economic Forum and the Boston Consulting Group noted:

> Despite today's high unemployment rates, the global talent risk is growing. Soon staggering talent gaps will appear in large parts of the world, threatening economic growth. Economies will struggle to remain competitive while organizations will compete for talent on an unprecedented scale. Now human capital is replacing financial capital as the engine of economic prosperity (p. 7).[48]

An ongoing challenge for multinational corporations, therefore, is to make the most of the global labor pool, wherever it exists. For both developed- and developing-nation multinationals, that often implies a corporate strategy of labor arbitrage—periodic moves to lower-wage locations as existing ones get too pricey. As wages rise in first-tier offshore cities like Bangalore, Shanghai, and Prague, U.S., European, and Asian multinationals alike are moving to places like Jaipur, India; Chengdu, China; and Kiev, Ukraine.

In developed countries, national labor markets can usually supply the skilled technical and professional people needed. However, developing countries and second-tier cities are characterized by severe shortages of qualified managers and skilled workers and by great surpluses of people with little or no skill, training, or education. Firms that plan to stay focus on two things: identifying top management potential early and providing lots of training to employees at all levels.[49] Unfortunately, most companies are far from having an accurate talent picture. Recent data indicate that only 9 percent of MNEs have adequately analyzed their future workforce supply and demand. A mere 6 percent have begun developing recruiting, retention, and talent-management strategies for the job families at greatest risk of a talent gap.[50]

## Recruitment

Broadly speaking, companies operating outside their home countries follow three basic models in the recruitment of executives: (1) They may select from the national group of the parent company only, (2) they may recruit only from within their own country and the country where the branch is located, or (3) they may adopt an international perspective and emphasize the unrestricted use of all nationalities.[51] Each of these strategies has both advantages and disadvantages.

### Ethnocentrism: Home-Country Executives Only

A strategy of **ethnocentrism** may be appropriate during the early phases of international expansion, because firms at this stage are concerned with transplanting a part of the business that has worked in their home countries. Hence, detailed knowledge of that part is crucial to success. On the other hand, a policy of ethnocentrism, of necessity, implies blocked promotional paths for local executives. Moreover, if there are many subsidiaries, home-country nationals must recognize that their foreign service may not lead to faster career progress. Finally, there are cost disadvantages to ethnocentrism as well as increased tendencies to impose the management style of the parent company.[52]

### Limiting Recruitment to Home- and Host-Country Nationals

Limiting recruitment may result from acquisition of local companies. In South Korea, for example, foreigners are clearly "outsiders," so acquisition of a local firm is a common market-entry strategy.[53] Hiring nationals has some clear advantages. It eliminates language barriers, expensive training periods, and cross-cultural adjustment problems of managers and their families. It also allows firms to take advantage of (lower) local salary levels while still paying a premium to attract high-quality employees.

Yet these advantages are not without cost. Local managers may have difficulty bridging the gap between the subsidiary and the parent company, because the business experience to which they have been exposed may not have prepared them to work as part of a global enterprise.[54] Finally, consideration of only home- and host-country nationals may result in the exclusion of some very able executives.

### Geocentrism: Seeking the Best Person for the Job Regardless of Nationality

At first glance it may appear that a strategy of **geocentrism** is optimal and most consistent with the underlying philosophy of a global corporation. Yet there are potential problems. Such a policy can be very expensive, it can take a long time to implement, and it requires a great deal of centralized control over managers and their career patterns. To implement such a policy effectively, companies must make it very clear that cross-national service is important and that it will be rewarded.

Colgate-Palmolive is an example of such a company. It has been operating internationally for more than 50 years, and its products (e.g., Colgate toothpaste, Ajax cleanser) are household names in more than 170 countries. Fully 60 percent of the company's expatriates are from countries other than the United States, and two of its last four CEOs were not U.S. nationals. In addition, all the top executives speak at least two languages, and important meetings routinely take place all over the globe.[55] Let's now consider a very serious problem that confronts many executives offered overseas assignments. See International Application on page 651.

## International Staffing

Recent reviews indicate that the selection process for international managers is, with few exceptions, largely intuitive and unsystematic.[56] A major problem is that the selection of people for overseas assignments often is based *solely* on their technical competence and job knowledge.[57] This is a mistake; technical competence per se has nothing to do with one's ability to adapt to a new environment, to deal effectively with foreign coworkers, or to perceive—and if necessary, imitate—foreign behavioral norms.[58] Keep this in mind as you consider various factors that determine success in an international assignment. Let us begin with general mental ability.

### General Mental Ability

**General mental ability** (GMA) may be defined broadly as the ability to learn. It includes any measure that combines two, three, or more specific aptitudes, or any measure that includes a variety of items that measure specific abilities (e.g., verbal, numerical, spatial relations).[59] As we noted in Chapter 7, the validity of GMA as a predictor of job performance as well as performance in training is

## INTERNATIONAL APPLICATION
### Job Aid for Spouses of Overseas Executives

Today, families in which both parents are working have become the majority among married couples with children.[a] In 2011 spouses accompanied 68 percent of expatriates, and 47 percent brought children with them.[b] With global companies expanding into areas such as Central and Eastern Europe and the Middle East, spouses of expatriates face particularly tough obstacles to finding jobs. Here is a scenario likely to become more and more common in the future. A company offers a promotion overseas to a promising executive. But the executive's spouse has a flourishing career in the United States. What should the company—and the couple—do?

Employers and employees are wrestling with this dilemma more often these days. As noted in Chapter 10, job aid for the so-called trailing spouse is already a popular benefit for domestic transfers. Not so for international transferees. While 60 percent of trailing spouses would like career assistance from the expatriate's employer, only 18 percent receive it. Actual interviews with 100 trailing spouses indicated that their greatest needs are for networking information to assist in their job search and for a go-to person for practical settling-in assistance.[c] That's good to know, because 51 percent of companies provide no financial support for dual-career couples.[d]

To fill their international needs, more firms are turning to short-term assignments (3 to 12 months) or "commuter assignments," in which spouses move to adjoining countries or regions. Another option is intercompany networking, in which one multinational employer (MNE) attempts to place an expatriate's spouse in a suitable job with another MNE in the same city or country. Sometimes this takes the form of a reciprocal arrangement, that is, "You find my expatriate's spouse a job and work visa and I will do the same for you."[e]

HR officers may try to find a job for the spouse within the company, press a spouse's current employer for a foreign post, provide job leads through customers and suppliers, or plow through costly government red tape to get work permits.

Despite company efforts, it is often very difficult to place spouses abroad. Where there are language barriers or barriers of labor laws, tradition, or underemployment, it can be almost impossible. Certain Middle Eastern nations frown on women working or even driving. In Switzerland and Kenya, expatriate spouses even need permission to work as volunteers.[f]

Moreover, an international assignment can slow a spouse's professional progress and sometimes stir resentment. On the other hand, some spouses find their overseas experiences as personally and professionally rewarding as their spouses do. One American tax lawyer received permission to work in Brussels as an independent legal consultant. A German travel executive followed his wife to Britain and, seven months later, landed a job organizing exhibitions between Britain and Germany. Since 91 percent of married female expatriates (and 50 percent of married male expatriates) are in dual-career marriages, it is not surprising that spousal income loss is a key factor determining an executive's decision to accept or reject an overseas position.[g]

[a]Galinsky, E., Aumann, K., and Bond, J. T. (2009). *Times Are Changing: Gender and Generation at Work and at Home.* New York, NY: Families & Work Institute.

[b]Brookfield GRS 2011 global relocation trends survey report. (2011, April 26). Downloaded from *www.relocatemagazine. com/relocation-news-blog-format/3-general-relocation-news/2212-brookfield-grs-2011-global-relocation-trends-survey-report* on September 5, 2011.

[c]Cole, N. D. (2008, June). Managing global talent: Solving the spousal adjustment problem. Final report to SHRM Foundation, Alexandria, VA.

[d]For dual-career expats, economic woes threaten benefits. (2009, Jan. 30). *HR News,* downloaded from *www.shrm.org/hrdisciplines/global/Articles/Pages/ForDualCareerExpats. aspx* on February 3, 2009.

[e]Dowling et al., 2009, op. cit.

[f]Jordan, M. (2001, Feb. 13). Have husband, will travel. *The Wall Street Journal,* pp. B1, B12. See also Weisbart, M. (2010, Nov. 8). South Korea: So fast, so dynamic—yet still hierarchical. *The Wall Street Journal,* p. R6.

[g]Tyler, K. (2003, May). Cut the stress. *HRMagazine,* pp. 101–106.

well established in the United States, on the basis of meta-analyses of hundreds of studies.[60] The estimated validity of GMA for predicting supervisory ratings of job performance is 0.57 for high-complexity jobs (17 percent of U.S. jobs), 0.51 for medium-complexity jobs (63 percent of U.S. jobs), and 0.38 for lowcomplexity jobs (20 percent of U.S. jobs). The estimated validity of GMA as a predictor of training success is 0.63.

Is GMA as robust a predictor of job performance and training in Europe as it is in the United States? The answer is yes. On the basis of a meta-analysis of 85 independent samples with job performance as the criterion and 89 independent samples with training success as the criterion, the validity of GMA as a predictor of job performance as well as performance in training across 12 occupational categories has been established in the European Community.[61] Findings were similar or somewhat larger than those in the United States for similar occupational groups.

In terms of job complexity, results were similar to those reported in the United States for job performance (0.64 for high-complexity jobs, 0.53 for medium-complexity, and 0.51 for low-complexity) and training (0.74 for high-complexity, 0.53 for medium-complexity, and 0.36 for low-complexity jobs). These results indicate that there is international validity generalization for GMA as a predictor of performance in training and on the job in the United States and in the European Community. Similar findings have been reported in meta-analyses of GMA as a predictor of job performance in the United Kingdom and in Germany.[62] GMA tests are therefore robust predictors for expatriate assignments across these two continents, although the same findings have not yet been demonstrated elsewhere.

### Personality

When success is defined in terms of completing the expatriate assignment and supervisory ratings of performance on the assignment, evidence indicates that three personality characteristics are related to ability to complete the assignment. These are **extroversion** and **agreeableness** (which facilitate interactions and making social alliances with host nationals and other expatriates), and **emotional stability. Conscientiousness** is a general work ethic that supervisors look for in their subordinates, and this affects their performance ratings. Expatriate assignments require a great deal of persistence, thoroughness, and responsibility—all of which conscientious people possess and use.[63]

Because personality characteristics are relatively immutable, organizations should think of selection (on the basis of personality) as the precursor to cross-cultural training: First identify expatriate candidates with the requisite personality characteristics, then offer cross-cultural training to those identified.[64] This sequence is reasonable, because cross-cultural training may only be effective when trainees are predisposed to success in the first place.

### Other Characteristics Related to Success in International Assignments

A recent study examined the validity of a broad set of predictors for selecting European managers for a cross-cultural training program in Japan.[65] The selection procedure assessed GMA, personality (in terms of the four characteristics described earlier, plus **openness**—the extent to which an individual is creative, curious, and has broad interests), and dimensions measured by an assessment center and a behavior-description interview. Two assessment-center exercises, an analysis-presentation exercise and a group-discussion exercise, were designed to measure the personal characteristics related to performance in an international context. The analysis-presentation exercise assessed the following:

- *Tenacity/resilience.* Keeps difficulties in perspective, stays positive despite disappointments and setbacks.
- *Communication.* Communicates clearly, fluently, and to the point; talks at a pace and level that holds people's attention, both in group and individual situations.
- *Adaptability.* Adapts readily to new situations and ways of working, receptive to new ideas, willing and able to adjust to changing demands and objectives.
- *Organizational and commercial awareness.* Alert to changing organizational dynamics, knowledgeable about financial and commercial issues, focuses on markets and business opportunities that yield the largest returns.

In addition to the dimensions of communication, adaptability, and organizational and commercial awareness, the group-discussion exercise assessed the following:

- *Teamwork.* Cooperates and works well with others in the pursuit of team goals, shares information, develops supportive relationships with colleagues, and creates a sense of team spirit.

Finally, in addition to tenacity, resilience, and teamwork, the behavior description interview was designed to assess:

- *Self-discipline.* Committed, consistent, and dependable; can be relied on to deliver what has been agreed; is punctual and conscientious.
- *Cross-cultural awareness.* Able to see issues from the perspective of people from other cultures.

Results indicated that GMA was significantly correlated with the test measuring language acquisition (corrected correlation of 0.27), openness was significantly related to instructors' ratings of cross-cultural training performance (corrected correlation of 0.33), and agreeableness correlated significantly negatively with instructors' ratings of cross-cultural training performance (corrected correlation of −0.26). Although agreeableness may be universally positive for forming social relationships, individuals who are too agreeable may be seen as "pushovers" in some cultures. Hence agreeableness may be culturally bound in terms of perceptions of professional competence.[66]

Finally, emotional stability correlated significantly negatively with the language proficiency test (corrected correlation of −0.29). All dimensions measured in the group-discussion exercise were significantly correlated with instructor ratings (corrected correlations ranged from 0.31 to 0.40) and from 0.33 to 0.44 with the language proficiency test.

Three dimensions, all measured by the group-discussion exercise, also predicted performance in cross-cultural training: teamwork, communication, and adaptability. This study also used a process of selecting people for cross-cultural training, providing the training to those selected, and then sending abroad those who passed the training. Performance in the cross-cultural training significantly predicted executives' performance in the Japanese companies (correlations of 0.38 for instructors' ratings and 0.45 for Japanese-language proficiency). An important advantage of this process is that it may reduce the costs of international assignees, because only people who pass the selection process, and who therefore are predisposed for expatriate success, are sent to the training and abroad.

What about motivation to succeed in an overseas assignment? High motivation has long been acknowledged as a key ingredient for success in missionary work. Who, for example, can forget the zeal of the Protestant missionaries in the book *Hawaii* by James Michener, as they set out from their native New England? While motivation is often difficult to assess reliably, firms should at the very least try to eliminate from consideration those who are only looking to get out of their own country for a change of scenery. One way to do that is to have candidates (and their spouses) complete self-assessments, in order to gauge their fit with the personality and lifestyle requirements of the international assignment. Here is an example.[67]

**HR BUZZ**

*Interviewing Potential Expatriates*

**AT&T**

AT&T is a worldwide player, spending about $4 billion since 2007 to improve its overseas network.[a] Here are some typical questions it uses to screen candidates for overseas transfers:[b]

- Would your spouse be interrupting a career to accompany you on an international assignment? If so, how do you think this will affect your spouse and your relationship with each other?
- Do you enjoy the challenge of making your own way in new situations?
- How able are you in initiating new social contacts?
- Are you prepared to have less contact with your extended family?
- How important is it for you to spend significant amounts of time with people of your own ethnic, racial, religious, and national background?
- As you look at your personal history, can you isolate any episodes that indicate a real interest in learning about other peoples and cultures?
- Has it been your habit to vacation in foreign countries?
- Do you enjoy sampling foreign cuisines?
- What is your tolerance for waiting for repairs?
- Upon reentry, securing a job will primarily be your responsibility. How do you feel about networking and being your own advocate?

---

[a]O'Brien, K. J. (2011, April 18). AT&T follows its customers overseas. *The New York Times*. Retrieved from *www.nytimes.com/2011/04/18/technology/18att.html?_r=1&scp=1&sq=AT&T%20 follows%20its%20customers%20overseas&st=cse* on September 7, 2011.

[b]Fuchsberg, G. (1992, Jan. 9). As costs of overseas assignments climb, firms select expatriates more carefully. *The Wall Street Journal*, pp. B1, B5.

### Applicability of U.S. Employment Laws to Multinational Employers (MNEs)

The following four employment laws may apply to United States citizens working abroad: Title VII of the Civil Rights Act, the Age Discrimination in Employment Act (ADEA), the Americans with Disabilities Act (ADA), and the Uniformed Services Employment and Reemployment Rights Act (USERRA). They also apply to U.S. citizens of foreign corporations doing business in the United States, even if those corporations employ fewer than 20 workers. However, they do not apply to foreign employees of a U.S.-based multinational who are not U.S. citizens.

USERRA applies only to veterans and reservists working overseas for the federal government or a firm under U.S. control. Title VII, the ADEA, and ADA are more far reaching, covering all U.S. citizens who are either employed outside the United States by a U.S. firm, or by a company under the control of a U.S. firm. In determining whether a non-U.S. firm is under U.S. control, the Equal Employment Opportunity Commission will review:

- The degree of interrelated operations.
- The extent of common management.
- The degree of centralized control of labor relations, common ownership, and financial control.
- The place of incorporation.[68]

Each of the four laws contains an exemption if compliance with the U.S. law would cause a company to violate a law of the country in which it is located. For example, if the laws of a particular country prohibit the hiring of women for certain jobs, a U.S. company operating within that country must follow that country's law. This is consistent with the general principle that MNEs are accountable to the laws of the countries where they operate.[69]

## Orientation

Orientation is particularly important in overseas assignments, both before departure and after arrival. Formalized orientation efforts—for example, elaborate multimedia presentations for the entire family, supplemented by presentations by representatives of the country and former expatriates who have since returned to the United States—are important. After all, in 2011, the top family challenges identified as very critical to companies were partner resistance (47 percent), family adjustment (32 percent), children's education (29 percent), and location difficulties (25 percent).[70]

Some firms go further. Federal Express, Colgate-Palmolive, and Apache Corp., for example, actually send prospective expatriates and their families on familiarization trips to the foreign location in question. While there, they have to live like the natives do by taking public transportation, shopping in local stores, and visiting prospective schools and current expatriates.[71] Said a journalist for *The Wall Street Journal* after turning down a transfer to the paper's Hong Kong Bureau after a week-long visit to Hong Kong, "I'm not going to relocate to the far side of the planet at the risk of making my wife miserable." Better to make that decision before incurring major costs and personal turmoil.[72]

In fact, there may be three separate phases to orientation, all of which are designed to provide potential expatriates and their families with realistic assignment previews.[73] The first is called *initial orientation,* which may last as long as two full days. Key components are as follows:

- *Cultural briefing.* Traditions, history, government, economy, living conditions, clothing and housing requirements, health requirements, and visa applications. (Drugs get a lot of coverage, both for adults and for teenagers—whether they use drugs or not. Special emphasis is given to the different drug laws in foreign countries. Alcohol use also gets special attention when candidates are going to Muslim countries, such as Saudi Arabia.)[74]
- *Assignment briefing.* Length of assignment, vacations, salary and allowances, tax consequences, and repatriation policy.
- *Relocation requirements.* Shipping, packing, or storage; home sale or rental; and information about housing at the new location.

During this time, it is important that employees and their families understand that there is no penalty attached to changing their minds about accepting the proposed assignment. It is better to bail out early than reluctantly to accept an assignment that they will regret later.

The second phase is *predeparture orientation,* which may last another 2 or 3 days. Its purpose is to make a more lasting impression on employees and their families and to remind them of material that may have been covered months earlier. Topics covered at this stage include

- Introduction to the language.
- Further reinforcement of important values, especially open-mindedness.
- En route, emergency, and arrival information.

The final aspect of overseas orientation is *postarrival orientation.* Upon arrival, employees and their families should be met by assigned company sponsors. This phase of orientation usually takes place on three levels, and a dedicated support staff may provide it. The purpose is to reduce the stress associated with clashing work and family demands:[75]

- *Orientation toward the environment.* Schools, housing, medical facilities, transportation, shopping, and other subjects that—depending on the country—may become understandable only through actual experience, such as dealing with local government officials.
- *Orientation toward the work unit and fellow employees.* Often a supervisor or a delegate from the work unit will describe host-office norms and politics, as well as introduce the new employee to his or her fellow workers, discuss expectations of the job, and share his or her own initial experiences as an expatriate. The ultimate objective, of course, is to relieve the feelings of strangeness or tension that the new expatriate feels.
- *Orientation to the actual job.* This may be an extended process that focuses on cultural differences in the way a job is done. Only when this process is complete can we begin to assess the accuracy and wisdom of the original selection decision.

Throughout the assignment, some companies arrange periodic company-sponsored social functions to provide opportunities for expatriates and their families to interact with host-country nationals. Doing so facilitates cross-cultural adjustment and overall satisfaction with the assignment.[76]

## Cross-Cultural Training and Development

**Cross-cultural training** refers to formal programs designed to prepare persons of one culture to interact effectively in another culture or to interact more effectively with persons from different cultures.[77] To survive, cope, and succeed, managers need training in three areas: the culture, the language, and practical day-to-day matters. Female expatriates (who accounted for 20 percent of expatriates in 2011, up from 10 percent in 1994) need training on the norms, values, and traditions that host nationals possess about women and also on how to deal with challenging situations they may face as women.[78] Reviews of research on cross-cultural training have reported mixed results in terms of the effects of such training on an

## INTERNATIONAL APPLICATION
### How to Stay Safe Abroad

Many parts of the world are dangerous, and becoming more so, including many cities in the United States. In Colombia, Venezuela, and Pakistan, kidnapping is almost a cottage industry. In China, extortion and other crimes are on the rise. In Paris, young hoodlums are boarding buses and holding up passengers and drivers. In Mexico, many cabs are driven by bandits who kidnap foreigners, force them to withdraw cash from an ATM, beat them, and dump them in remote locations. In Istanbul, bars catering to Westerners often present them with exorbitant bills, which they have no choice but to pay. According to experts in security, terrorism remains relatively rare, while crime is everywhere. Here are some tips to help keep you safe:

- Make photocopies of your passport, plane tickets, and other key documents. Leave a copy at home with family or friends. Take non-stop flights whenever possible, and don't show hotel details on your luggage.
- Familiarize yourself with the current political and health situations in the areas you are visiting. Check out free State Department warnings on the Internet (*www.travel.state. gov/travel/cis_pa_tw/tw/tw_1764.html*), as well as Travel Health Online (*www.tripprep. com/scripts/main/default.asp*).
- Divide your money in half and keep it in separate places, some in a wallet, some in a moneybelt or briefcase. Leave questionable reading material, expensive jewelry, and unneeded credit cards at home. Dress conservatively. Watch your drink being poured.
- In fundamentalist countries, do not proselytize or wear religious symbols. Remember to

smile, respect local customs, and mind your own business. Don't speak loudly in English, and keep strong opinions to yourself.
- Don't use unmarked taxis. Be careful about getting into a cab with other passengers. This practice is a no-no in some countries (Russia), but quite common in others (Morocco).
- Ask for directions in a hotel, restaurant, or airport, rather than querying a stranger on the street. In some countries you may ask the police, but in Colombia, Cambodia, and Mexico it is not recommended.
- At the hotel, use the chain and security lock when in your room. If anyone comes unexpectedly to your door, don't open it without calling the front seek to verify that the person is authorized.
- Use the safe deposit box at your hotel. Upon leaving your room, hang a "Do not disturb" sign outside your door.
- Stay in touch with your office, but keep your itinerary confidential. Give your schedule only to relatives and coworkers with a need to know it. If possible, have access to a 24-hour hotline to call in case of trouble.
- Above all, try not to look important or rich. Avoid luggage tags, dress, and behavior that may draw attention to yourself.[a]

---

[a]Pons, C. R., and Orozco, J. (2011, July 3). In Caracas, kidnappings spawn an industry. *BusinessWeek,* pp. 15, 16. See also U.S. State Department. (2008). A safe trip abroad. Retrieved from *travel.state.gov/travel/tips/safety/safety_1747. html* on September 5, 2011. See also Champion, M. (2002, Nov. 6). Hot lines for hot spots. *The Wall Street Journal,* pp. B1, B3. See also Jossi, F. (2001, June). Buying protection from terrorism. *HR Magazine,* pp. 155–160.

individual's development of skills, on his or her adjustment to the cross-cultural situation, and on his or her performance in such situations.[79] To an unknown extent, however, conclusions may well depend on moderating variables such as *training-design factors* (e.g., the duration of the cross-cultural training program, its timing—predeparture or postarrival—training rigor, and type of training content—cultural general or cultural specific), and *trainee characteristics* such as personality, previous international experience, and previous experience with cross-cultural training.[80] Evidence also indicates that training should take place prior to departure and also after arrival in the new location. Formal mentoring for expatriates by host-country nationals also shows organizational support, and it can help to improve both language skills and the ability to interact effectively.[81]

In a 2011 Global Relocation Trends survey, just 74 percent (versus 84 percent in 2008) of multinationals reported that they provide cross-cultural preparation of at least one day's duration, and that all family members are eligible to participate. While this benefit may be an easy one to cut to reduce costs, it is difficult to ensure the quality of Web-based or self-service cross-cultural preparation that is usually offered as an alternative.[82]

To a very great extent, expatriate failure rates can be attributed to the **culture shock** that usually occurs four to six months after arrival in the foreign country. The symptoms are not pleasant: homesickness, boredom, withdrawal, a need for excessive amounts of sleep, compulsive eating or drinking, irritability, exaggerated cleanliness, marital stress, family tension and conflict (involving children), hostility toward host-country nationals, loss of ability to work effectively, and physical ailments of a psychosomatic nature.[83]

To be sure, many of the common stresses of everyday living become amplified when a couple is living overseas with no support other than from a spouse. To deal with these potential problems, spouses are taught to recognize stress symptoms in each other, and they are counseled to be supportive. One exercise, for example, is

---

**HR BUZZ**

*Not Lost in Translation*

### SIEMENS

More and more U.S. companies are now owned by overseas parents—including Bertelsmann, Diageo PLC, and Anglo-Dutch Unilever PLC, to name a few. Yes, e-mails are written in English and English often is spoken at board meetings, even in Asian and European companies, but failing to speak the native language of a parent company could hamper a manager's advancement. Whether at companies based in the United States or overseas, executives can miss out on informal conversations or risk being misinterpreted if they don't speak the local language. Says an investment banker; "Speaking and understanding the local language gives you more insight, you can avoid misunderstandings, and it helps you achieve a deeper level of respect."

At Munich-based Siemens, country managers must learn the local language of their posts: The head of Siemens's China business speaks fluent Mandarin, for example. All managers must speak either German or English, but Siemens has an internal rule about corporate meetings: If one or more individuals doesn't speak German, the others are obliged to speak English. In France, however, meetings may take place in French even if one or more attendees does not speak French. As one global recruiter noted; "Language is always going to give somebody an edge, as long as they have the other requirements."[a]

---

[a]Bloomberg News. (2011, Aug. 31). Mandarin is top business language after English. Retrieved from *articles.boston.com/2011-08-31/business/29949956_1_official-language-american-sign-language-mandarin* on September 1, 2011. See also Lost in translation? (2004, May 18). *The Wall Street Journal*, pp. B1, B6. See also Tagliabue, J. (2002, May 20). As business borders fall, English rules. *International Herald Tribune*, pp. 1, 4.

## INTERNATIONAL APPLICATION
### Bridging the U.S.-India Culture Gap

When Axcelis Technologies, a maker of tools for manufacturing semiconductors, outsourced some jobs to India last year, the company worried that some of its employees might resent their new Indian colleagues. So it hired one of India's premier awareness trainers to offer a course on "Working Effectively with Indians." The day-long course starts with a quiz to assess how much students already know about India. The trainer then discusses aspects of India's religious and linguistic diversity and its differences with the United States, after which he divides the class into groups to analyze different case studies of working situations. He follows that up with a tutorial on communication tips, including pointers on shaking hands, business protocol, and business attire in India. Sometimes he ends the class with an Indian meal.

"At first I was skeptical and wondered what I'd get out of the class," says the firm's HR director. "But it was enlightening for me. Not everyone operates like we do in America." The knowledge the trainees gain may be basic, but it can help avoid business misunderstandings. For example, when Indians shake hands, they sometimes do so rather limply. That isn't a sign of weakness or dislike; instead, a soft handshake conveys respect. When an Indian avoids eye contact, that is also a sign of deference. Another tip that trainees learn is not to plunge right into business talk right away during meetings, but first to chat about current events and other subjects. The rationale? Culturally, Indians prefer a more roundabout way into business issues. Says the trainer: "When people understand these differences they're less likely to make mistakes with each other."[a]

---

[a] Tam, P. W. (2004, May 25). Culture course. *The Wall Street Journal*, pp. B1, B12. See also Cappelli, P., Singh, H., Singh, J., and Useem, M. (2010). *The India Way: How India's Top Business Leaders Are Revolutionizing Management*. Boston: Harvard Business School Press. See also Cappelli, P. (2011, Aug.). India's management mind-set. *HR Magazine*, 56(8), pp. 59–62.

for the couples periodically to list what they believe causes stress in their mates, what the other person does to relieve it, and what they themselves do to relieve it. Then they compare lists.[84] To help avoid, or at least minimize culture shock, some companies invest in awareness training. See International Application, this page.

A key characteristic of successful global managers is adaptability. Empirical research has revealed eight different dimensions of adaptability: handling emergencies or crisis situations; handling work stress; solving problems creatively; dealing with uncertain and unpredictable work situations; learning work tasks, technologies, and procedures; demonstrating interpersonal adaptability; cultural adaptability; and physically oriented adaptability.[85] This implies that an effective way to train employees to adapt is to expose them to situations like they will encounter in their assignments that require adaptation. Such a strategy has two benefits: (1) It enhances transfer of training, and (2) it is consistent with the idea that adaptive performance is enhanced by gaining experience in similar situations.

### Integration of Training and Business Strategy

Earlier, we noted that firms tend to evolve from domestic (exporters) to international (or multidomestic) to multinational to global, and, in some cases, to transnational. Not surprisingly, the stage of globalization of a firm influences both the type of training activities offered and their focus. In general, the more a firm moves away from the export stage of development, the more rigorous the training should be, including its breadth of content. At the multinational and global stages, managers need to be able to socialize host-country managers into the firm's corporate culture and other firm-specific practices. This added managerial responsibility intensifies the need for rigorous training.[86]

An example of such integration is FedEx Corporation. FedEx has integrated the latest information technology into its corporate strategy, the core of which is to use IT to help customers take advantage of international markets. In fact, the US$39.3 billion transportation giant sees itself more as an IT company than as a transporter of goods (operating 622 flights a week to and from Asian markets alone). Today, more than two-thirds of FedEx customers handle orders and deliveries online. "We decided years ago," says chairman and CEO Frederick W. Smith, "that the most important element in this business is information technology, and we have geared everything to that philosophy—recruitment, training, and compensation. Fail-safe precision is the key to it all."[87]

## International Compensation

Compensation policies can produce intense internal conflicts within a company at any stage of globalization. Indeed, few other areas in international HR management demand as much top-management attention as does compensation.

The principal problem is straightforward: *Salary levels for the same job differ among countries in which a global corporation operates.* Compounding this problem is the fact that fluctuating exchange rates require constant attention in order to maintain constant salary rates in home-country currency.

Ideally, an effective international compensation policy should meet the following objectives:

- Attract and retain employees who are qualified for overseas service.
- Facilitate transfers between foreign affiliates and between home-country and foreign locations.
- Establish and maintain a consistent relationship between the compensation of employees of all affiliates, both at home and abroad.
- Maintain compensation that is reasonable in relation to the practices of leading competitors.

Notice that none of these objectives links to performance, customer satisfaction, or quality, or ensures that the expatriate assignment is consistent with the organization's objectives. Those omissions are striking.[88]

As firms expand into overseas markets, they are likely to create an international division that becomes the home of all employees involved with operations outside the headquarters country. Three types of expatriate compensation plans typically found during this stage of development are:[89]

- Localization.
- "Higher-of-home-or-host" compensation.
- Balance sheet.

**Localization** refers to the practice of paying expatriates on the same scale as local nationals in the country of assignment. It implies paying a Saudi a

British salary and benefits in London, and an American an Argentine package in Buenos Aires. Salary and benefits may be supplemented with one-time or temporary transition payments.

Localization works well under certain conditions, for example, when transferring an employee with very limited home-country experience, such as a recent college graduate, to a developed country. It also works well in the case of permanent, indefinite, or extremely long (e.g., 10-year) transfers to another country. While it is designed to reduce costs, and may do so effectively in the short term, there can be long-term tax and retirement benefit complications that make localization less desirable, particularly for expatriates who plan to return to their home countries.[90]

**Higher-of-home-or-host compensation** localizes expatriates in the host-country salary program but establishes a compensation floor based on home-country compensation so that expatriates never receive less than they would be paid at home for a comparable position.

This approach frequently is used for transfers within regions—notably in Latin America and in the European Union—and for assignments of unlimited duration. It is less appropriate for expatriates on a series of assignments of two to three years.

The **balance-sheet approach** is by far the most common method used by North American, European, and Japanese global organizations to compensate expatriates. Its primary objective is to ensure that expatriates neither gain nor lose financially compared with their home-country peers. If there is no financial advantage to being in one country instead of another, then this objective will be realized. It also facilitates mobility among the expatriate staff in the most cost-effective way possible.[91]

Nonmonetary differences in the attractiveness of individual assignments (if they are not already reflected in base pay) may be compensated with separate allowances (premiums) and incentives. For example, expatriates often receive "hardship" allowances if they are sent to culturally deprived locations, war zones, or those with health or safety problems. Figure 16–1 illustrates this approach. Note the labels at the bottom of each of the four columns of Figure 16–1. The first is "home-country salary." Each of the four categories identified in this column is a "norm" that represents the typical proportion of income that someone at the stated income level and family size spends (e.g., a $100,000-a-year manager with a wife and two small children). Each category behaves differently as income increases and family size changes. In most countries, as income rises, income taxes and the reserve (net disposable income that can be saved, invested, or spent at home) increase at increasing rates, while housing and goods and services increase at decreasing rates.

*Host-country costs* of income taxes, housing, and goods and services tend to be higher abroad than in most home countries, while the reserve remains the same. The column labeled "host-country costs paid by organization and from salary" demonstrates that if expatriates are responsible for the same level of expenditures abroad as at home and overall purchasing power is maintained, the employer becomes responsible for costs that exceed "normal" expatriate home-country costs. Thus, if housing is more expensive abroad than at home, the employer is responsible for the remainder. These differentials are shown as lighter-colored blocks within column 3 of Figure 16–1.

The column labeled "home-country equivalent purchasing power" illustrates the objective of the balance sheet: to provide the expatriate with the same

Figure 16–1

The balance-sheet approach to international compensation.

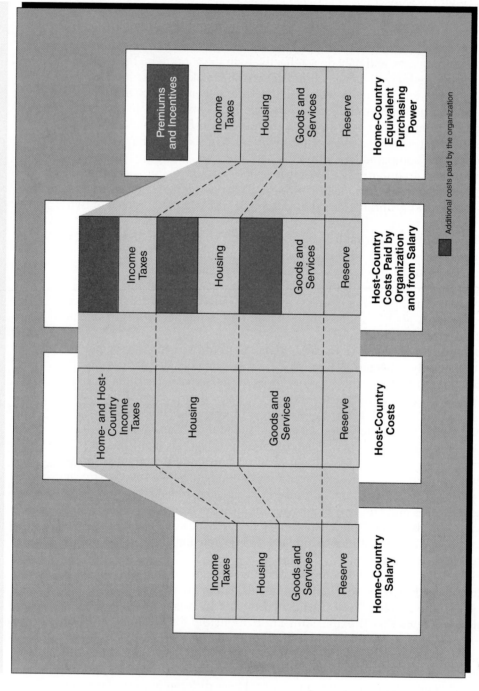

*Source: Reynolds, C. Compensation Basics for North American Expatriates: Developing an Effective Program for Employees Working Abroad. WorldatWork, formerly American Compensation Association, Contents © 1995, p. 8. Used with permission.*

purchasing power as a peer at home, plus any premiums and incentives necessary to induce an employee to accept a particular foreign assignment.

Two philosophies characterize the balance-sheet approach:

1. **Protection,** which is paying expatriates the supplements in home-country currency suggested by the darker-colored blocks in column 3 of Figure 16–1.
2. In a process known as **equalization,** the employer pays the reserve in home-country currency after deducting home-country norms from the expatriate's salary for income taxes, housing, and goods and services. The company pays all income taxes through the expatriate, while making payments to the expatriate in local currency to provide housing and purchasing power for goods and services comparable to the purchasing power of a home-country peer.

The most important advantages of the balance-sheet approach are

- It preserves the purchasing power of expatriates in a cost-effective manner.
- It facilitates mobility among expatriates.

This is not to imply that companies are not using alternative approaches. Small companies with very few expatriates, for example, may relay on *negotiation* of the overall compensation package on a case-by-case basis. Others use a **modified balance-sheet approach** that ties salary to a region (Asia-Pacific, Europe, North America) rather than to the home country.[92]

Two other major components of an international compensation package are (1) benefits and (2) pay adjustments and incentives. Let's consider each of these.

### Benefits

Benefits may vary drastically from one country to another. For example, most developed and emerging economies have some form of national health care supplied by employer- and employee-paid premiums. In Europe, employees have statutory rights that vary from country to country. These include pensions, sick pay, minimum wages, holiday pay, overtime pay, minimum work time, and dismissal procedures (including legally required severance benefits).

To deal with such variation, MNEs try to develop both qualitative and quantitative parity in benefits across countries. **Qualitative parity** is a commitment to offer employees worldwide something from each of the following categories of benefits:[93]

- *Core benefits*—basic items the company commits to making available to all employees worldwide, such as a certain level of health care insurance.
- *Required benefits*—a cash or noncash item required by local law (e.g., mandatory profit sharing).
- *Recommended benefits*—available wherever cost considerations permit, such as life insurance.
- *Optional benefits*—available if there is a competitive practice in a local market, such as local transportation or meal support. In India, for example, health-care coverage of aging parents is common, while some companies in Mexico City offer "pollution-escape trips."[94]

At Verizon Communications, **quantitative parity** is an effort to treat employees equitably from a total-cost perspective around the globe. If an employee is assigned to a country with a rich health care or pension system, such as France, for example, the company does not want to add a layer of benefits on top of the existing health-care and pension coverage, because that would create a situation where some employees are clearly getting more than others. To avoid that, Verizon reviews each country from a total-rewards perspective to ensure quantitative parity.[95]

Most U.S. multinationals also offer various types of premiums and incentives. Their purpose is to provide for the difference in living costs (i.e., the costs of goods, services, and currency realignments) between the home country and the host country. Premiums may include any one or more of the following components:

- *Housing allowance.* This can be substantial, especially since the monthly rent in 2011 in the world's top ten most expensive cities ranged from $164 per square foot in Tokyo (#1) to $84 per square foot in Zurich (#10). The other cities in the list, beginning with #2, were: London, Hong Kong, Dubai, Mumbai, New York, Moscow, Paris, and Milan.[96]
- *Education allowance.* This pays for schools, uniforms, and other educational expenses that would not have been incurred had the expatriate remained in the United States.
- *Income tax-equalization allowance* (as described earlier).
- *Hardship pay.* This is usually a percentage of base pay provided as compensation for living in an area with climactic extremes, political instability, or poor living conditions.
- *Hazardous-duty pay.* This compensates for living in an area where physical danger is present, such as a war zone. For example, contractors working to rebuild Iraq typically get bonuses that equal 100 percent of their salaries.[97]
- *Home leave.* Commonly one trip per year is provided for the entire family to the expatriate's home country. Hardship posts normally include more frequent travel for rest and relaxation.[98]

Finally, it is common practice for companies to pay for security guards in many overseas locations, such as in Middle Eastern countries, in the Philippines, and in Indonesia.

### Pay Adjustments and Performance Management

In the United States, adjustments in individual pay levels are based, to a great extent, on how well people do their jobs, as reflected in a performance review that is part of a broader performance management process. In most areas of the Third World, however, objective measures for rating employee or managerial performance are uncommon. Social status is based on characteristics such as age, religion, ethnic origin, and social class. Pay differentials that do not reflect these characteristics will not motivate workers.

Beyond those considerations, there are at least four broad constraints on expatriates with respect to the achievement of goals in the international context.[99] First, differences in local accounting rules or labor laws may make it difficult to compare the relative performance of host-country managers in different countries. Second, in turbulent international environments, objectives tend to be more fluid and flexible. Third, separation by time and distance may make it difficult for performance management systems to take into account country-specific factors. Fourth, market development in foreign subsidiaries is generally slower and more difficult than at home. Hence host-country managers of MNEs need more time to achieve results.

Some have argued that performance management systems are "broken."[100] Evidence from a 20-year review of 64 articles published in the academic literature on international performance management indicates, unfortunately, that while that may be the case domestically, the situation is even worse when those same systems are used in contexts and cultures outside the home countries where they were developed.[101]

With respect to performance management, three key cultural differences to consider are communications (gestures, eye contact, and body language in high-context cultures versus precision with words in low-context cultures), goal-setting, and reward systems (individual versus team-wide or organization-wide).[102] These concepts might be interpreted and implemented very differently in individualistic versus collectivistic cultures.

We know that concepts such as individual rewards for individual performance and making explicit distinctions in performance among employees are not universally accepted. Indeed, where the prevailing view is that it takes contributions from everyone to achieve continuous improvement (that is, the concept of *kaizen* in Japanese enterprises), the practice of singling out one employee's contribution may actually cause that employee to "lose face" among his or her fellow workgroup members. In other cultures, where nepotism is common and extended family members work together, the primary objective is to preserve working relationships. That objective may cause host- country managers to overlook results that more objective observers might judge to be inadequate. Implementation of performance feedback across cultures is fraught with even more difficulties.

In individualistic cultures, such as the United States, Great Britain, and Australia, a popular topic in first-level supervisory training programs is how to conduct appraisal interviews. Indeed the ability to conduct performance appraisal interviews well and the ability to communicate "bad news" are considered key skills for a successful manager in such cultures. By contrast, in collectivist societies, such as Korea, Guatemala, and Taiwan, discussing a person's performance openly with him or her is likely to clash head-on with the society's norm of harmony, and the subordinate may view it as an unacceptable loss of face. Such societies have more subtle, indirect ways of communicating feedback, as by withdrawing a normal favor or by communicating concerns verbally via a mutually trusted intermediary.[103]

In addition, the target of the feedback matters. In one study, for example, individual versus group performance feedback induced more positive evaluations from individualists and collectivists, respectively.[104] Little research, however, has been done on feedback in intercultural settings, although one study found that Japanese managers provide implicit and informal feedback, which caused frustration among Americans.[105] As these studies demonstrate, it is crucial to be sensitive to local customs with respect to the process used to communicate feedback. This is obviously an area that researchers and practitioners need to understand more deeply.

The general conclusion from this brief review is that it is unwise to presume that the approach that works well in one's own culture will work similarly elsewhere. Finally, managers who are not held accountable for effective implementation of performance management (for example, by being rated themselves on the extent to which they manage the performance of their subordinates effectively) have no incentive to execute that part of their jobs well. Unfortunately, fewer than 40 percent of multinational firms hold managers accountable for the effectiveness of their performance management systems.[106] Lack of accountability also invites political motives to dominate the process.[107] Conversely we know that when managers' own appraisals (and subsequent rewards) are on the line, they tend to take the process much more seriously. It is certainly possible to improve the process of performance management, but what is not realistic is the assumption that one size fits all.[108]

Despite such differences, research indicates that there are also important similarities in reward-allocation practices across cultures. The most universal of these seems to be the **equity norm,** according to which rewards are distributed to group members based on their contributions.[109] In general, the more expatriates perceive that the methods the parent organization uses to plan and implement decisions are fair (procedural justice), the better their adjustment and performance in overseas assignments.[110]

When implementing performance appraisal overseas, therefore, first determine the purpose of the appraisal. Second, whenever possible, set standards of performance against quantifiable assignments, tasks, or objectives. Third, allow more time to achieve results abroad than is customary in the domestic market. Fourth, keep the objectives flexible and responsive to potential market and environmental conditions.[111]

Perhaps the most important lesson from this brief review of this table is that a foreign manager could be completely misled by assuming that the approach that works in his or her own culture will work elsewhere.

Indeed, as firms evolve from multinational to global, they want their expatriates to understand that the greatest organizational growth—and their fastest career development opportunities—are outside their home or base country. Increasingly, therefore a large part of the compensation of these individuals will be performance-based, and not a package of costly allowances and premiums that represent fixed costs.[112]

## Labor Relations in the International Arena

Labor relations structures, laws, and practices vary considerably among countries.[113] Unions may or may not exist. Management or government may dictate terms and conditions of employment. Labor agreements may or may not be contractual obligations. Management may conclude agreements with unions that have little or no membership in a plant or with nonunion groups that wield more bargaining power than the established unions do. And principles and issues that are relevant in one context may not be in others, for example, seniority in layoff decisions or even the concept of a layoff.[114]

In general, unions may constrain the choices of global companies in three ways: (1) influencing wage levels to the extent that cost structures may become noncompetitive, (2) limiting the ability of companies to vary employment levels at their own discretion, and (3) hindering or preventing global integration of such companies (i.e., by forcing them to develop parallel operations in different countries).[115]

One of the most intriguing aspects of international labor relations is **transnational collective bargaining,** in which unions in more than one country negotiate jointly with the same company. Unions have found global corporations particularly difficult to deal with in terms of union power and difficult to penetrate in

## ETHICAL DILEMMA
### Bribery to Win Business?*

In the United States, the Foreign Corrupt Practices Act of 1977 (amended in 1988 to increase criminal fines for organizations and civil sanctions for individuals) prohibits payments by U.S. firms and their managers to win foreign business. It has cost them billions. In 1997, OECD member countries agreed to negotiate a binding international convention to criminalize the bribery of foreign public officials, "irrespective of the value or the outcome of the bribe, of perceptions of local custom, or of the tolerance of bribery by local authorities."[a] Worldwide, an estimated $1 trillion in bribes changes hands each year.[b] In the United States, officials have been pursuing violators aggressively. The Justice Department brought 24 enforcement actions in 2010, up from 5 in 2004. Penalties have increased as well, from $11 million in 2004 to nearly $2 billion in 2009–2010. German engineering conglomerate Siemens has paid the largest fines, $800 million in the U.S., almost $840 million in Germany, and another $100 million to the World Bank. Siemens does business in more than 200 countries, and apparently paid "commissions" to secure orders.[c] China was required to pass anti-corruption laws as a condition of joining the World Trade Organization in 2001. Since then it has turned into one of the world's most aggressive enforcers, prosecuting more than 21,000 cases of commercial bribery between 2005 and 2007. The problem in China is that a tradition of gift-giving in business often degenerates into serious graft. In the United Kingdom, the Bribery Act that took effect in 2011 outlaws "grease payments," small bribes that are common in some countries to get mail service, phone hookups, or other services that otherwise would be delayed.[d] Such payments are legal under the FCPA, as long as they are recorded. Conflicting requirements in antibribery laws across countries have created huge headaches and potential liabilities for U.S. companies that rely on local agents to get deals done. Are grease payments ethical?

---

*Source: Colvin, G. (2011, May 2). The biggest problem for developing economies: Corruption. *Fortune*, p. 48.

[a] Bray, N. (1997, May 27). OECD ministers agree to ban bribery as means for companies to win business. *The Wall Street Journal*, p. A2.

[b] Roberts, D., and Blum, J. (2010, July 18). Bribery is losing its charm in China. *BusinessWeek*, pp. 11, 12.

[c] Palazzolo, J., and Rubenfeld, S. (2011, Aug. 31). U.S. probes Oracle dealings. *The Wall Street Journal*, pp. B1, B2. See also Fuhrmans, V. (2009, July 5). Siemens settles with World Bank on bribes. *The Wall Street Journal*, p. B1.

[d] Searcey, D. (2010, Dec. 28). U.K. law on bribes has firms in a sweat. *The Wall Street Journal*, pp. B1, B2.

---

terms of union representation.[116] Here are some of the special problems that global corporations present to unions:

1. While national unions tend to follow the development of national companies, union expansion typically cannot follow the expansion of a company across national boundaries, with the exception of Canada. Legal differences, feelings of nationalism, and differences in union structure and industrial relations practices are effective barriers to such expansion.

2. The nature of foreign investment by global corporations has changed. In the past, they tended to invest in foreign sources of raw materials. As a result, the number of processing and manufacturing jobs in the home country may actually have increased. However, in recent years there has been a shift toward the development of parallel, or nearly parallel, operations in other countries.[117] Foreign investment of this type threatens union members in

the home country with loss of jobs or with a slower rate of job growth, especially if their wages are higher than those of workers in the host country.[118]

3.  When a global corporation has parallel operations in other locations, the firm's ability to switch production from one location shut down by a labor dispute to another location is increased. This, of course, assumes that the same union does not represent workers at each plant, or that, if different unions are involved, they do not coordinate their efforts and strike at the same time. Another assumption is that the various plants are sufficiently parallel that their products are interchangeable.

One solution to the problems that global corporations pose for union members is transnational collective bargaining. For this to work, though, coordination of efforts and the cooperation of the unions are required. That is beginning to occur. A recent investigation of the organization and policies of all 12 European industry federations since the early 1990s found that they have developed from providing forums for the exchange of information to becoming platforms for the definition of binding guidelines and minimum standards.[119] Yet persistent problems stand in the way of such collaboration:[120]

1.  National and local labor leaders would have to be willing to relinquish their autonomy to an international level. This is a major stumbling block because the local union or enterprise union is essentially an autonomous organization.
2.  National laws that restrict sympathy strikes, secondary boycotts, and affiliations of labor unions with international federations all hamper transnational cooperation.
3.  Language barriers, cultural, religious, and ideological differences, fear of losing domestic autonomy, legal constraints, differences in union structures and goals—not to mention employer resistance—make true transnational collective bargaining exceptionally rare.

## Toward International Labor Standards

In view of the lack of success with transnational collective bargaining, unions have taken a different tack. Labor unions in the United States, for example, are attempting to influence the international labor practices of U.S.-based corporations, arguing that U.S.-based employees are unable to compete with overseas workers who are paid below-market wages and benefits.[121]

Four forces are driving the trend toward adoption of international labor standards: labor unions, pressure from social-advocacy groups, resentment in some developing countries against multinationals, and U.S. and European proposals for linkages between trade policy and human rights. The international labor standards advocated by these groups include

- Prohibitions on child labor.
- Prohibitions on forced labor.
- Prohibitions against discrimination.
- Protection for workers' health.
- Payment of adequate wages.
- Provision of safe working conditions.
- Freedom of association.

Industry is making progress. Led by Hewlett-Packard, for example, Dell, IBM, Intel, and 12 other tech companies created the Electronic Industry Code of

Conduct in 2004 that incorporates many of the standards noted above, including some basic environmental standards. As of 2009, however, it leaves inspection and enforcement to each member company.[122] In the apparel industry, a Joint Initiative on Corporate Accountability & Workers' Rights is a 30-month pilot project sponsored by six anti-sweatshop activist groups and eight global apparel makers, including Nike, Gap, and Patagonia. The objective is to develop a common factory-inspection system and a single set of labor standards. More broadly, it is an effort to forge a private-industry solution rather than wait for government-imposed fixes.[123] Another strategic development is regional trading blocks, of which the North American Free Trade Agreement is just one example.

## The North American Free Trade Agreement

The North American Free Trade Agreement (NAFTA) is one of the most radical free-trade experiments in history. Begun in 1994, NAFTA eliminated trade barriers on goods and services within the United States, Canada, and Mexico over 15 years, and it created a region of 421 million consumers, melding two first-world economies (United States and Canada) with a struggling Third-World country (Mexico). It is North America's strategic response to the global economy.[124] NAFTA also incorporates a feature that is common in other free-trade agreements (except the European Union), namely, that companies are free to invest in all three NAFTA countries, but individuals are not free to work outside their home countries.[125]

How has NAFTA worked? Results have been mixed. Since the agreement took effect in 1994, trade among Canada, the United States, and Mexico has almost tripled, to about $800 billion annually. Of that amount, roughly 60 percent represents trade with Canada, and 40 percent trade with Mexico.[126] In general, NAFTA has been good to Mexico. According to former Mexican president Vicente Fox, "NAFTA gave us a big push—it gave us jobs, it gave us knowledge, experience, and technological transfer."[127]

In the United States, more than 200,000 auto-related jobs have left Michigan and Ohio since 1999, and more than three million manufacturing jobs have disappeared since the early 1990s. Certainly they cannot all be blamed on NAFTA. Investment in automation and information technology has led to massive reductions of factory workers everywhere—including in China. In the auto industry alone, investments in automation since NAFTA took effect have cut in half the number of hours needed to make a car, and soaring health-care costs have also killed many jobs in the auto industry. While some U.S. workers lose their jobs, new ones are also created in services and heavy manufacturing. Indeed, the world has changed so profoundly since 1994 that trying to tie specific job losses and gains directly to NAFTA is an exercise in futility. As experts have noted:

> Myriad free-trade deals, from bilateral pacts to the World Trade Organization, have been struck since. Nations in Asia, Latin America, and Central Europe have opened up to foreign investment and have deregulated local industries. China has emerged as the world's workshop. Emerging market crises and spendthrift U.S. policies have radically revalued currencies time and again.[128]

Mexican assembly plants get 82 percent of their components from U.S. suppliers. By contrast, factories in Asia use far fewer U.S. parts. If General Motors relies on a plant in Matamoros, Mexico, to build wire harnesses for car-audio systems, that's far better for the U.S. economy than if the carmaker buys its harnesses from, say, Taiwan. Says one economist, The real issue is globalization itself. NAFTA is just a proxy." In fact, countless American product lines have withstood the onslaught of Asian imports by integrating U.S. and Mexican operations. That process has saved thousands of U.S. jobs.[129]

## REPATRIATION

Consider these sobering **repatriation** statistics:[130]

- 68 percent of expatriates do not know what their jobs will be when they return home.
- 54 percent return to lower-level jobs. Only 11 percent are promoted.
- Only 5 percent believe their companies value overseas experience.
- 77 percent have less disposable income when they return home.

Furthermore, having become accustomed to foreign ways, upon reentry expatriates often find home-country customs strange and, at the extreme, annoying. Such **reverse culture shock** may be more challenging than the culture shock experienced when going overseas![131] Possible solutions to these problems fall into three areas: planning, career management, and compensation.

### Planning

Both the expatriation assignment and the repatriation move should be examined as parts of an integrated whole—not as unrelated events in an individual's career.[132] Unfortunately, while 95 percent of companies hold repatriation discussions, and 74 percent of them have written repatriation policies, only 14 percent have a formal repatriation strategy linked to career management and retention.[133] To improve this process, it is necessary to define a clear strategic purpose for the move. Prior to the assignment, therefore, the firm should define one or more of the three primary purposes for sending a particular expatriate abroad: executive development, coordination and control between headquarters and foreign operations, and to train local employees.[134] Research shows that unless there is a planned purpose in repatriation, the investment of as much as $1 million to send an expatriate overseas is likely to be squandered completely because turnover among repatriates is almost 50 percent within the first two years back in their home countries.[135]

Beyond that, returning expatriates need a crash course on how to live in their homelands again. Companies need to address the cultural gaps that repatriates and their families will encounter. Doing so will reduce the uncertainties and fear that often accompany the repatriation process.[136]

### Career Management

This is the number-one issue for expatriates. As an Australian expat living in Singapore noted, "Most expatriates are actually thinking that far ahead in terms of 'Where will this assignment take me in three years' time if I agree to go?'"[137] If companies want to retain this key talent, therefore, they need to give them a reason to stay beyond only financial rewards. They need to leverage their international experience in appropriate and challenging roles. Unfortunately, research with 111 expatriates from 23 countries who returned to their home countries within the previous year tells a different story. Compared to their expatriate job assignments, 16 percent of the repatriates were in a job that they considered a demotion, 57 percent were in a job considered a lateral move, and 27 percent were in a job considered a promotion. Receiving a promotion upon repatriation, however, signaled that the organization values international experience and it contributed to repatriates' beliefs that the organization met their expectations regarding training and career development. These two perceptions, in turn, related positively to career satisfaction and to intentions to stay.[138]

## Compensation

The loss of a monthly premium to which the expatriate has been accustomed is a severe shock financially, whatever the rationale. To overcome this problem, some firms have replaced the monthly foreign-service premium with a one-time **mobility premium** (e.g., three months' pay) for each move—overseas, back home, or to another overseas assignment. A few firms also provide low-cost loans or other financial assistance so that expatriates can get back into their hometown housing markets at a level at least equivalent to what they left. Finally, there is a strong need for financial counseling for repatriates. Such counseling has the psychological advantage of demonstrating to repatriates that the company is willing to help with the financial problems that they may encounter in uprooting their families once again to bring them home.[139]

---

## *WHAT'S IT LIKE TO BE A GLOBAL MANAGER?*

*Human Resource Management in Action: Conclusion*

Says Kelly Brookhouse, an industrial/organizational psychologist who directs Motorola's executive development program, "We put people into a simulated environment and throw business challenges at them to see how they respond. We get a fairly comprehensive picture of people's leadership profile."

---

## IMPACT OF INTERNATIONAL HRM ON PRODUCTIVITY, QUALITY OF WORK LIFE, AND THE BOTTOM LINE

The ways in which a company operates overseas can have fundamental, long-term impacts on all three of these indicators. Economic theory says that increased economic integration, free trade, and international capital mobility improve aggregate welfare in the long run, while short-run issues are dismissed as "adjustment costs." The economics of globalization are certainly important, but it also is critical not to overlook its broader effects on individuals, communities, cultures, and the environment. Globalization has brought many benefits to people around the world, but it also has closed U.S. factories, hollowed out entire communities, brought sweatshops to other countries, and placed great strains on the environment. It therefore raises impor-

tant ethical issues, and suggests that everyone—including corporations and consumers—has a moral obligation to address them.[a]

Many of these effects, by definition, are beyond the purview of HR management. Within organizations, however, adopting the kinds of enlightened HR policies that research has demonstrated to be most effective can go a long way toward improving the working lives of the millions of people who toil in the global economy every day. In short, progressive HR policies can enhance productivity, quality of work life, and profits—and that benefits everyone.

---

[a]Society for Human Resource Management. (2011). Global sustainability: Doing well by doing good (DVD). Alexandria, VA: SHRM Foundation. See also Budd, 2010, op. cit., p. 456.

## IMPLICATIONS FOR MANAGEMENT PRACTICE

No one has discovered a single best way to manage. But before a company can build an effective management team, it must understand thoroughly its own culture, the other cultures in which it does business, and the challenges and rewards of blending the best of each.

In the immediate future, there will certainly be international opportunities for managers at all levels, particularly those with the technical skills needed by developing countries. In the longer run, global companies will have their own cadres of **globalites,** sophisticated international executives drawn from many countries, as firms like Procter & Gamble, Schlumberger, Nestlé, and Sony do now. There is a bright future for managers with the cultural flexibility to be sensitive to the values and aspirations of foreign countries.[a]

Finally, there is one thing of which we can be certain. Talent—social, managerial, and technical—is needed to make global business work. Competent HR management practices can find that talent, recruit it, select it, train and develop it, motivate it, reward it, and profit from it. This will be the greatest challenge of all in the years to come.

[a]Dvorak, P. (2007, Mar. 12). Bridging the gap between here and there. *The Wall Street Journal,* pp. B1, B3.

"It was hard. A lot harder than I had expected," says Mandy Chooi, a Beijing-based HR executive at Motorola who recently went through the exercise. "It's surprising how realistic and demanding it is."

Companies that use such assessments often see a quick payoff. French food group Danone SA reduced its failure rate among expatriate managers to 3 percent from about 35 percent in the three years since it started using such assessment programs.

Back in suburban London (see the Human Resource Management in Action box that begins this chapter), I'm starting to sweat. Ms. Dubois is going to walk through the door in about 20 minutes, and I'm far from ready. There's a flip chart on an easel in the corner, but my handwriting is illegible. So I'm feverishly typing up a sheet of key points to hand her.

The phone rings. "Damn," I mutter. A persistent colleague wants me to send a team member to Holland for three months to help land a big new client. I put her off politely and promise to call back later. But I've lost precious time, and when Ms. Dubois strolls in, the presentation is still humming through the printer on my desk.

Sounds a lot like real life, doesn't it?

## SUMMARY

Foreign investment by the world's leading corporations is a fact of modern organizational life. For executives transferred overseas, the opportunities are great, but the risks of failure are considerable. This is because there are fundamental cultural differences that affect how different people view the world and operate in business. The lesson for companies doing business overseas is clear: Guard against the exportation of home-country bias, think in global terms, and recognize that no country has all the answers.

Recruitment for overseas assignments is typically based on one of three basic models: (1) ethnocentrism, (2) limiting recruitment to home- and host-country nationals, or (3) geocentrism. Selection is based on five criteria: personality, skills, attitudes, motivation, and behavior. Orientation for expatriates and their families often takes place in three stages: initial, predeparture, and postarrival. Cross-cultural training may incorporate a variety of methods and techniques, but to be most effective it should be integrated with the firm's long-range global strategy and business planning. International compensation presents special problems because salary levels differ among countries. To be competitive, firms normally follow local salary patterns in each country. Expatriates, however, receive various types of premiums (foreign service, tax equalization, cost-of-living) in addition to their base salaries—according to the balance-sheet approach. To deal with the wide variation in benefits across countries, MNEs try to provide both qualitative and quantitative parity. An overseas assignment is not complete, however, until repatriation problems have been resolved. These fall into three areas: personal finances, reacclimation to the U.S. lifestyle, and readjustment to the corporate structure. Finally, because global companies operate across national boundaries while unions typically do not, the balance of power in the multinational arena clearly rests with management. To provide a more level playing field, unions are pushing hard for international labor standards.

## KEY TERMS

multinational enterprise

global corporation

expatriate

home country

host country

third-country national

efficient-purchaser indexes

culture

local perspective

cosmopolitan perspective

norms of behavior

power distance

uncertainty avoidance

individualism

masculinity

long-term versus short-term orientation

transnational corporation

ethnocentrism

geocentrism

general mental ability

extroversion

agreeableness

emotional stability

conscientiousness

openness

cross-cultural training

culture shock

localization

higher-of-home-or-host compensation

balance-sheet approach

protection

equalization

modified balance-sheet approach

qualitative parity

| | |
|---|---|
| quantitative parity | reverse culture shock |
| equity norm | mobility premium |
| transnational collective bargaining | globalites |
| repatriation | |

## DISCUSSION QUESTIONS

**16–1.** What advice would you give to a prospective expatriate regarding questions to ask before accepting the assignment?

**16–2.** Discuss the special problems that women face in overseas assignments.

**16–3.** What effects might international labor standards have on workers, companies, and consumers?

**16–4.** Describe the conditions necessary in order for a geocentric recruitment policy to work effectively.

**16–5.** What key characteristics would you look for in selecting a prospective expatriate?

**16–6.** Describe the balance-sheet approach to international compensation.

**16–7.** Your boss asks for suggestions about ways to reduce the high rate of attrition among repatriates. What advice would you offer?

## APPLYING YOUR KNOWLEDGE

*Exercise 16–1*    ***Expatriate Orientation Role-Play***

Business is increasingly international in scope. Many problems can arise when citizens of one country attempt to conduct business in another without an awareness of the local culture and customs. The obvious solution to these problems is education and training—in particular, a series of briefings for expatriates before they are sent on overseas assignments.

The purpose of this exercise is to familiarize you with the culture and customs of one foreign country and with the process of developing and implementing a cultural-briefing program for expatriates.

### Procedure

Select a foreign country in which you have some interest. Then go to your college's library and use the Internet to find resources that discuss the customs and cultural dimensions of your chosen country that would be important for a businessperson to know.

On the basis of the information you have collected, develop a mock cultural briefing to be given to the rest of the class. Your cultural briefing should cover such topics as traditions, history, geography, living conditions, clothing and housing requirements, health requirements, drug and alcohol laws, and political and economic systems.

Collect visual aids for your briefing. For instance, your library or a campus professor may have posters, DVDs, videos, photos, or other visual aids available through on-line services that you can borrow to give students a visual overview of the country you have chosen. A local travel agency may have some brochures that you could pass around as part of your presentation. Another possibility is to develop a brief role-play that demonstrates a "rude" foreigner insulting his or her host through ignorance of local customs. Such a demonstration can be built right into your overall cultural briefing.

Be creative! The main idea is to teach the other students in your class about the conduct of business in another country and the importance of a cultural briefing for expatriates before they leave their home countries.

## REFERENCES

1. United Nations Conference on Trade and Development. (2010). *World Investment Report 2010.* Retrieved from *www.unctad.org/en/docs/wir2010_en.pdf* on September 5, 2011.
2. Fortune. (2011, July 14). Global 500. Retrieved from *money.cnn.com/magazines/fortune/global500/2011/full_list/* on September 5, 2011.
3. Tyrangiel, J. (2011, Jan. 2). Year in review. *BusinessWeek,* pp. 9–11. See also Borders are so 20th century. (2003, Sept. 22). *BusinessWeek,* pp. 68–70.
4. Friedman, T. L. (2005). *The World is Flat.* NY: Farrar, Straus, & Giroux.
5. Hof, R. D. (2005, June 20). The power of us. *BusinessWeek,* pp. 74–82.
6. Facebook. (2011). Statistics. Retrieved from *www.facebook.com/press/info.php?statistics* on September 6, 2011.
7. Wikinvest. Coca-Cola Company (KO). Retrieved from *www.wikinvest.com/stock/Coca-Cola_Company_(KO)* on September 6, 2011.
8. Briscoe, D. R., Schuler, R. S., and Claus, L. (2009). *International Human Resource Management* (3rd Ed.). London: Routledge.
9. Gunther, M. (2005, June 27). Cops of the global village. *Fortune,* pp. 158–166.
10. Linebaugh, K., and Hagerty, J. R. (2011, July 25). Business abroad drives U.S. profits. *The Wall Street Journal,* pp. B1, B2.
11. Wessel, D. (2011, April 19). Big U.S. firms shift hiring abroad—Data show work forces shrinking at home, sharpening debate on the impact of globalization. *The Wall Street Journal.* Retrieved from *online.wsj.com/article/SB100014240527487048217045762 70783611823972.html?KEYWORDS=Big+US+firms+shift+hiring+abroad* on April 30, 2011.
12. Sanders, P. (2010, July 19). Boeing brings in old hands, gets an earful. *The Wall Street Journal,* pp. B1, B5. See also Epstein, K., and Crown, J. (2008, Mar. 24). Globalization bites Boeing. *BusinessWeek,* p. 32. See also Miller, S. (2007). Collaboration is key to effective outsourcing. *2008 HR Trend Book.* Alexandria, VA: Society for Human Resource Management, pp. 58–61.
13. Moore, M. (2011, July 21). Apple, HP and Dell among companies responsible for "electronic sweatshops", claims report. *London Telegraph.* Retrieved from *www.telegraph.co.uk/technology/apple/8652295/Apple-HP-and-Dell-among-companies-responsible-for-electronic-sweatshops-claims-report.html* on July 22, 2011. See also Burrows, P. (2006, June 19). Stalking high-tech sweatshops. *BusinessWeek,* pp. 62, 63. See also Foust, D., and Smith, G. (2007, Jan. 23). "Killer Coke" or innocent abroad? *BusinessWeek,* pp. 46–48.
14. Hoshmand, L. T. (2003). Moral implications of globalization and identity. *American Psychologist* 58, pp. 814, 815. See also Schrage, M. (2000, Nov. 13). Nationality matters more than ever. That's no joke. *Fortune,* p. 462.
15. SHRM Foundation. (2011). *Global Sustainability: Doing Well by Doing Good* (DVD). Alexandria, VA: Society for Human Resource Management. See also Confronting anti-globalism. (2001, Aug. 6). *BusinessWeek,* p. 92.
16. United Nations Conference on Trade and Development, 2010, op. cit. See also Bhagwati, J. (2004). *In Defense of Globalization.* New York: Oxford University Press.
17. Ohmae, K. (1990). *The Borderless World.* New York: HarperBusiness.
18. Frauenheim, E. (2008, Jan. 14). Penny-wise, pound-foolish on expats? *Workforce Management.* Retrieved from *www.workforce.com/article/20090317/NEWS02/*

*303179989* on January 22, 2008. See also Sheridan, W. R., and Hansen, P. T. (1996, Spring). Linking international business and expatriate compensation strategies. *ACA Journal,* pp. 66–79.

19. Joinson, C. (2002a, July). Save thousands per expatriate. *HR Magazine,* pp. 73–77. See also Joinson, C. (2002b, Nov.). No returns. *HRMagazine,* pp. 70–77.

20. PricewaterhouseCoopers. (2010). Talent mobility 2020: The next generation of international assignments. Retrieved from *www.pwc.com/gx/en/managing-tomorrows-people/future-of-work/pdf/talent-mobility-2020.pdf* on September 6, 2011. See also International assignments increasing, Mercer survey finds. (2006, May 16). Retrieved from *www.moneycontrol.com/news/business/international-assignments-increasing-mercer-survey-finds_216435.html,* June 30, 2006. See also Carpenter, M. A., Sanders, G., and Gregersen, H. B. (2001). Bundling human capital with organizational context: The impact of international assignment experience on multinational firm performance and CEO pay. *Academy of Management Journal* 44, pp. 493–511.

21. Finfacts. Global/world cost-of-living rankings 2010/2011. Retrieved from *www.finfacts.ie/costofliving.htm* on September 6, 2011.

22. The Global Mobility Forum. (2011, Feb. 17). Smart implementation of international assignments Retrieved from *www.globalmobilityforum.co.uk/blog/?p=95* on September 6, 2011.

23. Dowling, P. J., Festing, M., and Engle, A. D., Sr. (2009). *International Human Resource Management* (5th Ed.). Mason, OH: Thomson/South-Western. See also Silverman, E. (2006, July 25). The global test. *Human Resource Executive Online.* Retrieved from *www.hreonline.com/HRE/story.jsp?storyId=5669803* on July 25, 2006.

24. Ibid. See also Shaffer, M. A., and Harrison, D. A. (1998). Expatriates' psychological withdrawal from international assignments: Work, nonwork, and family influences. *Personnel Psychology* 51, pp. 87–118.

25. Moran, R. T., Harris, P. R., and Moran, S. V. (2010). *Managing Cultural Differences: Global Leadership Strategies for the 21st Century* (8th Ed.). Oxford, UK: Butterworth-Heinemann. See also Ang, S., and Van Dyne, L. (Eds.). (2008). *Handbook of Cultural Intelligence: Theory, Measurement, and Applications.* Armonk, NY: M. E. Sharpe.

26. Ibid.

27. Ricks, D. A. (2006). *Blunders in International Business* (4th Ed.). Malden, MA: Blackwell.

28. Morrison, T., and Conaway, W. A. (2006). *Kiss, Bow, or Shake Hands* (2nd Ed.). Avon, MA: Adams Media.

29. Schmidt, P. L. (2003). *Understanding American and German Business Cultures.* Düsseldorf, Germany: Meridian World Press. See also Axtell, R. E. (1993). *Do's and Taboos around the World* (3rd Ed.). New York: John Wiley & Sons.

30. Needleman, S. E. (2008, July 31). Ivy Leaguers' big edge: Starting pay. *The Wall Street Journal.* Retrieved from *online.wsj.com/article/SB121746658635199271.html* on August 19, 2008. See also Rhee, Z., and Chang, E. (2002). *Korean Business and Management.* Elizabeth, NJ: Hollym International.

31. Moran et al., 2010, op. cit.

32. Ibid.

33. Ibid. See also Ralston, D. A., Gustafson, D. J., Elsass, P. M., Cheung, F., and Terpstra, R. H. (1992). Eastern values: A comparison of managers in the United States, Hong Kong, and the People's Republic of China. *Journal of Applied Psychology* 77, pp. 664–671.

34. Moran et al., 2010, op. cit.

35. Taras, V., Steel, P., and Kirkman, B. L. (2011). Three decades of research on national culture in the workplace: Do the differences still make a difference? *Organizational Dynamics* 40(3), pp. 189–198.

36. Gelfand, M. J., Erez, M., and Aycan, Z. (2007). Cross-cultural organizational behavior. *Annual Review of Psychology* 58, pp. 479–514.

**37.** Moran et al., 2010, op. cit.

**38.** Dowling et al., 2009, op. cit.

**39.** Briscoe et al., 2009, op. cit.

**40.** Beecham, H. (2010, Jan. 28). Expats should review cover. Retrieved from *www. expatmoneychannel.com/content/expats-should-review-cover* on September 7, 2011. See also Schwartz, N. D. (2004, Mar. 8). Caught in the crossfire. *Fortune,* pp. 178–190. See also Kissel, M. (2004, May 13). Americans consider terror risks before taking jobs abroad. *The San Diego Union-Tribune,* p. A18.

**41.** Discovery Channel. (2010). Worldwide kidnapping: Facts and Stats. Retrieved from *www.yourdiscovery.com/crime/kidnapandrescue/factsandstats* on September 7, 2011.

**42.** Baruch, Y., and Bozionelos, N. (2011). Career issues. In S. Zedeck (Ed.), *APA Handbook of Industrial and Organizational Psychology,* Vol. 2. Washington, DC: American Psychological Association, pp. 67–113. See also Kraimer, M. L., Shaffer, M. A., and Bolino, M. (2009). The influence of expatriate and repatriate experiences on career advancement and repatriate retention. *Human Resource Management* 48, pp. 27–47. See also The next CEO's key asset: A worn passport. (1998, Jan. 19). *BusinessWeek,* pp. 76, 77. See also Lublin, J. S. (1996, Jan. 29). An overseas stint can be a ticket to the top. *The Wall Street Journal,* pp. B1, B5.

**43.** Carpenter et al., 2001, op. cit.

**44.** Briscoe et al., 2009, op. cit. See also Sheridan and Hansen, 1996, op. cit. See also Reynolds, C. (1995a). *Compensating Globally Mobile Employees.* Scottsdale, AZ: American Compensation Association.

**45.** Friedman, 2005, op. cit. See also Borders are so 20th century, 2003, op. cit.

**46.** Dvorak, P. (2007, Nov. 19). Why multiple headquarters multiply. *The Wall Street Journal,* pp. B1, B3.

**47.** Lawler, E. E. III, and Worley, C. G., with Creelman, D. (2011). *Management Reset: Organizing for Sustainable Effectiveness.* San Francisco: Jossey-Bass.

**48.** World Economic Forum, in collaboration with The Boston Consulting Group. (2011). *Global Talent Risk—Seven Responses.* Geneva: Author.

**49.** Medland, M. E. (2004, Jan.). Setting up overseas. *HR Magazine,* pp. 68–72. See also Spreitzer, G. M., McCall, M. W., Jr., and Mahoney, J. D. (1997). Early identification of international executive potential. *Journal of Applied Psychology* 82, pp. 6–29.

**50.** World Economic Forum, in collaboration with The Boston Consulting Group, 2011, op. cit.

**51.** Dowling et al., 2009, op. cit. Briscoe et al., 2009, op. cit.

**52.** Ibid. See also Reynolds, 1995a, op. cit.

**53.** Weisbart, M. (2010, Nov. 8). South Korea: So fast, so dynamic—yet still hierarchical. *The Wall Street Journal,* p. R6.

**54.** Jossi, F. (2002, Oct.). Successful handoff. *HR Magazine,* pp. 48–52. See also Solomon, C. M. (1994, Jan.). Staff selection impacts global success. *Personnel Journal,* pp. 88–101.

**55.** Ibid. See also Jossi, 2002, op. cit.

**56.** Cascio, W. F., and Aguinis, H. (2011). *Applied Psychology in Human Resource Management* (7th Ed.). Upper Saddle River, NJ: Prentice-Hall. See also Caligiuri, P., and Tarique, I. (In press). International assignee selection and cross-cultural training and development. In I. Bjorkman, G. Stahl, and S. Morris (Eds.), *Handbook of Research in International Human Resource Management* (2nd Ed.). London: Edward Elgar Ltd. See also Sinangil, H. K., and Ones, D. S. (2001). Expatriate management. In N. Anderson, D. S. Ones, H. K. Sinangil, and C. Viswesvaran (Eds.), *Handbook of Industrial, Work, and Organizational Psychology,* Vol. 1. London: Sage, pp. 425–443.

**57.** Aryee, S. (1997). Selection and training of expatriate employees. In N. Andersonand P. Herriot (Eds.), *International Handbook of Selection and Assessment.* Chichester, UK: Wiley, pp. 147–160. See also Schmit, N., and Chan, D. (1998). *Personnel Selection: A Theoretical Approach.* Thousand Oaks, CA: Sage.

58. Mendenhall, M. E., and Oddou, G. (1995). The overseas assignment: A practical look. In Mendenhall and G. Oddou (Eds.). *Readings and Cases in International Human Resource Management* (2nd Ed.). Cincinnati, OH: South-Western, pp. 206–216.

59. Schmidt, F. L. (2002). The role of general cognitive ability and job performance: Why there cannot be a debate. *Human Performance* 15, pp. 187–210.

60. Schmidt, F. L., and Hunter, J. E. (1998). The validity and utility of selection methods in personnel psychology: Practical and theoretical implications of 85 years of research findings. *Psychological Bulletin* 124, pp. 262–274.

61. Salgado, J. F., Anderson, N., Moscoso, S., Berua, C., de Fruyt, F., and Rolland, J. P. (2003). A meta-analytic study of general mental ability validity for different occupations in the European Community. *Journal of Applied Psychology* 88, pp. 1068–1081.

62. Hülsheger, U. R., Maier, G. W., and Stumpp, T. (2007). Validity of general mental ability for the prediction of job performance and training success in Germany: A meta-analysis. *International Journal of Selection & Assessment* 15, pp. 3–18. See also Bertua, C., Anderson, N., and Salgado, J. F. (2005). The predictive validity of cognitive ability tests: A UK meta-analysis. *Journal of Occupational & Organizational Psychology* 78, pp. 387–409.

63. Caligiuri, P. M. (2000). The big five personality characteristics as predictors of expatriates' desire to terminate the assignment and supervisor-rated performance. *Personnel Psychology* 53, pp. 67–88. See also Silverman, 2006, op. cit.

64. Caligiuri and Tarique, in press, op. cit.

65. Lievens, F., Harris, M. M., Van Keer, E., and Bisqueret, C. (2003). Predicting cross-cultural training performance: The validity of personality, cognitive ability, and dimensions measured by an assessment center and a behavior description interview. *Journal of Applied Psychology* 88, pp. 476–489.

66. Caligiuri, 2000, op. cit.

67. Caligiuri, P., and Phillips, J. (2003). An application of self-assessment realistic job previews to expatriate assignments. *International Journal of Human Resource Management* 14, pp. 1102–1116.

68. Lau, S. (2008, Feb.). HR solutions: U.S. laws abroad. *HR Magazine*, p. 32.

69. Briscoe et al., 2009, op. cit. See also Carmell, W. A. (2001, May–June). Application of U.S. antidiscrimination laws to multinational employers. *Legal Report.* Alexandria, VA: Society for Human Resource Management.

70. Brookfield GRS 2011 global relocation trends survey report, 2011, op. cit. See also Shaffer, M. A., Harrison, D. A., Gilley, K. M., and Luk, D. M. (2001). Struggling for balance amid turbulence on international assignments: Work-family conflict, support, and commitment. *Journal of Management* 27, pp. 99–121.

71. Evans, P., Pucik, V., and Björkman, I. (2011). *The Global Challenge: International Human Resource Management* (2nd Ed.). New York, NY: McGraw-Hill Irwin. See also Pucik, V., and Saba, T. (1999). Selecting and developing the global versus the expatriate manager: A review of the state of the art. *Human Resource Planning*, pp. 40–54.

72. Opdyke, J. D. (2008, June 22). A trip—and a change of heart. *The Wall Street Journal.* Retrieved from *online.wsj.com/article/SB121408502764094609.html* on August 22, 2008.

73. Caligiuri and Tarique, in press, op. cit. See also Shaffer and Harrison, 1998, op. cit. See also Black, J. S., Gregersen, H. B., and Mendenhall, M. E. (1992). *Global Assignments.* San Francisco: Jossey-Bass.

74. Marino-Nachison, D. P. (2005, Feb.). Cultural briefing can prepare expats for challenges. Retrieved from *www.shrm.org/global* on August 21, 2008.

75. Krell, E. (2005, June). Budding relationships. *HR Magazine*, pp. 114–118. See also Aryee, S., Fields, D., and Luk, V. (1999). A cross-cultural test of a model of the work-family interface. *Journal of Management* 25, pp. 491–511.

76. Evans et al., 2011, op. cit. See also Shaffer, M. A., and Harrison, D. A. (2001). Forgotten partners of international assignments: Development and test of a model of spouse adjustment. *Journal of Applied Psychology* 86, pp. 238–254. See also Shaffer and Harrison, 1998, op. cit.

77. Kraiger, K. (2003). Perspectives on training and development. In W. C. Borman, D. R. Ilgen, and R. J. Klimoski (Eds.), *Handbook of Psychology: Industrial and Organizational Psychology,* Vol. 12. Hoboken, NJ: Wiley, pp. 171–192. See also Bhawuk, D. P. S., and Brislin, R. W. (2000). Cross-cultural training: A review. *Applied Psychology: An International Review* 49, pp. 162–191.

78. Brookfield GRS 2011 global relocation trends survey report, 2011, op. cit. See also Napier, N. K., and Taylor, S. (2002). Experiences of women professionals abroad: Comparisons across Japan, China, and Turkey. *International Journal of Human Resource Management* 13, pp. 837–851. See also Caligiuri, P., and Cascio, W. F. (2000). Sending women on global assignments. *WorldatWork Journal* 9(2), pp. 34–40. See also Fisher, A. (1998, Sept. 28). Overseas, U.S. businesswomen may have the edge. *Fortune,* p. 304.

79. Caligiuri and Tarique, in press, op. cit. Harrison, J. K. (1992). Individual and combined effects of behavior modeling and the cultural assimilator in cross-cultural management training. *Journal of Applied Psychology* 77, pp. 952–962. See also Black, J. S., and Mendenhall, M. (1990). Cross-cultural training effectiveness: A review and a theoretical framework for future research. *Academy of Management Review* 15, pp. 113–136.

80. Caligiuri and Tarique, in press, op. cit.

81. Kraimer, M. L., Wayne, S. J., and Jaworski, R. A. (2001). Sources of support and expatriate performance: The mediating role of expatriate adjustment. *Personnel Psychology* 54, pp. 71–99.

82. Brookfield GRS 2011 global relocation trends survey report, 2011, op. cit.

83. Moran et al., 2010, op. cit.

84. Tyler, K. (2003, May). Cut the stress. *HR Magazine*, pp. 101–106.

85. Pulakos, E. D., Arad, S., Donovan, M. A., and Plamondon, K. E. (2000). Adaptability in the workplace: Development of a taxonomy of adaptive performance. *Journal of Applied Psychology* 85, pp. 612–624.

86. Distefano, M., and Schulman, S. (2011, 3rd Quarter). Building global cultures. *Korn/Ferry Institute Briefings on Talent and Leadership,* pp. 46–52. See also Dowling et al., 2009, op. cit. See also Briscoe et al., 2009, op. cit.

87. Cassidy, W. B. (2011, June 22). FedEx annual revenue rises to $39.3 billion. *The Journal of Commerce.* Retrieved from *www.joc.com/parcel-package/fedex-annual-revenue-rises-393-billion* on September 8, 2011. FedEx. (2011). FedEx innovation. Retrieved from *about.van.fedex.com/our_company/fedex_innovation* on September 8, 2011. See also Boyle, M. (2004, Nov. 1). Why FedEx is flying high. *Fortune,* pp. 145–150.

88. Wright, G. (2011, June). Deliver pay worldwide. *HR Magazine* 56(6), pp. 111–114. See also Sheridan and Hansen, 1996, op. cit. See also Milkovich, G. T., Newman, J. M., and Gerhart, B. (2011). *Compensation* (10th Ed.). Burr Ridge, IL: McGraw-Hill/Irwin.

89. Milkovich et al., 2011, op cit.

90. Ibid.

91. Froymovich, R. (2011, June 20). Before you get on that plane . . . *The Wall Street Journal,* p. R6. See also Dwyer, T. (2004, June). Localization's hidden costs. *HR Magazine*, pp. 135–144.

92. Milkovich et al., 2011, op. cit.

93. Briscoe et al., 2009, op. cit.

94. McGregor, J. (2008, Jan. 28). The right perks. *BusinessWeek,* pp. 42, 43.

95. Woodward, N. H. (2007, Aug.). Using "cost of living adjustments" to compensate expats. *Global HR News.* Retrieved from *www.shrm.org* on August 15, 2007.

96. Cushman & Wakefield. (2011). The world's most expensive office rents. Retrieved from *www.cnbc.com/id/35581867/The_World_s_Most_Expensive_Office_Rents* on September 8, 2011.

97. Schwartz, 2004, op. cit.

98. Woodward, 2007, op. cit.

99. Dowling et al., 2009, op. cit.

100. Pulakos, E. D., and O'Leary, R. S. (2011). Why is performance management broken? *Industrial and Organizational Psychology: Perspectives on Science and Practice* 4(2), pp. 146–164.

101. Claus, L., and Briscoe, D. (2009). Employee performance management across borders: A review of relevant academic literature. *International Journal of Management Reviews* 11(2), pp. 175–196

102. Cascio, W. F. (2011). The puzzle of performance management in multinational enterprises. *Industrial and Organizational Psychology: Perspectives on Science and Practice* 4(2), pp. 190–193.

103. Hofstede, G. 2001. *Culture's Consequences: Comparing Values, Behaviors, Institutions, and Organizations across Nations* (2nd Ed.). Thousand Oaks, CA: Sage. See also Hofstede, G., and Hofstede, G. J. (2005). *Cultures and Organizations: Software of the Mind* (revised and expanded 2nd Ed.). New York: McGraw-Hill.

104. Van de Vliert, E., Shi, K., Sanders, K.,Wang, Y., and Huang, X. 2004. Chinese and Dutch interpretations of supervisory feedback. *Journal of Cross-Cultural Psychology* 35, pp. 417–435.

105. Matsumoto, T. (2004). Learning to "do time" in Japan: A study of U.S. interns in Japanese organizations. *International Journal of Cross-Cultural Management* 4, pp. 19–37.

106. Bernthal, P. R., Rogers, R.W., and Smith, A.B. (2003). *Managing Performance: Building Accountability for Organizational Success.* Pittsburgh, PA: Development Dimensions International, Inc.

107. Shore, T., and Strauss, J. (2008). The political context of employee appraisal: Effects of organizational goals on performance ratings. *International Journal of Management* 25(4), pp. 599–612.

108. Cascio, 2011, op. cit. See also Lawler, E. E. (2003). Reward practices and performance management system effectiveness. *Organizational Dynamics* 32(4), pp. 396–404.

109. Toh, S. M., and DeNisi, A. S. (2003). Host-country national reactions to expatriate pay policies: A model and implications. *Academy of Management Review* 28, pp. 606–621. See also Kim, K. I., Park, H. J., and Suzuki, N. (1990). Reward allocations in the United States, Japan, and Korea: A comparison of individualistic and collectivistic cultures. *Academy of Management Journal* 33, pp. 188–198.

110. Minton-Eversole, T. (2009). Best expatriate assignments require much thought, even more planning. *HR Trendbook,* pp. 74–75. Garonzik, R., Brockner, J., and Siegel, P. A. (2000). Identifying international assignees at risk for premature departure: The interactive effect of outcome favorability and procedural fairness. *Journal of Applied Psychology* 85, pp. 13–20.

111. Engle, A. D., Sr., Dowling, P. J., and Festing, M. (2008). State of origin: Research in global performance management, a proposed research domain, and emerging implications. *European Journal of International Management* 2, pp. 153–169. See also Cascio, W. F. (In press). Global performance management systems. In I. Bjorkman, G. Stahl, and S. Morris (Eds.), *Handbook of Research in International Human Resource Management* (2nd Ed.). London: Edward Elgar Ltd.

112. Rosman, K. (2007, Oct. 26). Expat life gets less cushy. *The Wall Street Journal,* pp. W1, W10. See also White, E. (2005, Jan. 25). Executives with global experience are among the most in-demand. *The Wall Street Journal,* p. B6.

113. Budd, J. W. (2010). *Labor Relations: Striking a Balance* (3rd Ed.). Burr Ridge, IL: McGraw-Hill/Irwin.

114. Lauffs, A. (2008, June). Chinese law spurs reforms. *HR Magazine*, pp. 92–98. See also Koen, C. (2005). *Comparative International Management.* Berkshire, UK: McGraw-Hill.

115. Dowling et al., 2009, op. cit. See also Movassaghi, H. (1996). The workers of nations: Industrial relations in a global economy. *Compensation & Benefits Management* 12(2), pp. 75–77.

116. Katz, H. C., Kochan, T. A., and Colvin, A. J. S. (2008). *An Introduction to Collective Bargaining and Industrial Relations* (4th Ed.). Burr Ridge, IL: McGraw-Hill/ Irwin. See also Servais, J. M. (2000). Labor law and cross-border cooperation among unions. In M. E. Gordon and L. Turner (Eds.), *Transnational Cooperation among Labor Unions.* Ithaca, NY: ILR Press.

117. Budd, 2010, op. cit. See also Briscoe et al., 2009, op. cit. See also Sera, K. (1992). Corporate globalization: A new trend. *Academy of Management Executive* 6(1), pp. 89–96.

118. Katz et al., 2008, op. cit. See also Batson, A. (2007, May 23). How U.S. labor leaders chart a global course. *The Wall Street Journal,* p. A6.

119. Mueller, T., Platzer, H. W., and Rueb, S. (2010). Transnational company policy and coordination of collective bargaining—New challenges and roles for European industry federations. *European Review of Labour and Research* 16(4), pp. 509–524.

120. Budd, 2010, op. cit. See also Katz et al., 2008, op. cit.

121. One big union? (2008, June 9). *BusinessWeek,* p. 6. See also Batson, 2007, op. cit.

122. Electronic Industry Code of Conduct, Version 3 (2009, June). Retrieved from *www.celestica.com/uploadedFiles/Corporate_Responsibility/Corporate_Social_ Responsibility/2009_EICC_Code.pdf* on September 8, 2011. See also Burrows, P. (2006, June 19). Stalking hi-tech sweatshops. *BusinessWeek,* pp. 62, 63.

123. Bernstein, A. (2005, May 23). A major swipe at sweatshops. *BusinessWeek,* pp. 98, 100. See also Stamping out sweatshops. (2005, May 23). *BusinessWeek,* p. 136.

124. Engardio, P., Smith, G., and Sasseen, J. (2008, March 31). Refighting NAFTA. *BusinessWeek,* pp. 55–59. See also Smith, G., and Lindblad, C. (2003, Dec. 22). Mexico: Was NAFTA worth it? *BusinessWeek,* pp. 66–72.

125. Budd, 2010, op. cit.

126. Bonney, J. (2011, March 17). NAFTA trade jumped record 24.3 percent in 2010. *The Journal of Commerce.* Retrieved from *www.joc.com/logistics-economy/nafta-trade-jumped-record-243-percent-2010* on September 8, 2011.

127. Smith and Lindblad, 2003, op. cit., p. 70.

128. Engardio et al., 2008, op. cit.

129. Welch, J., and Welch, S. (2008, March 31). A punching bag named NAFTA. *BusinessWeek,* p. 58.

130. Milkovich et al., 2011, op. cit.

131. Andors, A. (2010, March). Happy returns. *HR Magazine* 55(3), pp. 61–63. See also Gregersen, H. B. (1992). Commitments to a parent company and a local work unit during repatriation. *Personnel Psychology* 45, pp. 29–54.

132. Andors, 2010, op. cit. Minton-Eversole, 2009, op. cit. See also Before saying yes to going abroad. (1995, Dec. 4). *BusinessWeek,* pp. 130, 132.

133. Brookfield GRS 2011 global relocation trends survey report, 2011, op. cit.

134. Milkovich et al., 2011, op. cit.

135. Ibid. See also Baruch and Bozionelos, 2011, op. cit.

136. Andors, 2010, op. cit.

137. Ibid.

138. Kraimer, M. L., Shaffer, M. A., Harrison, D. A., and Ren, H. (In press). No place like home? An identity-distress perspective on repatriate turnover. *Academy of Management Journal.* See also Kraimer et al., 2009, op. cit. See also Baruch and Bozionelos, 2011, op. cit.

139. Woodward, 2007, op. cit. See also Thompson, R. W. (1998, Mar.). Study refutes perception that expatriation often fails. *HR News,* p. 2.

# GLOSSARY

**absenteeism**  Any failure of an employee to report for or to remain at work as scheduled, regardless of reason.

**absolute rating systems**  Rating formats that evaluate each employee in terms of performance standards, without reference to other employees.

**acceptability**  The extent to which a performance measure is deemed to be satisfactory or adequate by those who use it.

**accepting diversity**  Learning to value and respect styles and ways of behaving that differ from one's own.

**action learning**  A process in which participants learn through experience and application.

**action programs**  Programs, including the activities of recruitment, selection, performance appraisal, training, and transfer, that help organizations adapt to changes in their environments.

**active listening**  Listening in which five things are done well: taking time to listen, communicating verbally and nonverbally, not interrupting or arguing, watching for verbal and nonverbal cues, and summarizing what was said and what was agreed to.

**adjustment**  The managerial activities intended to maintain compliance with the organization's human resource policies and business strategies.

**adverse-impact discrimination**  Unintentional discrimination that occurs when identical standards or procedures are applied to everyone, despite the fact that such standards or procedures lead to a substantial difference in employment outcomes for the members of a particular group.

**affirmative action**  Action intended to overcome the effects of past or present discriminatory policies or practices, or other barriers to equal employment opportunity.

**age grading**  Subconscious expectations about what people can and cannot do at particular times of their lives.

**agency shop**  A union-security provision stipulating that although employees need not join the union that represents them, in lieu of dues they must pay a service charge for representation.

**agreeableness**  The degree to which an individual is cooperative, warm, and agreeable, versus cold, disagreeable, and antagonistic.

**alternation ranking**  A ranking method in which a rater initially lists all employees on a sheet of paper and then chooses the best employee, worst employee, second best, second worst, and so forth until all employees have been ranked.

**alternative career paths**  Part-time work arrangements that may be available to professionals in law, accounting, or consulting as a way to retain talent.

**alternative dispute resolution (ADR)**  A formal, structured policy for dispute resolution that may involve third-party mediation and arbitration.

**annuity problem**  The situation that exists when past merit payments, incorporated into an employee's base pay, form an annuity (a sum of money received at regular intervals), allowing formerly productive employees to slack off for several years while still earning high pay.

**anti-discrimination rule**  A principle that holds that employers can obtain tax advantages only for those benefits that do not discriminate in favor of highly compensated employees.

**applicant group**  Individuals who are eligible for and interested in selection or promotion.

**assessment-center method**  A process that evaluates a candidate's potential for management on the basis of multiple assessment techniques, standardized methods of making inferences from such techniques, and pooled judgments from multiple assessors.

**assessment phase of training**  The phase whose purpose is to define what the employee should learn in relation to desired job behaviors.

**attitudes**  Internal states that focus on particular aspects of or objects in the environment.

**authority**  For managers at all levels, the organizationally granted right to influence the actions and behavior of the workers they manage.

**authorization cards**  Cards, signed by employees, that designate the union as the employee's exclusive representative in bargaining with management.

682

**baby-boom generation** People born between 1946 and 1964, currently 54 percent of the workforce, who believe that the business of business includes leadership in redressing social inequities.

**balance** In a pay system, the relative size of pay differentials among different segments of the workforce.

**balance-sheet approach** A method of compensating expatriates in which the primary objective is to ensure that the expatriates neither gain nor lose financially compared with their home-country peers.

**bargaining impasse** The situation that occurs when the parties involved in negotiations are unable to move further toward settlement.

**bargaining unit** A group of employees eligible to vote in a representation election.

**behaviorally anchored rating scales (BARS)** Graphic rating scales that define the dimensions to be rated in behavioral terms and use critical incidents to describe various levels of performance.

**behavior costing** An approach to assessing human resource systems that focuses on dollar estimates of the behaviors of employees, measuring the economic consequences of their behaviors.

**behavior modeling** Acting as a role model. The fundamental characteristic of modeling is that learning takes place by observation of the role model's behavior or by imagining his or her experience.

**behavior-oriented rating method** An appraisal method in which employee performance is rated either by comparing the performance of employees to that of other employees or by evaluating each employee in terms of performance standards without reference to others.

**benchmark jobs** Jobs that are characterized by stable tasks and stable job specifications; also known as *key jobs*.

**blended life course** A lifestyle with balance in the ongoing mix of work, leisure, and education.

**bona fide occupational qualification (BFOQ)** Otherwise prohibited discriminatory factors that are exempted from coverage under Title VII of the Civil Rights Act of 1964 when they are considered reasonably necessary to the operation of a particular business or enterprise.

**break-even value** The length of time an observed training effect must be maintained in order to recover the cost of the training program.

**business game** A situational test in which candidates play themselves, not an assigned role, and are evaluated within a group.

**business strategy** The means that firms use to compete in the marketplace (e.g., cost leadership). It provides an overall direction and focus for the organization as a whole, as well as for each functional area.

**cafeteria benefits** A package of benefits offered to workers; both "basic" and "optional" items are included, and each worker can pick and choose among the alternative options.

**card check** A process in which a union secures authorization cards from more than 50 percent of employees, giving it the right to ask management directly for the right to exclusive representation.

**career** A sequence of positions occupied by a person during the course of a lifetime; also known as one's *objective career*.

**career paths** Logical and possible sequences of positions that could be held in an organization, based on an analysis of what people actually do in the organization.

**career planning** A support mechanism to help employees plan out their long-term career goals.

**career sponsor** An individual (usually a group vice president or higher) who is appointed to look out for an expatriate's career interests while she or he is abroad, to keep the expatriate abreast of company developments, and to counsel the expatriate when she or he returns home.

**career success** The measure of career development and satisfaction over a period of time.

**case law** The courts' interpretations of laws and determination of how those laws will be enforced, which serve as precedents to guide future legal decisions.

**cash-balance plan** A pension plan in which each employee receives steady annual credit toward an eventual pension, adding to his or her pension account "cash balance."

**central tendency** In rating employees, a tendency to give employees an average rating on each criterion.

**certiorari** Discretionary review by the Supreme Court when conflicting conclusions have been reached by lower courts or when a major question of constitutional interpretation is involved.

**change facilitator** An individual who anticipates the need for change in strategy and prepares the organization for that change; a key role of a human resource professional.

**Change to Win** A federation of four U.S. labor unions that represent about 5.5 million workers.

**checkoff** A union-security provision under which an employee may request that union dues be deducted from her or his pay and be sent directly to the union.

**choice-of-law provision** Specifies that the laws of a particular state will be used to interpret a contract.

**circumstantial evidence** Statistical evidence used as a method of proving the intention to discriminate systematically against classes of individuals.

**closed shop** A union-security provision stipulating that an individual must join the union that represents employees in order to be considered for employment.

**collaborator**  An individual who works well both inside and outside an organization, and who shares information rather than promoting competition; a key role of a human resources professional.

**collective bargaining unit**  The group of employees eligible to vote in a representation election.

**collectivism**  The extent to which members of a culture give preference to group over individual goals.

**community of interest**  A defined unit that reflects the shared interests of the employees involved.

**comparison quitters**  Those who rationally evaluate alternative jobs and are relatively free of strong negative emotions toward their former employers.

**compensable factors**  Common job characteristics that an organization is willing to pay for, such as skill, effort, responsibility, and working conditions.

**compensation**  The human resource management function that deals with every type of reward that individuals receive in return for performing work.

**compensatory damages**  In civil cases, damages that are awarded to reimburse a plaintiff for injuries or harm.

**competencies**  Characteristics of individuals that are necessary for successful performance, with behavioral indicators associated with high performance.

**competency-based pay system**  A pay system under which workers are paid on the basis of the number of jobs they are capable of doing, that is, on the basis of their skills or their depth of knowledge.

**competency models**  Attempt to identify variables related to overall organizational fit and to identify personality characteristics consistent with the organization's vision.

**competitive strategies**  The means that firms use to compete for business in the marketplace and to gain competitive advantage.

**conciliation agreement**  An agreement reached between the Office of Federal Contract Compliance Programs and an employer to provide relief for the victims of unlawful discrimination.

**concurrent engineering**  A design process that relies on teams of experts from design, manufacturing, and marketing working simultaneously on a project.

**conditional quitters**  Those who will quit their jobs as soon as they get another job offer that meets certain conditions.

**conscientiousness**  The degree to which an individual is hard-working, organized, dependable, and persevering versus lazy, disorganized, and unreliable.

**conspiracy doctrine**  A claim by employers that employees are conspiring against them in restraint of trade (for instance, by striking for higher wages).

**constitutional due-process rights**  Such rights, such as notice of charges or issues prior to a hearing, representation by counsel, and the opportunity to confront and

to cross-examine adverse witnesses and evidence, protect individuals with respect to state, municipal, and federal government processes. However, they normally do not apply to work situations.

**consumer-driven health plan**  Such plans involve a high-deductible insurance plan combined with a health-care spending account from which unreimbursed health-care costs are paid.

**contract compliance**  Adherence of contractors and subcontractors to equal employment opportunity, affirmative action, and other requirements of federal contract work.

**contrast effects**  A tendency among interviewers to evaluate a current candidate's interview performance relative to the performances of immediately preceding candidates.

**contrast error**  A rating error occurring when an appraiser compares several employees with one another rather than with an objective standard of performance.

**contributory plans**  Group health-care plans in which employees share in the cost of the premiums.

**control-group design**  A study design in which training is provided to one group but not to a second group that is similar to the trained group in terms of relevant characteristics.

**controllable costs**  Costs such as salary or benefits that are under the control of an organization.

**cosmopolitan managers**  Managers who are sensitive to cultural differences, respect the distinctive practices of others, and make allowances for such factors when communicating with representatives of different cultural groups.

**cosmopolitan perspective**  A perspective that comprises sensitivity to cultural differences, respect for distinctive practices of others, and making allowances for such factors in communicating with representatives of different cultural groups.

**cost control**  The practice of keeping business costs at the lowest possible level in order for the business to be competitive.

**cost shifting**  In health care, a situation in which one group of patients pays less than the true cost of their medical care.

**cost-reduction strategy**  A competitive strategy with the primary objective of gaining competitive advantage by being the lowest-cost producer of goods or provider of services.

**criteria**  The standards used to measure performance.

**critical incidents**  In job analysis, vignettes consisting of brief actual reports that illustrate particularly effective or ineffective worker behaviors; a behavior-oriented rating method consisting of such anecdotal reports.

**cross-cultural training**  Formal programs designed to prepare persons of one culture to interact effectively in another culture or to interact more effectively with persons from different cultures.

**cross-training**   Providing exposure to and practice with the tasks, roles, and responsibilities of an employee's teammates in an effort to increase shared understanding and knowledge among team members.

**culture**   The characteristic customs, social patterns, beliefs, and values of people in a particular country or region, or in a particular racial or religious group.

**culture shock**   The frustrations, conflict, anxiety, and feelings of alienation experienced by those who enter an unfamiliar culture.

**debarment**   The act of barring a contractor or subcontractor from any government-contract work because of violations of equal employment opportunity and affirmative action requirements.

**decertification**   Revocation of a union's status as the exclusive bargaining agent for the workers.

**decision support system (DSS)**   An interactive computer program designed to provide relevant information and to answer what-if questions; may be used to enhance communication about and understanding of employee benefit programs.

**defined-benefit plans**   Pension plans under which an employer promises to pay a retiree a stated pension, often expressed as a percentage of preretirement pay.

**defined-contribution plan**   A type of pension plan that fixes a rate for employer contributions to a pension fund; future benefits depend on how fast the fund grows.

**demographic analysis**   In the analysis of training needs, such analysis is helpful in determining the special needs of a particular group, such as older workers, women, or managers at different levels.

**demotions**   Downward internal moves in an organization that usually involve cuts in pay and reduced status, privileges, and opportunities.

**dental HMOs**   Health maintenance plans for dental care that operate in the same way as medical HMOs.

**desirable qualifications**   In job specifications, those qualities and skills that are advantageous but are not absolutely necessary for the performance of a particular job.

**destructive criticism**   Criticism that is general in nature; that is frequently delivered in a biting, sarcastic tone; and that often attributes poor performance to internal causes.

**development**   The managerial function of preserving and enhancing employees' competence in their jobs by improving their knowledge, skills, abilities, and other characteristics.

**direct contracting**   In health care, a system in which doctors are free to charge, organize, and treat patients as they choose.

**direct evidence**   In a discrimination case, an open expression of hatred, disrespect, or inequality, knowingly directed against members of a particular group, revealing pure bias.

**direct measures**   Measures that deal with actual costs, such as accumulated direct costs of recruiting.

**direct measures of training outcomes**   Value of a training program expressed in terms of objective measures of performance.

**disability**   A physical or mental impairment that substantially limits one or more major life activities.

**disability management**   A method of controlling disability-leave costs that emphasizes a partnership among physician, employee, manager, and human resources representative.

**discrimination**   The giving of an unfair advantage (or disadvantage) to the members of a particular group in comparison with the members of other groups.

**disease management**   A combination of strategies developed to reduce the cost of chronic conditions that require significant changes in behavior.

**distributed practice**   Practice sessions with rest intervals between the sessions.

**distributive bargaining**   In negotiations, the bargaining posture that assumes that the goals of the parties are irreconcilable; also known as *win–lose bargaining.*

**distributive justice**   Justice that focuses on the fairness of the outcomes of decisions, for example, in the allocation of bonuses or merit pay, or in making reasonable accommodations for employees with disabilities.

**diversity-based recruitment with preferential hiring**   An organization's recruitment policy that systematically favors women and minorities in hiring and promotion decisions; also known as *soft-quota system.*

**doctrine of constructive receipt**   The principle that holds that an individual must pay taxes on benefits that have monetary value when the individual receives them.

**downsizing**   The planned elimination of positions or jobs in an organization.

**due process**   In legal proceedings, a judicial requirement that treatment of an individual may not be unfair, arbitrary, or unreasonable.

**dynamic characteristics of jobs**   Characteristics of jobs that change over time, like those of public accountants or lifeguards.

**economic strikes**   Actions by a union of withdrawing its labor in support of bargaining demands, including those for recognition or organization.

**efficiency wage hypothesis**   The assumption that payment of wage premiums by employers to attract the best talent available will enhance productivity and thus offset any increase in labor costs.

**efficient-purchaser indexes**  Those that assume that a person is not completely new to a situation and has learned about some local brands and outlets and therefore pays prices that are lower than someone who is not familiar with the location.

**emotional intelligence**  The ability to perceive, appraise, and express emotion. It includes four domains, each with associated competencies: self-awareness, self-management, social awareness, and relationship management.

**emotional stability**  The opposite pole of neuroticism, which is being anxious, depressed, angry, emotional, worried, and insecure.

**employee assistance programs**  Programs that offer professional counseling, medical services, and rehabilitation opportunities to all troubled employees.

**employee relations**  All the practices that implement the philosophy and policy of an organization with respect to employment.

**employee stock-ownership plans (ESOPs)**  Organizationwide incentive programs in which employees receive shares of company stock, thereby becoming owners or part owners of the company; shares are deposited into employees' accounts and dividends from the stock are added to the accounts.

**employee voice**  A method of ensuring procedural justice within an organization by providing individuals and groups with an opportunity to be heard—a way to communicate their interests upward.

**employment at will**  An employment situation in which an employee agrees to work for an employer but there is no specification of how long the parties expect the agreement to last.

**engineering controls**  Modifications of the work environment that attempt to eliminate unsafe work conditions and neutralize unsafe worker behaviors.

**enterprise unions**  Unions in which membership is limited to regular employees of a single company regardless of whether they are blue-collar or white-collar employees.

**entrepreneurs**  Enterprising, decisive managers who can thrive in high-risk environments and can respond rapidly to changing conditions.

**equal employment opportunity (EEO)**  Nondiscriminatory employment practices that ensure evaluation of candidates for jobs in terms of job-related criteria only, and fair and equal treatment of employees on the job.

**equal employment opportunity (EEO) for women**  The raising of awareness of issues among both men and women so that women can be given a fair chance to think about their interests and potential, to investigate other possibilities, to make intelligent choices, and then to be considered for openings or promotions on an equal basis with men.

**equalization**  An approach to international compensation in which an employer deducts standard home-country amounts from an expatriate's salary for income taxes, housing, and goods and services, and then pays the balance, in home-country currency.

**equity**  The fairness of a pay system, assessed in terms of the relative worth of jobs to the organization, competitive market rates outside the organization, and the pay received by others doing the same job.

**equity norm**  A reward-allocation practice, common across cultures, in which rewards are distributed to group members on the basis of their contributions.

**erroneous acceptance**  In the selection of personnel, the selection of someone who should have been rejected.

**erroneous rejection**  In the selection of personnel, the rejection of someone who should have been accepted.

**essential functions**  Job functions that require relatively more time and have serious consequences of error or nonperformance associated with them.

**ethical decisions about behavior**  Decisions that concern a person's conformity to moral standards or to the standards of conduct of a given profession or group; decisions that take into account not only a person's own interests but also, equally, the interests of all others affected by the decisions.

**ethical dilemmas**  Situations that have the potential to result in a breach of acceptable behavior.

**ethnic**  Pertaining to groups of people classified according to common traits and customs.

**ethnic minorities**  People classified according to common traits and customs.

**ethnocentrism**  The view of an organization that the way things are done in the parent country is the best way, no matter where the business is conducted.

**evaluation phase of training**  A twofold process that involves establishing indicators of success in training as well as on the job, and determining exactly what job-related changes have occurred as a result of the training.

**exclusive bargaining representative**  In a union-representation election, if a union receives a majority of the ballots cast, that union is certified as the sole representative of all employees in the bargaining unit.

**exclusive representation**  The concept that one and only one union, selected by majority vote, will exist in a given job territory, although multiple unions may represent different groups of employees who work for the same employer.

**exempt employees**  Employees who are exempt from the overtime provisions of the Fair Labor Standards Act.

**expatriate**  Anyone working outside her or his home country with a planned return to that or a third country; also known as a *foreign-service employee*.

**experience-based interview** An employment interview in which candidates are asked to provide detailed accounts of how they reacted in actual job-related situations.

**expert system (ES)** An interactive computer program that combines the knowledge of subject-matter experts and uses this information to recommend a solution for the user; may be used to enhance communication about and understanding of employee benefit programs.

**extended leave** A policy in some companies to grant longer leaves of absence, with or without pay, as a way to retain talent.

**external criteria** Measures of behavior and results that indicate the impact of training on the job.

**external equity** "Fairness" in the wages paid by an organization, in terms of competitive market rates outside the organization.

**externalities** Social costs of production that are not necessarily included on a firm's profit-and-loss statement.

**extroversion** Gregariousness, assertiveness, and sociability in an individual, as opposed to reservation, timidness, and quietness.

**fact-finding** A dispute-resolution mechanism in which each party submits whatever information it believes is relevant to a resolution of the dispute, and a neutral fact finder then makes a study of the evidence and prepares a report on the facts.

**fairness** As it pertains to employee-performance rewards, the employees' perceptions that rewards are given honestly and impartially, without favoritism or prejudice; an employee's perception depends on a comparison with the reward received and some comparison standard, such as rewards received by others, rewards received previously, or rewards promised by the organization.

**family-friendly firms** Organizations with policies, such as on-site child care and flexible work schedules, that take into account the families of employees.

**featherbedding** Requiring an employer in a labor contract provision to pay for services that are not performed by hiring more employees than are needed or by limiting production.

**feedback** Evaluative or corrective information transmitted to employees about their attempts to improve their job performance.

**femininity** The extent to which members of a culture consider sex-role distinctions to be minimal and emphasize quality of life, as opposed to work, as the central value in a person's life.

**fiduciaries** Pension trustees.

**fiduciary duty of loyalty** An obligation by employees to maintain all trade secrets with which their employers have entrusted them; also provides a former employer with legal recourse if an executive joins a competitor and reveals trade secrets.

**financial rewards** The component of an organizational reward system that includes direct payments, such as salary, and indirect payments, such as employee benefits.

**flexible benefits** Benefits provided under a plan that allows employees to choose their benefits from among the alternatives offered by the organization.

**flexible scheduling** An option granted to workers to set the times they will work, within specified boundaries.

**flexible-spending accounts** Accounts into which employees can deposit pretax dollars (up to a specified amount) to pay for additional benefits.

**flextime** A strategy that allows any employee the right, within certain limitations, to set his or her own workday hours.

**forced distribution** A rating method in which the overall distribution of ratings is forced into a normal, or bell-shaped, curve, under the assumption that a relatively small portion of employees is truly outstanding, a relatively small portion is unsatisfactory, and all other employees fall in between.

**foreign-service employee** Anyone working outside her or his home country with a planned return to that or a third country; also known as an *expatriate.*

**formal recruitment sources** External recruitment channels, including university relations, executive search firms, employment agencies, and recruitment advertising.

**401(k) plan** A defined-contribution pension plan in which an employee can deduct a certain amount of his or her income from taxes and place the money into a personal retirement account; if the employer adds matching funds, the combined sums grow tax free until they are withdrawn, usually at retirement.

**frame-of-reference (FOR) training** A form of rater training that attempts to establish a common perspective and standards among raters.

**free-speech clause** The right of management to express its opinion about unions or unionism to employees, provided that it does not threaten or promise favors to employees to obtain antiunion actions.

**functional HR skills** Those, for example, in recruitment, selection, performance management, training and development, labor relations, and compensation.

**gain sharing** An organizationwide incentive program in which employee cooperation leads to information sharing and employee involvement, which in turn lead to new behaviors that improve organizational productivity; the increase in productivity results in a financial bonus (based on the amount of increase), which is distributed monthly or quarterly.

**gatekeeper**   A primary-care physician who monitors the medical history and care of each employee and his or her family.

**general mental ability**   The ability to learn. It includes any measure that combines two, three, or more specific aptitudes, or any measure that includes a variety of items that measure specific abilities (e.g., verbal, numerical, or spatial relations).

**Generation X**   People born between 1965 and 1980, who grew up in times of rapid change, both social and economic; also known as baby busters.

**Generation Y**   People born between 1981 and 1995; includes offspring of baby boomers as well as an influx of immigrants through the 1990s. These people have grown up and are growing up with sophisticated technologies, having been exposed to them much earlier in life than members of Generation X.

**generational diversity**   Important differences in values, aspirations, and beliefs that characterize the swing generation, the silent generation, the baby boomers, Generation X, and Generation Y.

**geocentrism**   In the recruitment of executives for multinational companies, a strategy with an international perspective that emphasizes the unrestricted use of people of all nationalities.

**glass ceiling**   The barrier faced by women in breaking through to senior-management positions, so called because, although women can see the top jobs, they cannot actually reach them.

**global challenge**   Training needs stimulated by the expansion of many firms into global markets. Such needs involve the training of local nationals, as well as preparing employees from the home country to work in foreign markets.

**global corporation**   A corporation that has become an "insider" in any market or nation where it operates and is thus competitive with domestic firms operating in local markets.

**globalites**   Sophisticated international executives drawn from many countries.

**globalization**   The interdependence of business operations internationally; commerce without borders.

**goal theory**   The theory that an individual's conscious goals or intentions regulate her or his behavior.

**goals and timetables**   Flexible objectives and schedules for hiring and promoting underrepresented group members to ensure compliance with equal opportunity employment and affirmative action requirements.

**graphic rating scales**   Those that identify, and may define, each dimension to be rated, and present the rater with alternative scale points (response categories) that may or may not be defined.

**grievance**   An alleged violation of the rights of workers on the job.

**grievance arbitration**   The final stage of the grievance process, which consists of compulsory, binding arbitration; used as an alternative to a work stoppage and to ensure labor peace for the duration of a labor contract.

**grievance procedures**   Procedures by which an employee can seek a formal, impartial review of a decision that affects him or her; a formal process to help the parties involved resolve a dispute.

**group life insurance**   Life insurance benefits, usually yearly renewable term insurance, provided for all employees as part of a benefits package.

**guided team self-correction**   Providing guidance to team members in reviewing team events; identifying errors and exchanging feedback; developing plans for the future.

**halo error**   A rating error occurring when an appraiser rates an employee high (or low) on many aspects of job performance because the appraiser believes the employee performs well (or poorly) on some specific aspect.

**hard quotas**   In an organization's recruitment and selection process, a mandate to hire or promote specific numbers or proportions of women or minority-group members.

**harmful patterns of drinking**   Drinking too much, too fast (more than 4 drinks in two hours for men, and more than 3 in two hours for women) or too much *and* too often (more than 14 drinks per week for men, and more than 7 for women).

**headhunter**   An executive recruiter.

**health awareness**   Knowledge of the present and future consequences of behaviors and lifestyles and the risks they may present.

**health maintenance organization (HMO)**   An organized system of health care, with the emphasis on preventive medicine, that assures the delivery of services to employees who enroll voluntarily under a prepayment plan, thereby committing themselves to using the services of only those doctors and hospitals that are members of the plan.

**health promotion**   A corporation's promotion of health awareness through four steps: educating employees about health-risk factors; identifying health-risk factors faced by employees; helping employees eliminate these risks; and helping employees maintain the new, healthier lifestyle.

**higher-of-home-or-host compensation**   Localizes expatriates in the host-country salary program but establishes a compensation floor based on home-country compensation so that expatriates never receive less than what they would be paid at home for a comparable position.

**high-performance work practices** Generally include the following features: instill learning as a priority throughout the organization, push responsibility down to employees operating in flat organizations, decentralize decision making, and link measures of employee performance to financial outcomes.

**high-performance work systems challenge** Increasingly sophisticated technological systems that will impose training and retraining requirements on the existing workforce.

**home country** An expatriate's country of residence.

**host country** The country in which an expatriate is working.

**hostile-environment harassment** Verbal or physical conduct that creates an intimidating, hostile, or offensive work environment or interferes with an employee's job performance.

**"hot cargo" agreements** Refusals by the management or union members of a company to handle another employer's products because of that employer's relationship with a particular union.

**HR strategy** One that parallels and facilitates implementation of the strategic business plan.

**human capital metrics** People-related measures that focus on outcomes that are directly relevant to the strategic objectives of a business.

**human resource accounting** An approach to assessing human resource systems that considers only the investments made in managers and not the returns on those investments.

**human resource forecasts** The human resource planning activity that predicts future human resource requirements, including the number of workers needed, the number expected to be available, the skills mix required, and the internal versus external labor supply.

**human resources information system** The method used by an organization to collect, store, analyze, report, and evaluate information and data on people, jobs, and costs.

**human resource management (HRM) system** An overall approach to management, comprising staffing, retention, development, adjustment, and managing change.

**human resource planning (HRP)** An effort to anticipate future business and environmental demands on an organization, and to provide qualified people to fulfill that business and satisfy those demands; HRP includes talent inventories, human resource forecasts, action plans, and control and evaluation.

**implied promises** Oral promises and implied and explicit covenants of good faith and fair dealing.

**impulsive quitters** Workers who quit on the spot without any advance planning.

**in-basket test** A situational test in which an individual is presented with items that might appear in the in-basket of an administrative officer, is given appropriate background information, and then is directed to deal with the material as though he or she were actually on the job.

**in-house temporaries** Temporary workers who work directly for the hiring organization, as opposed to those supplied from temporary agencies.

**in-plant slowdowns** The action of union workers of staying on the job instead of striking, but carrying out their tasks "by the book," showing no initiative and taking no shortcuts.

**incentives** One-time supplements, tied to levels of job performance and to the base pay of employees, including nonexempt and unionized employees.

**income-maintenance laws** Laws designed to provide employees and their families with income security in case of death, disability, unemployment, or retirement.

**indirect costs of accidents** Costs that cannot be avoided by a corporation when an employee has an accident, such as wages paid for time lost, cost of damage to material or equipment, and any other expense created in conjunction with the accident.

**indirect labor** Workers who provide essential services to line workers.

**indirect measures** Measures that do not deal directly with cost; expressed in terms of time, quantity, or quality.

**indirect measures of training outcomes** Improvements in job performance or decreases in error, scrap, and waste.

**individual analysis** In the assessment of training needs, the level of analysis that determines how well each employee is performing the tasks that make up his or her job.

**individual equity** Determination of whether or not each individual's pay is fair relative to that of other individuals doing the same or similar jobs.

**individualism** The extent to which members of a culture emphasize personal rather than group goals.

**informal recruitment sources** Recruitment sources such as walk-ins, write-ins, and employee referrals.

**informational justice** Justice expressed in terms of providing explanations or accounts for decisions made.

**initial screening** In the employee recruitment and selection process, a cursory selection of possible job candidates from a pool of qualified candidates.

**innovation strategy** A competitive strategy with the primary objective of developing products or services that differ from those of competitors.

**innovator** An individual who creates new approaches to motivating and managing people rather than relying on past procedures; a key role of a human resource professional.

**institutional memories** Memories (primarily of workers with long service) of corporate traditions and of how and why things are done as they are in an organization.

**integrative bargaining** In negotiations, the bargaining posture that assumes that the goals of the parties are not mutually exclusive, that it is possible for both sides to achieve their objectives; also known as *win–win bargaining.*

**integrity tests** (1) Overt (clear-purpose) tests that are designed to assess directly attitudes toward dishonest behaviors, and (2) personality-based (disguised-purpose) tests that aim to predict a broad range of counterproductive behaviors at work.

**interactional justice** The quality of interpersonal treatment that employees receive in their everyday work.

**interest arbitration** A dispute-resolution mechanism in which a neutral third party hears the positions of both parties and decides on binding settlement terms.

**internal criteria** Measures of reaction and learning that are concerned with outcomes of the training program per se.

**internal equity** Determination of whether or not pay rates are fair in terms of the relative worth of individual jobs to an organization.

**international alliance** A collaboration between two or more multinational companies that allows them jointly to pursue a common goal.

**interpersonal challenge** The need, as more firms move to employee involvement and teams in the workplace, for team members to learn behaviors such as asking for ideas, offering help without being asked, listening and providing feedback, and recognizing and considering the ideas of others.

**interrater reliability** An estimate of reliability obtained from independent ratings of the same sample of behavior by two different scorers.

**job analysis** The process of obtaining information about jobs, including the tasks to be done on the jobs as well as the personal characteristics necessary to do the tasks.

**job description** A written summary of task requirements for a particular job.

**job design** The processes and outcomes that describe how work is structured, organized, experienced, and enacted.

**job evaluation** Assessment of the relative worth of jobs to a firm.

**job families** Job classification systems that group jobs according to their similarities.

**job posting** The advertising of available jobs internally through the use of bulletin boards (electronic or hardcopy) or in lists available to all employees.

**job satisfaction** A pleasurable feeling that results from the perception that a job fulfills or allows for the fulfillment of its holder's important job values.

**job sharing** An approach that allows two employees to share the job responsibilities normally handled by only one employee, and to receive salary and benefits in proportion to their contribution.

**job specification** A written summary of worker requirements for a particular job.

**just cause** As it pertains to arbitration cases, the concept that requires an employer not only to produce persuasive evidence of an employee's liability or negligence, but also to provide the employee a fair hearing and to impose a penalty appropriate to the proven offense.

**justice** The maintenance or administration of what is just, especially by the impartial adjustment of conflicting claims or the assignment of merited rewards or punishments.

**key jobs** Jobs that are characterized by stable tasks and stable job specifications; also known as benchmark jobs.

**knowledge capital** The value of the knowledge possessed by people at all levels of an organization.

**labor market** A geographical area within which the forces of supply (people looking for work) interact with the forces of demand (employers looking for people) and thereby determine the price of labor.

**labor union** A group of workers who join together to influence the nature of their employment.

**LAMP** *Logic, analytics, measures,* and *process*—four critical components of a measurement system that drives strategic change and organizational effectiveness.

**leaderless group discussion (LGD)** A situational test in which a group of participants is given a job-related topic and is asked to carry on a discussion about it for a period of time, after which observers rate the performance of each participant.

**leniency** The tendency to rate every employee high or excellent on all criteria.

**liability without fault** The principle that forms the foundation for workers' compensation laws, under which benefits are provided not because of any liability or negligence on the part of the employer, but as a matter of social policy.

**lifestyle discrimination** Firing of workers for engaging in legal activities outside of work, such as refusing to quit smoking, living with someone without being married, using a competitor's product, and motorcycling.

**Likert method of summed ratings**   A type of behavioral checklist with declarative sentences and weighted response categories; the rater checks the response category that he or she thinks best describes the employee and sums the weights of the responses that were checked for each item.

**local perspective**   A viewpoint that includes no appreciation for cultural differences.

**localization**   The practice of paying expatriates on the same scale as local nationals in the country of assignment.

**lockout**   The shutting down of plant operations by management when contract negotiations fail.

**long-term disability (LTD) plans**   Disability insurance plans that provide benefits when an employee is disabled for 6 months or longer, usually at no more than 60 percent of base pay.

**long-term versus short-term orientation**   Refers to the extent to which a culture programs its members to accept delayed gratification of material, social, and emotional needs.

**loss-control program**   A way to sustain a safety policy through four components: a safety budget, safety records, management's personal concern, and management's good example.

**lump-sum bonus**   An end-of-year bonus given to employees that does not build into base pay.

**maintenance of membership**   A union-security provision stipulating that an employee must remain a member of the union once he or she joins.

**managed care**   A health-care system in which a doctor's clearance for treatment is required for the employee before he or she enters the hospital.

**managed-disability programs**   Disability-insurance plans that focus on making sure that employees with disabilities receive the care and rehabilitation they need to help them return to work quickly.

**management by objectives (MBO)**   A philosophy of management with a results-oriented rating method that relies on goal-setting to establish objectives for the organization as a whole, for each department, for each manager, and for each employee, thus providing a measure of each employee's contribution to the success of the organization.

**management controls**   Measures instituted by management in an attempt to increase safe worker behaviors.

**managing change**   The ongoing managerial process of enhancing the ability of an organization to anticipate and respond to developments in its external and internal environments, and to enable employees at all levels to cope with the changes.

**managing diversity**   Establishing a heterogeneous workforce (including white men) to perform to its potential in an equitable work environment where no member or group of members enjoys an advantage or suffers a disadvantage.

**market-based pay system**   A pay system that uses a direct market-pricing approach for all of a firm's jobs.

**masculinity**   The extent to which members of a culture differentiate very strongly by gender, and the dominant cultural values are work-related.

**massed practice**   Practice sessions that are crowded together.

**meaningfulness of material**   Material that is rich in associations for the trainees and is therefore easily understood by them.

**mediation**   A process by which a neutral third party attempts to help the parties in a dispute reach a settlement of the issues that divide them.

**mentor**   One who acts or is selected to act as teacher, advisor, sponsor, and confidant for a new hire—or a small group of new hires—in order to share his or her knowledge about the dynamics of power and politics, to facilitate socialization, and to improve the newcomers' chances for survival and growth in the organization.

**merit-guide charts**   Charts that are used to determine the size of an employee's merit increase for a given level of performance; the intersection on the chart of the employee's performance level and his or her location in a pay grade identifies the percentage of pay increase.

**merit-pay systems**   Pay systems, most commonly applied to exempt employees, under which employees receive permanent increases, tied to levels of job performance, in their base pay.

**meta-analysis**   A statistical cumulation of research results across studies.

**mid-career plateaus**   Performance by mid-career workers at an acceptable but not outstanding level, coupled with little or no effort to improve performance.

**mixed-motive case**   A discrimination case in which an employment decision was based on a combination of job-related as well as unlawful factors.

**mobility premium**   A one-time payment to an expatriate for each move—overseas, back home, or to another overseas assignment.

**modified balance-sheet approach**   In terms of international compensation, linking salary to a region rather than to the home country.

**modular corporation**   A new organizational form in which the basic idea is to focus on a few core competencies—those a company does best—and to outsource everything else to a network of suppliers.

**mommy wars**   Personal conflicts experienced by women in the workforce, especially those in demanding executive positions, as they juggle work and family roles.

**money-purchase plan** A defined-contribution pension plan in which the employer contributes a set percentage of each vested employee's salary to his or her retirement account; annual investment earnings and losses are added to or subtracted from the account balance.

**multinational enterprise** Any public- or private-sector organization that operates in more than one country.

**narrative essay** Simplest type of absolute rating system, in which a rater describes, in writing, an employee's strengths, weaknesses, and potential, together with suggestions for improvement.

**needs assessment** The process used to determine whether training is necessary.

**negligent hiring** The failure of an employer to check closely enough on a prospective employee, who then commits a crime in the course of performing his or her job duties.

**neuroticism** The degree to which an individual is insecure, anxious, depressed, and emotional, versus calm, self-confident, and cool.

**noncompete agreements** Clauses in a contract that bar an individual from working for a competitor for a fixed period of time if he or she is fired, if the job is eliminated, or if the individual leaves voluntarily.

**noncontributory plan** One in which the employer pays the full cost of insurance premiums for employees.

**nonfinancial rewards** The component of an organizational reward system that includes everything in a work environment that enhances a worker's sense of self-respect and esteem by others, such as training opportunities, involvement in decision making, and recognition.

**nonunion arbitration of grievances** Grievance arbitration in a nonunion firm. May provide fewer due-process rights than unionized grievance arbitration; for example, if there are limitations on discovery (how much information the grievant can collect from the company).

**norms of behavior** Local customs created from a culture's value system.

**objective career** A sequence of positions occupied by a person during the course of a lifetime; commonly referred to simply as one's *career*.

**obsolescence** As it pertains to human resource management, the tendency for knowledge or skills to become out of date.

**ombudspersons** People designated to investigate claims of unfair treatment or to act as intermediaries between an employee and senior management and recommend possible courses of action to the parties.

**open-door policies** Organizational policies that allow employees to approach senior managers with problems that they may not be willing to take to their immediate supervisors.

**openness** Publication of certain information, such as salary ranges, that acts as a public show of trust in employees.

**openness to experience** The degree to which an individual is creative, curious, and cultured, versus practical with narrow interests.

**operational planning** Short- to middle-range business planning that addresses issues associated with the growth of current or new operations, as well as with any specific problems that might disrupt the pace of planned growth; also known as *tactical planning*.

**operations analysis** In the assessment of training needs, the level of analysis that attempts to identify the content of training—what an employee must do in order to perform competently.

**organization** In business, a group of people who perform specialized tasks that are coordinated to enhance the value or utility of some good or service that is wanted by and provided to a set of customers or clients.

**organization analysis** In the assessment of training needs, the level of analysis that focuses on identifying where within the organization training is needed.

**organization development** Systematic, long-range programs of organizational improvement.

**organizational citizenship behaviors** Discretionary behaviors performed outside an employee's formal role, which help other employees perform their jobs or which show support for and conscientiousness toward an organization.

**organizational commitment** The degree to which an employee identifies with an organization and is willing to put forth effort on its behalf.

**organizational culture** The pattern of basic assumptions developed by an organization in learning to adapt to both its external and its internal environments.

**organizational entry** The process of becoming more involved in a particular organization.

**organizational reward system** A system for providing both financial and nonfinancial rewards; includes anything an employee values and desires that an employer is able and willing to offer in exchange for employee contributions.

**organizational support** The extent to which an organization values employees' general contributions and cares for their well being.

**orientation** Familiarization with and adaptation to a situation or an environment.

**outsourcing** Shifting work other than the organization's core competencies to a network of outside suppliers and contractors.

**overlearning** Practicing far beyond the point where a task has been performed correctly only several times to the point that the task becomes "second nature."

**paired comparisons** A behavior-oriented rating method in which an employee is compared to every other employee; the rater chooses the "better" of each pair and each employee's rank is determined by counting the number of times she or he was rated superior.

**paradigm shift** In management philosophy, a dramatic change in the way of thinking about business problems and organizations.

**parallel forms reliability estimate** The coefficient of correlation between two sets of scores obtained from two forms of the same test.

**passive nondiscrimination** An organization's commitment to treat all races and both sexes equally in all decisions about hiring, promotion, and pay, but with no attempt to recruit actively among prospective minority applicants.

**pattern bargaining** Negotiating the same contract provisions for several firms in the same industry, with the intent of making wages and benefits uniform industrywide.

**Paul principle** The phenomenon that over time, people become uneducated, and therefore incompetent, to perform at a level at which they once performed adequately.

**pay compression** A narrowing of the ratios of pay between jobs or pay grades in a firm's pay structure.

**pay openness** Disclosure of pay-related information on a scale from very little (work- and business-related rationale on which the system is based), to very much (availability of pay-related data from the compensation department).

**peer-review panel** Common in nonunion settings, a panel in which employees (not managers) comprise a majority of the panel members.

**pension** A sum of money paid at regular intervals to an employee who has retired from a company and is eligible to receive such benefits.

**performance-accelerated shares** Stock that vests sooner if the executive meets goals ahead of schedule.

**performance appraisal** A review of the job-relevant strengths and weaknesses of an individual or a team in an organization.

**performance definition** A way to ensure that individual employees or teams know what is expected of them, and that they stay focused on effective performance by paying attention to goals, measures, and assessment.

**performance encouragement** Provision of a sufficient amount of rewards that employees really value, in a timely, fair manner.

**performance facilitation** An approach to management in which roadblocks to successful performance of employees are eliminated, adequate resources to get a job done right and on time are provided, and careful attention is paid to the selection of employees.

**performance management** A broad process that requires managers to define, facilitate, and encourage performance by providing timely feedback and constantly focusing everyone's attention on the ultimate objectives.

**performance shares** Essentially stock grants awarded for meeting goals.

**performance standards** Criteria that specify *how well,* not *how,* work is to be done, by defining levels of acceptable or unacceptable employee behavior.

**personality** The set of characteristics of a person that account for the consistent way he or she responds to situations.

**placement** In the employee recruitment and selection process, the assignment of individuals to particular jobs.

**plateaued workers** Employees who are at a standstill in their jobs, either organizationally, through a lack of available promotions, or personally, through lack of ability or desire.

**point-of-service (POS) plans** Health-care plans that offer the choice of using the plan's network of doctors and hospitals (and paying no deductible and only small copayments for office visits) or seeing a physician outside the network (and paying 30 to 40 percent of the total cost); an in-network gatekeeper must approve all services.

**portability** Tax-free transfer of vested benefits to another employer or to an individual retirement account if a vested employee changes jobs and if the present employer agrees.

**power distance** The extent to which members of a culture accept the unequal distribution of power.

**practicality** Implies that appraisal instruments are easy for managers and employees to understand and use.

**pre-employment training programs** Programs developed by industry-specific, community-based coalitions, where member companies contribute time, money, and expertise to design training, and they also contribute employees to teach courses.

**preferential shop** A union-security provision stipulating that union members be given preference in hiring.

**preferred provider organization (PPO)** A health-care system, generally with no gatekeeper, in which medical care is provided by a specified group of physicians and hospitals; care from outside the network is available at additional cost to the individual employee.

**premium-price options** Stock options granted at a price higher than the market price.

**preplanned quitters** Workers who plan in advance to quit at a specific time in the future.

**pretest–posttest only design**   A study in which a control group is not used and the performance of the trained group is evaluated before and after the training program.

**prima facie case**   A case in which a body of facts is presumed to be true until proved otherwise.

**privacy**   The interest employees have in controlling the use that is made of their personal information and in being able to engage in behavior free from regulation or surveillance.

**procedural justice**   Justice that focuses on the fairness of the procedures used to make decisions—the extent to which the decisions are consistent across persons and over time, free from bias, based on accurate information, correctable, and based on prevailing moral and ethical standards.

**process**   In a process-based organization of work, a collection of activities cutting across organizational boundaries and traditional business functions that takes one or more kinds of input and creates an output that is of value to a customer.

**productivity**   A measure of the output of goods and services relative to the input of labor, material, and equipment.

**profit sharing**   An organizationwide incentive program in which employees receive a bonus that is normally based on some percentage of the company's profits beyond some minimum level.

**progressive discipline**   A discipline procedure that proceeds from an oral warning to a written warning to a suspension to dismissal.

**promotions**   Upward internal moves in an organization that usually involve greater responsibility and authority along with increases in pay, benefits, and privileges.

**protected health information**   Medical information that contains any of a number of patient identifiers, such as name or social security number.

**protection**   Paying supplements to expatriates in home-country currency.

**psychological success**   The feeling of pride and personal accomplishment that comes from achieving one's most important goals in life.

**public policy exception**   An exception to employment at will; an employee may not be fired because he or she refuses to commit an illegal act, such as perjury or price fixing.

**punitive damages**   In civil cases, damages that are awarded to punish a defendant or to deter a defendant's conduct.

**pure diversity-based recruitment**   An organization's concerted effort to expand actively the pool of applicants so that no one is excluded because of past or present discrimination; the decision to hire or to promote is based on the best-qualified individual regardless of race or sex.

**Pygmalion effect**   The phenomenon of the self-fulfilling prophecy; with regard to training, the fact that the higher the expectations of the trainer, the better the performance of the trainees.

**qualified individual with a disability**   An individual with a disability who is able to perform the essential functions of a job with or without accommodation.

**qualified job applicants**   Applicants with disabilities who can perform the essential functions of a job with or without reasonable accommodation.

**qualitative parity**   In terms of benefits provided by multinationals, a commitment to offer employees worldwide something from each of four categories of benefits: core, required, recommended, and optional.

**quality challenge**   Ongoing needs to meet the product and service needs of customers.

**quality of work life (QWL)**   A set of objective organizational conditions and practices designed to foster quality relationships within the organization; employees' perceptions of the degree to which the organizational environment meets the full range of human needs.

**quality-enhancement strategy**   A competitive strategy with the primary objective of enhancing product or service quality.

**quantitative parity**   In terms of benefits provided by multinationals, an effort to treat employees around the globe equitably from a total-cost perspective.

**quid pro quo harassment**   Sexual harassment—when sexual favors are a condition of gaining or keeping employment.

**quotas**   Inflexible numbers or percentages of underrepresented group members that companies must hire or promote to comply with equal employment opportunity and affirmative action requirements.

**race-norming**   Within-group percentile scoring of employment-related tests.

**realistic job preview (RJP)**   A recruiter's job overview that includes not only the positive aspects but also the unpleasant aspects of a job.

**reasonable accommodations**   Adjustments in the work environment to allow for the special needs of individuals with disabilities.

**recency error**   A rating error occurring when an appraiser assigns a rating on the basis of the employee's most recent performance rather than on long-term performance.

**recruitment**   A market-exchange process in which employers attempt to differentiate their "products" (job opportunities) among "consumers" (job applicants) who vary in their levels of job-relevant knowledge, abilities, and skills.

**recruitment pipeline** The time frame from the receipt of a résumé to the time a new hire starts work.

**red-hot-stove rule** The theory that discipline should be immediate, consistent, and impersonal, and should include a warning.

**redeployment** Transfer of an employee from one position or area to another—often resulting from a business slowdown or a reduced need for certain skills and usually coupled with training for the transition to new job skills and responsibilities.

**reengineering** Review and redesign of work processes to make them more efficient and to improve the quality of the end product or service.

**relative rating systems** Rating formats that compare the performance of an employee with that of other employees.

**relevance** In an effective appraisal system, a requirement that there be clear links between the performance standards for a particular job and the organization's goals, and clear links between the critical job elements identified through a job analysis and the dimensions to be rated on an appraisal form.

**relevant labor market** Determined by which jobs to survey and which markets are relevant for each job, considering geographical boundaries as well as product-market competitors.

**reliability** The consistency or stability of a measurement procedure.

**repatriation** The process of reentering one's native culture after being absent from it.

**repetitive-motion injuries** Injuries caused by performing the same task (or similar tasks) repeatedly, such as typing or using a computer mouse, for extended periods of time.

**representation election** A secret-ballot election to determine whether a particular union will be certified as the exclusive bargaining representative of all the employees in the unit.

**required qualifications** In job specifications, those qualities and skills that are absolutely necessary for the performance of a particular job.

**restricted stock** Common stock that vests after a specified period.

**restricted stock units** Shares awarded after time to defer taxes.

**restructuring** The process of changing a company by selling or buying plants or lines of business, or by laying off employees.

**results-oriented rating methods** Rating formats that place primary emphasis on what an employee produces.

**retaliatory discharge** Retaliation for filing a claim or bringing a charge against an employer; in such cases, the employee may seek damages under an exception to the employment-at-will doctrine.

**retention** Initiatives taken by management to keep employees from leaving, such as rewarding employees for performing their jobs effectively; ensuring harmonious working relations between employees and managers; and maintaining a safe, healthy work environment.

**return on investment (ROI)** A measure comparing a training program's monetary benefits with its cost.

**reverse culture shock** A condition experienced by an expatriate who has become accustomed to foreign ways and who, upon reentry, finds his or her home country customs strange and even annoying.

**reverse discrimination** Discrimination against whites (especially white males) and in favor of members of protected groups.

**reverse mentoring** A mentoring program in which an older manager meets with a younger subordinate to learn about technologies such as the Internet and e-commerce.

**right-to-work laws** Laws that prohibit compulsory union membership as a condition of continued employment.

**secondary boycott** A boycott occurring when a union appeals to firms or other unions to stop doing business with an employer who sells or handles struck products.

**secret-ballot election** An election supervised by the National Labor Relations Board, in which each eligible member of a bargaining unit casts a secret ballot for or against union representation.

**selection** The process of choosing among candidates or employees for hire or promotion.

**selection ratio** The percentage of applicants hired, which is used in evaluating the usefulness of any predictor.

**self-assessment** In career management, a process in which employees focus on their own career goals.

**seniority** Privileged status attained by length of employment.

**seniority system** An established business practice that allots to employees ever-improving employment rights and benefits as their relative lengths of pertinent employment increase.

**sensitivity** The capability of a performance appraisal system to distinguish effective from ineffective performers.

**severity** The tendency to rate every employee low on the criteria being evaluated.

**severance pay**   Payments, usually based on length of service, organization level, and reason for termination, provided to employees whose employment is terminated.

**sexual harassment**   Unwelcome sexual advances, requests for sexual favors, and other verbal or physical conduct of a sexual nature when submission to or rejection of this conduct explicitly or implicitly affects an individual's employment; unreasonably interferes with an individual's work performance; or creates an intimidating, hostile, or offensive work environment.

**short-term disability**   An insurance plan that provides income replacement for employees whose illness or injury causes absence from work. Short-term disability usually starts after a one- to two-week absence.

**shrinkage**   Losses due to bookkeeping errors and employee, customer, and vendor theft.

**silent generation**   People born between 1930 and 1945, who dedicated themselves to their employers, made sacrifices to get ahead, and currently hold many positions of power.

**simple ranking**   Requires only that the rater order all employees from highest to lowest, from "best" employee to "worst" employee.

**sit-down strike**   One in which workers refuse to leave the premises until employers agree to meet their demands for recognition.

**Six Sigma**   An effort to make error-free projects 99.9997 percent of the time, or just 3.4 errors per million opportunities. It is based on 5 steps: define, measure, analyze, improve, and control (or DMAIC, pronounced "dee-may-ic").

**simplified employee pension**   A defined-contribution pension plan under which a small-business employer can contribute a certain percentage or amount of an employee's salary tax-free to an individual retirement account; the employee is vested immediately for the amount paid into the account but cannot withdraw any funds before age 59 1/2 without penalty.

**situational interview**   An employment interview in which candidates are asked to describe how they think they would respond in certain job-related situations.

**situational tests**   Standardized measures of behavior whose primary objective is to assess the ability to *do* rather than the ability to *know,* through miniature replicas of actual job requirements; also known as *work-sample tests.*

**skip-level policy**   An employee-voice mechanism that allows an employee with a problem to proceed directly to the next higher level of management above his or her supervisor.

**SMART objectives**   Objectives that are Specific, Measurable, Appropriate (consistent with the vision and mission), Realistic (challenging but doable), and Timely.

**social learning theory**   The theory that individuals in groups learn appropriate behaviors and attitudes from one another.

**socialization**   In the employee recruitment and selection process, the introduction of new employees to company policies, practices, and benefits through an orientation program; the mutual adaptation of the new employee and the new employer to one another.

**soft-quota system**   An organizational recruitment policy that systematically favors women and minorities in hiring and promotion decisions; also known as *diversity-based recruitment with preferential hiring.*

**sorting effect**   An effect of variable pay, in which people who do not want to have their pay tied to their performance don't accept jobs at companies that offer it, or else they leave when pay for performance is implemented.

**spatial-relations ability**   The ability to visualize the effects of manipulating or changing the position of objects.

**speed strategy**   A competitive strategy with the primary goal of being the fastest innovator, producer, distributor, and responder to customer feedback; also known as a *time-based strategy.*

**spillover effect**   A situation in which employers seek to avoid unionization by offering the workers the wages, benefits, and working conditions that rival unionized firms do.

**spot bonus**   If an employee's performance has been exceptional, the employer may reward him or her with a one-time bonus shortly after the noteworthy actions.

**staffing**   The managerial activities of identifying work requirements within an organization; determining the numbers of people and the skills mix necessary to do the work; and recruiting, selecting, and promoting qualified candidates.

**status**   In an organization, the value ascribed to an individual because of his or her position in the organization's hierarchy.

**stock options**   The right (primarily of executives) to buy a company's stock sometime in the future at a fixed price, usually the price on the day the options are granted.

**strategic human resource management (HRM)**   An approach to HRM that has the goal of using people most wisely with respect to the strategic needs of the organization.

**strategic job analyses**   Future-oriented analyses that identify skill and ability requirements for jobs that do not yet exist.

**strategic partner**   An individual who works with managers to help them better understand the value of people and the consequences of ineffective or effective HRM; a key role of an HR professional.

**strategic planning** Long-range business planning that involves fundamental decisions about the very nature of the business, including defining the organization's philosophy; formulating statements of identity, purpose, and objectives; evaluating strengths, weaknesses, and competitive dynamics; determining organizational design; developing strategies; and devising programs.

**strategic workforce planning** Identification of the numbers of employees and the skills needed to perform available jobs, based on an understanding of available competencies and changes in jobs required by corporate goals.

**subjective career** A sense of where one is going in one's work life based on one's perceived talents and abilities, basic values, and career motives and needs.

**succession planning** The process of identifying replacement candidates for key positions, assessing their current performance and readiness for promotion, identifying career-development needs, and integrating the career goals of individuals with company goals to ensure the availability of competent executive talent.

**sympathy strikes** Refusals by employees of one bargaining unit to cross a picket line of a different bargaining unit.

**system** A network of interrelated components.

**systemic discrimination** Any business practice that results in the denial of equal employment opportunity.

**systems approach** An approach to managing human resources that provides a conceptual framework for integrating the various components within the system and for linking the human resource management (HRM) system with larger organizational needs.

**talent inventory** The human resource planning activity that assesses current human resources skills, abilities, and potential, and analyzes how those resources are currently being used.

**team** A group of individuals who are working together toward a common goal.

**team-coordination training** Focusing on teamwork skills that facilitate information exchange, cooperation, and coordination of job-related behaviors.

**teleworking** Work carried out in a location that is remote from central offices or production facilities, where the worker has no personal contact with co-workers but is able to communicate with them using electronic means.

**telecommuting** An approach made possible by the use of computer and electronic technology, in which an employee works either full-time or part-time from his or her home.

**test-retest reliability** An estimate of reliability obtained from two administrations of the same test at two different times.

**third-country national** An expatriate who has transferred to an additional country while working abroad.

**360-degree feedback** Performance assessments from above, below, and at the same level as an employee. It may also include feedback from customers.

**"Three-C" logic** An approach to organizational design based on the strategies of command, control, and compartmentalization.

**time study** A study conducted to determine how fast a job should be done.

**time-based strategy** A competitive strategy with the primary goal of being the fastest innovator, producer, distributor, and responder to customer feedback; also known as a *speed strategy*.

**total health and productivity management** A developing trend toward integrating disability coverage with workers' compensation and, eventually, with group health care; also known as *managed health*.

**tournament model of upward mobility** A model of career success based on the assumption that an individual must have a challenging first job and receive quick, early promotions in order to be successful in his or her career; so called because, as in a tournament, everyone has an equal chance in the early contests but the losers are not eligible for the later, major contests.

**training** Planned programs designed to improve performance at the individual, group, and/or organizational levels.

**training and development phase of training** The phase of training whose purpose is to design the environment in which to achieve the objectives defined in the assessment phase by choosing methods and techniques and by delivering them in a supportive environment based on sound principles of learning.

**training outcomes** The effectiveness of a training program based on cognitive, skill-based, affective, and results outcomes.

**training paradox** The seemingly contradictory fact that training employees to develop their skills and improve their performance increases their employability outside the company while simultaneously increasing their job security and desire to stay with their current employer.

**transfer** The extent to which competencies learned in training can be applied on the job.

**transfer of trained skills**   The use of knowledge, skills, and behaviors learned in training on the job.

**transnational collective bargaining**   Unions in more than one country negotiate jointly with the same company.

**transnational corporation**   A corporation that uses geodiversity to great advantage, placing its top executives and core corporate functions in different countries to gain a competitive edge through the availability of talent, capital, low costs, or proximity to its most important customers.

**troubled employee**   An individual with unresolved personal or work-related problems.

**trust gap**   A frame of mind in which employees mistrust senior management's intentions, doubt its competence, and resent its self-congratulatory pay.

**turnover**   Any permanent departure of employees beyond organizational boundaries.

**type A behavior pattern**   A hard-driving, aggressive, competitive, impatient pattern of behavior.

**unauthorized aliens**   Foreign-born U.S. residents not legally authorized to work in the United States.

**uncertainty avoidance**   The extent to which members of a culture feel threatened by ambiguous situations and thus emphasize ritual behavior, rules, and stability.

**uncontrollable costs**   Costs that are beyond the control of an organization.

**unequal treatment**   Disparate treatment of employees based on an intention to discriminate.

**unfair labor practice strikes**   Strikes that are caused or prolonged by unfair labor practices of the employer.

**union shop**   A union-security provision stipulating that, as a condition of continued employment, an individual must join the union that represents employees after a probationary period.

**union-security clause**   In a contract, a clause designed to force all employees to join the union in order to remain working.

**unprotected strikes**   Both lawful and unlawful work stoppages, such as sit-down strikes, slowdowns, and wildcat strikes, in which participants' jobs are not protected by law; thus the participants may be discharged by their employer.

**utility analysis**   A method of converting measures of staffing or training outcomes into the metric of dollars.

**validity**   Evidence regarding the appropriateness or meaningfulness of inferences about scores from a measurement procedure.

**validity generalization**   The assumption that the results of a validity study conducted in one situation can be generalized to other similar situations.

**variable-pay systems**   Pay programs that are linked to profit and productivity gains.

**vesting**   The legal right of an employee to receive the employer's share of retirement benefits contributed on his or her behalf after a certain length of employment.

**virtual corporation**   A new organizational form in which teams of specialists come together to work on a project and then disband when the project is finished.

**virtual job fair**   Computer-based use of video, voice, and text to connect job seekers with recruiters. Online visitors can listen to presentations; visit booths; leave résumés and business cards; participate in live chats; and get contact information from recruiters, HR managers, and even hiring managers.

**virtual organization**   An organizational form in which teams of specialists come together through technology to work on a project, and disband when the project is finished.

**virtual workplace**   A new organizational form based on the idea of working anytime, anywhere—in real space or in cyberspace.

**voice systems**   Organizational systems that provide individuals and groups with the capacity to be heard, with a way to communicate their interests upward.

**Weingarten rights**   Rights defined by the Supreme Court in *NLRB v. J. Weingarten, Inc.,* stating that a union employee has the right to demand that a union representative be present at an investigatory interview that the employee reasonably believes may result in disciplinary action.

**wellness programs**   Programs that focus on prevention to help employees build lifestyles that will enable them to achieve their full physical and mental potential.

**whistle-blowing**   Disclosure by former or current organization members of illegal, immoral, or illegitimate practices under the control of their employers.

**willful violations**   Violations of OSHA requirements in which an employer either knew that what was being done constituted a violation of federal regulations or was aware that a hazardous condition existed and made no reasonable effort to eliminate it.

**win–lose bargaining**   In negotiations, the bargaining posture that assumes that the goals of the parties are irreconcilable; also known as *distributive bargaining.*

**win–win bargaining**   In negotiations, the bargaining posture that assumes that the goals of the parties are not mutually exclusive, that it is possible for both sides to achieve their objectives; also known as *integrative bargaining.*

**work-life program**   An employer-sponsored benefit or working condition that helps employees to balance work and nonwork demands.

**work planning and review**   Emphasizes periodic review of work plans by both supervisor and subordinate in order to identify goals attained, problems encountered, and needs for training.

**work-sample tests**   Standardized measures of behavior whose primary objective is to assess the ability to *do* rather than the ability to *know* through miniature replicas of actual job requirements; also known as *situational tests.*

**workers' compensation programs**   Programs that provide payments to workers who are injured on the job, or who contract a work-related illness.

**workforce forecasting**   The estimation of labor requirements at some future time period.

**workplace aggression**   Efforts by individuals to harm others with whom they work or have worked, or their organization.

**yearly renewable term insurance**   Group life insurance in which each employee is insured one year at a time.

# CREDITS

## PHOTO CREDITS

# NAME INDEX

# SUBJECT INDEX

**709**